ISBN 978-1-5281-8937-8
PIBN 10165040

AMERICAN BOOKS

IN THE

BRITISH MUSEUM

A TALOGUE

OF

HE AMERICAN BOOKS IN

THE LIBRARY OF

THE BRITISH MUSEUM AT
Christmas MdcccLvi

By HENRY STEVENS GMB MA FSA ETC

Bibliography   The Tree of Knowledge

LONDON

PRINTED BY CHARLES WHITTINGHAM AT THE CHISWICK PRESS FOR
HENRY STEVENS 4 TRAFALGAR SQUARE
MdcccLxvi

To

The SEVEN ITALIANS who

BY THEIR INTELLIGENT ENTERPRISE IN FOREIGN COUNTRIES
ACHIEVED THE LASTING REMEMBRANCE
AND GRATITUDE
OF

AMERICA

THIS VOLUME IS EARNESTLY AND REVERENTLY
INSCRIBED.

To

CHRISTOPHER COLUMBUS of Genoa who gave a New World to
Castile and Leon ;

To

JOHN CABOT the Venetian who planted the Flags of St Mark and
St George side by side on the New Continent ;

To

AMERIGO VESPUCCI whose name given to the New Hemisphere
is a perpetual memorial of that enterprising Florentine ;

To

PETER MARTYR of Anghiera whose Letters and Decades comprise the first History of America ;

To

JEAN VERRAZZANO of Florence who in the service of France
checkmated Spain in her grasping policy West
of the Line of Demarcation ;

To

JEROME BENZONI of Milan who published the first Book of Travels
in America after a residence there of fourteen years ;

And

And, last not least, to ANTONIO PANIZZI of Brescello, of the University of Parma, and of the British Museum, who, while Keeper of the Department of Printed Books, fully alive to the importance of the subject, and the necessity of collecting the literature of new countries while there was a reasonable probability of securing it with tolerable completeness, and, lest the literary acquisitions in all foreign languages might together dwarf those in the English, initiated the unrivalled collection of American Books described in this Catalogue. It was possible then with pains and economy to form the nucleus of such a department for the National Library of England, an opportunity now passed.

To these ITALIANS therefore is due

The Sevenfold Homage of Americans, and especially from one who has made American History and American Literature his life-long study.

HENRY STEVENS of Vermont.

London, the fourth of July, 1865.

EXPLANATORY

AVING for some years quietly indulged in an ill-defined notion that I might some day endeavour to achieve A HISTORY OF AMERICAN LITERATURE, including books relating to America, together with an account of American books above and below these levels; and well knowing the paucity of materials existing in the chief repositories, public and private, on both sides of the Atlantic; and feeling, at the same time, the inadequacy of existing catalogues, I consulted in the autumn of 1855 Mr Panizzi, the Keeper of the Printed Books in the British Museum, and after much discussion submitted to him in writing, at his request, on the 25th of January, 1856, a preliminary proposition for editing and printing a complete catalogue of the American books in the Library of the British Museum up to Christmas of that year, with the double purpose of letting the world know how rich, and the authorities how poor, was the National Library of England in this foreign department of literature in the English language.

In this memorandum Mr Panizzi was reminded that in the autumn of 1845, shortly after I had drifted into the Museum from Vermont, with letters of introduction from my good friend Mr Jared Sparks, the historian, an amateur report upon American books not then in the Museum, was drawn up by me for him, at his particular request, the result of which was the accession to the library, through me, in that and the following year, of some ten thousand volumes. It was subsequently ascertained that in

1840 the Museum contained only about one thousand volumes
of American books. Soon after Mr Panizzi's famous report of
1843, considerable orders were sent to Philadelphia through Mr
Pickering, and some few American books were acquired in 1844
and 1845 through Messrs Wiley and Putnam. But down to the
time of my report it is certain that the Library did not contain
four thousand volumes of American books all told. From 1847
to 1855 the Museum acquired through me about six thousand
volumes more, and some few volumes drifted in by presents.
So that, at the time of my proposition to print, the Library of
the British Museum contained about twenty thousand volumes
of books printed in America, not including reprints of American
books or books in various languages relating to America.

In April, 1856, Mr Panizzi left the Department of Printed Books
and became the Principal Librarian and Secretary, Mr J. Winter
Jones taking his place as Keeper of the Printed Books. These
changes, however, did not affect my proposition, as appears by
the following letter, given in full, which explains itself:

VERMONT HOUSE, CAMDEN SQUARE,
LONDON, *April* 24, 1856.

J. WINTER JONES, Esquire,
     British Museum.

MY DEAR SIR,

     At your desire I embody in letter form the result of our several
conversations respecting the American books in the library of the British
Museum, and submit herewith my proposals for printing a catalogue of them.

I estimate that at present there are about 20,000 volumes of American books
in the Museum, about four-fifths of which have been supplied by me since the
year 1845. In three years I am confident 20,000 volumes more may be procured, including the publications of the Southern and Western States, California, Canada, and Mexico.

Considering these estimates I am of opinion that the printing of a catalogue
of all the American books in the library, to be completed within the present
year, will yield so many advantages that I am willing to undertake and execute
it at my own expense and responsibility. I propose to do the editing, proof
reading, etc. in the Museum, and all that I ask is a free and proper use of the
Museum titles, of course under all necessary restrictions. Mr Whittingham
(of the Chiswick Press), a gentleman well known to Mr Panizzi and yourself,
would do the printing, and probably would never require more than three or
four hundred titles in hand at one time.

I will not now venture to enumerate the advantages of such a catalogue both
to the Museum and to other libraries, and will only add, that if such a work is

to be done at all, there are many reasons for doing it at the present time, when all the American books purchased have been catalogued and before any more considerable accessions are made.

Trusting that the contents of this note will meet not alone your approval but that of the Trustees,   I remain, My Dear Sir,

Yours faithfully,

HENRY STEVENS.

The proposition having been submitted to the Trustees was accepted, and the result is seen in these four printed catalogues :

1st, of American books printed in the United States,

2d, of the Canadian and British North American books,

3d, of Mexican, Spanish American, and West Indian books, and

4th, of American Maps printed in the United States.

It was deemed preferable to print these imperfect catalogues at once rather than wait for better ones.   The work was therefore cut off square at Christmas, 1856, and hurried through the press with all possible despatch, condensing everything to the lowest point of clearness. Being only a special list of a single department, and not very bulky, the main titles only were printed, all cross-references and explanatory titles being omitted, to be hereafter condensed into a full and common-sense index. To save space and confusion headings are not repeated or represented by dashes, but by small numbers, in order that the proposed index might direct one to a precise title instead of a page of titles.   In case of supplementary volumes, these numbers are to be carried on, and thus indicate whether or not a heading found in the supplement has been given before.

The British Museum rules for cataloguing were of course followed, but with some important modifications necessary to adapt them from a general to a special catalogue of titles almost all in the English language. Transactions of academies and periodicals have each title placed under its own name in the general alphabet, with indexes under the headings ACADEMIES and PERIODICALS. Laws, journals, reports, and legislative documents are collected and given chronologically under the headings of each of the several States.

The catalogues will probably explain themselves, but a few particulars may be named. The printing was finished in June,

1857, but the publication has been unavoidably delayed. On the whole, the American collections in the British Museum, as indicated by these lists, are extraordinary, and one is hardly more surprised by what is found in them than by the omissions. It at first required some courage to show to the world such wealth and poverty side by side. But the printing of the catalogues was the best means of remedy, for from July, 1857, to July, 1862, the collections have been doubled, that is, the American department has been increased from twenty to forty thousand volumes.

It will be noticed that only books printed in America are given. The Museum Library is very rich in all kinds of works in all languages relating to America, as well as in American books reprinted in this country.

To the Trustees, Officers, Assistants, and Attendants of the Library my acknowledgment and thanks are due for unvarying kindness, and every facility necessary for carrying out this work, especially to Mr Panizzi, Mr Jones, and Mr Watts. They have all done much for me and my work, and I thank them. On the other hand I trust that this my work is a slight return to them and the British Museum.

I am permitted by the Trustees and Officers to append to this Preface—

I. The British Museum Rules for Cataloguing Books, Maps, and Music (first published in 1841), as revised and codified down to July, 1862.

II. The British Museum System of Classification of Books on the Shelves.

No doubt both the Rules and the Classification have been since somewhat modified and improved from time to time as occasion required. They are valuable additions to these catalogues, and, as they cover all departments, may do good service in libraries generally.

HENRY STEVENS of Vermont.

London, 1865.

RULES FOR THE COMPILATION OF THE

CATALOGUE OF PRINTED BOOKS IN THE LIBRARY OF

THE BRITISH MUSEUM.

ITLES to be written on slips, uniform in size.

The entries of works in the collection of George the Third presented by George the Fourth to the Nation to be distinguished by a crown.

II. Titles to be arranged alphabetically, according to the English alphabet only (whatever be the order of the alphabet in which a foreign name might have to be entered in its original language) under the surname of the author, whenever it appears printed in the title, or in any other part of the book. If the name be supplied in manuscript, the work must nevertheless be considered anonymous or pseudonymous, as the case may be, and the manuscript addition deemed merely a suggestion to which the librarian will attach such importance as he may think proper, on his own responsibility, in supplying the author's name between brackets, as hereafter directed.

In the alphabetical arrangement, initial prepositions, letters, or articles to be taken in connection with the rest of the name.

III. If more than one name occur in the title, by which it may appear that the work is the production of more than one person, the first to be taken as the leading name.

IV. Sovereigns, or princes of sovereign houses, and saints, to be entered under their Christian or first name, *in their English form.*

b

Acts of the pope, as head of the Church, to be entered under "Rome, Church of," with a sub-heading of the name of the pope. Acts by him as a temporal sovereign, to be entered under "States of the Church," and the name of the pope as a sub-heading. Acts of bishops, who, as such are sovereign princes, to be entered under the name of their respective bishoprics.

V. Works of Jewish Rabbis before 1700, as well as works of Oriental writers in general, to be entered under their first name.

VI. Works of friars, who, by the constitution of their order, drop their surname, to be entered under the Christian name; the name of the family, if ascertained, to be added in brackets. The same to be done for those known under their first name only, to which, for the sake of distinction, they add that of their native place, or profession, or rank. Patronymics, or denominations, derived from the ancestors or names of other persons, to be used as surnames.

VII. The respondent or defender in a thesis to be considered its author, except when it unequivocally appears to be the work of the Præses.

VIII. When an author uses a Christian or first name only (either real or assumed), such name to be taken as a heading; and if more than one be used, the first to be preferred for the principal entry. The surname, or family name, when known, to be added in brackets after the first name.

IX. Any act, resolution, or other document purporting to be agreed upon, authorized, or issued by assemblies, boards, or corporate bodies (with the exception of academies, universities, learned societies, and religious orders, respecting which special rules are to be followed), to be entered in distinct alphabetical series, under the name of the country or place from which they derive their denomination, or, for want of such denomination, under the name of the place whence their acts are issued.

X. Names of persons that may have been altered by being used in various languages, to be entered under their vernacular form, if any instance occur of such persons having used it in any of their printed publications. With respect to places, the English form to be preferred.

XI. Works of authors who change their name or add to it a second, after having begun to publish under the first, to be entered under the first name, noticing any alteration which may have subsequently taken place.

XII. Foreign names, excepting French, preceded by a preposition, an article, or by both, to be entered under the letter immediately following. French names, preceded by a preposition only, to follow the same rule; those preceded by an article, or by a preposition and an article, to be entered under the initial letter of the article. English surnames, of foreign origin, to be entered under their initial, even if originally belonging to a preposition. Foreign compound surnames to be entered under the initial of the first of them. In compound Dutch and English surnames the last name to be preferred, if no entry of a work by the same person occur in the catalogue under the first name only.

XIII. German names, in which the letters ä, ö or ü occur, to be spelt with the diphthong ae, oe and ue respectively.

XIV. Surnames of noblemen, though not expressed in the book, to be ascertained and written out as the heading of the entry. A person who has assumed titles not generally acknowledged, to have the words " calling himself," between brackets, to precede the assumed title.

XV. The same rule to be followed with respect to archbishops and bishops.

XVI. Christian names, included in parentheses, to follow the surname, and all to be written out in full, as far as they are known. In case of doubt, on this or any other point, when the librarian is directed to supply any information in cataloguing, a note of interrogation to follow in such a position as to indicate clearly the point on which any doubt is entertained.

XVII. An author's rank in society, in cases in which he enjoyed any eminent honorary distinction, or office for life, not lower than that of knight, admiral or general, to be stated in italics. Younger sons of dukes and marquesses, and all daughters of dukes, marquesses and earls, when not enjoying a distinct title, to have the designation Lord or Lady prefixed to the Christian name. All other younger branches of the nobility to have the word Hon. prefixed. The words Right Hon., in the same situation, to distinguish privy councillors. Knights to be indicated merely by the appellation Sir prefixed to their first name. Titles of inferior rank, whether ecclesiastical, military, or civil, to be given only when necessary to make a distinction between authors having the same surname and Christian name.

Proper names commencing with Mc. or M' to be entered under Mac, with cross-references from the other forms.

Where a person is referred to in a title-page by a description sufficiently clear to render his or her identity obvious, the proper name of such person to be adopted as a heading, whether the work be historical or otherwise.

XVIII. The title of the book next to be written, and that expressed in as few words, and those only of the author, as may be necessary to exhibit to the reader all that the author meant to convey in the titular description of his work; the original orthography to be preserved. The number of the edition to be stated when appearing in the title.

In cataloguing sermons, the text always to be specified. The date at which preached to be inserted when it differs from that of publication.

XIX. Any striking imperfection in a book to be carefully noted; and any remarkable peculiarity, such as that of containing cancelled or duplicate leaves, &c., to be stated.

XX. When the book is without a title-page, its contents to be concisely, but sufficiently, stated in the words of the head-title, preceded by the word *begin.* (*beginning*) in italics; if there be no head-title, in those of the colophon, preceded by the word *end.* (*ending*); and when the want of title is owing to an imperfection, the words taken from either head-title or colophon to be included between parentheses. If both head-title and colophon be wanting or insufficient, then some idea of the work to be briefly given in English, between brackets, and the edition so accurately described as to be easily identified without fear of mistake.

XXI. Whenever one or more separate works are mentioned in the title of any publication, as forming part of it, the same to be particularly noticed in cataloguing the principal publication; and, if not mentioned in the title-page, this information to be added to the title between brackets or parentheses, as the case may be.

XXII. All works in Oriental characters or languages to be separately catalogued in supplementary volumes, according to special rules to be framed. The Bible and its parts, however, in whatever language or characters, to be entered in the general catalogue as hereafter directed.

XXIII. Works in more languages than one, accompanied by the original, to be entered in the original only, unless the title be accompanied by a translation or translations, in which case such translation also to be given. If no original text occur, the first language used in the title to be preferred. In all cases the several languages used in the book to be indicated at the end of the title in italics.

XXIV. Works with a title in a language different from that used in the body of the book to be entered according to the above rule, merely stating at the end of the title, in italics, in what language the work is written.

XXV. The number of parts, volumes, fasciculi, or whatever may be the peculiar divisions of each author's work, to be next specified, in the words of the title.

XXVI. When nothing is said in the title respecting this point, if a work be divided into several portions, but the same pagination continue, or when the pages are not numbered, if the same register continue, the work to be considered as divided into parts; if the progressive number of the pages or the register be interrupted, then each series of pages or letters of the register to be designated as a volume.

XXVII. Then the place where the book was printed; and, in particular cases, as in the instance of early or very eminent typographers, the printer's name to be specified. Next the date: when no date or place is specified, then either or both to be given, if known to, or conjectured by, the librarian; but in these instances to be included in brackets. The form to follow, whether fol., 4to, 8vo, &c.

XXVIII. If an early printed book, and in Gothic or black letter, the circumstance to be mentioned at the end of the title, thus: —G. L. or B. L.

XXIX. If printed on vellum, satin, on large or fine paper, or if an *editio princeps* of a classical or very distinguished writer, who flourished before 1700, or if privately printed, or a fac-simile or reprint of an early edition; if only a small number of copies were struck off, or if there be any manuscript notes, these peculiarities to be stated.

XXX. If the author of the manuscript notes be known, this information to be added between brackets. If the volume belonged to some very distinguished personage, the fact to be recorded in few words at the end of the entry, also between brackets.

XXXI. An *editio princeps* to be designated by the words *ED. PR.* in italic capitals, at the end of the title. Manuscript notes to be indicated in italics at the end of the title, previous to the size of the volume, as follows:—*MS. NOTES.* If the notes be remarkably few, or the reverse, the circumstance to be noticed by prefixing to the above the word *FEW* or *COPIOUS*. Works printed *ON VELLUM* to be distinguished by these words, in small italic capitals, at the end of the title. The letters *L.P.* or *F.P.* in the same situation, to indicate copies on large or fine paper.

XXXII. Works published under initials, to be entered under the last of them: and should the librarian be able to fill up the blanks left, or complete the words which such initials are intended to represent, this to be done in the body of the title, and all the supplied parts to be included between brackets.

The rules applicable to proper names to be extended to initials.

XXXIII. When the author's name does not appear on the title or any other part of the work, the following rules to be observed. Anonymous publications, relating to any act, or to the life of a person whose name occurs on the title of a work, to be catalogued under the name of such person. The same rule to be followed with respect to anonymous publications addressed (not merely dedicated) to any individual whose name occurs on the title.

XXXIV. When no such name of a person appears, then that of any assembly, corporate body, society, board, party (sect under the English form of the name), or denomination, including all bodies exercising their profession or calling by commission, certificate, licence, or other authority granted by virtue of any law or charter, and also creeds, religious or political, appearing on the title to be preferred, subject to the arrangement of Rule IX.; and if no such name appear, then that of any country, province, city, town or place so appearing, to be adopted as the heading.

Proper name of a single colony to be taken, as *Barbadoes*, &c. Collective title of a colony to refer the work to the mother country, as West Indian Colonies, East Indian Possessions, to be catalogued under Great Britain, *Colonies*, &c. The colonies of Spain to be catalogued under Spain, *Colonies of Spain*. East and West Indies, *East Indies*, *West Indies*, according to the circumstances. America, East Indies, West Indies, &c. &c., to be adopted as a heading. Particular province, under such province, Lower or Upper House, &c.

Articles to be inquired of within an ecclesiastical district to be entered under the name of such district. Synods and ecclesiastical councils to be entered under the name of the place where held, without any sub-heading.

The word COUNCILS to be adopted as a heading, in whatever language the work may be written. All courts of justice including minor courts, as courts baron, leet, hundred courts, &c. to come under the name of the country.

Convocation generally under '*England, Church of, Convocation.*'

XXXV. If no name of any assembly or country, to be preferred as above, appear on the title, the name of the editor (if there be any), to be used as a heading; or, if no editor's name appear, that of the translator, if there be one. Reporters to be considered as editors.

Anonymous publications relating to armies to be catalogued under the countries to which the armies respectively belong. Regiments, or other divisions of an army, to follow the same rule (with a cross-reference from the name of such regiment or division), unless such regiment or division be named after some place or person, in which case the name of such person or place to be adopted, subject to Rule XXXVI.

The above to be subject to Rule XXXIII., and to be applied to Naval Armaments as far as practicable.

XXXVI. Adjectives formed from the name of a person, party, place or denomination, to be treated as the names from which they are formed.

XXXVII. If two names occur seeming to have an equal claim, the first to be chosen.

Reports of civil actions to be catalogued under the name of that party to the suit which stands first upon the title-page.

In criminal proceedings the name of the defendant to be adopted as a heading.

Trials relating to any vessel to be entered under the name of such vessel.

Patents for inventions to be entered under the names of the patentees.

The points of the compass adopted as headings.

Treaties to be entered under the country of the first contracting power. A preference to be given to England.

XXXVIII. In the case of anonymous works, to which none of the foregoing rules can be applied, the first substantive in the title (or if there be no substantive, the first word) to be selected as the heading. A substantive, adjectively used, to be taken in conjunction with its following substantive as forming one word; and the same to be done with respect to adjectives incorporated with their following substantive. The entries which may occur under the same heading, to succeed each other in strict alphabetical order.

XXXIX. Whenever the name of the author of an anonymous publication is known to, or conjectured by, the librarian, the same to be inserted at the end of the title, between brackets.

XL. Works without the author's name, and purporting to comment or remark on a work of which the title is set forth in that of such publication, to be catalogued under the same heading as the work remarked or commented upon.

XLI. In the case of pseudonymous publications, the book to be catalogued under the author's feigned name; and his real name, if discovered, to be inserted in brackets, immediately after the feigned name, preceded by the letters *i. e.*

XLII. Assumed names, or names used to designate an office, profession, party, or qualification of the writer, to be treated as real names. Academical names to follow the same rule. The works of an author not assuming any name, but describing himself by a circumlocution, to be considered anonymous.

Descriptions taken from the name of a country or place of habitation, as "Un François, Ein Zürcher," &c. to be translated, unless they be in Latin, or used as a proper name, as by "Anglus, Lipsiensis," &c.

XLIII. Works falsely attributed in their title to a particular person, to be treated as pseudonymous.

Continuations to be entered under the name of the original work, when printed with it; otherwise, under the name of the author.

XLIV. Works of several writers, collectively published, to be entered according to the following rules, and the separate pieces of the various authors included in the collection to be separately entered in the order in which they occur; excepting merely collections of letters, charters, short extracts from larger works, and similar compilations.

XLV. In any series of printed works, which embraces the collected productions of various writers upon particular subjects, such as Ugolini Thesaurus Antiq. Sacrarum, Gronovii Thesaurus Antiq. Græcarum, the work to be entered under the name of the editor.

Works of several authors published together, but not under a collective title, to be catalogued under the name of the first author, notwithstanding an editor's name may appear on the work.

XLVI. If the editor's name do not appear, the whole collection to be entered under the collective title, in the same manner as anonymous works.

In cataloguing collections without an editor's name, and having

RULES FOR CATALOGUING. xvii

a collective title, the heading to be taken from such collective title without reference to that portion of the title which may follow.

XLVII. General collections of laws, edicts, ordinances, or other public acts of a similar description, to be entered under the name of the state or nation in which or by whom they were sanctioned, signed, or promulgated. Collections extending only to one reign or period of supreme government by one person, as well as detached laws and documents separately enacted and issued, to be catalogued under the name of the person in whose name and by whose authority they are enacted or sanctioned, and, where enacted as sovereign of two or more independent states, the name of the principal state to be adopted; such names to be entered alphabetically under the principal entry of the state or nation, after the general collections. When more than one name occurs, the first to be preferred.

.XLVIII. Collections of laws, edicts, &c., of several countries or nations to be catalogued according to Rules XLV. and XLVI.

XLIX. The same to be done with respect to laws on one or more particular subjects, either merely collected or digested in some particular order, or used as text to some particular comment or treatise.

L. The names of translators or commentators to be stated in cataloguing and entering a work, if they occur in the title-page; and when they do not occur, but are known to or conjectured by the librarian, to be supplied between brackets.

LI. The works of translators to be entered under the name of the original author. The same rule to be observed with respect to the works of commentators, if the same be accompanied with the text complete.

LII. Translations to be entered immediately after the original, generally with only the indication of the language into which the version has been made, in italics; but if any material alteration in the title have been introduced, so much of the title of the translation to be given as may be deemed requisite, or a short explanation in English added, between brackets.

LIII. Commentaries unaccompanied by the text, to be entered under the commentator's name; if without a name, or with an assumed name, then according to the rules laid down for anonymous or pseudonymous works.

LIV. No work ever to be entered twice at full length. Whenever requisite, cross-references to be introduced.

LV. Cross-references to be divided into three classes, from

name to name, from name to work, and from work to work. Those of the first class to contain merely the name, title, or office of the person referred to as entered; those of the second, so much of the title referred to besides, as, together with the size and date, may give the means of at once identifying, under its heading, the book referred to; those of the third class to contain moreover so much of the title referred from, as may be necessary to ascertain the object of the reference.

LVI. Cross-references of the first class to be made in the following instances :—

From the titles of noblemen, and from the sees of archbishops or bishops, to the family name, or the first name under which the works of such personages are to be entered according to the foregoing rules.

LVII. From the family name of persons whose works are to be entered under the Christian or first name, to such Christian or first name; excepting in the case of sovereigns, or princes belonging to sovereign houses.

LVIII. From any surnames either spelt, or in any way used, in a manner differing from the form adopted in the principal entry, to such entry.

LIX. From any of the names or surnames used by an author besides that under which the principal entry is made, to the one so preferred.

LX. From the real to the assumed name of authors; adding *pseud.* to the entry referred to in the cross-reference.

LXI. Cross-references of the second or third class, according to circumstances, to be made in the following instances :—

From the names of editors, or of biographers who have prefixed an author's life to his works (provided such names appear in the book), to the principal entry. But not from contributors of separate articles.

LXII. From the names of authors of anonymous or pseudonymous works supplied in the title, as well as from the names of authors who have shared with another in writing a work, or have continued it, and also from the names of translators, commentators, or annotators, either appearing on the title, or supplied as above directed, to the main entry.

LXIII. From the name of any person the subject of any biography or narrative, to its author; stating briefly, in italics, after the name referred from, the peculiar designation of the biography in the work referred to ; or, if this cannot be done, using the nearest English word, in brackets and italics, that may give an idea of the object of the cross-reference.

In this description of cross-reference the first words of the title of the work referred to to be given, but not its date or size, so that the cross-reference may serve equally for all editions.

LXIV. From any name which may be reasonably conceived to have an equal claim to that selected for the principal entry, to such entry.

LXV. From any author, any whole work of whom or any considerable part of it may be the subject of a commentary, or notes, to the name of the commentator or annotator. No notice to be taken of the name of authors, fragments or inconsiderable parts of whose works are observed upon by the commentator or annotator.

LXVI. From any author whose works, or considerable part of them contained in a collection, are considered so important as to be distinctly specified in the entry of the collection itself, to the principal entry ; the volume, or part of the collection in which the article so referred to is found, to be specified.

Cross-references to be made from separate works forming part of a series of works published by a society, and catalogued according to Rule LXXX.

LXVII. From the names of authors whose entire works or any considerable part of them are included among the collected works of a polygraphic writer, or translator, to the principal entry.

LXVIII. From the name of a state or nation to which a collection of laws, entered under any other heading, belongs, to the main entry.

From the name of the superior of any ecclesiastical district who promulgates articles for inquiry to the name of such district.

From the name of any party to a civil action to the principal entry.

LXIX. Entries to be made in the following order :—

Cross-references to be placed at the beginning of the entry, from which they are made, in the alphabetical order of the entries referred to.

LXX. Collections of all the works of an author in their original language only, to be entered immediately after the cross-references ; the editions without date, and those of which the date cannot be ascertained even by approximation, to precede all those bearing date, or of which the date can be supplied either positively or by approximation. The latter to follow according to their date, whether apparent in any part of the book, or supplied. Editions by the same editor, or such as are expressly stated to follow a specific text or edition, and editions with the same notes or commentary, to succeed each other immediately in their chronological order after the entry of that which is, or is considered to be, the earliest.

LXXI. The text of the collected works, accompanied by a translation, to follow those having the text only, and in the same order.

LXXII. The translations of such collected works into the Latin language only to precede those in any other language in the above order; the Latin translations to be followed by those in English. Translations in any other language to follow according to the alphabetical order of the name of the language in English. If the volume contain two or more translations, without the text, the entry to be made according to the alphabetical order of the first of the languages employed. Translations into the same language, and their several editions, to be entered in conformity with the rules laid down for the entries of the originals.

LXXIII. Collections of two or more works of an author to be entered in the order and according to the rules laid down for the collections of all the works of a writer, after the translations of the whole works; such partial collections to precede, as are known or are supposed to contain the largest number of an author's works.

LXXIV. Selections, or collected fragments, from the works of an author, to follow the partial collections of his works, and to be entered according to the above rules.

LXXV. Separate works of an author to succeed each other alphabetically; the several editions and translations of each of them to be entered in the same manner as directed for the collected works of a writer.

LXXVI. Entire portions of a separate work to succeed the work from which they are taken, in the order above directed. If the whole work to which they belong do not occur, such portions to be entered after all the separate works, but according to the principles laid down for the latter.

LXXVII. Works not written by the person under whose name they are to be catalogued according to the foregoing rules, to be entered alphabetically as an appendix, and in chronological succession, when more than one article occurs in the same alphabetical series, after all the works of the person whose name is selected, if any occur in the catalogue. Volumes without date, or the date of which cannot be supplied, to be entered first.

LXXVIII. The same rule as to the alphabetical and chronological arrangement to apply to works entered under any other heading than the name of a person.

LXXIX. The Old and New Testament and their parts, to be catalogued under the general head " Bible," and arranged in the following order:—

1st. The Old and New Testaments in the original Hebrew and Greek only, chronologically arranged.

2nd. The same, in polyglot editions, which include the original texts; beginning with those editions which contain most translations.

3rd. The same, translated into other languages, but without the original; those editions to precede which contain most languages; then translations into one language only, arranged as directed in Rule LXXII.

4th. Editions, with comments, to follow those having the text only, in the same order and according to the same principles. Bibles accompanied by the same comment to follow each other immediately in chronological succession.

5th. The Old Testament only to be next entered, according to the same principles and rules.

6th. Detached parts of the Old Testament then to follow, in the same order in which they are arranged in the English authorized version of the Scriptures, and to be entered as directed for the whole Bible.

7th. The Apocrypha, as declared by the Church of England, to be next catalogued and entered according to the same rules.

8th. The New Testament to be next catalogued, and then its parts, according to the foregoing rules. Concordances and Harmonies to be entered in the Appendix to " Bibles."

9th. General cross-references to be made from the several names of the inspired writers, as well as from the names of the several parts of Scripture, to the general head "Bible." Particular cross-references to be made from the names of editors, commentators, translators, &c., to the precise entry under which the part of Holy Writ referred from in the cross-reference occurs.

10th. The names of parts of the Bible, as well as of inspired writers, to be expressed in the form adopted in the authorized English version of the Scriptures.

LXXX. All acts, memoirs, transactions, journals, minutes, &c., of academies, institutes, associations, universities, or societies learned, scientific, or literary, by whatever name known or designated, as well as works by various hands, *forming part of a series of volumes* edited by any such society, to be catalogued under the general name " Academies " and alphabetically entered, according to the English name of the country and towns at which the sittings of the society are held, in the following order.   The primary division to be of the four parts of the world in alphabetical succession, Australia and Polynesia being considered as appendixes to Asia ; the first subdivision to be of the various empires, kingdoms, or other independent governments into which any part of the world is divided, in alphabetical order ; and a second subdivision of each state to follow, according to the various cities or towns, alphabetically disposed, belonging to each state, in which any society of this description meets (other bodies under the name of the city or place where situated).   The acts, &c., of each society, when more than one meet at the same place, to be entered according to the name under which the society published its first work, in alphabetical series ; and the acts, memoirs, &c., of each society to be entered chronologically. Continuations to follow the original entry.

Works of the nature of periodical publications, issued by an academy to be entered under " Academies."

Institutions, societies, &c., not coming under the head " Academies," deriving their title from a proper name not being that of a country or place, to be entered under such proper name, as " Addenbrooke's Hospital."

The words "*forming part of a series of Volumes*" to be construed strictly, and to apply only to collective works, or to a series of works on one subject.

LXXXI. The same rule and arrangement to be followed for " Periodical Publications," which are to be catalogued under this general head, embracing reviews, magazines, newspapers, journals, gazettes, annuals, and all works of a similar nature, in whatever language and under whatever denomination they may be published.   The several entries under the last subdivision to be made in alphabetical order according to the first substantive occurring in the title.

Translations of periodicals to be entered under the place where the originals were published.

LXXXII. All almanacs, calendars, ephemerides, of whatever description they be, as well as their companions, appendixes, &c., to be entered under the general head "Ephemerides." The several works under this head to be entered alphabetically according to the first substantive occurring in the title.

Directories to be catalogued on their own merits, and not under any special head.

Calendars, to include periodical publications (excepting directories), each number of which contains information connected with a year to come, whether accompanied by an almanac or not. The mere insertion of an almanac not to bring a work under "Ephemerides." Law lists to be catalogued under the head, LAW LIST, with a cross-reference from the editor.

LXXXIII. There shall be cross-references from the name of any author, editor, or contributor to any of the above works, appearing in any of the title-pages of any of the volumes, as well as from the peculiar name or designation of any of the societies, from the place at which they hold their meetings, from any place forming part of the peculiar name of a journal, almanac, calendar, &c., from the name under which such publications are generally known, to the main entries of such works.

LXXXIV. Religious and military orders to be designated by the English name under which they are generally known, and entries to be made accordingly.

LXXXV. Anonymous catalogues, whether bearing the title catalogue or any other intended to convey the same meaning, to be entered under the head "Catalogues," subdivided as follows :— 1st. Catalogues of public establishments (including those of societies, although not strictly speaking *public*). 2nd. Catalogues of private collections, drawn up either for sale or otherwise (no cross-reference from possessor). 3rd. Catalogues of collections not for sale, the possessors of which are not known. 4th. General as well as special catalogues of objects, without any reference to their possessor. 5th. Dealers' catalogues. 6th. Sale catalogues not included in any of the preceding sections.

LXXXVI. Catalogues of the first subdivision to be entered under the name of the place at which the collection exists, as directed for Academies : those of the second, under the name of the collector or possessor, or if the name of the collector or possessor be not stated, under that of the place where the library, &c., is deposited, if mentioned in the catalogue: those of the third, in strict alphabetical order, according to the first substantive of the title: those of the fourth, to follow the same rule: those of the fifth, under the dealer's name: those of the sixth, strictly chronologically, supplying the year in brackets whenever omitted, but known to, or conjectured by, the librarian; and when it is impossible to ascertain the precise day and month, for catalogues coming under the same year, in strict alphabetical order before those having a precise date. Catalogues without any date, and the date of which cannot be supplied, to be entered at the beginning of this subdivision in strict alphabetical order, as just directed. With respect to mere dealers' and sale catalogues compiled since the beginning of the present century, such only to be catalogued and entered as may be considered of peculiar interest.

LXXXVII. Cross-references of the second class to be made from the name of the compiler of a catalogue (when supplied by the librarian, and other than the collector or possessor of a collection, a dealer or an auctioneer) to the principal entry.

LXXXVIII. Anonymous dictionaries of any description, including lexicons and vocabularies, to be catalogued under the general head " Dictionaries," and entered in strict alphabetical order according to the first substantive in the title, with cross-references from the author's name, when supplied.

Dictionaries having the name of the authors, or contributors on the title-page to be entered under the first name with cross-references. Names of contributors given otherwise than on the title not to be noticed. The editor's name to be adopted where the authors are not given on the title.

LXXXIX. The same rule to be applied to encyclopædias, the name of the editor of which does not appear on the title, and which shall be catalogued under the general head " Encyclopædias," with a cross-reference from the editor's name, when supplied in the principal entry, to such entry.

XC. Missals, Breviaries, Offices, Horæ, Prayer Books, Liturgies, and works of the same description (not compiled by private individuals and in their individual capacity, in which case they are to be catalogued and entered according to the general rules laid down for other works), to be entered under the general head " Liturgies," in one strict alphabetical series, according to the English denomination of the communion, sect, or religious order for whom they are specially intended; if drawn up for any particular church, congregation, or place of worship, then according to the English name peculiar to such church, congregation, or place of worship; if any work of this description occur not coming under either of these two classes, then the first substantive in the title to be preferred as a heading. Entries under the same heading to be made in strict alphabetical order. Catechisms and Confessions of Faith not to be catalogued under the head of Liturgies, but according to the general rules. The Liturgy of the Church of England to have a sub-heading of *Common Prayer*, and separate services that of *Prayers*.

XCI. Cross-references of the second class to be made from the peculiar name or designation of any of the churches, communions, sects, religious orders, or places of worship, as well as from the name under which any of the works mentioned in the preceding article is generally known, to the main entry.

Churches dedicated to St. Paul to be entered under PAUL, ST. The same rule to be followed in the case of Churches dedicated to other saints.

Places, such as towns, parishes, streets, &c., named after saints, to be entered under SAINT, as St. Pancras Parish.

Cathedrals named from the city to which they are attached, as Rochester Cathedral, &c., to be entered under ROCHESTER, &c., with cross-reference from the names of the saints to whom dedicated.

MAPS.

In the Map Catalogue the maps are entered under the name of the country, town, fort, or place represented; or if there are more countries or places than one mentioned in the title, then under the first, with cross-references from the rest, as well as from the names of places represented in side-maps. Cross-references are also made from authors' names; or failing authors', from editors', publishers', or engravers' names. All the headings are entered in the catalogue in one alphabetical series.

MUSIC.

The Catalogue of the collection of Music is in two parts, each in alphabetical order; one containing the titles and cross-references of music, the other, nothing but cross-references from the authors of words.

Music to be catalogued under the name of the composer, with cross-references from arrangers, adapters, &c., and in case of vocal music, from the authors of the words. The rules of the New General Catalogue [of Books] to regulate the forms of names.

The slips on which are written cross-references from the authors of words to be distinguished by a W, to prevent their being mixed with the others.

Collections of music by several composers to be entered under the name of the editor, if it appear; otherwise under the generic name of the music, or under the first substantive, with cross-references from the composers, authors, arrangers, &c., of the most important pieces. The names of oratorios, operas, &c., when they do not begin the title, to be inserted between brackets at the beginning of the title.

Titles and cross-references of pieces of music taken from any oratorio, opera, or larger work, to have the names of such work inserted between brackets, as in the foregoing rule.

Quadrilles, polkas, waltzes, fantasias, &c., founded on popular melodies, to be catalogued under the composers of such quadrilles, polkas, &c., with cross-references from the composers of the melodies.

Airs with variations to be entered under the composers of the airs, with cross-references from the composers of the variations.

Anonymous instrumental music to be catalogued under the English generic name of such music, as Polka, Waltz, Quadrille, March, &c., no account being taken of adjectives formed from proper names: for instance, the "Chinese Quadrilles" to be entered under "Quadrilles."

The first words of songs, preceded by the word "Begins," or "Beginning," to be supplied in brackets when they differ from the title.

In anonymous songs, the first word of the song to be taken as a heading, even if it be an article. The first few words of the song then to follow, after which the title in italics, cross-references being made from the title.

In cross-references from the authors of songs, the first words of the song are used. When these are the same as the title, they are not repeated after the heading referred to.

Songs of which the authors of the words appear, but not the composers of the music, to be entered under the first word of the song with a cross-reference from the author of the words.

The names of composers, authors of words, and the names of oratorios, operas, plays, entertainments, &c., from which pieces are taken, to be supplied in brackets when they do not appear on the piece of music.

Cross-references to be given from the titles of songs, overtures, or portions of operas or single pieces occurring in plays, &c., when the name of such opera or play does not appear upon the title.

Anonymous elementary works to be catalogued under the name of the instrument for which they are written.

THE BRITISH MUSEUM CLASSIFICATION.

The recent accessions of Printed Books in the Library of the British Museum are divided and arranged on the shelves in ten distinct Classes: viz. Class I, Theology; II, Jurisprudence; III, Natural History and Medicine; IV, Archæology and Arts; V, Philosophy; VI, History; VII, Geography; VIII, Biography; IX, Belles Lettres, and X, Philology. These ten Classes are subdivided and arranged on the shelves in five hundred and fifteen divisions, as follows:—

CLASS I, THEOLOGY.

1 Polyglot Bibles.
2 Hebrew Bibles.
3 Greek Bibles.
4 Latin Bibles.
5 French, Italian, Spanish, &c. Bibles.
6 German Bibles.
7 Dutch and Scandinavian Bibles.
8 English Bibles.
9 Bibles in Celtic Languages.
10 Slavonic Bibles.
11 Bibles in Oriental Languages.
12 American, Polynesian, &c. Bibles.
13 Concordances.
14 Commentaries on the entire Bible.
15 Commentaries on the Pentateuch.
16 Commentaries on other Historical Books.
17 Commentaries on the Psalms.
18 Commentaries on the Prophets and Hagiographa.
19 Commentaries on unfulfilled Prophecy.
20 Commentaries on the New Testament in general.
21 Commentaries on the Gospels and Acts.
22 Commentaries on the Epistles.
23 Liturgies of the Church of Rome and Eastern Churches.
24 Service-Books of the Diocese of Sarum.
25 English Liturgies.
26 Metrical Versions of the Psalms.
27 Hymns.
28 Private and Family Prayers.
29 Works on the Liturgy, Mass, &c.
30 Creeds and Catechisms.
31 Systems of Theology.

32 Theological Libraries.
33 Works of the Fathers.
34 Greek Fathers.
35 Latin Fathers.
36 Works of Foreign Divines (Southern Europe).
37 Foreign Divines (Northern Europe).
38 Works of Swedenborg and Boehme.
39 English Divines.
40 American Divines.
41 Mediæval Theologians.
42 Religious Controversy in Catholic Countries.
43 Religious Controversy in Germany.
44 Religious Controversy in Holland and Scandinavia.
45 Religious Controversy in Russia, &c.
46 Roman Catholic Controversy in England.
47 Roman Catholic Controversy in Scotland and Ireland.
48 Natural Theology.
49 Christian Evidences.
50 Works on the Jews.
51 Catholic Writers on Papal Supremacy, &c.
52 Catholic Writers on Confession, &c.
53 Catholic Writers on Priesthood and Monastic Orders.
54 Works on the Jesuits.
55 Tracts, etc. on Church of England.
56 Tracts, etc. Nonconformity in general.
57 Tracts, etc. Quakerism.
58 Tracts, etc. Church of Ireland.
59 Tracts, etc. Church of Scotland.
60 Tracts, etc. American Churches.
61 Tracts, etc. Missions.
62 Tracts, etc. Domestic Missions.
63 Works on the Trinity and Person of Christ.
64 Atonement and Justification.
65 Election and Grace.
66 Sacraments in general.
67 Baptism.
68 Lord's Supper.
69 Sabbath.
70 Universalism and Miscellaneous Theological Subjects.
71 Christian Practice and Edification.
72 Religious Fiction.
73 Religious Tracts.
74 Foreign Sermons.

75 Charges and Visitation Sermons.
76 Collected English Sermons.
77 Separate English Sermons.
78 Collected American Sermons.
79 Separate American Sermons.
80 Homiletics and Pastoral Duties.
81 Mythology.
82 Scriptures of non-Christian Religions.
83 Jewish History.
84 Christian Churches and Denominations.
85 History of the Early Church.
86 History of the Mediæval Church.
87 Ecclesiastical History of Italy.
88 Ecclesiastical History of Spain and Portugal.
89 Ecclesiastical History of France.
90 History of the Reformation in general.
91 Ecclesiastical History of Germany and Switzerland.
92 Ecclesiastical History of Netherlands.
93 Ecclesiastical History of Scandinavia.
94 Ecclesiastical History of Slavonic Countries.
95 Ecclesiastical History of England (Established Church).
96 Ecclesiastical History of England (Nonconformity).
97 Ecclesiastical History of Scotland.
98 Ecclesiastical History of Ireland.
99 Ecclesiastical History of America.
100 History of American and Polynesian Missions.
101 History of Asiatic and African Missions.
102 History of Roman Catholic Missions to Asia and Africa.
103 History of Religious Fraternities.
104 History of Freemasonry.
105 General Religious Biography.
106 Scripture Biography.
107 Lives of Saints.
108 Lives of Popes.
109 Lives of Cardinals.
110 Religious Biography. Southern Europe.
111 Religious Biography. Northern Europe.
112 Religious Biography. England.
113 Religious Biography. Scotland.
114 Religious Biography. Ireland.
115 Religious Biography. America.
116 Juvenile Religious Biography.
117 Theological Bibliography.

CLASS II, JURISPRUDENCE.

1 Papal Bulls.
2 History and Acts of Councils.
3 Canon Law.
4 English Ecclesiastical Law.
5 Scotch and Irish Ecclesiastical Law.
6 Law of Marriage.
7 Roman Law.
8 Mediæval Jurists.
9 Indian and Mohammedan Law.
10 Laws of the Italian Kingdom.
11 Laws of Northern Italy.

12 Laws of Tuscany.
13 Laws of the Papal States.
14 Laws of Naples and Sicily.
15 Laws of Spain and Portugal.
16 Laws of France.
17 Early German Law.
18 Laws of Austria.
19 Laws of Switzerland.
20 Laws of Southern Germany.
21 Laws of Northern Germany.
22 Laws of Prussia.

23 Laws of Modern German Empire.
24 Laws of Holland.
25 Laws of Belgium.
26 Laws of Scandinavia.
27 Laws of Russia.
28 Laws of Poland.
29 Elements of Jurisprudence.
30 General Questions of Jurisprudence.
31 Punishment of Crime.
32 Prison Discipline, &c.
33 Forensic Medicine.
34 Reports of English Law Cases.
35 Commentaries on English Law.
36 Commentaries on Equity.
37 Common Law Procedure.
38 Law of Real Property.
39 Law of Personal Relations.
40 Law of Legacies.
41 Law of Companies, Partnership, Patents, &c.

42 Law of Bankruptcy, County Courts, &c.
43 Municipal and Sanitary Law.
44 Criminal Law.
45 Trials.
46 Law of Ireland.
47 Law of Scotland.
48 Law of British Colonies.
49 United States Statutes.
50 United States Reports.
51 United States General Law.
52 United States. Laws of separate States (in alphabetical order).
53 Laws of South America.
54 Maritime Law.
55 Military Law.
56 Treaties and Conventions.
57 International Law.

CLASS III, NATURAL HISTORY AND MEDICINE.

1 Natural History in general.
2 Botany.
3 Horticulture.
4 Agriculture.
5 Mineralogy.
6 Geology.
7 Palæontology.
8 Zoology in general.
9 Mammalia.
10 Ornithology.
11 Herpetology.
12 Ichthyology.
13 Domestic Animals (with Veterinary Surgery).
14 Entomology.
15 Conchology, &c.
16 Dictionaries of Medicine.
17 Medical Principles and Practice.
18 Medical Theses.

19 Domestic Medicine, Dietetics, &c.
20 Physiology.
21 Phrenology, Animal Magnetism, &c.
22 Anatomy.
23 Pathology.
24 Therapeutics.
25 Mineral Waters.
26 Surgery.
27 Materia Medica.
28 Epidemics.
29 Diseases of Women and Children.
30 Diseases of special Parts of the Body.
31 Mental Disorders.
32 History of Medicine.
33 Tracts on Medical Subjects.
34 Climates, Endemic Diseases.
35 Hospitals.
36 Bill of Mortality.

CLASS IV, ARCHÆOLOGY AND ARTS.

1 Archæology.
2 Prehistoric and Mediæval Archæology.
3 Costumes.
4 Numismatics.
5 Fine Art in General.
6 Architecture.
7 Domestic Architecture.
8 Painting and Engraving.
9 Sculpture.

10 Music.
11 Field Sports.
12 Games of Chance.
13 Games of Skill.
14 Useful Arts.
15 Domestic Economy.
16 Industrial Exhibitions.
17 Publications of South Kensington Museum.

CLASS V, PHILOSOPHY.

1 Political Science.
2 Politics of India and the East.
3 Politics of Europe in general.
4 Politics of Turkey and Greece.
5 Politics of Italy.
6 Politics of Spain and Portugal.
7 Politics of France before Revolution.
8 Politics of France after Revolution.

9 Politics of Germany.
10 Politics of Austria and Hungary.
11 Politics of Scandinavia.
12 Politics of Slavonic Nations.
13 Politics of England before 1715.
14 Politics of England, 1715-1789.
15 Politics of England, 1789-1821.
16 Recent English Politics.

17 Politics of Scotland.
18 Politics of Ireland.
19 Politics of English Colonies.
20 Politics of Colonies of Foreign Nations.
21 Slavery.
22 Politics of the United States.
23 Politics of Spanish America.
24 Political Economy.
25 Finance.
26 Railway Administration.
27 Commerce.
28 Industrial Questions.
29 Public Charities.
30 Education.
31 Continental Schools, Universities, &c.
32 British Schools, Universities, &c.
33 American Schools, Universities, &c.
34 Moral Philosophy.
35 Marriage and Condition of Woman.
36 Peace, Duelling, Cruelty to Animals, &c.
37 Temperance.
38 Ancient Metaphysical Philosophy.
39 Modern Metaphysical Philosophy.

40 Logic.
41 History of Philosophy.
42 Arithmetic.
43 Mathematics.
44 Geometry.
45 Trigonometry.
46 Logarithms.
47 Astronomy.
48 Astrology.
49 Occult Sciences.
50 Spiritualism.
51 Physics.
52 Optics.
53 Meteorology.
54 Electricity.
55 Mechanics and Dynamics.
56 Hydrostatics and Hydraulics.
57 Nautical Sciences.
58 Arms and Military Engines.
59 Military Art.
60 Chemistry.
61 Spectral Analysis.
62 Photography.

CLASS VI, HISTORY.

1 Chronology.
2 Universal History.
3 History of Asia.
4 History of Asia, British India in particular.
5 History of Africa.
6 History of Europe in general.
7 History of Europe in the 18th century.
8 History of Europe in the 19th century.
9 Byzantine and Ottoman History, &c.
10 History of Italy.
11 History of Spain.
12 History of Portugal.
13 History of France in general.
14 History of France to the Revolution.
15 History of France, 1789-1847.
16 History of France, Recent.
17 History of Switzerland.
18 History of Austria.
19 History of the German Empire.
20 History of Southern Germany.
21 History of Northern Germany.
22 History of Prussia.
23 History of Holland.
24 History of Belgium.

25 History of Denmark.
26 History of Norway.
27 History of Sweden.
28 History of Russia.
29 History of Poland.
30 English History in general.
31 English History, Publications of Master of the Rolls.
32 Early English History.
33 English History under the Tudors and Stuarts.
34 English History, House of Brunswick.
35 Parliamentary Debates.
36 History of America in general.
37 History of Canada and West Indies.
38 History of the United States.
39 History of the United States, Separate States.
40 History of the United States, Congress.
41 History of Mexico and Central America.
42 History of South America.
43 History of Australia.
44 Heraldry.
45 Genealogy.
46 Pageants, Processions, &c.

CLASS VII, GEOGRAPHY.

1 Cosmography.
2 Ethnology.
3 Circumnavigations.
4 Voyages in two or more parts of the World.
5 Travels in (including Topography of) Eastern Asia.
6 Travels in Western Asia.
7 Travels in Africa.

8 Travels in Europe.
9 Travels in Turkey and Greece.
10 Travels in Italy in general.
11 Travels in Northern Italy.
12 Travels in Central Italy.
13 Travels in Southern Italy and Islands.
14 Travels in Spain and Portugal.
15 Travels in France.
16 Travels in Switzerland.

17 Travels in Austria.
18 Travels in Hungary, Bohemia, &c.
19 Travels in Germany in general.
20 Travels in Southern Germany.
21 Travels in Northern Germany.
22 Travels in Prussia.
23 Travels in Holland.
24 Travels in Belgium.
25 Travels in Scandinavia.
26 Travels in Russia, &c.
27 Travels in England in general.
28 Travels in London.
29 Travels in Northern England.
30 Travels in Southern and Western England.
31 Travels in Wales.
32 Travels in Scotland.
33 Travels in Ireland.
34 Travels in America in general.
35 Travels in the United States.
36 Travels in the Arctic Regions.
37 Travels in British America and West Indies.
38 Travels in South America.
39 Travels in Australasia and Polynesia.
40 Hydrography.

CLASS VIII, BIOGRAPHY.

1 Biographical Collections.
2 Classical and Oriental Biography.
3 Oriental Biography.
4 Italian Biography.
5 Spanish and Portuguese Biography.
6 Lives of French Sovereigns.
7 French Biography.
8 French Literary Biography.
9 Lives of German Sovereigns.
10 German Biography.
11 Dutch Biography.
12 Scandinavian Biography.
13 Slavonic Biography.
14 Collections of British Biography.
15 Lives of British Sovereigns.
16 Lives of Br. Statesmen and Commanders.
17 Miscellaneous British Biography.
18 Lives of British Men of Letters.
19 American Biography.
20 Latin Epistles.
21 Epistles in Languages of Southern Europe.
22 Epistles in Languages of Northern Europe (including English).

CLASS IX, BELLES LETTRES.

1 Classical Polygraphy.
2 Homer.
3 Greek Poets.
4 Latin Poets.
5 Greek Orators.
6 Latin Orator.
7 Modern Latin Poetry—Southern Europe.
8 Modern Latin Poetry—Northern Europe.
9 Collections of Italian Poetry.
10 Early Italian Poetry.
11 Dante.
12 Italian Poetry, 16th Century.
13 Italian Poetry, 17th Century.
14 Italian Poetry, 18th Century.
15 Italian Poetry, 19th Century.
16 Poetry in Italian Dialects.
17 Spanish Poetry.
18 Portuguese Poetry.
19 Early French Poetry.
20 Modern French Poetry.
21 Provençal and Patois Poetry.
22 Early German Poetry.
23 German Poetry of 18th Century.
24 German Poetry of 19th Century.
25 Dutch Poetry.
26 Scandinavian Poetry.
27 Slavonic and Hungarian Poetry.
28 Celtic Poetry.
29 Collections of English Poetry.
30 Works of Early English Poets.
31 Works of English Poets, 17th Century.
32 Works of English Poets, 18th Century.
33 Works of English Poets, 19th Century.
34 English Songs.
35 English Ballads, Chap-Books, &c.
36 English Poems of 16th Century.
37 English Poems of 17th Century.
38 English Poems of 18th Century.
39 English Poems of 19th Century, to 1830.
40 English Poems of 19th Century, from 1830 to 1850.
41 English Poems of 19th Century, since 1850.
42 American Poetry.
43 Greek Drama.
44 Latin Drama.
45 Modern Latin Drama.
46 Italian Drama.
47 Spanish Drama.
48 French Drama.
49 German Drama.
50 Dutch and Scandinavian Drama.
51 Russian Drama.
52 Shakspere.
53 English Drama, Collections.
54 English Drama, Separate Plays, 16th Century.
55 English Drama, Separate Plays, 17th Century.
56 English Drama, Separate Plays, 18th Century.
57 English Drama, Separate Plays, 19th Century.
58 American Drama.
59 Rhetoric.
60 Literary Criticisms and Æsthetics.

61 Literary History.
62 Typography.
63 Bibliography.
64 Catalogues.
65 Compendiums of General Knowledge.
66 Miscellaneous Libraries.
67 Encyclopædias.
68 Collected Works of Modern Latin Authors.
69 Collected Works of Italian Authors.
70 Spanish and Portuguese Authors.
71 French Authors.
72 German Authors.
73 Dutch and Scandinavian Authors.
74 Slavonic and Hungarian Authors.
75 Libraries of collected English Authors.
76 Collected works of English Authors.
77 Collected works of American Authors.
78 Speeches in Parliament and Congress.
79 Fables.
80 Proverbs.

81 Apophthegms and Anecdotes.
82 Satirical and Facetious Works.
83 Essays and Sketches.
84 Collections of Novels and Tales.
85 Folk Lore, Fairy Tales, &c.
86 Early Romances.
87 Italian Novels.
88 Spanish and Portuguese Novels.
89 French Novels.
90 German Novels.
91 Dutch and Scandinavian Novels.
92 Slavonic and Hungarian Novels.
93 Collected English Novels.
94 Waverley Novels.
95 Translations of English Novels.
96 Early English Novels.
97 Republications.
98 English Novels in general.
99 Minor Fiction.
100 American Novels.
101 Tales for Children.

CLASS X, PHILOLOGY.

1 Philology in general.
2 Semitic Languages.
3 Other Asiatic and African Languages.
4 American and Polynesian Languages.
5 Chinese and Japanese Languages.
6 Greek.
7 Latin.
8 Italian.
9 Spanish and Portuguese.

10 French.
11 German.
12 Dutch and Scandinavian.
13 Slavonic.
14 Celtic.
15 English.
16 Phonography.
17 Books for the Blind.

RECAPITULATION.

CLASS I, Theology 117
CLASS II, Jurisprudence 57
CLASS III, Natural History and Medicine 36
CLASS IV, Archæology and Arts . . 17
CLASS V, Philosophy 62
CLASS VI, History 46

CLASS VII, Geography 40
CLASS VIII, Biography 22
CLASS IX, Belles Lettres 101
CLASS X, Philology 17

Total Nº of Divisions   515

CATALOGUE OF AMERICAN BOOKS
IN THE LIBRARY OF THE
BRITISH MUSEUM.

Chriſtmas, 1856.

BBOT, HULL. The duty of God's people to pray for the peace of Jerusalem.. A Sermon [on Psalm cxxii. 6, 7] on occasion of the rebellion in Scotland. Preached at Charlestown in New England, Jan. 12, 1745-6. Boston, 1746. 8°

ABBOT, JOEL. Trial of lieut. J. Abbot by the General naval court martial. on allegations made against him by Capt. D. Porter, Navy Commissioner. Reported by F. W. Waldo .... To which is added an appendix, containing sundry documents in relation to the management of affairs on the Boston Station. Boston, 1822. 8°

ABBOTT, JACOB. The little Philosopher, for schools and families, *etc.* Boston, 1833. 12°

2 THE TEACHER; or, moral influences employed in the instruction and government of the young; *etc.* Boston, 1833. 12°

3 A SUMMER in Scotland. With engravings. New York, 1848. 12°

4 HISTORY of Alexander the Great. New York [1848]. 12°

5 HISTORY of King Charles the First of England. N. Y. [1848]. 12°

6 HISTORY of King Charles the Second of England. New York [1849]. 12°

7 HISTORY of Queen Elizabeth. New York [1849]. 12°

8 HISTORY of Hannibal the Carthagenian. New York [1849]. 12°

9 HISTORY of Julius Cæsar. New York [1849]. 12°

10 HISTORY of Mary Queen of Scots. New York [1849]. 12°

11 HISTORY of William the Conqueror. New York [1849]. 12°

12 HISTORY of Darius the Great. New York [1850]. 12°

13 HISTORY of Xerxes the Great. New York [1850]. 12°

14 HISTORY of Romulus. With engravings. New York, 1852. 12°

15 MARCO Paul's Voyages and Travels. Six Volumes. Vol. I. In New York. II. On the Erie Canal. III. In the Forests of Maine. IV. In Vermont. V. In Boston [*wanting*]. VI. At the Springfield Armory [*wanting*]. New York, 1852. 12°

B

16 YOUNG Christian Series. In four volumes, very greatly improved and enlarged. Vol. I. The Young Christian [wanting]. II. The Corner Stone, [wanting]. III. The Way to do good. IV. Hoaryhead and M'Donner [wanting]. New York, 1852. 8°

17 RODOLPHUS; A Franconian Story; by the author of the Rollo Books. New York, 1852. 16°

18 ROLLO on the Atlantic. London, [Boston printed], 1854. 8vo.

19 ROLLO in Paris. London [Boston printed], 1854. 12mo.

ABBOTT, JACOB and CHARLES EDWARD. The Mount Vernon Reader designed for middle claſses. Boston, 1839. 12°

2 THE MOUNT Vernon Reader; a course of leſsons designed for senior claſses. Boston, 1840. 12°

3 THE MOUNT Vernon Reader; a course of reading leſsons, etc. Boston, 1843. 12°

4 THE MOUNT Vernon Arithmetic. Part I. Elementary. Second Edition. New York, 1846. 12°

ABBOTT, JOHN STEVENS CABOT. The Young Astronomer; or, the facts developed by modern astronomy, collected for the use of schools, etc. New York, 1846. 12°

2 HISTORY of Madame Roland. New York [1850]. 12°

3 KINGS and Queens; or, Life in the Palace: consisting of historical sketches of Josephine and Maria Louisa, Louis Philippe, Ferdinand of Austria, Nicholas, Isabella II., Leopold, and Victoria. New York, 1850. 12°

ABBOTT, WILLIAM, Dramatic writer. Swedish Patriotism; or, the signal fire; a melodrama, in two acts, etc. [the dialogue in prose]. New York, 1823. 12°

ABEEL, DAVID. Journal of a residence in China, and the neighbouring countries, from 1829 to 1833. New York, 1834. 8vo.

2 THE MISSIONARY Convention at Jerusalem; or an exhibition of the claims of the world to the Gospel. New York, 1838. 12°

ABELL, MRS. L. G. Woman in her various relations; containing practical rules for American females, etc. New York, 1851. 12°

2 THE SKILFUL Housewife's Book: or complete guide to domestic cookery. . . . With valuable additions by an English Housekeeper. Thirty-fifth thousand. New York, 1853. 8°

ABERCROMBIE, JOHN, M. D. The Philosophy of the Moral Feelings. From the last Edinburgh edition; with questions for the examination of Students. New York, 1843. 12°

2 INQUIRIES concerning the Intellectual Powers, and the investigation of Truth. From the last Edinburgh edition. New York, 1846. 12°

ABERCROMBIE, R. M. Ecclesiastical Mnemonica, or aid to the memory in storing a correct knowledge of ecclesiastical dates, etc. New York, 1848. 12°

ABERT, JOHN J. Report . . . in reference to the Canal to connect the Chesapeake and Ohio Canal with the City of Baltimore. [With a map.] Washington, 1838. 8°

ABERT, JOHN J. and KEARNEY, JAMES. Report of J. J. Abert and J. Kearney, upon an examination of the Chesapeake and Ohio Canal, from Washington City to the "Point of Rocks," made by order of the Secretary of war. Washington, 1831. 8°

ABOLITION. Abolition a Sedition. By a northern man. Philadelphia, 1839. 12mo.

ABRAHAM, THE PATRIARCH. History of the Patriarch Abraham. Philadelphia, 1828. 12mo.

ACADEMICUS. A Friendly Debate; or, a Dialogue between Academicus and Sawney [W. Douglaſs, M.D.] and Mundungus, two eminent Physicians, about some of their late performances. Boston, 1722. 8vo.

ACADEMIES; COLLEGES;
LIBRARIES; LEARNED SOCIETIES; LI-
TERARY AND SCIENTIFIC INSTITUTIONS,
etc. See

ACADEMY of Medicine; Philadelphia.
ACADEMY of Natural Sciences; Phil.
ALBANY Female Academy; Albany.
ALBANY Institute; Albany, New York.
See SOCIETY for the Promotion of
Agriculture, etc.
AMERICAN Academy of Arts and
Sciences; Boston.
AMERICAN Academy of the Arts; New
York.
AMERICAN and Foreign Bible Society;
New York.
AMERICAN Antiquarian Society; Wor-
cester, Maſſachusetts.
AMERICAN Anti-Slavery Society.
AMERICAN Art Union; New York.
AMERICAN Aſſociation for the Ad-
vancement of Education.
AMERICAN Aſſociation for the Ad-
vancement of Science.
AMERICAN Asylum at Hartford for
the Deaf and Dumb.
AMERICAN Baptist Home Miſſion So-
ciety; New York.
AMERICAN Baptist Publication So-
ciety; New York.
AMERICAN Bible Society; New York.
AMERICAN Board of Commiſſioners
for Foreign Miſſions; Boston.
AMERICAN Colonization Society;
Washington.
AMERICAN Education Society; Boston.
AMERICAN Ethnological Society; New
York.
AMERICAN Geographical and Statisti-
cal Society; New York.
AMERICAN Institute; New York.
AMERICAN Institute of Instruction;
Boston.
AMERICAN Literary, Scientific and
Military Academy; Norwich, Vt.
AMERICAN Oriental Society; Boston.
AMERICAN Peace Society; Boston.
AMERICAN Philosophical Society; Phil.
AMERICAN Seamen's Friend Society.
AMERICAN Shipwreck Society.
AMERICAN Society for Meliorating the
Condition of the Jews; New York.

AMERICAN Society for Educating Pious
Youth for the Gospel Ministry;
afterwards AMERICAN Education
Society; which see.
AMERICAN Statistical Aſſociation; Bos-
ton.
AMERICAN Temperance Society;
Boston.
AMERICAN Tract Society; Boston.
AMHERST College; Amherst, Maſſa-
chusetts.
ANDOVER Theological Seminary; An-
dover, Maſſachusetts.
ASSOCIATION of American Geologists
and Naturalists.
ASTOR Library; New York.
AUBURN Theological Seminary.
BAPTIST Board of Foreign Miſſions.
BOARD of Agriculture of the State of
New York; Albany.
BOSTON Academy of Music.
BOSTON Baptist Aſſociation.
BOSTON Society of Natural History.
BOWDITCH Library; Boston.
BOWDOIN College; Brunswick, Maine.
BRISTOL Collegiate Institute; Bristol,
Pennsylvania.
BROWN University; Providence.
BURLINGTON College; Burlington,
New Jersey.
BURLINGTON College. See UNIVER-
SITY of Vermont.
CATALOGUES of Libraries.
CHARLESTON Library Society:
Charleston, South Carolina.
CHESTER County Cabinet of Natural
Sciences; West Chester, Pennsyl-
vania.
CHRISTIAN Alliance; New York.
CINCINNATI Astronomical Society.
COLONIZATION Society of the City of
New York.
CONNECTICUT Academy of Arts and
Sciences; New Haven.
DARTMOUTH College; Hanover, New
Hampshire.
DICKINSON College; Carlisle, Penn-
sylvania.
DORCHESTER Antiquarian and Histori-
cal Society.
ESSEX South District Medical So-
ciety; Salem, Maſſachusetts.

EAST India Marine Society; Salem.

FEMALE Miſsionary Society of the Western Diſtrict; Utica, New York.

FOREIGN Evangelical Society; New York.

FRANKLIN College; Athens, Georgia.

FRANKLIN Institute; Philadelphia.

GENEVA College; Geneva, New York.

GEOLOGICAL Society of Pennsylvania; Philadelphia.

GEORGETOWN College; Georgetown, District of Columbia.

GEORGIA Female College; Macon.

HAMILTON College; Clinton, N. York.

HAMILTON Literary and Theological Institution.

HARVARD University; Cambridge.

HISTORICAL Society of Pennsylvania; Philadelphia.

HISTORICAL and Philosophical Society of Ohio; Cincinnati.

HORTICULTURAL Society of Pennsylvania; Philadelphia.

JEFFERSON College; Canonsburg, Pennsylvania.

LITERARY and Philosophical Society; New York.

LYCEUM of Natural History; New York.

MACLURIAN Lyceum; Philadelphia.

MAINE Historical Society; Portland.

MANHATTEN College; New York.

MARYLAND Academy of the Fine Arts; Baltimore.

MARYLAND Historical Society; Baltimore.

MASSACHUSETTS Anti-Slavery Society. See NEW England Anti-Slavery Society.

MASSACHUSETTS Historical Society; Boston.

MASSACHUSETTS Medical Society; Boston.

MASSACHUSETTS Society for Promoting Agriculture.

MEDICAL Society; New Haven.

MEDICAL Society; New York.

MERCANTILE Library Aſsociation; Baltimore.

MERCANTILE Library Aſsociation; Boston.

MERCANTILE Library Aſsociation; New York.

MIAMI University; Oxford, Ohio.

MICHIGAN State Agricultural Society.

MIDDLEBURY College; Middlebury, Vermont.

NATIONAL Academy of Design; New York.

NATIONAL Eclectic Medical Aſsociation; Rochester, New York.

NATIONAL Institution for the Promotion of Science; Washington.

NATIONAL Observatory; Washington.

NEWARK College; Newark, Delaware.

NEW ENGLAND Anti-Slavery Society; Boston: afterwards MASSACHUSETTS Anti-Slavery Society.

NEW ENGLAND Institution for the Education of the Blind; Boston: afterwards PERKINS Institution.

NEW ENGLAND Historic Genealogical Society; Boston.

NEW HAMPSHIRE Historical Society; Concord, New Hampshire.

NEW JERSEY College; Princeton, New Jersey.

NEW JERSEY Historical Society; Newark, New Jersey.

NEW YORK State Library; Albany.

NEW YORK Ecclesiological Society; New York.

NEW YORK Historical Society; New York.

NEW YORK Society Library; New York.

NEW YORK State Agricultural Society; Albany.

NORTHERN Baptist Education Society; Boston.

PENNSYLVANIA Society for promoting the Culture of Mulberry and the raising of Silk Worms; Philadelphia.

PERIODICAL Publications.

PERKINS Institution and Maſsachusetts Asylum for the Blind. See NEW ENGLAND Institution, etc.

PHI Beta Kappa Society (Φ. B. K.)

PHILADELPHIA SOCIETY for promoting Agriculture. See SOCIETY for promoting Agriculture, Philadelphia.

PHILADELPHIA Medical Society.

PRINCETON College. See NEW JERSEY College.

PRISON Discipline Society; Boston.

PROTESTANT Episcopal Historical Society; New York.

PROVIDENCE Athenæum; Providence, Rhode Island.

PSI Upsilon Society.

RHODE Island Historical Society; Providence, Rhode Island.

RUTGERS College; New Brunswick, New Jersey.

SALEM Athenæum; Salem.

SEVENTY-SIX Society; Philadelphia.

SMITHSONIAN Institution; Washington.

SOCIETY for Promoting Agriculture; Philadelphia.

SOCIETY for the Promotion of Agriculture, Arts and Manufacture; New York: afterwards, SOCIETY for the promotion of useful Arts; and subsequently, ALBANY INSTITUTE.

SOUTH CAROLINA. Agricultural Society of South Carolina.

TRANSYLVANIA University; Lexington, Kentucky.

UNION College; Schenectady, New York.

UNITED States Military Academy; West Point, New York.

UNIVERSITY of Alabama; Tuscaloosa.

UNIVERSITY of Maryland; Baltimore.

UNIVERSITY of Nashville; Nashville, Tennessee.

UNIVERSITY of North Carolina; Chapel Hill, North Carolina.

UNIVERSITY of Pennsylvania; Phil.

UNIVERSITY of the City of New York.

UNIVERSITY of the State of New York.

UNIVERSITY of Vermont; Burlington.

VIRGINIA Historical and Philosophical Society; Richmond, Virginia.

WASHINGTON College; Washington, Pennsylvania.

WASHINGTON College; Hartford.

WASHINGTON College; Chestertown, Maryland.

WATERVILLE College; Waterville, Maine.

WESLEYAN University; Middletown, Connecticut.

WESTERN Literary Institution; Cincinnati, Ohio.

WESTERN Reserve College; Hudson, Ohio.

WILLIAMS College; Williamstown, Massachusetts.

WISCONSIN State Agricultural Society.

YALE College; New Haven, Conn.

YOUNG Men's Institute; Hartford.

ACADEMY OF MEDICINE. Proofs of the origin of the Yellow Fever, in Philadelphia and Kensington, in . . 1797, from domestic exhalation, etc. In two letters, etc. Philadelphia, 1798. 8vo.

ACADEMY OF NATURAL SCIENCES, PHILADELPHIA. Journal. Vol. 1-6 and 7, part I. Philadelphia, 1817-1834. 8vo.

2 PROCEEDINGS. Vol. 4. Philadelphia, 1848-1850. 8vo.

3 REPORT of the Transactions of the Academy of Natural Sciences of Philadelphia during the years 1827 and 1828. Submitted by S. G. Morton. Philadelphia, 1829. 8°

ACTON; or, the Circle of Life. A collection of thoughts and observations, designed to delineate life, man, and the world. New York, 1849. 12°

ADAM, ALEXANDER. Adam's Latin Grammar: with numerous additions and improvements . . . . by C. D. Cleveland. Philadelphia, 1836. 12°

ADAM, WILLIAM, of Boston. The Law and Custom of Slavery in British India. In a series of letters to T. F. Buxton, Esq. Boston, 1840. 12°

ADAMS, A.C. Waiting upon God, the Way to secure our Country's Welfare. A Sermon [on Isa. xxx. 15]. Portland, 1845. 8vo.

ADAMS, ABIGAIL. Journal and correspondence of Miss Adams [afterwards Mrs. Smith] daughter of John Adams, second President of the United States. Written in France and England, in 1785. Edited by her daughter (C. A. de Windt). 2 vol. New York, 1841-2. 12°

ADAMS, CHARLES BAKER. First (Second and Third) Annual Report on the Geology of the State of Vermont. 3 Parts. Burlington, Vt. 1845-6. 8°

ADAMS, CHARLES, *Rev.* A System of English Grammar; constructed upon the basis of Murray's grammar, *etc.* Boston, 1838. 12°

ADAMS, DANIEL, *M.B.* The Thorough Scholar: or, the Nature of Language, with the reasons, principles and rules of English grammar, *etc.* Third edition. Montpelier, Vt. 1814. 12°

2 THE UNDERSTANDING Reader: or, Knowledge before Oratory. Being a new selection of lessons, *etc.* Tenth edition, improved. Leicester, [Mass.] 1821. 12°

3 ADAMS' new Arithmetic . . . Designed for the use of schools and academies in the United States. Keene, N. H. 1842. 12°

ADAMS, FREDERIC A. Arithmetic, in two parts . . . For common and high schools. Lowell, 1846. 12°

ADAMS, HANNAH. A summary History of New England . . . comprehending a general sketch of the American war. Dedham, [Mass.] 1799. 8°

2 A MEMOIR of Miss Hannah Adams written by herself; with additional notices, by a friend. [Edited by A. N. and J. T.] Boston, 1832. 12°

ADAMS, J. G. Our Day; a gift for the times. Edited by J.G.Adams. Boston, 1848. 12°

ADAMS, JASPER. Elements of Moral Philosophy. N. York, 1837. 8°

ADAMS, JOHN, *Sergeant at law.* A Treatise on the Principles and Practice of the action of Ejectment, and the resulting action for Mesne Profits. With notes of the decisions made by the . . Courts of the United States . . . together with the statutory provisions . . . of New York; and precedents of entries, pleadings and process adapted thereto, by J. L. Tillinghast. To which are added, annotations and references to more recent American decisions, by T. W. Clerke . . carefully collated . . . Together with additional notes of decisions in the Courts of the several United States, to the present time, by W. Hogan. New York, 1846. 8°

ADAMS, JOHN, *The Second President of the United States of America.*

1 THE WORKS of John Adams, . . . with a Life of the Author, notes and illustrations, by his grandson, C. F. Adams. Vol. II. to V. Large paper. Boston, 1850-51. 8°

2 TWENTY-SIX Letters upon interesting subjects, respecting the Revolution of America. New York, 1789. 8vo.

3 A DEFENCE of the Constitutions of Government of the United States of America, against the attack of M. Turgot, in his Letter to Dr. Price; March 1778. Third edition. 3 vols. Philadelphia, 1797. 8°

4 FOUR Letters: being an interesting correspondence between . . John Adams . . and Samuel Adams, late governor of Massachusetts, on the important subject of government. Boston, 1802. 8°

5 CORRESPONDENCE of the late President Adams. Originally published in the Boston Patriot. In a series of letters. No. 1 to 10. Boston, 1809. 8°

6 NOVANGLUS and Massachusettensis; or, political essays, published in . . . 1774 and 1775, on the principal points of controversy between Great Britain and her colonies; the former by J. Adams, the latter by J. Sewall. . . . To which are added, . . . letters lately written by President Adams to the Hon. W. Tudor; some of which were never before published. Boston, 1819. 8°

7 CORRESPONDENCE between . . J. Adams . . and the late W. Cunningham . . beginning in 1803, and ending in 1812. [Edited by E. M. Cunningham.] Boston, 1823. 8°

8 LETTERS of J. Adams, addressed to his wife. Edited by his grandson, C. F. Adams. 2 vol. Bost. 1841. 12°

9 A SELECTION of Eulogies, pronounced in the several States, in honour of J. Adams and T. Jefferson. [By J. Tyler, C. Cushing, etc., etc.] Hartford, 1826. 8°

ADAMS, JOHN DAY. The Charter Oak, and other poems. New York, 1839. 12°

ADAMS, JOHN QUINCY, The Sixth President of the United States of America.

1 AN ORATION, pronounced July 4, 1793, at . . . . . Boston, in commemoration of the anniversary of American Independence. Second Edition. Boston, 1793. 8°

2 AN ORATION, delivered at Plymouth, [in Maſſachusetts] Dec. 22, 1802, at the anniversary commemoration of the first landing of our ancestors at that place. Boston, 1802. 8°

3 AN ORATION, delivered at Plymouth, Dec. 22, 1802, at the anniversary commemoration of the first landing of our ancestors, at that place. Plymouth, [Maſſ.] 1820. 8°

4 AN ADDRESS to the Members of the Maſſachusetts Charitable Fire Society, at their annual meeting, May 28, 1802. Boston, 1802. 8°

5 AN INAUGURAL Oration, delivered at the author's installation, as Boylston profeſſor of rhetorick and oratory, at Harvard University, in Cambridge, Maſſachusetts, . . . 12 June, 1806. Boston, 1806. 8°

6 LETTER to the Hon. H. G. Otis, on the present State of our national Affairs: with remarks upon Mr. Pickering's Letter to the Governor of the Commonwealth. Boston, 1808. ` 8°

7 A LETTER to the Hon. H. G. Otis . . . . on the present State of our national Affairs; with remarks upon Mr. Pickering's Letter to the Governor of the Commonwealth. Second Edition. Boston, 1808. 8°

8 LECTURES on Rhetoric and Oratory, delivered in Harvard University. 2 vol. Cambridge, 1810. 8vo.

9 REPORT upon Weights and Mea-

sures. . . Prepared in obedience to a resolution of the Senate (of the United States) of the third of March, 1817. Washington, 1821. 8°

10 AN ADDRESS delivered . . . on the occasion of reading the Declaration of Independence, on the fourth of July, 1821. Washington, 1821. 8vo.

11 THE DUPLICATE Letters, the Fisheries and the Miſſiſſippi. Documents relating to transactions at the negotiation of Ghent. Collected and published by J. Q. Adams. Washington, 1822. 8°

12 CORRESPONDENCE between J. Q. Adams, . . . and several citizens of Maſſachusetts [H. G. Otis and others], concerning the charge of a design to diſſolve the Union alleged to have existed in that State. Boston, 1829. 8°

13 AN ORATION addreſſed. to the Citizens of the town of Quincy, on the fourth of July, 1831, the fifty-fifth anniversary of the independence of the United States of America. Boston, 1831. 8°

14 AN EULOGY on the Life and Character of James Monroe, Fifth President of the United States, delivered at . . Boston, . 25 Aug. 1831. Boston, 1831. 8°

15 DERMOT Mac Morrogh, or, The Conquest of Ireland; an historical tale of the twelfth century. In four cantos. Boston, 1832. 8°

16 DERMOT Mac Morrogh, or, The Conquest of Ireland; an historical tale of the twelfth century. In four cantos. Second Edition. Boston, 1832. 8vo.

17 LETTERS to Edward Livingston, General Grand High Priest of the General Grand Royal Arch Chapter of the United States, etc. [on the Masonic Institution, etc.] [Boston, 1833.] 12°

18 SPEECH, suppreſſed by the previous question [being put and carried] . . . on the removal of the public deposites, and its reasons; [intended to be addreſſed to the House of Representatives, April, 1834.] Washington, 1834. 8°

19 Supplement to the Daily Advertiser and Patriot: Speech [intended to be delivered in the House of Representatives, but] suppreſsed by the previous question [having been put and carried,] . . on the removal of the public deposites and its reasons. [Washington, 1834.] 8°

20 Oration on the Life and Character of Gilbert Mottier de Lafayette, delivered at the request of both Houses of the Congreſs of the United States, before them, . . 31 Dec. 1834. New York, 1835. 8°

21 An Eulogy on the Life and Character of James Madison, fourth President of the United States, delivered at Boston, Sept. 27, 1836. Boston, 1836. 8°

22 An Oration delivered before the inhabitants . . of Newburyport, . . on the sixty-first anniversary of the Declaration of Independence, July 4, 1837. [With an appendix.] [Newburyport, 1837.] 8°

23 Letters from J. Q. Adams to his constituents of the twelfth congressional district in Maſsachusetts [relative to the proceedings of the House of Representatives on the presentation by him of certain anti-slavery petitions]. To which is added his Speech in Congreſs delivered February 9, 1837. [With a preface and two poems against Slavery by J. G. Whittier.] Boston, 1837. 8°

24 Speech of J. Q. Adams . . . upon the right of the people . . to petition; on the freedom of speech and of debate in the House of Representatives of the United States; on the resolutions of seven State Legislatures, and the petitions . . relating to the annexation of Texas to this Union. Washington, 1838. 8°

25 The Jubilee of the Constitution, a discourse, etc. New York, 1839. 8°

26 Speech . . . in relation to the Navy Pension Fund; delivered in the House of Representatives, . Dec. 28, 1840. [Washington, 1840.] 8°

27 Letters on the Masonic Institution. Boston, 1847. 8vo.

28 Letters of J. Q. Adams to his Son, on the Bible and its Teachings. Auburn, 1850. 16°

29 The Lives of J. Madison and J. Monroe, fourth and fifth Presidents of the United States. With historical notices of their administrations. Rochester, Buffalo [printed] 1850. 12°

30 Remarks on the Hon. J. Q. Adams's Review of Mr. Ames's works, with some strictures on the views of the author. Boston, 1809. 8°

31 A Vindication of Mr. Adams's Oration. Concord, N. H. 1821. 8°

32 Token of a Nation's Sorrow: Addreſses in the Congreſs of the United States, and funeral solemnities on the death of J. Q. Adams, etc. [including a funeral sermon by R. R. Gurley.] Washington, 1848. 8°

ADAMS, John Quincy, and CONDICT, Lewis. Report of the minority of the Committee on Manufactures, submitted to the House of Representatives of the United States, Feb. 28, 1833. By J. Q. Adams and Lewis Condict. Boston, 1833. 8°.

ADAMS, John S. 5000 Musical Terms: a complete Dictionary of . . . such words, phrases, abbreviations, and signs as are to be found in the works of . . . musical composers . . . To which is added a treatise on playing the organ or pianoforte by figures, etc. Boston, [1851] 12°

ADAMS, Josiah. Letter to L. Shattuck, Esq. of Boston . . . in vindication of the claims of Capt. J. Davis, of Acton, to his just share in the honors of the Concord Fight. Also, depositions of witneſses, etc. [In answer to L. Shattuck's " History of Concord." Boston, 1850. 8°

ADAMS, Moses. A Sermon [on Matt. xiv. 12]. Preached . . . Dec. 30, 1802, at the funeral of Rev. P. Wright . . . To which is added, the character of the deceased, by the Rev. D. Chaplin. Boston, 1803. 8vo.

2 A Sermon [on Eccles. vii. 1.] . . .

occasioned by the death of Col. J. Edwards. Boston, 1804. 8vo.

ADAMS, NATHANIEL. Reports of cases argued and determined in the Superior Court of Judicature for the State of New Hampshire. Sept. 1816 to Feb. 1819: [vol. 1.] By N. Adams. (Feb. 1819 to May, 1823: vol. 2. collected by W. M. Richardson and L. Woodbury. Sept. 1823 to Jan. 1832: vol. 3-5. Feb. 1832 to July, 1834: vol. 6 published by B. B. French. Dec. 1834 to July, 1841: vol. 7-11.) 11 vol. Exeter, Chester, Newport and Concord. 1819-44. 8°

2 ANNALS of Portsmouth, comprising a period of two hundred years from the first settlement of the town; with biographical sketches of a few of the . . . inhabitants. Portsmouth, 1825. 8°

ADAMS, NEHEMIAH, D. D. A Sermon [on 1 Samuel xxv. 1] preached . . . the Sabbath after the interment of Hon. Daniel Webster. Second edition. Boston, 1852. 8°

ADAMS, WILLIAM. The Elements of Christian Science, a Treatise upon Moral Philosophy and Practice. Philadelphia, 1850. 8°

ADAMS, WILLIAM. A Discourse [on Heb. xi. 4] on the life and services of Professor Moses Stuart, etc. New York, 1852. 8vo.

ADDICKS, BARBARA O'SULLIVAN. Essay on Education, in which the subject is treated as a natural science, in a series of familiar Lectures. With notes. New York, 1837. 8°

ADDINGTON, L. A Digest of the Revenue Laws of the United States; wherein are arranged, under distinct heads, the duties of all persons connected with the imports. To which is added, an Appendix containing the Forms and Oaths. Philadelphia, 1804. 12mo.

ADDISON, ALEXANDER. Reports of Cases in the County Courts of the

Fifth Circuit, and in the High Court of Errors and Appeals, of the State of Pennsylvania [Sept. 1791—March, 1799]. Washington, 1800. 8vo.

ADDRESS to the clergy of all denominations, on colonization [in Africa]. [Washington, 1845?] 8°

ADELUNG, FREDERICK. [A Review of his "Survey of all the known Languages." An article from the North American Review.] 8vo.

ADET, PIERRE AUGUSTE. Notes adressées par le Citoyen Adet . . . au Secrétaire d'Etat des Etats Unis. Notes from Citizen Adet . . . to the Secretary of State of the United States. Philadelphia, 1796. 8°

ADLER, G. J. Deutscher Lesebuch, mit Rücksicht auf die Amerikanische Ausgabe der Ollendorffschen Methode bearbeitet, etc. A progressive German reader, ... with copious notes and a vocabulary. New York, 1848. 12°

ADLUM, JOHN. A Memoir on the Cultivation of the Vine in America, and the best mode of making Wine. Washington, 1823. 12°

2 A MEMOIR on the Cultivation of the Vine in America, and the best mode of making Wine. Second edition. Washington, 1828. 12°

ADMIRARI, NIL, Pseud. The Trollopiad; or, Travelling Gentlemen in America: a satire [in verse]. By Nil Admirari, Esq. N. York, 1837. 12°

ADVICE. Parting Advice to a Youth on leaving his Sunday School. Philadelphia, 1829. 12mo.

ADVOCATE OF PEACE. Published by the American Peace Society. June, 1837, to Dec. 1845. [Edited by G. C. Beckwith and E. Burritt.] Vol. 1 to 6 [wanting No. 6 of vol. 2. and Nos. 1 and 2 of vol. 4]. Boston, 1837-1845. [New Series], Jan. to Aug. 1846; E. Burritt, Editor, etc. Vol. 1. Worcester, 1846. 8°

ÆLFRIC, *Archbishop of Canterbury*. Natale Sancti Gregori Papæ. Ælfric's Anglo-Saxon Homily on the Birthday of St. Gregory, and collateral Extracts from King Alfred's version of Bede's Ecclesiastical History, and from the Saxon Chronicle, with a full rendering into English, notes critical and explanatory, and an index of stems and forms. By L. F. Klipstein. New York, 1849. 12°

ÆSCHYLUS. The Agamemnon of Æschylus, with notes. By C. C. Felton. *Greek*. Boston, 1847. 12°
2 THE PROMETHEUS and Agamemnon . . . . Translated into English Verse by H. W. Herbert. Cambridge, 1849. 12°
3 THE PROMETHEUS of Æschylus, with notes, for the use of colleges in the United States. By T. D. Woolsey. New edition, revised. Boston and Cambridge, 1850. 12°

ÆSOP, *the Phrygian*. Æsop in Rhyme; or, Old Friends in a new Drefs, by Marmaduke Park. Philadelphia, 1852. 12°

AFFIDAVIT; or, the Rueful Swaddler. A tragedy in twenty-four acts. Second edition. New York (!), 1836. 12mo.

AFRICAN COLONIZATION. Remarks on African Colonization, The Abolition of Slavery. By a Citizen of New England. Windsor [Vermont], 1833. 8°

AFRICAN CRUISER. Journal of an African Cruiser. Comprising Sketches of the Canaries, the Cape de Verds, Liberia, Madeira, Sierra Leone, *etc*. By an Officer of the United States Navy, [Horatio Bridge; rewritten and] edited by Nathaniel Hawthorne. London [New York printed], 1845. 8°

AFRICAN EDUCATION SOCIETY OF THE UNITED STATES. Report of the proceedings at the formation of the African Education Society instituted at Washington Dec. 28, 1829. With an Addrefs to the public, by the Board of Managers. Washington, 1830. 8°

AFRICAN REPOSITORY AND COLONIAL JOURNAL. [Edited by R. R. Gurley.] Vol. 1 to 32. Washington, 1825-1856. 8°

AFRICANER. The Life of Africaner, a Namacqua Chief of South Africa. Philadelphia. 12mo.

AGASSIZ, LOUIS. Twelve Lectures on Comparative Embryology, delivered before the Lowell Institute in Boston. Boston, 1849. 8°
2 LAKE Superior: its Physical Character, Vegetation, and Animals, compared with those of other and similar regions. By L. Agafsiz, with a Narrative of the Tour, by J. E. Cabot, and contributions by other gentlemen. Boston, 1850. 8°

AGASSIZ, LOUIS, and GOULD, AUGUSTUS A. Principles of Zoology, touching the structure, development, distribution, and natural arrangement of the races of animals, living and extinct, *etc*. Revised edition. Part I. Boston, 1851, *etc*. 12°

AGATONE. The Prairie Scout, or, Agatone the Renegade, a romance of border life. Third edition. New York, 1852. 12°

AGNEL, H. R. Chefs for Winter Evenings, containing the rudiments of the game, . also a series of chefs tales, *etc*. New York, 1848. 12°

AGNES, COUSIN. Cousin Agnes' Story. The boys and girls of Chester. New York, 1852. 12°

AGNEW, JAMES. An inaugural Difsertation on Perspiration. Philadelphia, 1800. 8vo.

AGUILAR, GRACE. שמעישראל The Spirit of Judaism . . . . Edited by J. Leeser. Philadelphia, 5602 [1842]. 8vo.

AHMAD bnu Hamdan, called Su-HAILI. Turkish Evening Entertainments. The wonders of remarkable incidents and the rarities of anecdotes, by Ahmed Ibn Hemdem . . called "Sohailee." Translated from the Turkish by J. P. Brown [and edited by E. E. Salisbury]. New York [printed; and] London, 1850. 8vo.

AIKIN, JOHN. Letters from a Father to his Son on various Topics relative to Literature and the Conduct of Life. Philadelphia, -1796. 12°
2 SELECT Works of the British Poets, in a chronological series from Falconer to Sir Walter Scott. With biographical and critical notices. Designed as a continuation of Dr. Aikin's British Poets. (Vol. 2, . from Southey to Croly.) [Edited by J. Frost.] 2 vol. Phil. 1846. 8°

AKERLY, SAMUEL. An Essay on the Geology of the Hudson River, and the adjacent regions: illustrated by a geological section of the country, from the neighbourhood of Sandy Hook, in New Jersey, northward, etc. New York, 1820. 12mo.

AINSWORTH, LUTHER. Ainsworth's Practical, Mercantile Arithmetic, etc. Providence, Hartford and Boston, 1832. 12°

ALABAMA. Baptist State Convention. Journal of the Proceedings of the Baptist State Convention, in Alabama, at its nineteenth anniversary. Marion, Alab. 1842. 8vo.

ALABAMA, State of.
1 REPORTS of Cases at Law and in Equity, argued and determined in the Supreme Court of Alabama, 1840 to 1844. New Series. Vol. I. to VI. By the Judges of the Court. Tuscaloosa, 1841-45. 8°
2 A DIGEST of the Laws of the State of Alabama; containing the statutes and resolutions in force at the end of the General Assembly in Jan. 1823.

To which is added, an appendix, containing the Declaration of Independence; etc. Compiled . . . under the authority of the General Assembly, by H. Toulmin, Esq. Cahawba [Printed at New York], 1823. 8vo.
3 A DIGEST of the Laws of the State of Alabama; containing all the statutes of a public and general nature, in force at the close of the session of the General Assembly, in January, 1833. To which are prefixed, the Declaration of Independence, etc. Compiled, under the authority of the General Assembly, by J. G. Aikin. Philadelphia, 1833. 8°
4 A DIGEST of the Laws of the State of Alabama: containing all the statutes . . in force . . in Jan. 1833. . . With an appendix, and . . a supplement containing the public acts for the years 1833, 1834, and 1835. Compiled . . by J. G. Aikin. Second edition. Tuscaloosa, 1836. 8°
5 A SUPPLEMENT to Aikin's Digest of the Laws of the State of Alabama: containing all the unrepealed laws of a public and general nature, passed by the General Assembly, since the second edition of the Digest, up to the close of the Called Session in April, 1841 . . Compiled by A. B. Meek. Tuscaloosa, 1841. 8°
6 A DIGEST of the Laws of the State of Alabama: containing all the statutes of a public and general nature in force at the close of the session of the General Assembly, in Feb. 1843; to which are prefixed, the Declaration of Independence, the Constitution of the United States, etc. Compiled, under the authority of the General Assembly, by C. C. Clay. Tuskaloosa, 1843. 8°
7 THE MILITIA and Patrol Laws of the State of Alabama. Cahawba, 1823. 8vo.
8 THE MILITARY Code of the State of Alabama. With an appendix . . . . Prepared and arranged by Generals G. W. Crabb and J. T. Bradford. Tuscaloosa, 1838. 8vo.
9 JOURNAL of the House of Repre-

sentatives of the General Afsembly of the State of Alabama, *etc.* (1819 to 1845, together with the Journals of the "Called Sefsions" of 1821, 1837, and 1841.) 30 Parts. Cahawba, 1820-1826, and Tuscaloosa, 1827-1846. 8°

10 JOURNAL of the Senate of the General Afsembly of the State of Alabama, *etc.* (1819, 1821; 1823 to 1845, together with the Journals of the Called Sefsions of 1837 and 1841. 27 Parts [*wanting* 1820; Called Sefsion 1821; and 1822]. Cahawba, 1820-1826, and Tuscaloosa, 1827-1846. 8°

11 ACTS passed at the Second (the Called, the third, fourth, and seventh) Sefsion of the General Afsembly of the State of Alabama, held in the town of Cahawba, Nov. 1820 (to 1825, and at the eighth to the thirteenth sefsions, 1826 to 1831; the extra and annual sefsion, 1832, and the annual sefsions, 1833 to 1845, held in the town of Tuscaloosa). Cahawba, 1820-1826, and Tuscaloosa, 1827-1846. 8°

12 BANK Charter. An Act to establish the Bank of the State of Alabama; approved Dec. 20, 1823. Tuskaloosa, 1828. 8°

13 A TABULAR statement, exhibiting all the Liabilities of the State of Alabama on account of the State Bonds ifsued for the purpose of creating Banking Capital, *etc.* [Tuscaloosa, 1839.] 1 sh. fol°

14 LIABILITIES of the President and Directors of the branch of the Bank of the State of Alabama, at Mobile, to said bank. (Liabilities of members of the Senate, *etc.* [Tuscaloosa, 1841.] 8°

15 LIABILITIES of Directors and Officers of the State Bank, Mobile, Montgomery, and Huntsville Branches. Tuscaloosa, 1843. 8°

16 A CONDENSED statement of the indebtednefs of the several counties in the State of Alabama to the Bank of the State of Alabama, and its several branches: clafsified, good, bad,

and doubtful. Tuscaloosa, 1844. 8°

17 CLASSIFICATION of the indebtednefs of each county to the State Bank and branches. Tuscaloosa, 1845. 8°

18 CLASSIFICATION [by a Joint Committee of the Senate and House of Representatives] of the indebtednefs in each county to the State Bank and branches, Jan. 13, 1846. Tuscaloosa, 1846. 8°

19 A BILL to be entitled, An act to appoint a president and two directors for the State Bank, and other purposes. [Tuscaloosa, 1844.] fol°

20 A BILL to be entitled, An act to settle the affairs of the several branch banks of this State. [Tuscaloosa, 1844!] fol°

21 A BILL to be entitled, An act to close the affairs of the banks, and to apply their afsets to the payment of the public debt. [Tuscaloosa, 1846!] 1 sh. fol°

22 A BILL to be entitled, An act to withdraw the Sixteenth Section fund from the State Bank and branches, and to provide for the future management thereof. [Tuscaloosa, 1844.] fol°

23 A BILL to be entitled, An act to provide for the safe-keeping and management of the Sixteenth Section fund, in this State. [Tuscaloosa, 1844.] fol°

24 A BILL to be entitled, An act to provide for the preservation and consolidation of the Sixteenth Section fund, and for the establishment of a system of common school education throughout the State. [Tuscaloosa, 1844.] fol°

25 A BILL to be entitled, An act to apply a part of the two per cent. fund according to the compact between the General Government and the State of Alabama. [Tuscaloosa, 1844.] fol°

26 A BILL to be entitled, An act to raise a revenue for the State government, and to maintain the faith and credit of the State of Alabama. [Tuscaloosa, 1844.] fol°

27 A BILL to be entitled, An act to secure to married women their separate estates, and for other purposes. [Tuscaloosa, 1844.] 1 sh. fol°

28 A BILL to be entitled, An act to regulate the rights and liabilities of husband and wife, in regard to property. [Tuscaloosa, 1844.] 1 sh. fol°

29 A BILL to be entitled, An act to incorporate the Coosa Canal and Manufacturing Company, at Wetumpka. [Tuscaloosa, 1844.] 1 sh. fol°

30 A BILL to be entitled, An act to incorporate the Warrior Manufacturing Company. [Tuscaloosa, 1844.] 1 sh. fol°

31 A BILL to be entitled, An act to incorporate the Southern Railroad Company. [Tuscaloosa, 1844.] fol°

32 A BILL to be entitled, An act to regulate the introduction of slaves into the state. [Tuscaloosa, 1845.] 1 sh. fol°

33 HOUSE of Representatives. Report of the Committee of Ways and Means [upon the finances]. [Tuscaloosa, 1828.] 8°

34 REPORT of the Joint Examining Committee on the condition of the State Bank and branches; with an exhibit of the debt incurred by the State for banking capital; and a statement of the condition of the debts due the State Bank and branches. Tuscaloosa, 1840. 8°

35 REPORT of the State Bank Committee in relation to the purchase of property, by the Bank of the State of Alabama and branches, during the year 1841. Dec. 7, 1841. Tuscaloosa, 1841. 8°

36 REPORT of the State Bank Committee, in relation to the sinking fund by the Bank of the State of Alabama and branches. Dec. 13, 1841. Tuscaloosa, 1841. 8°

37 REPORT of the Committee on the State Bank and branches. Dec. 19, 1842. [Tuscaloosa, 1842.] 8°

38 BANK Reports: Report of the Chairman of the State Bank Committee; and also, the reports of the presidents and commissioners of the State Bank and branches. Tuscaloosa, 1843. 8°

39 REPORT of the Committee on the State Bank and branches, in relation to the management and liquidation of the Banks. Tuscaloosa, 1844. 8°

40 STATEMENT of the liabilities of members of the Legislature and Directors to the State Bank and branches. Tuscaloosa, 1844. 8°

41 REPORT of the Committee on the Penitentiary, on the bill providing for leasing out the Penitentiary. Tuscaloosa, 1842. 1 sh. fol°

42 REPORT of the Select Committee to whom was referred the communication of the Secretary of State, together with the accompanying documents, relative to the proposed amendments to the constitution, providing for biennial sessions of the Legislature, and for other purposes. [Tuscaloosa, 184-.] 8°

43 REPORT of the Committee on Education, on the Report of the Trustees of the University of Alabama, etc. [Tuscaloosa, 184-.] 8°

44 REPORT of the Committee of ways and means, in relation to the State debt. Tuscaloosa, 1844. 8°

45 REPORT of the majority of the Committee on the Sixteenth Section fund. Tuscaloosa, 1845. 8°

46 REPORT of the minority of the Committee on the Sixteenth Section fund. Tuscaloosa, 1846. 8°

47 REPORT of the Committee on the Penitentiary. [Tuscaloosa, 1845.] 8°

48 REPORT of the Committee on the State Bank and branches. Tuscaloosa, 1846. 8°

49 RULES of the House of Representatives. [Tuscaloosa, 1840?.] 1 sh. fol°

50 RULES of the House of Representatives. [Tuscaloosa, 1841?] 1 sh. fol°

51 RULES of the Senate. [Tuscaloosa, 1840?] 1 sh. fol°

52 [Begin] Session of 1844-45. [A list of the Senators and of the House of Representatives.] [Tuscaloosa, 1844.] 1 sh. fol°

53 LIST of Officers elected on joint

ballot, by the General Aſſembly. [Tuscaloosa, 1845.] 8°

ALABAMA TERRITORY. Journal of the Legislative Council of the Alabama Territory, at the first seſſion of the first General Aſſembly, in the forty-third year of American Independence. St. Stephen's, 1818. 8°

2 JOURNAL of the House of Representatives of the Alabama Territory, at the first seſſion of the first General Aſſembly, in the forty-second year of American Independence. St. Stephens, 1818. 4°

3 ACTS paſſed at the second Seſſion of the first General Aſſembly of the Alabama Territory, etc. St. Stephens, 1818. 8°

4 JOURNAL of the Convention of the Alabama Territory, begun July 5, 1819. Huntsville, 1819. 8°

ALBANY. The Weſtern Traveller; embracing the canal and railroad routes from Albany and Troy to Niagara Falls; etc. New York, 1844. 12°

ALBANY AND SUSQUEHANNA RAILROAD COMPANY. Some considerations reſpecting the proposed construction of the Albany and Susquehanna Railroad. Albany, 1852. 8°

ALBANY ARGUS EXTRA. Mr. Van Buren and the War. [Albany, 1832.] 4to.

ALBANY DIRECTORY. Child's Albany Directory, 1835-6. Compiled by E. B. Child. Albany, 1835. 12°

2 HOFFMAN's Albany Directory and City Register, for the years 1838-9, 1839-40, 1840-41, 1841-42, 1842-43, 1844-5, 1845-6. 7 vol. Albany, 1838-45. 12°

3 ALBANY COUNTY and Troy Buſineſſ Directory .. By Whitney and Bliſs. [1852.] Albany, 1852. 16°

ALBANY FEMALE ACADEMY. Exercises of the Alumnæ of the Albany Female Academy, on their fifth Anniversary, July 16, 1846. Albany, 1846. 8°

ALBANY INSTITUTE. TRANSACTIONS. Vol. 1 & 2, No. 1. Albany, 1830-33. 8vo.

ALCOTT, A. BRONSON. Conversations with Children on the Gospels. Conducted and edited by A. B. Alcott. 2 vol. Boston, 1836-37. 12°

ALCOTT, WILLIAM A. The Young Housekeeper, or Thoughts on Food and Cookery . . . Fifth stereotype edition. Boston, 1842. 12°

2 THE YOUNG Huſband, or, Duties of Man in the Marriage Relation. Sixth stereotype edition. Boston, 1842. 12°

3 THE YOUNG Mother, or Management of Children in regard to Health. Ninth stereotype edition. Boston, 1842. 12°

4 THE YOUNG Man's Guide . . . Revised and enlarged. Sixteenth edition. Boston, 1846. 12°

5 THE YOUNG Woman's Guide to Excellence . . . Tenth stereotype edition. Boston, 1846. 12°

6 ALCOTT's New Series. Letters to a Sister; or, Woman's Miſſion. To accompany the Letters to Young Men. Buffalo, 1850. 12°

7 LECTURES on Life and Health; or, the Laws and Means of Physical Culture. Boston, 1853. 12°

ALDEN, ABNER. An Introduction to Spelling and Reading; . . . being the first and second parts of a Columbian Exercise. . . . Comprising an easy and systematical method of teaching and of learning the English language. Seventh edition. Vol. 2. Boston, 1816. 12mo.

2 THE READER. . . . Being the third part of a Columbian Exercise. The whole comprising an easy and systematical method of teaching and of learning the English language. . . Fifth edition. Boston, 1822. 12°

ALDEN, T. J. Fox, and VAN HOESEN, J. A. A Digest of the Laws of Miſſiſſippi, comprising all the laws of a general nature, including the acts of the session of 1839. New York, 1839. 8°

ALDEN, TIMOTHY. A Collection of American Epitaphs and Inscriptions, with occasional notes. Second edition. 5 vol. New York, 1814. 12mo.

ALEXANDER, A. The Fall of Aztalan, and other poems. Washington, 1839. 8°

ALEXANDER, ARCHIBALD, D. D. A brief Outline of the Evidences of the Christian Religion. Philadelphia, 1829. 12mo.

2 A POCKET Dictionary of the Holy Bible. Philadelphia, 1829. 12mo.

3 HISTORY of the Patriarchs. Philadelphia, 1833. 12mo.

4 BIOGRAPHICAL Sketches of the Founder and Principal Alumni of the Log College. Together with an account of the revivals of religion under their ministry. Collected and edited by Archibald Alexander, D.D. Philadelphia [1851]. 12°

5 OUTLINES of Moral Science. New York, 1852. 12°

6 A HISTORY of the Israelitish Nation, from their origin to their dispersion at the destruction of Jerusalem by the Romans. [Edited by J. W. Alexander.] Philadelphia, 1853. 8vo.

ALEXANDER, CALEB. A Sermon [on Psal. lxxxii. 6, 7] occasioned by the death of . . . . George Washington, etc. Boston, 1800. 8°

2 A NEW and Complete System of Arithmetic; intended for the use of schools and academies. Albany, 1802. 12°

3 A GRAMMATICAL System of the English Language, etc. Ninth edition, corrected. Boston, 1807. 12°

ALEXANDER, JAMES EDWARD. An Expedition of Discovery into the Interior of Africa, through the hitherto undescribed countries of the great Namaquas, Boschmans, and Hill Domaras. 2 vol. Philadelphia, 1838. 12°

ALEXANDER, JAMES W. The American Mechanic and Workingman. [A series of essays, ethical and economical.] 2 vol. New York and Philadelphia, 1847. 12°

2 CONSOLATION: in discourses on select topics, addressed to the suffering people of God. New York, 1853. 8°

ALEXANDER, JAMES W. and J. ADDISON. A Geography of the Bible. Philadelphia, 1830. 12mo.

ALEXANDER, JOHN H. Engineer. Report on the New. Map of Maryland; [containing: 1. Engineer's Report, by J. H. Alexander; 2. Geologist's Report, by J. T. Ducatel.] 1835. [Balt. 1836.] 8vo.

2 REPORT on the New Map of Maryland, 1835. [Report of the Geologist (J. T. Ducatel) on the progress of the geological survey, etc. with an appendix.] [Baltimore, 1836.] 8°

3 REPORT on the Manufacture of Iron; addressed to the Governor of Maryland. . . Printed by order of the Senate. Annapolis, 1840. 8vo.

4 SECOND Report on the Manufacture of Iron; addressed to the Governor of Maryland. Printed by order of the Senate. Annapolis, 1844. 8vo.

5 CONTRIBUTIONS to the History of the Manufacture of Iron. (Part first: Report on the manufacture of iron; addressed to the Governor of Maryland. Part second: An elementary treatise on iron-making : . by S. Rogers. Now . . . first published, with notes, and an appendix, by John H. Alexander.) Baltimore, 1840-44. 8°

6 ON A NEW form of Mountain or other Barometer. [An article extracted from the American Journal of Science, for Oct. 1843. New Haven, 1843.] 8vo.

7 REPORT on the Standards of Weight and Measure for the State of Maryland; and on the construction of yard-measures. [Baltimore, 1845.] 8vo.

8 UNIVERSAL Dictionary of Weights

and Measures, ancient and modern, reduced to the standards of the United States of America. Balt. 1850. 8°

ALEXANDRIA, *District of Columbia*. Letter from the Mayor of Alexandria . . (E. C. Dick,) inclosing sundry resolutions of the citizens of . . Alexandria, expreſsive of their disapprobation of a motion now depending before the House [of Representatives of the United States of America] to recede to the States of Virginia and Maryland . . parts of the . . District [of Columbia] etc. Washington, 1804. 8°

2 LETTER from G. W. Custis . . . enclosing sundry resolutions agreed to by the inhabitants of Alexandria . . relative to the receſsion of . . . . part of the territory of the District of Columbia, etc. Dec. 11, 1804. [Washington, 1804.] 8°

ALFIERI, VITTORIO, *Count*. The autobiography of Vittorio Alfieri . . . Translated, with an original eſsay on the genius and times of Alfieri, by C. E. Lester, etc. New York, 1845, 12mo.

ALGER, ISRAEL, jun. The English Teacher, or private learner's guide; containing a new arrangement of Murray's exercises and key, etc. Boston, 1824. 12°

ALI BEY, *Pseud.* Extracts from a Journal of Travels in North America; consisting of an account of Boston and its vicinity. By Ali Bey, etc. Translated from the original manuscript. Boston, 1818. 12°

ALIDA; or, town and country. By the author of " Allen Prescott," [Mrs. T. Sedgwick.] New York, 1844. 8°

ALISON, ARCHIBALD. History of Europe from the commencement of the French Revolution, in 1789, to the Restoration of the Bourbons, in 1815. . . . Abridged from the last London edition . . . by E. S. Gould. Fourth edition. New York, 1845. 8°

2 ANOTHER copy. Fourth edition. Large paper. New York, 1845. 8°

ALLEGHANY MAGAZINE; or, Repository of Useful Knowledge. By Rev. T. Alden. Numbers 1-12. Meadville, Pennsylvania, 1816-17. 8°

ALLEINE, Rev. JOSEPH. An Alarm to Unconverted Sinners. Philadelphia, 1829. 12mo.

2 MEMOIRS of the Life of J. Alleine, including a Narrative written by his widow, Mrs. Theodosia Alleine. Philadelphia, 1829. 12mo.

ALLEN, Rev. BENJAMIN. History of the Church of Christ. 2 vol. Philadelphia, 1823-24. 8°

ALLEN, ETHAN, *Green Mountain Boy*. Reason the only Oracle of Man: or, a compendious System of Natural Religion. . . . To which is added, Critical Remarks on the Truth and Harmony of the Four Gospels . . . By a Free-thinker. 2 Parts. New York and Philadelphia, 1836. 12°

2 ALLEN's Captivity, being a narrative of Colonel Ethan Allen, containing his voyages, travels, etc. Interspersed with political observations. Written by himself. [Edited by F. W. E.] Boston, 1845. 12°

ALLEN, J. FISK. A Practical Treatise on the Culture and Treatment of the Grape Vine . . . Third edition, enlarged and revised. New York, 1853. 12°

ALLEN, JOSEPH. The Day of Small Things. A Centennial Discourse, delivered in Northborough, June 1, 1846, in commemoration of the organization of the first Congregational Church in that place, and the ordination of the first minister. [Zech. iv. 10:] With an appendix. Boston, 1846. 8vo.

ALLEN, JOSEPH D. Oswego and Utica Railroad Company. Report of Joseph D. Allen, Esq. chief engineer to the board of directors, September, 1837. New York, 1837. 8vo.

ALLEN, Lewis F. Rural Architecture. Being a complete description of farm-houses, cottages, and outbuildings. . Also the best method of conducting water into cattle yards and houses. New York, 1852. 12mo.

ALLEN, Martha. Day-Dreams. Philadelphia, 1852. 12°

ALLEN, Nathan. An Essay on the Opium Trade. Including a sketch of its history, extent, effects, etc. as carried on in India and China. Boston, 1850. 8°

ALLEN, Paul. An Oration on the Death of R. W. Howell, who died Oct. 7, 1792. [*Imprint torn off.* 1792.] 8°
2 Noah, a Poem. Baltimore, 1821. 12°
3 A History of the American Revolution. To which are added, the most important Resolutions of the Continental Congress, and many of the most important Letters of General Washington. 2 vols. Baltimore, 1822. 8vo.

ALLEN, R. L. Domestic Animals: history and description of the horse, mule, cattle, sheep, swine, poultry, and farm dogs; with directions for their management . . . together with . . directions for the management of the dairy. New York, 1848. 12°
2 The American Farm Book; or, compend of American agriculture . . . . Illustrated by more than 100 engravings. New York, 1850. 12°

ALLEN, Thaddeus. An Inquiry into the Views, Principles, Services, and Influences of the Leading Men in the Origination of our Union, and in the Formation and Early Administration of our present Government. 3 vols. Vol. I. [*II. and III. wanting*]. Boston, 1847. 8°

ALLEN, William, *President of Dartmouth and Bowdoin Colleges.* An American Biographical and Historical Dictionary. [*With Robert Southey's autograph.*] Cambridge, 1809. 8vo.
2 An American Biographical and Historical Dictionary. Second edition. Boston, 1832. 8vo.
3 A Sermon [on Josh. i. 8.] preached before the Council, and Legislature of New Hampshire, June 4, 1818, being the anniversary election. Concord, 1818. 8°

ALLEN, William. Speech on the Bill to separate the Government from the Bank; delivered in the Senate, . . . Feb. 20, 1838. Washington, 1838. 8°
2 Speech . . on the Report of the Select Committee in Relation to the Assumption of the Debts of the States by the Federal Government. Senate . . . Feb. 11, 1840. Washington, 1840. 8°
3 Speech . . in the Senate,. March 15, 1842 [on the State of the Public Finances]. [Washington, 1842.] 8°

ALLEN, Zachariah. The Science of Mechanics as applied to the Present Improvements in the Useful Arts. Providence, 1829. 8vo.
2 The Practical Tourist, or Sketches of the State of the Useful Arts, and of Society, Scenery, etc. etc. in Great Britain, France and Holland. 2 vols. Providence, Boston, 1832. 12mo.

ALLIN, Abby. Home Ballads: a book for New Englanders, etc. Boston and Cambridge, 1851. 12°

ALLISON, Burgiss. The American Standard of Orthography and Pronunciation, and Improved Dictionary of the English Language, abridged for the Use of Schools. Burlington, 1815, 12°

ALLISON, J. Mesmerism: its pretensions as a Science physiologically considered. London [Burlington], 1844. 8vo.

c

ALLSTON, WASHINGTON. Monaldi, a Tale. Boston, 1841. 12°

2 LECTURES on Art, and poems . . . Edited by R. H. Dana, jun. New York, 1850. 12°

ALLYN, AVERY. A Ritual of Freemasonry, illustrated by numerous engravings. To which is added, a Key to the Phi Beta Kappa, the Orange, and Odd Fellows Societies. Philadelphia, 1831. 8vo.

ALNWICK CASTLE; with other Poems [by F. Halleck]. New York, 1827. 8°

2 ALNWICK Castle, with other Poems [by F. Halleck]. New York, 1836. 8°

ALSOP, SAMUEL. An Elementary Treatise on Algebra, etc. Philadelphia, 1847. 12°

AMARANTH, . a Christmas and New Year's Gift . . Edited by E. Percival. Boston, 1853. 12°

AMATEUR. Crayon Sketches. By an Amateur [W. Cox]. Edited by T. S. Fay. 2 vols. New York, 1833. 12mo.

AMATEUR. The New Mirror for Travellers, and Guide to the Springs. By an Amateur. New York, 1828. 12mo.

AMELIA. Poems by Amelia [Mrs. Welby, of Louisville Ky.] Second edition, enlarged. New York and Philadelphia, 1846. 12°

2 POEMS, by Amelia [Mrs. Welby]. Fourth edition, enlarged. New York, 1847. 12°.

AMERICA. The Patriots of North America; a Sketch, with Explanatory Notes. New York, 1775. 8vo.

2 THE Advantages which America derives from her Commerce, Connexion, and Dependence on Britain. 1775. 8vo.

3 COMMON Sense; addressed to the inhabitants of America. A new edition, with several additions. To which is added an appendix; together with an Address to the people called Quakers. [By T. Paine.] Philadelphia [1776]. 8°

4 RESEARCHES on America; being an attempt to settle some points relative to the Aborigines of America, etc. . By an officer of the United States' army, [J. H. Mac Culloh.] Baltimore, 1816. 8vo.

5 AMERICA: or, a General Survey of the political situation of the several powers of the Western Continent . . . By a citizen of the United States. Author of " Europe," etc. [Alexander H. Everett]. Philadelphia, 1827. 8°

6 A DETAIL of some particular Services performed in America during the years 1776-79. Compiled from Journals and Official Papers, supposed to be chiefly taken from the Journal kept on board the Rainbow, commanded by Sir G. Collier. [Edited by Ithiel Town.] New York, 1835, 12mo.

7 THE BATTLE Grounds of America, illustrated by stories of the Revolution; with fourteen engravings. Auburn, 1846. 12°

8 PROGRESS of America. [A series of papers statistical, ethical, and economical; including Cobbett's Advice to Lovers.] [New York, 1847.] 8°

9 THE WATER Cure in America: two hundred and twenty cases of various diseases treated with water ; . . . notices of the water-cure establishments; descriptive catalogue of hydropathic publications; . . . . Edited by a water patient. New York and London, 1848. 12°

10 THE WATER Cure in America: two hundred and twenty cases of various diseases treated with water, by Drs. Weſselhoefft, Shew, Bedortha, Shieferdecker, and others: with cases of domestic practice, notices of the Water Cure establishments, descriptive catalogue of Hydropathic Publications, etc. Edited by a water patient. Second edition. New York and London, 1848. 12mo.

11 THE WATER Cure in America: over three hundred cases of various diseases treated with water, by Drs. Weſſelhoeſt, Shew, Bedortha, ... and others. . . Edited by a water patient. New York, 1852. 8vo.

12 COSTUMES of America. Philadelphia, 1852. 12°

13 THE CHILD'S First History of America. By the author of " Little Dora." New York, 1853. 12°

14 SCENES and Thoughts in Europe. By an American [see George H. CALVERT, No. 3]. London [New York printed], 1847. 12mo.

AMERICA, ABORIGINES OF. Traits of the Aborigines of America. A poem. [By L. H. Sigourney.] Cambridge, 1822. 8°

AMERICAN. An Eſſay on the Rights and Duties of Nations, relative to fugitives from justice; considered with reference to the affair of the Chesapeake. By an American. Boston, 1807. 8°

2 POEMS, by an American. [Not published.] Boston, 1830. 8°

3 SKETCHES of Turkey, in 1831 and 1832. By an American [J. E. De Kay]. New York, 1833. 8°

4 THE AMERICAN in England. By the author of " A Year in Spain" [A. Slidell Mackenzie]. 2 vol. New York, 1835. 12°

5 SKETCHES of Switzerland. By an American [J. F. Cooper]. Part second. 2 vol. Phil. 1836. 12°

6 GLEANINGS in Europe: England. By an American [J. F. Cooper]. 2 vol. Philadelphia, 1837. 12°

7 DESULTORY Reminiscences of a Tour through Germany, Switzerland, and France. By an American. Boston, 1838. 8vo.

8 AN INQUIRY into the Condition and Prospects of the African Race in the United States: and the means of bettering its fortunes. By an American. Philadelphia, 1839. 12mo.

9 MUSCIPULA sive Cambromyomachia: The Mouse-trap, or the Battle of the Welsh and the Mice, in Latin and English, with other poems, in different languages. By an American [Dr. Prime]. New York [1840]. 12mo.

10 FRANCE, its King, Court, and Government, by an American [General L. Cass]. New York, 1840. 8vo.

11 NAPOLEON, his Army and his Generals, etc. With a Sketch of the French Revolution. By an American. New York, 1847. 12°

13 AMERICA Discovered. A Poem, in twelve books. By an American. New York, 1850. 16°

14 JOURNAL of a Voyage up the Nile made between the months of November, 1848 and April, 1849. By an American. Buffalo, 1851. 12°

AMERICAN (The). Vol. 2, No. 451. August 22nd, 1821. New York, 1821. Fol.

AMERICAN ACADEMY OF ARTS AND SCIENCES. Memoirs. Vol. 1 to 2. Boston and Charlestown, 1785-1804. 4to. New Series, Vol. 1 to 4 and 5, part 1. Cambridge and Boston, 1833-1853. 4to.

2 PROCEEDINGS, selected from the Records. Vol. 1 and 2 [both imperfect]. Boston, Cambridge, 1846-52. 8vo.

AMERICAN ACADEMY OF THE ARTS. The Charter and By-Laws. With an account of the statues, busts, and paintings belonging to the Academy. New York, 1815. 8vo

2 A DISCOURSE delivered before the American Academy of the Arts, by De Witt Clinton, 23rd October, 1816. New York, 1816. 8vo.

AMERICAN ADVENTURE by Land and Sea: being remarkable instances of enterprise and fortitude among Americans, [being Nos. 153 and 154 of Harper's School District Library. By E. Sargent,] etc. 2 vol. New York, 1843. 12°

AMERICAN ADVERTISER, designed for the cards and advertisements of the leading business establishments of the United States. New York, 1849. 12°

AMERICAN ADVERTISING DIRECTORY, for manufacturers and dealers in American goods; for the year 1831 and 1832. 2 vol. New York, 1831-32. 12°

AMERICAN ALMANAC AND REPOSITORY OF USEFUL KNOWLEDGE, for 1831 (to 1856, *wanting* 1830). [The Astronomical department by R. T. Paine and B. Peirce, and Geo. P. Bond.] Boston [1830-55]. 12°
2 COMPANION to the American Almanac, . for 1834. Boston [1833], 12mo.

AMERICAN ANNUAL REGISTER, for 1825-26 (to 1832-33). 8 Vol. [*wanting the vol. for* 1831-32]. New York and Boston, 1827-35. 8vo.

AMERICAN ANTIQUARIAN SOCIETY. Archæologia Americana: Transactions and Collections of the Society. Vol. 1, 2, & 3, part 1. Worcester and Cambridge, 1820-50. 8vo.
2 ADDRESS to the Members of the American Antiquarian Society; together with the laws and regulations of the Institution, and a list of donations, *etc.* Worcester, March, 1819. 8°
3 Fifty-third Semi-Annual Report of the Council of the American Antiquarian Society, May 29, 1839: with the Report of the Librarian (S. F. Haven). Worcester, 1839. 8°
4 PROCEEDINGS of the American Antiquarian Society, at their thirty-first annual meeting, held at Worcester, Oct. 23, 1843; with the Address of Hon. J. Davis. Worcester, 1843. 8°
5 PROCEEDINGS of the American Antiquarian Society at . . Boston, May 29, and . . in Worcester, Oct. 23, 1850. Worcester [1850]. 8vo.

6 PROCEEDINGS of the American Antiquarian Society Annual Meeting at . . Worcester, Oct. 23, 1849. Cambridge, 1850. 8vo.

AMERICAN ANTI-SLAVERY ALMANAC for 1841 (and 1843 . . Compiled by L. M. Child). 2 parts. New York, 1841-43. 8°

AMERICAN ANTI-SLAVERY SOCIETY. Constitution and Declaration of Sentiments of the American Anti-Slavery Society. [Philadelphia, 1833?] 12°

AMERICAN ANTI-SLAVERY SOCIETY. Second (to the Seventh) Annual Report of the American Anti-Slavery Society; with the Speeches delivered at the Anniversary Meeting. 6 parts. New York, 1835-40. 8vo.

AMERICAN ARCHIVES: consisting of a collection of authentic Records, State Papers, Debates, and Letters and other notices of public affairs ; . . . Fourth Series, containing a documentary history of the English Colonies in North America, from the King's message to Parliament, of March 7, 1774, to the Declaration of Independence by the United States. Published by M. St. C. Clarke and P. Force, under authority of an Act of Congress, passed . . . . 2 March, 1833. 5 vol. Washington, 1837-44. Fol.

AMERICAN ART UNION. Transactions of the American Art Union, for the Promotion of the Fine Arts in the United States; for the year 1844 (1847 and 1849). 3 parts. New York [1844-50]. 8°
2 RIP VAN WINKLE [by W. Irving] illustrated by F. O. C. Darley. New York, 1848. Oblong fol.
3 THE LEGEND of Sleepy Hollow [by W. Irving] illustrated by F. O. C. Darley. Published by the American Art-Union, for the members of 1849. [New York, 1849.] Fol.

AMERICAN ASSOCIATION FOR THE ADVANCEMENT OF EDUCATION. Proceedings of the National Convention at Philadelphia, Oct. 1849 (of the first Session of the Association held at Cleveland, Ohio, Aug. 1851. 2nd Session at Newark, N. J. Aug. 1852), 3 parts. Philadelphia, 1849-52. 8°

AMERICAN ASSOCIATION FOR THE ADVANCEMENT OF SCIENCE. Proceedings. Second Meeting, at Cambridge, Aug. 1849, and 4th Meeting, at New Haven, Aug. 1850. 6th Meeting, at Albany, Aug. 1851. 3 Vol. Boston, 1850, and Washington, 1851-52. 8°

AMERICAN ASYLUM AT HARTFORD FOR THE DEAF AND DUMB. First, (seventh, eighth, tenth to seventeenth, nineteenth, twenty-first, twenty-second, twenty-sixth to twenty-eighth) Report of the Directors of the American Asylum for the Education and Instruction of the Deaf and Dumb. May, 1823 (to May, 1844). 16 parts. Hartford, 1823-44. 8vo.

AMERICAN ATLAS. A complete Historical, Chronological, and Geographical American Atlas, being a Guide to the History of North and South America and the West Indies to the year 1822, according to the plan of Le Sage's Atlas, and intended as a Companion to Lavoisne's Improvement of that work. Philadelphia, 1823. Fol.

2 A COMPLETE Historical, Chronological, and Geographical American Atlas, being a Guide to the history of North and South America and the West Indies to the year 1826, according to the plan of Le Sage's Atlas, and intended as a Companion to Lavoisne's Improvement of that work. Philadelphia and London, 1827. Fol.

AMERICAN AUTHORS. Homes of American Authors, comprising anecdotical, personal, and descriptive Sketches, by various writers. Illustrated with views of their residences, etc. New York, 1853. 8°

AMERICAN BAPTIST HOME MISSION SOCIETY. Proceedings of the Convention held in the city of New York, on the 27th of April, 1832, for the formation of the American Baptist Home Mission Society, with the constitution of the Society, etc. New York, 1832. 8vo.

2 THE FIRST (to the fourteenth) Report of the Executive Committee of the American Baptist Home Mission Society, etc. 14 Parts. New York, 1833-46. 8°

3 Quarterly Paper. Nos. 3 and 4, 1838; and Nos. 5 and 6, 1840. New York, 1838-40. 8°

AMERICAN BAPTIST PUBLICATION SOCIETY. Seventh Annual Report of the . . . Society. Philadelphia [1846]. 8vo.

AMERICAN BAPTIST REGISTER for 1852. J. L. Burrows, Editor. Philadelphia, 1853. 8°

AMERICAN AND FOREIGN BIBLE SOCIETY. Annual Reports, (First to the ninth) 1838-46. 9 Parts. New York, 1838-46. 8vo.

AMERICAN BIBLE SOCIETY. Constitution of the American Bible Society, formed by a Convention of Delegates, held in . . . New York, May, 1816, . . with their Address to the People of the United States, a notice of their proceedings; and a list of their officers. New York, 1816. 8°

2 THE FIRST (to the thirtieth, 18th wanting) Annual Report of the American Bible Society, with an appendix [to each Report], containing extracts of correspondence, etc. 29 Parts. New York, 1817-46. 8°

3 ANNUAL Reports, First (to the Twenty-second, inclusive) of the American Bible Society, with an account of its organization; . extracts of correspondence, etc. 1817-1838. New York. Reprinted, 1838. 8vo.

4 A BRIEF Analysis of the System of the American Bible Society containing a full account of its principles and operations, and of the manner of organizing and conducting branch . . societies, etc. [With an appendix.] New York, 1830. 8°

5 BRIEF View of the Plans and Operations of the American Bible Society. New York, 1846. 8vo.

AMERICAN BIOGRAPHY. Biographia Americana; or an historical and critical account of the lives, actions and writings of the most distinguished persons in North America; from the first settlement to the present time. By a Gentleman of Philadelphia. New York, 1825. 8°

AMERICAN BOARD OF COMMISSIONERS FOR FOREIGN MISSIONS. First ten annual Reports of the American Board . . with other documents of the Board. Boston, 1834. 8°

2 REPORT of the American Board of Commissioners for Foreign Missions . . at the eleventh (thirteenth, twentieth, twenty-fourth to the thirty-sixth) annual meeting, etc. 16 parts. Boston, 1820-45. 8°

3 QUARTERLY Paper of the American Board of Commissioners for Foreign Missions. No: 5, 9, 14, 21-23. [Boston, 1830-35 ?] 8°

4 MISSIONARY Paper. No. 1 to 3, 5 to 8, 12 to 14, and 18 to 22. 15 parts. Boston, 1834-40. 12°

5 ON THE USE of Missionary Maps at the Monthly Concert. Boston, 1842. 12°

6 AN APPEAL of the Missionaries residing at Constantinople, to the friends and supporters of the Mission in that city. [Boston, 1842 ?] 12°

7 AMERICAN Board, etc. Report of the Committee on Anti-Slavery Memorials, Sept. 1845; with an historical statement of previous proceedings. Boston, 1845. 8°

8 MISSIONARY Paper. The Divine method of raising charitable Contributions. (By E. Yale.) Boston, 1845. 12°

9 MAPS and Illustrations of the Missions of the American Board, etc. [Boston,] 1846. 8°

10 MISSIONARY Tracts. No. 1. The Theory of Missions to the Heathen. No. 2. The promised Advent of the Spirit. Boston, 1846. 12°

11 ON RECEIVING donations from holders of Slaves. Boston [1846 ?] 12°

AMERICAN BOOK OF BEAUTY, or Token of Friendship. A gift for all seasons. Edited by a Lady. Hartford [1845]. 8°

AMERICAN CALENDAR, or United States Register, for the year 1794. Philadelphia, 1794. 12mo.

AMERICAN CHRISTIANS. Politics for American Christians; a word upon our example as a nation, our labour, our trade, elections, education and Congressional legislation. [By S. Colwell.] Philadelphia, 1852. 8°

AMERICAN CLASSICAL AND MILITARY LYCEUM. Prospectus of the American Classical and Military Lyceum, at Mount Airy, near Germantown. [1827.] 12°

AMERICAN COLONIZATION SOCIETY. The second (the sixth to the sixteenth, and the twenty-sixth) Annual Report of the American Society for colonizing the free people of colour in the United States. With an appendix. Second edition. 12 Parts. Washington, 1819, 1823-33 and 1843. 8vo.

2 REPORT made at an adjourned Meeting of the Friends of the American Colonization Society, . . held in Worcester, Dec. 8, 1830, by a committee appointed for that purpose; with the proceedings of the meeting, etc. Worcester, 1831. 8vo.

3 A VIEW of exertions lately made for the purpose of colonizing the free people of colour, in the United States, in Africa or elsewhere. Washington, 1817. 8vo.

AMERICAN CONGRESS. *See* UNITED STATES.

AMERICAN EDUCATION SOCIETY. Third (fourth, fifth; eighth to the twenty-fourth; twenty-sixth to the thirtieth) Report of the Directors 1818—1846. 25 Parts. [1*st*, 2*nd*, 6*tb*, 7*tb*, 25*tb*, *wanting*.] Andover, New York, and Boston. 1818— 1846. 8°

2 QUARTERLY Register and Journal of the American Education Society (July 1827—May 1831) conducted by E. Cornelius and B. B. Edwards. Vol. 1-3. [Continued as] The American Quarterly Register (August 1831—May 1838), conducted by B. B. Edwards (and W. Cogswell). Vol. 4-10. Andover; Boston, 1829-38. 8vo.

AMERICAN EPHEMERIS AND NAUTICAL Almanac for the year 1855. [Edited by C. H. Davis.] Washington, Cambridge printed, 1852. 8vo.

AMERICAN ETHNOLOGICAL SOCIETY. Transactions. Vol. 1 and 2. New York, 1845-48. 8vo.

AMERICAN FARMER, containing original essays and selections on rural economy and internal improvements, *etc.* J. S. Skinner, Editor. Vol. 1-4. Third edition, April, 1819—March, 1823. Baltimore, 1821-23. 4°

AMERICAN FARMERS. Politics for American Farmers; being a series of tracts, exhibiting the blessings of free government, as it is administered in the United States, compared with the boasted stupendous fabric of British Monarchy. [By W. Duane.!] Washington, 1807. 8°

AMERICAN GARDENERS' MAGAZINE, and Register of useful Discoveries and improvements in horticulture and rural affairs. [Continued as] The Magazine of Horticulture, Botany, *etc.* Conducted by C. M. Hovey and P. B. Hovey. Vol. 1-10. 1835-1844. New Series, by C. M. Hovey, 1845-

54. Vols. 1-10. Third Series, 1855-56. Vol. 1, 2. Boston, 1835-56. 8°

AMERICAN GEOGRAPHICAL and Statistical Society. The charter and by-laws of the American Geographical and Statistical Society. New York, 1852. 8°

2 BULLETIN of the American Geographical and Statistical Society. New York, 1852. 8°

AMERICAN GOVERNMENT: An Inquiry into the Moral and Religious Character of the American Government. New York, 1838. 8vo.

AMERICAN HISTORY. Tales from American History. By the author of " American Popular Lessons," *etc.* 3 vol. [No. 9—11 of *The Boy's and Girl's Library*.] New York, 1844. 12°

2 THE BEAUTIES of American History. By the author of Evenings in Boston, *etc.* Hartford, 1850. 12°

3 A CHAPTER of American History. Five years' progress of the slave power; a series of papers first published in the Boston " Commonwealth," in . . . 1851. Boston, 1852. 8°

AMERICAN INSTITUTE. REPORT of a special Committee of the American Institute, on the subject of cash duties, the auction system, &c. Jan. 12, 1829. New York, 1829. 8°

2 JOURNAL of the American Institute; a monthly publication, devoted to the interests of agriculture, commerce, manufactures, and the arts, *etc.* Edited by a committee, members of the Institute. Vol. 1-4. Oct. 1835— Sept. 1839. New York, 1836-40. 8°

3 REPORT of the Superintending Agent. [New York, 1840.] 8°

4 PREMIUMS awarded by the managers of the thirteenth (fourteenth, sixteenth and seventeenth) annual Fair of the American Institute, 1840 (1842 to 1844) [New York, 1840-44.] 8°

5 TRANSACTIONS of the NEW YORK State Agricultural Society [*which see*]; together with an Abstract of the Proceedings of the County Agri-

cultural Societies and the American Institute. 1844-45.

6 REPORT of the Committee on Horticulture, in conjunction with the Agricultural Board of the American Institute, at their 17th annual Fair, October, 1844. [New York, 1844.] 8°

7 THE SECOND and third Reports of the American Institute of the City of New York, made to the Legislature, for the years 1842 and 1843 (and Feb. 1846). Albany, 1844-46. 8°

8 DOCUMENTS in relation to the manufacture of silk and of cotton and woollen goods in the City of New York. Published by order of the American Institute. New York, 1844. 8°

9 REPORT of the Committee on Horticulture, in conjunction with the Agricultural Board of the American Institute, at their eighteenth annual Fair. New York, 1845. 8°

10 ADDRESS delivered at the close of the eighteenth annual Fair of the American Institute. . by the Hon. J. Tallmadge, President of the Institute. Together with a list of the premiums awarded. New York, 1845. 8°

11 CHARTER and by-laws of the American Institute of the City of New York. New York, 1845. 8°

12 ANNUAL Report of the Trustees of the American Institute, . . 1844. New York, 1845. 8°

13 ANNUAL Report . . to the New York State Agricultural Society, Feb. 1846. Albany, 1846. 8°

14 MEMORIAL . . to the Legislature of New York [for a share of the Literature Fund]. N. York, 1846. 8°

AMERICAN INSTITUTE OF IN-STRUCTION. The Introductory Discourse and Lectures delivered in Boston, before the Convention of Teachers and other friends of education, assembled to form the American Institute of Instruction, August, 1830 (1831, 1836 and 1837). Published under the direction of the Board of Censors, 4 vols. Boston, 1831-38. 8vo.

AMERICAN JOURNAL (AND LIBRARY) OF DENTAL SCIENCE, etc.

Editors, C. A. Harris, E. Parmly. (S. Brown, L. Mackall, A. Westcott, E. Maynard, E. J. Dunning, W. H. Dwinelle.) July, 1839—July, 1850. Vol. 1-10. New York [and Baltimore], 1839-50. New Series. Edited by C. A. Harris (A. A. Blandy, A. S. Piggot). Vol. 1-6. Philadelphia, Baltimore [printed], 1850-56. 8°

AMERICAN JOURNAL OF EDU-CATION. Vol. 3 and 4. Jan. 1828 to Dec. 1829, (edited by W. Russell;) and Vol. 5, New Series, vol. 1, Jan. to August, 1830, (conducted by W. C. Woodbridge.) [Continued as] American Annals of Education. W. C. Woodbridge, editor. Vol. 2, 3. Jan. 1832—Dec. 1833. Boston, 1828-33. 8vo.

AMERICAN JOURNAL of Education and College Review. Edited by H. Barnard. Vol. 1. New York, 1855-6. 8°

AMERICAN JOURNAL OF IN-SANITY. Edited by the officers of the New York Lunatic Asylum, Utica. Vol. 1-6. Utica, 1844-50. 8vo.

AMERICAN JOURNAL OF SCI-ENCE . . and . . Arts. . . conducted by B. Silliman, (aided [after vol. 33] by B. Silliman, jun.) Vol. 1. New York, 1818. Vol. 2-49. New Haven, 1820-45. Vol. 50, General Index to 49 Vols. Second Series, conducted by Professor Silliman, B. Silliman, jun. and J. D. Dana. Vol. 1-22. New Haven, 1846-56. 8°

AMERICAN JOURNAL OF THE MEDICAL SCIENCES. 1827-40. 26 vol. Phila. 1828-40. 8vo.

AMERICAN LABOURER. Devoted to the cause of Protection to home Industry, embracing the arguments, reports, and speeches of the ablest civilians of the United States, in favour of the policy of protection to American labour. . In monthly parts, and now . . published complete in one volume. April, 1842, to March, 1843. New York, 1843. 8°

AMERICAN LAW JOURNAL
and Miscellaneous Repertory. By
J. E. Hall. 6 vol. Philadelphia, Baltimore, 1808-17. 8vo.

AMERICAN LITERARY MA-
GAZINE, monthly. By T. D. Sprague.
Vol. 1 and 2. Albany, 1847-48. 8°

AMERICAN LITERARY, SCI-
ENTIFIC and Military Academy. Catalogue of the officers and cadets;
together with the prospectus and internal regulations of the Institution,
etc. Windsor, Vt. [1823.] 8°

AMERICAN LITERATURE.
Views and Reviews in American Literature, History, and Fiction. By
the author of "The Yemassee," etc.
[W. G. Simms.] London [New York
printed], 1846. 8vo.

AMERICAN MAGAZINE; etc.
Dec. 1787—Nov. 1788. [Edited by
Noah Webster.] New York [1787-
88]. 8°

AMERICAN MAGAZINE and
Monthly Chronicle for the British
Colonies. Oct. 1757 to Oct. 1758.
By a Society of Gentlemen. Vol. 1.
Philadelphia [1757-58]. 8°

AMERICAN MAGAZINE of
Useful and Entertaining Knowledge.
Vol. 1-3. Boston, 1839. 8°

AMERICAN MECHANIC'S MA-
GAZINE: containing useful original
matter on subjects connected with
manufactures, the arts and sciences,
as well as selections from . . domestic
and foreign journals. Conducted by
Associated Mechanics. Feb. 5, 1825
—Feb. 11, 1826. 2 Vol. [After-
wards incorporated with the Journal
of the Franklin Institute.] New York,
1825-26. 8°.

AMERICAN MEDICAL AND
PHILOSOPHICAL REGISTER; or, Annals of Medicine, Natural History,
Agriculture, and the Arts, 1810-
14. Conducted by D. Hosack . .
and J. W. Francis. Second edition.
4 vol. New York, 1814. 8°

AMERICAN MISSIONS. His-
tory of American Missions to the Heathen, from their commencement to
the present time. Worcester, 1840.
8vo.

AMERICAN MONTHLY MA-
GAZINE. Edited . . by H. W.
Herbert and A. D. Paterson [and afterwards by C. F. Hoffman, P. Benjamin and R. M. Walsh]. March,
1833—Oct. 1838. 12 Vol. New
York, 1833-38. 8°

AMERICAN MONTHLY MA-
GAZINE and Critical Review. May,
1817—Oct. 1818. [Edited by H.
Biglow and O. L. Holley.] Vol. 1-3.
New York, 1817-18. 8°

AMERICAN MONTHLY RE-
VIEW [Edited by S. Willard.] 4 vol.
Cambridge, Boston, 1832-33. 8°

AMERICAN MUSEUM; or, Re-
pository of Ancient and Modern Fugitive Pieces, etc. 1787-89. 6 Vol.
[Continued as] The American Museum; or, Universal Magazine. 1790-
92. 6 Vol. Philadelphia, 1790-88-
92. 8vo.

AMERICAN NATIONAL PREA-
CHER; or, Original Monthly Ser-
mons, from Living Ministers of the
United States. Edited by Austin
Dickinson, A. M. Vol. 1-8. New
York, 1826-34. 8vo.

AMERICAN NAVAL BATTLES;
being a complete history of the battles
fought by the navy of the United States,
from its establishment in 1794 to the
present time. [By H. Kimball!]. . .
With twenty . . engravings. Boston,
1837. 8°

AMERICAN ORIENTAL SO-
CIETY. JOURNAL. Vol. 1-4, and vol. 5,
No. 1. [wanting Nos. 2 and 4 in vol.
1.] Boston, 1843-55. 8°

AMERICAN PAINTERS. Poeti-
cal and Prose Illustrations of celebrated
American Painters; with eleven engravings on steel by J. Sartain. Philadelphia, 1852. 4°

AMERICAN PEACE SOCIETY.
Ninth Report of the American Peace
Society. Boston [1837]. 8°

2 TENTH anniversary of the American Peace Society. (Tenth Annual
Report, *etc.*) Boston, 1838. 8°

3 TENTH Annual Report of the American Peace Society. Boston,1838. 8°

4 PRIZE Essays on a Congreſs of
Nations, for the adjustment of international disputes, and for the promotion of Universal Peace without resort
to arms . . Together with a Sixth Essay comprising the substance of the
rejected Eſſays . . [Edited by .
Ladd and G. C. Beckwith.] Boston,
1840. 8vo.

5 [*Begin.*] No. 1. The Cause of
Peace. [A series of occasional tracts
on peace, by various authors; Nos.
1—61]. Boston [1840?]. 8vo.

6 CLAIMS of Peace on Cities. Boston [1840?]. 8vo.

7 THE DUTY of Ministers with respect to the Cause of Peace. Boston
[1840?]. 8vo.

8 TRACT No. III. . The Duty of
Women to promote the Cause of Peace.
By Philanthropos. Boston[1840?]. 8°

AMERICAN PEOPLE. Ideas necesarias a todo pueblo Americano independiente, que quiera ser libre.
Philadelphia, 1821. 16mo.

AMERICAN PHILOSOPHICAL
SOCIETY. Transactions of the American Philosophical Society, held at
Philadelphia, for promoting Useful
Knowledge, from Jan. 1769 to 1809,
with plates. 6 Vol. Philadelphia,
1771-1809. New Series. Vol. 1 to
9. Philadelphia, 1818-46. 4°

2 TRANSACTIONS of the Historical
and Literary Committee of the . .
Society. Vol. 1 and vol. 3, part I.
Philadelphia, 1819-43. 8vo.

AMERICAN PIONEER; a monthly periodical, devoted to the objects
of the Logan Historical Society; or,
to collecting and publishing sketches
relative to the early settlement and

succeſſive improvement of the country. Vol. 1-2. January, 1842—October, 1843. Cincinnati, 1843. 8°

AMERICAN POEMS, selected
and original. Vol. 1. Litchfield (Connecticut), 1793. 8vo.

AMERICAN POLYTECHNIC
JOURNAL; a monthly periodical, devoted to Science, mechanic Arts, and
Agriculture. Conducted by . . C. G.
Page, . J. J. Greenough, . C. L.
Fleischmann. No. 1-5. Washington
and New York. 1853. 8vo.

AMERICAN PRECEDENTS.
American precedents of declarations;
collected chiefly from manuscripts of
accomplished pleaders; digested and
arranged under distinct titles and divisions, and adapted to the most modern practice. With a prefixed digest
of rules and cases concerning declarations. Boston, 1802. 12°

AMERICAN PUBLISHERS'
CIRCULAR and Literary Gazette. Vol.
1-2. September 1855—December
1856. New York, 1855-1856. 4to.

AMERICAN PULPIT; a Series
of original Sermons, by Clergymen of
the Protestant Episcopal Church. Vol.
1. Boston, 1831. 8vo. [Continued
under the title of] The Protestant
Episcopal Pulpit, *etc.* Vol. 2. New
York, 1832. 8vo.

AMERICAN QUARTERLY OB-
SERVER. 3 vol. [Afterwards united
with the BIBLICAL REPOSITORY, *which
see.*] Boston. 1833-34. 8°

AMERICAN QUARTERLY RE-
VIEW. March 1827—Dec. 1837. Vol.
1-22. Philadelphia, 1827-37. 8vo.

AMERICAN QUARTERLY TEM-
PERANCE MAGAZINE. No. II. May,
1833. [Albany, 1833.] 8°

AMERICAN RAILROAD JOUR-
NAL and Advocate of Internal Improvement (D. K. Minor, editor. Vol.
1-4. D. K. Minor and G. C. Schæffer,
editors, vol. 5-6). [There are two

editions of vol. 4 and 5.] 6 Vol. New York, 1832-1838. 4° [United with the Mechanics' Magazine, and continued under the title of] American Railroad Journal and Mechanics' Magazine (D. K. Minor, and G. C. Schæffer, editors. Vol. 1-2. G. C. Schæffer and E. Hedge, editors, Vol. 3-7. G. C. Schæffer, editor, Vol. 8-9). 9 vol. New York, 1838-42. 8°. Third Series, (G. C. Schæffer and D. K. Minor, editors.) 2 vol. New York, 1843-44. 8°. [Further continued as] The American Railroad Journal and General Advertiser for Railroads, Canals, Steamboats (D. K. Minor, editor). Second Quarto Series, Vol. 1-3. New York and Philadelphia, 1845-47. 4°. [Further continued as] The American Railroad Journal and Iron Manufacturers and Mining Gazette (D. K.Minor, editor). Vol.4. Philadelphia, 1848. 4° [Further continued as] American Railroad Journal, Steam Navigation, Commerce, Mining, etc. H. V. Poor, editor. Vol. 5-12. New York, 1849-56. 4°

AMERICAN REGISTER; Or, General Repository of History, Politics, and Science. [Edited by C. B. B. i. e. C. Brockden Brown.] 1806-7-1810. 7 vol. Philadelphia, 1807-1811. 8°

AMERICAN REGISTER; Or, Summary Review of History, Politics, and Literature. [Edited by R. Walsh.] 2 Vol. Philadelphia, 1817. 8°

AMERICAN REVIEW AND LIterary Journal. 1801-1802. 2 vol. New York, 1801-2. 8°

AMERICAN REVIEW; a Whig Journal of Politics, Literature, Art, and Science. [Continued under the title of] The American Whig Review. 16 Vol. New York, 1845-1852. 8°

AMERICAN REVIEW OF HIStory and Politics, and General Repository of Literature and State Papers.

Jan. 1811—Oct. 1812. 4 Vol. Philadelphia, 1811-12. 8°

AMERICAN REVOLUTION. The American Revolution; written in the style of ancient history. 2 vols. Philadelphia, 1793. 12°
- 2 STORIES of the American Revolution; comprising a complete anecdotic history of that . . . event. Philadelphia, 1847. 12°

AMERICAN SEAMEN. Remarks on the Scarcity of American Seamen, and the Remedy; the naval apprenticeship system; a home squadron, etc. etc. By a Gentleman connected with the New York press. New York, 1845. 8°

AMERICAN SEAMEN'S FRIEND SOCIETY. Second (to eighteenth) Annual Report; . with the Constitution, a list of Officers, etc. 13 Parts. [1st, 9th, 10th, 11th and 15th wanting.] New York, 1830—1846. 8vo.

AMERICAN SHIPWRECK SOCIETY. Constitution of the American Shipwreck Society. New York, 1844. 12mo.

AMERICAN SLAVERY. American Slavery as it is: Testimony of a thousand witnesses. New York, 1839. 8°

AMERICAN SOCIETY for EDucating Pious Youth, etc. Constitution and Address of the American Society. [See AMERICAN EDUCATION SOCIETY.] [Boston, 1816.] 8°

AMERICAN SOCIETY FOR MEliorating the Condition of the Jews. The Thirteenth (eighteenth to twenty-third) Report of the Board of Directors of the American Society, etc. 7 Parts. [1st to 12th; 14th to 17th wanting.] New York, 1836-1846. 8vo.

AMERICAN SOCIETY for the Encouragement of Domestic Manufactures. Addreſs to the people of the United States. New York, 1817. 8°

AMERICAN SONGS AND BAL-LADS. *See* SONGS AND BALLADS.

AMERICAN STAR. The American Star; being a choice collection of the most approved patriotic and other songs. Second edition. Richmond, 1817. 12°

AMERICAN STATISTICAL AS-SOCIATION. Collections of the American Statistical Aſsociations. Vol. 1. Boston, 1847. 8°

AMERICAN SYSTEM OF COOKERY. By a Lady of New York. New York, 1847. 12°

AMERICAN TEMPERANCE SOCIETY. Fourth (to sixth and ninth) Report of the American Temperance Society. 4 Parts. Boston, 1831-33 and 1836. 8°
2 VERBATIM Reprint of the Sixth Report of the American Temperance Society, presented at the meeting in New York, May, 1833. Boston, 1834. 8vo.

AMERICAN TRACT SOCIETY. Twenty-third, (twenty-fifth, twenty-seventh, twenty-eighth to thirty-second) Annual Report of the American Tract Society. 8 Parts. Boston, 1837-46. 8vo.

AMERICAN TURF REGISTER and Sporting Magazine. Vol. 1-7. [Vol. 1-6, edited .. by J. S. Skinner. Vol. 7, edited by A. J. Davie.] Sept. 1829—Aug. 1836. Baltimore, 1830-1836. 8°

AMERICAN UNITARIANISM. Review of American Unitarianism. Extracted from the Panoplist. [Boston, 1816?.] 8°

AMERICAN WEEKLY MES-SENGER; or, Register of State Papers, History, and Politics. 1813-14, 1814-15. 2 Vol. Philadelphia, 1814-15. 8°

AMERICAN WOMEN. The Duty of American Women to their Country. New York, 1845. 12°

AMERICANS. The other Side of the Question: or, A Defence of the Liberties of North America. In answer to a late Friendly Addreſs to all reasonable Americans. New York, 1774. 8vo.
2 A FRIENDLY Addreſs to all reasonable Americans, on the subject of our political confusions; in which the consequences of opposing the king's troops, and of a general non-importation, are fairly stated. America, 1774. 8vo.
3 STRICTURES on a pamphlet, entitled "A Friendly Addreſs to all reasonable Americans, on the subject of our Political Confusions," *etc.* New York, printed; Boston, reprinted, 1775. 12°
4 NOTIONS of the Americans: Picked up by a travelling bachelor [J. Fenimore Cooper]. A new edition. 2 vols. Philadelphia, 1838. 12°
5 NOTIONS of the Americans. Picked up by a travelling bachelor [J. Fenimore Cooper]. A new edition. 2 vols. Philadelphia, 1840. 12°

AMES, FISHER. Speech in the House of Representatives of the United States, April 28th, 1796, in support of the motion, That it is expedient to paſs the laws neceſsary to carry into effect the treaty lately concluded between the United States and the King of Great Britain. Boston [1796]. 8vo.
2 WORKS of Fisher Ames. Compiled by a number of his Friends. To which are prefixed notices of his Life. Boston, 1809. 8vo.
3 REMARKS on ... J. Q. Adams's Review of Mr. Ames's Works. Boston, 1809. 8vo.

AMHERST COLLEGE. [Annual] Catalogue of the Corporation, Faculty, and Students. Oct. 1831 (1833, 1838-9, 1839-40, 1840-41, 1841-2, 1845-46, and 1846-47). 8 Parts. Amherst, 1831-46. 8°

2 CATALOGUS eorum qui munera et officia gefserunt quique alicujus gradus laurea donati sunt in Collegio Amherstiensi, 1831 (1834 and 1839). 3 Parts. Amherstiæ, 1831-1839. 8°

AMICUS. Slavery among the Puritans. A Letter to the Rev. Moses Stuart [commenting on a pafsage in his Efsay on the Constitution]. Boston, 1850. 8°

AMISTAD. The African Captives. Trial of the prisoners of the Amistad on the writ of Habeas Corpus, before the Circuit Court of the United States, for the district of Connecticut, at Hartford. New York, 1839. 8°

AMOS, WILLIAM. Minutes in Agriculture and Planting. Boston, 1804. 4to.

ANACREON. Odes of Anacreon. Translated into English verse, with notes, by T. Moore. Philadelphia, 1804. 8°

ANALECTIC MAGAZINE; containing selections from foreign reviews and magazines, etc. Jan. 1813 —Dec. 1819. Vol. 1-14. New Series, Jan.—Dec. 1820. Vol. 1-2. Philadelphia, 1813-20. 8°

ANALYST. The Analyst: A collection of miscellaneous papers. New York, 1840. 12°

ANDERSON, CHRISTOPHER. The Annals of the English Bible. . . Abridged and continued by S. J. Prime. New York, 1849. 8°

ANDERSON, Rev. RUFUS. Observations on the Peloponnesus and Greek islands, made in 1829. Boston, 1830. 12°

2 MEMOIRS of Catharine Brown, a Christian Indian of the Cherokee Nation. Philadelphia, 1832. 12mo.

ANDERSON, WILLIAM WEMYSS. Jamaica and the Americans. New York, 1851. 8°

ANDOVER THEOLOGICAL SEMINARY. [Annual] Catalogue of the Officers and Students (for the years 1827, 1836, 1842, 1845, 1846). 5 Parts. Andover, 1827-46. 8°

2 TRIENNIAL Catalogue of the Theological Seminary. 1839 (and 1845). 2 Parts. Andover, 1839-45. 8°

ANDRAL, GABRIEL, the Younger. Pathological Hæmatology. An essay on the blood in disease, by G. A., . . . translated from the French by J. F. Meigs and A. Stillé. Philadelphia, 1844. 8°

ANDRE, JOHN, Major. Vindication of the Captors of Major André. [MS. note appended.] New York, 1817. 8vo.

ANDREW, JAMES O. Family Government; a treatise on conjugal, parental, and filial duties. Charleston, 1847. 12°

ANDREWS, CHARLES C. The History of the New York American Free Schools, from their establishment in 1837, to the present time ; . . . . Also, a brief account of the succefsful labours of the New York Manumifsion Society; with an appendix, etc. New York, 1830. 12°

ANDREWS, E. A. Slavery and the Domestic Slave-Trade in the United States. Boston, 1836. 12mo.

2 A copious and critical Latin-English Lexicon, founded on the larger Latin-German Lexicon of Dr. W. Freund; with additions and corrections. . By E. A. Andrews, etc. New York, 1852. 8°

ANDREWS, E. A. and STODDARD, SOLOMON. A Grammar of the Latin Language; for the use of schools and colleges. Tenth edition. Boston, 1844. 12°

ANDREWS, ELISHA. A Series of Letters upon this Question : Whether true saints are liable finally to fall from an estate of grace so as to perish everlastingly ? Containing a brief reply to a tract on that subject, supposed to be written by the late Rev. J. Wesley. Plattsburgh, 1821. 8vo.

ANGEL. The Angel over the Right Shoulder, or the beginning of a new year. By the author of "Sunny Side," [E. S. Phelps.] New York, Andover [printed !] 1853. 16mo.

ANGELL, JOSEPH K. A Practical Summary of the Law of Assignments in trust for the Benefit of Creditors; with an appendix of forms. Boston, 1835. 12°

2 A TREATISE on the Law of Watercourses; with an appendix, containing forms of declaration, *etc.* Third edition, revised and containing reference to many new adjudged cases. Boston, 1840. 8°

ANGELL, OLIVER. The Union, No. II; or, Child's Second Book. Being the second of a series of spelling and reading books, in six numbers. Providence, 1830. 12°

2 THE UNION, No. III; or, Child's Third Book. Being the third of a series of spelling and reading books, in six numbers. Providence, 1830. 12°

3 ANGELL's Union series. The Union, No. V; containing Lessons for Reading and Spelling, *etc.* Philadelphia, 1835. 12°

ANGLO-SAXON ORTHOGRAPHY. The American System of Education. A Hand-book of Anglo-Saxon Orthography. In 2 Parts. .... By a literary association. New York, 1853. 8°

ANNAPOLIS AND ELKRIDGE RAILROAD COMPANY. The First Annual Report of the Directors of the Annapolis and Elkridge Railroad Company. (Reports upon the surveys, location, and progress of construction of the Annapolis and Elkridge Railroad. By G. W. Hughes.) Annapolis [Maryland], 1839. 8°

ANNUAL LAW REGISTER OF

THE UNITED STATES. By W. Griffith. Vol. 3, 4. Burlington, N. J. 1822. 8vo.

ANNUAL OF SCIENTIFIC DISCOVERY; or, Year-book of Facts in Science and Art. . Edited by D. A. Wells and G. Bliss. 1850, 1851. 2 Vol. Boston, 1850-51. 12°

ANSLEY, E. A. Elements of Literature ; or, An Introduction to the Study of Rhetoric and Belles Lettres. Philadelphia, 1849. 12°

ANTHON, CHARLES. A Classical Dictionary; containing an account of the principal proper names mentioned in ancient authors. Together with an account of Coins, Weights, and Measures. New York, 1841. 8vo.

2 A SYSTEM of Greek Prosody and Metre . . together with the choral scanning of the Prometheus vinctus of Æschylus, *etc.* To which are appended remarks on Indo-Germanic analogies. New York, 1842. 12°

3 A SYSTEM of Latin Prosody and Metre, from the best authorities, ancient and modern. New York, 1844. 12°

4 A SYSTEM of Latin Versification, in a series of progressive exercises, including specimens of translation from English and German poetry into Latin verse. For the use of schools and colleges. New York, 1845. 12°

5 ANTHON's Greek Lessons. Part I. First Greek Lessons, containing all the inflections of the Greek language. Together with appropriate Exercises in the translating and writing of Greek, for the use of beginners. (Part II. An Introduction to Greek Prose Composition, with explanatory Exercises, in which the principles of Greek Syntax are elucidated.) 2 parts. New York, 1845. 12°

6 ANTHON's Latin Grammar. Part II. An Introduction to Latin Prose Composition, with a complete course of Exercises, illustrative of all the im-

portant principles of Latin syntax. New York, 1845. 12°

7 ANTHON's Latin Grammar. Part I. First Latin Leſsons, containing the most important parts of the Grammar of the Latin language, etc. New York, 1846. 12°

8 A GRAMMAR of the Greek Language, for the use of schools and colleges. New York, 1846. 12°

9 A GRAMMAR of the Greek Language, principally from the German of Kühner. With selections from Matthiæ, Buttmann, Thiersch, and Rost. For the use of schools and colleges. New York, 1846. 12°

10 A GREEK Reader, selected principally from the work of F. Jacobs . . with English notes, critical and explanatory, a metrical index to Homer and Anacreon, and a copious lexicon. New York, 1846. 12°

11 A SYSTEM of Ancient and Mediæval Geography, for the use of schools and colleges. New York, 1850. 8°

12 A MANUAL of Roman Antiquities. New York, 1851. 12°

ANTHON, GEORGE C. Narrative and documents connected with the displacement of the Profeſsor of the Greek language and literature in the University of the city of New York. New York, 1851. 8°

ANTHON, JOHN. A digested Index to the reported Decisions of the several Courts of Law in the United States. By John Anthon [continued by T. Day, T. J. Wharton, T. S. Smith, and F. J. Troubat]. 5 vols. Philadelphia, 1813-30. 8°

2 THE LAW of Nisi Prius, being reports of cases determined at Nisi Prius in the Supreme Court of the State of New York, with notes and commentaries on each case. To which is prefixed an introductory eſsay on the studies preparatory to the active duties of the bar. New York, 1820, 8°

3 THE LAW Student; or, Guides to the Study of the Law in its Principles. New York, 1850. 8°

ANTI-MASONIC CONVENTION. The proceedings of the United States Anti-Masonic Convention, held at Philadelphia, September 11, 1830. Embracing the Journal of proceedings, the reports, the debates, and the addreſs to the people. 2 parts. Philadelphia, 1830. 8vo.

2 PROCEEDINGS of the Second Convention at Baltimore, September 1831. Journal and reports, nomination of candidates for the President and Vice-President of the United States, letters of acceptance, resolutions, and the addreſs to the people. Boston, 1832. 8vo.

ANTI-MASONIC REVIEW AND MAGAZINE; intended to take note of the origin and history, of the pretensions and character, and of the standard works and productions of Freemasonry. By H. D. Ward. 2 vol. New York, 1828-30. 8vo.

ANTI-SLAVERY EXAMINER. Nos. 2, 3, 5 to 13. New York, 1836-1845. 8vo.

ANTI-SLAVERY RECORD FOR 1835 (-1837). . Published . . for the American Anti-Slavery Society. 3 vol. New York, 1835-38. 12°

ANTI-SLAVERY REPORTER; a Periodical. Vol. 1, No. 5 and 6. New York, 1833. 8°

APES, WILLIAM. Eulogy on King Philip, [Sachem of Pokanoket, Rhode Island,] as pronounced at the Odeon, in . . Boston, etc. Boston, 1836, 12°

APOSTLES. The Work claiming to be the Constitutions of the Holy Apostles, including the Canons; Whiston's version, revised from the Greek; with a prize eſsay . . . upon their origin and contents [by O. C. Krabbe]; translated from the German by J. Chase. New York, 1848. 8°

APPEAL to the Candid [in favour of Unitarianism], No. 1 to 3. [Boston ! 1814 !] 8°

APPLETON, DANIEL. Appleton's Library Manual; containing a Catalogue Raisonné of upwards of twelve thousand of the most important works in every department of knowledge, in all modern languages. [Compiled by T. Delf.] New York, 1847. 8vo.

2 APPLETON'S Dictionary of Machines, Mechanics, Engine-work, and Engineering. 2 vols. New York, 1852. 4°

3 APPLETON'S Mechanic's Magazine and Engineer's Journal... Edited by J. W. Adams. No. 1-10. New York, 1850. 8°

APPLETON, Rev. JESSE. Lectures delivered at Bowdoin College, and occasional Sermons. Brunswick, Maine, 1822. 8°

2 WORKS; embracing his Course of Theological Lectures, Academic Addresses and a Selection from his Sermons; with a Memoir of his Life and Character. [Edited by A. S. Packard.] 2 vols. Andover, 1837-36. 8vo.

APPLETON, NATHAN. Speech in reply to Mr. McDuffie, of South Carolina, on the Tariff; delivered in the House of Representatives, 30th May, 1842. Washington, 1832. 8°

2 SPEECH . . on the Bill to reduce and otherwise alter the Duties on Imports; delivered in the House of Representatives . . Jan. 23, 1833. Washington, 1833. 8°

3 REMARKS on Currency and Banking; having reference to the present derangement of the circulating medium in the United States. Boston, 1841. 8vo.

4 WHAT is a Revenue Standard ! and a review of Secretary Walker's Report on the Tariff. Bost. 1846. 8°

APPLETON, NATHANIEL, D. D. Isaiah's Mission consider'd and apply'd in a Sermon [on Isaiah vi. 8.] preached at the gathering of a church and ordination of their Pastor, Mr. J. Cotton, in Providence, Octob. 23, 1728. Boston, 1728. 8°

2 GOSPEL Ministers must be fit for the Master's use . . a sermon [on 2 Tim. ii. 21] at the ordination of Mr. J. Sargent. Boston, 1735. 8vo.

3 A DISCOURSE [on 2 Corinthians, viii. 18.] occasioned by the much lamented death of the Rev. E. Wigglesworth, etc. Boston, 1765. 8°

4 THE CROWN of eternal Life the sure Reward of the Faithful; exhibited in two discourses [on Rev. ii. 10] on the Lord's Day after the funeral of E. Holyoke. Boston, 1769. 8vo.

5 THE RIGHT Method of addressing the Divine Majesty in Prayer . . set forth in two discourses on . . the day of general fasting and prayer, etc. Boston, 1770. 8°

APPRENTICES. The Apprentices' Dialogues: written by the mother of an apprentice. Philadelphia [1829]. 12mo.

APRIL. The First of April [a religious tale]. Philadelphia, 1827. 12mo.

APTHORP, Rev. EAST. Considerations on the institution and conduct of the Society for the Propagation of the Gospel in Foreign Parts. Boston, 1763. 8°

2 THE FELICITY of the Times, a Sermon on Psalm cvi. 5. Boston, 1763. 4°

ARAGO, DOMINIQUE FRANCOIS JEAN. Tract on Comets; and particularly on the Comet that is to intersect the Earth's Path in October, 1832. Translated from the French, by J. Farrar. Boston, 1832. 12mo.

2 POPULAR Lectures on Astronomy, delivered at the Royal Observatory of Paris, with extensive additions and corrections by D. Lardner. Third edition. New York, 1848. 8°

ARAN, F. A. Practical Manual of the Diseases of the Heart and great

Veſſels . . Translated from the French by W. A. Harris. Philadelphia, 1843. 12°

ARATOR; being a series of Agricultural Eſſays, practical and political, in sixty-one numbers. By a citizen of Virginia [John Taylor]. Georgetown, D. C. 1813. 12°

ARCHDALE, JOHN. A New Description of that fertile and pleasant Province of Carolina: with a brief account of its Discovery and settling, and the Government thereof to this time. With several remarkable passages of Divine Providence during my time. London, printed in 1707. Charleston, reprinted, 1822. 8°

ARCHER, RICHARD, Pseud. The Island Home; or, the Young Castaways. Edited by C. Romaunt. Boston, 1852. 8°

ARCHIBALD, A. K. Poems. Boston, 1848. 12°

ARCTURUS; a Journal of Books and Opinion [edited by C. Mathews and E. A. Duyckinck]. Vol. 1, 2. New York, 1841. 8°

ARDEN. The Unfortunate Stranger, who was tried for the Murder of Miſſ Harriet Finch. . A true story. New York [1830?] 8°

ARIEL, JACK. Jack Ariel; or, Life on Board an Indiaman. By the author of the " Post Captain," " Travels in America," and " A Life of Chatterton." [By John Dix ?] New York, 1852. 8°

ARISTIDES, Pseud. A Letter [signed Aristides] to General Hamilton, occasioned by his letter to President Adams. By a Federalist. [Boston ! 1800.] 8°

2 AN EXAMINATION of the various Charges exhibited against A. Burr, Vice-President of the United States, and a Development of the Characters and Views of his Political Opponents.

A new edition, . with additions. By Aristides. [Washington ?] 1804. 8°

3 ESSAYS on the Spirit of Jacksonism, as exemplified in its deadly Hostility to the Bank of the United States, and in the odious Calumnies employed for its Destruction. By Aristides. Philadelphia, 1835. 8°

ARISTOPHANES. The Birds . . . With notes, and a metrical table ; by C. C. Felton. Cambridge, 1849. 12°

ARMSBY, JAMES H. Hospitals. Annual Addreſſ delivered before the Albany County Medical Society, November, 1852. Albany, 1853. 8vo.

ARMSTRONG, JOHN, Major-General. Notices of the War of 1812. 2 vol. New York, 1840. 12mo.

2 A TREATISE on Agriculture; comprising a concise History of its Origin and progreſſ; the present Condition of the Art, and the Theory and Practice of Husbandry. To which is added, a Diſſertation on the Kitchen and Fruit Garden. . With notes by J. Buel. New York, 1845. 12°

ARMSTRONG, Rev. LEBBEUS. The Temperance Reformation of this XIX. Century, the Fulfilment of Divine Prophecy. A Sermon [Isaiah lix. 19; Rev. xii. 15, 16]. New York, 1845. 8vo.

2 THE TEMPERANCE Reformation; its history from the organization of the first Temperance Society to the adoption of the liquor law of Maine, 1851 ; and the consequent influence of the promulgation of that law, etc. New York, 1853. 12°

ARMSTRONG, WILLIAM. Stocks and Stock-jobbing in Wall Street, with sketches of the brokers, and fancy stocks. . By a reformed stock-gambler (W. Armstrong). New York, 1848. 8°

ARMY AND NAVY CHRONICLE. Vol. 1-13. June 30, 1834— May 21, 1842. Edited by B. Homans.

Washington, 1834-42. Vol.1. 4° and 2-13 in 8°

ARMY AND NAVY CHRON-
ICLE AND SCIENTIFIC REPOSITORY.
W. Q. Force, editor. 3 vol. Wash-
ington, 1843-44. 8°

AROUET. The Poems of Arouet.
Charleston, S. C. 1786. 16mo.

ARTHUR, T. S. Heart-histories
and Life-pictures. N. York, 1853. 12°
   2 THE OLD Man's Bride. New
York, 1853. 12°
   3 THE Two Merchants; or, Sol-
vent and Insolvent. Philadelphia,
1853. 8°

ARTHUR, T. S. and CARPEN-
TER, W. H. The History of Georgia,
from its earliest Settlement to the present Time. By T. S. Arthur and W.
H. Carpenter. Philadel. 1852. 12°
   2 THE HISTORY of Kentucky, from
its earliest Settlement to the present
Time. By T. S. Arthur, and W. H.
Carpenter. Philadelphia, 1852. 12°

ARTHUR, T. S. and WOOD-
WORTH, FRANCIS C. The String of
Pearls, for Boys and Girls. By T. S.
Arthur and F. C. Woodworth. Au-
burn and Buffalo, 1853. 12°

ARTIST. The Artist's Afsistant
in Drawing, Perspective, Etching, etc.
Sixth edition. Philadelphia, 1794. 12°

ARVINE, A. KAZLITT. Cyclopæ-
dia of Moral and Religious Anecdotes.
. . With an introduction, by G. B.
Cheever, D.D. Fourth thousand.
New York, 1849. 8°
   2 THE CYCLOPÆDIA of Anecdotes
of Literature and the Fine Arts. . .
With illustrations. Boston, 1852. 8°

ASHMEAD, JOHN W. Reports
of Cases adjudged in the Courts of
Common Pleas, Quarter Sefsions,
Oyer and Terminer, and Orphans'
Court, of the first judicial district of
Pennsylvania: with notes and refer-
ences. 2 vol. Philadelphia, 1831-
1841. 8°

ASHMUN, GEORGE. Speech . . .
on the Mexican War; delivered in
the House of Representatives, . Feb.
4, 1847. Washington, 1847. 8°

ASIA. Letters from Asia; written
by a gentleman of Boston to his friend
in that place. New York, 1819.
12mo.

ASSOCIATION OF AMERICAN
GEOLOGISTS AND NATURALISTS. Reports of the first, second, and third
meetings of the Afsociation . . at
Philadelphia, in 1840 and 1841, and
at Boston, in 1842; embracing its
proceedings and transactions. Boston,
1843. 8vo.

ASTOR LIBRARY. Annual Re-
port of the Trustees of the Astor Library, Jan. 26, 1854. Albany, 1845.
8vo.
   2 ANNUAL Report of the Trustees
of the Astor Library, for 1854. Albany, 1855. 8vo.

ASTRO-MAGNETIC ALMANAC,
for 1843. By H. H. Sherwood.
Calendar, by D. Young, calculated
for the horizon .. of New Orleans. No.
1. New York [1842]. 12mo.

ASTRONOMICAL JOURNAL,
edited by B. A. Gould. Vol. 1-3.
Cambridge, 1851-53. 4°

.ATHANASION. Second Edition,
with notes and corrections. Also, Miscellaneous Poems. By the author of
"Christian Ballads," etc. [with a Dedication signed C., i. e. Arthur Cleaveland Coxe.] New York, 1842. 12°

ATHENS. Description of the
[panoramic] View of Athens and the
surrounding Country [exhibited at
Cambridge in Mafsachusetts. With
a plate]. Cambridge, 1842. 12°

ATHERTON, CHARLES GORDON.
Speech . . on the Twelve million
Loan Bill; delivered in the House of
Representatives, . July 12, 1841.
Washington, 1841. 8°
   2 SPEECH .. on the reference of

so much of the President's Message as relates to the Tariff; delivered in the House of Representatives, Dec. 23, 1841. Washington, 1841. 8°

3 SPEECH . . on the Loan Bill, and in favor of restoring to the Treasury the proceeds of the Public Lands, in House of Representatives, Mar. 30, 1842. [Washington, 1842.] 8°

4 SPEECH . . on the Apportionment Bill; delivered in the House of Representatives, May 3, 1842. Washington, 1842. 8°

5 SPEECH . . on the Tariff; delivered in the Senate . . May 25, 1844. Washington, 1844. 8°

ATLANTIC CLUB-BOOK: being sketches in prose and verse, by various authors. 2 vol. New York, 1834. 12°

ATLANTIC JOURNAL AND Friend of Knowledge; in eight numbers. By C. S. Rafinesque. Philadelphia, 1832-33. 8°

ATLANTIC MAGAZINE [and New York Review], May, 1824—April, 1825. Vol. 1, 2. New York, 1824-25. 8°

ATLANTIC SOUVENIR; a Christmas and New Year's Offering. Philadelphia [dates erased, 183-?]. 12°

ATTICUS, Pseud. Remarks on the proposed Canal from Lake Erie to the Hudson River. By Atticus. New York, 1816. 8vo.

2 HINTS on the subject of Interments within the City of Philadelphia, etc. Philadelphia, 1838. 8°

ATWATER, CALEB. Remarks made on a Tour to Prairie du Chien, thence to Washington City, in 1829. Columbus, Ohio, 1831. 12mo.

2 A HISTORY of the State of Ohio, Natural and Civil. Second edition. Cincinnati [1838]. 8vo.

AUBURN THEOLOGICAL SEMINARY. Catalogues of the officers and students of the Theological Semi-

nary, Auburn [New York], 1846-7. Auburn, 1847. 8vo.

AUDIN, J. M. V. History of the Life, Writings and Doctrines of Martin Luther. Translated from the French. Philadelphia, 1841. 8vo.

AUDUBON, JOHN W. Illustrated Notes of an Expedition through Mexico and California. No. 1. New York, 1852. Fol.

AUDUBON, JOHN JAMES. The Birds of America, from original drawings. 4 Vol. [containing 435 plates engraved, printed and coloured by R. Havell, except the first 10, which are by W. H. Lizars.] Large folio. London, 1827-38. Letterpress in 5 vol. Edinburgh. 1831-39.] 8vo.

2 THE BIRDS of America, from drawings made in the United States and their Territories. 7 Vols. New York, 1840-44. roy. 8vo.

AUDUBON, JOHN JAMES, and BACHMAN, JOHN. The Viviparous Quadrupeds of North America. 2 Vol. [containing 150 coloured plates]. New York, 1845-46. Fol. [With the Text. Vol. 1. London (New York printed), 1847]. 8vo.

AVERY, DAVID. The Lord is to be praised for the Triumphs of his Power, a Sermon [on Exodus xv. 11]. Norwich, 1778. 4°

2 A SERMON [on Job xix. 21] on the Duty of Christian Pity, preached at the interment of Mr. W. Moor, etc. Charlestown, 1799. 8vo.

AVERY, JOSEPH. An Oration, delivered at Holden, July 4, 1806, being the anniversary of the Independence of the United States of America. Boston, 1806. 8°

AVES, THOMAS. Case of the Slave-child, Med. Report of the arguments of counsel, and of the opinion of the Court, in the case of Commonwealth vs. Aves, . . in the Supreme

Judicial Court of Maſſachusetts. Boston, 1836. 8°

AUSTIN, BENJAMIN. Constitutional Republicanism, in opposition to fallacious Federalism; as published in the Independent Chronicle, under the signature of Old South. To which is prefixed, a Prefatory Addreſs to the Citizens of the United States. Boston, 1803. 8°

2 MEMORIAL to the Legislature of Maſſachusetts (relative to a charge delivered to the Grand Jury of the county of Suffolk, Nov. Term, 1806, by the Hon. T. Parsons, Esq. Chief Justice of the Commonwealth), [with the Report of a Committee of the Legislature thereon. Boston, 1808]. 8°

AUSTIN, J. M. A Voice to Youth; addreſſed to Young Men and Young Ladies. Eighth edition. New York, 1846. 12°

AUSTIN, JAMES TRECOTHICK. An Oration delivered .. July 4, 1829, at the celebration of American Independence, in the city of Boston. Boston, 1829. 8°

2 THE LIFE of Elbridge Gerry; with contemporary Letters: to the close of the American revolution. (The Life, etc. From the close of the American revolution.) 2 vol. Boston, 1828-29. 8°

3 AN ADDRESS delivered before the Maſſachusetts Society for the Suppreſſion of Intemperance. Boston, 1830. 8°

AUSTIN, IVERS J. An Addreſs delivered before the Corps of Cadets of the United States Military Academy. New York, 1842. 8°

AUSTIN, SAMUEL, D. D. The most promising Life and Death closely connected. A Sermon [on John xix. 41] delivered .. the Sabbath subsequent to the death .. of Miss H. Blair, etc. Worcester, Maſs. 1794. 8vo.

2 AN ORATION, pronounced at Worcester [in Maſſachusetts] .. July 4, 1798; the anniversary of the Independence of the United States of America. Worcester, Maſs. 1798. 8°

AUSTIN, WILLIAM. Letters from London, written during 1802 and 1803. Boston, 1804. 8vo.

AUTUMN LEAVES. A collection of Miscellaneous Poems, from various authors. N. York, 1837. 12°

AZUNI, DOMENICO ALBERTO. The Maritime Law of Europe. Translated from the French [by W. Johnson]. 2 vol. New York, 1806. 8°

ACHE, ALEX-ANDER DALLAS. Report to the Controllers of the Public Schools on the re-organization of the Central High Schools of Philadelphia. [Philadelphia, 1839.] 8°

2 ANOTHER edition [containing the semi-annual Report and other additional documents]. [Philadelphia, 1839.] 8°

3 REPORT on Education in Europe, to the Trustees of the Girard College for Orphans. Philadelphia, 1839. 8vo.

4 REPORT on the Organization of a High School for Girls and Seminary for Female Teachers. [Phila. 1840.] 8°

5 ADDRESS delivered at the close of the Twelfth Exhibition of American Manufactures held by the Franklin Institute of .. Pennsylvania ... 1842. [Philadelphia, 1842.] 8°

6 REPORT of the Principal of the Central High School to the Committee of the Board of Controllers of the Public Schools, for the year ending July 1842. Philadelphia, 1843. 8°

BACHE, ANNA. Clara Howell: or, the Little Housewife. London, Edinburgh, and New York, 1855. 16mo.

BACHE, FRANKLIN. Observations and Reflections on the Penitentiary System. A Letter to Roberts Vaux. Philadelphia, 1829. 8vo.

BACHE, WILLIAM. An Experimental Dissertation to ascertain the

Morbid Effects of Carbonic Acid Gas, or fixed air, on healthy animals, and the manner in which they are produced. Philadelphia, 1794. 8vo.

BACHI, PIETRO. A Grammar of the Italian language. A new edition revised and improved. Boston, Cambridge [printed].· 1838. 12mo.

BACKUS, GEORGE. A Digest of Laws relating to the Offices and Duties of Sheriff, Coroner, and Constable. 2 vol. New York, 1812. 8°

BACKUS, Rev. ISAAC. All true Ministers of the Gospel are called into that Work by the special Influences of the Holy Spirit. A Discourse shewing the nature and necessity of an internal call to preach the everlasting Gospel ... To which is added some short account of the experiences and dying testimony of Mr. N. Shepherd. Boston, 1754. 8vo.

2 A LETTER to .. Mr. B. Lord, .. occasioned by some harsh things .. published against those who have dissented from him about the Ministry, the Church, and Baptism. Providence, 1764. 8vo.

3 A HISTORY of New England, with particular reference to the denomination of Christians called Baptists. (A church history of New England, vol. 2, extending from 1690 to 1784.) 2 vol. Boston and Providence, 1777-84. 8vo.

BACON, DAVID FRANCIS. Lives of the Apostles of Jesus Christ. New York, 1846. 8°

BACON, EZEKIEL, and others. To the Hon. the Senate and House of Representatives of . . . Maſſachusetts, in General Court aſſembled, the memorial of the undersigned [E. Bacon and others], . sureties of T. J. Skinner, late Treasurer and Receiver-General of said Commonwealth, etc. Boston, 1811. 8°

2 MEMORIAL of the sureties of T. J. Skinner, late Treasurer of the Commonwealth ; together with a view of their case, and the grounds on which they claim to be exonerated from their liability for his defalcations. Pittsfield, [1812 ?] 8°

BACON, FRANCIS, Baron Verulam and Viscount St. Alban's. Essays, Moral, Economical, and Political. The Conduct of the Underſtanding, by J. Locke. With an introductory Eſſay by A. Potter. N. York, 1844. 12°

BACON, Rev. LEONARD. A Discourse on the Traffic in Spirituous Liquors. . With an appendix, exhibiting the present state and influence of the traffic in the City of New Haven. New Haven, 1838. 8°

2 THIRTEEN Historical Discourses, on the completion of 200 years, from the beginning of the first church in New Haven, with an appendix. New Haven, 1839. 8°

3 AN ADDRESS before the New England Society of . . New York, on Forefathers' Day, Dec. 22, 1838. New York, 1839. 8°

4 A DISCOURSE on the Early Constitutional History of Connecticut, delivered before the Connecticut Historical Society, Hartford, May 17, 1843. Hartford, 1843. 8°

5 ORATION before the Phi Beta Kappa Society of Dartmouth College, etc. Hanover, 1845. 8°

6 SLAVERY discuſſed in occasional Eſſays, from 1833 to 1846. New York, 1846. 12°

7 THE AMERICAN Church, a Discourse [on Titus i. 5] in behalf of the American Home Miſſionary Society, etc. New York, 1852. 8vo.

BACON, MATTHEW. A New Abridgment of the Law. [Continued by J. Sayer and O. Ruffhead.] . . With large additions and corrections by Sir H. Gwyllim and C. E. Dodd : and with the notes and references made to the edition published in 1809. by B. Wilson. To which are added notes and references to American law and decisions, by J. Bouvier. 10 vol. Philadelphia, 1846. 8°

BACON, Rev. SAMUEL. Memoir of Rev. Samuel Bacon, an early advocate of Sunday Schools. Revised by the Committee of Publication. Philadelphia, 1831. 12mo.

BACON, WILLIAM THOMPSON. A Poem by William Thompson Bacon. and the Valedictory Oration by C. A. Johnson, pronounced before the senior claſs of Yale College, July 5, 1837. New Haven, 1837. 8°

BAILEY, EBENEZER. The Young Lady's Claſs Book ; a selection of lessons for reading, in prose and verse . . . Revised stereotype edition. Boston, 1845. 12°

BAILEY, GAMALIEL. American Progreſs : a Lecture delivered before the Young Men's Mercantile Library Aſſociation of Cincinnati, etc. Cincinnati, 1846. 8°

BAILEY, HENRY, State Reporter. Reports of Cases argued and determined in the Court of Appeals of South Carolina, on appeal from the Courts of Law. May, 1828 to Jan. 1832. 2 vol. Charleston, 1833-34. 8°

2 REPORTS of Cases in Equity, argued and determined in the Court of Appeals of South Carolina. Vol. I., Jan. 1830 to April. 1831, inclusive. Charleston, 1841. 8°

BAILEY, J. T. An Historical Sketch of the City of Brooklyn, and the surrounding Neighbourhood ; . .

to which is added, an .. Account of the Battle of Long Island. Compiled from the best authorities. Brooklyn, 1840. 12°

BAILEY, JOHN J. Waldimar. A Tragedy, in five acts [and in verse]. Not published. N. York, 1834. 8vo.

BAILEY, ISAAC. American Naval Biography. Providence, 1815. 12°

BAILEY'S WASHINGTON ALMANAC, FOR .. 1823. Philadelphia [1823]. 12°

BAILEY, PHINEHAS. A Pronouncing Stenography, containing a complete system of Shorthand Writing; governed by the analogy of sounds, and adapted to every language. Second edition. Burlington, 1833. 8vo.

BAINES, EDWARD, the Elder, late M.P. for Leeds. History of the Wars of the French Revolution, from the breaking out of the War, in 1792, to the Restoration of a General Peace, in 1815; comprehending the civil History of Great Britain and France during that period. . Second edition. . With notes and an original history [by the American editor] of the late war between the United States and Great Britain. 4 vol. Philadelphia, 1824. 8°

BAIRD, ROBERT, D.D. Visit to Northern Europe: or, Sketches Descriptive, Historical, Political and Moral, of Denmark, Norway, Sweden and Finland, and the free cities of Hamburg and Lubeck; etc. 2 vol. New York, 1841. 12°

2 SKETCHES of Protestantism in Italy; past and present: including a notice of the Origin, History, and present State of the Waldenses. Boston, 1845. 12°

3 SKETCHES of Protestantism in Italy: past and present; including a notice of the Origin, History, and present State of the Waldenses. Second thousand, with an appendix. Boston, 1847. 12°

4 THE CHRISTIAN Retrospect and Register; a summary of the scientific, moral, and religious progress of the first half of the nineteenth century. Third edition. New York, 1851. 12°

BAIRD, ROBERT H. The American Cotton Spinner and Managers' and Carders' Guide. A practical treatise on Cotton Spinning, etc. Philadelphia, 1851. 12°

BAIRD, SPENCER F. On the Serpents of New York; with a notice of a species not hitherto included in the Fauna of the State. Albany, 1854. 8°

BAKER, JOHN M. A View of the Commerce between the United States and Rio de Janeiro, Brazil. Washington, 1838. 8°

BAKER, SARAH. Christian Effort; or, Facts and Incidents designed to enforce and illustrate the duty of Individual Labour for the Salvation of Souls. New York, 1850. 16°

BALCH, WILLIAM. A Public Spirit as express'd in praying for the Peace and seeking the Good of Jerusalem, recommended to Rulers and People. A Sermon [on Psalm cxxii. 6—9] preached before his Excellency W. Shirley, the Council, etc. of Massachusetts, May 31, 1749. Being the day for electing the Council. Boston, 1749. 8°

BALCH (WILLIAM S.) LECTURES on Language, as particularly connected with English Grammar. Providence, 1838. 12°

2 A GRAMMAR of the English Language, etc. Boston, 1839. 12°

3 IRELAND, as I saw it: the Character, Condition, and Prospects of the People. New York, 1850. 8°

4 ROMANISM and Republicanism incompatible. A Lecture .. in review of "The. Catholic Chapter in the History of the United States," . by .. J. Hughes, D. D. Archbishop of New York. New York, 1852. 8vo.

. BALDWIN. A Plan of Baldwin,

Maine] copied and reduced from the original in the Land Office. [Boston, 1815.] 8°

BALDWIN, EBENEZER. Annals of Yale College, in New Haven, Connecticut, from its foundation to 1831. With an appendix, containing statistical tables, and exhibiting the present condition of the Institution. New Haven, 1831. 8vo.

2 CATALOGUE of the Phenogamous Plants and the Ferns growing without cultivation, within five miles of Yale College, Connecticut. Extracted from the appendix to Mr. E. Baldwin's History of Yale College. New Haven, 1831. 8°

BALDWIN, ELIHU W. The Five Apprentices. (Procrastination; or, the History of Edward Crawford.) Philadelphia, 1828. 12mo.

2 THE YOUNG Freethinker reclaimed. Philadelphia, 1830. 12mo.

BALDWIN, HENRY. Reports of Cases determined in the Circuit Court of the United States, in and for the third circuit, comprising the eastern district of Pennsylvania, and the State of New Jersey. Vol. I. [All published.] Philadelphia, 1837. 8°

BALDWIN, LOAMMI. Report on introducing pure Water into the city of Boston. Second edition, with additions. Boston, 1835. 8°

2 REPORT on the Brunswick Canal and Railroad, Glynn County, Georgia, with an appendix containing the Charter and Commissioners Report. Boston, 1836. 8°

BALDWIN, MOSES. The Certainty of Death . . A Sermon [on Eccles. ix. 10] . . . occasioned by the death of Dr. A. Stone, etc. Boston, 1774. 8vo.

BALDWIN, SIMEON. An Oration pronounced . . July 4, 1788, in commemoration of the Declaration of Independence and establishment of the Constitution of the United States of America. New Haven, 1788. 8°

BALDWIN, THOMAS, D. D. A Sermon [on John i. 47] preached . . on the day of the interment of his Honour S. Phillips, Esq., Lieutenant Governor. Boston, 1802. 8vo.

2 THE PEACEFUL Reflections and glorious Prospects of the departing Saint. A Discourse [on 2 Tim. iv. 7, 8] delivered . . . at the interment of the Rev. S. Stillman, etc. Boston [1807]. 8vo.

BALDWIN, THOMAS. A Pronouncing Gazetteer, by T. Baldwin, assisted by several gentlemen. To which is added an appendix, containing more than 10,000 additional names chiefly of the small towns and villages, etc. of the United States and Mexico. Ninth edition, with a supplement. Philadelphia, 1851. 12°

BALDWIN, WILLIAM, M.D., U. S. Navy. Reliquiæ Baldwinianæ. Selections from the correspondence of the late W. Baldwin, with occasional notes and a short biographical memoir. Compiled by W. Darlington. Philadelphia, 1843. 12°

BALFOUR, WALTER, Rev. Some observations on searching the Scriptures. Charleston, 1810. 12°

BALL, BENJAMIN WEST. Elfin Land; and other Poems. Boston and Cambridge, 1851. 12°

BALLADS. See SONGS and Ballads.

BALLOU, HOSEA. The Ancient History of Universalism; from the Time of the Apostles to its Condemnation in the Fifth General Council, A.D. 553. With an appendix, tracing the doctrine down to the era of the Reformation. Boston, 1829. 12°

2 BALLOU's Miscellaneous Poems. Boston, 1852. 12°

BALLOU'S PICTORIAL. See GLEASON'S PICTORIAL.

BALL-ROOM INSTRUCTOR; containing a complete description of cotillons and other popular dances, etc. New York, 1841. 12°

BALTIMORE, MARYLAND. Remarks on the intercourse of Baltimore with the Western Country. With a view of the communications proposed between the Atlantic and the Western States. Baltimore, 1818. 8°

2 PROCEEDINGS of sundry citizens of Baltimore, convened for the purpose of devising the most efficient means of improving the intercourse between that city and the Western States. Baltimore, 1827. 8°

3 THE CONSTITUTION and addreſs of the Baltimore Temperance Society; to which is added, an Addreſs delivered before the Society, by N. R. Smith. Baltimore, 1830. 12°

4 REPORT of the Visitors and Governors of the Jail of Baltimore county. [Baltimore, 1831.] 8°

5 JOURNAL of the Internal Improvement Convention, which aſsembled in the city of Baltimore on the 8th day of December, 1834. Baltimore, 1835. 8vo.

6 AN ACCOUNT of the great Whig Festival, held in Baltimore, Nov. 12, 1835. Baltimore, 1835. 8°

7 MEMORIAL of the Citizens of Baltimore to the Mayor and City Council, in relation to the Baltimore and Ohio railroad. [With a statement of the receipts and disbursements of the Company.] [Baltimore, 1836.] 8°

8 CONCILIA Provincialia Baltimori [the Roman Catholic Diocese] habita ab anno 1829, usque ad annum 1840. Baltimori, 1842. 8°

9 PASTORAL Letter of . . the Archbishop of Baltimore, and . . the Bishops of the Roman Catholic church in the United States . . aſsembled in Provincial Council . . in Baltimore in . . May 1843, to the Clergy and Laity of their Charge. Baltimore ⌐1843⌐. 8°

10 PASTORAL Letter of the sixth Provincial Council of Baltimore, held in May 1846. Baltimore, 1846. 8°

11 PASTORAL letter of the first National Council of the United States, May 1852. Baltimore, 1852. 8°

BALTIMORE AND OHIO RAILROAD COMPANY. Report of the Engineers on the reconnoiſsance and surveys made in reference to the Baltimore and Ohio Railroad. Baltimore, 1828. 8°

2 [Begins] 20th Congreſs. House of Representatives. Documents accompanying a Memorial of the President and Directors of the Baltimore and Ohio Railroad Company. Washington, 1828. 8°

3 [Begins] 20th Congreſs. House of Representatives . . . Mr. Buchanan submitted the following Letter, etc. upon the subject of obtaining a supply of Iron for the Baltimore and O. Railroad. Washington, 1828. 8°

4 FOURTH Annual Report of the President and Directors to the Stockholders of the Baltimore and Ohio Railroad Comp. Baltimore, 1830. 8°

5 COMMUNICATIONS from the Baltimore and Ohio Railroad Company to the Mayor and City Council of Baltimore. Baltimore, 1831. 8°

6 DOCUMENTS submitted by the Baltimore and Ohio Railroad Company, in behalf of their application to the Legislature of Virginia. [With the reports of J. Knight, chief engineer, etc.] Richmond, 1838. 8°

BALTIMORE AND SUSQUEHANNA Railroad Company. Memorial of the President and Directors. [Baltimore, 1835.] 8vo.

BALTIMORE BOOK; a Christmas and New Year's Present. Edited by W. H. Carpenter and T. S. Arthur. Baltimore, 1838. 8°

BALTIMORE DIRECTORY for 1845. Baltimore, 1845. 8°

BALTIMORE MEDICAL AND PHYSICAL RECORDER; conducted by T. Watkins. Vol. 1. Baltimore, 1809. 8°

BANCROFT, Rev. AARON. An Eſsay on the Life of George Washington. Worcester, 1807. 8vo.

BANCROFT, GEORGE. Poems. Cambridge, 1823. 12°

2 AN ORATION delivered on the fourth of July, 1826, at Northampton. Northampton, 1826. 8°

3 A HISTORY of the United States, from the discovery of the American Continent to the present time. [1st edit.] Vol.1-3. Boston, 1834-40. 8°

4 HISTORY of the United States, from the discovery of the American Continent. Tenth edition. Vol. 1-3. Boston, 1842. 8vo.

BANGS, EDWARD. An Oration delivered at Worcester . . 4th July, 1791, being the anniversary of the Independence of the United States. Worcester, 1791. 4°

2 AN ORATION on the anniversary of American Independence, pronounced at Worcester, July 4, 1800. Worcester, 1800. 8°

BANGS, EDWARD D. An Oration pronounced at Springfield, Maſsachusetts, on the fourth of July, 1823, being the forty-seventh Anniversary of the declaration of American Independence. Springfield, 1823. 8°

BANGS, NATHAN. An Original Church of Christ : or, a Scriptural Vindication of the Orders and Powers of the Ministry of the Methodist Episcopal Church. . Second edition, revised. New York, 1840. 12°

2 A HISTORY of the Methodist Episcopal Church. 4 vol. [Vols. 1 and 2, third edition.] New York, 1845. 8°

3 THE PRESENT State, Prospects, and Responsibilities of the Methodist Episcopal Church. With an appendix of Ecclesiastical statistics. New York, 1850. 12°

BANKER'S ALMANACK for 1851. [Edited by J. Smith Homans.] Boston [1851]. 8°

BANKER'S MAGAZINE AND STATE FINANCIAL REGISTER, devoted to the diſsemination of Bank statis-

tics, sound principles of banking and currency, etc. Vol. 1-5. Baltimore, 1847-51. New Series, vol. 1-6. Boston, 1852-56. 8°

BANK OF THE UNITED STATES. Report of the proceedings of the triennial meeting of the stockholders of the Bank of the United States . . held September, 1831. Philadelphia, 1831. 8°

2 REPORT of the Bank of the United States to the Committee of Ways and Means of the House of Representatives, Jan. 28, 1833. [Philadelphia, 1833.] 8°

3 REPORT of the Committee of Investigation appointed at the Meeting of the Stockholders of the Bank of the United States, Jan. 4, 1841. Philadelphia, 1841. 8°

BANNING, EDWARD P. Explanation of the Principles and Action of Dr. Banning's Braces, Spinal Supporters, and Supporter Truſs, etc. New York, 1850. 8°

BANVARD, Rev. JOSEPH. Romance of American History, as illustrated by the early events connected with the French Settlement at Fort Carolina ; the Spanish Colony at St. Augustine, and the English Plantation at James's Town. . With illustrations. Boston, 1852. 12°

2 NOVELTIES of the New World ; or, The Adventures and Discoveries of the First Explorers of North America. Boston, 1852. 12°

3 THE AMERICAN Statesman ; or, Illustrations of the Life and Character of D. Webster. London [Boston printed, 1853]. 8vo.

BAPTIST BOARD OF FOREIGN MISSIONS for the United States. The First Annual Report of the Baptist Board of Foreign Miſsions for the United States. Philadelphia, 1815. 8°

2 REPORT of the Baptist Board of Foreign Miſsions, at its annual meeting, in Hartford, April 28, 1830. [Hartford, 1830.] 8°

BAPTIST GENERAL CONVEN-TION. Proceedings of the fifth triennial meeting, held at Boston, 1826 (and the seventh, held in New York, 1832). 2 parts. Boston and New York, 1826-1832. 8vo.

BARBE-MARBOIS, Francois, *Marquis de.* The History of Louisiana, particularly of the cefsion of that Colony to the United States of America; with an introductory efsay on the Constitution and Government of the United States. Translated from the French by an American citizen. Philadelphia, 1830. 8vo.

BARBER, John Warner. History and Antiquities of New Haven, Connecticut, from its earliest Settlement to the present Time. Collected and compiled from the most authentic sources. New Haven, 1831. 8°
2 Connecticut Historical Collections, containing a general collection of interesting facts . . relating to the History and Antiquities of every town in Connecticut, with geographical descriptions. Second edition. New Haven [1837]. 8vo.
3 Historical Collections, relating to the History and Antiquities of every town in Mafsachusetts, with geographical descriptions. Worcester, 1839. 8vo.
4 The History and Antiquities of New England, New York, and New Jersey, etc. Worcester, 1841. 8°
5 Pictorial History of the State of New York; being a general collection of the most interesting facts, biographical sketches, . . etc., relating to the past and present; with geographical descriptions, etc. Cooperstown, N. Y. 1846. 8°
6 Historical Collections of the State of New York; being a general collection of the most interesting facts, biographical sketches, etc. relating to the past and present; with geographical descriptions of the counties, cities and principal villages throughout the State. New York, 1851. 8vo.

BARBER, John Warner, and HOWE, Henry. Historical Collections of the State of New Jersey; . relating to its history and antiquities, with geographical descriptions of every township in the State. New York, 1845. 8°
2 Historical Collections of the State of New York; . relating to its history and antiquities, with geographical descriptions of every township in the State. New York, 1846. 8°
3 Historical Collections of the State of New Jersey, . relating to its History and Antiquities, with geographical descriptions of every township in the State. Newark, N. J. [1852]. 8vo.

BARBER, Jonathan. A Grammar of Elocution; containing the principles of the arts of reading and speaking; illustrated by appropriate exercises and examples, etc. New Haven, 1830. 12°

BARBOUR, Oliver Lorenzo. An Analytical Digest of the Equity Cases, decided in the Courts of the several States, and of the United States; in the Courts of Chancery and Exchequer in England and Ireland, and in the English Privy Council and House of Lords, since the year 1836. Springfield, Mafs. 1843. 8°
2 A Treatise on the Criminal Law of the State of New York, and upon the Jurisdiction, Duty and Authority of Justices of the Peace, and incidentally of the Power and Duty of Sheriffs, Constables, etc. in Criminal Cases. Second edition. Albany and New York, 1852. 4to.

BARBOUR, Oliver Lorenzo, and HARRINGTON, E. B. An analytical Digest of the Equity Cases decided in the Courts of the several States, and of the United States, from the earliest period; and of the decisions in Equity in . . England and Ireland . . from Hilary Term, 1822 . . to 1836. 3 vol. Springfield, Mafs. 1837. 8°

BARCLAY, James J. An Addrefs delivered at the laying of the Corner Stone of the House of Refuge for Coloured Juvenile Delinquents, . . July 1, 1848. Philadelphia, 1848. 8°

BARCLAY, Robert. Apologie . . . der wahren Christlichen Gottesgelahrheit, *etc.* ins Deutsche ubersetzt. Germantown, 1776. 8vo.

BARDWELL, Horatio. Memoir of Rev. Gordon Hall. Andover, 1834. 12°

BARHYDT, David Parish. Industrial Exchanges and Social Remedies, with a consideration of Taxation. New York, 1849. 12°
2 Life, a Poem. New York, 1851. 12°

BARKER, Jacob. Mr. J. Barker's Speech, in the Case of Barker vs. Barker, . before the Parish Court, in his own defence, against a claim preferred by H. Barker for 10,000 dollars damages, for an alleged malicious prosecution of said H. [Barker] for felony. [New York, 1843.] 8°

BARKER, James N. Sketches of the Primitive Settlements on the River Delaware. A Discourse delivered before the Society for the commemoration of the Landing of W. Penn, *etc.* Philadelphia, 1827. 8°

BARLOW, James. A New Theory, accounting for the dip of the magnetic needle, being an analysis of terrestrial magnetism. With a solution of the lines of variation and no variation, and an explanation of the nature of a magnet. 2 Parts. New York, 1835. 8vo.

BARLOW, Joel. The Vision of Columbus; a Poem. Hartford, 1787. 8vo.
2 Joel Barlow to his Fellow Citizens of the United States. Letter II. on certain political measures proposed to their consideration. [With an appendix.] Philadelphia, 1801. 8°
3 Two Letters to the Citizens of

the United States, and one to General Washington, written from Paris in the year 1799, on our political and commercial relations. New Haven, 1806. 12°
4 The Columbiad; a Poem. Philadelphia, 1807. 4°
5 The Vision of Columbus: a Poem, in nine books, with explanatory notes. . From a revised edition of the author. Baltimore, 1814. 12°
6 Hasty Pudding; a Poem. [By Joel Barlow.] 1815. 12mo.
7 The Hasty Pudding; a Poem, in three cantos. . With a memoir [on] maize, or Indian corn; compiled by D. J. Browne. New York, 1847. 12°
8 The Hasty Pudding; a Poem, in three cantos, written . . in . . 1793. . With a memoir on maize or Indian corn, compiled by D. J. Browne. New York [1850?]. 12°

BARNARD, Charles H. A Narrative of the Sufferings and Adventures of Captain C. H. Barnard, in a Voyage round the World, during the years 1812-16. . With six copperplate engravings, *etc.* New York, 1829. 8°

BARNARD, Daniel D. A Discourse on the Life, Services, and Character of Stephen Van Renfselaer. With an historical sketch of the colony and manor of Renfselaerwyck, in an Appendix. Albany, 1839. 8°
2 Speech . . on the Policy of a Protective Tariff; delivered in the House of Representatives, . . July 6, 1842. Washington, 1842. 8°
3 Anniversary Addrefs, delivered before the American Institute, at the Tabernacle in New York, 20th October, 1843. New York, 1843. 8°
4 An Address to the clafs of Graduates of the Albany Medical College, delivered at the commencement, January 27, 1846. Albany, 1846. 8vo.

BARNARD, Frederick A. P. A Treatise on Arithmetic, designed particularly as a text book for clafses, etc. Hartford, 1830. 12°

2 ANALYTIC Grammar; with symbolic illustration. N. York, 1836. 12°

BARNARD, HENRY. Legal Provision respecting the Education and Employment of Children in Factories, etc. . . Education and Labour; or, the Influence of Education on the Quality and Value of Labour; and its connection with Insanity and Crime. Hartford, 1842. 8°

2 REPORT on the condition and improvement of the Public Schools of Rhode Island. Nov. 1, 1845. By H. Barnard. Providence, 1846. 8vo.

3 SCHOOL Laws of Rhode Island. Acts relating to the Public Schools of Rhode Island, with remarks and forms. . . Revised edition. [Composed and edited by H. Barnard.] Providence, 1846. 8°

4 FIFTH (& Sixth) Annual Report of the Superintendent of Common Schools of Connecticut. New Haven and Hartford, 1850. 8°

5 SCHOOL Architecture; or Contributions to the Improvement of School Houses in the United States. Fourth edition. New York, 1850. 8°

6 NORMAL schools and other institutions, agencies, and means designed for the profefsional education of teachers. 2 Parts. Hartford, 1851. 8°

7 PRACTICAL Illustrations of the principles of School Architecture. Hartford, 1851, 8°

8 A DISCOURSE in commemoration of the Life, Character, and Services of the Rev. T. H. Gallaudet, etc. Hartford, 1852. 8°

9 TRIBUTE to Gallaudet. A Discourse in commemoration of the Life, Character, and Services of the Rev. T. H. Gallaudet . . With an appendix, containing a History of Deaf-Mute Instruction and Institutions. Hartford, 1852. 8°

BARNARD, SAMUEL. A polyglot grammar of the Hebrew, Chaldee, Syriac, Greek, Latin, English, French, Italian, Spanish and German languages, reduced to one common rule of syntax, and an uniform mode of declension and conjugation, as far as practicable. With notes explanatory of the idioms of each language, etc. Philadelphia, 1825. 8vo.

BARNARD, THOMAS. A Discourse [on Mark xiv. 7] delivered before the Humane Society of Mafsachusetts, June 20, 1794. [With an appendix of matters relative to that Society.] Boston, 1794. 8vo.

2 A SERMON [on Isa. v. 3—7] delivered on the day of national thanksgiving, February 19, 1795. Salem [Mafs.] 1795. 8vo.

3 A SERMON [on Isaiah xxviii. 26] preached December 29, 1799 . . the Lord's day after the melancholy tidings . . of the death of General G. Washington. Salem [1800]. 8°

BARNES, ALBERT. Questions on the Historical Books of the New Testament, designed for Bible Clafses and Sunday Schools. Vol. 1-4. (Vol. 5, Questions on the Epistle to the Romans.) 5 vol. New York [1830 -34]. 12°

2 NOTES explanatory and practical, on the Gospels. New York, 1833. 12mo.

3 TRIAL of the Rev. Albert Barnes before the Synod of Philadelphia, in sefsion at York, October 1835, on a charge of heresy, preferred against him by the Rev. G. Junkin: with all the pleadings and debate. As reported for the New York Observer, by A. J. Stansbury. (Appendix. Defence of Albert Barnes. Appeal, etc.) New York, 1836. 12°

4 AN ORATION on the Progrefs and Tendency of Science; delivered before the Connecticut Alpha of Phi, Beta, Kappa, at New Haven, etc. Philadelphia, 1840. 8°

5 AN INQUIRY into the Organization and Government of the Apostolic Church: particularly with reference

to the Claims of Episcopacy. Philadelphia, 1843. 12°

6 THE MISSIONARY Enterprise dependent on the Religion of Principle for Success : a Sermon [on Luke xiv. 28—32] preached . . before the American Board of Commissioners for Foreign Missions. Boston, 1844. 8°

7 AN INQUIRY into the Scriptural Views of Slavery. Philadel., 1846. 12°

8 PLEA in behalf of Western colleges. A Discourse [on Proverbs xix. 2] delivered before the Society for promoting Collegiate and Theological Education at the West, in the First Presbyterian church, Newark . . Oct. 29, 1845. Philadelphia, 1846. 8vo.

9 QUESTIONS on the first Epistle to the Corinthians ; . . adapted to the author's notes on that Epistle. New York, 1846. 12°

10 PRAYERS for the Use of Families, chiefly selected from various authors; with a preliminary Essay ; together with a selection of Hymns. Philadelphia, 1850. 12°

11 A. BARNES on the Maine Liquor Law. The Throne of Iniquity; or, Sustaining Evil by Law : a Discourse [on Psalm xciv. 20] in behalf of a law prohibiting the traffic in intoxicating drinks. Philadelphia [1852]. 8vo.

BARNES, CHARLOTTE M.S. Plays, Prose, and Poetry. Philadelphia, 1848. 12°

BARNES, DAVID, D. D. Thoughts on the Love of Life and Fear of Death: . . in a Sermon [on 2 Kings xx. 3]. Boston, 1795. 8vo.

2 THE WISDOM of God in appointing Men, Teachers of Men. A Sermon [on 2 Cor. iv. 7] delivered . . soon after the decease of . . Rev. J. Hawley, etc. Boston, 1801. 8vo.

BARNEY, MARY. A biographical Memoir of the late Commodore J. Barney, etc. Boston, 1832. 8°

BARNSTABLE, MASSACHUSETTS. A description of the Eastern coast of the county of Barnstable, from Cape Cod, or Race Point . . to Cape Mallebarre, or the sandy point of Chatham, pointing out the spots on which the trustees of the Humane Society have erected huts, etc. By a member of the Humane Society. Boston, 1802. 8°

BARNUM, PHINEAS TAYLOR. Barnum's Parnassus, being confidential disclosures of the Prize Committee on the Jenny Lind Song, with specimens of the leading American Poets in the happiest effulgence of their genius. New York, 1850. 12°

BARR, ROBERT M. Pennsylvania State Reports, containing cases adjudged in the Supreme Court, 1845-46. Vol.1, 2. Philadelphia,1846. 8°

BARRETT, G. The Boy in Prison. American Sunday School Union. Philadelphia, [1830!] 12mo.

BARRETT, S. A. Maintonomah, and other Poems. N. York,1849. 12°

BARRETT,SOLOMON, Theyounger. The Principles of Language : containing a full grammatical analysis of English poetry. Albany, 1837. 12°

BARRON, JAMES, Commodore. Proceedings of the general Court Martial for the trial of Commodore J. Barron, Captain Gordon, Mr. W. Hook, and Captain J. Hall, of the 'United States' ship Chesapeake . . Jan. 1808. 1822. 8vo.

BARROS Y SOUZA, MANOEL FRANCISCO DE, Viscount de Santarem. Researches respecting Americus Vespucius and his Voyages . . translated by E. V. Childe. Boston, 1850. 8°

BARROW, JOHN, F.R.S. A Memoir of the Life of Peter the Great. New York, 1845. 12°

BARROWS, E. P. Memoir of E. Judson. Boston, 1852. 8vo.

BARRY, P. The Fruit Garden ; a Treatise intended to explain and illustrate the Physiology of Fruit-trees, *etc.* New York, 1851. 12°

BARRY, WILLIAM. A History of Framingham, Maſsachusetts, including the plantation, from 1640 to the present time, with an appendix, containing a notice of Sudbury and its first proprietors; also, a register of the inhabitants of Framingham before 1800, with genealogical sketches. Boston, 1847. 8°

BARSTOW, GEORGE. The History of New Hampshire, from its discovery, in 1614, to the paſsage of the Toleration Aƈt, in 1819. Concord, N. H. June 4, 1842. 8°

BARTLETT, DAVID W. What I saw in London; or, Men and Things in the Great Metropolis. Auburn, 1852. 8°
2 THE LIFE of Gen. F. Pierce, of New Hampshire, the Democratic Candidate for President of the United States. Auburn, 1852. 12°

BARTLETT, ELISHA. The "Laws of Sobriety" and "The Temperance Reform:" an Addreſs delivered before the Young Men's Temperance Society in Lowell, Mar. 8, 1835. Lowell [1835]. 8°
2 AN ESSAY on the Philosophy of Medical Science. Philadelphia, 1844. 8vo.
3 THE HISTORY, Diagnosis, and Treatment of the Fevers of the United States. Philadelphia, 1847. 8°

BARTLETT, ICHABOD. Speech .. on the proposition to amend the Constitution of the United States; delivered in the House of Representatives, 30th Mar. 1826. Washington, 1826. 8°
2 SPEECH .. on the subjeƈt of Retrenchment; delivered in the House of Rep[resentative]s, Feb. 6, 1828. Second edition. Washing., 1828. 8°

BARTLETT, JOHN RUSSELL. The Progress of Ethnology; an account of recent archæological, philological,

and geographical researches in various parts of the globe, tending to elucidate the physical history of man. New York, 1848. 8°
2 DICTIONARY of Americanisms. A gloſsary of words and phrases usually regarded as peculiar to the United States. New York, 1848. 8°

BARTLETT, JOSEPH. Music as an Auxiliary to Religion: an Addreſs before the Handel Society of Dartmouth College, *etc.* Boston, 1841. 8°

BARTLETT, JOSIAH. Speech .. at the Republican Convention (of the County of Rockingham) at Kingston Plains, Sept. 10, 1812; with the Addreſs and Resolutions adopted by said Convention. Portsmouth, [N. H.] 1812. 8°
2 AN ORATION occasioned by the death of John Warren, .. delivered in the Grand Lodge of Maſsachusetts, .. in Boston, June 12, 1815. Boston, 1815. 8°

BARTLETT, MONTGOMERY R. The Common-school Manual; a regular and conneƈted course of elementary studies. Utica, 1827. 12°

BARTLETT, PHEBE. Memoir of Phebe Bartlett. Written for the American Sunday School Union. Philadelphia [1831]. 12mo.

BARTLETT, ROBERT. A Sermon [on Aƈts xvii. 28] delivered on the day of general eleƈtion, .. Oƈt. 13, .. before the .. Legislature of Vermont. Montpelier, 1825. 8°

BARTLETT, WILLIAM H. C. An Elementary Treatise on Optics. New York, 1839. 8vo.
2 ELEMENTS of Natural Philosophy, .. Seƈtion I. Mechanics, *etc.* New York, 1850. 8°

BARTOL, B. H. A Treatise on the Marine Boilers of the United States. Philadelphia, 1851. 8°

BARTOL, CYRUS A. Discourses on the Christian Spirit and Life. Se-

cond edition, revised, with an introduction. Boston, 1850. 12°

2 THE HAND of God in the Great
Man : A Sermon [on Psalm lxxv. 1,
6, 7] occasioned by the death of D.
Webster. Second edition. Boston,
1852. 8°

3 DISCOURSES on the Christian
Body and Form. Boston, 1853. 12°

BARTON, BENJAMIN SMITH. A
Memoir concerning the Fascinating
Faculty which has been ascribed to
the Rattle-snake, and other American
Serpents. Philadelphia, 1796. 8vo.

2 NEW VIEWS of the Origin of the
Tribes and Nations of America. Philadelphia, 1797. 8°

3 COLLECTIONS for an Essay towards a Materia Medica of the United
States. Philadelphia, 1798. 8vo.

4 NEW VIEWS of the Origin of the
Tribes and Nations of America. [With
an appendix, separately paged.] Philadelphia, 1798. 8vo.

5 FRAGMENTS of the Natural History of Pennsylvania. Part I. Philadelphia, 1799. fol.

6 SUPPLEMENT to a Memoir concerning the Fascinating Faculty which
has been ascribed to the Rattle-snake,
and other American Serpents. [Phila-
delphia ?] 1800. 8vo.

7 A MEMOIR concerning the Disease of Goitre, as it prevails in different parts of North America. Philadelphia, 1800. 8vo.

8 FACTS, Observations, and Conjectures, relative to the Generation of
the Opossum of North America. In
a Letter to Mons. Roume. Philadelphia, 1806. 8vo.

9 A DISCOURSE on some of the
principal Desiderata in Natural History, and on the best Means of promoting the Study of this Science in the
United States. Philadel., 1807. 8vo.

10 ADDITIONAL Facts, Observa-
tions, and Conjectures relative to the
Generation of the Opossum of North
America. In a Letter to Professor J.
A. H. Reimarus, of Hamburgh. Phi-
ladelphia, 1813. 8vo.

11 ARCHAEOLOGIAE Americanae
Telluris Collectanea et Specimina ;
or, Collections, with Specimens, for a
series of Memoirs on certain extinct
Animals and Vegetables of North
America. Together with facts and
conjectures relative to the ancient
condition of the lands and waters of
the Continent. Part I. Philadelphia, 1814. 8°

BARTON, IRA. An Oration delivered at Oxford [in Massachusetts],
on the Forty-sixth Anniversary of
American Independence. Cambridge,
1822. 8°

BARTON, K. Io : A Tale of the
Olden Fane. New York, 1851. 12°

BARTON, WILLIAM. Memoirs of
the late David Rittenhouse . . Interspersed with various notices of
many distinguished men. With an
appendix, containing sundry philosophical and other papers [by D. Ritten-
house], most of which have not hitherto been published. Philadelphia,
1813. 8°

BARTON, WILLIAM P. C. A
Treatise, containing a Plan for the
internal Organization and Government of Marine Hospitals in the
United States: together with a scheme
for amending and systematizing the
medical department of the Navy. Philadelphia, 1814. 8°

2 A BIOGRAPHICAL Sketch, read
before the Philadelphia Medical Society, Feb. 16, 1810, of their late
President, Professor Barton. [Phila-
delphia, 1816 ?] 8vo.

3 VEGETABLE Materia Medica of
the United States; or, Medical Botany:
Containing a botanical, general, and
medical history of medicinal plants
indigenous to the United States. Illustrated by coloured engravings. 2
vol. Philadelphia, 1817-18. 4to.

4 COMPENDIUM Floræ Philadel-
phicæ ; containing a description of
the indigenous and naturalized plants
found within a circuit of 10 miles

around Philadelphia. 2 vol. Philadelphia, 1818. 12mo.

5 A FLORA of North America. Illustrated by coloured figures. 2 vol.
Philadelphia, 1821-22. 4to.

BARTRAM, WILLIAM. Travels
through North and South Carolina,
Georgia, East and West Florida, the
Cherokee Country, the Territories of
the Muscogulges, or Creek Confederacy, and the Country of the Choctaws.
With copper plates. Philadelphia,
1791. 8vo.

BASCOM, HENRY B. The Me-
thodist Church Property Case. Report of the suit of H. B. Bascom and
others vs. G. Lane and others, heard
before the Hon. Judges Nelson and
Betts in the Circuit Court, United
States . . By R. Sutton. New York,
1851. 8°

BASSETT, FRANCIS. An Oration,
delivered . . July 5, 1834, in commemoration of American Independence, etc. Boston, 1824. 8°

BATCHELDER, J. P. Thoughts
on the connection of Life, Mind, and
Matter; in respect to Education.
Utica, New York, 1845. 8°

BATES, JOSHUA. An Inaugural
Oration, . . by J. Bates, President
of Middlebury College. Middlebury,
Vermont, 1818. 8°

BATES, ISAAC C. An Oration
pronounced at Northampton, July 4,
1805; the twenty-ninth anniversary
of American Independence, etc.
Northampton, [Maſs.] 1805. 8°

2 AN ORATION pronounced before
the Washington Benevolent Society,
. . on their first anniversary . . in
commemoration of the Nativity of
Washington. Northampton, 1812. 8°

3 SPEECH . . on the Tariff Bill;
delivered in the House of Representatives, . . March 26, 1828. Washington, 1828. 8°

BAUCHER, F. A Method of
Horsemanship, founded upon new

Principles . . Second American edition, revised and corrected from the
ninth Paris edition . . Engravings.
Philadelphia, 1852. 12°

BAXLEY, H. WILLIS. Introductory Lecture [on Medical Education].
Delivered . . Nov. 2, 1837. Baltimore, 1839. 8°

BAY, ELIHU HALL. Reports of
Cases argued and determined in the
Superior Courts of Law in the State
of South Carolina, since the Revolution. Second edition, with additional
notes and references, etc. 2 vol.
New York, 1809-11. 8°

BAYARD, JAMES. A Brief Exposition of the Constitution of the United
States; with an appendix, containing
the Declaration of Independence, and
the Articles of Confederation. Philadelphia, 1840. 12mo.

BAYARD, JAMES A. Speech . .
on the Bill received from the Senate,
entitled: " An Act to repeal certain
Acts respecting the Organization of
the Courts of the U[nited] States ;"
delivered in the House of Representatives, Feb. 19, 1802. [Washington,
1802.] 8°

2 MR. BAYARD's Speech on the
Bill received from the Senate, entitled : " An Act to repeal certain Acts
respecting the Organization of the
Courts of the United States ;" delivered in the House of Representatives
of the United States, Feb. 19, 20,
1802. Worcester, [Maſs.] April,
1802. 12°

BAYARD, NICHOLAS. An Account
of the Illegal Prosecution and Tryal
of Col. Nicholas Bayard, in the Province of New York, for supposed high
treason, in 1701-2. Collected from
Memorials taken by divers persons privately, the Commiſsioners having prohibited the taking of the tryal in open
Court. New York, 1702. Fol.

2 AN ACCOUNT of the Commitment,
Arraignment, Tryal, and Condemnation of Nicholas Bayard, Esq. for high

E

treason : in endeavouring to subvert the Government of the Province of New York, by signing and procuring others to sign scandalous libels called petitions . . to his late Majesty King William, the Parliament of England, and the Lord Cornbury. . . With a Copy of the Libels or Addreſſes. New York, 1703. fol.

BAYARD, SAMUEL. An Abstract of those Laws of the United States which relate chiefly to the Duties and Authority of the Judges of the Inferior State Courts, and the Justices of the Peace throughout the Union. Illustrated by Extracts from English Law Books. To which is added, an appendix, containing a variety of useful precedents. New York, 1804. 8°

BAYARD, WILLIAM. An Exposition of the Conduct of the Two Houses of G. G. and S. Howland, and Le Roy, Bayard and Company, in relation to the frigates Liberator and Hope, in answer to a Narrative, by A. Contostaolos. New York, 1826. 8°

BAYLE, ANTOINE LAURENT JESSE. An Elementary Treatise on Astronomy. Tranſlated from the fourth edition of the French, by A. S. Doane. New York, 1837. 12°

BAYLIES, FRANCIS, Nineteenth Congreſs, | First Seſsion. North West Coast of America. May 15, 1826. . . Mr. Baylies made the following Report. [Washington, 1826.] 8°

BAYLIES, FRANCIS. An Historical Memoir of the Colony of New Plymouth. 2 vol. in five parts. Boston, 1830. 8vo.

2 EULOGY on Lafayette, delivered in the Masonic Temple, Boston, Oct. 9, 1834, at the request of the Grand Lodge of Freemasons in Maſsachusetts. Boston, 1834. 8°

BAYLIES, FRANCIS. A NARRATIVE of Major-General Wool's Campaign in Mexico, in the years 1846, 1847, and 1848. Albany, 1851. 8°

BAYLIES, NICHOLAS. A Digested Index to the Modern Reports of the Courts of Common Law, in England and the United States. 3 vol. Montpelier, Vermont, 1814. 8°

BAYLY, WILLIAM. A Collection of the several Writings of that True Prophet, . W. Bayly. Philadelphia, New York. Printed 1676, reprinted 1830. 8°

BEACH, W. M.D. The American Practice of Medicine, revised, enlarged, and improved: . embracing the most useful portions of the former work, with corrections, additions, etc. Three hundred engravings. 3 vol. New York, 1850. 8°

BEACON HILL, a Local Poem, Historic and Descriptive. Book I. Boston, 1797. 4to.

BEAUMONT, GUSTAVE DE, and TOCQUEVILLE, ALEXIS DE, Count. On the Penitentiary System in the United States, and its Application in France ; with an appendix on Penal Colonies, and also statistical notes. . Translated from the French, with an introduction, notes, and additions. By F. Lieber. Philadelphia, 1833. 8vo.

BEAUMONT, WILLIAM, M. D. The Physiology of Digestion, with Experiments on the Gastric Juice. Second edition, corrected by S. Beaumont. Burlington, [Vt.] 1847. 12°

BECK, JOHN B. An Introductory Discourse before the Medico-Chirurgical Society of the University of the State of N. York. N. York, 1816. 8vo.

2 AN INAUGURAL Diſsertation on Infanticide. New York, 1817. 8vo.

3 RESEARCHES in Medicine and Medical Jurisprudence. Second edition. Albany, 1835. 8°

4 LECTURES on Materia Medica and Therapeutics, delivered in the College of Physicians and Surgeons of the University of the State of New York ; prepared for the preſs by C. R. Gilman, M. D. New York, 1851. 8vo.

BECKER, ABRAHAM. Addreſs before the Faculty and Students of the New York Conference Seminary and Citizens of Charlotteville, New York, July 5, 1852, at their celebration of the seventy-seventh anniversary of American Independence. Albany, 1852. 8°

2 ADDRESS delivered at Worcester, New York, on the occasion of the Burial of Captain Leslie Chase. . and Poem . . on the same occasion, by Robert F. Queal. Albany, 1852. 8vo.

BECKWITH, GEORGE C. Eulogy on William Ladd, late President of the American Peace Society. Boston, 1841. 8°

2 A UNIVERSAL Peace Society, with the Basis of co-operation in the cause of Peace. [A Letter to John Lee, LL.D., President of the London Peace Society.] Boston, 1844 ? 8°

BEDELL, GREGORY TOWNSEND. " Let it alone till to-morrow ;" or, The History of Robert Benton. Philadelphia, 1829. 12mo.

2 LIFE of Legh Richmond. Philadelphia, 1829. 12mo.

3 THE LIFE and Travels of St. Paul. Philadelphia [1830]. 12mo.

BEDINGER, HENRY. Speech . . on the War with Mexico; delivered in the House of Representatives, . Jan. 6, 1847. Washington, 1847. 8°

BEE. The Busy Bee. American Sunday School Union. Philadelphia, 1831. 12mo.

BEE, THOMAS. Reports of Cases adjudged in the Diſtrict Court of South Carolina. . To which is added, an appendix, containing decisions in the Admiralty Court of Pennsylvania, by the late F. Hopkinson ; and cases determined in other diſtricts of the United States. Philadelphia, 1810. 8°

BEECHER, MISS CATHARINE E. Arithmetic simplified, prepared for the use of Primary Schools, Female Semi-

naries and High Schools. In three parts. . Second edition. Hartford, 1833. 12°

2 THE EVILS suffered by American Women and American Children : the Causes and the Remedy. Presented in an Addreſs by Miſs C. E. Beecher, to Meetings of Ladies in Cincinnati, Washington. New York [1846]. 8°

3 THE EVILS suffered by American Women and . . Children ; the Causes and the Remedy. . Also, an Addreſs to the Protestant Clergy of the United States. New York [1846]. 8°

4 A TREATISE on Domestic Economy, for the Use of Young Ladies, etc. Revised edition, with numerous additions. New York, 1846. 12°

5 TRUTH stranger than Fiction ; a Narrative of recent Transactions, involving Inquiries in regard to the principles of Honour, Truth, and Justice, which obtain in a distinguished American University [Yale College]. New York, 1850. 12°

6 THE TRUE Remedy for the Wrongs of Woman ; with a History of an Enterprise having that for its object. Boston, 1851. 12°

BEECHER, CHARLES. A Review of the " Spiritual Manifestations," etc. New York, 1853. 12°

BEECHER, EDWARD, D.D. Narrative of Riots at Alton ; in connection with the Death of Rev. E. P. Lovejoy. Alton [Ohio], 1838. 12°

2 BAPTISM, with reference to its Import and Modes. New York, 1849. 12mo.

3 THE CONFLICT of Ages ; or, the Great Debate on the Moral Relations of God and Man. London [Boston printed], 1853. 12mo.

BEECHER, HENRY WARD. Lectures to Young Men, on various important subjects. . Seventh thousand. Salem, 1846. 12°

BEECHER, LUTHER F. On the Choice of a Profeſsion. An Addreſs delivered before the Theological Society of Union College, *etc.* Albany, 1851. 8°

BEECHER, LYMAN, *D.D.* A Reformation of Morals Practicable and Indispensable: a Sermon [on Ezek. xxxiii. 10] delivered . . Oct. 27, 1812. New Haven, 1813. 8°
2 REPLY to the Review of Dr. Beecher's Sermon (delivered at Worcester, Maſsachusetts), which appeared in the Christian Examiner for Jan. 1824. By the author of the Sermon. From the Christian Spectator for Feb. and March 1825. [Boston, 1825.] 8°
3 A PLEA for the West. Second edition. Cincinnati, 1835. 12mo.
4 BEECHER's Works. Vols. 1, 2, 3. Boston, 1852-3. 12°

BEEDE, SAMUEL. Questions Designed to aſsist the Pupil in acquiring a Knowledge of English Grammar, particularly adapted to Putnam's Grammar. Concord, 1831. 12°

BEEDE, THOMAS. A Sermon [on John vii. 48] preached . . before . . the Governor, . Council, *etc.* of . . New Hampshire. Concord, 1811. 8°
2 A DISCOURSE delivered in Dublin, N[ew] H[ampshire], at the Consecration of Altemont Lodge, . Sept. 18, 1816. Keene, N. H. 1817. 8°
3 A DISCOURSE [on Matt. xx. 9] delivered in the Representatives' Chamber in Concord, *etc.* Concord, N. H. 1820. 8vo.

BEERS, SETH P. Report of the Commiſsioner of the School Fund, (S. P. Beers) 1835, *etc.* Hartford, 1835, *etc.* 8vo.
2 ANNUAL Report of (S.P. Beers) the Superintendent of Common Schools of Connecticut to the General Assembly. [With an Appendix of School Returns, Reports, *etc.*] Hartford, 1846. 8vo.

BEETHOVEN, LUDWIG VAN. Louis Van Beethoven's Studies in Thorough-Baſs, Counterpoint, and the Art of Scientific Composition. . First published, together with Biographical Notices by J. Von Seyfried. Translated and edited by H. H. Pierson. 2 parts. Leipsic, Hamburgh, and New York, 1853. 8vo.

BELCHER, JOSEPH. The Clergy of America: Anecdotes Illustrative of the Character of the Ministers of Religion in the United States. Philadelphia, 1849. 12°

BELDEN, A. RUSSELL. Thrilling Incidents and Narratives for Christian Parents and their Children, .. edited by Rev. A. Ruſsell Belden. Auburn, N. Y. 1852. 12°

BELDEN, E. PORTER. New York; Past, Present, and Future. Second edition. New York, 1849. 8°
2 NEW York As It Is, *etc.* [A description of a carved Model of New York and Brooklyn, executed by E. P. Belden and others.] New York, 1849. 12mo.

BELGROVE, WILLIAM. A Treatise upon Husbandry and Planting. Boston, 1755. 4to.

BELKNAP, JEREMY, *D. D.* The History of New Hampshire. 3 vol. Philadelphia, 1784; Boston, 1792. 8vo.
2 THE HISTORY of New Hampshire. . Containing also, a Geographical description of the State, with Sketches of its Natural History, *etc.* Second edition, with large additions and improvements, published from the author's last manuscript. 3 vol. Boston, 1813. 8°
3 THE HISTORY of New Hampshire. . From a copy of the original edition, having the author's last corrections. To which are added notes, containing various corrections and illustrations of the text, and additional facts and notices of persons and events therein-mentioned. By J. Farmer. Vol. 1. [*all published.*] Dover, N. H. 1831. 8°

4 An Election Sermon [on Psalm cxliv. 11-15] preached before the General Court of New Hampshire, etc. Portsmouth, 1785. 8°

5 A Discourse intended to commemorate the Discovery of America by Christopher Columbus. To which are added, Four Dissertations. 1. On the Circumnavigation of Africa by the Ancients. 2. An Examination of the Pretensions of M. Behaim to a Discovery of America prior to that of Columbus, with a Chronological Detail of all the Discoveries made in the 15th Century. 3. On the Question whether the Honey-bee is a native of America? 4. On the Colour of the Native Americans and the recent Population of this Continent. Boston, 1792. 8vo.

6 American Biography; or, an Historical Account of those Persons who have been distinguished in America. 2 vols. Boston, 1794-98. 8vo.

7 American Biography . . With additions and notes by F. M. Hubbard. 3 vol. New York, 1846-44. 12°

8 Life of Jeremy Belknap, . with selections from his correspondence and other writings. Collected and arranged by his grand-daughter, (J. B.) [J. Belknap.] New York, 1847. 12°

BELL, Henry Glassford. Life of Mary, Queen of Scots. 2 vol. New York, 1844. 12°

BELL, John, of Tennessee. Speech . . on the Naval Appropriation Bill; delivered in the House of Representatives . . March . . 1836. Washington, 1836. 8°

BELL, Luther V. A Dissertation on the Boylston Prize Question for 1835: "What diet can be selected which will ensure the greatest probable health and strength to the labourer in the climate of New England?" etc. Boston, 1836. 8°

2 Eulogy of Gen. Z. Taylor . . delivered by the appointment of the

. . citizens of Cambridge, August 13, 1850. Cambridge, 1850. 8°

BELL, William H. Memorial to the Congress of the United States on the subject of a traverse board and elevating machine for working guns; . . with extracts of letters . . testifying in behalf of Captain Bell's Inventions. [Washington], 1836. 8°

BELLARMINO, Roberto, Cardinal, Archbishop of Capua. Dottrina Cristiana composta per ordine di Papa Clemente VIII. . (A Catechism of Christian Doctrine.) [Translated from the Italian, by C. B. Fairbanks.] Ital. and Engl. Boston, 1853. 12mo.

BELLOWS, Henry W. A Sermon [on Rom. viii. 2] occasioned by the late Riot in New York. New York, 1849. 12°

BELSHAM, Thomas. American Unitarianism; or, a Brief History of The Progress and Present State of the Unitarian Churches in America. Compiled . . by Thomas Belsham, extracted from his Memoirs of the Life of T. Lindsey. Fourth edition. Boston, 1815. 8°

BELTRAMI, J. C. La découverte des Sources du Missisippi, et de la Rivière Sanglante. Description du Cours " du Missisippi," Observations " sur les Mœurs . . . l'origine, etc. de plusieurs nations Indiennes," Coup d'œil sur les Compagnies Nord-ouest, et de la Baie d'Hudson, ainsi que sur la Colonie Selkirk. Preuves evidentes que le Missisippi est la première rivière du monde. Nouvelle Orleans. 1824. 8vo.

2 To the Public of New York, and of the United States, the author of " The Discovery of the Sources of the Missisippi," etc. (J. C. Beltrami) [An explanation and defence of that work.] New York [1825]. 8°

BEMENT, C. N. The American Poulterer's Companion; a practical Treatise on the breeding, rearing, fattening, and general management of the various species of Domestic Poultry. Fourth edition. New York, 1846. 12°

BENEDICT, DAVID. A General History of the Baptist Denomination in America, and other parts of the World. 2 vol. Boston, 1813. 8vo.

2 A GENERAL History of the Baptist Denomination in America, and other parts of the World. New York, 1850. 8°

BENEDICT, GEORGE W. An Oration, delivered at Burlington, Vt. . 4th July, 1826, being the Fiftieth Anniversary of American Independence. Burlington, Vt. 1826. 8°

BENEDICT, JOEL. A Short Enquiry why Death is appointed to men in general, and why to good men as well as to others: a Sermon [on Zech. i. 5], delivered at the funeral of . . L. Hart, *etc.* Norwich, Conn. 1809. 8°

BENEZET, ANTHONY. A Caution and Warning to Great Britain and her Colonies, in a Short Representation of the calamitous state of the enslaved Negroes in the British Dominions. To which is added, an Extract of a Sermon, preached by the Bishop of Gloucester. Philadelphia, 1767. 8vo.

2 A CAUTION and Warning to Great Britain and her Colonies, in a Representation of the State of the Enslaved Negroes in the British Dominions. [1780?] 8vo.

3 SOME HISTORICAL Account of Guinea, with an Inquiry into the Rise and Progress of the Slave Trade, also a Republication of the Sentiments of several authors of note, particularly an extract of a Treatise by G. Sharp. Philadelphia, 1771. 8vo.

BENGA PRIMER. The Benga Primer, containing Lessons for Beginners; a Series of Phrases and a Catechism. [Prepared by the Missionaries of the Presbyterian Board of the United States.] New London, Penn. 1855. 12mo.

BENJAMIN, ASHER. The Architect; or, Practical House Carpenter, *etc.* Boston, 1845. 4°

BENJAMIN, J. P. Address delivered before the Public Schools of Municipality Number Two of the city of New Orleans, *etc.* New Orleans, 1845. 8°

BENJAMIN, J. P. and SLIDELL, THOMAS. Digest of the Reported Decisions of the Superior Court of the late Territory of Orleans, and of the Supreme Court of the State of Louisiana. New Orleans, 1834. 8vo.

BENJAMIN, PARK. A Poem on the Meditation of Nature, spoken . . before the Association of the Alumni of Washington College. Hartford, 1832. 8°

2 POETRY: a Satire, pronounced before the Mercantile Library Association, at its twenty-second anniversary. New York, 1842. 8°

BENNET, JAMES. The American System of Practical Book-keeping. . With a copperplate engraving. . Twenty-first edition. New York, 1842. 8°

BENNETT, JOHN C. *M.D.* The History of the Saints; or, an Exposé of Joe Smith and Mormonism. Boston, 1842. 12mo.

BENNETT, JOSEPH. Permanence of the Pastoral Office: a Sermon [on 2 Kings, iv. 13] delivered . . Jan. 4, 1846, being the twenty-fifth anniversary of the author's ordination. Boston, 1846. 8°

BENNETT, S. A New Explanation of the ebbing and flowing of the Sea, upon the principles of Gravitation. New York, 1816. 8vo.

BENSON, EGBERT. Memoir read before the Historical Society of the State of New York, December 31, 1816. New York, 1817. 8°

BENT, N. T. A Discourse [on Prov. xxiii. 28] historical of St. Thomas' Church, Taunton, Maſſachusetts. Taunton, Maſs. 1844. 8vo.

BENTLEY, RENSSELAER. The Derivative Expositor; containing Rules for spelling Derivative Words, etc. Boston, 1832. 12°

BENTON, N. S. Annual Report of the Superintendent of Common Schools of the State of New York, . Jan. 5, 1848. Albany, 1848. 8vo.

BENTON, THOMAS HART. Speech . . on the Resolutions offered by Mr. Clay, . Dec. 26, [1833,] relative to the Removal of the Public Deposites from the Bank of the United States; delivered in the Senate, Jan. 2, 3, 6, and 7, 1834. Washington, 1834. 8°
2 SPEECH . . on the Bill designating and limiting the Funds receivable for the Revenues of the United States; delivered in the Senate, . Jan. 27, 1837. Washington, 1837. 8°
3 SPEECH . . on the Resolution of Mr. Ewing, for rescinding the Treasury Order [of July 11, 1836, for excluding Paper Money from the Land Offices, etc.] delivered in the Senate, Dec. 1836. Washington, 1837. 8°
4 SPEECH . . on the Bill to separate the Government from the Banks; delivered in the Senate, . . March 14, 1838. Washington, 1838. 8°
5 REMARKS on the Annual Expenditures of the Government. In Senate, . May 7 [1840]. Washington, 1840. 8vo.
6 SPEECH on his Motion to postpone the operation of the Bankrupt Aſt; delivered in the . . Senate, December 27, 1841. [Washington, 1841.] 8°
7 SPEECH . . on the Oregon Question; delivered in the Senate, . May, . 1846. Washington, 1846. 8°

BERANGER, PIERRE JEAN DE. Two Hundred of his Lyrical Poems, done into English Verse. By W. Young. New York, 1850. 12°

BERG, Rev. JOSEPH F. Trapezium; or, Law and Liberty versus Despotism and Anarchy. A Vindication of Protestantism from Papal Aſſailants, and Infidel Advocates. Philadelphia, 1851. 8°
2 THE JESUITS. A Leſture delivered . . Dec. 23, 1850. Philadelphia, 1851. 8°

BERKELEY, EVERARD. The World's Laconics; or, The Best Thoughts of the Best Authors. By E. Berkeley. With an introduſtion by W. B. Sprague. N. York, 1853. 12mo.

BERKELEY, GEORGE, Bishop of Cloyne. A Word to the Wise: or, the Bishop of Cloyne's Exhortation to the Roman Catholick Clergy of Ireland, 4th edition. Boston, 1750. 8°

BERKELEY, ROBERT. An Inquiry into the Modus Operandi of that claſſ of Medicines called Sedatives. Philadelphia, 1800. 8vo.

BERKENMEYER, WILLEM CHRISTOFFEL. W. C. Berkenmeyer's Herder-en Wachter-Stem, aan de Hoog-en Neder-Duitsche Lutheriaanen in dese Gewesten, eenstemmig te zyn vertoont, met twe brieven en andere redenen Lutherscher theologanten. Nieuw-York, J. Peter Zenger. 1728. 4to.

BERKSHIRE JUBILEE; celebrated at Pittsfield, Maſſachusetts, Aug. 22, 23, 1844. Albany, 1845. 8°

BERMINGHAM, JAMES. A Memoir of the Very Rev. Theobald Mathew; with an Account of the Rise and Progress of Temperance in Ireland. . Edited by P. H. Morris, . by whom is added, The evil Effeſts of Drunkenneſs, physiologically explained. New York, 1841. 12°

BERNARD, CHARLES DE, Pseud. [C. B. Dugrail de la Villette.] The Lion's Skin and the Lover Hunt. By C. de Bernard. [Translated from the French.] New York, 1853. 12°

BERRIAN, FRANCIS. Francis Berrian; or, The Mexican Patriot. [By Timothy Flint.] 2 vol. Boston, 1826. 12°

BERRIAN, WILLIAM. Travels in France and Italy, in 1817 and 1818. New York, 1821. 8vo.

2 AN HISTORICAL Sketch of Trinity Church, New York. New York, 1847. 8°

BERRIEN, JOHN MACPHERSON. Speech .. on the Joint Resolution to annex Texas to the United States; delivered in the Senate .. Feb. 1845. Washington, 1845. 8°

BERRY, R. T. A National Warning; a Sermon [on Micah vi. 9], preached .. as an improvement of the calamity that occurred on board .. the Steam-Frigate Princeton, etc. Philadelphia, 1844. 12°

BERZELIUS, JONS JACOB. The Kidneys and Urine. Translated from the German by M. H. Boyè and F. Learning. Philadelphia, 1843. 8°

2 THE USE of the Blow-pipe in Chemistry and Mineralogy. . Translated from the fourth enlarged .. edition, by J. D. Whitney. Boston, 1845. 12°

BETHUNE, Rev. GEORGE W. The Prospects of Art in the United States. An addrefs before the Artist's Fund Society of Philadelphia, . May, 1840. Philadelphia, 1840. 8°

2 THE DUTIES of Educated Men; an Oration before the Literary Societies of Dickinson College, Carlisle, Pennsylvania, July, 1843. Philadelphia, 1843. 8°

3 A PLEA for Study. An Oration before the Literary Societies of Yale College, August 19, 1845. Philadelphia, 1845. 8°

4 THE BRITISH Female Poets: with biographical and critical notices. Philadelphia, 1848. 8°

5 THE HISTORY of a Penitent: A Guide for the Inquiring; in a Com-

mentary on the One hundred and thirtieth Psalm. Philadel., 1848. 12°

6 ORATIONS and Occasional Discourses. New York [Andover, printed], 1850. 12°

BETTS, WILLIAM. The Causes of the Prosperity of New York. An Anniversary Addrefs delivered before the St. Nicholas Society of New York, Dec. 3, 1850. New York, 1851. 8°

BEVERIDGE, JOHN. Epistolæ Familiares et alia quædam Miscellanea. Familiar Epistles and other Miscellaneous Pieces. . Wrote originally in Latin Verse. . To which are added several translations into English verse, by different hands, etc. Philadelphia, 1765. 8vo.

BEZOUT, ETIENNE. Elements of Arithmetic, translated from the French of M. Bézout, and adapted to the use of American schools. By N. Haynes. Hallowell, Maine, 1824. 12°

2 FIRST Principles of the Differential and Integral Calculus; or, the Doctrine of Fluxions; intended as an introduction to the physico-mathematical sciences; taken chiefly from the Mathematics of Bézout, translated from the French, etc. Cambridge, 1824. 8°

BIBB, GEORGE M. Reports of Cases at Common Law and in Chancery, argued and decided in the Court of Appeals of the Commonwealth of Kentucky, etc. (Fall Term, 1808, to Spring Term, 1817.) Second edition. 4 vol. Frankfort, Ky., 1840. 8°

BIBLES, and PARTS thereof, arranged according to the order of the several Books.

1 THE HOLY Bible: containing the Old Testament and the New; translated [by J. Eliot] into the [Natick] Indian language [of Mafsachusetts.] [With a metrical version of the Psalms in the same language.] Cambridge, 1663-61. 4to.

2 THE HOLY Bible .. newly trans-

BIBLES *continued.*
lated out of the original Tongues, *etc.*
[Edited by R. Aitken.] Philadelphia,
1782-81. 12mo.

3 THE HOLY Bible : containing the
Old and New Covenant, commonly
called the Old and New Testament ;
translated from the Greek. By C.
Thomson. 4 vol. Philadel., 1808. 8vo.

4 THE HOLY Bible . . with Notes
. . prepared and arranged by G.
D'Oyly and R. Mant . . The first
American edition, with additional
notes, selected by J. H. Hobart. 2
vol. New York, 1818-20. 4to.

5 THE HOLY Bible . . the common
Version, with Amendments of the
Language, by Noah Webster. New
Haven, 1833. 8vo.

6 THE HOLY Bible . . arranged in
Paragraphs and Parallelisms, with
Philological and Explanatory Annotations. By T. W. Coit. Cambridge
and Boston, 1834. 8vo.

7 THE HOLY Bible . . the Text of
the common Translation . . arranged
in Paragraphs, such as the sense requires. By J. Nourse. Boston and
Philadel. [stereotyped] 1836. 12mo.

8 THE HOLY Bible . . according to
the authorized Version ; with the references and marginal readings of the
Polyglot Bible, with numerous additions from Bagster's Comprehensive
Bible. (The Psalms of David in
metre.) Philadelphia, 1841. 8vo.

9 BIBLIA . . nach der Deutschen
Uebersetzung, D. M. Luthers. Mit
eines jeden Capitels kurzen Summa-
rien, auch . . Parallelen. Philadelphia, [1846 ?] 4°

10 THE ILLUMINATED Bible ; containing the Old and New Testaments,
translated out of the original Tongues ;
. . with marginal readings, references,
and . . dates. Also. the Apocrypha.
To which are added, a chronological
index, *etc.* New York, 1846. 4°

11 THE HOLY Bible ; translated
from the Latin Vulgate . . The Old
Testament, first published by the
English College at Douay, A.D. 1609,
and the New Testament, first published by the English College, at
Rheims, A.D. 1582. With notes . .
selected . . by the Rev. G. L. Hay-
dock. No. 1. New York, 1852. 4to.

12 תורה נביאים וכתבים
Biblia Hebraica, secundum ultimam
editionem, J. Athiae a J. Leusden re-
cognita, recensita ab E. Van der
Hoogt. Editu prima Americana, sine
punctis. *Hebr.* 2 tom. Philadelphia,
1814. 8vo.

13 THE COLLATERAL Bible ; or, a
Key to the Holy Scriptures ; in which
all the corresponding texts are brought
into one view, and arranged in a familiar and easy manner. [Containing
the Old Testament only, the New
Testament not having been published
on this plan.] By W. M'Corkle, .
E. S. Ely, and G. T. Bedell. 3 vol.
Philadelphia, 1826-28. 4to.

14 NOTES, Critical and Practical,
on the Book of Genesis. By G. Bush.
[With the text.] Seventh edition.
2 vol. New York, 1844. 12mo.

15 THE FIRST Book of Moses,
called Genesis, translated in the Grebo
tongue. By the Rev. J. Payne. New
York, 1850. 12mo.

16 THE BOOKS of Joshua, Judges,
and Ruth, translated into the Choctaw
language. Choshua, nan apesa
vhleha ·micha Lulh holiĝo. New
York, 1852. 8vo.

17 NOTES, Critical and Practical,
on the Book of Joshua. By G. Bush.
[With the text.] New York, 1844.
12mo.

18 NOTES, Critical and Practical,
on the Book of Judges. . By G. Bush.
[With the text.] New York, 1844.
12mo.

19 THE FIRST and Second Books of
Samuel, and the First Book of Kings,
translated into the Choctaw language.
Samueli Holiĝo vmmona . . Hoke.
New York, 1852. 8vo.

20 AN AMENDED Version of the
Book of Job, with an introduction, and
notes, chiefly explanatory. By G.
R. Noyes. Cambridge, 1827. 8vo.

BIBLES *continued.*

21 A NEW Translation of the Book of Job, with an introduction and notes chiefly explanatory. By G. R. Noyes. Second edition, with corrections and additions. Boston, 1838. 12°

22 NOTES, Critical, Illustrative, and Practical, on the Book of Job; with a new translation, and an introductory Dissertation, by A. Barnes. 2 vol. [New York ?] London, 1849. 12mo.

23 THE MASSACHUSET Psalter; or, Psalms of David, with the Gospel according to John, in columns of Indian and English. [Translated by E. Mayhew.] Massachusee Psalter, *etc.* Boston, 1709. 8vo.

24 PSALTERIUM Americanum. The Book of Psalms, in a Translation exactly conformed unto the original; but all in Blank Verse; fitted unto the Tunes commonly used in our churches. Which pure offering is accompanied with Illustrations, digging for hidden treasures in it; and rules to employ it upon the glorious and various intentions of it. Whereto are added some other portions of the Sacred Scripture, to enrich the cantional. [By C. Mather.] Boston, 1718. 12mo.

25 THE PSALMS and Hymns and Spiritual Songs of the Old and New Testament, translated into English Metre. Twenty-fourth edition. Boston, 1737. 12mo.

26 THE PSALMS of David, with the Ten Commandments, Creed, Lord's Prayer, *etc.* in Metre. Also, the Catechism, Confession of Faith, Liturgy, *etc.* translated from the Dutch. For the use of the Reformed Protestant Dutch Church of the City of New York. [With the musical notes.] 2 parts. New York, 1767. 8vo.

27 THE PSALMS of David imitated in the Language of the New Testament, and applied to the Christian State and Worship. Together with a Collection of Hymns. By I. Watts. First Worcester edition. Worcester, Mass. 1786. 12°

28 A NEW Version of the Psalms of David .. by N. Brady and N. Tate. First Worcester edition. Worcester, Mass. 1788. 12°

29 A NEW Translation of the Book of Psalms, with an introduction. By G. R. Noyes. Boston, 1831. 8vo.

30 A NEW Translation of the Book of Psalms; with an introduction and notes, chiefly explanatory. By G. R. Noyes. Second ed. Boston, 1846. 12°

31 THE PSALMS, translated and explained by J. A. Alexander. [Formed chiefly upon the translation and commentaries of E. W. Hengstenberg.] Vol. 1-3. New York, 1850. 12°

32 HEBREW LYRICAL History; or, Select Psalms, arranged in the order of the Events to which they relate. With introductions and notes, by T. Bulfinch. Boston and Cambridge, 1853. 8vo.

33 A NEW Translation of the Proverbs, Ecclesiastes, and the Canticles; with introductions and notes, chiefly explanatory. By G. R. Noyes. Boston, 1846. 12°

34 THE EXCELLENT Woman, as described in the Book of Proverbs [xxxi. 31]. With an introduction by W. B. Sprague. Boston, 1852. 12°

35 A COMMENTARY on the Book of Proverbs. [With the text. By M. Stuart]. New York, 1852. 8°

36 A COMMENTARY on the Song of Solomon. [With the text.] By G. Burrowes. Philadelphia, 1853. 12°

37 A NEW Translation of the Hebrew Prophets, arranged in chronological order, by G. R. Noyes. 3 vol. Boston, 1833-37. 8vo.

38 NE KAGHYADONGHSERA ne Royadadokenghdy ne Isaiah. *Mobawk?* New York, 1839. 12°

39 NOTES, Critical, Explanatory, and Practical, on Isaiah; with a new translation, by A. Barnes. 3 vols. Boston, 1840. 8vo.

40 THE EARLIER Prophecies of Isaiah. [A Commentary with the text of the first thirty-nine chapters.] By J. A. Alexander. New York, 1846. 8°

BIBLES *continued.*

41 THE LATER Prophecies of Isaiah. [A Commentary, with the text of the last twenty-seven chapters of Isaiah.] By J. A. Alexander. N. York, 1847. 8°

42 NOTES, Critical, Explanatory, and Practical, on the Book of the Prophet Isaiah. By A. Barnes. [With the text.] Second edition, revised and corrected. 2 vol. N. York, 1847. 12°

43 THE NEW Testament. . Translated [by J. Eliot] into the [Natick] Indian Language [of Maſsachusetts]. Cambridge, 1661. 4to.

44 H Καινη Διαθηκη. Novum Testamentum Græce ex recensione J. J. Griesbachii. 2 tom. Lipsiæ, 1805. Cantabrigiæ Nov-Anglorum, 1809. 8vo.

45 THE NEW Testament, in an improved Version, upon the basis of Archbishop Newcome's new translation; with a corrected text, and notes critical and explanatory. Published by a Society for promoting Christian Knowledge and the practice of virtue by the distribution of books. From the London edition. Boston, 1809. 8vo.

46 A TRANSLATION of the New Testament: by G. Wakefield. From the second London edition. Cambridge, 1820. 8°

47 H Καινη Διαθηκη. The New Testament, in Greek and English; the Greek according to Griesbach, the English upon the basis of the fourth London edition of the improved Version; with an attempt to further improvement from the translations of Campbell, Wakefield, Scarlett, Macknight, and Thomson. By A. Kneeland. 2 vol. Philadel., 1823. 8°

48 THE NEW Testament. . The text of the common Translation arranged in paragraphs. By J. Nourse. New York, 1829. 12°

49 AN EXPOSITION of the Historical Writings of the New Testament [with the text]; with reflections subjoined to each section, by . . T. Kenrick. [Edited] With a memoir of the Author [by J. Kentish]. 3 vol. Boston, 1828. 8°

50 A NEW and Corrected Version of the New Testament ; . to which are subjoined a few, generally brief, critical, explanatory, and practical notes. By R. Dickinson. Boston, 1833. 8vo.

51 THE NEW Testament, . translated out of the Latin Vulgate, . and first published by the English College of Rheims, anno 1582. With the original preface, arguments and tables, marginal notes, and annotations. To which are now added, an introductory eſsay and a complete topical and textual index. New York, 1834. 8vo.

52 JU OTOSHKI-KIKINDIUIN au Kitogimaminan gaie bemajiinvng Jesus Krist: ima Ojibue inueuining giizhitong. The New Testament of our Lord and Saviour Jesus Christ: translated into the language of the Ojibwa Indians. New York, 1844. 12°

53 JU OTOSHKI-KIKINDIUIN . . ima Ojibue inueuining giizhitong. The New Testament, . translated into the language of the Ojibwa Indians. New York, 1844. 8vo.

54 THE NEW Testament ; or, the Book of the Holy Gospel of our Lord and our God Jesus the Meſsiah. A literal translation from the Syriac Peshito Version. By J. Murdock. New York, 1851. 8°

55 THE HISTORY of our Lord and Saviour Jesus Christ: comprehending all that the four Evangelists have recorded concerning him; . in the very words of Scripture. By the Rev. S. Lieberkuhn. Translated into the Delaware Indian language, by the Rev. D. Zeisberger. New York, 1821. 12°

56 AMONOTESSARON ; or, the Gospel of Jesus Christ, according to the four Evangelists: Harmonized and chronologically arranged in a new translation from the Greek text of Griesbach. By the Rev. J. S. Thompson. 2 parts. Baltimore, 1828-29. 8°

57 A HELP to the Gospels ; con-

BIBLES *continued.*
taining a harmony, exercises, *etc.*
Philadelphia, 1830. 12mo.

58 NOTES, Explanatory and Practical, on the Gospels : designed for Sunday-School teachers and Bible-clafses. [With the text.] By A. Barnes. New York, 1833. 12mo.

59 NOTES and Illustrations of the Parables of the New Testament. [With the English text.] Revised edition. Boston, 1834. 8vo.

60 A HARMONY of the Four Gospels in Greek, according to the text of Hahn. Newly arranged, with explanatory notes, by E. Robinson. Boston, 1845. 8vo.

61 AN EXAMINATION of the Testimony of the Four Evangelists, by the rules of evidence administered in Courts of Justice. With an account of the trial of Jesus [and a harmony of the Gospels]. By S. Greenleaf. Boston, 1846. 8vo.

62 NOTES, Explanatory and Practical on the Gospels [with the text]. By A. Barnes. Seventeenth edition, revised and corrected. 2 vol. New York, 1846. 12°

63 THA HALGAN Godspel on Englise. The Anglo-Saxon Version of the Holy Gospels. Edited by B. Thorpe, . from the original manuscripts. Reprinted by L. F. Klipstein. New York, 1846. 12°

64 THE WORDS of Christ, from the New Testament. Boston, 1847. 12°

65 THE FOUR Gospels, translated from the Latin Vulgate, and diligently compared with the original Greek text, being a revision of the Rhemish translation, with notes critical and explanatory, by F. P. Kenrick, Bishop of Philadelphia. New York, 1849. 8°

66 THE FOUR Gospels, with a commentary. By A. A. Livermore. 2 vol. New edition. Boston, 1850. 12°

67 A NEW Harmony and Exposition of the Gospels, . with brief notes subjoined. Being the first period of the Gospel history. With a supplement containing extended chronological and topographical differtations, *etc.* New York, 1852. 8°

68 NOTES on the Gospels, Critical and Explanatory, incorporating with the notes, on a new plan, the most approved harmony of the four Gospels. By M. W. Jacobus. . Vol. 1-2. Matthew. Sixth edition. (Mark and Luke.) New York, 1853. 12°

69 NE RAARIHWADOGENHTI ne Shongwayaner Yesus Keristus, jinihorihoten ne Royatadogenhti Matthew, Kanyengehaga Kaweanondahkon kenwendeshon Tehaweanatenyou oni shogwatagwen ne J. A. Wilkes. (The Gospel of our Lord and Saviour Jesus Christ according to Saint Matthew, translated into the Mohawk language by A. Hill, and corrected by J. A. Wilkes.) New York, 1836. 12°

70 NE TSINIHHOWEYEA-NENDA-ONH orighwa do geaty, roghyadon royadado geaghty, Saint Luke. The Gospel according to Saint Luke, translated into the Mohawk tongue by H. A. Hill. New York, 1827. 12°

71 NE HOIWIYOSDOSHEH noyohdadogehdih ne Saint Luke, nenonodowogha nigawenohdah. The Gospel according to Saint Luke, translated into the Seneca tongue by T. S. Harris. New York, 1829. 12°

72 THE GOSPEL according to St. Luke, translated into the Grebo language by the Rev. J. Payne. . (Hanh Tibosa ne Luke kinena.) New York, 1848. 12mo.

73 NENE KARIGHYOSTON tsinihorighhoten ne Saint John. The Gospel according to Saint John. (In the Mohawk language.) New York, 1818. 12°

74 LUTHER's German Version of the Gospel of St. John, with an interlinear English translation, for the use of students. By C. Follen. Cambridge, 1835. 8°

75 NE ORIGHWADOGENHTY ne jinityawea-onh ne Royatadogenhty ne John. [The Gospel according to St. John, in the Mohawk Indian Lan-

BIBLES *continued.*
guage, *wanting title.*] [New York,
1836.] 12°

76 THE GOSPEL of Jesus Christ,
according to John. Translated into
the Cherokee language. Second
edition. Park Hill, Miſsion Preſs,
1841. 12°

77 THE GOSPEL according to St.
John, translated into the Grebo tongue
by the Right Rev. J. Payne, D.D.
New York, 1852. 12mo.

78 THE GOSPEL according to St.
John, translated into the Mpongwe
language by Miſsionaries of the American Board of Commiſsioners for Foreign Miſsions, Gaboon, Western
Africa. New York, 1852. 8vo.

79 A HELP to the Aſts of the Apostles, adapted to the Leſson System of
reading and teaching the Scriptures.
Philadelphia, 1831-32. 12mo.

80 NE ne Jinihodiyeren ne Rodi-
yatadogenhti, kanyengehaga kaweanondahkon ne Tehaweanatennyon
ne Kenwendeshon nok oni shodigwatagwen ne W. Heſs and J. A. Wilkes.
(The `Aſts of the Apostles, in the
Mohawk language, translated by H.
A. Hill, with correſtions by W. Heſs
and J. A. Wilkes.) Mohawk. New
York, 1835. 12°

81 THE ACTS of the Apostles.
Translated into the Cherokee lan-
guage. Second edition. Park Hill,
Miſsion Preſs, 1842. 12mo.

82 NOTES, Explanatory and Prac-
tical, on the Aſts of the Apostles.
[With the text.] By A. Barnes.
Tenth edition. • New York, 1846. 8°

83 Πραξεις των Αποστολων. The
Aſts of the Apostles; according to the
text of A. Hahn; with notes and a
lexicon, *etc.* New York, 1850. 12°

84 THE ACTS of the Apostles, with
Notes, chiefly explanatory. . By H.
J. Ripley. Boston [1850?]. 12°

85 THE ACTS of the Apostles, with
a Commentary. By A. A. Livermore. Boston, 1850. 12°

86 THE ACTS of the Apostles translated into the Arrawack tongue, by

the Rev. Th. Shultz, in eighteen hundred and two. N. York, 1850. 12mo.

87 THE ACTS of the Apostles (Apos-
lebo äh nunude), translated into the
Grebo tongue by the Rev. J. Payne,
Miſsionary. New York, 1851. 12mo.

88 A COMMENTARY on the Epistle
to the Romans, with a translation and
various excursus. By M. Stuart.
. . Second edition, correſted and enlarged. Andover, 1835. 8°

89 NE ne Shagohyatonni Paul ne
Royatadogenhti Jinonkadih ne Romans, kanyengehaga kaweanondahkon.
ne Tehaweanatennyon ne Kenwendeshon nok oni shodigwatagwen ne
W. Heſs and J. A. Wilkes. (The
Epistle of Paul the Apostle to the
Romans, in the Mohawk language,
translated by H. A. Hill, with correſtions by W. Heſs and J. A.
Wilkes.) New York, 1835. 12°

90 NOTES, Explanatory and Prac-
tical, on the Epistle to the Romans.
[With the text.] By A. Barnes.
Ninth edition, revised and correſted.
New York, 1846. 12°

91 NOTES, Explanatory and Practical, on the First Epistle of Paul to
the Corinthians. [With the text.] By
A. Barnes. Third edition. New York,
1846. 12°

92 NOTES, Explanatory and Prac-
tical, on the Second Epistle to the
Corinthians, and the Epistle to the
Galatians. [With the text.] By A.
Barnes. New York, 1846. 12°

93 THE EPISTLE of Paul the Apostle to the Corinthians, translated into
the Mohawk language by W. Heſs,
with correſtions by J. A. Wilkes.
(Ne Tyotyerenhtonh kahyatonhsera
ne Paul ne Royaladogenhti Shagohyatonni jinonka ne Corinthians, W.
Heſs, tehaweanatennyon oni shogwatagwen ne J. A. Wilkes.) New
York, 1836. 12mo.

94 NE ne shagohyatonni Paul ne
Royatadogenhti jinonkadih ne Galatians, kanyengehaga kaweanondahkon, ne tehaweanatennyon ne kenwendeshon nok oni shodigwalagwen

BIBLES *continued.*

ne W. Hefs and J. A. Wilkes. (The Epistle of Paul the Apostle to the Galatians, in the Mohawk language, translated by H. A. Hill, with corrections by W. Hefs and J. A. Wilkes.) Mohawk and English. New York, 1835. 12°

95 NE ne shagohyatonni Paul ne Royatadogenhti jinonkadih ne Ephesians, kanyengehaga kaweanondahkon, ne Tehaweanatennyon ne kenwendeshon nok oni shodigwalagwen ne W. Hefs and J. A. Wilkes. (The Epistle to the Ephesians, in the Mohawk language, translated by H. A. Hill, with corrections by W. Hefs and J. A. Wilkes.) Mohawk and Engl. New York, 1835. 12°

96 NOTES, Explanatory and Practical, on the Epistles of Paul to the Ephesians, Philippians, and Colossians. [With the text.] By A. Barnes. New York, 1846. 12mo.

97 NE YEHOHYATON ne Royatadogenhti Paul jinonka ne Philippians, W. Hefs, tehaweanatennyon oni shogwatagwen ne J. A. Wilkes. (The Epistle of Paul the Apostle to the Philippians, translated into the Mohawk language by W. Hefs, with corrections by J. A. Wilkes.) Mohawk, New York, 1836. 12°

98 NE YEHOHYATON ne Royatadogenhti Paul jinonka ne Colofsians, W.Hess, tehaweanatennyon oni Shogwatagwen, ne J. A. Wilkes. (The Epistle of Paul the Apostle to the Colofsians, translated into the Mohawk language by W. Hefs, with corrections by J. A. Wilkes.) Mohawk, New York, 1836. 12°

99 NE Tyotyerenhton ne Royatadogenhti Paul Yehohyaton jinonka ne Thefsalonians, W. Hefs, tehaweanatennyon oni Shogwatagwen ne J. A. Wilkes. (The Epistle of Paul the Apostle to the Thefsalonians, translated into the Mohawk language by W. Hefs, with corrections by J.A.Wilkes.) Mohawk, New York, 1836. 12°

100 NOTES, Explanatory and Prac-

tical, on the Epistles of Paul to the Thefsalonians, to Timothy, to Titus, and to Philemon. By A. Barnes. [With the text.] New York, 1845. 12mo.

101 NOTES, Explanatory and Practical, on the Epistles of Paul to the Thefsalonians, to Timothy, to Titus, and to Philemon. By A. Barnes. [With the text.] N. York, 1846. 12°

102 NE ne tyotyerenhton ne Royatadogenhti Paul Yehohyatonni ne Timothy, W. Hefs, tehaweanatennyon oni shogwatagwen ne J.A.Wilkes. (The Epistle of Paul the Apostle to Timothy, translated into the Mohawk language by W. Hefs, with corrections by J. A. Wilkes.) Mohawk, New York, 1836. 12°

103 THE EPISTLES of Paul to Timothy. Translated into the Cherokee language. Park Hill, Mifsion Prefs, 1844. 12mo.

104 NE YEHOHYATON ne Royatadogenhti Paul jinonka ne Titus, W. Hefs, tehaweanatennyon oni shogwatagwen ne J. A. Wilkes. (The Epistle of Paul the Apostle to Titus, translated into the Mohawk language by W. Hefs, with corrections by J. A. Wilkes.) Mohawk. New York, 1836. 12°

105 NE YEHOHYATON ne Royatadogenhti Paul jinonka ne Philemon, W. Hefs, tehaweanatennyon oni shogwatagwen, ne J. A. Wilkes. (The Epistle of Paul the Apostle to Philemon, translated into the Mohawk language by W. Hefs, with corrections by J. A. Wilkes.) Mohawk. New York, 1836. 12°

106 A COMMENTARY on the Epistle to the Hebrews, by M. Stuart. [With the text.] 2 vol. Andover, 1827-28. 8°

107 A COMMENTARY on the Epistle to the Hebrews. [With the text.] By M. Stuart. Second edition, corrected and enlarged. Andover, 1833. 8°

108 NE YEHOHYATON ne Royatadogenhti Paul jinonka ne Hebrews, W. Hefs, tehaweanatennyon oni shogwatagwen ne J. A. Wilkes. (The

BIBLES *continued.*

Epistle of Paul the Apostle to the Hebrews, translated into the Mohawk language by W. Heſs, with corrections by J. A. Wilkes.) Mohawk. New York, 1836. 12°

109 NOTES, Explanatory and Practical, on the Epistle to the Hebrews. [With the text.] By A. Barnes. New York, 1846. 12°

110 THE EPISTLE to the Hebrews in Greek and English, with an Analysis and English Commentary, by S. H. Turner. New York, 1852. 8vo.

111 NE YEHHONWAGHYADONNYH ne James. Ne tyutyerenghdonh yehhonwaghyadonnyh orighwakwekonh ne Kwiter. Ne tekenihhadond yehhonwaghyadonnyh rayadakwe-niyu Kwiter. Ne tyutyadonghseratyerenghdonh rayadakwe-niyu ne Janyh. Ne ne tekaghyadonghserakehhadont ne Janyh. Ne aghsenhhadont nikaghyadongserakeh ne Janyh. [The general Epistle of St. James, the first and second Epistles of St. Peter, and the first, second, and third Epistles of St. John, in the Mohawk Indian language.] 3 parts. [*wanting titles.*] [New York, 1836.] 12°

112 NEK nechenenawachgiſbitschik bambilak naga geschiechauhsitpanna Johanneſsa elekhangup. Gischilak elleniechsink Untschi C. F. Dencke. (The three Epistles of the Apostle John. Translated into Delaware Indian, by C. F. Dencke.) New York, 1818. 12°

113 THE EPISTLES of John. Translated into the Cherokee language. Second edition. Park Hill, Miſsion Preſs, 1843. 12mo.

114 NE rayadakwe-niyu yehhonwaghyadonnyh ne Jude. [The General Epistle of St. Jude, in the Mohawk Indian language,] [*wanting title.*] Mohawk. [New York, 1836.] 12°

115 AN ATTEMPT to translate the Prophetic part of the Apocalypse of Saint John, into familiar Language, by divesting it of the Metaphors in which it is involved. By James Winthrop. Boston, 1794. 8vo.

116 NE ne Revelation konwayats. [The book of Revelations in the Mohawk Indian language.] Mohawk. [New York, 1836.] 12°

117 A COMMENTARY on the Apocalypse. [With the text.] By M. Stuart. 2 vol. Andover, 1845. 8°

118 AN EXPOSITION of the Apocalypse. By D. N. Lord. [With the text.] New York, 1847. 8°

119 AN EXPOSITION of the Revelation of John from the Fourth Chapter. [With the text.] By J. Mann. New York, 1851. 12°

120 THE APOCALYPSE unveiled; the Day of Judgment, the Resurrection, and the Millenium, presented in a New Light, *etc.* [With the text, with the exception of the first four chapters.] 2 vol. London [Boston ! printed], 1853. 12mo.

121 A DISCOURSE on the Genuineneſs and Authenticity of the New Testament; delivered at New Haven, Sept. 10th, 1793, at the Annual Lecture, appointed by the General Aſsociation of Connecticut, *etc.* New York, 1794. 8vo.

122 INDEX to the Bible, in which the various subjects which occur in the Scriptures are alphabetically arranged, *etc.* Philadelphia, 1804. 8°

123 BIBLE PICTURES. American Sunday School Union, Philadelphia. [1830 ?] 12mo.

124 FIRESIDE Conversations on some of the principal Doctrines of the Bible. Philadelphia, 1830. 12mo.

125 SKETCHES from the Bible. Philadelphia, 1830. 12mo.

126 BIBLE Anecdotes, illustrative of the value and influence of Divine Truth. Philadelphia [1833 ?] 12mo.

127 THE BIBLICAL Reader; consisting of Rhetorical Extracts from the Old and New Testaments, to which is applied a Notation. . By E. Porter. Andover, 1834. 12°

128 SUPPLEMENT to the Comprehensive Commentary. [Edited by W.

BIB

BIBLES *continued.*

Jenks.] (A new Concordance .. By .. J. Butterworth .. with .. improvements by A. Clark .. the Definitions of Cruden, and .. engravings, under the superintendence of W. Jenks. A Guide to the .. Study of the Bible .. by W. Carpenter .. abridged, with additions .. by J. W. Jenks. Biography of Biblical Writers and others quoted in the Comprehensive Commentary.) 3 parts. Brattleboro' [1838.] 8vo.

129 סבר הישר; or, the Book of Jasher; referred to in Joshua and Second Samuel, [with the preface of Joseph ben Samuel the little,] translated from the original Hebrew [by M. M. Noah.] Engl. New York, 1840. 8°

130 THE BIBLE Reader; being a new Selection of Reading Lessons from the Holy Scriptures, for the Use of Schools and Families; by W. B. Fowle. Boston, 1843. 12°

131 SELECT Passages from the Holy Scriptures. Cherokee. [Park Hill, Mission Press, 1843!] 12mo.

132 A NEW- Concordance to the Holy Scriptures in a Single Alphabet. .. A new edition, with considerable improvements, by A. Clarke, to which are added the Definitions of Cruden .. under the superintendence of Rev. W. Jenks. Philadelphia, 1851. 8°

133 EVERY-DAY Scripture Readings; with Brief Reviews and Practical Observations .. By J. L. Blake, D.D. New York, 1853. 12°

134 A COMPLETE Analysis of the Holy Bible, containing the whole of the Old and New Testaments, collected and arranged systematically in thirty books (based on the work of .. Talbot); together with an introduction, setting forth the character of the work. . Tables of Contents .. and a General Index . By . N. West. Fifth edition. London, New York [printed!] 1854. 8vo.

·BIBLICAL REPERTORY. A

Collection of Tracts in Biblical Literature, by C. Hodge. 4 vol. Princeton and New York, 1825-27. 8vo. [Continued under the title of] The Biblical Repertory and Theological Review, edited by an Association of Gentlemen in Princeton and its Vicinity. New Series. [Continued under the title of] The Biblical Repertory and Princeton Review. Edited by C. Hodge. Vol. 1-28. Princeton, Philadelphia, 1829-56. 8°

2 THEOLOGICAL Essays, reprinted from the Princeton Review. [First Series.] New York and London, 1846. 8°

3 ESSAYS, Theological and Miscellaneous. Reprinted from the Princeton Review. Second Series; including the contributions of.. A. B. Dod. N. York and London, 1847. 8°

BIBLICAL REPOSITORY, conducted by E. Robinson. Vol. 1-4. Andover, 1831-34. 8vo. [Then united with the American Quarterly Observer, and continued under the title of] The Biblical Repository and Quarterly Observer, conducted by B. B. Edwards. Vol. 5-8. Andover and Boston, 1835-36. 8vo. [Continued as] The American Biblical Repository. Vol. 9-10, conducted by B. B. Edwards; vol. 11-12, by A. Peters. New York and Boston, 1837-38. 8vo. Second Series. Vol. 1-3; conducted by A. Peters; vol. 4-6, by A. Peters and S. B. Treat; vol. 7, by A. Peters and J. H. Agnew; vol. 8-12, by J. H. Agnew. New York and Boston, 1839-44. 8° General Index, 1839-44, by J. H. Agnew. New York, 1845. 8° [Continued as] The Biblical Repository and Classical Review; edited by J. H. Agnew. Third Series. 6 vol. [Then united with the Bibliotheca Sacra.] New York, 1845-50. 8°

BIBLIOTHECA SACRA; or, Tracts and Essays on Topics connected with Biblical Literature and Theology. Editor, E. Robinson.

New York and London, 1843. 8°
[Continued under the title of] Bibliotheca Sacra and Theological Review.
Conducted by B. B. Edwards and E.
A. Park, with the co-operation of Dr.
Robinson and Profeſsor Stuart. Vol.
1-7. London, Andover [printed],
1844-50. 8° [The Biblical Repository was then combined with this
work, and it was continued as] Bibliotheca Sacra and American Biblical
Repository; conducted by B. B. Edwards and E. A. Park, with the co-
operation of Dr. Robinson and Profeſsor Stuart, etc. Vol. 8. Conducted
by E. A. Park and S. H. Taylor. Vol.
9-13. Andover, 1851-56. 8°

BICHENO, JAMES. The Signs of
the Times; or, the Overthrow of the
Papal tyranny in France, the pre-
lude of destruction to Popery and
Despotism, but of peace to mankind.
First American edition, from the se-
cond European. Providence (R.
Island), 1794. 8°

BICKERSTETH, EDWARD, Rec-
tor of Watton, Herts. The Christian
Hearer, abridged. . Edited, with additional matter, by C. Cotton. Columbus, 1838. 12°

BIDDLE, JOHN B. Review of
Materia Medica, for the Use of Students. Philadelphia, 1852. 12mo.

BIDDLE, NICHOLAS. Eulogium
on T. Jefferson, delivered before the
American Philosophical Society, . .
April, 1827. Philadelphia, 1827. 8°

BIDWELL, BARNABAS. Com-
monwealth of Maſsachusetts. The
Attorney-General's Report respecting
claims for confiscated Debts. Boston,
1808. 8°

BIGELOW, ABIJAH. The Sab-
bath; a Poem, in two parts. Worcester [Maſs.] 1842. 12°

BIGELOW, ANDREW. An Ora-
tion, delivered before the Washington
Benevolent Society, at Cambridge,
July 4, 1815. Cambridge, 1815. 8°

2 LEAVES from a Journal; or,
Sketches of Rambles in some parts of
North Britain and Ireland, chiefly in
. . 1817. [With MS. notes and
corrections by the Author.] Boston,
1821. 12mo.

3 TRAVELS in Malta and Sicily, with
Sketches of Gibraltar in MDCCCXXVII.
Boston, 1831. 8°

4 GOD'S Charge unto Israel: a
Sermon [Exod. xiv. 15], preached
before . . the Legislature of Maſsachusetts, at the annual election . .
Jan. 6, 1836. Boston, 1836. 8°

BIGELOW, HENRY JACOB. Fragments of Medical Science and Art:
an Addreſs delivered before the Boylston Medical Society of Harvard
University. Boston, 1846. 8°

BIGELOW, JACOB. Florula Bostoniensis. A collection of Plants of
Boston and its environs, etc. Boston,
1814. 8vo.

2 FLORULA Bostoniensis: a collection of the Plants of Boston and
its vicinity, etc. Third edition, enlarged, and containing a Gloſsary of
botanical terms. Boston, 1840. 12°

3 SOME Account of the White
Mountains of New Hampshire [1817].
8vo.

4 INAUGURAL Addreſs, delivered in
the chapel of the University at Cambridge, Dec. 11, 1816. Boston, 1817.
8vo.

5 AMERICAN Medical Botany, being a collection of the native Medicinal Plants of the United States, containing their botanical history and
chemical analysis and properties and
uses in medicine, diet, and the arts.
3 vol. Boston, 1817-20. 8°

6 FACTS serving to show the comparative forwardneſs of the Spring
in different parts of the United States.
Cambridge, 1818. 4to.

7 ELEMENTS of Technology; taken
chiefly from a course of Lectures . .
on the Application of the Sciences to
the Useful Arts. Second edition,
with additions. Boston, 1831. 8°

8 THE USEFUL Arts, considered in connexion with the Applications of Science. 2 vols. Boston, 1840. 12mo.

9 AN INTRODUCTORY Lecture on the Treatment of Disease, delivered . . at the Massachusetts Medical College, etc. Boston, 1853. 8vo.

BIGELOW, JOHN. Jamaica in 1850; or, the effects of sixteen years of freedom on a Slave Colony. New York [printed] and London, 1851. 12°

BIGELOW, JOHN PRESCOTT. Statistical Tables; exhibiting the condition and products of certain branches of industry in Massachusetts for the year ending April 1, 1837. Boston, 1838. 8°

2 INAUGURAL Address to the Aldermen and Common Council . . of Boston, January 7, 1850. Boston, 1850. 8vo.

BIGELOW, LEWIS. An Oration, pronounced at Templeton, July 5, 1813, in commemoration of the thirty-seventh anniversary of American Independence, before the Washington Benevolent Societies, etc. Worcester, 1813. 8°

2 A DIGEST of the Cases argued and determined in the Supreme Judicial Court of . . Massachusetts, from Sept. 1804 to Nov. 1815, as contained in the twelve first Volumes of the Reports. Cambridge, 1818. 8°

BIGELOW, TIMOTHY. An Eulogy on the Life, Character, and Services of Brother George Washington, . pronounced before the Fraternity of free and accepted Masons, . at . . Boston, . Feb. 11, 1800, being the day set apart by them to pay funeral honours to their deceased brother. To which are added, two addresses to the deceased, when President of the United States, and his answers, etc. Boston [1800]. 8°

BIGLOW, HOSEA, Pseud. [i. e. James Russell Lowell.] Melibœus-

Hipponax. The Biglow papers, edited with an introduction, notes, glossary, and copious index, by H. Wilbur. Cambridge, 1848. 12°

BIGLOW, WILLIAM. History of the town of Natick, Mass., from the days of the apostolic Eliot, 1650, to the present time, 1830. Boston, 1830. 8°

BIGLY, CANTELL, A. [i. e. CAN TELL A BIG LYE], Pseud. Aurifodina; or, Adventures in the Gold Region. New York, 1849. 12°

BINGHAM, CALEB. The Young Lady's Accidence; or, a short and easy Introduction to English Grammar. . The seventeenth edition. Boston, 1808. 12°

BINGHAM, H. Missionary to the Sandwich Islands. Bartimeus, of the Sandwich Islands. [A memoir of B. Puaaiki, afterwards called Lalana.] Boston [1852 ?] 16mo.

BINNEY, HORACE. Speech . . on the Question of the Removal of the Deposites; delivered in the House of Representatives, Jan. 1834. Washington, 1834. 8°

2 AN EULOGY upon the Life and Character of J. Marshall, Chief Justice of the Supreme Court of the United States, etc. Philadelphia, 1835. 8°

3 REMARKS upon Mr. Binney's Letter of January 3, 1840, to the Presidents of the Councils of the city of Philadelphia. By the writer of the Letter. Philadelphia, 1840. 8°

4 ARGUMENT of H. Binney, . in the case of Vidal v. the city of Philadelphia, in the Supreme Court of the United States, Feb. 1844. Philadelphia, 1844. 8°

5 REPORTS of Cases adjudged in the Supreme Court of Pennsylvania [1799-1814]. 6 vol. [vol. 1 and 6, 2nd edit.]. Phil., 1844-10-23. 8°

BIOGRAPHY of the Signers to the Declaration of Independence. Second edition. Revised, improved, and enlarged. 5 vol. Philadel., 1828. 8vo.

BIOGRAPHY of Two Little Children. American Sunday School Union. Philadelphia, 1831. 12mo.

BIOT, JEAN BAPTISTE. Elements of Electricity, Magnetism, and Electro-Magnetism, embracing the late discoveries and improvements; [Selected and translated from Biot's Précis elémentaire de physique;] digested into the form of a treatise; being the second part of a course of natural philosophy, . by J. Farrar. Cambridge, 1826. 8°

2 AN ELEMENTARY Treatise on Analytical Geometry; translated from the French . . and adapted to the present state of mathematical instruction in the colleges of the United States, by F. H. Smith. New York, 1840. 8°

BIRKBECK, MORRIS. Notes on a Journey in America, from the coast of Virginia to the territory of the Illinois, with proposals for the establishment of a colony of English. Philadelphia, 1817. 12°

BISBEE, JOHN H. A Sermon [on 2 Sam. xxiii. 3], delivered before . . the . . council and . . legislature of Massachusetts, at the annual election, . Jan. 6, 1847. Boston, 1847. 8°

BISHOP, ABRAHAM. Oration in honour of the election of President Jefferson, and the peaceable acquisition of Louisiana, delivered at the national festival in Hartford . . May 11, 1804. Printed for the general committee of Republicans. [Hartford,] 1804. 8°

BISHOP, JOEL PRENTISS. Commentaries on the Law of Marriage and Divorce, and evidence in matrimonial suits. Boston, Cambridge printed, and London, 1852. 8vo.

BLACHETTE, L. J. and ZOEGA, FREDERIC. A Manual of the Art of making and refining Sugar from Beets, including the cultivation of the plant, and the various improvements in the manufacture. Translated from portions of the treatise of MM. Blachette and Zoega, as published, with additions by J. De Fontenelle. Boston, 1836. 12mo.

BLACK, F. G. Lectures and Sermons, embracing the sovereignty, holiness, wisdom, and benevolence of God, etc. Cincinnati, 1851. 12°

BLACK HAWK. Life of Ma-ka-tai-me-she-kia-kiak, or Black Hawk. With an account of the late war. Dictated by himself. J. B. Patterson, editor. Boston, 1834. 12mo.

BLACKBEARD. A Page from the Colonial History of Philadelphia. 2 vol. New York, 1835. 12°

BLACKFORD, ISAAC. Reports of Cases argued and determined in the Supreme Court of Judicature of the state of Indiana, etc. May term, 1817—May term, 1845. Vol. 1-7. Indianapolis, 1830-44-47. 8°

BLACKSTONE, SIR WILLIAM. Blackstone's Commentaries: with notes of reference to the constitution and laws of the federal government of the United States, and of the commonwealth of Virginia; with an appendix to each volume, containing . . a connected view of the laws of Virginia as a member of the federal union. By St. George Tucker. 5 vol. Philadelphia, 1803. 8°

2 THE MOST important parts of Blackstone's Commentaries reduced to Questions and Answers, by Asa Kinne. Second edition. New York, 1839. 8°

3 COMMENTARIES. . With the last corrections of the author, and notes, from the twenty-first London edition, . by J. F. Hargrave, . G. Sweet, . R. Couch, . W. N. Welsby; together with notes, adapting the work to the American student, by J. L. Wendell. 4 vol. New York, 1847. 8°

BLACKWELL, Elizabeth, *M.D.* The Laws of Life; with special reference to the physical education of girls. New York, 1852. 12°

BLAGDEN, G. W. The Effects of Education upon a country village: an address delivered before the Brighton school fund corporation, March 30, 1828. Boston, 1828. 8°

BLAIR, David. Anniversary Address delivered before the Washington Literary Society of Washington College, Pa. [Washington, Pa. 1836.] 8°

BLAIR, Hugh. An Abridgment of Letters on Rhetoric. . Revised and corrected. Boston, 1803. 12°

BLAKE, Alexander V. The American Bookseller's Complete Reference Trade List, and alphabetical catalogue of books published in this country; with the publishers' and authors' names and prices arranged in classes. . Compiled by A. V. Blake. To which is added, an article [by P. T. Washburn] on the law of copyright. Claremont, N. H. 1847. 4°

BLAKE, D. T. Practice of the Court of Chancery of the State of New York; modified, corrected, and improved in conformity to the present constitution and laws. To which is added, the practice of the several district equity courts. Second edition. Albany, 1824. 8°

BLAKE, George. An Oration, pronounced July 4, 1795, at . . Boston, in commemoration of the anniversary of American Independence. Boston, 1795. 8°

BLAKE, John L. *D.D.* The Juvenile Companion, being an introduction to the historical reader. Boston, 1827. 12°

2 The High School Reader, . consisting of extracts in prose and poetry. Boston, 1832. 12°

3 The First Reader; a class-book for schools, *etc.* Concord, N. H. [1832.] 12°

4 The Historical Reader, designed for the use of schools and families. On a new plan. Concord, N. H. 1834. 12°

5 A General Biographical Dictionary, . including more than one thousand articles of American biography. . Fourth edition. Philadelphia, 1840. Roy. 8vo.

6 A Family-text Book for the Country; or, The Farmer at Home: being a cyclopædia of the more important topics in modern agriculture, *etc.* New York, 1852. 8°

7 The Modern Farmer; or, Home in the Country: [a collection of extracts in prose and verse,] *etc.* Auburn, 1853. 12°

BLANCHARD, J. On the Importance and Means of cultivating the Social Affections among Pupils; . delivered before the American Institute of Instruction. [With an appendix.] [Boston, 1835.] 8°

2 A Debate on Slavery, held in the city of Cincinnati, . October, 1845, upon the question: Is slaveholding in itself sinful, and the relation between master and slave a sinful relation? Affirmative: . J. Blanchard. Negative: N. L. Rice. Cincinnati, 1846. 12°

BLAND, Theodorick. Reports of Cases decided in the High Court of Chancery of Maryland. Vol. 1. Baltimore, 1836. 8°

2 The Bland Papers: being a selection from the manuscripts of Col. T. Bland. To which are prefixed an introduction, and a memoir of Col. Bland. Edited by C. Campbell. 2 vol. Petersburg (Virginia), 1840, 43. 8°

BLEDSOE, Albert Taylor. An Examination of President Edwards' Inquiry into the Freedom of the Will. Philadelphia, 1845. 12°

BLESSEDNESS. "Single Blessedness;" or, Single Ladies and Gentlemen against the Slanders of the Pulpit, the Press, and the Lecture-room. New York, 1852. 12°

BLISS, Mrs. The Practical Cook Book, containing upwards of one thousand receipts, etc. Philadelphia, 1850. 12°

BLISS, Daniel. The Gospel hidden to them that are lost: being the substance of two sermons [on 2 Cor. iv. 3] preached at Concord; showing when and whence the Gospel is hid to any under the dispensation of it, etc. Boston, 1755. 8vo.

BLISS, George. An Address to the Members of the Bar of the counties of Hampshire, Franklin, and Hampden, at their annual meeting, etc. Springfield, [Mass.] 1827. 8°

2 An Address delivered at the opening of the Town-Hall in Springfield, March 24, 1828, containing sketches of the early history of that town, and those in its vicinity. With an appendix. Springfield, 1828. 8°

BLISS, Leonard. The History of Rehoboth, Bristol County, Massachusetts. Boston, 1836. 8vo.

BLODGET, Samuel. Economica: a statistical manual for the United States of America. Washington, 1806. 8°

BLOIS, John T. Gazetteer of the State of Michigan; in three parts; ... with a succinct history of the State: .. an appendix, containing the usual Statistical Tables, and a Directory for Emigrants, etc. Detroit, 1840. 12°

BLOODGOOD, S. De Witt. A Treatise on Roads, their History, Character, and Utility; being the substance of two lectures, etc. Albany, 1838. 8vo.

BLUNT, Edmund M. Blunt's Stranger's Guide to the City of New York. . With an appendix, . a plan of the city, and engravings of public buildings. New York, 1817. 12°

2 The American Coast Pilot: containing directions for the principal harbours, capes, and headlands, on the coasts of North and South America; . together with a tide table. Fourteenth edition, improved, by E. and G. W. Blunt. N. York, 1842. 8°

3 The American Coast Pilot. . Sixteenth edition, by E. and G. W. Blunt. New York. 1850. 8vo.

BLUNT, Joseph. An Historical Sketch of the Formation of the Confederacy, particularly with reference to the provincial limits and the jurisdiction of the general government over Indian tribes and the public territory. New York, 1825. 8°

2 The Shipmaster's Assistant and Commercial Digest: containing information useful to merchants, owners, and masters of ships. New York, 1837. 8vo.

3 Speeches, reviews, reports, etc. New York, 1843. 8°

BOARD OF AGRICULTURE OF the State of New York. Memoirs. Vol. 2-3. Albany, 1823-26. 8vo.

BOARDMAN, Charles A. The Agency of God, illustrated in the achievement of the Independence of the United States: a sermon [on Psal. cxxiv. 1-7] delivered July 4, 1826, being a religious celebration of that day. New Haven, 1826. 8°

BOARDMAN, Henry A. D. D. Suggestions to young men engaged in mercantile business. A discourse [on Matt. vi. 33] occasioned by the death of Mr. A. Sloan, etc. Philadelphia, 1851. 8°

2 The American Union: a discourse delivered . : Dec. 12, 1850, the day of the annual thanksgiving in Pennsylvania. . Sixth edition. Philadelphia, 1851. 8°

3 The New Doctrine of Intervention tried by the Teachings of Washington: an address delivered in the Tenth Presbyterian church, Philadelphia, on . . the 23rd and 24th of February, 1852. Phil., 1852. 8°

4 The Bible in the Counting House: a course of lectures to mer-

chants. London [Philadelphia printed], 1853. 12mo.

5 A DISCOURSE on the Life and Character of D. Webster. Philadelphia, 1852. 8°

BOCKSHAMMER, GUSTAV FERDINAND. Bockshammer on the Freedom of the Human Will. Translated from the German, with additions, by A. Kaufman, Jr. Andover, 1835. 12°

BOENNINGHAUSEN, CLEMENS MAX FRIEDRICH VON. Therapeutic Pocket-book for Homœopathic Physicians. . Edited by C. J. Hempel. New York, 1847. 8vo.

BOGUE, DAVID, D. D. Objections against a Miſſion to the Heathen, stated and considered : a sermon [on Hagg. i. 2] preached . . before the founders of the [London] Miſſionary Society, Sept. 24, 1795. . First American edition. Camb., 1811. 8°

BOIARDO, MATTEO MARIA, Count di Scandiano. The Enchanted Lake of the Fairy Morgana ; [translated] from the Orlando Inamorato of F. Berni [by R. A. i. e. Richard Alsop ?] New York, 1806. 8vo.

BOKER, GEORGE HENRY. Calaynos : a tragedy [in five acts and in verse]. Philadelphia, 1848. 12°

2 ANNE BOLEYN : a tragedy [in five acts and in verse]. Philadelphia, 1850. 8°

- 3 THE PODESTA's Daughter and other miscellaneous Poems. Philadelphia. 1852, 12°

BOKUM, HERMANN. A Public Lecture on the German Language and Literature, introductory to a course of six lectures, etc. Boston, 1836. 8°

BOLLES, JOHN R. Solitude and Society ; with other poems. Second edition. New London, 1847. 12°

BOLTON, CORNELIUS WINTER. A Shepherd's Call to the Lambs of his Flock. New York, 1853. Square 16°

· BOLTON, ROBERT, the Younger.

A History of the County of West Chester, from its first settlement to the present time. 2 vol. New York, 1848. 8°

BONAPARTE, Family of. The Napoleon Dynasty ; or, The History of the Bonaparte Family. . By the Berkeley Men. With . . portraits. New York, 1852. 8°

BONAPARTE, CHARLES JULES LAURENT LUCIEN, Prince of Canino. American Ornithology ; or, The Natural History of Birds inhabiting the United States, not given by Wilson. 4 vol. Philadelphia, 1825-33. fol.

BOND. The New Bond of Love. New York, 1853. 12mo.

BOND, ALVAN. Two Discourses [on Isa. xxvi. 15, and Prov. xiv. 26] delivered on the annual fast, April 1, 1836. Norwich [Conn.], 1836. 8°

BOND, WILLIAM K. Speech . . upon the resolution to correct abuses in the public expenditures, and to separate the government from the preſs ; delivered in the House of Representatives April, 1838. [Waſhington, 1838.] 8°

BONNECHOSE, EMILE DE. The Reformers before the Reformation. The fifteenth century. John Huſs and the Council of Constance. . translated from the French by C. Mackenzie. 2 vols. New York, 1844. 12°

BONNEVILLE, B. L. E. Captain. The Rocky Mountains ; or, Scenes, Incidents, and Adventures in the far West ; digested from the journal of Captain B. L. E. Bonneville, . and illustrated from various other sources. By Washington Irving. 2 vol. Philadelphia, 1843. 12°

BONNYCASTLE, JOHN, of the Royal Military Academy, Woolwich. The Scholar's Guide to Arithmetic. . Second American, from the tenth London edition, etc. Philadelphia, 1818. 12°

2 An INTRODUCTION to Algebra; . . to which is added, an appendix on the application of Algebra to Geometry. . Third New York, from the last London edition. Revised, corrected, and enlarged, . . by J. Ryan. New York, 1825. 12°

BOOK. The Book of Commerce by Sea and Land. . To which are added, a history of commerce, and a chronological table. . a map and numerous engravings. Boston, 1834. 4°

2 THE FIRST Book of History, for Children and Youth. By the author of Peter Parley's tales [S. G. Goodrich]. With sixty engravings and sixteen maps. Revised edition. Boston, 1846. 4°

3 THE SECOND Book of History, including the Modern History of Europe, Africa, and Asia. Illustrated by engravings and sixteen maps, and designed as a sequel to the "First Book of History, by the author of Peter Parley's tales." [S. G. Goodrich.] Eleventh edition. Boston, 1836. 4°

4 THE THIRD Book of History; containing ancient history in connection with ancient geography. Designed as a sequel to the "First and Second Books of History," by the author of "Peter Parley's tales." [S. G. Goodrich.] Third edition. Boston, 1836. 4°

5 THE FIRST Book; or, Spelling Lessons for primary Schools. Boston, 1841. 12°

6 BOOK of the Telegraph. [By D. Davis.] (Catalogue of apparatus to illustrate magnetism, . . manufactured and sold by D. Davis, . . 1848.) Boston, 1851. 12°

7 THE BOOK of the Heart; or, Love's Emblems. Illustrated, etc. New York, 1853. 4°

BOONE, Rev. WILLIAM J. An Address in behalf of the China Mission. New York, 1837. 8°

BOORN, STEPHEN. Trial of S. and J. Boorn, for the murder of R.

Colvin, before . . the Supreme Court of Vermont. . To which is subjoined . . the wonderful discovery thereafter of the said Colvin's being alive, etc. Rutland, Vt. [1819.] 8°

BOOTH, JAMES C. Memoir of the Geological Survey of the State of Delaware, including the application of the geological observations to agriculture. Dover [Delaware], 1841. 8°

2 THE ENCYCLOPÆDIA of Chemistry, practical and theoretical. By J. C. Booth, . . assisted by C. Morfit. Philadelphia, 1850. 8°

3 THE ENCYCLOPÆDIA of Chemistry. . By J. C. Booth, assisted by C. Morfit. Second edition. London, Philadelphia [printed] 1853. 8vo.

BORDLEY, JOHN BENJAMIN. Essays and Notes on Husbandry, and Rural Affairs. Philadel., 1799. 8vo.

BOSTON. Propositions concerning the subject of Baptism and Consociations of Churches, collected and confirmed out of the Word of God, by a Synod of elders and messengers of the churches in Massachusetts colony in New England, at a general court held at Boston. Whereunto is anext the answer of the dissenting brethren and messengers of the churches of New England, etc. 2 pts. [separately paged.] [Cambridge], 1662. 4to.

2 A DEFENCE of the Answer and Arguments of the Synod met at Boston in the year 1662, concerning the subject of baptism and consociation of churches, against the reply of John Davenport, entituled "Another Essay for the Investigation of the Truth," etc. Together with an answer to the apologetical preface set before that essay. By some of the elders who were members of the synod abovementioned. Cambridge, 1664. 4to.

3 A PROJECTION for erecting a Bank of Credit in Boston, New England, founded on land security. [Boston?] 1714. 12mo.

4 A VINDICATION of the Ministers of Boston from the abuses and scan-

dals lately cast upon them, in diverse printed papers. By some of their people. Boston, 1722. 8vo.

5 AN APPEAL to the World; or, a Vindication of the town of Boston, from many false and malicious aspersions, contained in letters and memorials, written by Governor Bernard, General Gage, Commodore Hood, and others. Boston, 1769. 8vo.

6 A SHORT Narrative of the horrid Maſsacre, perpetrated 5th of March 1770, by Soldiers of the 29th Regiment. Boston, 1770. 8vo.

7 ADDITIONAL Observations to a " Short Narrative of the Horrid Massacre in Boston, perpetrated 5th March, 1770." Boston. 1770. 8vo.

8 A LETTER from a Veteran to the Officers of the Army encamped at Boston. America, 1774. 8vo.

9 MEMORIAL of the Merchants of . . Boston [relative to the violation by Great Britain of the rights of neutrals]. January 20, 1806. Washington, 1806. 8°

10 PROCEEDINGS of the Aſſociation of Citizens to erect a monument in honour of Gen. G. Washington. Boston, 1811. 12°

11 PAPERS on the Defence of Boston, and other places. [Boston, 1813.] 8°

12 A MEMORIAL to the Congreſs of the United States on the subject of restraining the increase of Slavery in new States to be admitted into the Union. Prepared in pursuance of a vote of the inhabitants of Boston and its vicinity, aſsembled at the State House . . 3rd December, 1819. Boston, 1819. 8°

13 ADDRESS of the Committee appointed at a public meeting held in Boston, December 19, 1823, for the relief of the Greeks, to their fellow citizens. [With an extract from a Boston newspaper of January 21, 1824, on the same subject.] Boston, 1824. 8°

14 REPORT of a Committee of the Citizens of Boston and Vicinity, op-

posed to a further increase of Duties on Importations. Boston, 1827. 8°

15 FIFTH Annual Report of the Directors of the House of Reformation. Boston, 1831. 12°

16 CITY of Boston. Report of the Standing Committee of the Common Council on the subject of the House of Reformation for juvenile offenders. [Boston], 1832. 8°

17 REMARKS on a Report of the Standing Committee of the Common Council, on the subject of the House of Reformation for juvenile offenders. By the Directors. Boston, 1833. 8°

18 TENTH Annual Report of the House of Industry to the City Council. (April 1, 1833.) [Boston, 1833.] 8°

19 THE CHARTER and Ordinances of the city of Boston, together with the acts of the legislature relating to the city. Collated and revised . . by T. Wetmore and E. G. Prescott. Boston, 1834. 8°

20 SELECTIONS from the Court Reports, originally published in the Boston Morning Post, from 1834 to 1837. Arranged and revised by the reporter of the Post. Boston, 1837. 12mo.

21 REMARKS on the Seventh Annual Report of . . H. Mann, secretary of the Maſsachusetts Board of Education. By the Aſsociation of Masters of the Boston Public Schools. Boston, 1844. 8°

22 REJOINDER to the " Reply". of . . H. Mann . . to the " Remarks" of the Aſsociation of Boston Masters, upon his seventh annual report. Boston, 1845. 8°

23 CITY Document, No. 10. List of persons, copartnerships, and corporations, who were taxed twenty-five dollars and upwards in the city of Boston in 1844, specifying the amount of tax on real and personal estate, severally, etc. Boston, 1845. 8°

24 LOCAL Loiterings and Visits in the vicinity of Boston. By a looker-on [J. Dix Roſs]. Boston, 1846. 12mo.

25 CITY Document, No. 40. Reports of the annual visiting commit-

tees of the public schools of . . Boston, 1847. Boston, 1847. 8°

26 MUNICIPAL Register, containing rules and orders of the city council, and a list of the officers of . . Boston, for 1847. Boston, 1847. 12°

27 MEASURES adopted in Boston, Maſſachusetts, for the relief of the suffering Scotch and Irish. Boston, 1847. 8vo.

28 THE REPORT of the Annual Examination of the Public Schools of the City of Boston. [By J. Codman.] 1848. Boston, 1848. 8vo.

29 THE ARISTOCRACY of Boston; who they are, and what they were: being a history of the busineſs and busineſs men of Boston, for the last forty years. By one who knows them. Boston, 1848. 8°

30 REPORT of the Committee of Internal Health on the Asiatic Cholera, together with a report of the city physician on the cholera hospital. Boston, 1849. 8vo.

31 MUNICIPAL Registeɛ, containing rules and orders of the city council, the city charter, recent laws and ordinances, and a list of the officers of the city of Boston, for 1850. Boston, 1850. 8vo.

32 SKETCHES of Boston, past and present, and of some few places in its vicinity. Boston, 1851. 12°

33 CITY Document, No. 14. List of persons, copartnerships, and corporations, who were taxed on six thousand dollars and upwards, in the city of Boston, in the year 1852, specifying the amount of tax, etc. Boston, 1853. 8°

BOSTON ACADEMY OF MUSIC. First (to the twelfth) Annual Report of the Boston Academy of Music (1833-1844). (Report of the Government of the Boston Academy of Music for the years 1845 and 1846.) 13 parts. Boston, 1835-46. 8vo.

BOSTON ALMANAC [1836-56]. By S. N. Dickinson. Boston [1835-1855]. 12°

BOSTON AND WORCESTER RAILROAD CORPORATION. Report of the Directors of the Boston and Worcester Railroad Corporation to the Stockholders; together with the report of J. M. Feſſenden, Esq., civil engineer, and a plan and profile of the location of the railroad. Boston 1832. 8°

BOSTON BAPTIST ASSOCIATION. Minutes of the Boston Baptist Aſſociation, held . . in Danvers, Sept. 17 and 18, 1817. Boston, [1817]. 8°

BOSTON BOOK, 1837. Being specimens of metropolitan literature. Edited by B. B. Thatcher. Boston, 1837. 12mo.

2 THE BOSTON BOOK. Being specimens of metropolitan literature. [Third series.] Boston, 1844. 12°

3 THE BOSTON Book. Being specimens of metropolitan literature. Boston, 1850. 12°

BOSTON CHRONICLE, for the year 1768. With many supplements and extraordinary papers. Vol. 1. Prefixed are the proposals for printing the Boston Chronicle. Boston [1768]. 4to. Vol. 2. Bost., 1769. Fol.

BOSTON DIRECTORY, etc. 1798; 1821, 1822, 1823, 1826, 1827, 1829, 1830. [Continued under the title] Stimpson's Boston Directory, etc., 1831, 1833 to 1842, 1844, 1845. 21 vol. Boston, 1798, 1821-45. 12°

2 ADAMS's New Directory of the City of Boston, from 1846 to 1847. Boston, 1846. 8° [Continued under the title of] Adams's Boston Directory, 1847-48. Boston, 1847. 8° [Continued under the title of] The Boston Directory, by G. Adams. Boston, 1848-1853. 8°

BOSTON DISPENSARY. Institution of the Boston Dispensary for the Medical Relief of the Poor. Incorporated 1801. Boston, 1837. 12°

BOSTON EVENING POST. Nos. 1737 to 2063; Jan. 9th, 1769, to April 10th, 1775. [*wanting numbers* 1738, 1756, 1773, 1775, 1950, 1958 to 1960, 1962, 1964, 1967, 1968, 1971, 2002, 2024, 2049 to 2054, 2057, 2059 and 2060.] Boston, 1769-1775. Fol.

BOSTON FARM SCHOOL. A Report of the Directors of the Boston Farm School, on the proposed union of this institution with the Boston Asylum for Indigent Boys. May, 1834. [Boston, 1834.] 8°

BOSTON FEMALE ANTI-SLAVERY SOCIETY. Eleventh Annual Report of the Boston Female Anti-Slavery Society. Adopted Oct. 9, 1844. New York [1844]. 12mo.

BOSTON GAZETTE AND COUNTRY JOURNAL. Numbers 720, 723 to 725, 730, 733 to 736, 745 to 747, 754, 756 to 759, 761 to 765, 767, 769 to 774, 783, 785, 787, 792, 794, 803, 804, 807, 815, 818, 827, 831, 842, 849, 890, *etc.* 861, 865, 874 to 889, 891, 892, 894 to 913, 916 to 922, 928, 929, 931, 933, 943 to 945, 948, 950 to 952, 954, 965, 968, 969, 971, 973, 975, 976, 982 to 987, 994 to 996, 1002 to 1004, 1008 to 1010, 1012 to 1017, 1019, 1020, 1023, 1024, 1026, 1029 to 1033, 1036. 1769 to Feb. 20th, 1775. Boston, 1769-1775. Fol.

BOSTON JOURNAL OF PHILOSOPHY AND THE ARTS; intended to exhibit a view of the progress of discovery, *etc.* Conducted by J. W. Webster, J. Ware, and D. Treadwell. May, 1823—Dec. 1826. 3 Vol. Boston, 1823-26. 8°

BOSTON MONTHLY MAGAZINE. Samuel L. Knapp, editor. June, 1825—July, 1826. Vol. 1 and vol. 2, No. 1, 2. Boston, 1825-26. 8°

BOSTON NOTION. By G. Roberts. Vol. 1. No. 7. (Nov. 16, 1839.) Boston, 1839. Fol.

BOSTON POST BOY AND ADVERTISER [continued under the title of] The Massachusetts Gazette and Boston Post Boy. Nos. 594, 598, 600, 601, 614, 622, 630, 634, 636 (Oct. 16, 1769) 636, (Oct. 23), 638 (Nov. 6th), 637 (Nov. 13th), 638 (Nov. 20th), 639 to 643, 806, 825, 838, 883, 887, 888, 892, 894, 895, 896, 898, 899, 900, 902, 903, 904, 906, 907, 909, 910, 912, 915, 916. Boston, 1769-1775. Fol.

BOSTON PRIZE POEMS. Boston Prize Poems and other specimens of Dramatic Poetry. Bost., 1824. 12°

BOSTON QUARTERLY REVIEW. 1838-1842. 5 Vol. [Edited by O. A. Brownson.] Boston, 1838-42. 8° [Then merged in the United States Magazine and Democratic Review, but afterwards resumed as] Brownson's Quarterly Review. 3 vol. 1844-46. New Series. 6 vol. 1847-52. Third Series. 3 vol. 1853-55. New York Series. Vol. 1. 1856. Boston and New York. 1844-56. 8°

BOSTON SCHOOL ATLAS. The Boston School Atlas, with elemental geography and astronomy. Boston, 1831. 4to.

BOSTON SOCIETY OF NATURAL HISTORY. Boston Journal of Natural History, containing papers and communications read to the Society. Vol. 1-5 and Vol. 6, No. 1-3. Boston, 1834-53. 8vo.

BOSTON TEA PARTY. A Retrospect of the Boston Tea Party, with a memoir of G. R. T. Hewes. . By a citizen of New York [J. Hawkes!]. New York, 1834. 12°

BOSTON WEEKLY NEWS-LETTER, [continued under the title of] The Massachusetts Gazette and Weekly News-letter. Nos. 3409, 3420, 3422, 3432-3434, 3445-46, 3449-56. Boston, 1769. Fol.

BOSTONIAN. Traits of the Tea Party; being a memoir of G. R. T. Hewes, one of the last of its survivors;

with a history of that transaction; reminiscences of the maſsacre, and the siege; and other stories of old times. By a Bostonian. New York, 1835. 12°

2 THE SCHOLIAST Schooled: an examination of the review of the reports of the annual visiting committees of the public schools of . . Boston, for 1845, by " Scholiast." By a Bostonian. Cambridge, 1846. 8°

BOSTWICK, HORNER. Medical Quackery; its origin, cause, and cure; with hints to young physicians in relation to . . consultation. New York, 1847. 8°

2 A TREATISE on the Nature and Treatment of Seminal Diseases, Impotency, and other kindred affections. Second edition. New York, 1848. 12°

BOSWELL, B. G. Cultivation of Fruit, including the Cranberry. [New York, 1840 !] 8°

BOSWELL, JAMES. Extracts from the Monthly Review . . [relative to a work entitled :] The Life of S. Johnson. . By J. Boswell. [Charlestown, 1807.] 8°

BOTHAM, P. E. BATES. Botham's Common School Arithmetic. . A revised, improved and enlarged edition. Hartford, 1833. 12°

BOTTA, CARLO. History of the War of the Independence of the United States of America. . Translated from the Italian by G. A. Otis. 3 vol. Philadelphia, 1820-21. 8vo.

BOUCHARD DE LA POTERIE, CLAUDE FLORENT. A Pastoral Letter from the Apostolic Vice-Prefect, curate of the Holy Croſs at Boston (C. F. Bouchard de la Poterie). (The solemnity of the holy time of Easter,) etc. [Boston, 1789.] 4°

BOUCHARLAT, J. L. An Elementary Treatise on Mechanics. Translated from the French, with additions and emendations; by E. H. Courtenay. New York, 1833. 8vo.

BOUDINOT, ELIAS. A Star in the West; or, a humble attempt to discover the long lost tribes of Israel, preparatory to their return to Jerusalem. (Appendix, historical sketches of Louisiana.) Trenton [New Jersey], 1816. 8°

BOUQUIER, GABRIEL. National Convention. Report on the organization of national schools, to complete a republican education. . Translated from an authentic original. Philadelphia, 1794. 8°

BOURDON, LOUIS PIERRE MARIE. Elements of Algebra: including Sturm's theorem. Translated from the French [by — Roſs]. . Adapted to the course of mathematical instruction in the United States, by C. Davies, LL. D. New York, 1845. 8°

BOURNE, BENJAMIN FRANKLIN. The Captive in Patagonia; or, Life among the Giants. A personal narrative. Boston, 1853. 12°

BOURNE, GEORGE. Picture of Slavery in the United States of America. Boston, 1838. 12°

BOURNE, W. OLAND. Poems of Hope and Action. New York, 1850. 8°

2 LITTLE Silverstring; or, Tales and Poems for the Young. New York, 1853. 12°

3 GEMS from Fable-Land: a collection of fables illustrated by facts. New York, 1853. 12°

BOUTON, NATHANIEL. Christian Patriotism: an addreſs delivered at Concord, July 4, 1825. Concord, 1825. 8°

2 THE RESPONSIBILITIES of Rulers: a sermon [on Luke xix. 13] delivered . . before the constituted authorities of . . New Hampshire. Concord, 1828. 8°

3 TWO SERMONS [on 1 Kings, viii. 57, 58] preached Nov. 21, 1830, in commemoration of the organizing of the first church in Concord, . Nov.

1730. [With a hymn, *etc.* and historical notes.] Concord, 1831. 8°

BOUVIER, John. A Law Dictionary, adapted to the constitution and laws of the United States of America, and of the several states of the American Union, with references to the civil and other systems of foreign law. 2 vols. Philadelphia, 1839. 8vo.

BOW. The Bow in the Cloud. American Sunday School Union, Philadelphia, 1831. 12°

BOWDITCH, Henry Ingersoll. The Young Stethoscopist; or, The Students' Aid to Auscultation. New York and Boston, 1846. 12°

BOWDITCH, Nathaniel. The New American Practical Navigator: being an epitome of navigation. . Continued by J. I. Bowditch. 15th stereotype edit. N. York, 1845. 8°

BOWDITCH, William Ingersoll. Slavery and the Constitution. Boston, 1849. 8°

BOWDITCH LIBRARY. Report of the Proprietors of the Bowditch Library. Boston, 1841. 8°

BOWDOIN, James. A Philosophical Discourse, addressed to the American Academy of Arts and Sciences, . Nov. 8, 1780, after the inauguration of the President into office. Boston, 1780. 8°

BOWDOIN COLLEGE, Brunswick, Maine. [Annual] Catalogue of the Officers and Students . . 1823 (1829, 1843, 1846-47). 4 parts. Brunswick, 1823-47. 8°

2 Catalogus [triennial] Senatus Academici et eorum qui munera et officia gesserunt, quique alicujus gradus laurea donati sunt in Collegio Bowdoinensis, *etc.* (1810, 1822, 1825, 1831, 1834, 1840). 6 parts. Brunsvici, 1810-40. 8°

3 Catalogue of the Athenæan Society of Bowdoin College. Instituted 1817; incorporated 1828. Brunswick, 1838. 8°

4 Catalogue of the Officers and Members of the Peucinian Society, Bowdoin College. [Brunswick,] 1843. 8°

BOWEN, A. The Naval Monument, containing official and other accounts of all the battles fought between the navies of the United States and Great Britain during the late war; and an account of the war with Algiers. . To which is annexed a naval register of the United States, . brought down to 1836. N. York [1836 ?]. 8°

BOWEN, Abel. Picture of Boston; or, The Citizen's and Stranger's Guide. . To which is affixed the annals of Boston. . Third edition. Boston, 1838. 12mo.

BOWEN, Eli. The United States Post Office Guide, *etc.* New York, 1851. 8°

BOWEN, Francis. Critical Essays on a few Subjects connected with the History and Present Condition of Speculative Philosophy. Boston, 1842. 8°

2 Critical Essays on a few Subjects connected with the History and Present Condition of Speculative Philosophy. Second edition. Boston, 1845. 12mo.

3 Lowell Lectures, on the application of metaphysical and ethical Science to the Evidences of Religion; delivered . . in the winters of 1848-49. Boston, 1849. 8°

BOWEN, Henry L. Memoir of Tristam Burges; with selections from his speeches and occasional writings. Providence, 1835. 8vo.

BOWEN, Nathaniel, *Bishop of the Diocese of South Carolina.* Sermons on Christian Doctrines and Duties. [To which is prefixed, a memoir of the author.] 2 vol. Charleston, 1842. 8°

BOWEN'S BOSTON NEWSLETTER, and City Record. Jan.—

Dec. 1826. J. V. C. Smith, Editor. 2 Vol. Boston, 1826. 8°

BOWER, ARCHIBALD. The History of the Popes, from the foundation of the see of Rome to A. D. 1758. With an introduction, and a continuation to the present time: by S. H. Cox. 3 vol. Philadel., 1844-5. 8°

BOWRON, JOHN S. Observations on planetary and celestial influences in the production of Epidemics, and on the nature and treatment of Diseases. New York, 1850. 8°

BOYD, JAMES ROBERT. Elements of Rhetoric; with copious practical exercises and examples. Fifth edition. New York, 1846. 12°

BOYKIN, B. Report of the President of the Branch of the Bank of the State of Alabama, at Mobile. Tuscaloosa, 1842. 8°

BOYLE, ISAAC. Apostolic Origin of Episcopacy: a sermon [on Ephes. ii. 20] preached . . before the annual convention of the Protestant Episcopal church in the State of Massachusetts. Boston, 1823. 8°
2 AN HISTORICAL Memoir of the Boston Episcopal Charitable Society. Boston, 1840. 8°

BOYNTON, CHARLES B. Our Country, the Herald of a new Era; a lecture delivered before the Young Men's Mercantile Library Association, of Cincinnati. Cincinnati, 1847. 8°
2 ORATION delivered before the New England Society of Cincinnati, on the anniversary of the landing of the pilgrims, Dec. 22, 1847. Cincinnati, 1848. 8°

BOYS. Bad Boys' Progress. Philadelphia [1833]. 12°

BOZMAN, JOHN LEEDS. A Sketch of the History of Maryland, during the three first years after its settlement: to which is prefixed a copious introduction. Baltimore, 1811. 8vo.

BRAAM-HOUCKGEEST, AN-

DREAS EVERHARD VAN. Voyage de l'Ambassade de la Compagnie des Indes Orientales Hollandaise vers l'Empéreur de la Chine, dans les années 1794 et 1795; où se trouve la description de plusieurs parties de la Chine inconnues aux Européens, . Le tout tiré du journal d'A. E. Van Braam-Houckgeest . publié en Français par M. L. E. Moreau de Saint Méry. 2 vol. Philadelphie, 1797-98. 4to.

BRACE, JACOB, *the younger*. The Principles of English Grammar, with copious exercises in parsing and syntax. Philadelphia, 1839. 12°
2 A KEY to Brace's Principles of English Grammar. Philadelphia, 1840. 12°

BRACKENRIDGE, HENRY M. Views of Louisiana; together with a Journal of a Voyage up the Missouri River in 1811. Pittsb., 1814. 8vo.
2 JOURNAL of a Voyage up the River Missouri performed in 1811. Second edition. Revised and enlarged. Baltimore, 1816. 12mo.
3 VOYAGE to South America, performed by order of the American government in the years 1817 and 1818, in the frigate Congress. 2 vol. Baltimore, 1819. 8°
4 RECOLLECTIONS of Persons and Places in the West. Philadelphia [1834]. 12mo.
5 AN ESSAY on Trusts and Trustees: in relation to the settlement of real estate . . the power of trustees. . and involving many of the most abstruse questions in the English and American law of tenures. Washington, 1842. 8°
6 HISTORY of the late War between the United States and Great Britain: comprising a minute account of the various military and naval operations. Philadelphia, 1844. 12°

BRACKENRIDGE, HUGH HENRY. Incidents of the Insurrection in the Western Parts of Pennsylvania, in 1794. 3 vol. Philadel., 1795. 8vo.

2 GAZETTE Publications. [A series of miscellaneous eſſays and pieces in prose and verse.] Carlisle [Pennsylvania], 1806. 12°

3 MODERN Chivalry ; or, The Adventures of Captain Farrago, and Teague O'Regan. . Second edition, since the author's death ; with a biographical notice, . and explanatory notes. 2 vol. Philadelphia, 1846. 12°

BRACKET, ADINO N. An Addreſs delivered before the Coos Agricultural Society. Concord, 1821. 8°

BRADFORD, ALDEN. Biography of the Hon. Caleb Strong, Governor of Maſſachusetts. Boston, 1820. 8vo.

2 HISTORY of Maſſachusetts, from 1764 to July 1775. Boston, 1822. 8°

3 HISTORY of Maſſachusetts, from July 1775 . . to the year 1789, inclusive, when the federal government was established under the present constitution. Boston, 1825. 8°

4 HISTORY of Maſſachusetts, from 1790 to 1820. Boston, 1829. 8°

5 HISTORY of Maſſachusetts, for two hundred years, from 1620 to 1820. Boston, 1835. 8vo.

6 MEMOIR of the Life and Writings of the Rev. J. Mayhew, Pastor of the West Church in Boston, from 1747 to 1766. Boston, 1838. 8vo.

7 HISTORY of the Federal Government for Fifty Years, from March 1789 to March 1839. Boston, July 1, 1840. 8°

8 BIOGRAPHICAL Notices of Distinguished Men in New England, etc. Boston, 1842. 12°

9 NEW England Chronology: from the discovery of the country by Cabot, in 1497, to 1800 [1820]. Boston, 1843. 12°

BRADFORD, ALEXANDER W. American Antiquities and Researches into the Origin and History of the Red Race. New York, 1841. 8vo.

2 AMERICAN Antiquities and Researches into the Origin and History of the Red Race. N.York, 1843. 8vo.

3 A DISCOURSE delivered before

the New York Historical Society, at its forty-first anniversary, November 20, 1845. New York, 1846. 8°

BRADFORD, DUNCAN. The Wonders of the Heavens ; being a popular view of astronomy, including a full illustration of the mechanism of the heavens, etc. Boston, 1845. 4°

BRADFORD, EBENEZER. The Nature and Manner of giving Thanks to God, illustrated. A Sermon [on Ephesians v. 20]. Boston, 1795. 8°

BRADFORD, EPHRAIM PUTNAM. A Sermon [on Isaiah xxi. 11] preached before the Council, and . . Legislature of . . New Hampshire, etc. Concord, 1821. 8°

BRADFORD, MOSES. A Sermon [on 1 Tim. i. 15] delivered . . before . . the Governor,ₐ. Council, etc. of . . New Hampshire, June 4, 1812. Concord, 1812. 8°

BRADFORD, THOMAS GAMALIEL. A Comprehensive Atlas, geographical, historical and commercial. Boston and New York [1835]. 4to.

BRADFORD, Rev. WILLIAM. An Enquiry how far the Punishment of Death is neceſſary in Pennsylvania, with notes and illustrations. To which is added (An account of the alteration and present State of the penal laws of Pennsylvania, containing an account of the gaol and penitentiary of Philadelphia and the management thereof. By Caleb Lownes. Appendix.) Philadelphia, 1793. 8°

BRADFORD, WILLIAM John Alden Notes on the North-West ; or, Valley of the Upper Miſſiſſippi. New York, 1846. 12°

BRADISH, LUTHER. Opening Addreſs of the Seventeenth Annual Fair of the American Institute of the City of New York. N.York, 1844. 8°

BRADLEY, CHARLES WILLIAM. Patronomatology ; from an eſſay on the philosophy of surnames, read before the Connecticut state Lyceum, Nov.13,1839. Baltimore,1842. 8vo.

BRADSHAW, CLINTON. Clinton Bradshaw; or, the Adventures of a Lawyer. [A tale.] Cincinnati, 1847. 8°

BRADSTREET, NATHAN. A Discourse [on Luke vii. 4, 5] delivered .. before .. the legislature of .. New Hampshire, at the annual election. Amherst, 1807. 8°

BRADY, WILLIAM. The Kedge-Anchor; or, Young Sailor's Assistant; appertaining to the practical evolutions of modern seamanship, etc. New York, 1848. 8°

BRAINARD, DYAR THROOP. The Annual Address to the Candidates for Degrees and Licenses, in the Medical Institution of Yale College, January 21, 1840. New Haven, 1840. 8°

BRAINARD, JOHN G. C. The Poems of J. G. C. Brainard. A new and authentic collection, with an original memoir of his life. Hartford, 1842. 12°

BRAINARD, WILLIAM F. Masonic Lecture spoken before the Brethren of the Union Lodge, New London, June 24, A. L. 5825. Third edition. New London printed 1825. Boston reprinted, 1830. 8vo.

BRAINERD, DAVID. Memoirs of D. Brainerd. Philadel., 1830. 12mo.

BRAINERD, THOMAS. The Lament of the Church at the Sepulchre of the Righteous. A sermon [on Acts viii. 2] on the death of F. A Raybold, Esq. etc. Philadelphia, 1851. 8vo.

BRANNAN, JOHN. Official Letters of the Military and Naval Officers of the United States during the War with Great Britain in the Years 1812-15. With some additional letters and documents elucidating the history of that period. Collected and arranged by J. Brannan. Washington, 1823. 8vo.

BRATTLE, WILLIAM. To the Public [An address, signed W. Brattle, in justification of his conduct in delivering certain military stores to General Gage]. Boston [1774], s. sh. fol.

BRAVO, The Bravo: A tale. By the author of "The Spy," etc. [J. F. Cooper.] A new edition. 2 vol. Philadelphia, 1836. 12°

BRAYMAN, JAMES O. Thrilling Adventures by Land and Sea. Being remarkable historical facts, etc. Buffalo, 1852. 12°

2, DARING Deeds of American Heroes, with biographical sketches. Buffalo, 1852. 12°

BRAZER, JOHN. A Discourse on the Life and Character of .. L. Saltonstall, etc. [With an appendix of biographical notices, etc.] Salem, 1845. 8°

BRECK, CHARLES. The Fox Chase. A comedy in five acts [and in prose]. New York, 1808. 12mo.

2 THE TRUST: a comedy in five acts [in prose and verse]. New York, 1808. 12mo.

BRECK, SAMUEL. Sketch of the Internal Improvements already made in Pennsylvania, with observations upon her .. means for their extension, particularly as they have reference to the growth and prosperity of Philadelphia. Illustrated by a map of Pennsylvania. Second edition, revised and enlarged. Philadelphia, 1818. 8°

2 DISCOURSE before the Society of the Sons of New England .. of Philadelphia, on the history of the early settlement of their country, etc. Philadelphia, 1845. 8°

BRECKINRIDGE, ROBERT J. Memoranda of Foreign Travel: containing notices of a pilgrimage through some of the principal states of Western Europe. 2 vol. Baltimore, 1845. 12°

BRENTON, JAMES J. Voices from

the Prefs; a collection of sketches, efsays, and poems, by practical printers. Edited by J. J. Brenton. New York, 1850. 8°

BREVARD, Joseph. An Alphabetical Digest of the Public Statute Law of South Carolina. 3 vol. Charleston, 1814. 8°

2 Reports of Judicial Decisions in the State of South Carolina, from 1793 to 1815 (1816). [Edited by W. Riley.] 3 vol. Charleston, 1839-40. 8°

BREWER, Josiah. A Residence at Constantinople, in the year 1827. With notes to the present time. . Second edition. N. Haven,1830. 12°

BREWSTER, Sir David. A Treatise on Optics. A new edition. With an appendix, containing an elementary view of the application of analysis to reflexion and refraction, by A.D. Bache. Philadel., 1844. 12°

2 The Martyrs of Science; or, the lives of Galileo, Tycho Brahè, and Kepler. New York, 1844. 12°

3 The Life of Sir Isaac Newton. New York, 1845. 12°

4 Letters on Natural Magic: addrefsed to Sir Walter Scott, bart. New York, 1845. 12°

BREWSTER, Francis E. The Philosophy of Human Nature. Philadelphia, 1851. 12°

BRICE, John. A Selection of all the Laws of the United States now in force relative to Commercial Subjects, with marginal notes and references . . clafsified under separate heads. Baltimore, 1814. 8°

BRIDGE, James, and others. To the Honourable Senate, and the House of Representatives, of the commonwealth of Mafsachusetts. [A memorial from the citizens of Maine, on its separation from Mafsachusetts Proper, and against its incorporation with any other district.] [Boston, 1820.] 8°

BRIDGEMAN, T. The Young Gardener's Afsistant: with practical directions for the cultivation of culinary vegetables and flowers. Third edition; with an appendix, containing directions for cultivating fruit-trees and the grape vine. N.York,1832. 12°

BRIDGMAN, Eliza J. Gillett. Daughters of China; or, Sketches of Domestic Life in the Celestial Empire. New York, 1853. 12°

BRIDGMAN, Thomas. Epitaphs from Copp's Hill Burial Ground, Boston. With notes. By T. Bridgman. [With an introduction, by J. H. Sheppard.] Boston and Camb.,1851. 12°

BRIGGS, Caroline A. Utterance; or, Private Voices to the Public Heart. A collection of home poems. Boston, 1852. 8°

BRIGGS, Ephraim. A Sermon [on Eccles. vii. 2] preached at the Interment of the Rev. N. Stone, etc. Boston, 1804. 8vo.

BRIGHAM, Amariah. Remarks on the Influence of Mental Cultivation and Mental Excitement upon Health. Second edition. Boston, 1833. 12°

2 Observations on the Influence of Religion upon the Health and Physical Welfare of Mankind. Boston, 1835. 12°

3 An Inquiry concerning the Diseases and Functions of the Brain, the Spinal Cord and the Nerves. New York, 1840. 12mo.

BRIGHAM, William. An Addrefs delivered before the Inhabitants of Grafton, on the first centennial anniversary of that town, April 25, 1835. Boston, 1835. 8vo.

2 The Compact with the Charter and Laws of the Colony of New Plymouth: together with the charter of the council at Plymouth, and an appendix, containing the articles of confederation of the united colonies of New England, and other valuable Documents, etc. Boston, 1836. 8vo.

BRIMBLECOMB, Nicholas, Pfeud! Uncle Tom's Cabin in Ruins. Triumphant defence of slavery ! in a series of letters to H. B. Stowe. Boston, 1853. 8vo.

BRINKERHOFF, Jacob. Speech .. on the Annexation of Texas ; delivered in the House of Representatives, Jan. 13, 1845, etc. Washington, 1845. 8°

BRINSMADE, N. H. A Geography for Children. . With . . engravings . . and . . maps. Fifth edition. Hartford, 1835. 16°

BRISBANE, Albert. Social Destiny of Man ; or, Aſſociation and Reorganization of Industry. Philadelphia, 1840. 8°

BRISSOT, Jean Pierre de Warville, and Claviere, Etienne. The Commerce of America with Europe, particularly with France and Great Britain, comparatively stated and explained. . Translated from the last French edition, revised by Briſſot, and called the second volume of his View of America. With the life of Briſſot, and an appendix by the translator. New York, 1795. 12°

BRISTED, Charles Astor. A Letter to the Hon. H. Mann [answer to his remarks on the character of J. J. Astor]. . Second edition. New York, 1850. 12°

2 Five Years in an English University. 2 vol. New York, 1852. 8°

3 The Upper Ten Thousand : sketches of American society. New York, 1852. 12°

BRISTED, John. Hints on the National Bankruptcy of Britain, and on her resources to maintain the present contest with France. New York, 1809. 8°

2 The Resources of the United States of America ; or, a View of the agricultural, . . political, literary, moral, and religious capacity and character of the American People. New York, 1818. 8vo.

BRISTOL. The Petition and Memorial of the Town of Bristol, Nobleborough, New-Castle, Edgcomb, and Boothbay, in the County of Lincoln, to the General Court of Maſſachusetts, A. D. 1810. Boston, 1811. 8°

BRISTOL COLLEGIATE INSTITUTE, Bristol, Pennsylvania. Course of Studies. [Philadelphia, 1832?] 8vo.

BRITISH ALBUM. Containing the Poems of Della Crusca [Merry], Anna Matilda [Mrs. Cowley], Arley, Benedict, the Bard [E. Jerningham],· etc. . First American edition. From the fourth London edition. Boston, 1793. 12°

BRITISH ESSAYISTS. The Modern British Eſſayists. 8 vol. Philadelphia, 1848-50. 8°

BRITISH Opinions on the Protecting System, being a reply to strictures on that system, which have appeared in several recent British publications. Reprinted, with a few alterations, from an article in the North American Review for January, 1830. Second edition. Boston, 1830. 8°

BRITISH SONGS AND BALLADS. See Songs and Ballads.

BROADDUS, Andrew, the elder. The Sermons and other Writings of the Rev. A. Broaddus. With a memoir of his life by J. B. Jeter. Edited by A. Broaddus. N. York, 1852. 12°

BROADWAY JOURNAL [Edited by C. F. Briggs, E. A. Poe, and H. C. Watson.] Jan. 4, 1845—Jan. 3, 1846. 2 Vol. New York, 1845-46. Fol°

BROCKENBROUGH, John W. Reports of Cases decided by the Hon. J. Marshall . . in the Circuit Court of the United States, for the district of Virginia and North Carolina, from 1802 to 1833, inclusive. Edited by J. W. Brockenbrough. (Memoir of J. Marshall. By J. Hopkinson.) 2 vol. Philadelphia, 1837. 8°

BROCKLEY, JOHN. Elements of Meteorology, with questions for examination. New York, 1851. 12°

2 VIEWS of the Microscopic World; designed for general reading and as a handbook for claſſes in natural science. New York, 1851. 16°

BRODHEAD, JOHN ROMEYN. An Addreſs delivered before the New York Historical Society, at its fortieth anniversary, November 20, 1844. New York, 1844. 8vo.

2 HISTORY of the State of New York. Vol. I. New York, 1853. 8°

3 ADDRESSES of J. R. Brodhead, Esq. and . . Gov. H. Seymour, delivered before the Clinton Hall Aſſociation, and Mercantile Library Association, at . . the removal of the library to Astor Place, etc. New York, 1854. 8vo.

BROMLEY, WALTER. An Appeal to the Virtue and Good Sense of the Inhabitants of Great Britain, etc., in behalf of the Indians of North America. [With an appendix.] Halifax [Nova Scotia], 1820. 12°

BRONSON, C. P. Elocution; or, Mental and Vocal Philosophy: involving the principles of reading and speaking ; . illustrated by . . anecdotes; . readings, etc. Sixth edition. Seventeenth thousand. Louisville, 1845. 8°

BROOKE, SAMUEL. Slavery and the Slaveholder's Religion, as opposed to Christianity. Cincinnati, 1846. 12°

BROOKS, Rev. CHARLES. A Family Prayer-Book, etc. Fifth edition. Boston, 1825. 12°

2 THE CHRISTIAN in his Closet ; or, Prayers for Individuals, adapted to the various ages, conditions, and circumstances of life. Bost., 1845. 12°

3 THE TORNADO of 1851, in Medford, West Cambridge, and Waltham, Middlesex County, Maſs. Being a report by Rev. C. Brooks, and reports by other committees. Bost., 1852. 12°

BROOKS, CHARLES T. German Lyrics [translations]. Bost., 1853. 12°

BROOKS, J. Commonwealth of Maſſachusetts. [A report on certain proposed alterations in the militia system of the commonwealth, with the draft of a new bill for regulating, governing, and training the militia.] [Boston, 1814.] 8°

BROOKS, JAMES GORDON, and Mrs. MARY ELIZABETH. The Rivals of Este, and other poems. New York, 1829. 12°

BROOKS, JOHN. An Oration, delivered to the Society of the Cincinnati, in the commonwealth of Massachusetts, July 4, 1787. Boston, 1787. 4°

2 A DISCOURSE delivered before the Humane Society of the commonwealth of Maſſachusetts. Boston, 1795. 4to.

BROOKS, NATHAN COVINGTON. The Utility of Claſſical Studies, an addreſs by N. C. Brooks. The uncertainty of literary fame, a poem ; by C. W. Thomson, Esq. Pronounced before the Philomathæan Society of Pennsylvania College . . on the anniversary, February 14, 1840. Baltimore, 1840. 8°

BROWN, AARON V. and others. The New Jersey contested Election. To the People of the United States [of America: an addreſs from A. V. Brown and others, members of the committee on elections of the House of Representatives]. [Washington, 1840.] 8°

BROWN, CHARLES. Remarks . . on the Pay of Navy Officers, and Whig Measures ; also on the bankrupt law and military academy. (Delivered in the House of Representatives, Feb. 3, 1843.) Washington, 1843. 8°

BROWN, CHARLES BROCKDEN. The Novels of C. B. Brown, Wieland,

Arthur Mervyn, Ormond, Edgar Huntly, Jane Talbot, and Clara Howard. With a memoir of the author. 7 vol. Boston, 1827. 12mo.

BROWN, ERASTUS. The Trial of Cain, the first Murderer: in poetry, by rule of court; in which a Predestinarian, a Universalian, and an Arminian, argue, etc. Boston, 1827. 12°

BROWN, GOOLD. A Key to the Exercises for Writing, contained in the institutes of English Grammar, etc. New York [1842]. 12°

2 THE FIRST Lines of English Grammar : being a brief abstract of the author's larger work, designed for young learners. New York, 1845. 12°

3 THE INSTITUTES of English Grammar, methodically arranged. . Stereotype edition, revised by the author. New York, 1846. 12°

4 BROWN'S GRAMMAR Improved. The Institutes of English Grammar methodically arranged : with . . . a Key to the Oral Exercises. To which are added Four Appendices. A new . . . edition, carefully revised. New York, 1856. 12mo.

BROWN, HENRY. The History of Illinois, from its first discovery and settlement, to the present time. New York, 1844. 8vo.

BROWN, J. A Letter to the Rev. W. E. Channing [on his sermon delivered at the ordination of the Rev. J. Sparks]. [Boston? 1820.] 8°

BROWN, J. NEWTON. The Obligation of the Sabbath : a discussion between J. N. Brown and W. B. Taylor. Philadelphia, 1853. 8vo.

BROWN, JAMES. An Application of " The Orb." Designed to illustrate the constructive principles of the English language, etc. Philadelphia, 1836. 12°

2 AN EXEGESIS of English Syntax, etc. Philadelphia, 1840. 12°

3 THE FIRST Part of the American

System of English Syntax, developing the constructive principles of the English language or phrenod, in three parts. Boston, 1841. 12°

BROWN, JOHN. In what sense the Heart is deceitful and wicked, a discourse from Jeremiah xvii. 9. Boston, 1754. 8°

2 A DISCOURSE [on Rom. xi. 33] delivered in the West Church at Boston, Aug. 24, 1766, . after the death of the Rev. Dr. Mayhew. Boston, 1766. 8°

BROWN, JOHN B. and BUCKMINSTER. Reports of Cases treated at the Boston Orthopedic Institution. . With some preliminary observations on the present state of the Institution, and on club foot, spinal curvature, etc. Boston, 1850. 8°

BROWN, JONATHAN, M. D. The History and Present Condition of St. Domingo. 2 vol. Philadelphia, 1837. 12mo.

BROWN, RICHARD. An Essay on the Truth of Physiognomy and its application to Medicine. Philadelphia, 1807. 8vo.

BROWN, S. and others. Commonwealth of Massachusetts. [Address to the committee appointed upon the subject of selling the Commonwealth's interest in the Boston and Union Banks.] [Boston? 1816.] 8°

BROWN, SAMUEL GILLMANN. The Studies of an Orator: an inaugural address, delivered at the annual commencement in Dartmouth College, July, 1840. New York, 1841. 8°

BROWN, SAMUEL R. An Authentic History of the Second War for Independence: comprising details of the military and naval operations from the commencement to the close of the recent war. 2 vol. Auburn, 1815. 12°

2 THE WESTERN Gazetteer; or, Emigrant's Directory; containing a geographical description of the West-

ern states and territories. . With an appendix. Auburn, N. Y. 1817. 8°

3 THE WESTERN Gazetteer; or, Emigrant's Directory. With an appendix, containing sketches of some of the western counties of New York, Pennsylvania, and Virginia; a description of the great northern lakes; Indian annuities and directions to emigrants. A new edition. Auburn, N. Y. 1820. 8°

BROWN, SOLYMAN. A Comparative View of the Systems of Pestalozzi and Lancaster: in an address delivered before the Society of Teachers of the city of New York. New York, 1825. 8°

BROWN, THOMAS. Account of the People called Shakers. . To which is affixed a history of their rise and progress to the present day. Troy, N. Y. 1812. 12°

BROWN, THOMAS, and others. Report of the Commissioners appointed by the Governor to examine the Branch Bank at Montgomery: also, the reports of the commissioners [J. Sanford, and others] appointed to examine the Merchants' and Planters' Bank; and [of P. Phillips, and others, appointed to examine] the Mobile Bank. Tuscaloosa, 1840. 8°

BROWN UNIVERSITY. [Annual] Catalogue of the Officers and Students, for the Academical year 1831-32 (1841-42, 1842-43). 3 parts. Providence, 1832-42. 12°

2 CATALOGUS Universitatis Brownensis. 1811. [Providence, 1811.] 12°

3 CATALOGUS Senatus Academici, et eorum qui munera et officia gesserunt, quique alicujus gradus laurea donati sunt, in Universitate Brunensi, etc. Bostoniæ, 1836. 8°

4 PREFACE to the Catalogue of the Library of Brown University, with the Laws of the Library. Providence, 1843. 8vo.

BROWNE. ARTHUR. A Compendious View of the Civil Law, and of the Law of the Admiralty; being the substance of a course of lectures read in the University of Dublin. . First American, from the second London edition, with additions. 2 vol. New York, 1840. 8°

BROWNE, D. J. The Sylva Americana; or, a Description of the Forest Trees indigenous to the United States, practically and botanically considered; illustrated by engravings. Boston, 1832. 8vo.

2 THE AMERICAN Bird Fancier, considered with reference to the breeding, rearing, feeding, management, and peculiarities of cage and house birds, etc. New York, 1851. 12°

3 THE AMERICAN Muck Book; treating of the nature, properties, . and operations of all the principal manures, etc. New York, 1852. 12°

BROWNE, J. ROSS. Etchings of a Whaling Cruise, with notes of a sojourn on the Island of Zanzibar. To which is appended a brief history of the whale fishery. . Illustrated by . . engravings. New York, 1850. 8°

2 YUSEF; or, the Journey of the Frangi. A crusade in the East. New York, 1853. 12°

BROWNE, PETER A. of Pennsylvania. Reports of Cases adjudged in the Court of Common Pleas of the First Judicial District of Pennsylvania. [With an appendix, separately paged.] Philadelphia, 1811. 8°

2 REPORTS of Cases adjudged in the District Court for the City and County of Philadelphia, and the Courts of Common Pleas of Pennsylvania. [With an appendix, separately paged.] Philadelphia, 1813. 8°

3 AN ATTEMPT to discover some of the Laws which govern Animal Torpidity and Hibernation. Philadelphia, 1847. 8vo.

BROWNELL, CHARLES DE WOLF. The Indian Races of North and South America. Boston, 1853. 8vo.

BROWNELL, HENRY HOWARD.

The Discoverers, Pioneers, and Settlers of North and South America, from the earliest period (982) to the present time. Boston, 1853. 8vo.

BROWNELL, T. C. *Bishop of Connecticut.* Review of the Errors of the Times: a charge, by the Rt. Rev. T. C. Brownell. Hartford, 1844. 8°

BROWNLEE, WILLIAM CRAIG. Letters in the Roman Catholic Controversy. New York. 1834. 8°

2 LIGHTS and Shadows of Christian Life. New York, 1837. 12°

3 POPERY, an Enemy to Civil and Religious Liberty; and dangerous to our Republic. . Fourth edition. New York, 1839. 12°

BROWNSON, ORESTES A. New Views of Christianity, Society, and the Church. Boston, 1836. 12°

2 CHARLES Elwood; or, the Infidel converted. Boston, 1840. 12°

3 AN ORATION on the Scholar's Mission. Boston, 1843. 8°

4 ESSAYS and Reviews chiefly on Theology, Politics, and Socialism. New York, 1852. 12°

5 BROWNSON's Quarterly Review. *See* BOSTON Quarterly Review.

BRUNSWICK, *Maine.* Proceedings of the Convention of Delegates, held in Brunswick, Maine, 1816. [On the question of the separation of the district of Maine from Massachusetts Proper.] [Brunswick, 1816.] 8°

BRUTUS, *Pseud.* Foreign Conspiracy against the Liberties of the United States. The numbers of Brutus originally published in the New York Observer revised and corrected, with notes, by the author [with an appendix]. New York, 1835. 12°

BRUUN, MALTHE CONRAD. A System of Universal Geography; or, a Description of all the Parts of the World, on a new plan, according to the great natural divisions of the globe; accompanied with analytical, synoptical, and elementary tables. With

additions and corrections by J. G. Percival. 3 vol. Boston, 1834. 4°

BRYAN, THOMAS. [*Begin.*] New York, Jan. 10, 1828, *etc.* [A circular letter, . relating to the customs' regulations affecting printed silks, *etc.*] [New York, 1828.] 8°

BRYANT, ALFRED. Millenarian Views: with reasons for receiving them. To which is added, a discourse on the fact and nature of the Resurrection. New York, 1852. 8°

BRYANT, EDWIN. What I saw in California: being the journal of a tour, by the emigrant route . . and through California, in the years 1846, 1847. Seventh edition. With an appendix, containing accounts of the gold mines, *etc.* New York, 1849. 12°

BRYANT, JOHN D. Pauline Seward. A tale of real life. . Fourth edition, carefully revised and corrected. Baltimore, 1848. 12°

BRYANT, WILLIAM CULLEN. Poems by W. C. Bryant. Cambridge, 1821. 12°

2 THE AMERICAN Landscape, No. I. . Engraved from original and accurate drawings, . With historical and topographical illustrations (by W. C. Bryant). New York, 1830. 4°

3 POPULAR Considerations on Homœopathia. New York [1841]. 8vo.

4 THE FOUNTAIN, and other Poems. New York, 1842. 12°

5 THE WHITE-FOOTED Deer, and other Poems. New York, 1844. 12°

6 SELECTIONS from the American Poets. New York, 1845. 12°

7 POEMS. . With illustrations by E. Leutze. . Third edition. Philadelphia, 1847. 8°

8 LETTERS of a Traveller; or Notes of Things seen in Europe and America. London [New York], 1850. 8vo.

BUCHANAN, CLAUDIUS, *D. D.* Memoir of . . the Expediency of an Ecclesiastical Establishment for British India, *etc.* Second Cambridge edition. [With notes by the American editor.] Cambridge, 1811. 8°

2 MEMOIRS of the Rev. Claudius Buchanan. By the author of Pierre and his Family. Philadel. 1827. 12mo.

BUCHANAN, JAMES. Last Letter of Mr. Buchanan to Mr. Pakenham, on the American title to Oregon [in reply to a statement by the latter]. Baltimore, 1845. 8°

BUCKE, CHARLES. On the Beauties, Harmonies, and Sublimities of Nature ; with notes, commentaries, and illustrations. . Selected and revised by . . W. P. Page. New York, 1843. 12°

2 RUINS of Ancient Cities ; with general and particular accounts of their rise, fall, and present condition. 2 vol. New York, 1845. 12°

BUCKINGHAM, CHARLES E. *M. D.* Circumstances affecting Individual and Public Health: a lecture, *etc.* Boston, 1848. 8vo.

BUCKINGHAM, EDGAR. An Oration delivered at Trenton, . July 4, 1842, being the sixty-sixth anniversary of the declaration of American Independence. Utica, 1842. 8°

BUCKINGHAM, JAMES SILK. Notes of the Buckingham Lectures, embracing sketches of the geography, antiquities, and present condition of Egypt and Palestine, compiled from the oral discourses. Together with a sketch of his life. By J. Hildreth. New York, 1838. 12mo.

BUCKINGHAM, JOSEPH T. Trial: Commonwealth vs. J. T. Buckingham, on an indictment for a libel before the municipal court of . . Boston, Dec. term, 1822. Boston [1822]. 8°

2 SPECIMENS of Newspaper Literature : with personal memoirs, anecdotes, and reminiscences. 2 vol. Boston, 1850. 12°

3 PERSONAL Memoirs and Recollections of Editorial Life. 2 vol. Boston, 1852. 12°

BUCKMINSTER, JOSEPH. A Sermon [on James i. 5] preached before . . the . . Council and . . House of Representatives of . . New Hampshire. Portsmouth, 1787. 8°

BUCKMINSTER, JOSEPH STEVENS. A Sermon [on Rom. xiv. 7] preached . . the Lord's day after the public funeral of his Excellency J. Sullivan, governor of the commonwealth of Massachusetts. Boston, 1809. 8vo.

2 SERMONS by. . J. S. Buckminster, with a memoir of his life and writings. Second edition. [With the autograph of Robert Southey.] Boston, 1815. 8vo.

BUDGET of Letters ; or, Things which I saw abroad. Boston, 1847. 12°

BUEL, JESSE. The Farmer's Companion ; or, Essays on the Principles and Practice of American Husbandry. With the address prepared to be delivered before the agricultural and horticultural societies of New Haven County ; and an appendix, containing tables. . Third edition, . enlarged. To which is added, an eulogy on the life and character of Judge Buel, by A. Dean. Boston, 1842. 12mo.

2 THE FARMER'S Instructor ; consisting of essays, practical directions, and hints for the management of the farm and the garden. Originally published in The Cultivator ; selected and revised for the school district library. 2 vol. New York, 1844. 12°

BUFFUM, E. GOULD. Six Months in the Gold Mines : from a journal of three years' residence in Upper and Lower California. 1847-8-9. Philadelphia, 1850. 12°

BUILDING ASSOCIATIONS ; their Deceptive Character and Ruinous Tendency exposed. By a Citizen. New York, 1852. 8°

BUIST, ROBERT. The American Flower Garden Directory ; containing .. directions for the culture of plants .. for every month in the year.. Second edition, with additions. Philadelphia, 1839. 8vo.

2 THE ROSE Manual; containing accurate descriptions of all the finest varieties of roses; . with directions for their propagation, *etc.* Second edition, with additions. Philadelphia, 1847. 12°

BULFINCH, THOMAS. Desultory Extracts and Observations, showing that the method of treatment, related in [a short account .. of the putrid bilious yellow fever, by J. Holliday], is agreeable to the rules laid down by Hippocrates and Galen, Sydenham and Boerhaave. Boston, 1796. 8vo.

BULKELEY, GERSHOM. The People's Right to Election or Alteration of Goverment in Connecticott, argued in a Letter; by G. Bulkeley, Esq. one of their Majesties Justices of the Peace in the county of Hartford. Together with a letter to the said Bulkeley, from a friend of his in the Bay. To which is added, the writing delivered to J. Rufsell of Charlestown, Esq. warning him and others concerned, not to meet to hold a court at Cambridge, within the county of Middlesex. By T. Greaves, Esq. Judge of their Majesties Inferior Court of Pleas, and one of their Majesties Justices of the Peace within the said county. And also his answer to Mr. Broadstreete, and the gentlemen mett at the Town-house in Boston, concerning the same. Published for the information and satisfaction of their Majesties loyall (but abused) subjects in New England. Philadelphia. Printed by afsigns of William Bradford, anno 1689. 4to.

BULKLEY, C. H. A. Niagara. A poem. New York, 1848. 12°

BULL, MARCUS. Experiments to determine the comparative value of the principal varieties of Fuel used in the United States, and also in Europe; and on the ordinary apparatus used for their combustion. Philadelphia, 1827. 8vo.

2 A DEFENCE of the Experiments to determine the comparative value of the principal varieties of Fuel used in the United States, and also in Europe; containing a correspondence with a committee of the American Academy of Arts and Sciences, their report, and remarks thereon, *etc.* Philadelphia, 1828. 8°

BULLARD, Mrs. A. T. J. Sights and Scenes in Europe: a series of letters [reprinted from the Mifsouri Republican]. St. Louis, 1852. 12°

BULLARD, HENRY A. and CURRY, THOMAS. A new Digest of the Statute Laws of the State of Louisiana, from the change of government [1812] to the year 1841, inclusive. Compiled by H. A. Bullard, and T. Curry. Vol. I. New Orleans, 1842. 8°

BULLIONS, PETER. Practical Lefsons in English Grammar and Composition, for young beginners, *etc.* New York, 1844. 12°

BUMSTEAD, J. F. Second Reading-Book in the Primary School, *etc.* Boston, 1845. 12°

2 THIRD Reading-Book in the Primary School. Boston, 1845. 12°

BUNCE, OLIVER B. The Romance of the Revolution, being a history of the personal adventures, heroic exploits, and romantic incidents, as enacted in the War of Independence. Edited by O. B. Bunce. New York, 1852. 8°

BUNGENER, LAURENCE LOUIS FELIX. The Preacher and the King; or, Bourdaloue in the Court of Louis XIV. . Translated from the French of L. Bungener. With an introduction by .. G. Potts. London [Boston printed], 1853. 8vo.

2 THE PRIEST and the Huguenot; or, Persecution in the Age of Louis XV. [Translated from the French,

by M. E.] 2 vol. London, [New York, printed ?] 1853. 12mo.

BUNKER HILL BATTLE. A Particular Account of the Battle of Bunker or Breed's Hill, on the 17th of June, 1775. By a citizen of Boston. Second edition. Boston, 1825. 8°

2 SKETCH of Bunker Hill Battle and Monument: with illustrative documents. Charlestown, 1843. 12°

BUNKER HILL MONUMENT. Panoramic View from Bunker Hill Monument. Engraved . . from a drawing by R. P. Mallory. [A folded engraving, with letter-preſs description.] Boston, 1848. 4°

BUNKER HILL MONUMENT ASSOCIATION. Circular [of the Directors, inviting contributions for erecting a monument to commemorate the battle of Bunker Hill]. By D. Webster ?] [Boston, 1824.] 8°

BUNNER, E. History of Louisiana, from its first discovery and settlement to the present time. New York, 1846. 12°

BURCH, SAMUEL. A Digest of the Laws of the Corporation of the City of Washington, to June, 1823; with an appendix, containing the acts of ceſsion from Maryland and Virginia; the laws of the United States, relating to the District of Columbia; the building regulations of the said city, etc. Compiled . . by S. Burch. Washington, 1823. 8°

BURCHARD, S. D. The Daughters of Zion. [Sketches of some of the women mentioned in the Scriptures.] New York, 1853. 12mo.

BURGES, BARTHOLOMEW. A Short Account of the Solar System, and of Comets in general: with a particular account of the comet that will appear in 1789. Boston, 1789. 12mo.

BURGES, TRISTAM. Addreſs to the Rhode Island Society for the Encouragement of Domestic Industry,

. Oct. 17, 1821. Providence,[R. I.] 1822. 8°

2 SPEECH . . delivered in the House of Representatives, . April 21, . 1828 on the Tariff. Washington, 1828. 8°

3 THE SPEECH of T. Burges, in the House of Representatives, . May 10, 1830, on the bill for the more effectual collection of the duties on imports, etc. Providence, 1830. 8°

4 SPEECH . . on the Motion to strike from the General Appropriation Bill the salary appropriated for the Minister to Ruſsia; delivered in the House of Representatives, Feb. 3, 1831. Washington, 1831. 12°

5 BATTLE of Lake Erie; with notices of Commodore Elliot's conduct in that engagement. Boston, 1839. 12°

BURK, JOHN. The History of Virginia, from its settlement to the commencement of the revolution. 3 vol. Petersburg, Virginia, 1822. 8vo.

BURKE, ÆDANUS. An Addreſs to the Freemen of the State of South Carolina. . By Caſsius. Supposed to be written by Æ. Burke. Philadelphia, 1783. 8°

BURKE, Right Hon. EDMUND. The Works of E. Burke. 9 vol. Boston, 1839. 8°

BURKE, EDMUND, of New Hampshire. Speech . . in the House of Representatives, June 13, 1840, on the independent treasury bill, etc. [Washington, 1840.] 8°

2 SPEECH . . on the Tariff Bill; delivered in the House of Representatives, July 8, 1842. Washington, 1842. 8°

3 THE PROTECTIVE System considered in connection with the present Tariff, in a series of twelve eſsays, originally published in the Washington Union, etc. Washington, 1846. 8°

BURKE, JOHN W. Life of R. Emmett, . with his speeches, etc.; also an appendix, containing valuable portions of Irish history. Third edition. Charleston, 1852. 12°

BURKE, WILLIAM. The Mineral Springs of Western Virginia: with remarks on their use, and the diseases to which they are applicable. New York, 1842.

2 THE MINERAL Springs of Western Virginia. . Second edition. . To which are added, a notice of the Fauquier White Sulphur Spring, and a chapter on taverns; also a review of a pamphlet published by Dr. J. J. Moorman. New York, 1846. 12°

BURLEIGH, JOSEPH BARTLETT. The American Manual: containing a brief outline of the origin and progreß of political power, and the laws of nations; a commentary on the constitution of the United States; with questions, definitions, and marginal exercises. Philadelphia, 1848. 12°

2 THE LEGISLATIVE Guide; containing all the rules for conducting busineß in Congreß; Jefferson's Manual; and the Citizen's Manual; . . with copious notes and marginal references. (Constitution of the United States. Original articles of confederation.) Second edition. Philadelphia, 1852. 8°

BURLEIGH, WILLIAM HENRY. Poems. Philadelphia, 1841. 12°

BURLINGTON COLLEGE. NEW JERSEY. Addreß of the Trustees; Prospectus of the Preparatory School. Burlington, 1846. 8vo.

2 ADDRESS of the Trustees [with General Statement, etc.] Burlington, 1848. 12mo.

3 BURLINGTON College [Addreßes, Claß Lists]. Burlington, 1848. 12mo.

4 PROCEEDINGS of the Fourth of July, 1850, at Burlington College. Burlington, 1850. 8vo.

5 NURTURE: together with the Catalogue and Prospectus of St. Mary's Hall. Winter Term, 1848-9. Burlington, 1849. 12mo.

BURLINGTON COLLEGE, VERMONT. See UNIVERSITY of Vermont.

BURNAP, GEORGE W. The Pro-

feßions: an oration delivered before the literary societies of Marshall College, Mercersburg, Pennsylvania, at their anniversary, September 27, 1842. Baltimore [1842]. 8°

2 MEMOIR of H. A. Ingalls. . With selections from his writings. Boston, 1846. 12°

3 THE SPHERE and Duties of Woman: a course of lectures. Baltimore, 1848. 12°

BURNAY, JACOB. A Sermon [on Psal. lxxxvii. 4-6] preached . . before . . the . . Senate and House of Representatives of . . New Hampshire. Concord, 1801. 8°

BURNBY, JOHN. Thoughts on the Freedom of Election. Rochester, 1785. 8vo.

BURNETT, Mr. Of Ohio. Speech . . in the Whig National Convention, giving a brief history of the life of Gen. W. H. Harrison. Washington, 1839. 8°

BURNET, JACOB. The Annual Addreß delivered before the Cincinnati Astronomical Society, June 3, 1844. . Together with the act of incorporation, the constitution of the society, the annual reports, etc. Cincinnati, 1844. 8°

2 NOTES on the Early Settlement of the North Western Territory. New York, 1847. 8°

BURNET, WILLIAM, Governor of Maßachusetts and New Hampshire. A Poem presented to his Excellency W. Burnet, Esq. on his arrival at Boston. [Boston, 1728.] 8vo.

BURNHAM, CHARLES G. A New System of Arithmetic, on the cancelling plan, etc. Second edition. Boston and Concord, 1841. 12°

BURNS, ROBERT. The Works of R. Burns; containing his life, by J. Lockhart; the poetry and correspondence of Dr. Currie's edition; biographical sketches . . by himself, G. Burns, Professor Stewart, and others;

Eſſay on Scottish poetry . . by Dr. Currie; Burns' songs, etc. Boston, 1846. 8°

BURNSIDE, Samuel M. Oration, delivered at Worcester [in Maſſachuſetts], . April 30, 1813, before the Washington Benevolent Society, . in commemoration of the first inauguration of General Washington as president of the United States. Worcester, 1813. 8°

BURR, Rev. Aaron. A Servant of God dismiſſed from Labour to Rest. A funeral sermon [on Dan. xii. 13], preached at the interment of J. Belcher, etc. New York, 1758. 4to.

BURR, Aaron. A Narrative of the Suppreſſion by Col. Burr, of the History of the Administration of J. Adams, late President of the United States, written by J. Wood. . To which is added a biography of T. Jefferson, president of the United States; and of General Hamilton : with strictures on the conduct of J. Adams, and on the character of General C. C. Pinckney. Extracted . . from the suppreſſed history. By a citizen of New York. New York, 1802. 8vo.

2 A View of the Political Conduct of A. Burr. By the author of the "Narrative." New York, 1802. 8vo.

3 The Trial of Col. A. Burr, on an Indictment for Treason, before the Circuit Court of the United States, . May term, 1807 : including the arguments and decisions on all the motions, and on the motion for an attachment against Gen. Wilkinson. Taken in shorthand by T. Carpenter. 3 vols. Washington City, 1807. 8vo.

4 The Private Journal of A. Burr, during his residence of four years in Europe; with selections from his correspondence. Edited by M. L. Davis. 2 vol. New York, 1838. 8vo.

BURR, David H. An Atlas of the State of New York ; . from documents deposited in the public offices of the state, . under the superintendence

and direction of S. De Witt ; . and also the physical geography of the State . . and statistical tables of the same. New York, 1829. Fol.

BURR, Jonathan. God's Presence removes the Fear of Death. A sermon [on Psalm xxiii. 4] preached . . at the interment of the Rev. O. Shaw, etc. Boston, 1807. 8vo.

BURRILL, Alexander M. A New Law Dictionary and Gloſſary ; containing full definitions of the principal terms of the common and civil law, together with translations and explanations of the various technical phrases in different languages occurring in the ancient and modern reports and standard treatises, embracing also all the principal common and civil law maxims. Compiled on the basis of Spelman's gloſſary. 2 parts. New York, 1850-51. 8°

BURRITT, Elihu. Sparks from the Anvil. [Miscellaneous eſſays and tales.] Worcester, 1846. 16°

BURRITT, Elijah Hinsdale. Logarithmic arithmetic, etc. Williamsburgh, 1818. 8°

2 The Geography of the Heavens and Claſs-Book of Astronomy ; accompanied by a celestial atlas. . Fifth edition. With an introduction by T. Dick, LL.D. New York, 1845. 12°

BURROUGHS, Charles. A Discourse delivered in the Chapel of the New Almshouse in Portsmouth, N. H. Dec. 15, 1834, on occasion of its being first opened for religious services. Portsmouth, 1835. 8°

BURROUGHS, Stephen. Memoirs of S. Burrroughs. Hanover, 1798. 8°

BURROWES, Thomas H. Draft of a revised Common School Law, and of a law relative to the preparation of Common School Teachers ; with explanatory remarks and a set of district regulations. Harrisburg, 1839. 8°

BURT, FEDERAL. An Addreſs delivered at Durham, N(ew) H(ampshire), . before the Old Hundred Sacred Music Society, on occasiori of their first annual meeting. Dover (New Hampshire), 1815. 8°

BURTON, ASA. A Discourse [on Psal. viii. 5] delivered before . . Governor, . Council, etc. of . . Vermont, . Oct. 8, . being the day of general election. Rutland, 1795. 8°

BURTON, WALTER HENRY. An Elementary Compendium of the Law of Real Property. From the last London edition. Philadel. 1839. 8°

BURTON, WARREN. The Scenery-Shower; with word paintings of the beautiful, the picturesque, and the grand in nature. Boston, 1844. 12°

2 THE DISTRICT School as it was; by One who went to it [i.e. W. Burton]. Revised edition. Boston, 1850. 12°

BURTON, WILLIAM EVANS. Waggeries and Vagaries; a series of sketches, humorous and descriptive. Philadelphia, 1848. 12°

BURWELL, WILLIAM A. Mr. Burwell's Motion [in the House of Representatives of the United States of America, relative to armaments]. Feb. 8, 1808. Washington, 1808. 8°

BUSBY, C. A. An Eſsay on the Propulsion of Navigable Bodies. Extracted from the American Monthly Magazine, with . . additions. New York, 1818. 8°

BUSH, GEORGE. A Grammar of the Hebrew Language. Second edition, corrected and enlarged. New York, 1839. 8°

2 ILLUSTRATIONS of the Holy Scriptures, derived principally from the manners, customs, rites, traditions, forms of speech, antiquities, climate, and works of art and literature, of the eastern nations; embodying all that is valuable in the works of Harmer,

Burder, Paxton, and Roberts, and the most celebrated Oriental travellers; embracing also the subject of the fulfilment of prophecy, as exhibited by Keith and others, etc. Edited by Rev. G. Bush. Brattelboro, Vermont, 1839. 8°

3 THE LIFE of Mohammed, founder of the religion of Islam, and of the empire of the Saracens. New York, 1844. 12°

4 THE VALLEY of Vision; or, the Dry Bones of Israel revived: an attempted proof (from Ezek. xxxvii. 1-14) of the restoration and conversion of the Jews. New York, 1844. 8vo.

5 THE SOUL; or, an Inquiry into Scriptural Psychology, as developed by the use of the terms, soul, spirit, life, etc., viewed in its bearings on the doctrine of the resurrection. New York, 1845. 12mo.

6 " DAVIS' Revelations" revealed; being a critical examination of the character and claims of that work in its relations to the teachings of Swedenborg. New York, 1847. 8°

BUSHE, GEORGE. A Treatise on the Malformations, Injuries, and Diseases of the Rectum and Anus. Illustrated with plates. New York, 1837. 8°. Plates in 4°

BUSHNELL, HORACE. A Discourse [from Acts xxvii. 41] on the Slavery Question; delivered in the North Church, Hartford, Jan. 10, 1839. Hartford, 1839. 8°

2 A DISCOURSE on the Moral Tendencies and Results of Human History, delivered before the Society of Alumni, in Yale College, etc. New York, 1843. 8°

3 VIEWS of Christian Nurture, and of subjects adjacent thereto. . Second edition. Hartford, 1848. 12°

4 AN ORATION delivered before the Society of Phi Beta Kappa, at Cambridge. . Third edition. Cambridge, 1848. 8°

5 GOD in Christ. Three discourses,

delivered at New Haven, Cambridge, and Andover, with a preliminary dissertation on language. Hartford, 1849. 12°

6 CHRIST in Theology ; being the answer of the author before the Hartford Central Aſſociation of Ministers, October, 1849, for the doctrines of the book entitled "God in Christ." Hartford, 1851. 12°

7 SPEECH for Connecticut. Being an historical estimate of the State, delivered before the Legislature and other invited guests at the festival of the Normal School in New Britain, June 4, 1851. Hartford, 1851. 8°

. BUTLER, BENJAMIN FRANKLIN. The Military Profeſſion in the United States, and the means of promoting its usefulneſſ and honour: an addreſſ, etc. New York, 1839. 8°

BUTLER, C. M. D.D. The Book of Common Prayer interpreted by its History. Boston, 1845. 12°

BUTLER, CALEB. History of the Town of Groton, including Pepperell and Shirley, from the first grant of Groton Plantation in 1655. With appendices, containing family registers, town and state officers, etc. Boston, 1848. 8°

BUTLER, Mrs. CAROLINE H. Life in Varied Phases : illustrated in a series of sketches. Boston, 1851. 12°

2 THE ICE King and the Sweet South Wind. Boston, 1852. sq. 16°

BUTLER, CHARLES. The American Gentleman. Philadelphia, 1849. 16°

2 THE AMERICAN Lady. Philadelphia, 1849. 16°

BUTLER, FREDERICK. A Complete History of the United States of America, embracing the whole period from the discovery of North America, down to the year 1820. 3 vol. Hartford, 1821. 8°

. BUTLER, JAMES DAVIE. Defi-

ciencies in our History ; an addreſſ delivered before the Vermont Historical and Antiquarian Society, at Montpelier. Montpelier, 1846. 8°

2 ADDRESSES on the Battle of Bennington, and the Life and Services of Col. Seth Warner, delivered Oct. 20, 1848, by J. D. Butler, and J. F. Houghton. [With an appendix to each addreſſ.] Burlington, 1849. 8°

BUTLER, MANN. A History of the Commonwealth of Kentucky. Louisville, Ky. 1834. 8°

2 A HISTORY of the Commonwealth of Kentucky. . Second edition, revised and enlarged. Cincinnati, 1836. 12mo.

BUTLER, P. M. Extracts from Reports made by P. M. Butler, United States Agent for the Cherokee Indians. [Fort Gibson ? 1845 ?] 12°

BUTLER, WILLIAM O. Speech . . on the Proposition to restore the fine to Gen. Jackson, delivered in the House of Representatives, Jan. 11, 1843. [Washington, 1843.] 8°

BUTT, Miſſ MARTHA HAINES. Antifanaticism: a tale of the South. Philadelphia, 1853. 12°

BUTTMAN, PHILIP CARL, and F. PASSOU. Practical Rules for Greek Accents and Quantity. From the German. By Moses Stuart. Andover, 1829. 8vo.

2 GREEK Grammar for the Use of Schools, from the German of P. Buttman [by E. Everett]. Third edition of the translation. Boston, 1831. 8°

3 BUTTMAN's Larger Greek Grammar. A Greek grammar for the use of High Schools and Universities. Translated from the German, with additions by E. Robinson. Andover, 1833. 8vo.

4 A GREEK Grammar for the use of High Schools and Universities, by P. Buttmann. Revised and enlarged by his son, A. Buttmann. Translated

from the eighteenth German edition,
by E. Robinson. New York, 1851.
8°

5 PRACTICAL Rules for Greek Accents and Quantity. From the German, . by M. Stuart. Andover, 1829.
12°

BYLES, MATHER. A Poem on the
Death of his late Majesty King George,
. and the Accefsion of . . George II.
[Boston, 1727.] 8°

BYNUM, JESSE A. Speech . .
on the Motion of Mr. Wagener, to
be excused from serving on the Investigating Committee, to examine
into the defalcation of S. Swartwout ;
in the House of Representatives, Jan.
1839. Washington, 1839. 8°

BYRD, WILLIAM, Colonel. The
Westover Manuscripts : containing
the history of the dividing line betwixt Virginia and North Carolina ;
a journey to the land of Eden, A. D.
1733 ; and a progrefs to the mines.
Written from 1728 to 1736, and now
first published. Petersburg [Virgi-
nia], 1841. 8°

BYRDSALL, F. The History of
the Loco-Foco, or Equal Rights Party,
its movements, conventions and proceedings. With short characteristic
sketches of its prominent men. New
York, 1842. 12°

BYRN, M. LAFAYETTE. The Repository of Wit and Humour ; comprising more than one thousand anecdotes. . Selected and arranged by
M. L. Byrn. Boston, 1853. 8°

2 THE COMPLETE Practical Distil-
ler, etc. Philadelphia, 1853. 12°

BYRNE, ALEXANDER S. Observations on the best means of Propel-
ling Ships. Second edition. New
York, 1841. 8vo.

BYRNE, JOHN. Anti-Phrenology;
or, a Chapter on Humbug. Washington, 1843. 8vo.

BYRNE, OLIVER. The Pocket
Companion for machinists, mechanics
and engineers. New York, 1851.
12°

2 THE PRACTICAL Metal-Worker's
Afsistant: containing the arts of working all metals and alloys, . with the
application of electro-metallurgy to
manufacturing procefses. . With . .
engravings on wood, etc. Philadelphia, 1851. 8°

3 THE PRACTICAL Model Calculator, for the engineer, mechanic, machinist, etc. Philadelphia, 1852. 8°

4 THE AMERICAN Engineer, Drafts-
man, and Machinist's Afsistant ; .
with engravings of recently constructed American machinery and
engine work. Philadelphia, 1853.
Fol°.

ABINET. The
Juvenile Ca-
binet; or, Pub-
lications of the
American Sun-
day School
Union. No.155-
157. Philadel-
phia, 1830-28-27. 12mo.

CADWALADER, Thomas. An
Eſſay on the West India Dry-Gripes,
. . . with the method of preventing
and curing that distemper . . to which
is added an extraordinary case in
physick. [Revised by A. Spencer.]
Philadelphia, 1745. 4to.

CADY (Hon. Judge). Opinion of
Hon. Judge Cady in Supreme Court.
The People of the State of New York
vs. George Clarke . . Judgment for
Defendant, G. Clarke. Albany, 1851.
8vo.

CÆSAR, Caius Julius. Caius
Julius Cæsar quæ extant, interpreta-
tione et notis illustravit J. Godrinus
. . in usum Delphini. The notes and
interpretations translated and improved by T. Clark. Fourth edition.
Philadelphia, 1824. 8°

2 Cæsar's Commentaries on the
Gallic War; and the first book of
the Greek paraphrase; with English
notes, critical and explanatory, plans
of battles, sieges, etc. and historical,
geographical, and archæological indexes, by C. Anthon. Lat. and Gr.
New York, 1845. 12°

CAHOONE, Sarah S. Visit to

Grand-papa; or, a Week at Newport. New York, 1840. 12°

CAIN, Jude. Memoir of J. Cain,
who died in Liverpool, Feb. 3, 1829,
aged twelve years. American Sunday School Union, Philadelphia, 1831.
12mo.

CAINES, George. A Summary
of the Practice of the Supreme Court
of the State of New York. New
York, 1808. 8°

2 Cases argued and determined
in the Court for the trial of Impeachments and correction of errors, in the
State of New York. [From Feb.
1801 to Feb. 1805.] 2 vol. in 1.
New York, 1810. 8°

3 New York Term Reports of
cases argued and determined in the
Supreme Court of that State [From
May Term 1803 to Nov. Term
1805]. Second edition, with corrections and additions. 3 vol. New
York, 1813-14. 8°

CALAVAR; or the Knight of the
Conquest; a romance of Mexico [by
R. M. Bird]. 2 vol. [Vol. 2, third
edition.] Philadel. 1834-37. 12°

CALDWELL, Charles, M.D.
An attempt to establish the original
sameneſs of three phenomena of fever
. . described . . under . . hydrocephalus internus, lynanche trachealis,
and diarrhœa infantum. Philadelphia,
1796. 8vo.

2 A semi-annual Oration, on the
origin of Pestilential Diseases. Philadelphia, 1799. 8vo.

3 An ELEGIAC Poem on the death of General Washington. Philadelphia, 1800. 8vo.

4 CHARACTER of General Washington. Philadelphia, 1801. 8vo.

5 A REPLY to Dr. Haygarth's letter to Dr. Percival, on infectious fevers, etc. Philadelphia, 1802. 8vo.

6 An EXPERIMENTAL Inquiry respecting the Vitality of the Blood. Philadelphia, 1805. 8vo.

7 An ORATION commemorative of the character and administration of Washington. Philadelphia, 1810. 8vo.

8 MEMOIRS of the life and campaigns of the Hon. Nathaniel Greene. Philadelphia, 1819. 8°

9 A DISCOURSE on the Genius and Character of the Rev. H. Holley, LL.D. late President of Transylvania University. . . With an appendix, containing copious notes, biographical and illustrative. Boston, 1828. 8°

10 PHRENOLOGY vindicated, and Anti-Phrenology unmasked. New York, 1838. 12°

CALDWELL, JOHN WILLIAM. Oration pronounced at Worcester, July 4, 1803. Worcester, 1803. 4°

CALHOUN, GEORGE A. Letters to the Rev. Leonard Bacon, in reply to his attack on the Pastoral Union and Theological Institute of Connecticut. Hartford, 1840. 8°

CALHOUN, JOHN CALDWELL. The works of J. C. Calhoun (edited by Richard K. Crallé). 6 vol. Charleston and New York, 1851-55. 8°

2 THE WORKS. Vol. 1. [another copy, differing only in the title-page]. Columbus, S. C. 1851. 8vo.

3 DEBATE in Congress. In Senate . . . February 15, 1833. Speech of Mr. Calhoun on the Bill further to provide for the collection of duties on imports. [Washington, 1833.] 8°

4 REMARKS . . in the Senate, . .

Jan. 13, 1834, on the removal of the deposites from the Bank of the United States. Washington, 1834. 8°

5 REMARKS . . in the Senate . . on . . the removal of the deposites from the Bank of the United States. Jan. 13, 1834. [Washington], 1834. 8°

6 REMARKS . . delivered in the Senate . . March 21, 1834, on the motion of Mr. Webster, for leave to introduce a bill to continue the Charter of the Bank of the United States, etc. [Washington, 1834.] 8°

7 REMARKS . . delivered in the Senate, . . May 6, 1834, on the President's protest [against a resolution of the Senate censuring the removal of the deposites]. Washington, 1834. 8°

8 SPEECH . . on Mr. Clay's resolutions in relation to the revenues and expenditures of the government: delivered in the Senate, . . March 16, 1842. Washington, 1842. 8°

9 LIFE of John Caldwell Calhoun, presenting a condensed history of political events from 1811 to 1843. Together with a selection from his speeches, reports, and other writings, etc. New York, 1843. 8°

10 SPEECH . . on the resolutions giving notice to Great Britain of the abrogation of the Convention of Joint Occupancy [of the Oregon Territory]: delivered in the Senate . . March 16, 1846. [Washington, 1846.] 8°

11 OBITUARY Addresses delivered on the occasion of the death of the Hon. John Caldwell Calhoun, in the Senate of the United States, April 1, 1850. With the funeral sermon of the Rev. C. M. Butler, etc. Washington, 1850. 8°

CALIFORNIA. The Statutes of California, passed at the first session of the Legislature, begun the fifteenth day of December, 1849, and ended the twenty-second day of April, 1850, at the city of Pueblo de San José. With an appendix and index. San José, 1850. 4°

2 REPORT of the Debates in the Convention of California, on the formation of the State Constitution, in September and October, 1849. By J. R. Browne. Washing. 1850. 8vo.

3 CALIFORNIA Sketches, with recollections of the Gold Mines. Albany, 1850. 12°

4 THE VOLCANO Diggings, a Tale of California Law. By a member of the Bar. New York, 1851. 12°

5 CALIFORNIA illustrated; including a description of the Panama and Nicaragua routes. By a returned Californian. New York, 1852. 8°

6 FIRST annual Report of the Superintendent of Public Instruction (J. G. Marvin) to the Legislature of the State of California. [Vallejo? 1852.] 8vo.

7 REPORT of Committee on Education. Presented March 8, 1852. [Vallejo? 1852.] 8vo.

8 THE LAW establishing and regulating Common Schools in the State of California, as amended during the fourth Session of the Legislature, 1853. With notes and explanatory forms. By J. G. Marvin . . Second edition. San Francisco, 1853. 8vo.

CALL, DANIEL. Reports of cases argued and adjudged in the Court of Appeals of Virginia [From April Term, 1797, to Dec. Term, 1818.] (Vol. 1-3. Second edition. To which are added notes referring to subsequent adjudications of the same court, and other authorities, . . by J. Tate.) 6 vol. Richmond, 1824-33. 8°

CALL, OSMAN. Call's decimal Arithmetic, on a new and improved plan throughout, etc. Hancock Factory, N. H., 1842. 12°

CALLENDER, JAMES THOMSON. Sketches of the history of America. Philadelphia, 1798. 8°

CALLENDER, JOHN. An Historical Discourse on the civil and religious affairs of the Colony of Rhode-

Island and Providence Plantations, in New-England in America, from the first settlement, 1638, to the end of first century [With the autograph of Robert Southey.] Boston, 1739. 8vo.

2 AN HISTORICAL Discourse on the civil and religious affairs of the Colony of Rhode Island. By John Callender, M.A. With a memoir of the author, biographical notices of some of his . . contemporaries, and annotations and original documents illustrative of the history of Rhode Island, etc. by Romeo Elton. Third edition. Boston, 1843. 8°

CALLENDER, JOHN. An Oration, pronounced July 4, 1797, at . . Boston, in commemoration of the anniversary of American Independence. Boston, 1797. 8°

CALLENDER, TOM. Letters to A. Hamilton, King of the Feds, etc. etc. etc. Being intended as a reply to a scandalous pamphlet lately published under the sanction, as it is presumed, of Mr. Hamilton, and signed with the signature of Junius Philænus. New York, 1802. 8°

CALPE, ADADUS, Pseud. [i.e. Antonio D. de Pascual]. The two Fathers; an unpublished original Spanish work . . translated into the English language by the Author and H. Edgar. 3 pts. New York, 1852. 8°

CALUMET; New series of the Harbinger of Peace. Published under the direction of the American Peace Society. 1831-1834. New York [1831-34]. 8°

CALVERT, GEORGE HENRY. Illustrations of Phrenology; being a selection of articles from the Edinburg Phrenological Journal, and the Transactions of the Edinburg Phrenological Society. Edited by George Henry Calvert. With an introduction. Baltimore, 1832. 12°

2 POEMS. Boston, 1847. 12°

3 SCENES and Thoughts in Europe.

(First Series.) By an American [George Henry Calvert]. London [New York printed], 1847. 12mo.

4 SCENES and Thoughts in Europe. (Second Series.) 2 vol. New York, 1852. 12°

CAMBRELENG, CHURCHILL C. Report of Mr. Cambreleng . . State of the Treasury and expenditures of Government. (In House of Representatives, Jan. 24, 1839. Mr. Cambreleng, from the Committee of Ways and Means, submitted the following Report.) [Washington, 1839.] 8°

CAMBRIDGE, MASSACHUSETTS. Epitaphs from the Old Burying-ground in Cambridge. With notes by William Thaddeus Harris. Cambridge, 1845. 12°

CAMBRIDGE AND SAYBROOK Platforms of Church Discipline ; with the Confeſſion of Faith of the New England Churches, adopted in 1680, and the heads of agreements aſſented to by the Presbyterians and Congregationalists in England in 1690. Illustrated with historical prefaces and notes. Boston, 1829. 12°

CAMBRIDGE PLATFORM of Church Discipline, adopted in 1648, and the Confeſſion of Faith adopted in 1680. Boston, 1850. 12°

CAMDEN, a Tale of the South. 2 vol. Philadelphia, 1830. 12°

CAMERON, ARCHIBALD. Archibald Cameron ; or, Heart Trials. New York, 1852. 12°

CAMP, GEORGE SIDNEY. Democracy [A treatise on popular government]. New York, 1845. 12°

CAMPBELL, ALEXANDER. A Debate on the Roman Catholic Religion . . between Alexander Campbell and the Rev. J. B. Purcell, Bishop of Cincinnati. Taken down by reporters, and revised by the parties. Cincinnati, 1837. 12°

CAMPBELL, GEORGE WASHINGTON. Motion respecting the establishment of a Post Road from Knoxville . . to New Orleans, etc. [submitted to the House of Representatives of the United States of America]. Washington, 1804. 8°

2 MR. G. W. CAMPBELL's motion [in the House of Representatives of the United States of America, relative to the commerce of Neutrals]. April 8, 1808. Washington, 1808. 8°

3 MR. G. W. CAMPBELL's motion, proposing an amendment to the Constitution of the United States relative to the Judges, etc. Jan. 30, 1808. Washington, 1808. 8°

CAMPBELL, JOHN. Negro-mania: being an examination of the falsely-aſſumed equality of the various races of men, etc. Philadelphia, 1851. 8°

CAMPBELL, JOHN, of South Carolina. Speech . . on the Bill relating to duties and drawbacks, delivered in the House of Representatives . . July 26, 1841. Washington, 1841. 8°

2 CONSIDERATIONS and Arguments proving the inexpediency of an international copyright law. New York, 1844. 8°

CAMPBELL, JOHN D. and CAMBRELENG, STEPHEN. The American Chancery Digest; being a digested index of all the reported decisions in equity in the United States Courts, and in the Courts of the several States. New York, 1828. 8°

CAMPBELL, J. W. A History of Virginia till 1781. With biographical sketches of all the most distinguished characters. Philadelphia, 1813. 12mo.

CAMPBELL, N. W. Mrs. Why should I be a Pastor? or, Conversations on the authority for the Gospel Ministry, etc. Philadelphia, 1852. 12mo.

CAMPBELL, THOMAS. The Poetry and History of Wyoming: containing Campbell's Gertrude; with a biographical sketch of the author, by W. Irving, and the history of Wyoming, from its discovery to the beginning of the present century, by W. L. Stone. New York and London, 1841. 12mo.

CAMPBELL, WILLIAM S. Report on the Alabama, Florida, and Georgia Railroad. [Philadelphia,] 1838. 8°

CAMPBELL, WILLIAM W. Lecture on the life and military services of General James Clinton, read before the New York Historical Society, Feb. 1839. New York, 1839. 8°

2 THE BORDER Warfare of New York during the Revolution; or, the annals of Tryon County. New York, 1849. 12°

3 AN HISTORICAL Sketch of Robin Hood and Captain Kidd. New York, 1853. 12°

CAMP MEETING CHORISTER; or, a collection of hymns and spiritual songs . . . to be sung at Camp Meetings, during revivals of religion, and on other occasions. Philadelphia, 1850. 16°

CANER, HENRY. God the only unfailing object of trust; being a discourse upon Psalm cxviii. 8, 9. . . upon occasion of the . . death of . . Frederick, Prince of Wales, etc. Boston, 1751. 8°

2 THE NATURE and Necessity of an habitual preparation for death and judgment. A sermon [on Matt. xxiv. 44] preached November 21, 1758, upon occasion of the death of Charles Apthorp. Boston, New England [1758]. 8vo.

CANNING, RIGHT HON. GEORGE. Select Speeches; with a preliminary biographical sketch, and an appendix of extracts from his writings and speeches. Edited by R. Walsh. Philadelphia, 1835. 8°

CANNING, JOSIAH D. The Harp and Plow. By the "Peasant Bard" (Josiah D. Canning). Greenfield, 1852. 12°

CANNON, CHARLES JAMES. Poems, dramatic and miscellaneous. New York, 1851. 12°

CAPEN, NAHUM. The Phrenological Library. Edited by N. Capen. Vol. 1-6 [all published. See GALL]. Boston [1835]. 12mo.

2 [Begin.] Twenty-eighth Congress, first Session. . . Memorial of N. Capen, on the subject of international copyright. [Bost. 1844.] 8°

CAREY, ALICE. Hagar, a story of to-day. New York, 1852. 12°

CAREY, EUSTACE. Memoir of W. Carey, D.D. . . with an introductory essay, by J. Chaplin. Hartford, 1837. 12°

CAREY, HENRY C. Essay on the rate of Wages; with an examination of the causes of the differences in the condition of the labouring population throughout the world. Philadelphia, 1835. 8°

2 PRINCIPLES of Political Economy. 2 parts. Philadelphia, 1837. 8vo.

3 THE PAST, the Present, and the Future. [A series of essays on Political Economy.] Philadelphia, 1848. 8°

4 THE SLAVE Trade, domestic and foreign: why it exists, and how it may be extinguished. Philadelphia, 1853. 12°

CAREY, MATTHEW. A short Account of the Malignant Fever lately prevalent in Philadelphia. . . Second edition. Philadelphia, 1793. 8vo.

2 A SHORT Account of the Malignant Fever lately prevalent in Philadelphia, . . with a statement of the proceedings that took place on the subject in different parts of the United States. Third edition. Philadelphia, 1793. 8vo.

3 HISTOIRE succincte de la Fièvre Maligne, qui a régné dernièrement à

Philadelphie, suivi d'un récit des mesures prises dans différentes parties des Etats Unis, au sujet de cette maladie. (Fourth edition.) Philadelphie [1794]. 8vo.

4 LETTERS to Dr. A. Seybert . . . on the subject of the renewal of the Charter of the Bank of the United States. Second edition, enlarged. Philadelphia, Jan. 7, 1811. 8°

5 CAREY's American Pocket Atlas, containing twenty maps, . . with a brief description of each State and Territory: also the Census . . for 1810, the Exports . . for twenty years. Fourth edition, . . enlarged. Philadelphia, 1813. 12°

6 LETTERS to the Bank Directors on the pernicious consequences of the prevailing system of Banking Operations, and on the facility of reducing discounts. Philadelphia, 1816. 8°

7 REFLECTIONS on the present system of Banking in Philadelphia, with a plan to revive confidence, trade, and commerce, and to facilitate the resumption of specie payments. Second edition. Philadelphia, 1817. 8°

8 VINDICLÆ Hibernicæ; or, Ireland Vindicated: an attempt to develop and expose a few of the multifarious errors and falsehoods respecting Ireland, in the histories of May, Temple, Whitelock, Borlase, Rushworth, Clarendon, Cox, Carte, Leland, Warner, Macaulay, Hume, and others: particularly in the legendary tales of the Conspiracy and pretended Massacre of 1641. Philadelphia, 1819. 8vo.

9 VINDICLÆ Hibernicæ, etc. Second edition, enlarged. Philadelphia, 1823. 8vo.

10 ADDRESS to the Farmers of the United States, on the ruinous consequences to their vital interests of the existing policy of this country. Philadelphia, 1821. 8°

11 ESSAYS on Political Economy; or the most certain means for promoting the wealth, power, resources, and happiness of nations, applied particularly to the United States. Philadelphia, 1822. 8vo.

12 ESSAYS on the Public Charities of Philadelphia, intended to vindicate the benevolent societies of this city from the charge of encouraging idleness, etc. . . Fourth edition, gratuitous. Philadelphia, 1829. 8vo.

13 MISCELLANEOUS Essays, etc. Philadelphia, Nov. 13, 1830. 8°

14 REFLECTIONS on the causes that led to the formation of the Colonization Society; with a view of its probable results, under the following heads: the increase of the coloured population; the origin of the Colonization Society; the manumission of slaves in this country; . . the advantages to the free coloured population by emigration to Liberia, etc. Philadelphia, 1832. 8°

15 LETTERS on the Colonization Society; with a view of its probable results, under the following heads: the origin of the Society; increase of the coloured population; manumission of slaves in this country, etc. Second edition, . . enlarged. Philadelphia, 1832. 8°

16 THE OLIVE Branch once more. Nº. 1-4. [Philadelphia, 1833.] 8°

CARLTON, ROBERT. The New Purchase; or seven and a half years in the Far West. 2 vols. New York, 1843. 12mo.

2 SOMETHING for Everybody; gleaned in the Old Purchase from fields often reaped. N. York, 1846. 12°

CARNAHAN, JAMES. The character and blessedness of the Good Man: a discourse [on Ps. i. 1, 2], etc. Princeton, 1831. 8°

CARNES, J. A. Journal of a Voyage from Boston to the west coast of Africa, with a full description of the manner of trading with the natives on the coast. Boston, 1852. 8°

CAROLINA HOUSEWIFE; or House and Home. By a lady of Charleston. Charleston, 1847. 12°

CAROLINIAN. Slavery in the Southern States. By a Carolinian. Second edition. Cambridge, 1852. 8°

CARPENTER, MARCUS T. Memories of the Past. Poems. New York, 1850. 12°

CARPENTER, STEPHEN CULLEN. Select American Speeches, forensic and parliamentary, with prefatory remarks : being a sequel to Dr. Chapman's 'Select Speeches.' 2 vol. Philadelphia, 1815. 8°

CARPENTER, THOMAS. The American Senator, or a copious and impartial Report of the Debates in the Congreſs of the United States, including all treaties, addreſses, proclamations, etc. Second Seſsion of Fourth Congreſs. 3 vol. Philadelphia, 1796-97. 8vo.

CARPENTER, WILLIAM H. Ruth Emsley, the Betrothed Maiden. A Tale of the Virginia Maſsacre. Philadelphia, 1850. 12°

CARPENTER, WILLIAM W. Travels and Adventures in Mexico. New York, 1851. 12°

CARROL, ELLEN. Ellen Carrol, written for the American Sunday-School Union, and revised by the Committee of Publication. Philadelphia [1834]. 12mo.

CARROL, JAMES. The American criterion of the English Language; containing the elements of pronunciation; in five sections. For the use of English schools and foreigners. New London, 1795. 12°

CARROLL, B. R. Historical Collections of South Carolina; embracing many rare and valuable pamphlets, and other documents, relating to the history of that State, from its first discovery to its independence, in the year 1776. Compiled, with various notes, and an introduction, by B. R. Carroll. 2 vol. New York, 1836. 8°

CARROLL, G. W. Report of the President of the Decatur Branch Bank. Tuscaloosa, 1844. 8°

CARSON, GEORGE LEDLIE. Memorials of the Family of the Rev. A. Carson, LL.D. By G. L. Carson and Mrs. M. C. Hanna. Philadelphia [1853]. 12mo.

CARSON, JOSEPH, M.D. Illustrations of Medical Botany; consisting of coloured figures of the plants affording the important articles of the Materia Medica, and descriptive letter-preſs, etc. Vol. 1 [wanting vol. 2]. Philadelphia, 1847. 4°

2 SYNOPSIS of the course of lectures on Materia Medica and Pharmacy, delivered in the University of Pennsylvania, by Joseph Carson. Philadelphia, 1851. 8vo.

CARTER, JAMES GORDON. Letters to the Hon. W. Prescott . . on the free schools of New England; with remarks upon the principles of instruction. Boston, 1824. 8°

2 ESSAYS upon popular Education; containing a particular examination of the schools of Maſsachusetts, etc. Boston, 1826. 8°

3 REMARKS upon Mr. Carter's Outline of an institution for the education of teachers. From the United States Review. Boston, 1827. 8°

CARTER, NATHANIEL HAZELTINE. Pains of the Imagination; a poem. New York, 1824. 8°

2 LETTERS from Europe; comprising the Journal of a Tour through Ireland, England, Scotland, France, Italy and Switzerland, in 1825-26 and 27. 2 vol. N. York, 1827. 8vo.

3 ADDRESS read before the New York Horticultural Society, at the anniversary celebration of the 28th of August, 1827. N. York, 1827. 8°

CARVER, JAMES. A Treatise on the age of the horse. Also, an eſsay on founder, contraction, and running thrush, etc. Philadel. 1818. 8vo.

CARVER, John. Sketches of New England; or, Memories of the Country. New York, 1842. 12°

CARY, Henry, *M.A. of Lincoln's Inn*. A practical Treatise on the Law of Partnership, with precedents of copartnership deeds. From the London edition. Philadel. 1834. 8°

CARY, Samuel. A Sermon [on Jeremiah xxiii. 28] delivered at King's Chapel, Boston, January 1, 1809, being the Sabbath of the author's ordination. Boston, 1809. 8°
2 A Sermon [on 2 Sam. xxiv. 16] preached before the .. Artillery Company, in Boston, June 6, 1814, being the 177th anniversary of their election of officers. Boston, 1814. 8°

CARY, Thomas Greaves. Letter to a Lady in France, on the supposed failure of a National Bank, the supposed delinquency of the National Government, the debts of the several States, and repudiation; with answers to enquiries concerning the books of Capt. Marryat and Mr. Dickens. [Second edition.] Boston, 1844. 8vo.
2 The Dependence of the Fine Arts for encouragement, in a Republic, on the security of property; with an enquiry into the causes of frequent failure among men of business; an address delivered before the Boston Mercantile Library Association, etc. Boston, 1845. 8°
3 A Practical View of the business of Banking; (an Address delivered before the Mercantile Library Association of Boston, etc.) [Boston], 1845. 8°
4 Profits of Manufactures at Lowell: a letter from (T. G. Cary) the Treasurer of a Corporation, etc. Boston, 1845. 8°
5 Memoir of T. H. Perkins; containing extracts from his Diaries and Letters. With an appendix. Boston, 1856. 8vo.

CARY, Virginia. Letters on Female Character, addressed to a young lady, on the death of her mother. Second edition, enlarged. Richmond, 1830. 12°

CASS, Lewis. A Discourse pronounced at the Capitol of the United States .. before the American Historical Society .. to which are prefixed its Constitution and the names of its officers. Washington, 1836. 8°
2 Speech .. on the defences of the country, delivered in the Senate .. Dec. 15, 1845. Washington, 1845. 8°
3 Speech .. on the Oregon question, delivered in the Senate .. March 30, 1846. [Washington, 1846.] 8°
4 Speech .. on the Bill providing for the prosecution of the war against Mexico; delivered in the Senate, .. May 12, 1846. Washing. 1846. 8°
5 Speech .. on the Bill to protect the rights of American settlers in Oregon, delivered in the Senate .. June 1, 1846. Washing. 1846. 8°
6 Substance of a speech delivered .. in Secret Session of the Senate of the United States, on the ratification of the Oregon treaty; with additions. July, 1846. Detroit, 1846. 8°
7 Gen. Cass' letter to the Harbour and River Convention. New York, 1848. 64°
8 Gen. Cass' Letter to the Harbour and River Convention. [Addressed to H. S. Whiting, with a facsimile of the letter.] Chicago, 1849. 64°

CASSIUS. *Pseud.* An Examination of Mr. Calhoun's Economy, and an apology for those members of Congress who have been denounced as Radicals. Part 1st [containing four numbers, each of which is subscribed 'Cassius.'] [Washington?] 1823. 8°

CASTANIS, Christophorus Plato. The Greek Exile; or, a narrative of the captivity and escape of Christophorus Plato Castanis during the massacre on the island of

Scio by the Turks, together with various adventures in Greece and America. Written by himself. Philadelphia, 1851. 12°

CASTE and Slavery in the American Church. By a Churchman. New York and London, 1843. 8°

CASWALL, Edward. Lyra Catholica : containing all the Hymns of the Roman Breviary and Miſſal, with others from various sources, arranged for every day in the week and the festivals and Saints' days throughout the year. With a selection of hymns, anthems, and sacred poetry. New York, 1851. 12°

CATALOGUES of Libraries.
1 A Catalogue of the books belonging to the Medical Library in the Pennsylvania Hospital. [Few MS. additions.] Philadelphia, 1790. 8°
2 Catalogus Bibliothecæ Harvardianæ, Cantabrigiæ Nov-Anglorum, 2 parts. Bostoniæ, 1790. 8°
3 A Catalogue of the books belonging to the Library Company of Philadelphia ; to which is prefixed, a short account of the Institution, with the charter laws and regulations. Philadelphia, 1807. 8°
4 Catalogue of the books, pamphlets, newspapers, maps, charts, manuscripts, etc. in the library of the Maſſachusetts Historical Society. Boston, 1811. 8°
5 Catalogue of the books, tracts, newspapers, maps, charts, views, portraits, and manuscripts, in the Library of the New York Historical Society. New York, Dec. 22, 1813. 8°
6 Catalogue of the . . . library of the New York Historical Society. (Appendix.) New York, 1813. 8vo.
7 Catalogue of the library of the United States. To which is annexed a copious index, alphabetically arranged. Washington, 1815. 4to.
8 A Catalogue of plants growing spontaneously within thirty miles of the city of New York. [Edited by J. Torrey !]. Albany, 1819. 8°

9 Catalogus Bibliothecæ Collegii Alleghaniensis. Meadville, 1823. 8°
10 A Catalogue of the Library of the American Philosophical Society, held at Philadelphia, for promoting Useful Knowledge. Philadelphia, 1824. 8°
11 A Catalogue of the books in the library of Dartmouth College. Concord, 1825. 8°
12 Catalogue of the books belonging to the Salem Athenæum, with the by-laws and regulations. Salem, 1826. 8°
13 A Catalogue of the books belonging to the Charleston Library Society. Charleston (S. Carolina), 1826. 8°
14 A Supplement to the Catalogue of the library of Congreſs. Washington, 1827. 8vo.
15 Catalogue of books in the Boston Atheneum ; to which are added the by-laws of the institution, and a list of its proprietors and subscribers. Boston, 1827. 8°
16 Library at Auction. Catalogue of . . . books ; the library of the late R. Peters, Esq. etc. Philadelphia, 1828. 8°
17 A Catalogue of the books belonging to the library of the New York Hospital : and the regulations for the use of the same. New York, 1829. 8°
18 Catalogue of the Medical Library of the Pennsylvania Hospital. (Supplement to the catalogue of the Medical Library of the Pennsylvania Hospital.) Philadelphia, 1829-37. 8°
19 Catalogue of the library of Congreſs. December 1830. Washington, 1830. 8vo.
20 Catalogue of the library of the Department of State of the United States. May 1830. [Washington, 1830.] 8°
21 A Catalogue of the Library of Harvard University in Cambridge. Maſſachusetts. [With a supplement.] 4 vol. Cambridge, 1830-34. 8°
22 A Catalogue of the maps and

charts in the Library of Harvard University in Cambridge, Maſsachuſetts. Cambridge, 1831. 8°

23 CATALOGUE of books belonging to the Society of Brothers in Unity; Yale College, Sept. 1832. [New Haven, 1832.] 8°

24 CATALOGUE of the Library of the State of Maryland. Dec. 1833. [By D. Ridgely.] Annapolis, 1833. 8°

25 A CATALOGUE of the Law Library of Harvard University, in Cambridge, Maſsachusetts. Cambridge, 1834. 8°

26 CATALOGUE of books in the library of the United Fraternity, Dartmouth College, April 1835. Windsor, Vt. [1835]. 8°

27 CATALOGUE of paintings [chiefly portraits] belonging to Yale College; deposited in the south room of the Trumbull Gallery. New Haven, 1835. 8°.

28 A SECOND Supplemental Catalogue, alphabetically arranged, of all the books, maps, and pamphlets, procured by the Charleston Library Society, since the publication of the first supplement in 1831, etc. Prepared by the Librarian. Charleston (S. Carolina), 1835. 8°

29 A CATALOGUE of the library of the State of Virginia, . . . to which are prefixed, the rules, etc. Richmond, 1835. 12°

30 A CATALOGUE of the books belonging to the Library Company of Philadelphia, with an account of the institution, charters, laws, and regulations. 2 vol. Philadelphia, 1835. 8vo.

31 CATALOGUE of a ſelect law library. [By S. Greenleaf.] Cambridge, 1836. 8°

32 CATALOGUE of the Library of the University of Vermont. Burlington, 1836. 8°

33 CATALOGUE of the Athenæum Library; with an appendix, containing the library regulations, and a list of the officers and proprietors. Providence, 1837. 8vo.

34 SYSTEMATIC Catalogue of books in the collection of the Mercantile Library Aſſociation of the city of New York. New York, 1837. 8°

35 A CATALOGUE of books in the library of the American Antiquarian Society, in Worcester, Maſsachusetts. Worcester, 1837. 8vo.

36 CATALOGUE of editions of the Holy Scriptures in various languages, and other biblical works, in the Library of the American Bible Society. New York, 1837. 8vo.

37 CATALOGUE of the books belonging to the Loganian Library: to which is prefixed a short account of the institution, with the law for annexing it to that belonging to "The Library Company of Philadelphia," and the rules of conducting the same. Philadelphia, 1837. 8°

38 CATALOGUE of the Library belonging to the Society of Brothers in Unity, Yale College, June, 1838. [MS. additions by Henry Stevens, the librarian.] New Haven, 1838. 8°

39 CATALOGUE of the Library of the Theological Seminary in Andover, Maſsachusetts. Andover, 1838. 8°

40 ALPHABETICAL and analytical Catalogue of the New York Society Library, with a brief historical notice of the Institution, the original articles of aſſociation in 1754, and the charter and laws of the Society. New York, 1838. 8°

41 ARTISTS' Fund Society of Philadelphia. Catalogue of the fourth annual exhibition, 1838. Philadelphia, 1838. 8°

42 FIRST Supplementary Catalogue of the Athenæum Library; with an appendix, etc. Providence, 1839. 8vo.

43 [Wǎn Tang Jin Wǔh] "Ten Thousand Chinese Things." A descriptive catalogue of the Chinese Collection in Philadelphia. With miscellaneous remarks upon the manners, customs, trade and government of the Celestial Empire. [By W. B. Langdon.] Philadelphia [1839]. 8vo.

44 SUPPLEMENTARY and analytic Catalogue of the New York Hospital Library, August, 1839. New York, 1839. 8°

45 A CATALOGUE of law books published and for sale by C. C. Little and J. Brown. Boston, 1840. 16mo.

46 CATALOGUE of the Library of the New Haven Young Men's Institute, with the charter, bye-laws, etc. New Haven, 1841, 8°

47 CATALOGUE of the Library of the New Haven Young Men's Institute. With the charter, bye-laws, etc. New Haven, 1841. 8°

48 CATALOGUE of the Library of the Calliopean Society, Yale College, October, 1841. New Haven, 1841. 8vo.

49 CATALOGUE of books in the Social Friends' Library, Dartmouth College, March 1841. Hanover, N. H. 1841. 8°

50 SUPPLEMENTARY Catalogue of the New York Society Library. New York, 1841. 8°

51 ANNUAL Catalogue of books published and for sale on the most favourable terms by A. V. Blake, No. 54, Gold, corner of Fulton Street, New York. No. 5. New York, 1842. 12mo.

52 A CATALOGUE of the Library of Brown University, in Providence, Rhode Island. Providence [Andover printed], 1843. 8vo.

53 CATALOGUE of the books belonging to the Company of the Redwood Library and Athenæum ; Newport, R. I. To which is prefixed a short account of the Institution, with the charter, laws and regulations. Providence, 1843. 8vo.

54 A CATALOGUE of the books of the Boston Library Society, in Franklin Place, January, 1844. Boston, 1844. 8°

55 CATALOGUE of the books of the Boston Library Society, Jan. 1844. Boston, 1844. 8°

56 CATALOGUE of the Mercantile

Library in New York. New York, 1844. 8°

57 CATALOGUE of the Medical Library of the Pennsylvania Hospital for the Insane, near Philadelphia. Philadelphia, 1844. 8°

58 CATALOGUE of the Library and Reading Room of the Young Men's Institute, Hartford. Hartford, 1844. 8°

59 GOULD, BANKS, and Co. Catalogue of ancient and modern law books, for sale by Gould, Banks and Co. New York, 1845. 12°

60 A CATALOGUE of the books belonging to the library of the New York Hospital, arranged alphabetically and analytically, and the regulations for the use of the same. New York, 1845. 8vo.

61 NEW and complete Catalogue of the books, Sunday School publications, and tracts, of the Methodist Episcopal Church, at reduced prices. 2 parts. New York, [1845?] 8°

62 CATALOGUE of the Philological, Classical and Law Library of the Hon. J. Pickering (sale catalogue). Boston, 1846. 8vo.

63 A CATALOGUE of the Law Library of Harvard University in Cambridge, Massachusetts. Fourth edition. Cambridge, 1846. 8°

64 A DESCRIPTIVE Catalogue of the Publications of the Massachusetts Sabbath School Society. Boston, 1846. 12mo.

65 CATALOGUE of the library of the Calliopean Society, Yale College, February, 1846. New Haven, 1846. 8vo.

66 CATALOGUE of the library of the Society of Brothers in Unity, Yale College. New Haven, 1846. 8vo.

67 A SUPPLEMENTARY Catalogue of books of the Mercantile Library Association of Boston. Together with the act of incorporation, bye-laws, and regulations ... and the Annual Report for 1845-6. May 1846. Boston, 1846. 8vo.

68 CATALOGUE of Congressional, law, medical, and miscellaneous works;

and of American and political history. By George Templeman. Washington, 1846. 12°

69 CATALOGUE of the New York State Library, Jan. 1, 1846. Prepared [by J. L. Tillinghast and G. Wood] and published in compliance with the provisions of an Act of the Legislature, etc. Albany, 1846. 8vo.

70 CATALOGUE of the library of the General Court. Boston, 1846. 8°

71 CATALOGUE of the Public School Library of Municipality, No. 2. New Orleans, 1848. 8°

72 CATALOGUE of books in the library of the Pawcattuck Library Association, Westerly, R. I.; with a sketch of the organization of the association, a copy of its constitution, and bye-laws, and hints respecting reading. Providence, 1849. 8°

73 THIRTY - SECOND Philadelphia Trade Sale. New Series. March, 1849. Catalogue of books, stereotype-plates, ... stationery, etc. to be sold ... by G. W. Lord, etc. Philadelphia, 1849. 8°

74 THIRTY - FOURTH Philadelphia Trade Sale. New Series. March 15, 1850. Catalogue of books, paper, stationery, etc. to be sold by G. W. Lord, etc. Philadelphia, 1850. 8°

75 THIRTY - FIFTH Philadelphia Trade Sale. New Series. August 30, 1850. Catalogue of books, ... stationery, etc. to be sold ... by G. W. Lord, etc. Philadelphia, 1850. 8°

76 FIRST Catalogue. Thirty-seventh Philadelphia Trade Sale. ... September 22, 1851. M. Thomas and Sons, auctioneers. Catalogue of books, copy-rights, etc. Philadelphia, 1851. 8°

77 FIRST Catalogue. Thirty-eighth Philadelphia Trade Sale, March, 1852. ... Catalogue of books, stereotype-plates, ... stationery, etc. to be sold at public sale. ... By M. Thomas and Sons. Philadelphia, 1852. 8°

78 G. W. LORD AND SON'S Thirty-eighth Philadelphia Trade Sale. New Series, March 15, 1852. Catalogue of books, stereotype-plates, binders'-tools, letter and cap paper. ... stationery, etc. to be sold at auction, etc. Philadelphia, 1852. 8°

79 JOHN KEESE, Auctioneer. September, 1851. Catalogue of books, paper, stationery, etc. New York, 1851. 8°

80 FIRST Catalogue. Catalogue of the Fifty-third New York Trade Sale of ... stationery, ... binders' materials, etc. to be sold at auction by Bangs, Brother and Co. etc. New York, 1851. 8°

81 FIRST Catalogue. Catalogue of the Fifty-fourth New York Trade-Sale of books, stereotype-plates, stationery, etc. to be sold at auction, ... by Bangs, Brother and Co. New York, 1851. 8°

82 CATALOGUE of the New York State Library. January 1, 1850. Albany, 1850. 8vo.

83 CATALOGUE of the Mercantile Library in New York. New York, 1850. 8°

84 A CATALOGUE of the Mercantile Library Company of Philadelphia. Philadelphia, 1850. 8°

85 CATALOGUE of foreign and American books; comprising . . . books in every class of literature, the fine arts, natural history, sciences, useful arts, etc. . . . for sale by G. P. Putnam. New York, [1851 ?] 8°

86 CATALOGUE of maps and surveys, in the offices of the Secretary of State, of the State Engineer and Surveyor, and in the New York State Library, etc. Albany, 1851. 8vo.

87 FIRST Supplement to the Catalogue of the Mercantile Library in the city of New York. January 1852. New York, 1852. 8°

88 CATALOGUE of books on the Masonic Institution, in public libraries of twenty-eight States of the Union, Antimasonic in arguments and conclusions, by ... citizens of the United States. With introductory remarks,

and a compilation of records, *etc.* Boston, 1852. 8vo.

89 CATALOGUE of the Mercantile Library of Boston. Boston, 1854. 8vo.

90 CATALOGUE of the ·Public Library of the City of Boston. Boston, 1854. 8vo.

91 CATALOGUE of books in the Astor Library relating to the languages and literature of Asia, Africa, and the Oceanic Islands. [With a preface by J. G. Cogswell.] New York, Astor Library Autographic Prefs, 1854. 8vo.

92 CATALOGUE of the New York State Library: 1855. General Library. Albany, 1856. 8°

93 CATALOGUE of the New York State Library: 1855. Law Library. Albany, 1856. 8°

94 CATALOGUE of the New York State Library: 1855. Manuscripts, maps, engravings, coins, *etc.* Albany, 1856. 8°

CATE, E. JANE. A Year with the Franklins; or, to suffer and be strong. New York, 1846. 12°

CATECHISM resolved into an easie and useful Method: wherein the Principles thereof are exhibited and explain'd in order, with inferences from and references to those Principles. Boston, 1723. 8vo.

CATECHIST; a Fragment. Philadelphia, 1827. 12mo.

CATHOLICUS. Letter [subscribed καθολικος] to .. A. Potter, .. Bishop of .. Pennsylvania, in vindication of the principle of Christian Union for the propagation of the Gospel. Philadelphia, 1850. 8°

CATO, DIONYSIUS. Cató's Moral Distichs Englished in couplets. Printed and sold by B. Franklin, Philadelphia, 1735. 4to.

CATULLUS, CAIUS VALERIUS. The Poems of Catullus, selected and prepared for the use of schools and

colleges. By F. M. Hubbard. Boston, 1836. 12°

CAULKINS, FRANCES MANWARING, *Mifs.* History of Norwich, Connecticut, from its settlement in 1660, to January, 1845. Norwich, Conn. 1845. 12°

2 COLPORTEUR Songs, written for the American Mefsenger. [New London? 1847?] 12mo.

3 HISTORY of New London, Connecticut, from the first survey of the coast in 1612, to 1852. New London, 1852. 8°

CAUSTIC, MRS. *Pfeud.* Matrimony; or, love affairs in our village twenty years ago. By Mrs. Caustic (authorefs of " Louisa Ralston; or, What can I do for the Heathen?") 2nd edition. N. York, 1853. 12°

CAUSTIC, CHRISTOPHER [THOMAS GREEN FESSENDEN]. Democracy Unveiled; or, Tyranny stripped of the garb of patriotism. [In verse.] By Christopher Caustic, LL.D. *etc.* Third edition. 2 vol. New York, 1806. 12mo.

CELNART, ELIZABETH FELICIE. Perfumery: its manufacture and use; with instructions in every branch of the art, and recipes ... from the French of Celnart and other late authorities; with additions and improvements, by C. Morfit. Philadelphia, 1847. 12°

CEYLON. Catalogue of pupils supported at Mifsion Schools (at Ceylon) by special donations. · [New York? 1838.] 8°

CHALLONER, RICHARD, *Bishop of Debras.* The Lives of the Fathers of the Eastern Deserts; or, the wonders of God in the wildernefs. [Edited by M. A. S.] To which is added an appendix [containing a collection of anecdotes of the Eastern solitaries]. New York, 1852. 12mo.

CHALMERS, GEORGE. An Introduction to the history of the Revolt of the American Colonies; being a comprehensive view of its origin, derived from the State Papers contained in the public offices of Great Britain. 2 vol. Boston, 1845. 8vo.

CHAMBERLAIN, Jason. An inaugural Oration [on the study of the Claßics] delivered at Burlington. Burlington, Vt. 1811. 8°

CHAMBERLAIN, William. An addreß delivered at Windsor, Vt. . . on the fiftieth anniversary of American Independence. Windsor, Vt. 1826. 8°

CHAMBERS, Joseph G. Elements of Orthography; or, an attempt to form a complete system of letters. Zanesville, Ohio, 1812. 8vo.

CHAMBERS, Robert. History of the English Language and Literature. To which is added, a history of American contributions to the English language and literature, by R. Robins. Hartford, 1837. 12mo.

CHAMBERS, William, and Robert. Chambers' Information for the People; a popular encyclopædia. First American edition, with numerous additions, etc. 2 vol. Philadelphia, 1848. 8°

CHANDLER, Adoniram. Addreß delivered at the close of the nineteenth annual fair of the American Institute. New York, 1846. 8°

CHANDLER, Peleg Whitmore. American Criminal Trials. 2 vol. Boston, 1841-1844. 12mo.

2 The Morals of Freedom: an Oration delivered before the authorities of . . . Boston, July 4, 1844. Boston, 1844. 8°

CHANDLER, Thomas Bradbury. An appeal to the public in behalf of the Church of England in America. New York, 1767. 8vo.

CHANG-ENG, the Siamese Twin

brothers. Begin. Introduction, etc. (Account of the Siamese Twin brothers.) [New York, 1836.] 8°

CHANNING, Edward Tyrrell. An Oration, delivered July 4, 1817, at . . Boston, in commemoration of the anniversary of American Independence. Boston [1817]. 8°

CHANNING, Walter. Thoughts on Peace and War: an addreß delivered before the American Peace Society, at its annual meeting, May 27, 1844. Boston, 1844. 8°

2 Cases of Inhalation of Ether in Labour. Second edition. Boston, 1847. 8vo.

3 A Treatise on Etherization in Childbirth. Illustrated by five hundred and eighty-one cases. Boston, 1848. 8°

CHANNING, William Ellery. A Sermon [on Matthew xvi. 3] preached in Boston, April 5, 1810, the day of the public fast. Boston, 1810. 8vo.

2 A Sermon [on Luke xix. 41, 42] preached in Boston, July 23, 1812, the day of the public fast, appointed by the Executive of the Commonwealth of Maßachusetts, in consequence of the declaration of war against Great Britain. Boston, 1812. 8vo.

3 A Discourse delivered in Boston at the solemn festival in commemoration of the goodneß of God in delivering the Christian world from military despotism, June 15, 1814. Boston, 1814. 8°

4 A Letter to S. C. Thacher, on the aspersions contained in a late number of the Panoplist on the ministers of Boston, etc. Second edition. Boston, 1815. 8°

5 Remarks on . . Dr. Worcester's letter to Mr. Channing, on the review of American Unitarianism in a late Panoplist. Boston, 1815. 8°

6 Remarks on . . Dr. Worcester's second letter to Mr. Channing on

American Unitarianism. Boston, 1815. 8°

7 A SERMON [on Isa. ii. 4] on War; delivered before the Convention of Congregational ministers of Maſſachusetts, May 30, 1816, etc. Boston, 1816. 12°

8 A SERMON [on 1 Theſſ. v. 21] delivered at the ordination of Jared Sparks, . . May 5, 1819. Eleventh edition. Boston, 1824. 12°

9 A DISCOURSE preached at the dedication of the second Congregational Unitarian Church, New York, December 7, 1826. New York, 1826. 8°

10 A REVIEW of . . Dr. Channing's Discourse preached at the dedication of the second Congregational Unitarian Church, New York, Dec. 7, 1826. Boston, 1827. 8°

11 N° 8. A DISCOURSE on the Evidences of revealed Religion. Third edition. Printed for the American Unitarian Aſſoc. Boston, 1826. 12°

12 A DISCOURSE [on Ephes. v. 1] delivered at the ordination of . . F. A. Farley, etc. Boston, 1828. 8°

13 A SERMON [on John viii. 31, 32, 36] preached at the annual Election, May 26, 1830, before . . L. Lincoln, Governor . . and the Legislature of Maſſachusetts. [Few MS. corrections.] Boston, 1830. 8°

14 DISCOURSES [with autograph of Channing]. Boston, 1832. 12°

15 THE FUTURE Life: a Sermon [on Ephes. i. 20] preached on Easter Sunday, 1834, etc. Boston, 1835. 8°

16 A SERMON [on James iv. 1] on War. . . . Second edition. Boston, 1835. 8°

17 SLAVERY. Boston, 1835. 12°

18 AN ADDRESS on Temperance. Boston, 1837. 8°

19 A LETTER to the Hon. Henry Clay, on the annexation of Texas to the United States . . Fifth edition. Boston, 1837. 12°

20 A TRIBUTE to the memory of the Rev. Noah Worcester; in a Discourse [on John xiii. 34], etc. Boston, 1837. 8°

21 SELF-CULTURE. An addreſs introductory to the Franklin lectures, delivered at Boston . . 1838. Boston, 1838. 8°

22 LECTURE on War. Boston, 1839. 8°

23 AN ADDRESS delivered before the Mercantile Library Company of Philadelphia, May 11, 1841. Philadelphia, 1841. 8°

24 EMANCIPATION. New York, 1841. 12°

25 THE DUTY of the Free States; or, remarks suggested by the case of the Creole. Boston, 1842. 12°

26 CONVERSATIONS in Rome, between an artist, a Catholic, and a critic. Boston, 1847. 16°

CHANNING, WILLIAM HENRY. The Gospel of To-Day; a discourse delivered at the ordination of T. W. Higginson, as minister of the first religious society in Newburyport, Maſſ. Sept. 15, 1847. . . Together with the charge, right hand of fellowship, and addreſs to the people. Boston, 1847. 8°

2 MEMOIR of William Ellery Channing, with extracts from his correspondence and manuscripts. 3 vol. Boston, 1848. 12°

CHAPIN, A. B. A Sermon in Christ Church, West Haven, Aug. 11, 1839, the hundredth anniversary of laying the foundation of the church. New Haven, 1839. 8vo.

2 ON the Study of the Celtic languages, etc. New York, 1840. 8°

CHAPIN, CALVIN. A Sermon [on Heb. xiii. 7, 8] delivered Jan. 14, 1817, at the funeral of the Rev. T. Dwight . . President of Yale College, etc. New Haven, 1817. 8°

CHAPIN, WILLIAM. Report on the benevolent institutions of Great Britain and Paris . . being supplementary to the ninth annual report of the Ohio Institution for the education of the blind. Columbus, 1846. 8°

CHAPMAN, DANIEL. Twenty

speeches and discourses on various subjects. London, Boston printed, 1855. 8vo.

CHAPMAN, George Thomas, D. D. Sermons to Presbyterians of all sects; supplementary to sermons upon the ministry, worship, and doctrines of the Protestant Episcopal church. Hartford, 1836. 8vo.

CHAPMAN, Isaac A. A Sketch of the history of Wyoming. To which is added an appendix, containing a statistical account of the valley and adjacent country. Wilkesbarre, Penn. 1830. 12mo.

CHAPMAN, J. G. The picture of the baptism of Pocahontas: painted by order of Congreſs, .. by J. G. Chapman. (Historical sketch and extracts from contemporary writers, relating to the subject of the picture.) Washington, 1840. 8°

CHAPMAN, John Ratcliffe. Instructions to young marksmen, in all that relates to the . . . improved American rifle. New York, 1848. 12°

CHAPMAN, Nathaniel. An Eſſay on the Canine state of Fever [Hydrophobia]. Philadel. 1801. 8vo.

2 Lectures on the more important eruptive Fevers, Hæmorrhages and Dropsies, and on Gout and Rheumatism. Philadelphia, 1844. 8vo.

3 Lectures on the more important diseases of the thoracic and abdominal viscera. Philadelphia, 1844. 8vo.

CHAPMAN, William. Facts and remarks relative to the Witham and the Welland, or . . . observations on their past and present state; on the means of improving the channel of the Witham and the Port of Boston, and on the impolicy of changing the course of the Welland: with an appendix containing remarks on the Bridge and Grand Sluice at Boston, and on Wainfleet Haven. Boston, 1800. 8vo.

CHAPTAL, Jean Antoine Claude, Count. Chymistry applied to agriculture. . . . With a preliminary chapter on the organization, structure, &c. of plants, by Sir H. Davy, and an eſſay on the use of lime as a manure, by M. Puvis; with introductory observations to the same by J. Renwick. Translated and edited by Rev. W. P. Page. New York, 1840. 12°

CHARGE delivered from the Bench to the Grand Inquest at a Court of Oyer and Terminer, and general Gaol Delivery held for the City and County of Philadelphia, April 13, 1736. B. Franklin, Philadelphia, 1736. 4to.

CHARLESTON. Port of Charles Town, in South Carolina, Nov. 1, 1736. An account of sundry goods, imported, and of sundry goods of the produce of this province exported, from 1724 to 1735. With the number of veſſels entered and cleared each year, and a particular account of the last year, etc. Charles Town, 1736. s. sh. fol.

2 An Account of sundry goods imported, and of sundry goods of the produce of this province exported, from several ports of Charles Town, George Town, and Port Royal, in South Carolina, from Nov. 1, 1736, to Nov. 1, 1737. With the number of veſſels entered and cleared in each port. Charles Town, 1737. s. sh. fol.

3 Port of Charles Town in South Carolina. An account of sundry goods imported, and of sundry goods of this province exported from this port, from Nov. 1, 1737, to Nov. 1, 1738. With the number of veſſels entered inwards, and from whence arrived, cleared outwards, and where bound. [Charles Town, 1738!] s. sh. fol.

CHARLESTON LIBRARY SOCIETY. The rules and bye-laws of the Charleston Library Society. Charleston, 1840. 8vo.

CHARLTON, ROBERT M. Reports of decisions made in the superior courts of the Eastern district of Georgia, [from Jan. 1811 to May 1837]. Savannah, 1838. 8°

CHASE, CARLTON, *Bishop of the Protestant Episcopal Church in New Hampshire.* The Faithful Saying. The sermon [on 1 Tim. i. 15] at the Consecration of J. M. Wainwright ... to the Episcopate, *etc.* New York, 1852. 8vo.

CHASE, HEBER. Treatise on the radical cure of Hernia by instruments. ... With numerous illustrations. Philadelphia, 1836. 8vo.

CHASE, LUCIEN B. History of the Polk Administration. New York, 1850. 8°

CHASE, PHILANDER, *Bishop of Ohio.* A Correspondence between Bishops Chase and M'Ilvaine. Detroit, 1834. 12mo.

2 BISHOP CHASE's Reminiscences: an autobiography. Second edition: comprising ... the author's life to A.D. 1847. With a portrait and four engravings. 2 vol. Boston, 1848. 8°

CHASE, PLINY E. The Elements of Arithmetic ... on the system of Pestalozzi. Part first. Philadelphia, 1844. 12°

2 THE Elements of Arithmetic; for schools and academies ... on the system of Pestalozzi. Part second. Philadelphia, 1844. 12°

3 KEY to the first and second parts of the Elements of Arithmetic. Philadelphia, 1845. 12°

CHASE, SALMON PORTLAND. Reclamation of fugitives from service: an argument, for the defendant, submitted to the supreme court of the United States, ... in the case of W. Jones *vs.* J. Vanzandt. Cincinnati, 1847. 8°

CHASE, SAMUEL. Articles of Impeachment exhibited against Samuel Chase, by the House of Representatives, *etc.* [Washington, 1805.] 8°

2 THE ANSWER and Pleas of Samuel Chase, one of the Associate Justices of the Supreme Court ... to the articles of impeachment exhibited against him ... by the House of Representatives of the United States, *etc.* Washington, 1805. 8°

3 EXHIBITS accompanying the answer and plea of Samuel Chase, *etc.* [Washington, 1805.] 8°

4 REPLICATION by the House of Representatives to the answer of Samuel Chase to the articles of impeachment, *etc.* [Washington, 1805.] 8°

5 REPORT of the Trial of the Hon. S. Chase before the High Court of Impeachment. Taken by E. Evans. Baltimore, 1805. 8vo.

CHASLES, VICTOR EUPHÉMON PHILARÈTE. Anglo-American Literature and Manners. New York, 1852. 12°

CHASSEBŒUF DE VOLNEY, CONSTANTIN FRANCOIS, *Count.* The Law of Nature, or Principles of Morality, deduced from the physical constitution of mankind and the universe [translated from the French]. Philadelphia, 1796. 12mo.

2 A VIEW of the soil and climate of the United States of America: with supplementary remarks upon Florida; on the French colonies .... and on the aboriginal tribes of America. Translated, with occasional remarks, by C. B. Brown. Philadelphia, 1804. 8°

CHAUDRON, SIMON. Funeral Oration of Brother George Washington, delivered January 1, 1800, in the French lodge, L'Amenité. *Fr. Engl.* Philadelphia, 1811. 8vo.

CHAUNCY, CHARLES. God's Mercy shewed to His People in giving them a Faithful Ministry and Schooles of Learning for the continual supplyes thereof. Delivered in a Sermon preached at Cambridg, the day after the Commencement, by

Charles Chauncy, B. D. President of Harvard Colledg in New - England. Published with some additions thereunto, at the request of diverse Honoured and much Respected friends, for publick benefit, as they judged. Printed by Samuel Green, at Cambridg in New - England. 1655. Small 8vo.

CHAUNCY, CHARLES, *D. D.* Seasonable thoughts on the state of Religion in New England . . . With a Preface, giving an account of the Antinomians, Familists and Libertines, who infected these Churches above an hundred years ago. Boston, 1743. 8vo.

2 ALL Nations of the Earth blessed in Christ, the Seed of Abraham. A Sermon [on Gen. xxiv. 18] preached at Boston at the Ordination of the Rev. Joseph Bowman to the ministry, more especially among the Mohawk Indians, . . . Aug. 31, 1762. Boston, 1762. 8°

3 A DISCOURSE [on Eccl. vii. 2] occasioned by the death of the Rev. Jonathan Mayhew, D. D. Boston, 1766. 8vo.

4 THE APPEAL to the Public answered, in behalf of the Non-Episcopal Churches in America; containing remarks on what Dr. T. B. Chandler has advanced on the four following points; The original and nature of the Episcopal office ; Reasons for sending Bishops to America ; The plan on which it is proposed to send them; and the objections against sending them. . . . Wherein the reasons for an American Episcopate are shown to be insufficient, *etc.* Boston, 1768. 8°

5 A REPLY to Dr. Chandler's Appeal defended : wherein his mistakes are rectified . . . and the objections against the planned American Episcopate shown to remain in full force, *etc.* [With an appendix.] Boston, 1770. 8°

6 CHRISTIAN love as exemplified

by the first Christian Church in their having all things in common, placed in its true . . . light : in a sermon . . . . from Acts iv. 32, *etc.* Boston, 1773. 8°

CHAUVENET, WILLIAM. A Treatise on Plane and Spherical Trigonometry. Second edition. Philadelphia, 1851. 8°

CHEESEMAN, LEWIS. Differences between Old and New School Presbyterians. . . . With an introductory chapter by J. C. Lord. Rochester [New York], 1848. 8°

CHEETHAM, JAMES. Nine letters on the subject of Aaron Burr's Political Defection, with an appendix. New York, 1803. 8°

2 THE LIFE of Thomas Paine. New York, 1809. 8vo.

CHEEVER, ABIJAH. History of a case of incisted dropsy ; with a dissection of the several cysts. Boston [1787]. 12mo.

CHEEVER, GEORGE BARRELL. God's Hand in America. . . With an essay [on patriotism] by the Rev. Dr. Skinner. Second edition. New York [printed] London, 1841. 12°

2 THE ELEMENTS of National Greatness : an address before the New England Society of New York, Dec. 22, 1842. N. York, 1843. 8°

3 THE HIERARCHICAL Despotism. Lectures on the mixture of civil and ecclesiastical power in the governments of the middle ages. In illustration of the nature and progress of despotism in the Romish Church. New York, 1844. 12°

4 LECTURES on the Pilgrim's Progress, and on the life and times of J. Bunyan. New York, 1844. 8vo.

5 THE PILGRIM in the shadow of the Jungfrau Alp. Part 2 [*part* 1 *wanting*]. London [N. York printed], 1846. 8vo.

6 THE JOURNAL of the Pilgrims at

Plymouth, in New England, in 1620;
reprinted from the original volume;
with historical and local illustrations
of providences, principles, and persons, by G. B. Cheever. New York,
1848. 8vo.

CHEEVER, HENRY T. The Is-
land World of the Pacific: being the
personal narrative and results of
travel through the Sandwich or Hawaiian Islands, and other parts of
Polynesia. New York, 1851. 12°
2 LIFE in the Sandwich Islands;
or, the heart of the Pacific, as it was
and is. . . With engravings. New
York, 1851. 12°
3 A REEL in a Bottle, for Jack in
the Doldrums; being the adventures
of two of the King's seamen in a
voyage to the celestial country.
Edited from the manuscripts of an
old salt. Second edition. New York,
1852. 12°
4 VOICES of Nature to her foster-
child the Soul of Man: a series of
analogies between the natural and
spiritual world. By the author of
" A Reel in a Bottle." Edited by
Rev. Henry T. Cheever. New York,
1852. 12°

CHELSEA, MASSACHUSETTS. Report of the School Committee, 1841
(1844, 1845, 1846). 4 parts. Chelsea, 1841-46. 8°

CHENEY, MRS. H. V. A Peep
at the Pilgrims in Sixteen hundred
thirty-six. A Tale of olden times.
Boston, 1850. 12°

CHEROKEE ALMANAC. Che-
rokee Almanac [partly in Cherokee
and partly in English]. 1845, 1846.
Park Hill Miſſion Preſs [1844-45].
12°

CHEROKEE ALPHABET. Che-
rokee Alphabet. Cherokee Baptist
Miſſion Preſs [Cherokee, 1845?] s.
sh. fol°

CHEROKEE CLAIMS. A Vin-
dication of the Cherokee Claims, ad-

dreſſed to the town meeting in Philadelphia, . . 11 Jan. 1830. [Phila-
delphia, 1830.] 8°

CHEROKEE HYMNS. Chero-
kee Hymns. Compiled from several
authors and revised. Seventh edition.
Park Hill Miſſion Preſs, 1844. 12°

CHEROKEE MESSENGER.
Edited by E. Jones. Jan. 1845. Vol. 1.
N° 4. [In the Cherokee language.]
Baptist Miſſion Preſs. Cherokee,
1845. 8°

CHEROKEE NATION. Laws
of the Cherokee Nation, adopted by
the Council at various periods. Knoxville, 1826. 12°
2 THE CASE of the Cherokee Nation against the State of Georgia;
argued and determined at the Supreme Court of the United States,
Jan. term, 1831. With an appendix,
etc. [Reported] by R. Peters. [With
a MS. letter by the Reporter.] Philadelphia, 1831. 8°
3 THE CONSTITUTION and Laws of
the Cherokee Nation: paſſed at Tah-
le-quah, 1839. Washing. 1840. 12°
4 THE CONSTITUTION and Laws of
the Cherokee Nation: paſſed at Tah-
le-quah, Cherokee Nation, 1839,
[1840 to 1844]. Washington, 1840-
44. 8°
5 LAWS of the Cherokee Nation,
paſſed at Tahlequah . . 1844-5.
Tahlequah, 1845. 12°
6 A FAITHFUL History of the Cherokee tribe of Indians, from the period of our firſt intercourse with them
down to the present time; . . with a
full exposition of . . their . . division
into three parties . . and of the nature
and extent of their present claims.
(The Commiſſioners' Report.) Washington, 1846. 8°

CHERRY VALLEY. The cen-
tennial celebration at Cherry Valley,
Otsego Co. N. Y. July 4th, 1840:
the addreſſes of W. W. Campbell,
and Gov. W. H. Seward; with letters,
toasts, etc. New York, 1840. 12°

CHESAPEAKE, *the United States frigate.* Peace without Dishonour —War without Hope: being a calm and dispaſsionate enquiry into the question of the Chesapeake, and the neceſsity and expediency of war. By a Yankee farmer. Boston, 1807. 8°

CHESAPEAKE AND DELAWARE CANAL COMPANY. [*Begins*] Observations respecting the Chesapeake and Delaware Canal. First (second; fifth, June 7, 1824; and ninth, 1828) General Report of the President and Directors of the Chesapeake and Delaware Canal Company. 4 Parts [*Part 1 wanting all before p.* 9]. [Philadelphia, 1805-28.] 8°

CHESAPEAKE AND OHIO CANAL COMPANY. Rules adopted by the President and Directors of the Chesapeake and Ohio Canal Company, for the government of the corps of Engineers. Washington, 1828. 8°
2 REPORTS and letters from [A. Cruger, N. S. Roberts, *etc.*] the Engineers employed in the revised location of the western section of the Chesapeake and Ohio Canal; with the estimates of the cost of the same. [Georgetown? 1829.] 8°
3 REGULATIONS for navigating the Chesapeake and Ohio Canal; Rules for the collection of tolls, *etc. etc.* Washington, 1831. 8°
4 REPORT of the probable revenue of the Chesapeake and Ohio Canal, made to the Baltimore Convention, Dec. 1834. [Baltimore, 1834.] 12°
5 MEMORIAL of a Committee of the Chesapeake and Ohio Canal Company to the Legislature of Maryland [with respect to an alleged misapplication of the funds of the Company]. [Annapolis? 1836.] 8°
6 REPORT of the general Committee of the Stockholders, *etc.* Washington, 1837. 8°

CHESEBRO', MISS CAROLINE. Dream-Land by Daylight. A Panorama of Romance. [Edited by

Mrs. E. F. Ellett.] Second edition. New York, 1852. 12°
2 ISA, a Pilgrimage. New York, 1852. 12°
3 THE CHILDREN of Light. A theme for the time. New York, 1853. 12°

CHESSMAN, DANIEL. A compendium of English Grammar... Third edition, corrected. Hallowell, 1821. 16°

CHESTER COUNTY CABINET OF NATURAL SCIENCE. Fourth Report. West Chester, Penn. 1831. 12mo.

CHEVALIER, MICHAEL. Society, Manners, and Politics in the United States; being a series of letters on North America. Translated from the third Paris edition [by T. G. Bradford]. Boston, 1839. 8vo.
2 MEXICO before and after the conquest. . . . . Translated from the French, by F. Robinson. Philadelphia, 1846. 8°

CHEVES, LANGDON. Cases at Law, argued and determined in the Court of Appeals of South Carolina. Vol. I. Nov. 1839 to May, 1840, both inclusive. Columbia, 1840. 8°

CHICKERING, JESSE. A Statistical View of the Population of Maſsachusetts from 1765 to 1840. Boston, 1846. 8°

CHICKERING, JOSEPH. A Sermon [on Ephes. i. 10] preached . . . before the American Society for Educating Pious Youth for the Gospel Ministry. Dedham, 1817. 8°

CHILD, DAVID LEE. Report of the case of alleged contempt and breach of the privileges of the House of Representatives of Maſsachusetts, tried before said House, on complaint of W. B. Calhoun, Speaker, against D. L. Child, a member; with notes by the latter. Boston, 1832. 8°

CHILD, MRS. LYDIA MARIA. An appeal in favour of that claſs of

Americans called Africans. Boston, 1833. 12°

2 AUTHENTIC anecdotes of American Slavery. Second edition, enlarged. Newburyport, 1838. 12°

3 ANTI-SLAVERY Catechism. Second edition. Newburyport, 1839. 12°

4 THE EVILS of Slavery, and the Cure of Slavery. The first proved by the opinions of Southerners themselves; the last shown by historical evidence. Second edition. Newburyport, 1839. 12°

5 LETTERS from New York. Second series. London, N. York, 1845. 12mo.

6 PHILOTHEA: a Grecian romance. A new and corrected edition. New York and Boston, 1845. 12°

7 BIOGRAPHIES of Good Wives .. Third edition, revised. New York, 1847. 12°

8 BRIEF History of the Condition of Women, in various ages and nations . . . revised and corrected . . . Fifth edit. 2 vol. New York, 1849. 12°

9 THE AMERICAN frugal Housewife. Thirty-second edition enlarged and corrected by the author. New York, 1850. 12°

CHILD OF PALLAS: devoted mostly to the Belles-Lettres. By C. Prentiss. Nº 1-8. Baltimore, 1800. 12°

CHILDREN. Children fifty years ago. Boston, 1853. 12°

CHILD'S (THE) ARITHMETIC, in which its most easy and simple rules and elements are brought down to the level of his comprehension. Stereotype edit. Washington, 1834. 12°

CHILD'S (THE) FIRST BOOK; being an easy introduction to spelling and reading. By the compiler of the Beauties of the Children's Friend. Boston, 1816. 12°

CHILD'S (THE) PAPER. . . . Published [monthly] by the American Tract Society. Vol. 1-4. New York, Boston, Philadelphia, 1852-56. Folº

CHINESE TREATISES. Summary of the principal Chinese Treatises upon the culture of the mulberry and the rearing of silkworms. Translated from the Chinese [by Stanislas Julien; with an introduction by C. Beauvais]. Washington, 1838. 8vo.

CHIPMAN, DANIEL. An Essay on the Law of Contracts, for the payment of specific articles. Middlebury, Vt. 1822. 8°

2 REPORTS of Cases argued and determined in the Supreme Court of the State of Vermont [Dec. 1789 to Feb. 1824]. Vol. 1. Middlebury, 1824. 8°

CHIPMAN, NATHANIEL. Sketches of the Principles of Government. Rutland, 1793. 12°

2 PRINCIPLES of Government: a treatise on free institutions, including the Constitution of the United States. Burlington, 1833. 8vo.

CHISHOLM, ALEXANDER. A case (A. Chisholm v. The State of Georgia) decided in the Supreme Court of the United States, in Feb. 1793; in which is discussed the question, "Whether a State be liable to be sued by a private citizen of another State?" Philadelphia, 1793. 8°

CHITTY, JOSEPH. A practical Treatise on the Criminal Law . . . Fourth American from the second . . . London edition, corrected and enlarged by the author. With notes and corrections by R. Peters and T. Huntington. To which are now added, notes and references to the cases decided in . . . the United States, ... as well as to the late English decisions, by J. C. Perkins. 3 vol. Springfield, 1841. 8°

CHIVERS, THOMAS H. Virginalia; or, songs of my summer nights, etc. Philadelphia, 1853. 12°

CHOATE, RUFUS. Speech . . . . on the case of A. McLeod, delivered in the Senate . . . June 11, 1841. Washington, 1841. 8°

2 SPEECH . . on the power and duty of Congreſs to continue the policy of protecting American Labour: delivered in the Senate . . . March 14, 1842. Washington, 1842. 8°

3 ABSTRACT of the arguments of R. Choate and C. T. Ruſſell for the petitioners . . for a railroad from Salem to Malden, before the Committee on Railways and Canals of the Maſſachusetts Legislature, Seſſion 1846. Boston, 1846. 8°

CHOCTAW INSTRUCTOR. Chahta Ikhananchi, or the Choctaw Instructor: containing a brief summary of Old Testament history and biography; with practical reflections, in the Choctaw language. By a Miſſionary. Utica, 1831. 12°

CHOULES, JOHN OVERTON, and SMITH, THOMAS. The Origin and History of Miſſions: a record of. the voyages, travels, labours, and succeſſes of the Miſſionaries sent forth by Protestant Societies to evangelize the heathen; compiled from authentic documents. Sixth edition. 2 vol. Boston, 1842. 4to.

2 YOUNG Americans abroad; or vacation in 'Europe: travels in England, France, Holland, Belgium, Pruſſia and Switzerland. Boston, 1852. 12°

CHRISTIAN ADVOCATE: being a continuation of the Presbyterian Magazine. Conducted by A. Green, D.D. Vol. 1-10. 1823-32. Philadelphia, 1823-32. 8°

CHRISTIAN ALLIANCE; its Constitution, List of Officers, and Addreſſ. [MS. note by T. H. Horne.] New York, 1843. 8°

2 THE CHRISTIAN Alliance Addreſſes of Rev. L. Bacon and Rev. E. N. Kirk, at the annual meeting . . . . . . with the addreſſ of the Society, and the bull [i. e. encyclical letter] of the Pope [Gregory XVI] against it [translated by Sir C. E. Smith]. New York, 1845. 8°

CHRISTIAN BALLADS. [By C. i. e. Arthur Cleaveland Coxe.] New York, 1840. 12°

CHRISTIAN BAPTIST. Edited by A. Campbell. . Revised by D. S. Burnet, from the second edition. 7 vols in 1. Cincinnati, 1835. 8°

CHRISTIAN DENOMINATION. An addreſſ to slaveholders, buyers and sellers, of every Christian Denomination. [Washington ? 1835.] 8°

CHRISTIAN DISCIPLE, 1813-18. 6 vol. [Continued as] The Christian Disciple and Theological Review; New Series, 1819-23. 5 vol. [Continued as] The Christian Examiner and Theological Review; 1824-28; vol. 1-5. [Continued as] The Christian Examiner and General Review; vol. 6-18; (New Series, vol. 1-13) 1829-35. Vol. 19-35. (Third Series, vol. 1-17) 1836-44. [Then united with the Monthly Miscellany and continued as] The Christian Examiner and Religious Miscellany; vol. 36-55 (Fourth Series. Vol. 1-26) 1844-56. Boston, 1813-56. 8°

2 A REPLY to the Review of Dr. Wyatt's Sermon and Mr. Sparks's Letters on the Protestant Episcopal Church, which originally appeared in the Christian Disciple at Boston, . . . in which it is attempted to vindicate the Church from the charges of that Review. By a Protestant Episcopalian. Boston, 1821. 8°

CHRISTIAN EXAMINER. See CHRISTIAN DISCIPLE.

CHRISTIAN HISTORY, containing accounts of the revival and propagation of religion in Great Britain and America for 1743 (1744). 2 vol. Boston, 1744-45. 8vo.

CHRISTIAN HISTORY. Scenes from Christian History. Boston, 1852. 12°

CHRISTIAN INQUIRER, devoted to the support of free inquiry,

religious liberty, and rational Christianity. New series. Vol. 1-2. New York, 1826. 8°

CHRISTIAN JOURNAL, and Literary Register. 14 vol. New York, 1817-30. 8°

CHRISTIAN PILGRIM; containing an account of the wonderful adventures and miraculous escapes of a Christian. [Abridged from the Pilgrim's Progress of J. Bunyan.] Philadelphia, 1829. 12°

CHRISTIAN REVIEW. Vol. 1-2, edited by J. D. Knowles; vol. 3, edited by J. D. Knowles and B. Sears; vol. 4-6, edited by B. Sears; vol. 7-13, edited by S. F. Smith; vol. 14, edited by E. G. Sears. Vol. 1-14, March, 1836—Dec. 1849. Boston, 1836-49. 8°. Vol. 15-17, S. S. Cutting, editor, assisted by W. Gammell, etc. Vol. 18-20, edited by R. Turnbull and J. N. Murdock. Vol. 21, editors, J. J. Woolsey, W. C. Ulyat. Assistant editors, R. Turnbull, J. N. Murdock, H. B. Hackett, J. J. Lincoln, W. R. Williams. Vol. 15-22, Jan. 1850—Dec. 1856. New York, 1850-56. 8°

CHRISTIANITY. Another Tongue brought in to confess the great Saviour of the World; or, some communications of Christianity put into a tongue used among the Iroquois Indians in America, and put into the hands of the English and Dutch traders... [A catechism.] Iroquois, Latin, English, Dutch. Boston, 1707. 8vo.

CHRISTIANS. History of the first Christians. Philadelphia, 1832. 12mo.

2 THE LAST Command; or, duty of Christians to the unevangelized world. Boston, 1834. 12mo.

CHRISTIAN'S, SCHOLAR'S, AND FARMER'S MAGAZINE, etc. By a number of gentlemen. April, 1789—March, 1791. 2 vol. Elizabethtown, 1789-91. 8°

CHRISTIE, ROBERT. The Military and Naval Operations in the Canadas during the late War with the United States; including also the political history of Lower Canada during the administration of Sir J. H. Craig and Sir G. Prevost, from . . 1807 until . . 1815. Quebec printed; New York reprinted, 1818. 12°

CHRISTY, DAVID. The Chemistry of Agriculture; or, the earth and atmosphere as related to vegetable and animal life. With new and extensive analytical tables. Cincinnati, 1852. 8vo.

CHRISTY, WILLIAM. Brief or argument of W. Christy, attorney of the appellee, in the case of Paterson vs. Gaines [arising out of the will of D. Clark] on appeal to the Supreme Court of the United States, etc. New Orleans, 1841. 8°

CHRONOLOGY; or, an Introduction and Index to Universal History, Biography, and Useful Knowledge. To which are added Valpy's Poetical Retrospect, Literary Chronology, and the latest statistical views of the world. With a Chart of History. [By G. P. Putnam.] New York, 1833. 12°

CHUBBUCK, afterwards JUDSON, EMILY C. Allen Lucas, the self-made Man. [A tale.] New York, 1847. 12°

2 THE GREAT Secret; or, how to be happy. [A tale.] Revised edition. New York, 1847. 12°

3 AN OLIO of domestic verses. New York, 1852. 12°

4 THE KATHAYAN Slave, and other papers connected with Missionary Life. Boston, 1853. 8vo.

CHURCH, ALBERT E. Elements of the differential and integral Calculus... Improved edition, containing the elements of the calculus of variations. New York, 1850. 8°

2 ELEMENTS of analytical Geometry. New York, 1851. 8°

CHURCH, BENJAMIN. An Oration, delivered March 5, 1773, at . . Boston, to commemorate the bloody tragedy of the 5th March, 1770. Boston, 1773. 4°

CHURCH, EDWARD. Notice on the Beet Sugar. Preceded by a few remarks on the origin and present state of the indigenous sugar manufactories of France. Translated from Dubrunfaut, De Domballe, etc. Northampton, 1837. 12mo.

CHURCH, JOHN. An inaugural differtation on Camphor. Philadelphia, 1797. 8°

CHURCH, JOHN HUBBARD. The First Settlement of New England: a sermon [on Psal. cv. 44. 45] delivered . . April 5. 1810, being the annual fast in Maffachusetts. Sutton, Maſs. 1810. 12°

2 A SERMON [on 2 Chron. xv. 2] preached . . before . . the Governor, . . Council, . . Senate, and House of Representatives of . . New Hampshire, June 3, . . being the anniversary Election. Concord, 1813. 8°

CHURCH, PHARCELLUS. Antioch; or, increase of moral power in the Church of Christ. . . With an introductory eſſay by the Rev. B. Stow. Boston, 1843. 12°

CHURCH, RODNEY SMITH. A digested Index of the Reports of the Supreme Court, and the Court for the Correction of Errors in the State of New York; including Coleman's Cases, Caines's Cases, 2 vol; Caines's Reports, 3 vol; Johnson's Cases, 3 vol; Johnson's Reports, 18 vol, and the 1st part of the 19th vol; Anthon's Nisi Prius. 2 vol. N. York, 1822. 8°

CHURCH, THOMAS. The entertaining History of King Philip's War, which began in . . 1675. As also of

expeditions more lately made against the common enemy and Indian rebels in the eastern parts of New England ; with some account of the Divine Providence towards Col. B. Church. Second edition. Newport, Rhode Island, 1772. 8vo.

2 THE HISTORY of Philip's War, commonly called the great Indian war, of 1675 and 1676; also of the French and Indian wars at the Eastward . . 1689-1704. . . With numerous notes . . and . . an appendix . . by S. G. Drake. Second edition. Exeter, N. H. 1829. 12°

CHURCH ALMANAC for the year of our Lord, 1844. New York [1843]. 12°

CHURCH REVIEW AND ECCLESIASTICAL REGISTER [Quarterly, Episcopalian]. 9 vol. New Haven, 1848-56. 8°

CHURCHILL, RUTH. Ruth Churchill; or, the true Protestant. A tale for the times. By a lady of Virginia. New York, 1851. 12°

CHURCHMAN, JOHN. An Explanation of the Magnetic Atlas or variation chart, projected on a plan entirely new. Philadel. 1790. 8vo.

2 THE MAGNETIC Atlas, or variation charts of the whole terraqueous globe; comprising a system of the variation and dip of the needle, by which the observations being truly made, the longitude may be ascertained. Third edition. New York, 1800. 4to.

CHURCHMAN'S ALMANAC for 1832. . . Calculated for the meridian of New York, by D. Young. With a table of the rising and setting of the sun, . . for Boston, Philadelphia, and Washington, by F. R. Haſſler. New York, 1832. 12mo.

CICERO, MARCUS TULLIUS. Marcus Tullius Cicero's Cato Major, or his discourse of Old Age; with explanatory notes [by J. Logan, the

translator; and a prefatory notice by
B. Franklin]. B. Franklin, Philadelphia, 1744. 4°

2 MARCI Tullii Ciceronis Opera
Omnia ex recensione noviſſima J. A.
Ernesti, cum eiusdem notis, et clave
Ciceroniana. Editio prima Ameri-
cana. 20 vol. Bostoniæ, 1815-16.
12°

3 THE REPUBLIC of Cicero, translated from the Latin, and accompanied with a critical and historical introduction. By G. W. Featherstonhaugh. New York, 1829. 12°

4 THE TUSCULAN Questions of
Marcus Tullius Cicero. In five books.
Translated by G. A. Otis. Boston,
1839. 12mo.

5 MARCI Tullii Ciceronis ad Quin-
tum Fratrem Dialogi tres de Oratore.
Cum excerptis ex notis variorum.
Editio tertia [by J. L. Kingsley].
Novi-Portus, 1839. 12°

6 SELECT Orations of Cicero. With
English notes, critical and explanatory, and historical, geographical, and
legal indexes, by C. Anthon. A new
edition, with improvements. New
York, 1845. 12°

7 THE DE SENECTUTE, De Amicitia,
Paradoxa, and Somnium Scipionis of
Cicero; and the life of Atticus, by
C. Nepos; with English notes, criti-
cal and explanatory; by C. Anthon.
New York, 1848. 12°

8 CICERO's Tusculan Disputations;
with English notes, critical and explanatory, by C. Anthon. New York,
1852. 8°

CINCINNATI. Report of the
Committee appointed by the citizens
of Cincinnati . . to inquire into the
causes of the explosion of the [steam-
boat] Moselle, etc. Cincin. 1838. 8°

2 PICTURE of Cincinnati. The
Cincinnati Almanack for 1839 (1840).
Cincinnati [1838-39]. 12°

3 THE CINCINNATI Almanack for
the year 1846; being a complete
picture of Cincinnati and its environs,
accompanied by a .. plan of the city.
First edition. Cincinnati, 1846. 12°

4 TWENTY-FIRST Annual Report of
the Board of Directors of the Young
Men's Mercantile Library Aſsociation
of Cincinnati. Cincin. 1856. 8vo.

CINCINNATI DAILY WHIG.
New series. Vol. 1, Nº 53. May 27,
1839. Cincinnati, 1839. Fol.

CINCINNATI DIRECTORY,
1834. Cincinnati, 1834. 12°

2 THE CINCINNATI Directory for
the years 1836-7. Cincin. 1836. 12°

3 THE CINCINNATI, Covington,
Newport and Fulton Directory, for
1840. By D. H. Shaffer. Cincinnati [1840]. 8°

4 THE CINCINNATI Directory for
. . 1842. C. Cist, compiler. Cincinnati [1842]. 12°

5 THE CINCINNATI Buſineſs Di-
rectory for 1844. As also, the City
Directory, with a supplement. 3 pts.
Cincinnati, 1844. 12mo.

6 ROBINSON and Jones' Cincinnati
Directory for 1846. .. First annual
issue. Cincinnati, 1846. 8°

CINCINNATI WEEKLY WHIG.
June 26, 1839. Cincin. 1839. Fol.

CINCINNATUS. A reply [signed
Cincinnatus] to A. Hamilton's Letter,
concerning the public conduct and
character of J. Adams, President of
the United States. By a Federal
Republican. New York, 1800. 8vo.

CIST, CHARLES. Cincinnati in
1841; its early Annals and future
Prospects. Cincinnati, 1841. 12°

2 SKETCHES and Statistics of Cincinnati in 1851. Cincin. 1851. 8°

CITY CHARACTERS; or, familiar scenes in town. . . With .. designs. Philadelphia, 1851. 16°

CLAESSE, LAWRENCE. The
Morning and Evening Prayer, the
Litany, Church Catechism, Family
Prayers, and Several Chapters of the
Old and New Testament, Translated
into the Mahaque Indian Language,
by Lawrence Claeſſe, Interpreter to
William Andrews, Miſſionary to the
Indians, from the Honourable and

Reverend the Society for the Propagation of the Gospel in Foreign Parts. Ask of me, and I will give thee the Heathen for thine Inheritance, and the Utmost Parts of the Earth for thy Poſſeſſion. Psalm ii. 8. Printed by William Bradford, in New York, 1715. [*The title in Mobawk.*] Ne Orhoengene neoni Yogaraskhagh Yondereanayendaghkwa, ne Ene Niyoh Raodeweyena, Onoghsadogeaghtige Yondadderighwanondoentha, Siyagonnoghsode Enyondereanayendaghkwagge, Yotkade Kapitelhogough ne Karighwadaghkweagh Agayea neoni Ase Testament, neoni Niyadegariwagge, ne Kanninggahaga Siniyewenoteagh. Tehoenwenadenyough Lawrence Claeſſe, Rowenagaradatsk William Andrews, Ronwanhaugh Ongwehoenwighne Rodirighhoeni Raddiyadanorough neoni Ahoenwadigonuyosthagge Thoderighwawaakhogk ne Wahooni Agarighhowanha Niyoh Raodeweyena Niyadegoghwhenjage. Eghtseraggwas Eghtjeeagh ne ongwehoonwe, neoni ne siyodoghwhenjooktannighhoegh etho ahadyeandough. 115 *pp.* 4to.

CLAGGETT, Rufus. The American Expositor, or intellectual definer. .. Second edition. Boston, 1836. 16°

CLAP, Thomas. A Letter from the Rev. Mr. Clap .. to the Rev. Mr. Edwards, of North-hampton, expostulating with him for his injurious reflections in his late Letter to a Friend, *etc.* Boston, 1745. 8°

2 The Annals or History of Yale College, in New Haven, in the Colony of Connecticut, from the first founding thereof, in the year 1700, to the year 1766: with an appendix, containing the present state of the College, the method of instruction and government, with the officers, benefactors, and graduates. By Thomas Clap, A. M. President of the said College. New Haven: Printed for John Hotchkiſs and B. Mecom. 1766. 8vo.

3 The Religious Constitution of Colleges, especially of Yale College, in New Haven, in the colony of Connecticut. New London, 1754. 4°

CLARK, Aaron. List of all the Incorporations in the State of New York, except religious Incorporations, with a recital of all their important particulars and peculiarities. Reported to the Aſſembly, pursuant to a resolution thereof. By A. Clark. Albany, 1819. Fol°

CLARK, Davis W. Elements of Algebra; embracing also the theory and application of logarithms; together with an appendix, containing infinite series, the general theory of equations, and the most approved methods of resolving the higher equations. New York, 1843. 8°

CLARK, Daniel Atkinson. The complete Works of the Rev. Daniel Atkinson Clark, edited by J. H. Clark; with a biographical sketch, and estimate of his powers as a preacher, by G. Shepard. (With introduction by W. Patton.) 2 vol. N. York, 1846. 8°

CLARK, John A. Glimpses of the Old World; or, excursions on the continent, and in the island of Great Britain. 2 vol. Philadelphia, 1840. 8°

CLARK, Joseph. An Oration delivered at Rochester [in New Hampshire] on the 4th July, 1794 (in commemoration of American Independence). Dover, 1794. 8°

CLARK, Joseph G. Lights and Shadows of Sailor Life, as exemplified in fifteen years' experience, including the more thrilling events of the United States Exploring Expedition, and reminiscences of an eventful life on the " Mountain Wave." Boston, 1848. 12°

CLARK, Joshua V. H. Onondaga; or, reminiscences of earlier and later times; being a series of historical sketches relative to Onondaga; with notes on the several towns in the county, and Oswego. 2 vol. Syracuse, N. Y. 1849. 8°

CLARK, LEWIS GAYLORD. Knick-
+ knacks from an Editor's Table. New York, 1853. 12°

CLARK, LINCOLN. An Eulogy upon the Life, Character, and Death of Gen. Andrew Jackson, delivered .. before the societies and citizens of Tuscaloosa, etc. Tuscaloosa, 1845. 8°

CLARK, O. An Addreſs delivered before the Cadets of Norwich University at their annual commencement, etc. Hanover, 1842. 8°

CLARK, PETER. A defence of the Divine Right of Infant Baptism... Being in reply to Dr. J. Gill's book, intitled, The Divine Right of Infant Baptism examined and disproved. And in vindication of .. J. Dickinson's brief illustration and confirmation of the Divine Right of Infant Baptism. Boston, 1752. 8vo.

CLARK, RUFUS W. A Review of the Rev. M. Stuart's Pamphlet on Slavery, entitled Conscience and the Constitution. Originally published in the Boston Daily Atlas. Boston, 1850. 12°

2 A MEMOIR of the Rev. J. E. Emerson... With extracts from his writings. Boston, 1852. 8°

3 FIFTY Arguments in favour of sustaining and enforcing the Maſſachusetts Anti-Liquor Law. Boston, 1853. 12mo.

4 HEAVEN and its Scriptural Emblems. Boston, 1853. 8°

CLARK, SCHUYLER. The American Linguist, or natural grammar, etc. Providence, 1830. 12°

CLARK, THOMAS. Naval History of the United States, from the commencement of the Revolutionary War to the present time. 2 vol. Philadelphia, 1814. 12°

2 NAVAL History of the United States, from the commencement of

the Revolutionary War to the present time. Second edition. 2 vol. Philadelphia, 1814. 12°

CLARKE, CHARLES L. Reports of Chancery Cases decided in the Eighth Circuit of the State of New York, by the Hon. F. Whittlesey, Vice Chancellor. Vol. 1. Rochester, 1841. 8°

CLARKE, FRANCIS L. The Life of the .. Marquis .. of Wellington, .. The first part by Francis L. Clarke. The second part, from the attack on the Castle of Burgos to the taking of Bordeaux, by W. Dunlap. Hartford, 1814. 8°

CLARKE, JAMES FREEMAN. Eleven Weeks in Europe; and what may be seen in that Time. Boston, 1852. 8°

2 THE CHRISTIAN Doctrine of Forgiveneſs of Sin; an eſſay. Boston, 1852. 12°

CLARKE, MATTHEW SAINT CLAIR, and HALL, D. A. Legislative and documentary History of the Bank of the United States; including the original Bank of North America. Compiled by Matthew Saint Clair Clarke, and D. A. Hall. Washington, 1832. 8°

2 CASES of contested Elections in Congreſs, from the year 1789 to 1834, inclusive. Compiled by Matthew Saint Clair Clarke and David A. Hall. Printed by order of the House of Representatives. Wash. 1834. 8°

CLARKE, afterwards LIPPINCOTT, SARA JANE, Mrs. Greenwood Leaves. A collection of sketches and letters. Third edition. By Grace Greenwood. Boston, 1851. 12°

2 HISTORY of my Pets. By Grace Greenwood. Boston, 1851. 16°

3 POEMS by Grace Greenwood. Boston, 1851. 16°

4 RECOLLECTIONS of my Childhood, and other stories. By Grace Greenwood. With engravings. Boston, 1852. 12°

CLASS BOOK. The general Claſs Book, or interesting leſſons in

prose and verse. . . By the author of
the Franklin Primer and the improved
Reader. Greenfield, 1828. 12°

2 THE GENERAL Claſs Book, or
interesting leſsons in prose and verse
on a great variety of subjeĉts, etc.
Twenty-first edition.   Greenfield,
Boston, and New York, 1842. 12°

CLAY, HENRY. To the people of
the Congreſsional diſtriĉt, composed
of the counties of Fayette, Woodford,
and Clarke, in Kentucky [in relation
to the Presidential Election, etc.]
[Washington? 1825.] 12°

2 AN ADDRESS . . to the Public;
containing certain testimony in refutation of the charges against him,
made by Gen. A. Jackson, touching
the last Presidential Eleĉtion. Washington, 1827. 8°

3 SPEECH . . in defence of the
American system, against the British
Colonial system; with an appendix
of documents referred to in the speech,
delivered in the Senate. . . Feb. . .
1832. Washington, 1832. 8°

4 SPEECH . . on the subjeĉt of the
removal of the Deposites, delivered
in the Senate, . . Dec. 26, 30, 1833.
Washington, 1834. 8°

5 SPEECH . . on the Bill imposing
additional duties, as depositaries, in
certain cases, on public officers. In
Senate, . . Sept. 25, 1837. Boston,
1837. 8°

6 SPEECH . . establishing a delibe-
rate design, on the part of the late
and present Executive, . . to break
down the whole Banking system of
the United States; . . and in reply to
the Speech of . . J. C. Calhoun. . .
Delivered in the Senate, . . Feb. 19,
1838. Washington, 1838. 8°

7 THE BEAUTIES of the Hon. Henry
Clay; to which is added a biographical and critical eſsay. New York,
1839. 12°

8 THE LIFE and Speeches of the
Hon. Henry Clay. Compiled and
edited by D. Mallory. 2 vol. New
York, 1843. Roy. 8vo.

9 OBITUARY Addreſses on the oc-

casion of the death of the Hon. Henry
Clay, a Senator of the United States
from the State of Kentucky, . . and
the Funeral Sermon of the Rev. C.
M. Butler, Chaplain of the Senate.
Washington, 1852. 8°

10 LIFE of Henry Clay, the Statesman and Patriot; containing numerous Anecdotes. Philadelphia, 1853. 8°

CLAY, JOHN CURTIS. Annals of
the Swedes on the Delaware; to
which is added, the Charter of the
United Swedish Churches. Philadelphia, 1835. 12mo.

CLAYDEN, PETER WILLIAM.
Christianity the Revolutionizer. A
discourse [on Ezek. xxi. 27]. London, Boston [printed], 1855. 8vo.

CLEAVELAND, NEHEMIAH. An
Addreſs delivered at Topsfield, in
Maſsachusetts, Aug. 28, 1850: the
two hundredth anniversary of the
Incorporation of the Town. New
York, 1851. 8°

CLEAVELAND, PARKER. An
Elementary Treatise on Mineralogy
and Geology. Boston, Cambridge
[printed], 1816. 8vo.

2 AN ELEMENTARY Treatise on
Mineralogy and Geology. Second
edition. 2 vol. Boston, Cambridge
[printed], 1822. 8vo.

CLEMENT I. SAINT, *Pope*. The
Lives of Clemens Romanus, Ignatius,
and Polycarp. Philadel. 1828. 18°

CLEMENT, J. Memoir of A.
Judson: being a sketch of his life and
miſsionary labours. Auburn, 1851.
12°

2 NOBLE deeds of American Women: with biographical sketches of
some of the more prominent. . . With
an introduĉtion by Mrs. L. H. Sigourney. Buffalo, 1851. 12°

CLEMENT, JONATHAN. An Addreſs delivered before the New Hampshire Lyceum, . . at their first annual
meeting, etc. (Officers of the Lyceum.) Concord, 1833. 8°

CLENNING, ARTHUR. The Life

and Adventures of Arthur Clenning. By the author of " Recollections of Ten Years in the Valley of the Missisippi," *etc.* [Timothy Flint.] 2 vol. Philadelphia, 1828. 12°

CLERGYMAN. The Island of Life. An allegory, by a Clergyman. Boston, 1851. 12°

CLERKE, THOMAS W. Rudiments of American Law and Practice, on the plan of Blackstone. Prepared for the use of students at law, and adapted to schools and colleges. New York, 1842. 8°

2 A PRACTICAL elementary Digest of the reported Cases in the Supreme Court of Judicature, and the Court for the Correction of Errors of the State of New York; together with the reported cases of the Superior Court for the city and county of New York, from the earliest period to the present time. 2 vol. in 4. New York, 1845. 8°

CLEVELAND, CHARLES. Exchange Tables : showing the value in dollars and cents of any sum of exchange on London. . . Second edition, with additional mercantile tables. Boston, 1844. 8°

CLEVELAND, CHARLES DEXTER. A Compendium of Grecian Antiquities. Boston, 1838. 12°

2 A COMPENDIUM of English Literature, chronologically arranged, from Sir John Mandeville to W. Cowper. . . By C. D. Cleveland. Stereotype edition. Philadelphia, 1850. 8vo.

CLEVELAND, EDWARD. The Glory of a House of Worship : a sermon [on Isa. lxiv. 11, and Hag. ii. 9]. Stoneham, Mass. 1840. 8°

CLEVELAND, PARKER. An Address . . before the Brunswick . . Society for the Suppression of Intemperance. Boston, 1814. 8°

CLEVELAND, RICHARD J. A Narrative of Voyages and Commercial Enterprises. 2 vol. Cambridge, 1842. 12mo.

CLIFFORD, CHARLES. Charles Clifford. [A tale.] Philadelphia, 1834. 16mo.

CLIFFORD, NATHAN. Speech .. on the Apportionment Bill; delivered in the House of Representatives, April 28, 1842. Washing. 1842. 8°

CLIFFORD FAMILY ; or, a Tale of the Old Dominion. By one of her daughters. New York, 1852. 12°

CLINTON, DE WITT. Speech in the Senate of the State of New York, Jan. 31, 1809, introductory to certain resolutions, which met the approbation of both Houses. New York, 1809. 8°

2 AN INTRODUCTORY Discourse delivered before the Literary and Philosophical Society of New York on the fourth of May, 1814. [With notes and illustrations.] N. York, 1815. 4to.

3 A MEMOIR of the Antiquities of the western parts of the State of New York, read before the Literary and Philosophical Society of New York, *etc.* Albany, 1818. 8vo.

4 REPORT of the Commissioners of the State of New York (De Witt Clinton, S. Van Rensselaer, Samuel Young, Myron Holley) on the Canals from Lake Erie to the Hudson River, and from Lake Champlain to the same. Albany, 1818. 8vo.

CLINTON, DICK. Companion to "Jack Sheppard." The Life and Adventures of Dick Clinton, the Masked Highwayman. . . By the author of " Nat Blake," " Ned Scarlet," *etc.* New York, 1852. 8°

CLINTON, GEORGE W. A Digest of the Decisions at Law and in Equity, of the several Courts of the State of New York, contained in the one hundred and nine volumes of Reports by Johnson, Caines, Cowen, Wendell, Hill, Denio, Comstock, Hopkins, Paige, Barbour, and Sandford, *etc.* 3 vol. Albany, 1852. 8°

CLOPTON, John. Mr. Clopton's Motion, proposing an amendment to the Constitution of the United States [submitted to the House of Representatives of the United States of America], Feb. 29, 1808. Washington, 1808. 8°

CLOUDS AND SUNSHINE. By the author of " Musings of an Invalid," etc. New York, 1853. 12°

COATES, Reynell. Physiology for Schools. Fourth edition, revised. Philadelphia, 1845. 12°

COBB, Enos. A Self-explaining Grammar of the English Language. Second edition. Boston, 1821. 12°

COBB, Howell. Speech .. on the Oregon Question; delivered in the House of Representatives, Jan. 8, 1846. Washington, 1846. 8°

COBB, J. H. A Manual containing information respecting the growth of the Mulberry Tree, with suitable directions for the culture of Silk. In three parts. New edition. Boston, 1833. 12°

2 A Manual containing information respecting the growth of the Mulberry Tree, with suitable instructions for the culture of Silk, etc. Fourth edition, enlarged. Boston, 1839. 12°

COBB, Joseph B. The Creole; or, siege of New Orleans. An historical romance. Phil. 1850. 8°

2 Mississippi Scenes; or, sketches of Southern and Western life and adventure; .. including the legend of Black Creek. Phil. 1851. 12°

COBB, Lyman. A Critical Review of the Orthography of Dr. Webster's series of books for systematic Instruction in the English Language, etc. (specimens of Webster's Orthography). New York, 1831. 8°

2 Cobb's New Spelling Book, in six parts. Philadelphia and Harrisburg, 1844. 12°

3 Cobb's Speaker; containing

ample exercises in Elocution in prose, poetry, and dialogues. .. Also an introduction, containing the principles of Elocution, etc. N. York, 1852. 12°

COBBETT, William. Le Tuteur Anglais, ou grammaire régulière de la langue Anglaise. Philadelphie, 1795. 8vo.

2 Letters on the late War between the United States and Great Britain; together with other miscellaneous writings on the same subject. New York, 1815. 8°

3 A Year's Residence in the United States of America, etc. 3 parts. New York, 1818-19. 12°

4 Advice to Young Men, and (incidentally) to Young Women, in the middle and higher ranks of life. Andover, 1829. 12mo.

5 The English Gardener; or, a treatise on .. kitchen gardens, .. hot beds, greenhouses, etc. Andover, 1829. 12mo.

COCHRAN, Peter. The Columbian Grammar; or, a concise view of the English language. Boston, 1802. 12°

COCK, Micajah R. The American Poultry Book; being a practical treatise on the Management of Domestic Poultry. New York, 1844. 12°

COCKE, Charles. An Original Dissertation; being an attempt to prove the Identity of Gout and Rheumatism, etc. Philadelphia, 1806. 8vo.

COCKINGS, George. War: an heroic poem, from the taking of Minorca by the French to the reduction of the Havannah. The second edition, to the raising the siege of Quebec; with large amendments and additions. [After the poem there follow several minor pieces.] 2 vol. in 1. Boston, 1762. 8vo.

2 The Conquest of Canada; or, the siege of Quebec. An historical tragedy. Albany, 1773. 8vo.

CODMAN, John. A Narrative of a Visit to England. Bost. 1836. 12°

2 An Exposition of the pretended Claims of W. Vans on the Estate of J. Codman; with an appendix of original documents, correspondence, and other evidence. [By J., C. R. and F. Codman.] 2 vol. Bost. 1837. 8°

3 The Importance of Moderation in Civil Rulers. A sermon [on Philippians iv. 5] delivered before His Excellency, E. Everett, governor, the honourable Council, and the Legislature of Maſſachusetts, at the annual Election, January 1, 1840. Boston, 1840. 8°

COE, Benjamin H. Coe's new Drawing-cards for Schools. N° 1-10. [New York, 1850?] 12°

2 Coe's new Drawing-leſſons... Drawing for Schools. Series 1-3. New York, 1852. 12° and obl. 4°

COFFIN, John G. An Addreſs delivered before the contributors of the Boston Dispensary, at their seventeenth anniversary, etc. Boston, 1813. 8°

COFFIN, Joshua. A Sketch of the History of Newbury, Newburyport, and West Newbury, from 1635 to 1845. Boston, 1845. 8°

COGHLAN, Margaret. Memoirs of Mrs. Coghlan,.. written by herself, and dedicated to the British nation, etc. New York, 1795. 12°

COGSWELL, William. Religious Liberty: a sermon [on Gal. v. 1] preached on the day of the annual fast in Maſſachusetts. Bost. 1828. 8°

2 A Valedictory Discourse [on 2 Cor. xiii. 2 and Phil. i. 27] preached in Dedham, Dec. 20, 1829. Boston, 1830. 8°

3 The Harbinger of the Millennium; with an appendix. Boston, 1833. 12°

4 Assistant to Family Religion; or, manual of theology and devotions. Third edition. Boston, 1836. 8vo.

5 The Christian Philanthropist; or, harbinger of the millennium. With an introductory eſſay by J. Matheson. Second edition. Boston, 1839. 12°

COHEN, M. M. Notices of Florida and the Campaigns. Charleston and New York, 1836. 12°

COIT, Thomas W. Puritanism; or, a Churchman's defence against its aspersions, by an appeal to its own history. New York, 1845. 12mo.

COKE, Edward Thomas. A Subaltern's Furlough: descriptive of scenes in various parts of the United States, Upper and Lower Canada, New Brunswick and Nova Scotia during the summer and autumn of 1832. 2 vol. New York, 1833. 12°

COLBURN, Warren. A Key containing the answers to the examples in the Introduction to Algebra, upon the inductive method of instruction. Boston, 1827. 12mo.

2 Arithmetic upon the inductive method of instruction; being a sequel to Intellectual Arithmetic. Boston, 1828. 12mo.

3 Arithmetic upon the inductive method of instruction; being a sequel to Intellectual Arithmetic. Philadelphia and Boston, 1830. 12°

4 An Introduction to Algebra upon the inductive method of instruction. Boston, 1829. 12mo.

5 An Introduction to Algebra upon the inductive method of instruction. Boston, 1844. 12°

6 First Leſſons in Reading and Grammar, for the use of schools: chiefly from the works of Miſs Edgeworth. Selected and prepared by W. Colburn. Boston, 1836. 12°

7 Second Leſſons in Reading and Grammar, for the use of schools: chiefly from the works of Miſs Edgeworth. Boston, 1844. 12°

8 Third Leſſons in Reading and Grammar, for the use of schools: chiefly from the works of Miſs Edgeworth. Boston, 1838. 12°

9 Fourth Leſſons in Reading and Grammar, for the use of schools:

chiefly from the works of Mifs Edgeworth. Boston, 1838. 12°

10 COLBURN's First Lefsons. Intellectual Arithmetic, upon the inductive method of instruction. Boston, [1845?] 12°

COLBURN, ZERAH. A memoir of him, written by himself. . . With his peculiar methods of calculation. Springfield, 1833. 12mo.

2 THE LOCOMOTIVE Engine: including a description of its structure, rules for estimating its capabilities, and practical observations on its construction and management. Boston, 1851. 12°

COLBY, H. G. O. Anniversary Addrefs before the American Institute . . during the fifteenth annual fair. New York, 1843. 8°

COLBY, PHILIP. The Conversion and Restoration of the Jews: a sermon [on Isa. lxv. 8-10] delivered . . before the Palestine Mifsionary Society, June 17, 1835. [With the Treasurer's report, etc.] Boston, 1836. 12°

COLDEN, CADWALLADER. The History of the Five Indian Nations depending on the Province of New York in America. New York, 1727. 12mo.

2 AN EXPLICATION of the first Causes of Action in Matter, and of the Cause of Gravitation. New York, 1745. 12mo.

COLDEN, CADWALLADER D. The Life of Robert Fulton; comprising some account of the invention, progrefs, and establishment of steamboats, of improvements in . . canals, etc. With an appendix. New York, 1817. 8vo.

2 MEMOIR [on the construction, etc. of the New York Canals] prepared at the request of a Committee of the Common Council, etc. (Appendix, containing an account of the commemoration of the completion of the Erie Canal, by the Corporation of . .

New York, etc. Narrative of the festivities observed in honour of the completion of the grand Erie Canal; . . by W. L. Stone.) New York, 1825. 4to.

COLEMAN, LYMAN. Reply to a " Review of Coleman's Antiquities of the Christian Church, by H. W. D." By the author of the Antiquities. Andover, 1841. 8°

2 AN HISTORICAL Geography of the Bible. New edition, with additions. Philadelphia, 1850. 12°

3 ANCIENT Christianity exemplified in the private, domestic, social, and civil life of the primitive Christians, and in the original institutions, offices, ordinances, and rites of the Church. Philadelphia, 1852. 8vo.

4 AN HISTORICAL Text-book and Atlas of Biblical Geography. London, Philadelphia [printed], 1854. 8vo.

COLERIDGE, SAMUEL TAYLOR. The complete works of Samuel Taylor Coleridge; with an introductory efsay upon his philosophical and theological opinions. Edited by Profefsor Shedd. In seven volumes. Vol. 1. New York, 1853. 8°

COLLAMER, JACOB. Speech . . delivered in the House of Representatives, . . on the constitutional validity of the act of Congrefs requiring the election of Representatives to be by districts, Feb. 8, 1844. Washington, 1844. 8°

2 SPEECH . . on wool and woollens; delivered before the House of Representatives in Committee . . upon the tariff, April 29, 1844. Washington, 1844. 8°

3 SPEECH . . on the annexation of Texas; delivered in the House of Representatives, . . Jan. 23, 1845. Washington [1845]. 8°

4 SPEECH . . on the tariff, delivered in the House of Representatives, . . June 26, 1846. Washing. 1846. 8°

COLLECTIONS, Topographical, Historical, and Biographical, relating principally to New Hampshire. Vol.

1. (Vol. 2, 3, Collections, historical and miscellaneous; and Monthly Literary Journal.) Edited by J. Farmer and J. B. Moore. Vol. 1-3. Concord, 1822; reprinted 1831. 1823-24. 8°

COLLEGE OF PHYSICIANS, PHILADELPHIA. The Charter, Constitution, and Bye-laws. Philadelphia, 1790. 8vo.

2 PROCEEDINGS of the College .. relative to the prevention of the introduction and spreading of contagious diseases. Philadel. 1798. 8vo.

3 FACTS and Observations relative to the nature and origin of the pestilential Fever which prevailed in this city, in 1793, 1797, and 1798. Philadelphia, 1798. 8vo.

4 ADDITIONAL Facts and Observations relative to the nature and origin of the pestilential Fever. Philadelphia, 1806. 8°

COLLIER, WILLIAM. Miniature Arithmetic. . . A new edition, with improvements. Charlestown, 1817. 24°

COLLIN, JOHN F. Speech . . . delivered in the House of Representatives, . . June 19, 1846, . . on the Bill reported from the Committee of Ways and Means, amendatory of the tariff law of 1842. [Washington, 1846.] 8°

COLLINS, MRS. A. M. Mrs. Collins' Table Receipts, adapted to Western housewifery. New Albany, Indiana, 1851. 12°

COLLINS, LEWIS. Historical Sketches of Kentucky; embracing its history, antiquities, and natural curiosities, geographical, statistical, and geological descriptions, with anecdotes of pioneer life . . and biographical sketches. Cincin. 1850. 8°

COLLINS, STEPHEN. Miscellanies. Second edition. Philadelphia, 1845. 8°

COLLOT, A. G. New and improved standard French and English and English and French Dictionary . . the whole preceded by a complete treatise on Punctuation and a table of all the irregular verbs, and followed by . . vocabularies of mythological, historical, and geographical names, etc. Philadelphia, 1852. 8°

COLLOT, GEORGES HENRI VICTOR. Précis des événemens qui se sont passés à la Guadeloupe pendant l'administration de G. H. V. Collot, depuis le 20 Mars 1793, jusqu'au 22 Avril, 1794. Présenté à la Convention Nationale. (Pièces justificatives.) Philadelphie, 1795. 4to.

COLLYER, JOHN, of Lincoln's Inn, Barrister at Law. A Practical Treatise on the Law of Partnership. Second American, from the last London edition, containing the American notes of the former edition, by W. Phillips and E. Pickering. To which are now added notes of recent American and English decisions, by O. L. Barbour. Springfield, 1839. 8°

COLMAN, BENJAMIN. A Sermon [on 2 Tim. ii. 1] preached at the ordination of Mr. W. Cooper, in Boston, May 23, 1716. . . With Mr. Cooper's Confession of Faith and his answers to the questions proposed to him upon that occasion. 2 parts [separately paged]. Printed by B. Green, for Samuel Gerrish and Daniel Henchman. Boston, 1716. 16mo.

2 A SERMON [on 1 Kings x. 9] preached . . . the 23rd of August, 1716, being the day of public Thanksgiving for the suppression of the late . . rebellion in Great Britain. Boston, 1716. 12°

3 A SERMON [on John ix. 4] at the lecture in Boston after the funerals of . . W. Brattle and E. Pemberton. Boston, 1717. 8vo.

4 SERMON on [Heb. xi. 22] on the death of Joseph Dudley, Esq. Boston, 1720. 8vo.

5 SOME Observations on the new method of receiving the Small Pox,

by ingrafting or inoculating. By Mr. Colman. Containing also the reasons which first induced him to, and have since confirmed him in, his favourable opinion of it. Boston, 1721. 8vo.

.6 MOSES a witneſs to our Lord and Saviour Jesus Christ. A Discourse [on John v. 46] had . . before the baptism of R. J. Monis. Boston 1722. 12°

7 THE RENDING of the Vail of the Temple at the Crucifixion of our Lord and Saviour Jesus Christ, considered in a Sacramental discourse [on Mark xv. 38] had at Boston. Second edition. Boston, 1722. 16mo.

8 PARENTS and Grown Children should be together at the Lord's Table: a sermon [on Luke ii. 41, 42]. Boston, 1727. 8°

9 THE FRIEND of Christ and of His People. A sermon [on John xi. 11] preached . . upon . . the death of . . T. Hollis, Esq. Boston, 1731. 8vo.

10 MINISTERS and People under special obligations to sanctity, humility, and gratitude, for the great grace given them in the preached Gospel. A sermon [on Ephes. iii. 8]. Boston, 1732. 8°

11 ONE chosen of God and called to the work of the ministry, willingly offering himself. A sermon [on Isaiah vi. 8] preached at the ordination of Mr. S. Cooper to the Pastoral office n the Church . . in Brattle Street, Boston. To which are added the charge then given by the Rev. Dr. Sewall, etc. Boston, 1746. 8°

COLMAN, HENRY. Sermons on various subjects. Boston, 1833. 12°

2 TERMS of Peace: a sermon [on 1 Cor. iii. 3] at the dedication of the church in South Orange, Maſs. Greenfield, 1834. 8°

3 FIRST Report on the Agriculture of Maſsachusetts. County of Eſsex. 1837. Boston, 1838. 8°

4 SECOND Report on the Agriculture of Maſsachusetts. County of Berkshire, 1838. Boston, 1839. 8°

5 FOURTH Report of the Agriculture of Maſsachusetts. Counties of Franklin and Middlesex. Boston, 1841. 8°

6 THE IMPROVEMENT of Agriculture as an art and a profeſsion: an addreſs at the annual cattle-show and fair . . in Rochester, New York. Rochester, 1842. 8°

7 EUROPEAN Life and Manners; in familiar letters to friends. 2 vol. Boston, 1850. 12°

COLOMBAT, MARC. A Treatise on the Diseases and special Hygiène of Females. Translated from the French, with additions. By C. D. Meigs. Philadelphia, 1845. Roy. 8vo.

COLOMBIA. Notes on Colombia, taken in the years 1822-3. With an itinerary of the route from Caracas to Bogotà, and an appendix. By an officer of the United States [R. Bache]. Philadelphia, 1827. 8vo.

COLONIZATION. A VIEW of exertions lately made for the purpose of colonizing the free people of colour in the United States, in Africa or elsewhere. Washington, 1817. 8vo.

2 ANOTHER Edition. Washington, 1817. 8vo.

COLONIZATION HERALD and General Register. No. 36, 53. Philadelphia, 1848. Fol.

COLONIZATION SOCIETY OF THE CITY OF NEW YORK. Proceedings at their third annual meeting, May 14, 1835. N. Y. 1835. 8vo.

2 SEVENTH Annual Report. New York, 1839. 8vo.

COLONIZATIONIST, AND JOURNAL OF FREEDOM. April 1833 to April 1834. Boston, 1833-34. 8°

COLTON, CALVIN. Four Years in Great Britain. New and improved edition. New York, 1836. 12°

COLTON, CHAUNCEY. An Addreſs delivered at the Inauguration of the Faculty of . . Bristol College, . . Pennsylvania. . . Second edition, with an appendix, embracing the first annual catalogue of Bristol College. Philadelphia, 1834. 8°

COLTON, GEORGE HOOKER. Tecumseh; or, the West thirty years since. A poem. New York, 1842. 12°

COLTON, WALTER. Visit to Constantinople and Athens. New York, 1836. 12mo.

2 DECK and Port; or, Incidents of a Cruise in the United States frigate Congress to California, with sketches of Rio Janeiro, Valparaiso, Lima, etc. New York, 1850. 12°

3 THREE years in California . . . With illustrations. N. York, 1850. 12°

4 SHIP and Shore in Madeira, Lisbon, and the Mediterranean. . . Revised from the " Journal of a Cruise in the frigate Constellation," by Rev. H. T. Cheever. N. York, 1851. 12°

COLUMBIA COLLEGE, NEW YORK CITY. Catalogue of Columbia College, . . embracing the names of its trustees, officers, and graduates; together with a list of all academical honours conferred . . from 1758 to 1826, inclusive. N. York, 1826. 8°

2 CATALOGUE of Columbia College, . . embracing the names of its trustees, officers, and graduates; together with a list of all academical honours conferred . . from . . 1758 to . . 1836, inclusive. New York, 1836. 8°

3 STATUTES of Columbia College, revised and passed by the Board of Trustees, May, 1836. To which is prefixed an historical sketch of the College. New York, 1836. 8°

COLUMBIAN COLLEGE, WASHINGTON. Catalogue of the Columbian College in the District of Columbia; embracing the names of its trustees, officers, and graduates; together with a list of all academical honours conferred, etc. Washington, 1839. 8°

COLUMBIAN HORTICULTURAL SOCIETY. Constitution and Byelaws, etc. (Officers and Council of the Society.) Aug. 1833. Washington, 1833. 8°

COLUMBIAN MAGAZINE; or Monthly Miscellany. (Sept. 1786—June, 1790.) Vol. 1-4. [Continued under the title of] The Universal Asylum and Columbian Magazine. Vol. 5-9. July, 1790—Dec. 1792. Philadelphia, 1786-92. 8°

COLUMBIAN PHENIX and BOSTON REVIEW; containing useful information on Literature, Religion, Morality, Politics, and Philosophy, etc. [Edited by J. Hawkins.] Vol. 1, for 1800. Boston [1800]. 8°

COLUMBUS, CHRISTOPHER. Personal Narrative of the First Voyage of Columbus to America. From a manuscript recently discovered in Spain. Translated from the Spanish. Boston, 1827. 8°

COLVOCORESSES, GEORGE M. Four Years in a Government Exploring Expedition; to the Island of Madeira, Cape Verd Islands, Brazil, Coast of Patagonia, Chili, Peru, etc. New York, 1852. 8°

COLWELL, STEPHEN. New Themes for the Protestant Clergy: Creeds without Charity, Theology without Humanity, and Protestantism without Christianity. With notes on the literature of charity, population, pauperism, political economy, and Protestantism. Second edition. Philadelphia, 1852. 12°

2 CHARITY and the Clergy; being a Review by a Protestant Clergyman of the " New Themes" [by Stephen Colwell] Controversy; together with sundry serious reflections upon the religious press, etc. Philadelphia, 1853. 8°

COMAN, J. M. Report of the President of the Decatur Branch Bank (J. M. Coman). Tuscaloosa, 1845. 8°

COMBE, ANDREW. The Principles of Physiology applied to the Preservation of Health, and to the Improvement of Physical and Mental Education. From the seventh Edinburgh edition. N. York, 1845. 12°

COMBE, GEORGE. An Address delivered at the Anniversary Celebration of the Birth of Spurzheim, and the organization of the Boston Phrenological Society, 31st December, 1839. Boston, 1840. 8vo.

2 LECTURES on Moral Philosophy. Boston, 1840. 12mo.

COMLY, JOHN. Comly's Spelling and Reading Books, with notes for parents and teachers, etc. Philadelphia, 1842. 12°

COMMERCIAL REVIEW OF THE SOUTH AND WEST. A Monthly Journal of Trade, etc. J. D. B. De Bow, Editor, etc. Vol. 1-8. [Continued as] De Bow's Review of the Southern and Western States. Vol. 9-22, Jan. 1846 to Dec. 1856. New Orleans, 1846-56. 8°

COMMON SCHOOL JOURNAL. Edited by Horace Mann. Vol. 1-7. Boston, 1839-45. 8vo.

COMMUCK, THOMAS. Indian Melodies... Harmonized by T. Hastings. New York, 1845. Obl. 8°

COMPANIONS. My Youthful Companions. By the author of ' My School-boy Days.' N. York, 1849. 12°

COMSTOCK, ANDREW. A System of Elocution, with special reference to gesture, to the treatment of stammering, and defective articulation. Philadelphia, 1844. 12°

COMSTOCK, F. G. A Practical Treatise on the Culture of Silk, adapted to the soil and climate of the United States... Second edition, revised and improved. Hartford, 1839. 12°

COMSTOCK, JOHN L. Natural History of Quadrupeds; with engravings .. exhibiting their comparative size; .. authentic anecdotes, illustrating the habits and characters of the animals, etc. Hartford, 1829. 12°

2 OUTLINES of Geology. . . With an examination of the question, Whether the days of Creation were indefinite periods. Hartford, 1834. 12°

3 OUTLINES of Geology: intended as a popular treatise on the most interesting parts of the science. Together with an examination of the question, Whether the days of Creation were indefinite periods. Fifteenth edition. New York, 1845. 12°

4 AN INTRODUCTION to Mineralogy; adapted to the use of Schools, etc. Third edition, improved. New York, 1841. 8°

5 OUTLINES of Physiology, both comparative and human, etc. Third edition. [To which is prefixed, Report on the method of teaching English Grammar, etc. By R. K. Finch.] New York, 1844. 12°

6 AN INTRODUCTION to the Study of Botany, including a treatise on Vegetable Physiology, and descriptions of the most common plants in the middle and northern States. Eleventh edition. New York, 1845. 12°

7 ELEMENTS of Chemistry, etc. Fifty-fifth edition. N. York, 1845. 12°

8 A SYSTEM of Natural Philosophy, etc. Seventy-first edition. New York, 1846. 12°

9 A HISTORY of the Precious Metals, from the earliest periods to the present time, with directions for testing their purity, and statements of their comparative value, estimated costs and amount at different periods; together with an account of the products of various mines ; a history of the Anglo-Mexican Mining Companies, and speculations concerning the mineral wealth of California. Hartford, 1849. 12°

COMTE, AUGUSTE. The Philosophy of Mathematics, translated from the Cours de Philosophie Positive of Auguste Compte, by W. M. Gillespie. New York, 1851. 8°

CONANT, Mrs. H. C. The English Bible. History of the translation of the Holy Scriptures into the English Tongue. With specimens of the Old English versions. London, [New York printed] 1856. 12mo.

CONANT, Sylvanus. An Anniversary Sermon preached at Plymouth [Massachusetts], Dec. 23, 1776, in grateful memory of the first landing of our worthy ancestors in that place, A.D. 1620. Boston, New England, 1777. 8°

CONANT, T. J. Defence of the Hebrew Grammar of Gesenius against Professor Stuart's Translation. By the original translator. New York, 1847. 8°

CONCORD POCKET ALMANACK .... and Register of New Hampshire, etc. (1811, 1813). Concord [1810-12]. 12°

CONDICT, Lewis, Resp. An Inaugural Dissertation on the Effects of Contagion upon the Human Body. Philadelphia, 1794. 8°

CONDIT, J. B. An Address delivered before the Literary Societies of Dartmouth College, etc. Portland, 1841. 8°

CONFESSION and Renewal of Covenant, Jan. 26, 1837. [New York !] 1837. 8°

CONFESSION; or, The Blind Heart. A domestic story. By the author of " The Kinsmen," etc. [W. G. Simms]. 2 vol. Philadelphia, 1841. 12°

CONGAR, Obadiah. The Autobiography and Memorials of Captain Obadiah Congar, for fifty years mariner and shipmaster from the port of New York. [Edited] by .. H. T. Cheever. New York, 1851. 12°

CONGRESS. History of Congress; exhibiting a classification of the proceedings of the Senate, and House of Representatives. Volume 1.

from March 4, 1789, to March 3, 1793, embracing the first term of the Administration of General Washington. Philadelphia, 1834. 8°

2 CONGRESS. See UNITED STATES.

CONGRESS CANVASSED: or an Examination into the Conduct of the Delegates, at their Grand Convention, held in Philadelphia Sept. 1, 1774. By A. W. Farmer. 1774. 8vo.

CONGRESSIONAL GLOBE: containing sketches of the Debates and proceedings of.. Congress. (Appendix to the Congressional Globe.) 23rd - 33rd Congress. Vol. 1 - 31. Washington, 1834-55. 4°

CONKLING, Alfred. A Treatise on the Organization, Jurisdiction and Practice of the Courts of the United States: to which is added an appendix, . and also a few practical forms. Albany, 1831. 8°

2 OPINION of .. Alfred Conkling, District Judge of the United States, on a motion .. for a new trial, in the case of M. Bradstreet vs. H. Huntington [the latter a claimant to a portion of certain premises in Utica]. Utica, 1834. 8°

3 OPINION .. upon the Question of Copyright in Manuscripts in the case of Little and Company against Hall, Goulds, and Banks, respecting the 4th vol. of Comstock's Reports. Albany, 1852. 8vo.

CONKLING, Margaret C. Memoirs of the mother and wife of Washington. . . . Second edition, revised and enlarged. Auburn, 1850. 12°

CONNECTICUT. Acts and Laws of His Majesty's Colony of Connecticut in New England. Boston, 1702. Fol.

2 ACTS and Laws of His Majesty's Colony of Connecticut, in New England. New London, 1715. Fol.

3 THE CHARTER granted by His Majesty King Charles II to the Governour and Company of the English

Colony of Connecticut, in New England in America. New London, 1718. Fol,

4 Acts and Laws of His Majesty's English Colony of Connecticut, etc. New London, 1750. Fol.

5 A CONFESSION of Faith, owned and consented to by the Elders and Messengers of the Churches in the Colony of Connecticut, assembled by delegation at Say Brook, Sept. 9th, 1708. (The Heads of Agreement assented to by the United Ministers formerly called Presbyterian and Congregational, and also Articles for the administration of Church Discipline.) New London, 1760. 12mo.

6 Acts and Laws of the State of Connecticut in America. New London, 1784. Fol°

7 Acts and Laws of the State of Connecticut in America. Hartford, 1805. 8°

8 THE PUBLIC Statute Laws of the State of Connecticut. Book I [Edited by J. Treadwell, E. Perkins, and T. Day.] Published by authority of the General Assembly. Hartford, 1808. 8°

9 THE CODE of 1650, being a compilation of the earliest laws and orders of the General Court of Connecticut: also the Constitution, or Civil Compact adopted by the towns of Windsor, Hartford and Wethersfield in 1638-9. To which is added, some extracts from the laws and judicial proceedings of New Haven Colony, commonly called Blue Laws. Hartford, 1822. 12mo.

10 THE PUBLIC Statute Laws of the State of Connecticut. To which are prefixed the Declaration of Independence, the Constitution of the United States and the Constitution of Connecticut. Hartford, 1824. 8vo.

11 THE PUBLIC Statute Laws of the State of Connecticut as revised and enacted by the General Assembly, in May, 1821, with the acts of the three subsequent sessions incorporated ; . . Prepared and published under the

authority of the General Assembly [by S. P. Beers, T. Day, and L. Whitman]. Hartford, 1824. 8°

12 MESSAGE of Oliver Wolcott to the Senate and House of Representatives of . . Connecticut, at the commencement of the Session of . . May, . . 1826. New Haven, 1826. 8°

13 A GENERAL history of Connecticut, including a description of the country, and many curious and interesting anecdotes. With an appendix. . . By a gentleman of the province [the Rev. S. Peters] . . To which is added a supplement, verifying many important statements made by the author. Illustrated with eight engravings. New Haven, 1829. 12°

14 REPORT of the Directors and Warden of the Connecticut State Prison, submitted to the Legislature, May Session, 1829. Printed by order of the Legislature. Hartford, 1829. 8vo.

15 REPORT of the Directors and Warden of the Connecticut State Prison ; submitted to the Legislature, May Session, 1830. Printed by order of the Legislature. N. Haven, 1830. 8vo.

16 MESSAGE of His Excellency John S. Peters, addressed to the Legislature of the State of Connecticut, May Session, 1831. Hartford [1831]. 8°

17 MINUTES of the testimony taken before J. Q. Wilson [and others] Committee from the General Assembly, to inquire into the condition of Connecticut State Prison. Together with their report, and remarks upon the same. Hartford, 1834. 8°.

18 MESSAGE from His Excellency Henry W. Edwards to the Legislature of Connecticut, May, 1835. Hartford, 1835. 8vo.

19 EXTRACTS from the Journal of the Annual Convention of the Diocese of Connecticut, held at Middletown: with an appendix, containing documents relating to Washington College and the Church Scholarship Society. Middletown, 1835. 8vo.

20 REPORT of the Directors of the

Connecticut State Prison, made to the General Aſsembly, 1835; 1837-8; 1843-4; 1846. Hartford and New Haven, 1835-46. 8vo.

21 REPORT of the Commiſsioner of the School Fund (S. P. Beers) 1835, 1837, 1839, 1841 to 1846. 9 parts. Hartford and New Haven, 1835-46. 8vo.

22 THE PUBLIC Statute Laws of the State of Connecticut. To which is prefixed the Declaration of Independence, Constitution of the United States, and Constitution of the State of Connecticut. Hartford, 1835. 8vo.

23 MESSAGE of the Governor (H. W. Edwards) to the General Aſsembly, May Seſsion, 1837. Hartford [1837]. 8vo.

24 RESOLVES and Private Laws of the State of Connecticut, from 1789 to 1836. 2 vol. Hartford, 1837. 8vo.

25 RESOLVES and Private Acts of the State of Connecticut, 1837-41. Hartford, 1837-41. 8vo.

26 REPORT of the Committee appointed by the Legislature to visit and examine the Banks in Connecticut, made, Seſsion, 1837. Hartford, 1837. 8vo.

27 REPORT of the Special Committee concerning the City Bank of New Haven. Hartford, 1839. 8vo.

28 [Begins.] BY His Excellency Henry W. Edwards, Governor . . A Proclamation [for a General Fast, on March 24th, 1837]. [New Haven, 1837.] s. sh. fol.

29 JOURNAL of the House of Representatives of the State of Connecticut, 1837 to 1840; 1842 to 1846. 9 parts. Hartford and New Haven, 1837-46. 8vo.

30 AN ACT to aid the construction of certain Railroads. New Haven, 1838. 8vo.

31 BOARD of Commiſsioners of Common Schools. Addreſs to the people of Connecticut by the Board of Commiſsioners of Common Schools. [Hartford, 1838.] 8º

32 THE PUBLIC Statute Laws of the State of Connecticut. To which is prefixed the Declaration of Independence, Constitution of the United States, and Constitution of the State of Connecticut. Hartford, 1839. 8vo.

33 [Begins] COPY of the Report of the Joint Committee of the Legislature of Connecticut on the Petition of C. Stockbridge and others against the Hartford Bridge Company, Session, 1836. [Hartford, 1839.] 8vo.

34 REPORT of Committee on Housatonic Railroad Company. . . General Aſsembly, . . The Joint Select Committee, etc. [With a draught of the Act for the Construction of the Railroad, etc.] [Hartford, 1839.] 8vo.

35 REPORT of the Joint Committee on Internal Improvements, presented Seſsion 1838, and continued to the next General Aſsembly. [To which is added an Act to aid in the construction of certain Railroads.] [Hartford, 1839.] 8vo.

36 REPORT of the Adjutant-General to the Governor of Connecticut. Session 1839. Hartford, 1839. 8vo.

37 FIRST (to fourth) Annual Report of the Board of Commiſsioners of Common Schools. . . Together with the first (to fourth) annual Report of the Secretary (H. Barnard). Hartford, 1839-42. 8º

38 SPEECH from His Excellency William W. Ellsworth to the Legislature, . . May, 1840. New Haven, 1840. 8vo.

39 JOURNAL of the Senate of the State of Connecticut, 1840 to 1846. Hartford and N. Haven, 1840-46. 8vo.

40 MINUTES of the General Aſsociation of Connecticut, at their Meeting in New Haven, . . June, 1840; with an appendix, containing the Report on the State of Religion, etc. Hartford, 1840. 8º

41 REPORT of the Joint Standing Committee, to whom was referred the several Petitions relative to the employment of mechanic labour in Connecticut State Prison. Hartford, 1841. 8vo.

42 THE PUBLIC Statute Law of the State of Connecticut respecting Common Schools. Hartford, 1841. 8vo.

43 MESSAGE from His Excellency Chauncey F. Cleveland to the Legislature of Connecticut, at the extra Session, Oct. 1842. New Haven, 1842. 8vo.

44 [Begins] BY His Excellency Chauncey F. Cleveland. . . A Proclamation [for a General Thanksgiving on Nov. 17th, 1842]. [Hartford, 1842.] s. sh. fol.

45 BOARD of Commissioners of Common Schools. Legal Provision respecting the education and employment of children in factories. Education and Labour; or the influence of education on the quality and value of labour, and its connection with insanity and crime. Hartford, 1842. 8vo.

46 RESOLUTIONS and Private Acts passed by the General Assembly of the State of Connecticut, 1842-47 [wanting 1846]. Hartford and New Haven, 1842-47. 8vo.

47 SCHOOL House Architecture: [Secretary's (Henry Barnard) Report to the Board.] Hartford, 1842. 8vo.

48 REPORT of the Joint Select Committee on so much of the Governor's Message as relates to Capital Punishment, with the petition of sundry citizens that it may be abolished. Hartford, 1843. 8vo.

49 PUBLIC Acts relating to Common Schools in force in the State of Connecticut, 1843. Hartford, 1843. 8vo.

50 [Begins] RESOLUTION for amendment of 6th Article, Section 2nd, Constitution. [Hartford, 1843.] 8vo.

51 REPORT of the Bank Commissioners to the General Assembly, 1843. Hartford, 1843. 8vo.

52 REPORT of the Joint Select Committee on so much of His Excellency's Message as relates to Resolutions received from the States of Georgia, Alabama, and New Jersey,

on the repudiation of State Debts, etc. Hartford, 1843. 8vo.

53 REPORT of the Commissioners on the Housatonic Railroad to the General Assembly, Session 1843. Hartford, 1843. 8vo.

54 REPORT of the Comptroller of Public Accounts to the General Assembly, Session 1843. Hartford, 1843. 8vo.

55 REPORT of the Committee appointed at the last Session of the General Assembly, to revise the Laws in relation to the collection of Debts and Attachment Laws; also the Bills relating to Imprisonment for Debt. Hartford, 1843. 8vo.

56 REPORT of the Committee on the Petition of the town of East Hartford and others, against the Hartford Bridge Company. Hartf. 1843. 8vo.

57 REPORT of the Committee to whom was referred the Bill for a Public Act to divide the city of New Haven into wards for the election of officers. Hartford, 1843. 8vo.

58 MESSAGE from His Excellency Chauncey F. Cleveland to the Legislature of Connecticut, May Session, 1843. Hartford, 1843. 8vo.

59 [Begins] BY His Excellency Chauncey F. Cleveland, a Proclamation [for a General Fast, April 14, 1843]. [Hartford, 1843.] s. sh. fol.

60 [Begins] BY His Excellency Chauncey F. Cleveland, . . a Proclamation [for a General Thanksgiving, Nov. 30, 1843]. [Hartford] s. sh. fol.

61 REPORT of the Committee on the Punishment and Reformation of Juvenile Offenders. New Haven, 1844. 8vo.

62 SPEECH of Roger S. Baldwin, Governor of Connecticut, to the Legislature of the State, May, 1844. New Haven, 1844. 8vo.

63 PUBLIC Acts passed by the General Assembly of the State of Connecticut, 1839-1847. 5 parts. Hartford and N. Haven, 1845, 44-47. 8vo.

64 [32 BLANK Forms of Appointment to Military Commissions and

Civil Offices; sundry voting papers, etc.] [Hartford, New Haven, etc. 1845.] 4to. and fol.

65 REPORT of the Joint Standing Committee on Banks, to whom was referred the Bank Commiſſioners' Report, Seſſion 1845. Hartford, 1845. 8vo.

66 SPEECH of .. Roger S. Baldwin, Governor of Connecticut, to the Legislature of the State, May, 1845. Hartford, 1845. 8vo.

67 REPORT of the Committee on Education, appointed under a Resolution of the General Aſſembly of 1844. Hartford, 1845. 8vo.

68 STATE of Connecticut. Statistics of certain branches of Industry. 1845. [Blank forms of return.] [Hartford] 1845. Fol.

69 [Begins] BY His Excellency Roger S. Baldwin, Governor, . . . a Proclamation [for a General Thanksgiving, Nov. 27, 1845]. [New Haven, 1845.] Fol.

70 [Begins] BY His Excellency Roger S. Baldwin, Governor, . . a Proclamation [for a General Fast, April 10, 1846]. [New Haven, 1846.] s. sh. fol.

71 REPORT of the Bank Commissioners to the General Aſſembly, 1846. New Haven, 1846. 8vo.

72 MESSAGE of the Governor (Isaac Toucey) in relation to the War with Mexico, together with the Report of the Select Committee, to whom the subject was referred, May Seſſion, 1846. New Haven, 1846. 8vo.

73 MESSAGE of the Governor to the Legislature [of Connecticut], returning the Bill chartering the New York and Boston Railroad Company. [New Haven, 1846.] 8vo.

74 MESSAGE from His Excellency Isaac Toucey to the Legislature of Connecticut, May Seſſion, 1846. New Haven, 1846. 8vo.

75 [Begins] LAWS relating to the sale of Wines and Spirituous Liquors in Connecticut, in force A. D. 1812; together with all subsequent Acts

relating thereto. [New Haven, 1846.] 8vo.

CONNECTICUT ACADEMY OF ARTS AND SCIENCES. A statistical Account of the Towns and Parishes in the State of Connecticut. Published by the Connecticut Academy of Arts and Sciences. Vol. I. Nº 1 [Containing] (A statistical account of the city of New Haven, by T. Dwight.) New Haven, 1811. 8º

CONNECTICUT ASYLUM FOR THE DEAF AND DUMB. See AMERICAN Asylum at Hartford.

CONNECTICUT BAPTIST CONVENTION. Seventeenth [and eighteenth] annual meeting of the Connecticut Baptist Convention, held at Eſſex, June, 1840 [and Hartford, June, 1841]. 2 parts. Hartford, 1840-41. 8vo.

CONNECTICUT COMMON SCHOOL JOURNAL. Published under the direction of the Board of Commiſſioners of Common Schools. From 1838 to 1842. Vol. 1-4. Edited by H. Barnard. Hartford, 1838-42. 4º

CONNECTICUT ÉVANGELICAL MAGAZINE. July, 1800, to June, 1804. 4 vol. [vol. 1, 2nd edition]. Hartford [1800-1804]. 8º

CONNECTICUT GAZETTE and the Universal Intelligencer. Nov. 1, 1782. Nº 990. New London, 1782. Fol.

CONNECTICUT PEACE SOCIETY. Tract Nº II of the Connecticut Peace Society. Reflections on the nature and dignity of the enterprise for establishing universal and permanent Peace. Hartford, 1835. 8º

CONNECTICUT REGISTER; being an official State Calendar of Public Officers and Institutions in Connecticut. 1847. By C. W. Bradley. Hartford [1846]. 16mo.

CONNECTICUT REPORTS. See Thomas DAY.

CONOVER, James F. A digested Index of all the reported Decisions in Law and Equity of the Supreme Courts of the States of Ohio, Indiana, and Illinois; with an appendix, etc. Philadelphia, 1834. 8°

CONRAD, Robert T. Aylmere; or, the Bondman of Kent, and other Poems. Philadelphia, 1852. 12°

CONRAD, T. A. New Fresh Water Shells of the United States. With coloured illustrations, etc. Philadelphia, 1834. 12°

2 Monography of the Family Unionidæ, or Naiades of La Marck (fresh-water bivalve shells) of North America. N° 1-12. Philadelphia, 1836-40. 8vo.

3 Fossils of the Tertiary Formations of the United States. Illustrated by figures. N° 1, 2. Philadelphia, 1838. 8vo.

CONSECRATED TALENTS; or, the Mifsion of the Children of the Church. By the author of ' Wreaths and Branches,' ' Christian Ornaments,' etc. New York, 1852. 12°

CONSIDERATIONS on some recent Social Theories. [By C. Norton?] Boston, 1853. 12°

CONSTANTINOPLE and its Environs. In a series of Letters. By an American [Commodore Porter] long resident at Constantinople. 2 vol. New York, 1835. 12°

CONTINENTAL CONGRESS. See United States.

CONTOSTAVLOS, Alexander. A Narrative of the material Facts in relation to the building of the two Greek Frigates. N. York, 1826. 8°

CONVERS, Charles C. [Begins] Court in Bank, Dec. term, 1846: J. Keen, vs. H. Mould. In Afsumpsit, etc. Reserved in the County of Muskingum. (Argument for Defendant.) [Zanesville? 1846.] 8°

2 Court in Bank, Dec. term, 1846.

D. B. Webster, et al. vs. M. E. Harris and F. A. Cleveland. In Chancery. . . Argument for Respondents [in a case of claim to lands in Ohio]. [Zanesville? 1846.] 8°

3 Court in Bank, Dec. term, 1846. S. Hyatt, vs. L. Robinson . . and J. Robinson. In debt. (Argument for Defendants.) [Zanesville? 1846.] 8°

4 Supreme Court of the United States, Dec. term, 1846. . . The . . Company of the Commercial Bank of Cincinnati, Plaintiffs in error, vs. the Executors of Eunice Buckingham, Defendants in error. Abstract and Brief [subscribed Charles C. Convers]. [Zanesville? 1847.] 8°

CONVERSATIONS on the Present Age of the World in connection with Prophecy. Albany, 1853. 8vo.

CONVERTED UNITARIAN. A short Memoir of E. E. Philadelphia [1852?]. 16°

COOK, George W. The Mariner's Physician and Surgeon; or, a Guide to the Homœopathic treatment of those diseases to which seamen are liable, comprising the treatment of syphilitic diseases, etc. New York, 1848. 12°

COOK, Zebedee. An Addrefs pronounced before the Mafsachusetts Horticultural Society, in commemoration of its second annual Festival, the 10th of Sept. 1830. Boston, 1830. 8°

COOKE, John E. M. D. Answer to the Review of an Efsay on the Invalidity of Presbyterian Ordination, published in the . . Biblical Repertory . . of Princeton, etc. Lexington, Kentucky, 1830. 8°

COOKE, Parsons. Moral Machinery simplified: a discourse delivered at Andover, Mafsachusetts. Andover, 1839. 8°

COOKE, Philip Pendleton. Froifsart Ballads, and other poems. Philadelphia, 1847. 12°

COOKE, Phinehas. Reciprocal Obligations of Religion and Civil Government: a discourse [on Matt. xxii. 21] delivered .. before the constituted authorities of .. New Hampshire, on the day of the anniversary Election, June 2, etc. Concord, 1825. 8°

2 A Discourse on Acts xx. 32. (A farewell sermon on Luke xvi. 32.) Delivered at Acworth, etc. Windsor, Vt. 1829. 8°

COOKE, Samuel. Divine Sovereignty in the Salvation of Sinners, considered and improved. In a sermon [on Exod. xxxiii. 19]. Boston, 1741. 12°

COOLEY, James Ewing. The American in Egypt, with rambles through Arabia Petræa and the Holy Land during the years 1839 and 1840. New York, 1842. 8°

COOLEY, Timothy Mather. Sketches of the Life and Character of the Rev. L. Haynes, . . with some introductory remarks by W. B. Sprague. New York, 1837. 12°

COON, Reune R. The Doctrine of Future and Endless Punishment logically proved in a critical examination of such passages of Scripture as relate to the final destiny of man. Cincinnati, 1850. 8vo.

COOPER, Rev. Mr. The History of North America, containing a review of the customs and manners of the original inhabitants; the first settlement of the British Colonies, their rise and progress .. to the time of their becoming United, free and independent States. Second American edit. Lansingburgh, 1795. 12°

COOPER, C. Campbell. Identities of light and heat, of caloric and electricity. Philadelphia, 1848. 8°

COOPER, James Fenimore. Precaution, a novel. [By J. F. Cooper.] 2 vol. New York, 1820. 12°

2 Lionel Lincoln; or, the Leaguer of Boston. By the author of the Pioneers, Pilot, etc. [J. F. Cooper.] 2 vol. New York, 1825-24. 12°

3 A Reply to the Letter of J. F. Cooper [on the dissension between the President and Senate of the United States]. By one of his countrymen. Boston, 1834. 8°

4 The Wept of Wish-Ton-Wish: a tale. By the author of "The Pioneers," etc. [J. F. Cooper]. A new edition. 2 vol. Philadelphia, 1836. 12°

5 The Last of the Mohicans; a narrative of 1757. By the author of "The Pioneers" [J. F. Cooper]. A new edition. 2 vol. Philadelphia, 1836. 12°

6 The Red Rover, a tale. By the author of "The Pilot," etc. [J. F. Cooper]. A new edition. 2 vol. Philadelphia, 1836. 12°

7 Lionel Lincoln: or, the Leaguer of Boston. By the author of "The Spy" [J. F. Cooper]. A new edition. 2 vol. Philadelphia, 1836. 12°

8 The Heidenmauer; or, the Benedictines. A legend of the Rhine. By the author of "The Prairie," etc. [J. F. Cooper]. A new edition. 2 vol. Philadelphia, 1836. 12°

9 The Prairie; a tale. By the author of "The Pioneers," and "The Last of the Mohicans" [J. F. Cooper]. A new edition. 2 vol. Philadelphia, 1836. 12°

10 The Bravo; a tale. By the author of "The Spy," etc. [J. F. Cooper]. A new edition. 2 vol. Philadelphia, 1836. 12°

11 The Headsman; or, the Abbaye des Vignerons. A tale. By the author of "The Bravo," etc. [J. F. Cooper]. A new edition. 2 vol. Philadelphia, 1836. 12°

12 The Pilot; a tale of the sea. By the author of "The Pioneers," etc. [J. F. Cooper]. A new edition. 2 vol. Philadelphia, 1836. 12°

13 THE PIONEERS; or, the sources of the Susquehanna; a descriptive tale. By the author of " The Spy" [J. F. Cooper]. A new edition. 2 vol. Philadelphia, 1836. 12°

14 GLEANINGS in Europe : England. By an American [J. F. Cooper]. 2 vol. Philadelphia, 1837. 12°

15 THE WATER-WITCH ; or, the Skimmer of the Seas. A tale. By the author of " The Pilot," etc. [J. F. Cooper]. A new edition. 2 vol. Philadelphia, 1838. 12°

16 THE AMERICAN Democrat; or, hints on the social and civic relations of the United States of America. Cooperstown, 1838. 12mo.

17 HOME as Found. By the author of " Homeward Bound," etc. [J. F. Cooper]. 2 vol. Philadelphia, 1838. 12°

18 NOTIONS of the Americans. Picked up by a Travelling Bachelor [J. F. Cooper]. A new edition. 2 vol. Philadelphia, 1838. 12°

19 NOTIONS of the Americans. Picked up by a Travelling Bachelor [J. F. Cooper]. A new edition. 2 vol. Philadelphia, 1840. 12°

20 HISTORY of the Navy of the United States of America. Second edition, with corrections. 2 vol. Philadelphia, 1840. 8°

21 THE MONIKINS. [A tale.] Edited by the author of " The Spy" [J. F. Cooper]. 2 vol. Philadelphia, 1841. 12°

22 THE WING-AND-WING; or, le feu-follet. A tale. By the author of " The Pilot," etc. (J. F. Cooper). 2 vol. Philadelphia, 1842. 12°

23 HOMEWARD Bound; or, the Chase. A tale of the sea. By the author of " The Pilot," etc. [J. F. Cooper]. A new edition. 2 vol. Philadelphia, 1842. 12°

24 NED Myers; or, a life before the mast. Edited by J. F. Cooper. Philadelphia, 1843. 12°

25 WYANDOTTÉ; or, the Hutted Knoll. A tale. By the author of " The Pathfinder," [J. F. Cooper]. 2 vol. Philadelphia, 1843. 12°

26 THE TWO Admirals. By the author of " The Pilot," [J. F. Cooper]. 2 vol. Philadelphia, 1843. 12°

27 THE BATTLE of Lake Erie ; or, answers to Messrs. Burges, Duer, and Mackenzie. Cooperstown, 1843. 12°

28 THE PATHFINDER; or, the inland sea. [A tale.] By the author of " The Pioneers," etc. [J. F. Cooper]. 2 vol. Philadelphia, 1845. 12°

29 THE DEERSLAYER; or, the first war-path. A tale. By the author of " The Last of the Mohicans," etc. [J. F. Cooper]. 2 vol. Philadelphia, 1845. 12°

30 ELINOR Wyllys; or, the young folk of Longbridge. A tale, by Amabel Penfeather. Edited by J. F. Cooper. 2 vol. Philadelphia, 1846. 12°

31 LIVES of distinguished American Naval Officers. 2 vol. Vol. 1 : Bainbridge, Somers, Shaw, Shubrich, Preble. Vol. 2 : Jones, Woolsey, Perry, Dale. Philadel. 1846. 12°

32 MEMORIAL of J. F. Cooper; [consisting of a discourse on the Life and Genius of Cooper, by W. C. Bryant ; Speeches by Daniel Webster and others, etc.] New York, 1852. 8°

COOPER, J. G. Rev. The Scholar's Assistant ; or, a plain comprehensive and practical system of Arithmetic, etc. Philadelphia, 1830. 12°

COOPER, JOHN. An Oration delivered at Machias, Feb. 11, 1794, at the celebration of the birth-day of President Washington. Boston, 1794. 8°

COOPER, S. A concise System of Instructions and Regulations for the Militia and Volunteers of the United States, comprehending the exercises and movements of the Infantry, . . Cavalry, and Artillery. . . Prepared and arranged by . . S. Cooper, under the supervision of . . A. Macomb, commanding the army of the United States. Phil. 1836. 12°

COOPER, SAMUEL, *Senior Surgeon to University College Hospital, etc.* A Diſſertation on the Properties and Effects of the Datura Stramonium, or common Thorn Apple ; and on its use in Medicine. Phil. 1797. 8vo.

2 A DICTIONARY of Practical Surgery. . . From the seventh London edition, revised, corrected, and enlarged. With numerous notes and additions, . . together with a supplementary index, in which the science . . is brought down to the present period, . . by D. M. Reese. New York, 1845. 12°

COOPER, THOMAS. The Opinion of Judge Cooper on the effect of a Sentence of a Foreign Court of Admiralty. Published . . by A. J. Dallas. Philadelphia, 1810. 8°

COOPER, THOMAS, *M. D.* A Practical Treatise on Dyeing and Calico Printing. Philadelphia, 1815. 8vo.

COOPER, WILLIAM, *Minister of Sion Chapel, Whitechapel.* The Promised Seed : a Sermon [on Gen. xxii. 18] preached to . . the Jews at Sion Chapel, Whitechapel [London]. . . To which are added the hymns, *etc.* Boston, 1796. 8°

COPE, THOMAS P. Speech . . on Banks and Currency. Delivered Dec. 20, 1837. [Philadelphia,] 1838. 8°

COPWAY, GEORGE, *Chief, Ojibway Nation.* The Life, Letters, and Speeches of Kah-ge-ga-gah-bowh, or George Copway, Chief, Ojibway Nation. New York, 1850. 12°

2 RUNNING Sketches of Men and Places, in England, France, Germany, Belgium, and Scotland: New York, 1851. 12mo.

3 THE TRADITIONAL History and Characteristic Sketches of the Ojibway Nation. By George Copway, or Kah-ge-ga-gah-bowh, Chief of the Ojibway nation. Boston, 1851. 12°

CORAM, ROBERT. Political Inquiries ; to which is added, a plan for the general establishment of schools throughout the United States. Wilmington, 1791. 8°

CORCORAN, D. Pickings from the Portfolio of the Reporter of the New Orleans " Picayne." Philadelphia, 1847. 12°

CORDA, AUGUST CARL JOSEPH. Contribution to the knowledge of the different kinds of Brand in the Cereals, and Blight in Grain ; . . translated from the German by E. G. Smith. Albany, 1847. 4to.

COREY, DANIEL H. Report of the Trial of Daniel H. Corey, . . for the murder of Mrs. M. Nash. . . By J. Parker. Newport, N. H. 1830. 8°

CORNELL, WILLIAM M. Consumption, forestalled and prevented. Boston, 1846. 16°

CORNWALL, N. E. Music : as it was and as it is. N. York, 1851. 12°

CORNWALL, SUSAN PEYTON. The Finland Family ; or, Fancies taken for Facts : a tale. New York, 1853. 8°

CORNYN, JOHN K. Dick Wilson, the Rumseller's Victim ; or, Humanity pleading for the " Maine Law." A temperance story. . . With an introduction, by T. W. Brown. Auburn and Buffalo, 1853. 12°

CORONAL and Young Lady's Remembrancer. Edited by Rev. F. James. New York, 1853. 8°

CORSAIR ; a Gazette of literature, art, dramatic criticism, fashion, and novelty. N° 1-52. March 16, 1839 to March 7, 1840. Edited by N. P. Willis and T. O. Porter. Vol. 1. New York, 1839-40. Fol°

CORSON, JOHN W. Loiterings in Europe ; or, Sketches of Travel in France, Belgium, Switzerland, Italy, Austria, Prussia, Great Britain, and Ireland. With an appendix, containing observations on European charities and medical institutions. Second edition. New York, 1848. 8°

CORTES, HERNANDO. Historia de Méjico .. aumentada .. por D. F. A. Lorenzana .. revisada .. por D. M. Del Mar. Neuva York, 1828. 8vo.

2 THE DESPATCHES of Hernando Cortes, the conqueror of Mexico, addressed to Charles V; written during the conquest, and containing a narrative of its events. Translated from the Spanish, with introduction and notes, by George Folson. New York, 1843. 8vo.

COSMOPOLITE. Tales and Sketches, by a Cosmopolite. New York, 1830. 12°

2 A REVIEW of the Prosecution against Abner Kneeland, for blasphemy. By a Cosmopolite. Boston, 1835. 8°

COTTAGE BEE KEEPER. Saxton's Cottage and Farm Library. The Cottage Bee Keeper; or, suggestions for the practical management of amateur cottage and farm Apiaries. By a Country Curate. New York, 1851. 12°

COTTING, B. E. Nature in Disease. An address before the Norfolk District Medical Society of Massachusetts, etc. Boston, 1852. 8vo.

COTTON, JOHN, Pastor of the Church in Halifax. The Separation of the Tares and Wheat reserved to the Day of Judgment. A sermon preached .. from Matthew xiii. 24, 30. Boston, 1746. 12°

COTTON, JOHN, M.A. of Plymouth, Massachusetts. The General Practice of the Churches of New England, relating to Baptism Vindicated, etc. Boston [1771 ?] 8°

COVELL, L. T. A Digest of English Grammar .. adapted to the use of Schools. New York, 1852. 8°

COVENTRY, C. B. Epidemic Cholera; its history, causes, pathology, and treatment. Buffalo, 1849. 12mo.

COVERLEY, SIR ROGER DE, Pseud. A Cure for the Spleen; or, amusement for a winter's evening. Being the substance of a conversation on the Times, over a friendly tankard and pipe, etc. America, 1775. 8vo.

COUES, SAMUEL ELLIOTT. War and Christianity: an address before the American Peace Society, on the fourteenth anniversary, etc. Boston, 1842. 8°

2 OUTLINES of a System of Mechanical Philosophy: being a research into the laws of force. Boston, 1851. 12°

COULTAS, HARLAND. The Principles of Botany, as exemplified in the Cryptogamia, etc. Philadelphia, 1853. 12°

COUSIN, VICTOR. Introduction to the History of Philosophy. Translated from the French, by H. G. Linberg. Boston, 1832. 8vo.

2 ELEMENTS of Psychology; included in a critical examination of Locke's Essay on the Human Understanding. Translated from the French, with an introduction, notes, and additions, by C. S. Henry. Hartford, 1834. 8vo.

3 ELEMENTS of Psychology: .. with additional pieces... Translated from the French, with an introduction and notes, by C. S. Henry. Third edition. New York, 1842. 12°

4 THE PHILOSOPHY of the Beautiful, from the French of Victor Cousin. Translated, with notes and an introduction, by J. C. Daniel. New York, 1849. 12°

COUTHOUY, JOSEPH P. Remarks upon coral formations in the Pacific; with suggestions as to the causes of their absence in the same parallels of latitude on the coast of South America. Extracted from the Journal of the Boston Society of

Natural History for January, 1842. Boston, 1842. 8°

COWELL, JOSEPH. Thirty Years passed among the Players in England and America: interspersed with anecdotes and reminiscences of a variety of persons directly or indirectly connected with the drama during the theatrical life of J. Cowell, comedian. Written by himself. 2 parts. New York, 1845. 8°

COWEN, ESEK. Reports of Cases argued and determined in the Supreme Court and in the Court for the trial of Impeachments and the Correction of Errors of the State of New York; from May term, 1823, to Aug. term, 1828. 9 vol. Second edition. Albany, 1835-1839. 8vo.

COX, SAMUEL HANSON. Quakerism not Christianity; or, reasons for renouncing the doctrine of Friends. New York and Boston, 1833. 8vo.

COX, SAMUEL S. A Buckeye Abroad; or, wanderings in Europe and in the Orient. N. York, 1852. 8°

COXE, JOHN REDMAN. An inaugural Essay on Inflammation. Philadelphia, 1794. 8vo.

COXE, JOHN REDMAN. Considerations respecting the recognition of Friends in another World; on the affirmed descent of Jesus Christ into Hell; on Phrenology in connexion with the Soul, and on the Existence of a Soul in Brutes. Philadelphia, 1845. 12mo.

COXE, MARGARET. The Young Lady's Companion, in a series of letters. Columbus, 1839. 12°

COXE, RICHARD S. Reports of Cases argued and determined in the Supreme Court of New Jersey; from April term, 1790, to November term, 1795, both inclusive. Vol. 1. Burlington, 1816. 8°

COXE, TENCH. [Begins] Memoir

of February, 1817, upon the subject of the Cotton Wool cultivation, the Cotton trade, and the Cotton manufactures of the United States of America. [Philadelphia.] 8°

2 [Begins.] AN ADDITION of December, 1818, to the Memoir of February and August, 1817, on the subject of the Cotton culture, the Cotton commerce, and the Cotton manufacture of the United States. [Philadelphia.] 8°

COXE, WILLIAM. A View of the cultivation of Fruit Trees and the management of Orchards and Cider; with accurate descriptions of the most estimable varieties of native and foreign apples, pears, peaches, plums, and cherries, cultivated in the middle States of America. Philadelphia [Burlington printed], 1817. 8vo.

COYLE, THOMAS C. Certificates and Letters recommending the American Hydraulic Cement; patented by Thomas C. Coyle. Baltimore, 1838. 8°

COZZENS, ISSACHAR, Jun. A Geological History of Manhattan or New York Island, together with a map of the island, etc. New York, 1843. 8°

CRAFTS, THOMAS. An Oration, pronounced July 4, 1791, at .. Boston, in commemoration of the anniversary of American Independence. Boston, 1791. 4°

CRAFTS, WILLIAM. A Selection, in prose and poetry, from the miscellaneous writings of the late W. Crafts. To which is prefixed, a memoir of his life. Charleston, 1828. 8°

CRANCH, WILLIAM. Reports of Cases argued and adjudged in the Supreme Court of the United States; [from Aug. term 1801 to Feb. term 1815.] 9 vol. Washington, 1804-17. 8vo.

2 MEMOIR of the Life, Character, and Writings of John Adams; read

in the Capitol, in the City of Washington, at the request of the Columbian Institute. Washing. 1827. 8°

3 CONDENSED Reports of Cases argued and adjudged in the Supreme Court of the United States, January Term, 1834. Edited by W. Cranch, assisted by Rufus Dawes. Washington, 1835. 8°

CRANE, JOHN, D.D. A Sermon [on 1 Tim. iv. 16] delivered at the installation of . . E. Rich to the pastoral care of the Church . . in Troy, New Hampshire, Dec. 20, 1815. (Charge by S. Payson. Right hand of Fellowship by . . W. Fay.) Keene, 1816. 8°

CRANE, WILLIAM. Observations on, and a reply to, a Card (published by Dr. Knolton) addressed to Dr. Crane and others. Boston, 1795. 8vo.

CRANMER, THOMAS, Archbishop of Canterbury. The Life and Times of Cranmer. By the author of "Three Experiments of Living," etc. [Mrs. H. Lee]. Boston, 1841. 12°

CRAWFORD, CHARLES, calling himself Earl of Crawford and Lindsay. An Essay on the Propagation of the Gospel; in which there are numerous facts and arguments adduced to prove that many of the Indians in America are descended from the Ten Tribes. Philadel. 1801. 12mo.

CRAYON, GEOFFREY. See IRVING, Washington.

CREAMER, DAVID. Methodist Hymnology; comprehending notices of the poetical works of John and Charles Wesley, etc. New York, 1848. 12°

CREAMER, HANNAH GARDNER. Delia's Doctors; or, a glance behind the scenes. New York, 1852. 12°

CREATION. The Words of the Creation: an oratorio, by Joseph Haydn. Baltimore [1841]. 8vo.

CRESUS, Pseud. Comparative Value of the Peace Cause. [A Dialogue between Cresus, Pacis, and others.] [Boston! 1840?] 8°

CREYTON, PAUL. Father Brighthopes; or, an old clergyman's vacation. Boston, 1853. 12°

CRICHTON, ANDREW. The History of Arabia, ancient and modern. 2 vol. New York, 1845. 12°

CRISIS. The Crisis: or, the origin and consequences of our political dissensions. To which is annexed, the late Treaty between the United States and Great Britain. By a citizen of Vermont. Albany, 1815. 8°

CRISWELL, ROBERT. "Uncle Tom's Cabin" [by H. B. Stowe] contrasted with Buckingham Hall, The Planter's Home; or, a fair view of both sides of the Slavery question. New York, 1853. 12°

CRITERION (THE). Art, Science, and Literature. Vol. 1 and 2. From November 3, 1855, to July 12, 1856. New York, 1855-6. 4°

CRITIC (THE), a weekly Review of literature, fine arts, and the drama. Edited by W. Leggett. Vol. 1, Nov. 1, 1828—May 2, 1829. New York [1828-29]. 8°

CRITTENDEN, JOHN J. Speech . . on the Oregon question; delivered in the Senate . . . April 16, 1846. [Washington, 1846.] 8°

CROCKER, H. MATHER. Observations on the real Rights of Women; with their appropriate duties, agreeable to Scripture, reason, and common sense. Boston, 1818. 12°

CROCKETT, DAVID. Sketches and Eccentricities of Col. D. Crockett, of West Tennessee. New edition. New York, 1833. 8°

2 AN ACCOUNT of Col. Crockett's tour to the North and down East, etc.

Written by himself. Philadelphia, 1835. 12°

3 THE LIFE of M. Van Buren, containing every authentic particular by which his extraordinary character has been formed; with a concise history of the events which have occasioned his .. elevation; together with a review of his policy as a statesman. Sixteenth edition. Phil. 1837. 12°

4 PICTORIAL Life and Adventures of D. Crockett. Written by himself. Embellished .. from original designs in the finest style of art. .. This work will in future times .. be prized almost beyond its weight in gold, etc. Philadelphia [1852]. 8°

CROES, ROBERT B. The Anniversary Lecture, pronounced before the Historical Society of the county of Vigo, 14th March, 1844. Cincinnati, 1845. 8vo.

2 Two Essays on the Two-Witness principle. New York, 1847. 12mo.

CROLY, GEORGE. Life and Times of his late Majesty George the Fourth, with anecdotes of distinguished persons of the last fifty years. New and improved edition. N. York, 1845. 12°

CROMWELL, C. T. Mrs. Over the Ocean; or, glimpses of travel in many lands. New York, 1849. 12°

CROOKER, TURNER, and others. To His Excellency the Governor .. of Massachusetts, and to his Hon. Council. [A memorial from certain officers of the militia; with a minute of the Council thereon; a Message from the Governor to the Legislature; and the resolutions of the Legislature on the militia, of June, 1798. Boston! 1808.] 8°

CROSBY, ALPHEUS. Tables illustrative of Greek Inflection. Boston, 1841. 12°

2 A GRAMMAR of the Greek Language: Part first, a practical grammar of the Attic and common dialects, with the elements of general grammar. Boston, 1844. 12°

CROSBY, JAAZANIAH. The tendency of Religious Obedience to promote National Prosperity: a sermon [on Deut. xxviii. 1] preached .. before .. the Governor, .. Council, and .. Legislature of New Hampshire, June 3, 1830, being the anniversary Election. Concord, 1830. 8°

2 HISTORY of Charlestown, in New Hampshire, ... to the year 1833. Concord, 1833. 8°

CROSS, MARCUS E. The Museum of Religious Knowledge: designed to illustrate religious truth. Philadelphia, 1839. 12°

CROSS, TRUEMAN. Military Laws of the United States; including those relating to the Marine Corps. To which is prefixed, the Constitution of the United States. Second edition. Washington City, 1838. 8vo.

CROSWELL, HARRY. National Sin Rebuked. A discourse [on Job v. 6] on the death of the President of the United States [W. H. Harrison]. New Haven, 1841. 8°

CROSWELL, WILLIAM. Tables for readily computing the Longitude by the Lunar Observations, partly new, and partly taken from the requisite Tables of Dr. Maskelyne. Boston, 1791. 8°

CROWELL, ROBERT. Interment of the Dead, a dictate of natural affection, sanctioned by the word of God, and the examples of the good in every age: a sermon [on John xx. 13], etc. Andover, 1818. 8°

CROWNINSHIELD, JACOB. Mr. Crowninshield's Motion [in the House of Representatives of the United States of America, relative to commercial restrictions] 23 Jan. 1805. [Washington, 1805.] 8°

2 MR. CROWNINSHIELD's Motion [in the House of Representatives, imposing restrictions, in certain cases, on the commerce of European Colonies with the United States]. Feb. 10, 1806. Washington, 1806. 8°

CRUSIUS, GOTTLIEB CHRISTIAN. A Complete Greek and English Lexicon of the Poems of Homer and the Homeridæ... Translated, with corrections and additions, by H. Smith. Hartford, 1844. 8°

CUBA and the Cubans; comprising a history of the Island,.. its present.. condition; also its relation to England and the United States. New York, 1850. 12°

CULTIVATOR (THE), a Monthly Publication, published by the New York State Agricultural Society, and conducted by J. Buel, J. P. Beekman, and J. D. Wafson. Vol. 1, second edition; (vol. 2, 3, second edition; vol. 4, conducted by J. Buel. March, 1834 to February, 1838.) Albany, 1838. 4to. [Continued as]

2 THE CULTIVATOR, a Monthly Publication... conducted by J. Buel. Vol. 5, 6. Albany, 1838-9, 1839-40. Fol. [Continued as]

3 THE CULTIVATOR, a consolidation of Buel's Cultivator and Genesee Farmer... W. Gaylord and L. Tucker, editors. Vol. 7-10. Albany, 1840-43. Fol. [Continued as]

4 THE CULTIVATOR... New series... Published by L. Tucker, editor. Albany, 1844-52. 8vo. [Continued as]

5 THE CULTIVATOR... Third series. Vol. 1-4. Albany, 1853-56. 8vo.

CUMBERLAND, Brothers. Hints to Engineers and others for the use of "Cumberland Brothers' patent Metallic Oil" for machinery. New York, 1852. 8°

CUMBERLAND BAPTIST ASSOCIATION. Minutes of the Cumberland (Baptist) Afsociation, holden in .. Jay (Maine), Sept. 29 and 30, 1813; together with their circular and corresponding letters. Hallowell, 1813. 8°

CUMING, F. Sketches of a Tour to the Western Country, through Ohio and Kentucky, a Voyage down the Ohio and Mifsifsippi, and a Trip through the Mifsifsippi territory and part of West Florida. Commenced 1807, and concluded 1809. With notes and an appendix, containing some interesting facts; together with a notice of an expedition through Louisiana. Pittsburg, 1810. 12mo.

CUMINGS, HENRY. A Sermon [on Job v. 12-16] preached at Billerica, Nov. 29, 1798, being the day of anniversary Thanksgiving throughout Mafsachusetts. Boston, 1798. 8°

CUMINGS, SAMUEL. The Western Pilot; containing charts of the Ohio River and of the Mifsifsippi, from the mouth of the Mifsouri to the Gulf of Mexico; with directions for navigating the same, and a Gazetteer. Cincinnati, 1832. 8°

CUMMING, HOOPER, D. D. An Oration, delivered at Newark, New Jersey. Newark, 1823. 8°

CUMMING, JOHN, D. D. Minister of the Scotch Church, London Wall. A Discourse [on Jude 3] to a Society of Young Men in London, preached in .. 1719. Boston, 1805. 8°

CUMMINGS, ASA. A Discourse [on Jer. xiv. 7] delivered .. April 6, 1820, the day of the annual Fast in Maine and Mafsachusetts. Brunswick, 1820. 8°

CUMMINGS, EBENEZER E. Annals of the Baptist Churches in New Hampshire; a sermon [on Deut. xxxii. 7-10] preached before the New Hampshire Baptist State Convention, etc. Concord, 1836. 8°

CUMMINGS, JACOB ABBOT. An Introduction to Ancient and Modern Geography... With an Atlas... Ninth edition. Boston, 1823. 12° Atlas, 1815. 8°

2 THE PRONOUNCING Spelling Book, adapted to Walker's Critical Pronouncing Dictionary... Revised and improved from the fourth edition. Concord, 1840. 12°

CUNNINGHAM, ALLAN. The

Lives of the most eminent British Painters and Sculptors. 5 vol. New York, 1844. 12°

CURRAN, Right Hon. John Philpot. Speeches of John Philpot Curran; with the speeches of Grattan, Erskine, and Burke. To which is prefixed a brief sketch of the history of Ireland, and a biographical account of Mr. Curran. 2 vol. New York, 1809. 8vo.

CURRIE, William. An Historical Account of the Climates and Diseases of the United States of America, and of the remedies and methods of treatment. Philadel. 1792. 8°

2 Memoirs of the Yellow Fever, which prevailed in Philadelphia and other parts of the United States of America, in the summer and autumn of the present year, 1798; including, tables of the weather, a collection of facts respecting the origin of the fever, etc. Philadel. 1798. 8vo.

3 A Sketch of the Rise and Progress of the Yellow Fever, and of the proceedings of the Board of Health in Philadelphia in the year 1799, etc. Philadelphia, 1800. 8vo.

CURTIS, Charles Pelham. An Oration delivered .. 4th July, 1823, in commemoration of American Independence, etc. Boston, 1823. 8°

CURTIS, George Ticknor. A Digest of Cases adjudicated in the Courts of Admiralty of the United States, and in the High Court of Admiralty in England; together with some topics from the works of Sir Leoline Jenkins, Judge of the Admiralty in the reign of Charles II. Boston, 1839. 8vo.

2 The American Conveyancer, containing a large variety of legal forms and instruments, adapted to popular wants and professional use throughout the United States, etc. Boston, 1839. 12mo.

3 A Treatise on the Rights and

Duties of Merchant Seamen, according to the general Maritime Law and the Statutes of the United States. Boston, 1841. 8°

4 Equity Precedents; supplementary to Mr. Justice Story's Treatise on Equity Pleadings. Boston, 1850. 8°

5 Digest of the Decisions of the Courts of Common Law and Admiralty in the United States. Vol. 1, by Theron Metcalf and J. C. Perkins. Vol. 2, 3, by George Ticknor Curtis. See Metcalf, Theron.

6 The Inventor's Manual of Legal Principles, and Guide to the Patent Office. Boston, 1851. 12°

CURTIS, George William. Lotus-eating: a summer-book. New York, 1852. 12°

CURTIS, J. T. and Lillie J. An Epitome of Homœopathic Practice; compiled chiefly from Jahr Rückert, Beauvais, etc. N. York, 1843. 12mo.

CURTIS, Newton M. The Doom of the Tory's Guide. A tale. New York, 1843. 8vo.

2 The Scout of the Silver Pond. [A tale.] New York, 1848. 8°

CURTIS'S Pocket Almanack, and Register of New Hampshire for .. 1809, etc. Amherst [1808]. 12°

CURTISS, Daniel S. Western Portraiture, and Emigrants' Guide: a description of Wisconsin, Illinois and Iowa; with remarks on Minnesota, and other Territories. New York, 1852. 12°

CURWEN, Samuel. Journal and Letters of the late Samuel Curwen, an American refugee in England from 1775 to 1784, comprising remarks on the prominent men and measures of that period. To which are added, biographical notices of many American Loyalists and other eminent persons, by G. A. Ward. London [New York printed]. 1842. 8vo.

CUSHING, Abel. Historical Letters on the First Charter of

L

Maſſachusetts Government. Boston, 1839. 12°

CUSHING, CALEB. An Addreſs delivered at Lynn [Maſs.] before the [Masonic] Aſſociated Lodges, etc. Newburyport, 1826. 8°·

2 THE HISTORY and Present State of the town of Newburyport. Newburyport, 1826. 12°

3 REMINISCENCES of Spain; the country, its people, history, and monuments. 2 vol. Bost. 1833. 12mo.

4 AN ORATION pronounced at Boston before the Colonization Society of Maſſachusetts, on the Anniversary of American Independence, July 4, 1833. Boston, 1833. 8°

5 REVIEW, historical and political, of the late revolution in France, and of the consequent events in Belgium, Poland, Great Britain, and other parts of Europe. 2 vol. Boston, 1833. 12°

6 SPEECH . . on the Right of Petition, as connected with petitions for the abolition of slavery and the slave trade in the Diſtrict of Columbia; in the House of Representatives, Jan. 25, 1836. Washington, 1836. 8°

7 SPEECH . . on the proposition to censure Mr. John Quincy Adams, for an alleged disrespect to the House of Representatives, Feb. 7, 1837. [Washington, 1837.] 8°

8 SPEECH. . on the Meſſage of the President of the United States, at the opening of the twenty-fifth Congreſs; delivered in the House of Representatives, Sept. 25, 1837. Washington, 1837. 8°

9 SPEECH . . on Executive Powers; delivered in the House of Representatives, Dec. 19, 1837. [Washington, 1837.] 8°

10 SPEECH on the Treasury Note Bill; delivered in the House of Representatives, Oct. 6, 1837. Washington, 1838. 8°

11 SPEECH . . on the continuation of the Cumberland road; delivered in the House of Representatives, April 19, 1838. Washing. 1838. 8°

12 SPEECH . . on the subject of the Oregon Territory; delivered in the House of Representatives, . . May 17 and 22, 1838. Washington, 1838. 8°

13 AN ORATION, on the material growth and territorial progreſs of the United States, delivered at Springfield, Maſs... July 4, 1839. Springfield, 1839. 8°

14 SPEECH . . on the Sub-Treasury Bill; delivered in the House of Representatives, May 20 and 21, 1840. [Washington, 1840.] 8°

15 SPEECH . . on the case of A. McLeod; delivered in the House of Representatives, June 24 and 25, 1841. Washington, 1841. 8°

16 REMARKS . . on the Navy Appropriation Bill. (In the House of Representatives, May 17, 1842.) Washington, 1842. 8°

17 TARIFF vs. [versus] Distribution. [A speech, delivered in the House of Representatives.] [Washington, 1842.] 8°

CUSHING, JACOB. A Discourse [on Luke xii. 35-37] occasioned by the death of the Rev. . J. Jackson, etc. Boston, 1797. 8°

CUSHING, LUTHER STEARNS. A practical treatise on the Trustee Proceſs, or Foreign Attachment of the laws of Maſſachusetts and Maine; with an appendix, containing the Statutes of Maſſachusetts, Connecticut, Rhode Island, New Hampshire, Vermont, and Maine, on that subject. Cambridge, 1833. 8°

2 REPORTS of Contested Elections, in the House of Representatives of the Commonwealth of Maſſachusetts; from 1780 to 1834 inclusive: compiled from the journals, files, and printed documents of the House, in pursuance of an order thereof, etc. Boston, 1834. 8°

3 AN ACT for the relief of Insolvent Debtors, and for the more equal distribution of their effects; paſſed by the legislature of Maſſachusetts, April

23, 1838; with an outline of the system thereby introduced, and forms of proceeding under the same by L. S. Cushing. Boston, 1838. 12°

4 REPORTS of cases argued and determined in the Supreme Judicial Court of Maſſachusetts. Boston, 1850. 8°

5 MANUAL of Parliamentary Practice. Rules of proceeding and debate in deliberative aſſemblies. Boston, 1853. 16mo.

CUSHMAN, ROBERT. Self-Love. 1621. The first Sermon preached in New England, and the oldest extant of any delivered in America [on 1 Cor. x. 24]. New York, 1847. 12°

CUTLER, CALVIN. Our Liberties in Danger: a sermon [on 2 Cor. iii. 17] preached in Windham, New Hampshire, on the day of the annual Thanksgiving,etc. Concord, 1835. 8°

CUTTER, CHARLES WILLIAM. An Oration pronounced before the Whigs of Portsmouth, . . July 4, 1834. Portsmouth, N. H. 1834. 8°

CUTTER, WILLIAM. The Life of Israel Putnam, Major-General in the army of the American Revolution. Compiled from the best authorities. Third edition. New York, 1847. 12°

CUTTS, JAMES MADISON. The Conquest of California and New Mexico, by the forces of the United States, in the years 1846 and 1847. Philadelphia, 1847. 12°

CUTTS, MARY. The Autobiography of a Clock, and other Poems. Boston, 1852. 12°

CUVIER, GEORGES LEOPOLD CHRETIEN FREDERIC DAGOBERT DE, Baron. Eſſay on the Theory of the Earth . . [translated from the French by R. Kerr]. With mineralogical notes, and an account of Cuvier's geological discoveries, by Profeſſor Jameson. To which are . . added, observations on the geology of North America . . by S. L. Mitchill. New York, 1818. 8vo.

2 THE ANIMAL Kingdom, arranged in conformity with its organization . . Translated from the French and abridged . . by H. M'Murtrie. New York, 1833. 8vo.

CUYLER, CORNELIUS C. The LAW of God with respect to Murder: a sermon [on Genesis ix. 5, 6]. Philadelphia, 1842. 8°

2 THE Impropriety of Capital Punishments: or the report of a committee on Dr. Cuyler's sermon entitled "The Law of God with respect to Murder." Philadelphia, 1842. 8°

CYR, N. Memoir of the Rev. C. H. O. Cote, with a memoir of Mrs. M. Y. Cote, and a history of the Grande Ligne Miſſion, Canada East. [Edited by J. N. B.] Philadelphia [1853]. 12mo.

ADD, GEORGE H. The Advocate of Veterinary Reform, and outlines of Anatomy and Physiology of the Horse. . . . Containing also a Veterinary Dictionary selected from the works of R. [J.] White, of London, and adapted to the present state of the reformed practice in the United States. Boston, 1850. 8vo.

2 THE AMERICAN Cattle Doctor. New York, 1853. 12°

DAGGET, DAVID. Sunbeams may be extracted from Cucumbers, but the process is tedious. An Oration pronounced on the fourth of July, 1799. New Haven, 1799. 8°

DAGGETT, JOHN. Sketch of the History of Attleborough, from its settlement to the present time. Dedham, 1834. 8vo.

DAGGETT, NAPHTALI. The Excellency of a good Name: a sermon [on Eccl. vii. 1] delivered in . . Yale College, . . occasioned by the death of . . J. Lane, one of the Tutors, etc. New Haven [1768]. 8°

DAILY ADVERTISER. N° 458. Aug. 15, 1786. N. York, 1786. Fol.

DAILY EVENING TRAN-SCRIPT. Lynde M. Walter, Editor. Sept. 24, 1839. Boston, 1839. Fol.

DAILY HERALD. Vol. 8. N° 49. Newburyport, 1839. Fol.

DAILY SUN. Vol. 1. N° 151. May 22nd, 1839. Cincinnati, 1839. Fol.

DALCHO, FREDERICK. An Historical Account of the Protestant Episcopal Church in South Carolina, from the first settlement of the Province to the war of the Revolution; with notices of the present state of the Church in each parish; and some account of the early civil history of Carolina, never before published. To which are added, the laws relating to religious worship; the journals and rules of the Convention of South Carolina, *etc.* Charleston, 1820. 8°

DALLAS, ALEXANDER JAMES. Reports of Cases ruled and adjudged in the Courts of Pennsylvania, before and since the Revolution. Vol. 1, third edition, with notes and additions by T. I. Wharton; (vol. 4, second edition, with notes and additions by B. Gerhard). 4 vol. Philadelphia, 1830, 1798-99, 1835. 8vo.

DALLAS, GEORGE MIFFLIN. An Address delivered . . before the annual commencement of the College of New Jersey. Princeton, 1831. 8°

DALRYMPLE, JOHN, *second Earl of Stair.* A Bill in the Chancery of New Jersey at the suit of John, Earl of Stair, and others, Proprietors of the Eastern Division of New Jersey, against B. Bond and some other persons . . distinguished by the name of Clinker Lot Right men. With three . . maps. To which is added, the publications of the Council of Proprietors . . concerning the riots . . in New Jersey, *etc.* Published by subscription. New York, 1747. Fol.

DANA, ALEXANDER H. Before the Board of Commiſſioners on claims against Mexico. Claim of J. Haggerty and others. Argument for claimants on the rehearing. New York, 1851. 8°

DANA, DANIEL. The Deity of Christ: a sermon [on Rom. ix. 5], *etc.* Haverhill, 1810. 8°

2 A SERMON [on 1 Tim. ii. 4] delivered before the Gloucester Female Society for promoting Christian Knowledge, *etc.* Newburyport, 1815. 8°

3 THE CONNECTION between Moral and Intellectual Improvement: an addreſs delivered at the anniversary of the New Hampshire Alpha of the Phi Beta Kappa Society, Dartmouth College, *etc.* Exeter, 1817. 8°

4 A SERMON [on Gen. xxviii. 17] preached Dec. 30, 1819, at the dedication of the house of worship . . in Dedham. Second edition. Dedham, 1820. 8°

5 AN ELECTION Sermon [on Prov. xiv. 34] preached before . . . the Council, Senate, and House of Representatives of . . New Hampshire. Concord, 1823. 8°

6 EVANGELICAL Preaching is rational Preaching: a sermon [on Acts xxvi. 25] delivered Nov. 2, 1825, at the ordination of . . W. K. Talbot. (The charge by J. H. Church. The right hand of fellowship by . . E. L. Parker.) Concord, 1826. 8°

7 A SERMON [on John xiv. 2, 3] occasioned by the death of Mrs. H. Putnam. Portsmouth, 1832. 8°

DANA, E. Geographical Sketches on the Western Country; designed for emigrants and settlers, *etc.* Cincinnati, 1819. 12°

DANA, J. FREEMAN *and* SAMUEL L. Outlines of the Mineralogy and Geology of Boston and its Vicinity. Boston, 1818. 8vo.

DANA, JAMES. The Heavenly Mansions; a sermon [on John xiv. 2] preached at the interment of the Rev. E. Stiles. New Haven [1795]. 8vo.

DANA, JAMES DWIGHT. United States Exploring Expedition. . . Zoophytes, by J. D. Dana. With a folio atlas of sixty-one plates.

2 GEOLOGY. By J. D. Dana. With a folio atlas of twenty-one plates.

3 CRUSTACEA. By J. D. Dana. *See* WILKES, Charles, Narrative of the United States Exploring Expedition, *etc.* Vol. 7, 10, 13, 14.

4 A SYSTEM of Mineralogy, comprising the most recent discoveries. Second edition. N. York, 1844. 8vo.

5 A SYSTEM of Mineralogy. . . Third edition, rewritten, rearranged, and enlarged. New York and London, 1850. 8vo.

6 CONSPECTUS Crustaceorum, quæ in Orbis Terrarum circum navigatione, C. Wilkes è Claſſe Reipublicæ Fœderatæ duce, lexit et descripsit J. D. Dana. [Ex Academiæ Scientiarum Naturalium Philadelphiensis Nuntiis, anno 1851, vol. 5.] [Philadelphia, 1851.] 8vo.

7 EXTRACTED from the American Journal of Science and Arts, vol. 12. Second series, Sept. 1851. On the claſſification of the Crustacea Grapsoidea. [New Haven, 1851.] 8°

8 MINERALOGICAL Notices. N° 3 (Notes on heteronomic isomorphism), [two articles by J. D. Dana, extracted from the " American Journal of Science and Arts."] [New Haven, 1851.] 8vo.

9 NOTE on the eruption of Mauna Loa. [From the " American Journal of Science and Arts." Vol. 14. Sept. 1852, pp. 254-259.] [New Haven, 1852.] 8vo.

10 CONSPECTUS Crustaceorum, *etc.* Conspectus of the Crustacea of the Exploring Expedition under Capt. Wilkes, *etc.* [From the proceedings of the Academy of Natural Sciences of Philadel.] [Philadel. 1852.] 8vo.

11 FROM the American Journal of Science and Arts. . . . On lettering figures of crystals. [New Haven, 1852.] 8vo.

12 ON the Claſsification of the Coristoidea, Paguridea, *etc.* [From the American Journal of Science and Arts. Second series, vol. 13. Jan. 1852.] [New Haven] 1852. 8vo.

13 ON Coral Reefs and Islands . . from the author's Exploring Expedition Report on Geology, with additions. New York, 1853. 8°

DANA, JAMES FREEMAN. Report on a Disease afflicting neat Cattle, in Burton, New Hampshire, *etc.* Read before the New Hampshire Medical Society, *etc.* Concord, 1822. 8°

DANA, JAMES G. Reports of select Cases decided in the Court of Appeals of Kentucky. 1833-1840. 9 vol. Frankfort, 1834-40. 8°

DANA, JOSEPH, *A.M.* A new American selection of leſsons in Reading and Speaking.' Bost. 1792. 12°

2 QUÆSTIONES Grammaticæ: or, grammatical exercises, by questions only . . particularly adapted to Adam's Latin Grammar. With an appendix. . . Second edition, corrected, *etc.* Boston, 1828. 12°

DANA, MARY S. B. Letters addreſsed to Relatives and Friends, chiefly in reply to arguments in support of the doctrine of the Trinity. Boston, 1845. 12°

2 FORECASTLE TOM; or, the Landsman turned sailor. N.York, 1846. 12°

3 THE YOUNG Sailor; a narrative founded on fact. N.York, 1846. 12°

DANA, RICHARD HENRY. Poems and Prose Writings. Philadelphia, 1833. 8vo.

2 POEMS and Prose Writings. 2 vol. New York, 1850. 8°

DANA, RICHARD HENRY. Two Years before the Mast. A personal narrative of life at sea. [By R. H. D. *i. e.* R. H. Dana, the younger.] New York, 1844. 12°

2 THE SEAMAN'S Friend. Containing a treatise on practical seamanship, *etc.* Fourth edition. Boston, 1845. 12°

DANA, SAMUEL. An Oration pronounced at Groton, in . . Maſsachusetts, . . 4th July, 1807, in commemoration of the Independence of the United States of America, before the republican citizens of . . Groton, *etc.* Amherst, N. H. 1807. 8°

DANA, SAMUEL LUTHER. A Muck Manual for Farmers. . . Second edition, with additions. Lowell, 1843. 12°

DANE, JOHN. A Declaration of Remarkable Providences in the Course of my Life. By John Dane. . . To which is added, a pedigree of the Dane family, and a few notes. By a member of the New England Historic-Genealogical Society. Boston, 1854. 8vo.

DANE, NATHAN., A General Abridgment and Digest of American Law, with occasional notes and comments. 9 vol. Boston, 1823-29. 8vo.

DANFORTH, JOSHUA, N. Gleanings and Groupings from a Pastor's Portfolio. New York, 1852. 12°

D[ANFORTH], S[AMUEL]. An Astronomical Description of the late Comet or Blazing Star, as it appeared in New England in the 9th, 10th, 11th, and in the beginning of the 12th Moneth, 1664. Together with a brief Theological Application thereof. By S[amuel] D[anforth.] Cambridge, printed by Samuel Green, 1665. 16mo.

DANFORTH, THOMAS. An Oration pronounced July 4, 1804, at . . Boston, in commemoration of the anniversary of American Independence. Boston, 1804. 8°

DANIELL, JOHN FREDERICK. Familiar Illustrations of Natural Philosophy. Selected principally from Daniell's Chymical Philosophy. By J. Renwick. New York, 1840. 12°

DANTE, ALIGHIERI. The first ten Cantos of the Inferno of Dante Alighieri. Newly translated into English verse [by T. W. Parsons]. Boston, 1843. 8°

DANVERS, JOHN THIERRY. A Picture of a Republican Magistrate of the New School, being a full length likeness of T. Jefferson. To which is added a short criticism on the characters and pretensions of Mr. Madison, Mr. Clinton, and Mr. Pinckney. New York, 1808. 8°

DARBY, WILLIAM. A Geographical Description of the State of Louisiana, with an account of the inhabitants. Philadelphia, 1816. 8vo.

2 A GEOGRAPHICAL Description of the State of Louisiana, the southern part of the State of Missisippi, and Territory of Alabama; presenting a view of the soil, climate, animal, vegetable, and mineral productions; illustrative of their natural physiognomy, their geographical configuration, and relative situation : with an account of the character and manners of the inhabitants. Together with a map, from actual survey and observations, projected on a scale of ten miles to an inch, of the State of Louisiana, and adjacent countries. Second edition, enlarged and improved. By William Darby. N. York, 1817. 8°

3 THE EMIGRANT's Guide to the Western and South-western States and Territories : comprising a geographical and statistical description of the States of Louisiana, Missisippi, Tennessee, Kentucky, and Ohio; the Territories of Alabama, Missouri, Illinois, and Michigan, and the western parts of Virginia, Pennsylvania, and New York. New York, 1818. 8vo.

4 A TOUR from the City of New York to Detroit, in the Michigan Territory. New York, 1819. 8vo.

5 MEMOIR of the Geography and Natural and Civil History of Florida. Attended by an appendix, containing the Treaty of Cession and other papers. Philadelphia, 1821. 8°

6 VIEW of the United States, historical, geographical, and statistical. Philadelphia, 1828. 12mo.

7 LECTURES on the Discovery of America, and Colonization of North America by the English. Baltimore, 1828. 12°

8 MNEMONIKA, or, the tablet of memory; being a register of events from the earliest period to .. 1829. .. The matter furnished by William Darby. Revised, with additions, by the Publisher (E. J. Coale) and other persons. Baltimore, 1829. 12°

9 ATCHAFALAYA Railroad. From the National Intelligencer. [Reasons in favour of that railroad.] [Washington, 1836.] 8°

DARBY, WILLIAM, and DWIGHT, THEODORE. A New Gazetteer of the United States of America. Hartford, 1833. 8°

DARLINGTON, WILLIAM N. Florula Cestrica : an essay towards a catalogue of the Phænogamous Plants .. growing in the vicinity of .. West Chester, in .. Pennsylvania ; with notices of their properties and uses. .. To which is subjoined an appendix of the useful cultivated plants of the same district. West Chester, 1826. 8vo.

DARTMOUTH (The). Conducted by Undergraduates in Dartmouth College. Nov. 1839 to July, 1844. 5 vol. Hanover, 1840-44. 8°

DARTMOUTH COLLEGE. Catalogus [triennial] eorum qui in Universitate Dartmuthensi .. in Republica Neo-Hantoniæ ab anno 1771 ad annum 1798, alicujus gradus laurea donati sunt. 1798, (1801, 1804, 1807, 1810, 1813, 1814, 1819. 1822, 1825, 1828, 1831, 1834, 1837, 1840, 1843, 1846, and 1852: wanting for the year 1849). 18 parts. Leuphanæ, Concordiæ, Andoverii, Portimuthi, Bostoniæ, et Hanoveræ, 1798-1852. 8°

2 CATALOGUE of the Members of the New Hampshire Alpha of the ΦBK Society, Dartmouth University. 1815 (1838, 1839, and 1844). 4 parts. Andover, Concord, and Hanover, 1815-44. 8°

3 SKETCHES of the History of Dartmouth College and Moors' Charity School; with a particular account of some late remarkable proceedings of the board of trustees, from .. 1779 to .. 1815. [Hanover! 1815?] 8°

4 A CANDID, Analytical Review of the "Sketches of the History of Dartmouth College," etc. [Hanover? 1815?] 8°

5 THE CHARTER of Dartmouth College. Hanover, 1816. 8°

6 REPORT of the Case of the Trustees of Dartmouth College against W. H. Woodward. Argued and determined in the Superior Court of Judicature of .. New Hampshire, Nov. 1817, and on Error in the Supreme Court of the United States, Feb. 1819. By T. Farrar. Portsmouth [1819]. 8°

7 [ANNUAL] Catalogue of the Officers and Students... 1820 (to 1853; wanting the years 1822, 1825, 1829, 1832, 1848 to 1852). 25 parts. Hanover, Concord, Boston, Windsor, Haverhill, Newport, and Claremont, 1820-1853. 8°

8 A CATALOGUE of the Officers and Students. 1838-9. Second edition. Concord, 1838. 12°

9 A CATALOGUE of the Officers and Students. .. Sept. 1840. Concord, 1840. 8°

10 COMMENCEMENT, etc. August, 1823... Order of Exercises. [Hanover, 1823.] 8°

11 ORDER of Exercises at Commencement. .. July 29, 1835 (July 27, 1836; July 26, 1837; July 28, 1842; July 27, 1843; July 25, 1844). 6 parts. [Hanover, 1835-44.] 8°

12 ORDER of Declamations for the Prizes at Dartmouth College, July 30, 1835 (July 28, 1836; July 27,

1837). 3 parts. [Hanover, 1835-37.] 8°

13 NEW Hampshire Medical Institution, Dartmouth College, Hanover. [Rules and regulations.] [Hanover] 1826. 8°

14 LAWS of Dartmouth College. Hanover, 1828. 8°

15 LAWS of Dartmouth College. Hanover, 1837. 8°

16 LAWS of Dartmouth College. Concord, 1842. 8°

17 CATALOGUE of the Officers and Members of the Society of Social Friends, .. Dartmouth College, 1839. Concord, 1839. 8°

18 CATALOGUE of the Officers and Members of the Society of United Fraternity, .. Dartmouth College, 1840. Concord, 1840. 8°

DASHIELL, GEORGE. A Sermon [on Job iii. 7] occasioned by the burning of the Theatre, Richmond, Virginia, delivered January 12, 1812. Baltimore. 8°

DAVEIS, CHARLES STEWART. Address delivered before the Alumni of Bowdoin College, .. Sept. 1, 1835. Portland, 1835. 8°

DAVENPORT, AMZI BENEDICT. The History and Genealogy of the Davenport Family, in England and America, from A. D. 1086 to 1850. [With an appendix.] New York, 1851. 12°

DAVENPORT, BISHOP. A New Gazetteer; or, geographical dictionary of North America and the West Indies. Baltimore, 1833. 8°

2 A POCKET Gazetteer; or, traveller's guide through North America and the West Indies. .. Compiled from the most recent and authentic sources. Trenton, 1833. 12°

3 A HISTORY and New Gazetteer; or, geographical dictionary of America and the West Indies. .. A new and much improved edition. New York, 1842. 8°

DAVENPORT, RICHARD ALFRED. Perilous Adventures: or, remarkable instances of courage, perseverance, and suffering. New York, 1846. 12°

DAUGHTER - IN - LAW. The affectionate Daughter-in-law. Written for the American Sunday-School Union, and revised by the committee of publication. Philadelphia [1833]. 12mo.

DAVID, *King of Israel*. The Life of David, King of Israel. By the author of "Bible Sketches." Philadelphia [1832]. 12mo.

DAVIDGE, Francis H. Address delivered before the Horticultural Society of Maryland, at its third anniversary celebration, etc. [With lists of officers and members.] Baltimore, 1835. 8°

DAVIDSON, JAMES, *Treasurer of the State of Kentucky*. Report of the Treasurer of the State, made in compliance with a resolution of the House of Representatives, of Dec. 16, 1839. [Frankfort, Ky. 1840.] 8°

DAVIDSON, LUCRETIA MARIA, *Miß*. Poetical remains of the late L. M. Davidson, collected and arranged by her mother (Margaret Davidson); with a biography by Miß Sedgwick. Philadelphia, 1841. 8vo.
2 POETICAL remains of the late L. M. Davidson, collected and arranged by her mother (M. Davidson); with a biography by Miß Sedgwick. A new edition, revised. New York, 1851. 8°

DAVIDSON, ROBERT G. W. An inaugural dissertation on the Suffocatio Stridula, or croup. Philadelphia, 1794. 8°

DAVIDSON, R. An excursion to the Mammoth Cave, and the Barrens of Kentucky. With some notices of the early settlement of the State. Lexington, 1840. 12mo.

DAVIES, CHARLES. Mental and practical Arithmetic, designed for the use of academies and schools. Hartford, 1838. 12°
2 FIRST Lessons in Arithmetic, etc. designed for beginners. Philadelphia, 1842. 12°
3 FIRST Lessons in Arithmetic, etc. New York, 1846. 12°
4 FIRST Lessons in Arithmetic, etc. New York, 1847. 12°
5 ARITHMETIC, designed for academies and schools (with answers). Philadelphia, 1843. 12°
6 ARITHMETIC, designed for academies and schools (with answers). [*The edition of* 1843, *with a new title-page.*] New York, 1846. 12°
7 PRACTICAL Geometry: with selected applications in mensuration, in artificers' work and mechanics. Philadelphia, 1844. 12°
8 ELEMENTS of Analytical Geometry: embracing the equations of the point, the straight line, the conic sections, and surfaces of the first and second order. Revised edition. New York, 1845. 8°
9 KEY to Davies' Arithmetic: with additional examples. For the use of teachers only. New York, 1845. 12°
10 ELEMENTS of Drawing and Mensuration, applied to the mechanic arts. New York, 1846. 12°
11 ELEMENTARY Geometry, with applications in mensuration. New York, 1846. 12°
12 ELEMENTARY Algebra: embracing the first principles of the science. New York, 1846. 12°
13 A KEY, containing the statements and solutions of questions in Davies' Elementary Algebra; for the use of teachers only. New York, 1846. 12°
14 ELEMENTS of Surveying and Navigation; with a description of the instruments and the necessary tables. Fifteenth edition. N. York, 1846. 8°
15 ELEMENTS of Descriptive Geometry, with their application to spherical trigonometry, spherical projections, and warped surfaces. New York, 1846. 8°

16 ELEMENTS of the differential and integral Calculus. Improved edition. New York, 1846. 8°

17 A TREATISE on Shades and Shadows, and linear perspective. New York, 1846. 8°

18 GRAMMAR of Arithmetic; or, an analysis of the language of figures and science of numbers. New York, 1850. 12°

19 THE LOGIC and utility of Mathematics, with the best methods of instruction explained and illustrated. New York, 1850. 8°

20 PRACTICAL Mathematics, with drawing and mensuration, applied to the mechanic arts. New York, 1852. 12°

DAVIES, SAMUEL, *President of Princeton College, New Jersey.* A Sermon [on 2 Sam. i. 19] .. on the death of .. King George.II... To which is prefixed, a brief account of the life, character, and death of the author, by D. Bostwick. Boston [1761]. 8°

2 SERMONS on important subjects. .. With an essay on the life and times of the author, by A. B. Stereotype edition, *etc.* 3 vol. New York, 1851. 12°

DAVILA, ENRICO CATERINO. Discourses on Davila, a series of papers on political history .. By an American citizen [J. Adams, President of the United States]. Boston, 1805. 8°

DAVIS, ANDREW JACKSON. The Principles of Nature, her Divine Revelations, and a voice to mankind by and through A. J. Davis. [Edited by W. Fishbough.] Fourth edition. New York, 1847. 8°

2 THE GREAT Harmonia; being a philosophical revelation of the natural, spiritual and celestial universe. Fourth edition. 2 vol. Boston, 1851. 12°

3 THE PHILOSOPHY of Spiritual Intercourse, being an explanation

of modern mysteries. New York, 1851. 8°

DAVIS, CHARLES GIDEON. United States vs. Charles Gideon Davis. Report of the proceedings at the examination of Charles Gideon Davis, on a charge of aiding and abetting in the rescue of a fugitive slave. Held in Boston in February 1851. Boston, 1851. 8°

DAVIS, DANIEL. An Oration delivered at Portland, July 4, 1796, in commemoration of the anniversary of American Independence. Portland [1796]. 8°

DAVIS, DANIEL. Davis's Manual of Magnetism; including also electro-magnetism, magneto-electricity, and thermo-electricity. With a description of the electrotype process. Boston, 1840. 12°

2 MANUAL of Magnetism. Including also electro-magnetism, magneto-electricity, and thermo-electricity. With a description of the electrotype process. Boston, 1842. 12mo.

DAVIS, DAVID. Blaengwawr Merthyr Steam Coal, Cardiff. Proprietor, D. Davis. N. York, 1852. 8°

DAVIS, EMERSON. The Half-Century: or, a history of changes that have taken place, and events that have transpired, chiefly in the United States, between 1800 and 1850. With an introduction by M. Hopkins. Boston, 1851. 12°

DAVIS, GARRETT. Speech .. against the motion to reconsider the vote by which the bill to repeal the bankrupt act passed the House of Representatives; delivered [in that House] Jan. 19, 1843. [Washington, 1843.] 8°

DAVIS, HENRY, *M.A., President of Middlebury College.* An Inaugural Oration, delivered Feb. 21, 1810, *etc.* Boston, 1810. 8°

DAVIS, HENRY WINTER. The War of Ormuzd and Ahriman in the Nineteenth Century. Baltimore, 1852. 8°

DAVIS, JOHN. The First Settlers of Virginia, an historical novel, exhibiting a view of the rise and progreſs of the colony at James Town, a picture of Indian manners, the countenance of the country, and its natural productions. Second edition. New York, 1806. 12°

DAVIS, JOHN, *Judge of the United States Diſtriƈt Court for Maſsachuſetts.* A Discourse before the Massachusetts Historical Society, .. at their anniversary commemoration of the first landing of our ancestors at Plymouth, in 1620. Boston, 1814. 8°

2 AN ORATION pronounced at Worcester (Maſs.) on the fortieth anniversary of American Independence. Worcester, July 1816. 8°

DAVIS, JOHN, *of Maſsachuſetts, called ' Honest John.'* Speech .. upon the bill reported by the committee of finance, and commonly called the Sub-treasury Bill. Delivered in the Senate .. Feb. 28 and Mar. 1, 1838. Washington, 1838. 8°

2 GOVERNMENT Expenditures: remarks .. in the Senate, Dec. 21, 1838, in relation to the wasteful expenditures of the federal government, under the last and present administrations. [Washington, 1838.] 8°

3 SPEECH .. on the Sub-treasury Bill; delivered in the Senate .. Jan. 23, 1840. Washington, 1840. 8°

4 REPLY .. to the charge of misrepresenting Mr. Buchanan's argument in favour of the hard-money system, and the consequent reduƈtion of wages. Delivered in the Senate .. March 6, 1840. Washington, 1840. 8°

DAVIS, JOHN, *of Pennsylvania.* Speech .. in the House of Representatives, June 27, 1840, on the Independent Treasury Bill. [Washington, 1840.] 8°

DAVIS, JOHN, *of Providence, Rhode Island.* The Measure of the Circle, perfeƈted in January, 1845. Providence, 1854. 8°

DAVIS, JOHN CHANDLER BANCROFT. Report upon the Condition and Sources of Busineſs of the Illinois Central Railroad, made at the request of the Board of Direƈtors, by J. C. Bancroft Davis, January 26th, 1855. New York, 1855. 8°

DAVIS, SIR JOHN FRANCIS; *Bart.* The Chinese: a general description of the empire of China and its inhabitants. 2 vol. New York, 1845, 1844. 12°

DAVIS, MATTHEW L. Memoirs of Aaron Burr. With miscellaneous seleƈtions from his correspondence. 2 vol. New York, 1836-37. 8vo.

DAVIS, PARIS M. An authentic History of the late War between the United States and Great Britain, with a full account of every battle by sea and land; the maſsacre at the River Raisin; the deſtruƈtion of the City of Washington; the treaty of peace in 1815. To which will be added the war with Algiers .. The treaties of peace with the various tribes of North American Indians and the United States Army Register and Peace Establishment. Ithaca, N. Y. 1829. 12°

2 AN AUTHENTIC History of the late War between the United States and Great Britain, with a full account of every battle by sea and land. New York, 1836. 12°

DAVIS, MRS. TAMAR. A general History of the Sabbatarian Churches: embracing accounts of the Armenian, East Indian and Abyſsinian Episcopacies in Asia and Africa, the Waldenses, Semi-Judaisers and Sabbatarian Anabaptists of Europe, with the Seventh-day Baptist denomination in the United States. Philadelphia, 1851. 12°

DAVIS, TIMOTHY. Popery shown to dishonour the Word of God. A sermon. Worcester, 1835. 8vo.

2 ANTI-CHRISTIAN Religion delineated, in a treatise on the Millenium; or, the fulfilment of the Old Testament prophecies completed. Leominster, 1807. 12°

DAVIS, Z. A. The Freemason's Monitor; containing a delineation of the fundamental principles of Freemasonry, with explanations of all the emblems .. Notes and remarks; also charges and songs. Philadelphia, 1847. 12°

DAVISON, DARIUS. Progreſs of Naval Architecture .. Being a popular and brief explanation of the principles and advantages of Darius Davison's New American model for ocean steamers, clipper ships, etc. New York, 1852. 8°

DAVY, SIR HUMPHREY, Bart. Elements of Agricultural Chemistry, in a course of lectures for the Board of Agriculture, by Sir Humphrey Davy .. To which is added, a treatise on soils and manures .. in which the theory and doctrines of Sir Humphrey Davy .. are rendered familiar to the experienced farmer; by a practical agriculturist. 2 parts. Philadelphia, 1821. 8vo.

DAVY, J. Chemistry and Familiar Science. Containing in a condensed form the elementary principles and all the most important facts of that science. Albany, 1851. 12°

DAWES, RUFUS. The Valley of the Nashaway; and other Poems. Boston, 1830. 12°

2 GERALDINE, Athenia of Damascus, and miscellaneous Poems. New York, 1839. 12°

DAWES, THOMAS. An Oration, delivered July 4, 1787, at .. Boston,

in celebration of the anniversary of American Independence. Boston, 1787. 8°

2 AN ADDRESS to the Maſſachusetts Peace Society, at their second Anniversary, Dec. 25, 1817. To which are added, the second annual report of the executive committee, .. votes of the trustees, etc. Boston, 1818. 8°

DAWSON, MOSES. An Historical Narrative of the Civil and Military Services of Major-General W. H. Harrison; and a vindication of his character and conduct as a statesman, a citizen, and a soldier. With a detail of his negotiations and wars with the Indians, until the final overthrow of the celebrated Chief Tecumseh, and his brother the prophet. Cincinnati, 1824. 8°

DAY, GEORGE EDWARD. Report on the Institutions for the Deaf and Dumb in central and western Europe. .. By Rev. George Edward Day, etc. New York, 1845. 8vo.

DAY, HENRY NOBLE. The Art of Elocution, exemplified in a systematic course of exercises. New Haven, 1844. 12°

DAY, JEREMIAH, President of Yale College. An Inquiry respecting the self-determining Power of the Will; or contingent volition. New Haven, 1838. 12°

2 A COURSE of Mathematics: containing the principles of plane trigonometry, mensuration, navigation, and surveying, etc. 3 parts. New Haven, 1839. 8°

3 AN EXAMINATION of President Edwards' Inquiry on the Freedom of the Will. New Haven, 1841. 12mo.

4 AN INTRODUCTION to Algebra: being the first part of a course of mathematics, adapted to the method of instruction in the American colleges. A new edition. Fifth thousand. With additions and alterations, by the author, and Profeſſor Stanley

of Yale College. N. Haven [printed], Philadelphia, 1853. 8vo.

DAY, ROBIN. The Adventures of Robin Day. [A romance.] By the author of " Calavar," etc. [R. M. Bird]. 2 vol. Philadelphia, 1839. 12°

DAY, SARAH. Divorce Case. Mrs. Sarah Day, complainant, and H. H. Day, defendant. Containing complaint, answer, proofs, and decree of the Court of the State of New Jersey. [Trenton, 1852.] 8°

DAY, SHERMAN. Historical Collections of the State of Pennsylvania. With topographical descriptions of every county and all the larger towns in the State. Philadel. [1843]. 8vo.

DAY, THOMAS. Reports of Cases argued and determined in the Supreme Court of Errors of the State of Connecticut, 1802-1813. 5 vol. (Vol. 1. Second edition, Philadelphia, 1830; vol. 2-5, N. York [and] Hartford, 1809-23. [Vol. 6 wanting.] Vol. 7-14, 1828-42. Hartf. 1831-43. 8°

2 A DIGEST of the Reported Cases decided by the Supreme Court of Errors of the State of Connecticut, from 1786 to 1838 inclusive. Hartford, 1840. 8vo.

3 AN HISTORICAL Discourse, delivered before the Connecticut Historical Society, . . . Dec. 26, 1843. Hartford, 1844. 8°

DAYSPRING (The). N° 1, 2, 3. [Published by the American Board of Commissioners for Foreign Missions] Aug. Oct. Nov. 1841. Boston, 1841. Fol°

2 THE DAYSPRING. Jan. 1842— Oct. 1846. Vol. 1-5. Published by the American Board of Commissioners for Foreign Missions. [A new series of the preceding, but not so described. The enumeration begins vol. 1, N° 1.] Boston, 1842-46. Fol°

DEAN, AMOS. Lectures on Phrenology. Albany, 1834. 12mo.

2 THE PHILOSOPHY of Human Life, etc. Boston, 1839. 12mo.

3 PRINCIPLES of Medical Jurisprudence. Albany [printed], N. York, 1850. 8vo.

DEAN, CYRUS B. The Trial of Cyrus B. Dean for the Murder of J. Ormsby and A. Marsh; before the Supreme Court of . . Vermont, etc. Burlington, 1808. 8°

DEAN, JAMES. An Alphabetical Atlas; or gazetteer of the State of Vermont. Affording a summary description of the State, its several counties, towns, and rivers, etc. Montpelier, Jan. 1808. 8°

DEAN, SARAH. A Plain and Candid Statement of Facts of the Difficulty existing between Mr. B. L. Hamlen and Mrs. Sarah Dean; being an appeal to the moral and religious community from a defenceless and injured widow for justice and protection. New Haven, 1843. 8°

DEANE, SAMUEL. The New England Farmer; or, Georgical dictionary, etc. Third edition, corrected, improved, .. and adapted to the present state .. of agriculture. Boston, 1822. 8°

2 HISTORY of Scituate, Massachusetts, from its first settlement to 1831. Boston, 1831. 8°

DEARBORN, BENJAMIN. The Columbian Grammar: or, an essay for reducing a grammatical knowledge of the English language to a degree of simplicity, etc. Boston, 1795. 12°

DEARBORN, HENRY ALEXANDER SCAMMELL, General. A Memoir on the Commerce and Navigation of the Black Sea, and the trade and maritime geography of Turkey and Egypt. 2 vol. Boston, 1819. 8°

2 DEFENCE of Gen. H. Dearborn against the Attack of Gen. W. Hull. Boston, 1824. 8°

3 AN ADDRESS delivered before the Massachusetts Horticultural Society,

on the celebration of their first anniversary, Sept. 19, 1829. [To which is added, a report of the Society's proceedings.] Second edition. Boston, 1833. 8°

DEARBORN, NATHANIEL. Boston Notions: being an authentic and concise account of " that village," from 1630 to 1847. Boston, 1848. 12°

2 DEARBORN'S Reminiscences of Boston, and guide through the City and environs. Boston [1851]. 12°

3 DEARBORN'S Guide through Mount Auburn (Cemetery), with engravings of the Monuments, etc. Boston, 1852. 8°

DE BOW, J. D. B. The Industrial Resources, etc. of the Southern and Western States: embracing a view of their commerce, agriculture, and manufactures... Together with historical and statistical sketches of the different States and cities of the Union, etc. 3 vol. New Orleans, 1852. 8°

2 ENCYCLOPÆDIA of the Trade and Commerce of the United States... First supplementary volume [containing the 14th volume of J. D. B. De Bow's " Review," from January to June, 1853.] [N. Orleans printed], London, 1854. 8vo.

3 ENCYCLOPÆDIA of the Trade and Commerce of the United States, more particularly of the Southern and Western States... With appendices. .. Second edition. 3 vols. [Another copy of De Bow's " Industrial Resources, etc. of the Southern and Western States. New Orleans, 1852."] [New Orleans printed], London, 1854. 8vo.

DE BRAHM, JOHN GERAR WILLIAM. History of the Province of Georgia; with maps of original surveys. Now first printed. [Edited by G. Wymberley-Jones. Only 49 copies printed.] Wormsloe, Georgia, 1849. Fol.

DEBTOR AND CREDITOR. [Remarks on the laws affecting the same.] Philadelphia, 1810. 12°

DECATUR, SUSAN. Documents relative to the claim of Mrs. Decatur, etc. Washington, 1834. 8°

DECATUR, STEPHEN. Correspondence between the late Commodore Stephen Decatur and Commodore J. Barron, which led to the unfortunate meeting of the 22nd of March. Charleston, 1820. 8°

DECATUR BANK, ALABAMA. Preamble and Resolutions of the Decatur Bank. [Tuscaloosa? 1839.] 8°

DECLARATION OF INDEPENDENCE. A Facsimile of the Original Rough Draft of the Declaration of Independence: the body of the work in the handwriting of T. Jefferson; alterations in the hands of J. Adams and B. Franklin; also a facsimile of the signatures thereto. [New York, 1847!] s. sh. fol.

DEEMS, CHARLES F. What Now? For young ladies leaving school. New York, 1852. 12°

DEFENCE of the Drama, containing Mansel's Free Thoughts; extracts from the most celebrated writers, and a discourse on the lawfulnefs and unlawfulnefs of Plays. By Father Caffaro. New York, 1826. 16mo.

DEFENCE of the Exposition of the Middling Interest on the right of Constituents to give Instructions to their Representatives, and the obligation of these to obey them. Boston, July, 1822. 8°

DE GRAFF, SIMON. The Modern Geometrical Stair Builder's Guide... Together with the use of the most important principles of practical geometry. New York, 1845. 8°

DE HART, WILLIAM C. Observations on Military Law, and the Constitution and Practice of Courts

Martial. With a summary of the law of evidence, as applicable to military trials; adapted to the laws, regulations, and customs of the army and navy of the United States. New York, 1846. 8°

DE HASS, WILLS. History of the Early Settlement and Indian Wars of Western Virginia; embracing an account of the various expeditions in the West, previous to 1795. Wheeling, Philadelphia [printed], 1851. 8°

DELAFIELD, JOHN, the Younger. An Inquiry into the Origin of the Antiquities of America. . . With an appendix, containing notes, and "A View of the causes of the Superiority of the Men of the Northern over those of the Southern Hemisphere." [With a preface by C. P. Mac Ilvaine, and plates.] Cincinnati, 1839. 4to.

DELANO, AMASA. A Narrative of Voyages and Travels in the Northern and Southern Hemispheres. Boston, 1817. 8vo.

DELAPLAINE, JOSEPH. Repository of the Lives and Portraits of distinguished American Characters. Vol. 1. Philadel. 1815 [1816]. 4to.

DELATOUR, ALBERT J. A Daily Record of the Thermometer for ten years, from 1840 to 1850, as kept at Delatour's, . . New York. New York, 1850. 12°

DELAWARE, State of. Laws of the State of Delaware, from Oct. 14, 1700, to Aug. 18, 1797. 2 vol. Newcastle, 1797. 8°
    2 LAWS of the State of Delaware, to the year . . 1829, inclusive. To which are prefixed the Declaration of Independence and Constitution of the United States. Revised edition. Arranged and published under the authority of the General Assembly [by W. Hall]. Wilmington, 1829. 8°

DELAWARE AND RARITAN CANAL COMPANY. An Investigation into the Affairs of the Delaware and Raritan Canal and Camden and Amboy Railroad Companies, in reference to certain charges by "a Citizen of Burlington." Newark, 1849. 8°

DEMOCRACY OF CHRISTIANITY; or, an analysis of the Bible and its doctrines in their relation to the principle of Democracy. By a Citizen of the United States. Vol. i [all published]. N. York, 1849. 12°

DEMOCRATS. An Appeal to the good Sense of the Democrats and the Public Spirit of the Federalists. By a Citizen of Massachusetts. Boston, 1814. 8°

DEMOPHILUS, Pseud. The Genuine Principles of the Ancient Saxon or English constitution, etc. Philadelphia, 1776. 8°

DENIS, ALEXANDER. "Tammany Hall," and other miscellaneous poems. New York, 1847. 12°

DENNIS, RICHARD, the Younger. Report of the Trial of Richard Dennis, the younger, for the Murder of James Shaw. By S. C. Carpenter. Charleston, 1805. 8vo.

DENNY, AUSTIN. An Oration, delivered at Worcester, Massachusetts, July 4, 1818 [in commemoration of American Independence]. Worcester, July, 1818. 8°

DENTON, DANIEL. A Brief Description of New York, formerly called New Netherlands, with the places thereunto adjoining. Likewise a brief relation of the customs of the Indians there. A new edition, etc. By G. Furman. New York, 1845. 4°

DE PUY, HENRY W. Louis Napoleon and his Times, with notices of his writings; a memoir of the Bonaparte family, and a sketch of French history. . . With portraits. Buffalo, 1852. 12°
    2 KOSSUTH and his Generals; with a brief history of Hungary, select

speeches of Koßuth, *etc.* With an introduction by Hon. Henry J. Raymond, *etc.* Buffalo, 1852. 8°

DE QUINCEY, Thomas. Letters of De Quincey to a Young Man whose Education has been neglected. Philadelphia, 1843. 12°

2 Confessions of an English Opium Eater, and Suspira de Profundis. Boston, 1851. 12°

3 Biographical Essays. Boston, 1851. 12°

4 Miscellaneous Essays. Boston, 1851. 12°

5 The Cæsars. Boston, 1851. 12°

6 Life and Manners; from the autobiography of an English Opium-Eater. Boston, 1851. 12°

7 Essays on the Poets. Boston, 1853. 12°

8 Historical and Critical Essays. 2 vol. Boston, 1853. 12°

9 Essays on Philosophical Writers and other Men of Letters. 2 vol. Boston, 1854. 12°

10 Letters to a Young Man, and other papers. Boston, 1854. 12°

11 Theological Essays and other papers. 2 vol. Boston, 1854. 12°

12 Narrative and Miscellaneous Papers. 2 vol. Boston, 1854. 12°

13 The Note-book of an English Opium-Eater. Boston, 1855. 12°

DERBY, Elias Hasket. Two Months Abroad: or, a trip to England, France, Baden, Prußia, and Belgium. . . By a railroad Director of Maßachusetts [i.e. E. H. Derby?] Boston, 1844. 8°

DESAUSSURE, Henry William. Reports of Cases argued and determined in the Court of Chancery of the State of South Carolina, from the Revolution, to Dec. 1813, inclusive [continued to Dec. 1816]. 4 vol. Columbia, 1817-19. 8°

DESHLER, Charles D. Selections from the Poetical Works of G.

Chaucer; with a concise life . . and remarks, by C. D. Deshler. London [New York printed], 1847. 8vo.

DE SMET, P. J. Oregon Missions and Travels over the Rocky Mountains, in 1845-46. New York, 1847. 12°

DES MOULINS, Charles. General Considerations on restricting the number of species of the Genera Unio and Anodonta. Translated from the French by Philip H. Nicklin. [From the American Journal of Science and Arts, vol. 41, No 1. New Haven, 1841.] 8vo.

DEVELOPMENT. A brief Development of the great Secret of giving and receiving Instruction, and maintaining School Government; applied to the cardinal branches of education. By an experienced teacher [Alison Wrifford]. Concord, 1835. 8°

DEVEREUX, John C. Addreß on the anniversary of American Independence, celebrated July 5, 1852, at Jamaica, New York, by the Catholic Temperance Societies of Long Island. New York, 1852. 8°

DEVEREUX, Thomas P. Cases argued and determined in the Supreme Court of North Carolina. Dec. 1826 to June, 1834. 4 vol. Raleigh, 1829-36. 8°

2 Equity Cases argued and determined in the Supreme Court of North Carolina. June, 1828 to June, 1834. 2 vol. Raleigh, 1831-36. 8°

DEVEREUX, Thomas P. and BATTLE, William H. Reports of Cases at law argued and determined in the Supreme Court of North Carolina. Dec. 1834 to Dec. 1839, both inclusive. 4 vol. Raleigh, 1837-40. 8°

2 Reports of Cases in Equity argued and determined in the Supreme Court of North Carolina. Dec. 1834 to Dec. 1839, both inclusive. 2 vol. Raleigh, 1838-40. 8°

M

DEVOTION, Ebenezer. A Mourning Piece. Being a discourse [on Job xvii. 13] .. occasioned by the .. death .. of .. Mr. E. Avery, etc. Boston, 1755. 8vo.

DEW, Thomas. A Digest of the Laws, Customs, Manners, and Institutions of the Ancient and Modern Nations. New York, 1853. 8vo.

DEW, Thomas R. Lectures on the Restrictive System, delivered to the senior political class of William and Mary College. Richmond, 1829. 8°

DEW-DROP: a tribute of affection. 1853. Philadelphia, 1853. 12°

DEWEES, William P. An Essay on the means of lessening Pain and facilitating certain cases of difficult Parturition. Philadelphia, 1806. 8vo.
2 A Practice of Physic, comprising most of the diseases not treated of in " Diseases of Females" and " Diseases of Children." 2 vol. Philadelphia, 1830. 8vo.
3 A Treatise on the Diseases of Females. Seventh edition. Philadelphia, 1840. 8vo.
4 A Treatise on the Diseases of Females. Eighth edition. Philadelphia, 1843. 8vo.
5 A Treatise on the Physical and Medical Treatment of Children. Eighth edition. Philadel. 1842. 8vo.
6 A Compendious System of Midwifery: illustrated by occasional cases. Tenth edition. Philadel. 1843. 8vo.

DEWEY, Orville. The Old World and the New; or, a Journal of reflections and observations made on a Tour in Europe. 2 vol. New York, 1836. 12°
2 Discourses on Human Life. New York, 1841. 12°
3 The Laws of Human Progress and Modern Reforms. A lecture delivered before the Mercantile Library Association of the City of New York. New York, 1852. 8°
4 A Discourse [on Deut. xxxii.

45, 46] on Obedience, preached in the City of Washington. New York, 1852. 8°

DE WITT, Benjamin, M.D. A Chemico-medical Essay, to explain the operation of Oxigene, or the base of vital air on the human body. Philadelphia, 1797. 8vo.

D'HOMERGUE, John. The Silk Culturist's Manual: or, a popular treatise on the planting and cultivation of mulberry trees, the rearing and propagating of silkworms, and the preparation of the raw material for exportation: addressed to the farmers and planters of the United States. Philadelphia, 1839. 12°

D'HOMERGUE, John, and DUPONCEAU, Peter Stephen. Essays on American Silk, and the best means of rendering it a source of individual and national wealth; with directions to farmers for raising silkworms. Philadelphia, 1830. 8°

DIAL (The): a Magazine for Literature, Philosophy, and Religion. [Edited by Miss S. Margaret Fuller, afterwards Ossoli, R. W. Emerson, and G. Ripley.] 4 vol. Boston, 1841-44. 8°

DIALOGUE between a One Thousand-dollar Clerk and a Member of Congress [relative to official salaries]. Washington, 1836. 8°

DIALOGUES. Familiar Dialogues; or, a companion for young ladies and gentlemen. .. In two parts; with a preface by P. Doddridge. Philadelphia, 1829. 12mo.

DIBBLE, Sheldon. History and general views of the Sandwich Islands Mission. N. York, 1839. 12°

DICK, Thomas. The Sidereal Heavens, and other subjects connected with astronomy, as illustrative of the character of the Deity and of an infinity of worlds. N. York, 1844. 12°
2 Celestial Scenery; or, the

wonders of the planetary system displayed; illustrating the perfections of Deity and a plurality of worlds. New York, 1845. 12°

3 ON the Improvement of Society by the Diffusion of Knowledge; or, an illustration of the advantages which would result from a more general dissemination of rational and scientific information among all ranks. New York, 1846. 12°

DICKENS, CHARLES. The Life and Adventures of Martin Chuzzlewit . . . with illustrations by Phiz. New York, 1844. 8°

DICKERSON, MAHLON. Address delivered at the opening of the nineteenth Annual Fair of the American Institute. New York, 1846. 8°

DICKINSON COLLEGE. Catalogus Senatus Academici, et eorum, qui munera et officia Academica gesserunt quique alicujus gradus laurea donati sunt, in Collegio Dickinsoniensi, etc. [M.S. additions and corrections.] Carleoli, 1840. 8°

DICKINSON, ANDREW. My first Visit to Europe; or, sketches of society, scenery, and antiquities, in England, Wales, Ireland, Scotland, and France. Second edition. New York, 1851. 12°

DICKINSON, DANIEL S. of New York. Speech . . in reply to . . D. Webster, on the North-Eastern Boundary, the Right of Search, and the destruction of the Caroline, delivered in the Senate, . . . April 9, 1846. [Washington, 1846.] 8°

DICKINSON, JOHN. The Political Writings of J. Dickinson. 2 vol. Wilmington, 1801. 8°

DICKINSON, JONATHAN, President of New Jersey College. A sermon [on 2 Tim. iii. 17] preached at the opening of the [Presbyterian] Synod at Philadelphia, Sept. 19,

1722, wherein is considered the Character of the Man of God, etc. Boston, 1723. 8vo.

2 A DEFENCE of a book lately reprinted at Boston, entituled, A Modest Proof of the Order, etc. in reply to a book entituled, Sober remarks on the Modest Proof, etc. With some strictures on J. Dickinson's defence of Presbyterian Ordination, by way of postscript. Also, Animadversions upon two pamphlets, the one entituled, An Essay upon that Paradox, Infallibility may sometimes mistake. The other, The ruling and ordaining power of Congregational Bishops or Presbyters defended, etc. 2 parts. Boston, 1724. 8vo.

3 THE DANGER of Schisms and Contentions with respect to the ministry and ordinances of the Gospel, represented in a sermon [on 1 Cor. iii. 4]. New York, 1739. 12°

4 A BRIEF Illustration . . of the Divine Right of Infant Baptism; in a . . dialogue between a minister and one of his parishioners. Providence, New England, 1763. 8vo.

DICKINSON, MOSES. An Inquiry into the consequences both of Calvinistic and Arminian Principles, compared together. In which the principal things in Mr. Beach's second reply to the late Mr. J. Dickinson's second vindication of God's sovereign free grace are particularly considered. Occasioned by a manuscript intitled, An Inquiry into the consequences of Calvinistic Principles, in a letter to Liberius, author of that piece. Boston, 1750. 8°

DICKINSON, PLINY. A Discourse [on Psal. xii. 1] delivered at the funeral of the Rev. T. Fessenden, etc. Brattleborough, 1813. 8°

2 A SERMON [on 2 Chron. xxiv. 2] preached . . before . . the Senate and House of Representatives of . . New Hampshire, June 16, . . being the anniversary Election. Concord, 1816. 8°

DICKINSON, RODOLPHUS. A Geographical and Statistical View of Mafaachusetts Proper. Greenfield, 1813. 8°

2 A DIGEST of the Common Law, the Statute Laws of Mafaachusetts and of the United States, and the decisions of the Supreme Judicial Court of Mafaachusetts, relative to the powers and duties of Justices of the Peace; to which is subjoined an extensive appendix of forms. Deerfield, 1818. 8°

DICKINSON, SAMUEL N. A Help to Printers and Publishers: being a series of calculations showing the quantity of paper required for a given number of signatures in book-work. . . . Also an extensive table for jobwork. Boston, 1835. 8vo.

DICKSON, SAMUEL HENRY. An Oration delivered at New Haven, before the Phi Beta Kappa Society. New Haven, 1842. 8vo.

2 ESSAYS on Life, Sleep, Pain, etc. Philadelphia, 1852. 12°

DIDIER, FRANKLIN J. Letters from Paris and other cities of France, Holland, etc. written during a tour and residence in these countries in 1816, 17, 18, 19 and 20, with Remarks on the conduct of the Ultra-Royalists since the Restoration. New York, 1821. 8vo.

DIDIMUS, H. Pseud. New Orleans as I found it. N. York, 1845. 8°

DIDO. The New Dido. [In verse.] New York, 1851. 12°

DILLON, JOHN B. The History of Indiana, from its earliest exploration by Europeans, to the close of the territorial government in 1816; with an introduction containing historical notes of the discovery and settlement of the territory of the United States north-west of the River Ohio. Vol. 1. Indianapolis, 1843. 8°

DILWORTH, THOMAS. The Federal Calculator; or, American Schoolmaster's Afaistant and Young Man's Companion. Being a compendium of federal arithmetic, both practical and theoretical. In five parts. Originally compiled by T. Dilworth. Revised, improved, and adapted to the currency of the United States, by D. Hawley. Troy, 1803. 12°

2 A KEY to Dilworth's Arithmetic. . . By a teacher of arithmetic in New York. New York, 1812. 12°

3 THE SCHOOLMASTER'S Afaistant; being a compendium of arithmetic . . in five parts. . . To which is prefixed, an efay on the education of youth, etc. New York, 1815. 12°

DINGLEY, AMASA. An Oration on the Improvement of Medicine. New York [1794]. 8vo.

DINKS. The Sportsman's Vade Mecum, by Dinks. Edited by F. Forester (H. W. Herbert), containing full instructions in all that relates to the breeding, rearing, breaking . . of dogs . . as also a few remarks on guns, etc. New York, 1850. 12°

D'ISRAELI, ISAAC. Curiosities of Literature, and the literary character illustrated. . . . With Curiosities of American Literature, by R. W. Griswold. New York, 1847. 8°

DISTRICT OF COLUMBIA. Memorial of the Delegates appointed by various sections of the District of Columbia. Jan. 22, 1805. [Washington, 1805.] 8°

DISTURNELL, JOHN. Summer Arrangements. Guide through the Middle, Northern, and Eastern States; containing a description of the principal places; canal, railroad, and steamboat routes; tables of distances, etc. Compiled from authentic sources. With a map. [The printed cover reads: " Disturnell's Railroad and Steamboat Book: Ninth edition."] New York, July, 1848. 12°

2 DISTURNELL'S Railroad, Steamboat, and Telegraph Book, being a Guide through the United States and

Canada; also giving the Ocean Steam-packet arrangements, telegraph lines and charges, list of hotels, *etc.* With a map of the United States and Canada, showing all the Canals, Railroads, *etc.* New York, 1851. 12°

3 DISTURNELL's United States National Register and Calendar for 1851-52, containing authentic political and statistical information relating to the United States, Canada, *etc.* New York, 1851-52. 8°

4 DISTURNELL's American and European Railway and Steamship Guide, ... through the United States and Canada; acrofs the Atlantic Ocean, and through Central Europe. New York, 1851. 12°

DITSON, GEORGE LEIGHTON. Circafsia; or, a tour to the Caucasus. New and revised edition. New York, 1850. 12°

DIUHSAWAHGWAH GAYA-DOSHAH. Diuhsáwahgwah Gayádoshah. Gówahás Goyádoh. Sgãóyadih Dówánandenyo. [An elementary reading-book in the language of the Seneca Indians. By the Rev. A. Wright.] Boston, 1836. 12mo.

DIX, MISS D. L. Memorial [to the Legislature of Mafsachusetts, on the condition of Idiots and Lunatics in Prisons and Asylums, *etc.* Boston, 1843. 8°

2 REMARKS on Prisons and Prison Discipline in the United States. Boston, 1845. 8°

DIX, JOHN A. Sketch of the Resources of the City of New York. ... [By J. A. Dix.] N. York, 1827. 8vo.

2 A WINTER in Madeira, and a Summer in Spain and Florence. ... Second edition. N. York, 1851. 12°

3 THE CITY of New York: its growth, destinies, and duties. A lecture, *etc.* New York, 1853. 8°

DIX, WILLIAM. An Inaugural Differtation on the Dropsy. Worcester, 1795. 8vo.

DIX, WILLIAM GILES. The Deck of the Crescent City: a picture of American life. New York, 1853. 8°

DIXON, EDWARD H. A Treatise on Diseases of the Sexual System; adapted to popular and profefsional reading, and the exposition of quackery. Sixth edition. New York, 1847. 12°

DOANE, AUGUSTUS SIDNEY. Surgery Illustrated; compiled from the works of Cutler, Hind, Velpeau, and Blasius. ... Second edition. New York, 1837. 8°

DOANE, GEORGE WASHINGTON, *Bishop of the Protestant Episcopal Church in New Jersey.* Songs by the Way, chiefly Devotional; with translations and imitations. New York, 1824. 8vo.

2 THE VOICE of the Departed: a sermon [on Hebrews xi. 4] on occasion of the death of the Rev.·J. S. J. Gardiner. Boston, 1830. 8vo.

3 EPISCOPAL Addrefs, delivered at the Convention of the Protestant Episcopal Church in the diocese of New Jersey. Camden, 1833. 8vo.

4 THE EDIFICATION of the Church for the Salvation of Souls, the Office and Duty of the Christian Ministry: the primary charge to the clergy of the Protestant Episcopal Church in the diocese of New Jersey. Camden, 1833. 8vo.

5 THE MISSIONARY Argument. A sermon [on Mark xvi. 15]. Boston, 1830. Reprinted Burlington, 1835. 8vo.

6 THE MISSIONARY Spirit. Boston, 1831. Reprinted Burling.1835. 8vo.

7 SERMON at the Consecration of Jackson Hemper, D. D. Mifsionary Bishop for Mifsouri and Indiana. Burlington, 1835. 8vo.

8 THE RECTOR's Christmas Offering for 1835: being a second pastoral addrefs to the parishioners of St. Mary's Church. Burlington [1835]. 8vo.

9 THE CHURCH's Care for Little Children. The second charge to the clergy of the diocese of New Jersey, at the opening of the annual convention, . . May 25, 1836. Burlington, 1836. 8vo.

10 THE PATH of the Just. A sermon [on Proverbs iv. 18] in commemoration of the Right Rev. W. White, Senior Bishop of the Protestant Episcopal Church. Burlington, 1836. 8vo.

11 THE APOSTOLICAL Commission the Missionary Charter of the Church. Sermon at the ordination of Joseph Wolff, Newark, Sept. 26, 1837. Burlington, 1837. 8vo.

12 EPISCOPAL Address to the Annual Convention of the Diocese of New Jersey, June, 1837. [To which is added, an appendix of documents.] Burlington, 1837. 8vo.

13 THE BEAUTY and the Blessedness of Early Piety: an address to the persons confirmed in St. Mary's Church, Burlington, . . 1839. Burlington, 1839. 8vo.

14 LOOKING unto Jesus: a sermon preached after the decease of the Rev. Benjamin Davis Winslow. [To which are added, obituary notices.] Burlington, 1839. 8vo.

15 EPISCOPAL Address to the Annual Convention of the Diocese of New Jersey, May, 1839. [To which is added, report of Episcopal Services in the Diocese of Maryland.] Burlington, 1839. 8vo.

16 THE PASTORAL Office : a charge to the clergy, May 29, 1839. Burlington, 1839. 8vo.

17 [Begins] A PASTORAL Letter to the clergy and laity of the Diocese of New Jersey on the rights and duties of Churchwardens and Vestrymen. 1840. 8vo.

18 ISAIAH's Prospect of the Church: the sermon at the consecration of the Right Rev. Christopher Edwards Gaddesden, Bishop of South Carolina, 1840. Burlington, 1840. 8vo.

19 THE FAITH once Delivered to the Saints : the sermon before the Northern Convocation of the Clergy [on Jude, 3], October 28, 1840. Burlington, 1840. 8vo.

20 AN APPEAL to Parents for Female Education on Christian Principles ; with a prospectus of St. Mary's Hall, Burlington. Fourth edition. Burlington, 1840. 8vo.

21 EPISCOPAL Address to the Annual Convention of the Diocese of New Jersey, May, 1840. [To which is added, Episcopal Address to the annual convention of the diocese of Maryland.] Burlington, 1840. 8vo.

22 THE NATION's Grief: a funeral address on occasion of the death of William Henry Harrison, late President of the United States. Burlington, 1841. 8vo.

23 THE BUSH that burned with Fire : the sermon at the consecration of St. John's Church, Elizabethtown [on Exod. iii. 5]. Burling. 1841. 8vo.

24 A BRIEF Examination of the Proofs by which the Rev. Mr. Boardman attempts to sustain his charge, that " A large and learned body of the Clergy of the Church (of England) have returned to some of the worst errors of Popery;" with a word or two as to his attempt to cast the suspicion of Popery on the Protestant Episcopal Church in the United States of America. Burlington, 1841. 8vo.

25 THE PENTECOSTAL Pattern: the fourth charge to the clergy of the diocese. Burlington, 1842. 8vo.

26 THE GLORIOUS Things of the City of God: the first sermon in St. Mary's Church, Burlington, after a brief pilgrimage to the Church of England [on Psalm lxxxvii. 1, 2]. Burlington, 1842. 8vo.

27 THE TRUE Catholic Pastor of the Church of Jesus Christ : the sermon at the funeral of the Rev. D. Butler. Burlington, 1842. 8vo.

28 EPISCOPAL Address to the Sixtieth Annual Convention, June, 1843. Burlington, 1843. 8vo.

29 THE SHEPHERD of the Sheep:
a sermon commemorative of the Rev.
E. G. Prescott [on John x. 1-16].
Burlington, 1844. 8vo.

30 JESUS of Nazareth, who went
about doing good, the Model for the
Church and Ministry: the sermon
at the annual commencement of the
General Theological Seminary [on
Acts x. 38]. Burlington, 1845. 8vo.

31 CIVIL Government a Sacred
Trust from God. The anniversary
oration before the New Jersey State
Society. Burlington, 1845. 8vo.

32 THE CHURCH, a Debtor to all
the World. [A sermon on Romans i.
14.] Burlington, 1845. 8vo.

33 EPISCOPAL Address to the sixty-
second Annual Convention, in May,
1845. Burlington, 1845. 8vo.

34 INCORPORATION with Christ, the
Source and Channel of the Spiritual
Life. The fifth charge. Burlington,
1845. 8vo.

35 AMERICA and Great Britain.
The address at Burlington College,
on the seventy-second anniversary of
American Independence. Burlington,
1848. 8vo.

36 THE GOODLY Heritage of Jer-
seymen: the first annual address before the New Jersey Historical Society, Jan. 15, 1846. Burlington,
1846. 8vo.

37 THE BISHOP'S Address to the
Members of the Senior Class [St.
Mary's Hall] at the closing exercises
of the winter term, 1846. To which
is added, the catalogue and prospectus
for the summer term. [Burlington?
1846?] 12mo.

38 DIOCESE of New Jersey: Episcopal Address to the sixty-third Annual Convention. Burlington, 1846.
8vo.

39 CHRIST Crucified; the hope,
the theme, and the model of the
Christian Minister. The sixth charge
to the clergy of the diocese. Burlington, 1848. 8vo.

40 THE ENDS and Objects of Burlington College: an address, intro-

ductory to a course of lectures, etc.
Third edition. Burlington, 1848. 8°

41 A BRIEF Narrative [relative to
the Condition of the Diocese of New
Jersey, etc.] [Burlington,1849.] 8vo.

42 THE BEAUTY of Holiness: the
sermon [on Psalm xciv. 9] at the
consecration of Grace Church, Newark, Oct. 5, 1848. Burling. 1849. 8vo.

43 THE MEN to make a State;
their making and their marks. An
address before the trustees, teachers,
and students of Burlington College,
.. July 4, 1849. Burling. 1849. 8vo.

44 A GREAT Man fallen in Israel:
the sermon [on 2 Sam. iii. 38] .. on
the .. Sunday .. next after the death
of Z. Taylor, President of the United
States. Burlington, 1850. 8vo.

45 THE DEVELOPMENT of the
Practical, in Subordination to the
Spiritual, the true end of academic
education. The second baccalaureate
address to the graduates of Burlington
College. Philadelphia, 1851. 8vo.

46 THE GOSPEL in the Church,
triumphant everywhere: the jubilee
sermon [of the Society for the Propagation of the Gospel; on 2 Cor. ii.
14; and a correspondence on the
occasion with the Archbishop of Can-
terbury]. Philadelphia, 1851. 8vo.

47 THE CHRISTIAN Minister: the
messenger, the watchman, and the
steward of the Lord. The seventh
[visitation] charge to the clergy of
the diocese of New Jersey, etc. Philadelphia, 1851. 8vo.

48 THE DIFFUSION of Useful Knowledge: the introductory lecture before the Mechanic's Library and Reading Room Association of the City of
Burlington. Burlington, 1851. 8vo.

49 THE SACRED Sympathy of Sorrow. The discourse commemorative
of the Rev. W. Croswell, etc. Boston, 1852. 8vo.

50 PRAYER for the Bishops and
other Clergy: the sermon [on 1
Thess. v. 25] at the opening of the
special convention of the diocese of
New Jersey. Burling. 1852. 8vo.

51 THE PROTEST and Appeal of George Washington Doane, . . as aggrieved by . . W. Meade, . . G. Burgefs, . . and C. P. Mc Ilvaine ; and his reply to the false, calumnious, and malignant representations of W. Halsted, C. Perkins, P. V. Coppuck, and B. Gill, on which they ground their uncanonical, unchristian, and inhuman procedure in regard to him. Philadelphia, 1852. 8vo.

52 THE RECORD of the Proceedings of the Court of Bishops afsembled for the Trial of George Washington Doane. New York, 1852. 8°

53 DIOCESE of New Jersey: Episcopal Addrefs to the special convention held in St. Mary's Church, Burlington, . . March 17, 1852, etc. Burlington, 1852. 8vo.

54 THE ARGUMENT of the Bishop of New Jersey in reply to the Paper read before the Court of Bishops, in Sefsion, at Burlington, on Monday, October 11, by the Bishops of Ohio and Maine, etc. Newark, 1852. 8vo.

55 THE YOUNG American; his dangers, his duties, and his destinies : the addrefs at Burlington College, July 4, 1853, etc. Philadelphia, 1853. 8vo.

56 THE CHURCH Aggrefsive: the triennial sermon [on 1 Cor. xiv. 8] before the afsociated alumni of the General Theological Seminary of the Protestant Episcopal Church in the United States of America, . . on . . Oct. 13, 1853. N. York, 1853. 8vo.

57 THE CHURCH Sufficient, through the Crofs, for the Salvation of the World: the eighth triennial charge to the clergy of the diocese of New Jersey, etc. Philadel. 1854. 8vo.

DOBBIN, JAMES C. of North Carolina. Speech . . on the Oregon Question, delivered in the House of Representatives, . . Jan. 15, 1846. [Washington, 1846.] 8°

DOBBINS, PETER, Pseud. [i. e. William Fefsenden?]. The Political Farrago ; or, a miscellaneous review of politics in the United States, from the administration of Washington to that of Mr. Jefferson, in 1806. Brattleboro, January, 1807. 12°

DODD, JAMES B. Elementary and Practical Algebra : in which have been attempted improvements in general arrangement and exposition. . . Second edition. N. York, 1852. 8vo.

DODD, STEPHEN. Revolutionary Memorials : embracing poems by Rev. Wheeler Chase, published in 1778, and an appendix containing General Burgoyne's proclamation (in burlesque), . . an account of the death of Mifs Jane Mc Crea, the American hero, . . by N. Niles, A. M. etc. New York, 1852. 8°

DODDRIDGE, PHILIP. The Life of Col. James Gardiner, who was slain at the Battle of Preston-Pans, Sept. 21, 1745. Phil. 1828. 12mo.

2 A PLAIN and Serious Addrefs to the Master of a Family on the important subject of Family Religion. London, printed; Hartford, reprinted, 1778. 8°

DODGE, ROBERT. Memorials of Columbus : read to the Maryland Historical Society, . . April 3, 1851. Baltimore, 1851. 8°

DODS, JOHN BOVEE. Immortality Triumphant. The existence of a God and human immortality philosophically considered, and the truth of divine revelation substantiated, etc. New York, 1852. 12mo.

DOMAT, JEAN. The Civil Law in its Natural Order. . . Translated from the French by W. Strahan. . . Edited from the second London edition, by L. S. Cushing. 2 vol. Boston, 1850. 8°

DOMESTIC INDUSTRY. Journal of the Proceedings of the Friends of Domestic Industry, in General Convention . . at . . New York, Oct. 26, 1831. Baltimore, 1831. 8°

DONKIN, *Major.* Military Collections and Remarks. New York, 1777. 8vo.

DONNEGAN, JAMES. A new Greek and English Lexicon. . . Arranged from the last London edition, by J. M. Cairns. New edition. Philadelphia, 1843. 12°

DOOLITTLE, MARK. Historical Sketch of the Congregational Church in Belcher Town, Maſs. . . With notices of the pastors and officers, and list of communicants chronologically arranged. Northampton [Springfield printed], 1852. 12mo.

DORCHESTER, MASSACHUSETTS. Proceedings of the Second Church and Parish in Dorchester [against J. Codman their Pastor] exhibited in a Collection of Papers. Published agreeably to a vote of the Church. Second edition. Boston, 1812. 8°
2 REVIEW of two Pamphlets, which were published on the subject of the Ecclesiastical Controversy in Dorchester [viz. 1. " Proceedings," *etc.* 2. " The Memorial of the Proprietors," *etc.*] (From the Panoplist.) Boston, 1814. 8°

DORCHESTER ANTIQUARIAN AND HISTORICAL SOCIETY. Collections of the Dorchester Antiquarian and Historical Society: Nº 1. Memoirs of Roger Clap. 1630. [A reprint of the edition by T. Prince, 1731.] Boston, 1844. 12°
2 NUMBER TWO. Annals of the Town of Dorchester, by J. Blake, 1750. Boston, 1846. 12°

DORR, BENJAMIN, *D.D.* An Historical Account of Christ Church, Philadelphia, from its foundation, A. D. 1695, to A. D. 1841; and of St. Peter's and St. James's, until the separation of the Churches. New York and Philadelphia, 1841. 12°
2 THE RECOGNITION of Friends in another World. . . Seventh edition. New York, 1850. 16°

DORSEY, MRS. ANNA HANSON. Woodreve Manor; or, six months in town; a tale of American life. Philadelphia, 1852. 8°

DORSEY, CLEMENT. Speech . . on the subject of Retrenchment, delivered in the House of Representatives . . . Jan. 1828. Washington, 1828. 12°

DORSEY, GREENBERRY. Dorsey Neville, et al. vs. Executors of Alice Packwood. Appeal from the Court of Probates. [N. York ! 1846 ?] 8°

DOUBOURG, J. HUEN. Life of the Cardinal de Cheverus, Archbishop of Bordeaux. Translated from the French by R. M. Walsh. Philadelphia, 1839. 12mo.

DOVE. The Dove and the Eagle. [A poem.] Boston, 1851. 12°

DOVECOTE; or, the Heart of the Homestead. By the author of " Cap Sheaf." Boston, 1854. 12mo.

DOUGLASS, FREDERICK. Narrative of the Life of F. Douglaſs, an American slave. Written by himself. [With a Preface by W. L. Garrison.] Boston, 1845. 8ᵇ

DOUGLASS, STEPHEN A. Speech . . on the Annexation of Texas; delivered in the House of Representatives, Jan. 6, 1845. [Washington, 1845.] 8°

DOUGLASS, WILLIAM. Inoculation of the Small Pox, as practised in Boston, considered. . [By W. Douglaſs.] Boston, 1722. 12mo.
2 A PRACTICAL Eſſay concerning the Small Pox. Boston, 1730. 8vo.
3 A SUMMARY, historical and political, of the first Planting, progreſſive Improvements, and present State of the British Settlements in North America: with some transient accounts of the bordering French and Spanish settlements. By W[illiam] D[ouglaſs], M.D. Nº 1. Boston, 1747. 8°

4 A SUMMARY, historical and political, of the first Planting, progressive Improvements, and present State of the British Settlements in North America. 2 vol. Bost. 1749-50. 8°

DOW, JR. *Pseud.* Short patent Sermons, by " Dow, Jr." Originally published in the New York Sunday Mercury. Revised and corrected. New York, 1841. 8°

DOW, D. A Wreath for . . D. Dow, . . . on the publication of his Familiar Letters, in answer to . . . J. Sherman's treatise of One God in one Person only, *etc.* By A. O. F. Utica, 1806. 8°

DOW, JOSEPH. An Historical Address, delivered at Hampton, New Hampshire . . Dec. 25, 1838, in commemoration of the settlement of that town, *etc.* Concord, 1839. 8°

DOW, LORENZO. The Dealings of God, Man, and the Devil, as exemplified in the life, experience, and travels of L. Dow. . . Together with his writings complete. · To which is added, the vicissitudes of life, by Peggy Dow. With an introductory essay by J. Dowling, *etc.* 2 vol. New York, 1850. 8°

DOWLING, JOHN. The History of Romanism : from the earliest corruptions of Christianity to the present time. With full chronological table, *etc.* Illustrated by numerous . . . engravings, *etc.* Third edition. New York, 1845. Roy. 8vo.

DOWNING, ANDREW JACKSON. A Treatise on the Theory and Practice of Landscape Gardening, adapted to North America, with a view to the improvement of country residences. With remarks on rural architecture. New York, 1841. 8vo.

2 COTTAGE Residences ; or, a series of designs for rural cottages and cottage villas and their gardens and grounds, adapted to North America. New York and London, 1842. 8vo.

3 A TREATISE on the Theory and Practice of Landscape Gardening, adapted to North America ; with a view to the improvement of country residences. Comprising historical notices and general principles of the art, etc. with remarks on rural architecture. Second edition, enlarged, revised, and newly illustrated. New York, 1844. Roy. 8vo.

4 A TREATISE on the Theory and Practice of Landscape Gardening, with a view to the improvement of country residences. With remarks on rural architecture. London [New York printed], 1849. 8vo.

5 THE ARCHITECTURE of Country Houses ; including designs for cottages, farm-houses, and villas. . . . With illustrations. N. York, 1850. 8°

6 RURAL Essays. . . Edited, with a memoir of the author, by G. W. Curtis ; and a letter to his friends, by F. Bremer. New York, 1853. 8°

DOWNING, JACK, *Major. Pseud.* [*i.e.* Seba Smith]. Letters of Jack Downing, Major, Downingville Militia, second brigade, to his old friend, Mr. Dwight, of the New York Daily Advertiser. New York, 1834. 12°

2 THE LIFE and Writings of Major Jack Downing [Seba Smith] of Downingville, *etc.* Second edition. Boston, 1834. 12°

DRAKE, BENJAMIN. The Life and Adventures of Black Hawk : with sketches of Keokuk, the Sac and Fox Indians, and the late Black Hawk War. Sixth edition, improved. Cincinnati, 1841. 12°

DRAKE, DANIEL, *M.D.* Natural and Statistical View, or picture of Cincinnati and the Miami Country, *etc.* Cincinnati, 1815. 8vo.

2 A SYSTEMATIC Treatise, Historical, Etiological, and Practical, on the principal Diseases of the Interior Valley of North America, as they appear in the Caucasian, African, Indian, and Esquimaux varieties of its population. Cincinnati, 1850. 8vo.

3 DISCOURSES delivered before the Cincinnati Medical Library Association. Cincinnati, 1852. 8vo.

DRAKE, SIR FRANCIS. Lives and Voyages of Drake, Cavendish, and Dampier; including an introductory view of the earlier discoveries in the South Sea, and the history of the Bucaniers. New York, 1846. 12°

DRAKE, JOSEPH RODMAN. The Culprit Fay, and other poems. New York, 1836. 8°

DRAKE, SAMUEL GARDNER. Biography and History of the Indians of North America. . . Also a history of their wars. . . Likewise exhibiting an analysis of the . . authors, who have written upon . . the first peopling of America. Third edition, with . . additions . . corrections and . . engravings. Boston, 1834. 8°

2 BIOGRAPHY and History of the Indians of North America. . . Also, a history of their wars. . . With an account of their manners, antiquities . . and customs. . . Seventh edition, with . . additions, corrections, and . . engravings. Boston, 1837. 8vo.

3 BIOGRAPHY and History of the Indians of North America, from its first discovery. Eleventh edition. Boston, 1851. 8°

4 THE OLD Indian Chronicle; being a collection of rare tracts written and published in the time of King Philip's War; to which are added notes and chronicles of the Indians, from the discovery of America to the present time. Boston, 1836. 12mo.

5 INDIAN Captivities; a collection of the most remarkable narratives of persons taken captive by the North American Indians. To which are added notes, historical, biographical, etc. Boston, 1839. 12mo.

6 GENEALOGICAL and Biographical Account of the Family of Drake in America. With some notices of the antiquities connected with the early times of persons of the name in Eng-

land. *Privately printed.* [Boston,] 1845. 12°

DRAPER, BOURNE HALL. Bible Histories. Philadelphia, 1830. 12mo.

2 SCRIPTURE Stories. Philadelphia, 1830. 12mo.

3 THE YOUTH'S Instructor. Philadelphia, 1830. 12mo.

4 THE SUNDAY School Story-Book. Philadelphia, 1832. 12mo.

DRAPER, JOHN WILLIAM. A Treatise on the Forces which produce the Organization of Plants. With an appendix, containing several memoirs on capillary attraction, electricity, and the chemical action of light. New York, 1844. Roy. 4to.

2 A TEXT-BOOK on Natural Philosophy; containing the most recent discoveries and facts, etc. With . . illustrations. Third edition. New York, 1851. 12°

3 A TEXT-BOOK on Chemistry. . With . . illustrations. Sixth edition. New York, 1851. 8°

DRAWING-MASTER. The Common School Drawing-Master. Part 1, containing Schmid's Practical Perspective. Boston, 1846. 8°

DRAYTON, JOHN. A View of South Carolina, as respects her natural and civil concerns. Charleston, 1802. 8vo.

2 MEMOIRS of the American Revolution to 1776, as relating to the State of South Carolina, and occasionally referring to the States of North Carolina and Georgia. 2 vol. Charleston, 1821. 8vo.

DREAMS and Reveries of a Quiet Man; consisting of the Little Genius, and other essays. By one of the editors of the New York Mirror [Theodore S. Fay]. 2 vol. New York, 1832. 12°

DRYSDALE, ISABEL. Scenes in Georgia. Written for the American Sunday School Union. Philadelphia, 1830. 18mo.

2 EVENING Recreations: a series of dialogues on the history and geography of the Bible. 4 parts. Philadelphia, 1832. 18mo.

DUANE, WILLIAM. Sampson against the Philistines; or, the reformation of lawsuits; and justice made cheap, *etc.* The second edition. Philadelphia, 1805. 8°

2 A MILITARY Dictionary; or, explanation of the several systems of discipline of different kinds of troops, .. the principles of fortification, and all the modern improvements in the science of tactics, *etc.* Philadelphia, 1810. 8°

3 A VISIT to Colombia in 1822 and 1823, by Laguayra and Caracas, over the Cordillera to Bogota, and thence by the Magdalena to Cartagena. Philadelphia, 1826. 8vo.

DUANE, WILLIAM JOHN. The Law of Nations, investigated in a popular manner, *etc.* Philadelphia, 1809. 8°

DUBLIN. Proceedings of the Society of United Irishmen of Dublin. Philadelphia, 1795. 12mo.

DU BOIS, WILLIAM E. Pledges of History. A brief account of the collection of coins belonging to the Mint of the United States, more particularly of the antique specimens. Philadelphia, 1846. 12°

DUCACHET, HENRY WILLIAM. An Inaugural Essay on the action of poisons. New York, 1817. 8vo.

DUCATEL, J. T., *Geologist of the State of Maryland.* Report on the New Map of Maryland, 1836. [Containing, 1. Report of the Geologist, J. T. Ducatel; 2. Engineers' Report, by J. H. Alexander.] [Baltimore, 1837.] 8vo.

2 ANNUAL Report of the Geologist of Maryland, 1837-1840. 4 parts. [Baltimore, 1837-41.] 8vo.

DUCATEL, J. T., *Geologist of the*

State of Maryland, and ALEXANDER, J. H. Report on the Projected Survey of the State of Maryland, pursuant to a resolution of the General Assembly. Annapolis, 1834. 8°

2 REPORT on the Projected Survey of Maryland, pursuant to a resolution of the General Assembly. [Annapolis! 1840!] 8°

DUDLEY, C. W. Reports of Cases at Law, argued and determined in the Court of Appeals of South Carolina, .. Dec. 1837, .. Feb. 1838, and .. May 1838. Columbia, 1838. 8°

DUDLEY, DEAN. Pictures of Life in England and America; prose and poetry. Boston, 1851. 12°

DUDLEY, PAUL. Objections to the Bank of Credit, projected at Boston. Being a letter upon that occasion to J. Burril, Esq. *etc.* Boston, 1714. 8°

DUER, JOHN. A Lecture on the Law of Representations in Marine Insurance, with notes and illustrations; and a preliminary Lecture on the question whether Marine Insurance was known to the ancients. New York, 1844. 8vo.

2 THE LAW and Practice of Marine Insurance, deduced from a critical examination of the adjudged cases, the nature and analogies of the subject, and the general usage of commercial nations. Vol. 1. New York, 1845. 8vo.

3 A DISCOURSE on the Life, Character, and Public Services of James Kent, late Chancellor of the State of New York; delivered .. before the judiciary and bar, *etc.* New York, 1848. 8°

DUER, JOHN, and SEDGWICK, ROBERT. An Examination of the Controversy between the Greek Deputies and two mercantile houses of New York: together with a review of the publications on the subject by Messrs.

Emmet and Ogden and W. Bayard. New York, 1826. 8°

DUER, WILLIAM ALEXANDER. Outlines of the Constitutional Jurisprudence of the United States. New York, 1833. 12mo.

2 A COURSE of Lectures on the Constitutional Jurisprudence of the United States; delivered annually in Columbia College, New York. New York, 1845. 12°

DUFFIELD, GEORGE. Dissertations on the Prophecies relative to the Second Coming of Jesus Christ. New York, 1842. 12°

DUFFIELD, JOHN T. The Princeton Pulpit. Edited by J. T. Duffield. New York, 1852. 8°

DUGGAN, GEORGE. Specimens of the Stone, Iron and Wood Bridges, . . of the United States Railroads . . accompanied by . . an appendix, illustrative of the art of bridge-building as at present practised in Europe, etc. Part 1-6. N. York, 1850. Fol°

DUKES, JOSEPH H. An Oration delivered before the firemen of Charleston, on the fourth of July, 1844. Charleston, 1844. 8°

DUMAS, DAVY DE LA PAILLETERIE ALEXANDRE, the Elder. The Fencing-Master: or, eighteen months at St. Petersburg. Translated from the French . . by G. Griswold. Cincinnati, 1850. 8°

DUMMER ACADEMY, BYFIELD. Catalogue of the Officers and Students of Dummer Academy, etc. [Salem,] 1844. 8°

DUMONT, HENRIETTA. The Lady's Oracle: an elegant pastime for social parties, etc. Philadelphia, 1852. 12°

DUNBAR, EDWARD E. Statement of the Controversy between Lewis Tappan and E. E. Dunbar [consequent on the dissolution of their mer-

cantile copartnership]. New York, 1846. 8°

DUNCAN, ALEXANDER, of Ohio. Speech of Mr. Duncan, of Ohio. (In the House of Representatives, Jan. 17, 1839, on a resolution providing for the appointment of a committee to inquire into the defalcations of S. Swartwout.) [Washington, 1839.] 8°

2 SPEECH . . on the Oregon Bill; delivered in the House of Representatives, Jan. 29, 1845. [Washington, 1845.] 8°

DUNCOMBE, CHARLES. Duncombe's Free Banking: an essay on Banking, Currency, Finance, Exchanges, and Political Economy. Cleveland, 1841. 16°

DUNGLISON, ROBLEY. Human Physiology; illustrated by numerous engravings. 2 vol. Philadelphia, 1832. 8vo.

2 ON the Influence of Atmosphere and Locality; change of air and climate; seasons, food, clothing, bathing, exercise, sleep, corporeal and intellectual pursuits, etc. on human health; constituting elements of hygiène. Philadelphia, 1835. 8°

3 GENERAL Therapeutics, or principles of medical practice; with tables of the chief remedial agents, etc. and their preparations, and of the different poisons and their antidotes. Philadelphia, 1836. 8vo.

4 GENERAL Therapeutics and Materia Medica, adapted for a Medical Text-Book. 2 vol. Philadelphia, 1843. 8vo.

5 THE MEDICAL Student; or aids to the study of Medicine, including a glossary . . bibliographical notices of medical works, etc. Philadelphia, 1837. 8vo.

6 HUMAN Physiology; illustrated by engravings. Second edition, with . . additions and modifications. 2 vol. Philadelphia, 1836. 8vo.

7 HUMAN Physiology. 4th edition. 2 vol. Philadelphia, 1841. 8vo.

8 HUMAN Physiology. 5th edition. 2 vol. Philadelphia, 1844. 8vo.

9 MEDICAL Lexicon. A new Dictionary of Medical Science, containing a concise account of the various subjects and terms; with the French and other synonymes, and formulæ for preparations, etc. 3rd edition. Philadelphia, 1842. 8vo.

10 NEW Remedies: pharmaceutically and therapeutically considered. 4th edition. Philadelphia, 1843. 8vo.

11 A PUBLIC Discourse in commemoration of P. S. du Ponceau, late President of the American Philosophical Society, delivered before the Society pursuant to appointment . . 25th of October, 1844. Philadelphia, 1844. 8°

12 HUMAN Health: or the influence of atmosphere and locality, change of air and climate, seasons, food, clothing, etc. on healthy man; constituting elements of hygiène. New edition. Philadel. 1844. 8vo.

13 A DICTIONARY of Medical Science, containing a concise account of the various subjects and terms; with the French and other synonymes; notices of climate, and of celebrated mineral waters, formulæ, etc. Philadelphia, 1844. 8vo.

14 THE PRACTICE of Medicine, a treatise on special pathology and therapeutics. Third edition. 2 vol. Philadelphia, 1848. 8vo.

DUNHAM, JOSIAH. An Oration for the fourth of July, 1798, . . at Hanover, in New Hampshire, etc. Hanover [1798]. 8°

2 A FUNERAL Oration on George Washington, late general of the armies of the United States, pronounced at Oxford, Maßachusetts, . . Jan. 15, 1800, etc. Boston [1800]. 8vo.

3 AN ORATION in commemoration of the birth of . . Washington, pronounced at Windsor [in Vermont], Feb. 22, 1814, etc. Windsor, 1814. 8°

DUNLAP, ANDREW. A Speech . . before the Municipal Court of . . Boston, in defence of A. Kneeland,

on an indictment for blasphemy. Jan. term, 1834. Boston, 1834. 8°

DUNLAP, JOHN A. A Treatise on the practice of the Supreme Court of New York, in civil actions, together with the proceedings in error. 2 vol. Albany, 1821-23. 8vo.

DUNLAP, WILLIAM. The Life of Charles Brockden Brown; together with selections from the rarest of his printed works, from his original letters, and from his manuscripts, before unpublished. 2 vol. Philadelphia, 1815. 8°

2 A HISTORY of the American Theatre. New York, 1832. 8°

3 HISTORY of the Rise and Progreß of the Arts of Design in the United States. 2 vol. New York, 1834. 8vo.

4 HISTORY of the New Netherlands, Province of New York, and State of New York, to the adoption of the Federal Constitution. 2 vol. New York, 1839-40. 8°

5 A HISTORY of New York, for schools. 2 vol. New York, 1840. 12°

DUNLAP'S MARYLAND GAZETTE. Nos. 156, 158, 160, 161, 174-176. April 21st to Sept. 8th, 1778. [Continued under the title of] The Maryland Gazette, etc. Nos. 177-183. Sept. 15th to Oct. 27th, 1778. [New Series] Nos. 116, 125, 191, 325, 334. June 28th, 1786, to Dec. 18th, 1787. Baltimore, 1778-87. Fol.

DUNLAP'S PENNSYLVANIA PACKET, or the General Advertiser. N° 212. Nov. 13, 1775. Philadel. 1775. Fol.

DUNLAP'S PENNSYLVANIA PACKET. Nos. 257, 277, 290. [Continued under the title of] The Pennsylvania Packet. For March 13th, 30th, April 1st, 3rd, 8th, 10th, 13th, 1779. Nov. 4th, 18th, 1780. Jan. 13th, 16th, Dec. 28th, 1781. Philadelphia, 1776-81. Fol.

DUNN, HENRY. Guatemala, or, the United Provinces of Central America in 1827-8; being sketches and memorandums made during a twelvemonth's residence in that Republic. New York, 1828. 8vo.

DUNN, THOMAS, *Rev.* Equality of Rich and Poor: a sermon [on Prov. xxii. 2] preached in the prison of Philadelphia, . . Dec. 12, 1793, being the day appointed for . . thanksgiving, on the ceasing of the late epidemical fever. Philadelphia, 1793. 8°

DUPIN, ANDRE MARIE JEAN JACQUES. The Trial of Jesus before Caiaphas and Pilate. Being a refutation of Mr. Salvador's Chapter entitled " The Trial and Condemnation of Jesus." . . Translated from the French by a member of the American Bar [John Pickering]. Boston [Cambridge printed], 1839. 8vo.

DU PONCEAU, PETER STEPHEN. A Discourse on the Early History of Pennsylvania; being an annual oration delivered before the American Philosophical Society, . . . June 6, 1821. Philadelphia, 1821. 8°

2 A DISSERTATION on the Nature and Extent of the Jurisdiction of the Courts of the United States. . . To which are added a brief sketch of the national judiciary powers exercised in the United States prior to the adoption of the present federal constitution, by T. Sergeant, and the author's discourse on legal education. With an appendix and notes. Philadelphia, 1824. 8vo.

3 EULOGIUM in commemoration of . . W. Tilghman, Chief Justice of the Supreme Court of Pennsylvania, . . delivered . . Oct. 11, 1827. Philadelphia, 1827. 8°

4 AN HISTORICAL Discourse delivered before the Society for the Commemoration of the Landing of W. Penn, Oct. 24, 1832, being the one hundred and fiftieth anniversary of that event. Philadel. 1832. 8°

5 A BRIEF View of the Constitution of the United States. Philadelphia, 1834. 12mo.

6 THE HISTORY of the Silk Bill, in a letter . . to D. B. Warden. Philadelphia, 1837. 8°

7 A DISSERTATION on the Nature and Character of the Chinese System of Writing. . . To which are subjoined, a vocabulary of the Cochin Chinese language, by J. Morrone. . . With notes showing the degree of affinity existing between the Chinese and Cochin Chinese languages, and . . their common system of writing, by M. de la Palun, and a Cochin Chinese and Latin dictionary. Philadelphia, 1838. 8vo.

8 CASE and Opinion of Peter Stephen Duponceau and A. Davezac, on the contested seat of the Hon. D. Levy, delegate from the Territory of Florida to the Congress of the United States. Alexandria, 1842. 8°

DUPONCEAU, PETER STEPHEN, and FISHER, JOSHUA FRANCIS. A Memoir on the History of the celebrated Treaty made by W. Penn with the Indians . . in 1682. Philadelphia, 1836. 8°

DU PUI, JAMES. An Exposition of the Prophecies of Apocalypse. Philadelphia, 1853. 12°

DUPUY, A. E. The Conspirator. [A tale.] New York, 1850. 12°

DUPUY, ELIZA A. *Miß.* The Adventures of a Gentleman in Search of Miß Smith. (Blanche de Beaulieu, by Dumas. A Masked Ball; James I. and James II. historical fragments.) Cincinnati, 1852. 8°

DURANG, C. Durang's Terpsichore; or, ball room guide: being a compendium of the theory, practice, and etiquette of dancing, *etc.* Philadelphia [1847]. 12°

DURBIN, JOHN PRICE. Observations in Europe, principally in France and Great Britain. 2 vol. New York, 1844. 12°

2 OBSERVATIONS in the East, chiefly in Egypt, Palestine, Syria, and Asia Minor. 2 vol. New York, 1845. 12°

DURFEE, Job. A Discourse [on the History of Rhode Island] delivered before the Rhode Island Historical Society. (Poem [in honour of Roger Williams] by S. H. Whitman.) Providence, 1847. 8°

DURIVAGE, Francis A. Stray Subjects Arrested and Bound Over; being the fugitive offspring of the "Old 'Un" (F. A. Durivage), and the "Young 'Un" (G. P. Burnham), that have been "lying round loose," and are now "tied up" for fast keeping. Philadelphia, 1848. 12°

DUSENBERY, B. M. Monument to the Memory of General Andrew Jackson; containing twenty-five eulogies and sermons delivered on occasion of his death. To which is added an appendix, containing General Jackson's proclamations, his farewell address, and a copy of his last will; preceded by a sketch of his life. Compiled by B. M. Dusenbery. Philadelphia, 1846. 12°

DUY, Albert William. Sermons .. [edited], with a biographical sketch of the author; containing extracts from his papers. By S. A. Clark. Philadelphia, 1846. 8°

DUYCKINCK, Evert A. and George L. Cyclopædia of American Literature; embracing personal and critical notices of authors, and selections from their writings, from the earliest period to the present day; with portraits, autographs, and other illustrations. By Evert A. Duyckinck and George L. Duyckinck. 2 vol. New York, 1855. Roy. 8°

DWIGHT, H. G. O. Memoir of Elizabeth B. Dwight, including an account of the plague of 1837. With a sketch of the life of Judith S. Grant, missionary to Persia. New York, 1840. 12mo.

2 Christianity Revived in the East; or, a narrative of the Work of God among the Armenians of Turkey. New York, 1850. 12°

DWIGHT, Henry Edwin. Travels in the North of Germany, in 1825 and 1826. N. York, 1829. 8vo.

DWIGHT, M. A. Grecian and Roman Mythology. With an introductory notice by .. T. Lewis, and a series of illustrations in outline. New York, 1849. 12°

DWIGHT, Sereno Edwards. The Greek Revolution. An address delivered in Park Street Church, Boston, on Thursday, April 1, ... 1824. Second edition. Boston, 1824. 8°

2 The Hebrew Wife; or, the law of marriage examined in relation to the lawfulness of polygamy, and to the extent of the law of incest. New York, 1836. 12°

3 Select Discourses of Sereno Edwards Dwight, D. D. .. With a memoir of his life, by W. T. Dwight. Boston, 1851. 12°

DWIGHT, Theodore, the Elder. An Oration, spoken at Hartford, in .. Connecticut, on the anniversary of American Independence, July 4, 1798. Hartford, 1798. 8°

2 History of the Hartford Convention; with a review of the policy of the United States Government, which led to the war of 1812. [With an appendix.] New York and Boston, 1833. 8vo.

DWIGHT, Theodore, the Younger. Lessons in Greek: a familiar introduction to the Greek language as a living tongue. Springfield, 1833. 12°

2 The Character of T. Jefferson, as exhibited in his own writings. Boston, 1839. 12°

3 The History of Connecticut, from the first settlement to the present time. New York, 1845. 12°

4 Summer Tours; or, notes of a traveller through some of the middle and northern States. Second edition. New York, 1847. 12°

5 The Roman Republic of 1849, with accounts of the inquisition and the siege of Rome, and biographical

sketches, with original portraits. New York [1851]. 12°

DWIGHT'S AMERICAN MAGAZINE, and Family Newspaper, *etc.* Edited by Theodore Dwight. Feb. 8, 1845 to Dec. 25, 1847. Vol. 1-3. New York, 1845-47. 8°

DWIGHT, TIMOTHY. Greenfield Hill: a poem, in seven parts. New York, 1794. 8°

2 THE DUTY of Americans at the Present Crisis; illustrated in a discourse [on Rev. xvi. 15], *etc.* New Haven, 1798. 8°

3 A DISCOURSE [on Isa. xxi. 11,12] in two parts, delivered July 23, 1812 [and Aug. 20, 1812, on Isa. xxi. 11, 12] on the public fast, in .. Yale College, *etc.* Second edition. Boston [Andover printed], 1813. 8°

4 TRAVELS in New England and

New York, *etc.* 4 vol. New Haven, 1821-22. 8°

DWIGHT, WILLIAM THEODORE. An Address delivered before the Association of Alumni of Yale College, Aug. 14,1844. N. Haven, 1844. 8vo.

DYER, SIDNEY. Voices of Nature, and Thoughts in Rhyme, *etc.* Louisville, 1849. 12°

DYMOND, JONATHAN. Essays on the Principles of Morality, and on the private and political rights and obligations of mankind. . . With a preface, by the Rev. G. Bush. New York, 1834. 8°

2 AN INQUIRY into the accordancy of war with the principles of Christianity, *etc.* Fourth edition, corrected and enlarged. Philadel. 1835. 8°

3 ON Military Glory. Philadelphia [1840?]. 8vo.

ARL, MARY. A short but comprehensive English Grammar, .. by familiar questions and answers. Boston, 1816. 12°

EARLE, PLINY. A Visit to Thirteen Asylums for the Insane in Europe: to which are added, a brief notice of similar institutions in Transatlantic countries and in the United States, and an eſſay on the causes, duration, termination, and moral treatment of insanity. With copious statistics. Philadelphia, 1841. 8vo.

EARLE, THOMAS. A Treatise on Railroads and Internal Communications, etc. Philadelphia, 1830. 8°

EASTBURN, JAMES WALLIS. Yamoyden, a tale of the wars of King Philip: in six cantos. By James Wallis Eastburn and his Friend. New York, 1820. 12mo.

EASTBURN, MANTON, Bishop. Lectures, explanatory and practical, on the Epistle of St. Paul to the Philippians. . . . Second edition. New York, 1836. 12°

2 THE VOICE of God in the recent National Bereavement; a sermon [on Proverbs viii. 33] delivered . . the Sunday after the interment of the Hon. D. Webster. Boston, 1852. 8°

EASTERN ARGUS. Vol. 5, N° 224. Sept. 24, 1839. Portland, 1839. Fol.

EASTERN TOURIST; being a Guide through the States of Connecticut, Rhode Island, Maſſachusetts, Vermont, New Hampshire, and Maine; also a Dash into Canada, .. etc. [By J. D. i. e. J. Disturnell.] New York, 1848. 12°

EAST INDIA MARINE SOCIETY. [Begins] The East India Marine Society of Salem. [Containing, an account of the Society, the act of incorporation, the bye-laws, lists of the members and officers, and catalogues of the library and museum.] [Salem, 1831.] 8°

EASTMAN, F. S. A History of the State of New York, from the first discovery of the country to the present time. New York, 1828. 12°

EASTMAN, MARY H. Dahcotah; or, life and legends of the Sioux around Fort Snelling. With preface, by Mrs. C. M. Kirkland. Illustrated from drawings, by Capt. Eastman. New York, 1849. 12°

2 AUNT Phillis's Cabin; or, Southern life as it is. Philadel. 1852. 12°

EASTWOOD, MARVIN. The Wise and Foolish Builders; or, true and false Christians compared and distinguished. New York, 1852. 12°

EATON, AMOS. A Manual of Botany for the Northern and Middle States. Second edition, enlarged. 2 parts. Albany, 1818. 12mo.

2 AN INDEX to the Geology of the Northern States, with transverse sec-

tions, extending from Susquehanna river to the Atlantic, crofsing Catskill Mountains. To which is prefixed a geological grammar. Second edition, .. written anew, *etc.* Troy, 1820. 12°

3 GEOLOGICAL Text Book, prepared for popular Lectures on North American Geology; with applications to agriculture and the arts. Albany, 1830. 8vo.

4 NORTH American Botany; comprising the native and common cultivated Plants north of Mexico... Eighth edition. In the present edition the author is afsociated with J. Wright, M.D... With the very valuable additions of the properties of plants, from Lindley's New Medical Flora. Troy, 1840. 8°

EATON, HORACE. Circular of the State Superintendent of Common Schools (Horace Eaton) to the County Superintendents; and an addrefs to the teachers of common schools in the State of Vermont. St. Albans, 1845. 8°

2 FIRST Annual Report of the State Superintendent of Common Schools, made to the Legislature, Oct. 1846. Montpelier, Vt. [1846]. 8°

EATON, JOHN HENRY. The Life of Andrew Jackson, Major-General in the service of the United States; comprising a history of the war in the South, from the commencement of the Creek campaign to the termination of hostilities before New Orleans. Philadelphia, 1824. 8vo.

2 CANDID Appeal to the American Public, in reply to Mefsrs. Ingham, Branch, and Berrien, on the difsolution of the late Cabinet. Washington, 1831. 8°

EATON, REBECCA. A Geography of Pennsylvania, for the Use of Schools. Philadelphia, 1835. 12°

2 A GEOGRAPHY of Pennsylvania, for the Use of Schools... Second edition, with .. additions. Philadelphia, 1837. 12°

EATON, WILLIAM, *General.* The Life of the late Gen. William Eaton. Principally collected from his correspondence and other manuscripts. Brookfield, 1813. 12mo.

EBERLE, FREDERICK. Trial of Frederick Eberle and others, at Philadelphia, July, 1816, for illegally conspiring together, by all means lawful and unlawful, to prevent the introduction of the English Language into the service of St. Michael's and Zion Churches, belonging to the German Lutheran Congregation, Philadelphia. Taken by J. Carson. Philadelphia, 1817. 8vo.

EBERLE, JOHN. Botanical Terminology; or, a pocket companion for students in Botany. Philadelphia, 1818. 12mo.

2 A TREATISE on the Practice of Medicine... Second edition, revised and enlarged. 2 vol. Philadelphia, 1831. 8vo.

3 A TREATISE on the Diseases and Physical Education of Children.... Third edition. Philadelphia, 1841. 8°

ECKFELDT, JACOB R. and DU BOIS, WILLIAM E. A Manual of Gold and Silver Coins of all Nations, struck within the last Century... Illustrated by numerous engravings, .. by .. J. Saxton. Philadel. 1842. 4°

ECLECTIC REPERTORY, and Analytical Review, Medical and Philosophical. Edited by a Society of Physicians. 10 vol. Philadel. 1811–20. 8°

EDA, *Pseud.* A Letter to a Friend on some important points of Christian Truth. Boston [printed], London, 1855. 12mo.

EDDOWES, RALPH. Sermons delivered before the first Society of Unitarian Christians in .. Philadelphia; wherein the principal points on which that denomination of believers differ from the majority of their brethren, are occasionally elucidated. Philadelphia, 1817. 12mo.

EDDY, Daniel C. Heroines of the Missionary Enterprise; or, sketches of prominent female missionaries. Boston, 1850. 16°

EDDY, Thomas. Hints for introducing an improved mode of treating the Insane in the Asylum, etc. New York, 1815. 8°

EDMOND, Amanda M. The Broken Vow, and other poems. Boston, 1845. 12°

EDNEY, Richard. Richard Edney and the Governor's Family; a Rus-Urban tale, simple and popular, yet cultured and noble of morals, sentiment and life, practically treated and pleasantly illustrated: containing also, Hints on being good and doing good. By the author of " Margaret" and "Philo"[S. Judd]. Boston, 1850. 12°

EDSON, Theodore. Christ the true Light: a sermon [on John i. 9] preached at the convention of the Protestant Episcopal Church of the Eastern diocese. Boston, 1827. 12°

EDUCATION. Thoughts on the Condition and Prospects of Popular Education in the United States. By a Citizen of Pennsylvania [F. A. Packard?]. Philadelphia, 1836. 8°

EDWARD'S First Lessons in Grammar. By the author of " Theory of Teaching." Boston, 1843. 12°

EDWARD, David B. The History of Texas; or, the emigrant's, farmer's and politician's guide to the character, soil, and productions of that country, etc. Cincinnati, 1836. 12mo.

EDWARDS, Ann. The Cottage Girl; or, an account of Ann Edwards. Philadelphia [1818?]. 12mo.

EDWARDS, Bela Bates. The Missionary Gazetteer; comprising a geographical and statistical account of the various stations of the American and Foreign Protestant Missionary Societies of all denominations; with their progress in evangelization and civilization. Boston, 1832. 12°

2 Memoir of the Rev. Elias Cornelius. Boston, 1833. 12°

3 The Eclectic Reader, designed for Schools and Academies. Boston, 1835. 12°

4 Selections from German Literature. Andover, 1839. 8vo.

5 Biography of Self-taught Men: with an introductory essay. [Continued by S. G. B.] 2 vol. Boston, 1846-7. 12°

6 Writings of Professor Bela Bates Edwards; with a memoir, by E. A. Park. 2 vol. Boston [Cambridge printed], 1853. 12°

EDWARDS, Charles. The Juryman's Guide throughout the State of New York; and containing general matter for the lawyer and law officer. New York, 1831. 8°

2 Reports of Chancery Cases decided in the First Circuit of the State of New York. Vol. 1-3. [Vol. 1, second edition.] [May, 1831—Oct. 1842.] By the Hon. William T. M'Coun, Vice Chancellor. N. York, 1844, 37, 43. 8°

EDWARDS, Frank S. A Campaign in New Mexico with Colonel Doniphon. Philadelphia, 1847. 8°

EDWARDS, John. An Address to all Play-actors, Play-hunters, Legislators, Governors, Magistrates, Clergy, .. and the world at large. New York, 1812. 8°

EDWARDS, Jonathan. A Divine and Supernatural Light, immediately imparted to the Soul by the Spirit of God, shown to be both a Scriptural and Rational Doctrine: a sermon [on Matt. xvi. 17] preached .. in 1734. Boston [1734]. 12°

2 A Treatise concerning Religious Affections [with MS. corrections]. Boston, 1746. 4°

3 The Life and Character of .. Jonathan Edwards. .. Together with a number of his sermons, etc. Boston, 1765. 8vo.

4 Memoirs of the Rev. D. Brainerd,

Miffionary to the Indians on the borders of New York, New Jersey, and Pennsylvania: chiefly taken from his own diary, .. including his journal, now for the first time incorporated... By S. E. Dwight. N. Haven, 1822. 8°

5 The Works of President Edwards (Life of President Edwards). By S. E. Dwight. 10 vol. N.York, 1830. 8vo.

6 The Works of President Edwards. A reprint of the Worcester edition, with valuable additions, *etc.* 4 vol. New York. 1844. 8°

7 Charity and its Fruits; or, Christian love as manifested in the heart and life. Edited from the original manuscripts, with an introduction, by T. Edwards. New York, 1852. 12°

EDWARDS, Jonathan, *the Younger.* Observations on the Language of the Muhhekaneew Indians; in which the extent of that language in North America is shown; its genius ..traced, *etc.* New Haven, 1789. 8vo.

2 The Injustice and Impolicy of the Slave Trade, and of the Slavery of the Africans: illustrated in a sermon [on Matthew vii. 12], *etc.* [New Haven], 1791. 8°

3 The Injustice and Impolicy of the Slave Trade, and of the Slavery of the Africans: illustrated in a sermon [on Matthew vii. 12] preached before the Connecticut Society for the Promotion of Freedom, .. at their annual meeting in New Haven, September 15, 1791. Third edition. New Haven, 1833. 8vo.

EDWARDS, Justin. Christian Communion: a sermon [on Rom. xv. 7] .. at the installation of .. T. Pomeroy, as Pastor of the Congregational Church in Gorham. (The Charge .. by A. Rand, *etc.*) Portland, 1822. 8°

EDWARDS, William H. A Voyage up the River Amazon, including a residence at Pará. N.York, 1847. 12°

EELLS, William Woodward. A

Discourse occasioned by the Death of D. Webster. Newburyport, 1852. 8°

ELDRIDGE, Joseph. Reform and Reformers: a sermon [on 2 Timothy ii. 24, 25] delivered at Norfolk, Conn. Nov. 30,1843. New Haven,1844. 8°

ELECTION DAY. Written for the American Sunday School Union. Philadelphia, 1827. 12mo.

ELIOT, Andrew. An Evil and Adulterous Generation: a sermon [on Matth. xii. 39] preached on the public fast, April 19,1753. Boston,1753. 8°

2 A Discourse on Natural Religion [on Acts xvii. 27]. Boston, 1771. 8°

ELIOT, John. The Indian Grammar Begun: or, an Efsay to bring the Indian Language into Rules, for the help of such as desire to learn the same, for the furtherance of the Gospel among them. By John Eliot. Printed by Marmaduke Johnson. Cambridge, 1666. 4to.

2 A Grammar of the Mafsachusetts Indian Language...A new edition, with notes and observations by P. S. Du Ponceau. .. and an introduction and supplementary observations, by J. Pickering, as published in the Mafsachusetts Historical Collections. Boston, 1822. 8vo.

3 The Logick Primer. Some logical notions to initiate the Indians in the knowledge of the Rule of Reason, .. especially for the instruction of such as are teachers among them. Composed by J. E[liot] for the use of the Praying Indians. [Cambridge?] 1672. 36mo.

4 The Holy Bible, in the Indian language, *etc. See* Bibles, N° 1, 43.

ELIOT, John, *D. D.* A Biographical Dictionary, containing a brief account of the first settlers and other eminent characters in New England. Boston, 1809. 8vo.

ELIOT, Samuel. History of Liberty. Part 1. The ancient Romans. A new edition. 2 vol. Boston [Cambridge printed], 1853. 12°

ELIOT, Samuel Atkins. An Address before the Boston Academy of Music, on the opening of the Odeon, *etc.* Boston, 1835. 8°

2 Sketch of the History of Harvard College, and of its present State. Boston, 1848. 12°

ELIOT, T. D. Anniversary Address delivered before the American Institute of the city of New York. New York, 1845. 8°

ELIOT, William G. Discourses on the Unity of God, and other subjects. Printed for the American Unitarian Association. Boston [Cambridge printed], 1853. 12°

ELKSWATAWA; or, the Prophet of the West. A tale of the frontier. [By Mr. French.] 2 vol. New York, 1836. 12°

ELLA, V——, or, the July tour. [A tale.] By one of the party [F. Taylor]. New York, 1841. 12°

ELLEN; or, the disinterested girl. [Published by the American Sunday School Union.] Phil. 1831. 12mo.

ELLET, Charles. The Mississippi and Ohio Rivers: containing plans for the protection of the Delta from inundation; and investigations of the practicability and cost of improving the navigation of the Ohio and other rivers, by means of reservoirs. With an appendix on the bars of the mouths of the Mississippi. Plates. Philadelphia, 1853. 8°

ELLET, Elizabeth Fries, *Mrs.* Poems, translated and original. Philadelphia, 1835. 12°

2 The Characters of Schiller. Boston, 1839. 12mo.

3 Scenes in the Life of Joanna of Sicily. Boston, 1840. 12°

4 Rambles about the Country. New York, 1847. 12°

5 The Charm: a series of elegant coloured groups. With descriptive illustrations, by Elizabeth F. Ellet. Philadelphia, 1848. Fol°

6 Evenings at Woodlawn. New York, 1849. 12°

7 Domestic History of the American Revolution. N. York, 1850. 12°

8 Watching Spirits. New York, 1851. 8°

9 Pioneer Women of the West. New York, 1852. 12°

10 Summer Rambles in the West. New York, 1853. 12°

ELLICOTT, Andrew. The Journal of A. Ellicott, late Commissioner on behalf of the United States for determining the boundary between the United States and the possessions of his Catholic Majesty in America. . . With six maps. . . To which is added an appendix, containing all the astronomical observations made, *etc.* Philadelphia, 1803. 4to.

ELLINGWOOD, John W. The Duty of using means for the reformation of immoral Persons. A sermon [on Levit. xix. 17], *etc.* Boston, 1815. 8°

ELLIOT, Jonathan. The Debates, Resolutions, and other Proceedings, in Convention, on the adoption of the Federal Constitution, as recommended by the general Convention at Philadelphia . . Sept. 17, 1787; with the yeas and nays on the decision of the main question. Collected and revised from contemporary publications. (Journal and Debates of the Federal Convention, *etc.*) 4 vol. [vol. 1, in 2 pts.] Washing. 1827-30.

2 The American Diplomatic Code, exhibiting a collection of treaties and conventions between the United States and foreign powers, from 1778 to 1834, with an abstract of important judicial decisions on points connected with our foreign relations. Also, a concise diplomatic manual, containing a summary of the law of nations, and other diplomatic writings on questions of international law. 2 vol. Washington, 1834. 8vo.

3 THE DEBATES in the several State Conventions, on the adoption of the Federal Constitution, as recommended by the general Convention at Philadelphia in 1787. Together with the Journal of the Federal Convention, Luther Martin's Letter, Yates's Minutes, Congreſſional Opinions, Virginia and Kentucky Resolutions of '98-'99, and other illustrations of the Constitution. Second edition, with considerable additions. 4 vol. Washington, 1836. 8vo.

4 THE DEBATES in the several State Conventions, on the adoption of the Federal Constitution, as recommended by the General Convention at Philadelphia, in 1787; together with the Journal of the Federal Convention, Luther Martin's Letter, Yates's Minutes, Congreſſional Opinions, Virginia and Kentucky Resolutions of '98-'99, and other illustrations of the Constitution. Second edition, with considerable additions. Collected and revised from contemporary publications, by J. Elliot. Published under the sanction of Congreſs. 4 vol. Washington, [1836!] 8°

5 DEBATES on the adoption of the Federal Constitution, in the Convention held at Philadelphia, in 1787; with a diary of the debates of the Congreſs of the Confederation; as reported by J. Madison. Revised and newly arranged by J. Elliot.. Supplementary to Elliot's Debates. (Vol. 5.) Washington, 1845. 8°

ELLIOT, SAMUEL. Oration pronounced at West Springfield, Maſſ. July 4, 1803. Bennington, 1803. 8°

2 AN ADDRESS to the members of the Washington Benevolent Society, etc. Brattleborough, 1812. 8°

3 AN ORATION pronounced at Brattleboro, Vermont, before the Washington Benevolent Societies .. July 6, 1813, in commemoration of the thirty-seventh anniversary of American Independence. Brattleborough, 1813. 8°

4 A VOICE from the Green Mountains on the subject of Masonry and antimasonry. Brattleboro, 1834. 8°

5 AN HUMBLE Tribute to my Country: or, practical eſſays, political, legal, moral, and miscellaneous; including a brief account of the life, sufferings, and memorable visit of General Lafayette. Bost. 1842. 12°

ELLIOT, WILLIAM. Addreſs delivered before the Columbian Society, at Marblehead, on their sixth anniversary, etc. Boston, 1830. 8°

ELLIOT, WILLIAM. The Washington Guide, etc. Washington City, 1837. 12°

ELLIOTT, C. W. Cottages and Cottage Life, containing plans for country houses. Cincinnati, 1848. 8°

ELLIOTT, CHARLES, D.D. Delineation of Roman Catholicism .. in which the peculiar doctrines .. of the Church of Rome are stated ... and confuted. 2 vol. N. York, 1842. 8°

2 SINFULNESS of American Slavery. . . . Together with observations on emancipation and the duties of American citizens in regard to slavery; edited by Rev. B. F. Tefft. 2 vol. Cincinnati, 1851. 8vo.

ELLIOTT, CHARLES WYLLYS. Mysteries; or, glimpses of the supernatural. Containing accounts of the Salem witchcraft, the Cock-Lane ghost, etc. New York, 1852. 12°

ELLIOTT, STEPHEN, LL.D. A Sketch of the Botany of South Carolina and Georgia. 2 vol. Charleston, 1821-24. 8vo.

ELLIOTT, STEPHEN, the younger, D.D. A high Civilization the Moral Duty of Georgians: a discourse delivered before the Georgia Historical Society, on ... its fifth anniversary, etc. Savannah, 1844. 8°

ELLIOTT, WILLIAM of Beaufort, South Carolina. Carolina Sports, by land and water; including incidents of devil fishing, etc. Charleston, 1846. 12°

ELLIS, CHARLES MAYO. The History of Roxbury Town. Boston, 1847. 8°

ELLIS, FERDINAND. Civil Government an Ordinance of God: a sermon [on Psal. lxxxii. 6, 7] delivered .. before .. the Governor, .. Council, and .. Legislature of .. New Hampshire, etc. Concord, 1826. 8°

ELLIS, GEORGE EDWARD. An Oration delivered at Charlestown, Maſſachusetts, on the 17th of June, 1841, in commemoration of the battle of Bunker Hill. Boston, 1841. 8°
   2 A DISCOURSE [on Matt. v. 9] delivered in .. Boston, before the ancient and honourable Artillery Company, June 1, 1846, being the two hundred and eighth anniversary. Boston, 1846. 8°
   3 THE ORGAN, and Church Music. Two discourses [on 1 Chron. xvi. 4, 5; and Ephes. v. 19], etc. Boston, 1852. 8vo.
   4 THE EVANGELICAL and the Philosophical Spirit in Religion. A discourse [on 1 Pet. iii. 15] preached at the Unitarian Convention at Baltimore, October 27, 1852. Boston, 1853. 8°

ELLIS, GEORGE JAMES WELBORE AGAR, Baron Dover. The Life of Frederic the Second, King of Prussia. 2 vol. New York, 1841. 12°

ELLSWORTH, HENRY WILLIAM. Valley of the Upper Wabash, Indiana, with hints on its agricultural advantages, .. estimates of cultivation, and notices of labour-saving machines. New York, 1838. 8°
   2 THE AMERICAN Swine Breeder; a practical treatise on the selection, rearing, and fattening of swine. Boston, 1840. 16°

ELMORE, D. W. English Grammar; or, a natural analysis of the English language. Troy, 1830. 12°

EL-MUKATTEM. Pseud. Lands of the Moslem. A narrative of Oriental travel. New York, 1851. 8°

ELNATHAN, a narrative illustrative of the manners of the ancient Israelites. (An account of the death of a Jewish girl.) Philadelphia, 1827. 12mo.

ELTON, ROMEO, D.D. Life of Roger Williams, the earliest Legislator and true Champion for a full and absolute liberty of conscience. Providence, 1853. 8°

ELVILLE. Behind the Curtain. A tale of Elville. Dansville, 1853. 12°

ELWELL, ODELL. A new and complete American Dictionary of the English and German Languages. With the pronunciation and accentuation according to Webster's method. (Neuestes vollständiges Amerikanisches Wörterbuch, etc.) 2 parts. New York, 1850. 12°

ELY, ZEBULUN. The Death of Moses, the Servant of the Lord; a sermon [on Deut. xxxiv. 5] preached at the funeral solemnity of . . . J. Trumbull, etc. Hartford, 1786. 8°

EMERALD, or, Miscellany of Literature, containing sketches of the manners, principles and amusements of the age. May 3, 1806, to Oct. 17, 1807. [Edited by Meſſrs. Belcher and Armstrong.] New series, Oct. 24, 1807 to Oct. 15, 1808. [Edited by O. C. Greenleaf.] 3 vol. Boston, 1806-1808. 8°

EMERICK, ALBERT G. Songs for the People; comprising national, patriotic, sentimental, comic and naval songs. Edited by A. G. Emerick, etc. Vol. 1. Philadelphia, 1848. 8°

EMERSON, B. D. The Second-Claſs Reader: designed for the use of the middle clafs of schools in the United States. Mobile, 1833. 12°

2 THE NEW National Spelling Book, and Pronouncing Tutor, *etc.* Claremont, N. H. [1834?] 12°

3 THE FIRST-CLASS Reader . . For the use of schools in the United States. Philadelphia, 1841. 12°

4 INTRODUCTION to the National Spelling-Books . . New edition, revised and enlarged. Claremont, N. H. 1844. 12°

5 THE NATIONAL Spelling-Book and Pronouncing Tutor, *etc.* One hundred and seventieth edition. Boston, [1844?] 12°

6 THE THIRD-CLASS Reader; designed for the use of the younger clafses in the schools of the United States. Philadelphia, 1844. 12°

EMERSON, FREDERICK. Outlines of Geography and History; presenting a concise view of the world. Philadelphia, 1843. 12°

2 EMERSON'S First Part. The North American Arithmetic, part first, for young learners. New York, 1845. 12°

3 EMERSON'S Second Part. The North American Arithmetic, *etc.* Philadelphia, 1845. 12°

4 KEY to the North American Arithmetic; part second and part third. For the use of teachers. Boston, 1845. 12°

5 EMERSON'S Third Part. The North American Arithmetic, part third, for advanced scholars. Boston, 1846. 12°

EMERSON, GEORGE B. A Report on the Trees and Shrubs growing naturally in the Forests of Mafsachusetts. Published agreeably to an Order of the Legislature, by the Commifsioners on the Zoological and Botanical Survey of the State. Boston, 1846. 8°

EMERSON, JOSEPH. Questions, adapted to Whelpley's Compend of History. Tenth edition. Boston, 1832. 12°

2 THE POETIC Reader; containing selections from the most approved authors, . . To which are prefixed, directions for reading. Wethersfield, 1832. 8°

3 QUESTIONS and Supplement to Goodrich's History of the United States . . A new edition, revised, *etc.* Boston, 1845. 12°

EMERSON, RALPH WALDO. An Oration delivered before the literary societies of Dartmouth College, July 24, 1838. Boston, 1838. 8°

2 AN ORATION, delivered before the Phi Beta Kappa Society, at Cambridge, Aug. 31, 1837. Second edition. Boston [printed at Cambridge], 1838. 8°

3 THE METHOD of Nature: an oration delivered before the society of the Adelphi, in Waterville College, in Maine, Aug. 11, 1841. Boston, 1841. 8°

4 AN ADDRESS delivered in the Court House in Concord, Mafsachusetts, . . Aug. 1, 1844, on the anniversary of the Emancipation of the Negroes in the British West Indies. Boston, 1844. 8°

5 ESSAYS: Second series. Boston, 1845. 12°

6 POEMS. Boston. 1847. 8°

EMERSON, REV. WILLIAM. An Historical Sketch of the First Church in Boston from its formation to the present period. To which are added, two sermons, *etc.* (Sketch of the life and character of the late Rev. Dr. Clarke. Character of Rev. Mr. Emerson . . Extracted from Rev. J. S. Buckminster's sermon at his funeral.) Boston, 1812. 8°

EMMA and her Nurse. Philadelphia, 1830. 12mo.

EMMONS, NATHANIEL. Christ the Standard of Preaching. A sermon [on John vii. 46] preached at the Installation of C. Alexander to the pastoral care of the Church in Mendon, April 12, 1786. New York, 1786. 12°

2 A SERMON [on Acts xx. 24] delivered at the ordination of the Rev. J. Robinson to the pastoral care of the church in Northborough, Jan. 14, 1789. Providence [1789]. 8°

3 A DISCOURSE [on Eccl. xii. 11] preached at the ordination of . . E. Smith . . Nov. 27, 1793. (The charge by . . S. Dix ; the right hand of fellowship by . . J. Bullard.) Worcester, 1794. 8°

4 A SERMON [on Dan. vi. 28] preached before . . the Council, Senate, and House of Representatives, of . . Massachusetts, . . the day of general Election. Boston, 1798. 8°

5 A DISCOURSE [on 2 Kings, xvii. 21] delivered on the annual fast in Massachusetts, April 9, 1801. Hartford, reprinted, 1801. 8°

6 THE GIVER more blessed than the Receiver : a discourse [on Acts xx. 35], etc. Boston, 1809. 8°

7 A DISCOURSE [on 2 Tim. i. 13] addressed to the Norfolk Auxiliary Society for the Education of Pious Youth for the Gospel Ministry, etc. Dedham, 1817. 8°

8 THE WORKS of Nathaniel Emmons, with a Memoir of his Life. Edited by J. Ide. 6 vol. Boston, 1842. 8°

EMMONS, RICHARD. The Fredoniad or Independence preserved, an epic poem on the late war of 1812. 4 vol. Boston, 1827. 12°

EMMONS, SAMUEL B. The Grammatical Instructer ; containing an exposition of all the essential rules of English grammar, etc. Boston, 1832. 12°

EMMONS, WILLIAM. Biography of Martin Van Buren, Vice President of the United States ; with an appendix, containing selections from his writings, . . speeches, etc. Compiled and edited by William Emmons. Washington, 1835. 12°

EMORY, WILLIAM H. Notes of a Military Reconnoissance from Fort Leavenworth in Missouri to San Diego in California, including parts of the Arkansas, del Norte and Gila Rivers. [With a map and plates.] New York, 1848. 8°

EMPEROR. The Philosophical Emperor : a political experiment ; or the progress of a false position. New York, 1841. 12mo.

EMPORIUM (THE) of Arts and Sciences, conducted by J. R. Coxe. 2 vol. Philadelphia [1812]. 8vo. New Series conducted by T. Cooper. 2 vol. Philadelphia, 1813. 8vo.

ENCYCLOPÆDIA AMERICANA. A popular Dictionary . . on the basis of the seventh edition of the German Conversations Lexicon. Edited by F. Lieber, assisted by E. Wigglesworth (and T. G. Bradford). 13 vol. Vol. 14, 1848 (Supplementary volume . . edited by H. Vethake.) Philadelphia, 1829-33, 1848. 8vo.

ENGELHARDT, G. Narrative of the Expedition to the Polar Sea, in the years 1820-23 ; commanded by Lieut, now Admiral, F. Wrangell, of the Russian imperial navy. New York, 1845. 12°

ENGLAND. A Sketch of Old England ; by a New England Man [J. K. Paulding]. 2 vol. New York, 1822. 12mo.

ENGLAND, Church of, Homilies. Certain Sermons or Homilies appointed to be read in Churches in the time of Queen Elizabeth, and reprinted by authority from King James I. A. D. 1623 ; to which are added, the constitutions and canons of the Church of England, set forth A. D. 1603. With an appendix, containing the Articles of Religion, constitution and canons of the Protestant Episcopal Church in the United States of America. Third American . . edition. Philadelphia, 1844. 8°

ENGLISH, George Bethune. A Narrative of the expedition to Dongola and Sennaar, under the command of .. Ismael Pasha... First American edition. [With an appendix.] Boston, 1823. 8°

ENGLISH, Thomas Dunn. The Power of the S. F. A tale, developing the secret action of parties during the presidential campaign of 1844. New York, 1847. 12°

ENGLISH CHURCHWOMEN of the Seventeenth Century. New York, 1846. 8vo.

ENGLISH GRAMMAR. A Catechism of English Grammar, with practical exercises; prepared for the use of the School of Mutual Instruction in Boston. By the Instructor. Boston [1823?]. 12°

ENGLISH LANGUAGE. Interrogative Grammar, .. illustrating the principles of the English Language, etc. Boston, 1832. 12°

ENGLISHMAN'S Sketch-book; or, letters from New York. New York, 1828. 8°

ENGLISH WORDS. The Scholar's Companion; containing exercises in the orthography, derivation, and classification of English words. Arranged on the basis of Butter's Etymological Expositor. A new edition, enlarged and improved. Philadelphia, 1842. 12°

ENQUIRY. A free Enquiry into the Causes, both real and pretended, for Laying the Embargo. By a Citizen of Vermont. Windsor, 1808. 8°

EPHEMERA. [In verse. By G. E. R. and J. H. Wainwright.] Boston, 1852. 8°

EPISCOPAL MANUAL; or, an attempt to explain and vindicate the doctrine, discipline, and worship of the Protestant Episcopal Church, as taught in her public formularies and the writings of her approved divines. (Directions for .. behaviour in the public worship of God, etc.) .. By a Clergyman of the Protestant Episcopal Church. Philadelphia, 1815. 12°

EPISCOPUS. Hints to a Layman. [A vindication of S. Colwell's " New Themes for the Protestant Clergy," in reply to the " Review of New Themes, by a Layman."] Philadelphia, 1853. 8°

ERNESTI, Johann August. Elements of Interpretation, translated from the Latin of Johann August Ernesti, and accompanied by notes; with an appendix, containing extracts from Morus, Beck, and Keil, by M. Stuart. Andover, 1822. 12°

ERRO Y AZPIROZ, Juan Bautista de. The Alphabet of the Primitive Language of Spain, and a Philosophical Examination of the Antiquity and Civilization of the Basque People: an extract from the works of .. Juan Bautista de Erro. [Translated and edited by G. W. Erving.] Boston, 1829. 8vo.

ERSKINE, Thomas, Baron Erskine. A View of the Causes and Consequences of the present war with France. From the twenty-fourth London edition. Boston [1797]. 8°

ESCHENBURG, Johann Joachim. Manual of Classical Literature: from the German. With additions, by N. W. Fiske. Third edition. Philadelphia, 1839. 8vo.

2 Manual of Classical Literature: from the German. With additions, by N. W. Fiske. Fourth edition. Philadelphia, 1844. 8vo.

ESPY, James P. The Philosophy of Storms. Boston, 1841. 8vo.

2 (Second Report on Meteorology. Third report on meteorology, with directions for mariners, etc.) Maps. [Washington, 1850.] Obl. fol°

ESQUIROL, Jean Etienne Do-

MINIQUE. Mental Maladies: a treatise on insanity. . . Translated from the French, with additions, by E. K. Hunt. Philadelphia, 1845. 8vo.

ESSAYS on the Spirit of Legislation, in the Encouragement of Agriculture, Population, Manufactures, and Commerce. Translated from the original French, which gained the premiums offered by the Œconomical Society of Berne. Newark, 1800. 8°

ESSAYS on the Primitive Church Offices. Reprinted . . from the Princetown Review. New York, 1851. 12°

ESSEX COUNTY, Maßachusetts. Abstract of the Laws for the Regulation of Licensed Houses. Published by order of the Court of Sefsions for the county of Eßex. Salem, 1821. 12°

ESSEX SOUTH DISTRICT MEDICAL SOCIETY. Memoir of E. A. Holyoke; [with paßages from his diary, etc.]. . . Prepared in compliance with a vote of the Eßex South District Medical Society [by a Committee thereof]. Boston, 1829. 8vo.

ESTABROOK, JOSEPH. Popular Education: an addreß delivered at the annual commencement of East Tennefsee College. Knoxville, 1838. 8°

ESTRAY, a collection of Poems. [Edited by H. W. Longfellow.] Boston, 1847. 12°

ETIENNE DE JOUY, VICTOR JOSEPH. Sylla, a tragedy, in five acts [and in verse]. . . Translated from the French, and adapted . . by a Citizen of New York. New York, 1827. 12mo.

EULER, LEONHARD. An introduction to the elements of Algebra. . . Selected from the Algebra of Euler [by J. Farrar]. Cambridge. 1818. 8°

2 LETTERS of Euler on different subjects in Natural Philosophy. Addreßed to a German princeß. [Translated from German by H. Hunter.] With notes, and a life of Euler, by

D. Brewster. . . Containing a gloßary of scientific terms, with additional notes, by J. Griscom. 2 vol. New York, 1846. 12°

EUSTIS, WILLIAM. Mr. Eustis's motion [in the House of Representatives of the United States of America, relating to the Navy yards of the United States.] Jan. 22, 1805. [Washington, 1805.] 8°

EVANS, ESTWICK. A Pedestrious Tour of four thousand miles through the Western States and Territories, during the winter and spring of 1818. Interspersed with reflections. Concord, N. H. 1819. 12mo.

EVANS, GEORGE. Speech . . in relation to the failure of the bill making appropriations for fortifications at the last Sefsion of Congreß; delivered in the House of Representatives, Jan. 28, 1836. Washington, 1836. 8°

2 SPEECH . . on the Oregon question, . . in the Senate . . March . . 1846. Washington, 1846. 8°

EVANS, GURDON. The Dairyman's Manual: being a complete guide for the American dairyman. Utica, 1851. 8°

EVANS, ISRAEL. A Sermon [on Gal. v. 1] delivered at Concord, before the . . General Court of . . New Hampshire, at the annual Election, etc. Concord, 1791. 8°

EVANS, LEWIS. Geographical, Historical, Political, Philosophical, and Mechanical Eßays. The first, containing an analysis of a general map of the middle British Colonies in America, etc. Second edition. (Number II. containing a letter, representing the impropriety of sending forces to Virginia, etc. with an answer by L. W.) Philadelphia, 1755-56. 4to.

EVANS, NATHANIEL. Poems on several occasions, with some other compositions. Philadelphia, 1772. 8°

EVANS, OLIVER. The Young Mill - Wright and Miller's Guide ; illustrated by twenty-eight descriptive plates. . . The eleventh edition, with additions and corrections by T. P. Jones, . . and a description of an improved merchant flour-mill, with engravings, by C. and O. Evans, Engineers. Philadelphia, 1846. 8°

EVANS, R. M. The Story of Joan of Arc : . . with . . plates. New York [and] Philadelphia, 1847. 12°

EVE. Our First Mother. New York, 1852. 12°

EVELETH, EPHRAIM. History of the Sandwich Islands : with an account of the American Miſſion established there in 1820. Philadelphia, 1831. 12mo.

EVELYN, CHETWOOD. The Companion. After Dinner Table Talk. New York, 1850. 12°

EVENING MIRROR. Oct. 7. 1844 to Oct. 6, 1847. N° 1-862, Vol. 1-6. New York [1844-47]. Fol°

EVEREST, CHARLES W. The Poets of Connecticut ; with biographical sketches. Edited by Rev. C. W. Everest. Hartford, 1843. 8°

2 THE SNOW-DROP : a gift for a friend, edited by C. W. Everest. New York, 1845. 12°

3 THE MEMENTO : a Gift of Friendship. Edited by C. W. Everest. New York, 1848. 12°

EVEREST, CORNELIUS BRADFORD. An English Grammar . . for schools, academies and private learners. Norwich, 1835. 12°

EVERETT, ALEXANDER HILL. An Oration, delivered at the request of the City Government, before the citizens of Boston, . . July 5, 1830. Boston, 1830. 8°

2 AN ADDRESS, delivered before the Maſſachusetts Historical Society, at their fifth annual festival, Sept. 18, 1833. [With a report of the Society's proceedings, etc.] Boston, 1833. 8vo.

3 AN ADDRESS delivered at Charlestown, . . June 17, 1836, . . in commemoration of the battle of Bunker Hill. Boston, 1836. 8°

4 AN ADDRESS to the Literary Societies of Dartmouth College, on the character and influence of German literature, etc. Boston, 1839. 8°

5 CRITICAL and Miscellaneous Essays. To which are added, a few poems. Boston, 1845. 12mo.

6 CRITICAL and Miscellaneous Essays ; to which are added a few poems. Boston, 1845. 12°

7 CRITICAL and Miscellaneous Essays. Second series. Boston, 1846. 12°

8 AMERICA : a general survey, etc. [By A. H. Everett.] See AMERICA, N° 5. 1827. 8°

EVERETT, EDWARD. A Defence of Christianity against the work of G. B. English . . intitled, The Grounds of Christianity examined, by comparing the New Testament with the Old. Boston, 1814. 12°

2 AN ORATION pronounced at Cambridge, before the Society of Phi Beta Kappa. New York, 1824. 8°

3 AN ORATION delivered at Cambridge [Maſſachusetts], on the fiftieth anniversary of the Declaration of the Independence of the United States of America. Boston, 1826. 8°

4 AN ADDRESS delivered at Charlestown, August 1, 1826, in commemoration of J. Adams and T. Jefferson. Boston, 1826. 8°

5 AN ORATION delivered before the citizens of Charlestown on the fifty-second anniversary of the Declaration of the Independence of the United States of America. Charlestown, 1828. 8°

6 SPEECH . . on the subject of Retrenchment ; . . in the House of Representatives, . . . Feb. 1, 1828. Washington, 1828. 8°

7 AN ADDRESS delivered . . June 28, 1830, the anniversary of the arrival of Governor Winthrop, at Charlestown. Charlestown, 1830. 8°

8 A LECTURE on the Working Men's Party, . . delivered . . before the Charlestown Lyceum, *etc.* Boston, 1830. 8°

9 SPEECH . . in the House of Representatives . . Feb. 1831, on the execution of the laws and treaties in favour of the Indian Tribes. [Washington, 1831.] 8°

10 AN ADDRESS delivered before the citizens of Worcester, on the fourth of July, 1833. Boston, 1833. 8°

11 AN ADDRESS delivered before the Phi Beta Kappa Society in Yale College, *etc.* New Haven, 1833. 8°

12 THOUGHTS on "The Excitement" [relating to Freemasonry]; in reply to a letter to Hon. E. Everett, first published in the 'National Ægis and Massachusetts Yeoman' [by Rev. G. Allen.] Worcester, 1833. 8°

13 EULOGY on Lafayette, delivered in . . Faneuil Hall, . . Sept. 6, 1834. (Second edition.) Boston, 1834. 8°

14 ORATION delivered on the fourth day of July, 1835, before the citizens of Beverly. Boston, 1835. 8°

15 REMARKS . . on the French question, in the House of Representatives; . . with the Reports of the majority and minority of the Committee of Foreign Affairs, on the same subject. Boston, 1835. 8°

16 AN ADDRESS delivered at Lexington, on the 19th (20th) of April, 1835 [in commemoration of the battle of Lexington. First edition]. Charlestown, 1835. 8°

17 AN ADDRESS delivered at Lexington, on the 19th (20th) of April, 1835 [in commemoration of the battle of Lexington]. Second edition. Charlestown, 1835. 8°

18 ORATIONS and Speeches, on various occasions. Boston, 1836. 8vo.

19 AN ADDRESS delivered before the Adelphic Union Society of Williams College on Commencement day, *etc.* Boston, 1837. 8°

20 AN ADDRESS delivered before the Mercantile Library Association, . . in Boston, *etc.* Boston, 1838. 8°

21 A MEMOIR of Mr. J. Lowell, Jun. delivered as the introduction to the lectures on his foundation . . December 31st, 1839. Bost. 1840. 8°

22 IMPORTANCE of Practical Education and Useful Knowledge; a selection from orations and other discourses. Boston, 1840. 12mo.

23 ADDRESSES at the Inauguration of the Hon. Edward Everett as President of the University at Cambridge, April 30, 1846. Boston, Cambridge [printed], 1846. 8vo.

24 AN EULOGY on the Life and Character of J. Q. Adams. Boston, 1848. 8vo.

25 SPEECH in support of the Memorial of Harvard, Williams, and Amherst Colleges, in the Hall of the House of Representatives, Boston. Cambridge, 1849. 8vo.

26 ORATIONS and Speeches on various occasions. Second edition. 2 vol. [vol. 1 only, 2nd edit.] Boston, 1850. 8°

27 THE DISCOVERY and Colonization of America, and immigration to the United States. A lecture delivered before the New York Historical Society, *etc.* Boston [Cambridge printed], 1853. 8°

EVERETT, ERASTUS. A System of English Versification; containing rules for the structure of the different kinds of verse; with numerous examples from the best poets. New York, 1848. 12°

EVERETT, HORACE. Speech . . in the House of Representatives . . . on the Indian Annuity Bill, . . June 3, 1836. [With an appendix of documents.] Washington, 1836. 8°

EVERETT, JOHN. An Oration, delivered July 5, 1824. Boston, 1824. 8°

EVERYBODY'S BOOK: or, something for all. . First series. New York, 1841. 12°

EWBANK, THOMAS. A Descriptive and Historical Account of Hy-

draulic and other Machines for raising
Water, ancient and modern : with observations on various subjects connected with the mechanic arts, including the progressive development
of the steam engine, *etc.* In five
books. New York, 1842. 8vo.

2 A DESCRIPTIVE and Historical
Account of Hydraulic and other Machines for raising Water, ancient and
modern ; with observations on various
subjects connected with the mechanic
arts, including the progressive development of the steam engine. . . Second edition, to which is added a supplement. New York, 1847. 8°

3 REPORT of T. Ewbank, the Commissioner of Patents, for . . . 1849.
Part 1, Arts and Manufactures ; embracing the Commissioner's views of
the origin and progress of invention ;
the motors—chief levers of civilization ; proposed applications of the
patent fund ; . . and on the propulsion of steamers. With an introduction, by H. Greeley. New York,
1850. 8°

EWING, GREVILLE. A Memoir
of Barbara Ewing ; by her husband,
G. Ewing. Philadelphia, 1830. 12°

EWING, STEPHEN S. Report of
the President of the Branch of the
Bank of the State of Alabama, at
Huntsville. Nov. 3, 1841. Tuscaloosa, 1841. 8°

2 REPORT of the President of the
Huntsville Branch Bank (S.S. Ewing).
Tuscaloosa, 1845. 8°

EWING, THOMAS, *of Ohio.* Speech

. . . on the removal of the deposites ;
delivered in the Senate. . Jan. 1834.
Washington, 1834. 8°

2 SPEECH . . . on introducing the
Bill to settle and determine the Northern Boundary line of . . Ohio ; delivered in the Senate . . Dec. 21, 1835.
Washington, 1835. 8°

3 SPEECH . . on the Bill to appropriate for a limited time the proceeds
of the sales of the public lands : delivered in the Senate . . . March 15
and 16, 1836. Washington, 1836. 8°

EXAMINATION of the Reasons
why the present System of Auctions
ought to be abolished, as set forth by
the Committee of New York merchants, opposed to the auction system.
Boston, 1828. 8°

EXCHANGE ADVERTISER, N°
94-95. Boston, 1786. Fol.

EXPERIENCE the Test of Government ; in eighteen essays. . . [By
W. Duane !] Philadelphia, 1807. 8°

EXTRACTS in Prose and Verse,
by a lady of Maryland. Together
with a collection of original poetry,
never before published ; by citizens
of Maryland. 2 vol. Annapolis, 1808.
12°

EYRE, JOHN. The Christian
Spectator : being a journey from England to Ohio, two years in that state,
travels in America, *etc.* Albany,
1838. 12°

2 THE EUROPEAN Stranger in America. New York, 1839. 12°

ABENS, Jo-
sEPH W. The
Camel Hunt ;
a narrative of
personal ad-
venture. Bos-
ton and Camb.
1851. 12°

2 A Story of Life on the Isthmus.
New York, 1853. 12°

FABER, Martin. The Story of a
Criminal ; and other tales. By the
author of " The Yemaſsee," etc. [W.
G. Simms]. 2 vol. N.York, 1837. 12°

FABLE FOR CRITICS. Reader,
Walk up at once (it will soon be too
late), and buy .. at a perfectly ruinous
rate, a Fable for Critics ; or,.. a glance
at a few of our literary progenies. . .
by a Wonderful Quiz [i.e. J. R. Lowell.
In verse. Second edition]. New York,
1848. 12°

FACTS and Arguments on the
Transmiſsion of Intellectual and Moral
Qualities from Parents to Offspring.
New York, 1843. 12mo.

FADETTE : A Domestic Story.
From the French [of A. Dudevant].
By M. M. Hays. N. York, 1851. 12°

FAIR, E. Y. Report of the President of the Montgomery Branch
Bank (E. Y. Fair). Also, the expense
account of said bank. Tuscaloosa,
1845. 8°

FAIRBANK, Drury. A Sermon
[on Isa. xxix. 9, 10] delivered at Plymouth, New Hampshire, on fast day,
April 12, 1810. Hanover, 1810. 8°

FAIRFIELD, J. B. A Manual of
False Orthography, etc. Andover and
New York, 1841. 12°

FAIRFIELD, John. Reports of
Cases argued and determined in the
Supreme Judicial Court of the State
of Maine. 3 vol. [Being vol. 10, 11,
and 12 of Maine Reports.] Hallowell, 1835, 37. 8°

FAIRFIELD, Sumner Lincoln.
The Last Night of Pompeii : a poem:
and lays and legends. New York,
1832. 8°

2 The Poems and Prose Writings
of Sumner Lincoln Fairfield. Vol. 1.
Philadelphia, 1841. 8°

FAIRFIELD WEST, Connecticut.
Appeal of the Aſsociation of Fairfield
West to the Aſsociated Ministers connected with the General Aſsociation
of Connecticut. New York, 1852. 8°

FALCONER, Thomas, of Lincoln's
Inn. Expedition to Santa Fé. An
account of its journey from Texas
through Mexico, with particulars of
its capture. New Orleans, 1842. 8vo.

2 [Begins] Mr. Falconer's Reply
to Mr. Greenhow's Answer ; with Mr.
Greenhow's Rejoinder. [Washing-
ton ? 1845.] 8vo.

FALES, William R. Memoir of
William R. Fales, the Portsmouth
Cripple : [an autobiography ; with
memorandums and letters. Edited
by S. H. L.] Philadelphia, 1851. 12°

FAMILY CHRISTIAN ALMA-
nac for the United States, 1847. Calculated for Boston, New York, Balti-

more, and Charleston.   New York [1846].   18mo.

FAMILY PHYSICIAN, and the Farmer's Companion.   [Syracuse ! 1840 ?]   12°

FAMILY RECEIPTS: being a compilation from several publications, for cooking, dyeing, varnishing, painting, etc.   Syracuse [1840?].   12°

FAMILY TABLET; containing a selection of original poetry.   Boston, 1796.   12mo.

FANCIES of a Whimsical Man. By the author of " Musings of an Invalid."   New York, 1852.   8°

FANNING, EDMUND. Voyages Round the World; with sketches of voyages to the South Seas, North and South Pacific Oceans, China, etc. New York, 1833.   8vo.

FARLEY, HARRIET, Miß.   Shells from the Strand of the Sea of Genius. .. First Series.   Boston, 1847.   12°

FARLEY, STEPHEN.   Discourses and Eßays on theological and speculative topics.   Boston, 1851.   12°

FARMER, DANIEL DAVIS. Trial of Daniel Davis Farmer for the Murder of the widow Anna Ayer, at Goffstown. .. Reported by A. Rogers and H. B. Chase.   Concord, 1821.   8°

FARMER, JOHN. An Historical Sketch of Amherst. . . New Hampshire, etc.   Amherst, 1820.   8°

2 A GENEALOGICAL Register of the First Settlers of New England, etc. Lancaster, 1829.   8vo.

FARMER, JOHN, and MOORE, JACOB BAILEY.   A Gazetteer of the State of New Hampshire.   Concord, 1823.   12°

FARNHAM, ELIZA W. Mrs.   Life in Prairie Land.   N. York, 1847.   12°

FARNHAM, THOMAS J. History of the Oregon Territory: it being a demonstration of the title of these

United States of North America to the same.   Accompanied by a map.   New York, 1844.   8°

FARNUM, CALEB, the Younger. Practical Grammar .. of the English Language, etc. Providence, 1842. 12°

FARRAR, JOHN.   An Elementary Treatise on the application of Trigonometry to orthographic and stereographic projection, dialling, mensuration of heights and distances, navigation, nautical astronomy, surveying and levelling; together with logarithmic and other tables, etc.   Cambridge, 1822.   8°

2 AN ELEMENTARY Treatise on Mechanics, comprehending the doctrine of equilibrium and motion, as applied to solids and fluids, etc.   Cambridge, 1825.   8°

3 AN EXPERIMENTAL Treatise on Optics, comprehending the leading principles of the science, and an explanation of the more important and curious optical instruments and optical phenomena; being the third part of a course of natural philosophy, etc. Cambridge, 1826.   8°

4 AN ELEMENTARY Treatise on Astronomy, adapted to the present improved state of the science; being the fourth part of a course of natural philosophy.   Compiled for the . . University at Cambridge, New England.   Cambridge, 1827.   8°

FARRINT, JOHN.   Newport Gaol. Oct. 4, 1773. To the public. [Addreß by John Farrint on the illegality of his confinement.] Newport [1773]. s. sh. fol.

FAUCHET, JOSEPH. A Sketch of the present state of our political relations with the United States of North America. .. Translated by the editor of the Aurora. Philadelphia, 1797. 8°

FAUVEL-GOURAUD, FRANÇOIS. Phreno - Mnemotechnic Dictionary: being a philosophical claßification of all the homophonic words of the English language, *etc.* Part 1. New York, 1844. 8°

2 PHRENO-MNEMOTECHNY; or, the art of memory. The series of lectures explanatory . . of the system, . . delivered in New York and Philadelphia in the beginning of 1844, *etc.* New York, 1845. 8°

FAULTS on all Sides. The Case of Religion considered: showing the substance of true godlineſs. . . presented to the inhabitants (especially) . . of Rhode Island. . . To which is added, the prophecies . . . of . . . J. Usher, Lord Archbishop of Armagh, . . relating to the great persecution that is yet to break out in England, Scotland, and Ireland. Newport, 1728. 8vo.

FAY, H. A. Collection of the Official Accounts in detail, of all the Battles fought by Sea and Land, between the Navy and Army of the United States and the Navy and Army of Great Britain, during the years 1812-15. New York, 1817. 8°

FAY, THEODORE S. Hoboken: a romance of New York. 2 vol. New York, 1843. 12°

FAY, WARREN. The Obligations of Christians to the Heathen World: a sermon [on Mark xiv. 8, 9] delivered . . before the Auxiliary Foreign Miſsion Society of Boston, *etc.* Boston, 1825. 8°

FEARN, THOMAS, AND OTHERS. Report of the Commiſsioners appointed to examine the Branch of the Bank of the State of Alabama at Huntsville. Tuscaloosa, 1842. 8°

FEATHERSTONHAUGH, GEORGE WILLIAM. The Death of Ugolino. A tragedy. [In five acts, and in prose and verse.] Philadelphia, 1830. 8vo.

2 GEOLOGICAL Report of an Examination made in 1834 of the elevated country between the Miſsouri and Red Rivers. Washing. 1835. 8°

FEDERALIST: a Collection of Eſsays written in favour of the new Constitution, as agreed upon by the Federal Convention, Sept. 17, 1787. [By Alexander Hamilton, James Madison, and John Jay.] 2 vol. New York, 1788. 12mo.

2 THE FEDERALIST; or, the new Constitution. . . written in 1778, by Mr. Hamilton, Mr. Jay, and Mr. Madison. New edition. Philadelphia, 1817. 8°

3 THE FEDERALIST; or, the new Constitution. . . with an appendix, containing the Letters of Pacificus [A. Hamilton], and Helvidius [J. Madison], on the Proclamation of Neutrality of 1793; also the original Articles of Confederation and the Constitution of the United States, with the amendments made thereto. A new edition. The numbers written by Mr. Madison corrected by himself. Hallowell, 1837. 8vo

4˙ THE FEDERALIST; on, the new Constitution. Written in the year 1788, by A. Hamilton, J. Madison, and J. Jay. With an appendix, containing the Letters of Pacificus [A. Hamilton], and Helvidius [J. Madison], on the Proclamation of Neutrality of 1793; the original Articles of Confederation; the letters of . . Washington, as President of the Convention, to the President of Congreſs; the Constitution of the United States, *etc.* Sixth edition. 2 parts. Philadelphia, 1847, 1845. 8°

FEDERALIST. A Letter to a Federalist, in reply to some of the popular objections to the motives and tendency of the measures of the present administration. Feb. 1805. [Boston, 1805.] 8°

2 AN ANSWER to the questions, Why are you a Federalist! and, Why shall you Vote for Gov. Strong! [Boston], 1805. 8°

FEIJO, DIOGO ANTONIO. Demonstration of the neceſsity of abolishing a constrained Clerical Celibacy; exhibiting the evils of that institution, and the remedy .. Translated from the Portuguese, with an introduction and appendix, by D. P. Kidder. Philadelphia, 1844. 12°

FELICE, G. DE. History of the Protestants of France from the commencement of the Reformation to the present time .. Translated with an introduction by H. Lobdell. New York, 1851. 8°

FELCH, W. A Comprehensive Grammar, presenting some new views of. the structure of language, etc. Boston, 1837. 12°

FELLOWS, JOHN. An Exposition of the mysteries, or religious dogmas and customs of the ancient Egyptians, Pythagoreans, and Druids. Also, an inquiry into the origin, history, and purport of Freemasonry. New York, 1835. 8°

2 THE VEIL Removed; or, Reflections on D. Humphreys' Essay on the Life of I. Putnam. Also, notices of O. W. B. Peabody's Life of the same ; S. Swett's Sketch of Bunker Hill Battle, etc. New York, 1843. 12°

FELT, JOSEPH B. The Annals of Salem, from its first settlement. Salem, 1827. 8°

2 ANNALS of Salem. Second edition. 2 vol. Salem, 1845-49. 12°

3 HISTORY of Ipswich, Essex, and Hamilton. Cambridge, 1834. 8°

4 AN HISTORICAL Account of Massachusetts Currency. Boston, 1839. 8vo.

5 MEMORIALS of W. S. Shaw. Boston, 1852. 12°

6 SELECTIONS from the New England Fathers. Nº 1. John Norton, 1652. Boston, 1851. 8°

FELTON, CORNELIUS CONWAY. A Discourse pronounced at the Inauguration of the author as Eliot Professor of Greek Literature in Harvard University. Cambridge, 1834. 8°

FELTON, JOHN BROOKS. The

Horse-Shoe : a poem, spoken before the Phi Beta Kappa Society in Cambridge. Cambridge, 1849. 12°

FELTON, O. C. The Analytic and Practical Grammar. A concise manual of English Grammar, etc. Salem, 1843. 12°

FEMALE MISSIONARY SOCIETY of the Western District, Utica, N. Y. The first (fifth to eighth, tenth and eleventh) annual report of the Trustees, etc. Utica, 1817-27. 8°

FENDERICH, CHARLES. Portfolio of Living American Statesmen, drawn and lithographed by C. Fenderich. Washington [1837]. Fol.

FENELON, FRANCOIS DE SALINAC DE LA MOTHE. Selections from the writings of Fenelon, with a Memoir of his Life. By a Lady [E. L. Follen]. Second edition. Boston, 1829. 12°

2 LIVES of the Ancient Philosophers. Translated from the French of Fenelon, with notes, and a life of the author, by J. Cormack. New York, 1844. 12°

FENNEL, JAMES. Report of the President of the branch of the Bank of the State of Alabama, at Decatur (J. Fennel). Nov. 8, 1841. Tuscaloosa, 1841. 8°

2 DECATUR branch [of the State Bank of Alabama] President's Report. (Nov. 29, 1842.) [Tuscaloosa, 1842.] 8°

FENNELL, JAMES. An Apology for the Life of J. Fennell, written by himself. Philadelphia, 1814. 8°

FENNER, ROBERT, AND OTHERS. Report of the Commissioners appointed to examine the Branch of the Bank of the State of Alabama at Decatur. Tuscaloosa, 1841. 8°

FENOLLOSA, MANUEL. The Piano-Forte ; a complete .. instruction book .. compiled .. principally from the works of Hunten, Burgmuller, Bertini .. etc. To which is added an extensive . . selection of . . airs, waltzes, etc. Boston, 1852. 4°

FERGUSON, JAMES, F.R.S. Ferguson's Lectures on select subjects in Mechanics, etc. A new edition, corrected and enlarged; with notes and an appendix . . by D. Brewster. . . This American edition, . . revised and corrected by R. Patterson. 2 vol. Philadelphia, 1806. 8° Plates. 4°

FERGUSON, PETER K. Uglineß and its Uses; a lecture delivered before the " Y. L. Circulating Library Aßociation," by Jak. Wonder (P. K. Ferguson). N. York, 1852. 8°

FERN, FANNY, Pseud. [i. e. Sarah Payson Willis, afterwards Eldredge, afterwards Farrington]. Fern Leaves from Fanny's Portfolio; with original designs by F. M. Coffin. Auburn, Buffalo, Cincinnati, 1853. 8°

2 FERN Leaves from Fanny's Portfolio. Second series. Auburn [printed] Buffalo [and] London. 1854. 8vo.

FERRETTI. La Cenerentola. Cinderilla, or the Triumph of Goodneß, a comic opera, in two acts. Italian and English. New York, 1826. 12°

FERRIS, BENJAMIN. A History of the original settlements on the Delaware, from its discovery by Hudson to the colonization under William Penn. To which is added, an account of the ecclesiastical affairs of the Swedish settlers, and a history of Wilmington, from its first settlement to the present time. Wilmington, 1846. 8°

FESSENDEN AND CO'S Encyclopædia of Religious Knowledge, or Dictionary of the Bible, Theology, etc. To which is added, a Mißionary Gazetteer, by Rev. B. B. Edwards; the whole . . edited by Rev. J. N. Brown. Brattleboro, 1837. 8vo.

FESSENDEN, THOMAS. A Theoretic Explanation of the Science of

Sanctity . . containing an idea of God, of His Creations, etc. Brattleboro, 1804. 8vo.

FESSENDEN, THOMAS GREEN. Democracy Unveiled; or, Tyranny stripped of the garb of Patriotism. Boston, 1805. 12°

2 ORIGINAL Poems. Philadelphia, 1806. 12°

3 THE AMERICAN Clerk's Companion and Attorney's Prompter; a collection of . . forms of legal instruments, precedents in pleading, etc.; with observations relative to the varieties of practice . . sanctioned by the statutes and courts of different States. Brattleborough, 1815. 12°

4 THE LADIES' Monitor; a poem. Bellows Falls, Vt. 1818. 12°

5 AN ESSAY on the Law of Patents and new Inventions. Second edition. Boston, 1822. 8vo.

6 ADDRESS delivered before the Charlestown Temperance Society, etc. Charlestown, 1831. 8°

7 TERRIBLE Tractoration, and other poems. By C. Caustic, M.D. Fourth American edition. To which is prefixed, Caustic's Wooden Booksellers and Miseries of Authorship. Boston, 1837. 12°

8 THE COMPLETE Farmer and Rural Economist. . . Fifth edition, revised, improved and enlarged. Boston and Philadelphia, 1840. 12°

9 THE AMERICAN Kitchen Gardener. . . Revised from the 35th edition, and adapted to the use of families. By a practical Gardener. New York. 1852. 12°

FEUCHTWANGER, LEWIS. A Treatise on Gems, in reference to their practical and scientific value; . . accompanied by a description of the most interesting American gems, and ornamental and architectural materials. New York, 1838. 8°

FIALIN DE PERSIGNY, JEAN GILBERT VICTOR, Viscount. Relation de l'entreprise du Prince Napoleon

Louis .. Troisième édition, augmentée de la Relation de l'enlevement du Prince, de la prison de Strasbourg. New York, 1837. 8vo.

FICKLIN, O. B. Speech .. on the Annexation of Texas; .. delivered in the House of Representatives, Jan. 23, 1845. Washington, 1845. 8°

FIELD, BARNUM. The American School Geography .. With an Atlas .. Fourteenth edition. Boston, 1844. 12°. Atlas, 4°

FIELD, DAVID DUDLEY, *Rev.* A Statistical Account of the County of Middlesex, in Connecticut. Middletown, 1819. 8°
2 A HISTORY of the County of Berkshire, Maßachusetts. . . . By Gentlemen in the Country. [Edited by D. D. Field.] Pittsfield, 1829. 12°

FIELD, DAVID DUDLEY. What shall be done with the Practice of the Courts? Shall it be wholly reformed? Questions addreßed to lawyers. New York, 1847. 8°

FIELD, HENRY M. The Irish Confederates and the Rebellion of 1798. New York, 1851. 12°

FIELD, J. M. The Drama in Pokerville; the Bench and Bar of Jury Town, and other stories. By " Everpoint " (J. M. Field). Philadelphia, 1847. 12°

FIELDS, JAMES T. Anniversary Poem, delivered before the Mercantile Library Aßociation of Boston. Boston, 1838. 8°

FIGLIA. La Figlia dell' Aria. The Daughter of the Air: a semi-tragic opera, in two acts. *Ital.* and *Engl.* New York, 1826. 12°

FILISOLA, VICENTE, *General.* Evacuation of Texas. Translation of the Representation addreßed to the Supreme Government in defence of his honour, and explanation of his operations as Commander in Chief of the Army against Texas. [Translated

by G. L. H.] [*The first book printed in Texas.*] Columbia, 1837. 8vo.

FILLEBROWN, THOMAS. Circular [in relation to his Claims against the Navy Hospital Fund of the United States, for certain official services]. [Washington, 1833.] 8°

FILLMORE, MILLARD. Speech .. on the Revenue Bill, delivered in the House of Representatives .. July 24, 1841. [Washington, 1841.] 8°

FILSON, JOHN. The Discovery, Settlement, and present state of Kentucke; and an eßay towards the topography and natural history of that important country. To which is added, an appendix, containing .. The Adventures of Col. D. Boon; .. An account of the Indian nations, *etc.* Wilmington, 1784. 8°

FINANCIAL REGISTER of the United States; devoted chiefly to finance and currency, and to banking and commercial statistics. July, 1837 to Dec. 1838. Vol. 1, 2. Philadelphia, 1837-38. 8°

FINDLEY, WILLIAM. History of the Insurrection in the four western counties of Pennsylvania, 1794, and an historical review of the previous situation of the country. Philadelphia, 1796. 8°

FINLEY, AMELIA. Amelia Finley; or, the careleß reading of the Bible reproved. Philadel. [1833]. 12mo.

FINLEY, JAMES B. History of the Wyandott Mißion at Upper Sandusky, Ohio, under the direction of the Methodist Episcopal Church. Cincinnati, 1840. 12°

FINLEY, SAMUEL. A Vindication of the Charitable Plea for the Speechless: in answer to Mr. A. Morgan's Antipædorantism, *etc.* Philadelphia, 1748. 8vo.
2 THE APPROVED Minister of God. A sermon [on 2 Corinthians, vi. 4] preached at the ordination of the Re-

verend J. Rodgers. Philadelphia,
1749. 8°

FINNEY, CHARLES G. A Sermon
[on Amos iii. 3] preached in the
Presbyterian Church at Troy, *etc.*
Troy, 1827. 8°

  2 SKELETONS of a Course of Theological lectures. Vol. 1. Oberlin,
1840. 8°

  3 VIEWS of Sanctification. Oberlin,
1840. 12°

FISCHER, E. S. Elements of
Natural Philosophy; . . . Translated
into French, with notes and additions,
by M. Biot . . . and now translated
from the French into English. . .
Edited by J. Farrar. Bost. 1827. 8°

FISH, ELISHA. Japheth dwelling
in the Tents of Shem; or, infant baptism vindicated, in a discourse [on
Genesis ix. 27]. . . With an appendix,
taken from the Rev. Mr. D. Bostwick's fair and rational vindication.
Boston, 1772. 8°

FISH, FRANKLIN W. The Mind
and the Heart. N. York, 1851. 12°

FISHER, GEORGE. The Instructor;
or, American Young Man's Best
Companion. Philadelphia, 1801. 12°

FISHER, HUGH. The Divine
Right of Private Judgment set in a
true light. A Reply to the Reverend Mr. J. Smith's answer to a postscript . . . to a sermon, entituled, A
Preservative from Damnable Errors,
etc. Together with remarks on . . .
Mr. N. Bassett's appendix. Boston,
1731. 8vo.

FISHER, JAMES. An Inaugural
Dissertation on that grade of the intestinal state of Fever known by the
name of Dysentery. Philadelphia
[1797]. 8vo.

FISHER, J. FRANCIS. A Discourse
delivered before the Historical Society of Pennsylvania . . April, 1836,
on the private life and domestic habits
of W. Penn. Philadelphia, 1836. 8°

FISHER, JOHN DIX. Description
of the distinct, confluent, and inoculated Small Pox, Varioloid Disease,
Cow Pox, and Chicken Pox. Boston,
1829. 4to.

FISHER, NATHANIEL. A Sermon
[on Psalm cxii. 6] preached December 29, 1799 . . the Sunday after the
melancholy tidings . . of the death of
Gen. Washington. Salem [1800]. 8°

FISHER, RICHARD S. The Seventh Census of the United States of
America, 1850. Compiled . . by R.
S. Fisher. Fourth edition. N. York,
1851. 12°

FISHER, SAMUEL W. The Three
great temptations of young men.
With several lectures . . to business
and professional men. Cincinnati,
1852. 8°

FISHER, THOMAS. Songs of the
Sea Shells, and other poems. Philadelphia, 1851. 8°

FISHERMAN. The Fisherman
and his Boy. By a Clergyman of
England. Also, John Pascal; or,
temptation resisted. Philadelphia,
1828. 12mo.

FISK, BENJAMIN FRANKLIN. A
Grammar of the Greek Language. .
Stereotype edition. Bost. 1840. 12°

FISK, CHARLES B. and HUGHES,
GEORGE W. Report on the examination of Canal Routes from the Potomac River to . . . Baltimore, especially in relation to the supply of
water for their summit levels; by C.
B. Fisk and G. W. Hughes, to the
Governor of Maryland. Annapolis,
1837. 8°

FISK, WILLBUR, *D.D.* Substance
of an Address delivered before the
Middletown Colonization Society, at
their annual meeting, July 4, 1835.
Middletown, 1835. 8vo.

  2 TRAVELS on the Continent of
Europe, in England, Ireland, Scotland,
etc. New York, 1838. 8vo.

FISKE, NATHAN. A Sermon [on
2 Sam. iii. 34] preached at . . . the
interment of Mr. J. Spooner, etc.
Boston, 1778. 8vo.

2 THE CHARACTER and Bleſſedneſs
of a diligent and faithful Servant. A
sermon [on Luke xii. 43] . . . at the
funeral of J. Foster. Providence
[1779]. 8vo.

3 THE SOVEREIGNTY of God in determining the Boundaries of Human
Life. A sermon [on Job xiv. 5]
preached . . . at the funeral of J.
Hobbs . . who was killed by lightning,
etc. Worcester, 1784. 8vo.

FISKE, OLIVER. An Oration pronounced at Worcester, on the anniversary of American Independence;
July 4, 1797. Worcester, 1797. 4°

2 ADDRESS delivered before the
Worcester Agricultural Society, Oct.
8, 1823, etc. Worcester, 1823. 8°

FITCH, ABEL F. Report of the
Great Conspiracy Case. The people
of the State of Michigan, versus A.
F. Fitch and others, commonly called
the Railroad Conspirators, etc. Detroit, 1851. 8°

FITCH, ASA. An Eſſay upon the
Wheat Fly and some species allied
to it. [From the Transactions of the
New York State Agricultural Society.
1845.] Albany, 1846. 8vo.

2 [Begins] WINTER Insects of
Eastern New York. From the "American Quarterly Journal of Agriculture
and Science." Vol. 5.] [Albany,
1847.] 8vo.

3 THE Heſſian Fly; its history,
character, transformations, and habits.
[From the "Transactions of the New
York State Agricultural Society."]
Albany, 1847. 8vo.

FITCH, JOHN. The Original
Steamboat supported; or, a reply to
Mr. J. Rumsey's pamphlet, showing
the true priority of J. Fitch and the
false datings, etc. of J. Rumsey. (A
plan wherein the power of steam is

fully shown by J. Rumsey.) 2 parts.
Philadelphia, 1788. 8vo.

FITCH, JOHN. A Sermon [on 1
Kings, iii. 9] delivered before . . the
Governor, . . Council, and House of
Representatives of Vermont, . . Nov.
10, . . being the day of general Elec-
tion. Peacham, 1805. 8°

FITCH, SAMUEL SHELDON. Six
Discourses on the Functions of the
Lungs, . . and on the mode of preserving . . . health to an hundred
years. London-[New York printed],
1852. 12mo.

FITZPATRICK, BENJAMIN. Message of His Excellency Gov. B. Fitzpatrick to the General Aſſembly of
the State of Alabama, . . . Dec. 3,
1844. Tuscaloosa, 1844. 8°

2 MESSAGE of His Excellency Gov.
B. Fitzpatrick to the General Aſſembly of the State of Alabama, . . Dec.
2, 1845. Tuscaloosa, 1845. 8°

FLACCUS, Pseud. [i.e. THOMAS
WARD]. Paſſaic; a group of poems
touching that river: with other musings. New York, 1842. 12°

FLAGG, HENRY. The Case of
H. Flagg, in Equity, versus S. H.
Mann and others. Supreme Judicial
Court. Middlesex (Maſſachusetts),
April term, 1832. Bost. 1832. 4°

FLANDERS, HENRY. A Treatise
on Maritime Law. Bost. 1852. 8vo.

FLEET, JOHN, M.D. Diſſertatio
inauguralis medica sistens observa-
tiones ad chirurgiæ operationes per-
tinentes. J. Willard, Præs. Bostoniæ, 1795. 4to.

2 A DISCOURSE relative to the
subject of Animation, delivered before
the Humane Society of . . . Maſſachusetts, etc. Boston, 1797. 4to.

FLEET, THOMAS and JOHN. A
Pocket Almanack for the year of our
Lord 1787 . . calculated for the use
of the commonwealth of Maſſachu-

setts. [By T. and J. Fleet.] Boston [1786]. 12°

2 FLEET's Pocket Almanack for the Year of our Lord 1788 (to 1800). .. To which is annexed the Maſſachusetts Register. 13 vol. Boston [1787-99]. 12°

FLEMING and TIBBINS. A New and Complete French and English and English and French Dictionary, on the basis of the Royal Dictionary. With complete tables of the verbs, by C. Picot. The whole prepared with the addition of a number of terms in the Sciences, by J. Dobson. Second edition. Philadelphia, 1845. 8vo.

FLETCHER, BENJAMIN, *Governor of New York*. An Account of the Treaty between His Excellency Benjamin Fletcher, Captain General and Governor in Chief of the Province of New York and the Indians of the Five Nations: viz. the Mohaques, Oneydes, Onnondages, Cajonges, and Sennekes, at Albany, beginning the 15th of August, 1694. Printed and sold by William Bradford, printer to their Majesties, King William and Queen Mary, at the sign of the Bible, in New York, 1694. 4to.

2 A JOURNAL of what paſſed in the Expedition of His Excellency Colonel Benjamin Fletcher, Captain General of New York, to Albany, to renew the Covenant Chain with the five Canton Nations of Indians, *etc.* [New York, 1696.] 4to.

FLETCHER, JAMES, *of Trinity College, Cambridge*. The History of Poland, from the earliest period to the present time. With a narrative of the recent events, obtained from a Polish patriot nobleman. New York, 1845. 12°

FLETCHER, JOHN. The Mirror of Nature. Part I. Presenting a brief sketch of the science of Phrenology. Baltimore, 1840. 12mo.

FLETCHER, JOHN, *of Louisiana*.

Studies on Slavery, in easy leſſons... Fifth thousand. Natchez, 1852. 8°

FLETCHER, RICHARD. Speech of Richard Fletcher [on currency and banking systems] to his Constituents, .. in Faneuil Hall, .. Nov. 6, 1837. [Boston, 1837.] 8°

2 MR. FLETCHER's Addreſs to his Constituents relative to the speech delivered by him in Faneuil Hall. [Boston, 1837.] 8°

FLINT, AUSTIN. Clinical Reports on Continued Fever, based on analyses of one hundred and sixty-four cases... To which is added, a memoir on the transportation and diffusion by contagion of typhoid fever, as exemplified in the occurrence of the disease at North Boston, Erie County, New York. Buffalo, 1852. 8vo.

FLINT, JAMES, *D. D.* Sermons. Boston, 1852. 12°

FLINT, JOSHUA BAKER. An Addreſs delivered before the Maſſachusetts Society for the Suppreſſion of Intemperance, May 29, 1828. Boston, 1828. 8°

FLINT, TIMOTHY. Recollections of the Last Ten Years, paſſed in occasional residences and journeyings in the Valley of the Miſſiſſippi. Boston, 1826. 8vo.

2 A CONDENSED Geography and History of the Western States or the Miſſiſſippi Valley. 2 vol. Cincinnati, 1828. 8°

3 THE HISTORY and Geography of the Miſſiſſippi Valley. To which is appended a condensed physical geography of the Atlantic United States, and the whole American continent. Second edition. 2 vol. Cincinnati, 1832. 8vo.

4 LECTURES upon Natural History, Geology, Chemistry, the application of Steam, and interesting discoveries in the Arts. Boston, 1833. 12°

5 INDIAN Wars of the West; containing biographical sketches of those pioneers who headed the Western

Settlers in repelling the attacks of the Savages, together with a view of the character, manners, monuments, and antiquities of the Western Indians. Cincinnati, 1833. 12mo.

6 THE BACHELOR Reclaimed; or, celibacy vanquished. From the French. Philadelphia, 1834. 12°

7 BIOGRAPHICAL Memoir of D. Boone, the first settler of Kentucky: interspersed with incidents in the early annals of the country. Cincinnati, 1845. 12°

FLINT, WALDO. An Address delivered before the Worcester Agricultural Society, Oct. 10, 1832, being their fourteenth anniversary cattle show and exhibition of manufactures. Worcester, 1832. 8°

FLORIDA. Rules of the Superior Court for the Southern Judicial District in Florida. In admiralty. [The law of salvage; being a judgment in the case of the ship Montgomery, by W. Marvin. Reprinted from Hunt's Merchant's Magazine.] New York, 1840. 8°

FLOWER BOOK. Written for the American Sunday School Union, and revised by the Committee of Publication. Philadel. [1830?]. 12mo.

FLYGARE, afterwards CARLEN, EMILIE. The Professor and his Favourites. Translated from the Swedish. New York, 1843. 8vo.

FLYNT, HENRY. An Appeal to the consciences of a degenerate people for the vindication of God's proceedings with them: a sermon [on Isa. v. 3-5]. Boston, 1729. 8vo.

FOLLEN, CHARLES. See FOLLEN, CARL THEODOR CHRISTIAN.

FOLLEN, CARL THEODOR CHRISTIAN. A Funeral Oration, delivered before the Citizens of Boston . . at the burial of G. Spurzheim. Boston, 1832. 8°

2 THE WORKS of C. Follen; with a memoir of his life [by E. L. Follen]. 5 vol. Boston, 1841. 12°

3 GERMAN Reader for Beginners. Deutsches Lesebuch, etc. Dritte Ausgabe. Boston, 1843. 12°

4 SKETCHES of Married Life. Revised edition. Boston, 1847. 12°

FOLLEN, ELIZA LEE, Mrs. Poems. Boston, 1839. 12mo.

2 THE WELL-SPENT Hour. New edition. [A tale for children.] Boston [printed at Greenfield], 1848. 12°

3 STORIES first published in the " Child's Friend." Edited by Mrs. Follen. [Being vol. 12 of the "Child's Friend," with a different title-page.] Boston, 1849. 12°

FOLSOM, GEORGE. History of Saco and Biddeford, with notices of other early Settlements, and of the Proprietary Governments in Maine, including the provinces of New Somersetshire and Lygonia. Saco, 1830. 12°

2 ADDRESS delivered at the nineteenth annual fair of the American Institute. New York, 1846. 8°

FOLSOM, NATHANIEL SMITH. Discourse before the R[hode] I[sland] State Temperance Society, delivered in Providence, Jan. 11, 1839. Providence, 1839. 12°

2 A CRITICAL and Historical Interpretation of the Prophecies of Daniel. Boston, 1842. 12°

FONTAINE, JACQUES, calling himself Abbé de la Roche. A Tale of the Huguenots; or, memoirs of a French refugee family. Translated and compiled from the original manuscripts of Jacques Fontaine, by one of his descendants. With an introduction, by F. L. Hawks. N. York, 1838. 12°

2 MEMOIRS of a Huguenot Family: translated and compiled from the original autobiography of Jacques Fontaine, by A. Maury. With an appendix, containing a translation of the Edict of Nantes, the Edict of Revocation, etc. New York, 1853. 8°

FOOT, SOLOMON, of Vermont. Speech . . on the Oregon Question, delivered in the House of Representatives, . . Feb. 6, 1846. [Washington, 1846.] 8°

2 SPEECH . . on the Origin and Causes of the Mexican War, delivered in the House of Representatives, . . July 16, 1846. Washing. 1846. 8°

FOOTE, HENRY STUART. Texas and the Texans ; or, advance of the Anglo-Americans to the South-west; including a history of leading events in Mexico, from the conquest of F. Cortes to the termination of the Texan Revolution. 2 vol. Phil. 1841. 12°

FOOTE, WILLIAM HENRY. Sketches of North Carolina, historical and biographical ; illustrative of the principles of a portion of her early settlers. New York, 1846. 8°

2 SKETCHES of Virginia, historical and biographical. Philadel. 1850. 8°

FORBES, JAMES GRANT. Sketches, historical and topographical, of the Floridas, more particularly of East Florida. New York, 1821. 8°

FORBES, R. B. Remarks on China and the China Trade. Boston, 1844. 8°

2 A NEW Rig for Ships and other Veſſels, etc. Boston, 1849. 8°

FORCE, PETER. Tracts and other Papers, relating principally to the origin, settlement, and progreſs of the Colonies in North America, from the discovery of the country to the year 1776. Vol. 1-4. Washington, 1836-46. 8°

2 GRINNELL LAND. Remarks on the English Maps of Arctic Discoveries, in 1850 and 1851, made at the Ordinary Meeting of the National Institute, Washington, in May, 1852. Washington [1852]. 8°

FORCE, WILLIAM Q. Picture of Washington and its vicinity for 1845. With forty-one embellishments on steel and lithograph. To which is added the Washington Guide, etc. Washington, 1845. 16°

FORD, DAVID EVERARD. Decapolis : or the individual obligation of Christians to save souls from death. An eſſay. Fifth American from the sixth London edition. New York, 1848. 16°

FOREIGN EVANGELICAL SOCIETY. First (to the Seventh) Annual Report of the Foreign Evangelical Society, etc. 1840-1846. 7 parts. New York, 1840-46. 8°

FOREIGN MISSIONARY CHRONICLE : containing a particular account of the proceedings of the Western Foreign Miſſionary Society, etc. N° 3, 4, 5. June—August, 1833. Pittsburgh, 1833. 8°

FORESTER, FANNY, Pseud. [Miſs Emily Chubbuck, afterwards Mrs. Judson]. Trippings in Author-Land, by Fanny Forester. New York, 1846. 12°

FORESTER, FRANK, Pseud. [i. e. Henry W. Herbert]. The Warwick Woodlands ; or, Things as they were there twenty years ago. By Frank Forester. New edition, revised and corrected, with illustrations by the author. New York, 1851. 12°

FORESTERS. The Foresters ; an American tale [by Jeremy Belknap]; being a sequel to the History of John Bull the Clothier. In a series of letters. Boston, 1792. 12mo.

FORGIVENESS of Sins. A discourse addreſſed to anxious inquirers. London published ; Boston printed, 1846. 12mo.

2 A DEFENCE of a Discourse on the Forgiveneſs of Sins. By the Author of the Discourse. London published ; Boston printed, 1846. 12mo.

FORREST, CATHARINE N. Report of the Forrest Divorce Case [Plaintiff, C. N. Forrest ; Defendant, Edwin Forrest.] New York [1852]. 8°

2 THE FORREST Divorce Case. C. N. Forrest against Edwin Forrest

fully .. reported by the Reporter of the National Police Gazette. New York, 1852. 8°

3 REVIEW of the Forrest Divorce, containing some remarkable disclosures of the secret doings of the Jury. By an Old Lawyer. New York, 1852. 8°

FORREST, EDWIN. Oration delivered at the democratic republican celebration of the Independence of the United States [of America], in .. New York, July 4, 1838. New York, 1838. 8°

FORREST, WILLIAM S. Historical and Descriptive Sketches of Norfolk and Vicinity, including Portsmouth and the adjacent counties, during a period of two hundred years. Also, Sketches of Williamsburg, Hampton, etc. Philadelphia, 1853. 8°

FORRESTI, FELIX. Crestomazia Italiana: a collection of selected pieces in Italian prose. N. York, 1847. 12°

FORRY, SAMUEL. The Climate of the United States and its endemic influences. Based chiefly on the records of the medical department and Adjutant General's office, United States' Army. New York, 1842. 8vo.

FORSTALL, EDMUND J. An Analytical Index of the whole of the Public Documents relative to Louisiana, deposited in the archives of the department " De la Marine et des Colonies" at Paris, etc. New Orleans, 1841. 8°

FORT, EDWARD. The Bride of Fort Edward [Jane M'Crea], founded on an incident of the Revolution. [By Miß Delia Bacon.] New York, 1839. 12°

FORTESCUE, F. Gonzalo, the Spanish Bandit. A melo-dramatic play, in five acts. [In prose and verse.] Boston, 1821. 8vo.

FOSDICK, DAVID. Introduction to the German Language: comprising a German Grammar, .. and a German Reader, consisting of selections from the claßic literature of Germany, accompanied by explanatory notes, and a vocabulary, etc. Andover, 1838. 12°

2 A GERMAN-ENGLISH and English-German Pocket Dictionary. .. Fourth edition. 2 parts. Boston, 1847. 16°

FOSGATE, BLANCHARD. Sleep psychologically considered, with reference to Sensation and Memory. New York, 1850. 12°

FOSTER, BENJAMIN FRANKLIN. The Merchant's Manual; comprising the principles of trade, commerce and banking; with merchants' accounts, etc. Boston, 1838. 12°

2 A PRACTICAL Summary of the Law and Usage of Bills of Exchange and Promißory Notes; .. To which are added, rates of commißion and storage; equation of payments; and general information connected with the busineß of the counting-house. Boston, 1840. 8°

FOSTER, C. An Account of the Conflagration of the principal part of the First Ward of the City of New York, on the night of the 16th of December, 1835. To which is added, a list of names of the persons burnt out, and of removals. [New York, 1835.] 8vo.

FOSTER, FESTUS. A Preached Gospel succeeded by the united efforts of Pastor and People: a sermon [on Psal. xlix. 1-3] etc. Greenfield, 1802. 8°

2 THE WATCHMAN'S Warning to the House of Israel: a sermon [on Ezek. xxxiii. 6, 7] delivered .. Nov. 21, 1811, being the day appointed for thanksgiving, etc. Worcester, 1811. 8°

3 AN ORATION pronounced .. July 5, 1813, in commemoration of the thirty-seventh anniversary of American Independence. Brattleborough, 1813. 8°

FOSTER, George G. Celio, or New York above ground and under ground. New York [1850]. 8°

2 New York by Gas-Light: with here and there a Streak of Sunshine. New York, 1850. 8°

FOSTER, Joel. An Oration, delivered at New Salem, July 4, 1797, being the anniversary of the Independence of the United States of America. Northampton, 1797. 8°

FOSTER, John, A.M. A Sermon [on Rom. x. 17] delivered at the installation of .. J. Foster .. to the pastoral office in East Sudbury. (The charge delivered by .. J. Bigelow, etc.) Cambridge, 1803. 8°

FOUCAUD, Edouard. The Book of Illustrious Mechanics of Europe and America .. Translated by J. Frost. New York, 1847. 12°

FOULHOUZE, James. A Philosophical Inquiry respecting the Abolition of Capital Punishment. Philadelphia, 1842. 12°

FOWLE, William Bentley. The Child's Arithmetic, or, the elements of calculation, in the spirit of Pestalozzi's method, etc. Boston, 1830. 12°

2 An Etymological Grammar of the English Language, etc. [Boston?] 1833. 12°

3 The Improved Guide to English Spelling, etc. Boston, 1840. 12°

4 The Common School Grammar, part first .. with illustrative engravings. Boston, 1842. 12°

5 The Common School Grammar, part second, etc. Boston, 1842. 12°

6 The Bible Reader; being a new selection of reading lessons .. by W. B. Fowle. Boston, 1843. 12° See Bible, N° 130.

7 The Companion to Spelling Books, etc. Boston, 1845. 12°

8 The Common School Speller .. Thirtieth edition. Boston, 1845. 12°

FOWLE, William Bentley, and Fitz, Asa. An Elementary Geography for Massachusetts' Children. Boston [1845]. 16°

FOWLER, Francis M. Testimony of F. M. Fowler, and E. Poultney, in the case of the Bank of Maryland vs. S. Poultney and W. M. Ellicott; tried before Harford County Court, March term, 1836. Baltimore, 1840. 8°

FOWLER, J. A. Analysis of Dramatic and Oratorical Expression; developing the associative relations of the elements of the voice and of gesture, and the adaptation of the English language .. to vocal and gesticulatory delineation. Philadelphia, 1853. 12°

FOWLER, Orson S. Hereditary Descent: its laws and facts applied to human improvement. New York, 1848. 12°

2 A Home for all; or, a new, cheap, convenient and superior mode of Building. New York, 1851. 8vo.

3 Fowler's Practical Phrenology, etc. New York, 1851. 8°

4 Phrenology Proved, illustrated and applied; accompanied by a Chart. .. By O. S. and L. N. Fowler, .. assisted by S. Kirkham. .. Sixty-second edition, enlarged and improved. New York, 1851. 8°

5 Physiology, Animal and Mental; applied to the preservation and restoration of health of body and power of mind. Sixth edition. New York, 1851. 12mo.

6 Self-Culture and Perfection of Character; including the management of Youth. .. Seventh thousand. New York, 1851. 12°

FOWLER, William Chauncy. English Grammar. The English language in its elements and forms; with a history of its origin and development. New York, 1850. 8°

FOX, Ebenezer. The Revolutionary Adventures of E. Fox, of Roxbury, Massachusetts. Boston, 1838. 8vo.

FOXCROFT, Thomas. The Day of a Godly Man's Death better than the day of his birth; shewed in a sermon [on Eccl. vii. 1]. (Two sermons shewing how to begin and end the year after a godly sort. To which is added, a discourse on Jer. xviii. 20.) Boston, 1722. 8°

2 Observations, historical and practical, on the rise and primitive state of New England. With special reference to the old or first gathered church in Boston. [A sermon on Matt.xiii.31,32.] A sermon preached . . Aug. 23, 1730. Being the last Sabbath of the first century since its settlement. Boston, 1730. 8°

3 An Apology in behalf of the Rev. Mr. Whitefield: offering a fair solution of certain difficulties, objected against some parts of his publick conduct, .. as the said objections are set forth in a late pamphlet, intituled, "A Letter to the Rev. Mr. G. Whitefield, publickly calling upon him to vindicate his conduct or confess his faults." Signed L. K. etc. Boston, 1745. 8°

4 Humilis Confessio: The Saints' United Confession, in disparagement of their own righteousness. A sermon [on Isaiah lxiv. 6, compared with Phil. iii. 8, 9]. Boston, 1750. 8°

FRANCE. Livre Rogue (sic), or Red Book; being a list of private pensions paid from the public treasury of France. Translated from the French, etc. New York, 1794. 8°

2 Characteristics applicable to and descriptive of the power and duration of the French Republic, etc. New York, 1798. 8°

3 Sketches of Conspicuous Living Characters of France. Translated by R. M. Walsh. Philadel. 1841. 12mo.

FRANCES, the Orphan Girl. Translated from the French, for the American Sunday School Union. Philadelphia [1828]. 12mo.

FRANCIS, Convers. Three Discourses preached before the Congregational Society in Watertown: two, upon leaving the old meeting-house, and one at the dedication of the new. Cambridge, 1836. 8°

FRANCIS, James B. Lowell Hydraulic Experiments; being a selection from experiments on hydraulic motors, . . . made at Lowell, Massachusetts. [With plates.] Boston, 1855. Fol.

FRANCIS, John William. An Inaugural Dissertation on Mercury; embracing its medical history, curative action, and abuse in certain diseases. New York, 1811. 8vo.

2 Cases of Morbid Anatomy. New York, 1815. 4to.

3 Letter on Febrile Contagion, addressed to D. Hosack, M.D. etc. New York, 1816. 8vo.

4 An Address delivered on the anniversary of the Philolexian Society of Columbia College. New York, 1831. 8°

FRANCKE, August Hermann. Vita B. A. H. Francke. Cui adjecta est narratio rerum memorabilium in ecclesiis Evangelicis per Germaniam, etc. Revisa, et cura S. Mather, .. cum dedicatione ejus, edita. Bostoni, 1733. 8°

2 Memoirs of A. H. Francke. [By R. B.] Philadelphia, 1831. 12mo.

FRANCO, Harry, Pseudonym. [Charles F. Briggs]. The Trippings of Tom Pepper; or, the results of romancing. An autobiography. New York, 1847. 12°

FRANKLIN, Benjamin. A Collection of the Familiar Letters and Miscellaneous Papers of B. Franklin. Now for the first time published. [Edited by J. Sparks.] Boston, 1833. 12°

2 The Works of B. Franklin, with notes and a life of the author by Jared Sparks. 10 vol. Boston, 1840. 8vo.

3 MEMOIRS of B. Franklin; written by himself. With his most interesting essays, letters, and miscellaneous writings, familiar, moral, political, economical, and philosophical, *etc.* 2 vol. New York, 1845. 12°

4 BENJAMIN FRANKLIN: his Autobiography; with a narrative of his public life and services, by H. H. Weld. New York, 1849. 8°

FRANKLIN'S Letters to his Kinsfolk, written during 1818-19 and 20, from Edinburgh, London, the Highlands of Scotland, and Ireland. 2 vol. Philadelphia, 1822. 12mo.

FRANKLIN COLLEGE, ATHENS, *Georgia.* Catalogue of the Trustees, Officers, and Graduates of Franklin College, from its establishment in 1801, to the annual commencement in 1836. Athens, 1837. 8°

FRANKLIN INSTITUTE, PHILADELPHIA. The Franklin Journal and American Mechanics' Magazine. Edited by T. P. Jones. 4 vol. [Continued as] Journal of the Franklin Institute of the State of Pennsylvania, and American Repertory of Mechanical and Physical Science. Edited by T. P. Jones. New series. 26 vol. Third series. Vol. 1-14. Edited by T. P. Jones (and J. J. Mapes. Vol. 15-18, by the Committee, *etc.* Vol. 19-29, by J. F. Frazer). Philadelphia, 1826-55. 8°

2 ADDRESS of the Committee on Premiums and Exhibitions of the Franklin Institute of the State of Pennsylvania. . . . With a list of the premiums offered . . at the exhibition . . 1831. Philadelphia, 1831. 8°

3 REPORT of the Committee of the Franklin Institute of the State of Pennsylvania, for the Promotion of the Mechanic Arts, on the explosions of steam-boilers. (Part 1, containing the first report of experiments; . . . Part 2, containing the general report of the Committee.) 2 parts. Philadelphia, 1836. 8vo.

FRANKS, JAMES. Sacred Literature; or, remarks upon the Book of Genesis, collected and arranged to promote the knowledge and evince the excellence of the Holy Scriptures. Halifax, 1802. 8vo.

FRASER, JAMES BAILLIE. Historical and Descriptive Account of Persia, from the earliest ages to the present time; . . including a description of Affghanistan and Beloochistan. New York, 1843. 12°

2 MESOPOTAMIA and Assyria, from the earliest ages to the present time; with illustrations of their natural history. New York, 1845. 12°

FRAZEE, BRADFORD. An Improved Grammar of the English Language, on the inductive system, *etc.* Philadelphia, 1844. 12°

FREDET, PETER. Ancient History; from the dispersion of the sons of Noe to the battle of Actium and change of the Roman Republic into an Empire. Baltimore, 1849. 12°

FREE GRACE maintained and improved. . . In two brief discourses, *etc.* Boston, 1706. 8°

FREEMAN. [*Begins*] A Freeman on Freemasonry. Boston! 8vo.

FREEMAN, JAMES, D.D. Sermons on Particular Occasions. Third edition. Boston, 1821. 12°

FREEMAN, N. CHAPMAN. The Twilight Dream, and Moments of Solitude [poems]. Philadel. 1853. 12°

FREEMAN, SAMUEL. The Massachusetts Justice: being a collection of the laws relative to the power and duty of Justices of the Peace. To which are added, a variety of forms, with an appendix. Boston, 1795. 8°

FREEMAN'S JOURNAL; or, the North American Intelligencer. N° 115, 118, 120. Philadelphia, 1783. Fol.

FREEMASONRY. Its Pretensions exposed in faithful Extracts of its standard authors; with a review of Town's Speculative Masonry; its liability to pervert the doctrines of revealed religion discovered; its dangerous tendency exhibited in extracts from the Abbé Barruel and Profeſsor Robinson, and further illustrated in its base service to the illuminati. By a Master Mason. N. York, 1828. 8vo.

2 "MASONRY the same all over the World." Another Masonic murder. [Containing the affidavit of S. G. Anderton concerning the murder of W. Miller.] [Boston, 1830.] 8vo.

3 A COLLECTION of Letters on Freemasonry, in chronological order. Boston, 1849. 8vo.

FRELINGHUYSEN, THEODORE. Speech .. on .. Sabbath Mails; in the Senate of the United States, May 8, 1830. Washington, 1830. 8°

2 SPEECH .. on the removal of the Deposites; delivered in the Senate of the United States, ... Jan. 1834. Washington, 1834. 8°

FREMONT, JOHN CHARLES. Report of the Exploring Expedition to the Rocky Mountains, in the Year 1842; and to Oregon and North California in .. 1843-44. .. Printed by order of the Senate of the United States. Washington, 1845. 8vo.

2 NOTES of Travel in California; comprising the .. geographical, agricultural, geological, and mineralogical features of the country; also the route from Fort Leavenworth, in Miſsouri, to San Diego, in California, including parts of the Arkansas, Del Norte, and Gila Rivers. From the official reports of Col. Fremont and Major Emory. New York, 1849. 8°

FRENCH, BENJAMIN F. Historical Collections of Louisiana, embracing many rare and valuable documents relating to the natural, civil, and political history of that State.

Compiled, with historical and biographical notes, and an introduction, by B. F. French. Parts 1 and 2. New York, Philadelphia, 1846-50. 8°

FRENCH, JONATHAN, the Elder. A Sermon [on 2 Cor. ii. 15,16] preached at the ordination of .. J. French, jun. .. Nov. 18, 1801. (The charge by .. J. Buckminster. The right hand of fellowship .. by S. Stearns.) Portsmouth, 1802. 8°

FRENCH, JONATHAN, the Younger, Northampton, New Hampshire. A Sermon [on 2 Chron. i. 10] preached .. before .. the .. Council, Senate, and House of Representatives of .. New Hampshire, June 6, .. being the anniversary Election. Concord, 1822. 8°

2 CHRIST the Believer's Life: a discourse [on Col. iii. 4] at the funeral of Mrs. H. Putnam, etc. Portsmouth, 1832. 8°

FRENCH GOVERNMENT. A Letter on the genius and dispositions of the French Government; including a view of the taxation of the French Empire. Addreſſed to a friend by an American recently returned from Europe. Philadelphia, 1810. 8°

FRENCH SPOLIATIONS. From the American Quarterly Review. French Spoliations prior to 1800. [Washington, 1832 !] 8°

FRENEAU, PHILIP. The Poems of Philip Freneau. Phil. 1786. 8°

2 THE MISCELLANEOUS Works of Mr. Philip Freneau, containing his eſſays and additional poems. Philadelphia, 1788. 8vo.

3 POEMS written between the years 1768 and 1794... A new edition, revised and corrected, .. including a considerable number of pieces never before published. Monmouth, N. J. 1795. 8vo.

4 POEMS. .. Third edition. 2 vol. Philadelphia, 1809. 12°

FRESENIUS, JOHANN PHILIPP,

Baron de Dybern. Narrative of the Conversion of Baron de Dyhern, *etc.* Written by Doctor Fresenicurs. Translated from German to French, and from French to English. [Boston, 1835?] 12mo.

FREUND, WILHELM. A Copious and Critical Latin-English Lexicon, founded on the larger Lexicon of Dr. Wilhelm Freund : with additions and corrections from the Lexicons of Gesner, .. Georges, *etc.* By E. A. Andrews. New York, 1852. 8°

2 ANOTHER copy, with new title-page, and editor's preface. London, 1852. 8vo.

FRICK, WILLIAM. An Address preparatory to opening the Department of the Arts and Sciences in the University of Maryland. Delivered on behalf of the trustees. Baltimore, 1831. 8°

FRIEDLANDER, JULIUS R. An Address to the Public at the First Exhibition of the Pupils of the Pennsylvania Institution for the Instruction of the Blind. Second edition. Philadelphia, 1833. 8°

FRIEND (The): a Religious and Literary Journal. Edited by R. Smith. Vol. 1-22. [Vol. 1 is of the second edition.] Philadelphia, 1820-49. 4°

FRIEND. The Best Friend. American Sunday School Union. Philadelphia, 1831. 12mo.

FRIEND OF PEACE. By Philo-Pacificus, author of " A Solemn Review of the custom of war." Vol. 1-4; Appendix, N° 1-3. Cambridge, 1816-28. 8°

FRIERSON, S. G. Report of the Treasurer of the State of Alabama (S. G. Frierson), Nov. 27, 1841. Tuscaloosa, 1841. 8°

2 ANNUAL Report of the State Treasurer, Dec. 14, 1843. [Tuscaloosa, 1843.] 8°

FRIES, JOHN. The two Trials of J. Fries on an indictment for Treason;

together with a brief report of the trials of several other persons, for treason and insurrection, in the . . . Circuit Court of the United States, .. at Philadelphia. . . To which is added a copious appendix. . . Taken in shorthand, by T. Carpenter. Philadelphia, 1800. 8°

FRIESE, PHILIP C. An Essay on Wages; discussing the means now employed for upholding them, and showing the necessity of a working man's tariff, *etc.* N. York, 1853. 12°

FRIEZE, JACOB. A Concise History of the Efforts to obtain an Extension of Suffrage in Rhode Island, from the year 1811 to 1842. Providence, 1842. 12°

FRISBIE, LEVI. A Collection of the Miscellaneous Writings of Professor Frisbie, with some notices of his life and character. By A. Norton. Boston, Cambridge [printed], 1823. 8vo.

FROISSART, JEAN. Chronicles... Translated from the French, .. by T. Johnes. To which are prefixed, a life of the author [by T. Johnes], an essay on his works, and a criticism on his history [by J. B. de la Curne de Ste Palaye]; with an original introductory essay on the character and society of the middle ages, by .. J. Lord. New York, 1847. 4°

FROST, BARZILLAI. The Church: a discourse [on 1 Tim. iii. 15] delivered at the dedication of the new church of the first parish in Concord, Mass. Dec. 29,1841. Boston,1842. 8°

FROST, JOHN, *LL.D. A. M.* Elements of English Grammar, with progressive exercises in parsing. Boston, 1829. 12°

2 FROST's Practical Grammar. A Practical English Grammar, with progressive exercises, *etc.* Philadelphia, 1842. 12°

3 THE BOOK of the Navy; comprising a general history of the American Marine, and particular accounts

of all the most celebrated naval battles, from the Declaration of Independence to the present time. With an appendix. New York, 1843. 8vo.

4 HISTORY of the United States, for the use of common schools... Illustrated with numerous engravings. Philadelphia, 1843. 12°

5 A HISTORY.of the United States, for the use of schools and academies. New edition, with additions and corrections. Philadelphia, 1846. 12°

6 THE PICTORIAL History of the United States of America, from the discovery by the Northmen in the tenth century to the present time. Embellished with .. engravings, from drawings by W. Croome. 4 vol. Philadelphia, 1843-44. 8°

7 AMERICAN Naval Biography, comprising lives of the commodores, and other commanders, distinguished in the history of the American navy. Philadelphia, 1844. 8°

8 THE BOOK of the Indians of North America: illustrating their manners, customs, and present state. [Compiled and] edited by John Frost. New York, 1845. 8°

9 THE BOOK of the Colonies; comprising a history of the Colonies composing the United States, etc. New York and Philadelphia, 1846. 12°

10 PICTORIAL History of the World. (Pictorial ancient history of the world, from the earliest ages to the death of Constantine the Great. Pictorial history of the middle ages, from the death of Constantine the Great to the discovery of America by Columbus. Pictorial modern history, from the discovery of America by Columbus to the present time.) 3 parts. Philadelphia, 1846. 8°

11 THE BOOK of Good Examples; drawn from authentic history and biography. Designed to illustrate the beneficial effects of virtuous conduct. N. York and Philadelphia, 1846. 12°

12 THE BOOK of Illustrious Mechanics... Translated by John Frost. 1847. 12mo.

13 THE BOOK of Travels in Africa, from the earliest ages to the present time. New York, 1847. 12°

14 LIFE of Major-General Zachary Taylor, with notices of the war in New Mexico, California, and in Southern Mexico; and biographical sketches of officers who have distinguished themselves in the war with Mexico. New York, 1847. 8°

15 PICTORIAL Life of G. Washington: `embracing a complete history of the seven years' war, the revolutionary war, the formation of the federal constitution, and the administration of Washington. Philadelphia, 1847. 8°

16 REMARKABLE Events in the History of America, from the earliest times to the year 1848 ; compiled from the best authorities. 2 vol. Philadelphia, 1848. 8°

17 THE BOOK of Anecdotes; or, the moral of history taught by real examples. Hartford, 1851. 12°

18 LIVES of Eminent Christians of various Denominations. Plates. Philadelphia, 1852. 8°

19 BORDER Wars of the West. Comprising the frontier wars of Pennsylvania, Virginia, Kentucky, Ohio, Indiana, Illinois, Tenneſsee and Wisconsin, etc. Auburn [Philadelphia printed], 1853. 8°

FROTHINGHAM, NATHANIEL LANGDON. The Shade of the Past, [a sermon on Job iv. 15] for the celebration of the close of the second century since the establishment of the Thursday Lecture. Boston, 1833. 8°

2 A SERMON [on Ecclesiasticus xlviii. 12] on the death of General Lafayette, etc. Boston, 1834. 8°

3 SERMONS, in the order of a twelvemonth. Boston, 1852. 12°

FROTHINGHAM, RICHARD, the Younger. The History of Charlestown, Maſsachusetts. Nº 1-6. Boston, 1845-47. 8vo.

2 HISTORY of the Siege of Boston,

and of the battles of Lexington, Concord, and Bunker Hill. Also, an account of the Bunker Hill Monument. With illustrative documents. Boston, 1849. 8°

3 THE COMMAND in the Battle of Bunker Hill; with a reply to "Remarks on Frothingham's History of the Battle, by S. Swett." Boston, 1850. 8°

FRY, HENRY. To the Hon. the House of Representatives .. the Memorial of H. Fry [relative to his dismiſsal as purser, with an appendix of documents]. [Philadel. 1835.] 8°

FRY, J. REESE. A Life of Gen. Zachary Taylor; comprising a narrative of events connected with his profeſsional career, derived from public documents and private correspondence, by J. R. Fry; and authentic incidents of his early years, from materials collected by R. T. Conrad. Philadelphia, 1847. 12°

FULFORD, FRANCIS, Bishop of Montreal. An Addreſs delivered in the chapel of the General Theological Seminary of the Protestant Episcopal Church in the United States .. Nov. 13. New York, 1852. 8vo.

FULLER, ALLEN. Grammatical Exercises, etc. Plymouth, 1822. 12°

FULLER, ANDREW. Memoirs of the late Rev. S. Pearce; with extracts from some of his .. letters .. a brief memoir of Mrs. Pearce, etc. Philadelphia, 1829. 12mo.

FULLER, METTA VICTORIA. Fresh Leaves from Western Woods. Buffalo, 1852. 8°

FULLER, RICHARD, Rev. Domestic Slavery considered as a Scriptural Institution: in a correspondence between the Rev. R. Fuller and the Rev. F. Wayland. . . Revised and corrected by the authors. New York and Boston, 1845. 12°

FULLER, afterwards OSSOLI,

SARAH MARGARET. Summer on the Lakes in 1843. Boston, 1844. 12°

2 PAPERS on Literature and Art. 2 parts. London [New York printed], 1846. 12mo.

3 MEMOIRS of M. Fuller Oſſoli. 2 vol. Boston, 1852. 8°

FULLER, TIMOTHY. An Oration pronounced at Watertown, July 4, 1809, .. in commemoration of the anniversary of American Independence. Boston, 1809. 8°

FUN and Earnest. By the author of "Musings of an Invalid," "Fancies of a Whimsical Man," etc. New York, 1853. 12°

FURMAN, GABRIEL. Notes, geographical and historical, relating to the town of Brooklyn, in King's County on Long-Island. Brooklyn, 1824. 12°

2 ADDRESS delivered before the American Institute, . . during the sixteenth annual fair. New York, 1843. 8°

FURMAN, GARRIT. Rural Hours, a poem. [Maspeth, Long Island, 1824.] 8°

FURMAN, RICHARD. A Sermon [on Matt. xxv. 21], occasioned by the decease of the Rev. Oliver Hart. Charleston, 1796. 8vo.

FURNESS, WILLIAM HENRY. A discourse [on 1 Cor. iii. 16] preached at the opening of the first Congregational Unitarian Church, Philadelphia, November 5, 1828. Philadelphia, 1828. 8°

2 A DISCOURSE [on Matt. xvi. 27] preached in the first Congregational Unitarian Church (Philadelphia) May 24, 1829; occasioned by the recent emancipation of the Roman Catholics throughout the British Empire. Philadelphia, 1829. 8°

3 REMARKS on the Four Gospels. Philadelphia, 1836. 12°

4 JESUS and His Biographers; or the remarks on the four Gospels re-

vised, with copious additions. Philadelphia, 1838. 8°

5 OUR Benevolent Institutions. A
discourse [on Job xxix. 15, 16] occasioned by the death of J. R. Friedlander, Principal of the Pennsylvania
Institution for the Blind. Philadelphia, 1839. 8°

6 A SERMON [on 1 Pet. v. 6] delivered May 14, 1841, on the occasion of the National Fast, recommended by the President. Philadelphia, 1841. 8°

7 A DISCOURSE [on Psalm xcii. 14]
delivered on the occasion of the death
of J. Vaughan, etc. Philadelphia,
1842. 8°

8 A DISCOURSE [on Prov. x. 7]
delivered on the occasion of the erection in the Church of Tablets, in
memory of J. Vaughan, R. Eddowes,
and W. Y. Birch, August 20, 1842.
[Philadelphia, 1842.] 8°

9 A FUNERAL Discourse [on Job
iv. 15] May 4th, 1845. Philadelphia, 1845. 8°

10 A HISTORY of Jesus. Boston,
1851. 12°

11 GEMS of German Verse, edited
by W. H. Furness. Philadelphia,
[1853!] 8°

FURNISS, WILLIAM. Waraga, or
the Charms of the Hill. New York,
1850. 12°

2 THE LAND of the Cæsar and the
Doge. Historical and artistic: inci-
dental, personal, and literary. New
York, 1853. 8°

ABOON MISSION. A Grammar of the Mpongwe Language, with vocabularies. By the miſsionaries of the A[meri-can] B[aptist] C[hurch] F[oreign] M[iſsions], Gaboon Miſsion, Western Africa, [or rather by J. L. Wilson, one of the same]. New York, 1847. 8vo.

GADSDEN, THEODORE. An Eſsay on the Life of the Right Rev. T. Dehon, late Bishop of the Protestant Episcopal Church in the Diocese of South Carolina; with an appendix. Charleston, 1833. 8vo.

GAGE, THOMAS. The History of Rowley, anciently including Bradford, Boxford and Georgetown, from 1639 to the present time. With an Addreſs, delivered at the celebration of the Second Centennial Anniversary of its settlement, by Rev. J. Bradford. Boston, 1840. 12mo.

GAILLARD, THOMAS. The History of the Reformation in the Church of Christ; continued from the close of the fifteenth century. New York, 1847. 8°

GAINES, GEORGE S. AND OTHERS. Report of the Affairs and Condition of the Branch of the Bank of the State of Alabama at Mobile, and accompanying documents. Tuscaloosa, 1837. 8°

GALL, FRANCOIS JOSEPH. [Works]

on the Functions of the Brain, and of each of its parts: with observations on the poſsibility of determining the instincts, propensities, and talents, or the moral and intellectual dispositions of men and animals, by the configuration of the brain and head. Translated from the French by Winslow Lewis, junior. 6 vol. [each with a distinct title]. [With a collective title: " The Phrenological Library. Edited by Nahum Capen," all ever published.] Boston, 1835. 12mo.

GALLAGHER, MASON. True Churchmanship Vindicated; or, the Protestant Episcopal Church not exclusive. Cincinnati, 1851. 12°

GALLAGHER, WILLIAM D. Selections from the Poetical Literature of the West. [Edited by W. D. G. i.e. William D. Gallagher.] Cincinnati, 1841. 12°

GALLATIN, ALBERT. Views of the Public Debt, Receipts and Expenditures of the United States. New York, 1800. 8°

2 REPORT of the Secretary of the Treasury (Albert Gallatin) on the subject of Public Roads and Canals; made in pursuance of a resolution of the Senate of March 2, 1807. [With communications on the same subject from B. H. Latrobe and R. Fulton.] Washington, 1808. 8°

3 CONSIDERATIONS on the Currency and Banking System of the United States [with notes and statements]. Philadelphia, 1831. 8vo.

4 THE RIGHT of the United States

of America to the North-Eastern boundary claimed by them. Principally extracted from the statements laid before the King of Netherlands, and revised by A. Gallatin, with an appendix and eight maps. New York, 1840. 8vo.

5 SUGGESTIONS on the Banks and Currency of the several United States, in reference principally to the suspension of specie payments. New York, 1841. 8°

6 INAUGURAL Addreſſ .. on taking the chair as President of the New York Historical Society, etc. [With a short account of the Society, etc.] New York, 1843. 8°

7 PEACE with Mexico. New York, 1848. 8°

GALLAUDET, THOMAS HOPKINS. Plan of a Seminary for the Education of Instructers of Youth. Boston, 1825. 8°

2 THE CHILD's Picture Defining and Reading Book. . . Third edition, etc. Hartford, 1833. 12°

GALLAUDET, THOMAS HOPKINS, AND HOOKER, HORACE. The Practical Spelling-Book; with reading leſſons. Hartford, [1840?] 12°

GALLERY of Illustrious Americans. . . C. Edwards Lester, Editor. Nº 1-5. New York, 1850. Folº

GALLISON, JOHN. Addreſſ delivered at the fourth anniversary of the Maſſachusetts' Peace Society, Dec. 25, 1819. Cambridge, 1820. 8°

2 REPORTS of Cases argued and determined in the Circuit Court of the United States, for the first Circuit. Second edition, with additional notes and references. 2 vol. 1812-1815. Boston, 1845. 8°

GALLITZIN, DEMETRIUS A. See GOLITSUIN, Dmetri A.

GALLOP, JOSEPH A. Outlines of the Institutes of Medicine: founded on the philosophy of the human economy, in health and in disease. 2 vol. Boston, 1839. 8°

GALT, JOHN. The Life of Lord Byron. New York, 1845. 12°

GAMMELL, WILLIAM. Addreſſ delivered before the Rhode Island Historical Society, at the opening of their Cabinet, etc.· Nov. 20, 1844. [With an appendix.] Providence, 1844. 8°

2 A HISTORY of American Baptist Miſſions in Asia, Africa, Europe, and North America. Boston, 1849. 12°

GANDS, P. A Key to the exercises in Ollendorff's New Method of learning .. the German Language. [Edited by G. J. Adler.] New York, 1847. 12°

GANNAL, J. N. History of Embalming, and of preparations in anatomy, pathology and natural history, including an account of a new proceſſ for embalming. Translated from the French, with notes and additions by R. Harlan. Philadelphia, 1840. 8vo.

GANNETT, EZRA STILES. The Religion of Politics. A sermon [on 1 Cor. x. 31] delivered before .. J. Davis, Governor, .. and the Legislature of Maſſachusetts, at the annual Election, January 5, 1842. Boston, 1842. 8°

2 AN ADDRESS delivered at the funeral of W. E. Channing .. October 7, 1842. Boston, 1842. 8°

3 A SERMON [on Rom. xiv. 7] delivered in the Federal Street Meeting House, in Boston, October 9, 1842, the Sunday after the death of W. E. Channing. Boston, 1842. 8°

4 PEACE, not War: a sermon [on Isaiah ii. 4] preached in the Federal Street Meeting House, Dec. 14, 1845. Boston, 1845. 8°

GARCIA DEL RIO, J. Documentos relativos a la denegacion de pasaporte para Mejico a J. G. del Rio. New York, 1828. 8vo.

GARDEN, ALEXANDER. Six Letters to the Rev. Mr. G. Whitefield, .. on the subject of Justification, etc. Together with Mr. Whitefield's answer to the first letter. The second edition. Boston, 1740. 4°

2 ANECDOTES of the Revolutionary War in America, with sketches of character of. persons the most distinguished in the Southern States for civil and military services. Charleston, 1822. 8°

3 ANECDOTES of the American Revolution, etc. Second series. Charleston, 1828. 12°

GARDINER, MARGUERITE, Countefs of Blefsington. The Works of Lady Blefsington. 2 vol. Philadelphia, 1838. 8°

GARDINER, WILLIAM HOWARD. An Addrefs, delivered before the Phi Beta Kappa Society of Harvard University, . . on Clafsical Learning and Eloquence. Cambridge, 1834. 8vo.

GARDNER, AUGUSTUS KINGSLEY. The French Metropolis. Paris ; as seen during the spare hours of a medical student. . . Second edition, revised, and illustrated by twenty fine steel engravings. New York [Boston printed], 1850. 8°

GARDNER, CHARLES K. A Dictionary of all Officers who have been commifsioned, or have been appointed and served in the army of the United States since 1789 to Jan. 1, 1853, etc. New York, 1853. 8°

GARDNER, D. P. Addrefs of Dr. D. P. Gardner before the National Convention of Farmers and Gardeners, held at the Repository of the American Institute. [New York, 1844.] 8°

GARLAND, HUGH A. The Life of John Randolph, of Roanoke. [With extracts from his speeches, etc.] 2 vol. New York, 1851. 12°

GARRETT, W. A Tabular Statement of the Census of Alabama, taken in the year 1844; also, the census or enumeration of 1838 and 1840, and an estimate showing the increase and decrease in each county since

1838. Compiled by W. Garrett. Tuscaloosa, 1844. 8°

GARRISON, WILLIAM LLOYD. An Addrefs delivered at the Broadway Tabernacle, New York, August 1, 1838, by request of the people of colour in that city, in commemoration of the complete emancipation of 600,000 slaves on that day, in the British West Indies. Boston, 1838. 12°

GASS, PATRICK. A Journal of the Voyages and Travels of a Corps of Discovery, under the command of Capt. Lewis and Capt. Clarke, of the army of the United States, from the mouth of the river Mifsouri, through the interior parts of North America, to the Pacific Ocean, during the years 1804, 1805 and 1806. . . With geographical and explanatory notes by the publisher . . D. M'Keehan. Pittsburgh, 1807. 12°

GASTON, WILLIAM, LL. D. An Addrefs delivered before the American Whig and Cliosophic Societies of the College of New Jersey, etc. . . Second edition. Princeton, 1835. 8°

GAUSSEN, S. R. LOUIS. The Parables of Spring. . . Translated from the French by P. Berry. New York, 1853. 12mo.

GAY, EBENEZER. A Beloved Disciple of Jesus Christ characterized : in a sermon [on John xxi. 20] preached . . in Boston July 27, 1766, the third Lord's-day from the decease of . . J. Mayhew, D.D. Boston, 1766. 8°

GAY, MARTIN, M. D. A Statement of the Claims of C. T. Jackson . . to the discovery of the applicability of sulphuric Ether to the prevention of pain in surgical operations. Boston, 1847. 8°

GAY, SOPHIE. Celebrated Saloons, by Madame Gay ; and Parisian Letters, by Madame Girardin. Translated from the French by L. Willard. Boston, 1851. 12°

GAYARRE, Charles. Romance of the History of Louisiana. A series of lectures. New York, 1848. 12°

2 Louisiana ; its colonial history and romance. New York, 1851. 8°

GAYLORD, Willis, and Tucker, Luther. American Husbandry: being a series of essays on agriculture. Compiled principally from "The Cultivator" and "The Genesee Farmer," with additions, by W. Gaylord and L. Tucker. 2 vol. New York, 1843. 12°

GAZETTE of the State of Georgia. N° 110, 111, 113, 116. [Savannah!] 1785. Fol.

GEM of the Season, for 1848. New York, 1848. 8°

GEM of the Western World, for all seasons. . . Edited by M. E. Hewitt. New York, [1850!] 8°

GEMS. The Illuminated Gems of Sacred Poetry. [Selection from English and American authors.] Philadelphia, [1848!] 8°

GENERAL REPOSITORY and Review. Jan. 1812 to Oct. 1813. Vol. 1-4. Cambridge, 1812-13. 8°

GENESEE COUNTRY. Description of the Settlement of the Genesee Country, in the State of New York, in a series of letters from a gentleman to his friend. New York, 1799. 8°

GENET, Edmond Charles. Memorial on the Upward Forces of Fluids, and their applicability to several arts, sciences, and public improvements. Albany, 1825. 8°

GENEVA COLLEGE. Geneva College Register, for the academical year 1842-3. Geneva [1842]. 8vo.

GENIN, J. N. An Illustrated History of the Hat, from the earliest ages to the present time. New York, 1848. 12°

GENIUS of Oblivion, and other original poems. By a lady of New Hampshire [Miss Sarah Josepha Buell, afterwards Mrs. S. J. Hale]. Concord, 1823. 12°

GENTRY, Meredith P. of Tennessee. Speech .. on the Tariff; delivered in the House of Representatives, .. July 2, 1846. Washington, 1846. 8°

GEOGRAPHICAL and Commercial Gazette. . . . Edited by an Association of practical and scientific gentlemen. New York, 1855. Fol°

GEOGRAPHICAL QUESTIONS. A complete series of Geographical Questions, etc. Boston, 1842. 12°

GEOLOGICAL SOCIETY of Pennsylvania. Transactions. Vol. 1. in 2 parts. Philadelphia, 1834-35. 8vo.

GEORGE III. The King's Speech [on opening Parliament, Nov. 30th, 1774]. Newport [1775], s. sh. fol.

2 His Majesty's .. Speech to both Houses of Parliament, October 26, 1775. Boston [1775]. Fol.

GEORGE, Anita. Annals of the Queens of Spain; from the period of the conquest of the Goths down to the reign of her present Majesty, Isabel II. etc. 2 vol. New York, 1850. 8vo.

GEORGE, Julia W. H. A History of the English and Scotch Rebellions of 1685, etc. New York, 1851. 12°

GEORGETOWN, District of Columbia. Petition of the Sisters of the Visitation of George Town, District of Columbia [to the Congress of the United States], praying that an Act of Incorporation may be passed in their favour. Washington, 1828. 8°

GEORGETOWN COLLEGE. Annals of the Astronomical Observatory of Georgetown College, District of Columbia. [Edited by J. Curley.] New York, 1852. 4to.

GEORGIA, *State of.* A Compilation of the Laws of the State of Georgia, paſſed by the General Assembly, since . . . 1819 to . . . 1829 inclusive, comprising all the laws paſſed within those periods, arranged under titles, with marginal notes. . . To which are added such concurred and approved resolutions as are either of general, local, or private nature. . By W. C. Dawson. Milledgeville, 1831. 4°

2 A DIGEST of the Laws of the State of Georgia : containing all statutes and the substance of all resolutions of a general and public nature, and now in force, which have been paſſed in this State, previous to . . . Dec. 1837. With . . notes, . . connecting references [and] . . an appendix, *etc.* Second edition. Compiled by . . O. H. Prince. Athens, 1837. 8°

3 MEMORIAL of the Legislature of the State of Georgia. Washington, 1806. 8°

GEORGIA BAPTIST CONVENTION. Minutes of the Twenty-first Anniversary of the Georgia Baptist Convention. Penfield, 1842. 8vo.

GEORGIA FEMALE COLLEGE. Catalogue of the Trustees, Officers, and Students of the Georgia Female College [at Macon]. N. York [1844]. 8vo.

GEORGIA SCENES, Characters, Incidents, etc. in the first half century of the Republic. By a native Georgian. Second edition. With original illustrations. New York, 1848. 12°

GERBET, PHILIPPE. The Life of the Bleſſed virgin Mary ; or, the Lily of Israel. Translated from the French of the Abbé Gerbet. To which is added, The Veneration of the Bleſſed Virgin Mary [No. 4 of " Sadlier's Fireside Library"]. New York, 1852. 12mo.

GERHARD, W. W. The Diagnosis, Pathology, and Treatment of the Diseases of the Chest. Third edition . . . enlarged. Philadelphia, 1850. 8vo.

GESENIUS, FRIEDRICH HEINRICH WILHELM. Hebrew Grammar of Gesenius, as edited by Roediger. Translated, with additions, and also a Hebrew Chrestomathy, by M. Stuart. Andover, 1846. 8°

2 GESENIUS' Hebrew Grammar. Fourteenth edition, as revised by Dr. E. Rödiger. Translated by T. J. Conant. . . With the modifications of the editions subsequent to the eleventh by Dr. Davies. . . To which are added, a course of exercises in Hebrew grammar, and a Hebrew Chrestomathy prepared by the translator. (A Hebrew reading-book . . . by B. Davies.) 3 parts. New York, 1847. 8°

GIBBES, LEWIS R. On the Carcinological Collections of the Cabinets of Natural History in the United States. With an enumeration of the species contained therein, and descriptions of new species. Charleston, 1850. 8vo.

GIBBES, ROBERT W. Description of the Teeth of a new Foſſil Animal found in the green sand of South Carolina. . . (From the proceedings of the Academy of Natural Sciences.) [Philadelphia,] 1845. 8vo.

*2 A MEMOIR of J. De Veaux, of Charleston, South Carolina. Columbia, 1846. 8°

GIBBS, CHARLES, *otherwise* JEFFERS, JAMES J. Mutiny and Murder. Confeſſions and life of C. Gibbs, alias J. J. Jeffers, who . . . was hung in New York, . . for the murder of the captain and mate of the brig Vineyard, *etc.* Dover, 1831. 12°

GIBBS, GEORGE. The Judicial Chronicle ; being a list of the Judges of the Courts of Common Law and Chancery in England and America, and of the contemporary reports, from

the earliest period .. to the present
time. Cambridge, 1834. 8°

GIBBS, JOSIAH WILLARD. A
Manual Hebrew and English Lexicon,
including the Biblical Chaldee. . . .
Second edition, revised and enlarged.
New Haven, 1832. 8°

GIBERT, PEDRO, AND OTHERS. A
Report of the Trial of P. Gibert and
J. Montenegro .. before the United
States Circuit Court, on an indictment
charging them with . . . piracy on
board the brig Mexican, etc. By a
Congreſsional stenographer. Boston,
1834. 8°

GIBSON, JOHN. Gibson's Guide
and Directory of the State of Louisiana and the cities of New Orleans
and Lafayette. N. Orleans, 1838. 12°

GIBSON, WILLIAM. Institutes
and Practice of Surgery, being outlines of a course of lectures. Sixth
edition. 2 vol. Philadel. 1841. 8vo.

2 RAMBLES in Europe in 1839.
With sketches of prominent surgeons,
physicians, medical schools, hospitals,
literary personages, scenery, etc.
Philadelphia, 1841. 12°

3 LECTURE introductory to a course
on Surgery in the University of Pennsylvania, containing a short account
of eminent British surgeons, physicians, etc. Philadelphia, 1847. 8°

4 LECTURE correlative to a course
on Surgery in the University of Pennsylvania, embracing a short account
of eminent Belgian surgeons, physicians, etc. Philadelphia, 1848. 8°

GIBSON, WILLIAM, of the United
States Navy. A Vision of Faery
Land and other Poems. Boston and
Cambridge [printed], 1853. 12°

GIDDINGS, JOSHUA R. Speeches
in Congreſs. Boston, 1853. 12°

GIERLOW, JOHN. Elements of
the Danish and Swedish Languages.
Cambridge, 1847. 12°

GIESELER, JOHANN CARL LUD-
WIG. Text-book of Ecclesiastical History. . . Translated from the third
German edition by F. Cunningham.
3 vol. Philadelphia, 1836. 8vo.

GIFT (THE): a Christmas and New
Year's Present for 1836. Edited by
Miſs Leslie. [For 1843.] 2 vol. Phi-
ladelphia [1835-42].

2 THE GIFT. Philadel. [1840!] 8°

GIFT for all Seasons, etc. New
York, 1853. 12mo.

GILES, HENRY, Rev. The Guilt
of Contempt. A sermon [on Matt.
v. 21, 22]. Bangor, 1847. 8°

2 CHRISTIAN Thought on Life, in
a series of discourses. Bost. 1850. 8°

3 LECTURES and Eſsays. 2 vol.
Boston, 1850. 16°

GILES, WILLIAM BRANCH. The
Speeches of Mr. Giles and Mr. Bayard,
in the House of Representatives of
the United States, Feb. 1802, on the
bill received from the Senate, entitled, An Act to repeal certain Acts
respecting the organization of the
Courts of the United States. Boston,
1802. 8°

2 Mr. GILES' Speech in the Senate
of the United States, on the Bill for
renewing the Charter of the United
States Bank. [Washington! 1811.] 8°

3 LETTER from W. B. Giles to the
Legislature of Virginia [concerning
its censure of his conduct in Congreſs, in relation to the subject of the
Bank of the United States.] [Wash-
ington! 1812.] 8°

GILL, C. Application of the An-
gular Analysis to the solution of the
indeterminate problems of the second
degree. New York and London,
1848. 12mo.

GILL, RICHARD W. and JOHN-
SON, JOHN. Reports of Cases argued
and determined in the Court of Appeals of Maryland. 1829-1842. 12
vol. Baltimore [and] Annapolis,
1830-45. 8°

GILL, Sarah. Sermon on her Death. Boston, 1771. 8vo.

GILLELAND, J. C. History of the late War between the United States and Great Britain, etc. Baltimore, 1817. 12°

GILLESPIE, William Mitchell. A Manual of the principles and practice of road-making; comprising the location, construction, and improvement of roads .... and railroads. Second edition, with additions. New York, 1848. 8°

GILLET, Eliphalet. Thanksgiving. A discourse [on Psalm lxxv. 1] delivered at Hallowell on the day of the annual thanksgiving in Massachusetts. Hallowell, 1819. 8°

GILLETTE, A. D. A Sketch of the Labours, Sufferings, and Death of the Rev. A. Judson. Philadelphia, 1851. 16°
2 Memoir of Joseph Wistar. Philadelphia, 1852. 16°

GILLIAM, Albert M. Travels over the Table lands and Cordilleras of Mexico, during the years 1843 and 44; including a description of California, the principal cities and mining districts of that republic, and the biographies of Iturbide and Santa Anna ... With maps and plates. Philadelphia, 1846. 8°

GILLISS, J. Melville. Magnetical and Meteorological Observations, made at Washington, under orders of the Hon. Secretary of the Navy, etc. Washington, 1845. 8vo.
2 Astronomical Observations made at the Naval Observatory, Washington, under orders of the Hon. Secretary of the Navy, etc. Washington, 1846. 8°
3 The United States Naval Astronomical Expedition to the Southern Hemisphere, during the years 1849-'50-'51-'52. Lieut. J. M. Gilliss, Superintendent. A. Mac Rae, S. L. Phelps, E. R. Smith, Assistants. 2 vol. Washington, 1855. 4to.

GILMAN, Caroline. The Poetry of Travelling in the United States; with additional sketches by a few friends, and a week among autographs, by .. S. Gilman. New York, 1838. 12°
2 Recollections of a Southern Matron. New York, 1838. 12mo.
3 Recollections of a Southern Matron. New York, 1839. 12°
4 Tales and Ballads. Boston, 1839. 12°
5 Oracles from the Poets: a fanciful diversion for the drawing-room. New York, 1845. 12°
6 The Sibyl; or, new Oracles from the Poets. New York, 1848. 12°
7 Oracles for Youth. A home pastime. New York, 1852. 12°
8 Recollections of a New England Bride and of a Southern Matron. .. New edition, revised. 2 parts. New York, 1852. 12°

GILMAN, S. Monody on the Victims and Sufferers by the late Conflagration in the city of Richmond, Virginia. Boston, 1812. 8°

GILMER, Francis W. Reports of Cases decided in the Court of Appeals of Virginia, from April 10, 1820, to June 28, 1821. Richmond, 1821. 8°

GILPIN, Henry D. Reports of Cases adjudged in the District Court of the United States for the Eastern District of Pennsylvania. Philadelphia, 1837. 8°

GILPIN, Joshua. A Memoir on the rise, progress, and present state of the Chesapeake and Delaware Canal, accompanied with original documents and maps. Wilmington, 1821. 8°
2 A Monument of Parental Affection to a dear and only son; or, a memoir of J. R. Gilpin. Philadelphia, 1830. 12°

GIRARD, Charles. Essays on the Classification of Nemertes and

Planariæ : preceded by some general consideration on the primary divisions of the animal kingdom. [New Haven, 1850.] 8°

2 AMERICAN Zoological, Botanical, and Geological Bibliography for the year 1851, etc. [From the "American Journal of Science and Arts." Second series. Vol. 13.] [N. Haven, 1852.] 8°

GIRARD, STEPHEN. The Will of the late S. Girard... With a short biography. Philadelphia, 1832. 8°

GIRARD COLLEGE, PHILADELPHIA. Account of the Proceedings on laying the Corner Stone of the Girard College for Orphans, on July 4, 1833 : together with the address pronounced on that occasion at the request of the Building Committee, by Nicholas Biddle. Phil. 1833. 8°

2 REPORT of the Special Committee appointed by the Common Council on a communication from the Board of Trustees of the Girard College, .. read .. August 27, 1840. Philadelphia, 1840. 8°

3 COMMUNICATIONS from the Board of Trustees of the Girard College for Orphans, to the Select and Common Councils of Philadelphia. Philadelphia, 1840. 8°

4 REPORT of a Special Committee to the Commissioners of the Girard estate, on the subject of opening the Girard College for Orphans. Philadelphia, 1847. 8°

GIRAUD, J. P. the Younger. The Birds of Long Island. New York, 1844. 8°

GLASS, FRANCIS. A Life of George Washington, in Latin prose. Edited by J. N. Reynolds. Third edition. New York, 1842. 12mo.

GLAUBER-SPA. Tales of Glauber-Spa. By several American authors [C. M. Sedgwick, J. K. Paulding, W. C. Bryant, W. Leggett, and R. C. Sands]. New York, 1832. 12°

GLEASON, BENJAMIN. An Oration pronounced at the Baptist Meeting House in Wrentham, Feb. 22, 1800, at the request of the Society, in memory of Gen. George Washington, etc. Wrentham, 1800. 8°

2 AN ORATION pronounced.. before the Republican Citizens of Charlestown, on the anniversary of American Independence, July 4, 1805. Second edition. Boston, 1805. 8°

GLEASON'S Pictorial Drawing-Room Companion. 6 vol. Boston, 1851-54. Fol° [Continued under the title of] Ballou's Pictorial Drawing-Room Companion. Vol. 7-10. Boston, 1854-56. Fol°

GLEIG, GEORGE ROBERT. The History of the Bible. 2 vol. New York, 1844. 12°

GLOVER, JOSEPH. An Attempt to prove that Digestion in Man depends on the united causes of Solution and Fermentation. Philadelphia, 1800. 8vo.

GLOW-WORM (THE). American Sunday School Union, Philadelphia, 1831. 12mo.

GODDARD, PAUL B. The Anatomy, Physiology, and Pathology of the Human Teeth ; with the most approved methods of treatment, including operations, etc. Aided in the practical part by J. E. Parker. Philadelphia, 1844. Imp. 4to.

GODDARD, THOMAS H. A General History of the most prominent Banks in Europe, .. and .. the United States. Compiled from various standard works, official sources, and private correspondence. Also, A. Hamilton's Report to Congress on currency, .. and Mc Duffie's Report on currency, presented to the last Congress. New York, 1831. 8°

GODDARD, WILLIAM GILES. An Address to the People of Rhode Island, delivered .. May 3, 1843, in

presence of the General Aſſembly, on
the occasion of the change in the
civil government of Rhode Island, by
the adoption of the constitution, which
superseded the charter of 1663. Providence, 1843. 8°

GODMAN, JOHN D. Introduc-
tory Lecture to the course of anatomy and physiology in Rutger's Medical College, New York. New York,
1826. 8°

2 AMERICAN Natural History. Vol.
1, 2. Philadelphia, 1826. 8vo.

GODMAN, STUART ADAIR. The
Ocean-Born: a tale of the Southern
Seas. New York [1852]. 8°

GODWIN, PARKE. Tales from the
German of H. Zschökke, translated
by P. Godwin. Series 1 and 2. London [New York printed], 1846. 8vo.

2 VALA: a mythological tale.
[Founded upon the life of Jenny
Lind.] New York, 1851. 4°

GOETHE, JOHANN WOLFGANG
VON. Eſſays on Art. Translated by
S. G. Ward. Boston, 1845. 16°

2 IPHIGENIA in Tauris: a drama in
five acts [and in verse]. Translated
from the German by G. J. Adler.
New York, 1850. 12°

GOLDER, JOHN. Life of the Hon.
William Tilghman, Chief Justice of
Pennsylvania. Compiled from the
eulogies of two distinguished members of the Philadelphia Bar. [With
an appendix.] Philadel. 1829. 8vo.

GOLDSBOROUGH, CHARLES W.
The United States Naval Chronicle.
Vol. 1. Washington, 1824. 8°

GOLDSBURY, JOHN. A Sequel
to the Common School Grammar, etc.
Boston, 1842. 12°

2 THE COMMON School Grammar.
.. Sixth edition. Boston, 1845. 12°

GOLDSMITH, OLIVER. Gold-
smith's Roman History abridged by
himself, for the use of schools. Re-

vised and corrected by William Grimshaw. Baltimore, 1818. 12mo.

GOLITSUIN, DMETRI A. A De-
fence of Catholic Principles, in a Letter to a Protestant Minister: to which
is added, an appeal to the Protestant
public. Fourth edition, corrected,
etc. Baltimore [1837]. 12°

2 A LETTER to a Protestant Friend
on the Holy Scriptures: being a continuation of the "Defence of Catholic
Principles." Baltimore [1847?]. 12°

GOOD BOOK, and Amenities of
Nature; or, annals of historical and
natural sciences: containing selections of observations, researches, and
novelties, in all the branches of physical and historical knowledge, . . .
chiefly on zoology, botany, etc. (N° 1.)
By C. S. Rafinesque. Philadelphia,
1840. 8°

GOODALE, EBENEZER. Record
of the Proceedings of a General Court
Martial, holden .. Sept. 28, 1812, ..
on the complaint of Lt. Col. S. Brim-
blecom and others, against E. Goodale, etc. Cambridge, 1812. 8°

GOODELL, WILLIAM, AND OTHERS.
Mr. Southgate and the Miſſionaries
at Constantinople. A letter from the
miſſionaries at Constantinople in reply to charges by Rev. H. Southgate.
[Signed by W. Goodell and six others.]
Boston, 1844. 8vo.

2 SLAVERY and Anti-Slavery; a
history of the great struggle in both
hemispheres; with a view of the
slavery question in the United States.
New York, 1852. 8vo.

3 THE AMERICAN Slave Code in
theory and practice. .. Second edition. New York, 1853. 12mo.

4 THE OLD and the New; or,
changes of thirty years in the East.
.. With an introduction by W.
Adams. New York, 1853. 12°

GOODENOW, SMITH B. A. M.
New England Grammar. A systematic text-book of English grammar,

on the eclectic plan; with progressive questions and exercises. . . Second edition, enlarged and improved. Boston, 1843. 12°

GOODENOW, STERLING. A brief topographical and statistical Manual of the State of New York. . . Second edition . . enlarged. New York, 1822. 8°

GOODRICH, CHARLES AUGUSTUS, *Rev.* A new Family Encyclopædia; or, compendium of universal knowledge, *etc.* Second improved edition. Philadelphia, 1831. 12°

2 OUTLINES of Modern Geography, on a new plan. . . Accompanied by an Atlas. [Wanting the Atlas.] Boston, 1837. 12°

3 A HISTORY of the United States of America; from the discovery of the continent by Christopher Columbus to the present time: embracing an account of the aboriginal tribes, *etc.* Hartford, 1840. 12°

4 LIVES of the Signers of the Declaration of Independence. Hartford, 1842. 8°

5 A HISTORY of the United States of America, on a plan adapted to the capacity of youth. . . Enlarged from the one hundredth edition. Boston, 1845. 12°

6 THE CHILD's History of the United States. Designed as a first book of history for schools. Illustrated by numerous anecdotes. Improved from the twenty-first edition. Philadelphia, 1846. 16°

GOODRICH, CHAUNCEY ALLEN. Elements of Greek Grammar. . . Used in Yale College. Heretofore published as the Grammar of C. F. Hachenbach. Stereotype edition. Hartford [1829]. 12°

2 SELECT British Eloquence, embracing the best speeches entire of the most eminent orators of Great Britain for the last two centuries, with sketches of their lives, *etc.* New York, 1852. 8°

3 ANOTHER copy, with new title-page. London, 1852. 8vo.

GOODRICH, SAMUEL GRISWOLD. A System of School Geography, chiefly derived from Malte Brun, and arranged according to the inductive plan of instruction. Hartford, 1830. 12° Atlas, 4°

2 A SYSTEM of Universal Geography, popular and scientific; comprising a physical, political, and statistical account of the world. . . Illustrated by engravings, *etc.* Boston, 1832. 8vo.

3 THE CHILD's Book of American Geography. . . With sixty engravings and eighteen maps. Bost. 1832. 4°

4 BIBLE Stories; or, a description of Manners and Customs peculiar to the East, especially explanatory of the Holy Scriptures. . . American edition, with many improvements. Philadelphia [1832 ?] 16°

5 PETER Parley's Universal History, on the basis of Geography. . . Sixth edition. N. York [1837]. 12°

6 PETER Parley's Universal History, on the basis of Geography. For the use of families. Eighth edition, 2 vol. New York, 1844. 12°

7 SKETCHES from a Student's Window. Boston, 1841. 12°

8 THE FIRST Reader for Schools. Boston, 1842. 12°

9 THE SECOND Reader for Schools. Boston, 1839. 12°

10 THE THIRD Reader for the use of schools. . . Sixth edition. Boston, 1841. 12°

11 THE FOURTH Reader for the use of schools. Boston, 1839. 12°

12 PETER Parley's common School History. Stereotype edition. Philadelphia, 1843. 12°

13 MAKE the best of it; or, cheerful Cherry, and other tales, *etc.* New York, 1843. 12°

14 THE LIFE of Benjamin Franklin, illustrated by tales, sketches, and anecdotes . . With engravings. Philadelphia, 1844. 12°

15 THE YOUNG American: or book of government and law; showing their history, nature, and necefsity. For the use of schools. Fourth edition. New York, 1844. 12°

16 THE LIFE of C. Columbus, illustrated by tales, sketches, and anecdotes. Adapted to the use of schools. With engravings. Philadel. 1844. 12°

17 THE LIFE of G. Washington. Illustrated by tales, sketches, and anecdotes. Adapted to the use of schools. With engravings. Philadelphia, 1844. 12°

18 PETER Parley's Bible Dictionary; containing illustrations of arts, manners, customs, .. and other things mentioned in the Bible. New York, 1844. 16°

19 PETER Parley's Illustrations of History and Geography. New York, 1844. 12°

20 PETER Parley's Illustrations of the Vegetable Kingdom; trees, plants, and shrubs. N. York, 1844. 12°

21 PETER Parley's Illustrations of Astronomy. New York, 1844. 16°

22 A TALE of Adventure; or, the Siberian sable hunter, etc. N. York, 1844. 16°

23 PETER Parley's Illustrations of the Animal Kingdom; beasts, birds, fishes, reptiles, and insects. New York, 1844. 12°

24 PETER Parley's Illustrations of Commerce. N. York, 1844. 16°

25 WIT Bought; or, the life and adventures of R. Merry. By Peter Parley. New York, 1844. 12°

26 WHAT to do, and how to do it; or, morals and manners taught by examples. By Peter Parley. New York, 1844. 16°

27 PETER Parley's Bible Gazetteer; containing illustrations of Bible geography. New York, 1844. 12°

28 THE TRUTH-FINDER; or, the story of inquisitive Jack, etc. Philadelphia, 1845. 16°

29 PETER Parley's Tales about Ancient Rome, with some account of modern Italy. Philadel. 1845. 12°

30 PETER Parley's Juvenile Tales. Revised edition. Philadel. 1845. 16°

31 DICK Boldhero; or, a tale of adventures in South America, etc. Philadelphia, 1845. 12°

32 PETER Parley's Winter Evening Tales. Revised edition. Philadelphia, 1845. 16°

33 PETER Parley's Tales about Ancient and Modern Greece. Philadelphia, 1845. 16°

34 A HOME in the Sea; or, the adventures of Philip Brusque: designed to show the nature and necessity of government. Philadelphia, 1845. 16°

35 A NATIONAL Geography for Schools: illustrated by 220 engravings and 33 maps. With a globe map on a new plan. New York, 1845. 4°

36 PETER Parley's Book of Anecdotes. Philadelphia, 1845. 12°

37 A TALE of the Revolution, and other sketches, etc. Philadelphia, 1845. 12°

38 PETER Parley's Tales of the Sea. Philadelphia, 1845. 12°

39 PETER Parley's Tales about the Islands in the Pacific Ocean. Philadelphia, 1845. 16°

40 THE TALES of Peter Parley about America. Revised edition. Philadelphia, 1845. 12°

41 RIGHT is Might, and other sketches. Philadelphia, 1846. 16°

42 Sow well and reap well; or, fireside education. . . Third edition. Albany, 1846. 12°

43 TALES of Sea and Land. Philadelphia, 1846. 16°

44 PARLEY's Cabinet Library: Biographical Department. 1. Lives of famous men of modern times; 2. Lives of famous men of ancient times; 3. Curiosities of human nature; 4. Lives of benefactors; 5. Lives of famous American Indians; 6. Lives of celebrated women. Historical department. 7. Lights and shadows of American history; 8. . . of European

history; 9... of Asiatic history; 10. .. of African history; 11. History of the American Indians; 12. Manners, customs, and antiquities of the American Indians. Miscellaneous. 13. A glance at the sciences; 14. Wonders of geology; 15. Anecdotes of the animal kingdom; 16. A glance at philosophy; 17. Book of literature, with specimens; 18. Enterprise, industry, and art of man; 19. Manners and customs of nations; 20. The world and its inhabitants. 20 vol. Philadelphia, 1846. 12°

45 POEMS. New York, 1851. 12°
46 *See* PARLEY, Peter.

GOODWIN, ISAAC. An Addreſs delivered at Worcester, Aug. 24, 1820, before the American Antiquarian Society at the opening of the Antiquarian Hall, *etc.* Worcester, Sept. 1820. 8°

2 ADDRESS delivered before the Worcester Agricultural Society, Oct. 13, 1824, being their anniversary cattle show and exhibition of manufactures. Worcester [1824]. 8°

GOODWIN, NATHANIEL. The Foote Family; or, the descendants of N. Foote... With genealogical notes of P. Foote, .. and J. Foote, and others of the name, who settled more recently in New York. [With portraits.] Hartford, 1849. 8vo.

GOODWIN, ROBERT M. The Case of R. M. Goodwin, charged with killing J. Stoughton, containing the whole of the proceedings, *etc.* By W. Sampson. [Another title-page, bearing date 1820, which reads, " Trial of R. M. Goodwin, *etc.* . . taken in shorthand by W. Sampson."] New York, 1821. 8°

GOOKIN, DANIEL. Historical Collections of the Indians in New England: of their several nations, numbers, customs, manners, religion, and government, before the English planted there... Now first printed from the original manuscript. Boston, 1792. 8°

GORDON, A. J. Addreſs (by A. J. Gordon) and Reply (by S. P. Chase) on the presentation of a testimonial to S. P. Chase by the coloured people of Cincinnati; with some account of the case of J. Watson. [Cincinnati, 1845.] 8°

GORDON, SAMUEL, *of New York.* Speech .. on the Bankrupt Law, delivered in the House of Representatives, Jan. 5, 1843. Washington, 1843. 8°

GORDON, THOMAS F. The History of Pennsylvania, from its discovery by Europeans to the Declaration of Independence in 1776. Philadelphia, 1829. 8°

2 A GAZETTEER of the State of Pennsylvania, *etc.* Philadel. 1833. 8°

3 THE HISTORY of New Jersey, from its discovery by Europeans to the adoption of the Federal Constitution. Trenton [published; Philadelphia printed], 1834. 8vo.

4 A GAZETTEER of the State of New Jersey; .. together with a topographical and statistical account of its counties, towns, *etc.* Trenton [published; Philadelphia printed], 1834. 8vo.

5 GAZETTEER of the State of New York, *etc.* Comprehending its colonial history, .. its political state, statistical tables, .. a map, *etc.* Philadelphia, 1836. 8vo.

GORDON, WILLIAM. Religious and Civil Liberty: a thanksgiving discourse. Boston, 1775. 8vo.

GORE, CHRISTOPHER, *of Maſſachusetts.* Who shall be Governor? The Contrast: containing sketches of the characters and public services of the two candidates for the office of Chief Magistrate of the Commonwealth of Maſſachusetts (C. Gore and L. Lincoln). Worcester, 1809. 12°

GORHAM, JOHN. Inaugural Addreſs, delivered in the Chapel of the University at Cambridge, Dec. 11, 1816. Boston, 1817. 8°

GORMAN, John B. Philosophy of Animated Existence; or, sketches of living physics, with discuſsions of physiology philosophical. To which is added, a brief medical account of the middle regions of Georgia. Philadelphia, 1845. 8vo.

GORRIE, P. Douglass. Episcopal Methodism, as it was, and is, .. in the United States. Embracing also, a sketch of Methodism in Europe, etc. Auburn, 1852. 12°

2 The Lives of Eminent Methodist Ministers; containing biographical sketches, etc. Auburn, 1852. 12°

GOTHAM, City of. Chronicles of the city of Gotham. From the papers of a retired Common Councilman. Edited by the author of the "Backwoodsman," etc. [J. K. Paulding]. New York, 1830. 12°

GOVE, Mary S. Lectures to Women on Anatomy and Physiology. With an appendix -on water cure. New York, 1846. 8°

GOUGE, William M. A Short History of Paper-Money and Banking in the United States. .. With considerations of its effects on morals and happineſs, etc. Philadelphia, 1833. 12mo.

2 The Fiscal History of Texas. .. from .. 1834 to 1851-52. With remarks on American debts. Philadelphia, 1852. 8°

GOUGH, John Parker. An Eſſay on Cantharides. Comprising a brief account of their natural history; an inquiry into their mode of operation, etc. Philadelphia, 1800. 8vo.

GOULD, Augustus Addison. Report on the Invertebrata of Maſſachusetts; comprising the mollusca, crustacea, annelida, and radiata. Published by the Commiſſioners of the Zoological and. Botanical Survey. Cambridge, 1841. 8vo.

GOULD, Benjamin Apthorp.

Report (to the Smithsonian Institution) on the History of the Discovery of the Planet Neptune. Washington City [Cambridge printed], 1850. 8°

GOULD, Hannah Flagg, Miſs. Poems. 3 vol. Boston, 1839-41. 12°
   2 New Poems. Boston, 1850. 12°

GOULD, James. A Treatise on the Principles of Pleading, in Civil Actions. Second edition, revised and corrected by the author. New York, 1836. 8°

GOULD, Marcus T. C. Gould's Universal Index, and everybody's own book, etc. Third edition, revised and stereotyped. New York, 1842. 4°

GOULD, William M. Zephyrs from Italy and Sicily. New York, 1852. 12°

GOULD, William Tracy. An Addreſs, introductory to the second course of lectures, in the Law-School, at Augusta, Georgia, etc. Augusta, 1835. 8°

GOULDING, F. R. Robert and Harold; or, the young Marooners on the Florida coast. Second edition. Philadelphia, 1853. 12°

GOURLIE, John H. An Addreſs, delivered before the Mercantile Library Aſſociation, at its eighteenth annual meeting, Jan. 8, 1839, embodying a history of the Aſſociation. New York, 1839. 8°

GOWANS, William. Gowans' Bibliotheca Americana. 1. (A brief description of New York, formerly called New Netherlands, with the places thereunto adjoining. Likewise a brief relation of the customs of the Indians there. By D. Denton. A new edition, with an introduction and notes. By G. Furman.) New York, 1845. 4to.

GOWEN, Alfred C. Addreſs delivered at the annual Commencement of Calvert College, New Windsor, Carroll County, Maryland, Sept. 18, 1851. Baltimore, 1851. 8°

GRAFF, SIMON DE. The Modern Geometrical Stair-Builder's Guide; being a plain practical system of hand-railing, etc. New York, 1845. Imp. 8vo.

GRAFTON, JOSEPH. "The Godly and Faithful Man" delineated. A sermon [on Psalm xii. 1], .. occasioned by the death of Mr. S. Richardson, etc. Boston [1804]. 8vo.

GRAHAM, DAVID, Junior. A Treatise on the Practice of the Supreme Court of the State of New York. New York, 1832. 8°
2 A TREATISE on the Organization and Jurisdiction of the Courts of Law and Equity, in the State of New York. New York, 1839. 8°

GRAHAM, GEORGE FREDERICK. English Synonymes classified and explained; with practical exercises. .. Edited, with an introduction and illustrative authorities, by H. Reed. New York, 1847. 12°

GRAHAM, ISABELLA. The Power of Faith exemplified in the Life and Writings of Isabella Graham, of New York. New York, 1816. 8vo.

GRAHAM, JOHN ANDREW. Memoirs of J. Horne Tooke, together with his .. speeches and writings: also, containing proofs identifying him as the author of the .. Letters of Junius. New York, 1828. 8vo.

GRAHAM, SYLVESTER. A Lecture to Young Men, on Chastity. Intended also for the serious consideration of parents and guardians. Boston, 1837. 8°
2 LECTURES on the Science of Human Life. 2 vol. Boston, 1839. 12°

GRAHAM, WILLIAM SLOAN. Remains of W. S. Graham, with a memoir. . . Edited by G. Allen. Philadelphia, 1849. 12°

GRAHAME; or, Youth and Manhood. A romance, by the author of Talbot and Vernon. [i. e. J. L. Mac Connel]. New York, 1850. 12°

GRAHAME, JAMES, LL.D. The History of the United States of North America, from the Plantation of the British Colonies till their Assumption of National Independence. Second edition, enlarged and amended. [Edited, with a memoir of the author, by J. Quincy.] 4 vol. Philadelphia, 1845. 8°

GRAMMAR. A Short but Comprehensive Grammar; designed for the use of schools. By a teacher of youth. Salem, 1818. 16°

GRAND D'HAUTEVILLE, PAUL DANIEL GONSALVE. Report of the D'Hauteville Case: The Commonwealth of Pennsylvania, at the suggestion of P. D. G. G. d'Hauteville, versus David Sears, Miriam C. Sears and Ellen Sears Grand d'Hauteville: Habeas Corpus for the custody of an infant child. Philadel. 1840. 8vo.

GRANGER, GIDEON. An Oration, spoken .. July 4, 1797, at the East Meeting House in Suffield, being the anniversary of American Independence. Suffield, 1797. 8°

GRANT, DUNCAN. Addresses .. to the children attending the Aberdeen Sabbath Schools. Philadelphia, 1829. 12mo.

GRÆTER, FRANCIS. Hydriatics: or, Manual of the Water Cure; especially as practised by V. Priessnitz in Græfenberg. Compiled and translated from the writings of C. Munde, Dr. Oertel, Dr. B. Hirschel, and other eye-witnesses and practitioners. New York, 1842. 16mo.

GRAVES, MRS. A. J. Woman in America; being an examination into the moral and intellectual condition of American female society. New York, 1843. 12°

GRAY, ALONSO. Elements of Scientific and Practical Agriculture; or, the application of biology, geology, and chemistry to agriculture and horticulture. Intended as a text-book for farmers and students in agriculture. Andover, 1842. 12°

2 ELEMENTS of Natural Philosophy. Designed as a text-book for academies, etc. New York, 1850. 12°

3 ELEMENTS of Geology. By A. Gray and C. B. Adams. New York, 1853. 8°

GRAY, ASA. Elements of Botany. New York, 1836. 8°

2 THE BOTANICAL Text-Book. . . Second edition, illustrated with more than a thousand engravings on wood. New York, 1845. 12°

3 A MANUAL of the Botany of the Northern United States, from New England to Wisconsin, and south to Ohio and Pennsylvania inclusive. (The Mosses and Liverworts by W. S. Sullivant.) Arranged according to the natural system; with an introduction, containing a reduction of the genera to the Linnæan classes. Boston [Cambridge printed], 1848. 12°

4 GENERA Floræ Americæ Boreali-Orientalis illustrata: The genera of the plants of the United States, illustrated by figures and analyses from nature, by J. Sprague, . . with descriptions, etc. by A. Gray. Vol. 1. Boston [Cambridge printed], 1848. 8°

5 GENERA Floræ Americæ Boreali-Orientalis illustrata. The genera of the plants of the United States illustrated by figures and analyses from nature. . . Superintended, and with descriptions, etc. by A. Gray. 2 vol. New York [Cambridge printed], 1849. 8°

GRAY, CATHARINE. Catharine Gray: written for the American Sunday School Union. Philadelphia [1833]. 16mo.

GRAY, EDWARD. An Oration, delivered July 5, 1790, at . . Boston,
in celebration of the anniversary of American Independence. Boston, 1790. 8°

GRAY, EDWIN. Mr. Gray's Motion [relative to members of the House of Representatives who shall become contractors for the public service.] Jan. 24, 1806. [Washington, 1806.] 8°

GRAY, ELLIS. The Fidelity of Ministers to themselves, and to the Flock of God, considered and enforced: a sermon [on Acts xx. 28] preached at the ordination of the Rev. Mr. T. Maccarty, etc. Boston, 1742. 8vo.

GRAY, FRANCIS CALLEY. Letter to Governor Lincoln in relation to Harvard University. . . Third edition. Boston, 1831. 8°

2 ORATION delivered before the Legislature of Massachusetts. . . on the hundredth anniversary of the birth of George Washington. Boston, 1832. 8°

3 SPEECH . . in the House of Representatives of Massachusetts, March 19, 1836, on the bill to abolish capital punishment. Boston, 1836. 8°

4 POEM spoken at Cambridge, before the Phi Beta Kappa Society of Harvard University, Aug. 27, 1840. Boston, 1840. 8°

GRAY, ROBERT. A Sermon [on Gen. xii. 2] delivered . . before the . . General Court of . . New Hampshire, at the annual Election . . in June, 1798. Dover, 1798. 8°

GRAY, THOMAS. The value of Life and Charitable Institutions. A discourse delivered before the Humane Society of the Commonwealth of Massachusetts [with an appendix]. Boston, 1805. 8°

GRAY, THOMAS. The Poetical Works of T. Gray. With illustrations . . edited, with a memoir, by H. Reed. Philadelphia, 1851. 12°

GRAYDON, Alexander. Memoirs of a Life, chiefly passed in Pennsylvania, within the last sixty years; with occasional remarks upon the general occurrences, character, and spirit of that eventful period. [By Alexander Graydon.] Harrisburgh, Pa. 1811. 12mo.

2 Memoirs of his own Time: with reminiscences of the men and events of the revolution. Edited by J. S. Littell. Philadelphia, 1846. 8°

GRAYDON, William. An Abridgment of the Laws of the United States; or, a complete Digest of all such acts of Congress as concern the United States at large. To which is added an appendix, containing all existing Treaties, and the Ordinance for the government of the Territory northwest of the Ohio. Harrisburgh, 1803. 8vo.

2 Graydon's Forms of Conveyancing, and of Practice in the Courts and the offices of the various civil officers, magistrates, etc. A new edition, revised, corrected, enlarged, and adapted to the present state of the law, with explanatory notes and references, by R. E. Wright. Philadel. 1845. 8°

GRAYSON, Eldred. Overing; or, the Heir of Wycherly. A historical romance. New York, 1852. 8°

GREAT BRITAIN. Observations on several Acts of Parliament, passed in the 4th, 6th, and 7th years of his present majesty's reign; and also on the conduct of the officers of the customs since those acts were passed, etc. Published by the merchants of Boston. [Boston], 1769. 4°

2 Dissertations on the grand dispute between Great Britain and America. [By] (Amor Patriae.) [1773-74.] 8°

3 A candid Examination of the mutual Claims of Great Britain and the Colonies; with a plan of accommodation on constitutional principles. [By J. Galloway.] N. York, 1775. 8vo.

4 The Treaty [between Great Britain and the United States of America, at London, 19 Nov. 1794], its merits and demerits fairly discussed and displayed. [With a copy of the treaty, and an appendix.] [Boston! 1795.] 8°

5 An Appeal to the People on the causes and consequences of a war with Great Britain. Boston, 1811. 8°

6 Famous Men of Britain. Philadelphia [1850?] 16°

GREAT METROPOLIS; or Guide to New York for 1848. New York [1847]. 16°

GREAT WESTERN CANAL. Considerations on the Great Western Canal, from the Hudson to Lake Erie. Second edition. Published by order of the New York Corresponding Association for the promotion of internal improvements. Brooklyn, 1818. 8vo.

GREBO LANGUAGE. Brief Grammatical Analysis of the Grebo Language. [By John Payne.] Fair Hope Station, Cape Palmas, 1838. 8vo.

GREEK GRAMMARS. Remarks on Greek Grammars. [By John Pickering.] Boston, 1825. 8°

GREEK MYTHOLOGY. Epitome of Greek and Roman Mythology, with explanatory notes, and a vocabulary, by J. S. Hart. Latin. [An American edition of an elementary Latin text-book used in France.] Philadelphia, 1853. 12°

GREELEY, Horace. Hints towards Reforms in Lectures, Addresses, and other Writings. New York, 1850. 12°

2 Glances at Europe; in a series of Letters from Great Britain, France, Italy, Switzerland, etc. during the summer of 1851, including notices of the Great Exhibition, or World's Fair. New York, 1851. 12°

GREELEY, Horace, and Raymond,

HENRY J. Affociation discuffed; or, the Socialism of the Tribune examined: being a controversy between the New York Tribune and the Courier and .Enquirer. New York, 1847. 8°

GREEN, ASHBEL. Practical Sermons, extracted from the Christian Advocate. Philadelphia [1820?] 8°
2 DISCOURSES delivered in the College of New Jersey, addreffed chiefly to candidates for the first degree in the Arts; with notes and illustrations, including a historical sketch of the college. Trenton, 1822. 8°
3 LECTURES on the Shorter Catechism of the Presbyterian Church in the United States of America. Philadelphia, 1829. 8°
4 THE LIFE of Ashbel Green, .. begun to be written by himself in his eighty-second year, and continued to his eighty-fourth [by the editor]. Prepared for the prefs .. by J. H. Jones. [With an appendix.] New York, 1849. 8°

GREEN, HENRY W. Reports of Cases determined in the Court of Chancery of the State of New Jersey. Vol. 1. January 1838 to Oct. 1841. Elizabethtown, 1842. 8°

GREEN, HORACE. A treatise on Diseases of the Air Paffages; comprising an inquiry into the history, pathology, causes, and treatment of .. affections of the throat, etc. New York and London, 1846. 8°
2 OBSERVATIONS on the Pathology of Croup: with remarks on its treatment by topical medications. New York, 1848. 12mo.
3 ON the Surgical Treatment of Polypi of the larynx and œdema of the glottis. New York, 1852. 8°

GREEN, JACOB, A. M. Spiritual Inability. Sinners' faultinefs and spiritual inability considered, in a sermon [on Rom. ix. 19]. N. York, 1767. 8°

GREEN, JACOB, M. D. Astrono-mical Recreations; or, sketches of the relative position and mythological History of the Constellations. [With plates.] Philadelphia, 1824. 4to.
2 A MONOGRAPH of the Trilobites of North America. Philadel. 1832. 12mo.
3 A SUPPLEMENT to the Monograph of the Trilobites of North America. Philadelphia, 1835. 12mo.

GREEN, JOHN ORNE. The Factory System, in its hygienic relations. An addreff at the annual meeting of the Maffachusetts Medical Society. Boston, 1846. 8vo.

GREEN, JONATHAN H. An Exposure of the Arts and Miseries of Gambling .. Fourth edition, improved. Philadelphia, 1847. 12°

GREEN, RICHARD W. Green's new Arithmetic .. for schools and academies .. Fourth edition, enlarged and improved. Philadel. 1842. 12°

GREEN MOUNTAIN BOYS: a historical tale of the early settlement of Vermont. By the author of "May Martin; or, the Money-diggers." [Daniel P. Thompson.] 2 vol. Montpelier, 1839. 12°
2 THE GREEN Mountain Boys: a historical tale of the early settlement of Vermont. By the author of "May Martin; or, the Money-diggers," .. etc. [D. P. Thompson]. Revised edition. Boston, 1848. 12°

GREEN MOUNTAIN Repository; for .. 1832. Edited by Zadok Thompson. Burlington, 1832. 12°

GREENE, DAVID. Ministerial Fidelity Exemplified: a sermon [on John xvii. 4] at the funeral of the Rev. D. Crosby, etc. Boston, 1843. 8°
2 MEMOIR and Sermons of W. J. Armstrong, D.D. .. Edited by H. Read. New York, 1853. 12°

GREENE, GEORGE WASHINGTON. Historical Studies. New York, 1850. 12°

GREENE, NATHANIEL. An Address delivered at Faneuil Hall, Boston, Jan. 8, 1828 [in celebration of the anniversary of the battle of New Orleans. Ode .. for the occasion, *etc.*] Boston, 1828. 8°

GREENE, ROSCOE G. A Grammatical Text-book, in which the several moods are clearly illustrated by diagrams, *etc.* Boston, 1833. 12°

GREENE, SAMUEL S.   Greene's Analysis. A treatise on the structure of the English language ; or, the analysis and clasification of sentences and their component parts, *etc.* Philadelphia, 1848. 12mo.

2 GREENE's Analysis. A treatise on the structure of the English language, . . . adapted to the use of schools. Philadelphia, 1851. 12°

GREENHOW, ROBERT. Memoir, historical and political, on the North-West coast of America and the adjacent territories ; illustrated by a map and geographical view. New York, 1840. 8vo.

2 ANSWER to the Strictures of Mr. T. Falconer, on the history of Oregon and California. [Washington, 1845.] 8vo.

3 THE HISTORY of Oregon and California and the other territories on the North-West coast of North America ; accompanied by a geographical view and map of those countries. . . Third edition. New York, 1845. 8°

GREENLEAF, ABNER. An Address delivered before the Society of Asociated Mechanics and Manufacturers of . . New Hampshire, at . . . their anniversary, *etc.* Portsmouth, 1826. 8°

GREENLEAF, BENJAMIN. A Key to the National Arithmetic, *etc.* Boston, 1844. 12°

2 A KEY to the Introduction to the National Arithmetic, *etc.* Boston, 1845. 12°

3 GREENLEAF's Mental Arithmetic

.. upon the inductive plan ; for beginners. Boston, 1845. 12°

4 GREENLEAF's Introduction .. to the National Arithmetic, on the inductive system. Boston, 1845. 12°

5 GREENLEAF's Arithmetic, improved stereotype edition, *etc.* Boston, 1846. 12°

GREENLEAF, JONATHAN. Sketches of the Ecclesiastical History of the State of Maine, from the earliest settlement to the present time. Portsmouth, 1821. 12°

2 A SERMON [on 2 Tim. ii. 1] delivered .. Oct. 25, 1826, at the ordination of J. Jefferds, *etc.* Concord, 1827. 8°

3 GRAMMAR Simplified ; or, an ocular analysis of the English language. . Twentieth edition, corrected, enlarged, and improved by the author. New York, 1846. 4°

4 A HISTORY of the Churches of all denominations in the City of New York, from the first settlement to the year 1846. New York, 1846. 12°

GREENLEAF, MOSES. A Statistical View of the District of Maine, more especially with reference to the value and importance of its interior. Addresed to the consideration of the legislators of Masachusetts. Boston, 1816. 8°

2 A SURVEY of the State of Maine, in reference to its geographical features, statistics, and political economy. Portland, 1829. 8°

GREENLEAF, SIMON. A Brief Enquiry into the origin and principles of Freemasonry. Portland, 1820. 8°

2 REPORTS of Cases argued and determined in the Supreme Judicial Court of the State of Maine (1820-1832), 9 vol. Hallowell [and] Portland, 1822-35. 8°

3 A DISCOURSE pronounced at the inauguration of the author as Royall Profesor of Law in Harvard University, *etc.* Cambridge, 1834. 8°

4 A DIGEST of Greenleaf's Reports

of Cases argued and determined in the Supreme Judicial Court of the State of Maine, . . 1820-1832, inclusive. Portland, 1835. 8°

5 CATALOGUE of a Select Law Library. [By S. Greenleaf.] 1836. 8°

6 A COLLECTION of Cases overruled, denied, doubted, or limited in their application: taken from American and English reports. Third edition, revised and enlarged. New York, 1840. 8°

7 A TREATISE on the law of Evidence. Second edition (vol. 1 only, 2nd ed.). 2 vol. Boston, 1844-46. 8°

8 A DISCOURSE commemorative of the life and character of the Hon. J. Story, . . pronounced . . at the request of the Corporation of the University, etc. Boston, 1845. 8°

9 AN EXAMINATION of the Testimony of the Four Evangelists, etc. By S. Greenleaf. Boston, 1846. 8°

GREENWOOD, FRANCIS WILLIAM PITT. A Sermon [on Revelation xxi. 1] delivered at the ordination of the Rev. W. P. Lunt as pastor of the second Congregational Unitarian Society in the City of New York. (A charge by the Rev. N. L. Frothingham. The right hand of fellowship and address to the Society by the Rev. W. Ware.) New York, 1828. 8°

2 A HISTORY of King's Chapel, in Boston . . . comprising notices of the introduction of Episcopacy into the Northern Colonies. Bost. 1833. 8vo.

3 A SERMON on the death of J. Lowell, delivered in King's Chapel, Boston, March 22, 1840. 8°

4 SERMONS. [With a memoir of the author.] 2 vol. Bost. 1844. 12°

5 THE MISCELLANEOUS Writings of F. W. P. Greenwood. [Edited by F. W. G. i.e. Greenwood.] Boston, 1846. 12°

6 LIVES of the Twelve Apostles. To which is prefixed, a life of John the Baptist. Third edition. Boston, 1846. 12°

7 SERMONS of Consolation. Third edition. Boston, 1847. 8°

GREENWOOD, FRANCIS WILLIAM PITT, and EMERSON, G. B. The Classical Reader: a selection of lessons in prose and verse, from the most esteemed English and American writers. Boston, 1830. 12°

GREER, S. D. Mrs. Vindication of Friends ,(by one not a member,) from slanders contained in a book just published, entitled "Quakerism; or, the story of my life." By an Irish Lady (Mrs. Greer). Philadelphia, 1852. 8°

GREGG, ANDREW. Mr. Gregg's Motion [in the House of Representatives of the United States, relative to grants of land],Dec. 6,1805. [Washington, 1805.] 8°

2 MR. GREGG's Motion [in the House of Representatives of the United States] to suspend commercial intercourse with Great Britain and her dependencies, Jan. 29, 1806. Washington, 1806. 8°

GREGG, JARVIS. An Address delivered before the New Hampshire State Lyceum, . . at their second annual meeting, etc. Concord, 1834. 8°

GREGG, JOSIAH. Commerce of the Prairies; or, the journal of a Santa Fé trader, during eight expeditions across the great Western Prairies, and a residence of nearly nine years in Northern Mexico. 2 vol. New York, 1844. 12mo.

GREGG, W. P. and POND, BENJAMIN. The Railroad Laws and Charters of the United States, now for the first time collated, arranged in chronological order, and published with a synopsis and explanatory remarks. 2 vol. Boston, 1851. 8°

GREGG, WILLIAM. Essays on Domestic Industry; or, an enquiry into the expediency of establishing cotton manufactures in South Carolina. Originally published in the Charleston Courier, *etc.* Charleston, 1845. 8°

GREGOIRE, HENRI, *Count, Bishop of Blois.* National Convention. Report on the means of completing and distributing the national library. . . [Translated from an authentic original.] Philadelphia, 1794. 8°

2 AN ENQUIRY concerning the Intellectual and Moral Faculties, and Literature of Negroes; followed with an account of the life and works of fifteen Negroes and Mulattoes, distinguished in science, literature, and the arts. . . . Translated [from the French] by D. B. Warden. Brooklyn, 1810. 8°

GREGORY. My Grandfather Gregory. [A tale.] Revised by the Committee of Publication [of the American Sunday School Union]. Philadelphia, 1830. 12mo.

GREGORY, SAMUEL. Man Midwifery exposed and corrected, *etc.* Boston, 1848. 8vo.

GRENVILLE, A. S. Introduction to English Grammar. To which are added exercises in parsing, *etc.* Boston, 1822. 12°

GREPPO, J. G. HONORE. Essay on the Hieroglyphic System of M. Champollion, Jun. and on the advantages which it offers to Sacred Criticism. . . Translated from the French by Isaac Stuart, with notes and illustrations [and a preface, by M. Stuart]. Boston, 1830. 8vo.

GREY, LADY JANE, calling herself *Queen of England.* The Life and Death of Lady Jane Grey. Philadelphia [1835?]. 12mo.

GREYLOCK, GODFREY, *Pseud.* [*i. e.* J. E. A. Smith?]. Taghconic; or, letters and legends about our summer home. By G. Greylock. Boston, 1852. 12°

GRIDLEY, JOHN. History of Montpelier: a discourse delivered . . on thanksgiving day, Dec. 8, 1842. Montpelier, Vt. 1843. 8°

GRIFFEN, AUGUSTUS R. An Essay on the Botanical, Chemical, and Medical Properties of the Fucus Edulis of Linnæus, *etc.* N.York, 1816. 8vo.

GRIFFIN, EDWARD D. A Sermon [on 2 Chron. vi. 18] preached Jan. 10, 1810, at the dedication of the Church in Park Street, Boston. Boston, 1810. 8°

2 A SERMON [on Acts ix. 6] in which is attempted a full . . answer to the . . question, " What wilt Thou have me to do ?" . . Second edition. Boston, 1824. 12°

3 REMAINS of the Rev. E. D. Griffin. Compiled by F. Griffin; with a biographical memoir of the deceased, by J. Mc Vickar. 2 vol. New York, 1831. 8vo.

4 THE DOCTRINE of Divine Efficiency defended against certain modern speculations. New York, 1833. 12mo.

GRIFFITH, MATTIE. Poems. Now first collected. N.York,1853. 12°

GRIFFITH, THOMAS W. Sketches of the early History of Maryland. Baltimore, 1821. 8°

2 ANNALS of Baltimore. Baltimore, 1824. 8°

GRIFFITH, WILLIAM. A Treatise on the Jurisdiction and Proceedings of Justices of the Peace in Civil Suits, in New Jersey; with an appendix, *etc.* Third edition, revised, corrected, and considerably enlarged. Burlington, 1813. 8°

2 HISTORICAL Notes of the American Colonies and Revolution, from 1754 to 1775. Published by his executors. Burlington, 1843. 8°

GRIFFITHS, JOHN W. Marine and Naval Architecture, or the Science of Ship-Building, condensed into a single lecture, and delivered before the shipwrights of the city of New York. New York, 1844. 8°

GRIMES, J. STANLEY. Etherology and the Phreno-Philosophy of Mesmerism and Magic Eloquence; including a new philosophy of sleep, and of consciousnefs, with a review of the pretensions of phreno-magnetism, electro-biology, etc. .. Revised and edited by W. G. Le Duc. Boston [printed] and Cambridge, 1850. 12°

GRIMKE, ANGELINA E. Letters to C. H. Beecher, in reply to an Effay on Slavery and Åbolitionism; addreffed to A. E. Grimke: revised by the author. Boston, 1838. 12°

2 APPEAL to the Christian Women of the South. [On slavery.] [New York, 1840!] 8°

GRIMKE, FREDERICK. Considerations upon the Nature and Tendency of Free Institutions. Cincinnati, 1848. 8°

GRIMKE, THOMAS SMITH. Reflections on the character and objects of all Science and Literature, and on the relative excellence and value of religious and secular education, etc. New Haven, 1831. 12°

2 ADDRESS on the Truth, Dignity, Power, and Beauty of the Principles of Peace; and on the unchristian character and influence of war and the warrior: delivered .. at the request of the Connecticut Peace Society, etc. Hartford, 1832. 8°

3 A LETTER to the Hon. J. C. Calhoun, Vice-President of the United States, R. Y. Hayne, Senator, etc. [on the importance of the Union, etc.] Philadelphia, 1832. 8°

GRIMSHAW, WILLIAM. History of the United States, from their first settlement as Colonies, to the Ceffion of Florida in 1821, etc. Third edition. Philadelphia, 1822. 12mo.

2 QUESTIONS adapted to Grim-

shaw's History of England. Philadelphia, 1823. 12°

3 AN ETYMOLOGICAL Dictionary and Expositor of the English Language. .. Second edition, carefully revised and enlarged. Philadelphia, 1826. 12°

4 THE MERCHANT'S Law Book; being a treatise on the law of account render, attachment, bailment, bills of exchange, .. etc. Illustrated by many thousand judicial decisions, etc. Philadelphia, 1831. 12°

5 HISTORY of the United States from their first settlement as Colonies, to the period of the fifth census, in 1830. .. Accompanied by a book of questions and a key. Philadelphia, 1846. 12°

GRISCOM, JOHN. A Year in Europe. Comprising a journal of observations in England, Scotland, Ireland, France, Switzerland, the north of Italy, and Holland. 2 vol. New York, 1823. 8vo.

2 MONITORIAL Instruction: an addreff pronounced at the opening of the New York High School, with notes and illustrations. New York, 1825. 12°

GRISCOM, JOHN H. Animal Mechanism and Physiology; being a plain and familiar exposition of the structure and functions of the human system. New York, 1840. 12°

2 THE SANITARY Condition of the Labouring Population of New York; with suggestions for its improvement. A discourse .. delivered .. at the Repository of the American Institute. New York, 1845. 8°

GRISWOLD, ALEXANDER V. D.D. Discourses on the most important doctrines and duties of the Christian Religion. Philadelphia, 1830. 8vo.

2 A DISCOURSE on the Apostolic Office [on Matt. xxviii. 18, 20] delivered .. on occasion of the ordination of the Rev. J. C. Richmond. Philadelphia, 1835. 8vo.

3 A LETTER in answer to the Rev.
D. Perry's Short View and Defence
of the Ecclesiastical Rights of Man.
Hartford [1796]. 8°

GRISWOLD, ROGER. Speech . .
on the Bill for the Repeal of the Internal Taxes; delivered in the House
of Representatives of the United
States, . . March 18 [1802]. Philadelphia, 1802. 8°

GRISWOLD, RUFUS WILMOT.
Scenes in the Life of the Saviour; by
the poets and painters. Edited by R.
W. Griswold. Philadelphia [1845]. 8°

2 THE POETS and Poetry of England, in the nineteenth century. Second edition. Philadelphia, 1845. 8°

3 THE POETS and Poetry of America. With an historical introduction.
Seventh edition, revised. Philadelphia, 1846. 8°

4 THE PROSE Writers of America;
with a survey of the intellectual history, condition, and prospects of the
country. Second edition, revised.
Philadelphia, 1847. 8°

5 THE PROSE Writers of America;
with a survey of the intellectual history, condition, and prospects of the
country. . . Illustrated with portraits.
. . Fourth edition, revised. Philadelphia, 1851. 8°

GRISWOLD, STANLEY. The Good
Land we live in: a sermon [on Deut.
viii. 7-14] delivered . . on the celebration of the anniversary of American
Independence. Suffield, 1802. 8°

GROSS, S. D. A Practical Treatise on the Diseases and Injuries of
the Urinary Bladder, the Prostate
Gland, and the Urethra. Philadelphia, 1851. 8vo.

GRUND, FRANCIS J. Exercises
in Arithmetic. . . Accompanied by a
key for the use of the teacher. Boston, 1833. 12°

2 THE AMERICANS in their Moral,
Social, and Political Relations. From
the London edition. Boston, 1837. 12°

GRUNDY, FELIX. Speech . . on
the Tariff, . . Feb. 15, 1832, in the
Senate, . . on Mr. Clay's resolution.
Washington, 1832. 12°

GUERNSEY, EGBERT. Homœopathic Domestic Practice; containing
also, chapters on anatomy, physiology,
hygiene, and an abridged materia
medica. New York, 1853. 12mo.

GUETZLAFF, CARL FRIEDRICH
AUGUST. The Journal of two Voyages along the coast of China in 1831
and 1832; . . with notices of Siam,
Corea, and the Loo-Choo Islands, and
remarks on the policy, religion, etc.
of China. New York, 1833. 8vo.

GUILD, WILLIAM. New York and
the White Mountains; with a complete map, and numerous views, etc.
Boston, 1852. 12°

GUILLERMIN, GILBERT. Journal Historique de la Révolution de la
Partie de l'Est se Saint Domingue,
commencée le 10 Aout, 1808, avec
des notes statistiques sur cette partie.
Philadelphie, 1810. 8vo.

GUIREY, WILLIAM. The Pattern
in the Mount: the substance of a
sermon [on Hebrews viii. 5] . . on
the ordination of J. Lockhart. . . Second edition. Raleigh, printed; Philadelphia, reprinted, 1808. 8°

GUMMERE, JOHN. An Elementary Treatise on Astronomy. In two
parts. The first, containing a clear
and compendious view of the theory;
the second, a number of practical
problems. To which are added, solar,
lunar, and other astronomical tables.
Third edition, improved. Philadelphia, 1842. 8°

2 A TREATISE on Surveying; containing the theory and practice. To
which is prefixed a perspicuous system of plane trigonometry. . . Fourteenth edition, carefully revised, and
enlarged by the addition of articles on
the theodolite, levelling, and topography. Philadelphia, 1846. 8°

GUNN, ALEXANDER. Memoirs of the Rev. John H. Livingston. New York, 1829. 8°

GUNN, THOMAS B. Mose among the Britishers; or, the B'hoy in London. [A series of comic plates,] drawn and engraved by T. B. Gunn. Philadelphia, 1850. Obl. 8°

GUNNISON, J. W. The Mormons, or Latter Day Saints, in the Valley of the Great Salt Lake : a history of their rise and progreſs, peculiar doctrines, present condition and prospects. London [Philadelphia printed], 1852. 8vo.

GURLEY, RALPH RANDOLPH. Life of Jehudi Ashmun, late Colonial Agent in Liberia. With an appendix, containing extracts from his journal and other writings, with a brief sketch of the life of the Rev. Lott Cary. Washington, 1835. 8vo.

2 LIFE of Jehudi Ashmun, late Colonial Agent in Liberia. With an appendix, containing extracts from his journal and other writings, with a brief sketch of the life of the Rev. Lott Cary. New York, Boston, Washington [printed], 1835. 8vo.

3 ADDRESS at the annual meeting of the Pennsylvania Colonization Society, Nov. 11, 1839. Philadelphia, 1839. 8vo.

4 MISSION to England on behalf of the American Colonization Society. Washington, 1841. 12°

5 LIFE and Eloquence of the Rev. S. Larned. New York, 1844. 12°

GURNEY, DAVID. The Columbian Accidence ; or, a brief introduction to the English languuge. . . Second edition. Boston, 1818. 12°

GUY, WILLIAM AUGUSTUS. Principles of Medical Jurisprudence; with so much of anatomy, physiology, pathology, and the practice of medicine and surgery, as are eſſential to be known by lawyers, coroners, magistrates, etc. First American edition, edited by C. A. Lee. New York, 1845. 8°

ABERSHAM, R. W. Speech .. on the Tariff Bills; delivered in the House of Representatives, June 22, 1842. Washington, 1842. 8°

HACKETT, HORATIO B. A Commentary on the original text of the Acts of the Apostles. Bost. 1852. 8°

HACKLEY, CHARLES W. Elements of Trigonometry, plane and spherical. Adapted to the present state of analysis. To which is added, their application to the principles of navigation and nautical astronomy. With logarithmical, trigonometrical, and nautical tables. N. York, 1838. 8°

2 A TREATISE on Trigonometry, plane and spherical, with its application to navigation and surveying .. astronomy and geodesy, with . . . . . tables, etc. A new edition, with extensive .. improvements. New York, 1851. 8°

HADDOCK, CHARLES BRICKET. A Discourse delivered before the New England Society of . . . New York, Dec. 22, 1841. New York, 1842. 8°

2 ADDRESSES and Miscellaneous Writings. Cambridge, 1846. 8°

HAGEN, JOHN COLE. Footprints of Truth; or, voice of humanity [poems], by J. C. Hagen. With illustrations by F. A. Chapman, J. Cranch, and W. Wallcutt. N. York, 1853. 8°

HAGUE, WILLIAM. An Historical Discourse delivered at the celebration of the second centennial anniversary of the first Baptist Church, in Providence, Nov. 7, 1839. Boston, 1839. 12°

2 THE BAPTIST Church transplanted from the Old World to the New, etc. New York, 1846. 12°

HAINES, CHARLES G. Public Documents relating to the New York Canals, which are to connect the Western and Northern lakes with the Atlantic Ocean; with an introduction. Printed under the direction of the New York Corresponding Association for the promotion of internal improvements. New York, 1821. 8°

HALDEMAN, S. STEHMAN. A Monograph of the Limniades and other fresh water univalve shells of North America. N° 1-5. Philadelphia, 1840-42. 8vo.

2 HISTORY and Transformations of Corydalus Cornutus, by S. S. Haldeman. With a plate. Internal anatomy of Corydalus Cornutus, in its three stages of existence. By J. Leidy, .. with two plates. Extracted from the Journal of the American Academy of Arts and Sciences. Boston and Cambridge, 1848. 4to.

HALE, BENJAMIN, D.D. An Inaugural Address, delivered at Gardiner, .. Jan. 1, 1823 [at the opening of the Gardiner Lyceum]. Hallowell, 1823. 8°

2 A SERMON [on Rom. xiv. 16]

preached at the opening of the Convention of the Protestant Episcopal Church in .. New Hampshire, holden in .. Hopkinton, Sept. 8, *etc.* Concord, 1830. 8°

3 SCRIPTURAL Illustrations of the daily morning and evening service and litany of the Protestant Episcopal Church. Boston, 1835. 12mo.

HALE, EDWARD E. Letters on Irish Emigration. First published in the Boston Daily Advertiser. Boston, 1852. 8°

HALE, NATHAN. Memoir of Captain Nathan Hale. New Haven, 1844. 8vo.

HALE, SALMA. An Oration delivered at Keene, Feb. 22, 1832, being the centennial anniversary of the birthday of Washington. Keene, 1832. 8°

2 HISTORY of the United States, from their first settlement as Colonies to the close of the administration of Mr. Madison in 1817. New York, 1845. 12°

HALE, SARAH JOSEPHA, *Mrs.* Sketches of American Character. Boston, 1829. 12°

2 THE LADIES Wreath; a selection from the female poetic writers of England and America. With original notices and notes. . Second edition . . enlarged. Boston, 1839. 12°

3 KEEPING House and Housekeeping. A story of domestic life. New York, 1845. 12°

4 NORTHWOOD ; or, Life North and South. . . Second edition. New York [1852]. 12°

5 THE LADIES' New Book of Cookery . . . . with . . . . engravings. Third edition. N. York, 1852. 12°

6 WOMAN'S Record ; or, Sketches of all distinguished women from " the beginning" till A.D. 1850, arranged in four eras. With selections from female writers of every age. New York, 1853. 8°

7 LIBERIA ; or, M. Peyton's Ex-

periments. Edited by S. J. Hale. London, New York [printed], 1854. 12mo.

HALES, JOHN G. A Survey of Boston and its Vicinity ; .. together with a short topographical sketch of the country, *etc.* Boston, 1821. 12°

HALL, A. OAKEY. The Manhattaner in New Orleans ; or, Phases of " Crescent City" Life. New York [and] New Orleans, 1851. 12°

HALL, AARON. A Sermon [on 2 Chron. xix. 6] preached June 2, 1803, before . . . the Governor, . . Council, *etc.* of . . . New Hampshire. Concord, 1803. 8°

HALL, BAYNARD R. Teaching, a science ; the teacher, an artist. New York, 1848. 12°

2 FRANK Freeman's Barber Shop. A tale. Illustrated by Rush B. Hall. New York, 1852. 12°

HALL, BENJAMIN F. The Landowner's Manual ; containing a summary of Statute regulations, in New York, Ohio, Indiana, Illinois, Michigan, Iowa, and Wisconsin, concerning land-titles, deeds, mortgages, wills of real estate. . . With an appendix, containing the constitutions of the said states. Auburn, 1847. 12°

HALL, EDWARD BROOKS. Memoir of M. L. Ware. Third thousand. Boston, 1853. 12°

HALL, EDWIN. An Exposition of the Law of Baptism, as it regards the mode and the subjects. Third edition, revised and enlarged. New York, 1846. 12°

2 THE PURITANS and their principles. Second edition. New York, 1846. 8°

HALL, FANNY W. Rambles in Europe ; or, a tour through France, Italy, Switzerland, Great Britain, and Ireland in 1836. 2 vol. New York, 1839. 12mo.

HALL, FREDERICK, *M.D.* An Oration on the importance of cultivating the Sciences; delivered at Dartmouth College, before the New Hampshire Alpha of the Phi Beta Kappa, *etc.* Baltimore, 1828. 8°

2 LETTERS from the East and from the West [on various subjects, including a series on the geology and mineralogy of the valley of the Connecticut river]. [Washing. 1840.] 8°

HALL, HILAND. Remarks . . . . made in the House of Representatives, May 5, 1834, on presenting a memorial from Windham County, Vermont, on the . . . removal of the public deposites. Washing. 1834. 8°

2 SPEECH . . . on the fortification Bill; delivered in the House of Representatives, May 24, 1836. [Washington, 1836.] 8°

3 SPEECHES . . . on the Virginia bounty land claims, delivered in the House of Representatives . . June . . 1842. Washington, 1842. 8°

HALL, JAMES, *Geologist of the State of New York.* On the Geological position of the Castoroides Ohioensis. Also, a description of the cranium of the same, by J. Wyman. [From the Boston Journal of Natural History.] Boston, 1846. 4to.

HALL, JAMES. The Harpe's Head; a legend of Kentucky. Philadelphia, 1833. 12°

2 LEGENDS of the West. Second edition. Philadelphia, 1833. 12°

3 SKETCHES of history, life, and manners in the West. Philadelphia, 1835. 12mo.

4 STATISTICS of the West, at the close of the year 1836. Cincinnati, 1836. 12mo.

5 THE WILDERNESS and the War Path. London [New York printed], 1846. 8vo.

6 THE WEST; its soil, surface, and productions. Cincinnati, 1848. 12°

HALL, MRS. JAMES. Phantasia, and other poems. N. York, 1849. 4°

HALL, JOHN. On the Education of Children, while under the care of parents or guardians. Second edition. Hartford, 1836. 12°

HALL, JOHN E. The Practice and Jurisdiction of the Court of Admiralty; in three parts: 1. An historical examination of the civil jurisdiction of the Court of Admiralty; 2. A translation of Clerke's Praxis. . . 3. A collection of precedents. Baltimore, 1809. 8°

HALL, JONATHAN PRESCOTT. Reports of Cases argued and determined in the Superior Court of the City of New York [from Aug. term, 1828 to Dec. term, 1829]. 2 vol. New York, 1831-33. 8°

HALL, JOSEPH. An Oration, pronounced July 4, 1800, at . . Boston, in commemoration of the anniversary of American Independence. Boston [1800]. 8°

HALL, JOSEPH SPARKES. The Book of the Feet: a history of boots and shoes, with illustrations. From the second London edition; with a history of boots and shoes in the United States, biographical sketches of eminent shoemakers, and Crispin anecdotes. New York, 1847. 12°

HALL, RICHARD WILMOTT. An Essay on the use of Electricity in Medicine. Philadelphia, 1806. 8vo.

HALL, S. R. The Grammatical Assistant. . . Second edition, revised and enlarged. Springfield, 1833. 12°

2 HALL'S Arithmetic, *etc.* Andover, 1836. 12°

HALL, S. R. and BAKER, A. R. School History of the United States; containing maps, a chronological chart, and an outline of topics for a more extensive course of study. Andover, 1839. 12°

HALL, W. W. Bronchitis and kindred Diseases, in language adapted to common readers. Second edition. New York, 1852. 8vo.

HALL, WILLARD. A Defence of the American Sunday School Union against the charges of its opponents, etc. Philadelphia, 1828. 8°

HALL, WILLIAM W. An Appeal to the Bar and the "Freemen of Maryland," for the refusal of Baltimore City Court to grant a rule requiring R. N. Allen , . to show cause why an information .. should not be exhibited against him for usurping the office of Commissioner of Insolvent Debtors, etc. Baltim. 1823. 12°

HALLECK, FITZ-GREENE. Selections from the British Poets. 2 vol. New York, 1845-43. 12°

2 THE POETICAL Works of F. Halleck, now first collected. New York, 1847. 8°

HALLECK, H. WAGER. Elements of Military Art and Science; or, course of instruction in strategy, fortification, tactics of battles, etc. N.York[and]Philadelphia, 1846. 12°

HALSEY, LEROY, J. Address to the Alumni Society of the University of Nashville on the Study of Theology. .. With an appendix, containing a catalogue of the Alumni, and certain proceedings of the society. Nashville, 1841. 8°

HALSTED, H. M.D. Exposition of Motorpathy: a new system of curing disease by statuminating, vitalizing motion. Rochester, 1853. 12mo.

HALSTED, WILLIAM, the younger. Report of Cases argued and determined in the Supreme Court of Judicature of the State of New Jersey [from Nov. term, 1821, to Sept. term, 1831]. 7 vol. [vol. 7, wanting]. Trenton, 1823-32. 8°

HAMBDEN, Pseud. First Reflections on reading the President's Message to Congress of Dec. 7,

1830. By "Hambden." Published originally in the National Intelligencer. Washington, 1831. 8°

HAMER, THOMAS L. Speech .. in the House of Representatives, March 2, 1837, on the bill making appropriations for the civil and diplomatic expenses of the government for the year 1837, etc. [Washington, 1837.] 8°

HAMERSLEY, ANDREW. A Dissertation on the remote and proximate causes of Phthisis Pulmonalis. With notes. New York, 1827. 12mo.

HAMILTON, Pseud. "Look before you leap." Addresses to the Citizens of the Southern States : being a solemn warning against a separation of the Union, advocated in the late message of .. G. McDuffie, governor of South Carolina, etc. Second edition, improved. By the author of "The Olive Branch," [signed "Hamilton"]. Philadelphia, 1835. 8°

HAMILTON, ALEXANDER. Letter from A. Hamilton concerning the public conduct and character of J. Adams, President of the United States. New York, 1800. 8vo.

2 LETTER from A. Hamilton, concerning the public conduct and character of J. Adams, Esq. etc. New York, printed ; Philadel. re-printed, 1800. 8°

3 A COLLECTION of Facts and Documents relative to the Death of Major-General A. Hamilton ; with comments, etc. By the editor of the Evening Post. New York, 1804. 8°

4 LETTER from A. Hamilton concerning the public conduct and character of J. Adams, Esq. President of the United States, written in .. 1800. New edition, with a preface. Boston, 1809. 8°

4 THE WORKS of A. Hamilton. 3 vol. New York, 1810. 12mo.

5 THE SOUNDNESS of the policy of protecting Domestic Manufactures,

fully established by A. Hamilton in his Report to Congreſs, and by T. Jefferson, in his Letter to B. Austin. Philadelphia, 1817. 8°

6 A. HAMILTON's Report on .. Manufactures, made in .. Dec. 1791. Sixth edition. To which are prefixed two prefaces by the editor, (M. C.) Philadelphia, 1827. 8°

7 THE OFFICIAL and other Papers of the late Major-General A. Hamilton, compiled chiefly from the originals in the poſſeſſion of Mrs. Hamilton. [By F. L. Hawks.] Vol. 1. New York, 1842. 8°

8 THE WORKS of A. Hamilton; comprising his correspondence, and his political and official writings, exclusive of the Federalist, civil and military. Published from the original manuscripts. Edited by J. C. Hamilton. 7 vol. N. York, 1851. 8°

HAMILTON, JAMES. The substance of General Hamilton's Remarks, delivered May 31, 1838, in the Senate of South Carolina, on the resolution of the House of Representatives respecting the sub-treasury. [Charleston, 1838.] 8°

HAMILTON, LUTHER. Worship God: a sermon [on Rev. xxii. 9], etc. Boston, 1830. 8°

HAMILTON, SCHUYLER. History of the National Flag of the United States of America. Phil. 1852. 8°

HAMILTON, WILLIAM. An Oration delivered in the African Zion Church, .. in commemoration of the abolition of domestic slavery in this state. New York, 1827. 8°

HAMILTON, WILLIAM T. The "Friend of Moses;" or, a defence of the Pentateuch as the production of Moses, and an inspired document, against the objections of modern scepticism. New York, 1852. 8°

HAMILTON COLLEGE, CLINTON, New York. Catalogus senatus

academici, et eorum qui munera et officia academica geſſerunt, quique aliquo gradu exornati fuerunt, in Collegio Hamiltonensi, etc. Romæ, 1840. 8°

HAMILTON Literary and Theological Institution. Catalogue of Officers and Students for 1839-40 (1840-41). 2 pts. [Hamilton, 1839-40.] 8°

HAMLIN, L. F. English Grammar in lectures, etc. Boston, New York, and Philadelphia, 1832. 12°

HAMMOND, ELISHA. A Treatise on the law of fire insurance and insurance on inland waters. 2 parts. New York, 1840. 8°

2 A PRACTICAL Treatise, or an abridgment of the law appertaining to the office of Justice of the Peace; and also relating to the practice in justices' courts, in civil and criminal matters, with appropriate forms of practice. In 3 parts. West Brookfield, 1841. 8°

HAMMOND, JAMES H. Governor Hammond's Letters on Southern Slavery: addreſſed to Thomas Clarkson, the English abolitionist. Charleston, 1845. 8°

HAMMOND, J. W. A tabular View of the Financial Affairs of Pennsylvania, from the commencement of her public works to the present time; in which are included the cost, revenue, and expenditures of the .. canals, .. railroads, etc. .. Prepared from the official records. Philadel. 1844. 8vo.

HAMMOND, JABEZ D. The History of Political Parties in the State of New York, from the ratification of the federal constitution to Dec. 1840. 2 vol. Albany, 1842. 8°

HAMMOND, M. C. M. An Oration on the duties and requirements of an American Officer, delivered before the Dialectic Society of the

United States Military Academy at West Point, June 5, 1852. New York, 1852. 8°

HANCOCK, JOHN. An Oration .. to commemorate the bloody Tragedy of the fifth of March, 1770. Boston, 1774. 4°

HANCOCK, JOHN, *M. A.* The Prophet Jeremiah's Resolution to get him unto great Men, and to speak unto them, considered and applied: in a Sermon [on Jer. v. 5], *etc.* Boston, 1734. 8°

HANDY, WILLIAM W. Speech .. delivered in the House of Delegates of Maryland, April 4, 1839, in the debate on the proposition to release the private stockholders from paying up their stock to the Eastern Shore Railroad Company. Baltimore, 1839. 8°

HANNA, WILLIAM. Life of T. Chalmers, D. D., LL. D. Edited by Rev. J. C. Moffat, M. A. *etc.* [Being an abstract of Hanna's Memoirs of Chalmers.] Cincinnati, 1853. 12°

HANNAH, the Mother of Samuel the Prophet and Judge of Israel. A sacred drama [in five acts, and in verse]. Boston, 1839. 8vo.

HANNEGAN, EDWARD A. Speech .. on the Oregon question; delivered in the Senate, .. Feb. 16, 1846. Washington, 1846. 8°

HANNIBAL, JULIUS CÆSAR, *Pseud.* Professor J. C. Hannibal's Scientific Discourses; originally published in the New York Picayune. New York, 1852. 8°

HANNING, JOHN. Lecture on Theology, History, and Moral Philosophy, *etc.* [a sermon, on Acts xxv. 22]. Lancaster, Pa. 1835. 12°

HAOLE. Sandwich Island Notes By a Haolé [A. Liholiho]. London [New York printed], 1854. 12mo.

HARBAUGH, H. Heaven: or,

an earnest and scriptural inquiry into the abode of the sainted dead. .. Second edition, revised and improved. Philadelphia, 1851. 12°
2 THE HEAVENLY Recognition; or, an earnest .. discussion of the question, Will we meet our friends in Heaven? .. Second edition. Philadelphia, 1852. 12°

HARDENBERG, FRIEDRICH LUDWIG VON, *Baron.* Henry of Ofterdingen. A romance from the German of Novalis (F. von Hardenberg). Cambridge, 1842. 12°

HARDIE, JAMES, *A. M.* The American Remembrancer, or Universal Tablet of Memory. Philadelphia, 1795. 12°
2 THE NEW Universal Biographical Dictionary and American Remembrancer of Departed Merit. 4 vol. New York, 1805. 8vo.
3 THE DESCRIPTION of the City of New York, *etc.* New York, 1827. 12°

HARDING, BENJAMIN. A Tour through the Western Country; .. published for the use of emigrants. New London, 1819. 8°
2 SPEECH .. on Mr. Adams's Resolutions, concerning the loss of the Fortification Bill of the last Session; delivered in the House of Representatives, Jan. 28, 1836. Washington, 1836. 8°

HARE, G. EMLEN. Christ to Return; a practical exposition of the prophecy recorded in the 24th and 25th chapters of .. St. Matthew. With a preface, by .. L. S. Ives. Philadelphia, 1840. 12°

HARE, J. I. CLARK, AND WALLACE, HORACE B. American Leading Cases: being select decisions of American courts in several departments of law; with especial reference to mercantile law. With notes by J. I. C. Hare, and H. B. Wallace. Second edition, with additional cases and notes. 2 vol. Philadelphia, 1851. 8°

HARE, Joseph T. The Life and Adventures of J. T. Hare, the bold Robber and Highwayman; with sixteen .. engravings. [By the author of the Life of J. A. Murrell.] New York, [1850?] 8°

HARE, Robert. Memoir on the Supply and Application of the Blow-Pipe; illustrated by engravings. Philadelphia, 1802. 8vo.

2 A New Theory of Galvanism. Philadelphia, 1819. 8vo.

3 A Brief Exposition of the Science of Mechanical Electricity, or Electricity proper; subsidiary to the course of chemical instruction in the University of Pennsylvania, etc. Philadelphia, 1840. 8°

4 A Compendium of the Course of Chemical Instruction in the Medical Department of the University of Pennsylvania. 2 parts. Fourth edition, with amendments and additions. Philadelphia, 1840-43. 8°

5 An Effort to refute the Arguments advanced in favour of the Existence in the Amphide Salts, of radicals, consisting, like Cyanogen, of more than one element. Philadelphia, 1842. 8°

6 Lecture, introductory to a course on Chemistry, in the University of Pennsylvania, delivered Nov. 7, 1843. Philadelphia, 1843. 8°

7 Of the Conclusion arrived at by a Committee of the Academy of Sciences of France, agreeably to which tornados are caused by heat; while agreeably to Peltier's Report to the same body, certain insurers had been obliged to pay for a tornado as an electrical storm; also abstracts from Peltier's Report; moreover, quotations showing the ignorance which existed in the Academy respecting .. the meteor in question; .. with objections to the opinions of Peltier and Espy. Second edition, revised. Philadelphia, 1852. 8°

HARLAN, J. A Memoir of India and Avghanistaun; with observations on the present exciting and critical state and future prospects of those countries, etc. Philadelphia, 1842. 12°

HARLAN, Richard. Fauna Americana: being a description of the mammiferous animals inhabiting North America. Philadelphia, 1825. 8vo.

2 Medical and Physical Researches: or original memoirs in medicine, surgery, physiology, geology, zoology, and comparative anatomy .. with plates. Philadelphia, 1835. 8vo.

HARPER and Brothers. Harper's Illustrated Catalogue of valuable Standard Works, in the several departments of general literature. New York, 1847. 8vo.

2 Harper's New Monthly Magazine, 1850-56. 13 vol. New York, 1850-56. 8°

3 Harper's New York and Erie Railroad Guide Book .. with one hundred and thirty-six engravings .. from original sketches made expressly for this work, by W. MacLeod. New York [1851]. 12°

HARPER, Robert Goodloe. Observations on the Dispute between the United States and France. Philadelphia, 1797. 8vo.

2 Mr. Harper's Speech on the Foreign Intercourse Bill; in reply to Mr. Nicholas and Mr. Gallatin; delivered in .. the House of Representatives of the United States, .. March 2, 1798. Washing. 1798. 8°

3 Observation on the Dispute between the United States and France, by R. G. Harper. .. Fourth American edition. To which is annexed, his Speech, in Congress, on the Foreign Intercourse Bill, .. delivered March 2, 1798. Boston, April 1798. 8°

4 Speech of R. G. Harper, Esq. at the celebration of the recent triumphs of the cause of mankind, in Germany, delivered at Annapolis, Maryland, Jan. 20, 1814. New Haven, 1814. 8°

5 Gen. Harper's Speech to the

citizens of Baltimore on the expediency of promoting a connexion between the Ohio, at Pittsburgh, and the Waters of the Chesapeake at Baltimore, by a canal through the District of Columbia; with his reply to some of the objections of Mr. Winchester: delivered . . Dec. 20, 1823. Baltimore, 1824. 8°

HARPER, WILLIAM. The South Carolina Society for the Advancement of Learning. Publication N° 2. Dec. 1836. Anniversary oration, delivered by W. Harper. Washington, 1836. 8°

HARRIET and her Scholars; a Sabbath-school story. Philadelphia, 1828. 12mo.

HARRINGTON, HENRY F. The Moral Influence of the American Government: an oration, delivered at Albany. . . before the Young Men's Association. Albany, 1846. 8°

HARRINGTON, SAMUEL M. Reports of Cases argued and adjudged in the Superior Court of Errors, and Appeals of the State of Delaware from the organization of those courts under the amended constitution; with references to some of the earlier cases. (To which are added, Select Cases from the Courts of Oyer and Terminer, etc. 3 vol. Dover (Delaware), 1837-1844. 8°

HARRIS, Judge. The Manor of Renſselaerwyck. Opinion of Judge Harris, in the case of the People against W. P. Van Renſselaer and others. Albany, 1852. 8vo.

HARRIS, CHAPIN A. The Principles and Practice of Dental Surgery. Second edition, revised, modified, and greatly enlarged. Philadelphia, 1845. Roy. 8vo.
2 THE PRINCIPLES and Practice of Dental Surgery. . . Fourth edition, revised, modified, and greatly enlarged. Philadelphia, 1850. 8vo.
3 A DICTIONARY of Dental Science,

Biography, Bibliography, and Medical Terminology. Philadel. 1849. 8vo.

HARRIS, THADDEUS MASON. The Journal of a Tour into the Territory North-west of the Alleghany Mountains, made in the . . year 1803: with a geographical and historical account of the State of Ohio. Illustrated with original maps and views. Boston, 1805. 8°
2 A DISCOURSE [on Josh. i. 2] delivered . . at the funeral of M. Everett, etc. Boston, 1813. 8°
3 A SERMON [on Isaiah lii. 7] at the ordination of . . L. Capen, etc. Boston, 1815. 8°
4 MEMORIALS of the First Church in Dorchester, from its settlement in New England, to the end of the second century: in two discourses [on Psalm lxxvii. 5, and lxxviii. 1-7], etc. Boston, 1830. 8°
5 BIOGRAPHICAL Memorials of James Oglethorpe, founder of the Colony of Georgia. Bost. 1841. 8vo.

HARRIS, THADDEUS WILLIAM. Remarks upon the North American Insects belonging to the genus Cychrus of Fabricius, with descriptions of some newly detected species. Cambridge [Boston printed], 1839. 8vo.

HARRIS, THOMAS. The Life and Services of Commodore William Bainbridge, United States Navy. Philadelphia, 1837. 8vo.

HARRIS, THOMAS, AND GILL, RICHARD W. Reports of Cases argued and determined in the Court of Appeals of Maryland, in 1826 . . [to 1829, inclusive]. 2 vol. Annapolis, 1828, 29. 8°

HARRIS, THOMAS, AND JOHNSON, REVERDY. Reports of Cases argued and determined in the General Court, and the Court of Appeals, of the State of Maryland. 1800-1826. 7 vol. Annapolis, 1821-27. 8°

HARRIS, THOMAS, AND MACHENRY, JOHN. Maryland Reports, being a series of the most important law cases, argued and determined in the Provincial Court and Court of Appeals of the then Province of Maryland, from the year 1700 down to the American Revolution. [Continued to 1799.] Selected from the records of the State and from notes of .. Counsel, *etc.* 4 vol. New York, 1809-40. 8°

HARRISON, EDMUND. President's Reply of the Branch Bank at Mobile, to the Resolution of the House of Representatives, of the 7th inst. [with other papers relative to the bank]. [Tuscaloosa, 1843.] 8°

HARRISON, EDMUND, AND OTHERS. Report of the Commissioners appointed to examine the bank of Mobile. Tuscaloosa, 1844. 8°

HARRISON, ELIAS. A Funeral Discourse [on 1 Sam. xxv. 1] delivered .. on the occasion of the death of .. J. Muir, *etc.* Alexandria, 1820. 8°

HARRISON, H. Hydraulicus; or, improvement of the Missisippi; offering a plan for the reduction of its overflow, and of that of its alluvial tributary streams, *etc.* Cincinnati, 1828. 12°

HARRISON, JOHN. An Essay towards a correct theory of the Nervous System. Philadelphia, 1844. Roy. 8vo.

HARRISON, JOSIAH. Reports of Cases decided in the Supreme Court of Judicature of the State of New Jersey, from February term, 1837, to November term, 1838, inclusive. [Continued to September term, 1842.] 4 vol. Camden, 1839-43. 8°

HARRISON, WILLIAM HENRY, *President.* The People's Presidential Candidate; or the life of W. H. Harrison, of Ohio. [By Caleb Cushing.] Boston, 1839. 12°

2 THE NORTHERN Man with Sou-

thern Principles, and the Southern Man with American Principles: or, a view of the comparative claims of .. W. H. Harrison, and M. Van Buren, candidates for the presidency, to the support of citizens of the Southern States. Washington, 1840. 8°

3 HARRISON Melodies, original and selected. Published under the direction of the Boston Harrison Club. Boston, 1840. 12°

4 THE LIFE of Major General W. H. Harrison: comprising a brief account of his important civil and military services, and an accurate description of the Council at Vincennes with Tecumseh, *etc.* Philadelphia, 1840. 8°

5 GENERAL HARRISON in Congress; [a pamphlet advocating his election to the presidency.] Washington, 1840. 8°

HARRISS, JULIA MILDRED. Wild Shrubs of Alabama; or, rhapsodies of restless hours. New York, 1852. 8°

HARRO-HARRING, PAUL. Harro-Harring's Werke. Auswuhl lezter hand. Band, 1, 2. New York, 1844-46. 8vo.

2 DOLORES. A novel of South America. New York, 1846. 8vo.

HARSHA, DAVID A. The Principles of Hydropathy; or, the invalid's guide to health and happiness, *etc.* Albany, 1852. 8°

HARSHA, JOHN W. The Nature, Effects, and Pardon of Sin. To which is added, a warning and exhortation to sinners. N. York [Albany printed], 1853. 12°

HART, ADOLPHUS M. History of the Valley of the Missisippi. Cincinnati, 1853. 12°

HART, JOHN S. The Female Prose Writers of America. With portraits, biographical notices, and specimens of their writings, *etc.* Philadelphia, 1852. 8°

HART, Levi. A Christian Minister described, .. in a discourse [on] Gal. i. 10, at the ordination of .. A. Holmes [to the pastoral care of the Church at Midway], Sept. 15, 1785; [with his pastoral letter. The charge by .. E. Williams; the right hand of fellowship by .. W. Williams]. New Haven, 1787. 8°

HARTFORD, *Connecticut*. Friends of Education in Greece. School at Athens. [A circular inviting subscriptions.] [Hartf. 1832.] s. sh. 4°

2 THE NINETEENTH Annual Report of the Officers of the Retreat for the Insane, Hartford. Hartf. 1843. 8vo.

HARTFORD CONVENTION. The Proceedings of a Convention of Delegates from the States of Massachusetts, Connecticut, and Rhode Island; the counties of Cheshire and Grafton, in the State of New Hampshire, and the county of Windham, in the State of Vermont; convened at Hartford, in the State of Connecticut, Dec. 15, 1814. Third edition, corrected and improved. Boston, 1815. 8°

2 PUBLIC Documents; containing proceedings of the Hartford Convention..; report of the Commissioners while at Washington; letters from Massachusett members in Congress; letters from the Governor of Pennsylvania; report and resolutions of Pennsylvania State; letter of Governor of New Jersey, inclosing sundry papers. Published by order of the Senate. [Boston] 1815. 8°

3 LETTERS developing the Character and Views of the Hartford Convention. By "One of the Convention." First published in the National Intelligencer, in Jan. 1820. Washington, 1820. 12°

HARTFORD DIRECTORY. Gardner's Hartford City Directory. Published annually. N° 1-4, 1838-1841. [Continued as] Geer's Hartford City Directory. N° 5-9, 1842-1846. Hartford, 1838-46. 12°

HARTLEY, ROBERT M. An historical, scientific, and practical Essay on Milk, as an article of human sustenance, *etc.* New York, 1842. 12°

HARTMANN, FRANZ. Practical Observations on some of the chief Homœopathic remedies. Translated from the German, with notes, by A. Howard Okie. 2 parts. Philadelphia, 1841-46. 12mo.

HARVARD UNIVERSITY, CAMBRIDGE, *Massachusetts*. The Testimony of the President, Professors, Tutors, and Hebrew Instructor of Harvard College, in Cambridge, against the Rev. Mr. G. Whitefield and his conduct. Boston, 1744. 8°

2 PIETAS et Gratulatio Collegii Cantabrigiensis apud Novanglos. [A collection of English and Latin verses on the accession of George III.] Bostoni, 1761. 4to.

3 CATALOGUS eorum qui in Collegio Harvardino, .. ab anno 1642, ad annum 1776 [continued to 1848], alicujus gradus laurea donati sunt. (Catalogus senatus academici, eorum, qui munera et officia gesserunt, quique alicujus gradus laurea donati sunt in Universitate Harvardiana, *etc.*) [Triennial: 1776 (1779 *wanting*) 1782-1848.] 24 parts. Bostoniæ et Cantabrigiæ, 1776-1848. 8°

4 [*Begins*] ILLUSTRISSIMO Johanni Hancock, .. Gubernatori, *etc.* [Theses for the public examination, 1788, 1789, 1792.] Bostoniæ [1788-92]. s. sh. fol°

5 LAWS of Harvard College. Boston, 1790. 8vo.

6 THE FOUNDATION of the Massachusetts Professorship of Natural History, at Harvard College, in Cambridge. Boston, 1805. 8vo.

7 THE STATUTES of the University in Cambridge relating to the degree of Doctor in Medicine. Bost.1817. 8°

8 LAWS of Harvard College. Cambridge, 1820. 8°

9 COURSE of Instruction for Undergraduates in Harvard College, Oct.

1821, for the ensuing year. [Cambridge, 1821.] 8°

10 CATALOGUE [annual] of the Officers and Students of the University in Cambridge, October, 1821 (1833-34; 1836-37 to 1847-48). 14 pts. Cambridge, 1821-48. 8°

11 REPORT upon the constitutional rights and privileges of Harvard College; and upon the donations that have been made to it by this Commonwealth. [Boston,] 1821. 8°

12 REPORT of a Committee of the Overseers of Harvard College on the memorial of the resident Instructors. [Cambridge,] 1825. 8° .

13 [Begins] Treasurer's Report, etc. [A collection of the annual reports and statements of the treasurer, from 1831 to 1842, inclusive.] 12 parts. [Cambridge, 1831-42.] 8vo.

14 SIXTH (seventh, eighth, ninth, tenth, eleventh, twelfth, thirteenth, fourteenth, fifteenth, sixteenth, seventeenth, nineteenth, twentieth) Report of the President of Harvard University (J. Quincy) to the Overseers, etc. Cambridge, 1832-46. 8°

15 PROCEEDINGS of the Overseers of Harvard University, the report accepted, and the resolutions adopted by them, .. Aug. 25, 1834, relative to the late disturbances in that seminary. Boston [1834]. 8°

16 PROCEEDINGS of the Overseers of Harvard University, the report accepted, and the resolutions adopted, .. Aug. 25, 1834, relative to the late disturbances in that seminary. Boston [1834]. 8°

17 CONSTITUTIONAL Articles and Legislative Enactments relative to the Board of Overseers and the Corporation of Harvard University; also, rules and regulations of the Overseers. Cambridge, 1835. 8°

18 A CATALOGUE of the Students of Law in Harvard University, from the establishment of the law school, 1836 (1839, 1842, 1845). 4 vol. Cambridge, 1836-45. 12°

19 ARRANGEMENT of Lectures and

Recitations in Harvard University for the second term of the academic year, 1838-9; 1840-41. Cambridge, 1839-40. 8°

20 THE REPORT of the Committee to whom was referred the report and resolutions of the President and Fellows of Harvard University, respecting the introduction of the voluntary system in the studies of the mathematics, Latin, and Greek. Cambridge, 1841. 8°

21 BYE-LAWS, Rules, and Regulations of the Overseers of Harvard University, now in force. Cambridge, 1842. 8°

22 ANNUAL Circular of the Massachusetts Medical College, with a history of the medical department of Harvard University, a catalogue of graduates, etc. Boston, 1846. 8°

23 LIBRARY of Harvard University. See CATALOGUES, N° 2, 21, 22, 25.

HARVEST. Philadelphia [1832]. 12mo.

HARVEY, H. Memoir of A. Bennett, first Pastor of the Baptist Church, Homer, New York .. Third edition. New York, 1852. 12mo.

HARVEY, JOSEPH. A Sermon [on Rev. xi. 15] preached .. before the Foreign Mission Society of Litchfield County. New Haven, 1815. 8°

HARWARD. The Fulness of Joy in the Presence of God; being the substance of a discourse preached lately in the Royal Chappel at Boston [on Psal. xvi. 11], etc. Boston, 1732. 8°

HARWOOD, EDWIN. A Contribution to the Church Question. An essay read before the Associate Alumni of the General Theological Seminary. New York, 1851. 8°

HASKEL, DANIEL. A Sermon [on Mark xvi. 15] delivered .. at the annual meeting of the Vermont Juvenile Missionary Society, etc. Middlebury, 1819. 8°

HASKEL, Daniel, and SMITH, J. Calvin. A complete descriptive and statistical Gazetteer of the United States of America; with an abstract of the census and statistics for 1840. New York, 1844. 8vo.

HASKINS, Roswell W. From the American Journal of Science and Arts . . Examination of the theory of a resisting medium, in which it is assumed that the planets and comets of our system are moved. [Buffalo ? 1840 ?] 8°

2 Astronomy for Schools; upon the basis of Mons. Arago's lectures at the Royal Observatory of Paris, and in which the leading truths of that science are clearly illustrated without mathematical demonstrations. New York, 1841. 12°

3 New England and the West: [their geology, agriculture, manufactures, etc.] Reprinted from the Boston Atlas. Buffalo, 1843. 8°

HASSLER, Ferdinand R. Elements of Arithmetic, theoretical and practical, etc. New York, 1826. 12°

2 Logarithmische und Trigonometrische Tafeln zu sieben dezimal Stellen . . . . . worin die . . Fehler voriger Tafeln verbeßert sind . . In stereotypen. Neu-York, 1830. 12mo.

3 Comparison of Weights and Measures of length and capacity, reported to the Senate of the United States, by the Treasury department, in 1832. Washington, 1832. 8vo.

4 Documents relating to the construction of Standards of Weights and Measures for the Custom-houses from March to Nov. 1835. New York, 1835. 8vo.

5 Second volume of the principal documents relating to the Survey of the Coast of the United States, from Oct. 1834 to Nov. 1835. New York, 1835. 8vo.

6 Third volume of the principal documents relating to the Survey of the Coast of the United States; and

the construction of uniform standards of weights and measures for the Custom-houses and States, from Nov. 1835 to Nov. 1836. New York, 1836. 8vo.

7 Documents relating to the construction of uniform Standards of Weights and Measures for the United States, from 1832 to 1835. New York, 1836. 8vo.

8 Sixth Report of the Survey of the Coast of the United States, and the construction of standards of weights and measures. [Washington], 1837. 8vo.

9 Coast Survey of the United States. [An answer to certain statements on that subject made in Congress.] [Philadelphia, 1842.] 8vo.

10 Report upon the Standards of the liquid capacity Measures of the system of uniform standards for the United States; with a description of a new original barometer, and of the balance for adjusting the half-bushels by their weight of distilled water. Washington, 1842. 8vo.

11 Survey of the Coast of the United States. Further rectification of facts alleged in the discußion of Congress, in December, 1842. [Washington, 1843.] 8vo.

HASTINGS, John, M. D. Lectures on Yellow Fever, its causes, pathology, and treatment. Philadelphia, 1848. 8vo.

HASTINGS, Lansford W. The Emigrant's Guide to Oregon and California. Cincinnati, 1845. 8°

HASTINGS, Thomas. Dissertation on Musical Taste; or, general principles of taste applied to the art of music. Albany, 1822. 8°

2 The Union Minstrel. Philadel. [1834]. 12mo.

HASTY-PUDDING. The Hasty-pudding; a poem, in three cantos . . [By Joel Barlow.] Together with the Ruling Paßion, by R. T. Paine. Hallowell, 1815. 12°

HATFIELD, Edwin F. St. Helena and the Cape of Good Hope; or, incidents in the miſſionary life of the Rev. J. M. Bertram .. With an introduction by G. B. Cheever. New York, 1852. 12°

HATFIELD, R.G. The American House-carpenter: a treatise upon architecture, cornices and mouldings, framing, doors, windows, and stairs. Together with the most important principles of practical geometry. New York, 1844. 8vo.

2 The American House-carpenter: a treatise upon architecture, cornices and mouldings, framing, doors, windows, and stairs, etc. Second edition. With an appendix. New York and London, 1845. 8°

HATT, George. Sketches of a Tract Miſſionary. New York, 1852. 16mo.

HAVEN, Nathaniel Appleton. The Remains of N. A. Haven. With a memoir of his life by G. Ticknor. [Privately printed.] [Boston,] 1827. 8vo.

HAVEN, Samuel. An Election Sermon [on Matt. xxiv. 45-47] preached before the General Court of New Hampshire, at Concord. Portsmouth, 1786. 8°

2 A Funeral Discourse [on 2 Tim. iv. 7, 8] delivered at the interment of .. B. Stevens. [Dover, 1791.] 12°

3 The Validity of Presbyterian Ordination, and the importance of candour and union among Christians, .. illustrated in a discourse [on Phil. i. 15-18] delivered at the Dudleian lecture of Harvard College. Boston, 1798. 8°

HAVEN, Samuel Foster, *the Elder*. An Historical Addreſs delivered before the citizens of the town of Dedham, .. Sept. 21, 1836, being the second centennial anniversary of the incorporation of the town. [Large paper.] Dedham, 1837. 8°

HAWES, Angelica H. *Mrs.* The Grafted Bud: a memoir of A. J. Hawes. New York, 1853. 12°

HAWES, Joel, *D. D.* Lectures to young men on the formation of character. .. Third edition; with an additional lecture on reading. Hartford, 1829. 12°

2 An Address delivered at the request of the citizens of Hartford, on the 9th of November, 1835, the close of the second century from the first settlement of the city. Hartford, 1835. 12°

3 A Tribute to the Memory of the Pilgrims, and a vindication of the Congregational Churches of New England. Second edition. Hartford, 1836. 12°

4 The Help of the Lord, the Seal of the Miſſionary Work: a sermon [on 1 Sam. vii. 12] preached .. before the American Board of Commissioners for Foreign Miſſions. Boston, 1846. 8°

5 Travels in the East. The Religion of the East, with impreſſions of foreign travel. Hartford, 1847. 12°

6 Reasons for not embracing the doctrine ʳof Universal Salvation, etc. New York [1853 ?] 16mo.

HAWES, Mrs. Joel. Memoirs of Mrs. M. E. Van Lennep, only daughter of the Rev. Joel Hawes .. and wife of the Rev. H. J. Van Lennep, miſſionary in Turkey, by her mother [with extracts from her correspondence and journal]. (A father's memorial of an only daughter. A discourse .. on the death of Mrs. M. E. Van Lennep .. by J. Hawes, D. D.) Hartford, 1851. 12°

HAWES, Noyes P. The United States Spelling-book and English Orthoepist, etc. 1831. 12°

HAWKS, Francis L. Contributions to the Ecclesiastical History of the United States of America; to which is added an appendix, containing the journals of the Conventions of the Protestant Episcopal Church in the Diocese of Virginia (from 1785 to 1835 inclusive). 2 vol. New York, 1836-1839. 8vo.

2 THE MONUMENTS of Egypt ; or, Egypt a witneſs for the Bible. . . Second edition, revised and enlarged. New York, 1850. 8°

HAWKSLEY, JOHN. The Security of God's People in times of trouble. A sermon [on Habakkuk iii. 18, 19]. Boston, 1846. 8vo.

HAWLEY, Z. K. Congregationalism and Methodism. New York, 1846. 12°

HAWLEY, ZERAH. A Journal of a Tour through Connecticut, Maſſachusetts, New York, the north part of Pennsylvania and Ohio, including a year's residence in that part of the State of Ohio, styled New Connecticut, or Western Reserve. New Haven, 1822. 12°

HAWN, WILLIAM. Answer of the Cashier of the Branch Bank at Mobile (W. Hawn) to the Resolutions of the House of Representatives in relation to the overpayments of officers, etc. [Tuscaloosa, 1842 ?] 8°

2 CASHIER's Reply of the Branch Bank of Decatur to the Resolution of the House of Representatives of the 7th inst. [i. e. Dec. 7, 1843]. [Tuscaloosa, 1843.] 8°

HAWTHORNE, NATHANIEL. Twice told Tales. 2 vol. Boston, 1842. 8°

2 MOSSES from an old Manse. Second part. London [New York printed], 1846. 8vo.

3 THE SCARLET Letter; a Romance. Boston, 1850. 16°

4 THE HOUSE of the Seven Gables: a Romance. Boston, 1851. 8° ´

5 TRUE Stories from History and Biography. Boston, 1851. 12°

6 LIFE of Franklin Pierce. Boston, 1852. 8°

7 A WONDER-BOOK for Girls and Boys. . . With engravings, etc. Boston, 1852. 12°

8 THE BLITHEDALE Romance. Boston, 1852. 12°

HAYDEN, WILLIAM B. The Two Revelations, Nature and the Word. A discourse delivered before the General Convention of the New Jerusalem Church, Boston, June 12, 1851. Boston, 1851. 8°

2 SCIENCE and Revelation : or, the bearing of modern scientific developments upon the interpretation of the first eleven chapters of Genesis. Boston, 1852. 12°

HAYMAKERS. The Haymakers. American Sunday School Union, Philadelphia, [1830?] 12mo.

HAYNE, ROBERT Y. of South Carolina. Speeches of Meſſrs. Hayne and Webster in the United States Senate, on the Resolution of Mr. Foot, January, 1830. Boston, 1852. 8°

HAYNER, Member of the House of Aſſembly of New York. Albany Freeholder-Extra. Speech .. on the anti-rent question, .. delivered in the House of Aſſembly : .. Jan. 17, 1846. [Albany,] 1846. 8°

HAYNES, SYLVANUS. A Sermon [on Prov. xiv. 34] delivered before .. the Governor, .. Council, and .. Representatives of Vermont .. Oct. 13, .. being the day of general Election. Randolph, 1809. 12°

HAYWARD, JOHN. The Columbian Traveller, and Statistical Register. Principally relating to the United States. Boston, 1833. Fol.

2 THE RELIGIOUS Creeds and Statistics of every Christian denomination in the United States and British Provinces; with some account of the religious sentiments of the Jews, American Indians, Deists, Mahometans, etc. alphabetically arranged. Boston, 1836. 12mo.

3 THE NEW England Gazetteer, *etc.* Tenth edition. Concord, 1839. 8°

4 THE BOOK of Religions; comprising the views, creeds, sentiments, or opinions of all the principal religious sects .. to which are added, Church and Missionary Statistics, together with biographical sketches. Boston, 1843. 12°

5 A GAZETTEER of Massachusetts. To which are added, statistical accounts of its agriculture, commerce and manufactures. Boston, 1847. 12°

HAYWOOD, JOHN. Reports of Cases adjudged in the Superior Courts of law and equity of the State of North Carolina, from .. 1789 to .. 1798. Second edition, with references to subsequent enactments .. and decisions .. by W. H. Battle. Raleigh, 1832. 8°

HAYWOOD, JOHN, AND COBBS, ROBERT L. The Statute Laws of the State of Tennessee, of a public and general nature; revised and digested by J. Haywood and R. L. Cobbs. [Continued and edited by J. A. Whiteside.] 2 vol. Knoxville, 1831. 8°

HAZARD, EBENEZER, Historical Collections; consisting of state papers and other authentic documents; intended as materials for an history of the United States of America. 2 vol. [Imperfect: wanting a portion of the index to the second volume, namely, from page 648, in the letter M, to the end.] Philadelphia, 1792-94. 4to.

HAZARD, W. P. The American Guide Book; being a hand-book for tourists and travellers through every part of the United States, *etc.* Part 1, Northern and Eastern States and Canada. Philadelphia, 1846. 12°

HAZEL, HARRY, *Pseud?* [i. e. J. JONES]. Yankee Jack: or, the perils of a privateersman. New York [1852]. 8°

2 THE FLYING Artillerist: or, the

child of the battle-field. A tale of Mexican treachery. New York, 1853. 8°

HAZELIUS, ERNEST L. History of the American Lutheran Church, from its commencement in .. 1685 to .. 1842, to which several appendices are added, *etc.* Zanesville, 1846. 12°

HAZEN, EDWARD. Popular Technology; or, professions and trades. 2 vol. New York, 1844, 1843. 12°

2 A PRACTICAL Grammar of the English language; or, an introduction to composition, *etc.* New York, 1844. 12°

3 THE SPELLER and Definer; or, class-book, N° 2, *etc.* Philadelphia, 1845. 12°

HAZLITT, WILLIAM, *A. M. of Boston.* A Thanksgiving Sermon [on Psalm cvii. 8]. Boston, 1786. 8°

HAZZI, JOSEPH VON. A Treatise on the Culture of Silk in Germany, and especially in Bavaria: or complete instruction for the management of mulberry trees, and the rearing of silkworms. . . Translated from the German. Together with other documents, reported to the Legislature of Kentucky, by Gov. Wickliffe. Frankfort, Ky. 1840. 8°

HEADLEY, JOEL T. Napoleon and his Marshals. Fourth edition. 2 vol. New York, 1846. 12°

2 LETTERS from Italy. London [New York printed], 1845. 8vo.

3 THE ALPS and the Rhine. London [New York printed], 1846. 8vo.

4 THE LIFE of Oliver Cromwell; [with an appendix.] New York, 1848. 12°

5 SACRED Scenes and Characters, .. with original designs by Darley. New York, 1850. 12°

6 SKETCHES and Rambles. New York, 1850. 12°

7 MISCELLANIES. . . Authorized edition. New York, 1850. 12°

8 THE ADIRONDACK; or, Life in the Woods. New York, 1851. 12°

9 THE LIVES of Winfield Scott and Andrew Jackson. N. York, 1852. 12°

10 THE IMPERIAL Guard of Napoleon from Marengo to Waterloo. New York, 1852. 12°

HEADLEY, P. C., *Rev.* The Life of L. Kofsuth. . . To which is added an appendix containing his principal speeches, *etc.* With an introduction by H. Greeley. Auburn, 1852. 12°

HEADSMAN. The Headsman; or, the Abbaye des Vignerons. A tale. By the author of " The Bravo," *etc.* [J. F. Cooper]. A new edition. 2 vol. Philadelphia, 1836. 12°

HEARD, F. C. AND OTHERS. Report of the Commifsioners appointed to examine the bank of Mobile. Tuscaloosa, 1845. 8°

HEART. The Heart delineated in its state by Nature, and as renewed by Grace. By a Presbyter of the Protestant Episcopal Church. New York, 1834. 8vo.

HEARTS of Oak. [*Begins*] The new Hearts of Oak. New York, 1834. s. sh. fol.

HEATH, JAMES P. Reply .. to a pamphlet .. by H. May .. [relative to an intended duel between J. A. Young and J. H. Sothoron]. [Baltimore? 1839.] 8°

HEATH, WILLIAM, *Major General.* Memoirs ; containing anecdotes, details of skirmishes, battles and other military events during the American War. Boston, 1798. 8vo.

HEATHEN. [*Begins*] Duty to the Heathen. [Boston, 183-?] 12mo.

HEBBE, GUSTAVUS C. An Universal History, in a series of letters: being a complete and impartial narrative of the most remarkable events of all nations, from the earliest period to the present time; forming a complete

history of the world. vol. 1 Ancient History. New York, 1848. 8°

HEBREW CUSTOMS; or, the mifsionary's return. Philad. [1834]. 12mo.

HEBREW GRAMMAR, collected chiefly from those of Mr. I. Lyons .. and the Rev. R. Grey. . . To which is subjoined, a praxis taken from the sacred clafsics, and containing a specimen of the whole Hebrew language; with a sketch of the Hebrew poetry, as retrieved by Bishop Hare. [By S. Sewall.] Boston, 1763. 8°

HECK, JOHANN GEORG. Iconographic Encyclopædia of Science, Literature, and Art, systematically arranged by J. G. Heck. Translated from the German, with additions, and edited by S. F. Baird. Illustrated by five hundred steel plates, containing upwards of twelve thousand engravings. 4 vol. New York, 1851. 8°. Plates, obl. 4°

HEDGE, FREDERICK H. Conservation and Reform: an oration pronounced before the Peucinian Society, Bowdoin College. Boston, 1843. 8°

2 PROSE Writers of Germany. . . Second edition. Philadel. 1849. 8°

HEDGE, LEVI. Elements of Logic, *etc.* New York, 1841. 12°

HEGENBERG Handbibliothek der reinen, höhern und niedern Mathematik. Bändch. I. II. [Lehrbuch der Zahlen-Arithmetik, Buchstaben Rechenkunst und Algebra (Zahlen-Arithmetik)]. Baltimore, 1834. 8vo.

HEGEWISCH, DIETRICH HERMANN. Introduction to Historical Chronology. . . Translated from the German, by J. Marsh. Burlington, 1837. 8°

HEIDENMAUER; or, the Benedictines. A legend of the Rhine. By the author of " The Prairie," *etc.* [J. F. Cooper]. A new edition. 2 vol. Philadelphia, 1836. 12°

HELEN and her Cousin. Philadelphia, 1831. 12mo.

HELEN MAURICE. By a Sunday School Teacher. Philadelphia, 1828. 12mo.

HELM, JAMES J. Memoir of M. T. Sharp. New York [1853]. 16mo.

HEMANS, FELICIA DOROTHEA, *Mrs.* The complete Works of Mrs. Hemans. Reprinted entire from the last English edition. Edited by her sister. 2 vol. New York, 1847. 12°

HEMMENWAY, MOSES. A Discourse concerning the Church; in which the several acceptations of the word are explained and distinguished; the Gospel covenant delineated, *etc.* Designed to remove the scruples and reconcile the differences of Christians. Boston, 1792. 8°

2 REMARKS on .. Mr. Emmons's Differtation on the scriptural qualifications for admiffion and acceſs to the Christian Sacraments; and on his Strictures on a discourse [by M. Hemmenway] concerning the Church. Boston, 1794. 8°

HEMPHILL, *Rev. Mr.* A Vindication of the Reverend Commiffion of the Synod, in answer to some observations on their proceedings against the Rev. Mr. Hemphill. Philadelphia, 1735. 8vo.

HEMPHILL, JOSEPH. Mr. Hemphill's Speech on the bill to construct a national road from Buffalo .. to New Orleans, delivered in the House of Representatives, .. March 23, 1830. [Washington,] 1830. 8°

HENDERSON, ALEXANDER, *of Belize, Honduras.* A Grammar of the Moskito Language. New York, 1846. 8vo.

HENGSTENBERG, ERNEST WILHELM. Christology of the Old Testament, and a commentary on the predictions of the Meffiah by the Prophets. Translated from the Ger-

man by M. Keith. 3 vol. Alexandria and Washington, 1836-39. 8vo.

2 EGYPT and the Books of Moses; or, the Books of Moses illustrated by the monuments of Egypt. With an appendix. From the German, by R. D.C. Robbins. Andover, 1843. 12mo.

HENING, WILLIAM W. and MUNFORD, WILLIAM. Reports of Cases argued and determined in the Supreme Court of Appeals of Virginia; with select cases, relating chiefly to points of practice, decided by the Superior Court of Chancery for the Richmond district [from 1806 to 1810]. Second edition, revised and corrected by the authors. 4 vol. [Vol. 1 only is of the second edition.] Flatbush [and] N.York, 1809-11. 8°

HENRY, ALEXANDER. Travels and Adventures in Canada and the Indian territories, between the years 1760 and 1776. In 2 parts. New York, 1809. 8vo.

HENRY, CALEB S. A Compendium of Christian Antiquities: being a brief view of the orders, rites, laws, and customs of the ancient Church in the early ages. [With an appendix.] Philadelphia, 1837. 8°

2 THE POSITION and Duties of the Educated Men of the country: a discourse pronounced before the Euglosſian and Alpha Phi Delta Societies of Geneva College, *etc.* New York, 1840. 8°

3 AN EPITOME of the History of Philosophy. . . Translated from the French, with additions, and a continuation, . . . by C. S. Henry. 2 vol. New York, 1842. 12°

HENRY, JAMES, *the Younger.* An Addreſs upon education and common schools, delivered at Cooperstown, Otsego County, Sept. 21, .. 1843. Albany, 1843. 8vo.

HENRY, JOHN JOSEPH. An accurate and interesting Account of the Hardships and Sufferings of that Band of Heroes who traversed the wilderneſs in the campaign against Quebec, in 1775. Lancaster, Pa. 1812. 12°

HENRY, Thomas Charlton. Etchings from the Religious World. Charleston, 1828. 8vo.

HENRY, W. S. Campaign Sketches of the War with Mexico. New York, 1848. 12°

HENSHAW, David. An Addreſs delivered before an aſſembly of Citizens from all parts of the Commonwealth [of Maſſachusetts] at Boston, July 4, 1836. Boston, 1836. 8°

HENSHAW, John Prentiss Kewley. Funeral Sermon [on Psalm cxii. 6] occasioned by the death of W. H. Harrison, late President of the United States. Baltimore, 1841. 8vo.

2 Memoir of the Life of R. C. Moore, Bishop of the Protestant Episcopal Church in the Diocese of Virginia. Accompanied by a selection from the sermons of the late bishop. Philadelphia, 1843. 8vo.

HENTZ, Caroline Lee, Mrs. De Lara; or, the Moorish bride. A tragedy, in five acts [and in verse]. Tuscaloosa, 1843. 12mo.

2 Aunt Patty's Scrap-bag. [A series of tales.] Philadel. 1846. 12°

3 Linda; or, the young pilot of the Belle Creole. A tale. Philadelphia, 1850. 12°

4 Eoline; or, Magnolia Vale. A novel. Philadelphia, 1852. 12°

5 Marcus Warland; or, the Long Moſs Spring. A tale of the South. Philadelphia, 1852. 12°

HERBERT, Henry William. My Shooting Box. Philadel. 1846. 12°

2 The Miller of Martigné. A romance. New York, 1847. 8°

3 The Captains of the Old World. New York, 1851. 12°

4 My Shooting Box. By F. Forester [H. W. Herbert]. Philadelphia, 1851. 12°

5 Frank Forester's Field Sports of the United States and British Provinces of North America. In 2 vols. Fourth edition. New York, 1852. 8°

6 The Auorndon Hounds; or, a Virginian at Melton Mowbray.... With illustrations by the author. Philadelphia, 1852. 12°

7 The Knights of England, France, and Scotland. New York, 1852. 12°

8 American Game in its Seasons, etc. New York, 1853. 12°

9 The Chevaliers of France, from the Crusaders to the Marechals of Louis XIV. New York, 1853. 12°

HERBERT, John C. An Addreſs delivered in .. Annapolis .. at the request of the Society of the Alumni of St. John's College, etc. Annapolis, 1828. 8°

HERDER, Joham Gollfried von. The Spirit of Hebrew Poetry. Translated by James Marsh. 2 vol. Burlington, 1833. 12°

HERNDON, Mary E. Mrs. Louise Elton; or, things seen and heard. A novel. Philadelphia, 1853. 12°

HERODOTUS. Ηροδοτου ιστοριων λογοι θ. From the text of Schweighaeuser; with English notes. Edited by C. S. Wheeler. Second edition. 2 vol. Boston, 1843. 12°

HERRICK, Jedediah. A Genealogical Register of the name and family of Herrick, from the settlement of Henerie Hericke, in Salem, Maſſachusetts, 1629, to 1846; with a concise notice of their English ancestry. Bangor, 1846. 8°

HERRING, James, and LONGACRE, James B. The National Portrait Gallery of distinguished Americans. Conducted by J. Herring and J. B. Longacre. 4 vol. New York and Philadelphia, 1834-39. 8°

HERSHBERGER, H. R. The Horseman. A work on Horsemanship, containing plain practical rules for riding, and hints to the readers on the selection of horses. To which is annexed a sabre exercise for mounted and dismounted service. New York, 1844. 12°

HERTTELL, Thomas. An Exposé of the causes of intemperate drinking, and the means by which it may be obviated. New York, 1819. 8vo.

2 Rights of Conscience defended, in a speech in the Aſſembly of the State of New York, May 7, 1835, on the bill relative to the rights and competency of witneſſes. Also, his reply to Mr. (Speaker) Humphrey's remarks against the bill, and in support of the religious Test Act. New York, 1835. 12mo.

HERTY, Thomas. A Digest of the Laws of the United States of America: being a complete system .. of all the public Acts of Congreſſ now in force, etc. Baltimore, 1800. 8°

HERTZOG. The Protestant Theological and Ecclesiastical Encyclopædia: being a condensed translation of Hertzog's " Real Encyclopædia." With additions from other sources. By the Rev. J. H. A. Bomberger. Part 1. Edinburgh, Philadel.[printed] [1856]. 8vo.

HERVEY, George Winfred. The Principles of Courtesy. With hints .. on manners and habits. New York, 1852. 8°

2 The Rhetoric of Conversation; or, bridles and spurs for the management of the tongue. London, New York [printed], 1854. 12mo.

HERVEY, N. The Memory of Washington; with biographical sketches of his mother and wife. Relations of Lafayette to Washington; with incidents and anecdotes in the lives of the two patriots. Boston and Cambridge, 1852. 12°

HERVEY, William, A.M. The Spirit of Missions: a sermon [on Mark xvi. 15] preached .. Dec. 13, 1839. [Edited by E. D. Griffin.] Williamstown, 1831. 8°

HESPERIAN (The) ; or Western Monthly Magazine. Edited by W. D. Gallagher and O. Curry. 3 vol. Columbus and Cincin. 1838-39. 4to.

HEUSTIS, Jabez W. Physical Observations and medical tracts and researches, on the topography and diseases of Louisiana. New York, 1817. 8°

HEWETT, D. A Gazetteer of the New England States, concise and comprehensive. New York, 1829. 12°

HEWITT, afterwards STEBBINS, Mary E. Mrs. The Songs of our Land, and other poems. Boston, 1846. 12°

2 The Memorial; written by the friends of the late Mrs. Osgood, and edited by M. E. Hewitt. With illustrations, etc. New York, 1851. 8°

3 Heroines of History illustrated. Edited by M. E. Hewitt. New York, 1852. 8°

HEWLETT, afterwards COPLEY, Esther, Mrs. Kind Words for the Kitchen; or, illustrations of humble life. New York, 1848. 12°

HEYWOOD, John H. Discourse [on 2 Samuel iii. 38] on the life and services of D. Webster, delivered in the Unitarian Church, Louisville, etc. Louisville, 1852. 8°

HIBERNICUS, Pseud. [i.e. De Witt Clinton]. Letters on the Natural History and internal resources of the State of New York. By Hibernicus. New York, 1822. 12°

HICHBORN, Benjamin. An Oration, delivered March 5, 1777, at .. Boston, to commemorate the bloody tragedy of March 5, 1770. Boston, 1777. 4°

2 An Oration, delivered July 5, 1784, at .. Boston, in celebration of the anniversary of American Independence. Boston [1784]. 4°

HICKMAN, Harris Hampden. Oration delivered at . . . Detroit, to

Zion Lodge, N° 1, .. on the anniversary of St. John the Evangelist, Dec. 27, A. L. 5810 [1810]. Pittsburgh, 1811. 12°

HICKOK, LAURENS P. The Sources of Military Delusion, and the practicability of their removal: an address before the Connecticut Peace Society, etc. Hartford, 1833. 8°
2 RATIONAL Psychology; or, the subjective idea and the objective law of all intelligence. Auburn, 1849. 8°

HICKS, REBECCA. The Lady Killer. Philadelphia, 1851. 12°

HIEROPHANT (The); or, monthly journal of sacred symbols and prophecy. Conducted by Geo. Bush. Complete in one vol. New York, 1844. 8vo.

HIESTAND, HENRY. Travels in Germany, Prussia, and Switzerland. Edited by a minister of the Gospel in New York. N. York, 1837. 12mo.

HIGGINS, WILLIAM MULLINGER. The Earth; its physical condition and most remarkable phenomena. New York, 1846. 12°

HIGGINSON, THOMAS WENTWORTH. Things new and old: an installation sermon [on Matthew xiii. 52]. Worcester, 1852. 8°

HIGHMORE, ANTHONY. A Treatise on the law of idiocy and lunacy. First American from the last London edition. To which is subjoined an appendix, comprising a selection of American cases. Exeter, N. H. 1822. 8°

HILDEBRANDT, C. Winter in Spitzbergen; a book for youth. From the German of C. Hildebrandt, .. by E. G. Smith. New York, 1852. 12°

HILDRETH, HOSEA. A View of the United States; with a map and engravings. . . Second edition. Boston, 1831. 12°

2 A BOOK for Massachusetts Children, in familiar letters from a father, for the use of families and schools. Second edition. Boston, 1831. 12°

HILDRETH, RICHARD. Despotism in America; or, an enquiry into the nature and results of the slave-holding system in the United States. By the author of "Archy Moore" (Richard Hildreth). Second edition. Boston, 1840. 12°
2 THE HISTORY of the United States of America, from the discovery of the Continent to the organization of government under the federal constitution. 3 vol. (From the adoption of the federal constitution to the end of the sixteenth Congress. 3 vol.) 6 vol. New York, 1849-52. 8°

HILDRETH, S. P. Biographical and historical Memoirs of the early pioneer settlers of Ohio, with narratives of incidents and occurrences in 1775. To which is annexed, "A Journal of occurrences which happened in the circles of the author's personal observation, in the detachment commanded by Col. Benedict Arnold . . . at Cambridge, Mass. in 1775; by Colonel R[eturn] J. Meigs. Cincinnati, 1852. 8°

HILL, ALONZO. . A Discourse [on 2 Tim. iv. 7-8] on the life and character of Aaron Bancroft, D.D. Worcester, 1839. 8°

HILL, BENJAMIN L. Lectures on the American Eclectic System of Surgery; with over one hundred engravings illustrating the practice of surgery. Cincinnati, 1850. 8vo. .

HILL, G. The Ruins of Athens; Titania's Banquet, a Mask; and other poems. Boston, 1839. 8vo.

HILL, ISAAC, of New Hampshire. An Address delivered .. Jan. 8, 1828, being the thirteenth anniversary of Jackson's victory at New Orleans.

(Addreſs by J. B. Thornton, *etc.*) Concord, 1828. 8°

2 AN ADDRESS delivered before the Republicans of Portsmouth [in New Hampshire] . . July 4, 1828. Concord, 1828. 8°

3 SPEECH [in the Senate] . . . on . . Mr. Clay's resolutions in relation to the tariff. 2 parts. [Washington, 1832.] 8°

4 SPEECH . . on the . . removal of the deposites from the Bank of the United States ; in the Senate, March 3 and 4, 1834. Washing. 1834. 8°

5 SPEECH . . on the Bill to provide compensation for French spoliations prior to 1800; delivered in the Senate, . . Dec. 22, 1834. Washington, 1834. 8°

6 SPEECH . . on Mr. Benton's expunging resolutions ; in Senate, May 27, 1836. [Washington, 1836.] 8°

7 SPEECH . . . [in the Senate] on Mr. Benton's resolution for setting apart the surplus revenue for the defence and permanent security of the country. Jan. 28, 1836. [Washington, 1836.] 8°

HILL, NICHOLAS. Reports of Cases argued and determined in the Supreme Court of the State of New York (and in the Court for the Correction of Errors). Vol. 1-6. [From Jan. term, 1841, to Dec. term, 1844.] Albany, 1842-45. 8°

HILL, RICHARD, *M. D.* Letters of Dr. R. Hill and his children. . . Collected and arranged by J. J. Smith. Privately printed. Philadel. 1854. 8vo.

HILL, W. R. Reports of Cases in Chancery argued and determined in the Courts of Appeals of South Carolina ; from Jan. 1833 to . . (May 1837), both inclusive. 2 vol. Columbia, 1834-37. 8°

2 REPORTS of Cases at Law, argued and determined in the Court of Appeals of South Carolina. 1833-37. 3 vol. Columbia, 1834-41. 8°

HILLARD, GEORGE STILLMAN.

The relation of the Poet to his age : a discourse delivered before the Phi Beta Kappa Society of Harvard University, . . Aug. 24, 1843. Second edition. Boston, 1843. 8vo.

2 EULOGY on the life and services of Daniel Webster. Boston, 1853. 8vo.

HILLHOUSE, JAMES ABRAHAM. Hadad, a dramatic poem. New York, 1825. 8vo.

2 AN ORATION on some of the considerations which should influence an epic or tragic writer in the choice of an era. New Haven, 1826. 8vo.

3 DRAMAS, Discourses, and other pieces. 2 vol. Boston, 1839. 8vo.

HILLIARD, FRANCIS. The Elements of Law : being a comprehensive summary of American civil jurisprudence. Boston, Cambridge [printed], 1835. 8vo.

2 A DIGEST of Pickering's Reports. Vol. 8-14 inclusive. Boston, 1837. 8°

3 AN ABRIDGMENT of the American Law of Real Property. 2 vol. Boston, 1838-9. 8vo.

4 A TREATISE on the Law of Sales of personal Property. New York, 1841. 8°

5 THE ELEMENTS of Law ; being a comprehensive summary of American jurisprudence. . . Second edition, revised, enlarged, and improved. New York, 1848. 8°

HILLIARD, HENRY W. Speech . . on the Mexican War ; delivered in the House of Representatives, Jan. 5, 1847. Washington, 1847. 8°

HILLIARD, TIMOTHY. Paradise promised by a dying Saviour to the penitent Thief on the Croſs. A sermon [on Luke xxii. 42, 43] . . . on . . the execution of A. White, R. Barrick, and J. Sullivan. With . . some account of their conversation, *etc.* Boston, 1785. 8vo.

2 A SERMON [on Rom. i. 4] delivered . . at the Dudleian lecture in . . Harvard College, *etc.* Bost. 1788. 8°

HILTON, NATHAN T. Practical

Arithmetic: or, a complete exercise-book, for the use of schools. Exeter, 1807. 12°

HINDOO CONVERT. The first Hindoo Convert: a memoir of Krishna Pal, *etc.* [The preface is signed B.] Philadelphia, 1852. 16mo.

HINDS, John. Hinds' Farriery and Stud-book. New edition .. with considerable additions and improvements .. by T. M. Smith .. With a supplement .. by J. J. Skinner. Philadelphia, 1848. 12°

HINES, Gustavus. Life on the Plains of the Pacific. Oregon: its history, condition, and prospects; containing a description of the geography, climate, and productions; with personal adventures among the Indians, during a residence .. on the plains bordering the Pacific, *etc.* .. Embracing extended notes of a voyage round the world. Buffalo, 1851. 12°

HINMAN, Royal R. Letters from the English Kings and Queens, Charles II, James II, William and Mary, Anne, George II, *etc.* to the Governors of the colony of Connecticut, together with the answers thereto, from 1635 to 1749, and other .. documents, compiled from files and records in the office of the Secretary of the State of Connecticut. By R. R. Hinman. Hartford, 1836. 12°

2 An Historical Collection, from official records, files, *etc.* of the part sustained by Connecticut during the war of the Revolution. With an appendix, containing important letters, depositions, *etc.* written during the war. Compiled by R. R. Hinman. Hartford, 1842. 8°

HINTON, John Howard, and others. The History and Topography of the United States of North America, from the earliest period to the present time .. A new and improved edition, with additions and corrections, by S. L. Knapp. 2 vol. Boston, 1834. 4°

HINTS. A few Hints on Monarchy and Republicanism. By a true friend to liberty. Boston, 1825. 12°

HIRST, Henry B. Endymion a tale of Greece [in verse]. Boston, 1848. 12°

2 The Penance of Roland: a romance of the Peine forte et dure; and other poems. Boston, 1849. 12°

HIRZEL, Hans Caspar, *the Elder*. The rural Socrates; or, an account of a celebrated philosophical farmer, lately living in Switzerland, and known by the name of Kliyogg. [Translated from the German of H. C. Hirzel; with notes from the French and English versions, and additions by the American editor.] Hallowell, 1800. 8°

HISTORICAL AND PHILOSOphical Society of Ohio. Transactions of the historical and philosophical society of Ohio. Part second, vol. 1. Cincinnati, 1839. 8°

HISTORICAL SOCIETY of Pennsylvania. Memoirs. Vol. 1-3, and vol. 4, part 1. Philadelphia, 1826-40. 8vo.

2 [*Begins*] The Historical Society of Pennsylvania. [An address to the public, with a list of subscribers to the publication fund.] [Philadelphia, 1855.] 8vo.

3 The History of an Expedition against Fort du Quesne, in 1755, under Major-General E. Braddock (Captain Orme's journal). Edited from the original manuscripts by W. Sargent. Philadelphia, 1855. 8vo.

HISTORY.
1 A General History of Quadrupeds. [By R. Beilby.] The figures engraved on wood, chiefly copied from the original of T. Bewick, by A. Anderson. First American edition, with an appendix, containing some American annals not hitherto described. New York, 1804. 8vo.

2 History of Edwin Judd. Philadelphia [1829]. 12mo.

3 HISTORY of John Wise, a poor boy. Philadelphia [1830]. 12mo.

4 HISTORY of George Hicks. By a Sunday-school teacher. Philadelphia, 1830. 12mo.

5 HISTORY of Little Henry and his Bearer. Philadelphia, 1832. 12mo.

6 LETTERS on Ecclesiastical History. Vol. 1. Philadelphia [1832]. 12mo.

7 HISTORY of Henry Fairchild and Charles Trueman. Philadel. [1832]. 12mo.

8 HISTORY of Thomas and Joseph. Philadelphia, 1832. 12mo.

9 HISTORY of a Pocket Prayerbook. Written by itself. [By B. D. i. e., Benjamin Dorr.] Philadelphia, 1839. 12°

10 THE NATURAL History of Insects. 2 vol. New York, 1843-46. 12°

11 NATURAL History of Quadrupeds. New York, 1844. 12°

12 NATURAL History: the elephant as he exists in a wild state, and as he has been made subservient, in peace and in war, to the purposes of man. New York, 1844. 12°

13 THE HISTORY and mystery of puffing; or, a few fragrant whiffs of the weed, evolving . . hints touching the poetry of smoking, etc. New York, 1844. 12°

14 NATURAL History of Birds; their architecture, habits, and faculties. New York, 1845. 12°

HITCHCOCK, EDWARD, President of Amherst College. An Essay on Temperance, addressed particularly to students, etc. Second edition. Amherst, 1830. 12°

2 REPORT of a geological Survey of Massachusetts, made under an appointment by the Governor, etc. [Part 1 only, containing " economical geology." Republished with the 3 remaining pts. in 1833.] Amherst, 1832. 8vo.

3 REPORT on the Geology, Mineralogy, Botany, and Zoology of Massachusetts; made and published by order of the Government of that State.

Amherst, 1833. 8vo. Plates. Obl. fol.

4 CATALOGUE of the Animals and Plants of Massachusetts (from the second edition of Professor Hitchcock's Report on the Geology . . of Massachusetts). Amherst, 1835. 8vo.

5 REPORT of a re-examination of the economical Geology of Massachusetts. Boston, 1838. 8vo.

6 ELEMENTARY Geology. Amherst, 1840. 12mo.

7 FIRST Anniversary Address before the Association of American Geologists, at their second annual meeting in Philadelphia, . . with an abstract of the proceedings of the Association at their Sessions in .1840 and 1841. New Haven, 1841. 8vo.

8 FINAL Report on the Geology of Massachusetts: in four parts. With an appended catalogue of the specimens of rocks and minerals in the State Collection. Amherst, 1841. 4to.

9 FINAL Report on the Geology of Massachusetts. 2 vol. Northampton, 1841. 4to.

10 ELEMENTARY Geology... Third edition, revised and improved: with an introductory notice by J. P. Smith. New York, 1842. 12°

11 SKETCH of the Scenery of Massachusetts. With plates: from the Geological Report of Prof. Hitchcock. Northampton, 1842. 4°

12 THE HIGHEST Use of Learning: an address delivered at . . Amherst College, etc. Amherst, 1845. 8°

13 ELEMENTARY Geology... Eighth edition, revised . . with an introductory notice by J. Pye Smith. New York, 1847. 12°

14 THE RELIGION of Geology and its connected Sciences. Boston, 1851. 12°

15 RELIGIOUS Lectures on peculiar phenomena of the Four Seasons. . . Third edition. Boston, 1853. 12°

HITCHCOCK, ENOS. A Discourse on the Dignity and Excellence of the Human Character; illustrated in the life of Gen. G. Washington, . .

in commemoration of the afflictive
event of his death, delivered Feb.
22, 1800. Providence, 1800. 8°

HITCHCOCK, Gad. A Sermon
[on Gen. i. 31] preached at Plymouth
. . in commemoration of the first
landing of our New England ancestors
in that place, *etc.* Boston, 1775. 8°

HOADLY, L. Ives. An Address
delivered at the Union Celebration of
Independence, at Sutton, Mass. July
5, 1824. Worcester [1824]. 8°

HOAR, Samuel. Remarks on the
Resolutions [touching the proposed
Abolition of Slavery in the District of
Columbia, *etc.*] introduced by Mr.
Jarvis, of Maine, and Mr. Wise, of
Virginia, delivered in the House of
Representatives, . . Jan. 21, 1836.
Washington, 1836. 8°

HOARE, Prince. My Grand-
mother; a musical farce, in two acts
[and in prose, with songs]. New
York, 1806. 12mo.

HOBART, Aaron. An Historical
Sketch of Abington, Plymouth County,
Massachusetts. With an appendix.
Boston, 1839. 8vo.

HOBART, John Henry, *Bishop
of New York.* The Origin, the
General Character, and the Present
Situation of the Protestant Episcopal
Church, in the United States of America: a sermon [on Psalm cxxii. 7]
preached . . on the . . opening of the
general convention of the said Church,
and of the consecration of . . Bishop
Moore, of Virginia. Philadelphia,
1814. 8°

2 A Charge to the Clergy of the
Protestant Episcopal Church in the
State of New York; delivered at the
convention of the Church, *etc.* New
York, 1815. 8°

3 Sunday School Address. The
beneficial effects of Sunday Schools
considered. . . To which is annexed,
the first annual report of the . . New
York Protestant Episcopal Sunday
School Society. New York, 1818. 8°

4 The Principles of the Churchman stated and explained, in distinction from the corruptions of the
Church of Rome, and from the errors of certain Protestant Sects; in a
charge delivered to the clergy of the
Protestant Episcopal Church in the
State of Connecticut. New York,
1819. 8vo.

5 A Letter to Bishop Hobart,
occasioned by the strictures on Bible
Societies, contained in his late charge
to the Convention of New York. By
a Churchman of the Diocese of New
York [*i. e.* W. Jay]. New York,
1823. 8°

6 The Church Catechism; and
the same broke into short questions
and answers, and enlarged, explained
and proved from Scripture. New
York, 1826. 12mo.

7 The High Churchman Vindicated; in a charge to the Clergy.
New York, 1826. 8vo.

8 An Address before a Convention
of the Church in New York. New
York, 1826. 8vo.

9 A Sermon at the Institution of
the Rev. George Upfold, M.D. New
York, 1828. 8vo.

10 The Posthumous works of J.
H. Hobart: with his life by W. Berrian. 3 vol. New York, 1833-32. 8vo.

HOBART, Noah. A Serious Address to the members of the Episcopal
Separation in New England; occasioned by Mr. Wetmore's Vindication
of the Professors of the Church of
England in Connecticut, *etc.* Boston,
1748. 8°

2 A Second Address to the Members of the Episcopal Separation in
New England; occasioned by the exceptions made to the former by Dr.
Johnson, Mr. Wetmore, Mr. Beach,
and Mr. Caner. To which is added,
by way of appendix, a letter from
Mr. Dickinson, in answer to some
things Mr. Wetmore has charged him
with. Boston, 1751. 8°

HOBBY, WILLIAM. An Inquiry into the Itinerancy and the Conduct of the Rev. Mr. G. Whitefield. .. vindicating the former . . and the latter. Boston, 1745. 4°

HODGE, CHARLES. A Commentary on the Epistle to the Romans. Philadelphia, 1835. 8vo.

HODGE, PAUL RAPSEYS. The Steam Engine; its origin and gradual improvement, from the time of Hero to the present day; as adapted to manufactures, locomotion, and navigation. New York, 1840. 8°. Plates, [1841]. Fol°

HODGES, SILAS H. Annual Report of the Auditor of Accounts of the State of Vermont; made to the Legislature, Oct. 8, 1846. Rutland, 1846. 8°

HOFFMAN, DAVID. A Course of Legal Study, addressed to students and the profession generally. .. Second edition, rewritten and much enlarged. 2 vol. Baltimore, 1836. 8vo.

2 LEGAL Outlines, being the substance of the first title of a course of lectures now delivering in the University of Maryland. Baltimore, 1836. 8vo.

HOFFMANN, CHARLES FENNO. The Vigil of Faith, and other Poems. . . Fourth edition. New York, 1845. 12°

2 THE VIGIL of Faith, and other Poems. [With a preface by R. W. Griswold.] Nurnberg and New York, [1846?] 24mo.

3 THE PIONEERS of New York: an anniversary discourse delivered before the St. Nicholas Society of Manhattan, Dec. 6, 1847. New York, 1848. 8°

4 LOVE's Calendar, Lays of the Hudson, and other Poems. New York, 1850. 16°

HOFFMANN, ERNST THEODOR WILHELM. Nutcracker and Mouse-King: translated .. by Mrs. St. Si-

mon. With illustrations on wood. New York, 1853. 12°

HOFFMANN, MURRAY. The Office and Duties of Masters in Chancery, and Practice in the Master's Office. With an appendix of precedents. New York, 1824. 8°

2 REPORTS of. Cases argued and determined in the Court of Chancery of the State of New York, before the Assistant Vice-Chancellor of the first circuit, the Hon. M. Hoffmann. Vol. 1. New York, 1841. 8°

3 A TREATISE on the Practice of the Court of Chancery; with an appendix of forms. Second edition. 3 vol. [The first volume only is of the second edition.] New York, 1843, 1839-40. 8°

4 A TREATISE on the Law of the Protestant Episcopal Church in the United States. New York, 1850. 8°

HOGAN, EDMUND. The Pennsylvania State Trials: containing the impeachment, trial, and acquittal of Francis Hopkinson and John Nicholson, Judge of the Court of Admiralty and Comptroller General of Pennsylvania. [Edited by E. Hogan.] Vol. 1. Philadelphia, 1794. 8vo.

HOGAN, WILLIAM, AND OTHERS. Report of the Commissioners of the Penitentiary. Nov. 3, 1841. Tuscaloosa, 1841. 8°

HOGE, MARGARETTA C. History of Margaretta C. Hoge. Philadelphia. 12mo.

HOLBROOK, JOHN EDWARDS, M.D. North American Herpetology; or, a description of the reptiles inhabiting the United States. Vol. 1. Philadelphia, 1836. 4to.

2 NORTH American Herpetology; or, a description of the reptiles inhabiting the United States. 5 vol. Philadelphia, 1842. 4°

3 ICHTHYOLOGY of South Carolina. N° 1-10. Charleston, 1855. 4to.

HOLCOMBE, HENRY. A Sermon

[on 2 Sam. iii. 38] occasioned by the death of Lieutenant-General Washington. [Savannah, 1800.] 4°

HOLCOMBE, James P. A Selection of Leading Cases upon commercial law, decided by the Supreme Court of the United States; with notes and illustrations. New York, 1847. 8°

2 A Digest of the decisions of the Supreme Court of the United States, from its organization to the present time. New York, 1848. 8°

HOLDEN, Horace. A Narrative of the Shipwreck, Captivity, and Sufferings of H. Holden and B. H. Nute, who were cast away in the American ship Mentor on the Pelew Islands 1832; and for two years afterwards were subjected to unheard of sufferings among the inhabitants of Lord North's Island. Fourth edition. Boston, 1839. 12mo.

HOLDICH, Joseph. The Life of W. Fisk, D.D. first President of the Wesleyan University. New York, 1842. 8°

HOLGATE, Jerome B. Atlas of American History, on a novel plan; comprising a complete synopsis of events, from the discovery of the American Continent by Columbus in 1492, to the year 1842. [Cambridge], 1842. Fol°

2 American Genealogy: being a history of some of the early settlers of North America and their descendants, from their first emigration to the present time. . . Illustrated by genealogical tables. N.York, 1851. 4°

HOLIDAY WEEK, and other Sketches, from the first series of " Shades of Character." By the author of " Charlie Burton," " George Austin," " The Widow's Son," etc. etc. From the edition of the Society for Promoting Christian Knowledge. New York, 1851. 12°

HOLLAND, Elihu Goodwin. Reviews and Essays. Bost.1849. 12°

2 Essays, and a Drama in five acts [intitled, " The Highland Treason."] Boston, 1852. 8°

HOLLAND, William H. The Life and Political Opinions of Martin Van Buren, Vice President of the United States. Second edition. Hartford, 1836. 12mo.

HOLLEY, Mary Austin, Mrs. Texas. Observations, historical, geographical, and descriptive, in a series of letters, written during a visit to Austin's Colony in 1831. . . With an appendix, containing . . answers to certain questions relative to colonization in Texas issued . . . by the London Geographical Society, etc. Baltimore, 1833. 12°

HOLLEY, O. L. The Picturesque Tourist; being a guide through the Northern and Eastern States, and Canada, etc. New York, 1844. 12°

HOLLICK, Frederick, M. D. Neuropathy; or, the true principles of the art of healing the sick : being an explanation of the action of galvanism, electricity, and magnetism, in the cure of disease, etc. Philadelphia, 1847. 12°

HOLLIDAY, John. A Short Account of the putrid bilious yellow fever, vulgarly called the black vomit, which appeared in the city of the Havanna in June, July, August, 1794. Boston, 1796. 8vo.

HOLLIS, Pseud. AND OTHERS. Facts and Documents in relation to Harvard College. Boston, 1829. 12°

HOLLISTER, Gideon Hiram. A Poem, by G. H. Hollister; and the valedictory oration, by C. F. Burnam. Pronounced before the senior class in Yale College, July 1, 1840. New Haven, 1840. 8°

HOLM, Thomas Campanius. Description of the Province of New Sweden, now called Pennsylvania. Compiled by T. C. Holm. Translated from the Swedish, with notes, by Peter S. Duponceau. Philadelphia, 1834. 8vo.

HOLMAN, JAMES T. A Digest of the reported cases ruled and adjudged in the Courts of Tennefsee, from the year 1796 to 1835. With a memorandum of the names of the judges, etc. Nashville, 1835. 8°

HOLMES, ABIEL. The Life of Ezra Stiles, President of Yale College. Boston, 1798. 8vo.

2 A SERMON [on Lamentations ii. 13] preached at Cambridge the Lord's day after the interment of . . J. Sumner, etc. Boston [1799]. 8°

3 AMERICAN Annals, or a chronological history of America, from its discovery in 1492 to 1806. . . With additions and corrections by the author. 2 vol. [With the autograph of Robert Southey.] Cambridge, 1808. 8vo.

4 THE ANNALS of America, from the year 1492 to 1826. 2 vol. Cambridge, 1829. 8vo.

5 A SERMON [on 2 Cor. ii. 14] delivered before the Maſsachusetts Missionary Society, etc. Camb. 1804. 8°

6 AN ADDRESS delivered before the American Antiquarian Society, in King's Chapel, Boston, on their second anniversary, Oct. 24, 1814. Boston, Nov. 1814. 8°

HOLMES, D. M. A. The Wesley Offering; or, Wesley and his times. Auburn, 1852. 12°

2 THE METHODIST Preacher; containing twenty-eight sermons on doctrinal and practical subjects. By Bishop Hedding, Dr. Fisk, Dr. Bangs, Dr. Durbin. Auburn, 1852. 8°

HOLMES, ELIAS B. Speech . . on the . . Mexican War; delivered in the House of Representatives, . . June 18, 1846. Washington, 1846. 8°

HOLMES, JOHN, of Maine. Speech . . in the Senate, on the nomi-

nation of J. J. Crittenden [to be an Aſsociate Judge of the Supreme Court], Feb. 4, 1829. Washington, 1829. 8°

2 SPEECH of Mr. Holmes, . . in the Senate, . . on his resolutions calling upon the President . . for the reasons of his removing from office, and filling the vacancies thus created, in the receſs of the Senate. Washing.1830. 8°

3 SPEECH . . delivered in the Senate, . . in the debate which arose upon Mr. Foot's resolution relative to the public lands. Washington, 1830. 8°

4 THE STATESMAN; or, principles of legislation and law. Augusta, 1840. 8°

HOLMES, OLIVER WENDELL. Boylston Prize Diſsertations for the years 1836-1837. Boston, 1838. 8°

2 ASTRÆA: the balance of illusions. A poem delivered before the Phi Beta Kappa Society of Yale College, August 14, 1850. Boston, 1850. 12°

3 POEMS. New and enlarged edition. Boston, 1851. 12°

HOLTHOUSE, HENRY JAMES. A New Law Dictionary. . . To which is added, an outline of an action at law, and of a suit in equity. . . Edited from the second . . London edition, with numerous additions, by Henry Penington. Philadelphia, 1847. 8°

HOLY LAND. Views of interesting places in the Holy Land (after the original sketches of L. Mayers); with a brief sketch of . . events aſsociated with them in the sacred Scriptures, and of their modern appearance and situation. Philadelphia [1830?]. Obl. 4to.

HOLYOKE, EDWARD AUGUSTUS, M.D. LL.D. Memoir of E. A. Holyoke. . . Prepared in compliance with a vote of the Eſsex South District Medical Society. Boston, 1829. 8°

HOME. The Pleasures of Home: a poem, in four parts. Boston, 1818. 12mo.

HOME BOOK of the Picturesque; or, American scenery, art, and literature. Comprising a series of essays by W. Irving, W. C. Bryant, F. Cooper, Miss Cooper, N. P. Willis, B. Taylor, H. T. Tuckerman, E. L. Magoon, A. B. Street, Miss Field, etc. New York, 1852.   8°

HOME CONVERSATIONS on what are commonly called Little Things. New York, 1852.   12°

HOMŒOPATHIC EXAMINER. By A. Gerald Hull. 3 vol. New York, 1840-44. 8vo. New series, edited by Drs. Gray and Hempel. Vol. 1, 2. New York, 1845-47. 8vo.

HOMER. Ὁμήρου Ἰλιάς. The Iliad of Homer... With English notes and Flaxman's illustrative designs. Edited by C. C. Felton. *Gr.* Boston, Cambridge printed, 1833. 8vo.

2 Ὁμήρου Ὀδυσσειας. The Odyssey of Homer, according to the text of Wolf; with notes: for the use of schools and colleges. By J. J. Owen. Fourth edition. N. York, 1846. 12°

3 HOMER's Iliad: translated by W. Munford. 2 vol. Boston, 1846. 8°

4 THE FIRST Three Books of Homer's Iliad, according to the ordinary text, and also with the restoration of the digamma. To which are appended, English notes, critical and explanatory, a metrical index, and Homeric glossary, by C. Anthon. New York, 1846. 8°

HOMER, JONATHAN, *the Elder.* The Mourner's Friend, or consolation and advice offered to Christian parents in the death of their little children... A sermon [on 2 Sam. xii. 23] preached Dec. 7, 1792. Boston, 1793. 8vo.

2 THE WAY of God Vindicated, in a sermon [on Psalm xviii. 30].. after the interment of his only child, Jonathan Homer... By J. Homer. Boston, 1804. 8vo.

HOMEWARD BOUND; or, the Chase. A tale of the sea. By the author of " The Pilot," *etc.* [J. F. Cooper]. A new edition. 2 vol. Philadelphia, 1842. 12°

HONEYWOOD, SAINT JOHN. Poems... With some pieces in prose. New York, 1801. 12°

HOOD, GEORGE. A History of Music in New England. With biographical sketches of reformers and psalmists. Boston, 1846. 8°

HOOD, JOHN W. The Principles and Practice of Medicine, in a series of essays. Philadelphia, 1848. 8vo.

HOOD, THOMAS. A series of Etchings, suggested by Hood's Bridge of Sighs. Designed and etched by J. W. Ehninger. [With the text.] New York [1850?]. Obl. 4°

HOOK, WALTER FARQUHAR. Hear the Church: a sermon preached in the Chapel Royal. Burlington, N. J. 1838. 8vo.

HOOKER, CHARLES. An Essay on the relation between the respiratory and circulating functions. (From the Boston Medical and Surgical Journal.) Boston, 1838. 8vo.

HOOKER, EDWARD W. Memoir of Mrs. Sarah Louman Smith, late of the mission in Syria. Second edition. Boston, 1840. 12mo.

HOOKER, HERMANN. Popular Infidelity... Second edition. Philadelphia, 1836. 12°

2 THE CHRISTIAN Life: a fight of faith. Philadelphia, 1848. 12°

3 USES of Adversity, and the Provisions of Consolation. Philadelphia, 1848. 12°

HOOPER, JOHNSON J. The Widow Rugby's Husband, a Night at the Ugly Man's, and other tales of Alabama. [Forming part of the " Library of humorous American Works."] Philadelphia, 1851. 12°

HOOPER, LUCY. Poetical Remains of the late L. Hooper. Collected and arranged, with a memoir, by J. Keese. New York, 1842. 12°

HOPKINS, DANIEL, A.M. A Sermon [on 2 Samuel iii. 38] preached Dec. 29, 1799, . . the Lord's day after the melancholy tidings . . of the death of General G. Washington. Salem [1800]. 8°

HOPKINS, HIRAM B. Renunciation of Freemasonry. Bost. 1830. 12mo.

HOPKINS, JAMES D. An Oration pronounced before the inhabitants of Portland, July 4, 1805, in commemoration of American Independence. Portland, 1805. 8°

HOPKINS, JOHN HENRY, Bishop of Vermont. Christianity Vindicated, in seven discourses on the external evidences of the New Testament, with a concluding dissertation. Burlington, 1833. 12°

2 THE PRIMITIVE Creed examined and explained, etc. Burlington, 1834. 8vo.

3 THE PRIMITIVE Church, compared with the Protestant Episcopal Church of the present day; with a dissertation on sundry points of theology and practice, connected with the subject of episcopacy. . . Second edition, revised and improved. Burlington, 1836. 12°

4 ESSAY on Gothic Architecture; with various plans and drawings for churches; designed chiefly for the use of the clergy. Burlington, 1836. 4°

5 THE NOVELTIES which disturb our Peace; a letter addressed to the bishops, clergy and laity of the Protestant Episcopal Church [of the United States of America]. Philadelphia, 1844. 12°

6 THE NOVELTIES which disturb our Peace; a second letter, etc. Philadelphia, 1844. 12°

7 THE NOVELTIES which disturb our Peace; a third letter, etc. Philadelphia, 1844. 12°

8 THE NOVELTIES which disturb our Peace; a fourth letter, etc. Philadelphia, 1844. 12°

9 THE HISTORY of the Confessional. New York, 1850. 12°

HOPKINS, JOHN HENRY, the Younger. The Burlington Drawing-Book of Flowers; progressively arranged from a single leaf up to large groups: accurately drawn and coloured from nature, etc. New York, [1846?] Fol°

2 THE BURLINGTON Drawing-Book of Figures; selected from the works of eminent masters. New York, [1846?] Fol°

HOPKINS, MARK, D.D. Burdens to be cast upon the Lord. A sermon [on Psalm lv. 22] before the American Board of Commissioners for Foreign Missions. Boston, 1845. 8vo.

2 LECTURES on the Evidences of Christianity before the Lowell Institute, Jan. 1844. Boston, 1846. 8vo.

3 MISCELLANEOUS Essays and Discourses. Boston, 1847. 8°

4 LECTURES on the Evidences of Christianity; before the Lowell Institute, Jan. 1844. Boston, 1847. 8°

HOPKINS, SAMUEL. Historical Memoirs relating to the Housatunnuk Indians; or, an account of the methods used . . for the propagation of the Gospel among that heathenish tribe, and the success thereof, under the ministry of the late Rev. Mr. J. Sergeant. Together with the character of that worthy missionary, etc. Boston, 1753. 4to.

2 THE SYSTEM of Doctrines contained in Divine Revelation explained and defended. . . To which is added, a treatise on the Millennium. 2 vol. Boston, 1793. 8vo.

3 MEMOIRS of Miss Susanna Anthony; consisting chiefly of extracts from her writings. Compiled by S. Hopkins. New edition, with a recommendatory preface by Dr. Ryland, Mr. Fuller and Mr. Sutcliff. Clipstone, 1802. 8°

4 SKETCHES of the Life of the Rev. S. Hopkins, Pastor of the first Congregational Church in Newport; written by himself, interspersed with marginal notes from his private Diary: to which is added, a Dialogue by the same, on the nature and extent of true Christian submifsion; also, a serious addreſs to profeſsing Christians, closed by Dr. Hart's Sermon at his funeral, with an introduction by the Editor, S. West. Hartf. 1805. 12mo.

5 THE SYSTEM of Doctrines contained in Divine Revelation explained and defended; showing their consistence and connexion with each other. To which is added, a treatise on the Millennium. Second edition. 2 vol. Boston, 1811. 8°

HOPKINS, SAMUEL M. Reports of Cases argued and determined in the Court of Chancery of the State of New York. Vol. 1. New York, 1827. 8°

HOPKINSON, FRANCIS. Miscellaneous Eſsays and Occasional Writings. 3 vol. Philadelphia, 1792. 8vo.

HOPKINSON, JOSEPH. Speeches of J. Hopkinson and C. Chauncy, on the Judicial Tenure; delivered in the Convention of Pennsylvania for revising the Constitution. Philadelphia, 1838. 8°

HORATIUS FLACCUS, QUINTUS. Q. Horatii Flacci Opera. Accedunt clavis metrica et notæ Anglicæ juventuti accomodatæ. Cura B. A. Gould. Bostoniæ, 1839. 12°

2 THE WORKS of Horace: Latin, with English notes .. by J. L. Lincoln. New York [1851]. 8°

HORNE, THOMAS HARTWELL. Mariolatry; or, facts and evidences demonstrating the worship of the Bleſsed Virgin Mary, by the Church of Rome; derived from the testimonies of her reputed saints and doctors, from her breviary, etc. First American, corrected and enlarged by the author, from the second London edition, and edited by the Rev. S. F. Jarvis. Hartford, 1844. 8vo.

HORNER, FRANCIS. Memoirs and Correspondence of F. Horner, .. edited by his brother, L. Horner. Second edition, with additions. 2 vol. Boston [Cambridge printed], London, 1853. 8vo.

HORNER, GUSTAVUS R. B. Medical Topography of Brazil and Uruguay, with incidental remarks. Philadelphia, 1845. 8vo.

HORRY, P. General, AND WEEMS, M. L. The Life of General Francis Marion, a celebrated partizan officer in the revolutionary war. Fourth edition. Philadelphia, 1816. 12°

2 THE LIFE of General F. Marion, a celebrated partisan officer in the revolutionary war against the British and Tories in South Carolina and Georgia. Philadelphia, 1837. 12mo.

HORSFIELD, THOMAS. An Experimental Diſsertation on the Rhus Vernix, Rhus Radicans, and Rhus Glabrum. Philadelphia, 1798. 8vo.

HORSMANDEN, DANIEL. The New York Conspiracy; or, a history of the Negro Plot, with the journal of the proceedings against the conspirators in 1741-2. [Second edition.] New York, 1810. 8vo.

HORTICULTURAL SOCIETY OF PENNSYLVANIA. Report of the Committee appointed by the Horticultural Society of Pennsylvania, for visiting the nurseries and gardens in the vicinity of Philadelphia, July 13, 1830. Philadelphia, 1831. 8°

HOSACK, DAVID. Syllabus of the Course of Lectures on Botany, delivered in Columbia College. New York, 1795. 8vo.

2 HORTUS Elginensis; or, a catalogue of plants, indigenous and exotic, cultivated in the Elgin Botanic Garden, in the vicinity of the city of New York. New York, 1811. 8vo.

3 OBSERVATIONS on Croup, or Hives. New York, 1811. 8vo.

4 OBSERVATIONS on the Establishment of the College of Physicians and Surgeons in the city of New York. New York, 1811. 8vo.

5 A STATEMENT of Facts relative to the establishment and progreſs of the Elgin Botanical Garden. New York, 1811. 8vo.

6 SYLLABUS of the Course of Lectures on Botany, delivered in Columbia College. New York, 1814. 8vo.

7 SYLLABUS of the Course of Lectures on the theory and practice of physic, delivered in the University of New York. New York, 1816. 8vo.

8 COURSE of Studies designed for the private medical school established in New York. New York, 1816. 8vo.

9 A FUNERAL Addreſs at the interment of Doctor James Tillary. New York, 1818. 8vo.

10 A TRIBUTE to the memory of the late Caspar Wistar, M.D. New York, 1818. 8vo.

11 A SYSTEM of practical Nosology; to which is prefixed a synopsis of the systems of Sauvages, Linnæus, Vogel .. and Young. With references to the best authors on each disease. New York, 1818. 8vo.

12 AN INAUGURAL Discourse, delivered before the New York Horticultural Society. New York, 1824. 8°

13 ESSAYS on various subjects of medical science. 3 vol. New York, 1824-30. 8°

14 AN INAUGURAL Discourse, delivered at the opening of Rutger's Medical College, in the city of New York. [With an appendix.] New York, 1826. 8°

15 MEMOIR of De Witt Clinton; with an appendix, containing numerous documents illustrative of the principal events of his life. New York, 1829. 4to.

HOSMER, WILLIAM. The Young Man's Book; or, self-education. Auburn, 1852. 12°

2 THE HIGHER Law, in its relations to civil government: with particular reference to slavery and the fugitive slave law. Auburn, 1852. 12°

HOSMER, WILLIAM H. C. The Months. [In verse.] Bost. 1847. 12°

HOTCHKIN, JAMES H. A History of the purchase and settlement of western New York, and of the rise, progreſs, and present state of the Presbyterian Church in that section. New York, 1848. 8° .

HOVEY, SYLVESTER. Letters from the West Indies, relating especially to the Danish island St. Croix, and to the British islands Antigua, Barbadoes, and Jamaica. New York, 1838. 12°

HOUGH, FRANKLIN B. A History of St. Lawrence and Franklin counties, New York, from the earliest period to the present time. Albany, 1853. 8°

HOUGH, HORATIO GATES. Diving, or an attempt to describe .. a method of supplying the diver with air under water. Hartford, 1813. 8vo.

HOUSEKEEPER. The American Matron; or, practical and scientific cookery. By a housekeeper. Boston and Cambridge, 1851. 12°

HOUSSAYE, ARSENE. Philosophers and Actreſses. 2 vol. New York, 1852. 12°

HOWARD and OSGOOD. Supreme Judicial Court, Oxford county. J. Bradley et al. plaintiffs in equity, vs. S. Chase, defendant [in a case of contract for the sale of land]. Argument for the defendant (Howard & Osgood, and S. H. Case, counsel for defendant). [Oxford, Maine, 1844.] 8°

HOWARD, BENJAMIN C. Reports of Cases argued and adjudged in the Supreme Court of the United States. 1843-1846. Vol. 1-4. Philadelphia, 1843-46. 8°

HOWARD, H. R. The History of V. A. Stewart, and his adventure in capturing and exposing the great " Western land pirate" (J. A. Murrell) ; .. also of the trials, confeſſions, and execution of a number of Murrell's aſſociates in the State of Miſſiſſippi .. and the execution of five profeſſional gamblers by the citizens of Vicksburg .. July, 1835. Compiled by H. R. Howard. New York, 1839. 12°

HOWARD, VOLNEY E. Reports of Cases argued and determined in the High Court of Errors and Appeals of the State of Miſſiſſippi. 7 vol. Philadelphia [and] Cincinnati, 1839-44. 8°

HOWARD, WILLIAM. Report on the survey of a canal from the Potomac to Baltimore. Baltim. 1828. 8°

HOWARD, WILLIAM, M. D. Narrative of a journey to the summit of Mont Blanc, made in July, 1819. Baltimore, 1821. 12mo.

HOWE, HENRY. Memoirs of the most eminent American mechanics ; also, lives of distinguished European mechanics ; together with a collection of anecdotes, descriptions, etc. relating to the mechanic arts. New York, 1841. 12mo.

2 HISTORICAL Collections of Virginia ... relating to its history and antiquities ; together with geographical and statistical descriptions. To which is appended, an historical and descriptive sketch of the Diſtriĉt of Columbia. Charleston, 1845. 8°

HOWE, JAMES B. A Sermon [on John ix. 29] preached .. before ... the .. Council and .. Legislature of .. New Hampshire, June 8, . being the anniversary Eleĉtion. Concord, 1820. 8°

HOWE, JOHN. An Addreſs delivered at the installation of officers in Washington Lodge. . . To which

are added an addreſs to the past master .. and charges to the officers installed. Boston, 1819. 8°

HOWE, SAMUEL. The Praĉtice of civil aĉtions and proceedings at law in Maſſachusetts. Edited by R. S. Fay and J. Chapman. Boston, 1834. 8°

HOWE, SAMUEL GRIDLEY. An Historical Sketch of the Greek Revolution. New York, 1828. 8°

2 AN ATLAS of the principal islands of the globe, for the use of the blind [in emboſſed outlines]. Bost.1838. 4°

3 A CYCLOPÆDIA for the use of the blind [in emboſſed typography]. Geography, vol.1-2. Boston,1846. 4°

HOWISON, ROBERT R. A History of Virginia, from its discovery and settlement by Europeans, to the present time. Vol. 1. Philadelphia, 1846. 8°

HOYT, E. Antiquarian Researches : comprising a history of the Indian wars in the country bordering Conneĉticut river and parts adjacent, etc. Greenfield, 1824. 8°

HOYT, RALPH. Sketches of life and landscape. New edition, enlarged. New York, 1849. 12°

2 SKETCHES of life and landscape. Fourth edition, enlarged. New York, 1852. 8°

HUBBARD, AUSTIN OSGOOD. Five Discourses on the moral obligation and the particular duties of the Sabbath. Hanover, 1843. 16°

HUBBARD, DAVID. Letter .. to the voters of the Second Congreſſional diſtriĉt of the State of Alabama. Washington, 1840. 8°

HUBBARD, HARVEY. Ixion, and other poems. Boston, 1852. 8°

HUBBARD, HENRY, of New Hampshire. Speech .. upon the Bill making further provisions for the persons engaged in the land and naval service of the U[nited] States during the Revolutionary war; delivered in the House of Representatives, Feb. 29, 1832. Washington, 1832. 8°

2 SPEECH .. on the Bill to authorize the iſſue of Treasury notes; delivered in Senate .. March 30, 1840. [Washington], 1840. 8°

3 SPEECH . . . on the permanent prospective pre-emption Bill. . . In Senate, on Feb. 2, 1841. [Washington, 1841.] 8°

HUBBARD, JOHN. The American Reader. . . designed for the use of schools. . . Fifth edition. Walpole, 1811. 12°

HUBBARD, WILLIAM. The Happineſs of a People in the Wisdome of their Rulers directing and in the obedience of their brethren attending unto what Israel ought to do: recommended in a sermon before the Honourable Governour and Council and the respected Deputies of the Mattachusetts Colony in New England. Preached at Boston, May 3d, 1676, being the day of Election there. By William Hvbbard, minister of Ipswich. Boston, printed by John Foster, 1676. 4to.

2 A NARRATIVE of the Troubles with the Indians in New England, from the first planting thereof, in the year 1607, to this present year, 1677. But chiefly of the late Troubles in the two last years, 1675 and 1676. To which is added, a Discourse about the Warre with the Pequods in the year 1637. By W. Hubbard, Minister of Ipswich. Published by Authority. Boston; Printed by John Foster, in the year 1677. 4to.

3 A NARRATIVE of the Indian Wars in New England, from 1607 to 1677. Worcester, 1801. 12°

4 A GENERAL History of New England, from the discovery to 1670. [Vol. 5 and 6 of the Maſſachusetts Historical Society Collections.] Cambridge, 1815. 8vo.

HUDSON, BENJAMIN, AND OTHERS. Report of the Commiſſioners appointed to examine the Branch Bank at Decatur. Tuscaloosa, 1845. 8°

HUDSON, CHARLES, of Maſſachusetts. Speech .. on .. discriminating duties; delivered in the House of Representatives, Dec. 27 and 28, 1841. Washington, 1842. 8°

2 SPEECH .. on the annexation of Texas; delivered in the House of Representatives . . . Jan. 20, 1845. [Washington, 1845.] 8°

3 SPEECH .. on the war with Mexico; delivered in the House of Representatives, May 14, 1846. [Washington, 1846.] 8°

4 SPEECH . . . on the tariff; delivered in the House of Representatives .. June 29, 1846. [Washington, 1846.] 8°

HUDSON, DAVID. History of Jemima Wilkinson, a preachereſs of the eighteenth century; containing an authentic narrative of her life and character, and of the rise, progreſs, and conclusion of her ministry. Geneva, N. Y. 1821. 12°

HUDSON, HENRY NORMAN. Lectures on Shakespeare. 2 vol. New York, 1848. 12°

HUDSON RIVER and the Hudson River Railroad, with a complete map and woodcut views. Boston, 1851. 8°

2 THE HUDSON, illustrated with pen and pencil .. together with the route to Niagara Falls. New York, 1852. 8°

HUFELAND, C. W. Enchiridion Medicum: or manual of the practice of medicine. The result of fifty years' experience. From the sixth German edition, translated by C. Bruchhausen, revised for the proprietor by R. Nelson. New York, 1842. 8vo.

HUGER, FRANCIS K. An Inaugural Diſſertation on gangrene and mortification. Philadelphia, 1797. 8vo.

HUGGINS, John Richard Des-borus. Hugginiana, or Huggin's Fantasy; showing how a mere barber may become an Emperor. New York, 1808. 12mo.

HUGHES, George W. *Civil Engineer.* Report on the location and survey of the Potomac and Annapolis Canal .. to the Governor of Maryland. Annapolis, 1837. 8°

HUGHES, John, *R. C. Archbishop of New York.* Controversy between Rev. Messrs. Hughes and Breckenridge on the subject, " Is the Protestant Religion the Religion of Christ ?" Third edition. Philadelphia [1833 ?]. 8°

2 A Lecture on the antecedent causes of the Irish Famine in 1847, delivered under the auspices of the general committee for the relief of the suffering poor of Ireland, *etc.* New York, 1847. 8°

3 Christianity the only source of moral, social, and political Regeneration: a sermon [on Matt. xx. 20] preached in the hall of the House of Representatives of the United States, .. Dec. 12, 1847. N. York, 1848. 8°

4 The Church and the World: a lecture delivered .. (for the benefit of St. John's Orphan Asylum). New York, 1850. 8°

5 The Decline of Protestantism and its cause: a lecture delivered .. Nov. 10, 1850. New York, 1851. 8°

6 The Catholic Chapter in the History of the United States: a lecture, *etc.* New York, 1852. 8°

HUGHES, William Carter. The American Miller and Millwright's Assistant. Philadelphia, 1851. 12°

HUGHS, Mrs. The Life of W. Penn. Compiled from the usual authorities, and also many original manuscripts. Philadelphia, 1828. 12°

HUGUENOTS in France and America. By the author of " Three Experiments of Living" [Mrs. H. F. Lee], *etc.* Cambridge, 1843. 12°

HULL, William. An Oration delivered to the Society of the Cincinnati, in the Commonwealth of Massachusetts, July 4, 1788. Bost. 1788. 4°

2 Defence delivered before the General Court Martial; with an address to the citizens of the United States. To which are prefixed, the charges against General Hull, as specified by the Government. Boston, 1814. 12°

3 Report of the Trial of Brigadier General W. Hull .. by a Court Martial, held at Albany, on Monday, Jan. 3, 1814, and succeeding days. Taken by Lieut. Col. Forbes. New York, 1814. 8°

4 Memoirs of the Campaign of the North Western Army of the United States, A. D. 1812. In a series of letters addressed to the citizens of the United States. With an appendix, *etc.* Boston, 1824. 8°

5 Revolutionary Services and Civil Life of General W. Hull. Prepared from his manuscripts by Maria Campbell; together with the history of the Campaign of 1812, and surrender of the Post of Detroit, by J. F. Clarke. New York, 1848. 8°

HUMBOLDT, Carl Wilhelm von, *Baron.* Religious Thoughts and Opinions. [Translated from the German. A reprint of the English edition, entitled " Thoughts and Opinions of a Statesman."] Boston, 1851. 12°

HUME, George Henry. Canada as it is; comprising details relating to the domestic policy, commerce, and agriculture of the Upper and Lower Provinces, *etc.* New York, 1832. 18°

HUMPHREY, Heman, *President of Amherst College.* An Address delivered at the opening of the Convention of Teachers, and of the Friends of Education, in the City Hall in Hartford, Nov. 10, 1830. Hartford, 1831. 8°

2 MISCELLANEOUS Discourses and Reviews. Amherst, 1834. 12°

3 A SERMON [on Psalm cii. 13-15] preached .. before the American Board of Commifsioners for Foreign Mifsions, etc. Boston, 1838. 8°

4 GREAT Britain, France, and Belgium: a short tour in 1835. 2 vol. New York, 1838. 8vo.

5 A DISCOURSE delivered before the Conneсticut Alpha of Φ. B. K. at New Haven, August 14, 1838. New Haven, 1839. 8°

6 DOMESTIC Education. Amherst, 1840. 12°

7 THIRTY-FOUR Letters to a Son in the Ministry. Amherst, 1842. 12°

8 VALEDICTORY Addrefs delivered at Amherst College, .. on leaving the presidential chair. Amherst, 1845. 8°

HUMPHREY, HOSEA. A Difsertation on Fire; or, miscellaneous inquiries and reflections concerning the operations of the laws of nature. With an appendix, containing thoughts on memory, reflection, decision, muscular motion, etc. Providence, 1814. 12mo.

HUMPHREYS, DAVID. An Efsay on the Life of the Honourable Major General Israel Putnam: addrefsed to the State Society of the Cincinnati in Conneсticut. By Col. David Humphreys. Hartford: printed by Hudson and Goodwin, 1788. 12mo.

2 A VALEDICTORY Discourse before the Cincinnati of Conneсticut, in Hartford, at the difsolution of the society. Boston, 1804. 8°

3 MISCELLANEOUS Works. New York, 1804. 8vo.

4 LETTERS from the Hon. David Humphreys .. to .. Sir J. Banks; .. containing some account of the serpent of the ocean, frequently seen in Gloucester Bay. [With cuttings from newspapers relative to General Humphreys and the Sea-serpent.] New York, 1817. 8vo.

5 AN ESSAY on the Life of General I. Putnam, with notes and additions.

With an appendix, containing an historical and topographical sketch of Bunker Hill Battle, by S. Swett. Boston, 1818. 12mo.

HUMPHREYS, HECTOR. Addrefs to the Alumni and Graduates of St. John's College, and to the Friends of Education in Maryland. Annapolis, 1835. 8vo.

HUMPHREYS, WEST H. Reports of Cases argued and determined in the Supreme Court of Tennefsee, 1839-45. Vol. 1-5. Nashville, 1841-45. 8°

HUNGARIAN CONTROVERSY: an exposure of the falsifications of the slanderers of Hungary. [By R. C. i.e. Robert Carter.] Boston, 1852. 8°

HUNT, D. History of Pomfret: a discourse [on Deut. xxxii. 7] delivered on the day of annual thanksgiving, Nov. 19, 1840. Hartford, 1841. 8°

HUNT, GILBERT J. The late War between the United States and Great Britain, from June, 1812, to February, 1815. . . Also, a sketch of the late Algerine war, etc. New York, 1816. 8vo.

2 THE HISTORICAL Reader; containing " The late War between the United States and Great Britain, from June, 1812, to February, 1815, in the scriptural style." Third edition. New York, 1819. 12°

HUNT, HIRAM P. Speech .. on the Fortification Bill, delivered in the House of Representatives, .. June 7, 1836. Washington, 1836. 8°

HUNT, JOHN. A Sermon [on Rev. vii. 14] on the death of Sarah Gill. Boston, 1771. 8vo.

HUNT, RICHARD S. and RANDEL, J. F. A New Guide to Texas: consisting of a brief outline of the history of its settlement, and the colonization and land laws; a general view of the country, etc. New York, 1846. 12°

HUNT, Thomas P. Death by Measure; or, poisons and their effects, found in intoxicating liquors. Philadelphia, 1846. 16°

HUNT, William, *Publisher, at Albany*. The American Biographical Sketch-Book. Vol.1. Albany,1848. 8°

HUNTINGTON, Ezra A. Strife for Supremacy in the Church: a sermon (on Mark ix. 33, 34) preached at the opening of the Synod of Albany. Albany, 1852. 8vo.

HUNTINGTON, F. D. The Christian Doctrine of Charity: a sermon [on 1 Cor. xiii. 3] delivered before the Howard Benevolent Society. Boston, 1844. 8vo.
2 THE GREAT Conflict of the Day: a discourse [on Exod. xxxii. 26], etc. Boston, 1846. 8°
3 THE FAMINE and the Sword. Brotherhood of Nations: a sermon [on Jer. xiv. 16]. Boston, 1847. 8°

HUNTINGTON, J. V. The Forest. New York, 1852. 12°

HUNTINGTON, Jedidiah. Poems. New York, 1843. 12°

HUNTINGTON, Joseph. Calvinism Improved; or, the Gospel illustrated as a system of real grace, issuing in the salvation of all men. New London, 1796. 8vo.

HUNTINGTON, Joshua. Memoirs of the Life of Mrs. Abigail Waters. . . To which is prefixed, the sermon [on Rev. xiv. 13] preached on occasion of her death. Second edition. Boston, 1817. 12°

HUNTINGTON, Nathaniel Gilbert. A System of Modern Geography. . . Illustrated by a variety of cuts and tables, and accompanied by a new . . Atlas. Hartford, 1835. 12° Atlas, 1836. 4°

HURD, Isaac. A Discourse delivered before the Humane Society of Massachusetts, June 11, 1799. Boston, 1799. 4to.

HURD, Seth T. A Grammatical Corrector; or, vocabulary of the common errors of speech, .. peculiar to the different States of the Union, etc. Philadelphia, 1847. 8°

HURLBUT, Elisha P. Essays on Human Rights and their Political Guaranties. New York, 1845. 12°

HURONS. The King of the Hurons. By the author of " The First of the Knickerbockers," etc. [P. H. Myers]. New York, 1850. 12°

HUTCHINS, Thomas. An Historical Narrative and Topographical description of Louisiana and West Florida. Philadelphia, 1784. 8vo.

HUTCHINSON, Thomas. The History of the Province of Massachusetts Bay [1628 to 1750]. 2 vol. Boston, 1764-67. 8°
2 A COLLECTION of Original Papers relative to the history of the Colony of Massachusetts Bay. [By T. Hutchinson.] Few MS. notes [by a son of the compiler]. Boston, 1769. 8°

HUTCHINSON, Titus. The Ex-Chief Justice and the Printer: being a report of a trial for libel: T. Hutchinson vs. B. F. Kendall, etc. Woodstock, Vt. 1836. 8°

HYDE, Alvan. Memoir of . . A. Hyde. Boston and Philadelphia, 1835. 12mo.

' HYMNS. Hymns for Infant Minds; chiefly by the author of Original Poems .. etc. [A. and J. Taylor]. Philadelphia, 1828. 12mo.
2 ANCIENT Hymns of Holy Church. [Partly extracted and translated from the Roman breviary. By J. W.] Hartford, 1845. 16°

HYNEMAN, Rebekah, *Mrs*. The Leper, and other Poems. Philadelphia, 1853. 12°

CELAND. An Historical and Descriptive Account of Iceland, Greenland, and the Faroe Islands. N. York, 1844. 12°

IDA. [A poem.] Boston, 1851. 12°

IDA, *Countess.* The Countess Ida: a tale of Berlin. By the author of " Norman Leslie," . . *etc.* [Theodore S. Fay.] 2 vol. N. York, 1840. 12°

IDLE MAN (The). [A Miscellany of Tales and Essays. By R.H. Dana.] Vol. 1, and vol. 2, part 1. [5 parts separately paged.] New York, 1821-22. 12°

ILLINOIS, STATE OF. Constitution of the State of Illinois. Adopted in Convention, *etc.* (26th Aug. 1818). Washington, 1818. 8°

2 THE REVISED Laws of Illinois: containing all laws of a general and public nature, passed by the eighth General Assembly, at their session held at Vandalia; . . together with all laws required to be republished by the said General Assembly. Vandalia, 1833. 8°

3 ILLINOIS in 1837: a sketch descriptive of the situation, productions, etc. of the State; together with a letter on the cultivation of the prairies, by the Hon. H. L. Ellsworth. To which are annexed the letters from a Rambler in the West. Philadelphia, 1837. 8°

4 SKETCHES of Illinois, descriptive of its geographical features, productions, and public lands. Philadelphia, 1838. 8°

INA, *Pseud.* Paragraphs on the subject of judicial reform in Maryland, showing the evils of the present system, and pointing out the only remedy, *etc.* Baltimore, 1846. 8°

INCEST. The Doctrine of Incest stated; with an examination of the question whether a man may marry his deceased wife's sister, in a letter to a clergyman of the Presbyterian Church. By Domesticus. Second edit. New York, 1837. 8°

INCHIQUIN. Inchiquin, the Jesuit's letters, during a late residence in the United States of America; being a fragment of a private correspondence. accidently discovered in Europe, containing a favourable view of the manners, *etc.* of the United States. By some unknown foreigner. [Charles J. Ingersoll.] New York, 1810. 8°

2 THE UNITED States and England: being a reply to the criticism [by R. Southey] on Inchiquin's Letters, contained in the Quarterly Review for Jan. 1815. Philadel. 1815. 8°

INDEPENDENCE DAY; or, two modes of spending it. Philadelphia, 1852. 16mo.

INDEPENDENT. A Discourse on Government and Religion, calculated for the meridian of the 30th of

January.   By an independent. Boston, 1750. 8vo.

INDEPENDENT CHRONICLE and the Universal Advertiser. N° 944-6, 989, 990, 993-6, 998-1001, Nov. 30, 1786, to Jan. 3, 1788. Boston, 1786-88. Fol.

THE INDEPENDENT GAZETTE and New York Journal. N° 9-19. New York, 1784. Fol.

INDEPENDENT GAZETTEER; or, the Chronicle of Freedom. N° 89-90, 93-94, 98, 101, 102, 103, 105, 106, 175. Philadel. 1783-85. Fol.

INDEPENDENT JOURNAL; or, the General Advertiser. N° 16, 18, 20, 22, 24. New York, 1784. Fol.

INDEPENDENT LEDGER and the American Advertiser. N° 456-57. Boston, 1786. Fol.

INDIA. Labourers in the East, or memoirs of eminent men, who were devoted to the service of Christ in India. By the author of Pierre and his Family. 2 vol. Philadelphia, 1827. 12mo.

INDIANA, TERRITORY OF. Memorial of the Citizens. . . of the Indiana Territory, praying for the interposition of Congrefs, to relieve them from certain opprefsions and embarrafsments. Washing. 1804. 8°

INDIANA, STATE OF. The revised Laws of Indiana; in which are comprised all such acts of a general nature as are in force in the said State, adopted and enacted by the General Afsembly at their fifteenth sefsion. To which are prefixed, . . sundry . . documents connected with the political history of . . Indiana, etc. Indianapolis, 1831. 8°

2 THE REVISED Statutes of the State of Indiana, adopted and enacted by the General Afsembly, at their twenty-second sefsion, etc. Indianapolis, 1838. 8°

3 THE REVISED Statutes of the State of Indiana, passed at the twenty-seventh sefsion of the General Assembly ; also sundry acts, ordinances, and public documents . . To which are prefixed the constitutions of the United States and of the State of Indiana. [Revised and edited by S. Bigger and G. H. Dunn.] Indianapolis, 1843. 8°

4 LAWS [annual] of the State of Indiana, pafsed and published at the sixteenth sefsion of the General Assembly, held at Indianapolis, . . in Dec. 1831 [and at the 17th, 19th, 23rd, 24th, 25th, 26th, 27th, 28th, 29th, 30th, and 31st sefsions]. 12 vol. Indianapolis, 1832-47. 8°

5 JOURNAL of the House of Representatives of the State of Indiana . . [from the 22nd to the 31st] sefsion of the General Afsembly, . . at Indianapolis, . . 1837 [to 1846, inclusive]. 10 vol. Indianapolis, 1837-46. 8°

6 JOURNAL of the Senate of the State of Indiana during the 22nd sefsion [continued to the 31st, inclusive] of the General Afsembly . . at Indianapolis . . 1837 [to 1846, inclusive]. 10 vol. Indianapolis, 1837-46. 8°

7 REPORTS made to the House of Representatives, at the twenty-fourth sefsion of the Legislature of Indiana, begun and held at Indianapolis, Dec. 2, 1839 [and 25th sefsion, 1840-41]. 2 vol. Indianapolis, 1840-41. 8°

8 DOCUMENTS of the House of Representatives, at the twenty-sixth sefsion of the General Afsembly of the State of Indiana, begun . . at . . Indianapolis, Dec. 6, 1841 [27th sefsion, 1842, 28th sefsion, 1843]. 3 vol. Indianapolis, 1842-44. 8°

9 DOCUMENTS of the Senate of Indiana. Twenty-fourth sefsion [begun Dec. 1839, the 25th sefsion, 1840, the 26th, 1841, the 27th, 1842, the 28th, 1843]. 5 vol. Indianapolis, 1840-44. 8°

10 DOCUMENTS of the twenty-ninth sefsion of the General Afsembly of

the State of Indiana, begun .. at ..
Indianapolis, Dec. 2, 1844. 2 vol.
[and of the 29th sefsion, 1845, 2 vol.
and the 30th sefsion, 1846, 2 vol.]
6 vol. Indianapolis, 1845-47. 8°

INDIANA ANNUAL REGISTER
and Pocket Manual for 1845. By
C. W. Cady. Indianapolis, 1844.
12°

INDIAN LIFE. Tales of the
North-west; or, sketches of Indian
life and character, by a resident beyond the frontier. Boston, 1830. 12°

INDIAN MISSIONARY. The
Good Indian Mifsionary [a Sunday-
school tale]. Philadel.[1833]. 12mo.

INDIAN PRIMER. Indiane
Primer asuh negonneyeuuk. Ne
naahpe Mukkiesog Woh tauog wun-
namuhkuttee og ketamunnate Indiane Unnontoowaonk. Kah Menin-
nunk wutch Mukkiesog (The Indian
Primer; or, the first book. By which
children may know truely to read the
Indian language. And Milk for Babes.)
Maſsachusetts-Indian and English.
Boston, 1720. 12mo.

INDIANS. A brief Account of
the Proceedings of the Committee,
appointed by the yearly meeting of
Friends, held in Baltimore, for promoting the improvement and civilization of the Indian natives. Baltimore, 1806. 8vo.

2 DOCUMENTS and proceedings relating to the formation and progreſs
of a Board in the city of New York,
for the emigration, preservation, and
improvement of the aborigines of
America. July 22, 1829. N. York,
1829. 8°

3 REVIEW of an Article in the North
American for Jan. 1830, on the present relations of the Indians. [Bos-
ton ! 1830 !] 8°

4 THE REMOVAL of the Indians:
an article from the American Monthly
Magazine; an examination of an
article in the North American Review; and an exhibition of the ad-

vancement of the southern tribes in
civilization and Christianity. Boston,
1830. 8°

5 RIGHTS of the Indians. [An account of the proceedings at a public
meeting held in Boston, Jan. 21,
1830, to consider the relations then
subsisting between the government
of the United States and the Indians;
with a memorial to Congreſs thereon.]
[Boston, 1830.] 8°

6 RIGHTS of the Indians. [Reso-
lutions, memorial, and circular letter on the relations between the government of the United States of
America and the Indians.] [Boston,
1830.] 8°

7 LAWS of the Colonial and State
Governments relating to Indians and
Indian affairs, from 1633 to 1831 inclusive; with an appendix containing
the proceedings of the Congreſs of
the Confederation, and the laws of
Congreſs, from 1800 to 1830, on the
same subject. Washington, 1832. 8°

8 PLEA for the Indians... Written
as a memorial .. to the Senate and
House of Representatives in Congreſs
afsembled. [Hartford ? 1845 !] 8°

INDUSTRY. Industry and Fru-
gality proposed as the surest means
to make us a rich and flourishing
people; and the linen manufacture
recommended as tending to promote
these among us. With some reflections on charity, *etc.* Boston, 1753.
8°

INFANT DIALOGUES. Infant
Dialogues, adapted to the use of infant and primary schools. By the
author of the Infant School Manual.
Worcester, 1833. 12°

INFANT SCHOOL GRAMMAR.
The Infant School Grammar, *etc.*
New York, 1830. 12°

INGERSOLL, CHARLES JARED.
Edwy and Elgiva: a tragedy. Philadelphia, 1801. 8vo.

2 A DISCOURSE concerning the influence of America on the mind, being

the annual oration before the American Philosophical Society. Philadelphia, 1823. 8°

3 A COMMUNICATION on the improvement of Government : read before the American Philosophical Society . . October 1st, 1824. Philadelphia, 1824. 8°

4 HISTORICAL Sketch of the second war between the United States of America and Great Britain, declared by act of Congress, the 18th of June, 1812, and concluded by peace, the 15th of February, 1815. 2 vol. Philadelphia, 1845-49. 8vo.

5 See INCHIQUIN.

INGERSOLL, CHARLES M. Conversations on English Grammar, . . illustrated by appropriate exercises ; adapted to the use of schools. Philadelphia, 1835. 12°

INGERSOLL, EDWARD. A Digest of the Laws of the United States of America from March 4th, 1789, to May 15th, 1820. Including also the Constitution and the old Act of Confederation, and excluding all acts relating to Columbia, acts establishing or discontinuing post-roads, and private acts. Philadelphia, 1821. 8vo.

2 AN ABRIDGEMENT of the Acts of Congress now in force, excepting those of private and local application, with notes of decisions, giving construction to the same, in the Supreme Court of the United States, etc. Philadelphia, 1825. 8°

INGERSOLL, GEORGE G. A Discourse [on Mark x. 42-44] delivered before the legislature of Vermont, on the day of general Election. Burlington, 1830. 8°

INGERSOLL, JOSEPH REED. An Address delivered at the opening of the Wills Hospital, for indigent blind and lame, March 3, 1834. Philadelphia [1834]. 8°

2 AN ADDRESS delivered before the Phi Beta Kappa Society, Alpha of

Maine, in Bowdoin College . . Sept. 7, 1837. Brunswick, 1837. 8°

INGLIS, CHARLES, *Bishop of Nova Scotia.* The Claim and Answer, with the subsequent proceedings, in the case of the Rt. Rev. C. Inglis against the United States, under the sixth article of the Treaty of Amity, Commerce, and Navigation, between His Britannic Majesty and the United States of America. Philadelphia, 1799. 4°

INGRAHAM, EDWARD D. A View of the Insolvent Laws of Pennsylvania. Second edition, with considerable additions. Philadelphia, 1827. 8°

2 A SKETCH of the Events which preceded the Capture of Washington by the British, on the 24th of August, 1814. Philadelphia, 1849. 8vo.

INOCULATION. The Imposition of Inoculation as a Duty, religiously considered. Boston, 1721. 8vo.

2 A LETTER to a Friend in the Country ; attempting a solution of the objections against Inoculation. Boston, 1721. 8vo.

3 A LETTER from one in the Country to his Friend in the City ; in relation to the distresses occasioned by Inoculation. Boston, 1721. 8vo.

4 INOCULATION of the Small Pox as practised in Boston, considered in a letter to A[lexander] S[tuart], M.D. and F.R.S. in London. [By W. Douglass.] Boston, 1722. 12mo.

5 THE ABUSES and Scandals of some late Pamphlets in favour of Inoculation of the Small Pox, modestly obviated ; and Inoculation further considered, in a Letter to A[lexander] S[tuart,] [by W. Douglass.] Boston, 1722. 12mo.

6 POSTSCRIPT to Abuses, etc. obviated [in a letter to A. Stuart, M.D. etc. by W. Douglass]. Being a short . . answer to matters of fact . . misrepresented in a late doggrel dialogue [between Academicus and Sawny, etc.] [Boston, 1722.] 8°

7 A DISSERTATION concerning Inoculation of the Small Pox. [By W. D. i.e. William Douglaſs.] Boston, 1730. 8vo.

INQUISITION, TRIBUNAL OF, SPAIN. Records of the Spanish Inquisition, translated from the original manuscripts. Boston, 1828. 8vo.

INSKIP, J. S. Methodism explained and defended. Cincinnati, 1851. 12°

INSTRUCTION for field Artillery, horse and foot. Compiled by a board of artillery officers. Baltimore, 1845. 12mo.

INSTRUCTOR. The Family Instructor... [By D. Defoe.] To which is added, several new dialogues and a number of prayers, etc. First American, altered and improved, from the seventeenth English edition. Georgetown, 1814. 12°

2 INDUCTIVE Grammar; designed for beginners. By an Instructor. Boston, 1829. 12°

INTEREST of City and Country to lay no duties; ... also how the Government may be easier and better supported than by duties. New York, 1726. 8vo.

INTERNATIONAL MONTHLY MAGAZINE of Literature, Art, and Science. Aug. 1850 to April, 1852. 5 vol. New York, 1850-52. 8°

INTRODUCTION to Popular Lessons, for the use of small children in schools. By the author of American Popular Leſsons. Ninth edition. New York, 1836. 12°

2 AN INTRODUCTION to Geometry, and the science of Form. Prepared from the most approved Pruſsian text books. Boston, 1843. 12°

INVALID. A Winter in the West Indies and Florida; containing general observations upon modes of travelling, manners and customs, climates and productions, with a particular description of St. Croix, Trinidad de Cuba, Havana, Key West and St. Augustine, as places of resort for northern invalids. By an Invalid. New York, 1839. 12°

INVESTIGATOR. The Triangle: a series of numbers upon three theological points, enforced from various pulpits in the city of New York. By Investigator. New York, 1832. 8°

IREDELL, JAMES. A Digest of all the reported Cases determined in the Courts of North Carolina, from the year 1778 to the year 1837 [continued to 1845] inclusive. 3 vol. Raleigh, 1839-46. 8°

2 REPORTS of Cases at Law argued and determined in the Supreme Court of North Carolina. June, 1840, to June, 1845. Vol. 1-5. Raleigh, 1841-45. 8°

3 REPORTS of Cases in Equity argued and determined in the Supreme Court of North Carolina. June, 1840, to June, 1845, both inclusive. Vol. 1-3. Raleigh, 1841-45. 8°

IRIS (THE), an illuminated Souvenir for 1852. Edited by J. S. Hart. Philadelphia, 1852. 8°

IROQUOIS INDIANS. Another Tongue brought in, to confeſs the Great Saviour of the World. Or some communications of Christianity, put into a tongue used among the Iroquois Indians, in America, and put into the hands of the English and the Dutch traders; to accommodate the great intention of communicating the Christian Religion unto the Salvages, among whom they may find anything of this language to be intelligible. Boston, printed by B. Green, 1707. Small 8°

IRVING, JOHN T. Addreſs delivered on the opening of the New York High School for females. New York, 1826. 8°

2 INDIAN Sketches taken during an expedition to the Pawnee tribes. 2 vol. Philadelphia, 1835. 12°

IRVING, THEODORE. The Conquest of Florida by Hernando de Soto. New York, 1851. 12°

IRVING, WASHINGTON. Bracebridge Hall, or the humourists: a medley. By Geoffrey Crayon, Gent. [W. Irving]. 2 vol. New York, 1822. 8°

2 TALES of a Traveller. By Geoffrey Crayon [W. Irving]. 4 parts. Philadelphia, 1824. 8°

3 LETTERS of Jonathan Oldstyle, Gent. By the author of " The Sketch Book" [W. Irving]. With a biographical notice. New York, 1824. 8°

4 THE CRAYON Miscellany. N° 1. A Tour on the Prairies. Philadelphia, 1835. 12mo.

5 ASTORIA, or anecdotes of an enterprize beyond the Rocky Mountains. 2 vol. Philadelphia, 1841. 8°

6 BIOGRAPHY and Poetical Remains of the late M. M. Davidson. Third edition. Philadel. 1842. 8vo.

7 THE LIFE of Oliver Goldsmith. With selections from his writings. 2 vol. New York, 1844. 12°

8 OLIVER Goldsmith: a biography . . With illustrations. New York [printed], London, 1849. 4°

9 THE SKETCH Book of Geoffrey Crayon, Gent. . . With a new introduction by the author (W. Irving). Illustrated, etc. London [New York printed], 1849. 8vo.

10 A BOOK of the Hudson; collected from the various works of D. Knickerbocker. Edited by Geoffrey Crayon. 1849. 12mo.

11 TALES of a Traveller. By Geoffrey Crayon, Gent. . . with illustrations by F. O. C. Darley. New York, 1850. 8°

12 TALES of a Traveller. By Geof-frey Crayon, Gent. London [New York printed], 1850. 8vo.

13 ILLUSTRATIONS of W. Irving's Dolph Heyliger, designed and etched by J. W. Ehninger. [With the text.] New York, 1851. Obl. 4°

14 A HISTORY of New York from the beginning of the World to the end of the Dutch Dynasty; . . by Diedrich Knickerbocker, with illustrations by F. O. C. Darley. New York, 1852. 8°

ISAAC, DANIEL. The Doctrine of Universal Restoration examined and refuted; and the objections to that of endless punishment considered and answered: being a reply to the most important particulars contained in the writings of Winchester, Vidler, Wright, and Weaver. New York, 1819. 8°

ISABEL, Pseud. [i. e. WILLIAM GILMORE SIMMS]. Pelayo; or, the cavern of Covadonga. A romance [in verse]. By Isabel. New York, 1836. 8°

ISOCRATES. The Panegyricus of Isocrates, from the text of Bremi, with English notes. By C. C. Felton. Greek. Cambridge, 1847. 12°

IZARD, GEORGE. Official Correspondence with the Department of War, relative to the military operations of the American army under the command of Major General Izard, on the northern frontier of the United States, in the years 1814 and 1815. Philadelphia, 1816. 8°

IZARD, RALPH. Correspondence of Mr. R. Izard, of South Carolina, from .. 1774, to 1804; with a short memoir. [Edited by Anne Izard, Deas?] Vol. 1. New York, 1844. 12°

ACKMAN, Joseph. The sham Robbery, committed by E. P. Goodridge on his own person, . with a history of his journey . . and his trial with Mr. E. Pearson, whom he maliciously arrested for robbery; also the trial of Levi and Laban Kenniston. Concord, N. H. 1819. 12°

JACKMAN, William. The Australian Captive; or, an authentic narrative of fifteen years in the life of W. Jackman. Edited by J. Chamberlaine. London [New York printed], 1853. 12mo.

JACKSON, Andrew, *President of the United States of America.* Some Account of some of the [tyrannical?] deeds of General Jackson. [With the account of an affray at Nashville between the same and Col. T. H. Benton, *etc.*] [Franklin? 1818.] s. sh. fol°

2 Correspondence between Gen. A. Jackson and J. C. Calhoun . . on the subject of the course of the latter, in the deliberations of the Cabinet of Mr. Monroe, on the occurrences in the Seminole war. [With an appendix. Published by J. C. Calhoun.] Washington, 1831. 8°

3 Annual Messages, Veto messages, Protest, *etc.* Second edition. Baltimore, 1835. 8°

JACKSON, Charles. A Treatise on the pleadings and practice in real actions; with precedents of pleadings. Boston, 1828. 8°

JACKSON, Charles T. *M.D.* Report on the geological and agricultural survey of the State of Rhode-Island, made under a resolve of Legislature in the year 1839. Providence, 1840. 8°

JACKSON, J. B. S. *M.D.* Discovery of the inhalation of sulphuric ether as a preventive of pain. By J. B. S. Jackson, M.D. [From the Boston Medical and Surgical Journal of June 30, 1847.] [Bost. 1847.] 8°

2 A descriptive Catalogue of the Anatomical Museum of the Boston Society for Medical Improvement. Boston, 1847. 8vo.

JACKSON, James, *M.D.* An Eulogy on the character of J. Warren, M.D. Boston, 1815. 8°

2 A Report founded on the cases of typhoid fever, or the common continued fever of New England, which occurred in the Massachusetts general Hospital, from the opening of that institution, in Sept. 1821, to the end of 1835: communicated to the Massachusetts Medical Society in June, 1838. Boston, 1838. 8vo.

JACKSON, James C. Hints on the reproductive organs: their diseases, causes, and cure on hydropathic principles. N. York, 1852. 12°

JACKSON, William, *Major.* Eulogium on the character of General Washington, . . . pronounced before the Pennsylvania Society of the Cincinnati, ... Feb. 22, 1800. Philadelphia, 1800. 8°

JACKSON, WILLIAM, Rev. Remains... With a brief sketch of his life and character, by .. W. M. Jackson. New York, 1847. 8°

JACOBINIAD. Remarks on the Jacobiniad. Boston, 1795. 8vo.

JACOBS, THOMAS JEFFERSON. Scenes, Incidents, and Adventures in the Pacific Ocean or the islands of the Australasian seas during the cruise of the clipper Margaret Oakley, under Capt. B. Morrell. N. York, 1844. 12°

JACOBS, WILLIAM STEPHEN. Experiments and Observations on urinary and intestinal calculi. Philadelphia, 1801. 8vo.

JACOCKS, ABEL B. The general features of the moral government of God. Boston, 1848. 12°
2 SUGGESTIONS in Mental Philosophy. Boston, 1853. 8vo.

JAHN, JOHN. Dissertations on the best method of studying the Bible by Jahn and others; translated, with notes, by M. Stuart. Andover, 1827. 8vo.
2 AN INTRODUCTION to the Old Testament; translated from the Latin and German works of John Jahn; with notes by S. H. Turner, D.D. and W. R. Whittingham, A.M. New York, 1827. 8vo.
3 BIBLICAL Archæology; translated from the Latin, with additions and corrections, by T. C. Upham. Andover, 1827. 8vo.

JAHR, G. H. G. New Homœopathic Pharmacopœia and Posology, or the preparation of homœopathic medicines and the administration of doses. Translated, with additions, by J. Kitchen. Philadelphia, etc. 1842. 8vo.

JAMES, EDWIN. Account of an Expedition from Pittsburgh to the Rocky Mountains, 1819-20, under the command of Major S. H. Long. From the notes of Major Long, T. Say, and other gentlemen of the party. 2 vol. Philadelphia, 1823. 8°

JAMES, GEORGE PAYNE RAINSFORD. The History of Chivalry. New York, 1843. 12°
2 FRANCE in the lives of her great men. (Vol. 1. The history of Charlemagne.) New York, 1845. 12°

JAMES, HENRY. Moralism and Christianity. In three lectures. New York, 1850. 12°
2 LECTURES and Miscellanies. New York, 1852. 8°

JAMES, J. J. The Sunday School Teacher's Guide. Philadelphia, 1832. 12mo.

JAMES, MARIA. Wales, and other poems... With an introduction, by A. Potter. New York, 1839. 16°

JAMESON, ANNA, Mrs. Memoirs of celebrated female sovereigns. 2 vol. New York, 1844-45. 12°
2 CHARACTERISTICS of women; .. from the last London edition. New York, 1847. 8°

JAMESON, R. G. Australia and her Gold Regions .. accompanied by a map. . The whole forming a complete guide-book to the gold mines. New York, 1852. 12°

JAMESON, ROBERT. Narrative of discovery and adventure in Africa, from the earliest ages to the present time: with illustrations of the geology, mineralogy, and zoology. By Prof. Jameson, J. Wilson .. and H. Murray. New York, 1844. 12°

JAMIESON, JOHN, D.D. of Edinburgh. The Use of Sacred History, especially as illustrating and confirming the great doctrines of revelation. To which are prefixed, two dissertations; the first, on the authenticity of

the history contained in the Pentateuch and in the book of Joshua; the
second, proving that the books ascribed to Moses were actually written
by him .. by divine inspiration. 2
vol. Hartford, 1810. 8vo.

JANE and her Teacher. Philadelphia [1832?] 12°

JANE Scott. Philadelphia [1832].
12mo.

JANNEY, SAMUEL M. The Life
of W. Penn: with selections from his
correspondence and autobiography. .
Second edition, revised. Philadelphia,
1852. 8°

JAPAN. The Claims of Japan
and Malaysia upon Christendom, exhibited in notes of voyages made in
1837 from Canton, in the ship Morrison and brig Himmaleh, under direction of the owners. 2 vol. New
York, 1839. 12mo.

JAPANESE. Manners and Customs of the Japanese in the nineteenth century; from the accounts of
recent Dutch residents in Japan, and
from the German work of Dr. P. F.
Von Siebold. New York, 1845. 12°

JARNAGIN, SPENCER. Speech
... on the treaty for the annexation
of Texas; delivered in the Senate ..
June 6, 1844. [Washing. 1844.] 8°

JARVIS, CHARLES. An improved
method of Instruction for the piano-
forte... Also a collection of the most
popular airs, and many original compositions, etc. Philadelphia, 1851. 4°

• JARVIS, JAMES JACKSON. History of the Hawaiian or Sandwich
Islands, from the earliest traditionary
period to the present time. Boston,
1843. 8vo.

JARVIS, LEONARD. Speech .. on
the Navy appropriation Bill; in House
of Representatives, .. April 4, 1836.
Washington, 1836. 8°

JARVIS, SAMUEL FARMAR. A
Discourse on the religion of the In-
dian tribes of North America. New
York, 1820. 8vo.

2 AN ADDRESS to the citizens of
Hartford, on the birthday of Linnæus,
May 26, 1836, in behalf of the ob-
jects of the Natural History Society.
[With notes.] Hartford, 1836. 8°

3 No Union with Rome. An address to the members of the Protestant Episcopal Church in the United
States of America, occasioned by the
unjust accusation of a tendency in
our Communion towards the errors of
the present Church of Rome. Hartford, 1843. 12mo.

4 A CHRONOLOGICAL Introduction
to the history of the Church, etc.
[Stereotyped in London, and reissued
in New York, with a new title-page.]
New York, 1845. 8°

5 REVIEW of "Kenrick on the
Primacy" [a reprint of an article in
the Churchman]. [New Haven,]
1846. 8vo.

6 A REPLY to Dr. Milner's "End
of Religious Controversy," so far as
the Churches of the English Communion are concerned. New York,
1847. 12°

7 DR. JARVIS's Vindication [of his
" Chronological Introduction to the
History of the Church;" from the
critique of Professor J. L. Kingsley].
[New Haven, 1848.] 8vo.

JARVIS, WILLIAM C. An Oration,
delivered at Pittsfield, before the Washington Benevolent Society of .. Berkshire, ... July, 1812. Pittsfield,
1812. 8°

JAY, JOHN CLARKSON. A Catalogue of the shells, arranged according to the Lamarckian system; together with descriptions of new or
rare species, contained in the collection of J. C. Jay. Third edition.
New York, 1839. 4to.

JAY, WILLIAM. A Letter to ...
Bishop Hobart, in reply to the pam-

phlet addressed by him to the author, under the signature of Corrector. New York, 1823. 8°

2 THE LIFE of John Jay; with selections from his correspondence and miscellaneous papers. 2 vol. New York, 1833. 8vo.

3 AN INQUIRY into the character and tendency of the American Colonization and American Anti-Slavery Societies. New York, 1835. 12°

4 A VIEW of the action of the Federal Government, in behalf of slavery. Second edition. N. York, 1839. 12°

5 WAR and Peace: the evils of the first, and a plan for preserving the last. New York, 1842. 12mo.

6 AN ADDRESS delivered before the American Peace Society, at its annual meeting, May 26, 1845. Boston, 1845. 8°

JEAN PAUL [FRIEDRICH RICHTER]. Walt and Vult, or the twins. Translated from the Flegeljahre of Jean Paul. By the author of the "Life of Jean Paul" [Eliza Lee]. 2 vol. Boston, 1846. 12°

JEFFERSON, THOMAS, *Third President of the United States of America.* Notes on the State of Virginia. Philadelphia, 1788. 8vo.

2 AUTHENTIC Copies of the correspondence of Thomas Jefferson, Esq. and George Hammond, Esq. on the non-execution of existing treaties. 2 pts. Philadelphia, 1794. 8vo.

3 MEMOIRS of the Hon. T. Jefferson, President of the United States; containing a concise history of those States from the acknowledgment of their independence; with a view of the rise and progress of French influence and French principles in'that country. New York, 1800. 8°

4 A CONCISE Account of the life of Tho. Jefferson. Philadel. 1801. 8vo.

5 NOTES on the State of Virginia. With an appendix. Ninth American edition. Boston, 1802. 12°

6 MESSAGE from the President of

the United States (Thomas Jefferson), communicating discoveries made in exploring the Missouri, Red River, and Washita, by Captains Lewis and Clark, Doctor Sibley and Mr. Dunbar. With a statistical account of the countries adjacent. Washington, 1806. 8vo.

7 MEMOIRS of the Hon. T. Jefferson,.. President of the United States of America; containing a concise history of those states, from the acknowledgment of their independence; with a view of the rise and progress of French influence, and French principles in that country. [By — Carpenter.] 2 vol. [N. York?] 1809. 8°

8 A MANUAL of Parliamentary Practice for the use of the Senate of the United States. Second edition, with the last additions. (Constitution of the United States of America; rules for conducting business in the Senate; rules .. for conducting business in the House of Representatives; joint rules and orders of the two Houses.) 4 parts. Washington, 1812. 12°

9 MEMOIR, Correspondence, and Miscellanies, from the papers of T. Jefferson. Edited by T. J. Randolph. 4 vol. Charlottesville, 1829. 8°

10 A MANUAL of Parliamentary Practice, for the use of the Senate of the United States. To which are added, the rules and orders. Philadelphia, 1840. 12mo.

11 THE WRITINGS of T. Jefferson, being his autobiography, correspondence, reports, messages, addresses, and other writings, official and private. Published by the order of the joint committee of Congress on the Library from the original manuscripts. .. With explanatory notes, .. by the editor, H. A. Washington. 9 vol. New York, 1853-54. 8°

JEFFERSON COLLEGE, CANONSBURG, *Pennsylvania.* Catalogue of the officers and students of Jefferson College, .. July, 1839. Washington, Pa. [1839]. 8°

JENKINS, Charles. Sermons. [Portland ?] 1832. 12°

JENKINS, John S. The Lives of Patriots and Heroes, distinguished in the battles for American Freedom. Auburn, 1847. 16°

2 The Life of General Andrew Jackson, seventh President of the United States; with an appendix, containing the most important of his state papers. Third edition. Buffalo, 1847. 8°

3 The Generals of the last war with Great Britain. Auburn, 1849. 12°

4 United States Exploring Expeditions. Voyage of the United States exploring squadron, commanded by Captain C. Wilkes, .. in 1838-42; together with explorations and discoveries made by Admiral D'Urville, Captain Rofs, and other navigators and travellers; and an account of the expedition to the Dead Sea, under Lieutenant Lynch... With numerous illustrations. Auburn, 1850. 8°.

5 The Life of Silas Wright, late Governor of the State of New York. With an appendix, containing a selection from his speeches, etc. Auburn, 1850. 12°

6 History of the War between the United States and Mexico, from the commencement of hostilities to the ratification of the treaty of peace. Auburn, 1851. 12°

7 Lives of the Governors of the State of New York. Auburn, 1851. 8°

JENKINS, Joseph. An Addrefs delivered before the [Masonic] Grand Lodge of Mafsachusetts, at the installation of officers, Dec. 28, 1829. Boston, 1830. 8°

2 An Address delivered before the [Masonic] Grand Lodge of Mafsachusetts, at the installation of officers, Dec. 28, 1829. Second edition. Boston, 1830. 8°

JENKINS, Warren. The Ohio Gazetteer and Traveller's Guide; con-taining a description of the several towns, townships, and counties. ... together with an appendix, or general register; embracing tables of roads and distances, etc. Revised edition, with a second appendix, containing the census of the State for 1840. Columbus, 1841. 8°

JENKS, Robert W. The Practical Telegraph. An original method of convening and signalizing on land and at sea, by means of the human arms. New York, 1852. 8vo.

JENKS, William. A Sermon [on Deut. xxxii. 29] delivered before the Mafsachusetts Society for the Suppreffion of Intemperance, at their annual meeting, June 1, 1821. With the annual report. Boston, 1821. 12°

JESUS CHRIST. A Glorious Espousal. A brief efsay to illustrate and prosecute the marriage, wherein our great Saviour offers to espouse unto himself the children of men, etc. Boston, 1719. 12°

2 A Right to the Lord's Supper, considered in a letter to a serious enquirer after truth. By a lover of the same [i. e. E. Mayhew?]. Boston, 1741. 12°

3 Jesus the Child's best Teacher. Philadelphia, 1830. 12mo.

JEW (The), being a defence of Judaism against all adversaries, and particularly against the insidious attacks of Israel's Advocate. Edited by S. H. Jackson. Vol. 1. New York, 1824. 8vo.

JEWETT, Charles C. Facts and Considerations relative to duties on books; addrefsed to the Library Committee of Brown University. Providence, 1846. 8vo.

2 Smithsonian Reports. Notices of public libraries in the United States of America, by C. C. Jewett. Printed by order of Congrefs, as an appendix to the fourth annual report of the Board of Regents of the Smithsonian Institution. Washington, 1851. 8°

JEWETT, Isaac Appleton. Passages in Foreign Travel. 2 vol. Boston, 1838. 12mo.

JEWISH CHRONICLE. Published under the direction of the American Society for meliorating the condition of the Jews, and edited by J. Lillie. Vol. 1, 2. July, 1844, to June, 1846. New York, 1844-46. 8°

JEWISH INTELLIGENCER (The). By J. S. C. F. Frey. Vol. 1. New York, 1837. 8°

JEWISH NATION (The); containing an account of their manners and customs, rites and worship, laws and polity. Revised by D. P. Kidder. New York, 1850. 12°

JEWITT, John R. A Narrative of the Adventures and Sufferings of John R. Jewitt, only survivor of the crew of the ship Boston, during a captivity of nearly three years among the savages of Nootka Sound. With an account of the manners, mode of living, and religious opinions of the Natives. Embellished with a plate, representing the ship in possession of the savages. New York, 1816. 12mo.

JOAN OF ARC, an epic Poem, by Robert Southey. Boston, 1798. 12mo.

JOHN. Pictures of John and George. American Sunday School Union. Philadelphia [1830?]. 12°

JOHNSON, A. B. A Treatise on language; in the relation which words bear to things. In four parts. New York, 1836. 8vo.

JOHNSON, C. B. Letters from North America. To which are added, the Constitution of the United States and of Pennsylvania, and extracts from the laws respecting aliens and naturalized citizens. New edition. Philadelphia, 1821. 12°

JOHNSON, George William. A Dictionary of Modern Gardening. . .

Edited, with numerous additions, by D. Landreth. Philadelphia, 1847. 12°

JOHNSON, J. C. The Palace of Industry : a juvenile oratorio, illustrative of the poetry of labour, with additional songs, etc. Boston, 1851. Obl. 12°

JOHNSON, Joseph, M.D. An Experimental Inquiry into the Properties of Carbonic acid Gas or Fixed Air. Philadelphia, 1797. 8vo.

JOHNSON, Louisa. Every Lady her own Flower Gardener. . . Revised from the fourteenth London edition, and adapted to the use of American Ladies. New York, 1852. 12°

JOHNSON, Reverdy. The Memorial of R. Johnson to the Legislature of Maryland; praying indemnity for the destruction of his property in . . Baltimore, by a mob, in August, 1835. [Annapolis, 1836.] 8°
2 The Memorial of R. Johnson, of the city of Baltimore, to the Legislature of Maryland: with an appendix. Baltimore, 1840. 8°

JOHNSON, Reverdy, and Glenn, John. A Final Reply to the Libels of E. Poultney, late President of the Bank of Maryland, and a further examination of the causes of the failure of that institution [with an appendix of letters]. Baltimore, 1835. 8°

JOHNSON, Richard Mentor, Vice President of the United States. Speech of Col. R. M. Johnson, of Kentucky, on a proposition to abolish imprisonment for debt, submitted by him to the Senate of the United States, Jan. 14, 1823. Boston, 1823. 8°
2 Authentic Biography of Colonel R. M. Johnson, of Kentucky [by W. Emmons?]. Boston, 1834. 8°

JOHNSON, Samuel, LL.D. Johnson's Dictionary, Improved by Todd; abridged . . with the addition of Walker's pronunciation . . and an appendix of Americanisms. Boston, 1839. 16°

2 THE LIFE and Writings of S. Johnson. [The life abridged from Gifford.] Selected and arranged by Rev. W. P. Page. 2 vol. New York, 1842-43. 12°

JOHNSON, SUSANNA. A Narrative of the Captivity of Mrs. Johnson [written by herself]. . . Together with an appendix, etc. Fourth edition. Lowell, 1834. 12°

JOHNSON, THEODORE T. Sights in the Gold Region, and Scenes by the way. . . With numerous illustrations . . Second edition, revised and enlarged. New York, 1850. 12°

JOHNSON, WALTER R. Notes on the Use of Anthracite in the Manufacture of Iron; with some remarks on its evaporating power. Boston, 1841. 12°

2 A REPORT to the navy department of the United States, on American Coals applicable to steam navigation and other purposes. Washington, 1844. 8°

3 THE COAL Trade of British America, with researches on the characters and practical values of American and foreign coals. Washington, 1850. 8vo.

JOHNSON, WILLIAM. A Digest of the Cases decided and reported in the Supreme Court of Judicature, and the Court for the Correction of Errors, in the State of New York, from Jan. term, 1799, to Oct. term, 1813, inclusive, etc. Albany, 1815. 8°

2 A DIGEST of the Cases decided and reported in the Supreme Court of Judicature, the Court of Chancery, and the Court for the Correction of Errors, of the State of New York, from 1799 to 1823; with tables of the names of the cases, and of titles and references. 2 vol. Albany, 1825. 8°

3 A DIGEST of Cases decided and reported in the Supreme Court of

Judicature, the Court of Chancery, and the Court for the Correction of Errors, of the State of New York; from 1799 to 1823. Second edition, corrected. 2 vol. Philadel. 1837. 8°

4 REPORTS of Cases adjudged in the Court of Chancery, of New York. March, 1814, to July, 1823. Second edition, revised and corrected. 7 vol. Philadelphia, 1836-39. 8°

5 REPORTS of Cases argued and determined in the Supreme Court of Judicature, and in the Court for the Trial of Impeachments and the Correction of Errors, in the State of New York. 20 vol. (Vol. 1-11, third edition, with additional notes and references: vol. 12-20, second edition, with additional notes and references.) [Vol. 19 is dated 1833.] Philadelphia, 1839. 8°

JOHNSON, WILLIAM. Sketches of the Life and Correspondence of Nathaniel Greene, Major-General of the armies of the United States, in the war of the Revolution. 2 vol. Charleston, 1822. 4to.

JOHNSTON, JOSIAH S. Letter . . to the Secretary of the Treasury; in reply to his circular of . . July 1, 1830, relative to the culture of the sugar-cane. [With an appendix.] Washington, 1831. 8°

2 LETTER . . to a Gentleman in New York; in reply to an article on the expediency of reducing the duty on sugar, particularly in relation to its effect upon the commercial and navigating interests of that city. Washington, 1831. 8°

3 SPEECH of Mr. J. S. Johnston, at a public dinner, given to him and . . E. D. White, in . . New Orleans, June 8, 1831. [New Orleans? 1831.] 8°

JONES, A. D. Illinois and the West: with a township map, containing the latest surveys and improvements. Boston, 1838. 12°

JONES, ALEXANDER. Historical

Sketch of the Electric Telegraph: including its rise and progress in the United States. New York, 1852. 8°

JONES, CHARLES COLCOCK. The Religious Instruction of the Negroes in the United States. Savannah, 1842. 12°

2 SUGGESTIONS on the Religious Instruction of the Negroes in the Southern States. . . with an appendix, etc. Philadelphia, 1847. 8°

JONES, DARIUS C. Temple Melodies: a collection of about two hundred popular tunes, adapted to nearly five hundred favourite hymns, selected with special reference to public, social, and private worship. New York, 1851. 12°

JONES, GEORGE. Excursions to Cairo, Jerusalem, Damascus, and Balbec, from the United States Ship, Delaware, during her recent cruise. With an attempt to discriminate . . the sacred places of the holy city. New York, 1836. 12°

2 ORATION on the National Independence, Richmond, Va. July 4, 1840, before the Franklin Society, at the City Hall. Written and pronounced by George Jones, Tragedian, author of the first Annual Oration (at Stratford-on-Avon), upon the Genius of Shakespeare, etc. etc. Richmond, 1840. 8°

JONES, GEORGE T. AND OTHERS. Report of the Commissioners appointed to examine the Huntsville Branch Bank; also, the expense accounts of said bank. Tuscaloosa, 1845. 8°

JONES, HENRY. American Views of Christ's Second Advent, consisting mostly of Lectures delivered before the late general conventions in . . Boston, Lowell, and New York; vindicating the Lord's personal and glorious appearing on earth, etc. Selected, and in part given, by H. Jones. New York, 1842. 8°

JONES, J. B. The Spanglers and Tinglers; or, the rival belles. A tale unveiling some of the mysteries of society and politics as they exist at the present time in the United States. Philadelphia, 1852. 8°

2 ADVENTURES of Col. Gracchus Vanderbomb of Sloughcreek, in pursuit of the Presidency: also the exploits of Mr. Numerius Plutarch Kipps, his private secretary. Philadelphia, 1852. 12°

3 THE MONARCHIST: an historical novel, etc. Philadelphia, 1853. 12°

JONES, JOHN. The Power of Deception Unveiled, and the Man of Sin Revealed in an analysis of the Book of Revelations. To which is prefixed an essay on the system of man. Philadelphia, 1829. 8°

JONES, JOHN PRINGLE. An Eulogium upon A. Laussat, etc. Philadelphia, 1834. 8°

JONES, JOHN SEAWELL. A Defence of the Revolutionary History of North Carolina from the aspersions of Mr. Jefferson. Boston, 1834. 8°

JONES, Jos., Major, Pseud. Major Jones's Sketches of Travel, comprising the scenes, incidents and adventures in his tour from Georgia to Canada. Philadelphia, 1848. 12°

JONES, S. Pittsburgh in the year eighteen hundred and twenty-six, containing sketches topographical, historical and statistical; together with a directory of the city. Pittsburgh, 1826. 12°

JONES, SAMUEL. An Inaugural Dissertation on Hydrocele. Philadelphia, 1797. 8vo.

JONES, SEABORN. Speech . . on the Oregon question, delivered in the House of Representatives [of the United States] Jan. 15, 1846. Washington, 1846. 8°

JONES, SILAS. Practical Phrenology. Boston, 1836. 12mo.

JONES, WILLIAM. Remarks on the proposed Breakwater at Cape Henlopen . . To which are added, the report of the board of engineers [on the same]. Third edition. Philadelphia, 1828. 8°

JONES, WILLIAM A. Literary Studies : a collection of miscellaneous essays. 2 vol. New York, 1847. 12°
2 MEMORIAL of the late Hon. David S. Jones, with an appendix, containing notices of the Jones family, of Queen's County. New York, 1849. 12°

JONES, WILLIAM BASIL. Wonderful Curiosity ; or, a correct narrative of the celebrated mammoth cave of Kentucky. Russellville, 1844. 16mo.

JOSEPH ; or, sketches of scripture history, illustrating his life and character. Philadel. 1827. 12mo.

JOSEPH, HENRY. The Trial of H. Joseph and A. Otis for the murder of J. Crosby . . on the high seas, in the Circuit-court of the United States . . at Boston, etc. Boston, 1834. 8°

JOSEPHUS, FLAVIUS. Destruction of Jerusalem ; abridged from the History of the Jewish Wars ; with sketches of the history of the Jews since their dispersion. Philadelphia, 1828. 12mo.

JOSLIN, B. F. Discourse on the evidence of the power of small doses and attenuated medicines, including a theory of potentization . . Read before the Homœopathic Society of New York, etc. [The half-title reads : " Dr. Joslin on Homœopathy."] [N. York, 1847.] 8°

THE JOURNAL OF HEALTH. Conducted by an association of physicians [i. e. J. Bell and D. F. Condie]. 4 vol. Philadelphia, 1830-33. 8°

JOURNAL (THE) of LAW. Conducted by an Association of members of the bar. [Vol. 1. all published, N° 1-24.] Philadelphia, 1833. 8°

JOURNAL of the Rhode Island Institute of Instruction for 1845-6-7, edited by H. Barnard. (Report and documents relating to the public schools of Rhode Island, for 1848. Educational Tracts, N° 1-7.) 3 vol. Providence, 1846-49. 8°

JUDSON, ADONIRAM. The young Lady's Arithmetic, etc. Boston, 1808. 12°

JUDSON, ANDREW T. An Address delivered at South Coventry, Connecticut, at the request of the Hale Monument Association, Nov. 25, 1836. Norwich, 1837. 8°

JUDSON, DAVID. Sermons on Church Government, in reply to a discourse on that subject delivered . . by Mr. Ross. To which is added a brief view of the Scripture texts subjoined to some of the most exceptionable articles in the Say-Brooke Platform . . And also an appendix. New Haven [1774]. 8°

JUDSON, EDWARD Z. C. The Mysteries and Miseries of New York. By Ned Buntline. 5 parts. New York [1851 ?]. 8°

JULIA. Living to Christ. A mother's memorial of a departed daughter, Julia. With an introduction by Rev. A. D. Smith. New York, 1853. 12°

JULIA changed : or, the true secret of a happy Christmas. Philadelphia, 1831. 12mo.

JULIAN ; or scenes in Judea. By the author of Letters from Palmyra and Rome. [W. Ware.] 2 vol. New York, 1842. 12°

JULIEN, STANISLAS. Summary of the principal Chinese treatises upon the culture of the mulberry and the rearing of silk-worms. Translated from the Chinese [into French by S. Julien, and from the French into English.]   Washington, 1838. 8°

JULIUS, *Pseud.* A Geographical Narrative, containing a concise description of the several States and provinces of the American Continent, *etc.* [By Julius.] Hanover, 1805. 8°

JUNIUS, *Pseud.* The posthumous works of Junius. To which is prefixed, an inquiry respecting the author: also, a sketch of the life of J. Horne Tooke [by J. Fellows]. New York, 1829.   8°

JUNIUS Tracts: Nº 1. The test, or parties tried by their acts. Nº 2. The currency. Nº 3. The tariff. Nº 4. Life of Henry Clay. Nº 5. Political abolition. Nº 6. Democracy. Nº 7. Labor and capital. Nº 8. The public lands. March, 1843, to May, 1844. New York, 1844. 8vo.

JUNKIN, D. X. The Oath, a divine ordinance and an element of the social constitution: its origin, nature, ends, *etc.* N. York, 1845. 12°

JUNKIN, GEORGE. The great Apostacy; a sermon [on Rev. xviii. 2] on Romanism, *etc.* Philadelphia, 1853. 12mo.

JURISCOLA. An examination of the conduct of Great Britain respecting neutrals, since the year 1791. [By Juriscola.] Second edition, with corrections and amendments. Boston, 1808. 8°

JUSTINIAN, *Emperor of Constantinople.* The Institutes of Justinian. With [Harris's version condensed, and] notes by T. Cooper. Second edition. New York, 1841. 8°

JUVENALIS, DECIUS JUNIUS. A new translation, with notes, of the Third Satire of Juvenal. *Latin and English.* To which are added, miscellaneous poems, original and translated. New York, 1806. 12mo.

ALTSCHMIDT J. H. A School Dictionary of the Latin Language. [One of the " Claſsical Series," edited by Drs. Schmitz and Zumpt. Reprinted from "Chambers's Educational Course."] Philadelphia [1851]. 12°

KANE, ELISHA KENT. Speech .. upon the arrangement of the colonial trade with Great Britain; delivered in the Senate, April 8, 1832. Washington, 1832. 8°

KANE, ELISHA KENT. The United States Grinnell Expedition in search of Sir J. Franklin: a personal narrative by E. K. Kent. [With an appendix.] London [New York printed], 1854 [1853]. 8vo.

KAVANAUGH, H. H. Annual Report of the Superintendent of Public Instruction (H. H. Kavanaugh), Jan. 3, 1840. [Frankfort, 1840.] 8°

KEAN, LAWRENCE. A plain and positive refutation of the Rev. Samuel Pelton's unjust and unfounded charges, entitled, " The Absurdities of Methodism," etc. New York, 1823. 12°

KEENE, RICHARD RAYNAL. A Letter from R. R. Keene to L. Martin, Esq. . . upon the subject of his " Modern Gratitude." Balt. 1802. 8°

KEEP, JOHN. Congregationalism and Church-action; with the principles of Christian union, etc. New York, 1845. 12°

KEEPSAKE (THE): a Gift for the Holidays. With illustrations. [Compiled from the English Keepsake and other sources, by W. T.] Vol. 9. New York, 1853. 8°

KEESE, JOHN. The Poets of America, illustrated by one of her painters. Edited by J. Keese. Fourth edition. 2 vol. N. York, 1811. 12mo.

KEIGHTLEY, THOMAS. The History of England, from the earliest period to 1839. From the second London edition. With notes, etc. by the American editor. 5 vol. New York, 1843-45. 12°

2 THE HISTORY of England... Revised and edited, with notes and additions, by J. T. Smith. 2 vol. New York, 1848. 8°

3 THE HISTORY of Greece... To which is added, a chronological table of contemporary history, by J. T. Smith. New York, 1848. 8°

4 HISTORY of the Roman Empire, from the acceſsion of Augustus to the end of the Empire of the West. Edited by J. T. Smith. New York, 1848. 8°

5 THE HISTORY of Rome... To which is added, a chronological table of contemporary history, by J. T. Smith. New York, 1848. 8°

KEITH, GEORGE, M. A. The Notes of the true Church; with the application of them to the Church of England, etc. a sermon [on Acts ii. 41, 42] preached ... Nov. 7, 1703. New York, 1704. 4to.

2 THE GREAT Neceſsity and Use of the Holy Sacraments: .. a sermon

[on 1 Cor. xii. 13] preached . . Nov. 28, 1703. New York, 1704. 4to.

KELL, RACHEL. Rachel Kell: By the author of " My Mother," etc. New York, 1853. 12°

KELLEY, HALL J. A Geographical Sketch of that part of North America called Oregon, etc. Second edition, enlarged with an appendix, embracing an account of the expedition, and directions for becoming an emigrant. Boston [1830 ?]. 8°

KELLOGG, E. H. Oration delivered . . before the Social Union Society of Amherst College. Amherst, 1836. 8°

KEMBLE, afterwards BUTLER, FRANCES ANNE. Poems. Philadelphia, 1844. 12°

KENDALL, AMOS. Morse's Patent. Full exposure of Dr. C. T. Jackson's pretensions to the invention of the American Electro-Magnetic telegraph. Washington, 1852. 8vo.

KENDALL, GEORGE WILKINS. The War between the United States and Mexico illustrated ; embracing pictorial drawings of all the principal conflicts, by C. Nebel. . . With a description of each battle, by G. W. Kendall. Coloured plates. N.York, 1851. Fol°

KENDALL, JONAS. An Address delivered to the Washington Benevolent Society of Leominster and Fitchburg, at . . their annual meeting, etc. Jaffrey, N. H. 1814. 8°

KENDRICK, ASAHEL C. Greek Ollendorff ; being a progressive exhibition of the principles of the Greek grammar, etc. New York [and] Philadelphia, 1851. 12°

KENNEDY, ANDREW, of Indiana. Remarks . . on the bankrupt law ; delivered in the House of Representatives, Dec. 28, 1842. Washington, 1842. 8°

2 SPEECH . . on the Oregon question ; delivered in the House of Re-

presentatives, Jan. 10, 1846. Washington, 1846. 8°

KENNEDY, DUNCAN. A Discourse delivered Oct. 1, 1851, on occasion of the inauguration of the Rev. W. H. Campbell, as professor of biblical literature in the Theological Seminary of the Reformed Dutch Church, New Brunswick, New Jersey. Albany, 1851. 8°

KENNEDY, EVORY. Observations on Obstetric Auscultation, with an analysis of the evidences of pregnancy, and an inquiry into the proofs of the life and death of the fœtus in utero. . . With an appendix, containing legal notes by J. Smith ; with notes and additional illustrations by J. E. Taylor. New York, 1843. 12mo.

KENNEDY, JOHN P. Address delivered on behalf of the Faculty of Arts and Sciences, on the occasion of the opening of the collegiate department of the University of Maryland. Baltimore, 1831. 8°

2 DISCOURSE on the life and character of George Calvert, the first Lord Baltimore. Baltimore, 1845. 8°

3 REVIEW of the Hon. J. P. Kennedy's Discourse on the life and character of G. Calvert, the first Lord Baltimore. Baltimore, 1846. 8vo.

4 REPLY of J. P. Kennedy to the review of his discourse on the life and character of Calvert, published in the United States' Catholic Magazine, April, 1846. Baltimore, 1846. 8°

5 MEMOIRS of the life of W. Wirt, Attorney General of the United States. . . A new and revised edition. 2 vol. Philadelphia, 1850. 8°

6 ADDRESS delivered before the Maryland Institute for the Promotion of the Mechanic Arts, on the occasion of the opening the fourth annual exhibition, 1851. Baltimore, 1851. 8°

7 SWALLOW Barn ; or, a sojourn in the Old Dominion. Revised edition. New York, 1851. 12°

KENNEDY, JOSEPH C. G. Statistics of American Railroads. Prepared by J. C. G. Kennedy. Washington, 1852. 8°

2 HISTORY and Statistics of the State of Maryland, according to the returns of the seventh census of the United States, 1850, etc. Washington, 1852. Fol.

KENNY, CHARLES. The Manual of Chefs containing the elementary principles of the game, etc. New York, 1847. 16°

KENRICK, FRANCIS PATRICK, Bishop. The Primacy of the Apostolic See, and the authority of General Councils vindicated. In a series of letters to the Right Rev. J. H. Hopkins. Philadelphia, 1838. 12mo.

2 THEOLOGIÆ dogmaticæ tractatus tres [xix] de revelatione, de ecclesia, et de verbo Dei [etc.], quos concinnavit Franciscus Patricius Kenrick. 4 vol. ' Philadelphiæ, 1839-40. 8vo.

3 THE PRIMACY of the Apostolic See vindicated. Philadel. 1845. 8°

KENRICK, PETER RICHARD. The Validity of Anglican Ordinations examined; or, a review of certain facts regarding the consecration of M. Parker, first Protestant Archbishop of Canterbury. Philadel. 1841. 12mo.

KENRICK, WILLIAM. The American Silk Grower's Guide. Boston, 1835. 12mo.

2 THE AMERICAN Silk Grower's Guide; or, the art of raising the mulberry and silk, and the system of successive crops in each season. Second edition, enlarged and improved. Boston, 1839. 12°

3 THE NEW American Orchardist; or, an account of the most valuable varieties of fruit of all climates, adapted to cultivation in the United States. Third edition, enlarged and improved. Boston, 1841. 12mo.

KENRICK, WILLIAM. Notes on Ogdensburg; its position, . . rivers and lakes, and proposed rail-road. Boston, 1846. 8°

KENT, GEORGE. The Characteristics and Claims of the Age in which we live : an oration pronounced . . before the New Hampshire Alpha of the Phi Beta Kappa Society. Concord, 1832. 8°

KENT, JAMES. An Addreſs delivered at New Haven, before the Phi Beta Kappa Society, Sept. 13, 1831. New Haven, 1831. 8°

2 COMMENTARIES on American Law. Second edition. 4 vol. New York, 1832. 8vo.

3 COMMENTARIES on American Law. Fifth edition. 4 vol. New York, 1844. 8°

4 AN ANALYTICAL Abridgment of Kent's Commentaries on American Law. With a full series of questions for examination, . . by J. E. Johnson. New York, 1839. 8°

5 A COURSE of Reading, drawn up by the Hon. J. Kent, for the use of the members of the Mercantile Library Aſsociation. New York, 1840. 12°

6 OUTLINE of a Course of English Reading, based on that prepared . . by the late Chancellor Kent; with additions by Charles King; edited with further additions and notes by H. A. Oakley. New York, 1853. 8°

KENT, JOSEPH. Speech [in the House of Representatives; in support of a resolution moved for restricting the veto power of the President, etc.] [Washington, 1834.] 8°

2 SPEECH . . . . in support of an amendment to the Constitution to restrain the veto power of the President . . . delivered in the Senate, . . Feb. 20, 1835. Washington, 1835. 8°

KENT, WILLIAM. An Addreſs pronounced before the Phi Beta Kappa Society of Union College, at Schnectady, etc. New York, 1841. 8°

KENTUCKY, State of. The Statute Law of Kentucky; with notes, prælections, and observations on the public acts; comprehending also, the laws of Virginia, and acts of Parliament in force in this commonwealth; the charter of Virginia, the federal and state constitutions, and .. a table of reference to the cases adjudicated in the Court of Appeals. By W. Littell. 3 vol. Frankfort, 1809-11. 8°

2 A DIGEST of the Statute Laws of Kentucky, of a public and permanent nature, from the commencement of the Government to the Session of the Legislature, ending .. 24 Feb. 1834. With references to judicial decisions. By C. S. Morehead and Mason Brown. 2 vol. Frankfort, 1834. 8vo.

3 MILITIA Law of Kentucky. An Act to amend the Militia Law; approved Feb. 9, 1837. (Digest of the militia laws of the United States.) Frankfort, 1837. 12°

4 ACTS passed at the first Session of the seventeenth General Assembly for the Commonwealth of Kentucky, begun and held in . . . Frankfort, .. Dec. 12, 1808. Frankfort, 1809. 8°

[Also at the]
18th Gen. Assembly, 1st Session, 1809-10
20th Gen. Assembly, 1st Session, 1811-12
21st Gen. Assembly, 1st Session, 1812-13
22nd Gen. Assembly, 1st Session, 1813-14
23rd Gen. Assembly, 1st Session, 1814-15
24th Gen. Assembly, 1st Session, 1815-16
25th Gen. Assembly, 1st Session, 1816-17
26th Gen. Assembly, 1st Session, 1817-18
27th Gen. Assembly, 1st Session, 1818-19
28th Gen. Assembly, 1st Session, 1819-20
29th Gen. Assembly, 1st Session, 1820
30th Gen. Assembly, 1st Session, 1821
30th Gen. Assembly, 2nd Session, 1822
31st Gen. Assembly, 1st Session, 1822
32nd Gen. Assembly, 1st Session, 1823-24
33rd Gen. Assembly, 1st Session, 1824-25
34th Gen. Assembly, 1st Session, 1825
35th Gen. Assembly, 1st Session, 1826-27
36th Gen. Assembly, 1st Session, 1827-28
37th Gen. Assembly, 1st Session, 1828-29
38th Gen. Assembly, 1st Session, 1829-30
39th Gen. Assembly, 1st Session, 1830-31
40th Gen. Assembly, 1st Session, 1831
41st Gen. Assembly, 1st Session, 1832-33
42nd Gen. Assembly, 1st Session, 1833-34
43rd Gen. Assembly, 1st Session, 1834-35
44th Gen. Assembly, 1st Session, 1835-36
Frankfort, 1810-37. 8°

5 ACTS of the General Assembly of the Commonwealth of Kentucky,

December Session, 1836 (1837, 1838, 1839, Called Session August, 1840, Dec. 1840, 1841, 1842, 1843, 1844, 1845). 11 vol. Frankfort, 1837-46. 8°

6 JOURNAL of the Senate of the Commonwealth of Kentucky, begun and held in .. Frankfort, .. Dec. 5, 1814 (Dec. 1, 1817; Dec. 7, 1818; Dec. 6, 1819; Oct. 16, 1820; Oct. 21, 1822; Nov. 3, 1823; Nov. 1, 1824; Nov. 7, 1825; Dec. 4, 1826; Dec. 3, 1827; Dec. 1, 1828; Dec. 7, 1829; Dec. 6, 1830; Nov. 7, 1831; Dec. 3, 1832; Dec. 31, 1833; Dec. 31, 1834; Dec. 28, 1835, with an appendix of documents; Dec. 5, 1836, with an appendix; Dec. 4, 1837: Dec. 3, 1838, with an appendix; Dec. 2, 1839, with an appendix; Dec. 7, 1840; Dec. 31, 1841; Dec. 31, 1842; Dec. 30, 1843; Dec. 31, 1844; Dec. 31, 1845). Frankfort, 1815-46. 8°

7 JOURNAL of the House of Representatives of the Commonwealth of Kentucky, begun and held in . . . Frankfort, Dec. 5, 1814 (1816, 1817, 1818, 1819, 1820, 1822, 1824, 1825, 1826, 1827, 1828, 1829, 1830, 1831, 1832, 1833, with an appendix; 1834, 1835, with an appendix; 1836 with an appendix; 1837, 1838, with an appendix; 1839 with an appendix; 1840, 1841, 1842, 1843, 1844).. Frankfort, 1814 [1815]-45. 8°

8 ANNUAL Report of the Commissioners of the Sinking Fund, etc. Communicated to the Legislature, .. Jan. 21, 1840. Frankfort, 1840. 8°

9 REPORT of the Committee on the Sinking Fund, communicated to the House, .. Feb. 12, 1840. Frankfort, 1840. 8°

10 REPORT of the Board of Internal Improvement, made in compliance with a resolution of the House of Representatives . . . of Dec. 9, 1839. [Frankfort, 1840.] 8°

11 REPORT of the Joint Committee appointed to visit the Deaf and Dumb Asylum, at Danville, and examine its condition and resources. Communi-

cated to the Legislature, . . Feb. 1, 1840. [Frankfort, 1840.] 8°

12 REPORT of the Select Committee, to whom was referred the response of the Treasurer. [Frankfort, 1840.] 8°

13 ANNUAL Report of the Board of Internal Improvement. Communicated to the Legislature, . . Jan. 16, 1840. Frankfort, 1840. 8°

14 REPORT of the Committee on the expenditures of the Board of Internal Improvement. [Frankfort, 1840.] 8°

15 REPORT of the Board of Internal Improvement, made in compliance with a resolution of the House of Representatives . . . of Jan. 20, 1840. [Frankfort, 1840.] 8°

16 REPORT of the Joint Committee appointed to examine the condition and resources of Transylvania University and the Lunatic Asylum. [Frankfort, 1840.] 8°

17 REPORT of the Joint Committee on Banks. Communicated to the Legislature, Jan. 28, 1840. [Frankfort, 1840.] 8°

18 REPORTS communicated to both branches of the Legislature of Kentucky, at the December Session, 1840 (1841, 1842, 1843, 1844, 1845). 6 vol. Frankfort, 1840-46. 8°

19 AN ADDRESS to the Presbyterians of Kentucky, proposing a plan for the instruction and emancipation of their slaves. By a Committee of the synod of Kentucky. Newburyport, 1836. 12°

20 A QUARTER Race in Kentucky, and other Sketches, illustrative of scenes, characters, and incidents throughout " the universal Yankee Nation." Edited by W. T. Porter. Philadelphia, 1847. 12°

KENTUCKY STATE REGISTER, for . . 1847. . . Edited by T. P. Shaffner. Louisville, 1847. 12°

KERSEY, JESSE. A Narrative of the early life, travels, and Gospel labours of J. Kersey, late of Chester County, Pennsylvania. Philadelphia, 1852. 12°

KETCHUM, HIRAM. A Eulogy on the late D. Webster, pronounced before the Faculty and Students of Yale College, etc. New Haven, 1853. 8°

KETTELL, THOMAS PRENTICE. Constitutional Reform: in a series of articles contributed to the Democratic Review, upon Constitutional Guaranties in political government; . . . to which are added, two letters of the Hon. M. Hoffman. . . Also, the correspondence of T. Jefferson on Constitutional Reform. Edited by T. P. Kettell. New York, 1846. 8°

KIDDER, DANIEL P. Mormonism and the Mormons: a historical view of the rise and progress of the sect self-styled Latter Day Saints. New York, 1844. 16°

KIDDER, FREDERIC, and GOULD, AUGUSTUS A. The History of New Ipswich, from its first grant in 1736, to the present time ; with genealogical notices of the principal families, etc. Boston, 1852. 8°

KIDDLE, HENRY. A Manual of Astronomy and the use of the globes. New York, 1852. 12°

KIENER, L. C. General Species and Iconography of recent shells comprising the Massena Museum, the collection of Lamarck, the collection of the Museum of Natural History, and the recent discoveries of travellers. Translated from the French by D. Humphreys Storer. N° 1. Boston, 1837. 8vo.

KILBOURN, JOHN. Public Documents concerning the Ohio canals, which are to connect Lake Erie with the Ohio River; comprising a complete official history of these great works of internal improvement, from their commencement down to the close of the

Seßion of the Legislature of 1831-32. Compiled by J. Kilbourn. Columbus, 1832. 8°

2 THE OHIO Gazetteer and Traveller's Guide; together with an appendix, or General Register. Revised edition. By W. Jenkins. Columbus, 1839. 12mo.

KIMBALL, RICHARD B. Romance of Student Life abroad. New York, 1853. 12°

KIMBALL and JAMES' Busineß Directory for the Mißißippi Valley; 1844... With a brief notice of the discovery and occupation of the Mississippi Valley. Cincinnati, 1844. 8°

KIMBER, EMMOR. Arithmetic made easy to children... The fourth edition, enlarged and improved. Philadelphia, 1809. 12°

KINE POCK. Constitution for the government of the New York Institution for the inoculation of the Kine Pock. New York, 1802. 12°

2 FACTS and Observations relative to the kine-pock, drawn up by the Medical Board of the New York Institution for the inoculation of the kine-pock. New York, 1802. 8vo.

KING, ALONZO. Memoirs of G. D. Boardman, late mißionary to Burmah. With an introductory eßay. Boston, 1839. 12mo.

KING, CHARLES. A Memoir of the construction, cost, and capacity of the Croton Aqueduct, compiled from official documents: together with an account of the civic celebration, .. Oct. 14, 1842, on occasion of the completion of the great work; preceded by a preliminary eßay on ancient and modern aqueducts. New York, 1843. 4°

2 PROGRESS of the City of New York during the last Fifty Years, with notices of the principal changes and important events. A lecture. New York, 1852. 8°

KING, D. S. The Riches of

Grace; or, the bleßing of perfect love, as experienced, enjoyed and recorded by living witneßes. Edited by D. S. King. Boston, 1847. 12°

KING, DANIEL P. An Addreß commemorative of seven young men of Danvers, who were slain in the battle of Lexington, delivered .. on the sixteenth anniversary of the battle. With notes. Salem, 1835. 8°

KING, DANIEL P. AND OTHERS. Answer of the Whig Members of the Legislature of Maßachusetts, constituting a majority of both branches, to the Addreß of His Excellency, M. Morton, [Governor of Maßachusetts] delivered in the . Convention of the two Houses. Jan. 22, 1840. Boston, 1840. 8vo.

KING, JOHN, M.D. AND NEWTON, ROBERT S. The Eclectic Dispensatory of the United States of America. Cincinnati, 1852. 8vo.

KING, JOHN ANTHONY. Twenty-Four Years in the Argentine Republic; embracing its civil and military history, and an account of its political condition before and during the administration of Governor Rosas, etc. [Edited by T. R. Whitney.] New York, 1846. 12°

KING, JOHN P. Speech .. in the . Senate, Sept. 23, 1837, upon the "Sub-Treasury Bill." [Washington? 1837.] 12°

KING, MITCHELL. A Discourse on the Qualifications and Duties of an Historian; delivered before the Georgia Historical Society, on .. its fourth anniversary, etc. Savannah, 1843. 8°

KING, RUFUS. Speech .. on the American Navigation Act; delivered in the Senate of the United States, etc. New York, 1818. 8°

KING, THOMAS BUTLER. Report on California. Washington, 1850. 8°

2 CALIFORNIA, the Wonder of the

Age. . . Being the report of T. B. King. New York, 1850. 8°

KING, THOMAS STARR. The Death of Mr. Webster ; a sermon [on Daniel vi. 3]. Second edition. Boston, 1852. 8°

2 THE LOSSES and Gains of a Church. A sermon [on Job xv. 10] . . on occasion of the death of Mr. D. Weld. Boston, 1852. 8°

KINGSBURY, C. P. An Elementary Treatise on Artillery and Infantry adapted to the service of the United States, etc. New York, 1849. 12°

KINGSLEY, JAMES LUCE. A Sketch of the History of Yale College, in Connecticut. Prepared by Professor Kingsley, and first published in the American Quarterly Register. Boston, 1835. 8°

2 A HISTORICAL Discourse, delivered by request before the citizens of New Haven, April 25, 1838, the two hundredth anniversary of the first settlement of the town and colony. New Haven, 1838. 8vo.

KINNE, WILLIAM. A Short System of Practical Arithmetic . . Second edition. Hallowell, Maine, 1809. 12°

KINSMAN, HENRY W. An Oration pronounced before the inhabitants of Boston, July 4, 1836, in commemoration of the sixtieth anniversary of American Independence. Boston, 1836. 8°

KINSMEN (THE); or, the black riders of Congaree. A tale, by the author of "The Partisan," etc. [W. G. Simms]. 2 vol. Philadelphia, 1841. 12°

KIP, FRANCIS M. Memoirs of an Old Disciple and his Descendants: C. Miller, S. S. Miller, I. L. K. Miller, Rev. J. E. Miller. . . with an introductory chapter by T. de Witt. New York, 1848. 12°

KIP, WILLIAM, INGRAHAM. The

History, Object, and proper Observance of the holy season of Lent. Second edition. Albany, 1844. 12°

2 THE EARLY Jesuit Missions in North America, compiled and translated from the Letters of the French Jesuits, with notes.. London [New York printed], 1847. 8vo.

3 THE DOUBLE Witness of the Church. . . Fifth edition. New York, 1851. 12°

KIRBY, EPHRAIM. Reports of Cases adjudged in the Superior Court of the State of Connecticut, from . . 1785, to May 1788 ; with some determinations in the Supreme Court of Errors. Litchfield, 1789. 8°

KIRK, EDWARD N. Great Men are God's Gift. A discourse [on Isaiah xlv. 6, 7] on the death of D. Webster. Boston, 1852. 8°

KIRKBRIDE, THOMAS S. Report of the Pennsylvania Hospital for the Insane. . . 1842-45. Philadelphia, 1843-46. 8°

2 ACCOUNT of the Pennsylvania Hospital for the Insane. From the American Journal of Insanity. (Extracted principally from the reports of T. S. Kirkbride.) [Utica, N. Y. 1845.] 8°

KIRKHAM, SAMUEL. English Grammar in familiar lectures; accompanied by a compendium, etc. Twenty-seventh edition, enlarged and improved. New York, 1835. 12°

KIRKLAND, CAROLINE MARY. Western Clearings. London [New York printed], 1846. 8vo.

2 SPENSER and the Faëry Queen. [Selections, with notes, etc.] London [New York printed], 1847. 8vo.

3 HOLIDAYS Abroad; or, Europe from the West. 2 vol. New York, 1849. 12°

4 THE EVENING Book or Fire-side Talk on Morals and Manners, with sketches of Western life. New York, 1852. 8°

5 GARDEN Walks with the Poets. [A collection of poems and extracts.] By Mrs. C. M. Kirkland. New York, 1852. 12°

6 THE BOOK of Home Beauty .. with twelve portraits of American ladies, from drawings by C. Martin. New York, 1852. 4°

7 A BOOK for the Home Circle; or familiar thoughts on various topics, literary, moral and social. New York, 1853. 4°

KIRKLAND, JOHN THORNTON. An Oration, delivered at the request of the Society of Phi Beta Kappa, in the Chapel of Harvard College, on the day of their anniversary, July 19, 1798. Boston, 1798. 8°

KIRWAN, *Pseud.* [i. e. Nicholas Murray, D.D.] Letters to the Rt. Rev. J. Hughes. By Kirwan. [Edited by S. I. Prime.] 2 parts. New York, 1848. 12°

2 ROMANISM at Home. Letters to the Hon. R. B. Taney... Sixth edition. New York, 1852. 12mo.

KLIPSTEIN, LOUIS F. Study of Modern Languages. Part first. French, Italian, Spanish, Portuguese, German and English. New York, 1848. 4°

2 A GRAMMAR of the Anglo-Saxon Language... Revised and enlarged edition; [with postscript and appendix.] New York, 1849. 12°

3 ANALECTA Anglo-Saxonica. Selections, in prose and verse, from the Anglo-Saxon Literature: with an introductory ethnological essay, and notes, critical and explanatory. 2 vol. New York, 1849. 12°

KNAPP, GEORGE CHRISTIAN. Lectures on Christian Theology. Translated by Leonard Woods, Jun. 2 vol. New York, 1821-33. 8vo.

KNAPP, SAMUEL LORENZO. Biographical Sketches of eminent lawyers, statesmen, and men of letters. Boston, 1821. 8vo.

2 AN ORATION pronounced before the society of Phi Beta Kappa, at Dartmouth College. Bost. 1824. 8°

3 THE GENIUS of Masonry, or a defence of the order. Providence, 1828. 12mo.

4 LECTURES on American Literature, with remarks on some passages of American history. New York, 1829. 8°

5 A MEMOIR of the Life of Daniel Webster. Boston, 1831. 12°

6 ADVICE in the pursuits of literature, containing historical, biographical, and critical remarks. Second edition. New York, 1832. 8°

7 AMERICAN Biography .. forming part VI of the Treasury of Knowledge and library of reference. New York, 1833. 12mo.

8 THE LIFE of Thomas Eddy; comprising an extensive correspondence with many of the most distinguished philosophers and philanthropists of this and other countries. New York, 1834. 8vo.

9 TALES of the GARDEN of Kosciuszo. New York, 1834. 12°

10 THE BACHELORS, and other tales, founded on American incidents and character. N. York, 1836. 12°

11 FEMALE Biography; containing notices of distinguished women, in different nations and ages. Philadelphia, 1846. 12°

KNEELAND, ABNER. The American definition spelling-book . . Hough's fourth edition. Concord, 1826. 12°

KNICKERBOCKER (THE); or New York Monthly Magazine. 1833 to 1856. 47 vol. New York, 1833-56. 8°

KNICKERBOCKER, DIEDRICH, *Pseud.* [i. e. Washington Irving]. A Book of the Hudson River, collected from the various works of D. Knickerbocker. Edited by G. Crayon [i. e. W. Irving]. New York, 1849. 12°

KNIGHT, JONATHAN. Eulogium

on N. Smith, M. D. . . pronounced at his funeral, *etc.* New Haven, 1829. 8°

KNIGHT, SARAH. The Journals of Madam Knight and the Rev. Mr. Buckingham, from the original manuscripts, written in 1704 and 1710. 2 parts. New York, 1825. 12°

KNOWLES, JAMES D. Life of Mrs. Ann H. Judson. Philadelphia, 1832. 12mo.

2 MEMOIR of Roger Williams, the founder of the State of Rhode Island. Boston, 1834. 12°

KNOWLES, JAMES SHERIDAN. Knowles's Elocutionist; a first-claſs rhetorical reader and recitation book. . . Enlarged and adapted to the purposes of instruction in the United States, by E. Sargent. Second edition. New York, 1844. 12°

KNOX, JOHN. Crumbs from the Land o'Cakes. Boston, 1851. 16°

KNOX, JOHN P. Historical Account of St. Thomas, W. I. with its rise and progreſs in commerce, missions and churches, climate . . and incidental notices of St. Croix and St. Johns, slave insurrections, *etc.* New York, 1852. 8°

KNOX, VICESIMUS. Eſsays, moral and literary. 2 vols. New York, 1793. 12mo.

2 ELEGANT Extracts; . . originally compiled by the Rev. V. Knox. A new edition . . prepared by J. G. Percival. 6 vol. Boston, 1842. 8°

KOHLMANN, ANTHONY. Unitarianism philosophically and theologically examined: in a series of periodical numbers; comprising a complete refutation of the leading principles of the Unitarian system. Third edit. 2 vol. Washington, 1821. 8°

KOLLOCK, SHEPARD K. Pastoral Reminiscences, . . with an introduction by A. Alexander. New York, 1849. 12°

KOLLOCK, SUSAN. Little Susan; or, a memoir of Susan Kollock, daughter of the Rev. Shepard K. Kollock. Philadelphia, 1831. 12mo.

KOSSUTH, LOUIS. Kossuth in New England: a full account of the Hungarian governor's visit to Maſsachusetts; with his speeches, and the addreſses that were made to him: . . with an appendix. Boston, 1852. 8°

2 THE FUTURE of Nations . . A lecture; revised and corrected by the author. New York, 1852. 8°

KOTZEBUE, AUGUST FRIEDRICH FERDINAND VON. The Virgin of the Sun: a play in five acts [and in prose]. From the German of A. von Kotzebue, with notes marking the variations from the original [translated by J. Lawrence]. New York, 1800. 8vo.

2 THE WILD-GOOSE Chace: a play in four acts [and in prose], with songs. From the German of A. von Kotzebue [by W. Dunlap]. With notes marking the variations from the original. New York, 1800. 8°

KRAITSIR, CHARLES. Gloſsology: being a treatise on the nature of language and on the language of nature. New York, 1852. 12°

KREBS, JOHANN PHILIP. Guide for writing Latin: consisting of rules and examples for practice. From the German by S. H. Taylor. Second edition. Andover, 1845. 12°

KREBS, JOHN M. The American Citizen. A discourse [on Deut. iv. 7, 8] on the nature and extent of our religious subjection to the government under which we live: including inquiry into the scriptural authority of that provision of the constitution of the United States which requires the surrender of fugitive slaves. New York, 1851. 8°

KRUMMACHER, FRIEDRICH WILHELM. The early days of Elisha: translated from the German of F. W. Krummacher . . With an introduction by G. Spring, *etc.*   New York, 1853. 8mo.

KUEHNER, Raphael. Elementary Grammar of the Latin language: with a series of Latin and English exercises for translation, and a collection of Latin reading lessons, with the requisite vocabularies . . Translated from the German by J. T. Champlin. Boston, 1845. 12°

KUHN, William. Speech pronounced by W. Kuhn, on the occasion of his graduation at Mount St. Mary's College, Emmitsburg.   Baltimore, 1837. 8°

KUNST, P. J. Ein Amerikanisches Wörterbuch der Englischen und Deutschen, Sprache. Th. 1. *Eng. Deutsch.* (An American dictionary of the German and English languages. Pt. 2, *Ger.* and *Eng.*) 2 parts. Harrisburg, 1850. 12°

ABARRAQUE, A. G. Instructions and observations concerning the use of the chlorides of soda and lime. Translated by Jacob Porter. Second edition. New Haven, 1831. 8vo.

2 METHOD of using the chloride of soda, either for dreſſing ill-conditioned sores, or as a means of purifying unhealthy places, and of disinfecting animal substances. Translated by Jacob Porter. Northampton, 1833. 8vo.

LABLACHE, LOUIS. Complete method of singing . . with examples for illustration, and progreſſive vocalizing exercises. Translated from the French. Boston, [1851 ?] 4°

LABOR and Love. A Tale of English life. Boston, 1853. 12°

LACO, Pseud. The writings of Laco, as published in the Maſſachusetts Centinel, etc. Boston, 1789. 8°

LACOMBE, JEAN BAPTISTE. A specimen of the patriotism of the Jacobins in France, or, the trial of Jean Baptiste Lacombe, late President of the Military Commiſſion at Bourdeaux, condemned to death as an exaſtor, an extortioner, a prevaricator, a corruptor of morality and of the public mind, and as such a traitor to his country, on the 27th Thermidor, second year of the French Republic, one and indivisible. Translated from the French. Philadelphia, 1795. 8°

LA CROIX, J. A. DE. Portrait of Colonel J. A. De la Croix, Baron de Vanden Boègard : written by his former secretary, and afterwards his adjutant-major. Translated from the French Military Magazine . . By Madame de la Croix. Baltimore, 1814. 12°

LACROIX, SILVESTRE FRANÇOIS. An elementary treatise on Arithmetic, taken principally from the Arithmetic of S. F. Lacroix, and translated into English [by J. Farrar] with . . alterations and additions, etc. Cambridge, 1818. 8°

2 AN ELEMENTARY treatise on plane and spherical Trigonometry, and on the application of algebra to geometry ; from the mathematics of Lacroix and Bézout. Translated from the French [by J. Farrar], etc.

3 ELEMENTS of Algebra : . . Translated from the French . . by J. Farrar. Fourth edition. Bost. 1833. 8°

4 AN ELEMENTARY treatise on Arithmetic, taken principally from the arithmetic of S. F. Lacroix. . . Translated from the French, with alterations and additions . . by J. Farrar. Fourth edition, revised and correſted. Boston, 1834. 8°

LADD, JOSEPH BROWN. An Essay on primitive, latent, and regenerated Light. Charleston [1790 ?] 12°

2 THE LITERARY remains of J. B.

Ladd, collected by . . E. Haskins . . to which is prefixed a sketch of the author's life by W. B. Chittenden. New York, 1832. 12°

LADY. Secret History; or the horrors of St. Domingo, in a series of letters written by a Lady at Cape François to Colonel Burr. Philadelphia, 1808. 12°

2 THE LADY of the farm-house. Philadelphia, 1828. 12mo.

3 FLORA's Dictionary. [A treatise on the language of flowers. With a series of poetical extracts.] By a Lady. Baltimore [1831]. 4°

4 THE YOUNG Lady's Friend. By a Lady. Boston, 1836. 12°

5 THE FLOWER People. A token of friendship. By a Lady. Hartford, 1846. 16°

6 THE LADY's Companion; or sketches of life, manners, and morals at the present day. Edited by a Lady. Philadelphia, 1851. 8°

7 RURAL Hours. By a Lady [Miſs Susan Fenimore Cooper]. Third edition. New York, 1851. 12°

LADY'S BOOK (THE), (a magazine of fashion and the arts.) Vol. 1 to 19. Philadelphia, 1830-39. 8° [Continued as] Godey's Lady's Book and Ladies' American Magazine, etc. Edited by Mrs. S. J. Hale, Mrs. L. H. Sigourney (M. McMichael) and L. A. Godey. Vol. 20 to 53. Philadelphia, 1840-56. 8°

LADIES' COMPANION (THE), a monthly Magazine of Literature and the Arts. [Edited by W. W. Snowden, J. H. Payne, A. S. Stephens, H. F. Harrington, L. H. Sigourney, and E. C. Embury.] May, 1834, to April, 1844. 20 vol. New York, 1834-44. 8° [Continued as] The Ladies' Companion and Literary Expositor; a monthly magazine, embracing every department of literature. New series, vol. 1. May to Oct. 1844. New York, 1844. 8°

LA FAYETTE. See MOTIER.

LAFEVER, MINARD. The Modern Builder's Guide . . Illustrated by ninety copper-plate engravings. New York, 1851. 4°

LA FONTAINE, JEAN DE. La Fontaine. A present for the young. [A selection of his fables, in English verse.] From the French [by J. S. Wright]. Boston, 1839. 12°

LA HAYE, LOUIS MARIE DE, Viscount de Cormenin. The public and private History of the Popes of Rome, from the earliest period to the present time; including the history of saints, martyrs, fathers of the church, . . and the great reformers. Translated from the French. 2 vol. Philadelphia [1846]. 8°

L'ALLEGRO. Pseud. "As good as a Comedy," or the Tenneſſean's Story. By an editor. (L'Allegro.) Philadelphia, 1852. 12°

LALLEMAND, HENRI DOMINIQUE, Baron. A Treatise on Artillery: to which is added, a summary of military reconnoitring, of fortification, of the attack and defence of places, and of castrametation. Translated from the manuscript of the author, by J. Renwick. 2 vol. New York, 1820. 8vo.

LAMARTINE, ALPHONSE DE PRAT DE. History of the Girondists . . [An abridgment only.] Translated by H. T. Ryde. 3 vol. New York, 1847. 12°

2 ENGLAND in 1850 . . Translated by W. C. Ouseley. N. York, 1851. 8°

LAMBERT, EDWARD R. History of the Colony of New Haven, before and after the union with Connecticut. . . Illustrated by engravings. New Haven, 1838. 12mo.

LAMBERT, ELI. A Treatise on Dower. Comprising a digest of the American decisions, and the provisions of the revised statutes of the State of New York. N. York, 1834. 8°

LAMBERT, T. S. *M. D.* Practical Anatomy, physiology, and pathology; hygiene and therapeutics, *etc.* Portland, 1851. 12mo.

2 POPULAR Anatomy and Physiology, adapted to the use of students and general readers, *etc.* Auburn, Rochester, 1852. 12mo.

LAMSON, ALVAN. The Memory of J. Robinson, a discourse [on Ezra viii. 21]. Boston, 1852. 8°

LANCASTER COUNTY, PENNSYLVANIA. The Voice of Lancaster county upon the subject of a national foundry. Lancaster, 1839. 8°

LANCASTER, JOSEPH, A comparative view of the two systems of Education of the Infant Poor, as recommended by Mr. Lancaster and Dr. Bell; with an account of the progress of Mr. Lancaster's plan, and comments on Dr. Marsh's sermon against the .. Lancasterian system: extracted from the Edinburgh Review, N° 37; *etc.* Boston, 1812. 8°

2 THE LANCASTERIAN System of Education; with improvements. By its founder, J. Lancaster. Baltimore, 1821. 8°

3 EPITOME of some of the chief Events and Transactions in the Life of J. Lancaster, containing an account of the rise and progress of the Lancasterian system of education; .. written by himself. New Haven, 1833. 8vo.

LANCASTERIAN SYSTEM. Manual of the Lancasterian System of Teaching as practised in the schools of the Free School Society of New York. New York, 1820. 8°

LANDER, RICHARD AND JOHN. Journal of an Expedition to explore the course and termination of the Niger; with a narrative of a voyage down that river to its termination. 2 vol. New York, 1844. 12°

LANDIS, ROBERT W. The Doctrine of the Resurrection of the Body asserted and defended, in answer to the exceptions recently presented by the Rev. G. Bush. Philadelphia, 1846. 12°

2 LIBERTY's Triumph. A poem. New York, 1849. 12°

LANE, BENJAMIN INGERSOL, *Rev.* Sabbath Evening Lectures; or the refuge of lies and the covert from the storm: being a series of thirteen lectures on the doctrine of future punishment. Troy, 1844. 12°

2 RESPONSES on the use of Tobacco. New York, 1846. 12mo.

3 THE MYSTERIES of Tobacco... With an introductory letter, addressed to the Hon. J. Q. Adams, by the Rev. S. H. Cox. New York, 1846. 12mo.

LANG, WILLIAM. Animal Magnetism, or Mesmerism; its history, phenomena and present condition; containing practical instructions, and the latest discoveries in the science, principally derived from a work by W. Lang. With a supplement, containing new and important facts, by C. H. Townshend. N. York, 1844. 12mo.

LANMAN, CHARLES. Essays for Summer Hours. 2nd edition. Boston, 1842. 16°

2 LETTERS from a landscape-painter. By the author of "Essays for Summer Hours." (C. Lanman.) Boston, 1845. 8°

3 A SUMMER in the Wilderness; embracing a canoe voyage up the Mississippi and around Lake Superior. New York, 1847. 12°

4 A TOUR to the River Saguenay in Lower Canada. Philadelphia, 1848. 16°

5 LETTERS from the Alleghany Mountains; [with addenda.] New York, 1849. 12°

6 HAW-HO-NOO; or, records of a Tourist. Philadelphia, 1850. 12°

7 THE PRIVATE Life of Daniel Webster. New York, 1852. 8°

LANMAN, JAMES H. History of Michigan, civil and topographical, in a compendious form; with a view of the surrounding lakes. With a map. New York, 1839. 8°

2 HISTORY of Michigan, from its earliest colonization to the present time. New York, 1842. 12mo.

3 HISTORY of Michigan, from its earliest colonization to the present time. New York, 1843. 12°

LANTERN (THE). N° 1-23. New York, 1852. 4°

LAPE, THOMAS. A Manual of the Christian Atonement. New York, 1851. 12°

LA PLACE, P. SIMON DE, *Marquis*. Mécanique Céleste. Translated, with a Commentary, by Nathaniel Bowditch, LL.D. 4 vol. Boston, 1829-39. 4to.

2 NEW Topographical Map of France, adapted to all the public services, and combined with the operations of the cadaster. (Extract of the opinion of the Marquis of La Place, Chamber of Peers, .. Mar. 21, 1817.) [Translated from the French, by F. R. Haßler.] [Washington, 1843.] 8vo.

LARDNER, DIONYSIUS, *LL.D.* Outlines of History [by T. Keightley]. .. Second American edition, with additions and a set of questions for examination of students, by J. Frost. Philadelphia, 1831. 12°

LARK'S (THE) NEST. American Sunday School Union, Philadelphia. [1830?] 12mo.

LA ROCHEFOUCAULD-LIAN-COURT, FRANCOIS ALEXANDRE FREDERIC DE, *Duke*. A Comparative View of Mild and Sanguinary Laws; and the good effects of the former exhibited in the present economy of the prisons of Philadelphia. Philadelphia, 1796. 12°

2 MORAL Reflections, Sentences, and Maxims .. newly translated from the French, with an introduction and notes. To which are added, moral sentences and maxims of Stanislaus, King of Poland. (A catalogue of books of Proverbs, sayings, maxims, .. and similitudes by ancient, intermediate and modern authors.) L. P. 2 parts. New York, 1851. 4to.

LARRABEE, CHARLES. Thoughts on Peace and War. Hartford, 1845. 12mo.

LATER YEARS. By the author of "The Old House by the River," [here subscribing himself W.] London [Boston printed], 1855. 8vo.

LATHROP, JOHN, *D.D.* A Discourse [on Luke ix. 56] before the Humane Society, in Boston [Massachusetts]. Boston, 1787. 8vo.

2 A DISCOURSE [on 1 Tim. vi. 9] before the Massachusetts Charitable Fire Society, at their annual meeting in Boston, 1796. Boston, 1796. 8vo.

3 GOD our Protector and Refuge in danger and trouble. A discourse [on Psalm cxx. 1]. Boston, 1797. 8vo.

4 A SERMON [on Amos iii. 2] preached in Boston, Sept. 27, 1798, a day religiously observed on account of the epidemic prevailing in that town and several other sea-ports in America. Boston, 1798. 8vo.

5 A DISCOURSE [on Psalm cxxviii. 2, 3, 6, 7] in two parts; preached at the commencement of the nineteenth century. Boston, 1801. 8vo.

6 PRAYER. Eulogy by Professor Webber, at the funeral of the Rev. Joseph Willard, President of the University of Cambridge, with a Sermon [on Dan. xii. 3] by the Rev. Mr. HOLMES. Cambridge, 1804. 8vo.

7 A DISCOURSE [on Rom. x. 13-15] before the Society for Propagating the Gospel among the Indians and others in North America; delivered January 19, 1804. Boston, 1804. 8vo.

8 A DISCOURSE delivered before

the members of the Boston Female Asylum. Boston, 1804. 8vo.

9 A Discourse [on 1 Thess. v. 12, 13] delivered at Milton, Oct. 3, 1804, the day on which the pastoral relation of the Rev. J. M'Kean to the Church of Christ in that town was .. dissolved. Boston, 1804. 8vo.

LATHROP, D. W. The Case of the General Assembly of the Presbyterian Church in the United States of America, before the Supreme Court of the commonwealth of Pennsylvania, impartially reported by disinterested stenographers, etc. Philadelphia, 1839. 8vo.

LATHROP, Edward. Metropolitan Influence. Cities in their relation to the world's evangelization. A discourse [upon Acts viii. 5 and 8] delivered at the opening of the .. Tabernacle Baptist Church, New York, Dec. 22, 1850. New York, 1851. 8°

LATHROP, John. A Discourse [on Psalm ci. 1] .. in thanksgiving to God for the blessings enjoyed; and humiliation on account of public calamities. Boston, 1774. 8°

2 An Oration, written at the request of the officers of the Boston regiment, and intended for delivery, Oct. 20, 1794. Boston, 1795. 8°

3 An Oration, pronounced July 4, 1796, at .. Boston, in commemoration of the anniversary of American Independence. Boston, 1796. 8°

4 An Oration, pronounced .. July 4, 1798, .. in commemoration of the anniversary of American Independence. Dedham, 1798. 8°

LATHROP, Joseph. A Discourse before the Humane Society in Boston [on Luke ix. 56]. Boston, 1787. 8°

2 The Works of God in relation to the Church in general, and our own land in particular, especially in the last century; considered in a sermon [on Psalm lxiv. 9] delivered in West Springfield, on the first day

of the nineteenth century. Springfield, 1801. 8°

3 Christ's Warning to the Churches to beware of false prophets, .. illustrated in two discourses [on Matt. vii. 15, 16]; with an appendix. Eleventh edition, revised, corrected, and much enlarged. Boston, 1811. 12°

4 Christ's Warning to the Churches; with an appendix on the apostolic succession. .. With an introductory notice by the Rev. J. M. Wainwright. New York, 1844. 12°

LATIMER, George. An Article on the Latimer Case; [viz. the arrest of G. Latimer as a fugitive slave.] From the .. Law Reporter. Boston, 1843. 8°

LA TOUR, A. La Carrière. Historical Memoir of the war in West Florida and Louisiana in 1814-15. With an atlas. .. Written originally in French, and translated. .. by H. P. Nugent. [With an appendix.] 2 parts. Philadelphia, 1816. 8°

LATROBE, B. Henry. Letter from the Surveyor of the Public Buildings at .. Washington (Dec. 30, 1804) .. accompanying a Bill, making an appropriation for completing the south wing of the capitol, etc. [Washington, 1804.] 8°

LATROBE, John H. B. Memoir of B. Banneker; read before the Maryland Historical Society, etc. Baltimore, 1845. 8°

2 The History of Mason and Dixon's Line. .. an address before the Historical Society of Pennsylvania, Nov. 8, 1854. [Philadel.] 1855. 8vo.

LAUREL HILL CEMETERY, near Philadelphia. Regulations of the Laurel Hill Cemetery, on the River Schuylkill. [Philadelphia,] 1837. 8°

2 Guide to Laurel Hill Cemetery, near Philadelphia. With numerous illustrations. Philadelphia, 1844. 8vo.

LAURIE, Joseph, M.D. Homœopathic Domestic Medicine. .. Sixth

American edition, enlarged and improved by A. G. Hull. New York, 1853. 12mo.

LAW, STEPHEN D. The Jurisdiction and Powers of the United States' Courts, and the Rules of Practice of the Supreme Court of the United States, and of the Circuit and District Courts of Equity and Admiralty; with notes and references, and an appendix containing the orders of the High Court of Chancery of England, etc. Albany, 1852. 8°

LAW REFORM TRACTS. Published under the superintendence of a Law Reform Association. New York, 1852. 8°

LAW REPORTER (THE). Edited by Peleg W. Chandler (and S. H. Phillips). Vol. 1-10. Boston, 1839-48. 8vo. [Continued as] The Monthly Law Reporter. Vol. 11-13 (New series, 1-3), edited by S. H. Phillips. Vol. 14-15 (vol. 4-5 new series), G. P. Sanger. Vol. 16 and 17 (New series, 6-7), G. P. Sanger and G. S. Hale. Vol. 18 (8), by G. S. Hale and J. Codman. Boston, 1849-56. 8vo.

LAWRENCE, ABBOTT. Letters from the Hon. Abbott Lawrence to Hon. Wm. C. Rives, of Virginia. [On the resources of Virginia.] Boston, 1846. 8°

LAWRENCE, AMELIA W. The Offering of Beauty; a present for all seasons. [A selection of pieces in prose and verse, chiefly from English authors.] Edited by A. W. Lawrence. Philadelphia, 1848. 8°

LAWRENCE, EDWARD A. *Pastor of the first Church, Marblehead, Massachusetts.* A Discourse on the death of .. D. Webster; delivered October 31, 1852. Boston, 1852. 8°

LAWRENCE, JONATHAN. A Selection from the Writings of the late J. Lawrence, junior. New York, 1833. 12°

LAWRENCE, WILLIAM BEACH. An Address delivered at the opening of the eleventh Exhibition of the American Academy of the Fine Arts, May 10, 1825. Second edition, with notes. New York, 1826. 8°

2 THE COLONIZATION and Subsequent History of New Jersey: a discourse pronounced before the Young Men's Association of New Brunswick, Dec. 1, 1842. Somerville, 1843. 8°

LAWSON, THOMAS. Statistical Report on the sickness and mortality in the army of the United States. Washington, 1840. 8°

2 METEOROLOGICAL Register for twelve years, .. 1831 to 1842; .. compiled from observations made by the officers of the medical department of the army at the military posts of the United States. Prepared under the direction of T. Lawson. Washington, 1851. 8°

LAY, HENRY C. Letters to a Man bewildered among many Counsellors. Second edition, revised and enlarged. New York, 1853. 12mo.

LAYMAN. Remarks on the proceedings of the Episcopal Conventions for forming an American Constitution... By a Layman. Boston, 1786. 8°

2 ARE you a Christian or a Calvinist? or, do you prefer the authority of Christ to that of the Genevan reformer! .. Suggested by the late review of American Unitarianism in the Panoplist, and by .. Worcester's Letter to .. Channing. To which are added, some strictures on both those works. By a Layman. Bost. 1815. 8°

3 AN INQUIRY into the right to change the Ecclesiastical Constitution of the Congregational Churches of Massachusetts. .. To which is prefixed, Dr. Morse's report to the General Association of Massachusetts, from the Panoplist of August, 1815. [By a Layman.] Boston, 1816. 8°

4 A FEW Remarks on Professor

Stuart's reply to Mr. Channing's sermon. By a Layman. Boston [1819?]. 8°

5 The Scripture Doctrine of Materialism. By a Layman. Philadelphia, 1823. 12°

6 Obstacles and Objections to the cause of permanent and universal peace considered. By a Layman. Boston, 1837. 8°

7 [Third thousand.] Remarks on Schism. By a Layman. London, Boston printed [1843]. 12mo.

8 The Sufferings of Christ. By a Layman. Second edition, revised and enlarged. New York, 1846. 12°

9 Puseyite Developments, or notices of the New York Ecclesiologists... By a Layman. New York, 1850. 8vo.

10 A Review, by a Layman [i. e. S. A. Allibone], of a work entitled, "New Themes for the Protestant Clergy: creeds without charity, theology without humanity, and Protestantism without Christianity" [by S. Colwell]. etc. Philadel. 1852. 12°

LAZARUS, M. Edgeworth. Comparative Psychology. Vol. 1. N. York, 1852. 12°

2 Love vs. Marriage. Part 1. New York, 1852. 12°

3 Involuntary Seminal Losses: their causes, effects, and cure. New York, 1852. 12°

4 Passional Hygiene and Natural Medicine; embracing the harmonies of man with his planet. New York, 1852. 12°

LEA, Albert M. Notes on Wisconsin Territory, with a map. Philadelphia, 1836. 12mo.

LEA, Henry C. Description of some new Fossil Shells, from the tertiary of Petersburg, Va. Read before the American Philosophical Society, May 29, 1843. [Reprinted from the "Transactions" of the Society.] Philadelphia [1843?]. 4to.

2 Catalogue of the Tertiary Testacea of the United States, .. etc. Philadelphia, 1848. 8vo.

LEA, Isaac. Contributions to Geology. Philadelphia, 1833. 8vo.

2 A Synopsis of the Family of Naïades. Philadelphia and London, 1836. 8vo.

3 Description of nineteen new species of Colimacea. [Article xxi of vol. 7 of the Transactions of the American Philosophical Society. New Series.] [Philadelphia, 1840.] 4to.

4 [Descriptions of new fresh-water and land shells.] [A fragment, pp. 281-290, apparently of the Transactions of the Natural History Society of Philadelphia.] [Philadel. 1840.] 8vo.

5 Notice of the Oolitic formation in America, with descriptions of some of its organic remains. [Article xvi of vol. 7 of the Transactions of the American Philosophical Society. New Series.] [Philadelphia, 1840.] 4to.

6 [Part of a volume of the Proceedings of the American Philosophical Society? containing the substance of a communication by I. Lea, entitled, "Descriptions of new fresh-water and land Shells." A fragment, consisting of pp. 281-290.] [Philadelphia, 1841?] 8vo.

7 Observations on the genus unio, together with descriptions of new species in the families Naïades, Colimacea, Lymnæana, Melaniana, and Peristomiana, etc. [Republished from the Transactions of the American Philosophical Society.] Vol. 4, 5. Philadelphia [1844-50?]. 4to.

8 [Communication from I. Lea "upon some reptilian footmarks recently discovered by him in the gorge of the Sharp Mountain, near Pittsville."] [Being pp. 89-96, vol. 5, of the Proceedings of the Academy of Natural Sciences of Philadelphia.] [Philadelphia, 1851?] 8vo.

9 [Begins] [From the Proceedings of the Academy of Natural Sciences of Philadelphia, Vol. v. N° 11, 1851.]

Mr. Lea announced the death of R. C. Taylor, *etc.* [A biographical notice of R. C. Taylor, delivered before the Academy of Natural Sciences of Philadelphia.] [Philadelphia, 1851.] 8vo.

10 [*Begins*] ART. XV. On the Genus Acostæa of D'Orbigny, *etc.* [pp. 125-131, of the " Journal of the Academy of Natural Sciences of Philadelphia," Nov. 1851]. [Philadelphia, 1851.] 4to.

11 ON the Fofsil Footmarks in the red sandstone of Pottsville, Pennsylvania. [From the Transactions of the American Philosophical Society.] Philadelphia, 1852. 4to.

12 A SYNOPSIS of the family of Naïades. Third edition. Philadelphia, 1852. 4to.

13 ON a Fofsil Saurian of the new red sandstone formation of Pennsylvania, with some account of that formation. Also, on some new fofsil molluscs in the carboniferous slates of the anthracite seams of the Wilkesbarre coal formation. [From the Journal of the Academy of Natural Sciences.] Philadelphia, 1852. 4to.

14 RECTIFICATION of Mr. T. A. Conrad's " Synopsis of the Family of Naïades of North America," published in the " Proceedings of the Academy of Natural Sciences of Philadelphia, February, 1853." [From the " Proceedings of the Academy, . . December, 1854."] Phil. 1854. 8vo.

15 FOSSIL Footmarks in the red sandstone of Pottsville, Pennsylvania. Large paper. Philadel. 1855. Fol.

LEA, THOMAS G. Catalogue of Plants, native and naturalized, collected in the vicinity of Cincinnati, Ohio, during the years 1834-1844. By T. G. Lea. Philadel. 1849. 8vo.

LEACH, JOSEPH. The Folly and Wickednefs of Duelling exposed. Andover, 1822. 8vo.

LEAKE, ISAAC Q. Memoir of the Life and Times of General John Lamb, an officer of the Revolution, who com-

manded the post at West Point at the time of Arnold's defection and his correspondence with Washington, Clinton, Patrick Henry, and other distinguished men of his time. Albany, 1850. 8°

LEARNED, JOSEPH D. A View of the policy of permitting slaves in the States west of the Mifsifsippi : being a letter to a member of Congrefs. Baltimore, 1820. 8°

LEAVITT, DUDLEY. Elements of Arithmetic made easy, *etc.* Exeter, 1813. 12°

LEAVITT, JONATHAN. A Summary of the Laws of Mafsachusetts, relative to the settlement, support, employment, and removal of paupers. Greenfield, 1810. 8°

LEAVITT, JOSHUA. Stereotype edition. Easy Lefsons in Reading. Keene, 1831. 12°

2 CHEAP Postage. Remarks and Statistics on the subject of cheap postage and postal reform in Great Britain and the United States. Boston, 1848. 8°

LEAVITT, WILLIAM. A New Method of finding the Longitude at Sunrise, Sunset, and at Noon. Second edition. Salem, 1853. 8vo.

LECTURES. The Spruce Street Lectures. With a lecture on the importance of Creeds, by Samuel Miller, D. D. Philadel. 1833. 4to.

LEE, ALFRED, *Bishop.* Life of the Apostle Peter, in a series of practical discourses. N. York, 1852. 12°

LEE, CHARLES A. The Elements of Geology, for popular use ; containing a description of the geological formations and mineral resources of the United States. New York, 1846. 12°

2 HUMAN Physiology, for the use of elementary schools. . . Seventh edition. New York, 1846. 12°

3 A CATALOGUE of the Medicinal Plants, indigenous and exotic, growing in the State of New York. With a brief account of their composition and medical properties. New York, 1848. 8°

LEE, D. and FROST, J. H. Ten Years in Oregon. N. York, 1844. 12°

LEE, DAY KELLOGG. Summerfield; or life on a farm. Auburn, 1852. 8°

2 THE MASTER Builder; or, life at a trade. New York, 1852. 12°

LEE, ELIZA BUCKMINSTER. Naomi, or Boston two hundred years ago. Second edition. Boston, 1848. 12°

2 MEMOIRS of Rev. J. Buckminster .. and of his son, Rev. J. S. Buckminster. Second edition. Boston, 1851. 12°

3 FLORENCE, the Parish Orphan; and a sketch of the village in the last century. Boston, 1852. 12°

LEE, HENRY, the Elder. Funeral Oration on the death of Gen. Washington, delivered at the request of Congreſs [Dec. 26, 1799]. Boston [1800]. 8°

2 FUNERAL Oration [on George Washington; pronounced before Congreſs, Dec. 26, 1799]. [Philadelphia ? 1800.] 8°

3 MEMOIRS of the War in the Southern department of the United States. 2 vol. Philadel. 1812. 8vo.

4 MEMOIRS of the War in the Southern department of the United States. A new edition, with corrections left by the author, and with notes and additions by Henry Lee. Washington, 1827. 8°

LEE, HENRY, the Younger. The Campaign of 1718 in the Carolinas; with remarks, historical and critical, on Johnson's Life of Greene. To which is added, an appendix of original documents. Philadel. 1824. 8vo.

2 OBSERVATIONS on the writings of T. Jefferson; with particular re-

ference to the attack they contain on the memory of Gen. H. Lee. In a series of letters. New York, 1832. 8°

3 OBSERVATIONS on the Writings of Thomas Jefferson; with particular reference to the attack they contain on the memory of the late Gen. H. Lee. In a series of letters. Second edition, with an introduction and notes, by C. C. Lee. Philadelphia, 1839. 8vo.

LEE, HENRY, of Maſſachusetts. An Exposition of Evidence in support of the Memorial to Congreſs, setting forth the evils of the existing Tariff of Duties, and asking .. a modification of the same... Prepared in pursuance of instructions from the Permanent Committee appointed by the Free Trade Convention aſſembled at Philadelphia, etc. Nº 4-11. Boston, 1832. 8°

LEE, RICHARD HENRY. Memoir of the Life of Richard Henry Lee, and his Correspondence with the most distinguished men in America and Europe. By his grandson, R. H. Lee. 2 vol. Philadelphia, 1825. 8vo.

2 LIFE of Arthur Lee. 2 vol. Boston, 1829. 8vo.

LEE, THOMAS J. A Spelling Book, containing the rudiments of the English language : with appropriate reading leſſons. Boston, 1830. 12°

LEECH, SAMUEL. Thirty Years from Home, or a Voice from the Main Deck; being the experience of S. Leech, who was for six years in the British and American Navies, etc. Fifteenth edition. Bost. [1843 ?] 12°

LEESER, ISAAC. The Jews and the Mosaic Law. Part the first : containing a defence of the revelation of the Pentateuch, and of the Jews for their adherence to the same. (Part the second : containing four eſſays on the relative importance of Judaism and Christianity. By a native of Germany, and a profeſſor of Christianity.) 2 parts. Philadelphia, 5594 [1833]. 8°

LEGARÉ, Hugh Swinton. Writings . . consisting of a diary of Brussels, and journal of the Rhine; extracts from his . . correspondence; orations and speeches; and contributions to the New York and Southern Reviews. Prefaced by a memoir of his life [signed E. W. J.] . . Edited by his sister (M. S. Legaré). 2 vol. Charleston, 1846. 8°

LEGARÉ, I. M. Orta-Undis, and other poems. Boston, 1848. 8°

LEGENDRE, Adrien Marie. Elements of Geometry; . . Translated from the French . . by J. Farrar. New edition, improved and enlarged. Boston, 1833. 8°
2 Elements of Geometry and Trigonometry. Translated from the French . . by D. Brewster. Revised and adapted to the course of mathematical instruction in the United States, by C. Davies. New York, 1846. 8°

LEGER, Theodore. Animal Magnetism, or Psycodunamy. New York, 1846. 12°

LEGGETT, William. Naval Stories. . . Second edition. New York, 1835. 16°
2 A Collection of the Political Writings of W. Leggett. Selected and arranged, with a preface by Theodore Sedgwick, Junior. 2 vol. New York, 1840. 12°

LEGION of Liberty! and Force of Truth; containing the thoughts, words and deeds of some prominent apostles, champions and martyrs. Second edition. New York, 1843. 12°

LEHIGH COAL AND NAVIGATION Company. A History of the Lehigh Coal and Navigation Company. Philadelphia, 1840. 8°

LEIDY, Joseph. Art. vi. History and Anatomy of the Hemipterous Genus Belostoma. [Extracted from the Proceedings of the Academy of Natural Sciences of Philadelphia, pp. 57-70.] [Philadelphia, 1845!] 4to.
2 [Begins] On a new genus and species of Fossil Ruminantia: Poebrotherium Wilsoni. [From the Proceedings of the Academy of Natural Sciences, Philadelphia, pp. 322-26.] [Philadelphia, 1847. 8vo.]
3 [Begins] On a new Fossil Genus and species of Ruminantoid Pachydermata: Merycoidodon Culbertsonii. [From the Proceedings of the Academy of Natural Sciences,] Philadelphia. [Philadelphia, 1848.] 8vo.
4 [Begins] On some bodies in the Boa Constrictor, resembling the Pacinian Corpuscles. [Philadelphia? 1848!] 8vo.
5 Art. xxvi. Descriptions of two species of Distoma with the partial history of one of them. (Plate 43.) [From the Proceedings of the Academy of Natural Sciences of Philadelphia, pp. 301-310.] [Philadelphia, 1848!] 4to.
6 On Entophyta in Living Animals. New species of Entozoa. On Glandulæ Odoriferæ. . . Extracted from the Proceedings of the Academy of Natural Sciences of Philadelphia, Oct. 1849 [pp. 225-236]. [Philadelphia, 1849.] 8vo.
7 On the Intimate Structure and History of the Articular Cartilages . . (With two plates.) [Extracted from the American Journal of the Medical Science for April 1849.] [Philadelphia, 1849.] 8vo.
8 [Begins] Art. xvii. Description of a new species of Crocodile from the Miocene of Virginia [pp. 135-138 of the " Journal of the Academy of Natural Sciences, vol. 2, of Philadelphia."] [Philadelphia, 1851.] 4to.
9 Descriptions of Three Filaria. [Extracted from the Proceedings of the Academy of Natural Sciences of Philadelphia, pp. 117-126.] [Philadelphia, 1851.] 8°
10 Special Anatomy of the Gas-

teropoda of the United States [with plates]. [From Boston Annals of Natural History.] [Boston, 1851.] 8vo.

11 ON the Extinct Species of American Ox. (From the Smithsonian Contributions to Knowledge, vol. 5.) Description of an extinct species of American lion, Felis atrox. A memoir on the extinct Dicotylinæ of America. From the Transactions of the American Philosophical Society, vol. 10. Philadelphia, 1852. 4to.

12 ON Bathygnathus Borealis, an extinct Saurian of the New Red Sandstone of Prince Edward's Island. [Extracted from the Journal of the Academy of Natural Sciences, vol. 2.] [Philadelphia, 1854?] 4to.

13 DESCRIPTIONS of some American Annelida Abranchia. [From the Journal of the Academy of Natural Sciences of Philadelphia.] [Philadelphia, 1854?] 4to.

14 DESCRIPTION of the Remains of Extinct Mammalia and Chelonia from Nebraska Territory, collected during the geological survey under the direction of Dr. D. D. Owen [pp. 539-572 of the memoir published in the "Report of a Geological Survey of Wisconsin," etc. by D. D. Owen; with a title-page]. Philadel. [1854]. 4to.

LEIGH, BENJAMIN WATKINS. Reports of Cases argued and determined in the Court of Appeals, and in the General Court, of Virginia. 9 vol. Richmond, 1830-40. 8°

2 SPEECH . . on the expunging resolution, delivered in the Senate, . . April 4, 1836. Washington, 1836. 8°

LEIGH, P. BRADY. An Abridgment of the Law of Nisi Prius. . . With notes and references to the latest American cases, by G. Sharswood. 2 vol. Philadelphia, 1838. 8°

LE MERCIER, ANDREW. The Church History of Geneva. As also a political and geographical account of that Republick. Boston, 1732. 8vo.

LEMPRIERE, JOHN. Bibliotheca

Clastica; or, a classical Dictionary. A new edition . . by C. Anthon. 2 vol. New York, 1833. 8vo.

LENDRUM, JOHN. A Concise and Impartial History of the American Revolution. To which is prefixed a general history of North and South America, etc. 2 vol. Boston, 1795. 12°

LENNEP, JACOB VAN. The Adopted Son. An historical novel... Translated from the Dutch, by E. W. Hoskin. 2 vol. New York, 1847. 8°

LE NORMAND, MARIANNE A. Historical and Secret Memoirs of the Empress Josephine, first wife of Napoleon Bonaparte. Translated by J. M. Howard. 2 vol. Philadelphia, 1848. 8°

LEONARD, CHARLES ELDREDGE. The Mechanical Principia; containing all the various calculations on water and steam power, and on the different kinds of machinery used in manufacturing; with tables, showing the cost of manufacturing different styles of cotton goods. New York, 1848. 12°

LEONARD, GEORGE, Jun. A Practical Treatise on Arithmetic. . . Fourth edition, stereotyped. Boston, 1841. 12°

LEONHARD, K. C. VON. Popular Lectures on Geology, treated in a comprehensive manner. Translated by J. G. Morris, and edited by F. Hall. Part 1, 2. Baltimore, 1839. 8vo.

LE POIVRE. Travels of a Philosopher; or observations on the manners and arts of various nations in Africa and Asia. Baltimore, 1818. 12mo.

LEPOUZÉ, CONSTANT. Poesies Diverses par Constant Lepouzé. Nouvelle Orleans, 1838. 8°

LESLIE, ELIZA, Miß. Althea Vernon; or, the embroidered handkerchief. To which is added, Hen-

rietta Harrison; or, the blue cotton
umbrella. [Tales.] Phil. 1838. 12°

2 DIRECTIONS for Cookery in its
various branches... Twentieth edition, with improvements, supplementary receipts, and a new appendix.
Philadelphia, 1845. 12°

LESLIE, HOPE; or, early times in
the Maſſachusetts. By the author of
" The Linwoods," etc. [Miſs Catherine M. Sedgwick]. 2 vol. New
York, 1842. 12°

LESLIE, JOHN. Narrative of
Discovery and Adventure in the Polar
Seas and Regions: with illustrations
of their climate, geology, and natural
history; and an account of the whale
fishery. By Profeſſor Leslie, Profeſſor Jameson, and H. Murray. New
York, 1844. 12°

LESLIE, NORMAN. Norman Les-
lie: a tale of the present times. [By
Theodore S. Fay.] 2 vol. New York,
1835. 12°

LESSONS. Secondary Leſſons,
or the improved reader: intended as
a sequel to the Franklin Primer. By
a friend of youth... Twenty-fourth
edition. Greenfield, 1835. 12°

LESTER, C. EDWARDS. The
Condition and Fate of England. Second edition. 2 vol. New York,
1843. 12°

2 THE ARTIST, the Merchant, and
the Statesman of the age of the Me-
dici, and of our own times. 2 vol.
New York, 1845. 12°

3 THE GLORY and the Shame of
England. 2 vol. N. York, 1845. 12°

4 THE ARTISTS of America: a
series of biographical sketches of
American artists. N. York, 1846. 8°

5 MY Consulship. 2 vol. New
York, 1853. 8°

LESTER, C. EDWARDS, and FOSTER,
ANDREW. The Life and Voyages of
Americus Vespucius; with illustra-
tions concerning the navigator, and

the discovery of the New World. New
York, 1846. 8°

LETTERS. A Father's Letters
to his Son. Philadel. 1829. 12mo.

2 FAMILIAR Letters on public cha-
raſters and public events, from the
peace of 1783 to the peace of 1815.
Boston, 1834. 8°

3 FAMILIAR Letters on public cha-
raſters and public events, from the
peace of 1783 to the peace of 1815.
Boston, 1834. 8°

4 LETTERS from the Old World.
By a Lady of New York [Mrs.
Haight?]. Second edition. 2 vol. New
York, 1840. 12mo.

5 LETTERS from abroad to kindred
at home. By the author of " Hope
Leslie," etc. [Miſs Catherine M.
Sedgwick]. 2 vol. New York, 1841.
12°

6 A LETTER to a lady in France
on the supposed failure of a National
Bank, the supposed delinquency of
the National Government, the debts
of the States, and repudiation; with
answers to enquiries concerning the
books of Captain Marryat and Mr.
Dickens. [By Thomas Greaves Cary.
See CARY, T. G.] Boston, 1843. 8vo.

LETTRE de Gros-Jean à son
curé. Philadelphie, 1789. 8vo.

LEUCHARS, ROBERT B. A Practical Treatise on the construſtion,
heating, and ventilation of hot-houses.
With engravings. Boston, 1851. 8°

LE VASSEUR, A. Lafayette in
America in 1824 and 1825; or
journal of travels in the United States.
Translated from the French. 2 vol.
New York, 1829. 12mo.

LEVERETT, F. P. An Abridgment of Leverett's Latin Lexicon...
By F. Gardner. Boston, 1840. 8°

2 A NEW and Copious Lexicon of
the Latin Language; compiled chiefly
from the Magnum totius Latinitatis
Lexicon of Facciolati and Forcellini,
and the works of Schiller and Luenemann. Boston, 1842. Roy. 8vo.

3 A NEW and Copious Lexicon of the Latin Language; compiled chiefly from the Magnum totius Latinitatis Lexicon of Facciolati and Forcellini, and the German works of Schiller and Luenemann. Boston, 1844. 8vo.

LEVIS, JEREMY. Sixty years of the Life of J. Levis. 2 vol. New York, 1831. 12°

LEWIS, ALONZO. The History of Lynn, including Nahant. Second edition. Boston, 1844. 8°

2 LOVE, Forest Flowers, and Sea Shells. [Poems.] Boston, 1845. 16°

LEWIS, ESTELLE ANNA. Myths of the Minstrel. New York, 1852. 8°

LEWIS, ISAAC, D. D. A Sermon [on 1 Tim. iv. 16] delivered in New Haven, at the ordination of . . J. Day, etc. New Haven, 1817. 8°

LEWIS, JOHN. Tables of Comparative Etymology and analogous formations in the Greek, Latin, Spanish, Italian, French, English, and German languages. . . The Greek by G. Long, the German by G. Blaettermann. Philadelphia, 1828. 4to.

LEWIS, MERIWETHER, and CLARK, WILLIAM. Discoveries made in exploring the Miſſouri, Red River, and Washita, by Captains Lewis and Clark, Doctor Sibley and W. Dunbar; with a statistical account of the countries adjacent. With an appendix, by Mr. Dunbar. Natchez, 1806. 8vo.

2 HISTORY of the Expedition under the command of Captains Lewis and Clarke, to the sources of the Miſſouri, thence acroſs the Rocky Mountains, and down the river Columbia to the Pacific Ocean, during 1804-6. Prepared for the preſs by Paul Allen. 2 vol. Philadelphia, 1814. 8°

3 HISTORY of the Expedition under the command of Captains Lewis and Clarke, to the sources of the Miſſouri, thence acroſs the Rocky Mountains, and down the River Columbia to the Pacific Ocean ; performed during the

years 1804, 1805, 1806, by order of the Government of the United States. Prepared for the preſs by Paul Allen. Revised and abridged, . . with an introduction and notes, by A. M'Vickar. 2 vol. New York, 1845. 12°

LEWIS, SETH. The Restoration of the Jews, with the political destiny of the nations of the earth as foretold in the Prophecies of Scripture. With a biographical sketch of the author [subscribed S.]. N. York, 1851. 12°

LEWIS, TAYLER. An Eſſay on the ground and reason of punishment, with special reference to the penalty of death. By T. Lewis. And a defence of capital punishment, by Rev. G. C. With an appendix, containing a review of Burleigh on the death penalty. New York, 1846. 12°

LEWIS, WILLIAM H. Sermons for the Christian Year. New York, 1851. 8°

2 CONFESSION of Christ. New York, 1852. 8vo.

LEWIS, ZECHARIAH. An Oration on the apparent and the real political situation of the United States, pronounced before the Connecticut Society of Cincinnati, . . at . . the celebration of American Independence, July 4, 1799. New Haven, 1799. 8°

LIBERATOR (THE); William Lloyd Garrison, Editor. Vol. 9, N° 40. Boston, 1839. Fol.

LIBERIA. To the Editor of the Rockingham. [Letter from T. S. in reply to certain charges against the above colony.] [Beverley, 1833.] s. sh. fol°

2 THE INDEPENDENT Republic of Liberia; its constitution, and Declaration of Independence : addreſs of the colonists to the free people of color in the United States, with other documents. [Drawn up by S. Greenleaf.] MS. note [by the Rev. T. H. Horne]. Philadelphia, 1848. Fol.

LIBERTAS, *Pseud.* The Fame and Glory of England vindicated : being an answer to " The Glory and Shame of England" [by C. E. Lester]. By Libertas. New York, 1842. 12°

LIBRARIES. Plans for Libraries. By a Friend of Education. Andover, 1833. 4to.

LICENSED HOUSES. An Examination of the License Law of the Commonwealth of Maſſachusetts. First published in the Boston Courier, Dec. 1832. By M. L. V. Boston, 1833. 8°

LIEBER, FRANCIS. A Constitution and Plan of Education for Girard College for Orphans, with an introductory report laid before the Board of Trustees. Philadelphia, 1834. 8vo.

2 THE STRANGER in America ; or, letters to a gentleman in Germany : comprising sketches of the manners, society, and national peculiarities of the United States. Philadelphia, 1835. 8vo.

3 LEGAL and Political Hermeneutics, or principles of interpretation and construction in law and politics. Enlarged edition. Bost. 1839. 12mo.

4 ON International Copyright, in a letter to the Hon. W. C. Preston. New York, 1840. 8vo.

5 GREAT Events described by distinguished historians, chroniclers, and other writers. Collected, and in part translated, by F. Lieber. Boston, 1840. 12mo.

6 COLUMBIA Athenæum Lecture. A lecture on the history and uses of Athenæums. Columbia, 1856. 8vo.

7 *See* ENCYCLOPÆDIA AMERICANA.

LIEBERKUEHN, SAMUEL. The History of our Lord and Saviour Jesus Christ. Translated into the Delaware Indian language by D. Zeisberger. New York, 1821. 12°

LIFE and its Aims : in two parts. London, Philadelphia [printed], 1854. 12mo.

LIFE on the Lakes ; being tales and sketches collected during a trip to the pictured rocks of Lake Superior. 2 vol. New York, 1836. 8vo.

LIFE'S LESSON. A tale. London [Boston? printed], 1854. 8vo.

LIFE INSURANCE, its nature and progreſs. . . Containing also tables of mortality, annuities, etc. New York, 1852. 12°

LIGHT, GEORGE W. Keep Cool, Go Ahead, and a few other poems. Boston, 1851. 12°

L——, LAMBERT. The early Hiſtöſyloſ the Southern States : Virginia, North and South Carolina, and Georgia. Illustrated by tales, sketches, anecdotes, and adventures. With numerous engravings. Philadel. 1832. 12°

2 THE HISTORY of the Middle States, illustrated by tales, sketches, and anecdotes. With numerous engravings. Boston, 1842. 12°

3 THE STORY of the American Revolution. Illustrated by tales, sketches, and anecdotes. With numerous engravings. Boston, 1842. 12°

4 THE HISTORY of New England. Illustrated by tales, sketches, and anecdotes. With numerous engravings. Boston, 1844. 12°

LILY OF THE VALLEY (THE). . . Edited by E. Doten. Boston, 1853. 12°

LINCOLN, ALMIRA H. Familiar Lectures on Botany, practical, elementary, and physiological. With an appendix, containing descriptions of the plants of the United States, and exotics, etc. Twenty-first edition, revised and enlarged. New York, 1844. 12°

LINCOLN, BARNABAS. Narrative of the Capture, Sufferings, and Escape of Capt. B. Lincoln and his Crew ; who were taken by a piratical schooner, December, 1821, off Key Largo, etc. . . Written by himself. Boston, 1822. 8°

LINCOLN, BENJAMIN. An Exposition of certain Abuses practised by some of the medical schools in New England; and particularly, of the agent-sending system, as practised by T. Woodward, M.D., etc. [with a letter from the latter, and comments thereon]. Burlington, 1833. 8°

LINCOLN, DANIEL WALDO. An Oration, pronounced at Boston, . . July 4, 1810, before the Bunker Hill Association, etc. [in commemoration of American Independence]. Boston, 1810. 8°

LINCOLN, LEVI. Address delivered before the Worcester Agricultural Society, Oct. 7, 1819, being their first anniversary cattle show and exhibition of manufactures. Worcester, Dec. 1819. 8°

LINCOLN, LIONEL. Lionel Lincoln; or, the leaguer of Boston. By the author of the Pioneers, Pilot, etc. [J. F. Cooper]. 2 vol. New York, 1825, 1824. 12°

2 LIONEL Lincoln; or, the leaguer of Boston. [A romance.] By the author of "The Spy" [J. F. Cooper]. A new edition. 2 vol. Philadelphia, 1836. . 12°

LINCOLN, LUTHER B. An Address delivered at Deerfield, before the Society of Adelphi, etc. (Poem [on the New Year] by J. Williams.) Greenfield, 1837. 8°

LINCOLN, SOLOMON. An Address delivered before the citizens of the town of Hingham, on the twenty-eighth of September, 1835, being the two hundredth anniversary of the settlement of the town. Hingham, 1835. 8°

LINCOLN, WILLIAM. An Address delivered before the American Antiquarian Society, at their annual meeting, Oct. 23, 1835, . . in relation to the character and services of their late librarian, C. C. Baldwin. Worcester, 1835. 8°

2 AN ADDRESS delivered before the Massachusetts Horticultural Society, at their ninth anniversary, Sept. 20, 1837. [With a report of the Society's proceedings, etc.] Boston, 1837. 8°

3 HISTORY of Worcester, Massachusetts, from its earliest settlement to September, 1836. With various notices relating to the history of Worcester county [and an appendix]. Worcester, 1837. 8vo.

LIND, afterwards GOLDSCHMIDT, JENNY. Programme of Madame Otto Goldschmidt's grand concert . . May 21, 1852. With the words of the songs, and translations. N[ew] Y[ork], 1852. 8°

LINEN, JAMES. Songs of the Seasons, and other poems. New York [1852]. 8°

LINFORD, HARRY. The Fatal Ladder; or, Harry Linford. Philadelphia, 1828. 12°

LINN, JOHN BLAIR. The Powers of Genius, a poem. . . (With an appendix.) Philadelphia, 1801. 8vo.

LINN, LEWIS F. Speech of . . L. F. Linn on his amendment to the land distribution bill, proposing to appropriate the revenue from the public lands to the national defences. In Senate, Aug. 11, 1841. Washington, 1842. 8°

LINN, WILLIAM. The Life of T. Jefferson. . . Second edition. Ithaca, 1839. 12°

2 THE LEGAL and Commercial Common-place Book, containing the decisions of the Supreme Court of the United States, and of the respective State Courts, on bills of exchange, checks, and promissory notes, etc. Ithaca, 1850. 8°

LINNÆAN SOCIETY of New England. Report of a Committee of the Linnæan Society of New England relative to a large marine animal supposed to be a serpent, seen near

Cape Ann, Maſſachuſetts, in August, 1817. Boston, 1817. 8vo.

LINTNER, G. A. *D. D.* A Memoir of the Rev. Walter Gunn. Albany, 1852. 12°

LINWOODS (The); or " Sixty Years since" in America. By the author of " Hope Leslie," *etc.* [Miſs Catherine M. Sedgwick]. 2 vol. New York, 1835. 12°

LIPPARD, GEORGE. Washington and his Generals ; or, legends of the Revolution. . . With a biographical Sketch of the author, by . . . C. C. Burr. Philadelphia, 1847. 8°

LIPPINCOTT, J. B. and Co. Lippincott's Cabinet Histories [of the States of the United States]. Georgia, Kentucky. 2 vol. [*See* ARTHER, T.S.] Philadelphia, 1852. 12°

LISLET, L. MOREAU. A General Digest of the acts of the Legislature of Louisiana : paſſed from . . 1804 to 1827 inclusive, and in force at this last period ; with an appendix, *etc.* 2 vol. New Orleans, 1828. 8°

LIST, FRIEDRICH. Appendix to the Outlines of American Political Economy, in three additional letters, N° 9, 10, 11. Addreſſed by Profeſſor F. List to C. J. Ingersoll, Esq. Philadelphia, 1827. 8°

LITERARY and Philosophical Society of New York. Transactions. Vol. 1. New York, 1815. 4to.

LITERARY and Scientific Repository, and Critical Review. July, 1820, to June, 1822. 4 vol. New York, 1820-22. 8°

LITERARY and Theological Review. Conducted by Leonard Woods, Jun. N° 1-2. N. York, 1834. 8vo.

LITERARY MAGAZINE, and American Register. Oct. 1803 to Oct. 1805. 4 vol. Philadel. 1803-5. 8°

LITERARY MISCELLANY ; including diſſertations and eſſays. . . published quarterly. 2 vol. Cambridge [1805], 1806. 8°

LITERARY WORLD (The): A Gazette for authors, readers, and publishers. Edited [at the outset— Feb. to April, 1847—by Edward A. Duyckinck, then] by Charles F. Hoffman. Feb. 6, 1847, to Jan. 29, 1848 [and from Oct. 1848 by E. A. and G. L. Duyckinck]. 13 vol. New York, 1847-53. 4°

LITERATURE of the World (The). The American Eclectic ; or, selections from the periodical literature of all foreign countries. Vol. 1, 2, conducted by A. Peters and S. B. Treat. Vol. 3 by A. Peters and J. H. Agnew. Vol. 4 by J. H. Agnew. New York, 1841-42. 8° [Continued under the title of] The Eclectic Magazine of Foreign Literature, Science, and Art. Vol. 5-7. Edited by J. H. Agnew. Vol. 8 [no editor's name appears]. Vol. 9-39. W. H. Bidwell, Editor. Vol. 1-39. New York, 1845-56. 8°

LITTLE DECEIVER reclaimed. Philadelphia [1832]. 12mo.

LITTLE EDWARD. Philadelphia [1834]. 12mo.

LITTLE ROBERT'S First Day at the Sunday School. Philadelphia, 1831. 12mo.

LITTLE, EZEKIEL. The Usher, comprising Arithmetic in whole numbers, *etc.* Exeter, 1799. 12°

LITTLE, GEORGE. Life on the Ocean; or twenty years at sea: being the personal adventures of the author. Boston, 1846. 12°
2 THE AMERICAN Cruiser's Own Book. New York, 1851. 12°

LITTLE, JOHN, *Rev.* Obedience to Law, a sermon [on Romans xiii. 5 and Acts v. 29]. N. York, 1851. 8°

LITTLE, JOHN A. The Auto-
biography of a New Churchman; or,
incidents and observations connected
with the life of J. A. Little. Philadelphia, 1852. 12mo.

LITTLETON, MARK, *Pseud.* [*i.e.*
JOHN P. KENNEDY]. Swallow Barn;
or, a sojourn in the Old Dominion. 2
vol. Philadelphia, 1832. 12°

2 HORSESHOE Robinson; a tale of
the Tory ascendancy. By the author
of "Swallow Barn." 2 vol. Philadelphia, 1835. 12°

LITURGIES. The Morning and
Evening Prayer, the Litany, Church
Catechism, Family Prayers, and several chapters of the Old and New
Testament, translated into the Mahaque Indian language. By L. Cla-
eſse. [*See* CLAESSE, L.] New York,
1715. 4to.

2 A LITURGY, collected principally
from the Book of Common Prayer,
for the use of the First Episcopal
Church in Boston; together with the
Psalter, or Psalms of David. [By the
Rev. J. Freeman.] Bost. 1785. 8vo.

3 A LITURGY collected for the use
of the Church at King's Chapel,
Boston. Second edition. Boston,
1811. 8°

4 THE BOOK of Common Prayer,
and administration of the Sacraments
and other rites and ceremonies of the
Church, according to the use of the
Protestant Episcopal Church in the
United States of America. Together
with the Psalter or Psalms of David.
Philadelphia, 1825. 8vo.

5 HYMNS of the Protestant Episcopal Church in the United States of
America... Set forth in General Conventions of the said Church, *etc.*
Philadelphia, 1827. 8vo.

6 A LITURGY for the use of the
Church at King's Chapel in Boston;
collected principally from the Book
of Common Prayer. Fourth edition.
With family prayers and services, by
F. W. P. Greenwood. Boston, 1831.
12mo.

7 A PRAYER-BOOK, in the language
of the Six Nations of Indians, containing the morning and evening service,
the Litany, Catechism, some of the
Collects, and the prayers and thanks-
givings upon several occasions, in the
Book of Common Prayer of the Protestant Episcopal Church; together
with forms of Family and Private Devotions. Compiled from various translations, and prepared for publication
.. by the Rev. S. Davis. New York,
1837. 12mo.

8 EXCERPTA ex Rituali Romano pro
administratione Sacramentorum, ad
commodiorem miſſionariorum diœcesum provinciæ Baltimorensis usum,
etc. Baltimore, 1842. 12°

9 COMPENDIUM Ritualis Romani,
ad usum Diœcesum Provinciæ Baltimorensis. Baltimori, 1842. 12°

10 THE BOOK of Common Prayer,
and Administration of the Sacraments,
together with the Psalter. [To which
are added, metrical psalms and hymns.]
New York [1843]. 8°

11 THE CHRISTIAN Liturgy, and
Book of Common Prayer, containing
the administration of the Sacraments
and other rites and ceremonies of the
Apostolic Catholic or Universal Church
of Christ. With ... extracts from
the Psalter. .... Also a collection of
psalms and hymns for public worship.
Boston, 1846. 12°

LIVE AND LET LIVE; or do-
mestic service illustrated. By the
author of "Hope Leslie," *etc.* [Miſs
Catherine M. Sedgwick]. New York,
1844. 12°

LIVERMORE, ABIEL ABBOT.
Lectures to Young Men on their
moral dangers and duties. New edition. Boston, 1847. 12°

2 THE WAR with Mexico Reviewed.
Boston, 1850. 12°

LIVERMORE, EDWARD SAINT
LOE. An Oration in commemoration
of the diſſolution of the political union
between the United States of America

and France, delivered . . . July 17, 1799, . . in Portsmouth, New Hampshire. Portsmouth, 1799. 4to.

LIVERMORE, Samuel. A Treatise on the law of principal and agent: and on sales by auction. 2 vol. Baltimore, 1818. 8°

LIVINGSTON, Edward. Introductory Report to the Code of prison discipline ; . . being part of the system of penal law, prepared for the State of Louisiana. Philadelphia, 1827. 8°

2 A System of Penal Law for the United States of America. Presented to the House of Representatives of the United States. Washington, 1828. Fol.

3 A System of Penal Law for the State of Louisiana, etc. Philadelphia [1833]. 8vo.

LIVINGSTON, John. Livingston's Law Register; containing the name, post-office, county, and state of every lawyer in the United States, etc. New York, 1851. 8vo.

2 Portraits of eminent Americans now living; with biographical and historical memoirs of their lives and actions. 2 vol. N. York [printed] and London, 1853. 8°

LIVINGSTON, Robert R. Essay on Sheep; their varieties; account of the Merinos of Spain, France, etc. . . . together with miscellaneous remarks on sheep and woollen manufactures. Second edition, much enlarged. New York, 1810. 12mo.

LIVINGSTON, Vanbrugh. An Inquiry into the merits of the Reformed doctrine of " Imputation," as contrasted with those of " Catholic Imputation," or the cardinal point of controversy between the Church of Rome and the Protestant High Church. Together with miscellaneous essays on the Catholic faith. With an introduction by the Right Rev. J. Hughes. New York, 1843. 12°

LIVINGSTON, William. A Funeral Eulogium on the Rev. Mr. Aaron Burr. New York, printed, Boston, re-printed, 1758.

LIVIUS, Titus. Selections from the first five books, together with the twenty-first and twenty-second books entire ; chiefly from the text of Alschefski ; with English notes . . by J. L. Lincoln. Second edition, revised. New York, 1847. 12°

LJUNGSTEDT, Anders. An Historical Sketch of the Portuguese settlements in China ; and of the Roman Catholic Church and mission in China, etc. Boston, 1836. 8vo.

LLOYD, James. Hon. Mr. Lloyd's Letter on Impressments. [Boston, 1813.] 8°

LLOYD, Thomas. The Congressional Register ; . . . Taken in shorthand by T. Lloyd. Vol. 1. New York, 1789. 8°

2 The System of Shorthand practised by Mr. T. Lloyd in taking down the debates of Congress, and now . . published for general use by J. C. Philadelphia, 1793. 12mo.

LLOYD, W. F. The Teacher's Manual. Philadelphia, 1826. 12mo.

LOBSTEIN, Johann Friedrich. A Treatise on the structure, functions, and diseases of the human sympathetic nerve. Translated from the Latin, with notes, by J. Pancoast. Philadelphia, 1831. 8vo.

LOCKE, John Goodwin. Book of the Lockes. A genealogical and historical record of the descendants of W. Locke, of Woburn. With an appendix, containing a history of the Lockes in England, also of the family of J. Locke of Hampton, New Hampshire, and kindred families and individuals. Boston and Cambridge, 1853. 8°

LOCKE, Richard Adams. The celebrated Moon Story. . . With a

memoir of the author and an appendix, containing, 1. An authentic description of the moon; 2. A new theory of the lunar surface in relation to that of the earth, by W. N. Griggs. New York, 1852. 12°

LOCKHART, JOHN GIBSON. The History of Napoleon Buonaparte. 2 vol. New York, 1843. 12°

LOCKWOOD, PETER. Memoir of J. D. Lockwood. Second edition. New York, 1852. 12°

LOEHER, FRANZ. Geschichte und Justände der Deutschen in Amerika. Cincinnati, Leipzig, 1847. 8vo.

LOEWIG, CARL. Principles of Organic and Physiological Chemistry. Translated by D. Breed. London [Philadelphia printed], 1853. 8vo.

LOGAN, GEORGE. An Addreſs on the natural and social order of the world, as intended to produce universal good: delivered before the Tammany Society. Philadel. [1798]. 8°

LOMAX, JOHN TAYLOR. Digest of the Laws respecting real property, generally adopted and in use in the United States; embracing, more especially, the law of real property in Virginia. 3 vol. Philadel. 1839. 8°

2 A TREATISE on the law of executors and administrators, generally in use in the United States; and adapted more particularly to the practice of Virginia. 2 vol. Philadelphia, 1841. 8°

LONG, GEORGE. A Treatise on the law relative to sales of personal property. Second American edition, with additions by B. Rand. Boston, 1839. 8°

LONGACRE, JAMES B. National Portrait Gallery, etc. See HERRING, JAMES.

LONGFELLOW, HENRY WADSWORTH. Voices of the Night. Second edition, Cambridge, 1840. 8vo.

2 POEMS. Philadel. 1845. 8vo.

3 THE POETS and Poetry of Europe. With introductions and biographical notices. Philadelphia, 1845. 8°

4 EVANGELINE, a tale of Acadie. [In verse.] Sixth edition. Boston, 1848. 12°

5 THE SEASIDE and the Fireside. [In verse.] Boston, 1850. 12°

6 KAVANAGH: a tale. Boston, 1851. 12°

7 THE GOLDEN Legend. Boston, 1852. 12°

8 THE POETS and Poetry of Europe. With introductions and biographical notices by H. W. Longfellow [aſsisted by C. C. Felton]. London, New York [printed]. 1855. 8vo.

LONGKING, JOSEPH. Notes, illustrative and explanatory, on the Holy Gospels, arranged according to Townsend's Chronological New Testament. 4 vol. N. York, 1851-49. 16°

LOOMIS, ELIAS. Astronomical Observations made at Hudson Observatory. Third series. [From the Transactions of the American Philosophical Society.] [Philadel. 1845?] 4to.

2 [Begins] HISTORICAL notice of the discovery of the Planet Neptune. [From the American Journal of Science and Arts. Second series. Vol. 5.] [New Haven, 1848.] 8vo.

3 THE RECENT Progreſs of Astronomy, especially in the United States. New York, 1851. 12°

4 ELEMENTS of Analytical Geometry, and of the differential and integral calculus. N. York, 1851. 8°

LOOMIS, JUSTIN. R. The Elements of Geology; adapted to the use of schools and colleges . . With numerous illustrations. Boston, 1852. 12°

LORD, DANIEL. A Vindication of the award between Boorman, Johnston, and Co. and J. Little and Co. By one of the referees (D. Lord). New York, 1842. 8°

LORD, DAVID N. An Exposition of the Apocalypse. New York, 1847. 8vo.

LORD, ELEAZAR. The Meſſiah in Moses and the Prophets. New York, 1853. 12°

LORD, JOHN. A modern History, from the time of Luther to the fall of Napoleon. For the use of schools and colleges. Philadel. [1849]. 8°

LORD, JOHN. An Addreſs delivered before the Peace Society of Amherst College. July 4, 1839. Amherst, 1839. 8°

LORD, JOHN C. D.D. Slavery in its relation to God. A review of Rev. Dr. Lord's Thanksgiving Sermon, in favour of domestic slavery, entitled the Higher Law, in its application to the Fugitive Slave Bill. By a Minister of the Gospel, etc. Buffalo, 1851. 8°
2 THE WAR of the Giants: the earth-born and the heaven-born. Delivered before the literary societies at the Commencement of Genesee College, etc. Buffalo, 1851. 8°
3 LECTURES on the Progreſs of Civilization and Government, and other subjeɛs. Buffalo, 1851. 8°
4 HUMAN Government and Laws based upon the Divine Law and Government. A discourse [on Rom. vii. 1], etc. Buffalo, 1852. 8°

LORD, JOHN KING. The Dangers of the Scholar: an addreſs delivered before the Gamma Sigma Society of Dartmouth College, etc. Boston, 1844. 8°

LORD, NATHAN. A Sermon [on 1 Cor. xiii. 5] preached at the annual Eleɛtion, . . June 2, 1831, before the executive and legislative authorities of . . New Hampshire. Concord, 1831. 8°
2 A LETTER to the Rev. D. Dana, D.D. on Profeſſor Park's Theology of New England. Boston, 1852. 8vo.

LORGNETTE (THE); or, studies of the Town. By an Opera goer.

[With a preface signed " John Timon," i. e. Donald G. Mitchell.] . . Second edition, set off with Mr. Darley's designs. N. York [1850]. 12°
2 THE OPERA Goer; or, studies of the town. By Ike Marvell. [With preface to the fourth edition, signed " Ik : Marvel," and also a preface signed " John Timon," i. e. Donald G. Mitchell.] Illustrated by Mr. Darley. 2 vol. [The same as the periodical entitled " The Lorgnette," with a new title-page.] London, [N. York, printed, 1852] 12mo.

LORING, JAMES SPEAR. The hundred Boston orators appointed by the municipal authorities and other public bodies, from 1770 to 1852; comprising historical gleanings, illustrating the principles and progreſs of our republican institutions. Boston, 1852. 8°

LORING, SAMUEL. Three Discourses on several subjeɛs: 1. The glories of the heavenly world displayed and improved from Psal. 73. 24. 2. A religious conversation, excited and aſſisted from Mal. 3. 16. 3. The great duty of self-examination urged on the profeſſors of religion . . 2 Cor. 13. 5. Boston, 1731. 12°

LOSSING, BENSON J. Outline History of the fine Arts ; embracing a view of the rise, progreſs, and influence of the arts among different nations, ancient and modern, with notices of the charaɛer and works of many celebrated artists. New York, 1843. 12°
2 SEVENTEEN hundred and seventy-six, or the war of Independence : a history of the Anglo-Americans, from the period of the union of the colonies against the French to the inauguration of Washington, the first President of the United States of America. New York, 1847. 8°
3 PICTORIAL Field Books of the Revolution ; or, illustrations, by pen

and pencil, of the history, scenery, biography, relics, and traditions of the war for Independence. N° 1 to 16. [New York, 1850.] 8°

4 SEVENTEEN hundred and seventy-six, or the war of Independence: a history of the Anglo-Americans from the period of the union of the colonies against the French to the inauguration of Washington . . illustrated by numerous engravings of plans of battles, etc. New edition. New York, 1850. 8°

LOTHROP, SAMUEL KIRKLAND. An Addreſs delivered before the Massachusetts State Temperance Society, May 31, 1835. Boston, 1835. 8°

2 A SERMON [on Job i. 19] preached . . Jan. 19, 1840, on the destruction of the Lexington by fire, January 13th. Boston, 1840. 8°

3 A HISTORY of the Church in Brattle Street, Boston. Boston, 1851. 12°

4 THE MORAL Power of Character. A sermon [on Romans xiv. 17] preached . . the Sunday after the funeral of Amos Lawrence. Boston, 1853. 8°

LOUD, MARGUERITE ST. LEON. Wayside Flowers. A collection of poems. Boston, 1851. 12°

LOUDON, JANE, Mrs. Gardening for Ladies; and companion to the flower-garden. First American, from the third London, edition. Edited by A. J. Downing. New York, 1848. 12°

LOVE'S Progreſs. [A tale.] By the author of " The Recollections of a New England Housekeeper," etc. [Mrs. Caroline Gilman]. New York, 1840. 12°

LOVE TOKEN. A Love Token for children. Designed for Sunday-school libraries. By the author of the Linwoods, etc. [Miſs Catherine M. Sedgwick]. N. York, 1844. 12°

LOVEJOY, JOSEPH C. Memoir of Rev. C. E. Torrey, who died in the Penitentiary of Maryland, where he was confined for showing mercy to the poor. Boston, 1847. 12°

LOVEJOY, JOSEPH C. and—OWEN. Memoir of the Rev. Elijah P. Lovejoy, murdered in defence of the liberty of the preſs at Alton, Illinois, Nov. 7, 1837. With an introduction by John Quincy Adams. New York, 1838. 12mo.

LOVELAND, J. S. The Spiritualist's Plea with the Bible Believer. A dialogue. Boston, 1853. 12mo.

LOVELL, JOHN. A funeral Oration . . occasioned by the death of . . P. Faneuil, Esq. . . The second edit. Boston, 1743. 4°

LOVELL, JOHN E. The young Pupil's Second Book, etc. Fourth edit. New Haven, 1844. 12°

LOUIS, P. CH. A. Researches on the Effects of Blood-letting in some inflammatory diseases, and on the influence of tartarized antimony and vesication in Pneumonitis. Translated by C. G. Putnam, with preface and appendix by J. Jackson. Boston, 1836. 8°

LOUISIANA. An Account of Louisiana, being an abstract of documents in the offices of the departments of State and of the Treasury. Philadelphia, 1803. 8°

2 AN ACCOUNT of Louisiana, being an abstract of documents in the offices of the departments of State and of the Treasury. [By W. Duane?] [Philadelphia, 1803?] 8°

3 APPENDIX to an Account of Louisiana, being an abstract of documents in the offices of the departments of State and of the Treasury. [Philadelphia, 1803!] 8°

4 REPRESENTATION and Petition of the Representatives elected by the freemen of the Territory of Louisiana [addreſsed to the Congreſs of the United States of America], (Sept. 29, 1804). Washington, 1805. 8°

5 TRAVELS in Louisiana and the

Floridas in the year 1802... Translated from the French, with notes, *etc.* by J. Davis. New York, 1806. 12mo.

6 REMARKS on a dangerous mistake made as to the Eastern Boundary of Louisiana. Boston, 1814. 8°

7 A GENERAL Digest of the Acts of the Legislature of Louisiana, passed from .. 1804 to 1827 inclusive, and in force at this last period. With an appendix and general index. By L. Moreau Lislet, Esq... Published according to an act of the Legislature. 2 vol. New Orleans, 1828. 8vo.

8 ACTS passed at the Second Session of the Eighth Legislature of .. Louisiana, *etc.* [In English and French.] New Orleans, 1828. 8°

Also at the

9th Legislature, 1st Session, 1828
9th Legislature, 2nd Session, 1830
10th Legislature, 1st Session, 1831
10th Legislature, Extra Session, 1831
10th Legislature, 3rd Session, 1832
11th Legislature, 1st Session, 1832
11th Legislature, 2nd Session, 1833
12th Legislature, 1st Session, 1835
12th Legislature, 2nd Session, 1836
13th Legislature, 1st Session, 1837
13th Legislature, 2nd Session, 1837
14th Legislature, 1st Session, 1839
14th Legislature, 2nd Session, 1840.
[In French and English.]
New Orleans, 1829-40. 8°

9 CIVIL Code of the State of Louisiana; with annotations, by W. S. Upton .. and N. R. Jennings. New Orleans, 1838. 8°

10 ADDRESS .. to the Citizens of Louisiana and the inhabitants of the United States [against the Naturalization Laws]. New Orleans, 1839. 8°

LOUISIANA LAW JOURNAL; devoted to the theory and practice of the Law. Edited by G. Schmidt. Vol. 1. May, 1841 to April, 1842. New Orleans, 1842. 8°

LOUISIANA REPORTS, *see* MILLER, Branch W.

LOUISVILLE, CINCINNATI, and Charleston Railroad Company. Proceedings of the Stockholders .. at their second meeting... With the

first annual report of the president and directors, the report of the .. engineers [W. G. M'Neill and W. G. Williams], and the bye-laws. Charleston, 1837. 8°

LOUISVILLE DAILY JOURNAL. Sept. 14, 1839. Louisville, 1839. Fol.

LOUISVILLE [Kentucky] DIRECTORY, for .. 1832. Louisville, 1832. 12mo.

LOWE, A. T. *M. D.* The Columbian Class-book, consisting of geographical, historical, and biographical extracts, *etc.* Second edition. Worcester, 1825. 8°

LOWE, B. M. and MARTIN, JOHN. Report [on the affairs of the State Bank of Alabama and its several branches]. [Tuscaloosa, 1839.] s. sh. fol°

LOWELL, ANNA C. *Mrs.* Thoughts on the Education of Girls. Boston, 1853. 12°

LOWELL, CHARLES. A Discourse [on Deut. iv. 32] delivered in the West Church, in Boston, Dec. 31, 1820. Boston, 1820. 8°

LOWELL, JAMES RUSSELL. A Year's Life. Boston, 1841. 8vo.

2 POEMS... Third edition. Cambridge, 1844. 12°

3 READER! Walk up at once (it will soon be too late), and buy at a perfectly ruinous rate; a Fable for Critics... By a Wonderful Quiz [*i. e.* J. R. Lowell]. [*See* FABLE.] New York, 1848. 12mo.

4 POEMS. 2 vol. Boston, 1849. 8°

LOWELL, JOHN. An Eulogy on the Hon. James Bowdoin, late President of the American Academy of Arts and Sciences. Boston, 1791. 4to.

2 AN ADDRESS delivered before the Massachusetts Agricultural Society. Boston, 1818. 8vo.

LOWELL, SAMUEL. Sermons on evangelical and practical subjects. Bristol, 1801. 8vo.

LOWELL DIRECTORY (THE).
.. By B. Floyd. (1834, 1838, 1840.)
Lowell, 1834-40. 12°

LOWELL OFFERING (THE): a
Repository of original articles, written
exclusively by females actively employed in the mills. [Succeſsively
edited by A. C. Thomas and H. Farley.] 5 vol. Lowell, 1841-45. 8vo.
[Continued under the title of] The
New England Offering. H. Farley,
editor. April, 1848 to March, 1850.
Lowell, 1848-50. 8°

LOWRIE, REV. WALTER M. Sermons preached in China. New York,
1851. 8°

LOWTH, ROBERT, Bishop. A
Short Introduction to English Grammar, with critical notes .. First American edition. Cambridge, 1811. 12°

LUCAS, ROBERT, Governor of
Obio. Governor's Special Meſsage.
[Signed R. Lucas.] [Columbus?
1834.] 8°

LUCY and her Dhaye. Philadelphia, 1827. 12mo.

LUDEWIG, HERMANN E. The
Literature of American Local His-
tory; a bibliographical eſsay. New
York, 1846. 8°

LUDLOW, J. L. A Manual of
Examinations upon anatomy and physiology, surgery, practice of medicine,
chemistry, materia medica, obstetrics,
etc. Philadelphia, 1844. 8vo.

LUNT, GEORGE. Poems. New
York, 1839. 12°

LUNT, WILLIAM PARSONS. Two
Discourses [on Deut. viii. 11-18, and
John iv. 20] delivered September 29,
1839, on occasion of the 200th anni-
versary of the .. first Congregational
Church, Quincy. With an appendix.
Boston, 1840. 8°

2 A DISCOURSE delivered in Quincy,
Maſsachusetts, on thanksgiving day,
Nov. 25, 1852, commemorative of
D. Webster. Boston, 1852. 8°

LYCEUM. Contributions of the
Maclurian Lyceum to the arts and
sciences. Vol. 1, N° 1, 2. Philadelphia, 1827. 8vo.

LYCEUM ARITHMETIC, in three
parts. .. By an experienced Teacher.
Boston, 1835. 12°

LYCEUM OF NATURAL HIS-
TORY of New York. Annals. Vol. 1-3;
vol. 4, N° 1-7; and vol. 6, N° 1-5.
2 vol. New York, 1824-55. 8°

LYFORD, W. G. The Western
Addreſs Directory; containing ...
Pittsburgh, Wheeling, Zanesville,
Portsmouth, Dayton, Cincinnati, Madison, Louisville, St. Louis; together
with historical, topographical, and
statistical sketches .. of those cities
and towns in the Miſsiſsippi Valley,
etc. Boston, 1837. 12°

LYMAN, ELIJAH. A Sermon [on
1 Pet. ii. 13-15] delivered on the day
of general Election, .. Oct. 13, 1814,
before the .. Legislature of Vermont.
Montpelier, 1814. 8°

LYMAN, GERSHOM C. A Sermon
[on 1 Kings iii. 9, 10] preached ..
before .. the .. Council and .. House
of Representatives of .. Vermont, on
the day of the anniversary Election,
Oct. 10, 1782. Windsor, 1784. 4°

LYMAN, THEODORE, tbe Younger.
The Political State of Italy. Boston,
1820. 8°

2 THE DIPLOMACY of the United
States. Being an account of the foreign relations of the country, from
the first treaty with France, in 1778,
to the treaty of Ghent, in 1814, with
Great Britain. [First edition. By
Theodore Lyman, junior.] Boston,
1826. 8vo.

3 THE DIPLOMACY of the United
States. Being an account of the foreign
relations of the country, from the first
treaty with France, in 1778, to the
present time. Second edition, with
additions. 2 vol. Boston, 1828. 8vo.

4 REPORT of a Trial in the Supreme
Judicial Court, .. at Boston, .. of

Theodore Lyman, jun. for an alleged libel on Daniel Webster, . . published in the Jackson Republican. . . Taken in shorthand by J. W. Whitman. Boston, 1828. 12°

LYNCH, *afterwards* BOTTA, Anne Charlotte, *Mrs.* Poems. . . With illustrations by Durand, Huntington, *etc.* New York, 1849. 8°

LYNCH, Eugene H. Addreſs delivered before the Philomathean Society of Mount Saint Mary's College, near Emmittsburg, Maryland, at the annual commencement, June 24, 1840. Baltimore [1840]. 8°

LYNCH, William F. Naval Life ; or, observations afloat and on ahore. New York, 1851. 8°
2 Official Report of the United States' Expedition to explore the Dead Sea and the River Jordan, *etc.* Baltimore, 1852. 4to.

LYND, James. The Claſs-book of Etymology designed to promote precision in the use, and facilitate the acquisition of a knowledge of the English language. Revised edition. Philadelphia, 1847. 12°

LYNN, David, and others. The Trial of D. Lynn, *etc.* indicted for the murder of P. Chadwick, *etc.* Augusta (Maine), 1809. 8°

LYON, F. S. and others. [*Begins*] Office of the Commiſsioners, *etc.* [A report to the Governor of Alabama, from F. S. Lyon and others, appointed Commiſsioners to settle the affairs of the State Bank and branches.] [Tuscaloosa, 1847.] s. sh. fol°

LYON, Lucius. A Treatise on Lightning Conductors; compiled from a work on Thunderstorms, by Sir W. Harris, F. R. S. and other standard authors. New York, 1853. 12mo.

ACALISTER
A. A Diſſertation on the
medical properties and injurious effeᶜts of
the habitual use
of tobacco ; . .
Second edition, . . enlarged ; with an
introduᶜtory preface, by M. Stuart,
etc. Boston, 1832. 12°

MACAULAY, Thomas Babington. Critical and Miscellaneous Essays, by T. Babington ˙Macaulay.
3 vol. [Second edition.] Philadelphia,
1842. 8°

2 Speeches. 2 vol. New York,
1853. 8°

MACAULEY, James. The Natural, Statistical, and Civil History of
the State of New York. 3 vol. New
York, 1829. 8°

MAC CALEB, Theodore H. An
Addreſs delivered at the request of
the direᶜtors of public schools, of the
second municipality of New Orleans,
. . Feb. 22, 1843. New Orleans,
1843. 8°

MAC CALL, Hugh. The History of Georgia, containing brief
sketches of the most remarkable
events, up to the present day. 2 vol.
Savannah, 1811-16. 8°

MACCARGO, Thomas. Supreme
Court. T. Maccargo versus the
Merchants' Insurance Company. [An
argument, in an aᶜtion for recovery of
the value of certain slaves, embarked

on board the brig Creole.] New Orleans [1842]. 8°

MACCARTNEY, Washington.
The Origin and Progreſs of the
United States. Philadelphia, 1847.
12°

2 The Principles of the Differential and integral Calculus, and their
application to geometry. Philadelphia, 1848. 12°

MAC CLELLAN, George. Principles and Praᶜtice of Surgery. Edited
by his son, J. H. B. M'Clellan. Philadelphia, 1848. 8°

MAC CLINTOCK, Samuel. A
Sermon [on Jer. xviii. 7-10] preached before the . . Council . . Senate,
and House of Representatives of . .
New Hampshire . . on occasion of
the commencement of the new constitution and foɋm of government.
Portsmouth, 1784. 8°

2 A Discourse [on Levit. x. 3]
on submiſſion to the Divine Will under affliᶜtion, delivered . . at the
funeral of . . A. Spring ; etc. Dover,
1791. 12°

MAC CLUNG, John A. Sketches
of western Adventure : containing an
account of the most interesting incidents conneᶜted with the settlement
of the West, from 1755 to 1794 : together with an appendix. Philadelphia, 1832. 12mo.

2 Sketches of western Adventure :
containing an account of the most interesting incidents˙conneᶜted with the

settlement of the West, from 1755 to 1794; with an appendix: revised and corrected. Cincinnati, 1838. 12°

MAC CLURE, A. W. The Translators revived ; a biographical memoir of the authors of the English version of the Holy Bible. New York, 1853. 12°

MAC CLURE, DAVID, and PARISH, ELIJAH. Memoirs of the Rev. Eleazer Wheelock, founder and president of Dartmouth College and Moor's Charity School ; with a summary history of the college and school. To which are added, copious extracts from Dr. Wheelock's correspondence. Newburyport, 1811. 8vo.

MAC CONNEL, J. L. The Glenns : a family history. New York, 1851. 12°

MAC CORD, DAVID JAMES. Reports of Cases determined in the Constitutional Court [and Court of Appeals] of South Carolina. 4 vol. Columbia, 1822-30. 8°

2 CHANCERY Cases argued and determined in the Court of Appeals of South Carolina, from Jan. 1825 to May 1826 [and from Jan. to May 1827], both inclusive. 2 vol. Philadelphia, 1827-29. 8°

MAC CORD, LOUISA S. Mrs. Caius Gracchus. A tragedy, in five acts. [In verse.] N. York, 1851. 12°

MAC COY, AMASA. Funeral Oration on the Death of D. Webster, etc. Boston, 1853. 8°

MAC COY, ISAAC. Remarks on the practicability of Indian Reform, embracing their colonization. Boston, 1827. 8°

2 REMARKS on the practicability of Indian reform, embracing their colonization; with an appendix. Second edition. New York, 1829. 8°

3 ADDRESS to Philanthropists in

the United States, generally, and to Christians, in particular, on the condition and prospects of the American Indians. [Washington ? 1831 ?] 8°

4 HISTORY of Baptist Indian Missions : embracing remarks on the former and present condition of the aboriginal tribes ; their settlement within the Indian territory, and their future prospects. Washington, 1840. 8°

MAC CRINDELL, R. The School Girl in France. New York, 1852. 8°

MAC CULLOH, JAMES H. M. D. Researches in America ; being an attempt to settle some points relative to the aborigines of America, etc. Baltimore, 1817. 8vo.

2 RESEARCHES, philosophical and antiquarian, concerning the aboriginal history of America. Baltimore, 1829. 4to.

3 ANALYTICAL Investigations concerning the credibility of the Scriptures, and of the religious system inculcated in them ; together with a historical exhibition of human conduct during the several dispensations under which mankind have been placed by their Creator. 2 vol. Baltimore, 1852. 8°

MAC DERMOND. Remarks upon the Report of the Case of M'Dermond v. Kennedy, in the Pennsylvania Law Journal for Dec. 1846, and upon the note to it [in that journal. By W.] Philadelphia, 1846. 8vo.

MACDUFFIE, GEORGE. Defence of a liberal construction of the Powers of Congress, as regards internal improvements, etc. Written .. in .. 1821. To which are prefixed, an encomiastic advertisement .. by Major .. Hamilton, and a preface by the Philadelphia editor. Second Philadelphia edition. Philadel. 1832. 8°

2 SPEECH .. on the .. removal of the Deposites, Dec. 19, 1833

[in the House of Representatives].
[Washington, 1833.] 8°

MAC FARLAND, ANDREW. The Escape or loiterings amid the scenes of story and song. Boston, 1851. 12°

MAC FARLAND, ASA. A Sermon [on 2 Pet. i. 19] preached . . before . . the Senate and House of Representatives of . . New Hampshire. Concord, 1808. 8°

MACFARLANE, ROBERT. History of Propellers and Steam Navigation. With biographical sketches of the early inventors. N. York, 1851. 12°

MAC GAVIN, JAMES R. The Loß of the Australia, . . by fire, on her voyage from Leith to Sydney. With an account of the sufferings, . . and . . rescue of the crew and paßsengers. New York, 1849. 12°

MAC GEE, THOMAS D'ARCY. Historical Sketches of O'Connell and his friends : including . . Drs. Doyle and Milner, T. Moore, J. Lawleß, T. Furlong, R. Lalor Shiel, T. Steele, Counsellor Brie, T. A. Emmet, W. Cobbett, Sir M. O'Loghlen, etc. with a glance at the future destiny of Ireland. Third edition. Bost. 1845. 12°

2 A HISTORY of the Irish Settlers in North America, from the earliest period to the census of 1850. Second edition. Boston, 1852. 8°

MACGILLIVRAY, WILLIAM. The Travels and Researches of Alexander von Humboldt ; being a condensed narrative of his journeys in the equinoctial regions of America, and in Asiatic Rußia : together with analyses of his more important investigations. By W. Macgillivray. New York, 1842. 12°

MAC GUFFEY, W. H. Revised and improved edition of the Eclectic Second Reader . . With engravings . .

Twenty-third edition. Cincinnati, [1838?] 12°

MAC GUIRE, E. C. The religious Opinions and Character of Washington. New York, 1836. 8vo.

MAC ILVAINE, CHARLES PETIT, Bishop. Select Family and Parish Sermons ; a series of evangelical discourses, selected [chiefly from British authors] for the use of families, and destitute congregations. With a preliminary addreß. 2 vol. Columbus, 1838-39. 8°

MAC INTOSH, MARIA JANE. Aunt Kitty's Tales . . Revised edit. New York, 1847. 12°

2 Two Lives : or, to seem and to be. Second revised edition. New York, 1847. 12°

3 WOMAN in America : her work and her reward. N. York, 1850. 12°

4 CHARMS and Countercharms. Sixth edition. New York, 1851. 12°

5 THE LOFTY and the Lowly ; or good in all and none all good. 2 vol. New York, 1853. 12°

MACK, EBENEZER. The Life of Gilbert Motier de Lafayetté, . . from numerous and authentic sources. Second edition. Ithaca, 1843. 12°

MAC KEAN, JOSEPH. A Sermon [on Rom. xii. 11] preached . . on the Lord's Day, after the decease of John Warren, M.D. etc. Boston, 1815. 8°

MACKELLAR, THOMAS. Tam's Fortnight Ramble, and other poems. Philadelphia, 1847. 12°

MAC KENNEY, THOMAS L. Sketches of a Tour to the Lakes, of the character and customs of the Chippeway Indians, and of incidents connected with the treaty of Fond du Lac. Also, a vocabulary of the Algic, or Chippeway language. Baltimore, 1827. 8vo.

· 2 MEMOIRS, official and personal ; with sketches of travels among the northern and southern Indians ; embracing a war excursion, and descriptions of scenes along the western borders. Second edition. (On the origin, history, chara&er, . . wrongs and rights of the Indians, *etc.*) 2 vol. New York, 1846. 8°

3 REPLY to Kosciusko Armstrong's Affault upon Colonel M⸱Kenney's narrative of the causes that led to General Armstrong's resignation of the office of secretary of war in 1814. New York, 1847. 8°

MAC KENNEY, THOMAS L. AND HALL, JAMES. History of the Indian Tribes of North America, with biographical sketches and anecdotes of the principal chiefs, embellished with portraits from the Indian Gallery at Washington. Vol. 1, 2. Philadelphia, 1836-42. Fol.

MACKENZIE, ALEXANDER SLIDELL. The Life of Paul Jones. 2 vol. Boston, 1841. 8vo.

2 THE LIFE of Commodore Oliver Hazard Perry. 2 vol. New York, 1841. 12mo.

3 CASE of the Somers' Mutiny. Defence of A. S. Mackenzie, Commander of the United States Brig Somers, before the Court Martial held at the Navy-yard, Brooklyn. New York, 1843. 8vo.

4 PROCEEDINGS of the Naval Court Martial, in the case of A. S. Mackenzie, . . including the charges and specifications of charges, preferred against him by the Secretary of the Navy. To which is annexed, an elaborate review, by J. F. Cooper. New York, 1844. 8°

MACKENZIE, WILLIAM L. The Lives and Opinions of B. F. Butler . . and J. Hoyt, . . with anecdotes or biographical sketches of S. Allen, G. P. Barker, *etc.* By W. L. Mackenzie. Boston, 1845. 8°

2 THE LIFE and Times of Martin Van Buren: the correspondence of his friends, family and pupils, together with brief notices, sketches and anecdotes illustrative of the public career of J. K. Polk, B. F. Butler, *etc.* Boston, 1846. 8°

MACKEY, ALBERT G. A Lexicon of Freemasonry: containing a definition of all its communicable terms, notices of its history, traditions, and antiquities; and an account of all the rites and mysteries of the ancient world. Charleston, 1845. 12°

MACKEY, JOHN. The American Teacher's Affistant and Self-instructor's Guide; containing all the rules of arithmetic, *etc.* Charleston, 1826. 12°

MACKINTOSH, DUNCAN. A plain, rational Effay on English Grammar: the main obje& of which is to point out a plain, rational and permanent standard of pronunciation. . . by D. Mackintosh and his two Daughters. Boston, 1797. 8vo.

MACK ORMSBY, R. The American Definition Spelling Book, on an improved plan. . . Improved edition. Bradford, Vt. 1844. 12°

MAC LAURIN, W. S. Currente Calamo. Mac Laurin's Series of Fine Hand Copy Books. In four parts. New York, 1853. Oblong 8vo.

2 MAC LAURIN's System of Writing [in 12 books]. New York, 1843. Oblong 8vo.

MACLEAN, JOHN. Reports of Cases argued and decided in the Circuit Court of the United States, for the seventh circuit. 2 vol. Cincinnati and Columbus, 1840-43. 8°

MAC LELLAN, HENRY B. Journal of a Residence in Scotland, and Tour through England, France, Germany, Switzerland and Italy. With a memoir of the author, and extra&s from his religious papers. Compiled by Isaac Mac Lellan, Junior. Boston, 1834. 12mo.

MAC LELLAN, ISAAC, *the Younger*. The Fall of the Indian, with other poems. Boston, 1830. 12°

2 MOUNT Auburn, and other poems. Boston, 1843. 8°

MAC LEOD, C. DONALD. Plasmion, a poem, delivered before the Philomathean and Eucleian Societies of the University of .. New York. [With notes.] New York, 1841. 8°

MAC LEOD, DONALD. Life of Sir Walter Scott. New York, 1852. 12°

2 PYNNSHURST; his wanderings and ways of thinking. New York, 1852. 8°

MACLINTOCK, *Captain.* John Beedle's Sleigh-ride, Courtship, and Marriage. Attributed to Capt. Maclintock [or rather, by J. Neal?] New York, 1841. 12°

MACLURE, WILLIAM. Observations on the Geology of the United States of America; with some remarks on the effect produced on the nature and fertility of soils, by the decomposition of the different classes of rocks; and an application to the fertility of every State in the Union. Philadelphia, 1817. 8vo.

2 OPINIONS on various subjects; dedicated to the industrious producers. 2 vol. New Harmony, Indiana, 1831. 8vo.

MACLURIAN LYCEUM. Contributions of the Maclurian Lyceum to the Arts and Sciences, N° 1, 2. [No more published.] Philadel. 1827. 8vo.

MAC MAHON, BERNARD. The American Gardener's Calendar; adapted to the climates and seasons of the United States, *etc.* Philadelphia, 1806. 8vo.

2 AMERICAN Gardener's Calendar; adapted to the climates and seasons of the United States. Second edition. Philadelphia, 1819. 8°

MAC MAHON, JOHN V. L. An Historical View of the Government of Maryland, from its colonization to the present day. Vol. 1. Baltimore, 1831. 8vo.

MAC MANUS, CHARLES, AND OTHERS. A Correct Account of the Trials of C. Mac Manus, J. Hauer, E. Hauer, P. Donagan, F. Cox, and others, at Harrisburgh, June oyer and terminer, 1798, for the murder of F. Shitz, .. containing the whole evidence, and the substance of all the law arguments in those celebrated trials. Harrisburgh, 1798. 8°

MAC MULLEN, THOMAS. Hand Book of Wines, practical, theoretical and historical; with a description of foreign spirits and liqueurs. New York, 1852. 8vo.

MAC MURRAY, WILLIAM. The Spiritual Contest of the Church: a sermon [on 2 Cor. x. 4] preached in Philadelphia .. before the American Board of Commissioners for Foreign Missions, at their twenty-fourth annual meeting. Boston, 1833. 8°

MAC MURTRIE, HENRY, *M.D.* Sketches of Louisville and its environs; including .. a Florula Louisvillensis .. To which is added an appendix, containing an accurate account of the earthquakes experienced here from the 16th December, 1811, to the 7th February, 1812, extracted principally from the papers of the late J. Brookes, Esq. Louisville, 1819. 8°

2 LEXICON Scientiarum. A Dictionary of terms used in the various branches of anatomy, astronomy, botany, chemistry, geology, geometry, hygiene, mineralogy, natural philosophy, physiology, zoology, *etc.* Third edition, revised and corrected, with an appendix. Philadelphia, 1851. 12°

MAC QUEEN, HUGH. The Orator's Touchstone; or, eloquence simplified. London [New York? printed], 1854. 12mo.

MACREADY, WILLIAM CHARLES. A Rejoinder to "The Replies from England, etc. to certain statements circulated in this country respecting Mr. Macready," together with an impartial history and review of the lamentable occurrences at the Astor Place Opera House, on the 10th of May, 1849. By an American Citizen. New York, 1849. 8°

MACROBERTS, SAMUEL. Speech .. on the Title of the United States to the territory of Oregon, and in favour of the Bill for its Occupation and Settlement; delivered in the .. Senate, Dec. 30, 1842, and Jan. 9, 1843. Washington, 1843. 8°

MAC SHERRY, JAMES. The History of Maryland from its first Settlement in 1634 to the year 1848. Baltimore, 1849. 12°

MAC SHERRY, RICHARD. El Puchero : or, a mixed dish from Mexico, embracing General Scott's Campaign, with sketches of military life, .. of the character of the country, etc. Philadelphia, 1850. 12°

MAC VEAN, CHARLES. Opinion of C. McVean, Surrogate of New York, on an application to compel the administrator of Isaac Lawrence, deceased, to sell certain parts of his real estate. Published by the Administrator (John L. Lawrence.) New York, 1847. 8vo.

MAC VICKAR, JOHN. A Domestic Narrative of the Life of Samuel Bard, M.D. New York, 1822. 8vo.
2 THE PROFESSIONAL Years of J. H. Hobart, D.D. Being a sequel to his "Early Years." [With extracts from his correspondence, etc.] New York, 1836. 12°

MAC WHORTER, ALWIN A. AND OTHERS. Report of the Commissioners appointed to examine the Branch of the Bank of the State of Alabama at Montgomery. [Tuscaloosa, 1841.] 8°

MADDEN, RICHARD ROBERT. A Letter to W. E. Channing, on the

subject of the Abuse of the Flag of the United States in the Island of Cuba, and the advantage taken of its protection in promoting the Slave Trade. Boston, 1839. 8vo.
2 A LETTER to W. E. Channing, in reply to one addressed to him by R. R. Madden, on the abuse of the flag of the United States in the Island of Cuba, for promoting the slave trade. By a Calm Observer. Boston, 1840. 8°

MADISON, JAMES, D.D. A Sermon [on John iv. 24] preached before the Convention of the Protestant Episcopal Church in the State of Virginia. Richmond, 1786. 4to.
2 A DISCOURSE [on 2 Tim. iv. 7] on the death of General Washington. New York, 1800. 8vo.
3 A DISCOURSE [on 2 Tim. iv. 7] on the death of General Washington, .. delivered on the 22nd of February, 1800, in the church in Williamsburgh. Third edition, with additions. Philadelphia, 1831. 8°

MADISON, JAMES, Fourth President of the United States of America. Mr. Madison's Motion for Commercial Restrictions, in a Committee of the whole House [of Representatives] on the Report of the Secretary of State (Mr. Jefferson) on the Privileges and Restrictions on the Commerce of the United States in foreign countries. Jan. 3, 1794. Washington, 1806. 8°
2 THE IMPARTIAL Inquirer: being a candid examination of the conduct of the President of the United States, in execution of the powers vested in him, by the Act of Congress of May 1, 1810. To which is added, some reflections upon the invasion of the Spanish territory of West Florida. By a Citizen of Massachusetts. [Boston?] 1811. 8°
3 THE REPUBLICAN Crisis: or, an exposition of the political Jesuitism of J. Madison. .. By an Observant Citizen of the District of Columbia. Alexandria, 1812. 8°

4 THE PAPERS of J. Madison; being his correspondence and reports of debates. Published from the original manuscripts by H. D. Gilpin. 3 vol. New York, 1841. 8vo.

MADISON, JAMES M. An Exposition of the forms and usages observed in the various lodges of the independent order of Odd Fellows, as organized in the United States; together with a full account of the awful and terrifying ceremonies attendant upon the initiation of a new member into the order. New York [1847]. 8°

2 AN EXPOSITION of the forms and usages observed in the various lodges of the independent order of Odd Fellows, as organized in the United States, etc. [A satire.] New York, 1848. 8°

MAFFIT, JOHN NEWLAND. Pulpit Sketches, Sermons, and Devotional Fragments. Boston, 1828. 12°

2 AN ADDRESS delivered before the literary societies of the Wesleyan University, August 3, 1841. Middletown, 1841. 8°

MAGIE, DAVID. The Spring Time of Life; or, advice to youth. New York, 1853. 12°

MAGNOLIA (THE). 1836 (1837). Edited by H. W. Herbert. 2 vol. New York [1835-37]. 8°

MAGNOLIA (THE); or, gift-book of friendship. Edited by C. Arnold. 1852. Boston [1852]. 12°

MAGOON, E. L. Orators of the American Revolution. Second edition. New York, 1848. 12°

2 REPUBLICAN Christianity; or true liberty as exhibited in the life, precepts, and early disciples of the Great Redeemer. Boston, 1849. 12°

3 PROVERBS for the People; or illustrations of practical godlineſs drawn from the book of wisdom. Boston, 1849. 12°

4 LIVING Orators in America. New York, 1849. 12°

MAHAN, ASA. The True Believer: his character, duty, and privileges, elucidated in a series of discourses. New York, 1847. 12°

2 A SYSTEM of Intellectual Philosophy. Second edition. New York, 1847. 12°

3 LECTURES on the Ninth of Romans: Election, and the influence of the Holy Spirit. Boston, 1851. 16°

MAHAN, D. H. A complete Treatise on Field Fortification; with the general outlines of the principles regulating the arrangement, .. attack, and .. defence of permanent works. New York, 1836. 12mo.

2 AN ELEMENTARY Course of Civil Engineering, for the use of the Cadets of the United States Military Academy. New York, 1837. 8vo.

3 AN ELEMENTARY Course of Civil Engineering, for the use of Cadets of the United States Military Academy. New edition, mostly rewritten, and augmented, etc. New York, 1846. 8°

4 AN ELEMENTARY Treatise on advanced guard, outpost, and detachment service of troops, and the manner of posting and handling them in presence of an enemy. With a historical sketch of the rise and progreſs of tactics, etc. New York, 1847. 12°

5 INDUSTRIAL Drawing; comprising the description and uses of drawing instruments, the construction of plane figures, the projections and sections of geometrical solids... With remarks on the method of teaching the subject, etc. New York, 1852. 8°

MAHAN, M. The Exercise of Faith in its relation to authority and private judgment. Philadel.1851. 12°

MAHOMED ALI BEY. A Brief Memoir of the Life of Mahomed Ali Bey, a learned Persian of Derbent. Philadelphia, 1827. 12mo.

MAHONEY, S. J. Six Years in the Monasteries of Italy, and two years in the Islands of the Mediterranean and in Asia Minor: containing a view of the manners and customs of the popish clergy. With anecdotes and remarks, illustrating some of the peculiar doctrines of the Roman Catholic Church. Philadelphia, 1836. 12mo.

MAINE, *District and State of.* Aggregate amount of each description of Persons within the District of Maine. [Washington? 1811.] Fol°

2 AN APPEAL to the People of Maine on the question of separation [from Massachusetts]. Second edition. [Portland,] 1816. 8°

3 CONSTITUTION for the State of Maine: formed in Convention, at Portland, Oct. 29, 1819... Published by order of the Convention. Portland, 1819. 8°

4 THE DEBATES, Resolutions, and other Proceedings of the Convention of Delegates, assembled at Portland 11th-29th of October, 1819, for the purpose of forming a constitution for the State of Maine. To which is prefixed the Constitution. Taken in convention by Jeremiah Perley. Portland, 1820. 8°

5 LAWS of the State of Maine passed by the Legislature at its Session, .. May—June, 1820. To which is prefixed the Constitution of the State. Portland, 1820. 8°

6 RESOLVES of the Legislature of the State of Maine, passed at its Session, May—June, 1820. Portland, 1820. 8°

7 LAWS of the State of Maine; to which are prefixed the Constitution of the United States, and of said State. 3 vol. Brunswick [and] Portland, 1821-31. 8°

8 RESOLVES of the Legislature, .. passed .. January—February, 1822. Portland, 1822. 8°

9 PRIVATE Acts of the State of Maine, passed by the Legislature, at its Session, January, 1822. [With the resolves of the Legislature, *etc.*] 2 parts. Portland, 1822. 8°

10 PRIVATE Acts of the State of Maine. [To which are added the public acts, and the resolves of the Legislature.] Passed by the third Legislature [continued to the sixteenth], *etc.* 1823-36. 6 vol. Portland [and] Augusta, 1823-36. 8°

11 JAN. Sess. 1828. Doc. N° 13. Report of the Joint Select Committee of the Senate and House of Representatives of the State of Maine, in relation to the North-Eastern Boundary of the State. [With an appendix.] 2 parts. Portland, 1828. 8°

12 LAWS of the State of Maine; to which are prefixed, the Constitution of the United States and of said State; with an appendix. 2 vol. [The title-page of vol. 2 reads: Laws of the State of Maine, from the separation to 1833 inclusive. This is in two parts, the second of which brings down the series of laws to 1838.] Hallowell, 1830-38. 8vo.

13 ADDRESS of Governor Kent to both branches of the Legislature of the State of Maine, Jan. 1841. Augusta, 1841. 8°

14 RESOLUTIONS on the decease of Joseph Story, .. presented to the Circuit Court of the United States for Maine district, .. Oct. term, 1845, by the members of the bar; with the replies of the justices. [Augusta, 1845.] 8°

MAINE HISTORICAL SOCIETY. Collections of the Maine Historical Society. Vol. 1. Portland, 1831. 8°

MALCOLM, HOWARD. Wickedness of War. [Boston, 1838?] 8°

2 TRAVELS in South-eastern Asia, embracing Hindustan, Malaya, Siam, and China. With notices of numerous missionary stations, and a full account of the Burman empire; with dissertations, tables, *etc.* Boston, 1839. 12°

MALTBY, ISAAC. The Elements of War. Boston, 1811. 8°

2 A TREATISE on Courts Martial and military law. Boston, 1813. 8vo.

MAN. The poor Rich Man and the rich Poor Man. By the author of " Hope Leslie," . . etc. [Miſs Catherine M. Sedgwick]. New York, 1845. 12°

MANAHAN, AMBROSE. The Catholic Church and Naturalism : a lecture. New York, 1853. 8vo.

MANCHESTER, New Hampshire. Reports of the Select Men, the superintendent of the alms-house, .. and the superintending school committee of the town of Manchester, for the year 1845-6. Manchester, 1846. 12°

2 THE MANCHESTER Directory, embracing the names of the citizens, etc. Manchester, 1852. 12°

MANDEVILLE, H. A Course of Reading for common schools and the lower claſses of academies. New York, 1846. 12°

MANHATTAN COLLEGE. Documents in the matter of an application to the Legislature of New York for a Charter for Manhattan College. New York, 1829. 8°

MANITOWOMPAE Pomantamoonk Sampwahanan Christianoh Uttoh woh au Pomantog Wuſhikkitteahonat God. 1 Tim. 4. 8. Manittooonk ohtooomoo quoshodinengash yeyueu ut pomantamocouganit kah ne paomocug. Cambridge. Printed for the right Honourable Corporation in London for the Gospellizing the Indians, in New England. 1685. Small 8vo.

MANN, ABIJAH. Original Letters . . of A. Mann . . and others, to J. W. Parkins, ex-sheriff of London, showing the causes of his [J. W. Parkins's] unjust confinement for five years [in the New York debtor's prison] ; including also certain letters from the latter person. New York, 1838. 8°

MANN, HORACE, Secretary to the Board of Education of the State of Maſsachusetts. Report of H. Mann, Secretary of the Board of Education,

on the subject of school houses, supplementary to his first annual report. Boston, 1838. 8°

2 ABSTRACT of the Maſsachusetts School Returns, for 1837. Boston, 1838. 8vo.

3 AN ORATION delivered before the authorities . . Boston, July 4, 1842. [Boston, 1842.] 8°

4 REPLY to the " Remarks" of thirty-one Boston schoolmasters, on the seventh annual report of the Secretary of the Maſsachusetts Board of Education. Boston, 1844. 8vo.

5 OBSERVATIONS on a pamphlet [by the Aſsociation of Masters of the Boston Public Schools], entitled, " Remarks on the Seventh Annual Report of . . H. Mann, Secretary of the Maſsachusetts Board of Education." [Boston, 1844.] 8°

6 PENITENTIAL Tears ; or, a cry from the dust by " the thirty-one" [i.e. the Aſsociation of the Masters of the Boston Public Schools], prostrated and pulverized by the hand of H. Mann, etc. Boston, 1845. 8°

7 ANSWER to the " Rejoinder" of twenty-nine Boston schoolmasters, part of the " thirty-one" who published " Remarks" on the seventh annual report of the Secretary of the Maſsachusetts Board of Education. Boston, 1845. 8°

8 SEQUEL to the so called Correspondence between the Rev. M. H. Smith and H. Mann, surreptitiously published by Mr. Smith ; containing a letter from Mr. Mann, suppreſsed by Mr. Smith, with the reply therein promised [on the subject of the proceedings of the Maſsachusetts Board of Education]. Boston, 1847. 8°

9 THE MASSACHUSETTS System of Common Schools ; being an enlarged and revised edition of the tenth annual report of the first Secretary of the Maſsachusetts Board of Education. Boston, 1849. 8vo.

10 A FEW Thoughts for a Young Man : a lecture delivered before the

Boston Mercantile Library Aſſociation. Boston, 1850.   12°
    11 SLAVERY: Letters and Speeches.
Boston, 1851.   12°

MANN, JOEL. Intemperance de-
ſtruſtive of National Welfare; an
essay. [Suffield?] 1828.   12°

MANNERS, MOTLEY, *Pseud.* [*i.e.*
A. J. Duganne]. Parnaſsus in Pil-
lory. A satire. New York, 1851. 12°

MANRIQUE, JORGE. Coplas,
translated from the Spanish; with an
introduſtory eſſay. By Henry W.
Longfellow. Boston, 1833. 12°

MANSFIELD, EDWARD D. The
Political Grammar of the United
States; or, a complete view of the
theory and praſtice of the general
and state governments, with the relations between them. New York,
1834. 12°
    2 THE POLITICAL Grammar of the
United States, or, a complete view of
the theory and praſtice of the general
and state governments. New edition, containing parliamentary rules;
also an appendix of questions. Cincinnati, 1840. 12mo.
    3 THE LEGAL Rights, Liabilities,
and Duties of Women. With an introduſtory history of their legal condition in the Hebrew, Roman, and
feudal civil systems, *etc.*   Salem,
1845. 12°
    4 THE LIFE of General Winfield
Scott. New York, 1846. 8°
    5 THE ONLY authentic edition.
Life and Services of General W.
Scott, *etc.* New York, 1852. 8°
    6 THE UTILITY and Services of the
United States' Military Academy.
(With notices of some of its graduates
fallen in Mexico,) *etc.* New York,
1847. 8°
    7 THE MEXICAN War: a history of
its origin; and a detailed account of
the viſtories which terminated in the
surrender of the capital; with the official despatches of the Generals.
New York, 1848. 12°

    8 AMERICAN Education, its princi-
ples and elements. Dedicated to the
teachers of the United States. New
York, 1851. 8°

MANUAL OF BOTANY for the
Northern States, comprising generic
descriptions of all phenogamous and
cryptogamous plants to the north of
Virginia hitherto described . . . each
genus illustrated by short descriptions of its most common species.
By the members of the Botanical
claſs in Williams' College (Maſs.)
From a manuscript system by the
author of Richards' Botanical Dictionary. [By Amos Eaton.] Albany,
1817. 12mo.

MANUAL of Politeneſs, comprising
the principles of etiquette and rules of
behaviour. Philadel. 1812. 16mo.

MAPLES, JAMES J. Addreſs delivered at the opening of the eighteenth annual fair of the American
Institute. New York, 1845. 8°

MAPLESON, T. W. GWILT.
Pearls of American Poetry [colleſted
and illuminated by T. W. G. Maple-
son]. New York [1847?] 4°
    2 A HAND BOOK of Heraldry. [With
illuminated illustrations.] New York
[1851]. 8°

MAPLETON; or, more work for
the Maine Law. [A tale.] Boston,
1853. 12°

MARBLE, SUSAN B. Memoir of
S. B. Marble, who died at New Haven,
February 4, 1821. American Sunday
School Union, Philadel. 1831. 12°

MARCH, CHARLES W. Remi-
niscences of Congreſs [chiefly a biography of D. Webster]. Second
edition. New York, 1850. 12°

MARCY, E. E. Homœopathy and
Allopathy: Reply to " An Examination of the doſtrines and evidences of
Homœopathy, by W. Hooker, M.D."
etc. New York, 1852. 12mo.

MARGARET, a tale of the Real and Ideal, blight and bloom... By the author of " Philo" [S. Judd]. 2 vol. Boston, 1851. 12°

MARIA. American Sunday School Union, Philadelphia [1830!] 12°

MARIE, JANE. The Case of J. Marie, exhibiting the cruelty and barbarous conduct of J. Rofs to a defenceless woman, etc. [Philadelphia,] 1808. 8°

MARRAST, JOHN. Report [to the Speaker of the House of Representatives] of the President of the Bank of the State of Alabama, at Tuscaloosa. Tuscaloosa, 1842. 8°

MARSH, DANIEL. A Sermon [on Ps. clxv. 13] preached on the day of general Election, .. before the .. Legislature of Vermont. Montpelier, 1813. 8°

MARSH, EBENEZER GRANT. An Oration, delivered before the Φ. B. K. Society, at their anniversary meeting in New Haven [Connecticut], .. Dec. 5, 1797. Hartford, 1798. 8°

2 AN ORATION on the truth of the Mosaic history of the Creation; delivered at New Haven, on the public commencement, September, 1798. Hartford, 1798. 8°

MARSH, GEORGE PERKINS. A Compendious Grammar of the Old-Northern or Icelandic language: compiled and translated from the Grammars of Rask by G. P. Marsh. Burlington, 1838. 12°

2 THE GOTHS in New England. A discourse delivered at the anniversary of the Philomathesian Society of Middlebury College, August 15, 1843. Middlebury, 1843. 12mo.

3 SPEECH .. on the Tariff Bill, .. in the House of Representatives .. April 30, 1844. Washington [1844]. 8°

4 Ἴωμεν 'εις 'Αθηνας: Addrefs delivered before the New England

Society of .. New York, Dec. 24, 1844. New York, 1845. 8°

5 SPEECH .. on the Bill for establishing the Smithsonian Institution, delivered in the House of Representatives, .. April 22, 1846. 8°

6 HUMAN Knowledge: a discourse delivered before the Mafsachusetts Alpha of the Phi Beta Kappa Society at Cambridge, etc. Boston, 1847. 8°

7 THE AMERICAN Historical School: a discourse delivered before the literary societies of Union College. Troy, 1847. 8°

8 ADDRESS delivered before the Agricultural Society of Rutland county [in the State of Vermont], Sept. 30, 1847. Rutland, 1848. 8°

MARSH, JAMES, President of the University of Vermont. The Remains of the Rev. J. Marsh, with a memoir of his life. [Edited by J. Torrey.] Second edition. New York, 1845. 8°

MARSH, JOHN. An epitome of general Ecclesiastical History, from the earliest period to the present time. With an appendix, giving a condensed history of the Jews, from the destruction of Jerusalem to the present day. Fifth edition. New York, 1839. 12°

MARSHALL, Mrs. A Sketch of my Friend's Family. Philadelphia, 1827. 12mo.

MARSHALL, CHRISTOPHER. Passages from the Remembrancer of C. Marshall, member of the committee of observation, etc. 1774-76. Edited by W. Duane, jun. Philadelphia, 1839. 12°

2 PASSAGES from the Diary of C. Marshall, kept in Philadelphia and Lancaster during the American Revolution. Edited by W. Duane. Vol. 1. 1774 to 1777. Philadelphia, 1839. 12mo.

MARSHALL, EDWARD C. The Book of Oratory: a new collection of extracts in prose, poetry, and dialogue, containing selections from distinguished American and English orators, divines, and poets, etc. New York, 1851. 12°

MARSHALL, ELIHU F. Marshall's new Spelling-book and elementary principles of the English language, etc. Concord, 1836. 12°

MARSHALL, HUMPHRY. Arbustrum Americanum : the American Grove, or an alphabetical catalogue of forest trees and shrubs, natives of the American United States, etc. Philadelphia, 1785. 8vo.

2 THE HISTORY of Kentucky : exhibiting an account of the modern discovery, settlement, progressive improvement; civil and military transactions, and the present state of the country. 2 vol. Frankfort, 1824. 8vo.

MARSHALL, JOHN, LL.D. Chief Justice of the United States of America. The Life of George Washington. . Compiled under the inspection of the Hon. B. Washington, from original papers bequeathed to him by his deceased relative . . To which is prefixed, an introduction, containing a compendious view of the colonies planted by the English on the continent of North America, from their settlement to the commencement of that war which terminated in their independence. 5 vol. Philadelphia, 1804-1807. 8°

2 A HISTORY of the Colonies planted by the English on the continent of North America, from their settlement to the commencement of that war which terminated in their independence. Philadelphia, 1824. 8vo.

3 THE LIFE of George Washington, first President of the United States. 2 vol. 8vo. Philadel. 1832. Atlas, 8vo.

4 WRITINGS upon the Federal Constitution. Boston, 1839. 8vo.

MARTELL, MARTHA. Second Love. New York, 1851. 12°

MARTEN and his two little Scholars at a Sunday-school. Philadelphia, 1827. 12mo.

MARTIN, FRANÇOIS XAVIER. Orleans Term Reports, or cases argued and determined in the Superior Court of the territory of Orleans. 1809-1812. 2 vol. New Orleans, 1811-13. 8°

2 LOUISIANA Term Reports, or cases argued and determined in the Supreme Court of that State. 1813-1823. 10 vol. New Orleans, 1816-23. 8°

3 LOUISIANA Term Reports, etc. New series. 8 vol. 1823-1830. New Orleans, 1824-30. 8°

4 REPORTS of Cases in the superior Court of the territory of Orleans, and in the Supreme Court of Louisiana ; containing the decisions of those courts from the autumn term, 1809, to the March term, 1830, and which were embraced in the twenty volumes of F.X. Martin's Reports ; with notes of Louisiana cases, wherein the doctrines are affirmed, contradicted, or extended, and of the subsequent legislation. Edited by J. B. Harrison. 4 vol. New Orleans, 1839-40. 8°

5 THE HISTORY of Louisiana, from the earliest period. 2 vol. New Orleans, 1827. 8vo.

6 THE HISTORY of North Carolina, from the earliest period. 2 vol. New Orleans, 1829. 8vo.

7 NORTH Carolina Reports: embracing " Notes of a few decisions in the Superior Courts of the State of North Carolina, and in the Circuit Court of the United States for the district of North Carolina. By F. X. Martin." Also, " Reports of cases adjudged in the . . State of North Carolina . . 1797-1806. By J. Haywood" . . (Vol. 2.) Second edition, with notes referring to subsequent enactments . . and decisions, . . by W. H. Battle. Raleigh, 1843. 8°

MARTIN, HORACE. Pictorial Guide to the Mammoth Cave, Kentucky. Illustrated . . by S. Wallen, J. Andrew, J. W. Orr, and N. Orr. New York, 1803. 8°

MARTIN, JOHN. Report of the President of the branch of the bank of the State of Alabama at Montgomery (J. Martin). Tuscaloosa, 1842. 8°

MARTIN, JOHN PAUL. The Triumph of Truth. History and visions of Clio. [A rhapsody.] Boston, 1791. 8°

MARTIN, JOSHUA L. Inaugural Addreſs of Governor J. L. Martin [as Governor of the State of Alabama]. [Tuscaloosa, 1845 ?] 8°

2 MESSAGE of his Excellency Gov. J. L. Martin to the General Assembly of the State of Alabama. Dec. 16, 1845. Tuscaloosa, 1845. 8°

MARTINEAU, HARRIET. Eastern Life, present and past. Philadelphia, 1848. 8°

MARTINET, ABBÉ. Religion in Society, or the solution of great problems ; placed within the reach of every mind . . . with an introduction by . . J. Hughes, D.D. 2 vol. New York, 1850. 12°

MARTYRS. Christian Martyrs. Philadelphia, 1828. 12mo.

2 THE MARTYRS of Lyons and Vienne, in France. Philadel. [1831]. 18mo.

MARVEL, IKE, Pseud. [i. e. DONALD G. MITCHELL]. The Battle Summer : being transcripts from personal observation in Paris, during the year 1848. New York, 1850. 12°

2 REVERIES of a Bachelor : or, a book of the heart. Twelfth edition. New York, 1851. 12°

3 REVERIES of a Bachelor : or, a book of the heart. Illustrated edit. New York, 1852. 4°

MARVIN, JOHN G. Legal Bibliography : or, a Thesaurus of American, English, Irish, and Scotch Law Books, together with some continent-

al treatises. Interspersed with critical observations upon their various editions and authority. To which is prefixed a copious list of observations. Philadelphia, 1847. 8vo.

2 AN ACT to establish a system of Common Schools, in the State of California ; and other acts providing for the revenue of the same, with explanatory forms. By J. G. Marvin, LL.B. superintendent of public instruction. Sacramento, 1852. 4to.

3 SECOND annual Report of the Superintendent of Public Instruction to the Legislature of California. 1853. 8vo.

MARY. The Story of Isaac, or the first part of a conversation between Mary and her mother, (Jacob and his sons, etc.) Simple scripture biographies, etc. Prepared [from the original English works] for the American School Union, by T. H. Gallaudet. 3 parts. Philadel. [1830]-32. 12mo.

MARY CARTER. Philadelphia [1832]. 12mo.

MARY and Archie Graham. Philadelphia, 1830. 12mo.

MARY EDMOND SAINT GEORGE, Lady Superior of the Ursuline Convent at Charlestown, Massachusetts. An Answer to " Six months in a convent" [by R. T. Reed] exposing its falsehoods and manifold absurdities. By the Lady Superior. With some preliminary remarks [and an appendix]. Second edition. Boston, 1835. 8°

MARYLAND, Province and State of. A complete collection of the Laws of Maryland, with an index and marginal notes, etc. Annapolis, 1727. Fol.

2 LAWS of Maryland, enacted at a Seſsion of Aſsembly . . held at the city of Annapolis, Oct. 10, 1727. Annapolis, 1727. Fol. Also at the

Seſsion, begun Oct. 3, 1728.
Seſsion, begun July 10, 1729.
Seſsion, begun May 21, 1730.

Seſſion, begun July 13, 1731.
Seſſion, begun Aug. 19, 1731.
Seſſion, begun March 13, 1732.
Seſſion, begun July 11, 1732.
Seſſion, begun March 20, 1734.
Seſſion, begun March 19, 1735.
Annapolis, 1728-36. Fol.

3 Votes and Resolves of the Lower House of Aſſembly of the Province of Maryland[July-August 1729]. N° 1 to 14. [Annapolis, 1729.] Fol.

4 Laws of Maryland at large, with proper indexes now first collected, together with notes and other matters relative to the constitution thereof. To which is prefixed, the charter, with an English translation. By T. Bacon. Annapolis, 1765. Fol.

5 Laws of Maryland, .. paſſed at a Seſſion of Aſſembly, .. begun .. Nov. 17, .. 1769 (and at the two Seſſions of 1770). Annapolis [1769-70]. Fol°. Also at the
Seſſion, begun June 15, 1773.
Seſſion, begun Nov. 16, 1773.
Seſſion, begun Feb. 5, 1777.
Seſſion, begun June 16, 1777.
Seſſion, begun Oct. 31, 1777.
Seſſion, begun March 17, 1778.
Seſſion, begun June 8, 1778.
Seſſion, begun Oct. 26, 1778.
Seſſion, begun March 9, 1779.
Seſſion, begun July 22, 1779.
Seſſion, begun Nov. 8, 1779.
Seſſion, begun March 23, 1780.
Seſſion, begun June 12, 1780.
Seſſion, begun May 10, 1781.
Seſſion, begun Nov. 5, 1781.
Seſſion, begun April 25, 1782.
Seſſion, begun April 21, 1783.
Seſſion, begun Nov. 3, 1783.
Seſſion, begun Nov. 1, 1784.
Annapolis, 1773-1784. Fol°

6 Laws of Maryland, made and paſſed at a Seſſion of Aſſembly, begun and held at .. Annapolis .. Nov. 3, .. 1800; (Nov. 2, 1801; Nov. 1, 1802; Nov. 7, 1803; Nov. 5, 1804; Nov. 4, 1805; Nov. 3, 1806; Nov. 2, 1807; Nov. 7, 1808; Nov. 6, 1809; Nov. 5, 1810; Nov. 4, 1811; Extra Seſſion, June 15, 1812; Nov. 2, 1812; Extra Seſſion, May 7, 1813; Dec. 6, 1813; Dec. 1814; Dec. 4, 1815; Dec. 2, 1816; Dec. 1, 1817) 20 parts. Annapolis, 1800-1810 in 4° and 1812-18 in 8°

7 Votes and Proceedings of the Lower House of Aſſembly of Maryland, October Seſſion, 1771 (and at the June Seſſion, 1773). 2 parts. Annapolis [1771-73]. Fol°

8 Votes and Proceedings of the Senate of .. Maryland. June Seſſion, 1777; (and at the October Seſſion, 1778) 2 parts. [Annapolis, 1777-78.] Fol°

9 Votes and Proceedings of the House of Delegates of .. Maryland. June Seſſion, 1777; (October Seſſion, 1777; March Seſſion, 1778; June Seſſion, 1778; October Seſſion, 1778) 5 parts. [Annapolis, 1777-78.] Fol°

10 The Laws of Maryland; to which are prefixed, the original charter, with an English translation; the Bill of Rights and Constitution of the State, as originally adopted by the convention, with the several alterations by acts of aſſembly; the Declaration of Independence; the Articles of Confederation; the Constitution of the general government, and the amendments made thereto. .. Revised and collected, under the authority of the legislature, by W. Kilty. 2 vol. [To vol. ii. is prefixed: Addreſs of G. Washington to the People of the United States, Sept. 17, 1796.] Annapolis, 1799-1800. 4°

11 The Laws of Maryland; with the Charter, the Bill of Rights, the Constitution, .. and its alterations. .. Revised by V. Maxey. 3 vol. Baltimore, 1811. 8°

12 Votes and Proceedings .. [at] an extra Seſſion held in June, 1812. Annapolis, 1812. 8°

13 Index to the Laws and Resolutions of the State of Maryland, from 1800 to 1813, inclusive. Annapolis, 1815. 8°

14 The Laws of Maryland, from the end of the year 1799, with a full index, and the constitution of this state, .. and an appendix containing the land laws; with the resolutions considered proper to be published. Revised .. by W. Kilty, T. Harris,

and J. N. Watkins. 2 vol. [vol. 6 and 7]. Annapolis [1820]. 8°

15 A COMPILATION of the Insolvent Laws of Maryland: together with the decisions of the Court of Appeals of Maryland, and of the Supreme Court of the United States, on the subject of insolvency. .. By a Member of the Baltimore Bar. Baltimore, 1831. 8°

16 THE GENERAL Public Statutory Law and Public Local Law of the State of Maryland, from the year 1692 to 1839 inclusive: with annotations thereto, and a copious index, by C. Dorsey. 3 vol. Baltimore, 1840. 8vo.

17 THE THREE Patriots; [T. Jefferson, J. Madison and J. Monroe] or the cause and cure of present evils: addressed to the voters of Maryland. Baltimore, 1811. 8°

18 REPORT of the Commissioners appointed to examine into the practicability of a canal from Baltimore to the Potomac. Together with the Engineer's Report. Baltimore, 1823. 8°

19 AN ACT to Incorporate the Baltimore and Ohio Rail Road Company, passed 1826. Baltimore, 1827. 8° Supplement [1828]. 8°

20 GENERAL Report of the Committee on Internal Improvement. [With an appendix of documents, N° 1-5.] Annapolis, 1831. 8°

21 THE ANNUAL Report of the Treasurer of the Western Shore for December Session, 1834, to the General Assembly of Maryland. Annapolis, 1834. 8vo.

22 REPORT on the New Map of Maryland, 1834. 8vo.

23 REPORT of the Committee of Ways and Means. Dec. 1, 1834. 8vo.

24 REPORT of the Joint Committee in relation to the State Library [Maryland]. 1834. 8vo.

25 MEMORIAL to the General Assembly of Maryland in behalf of the Baltimore and Susquehannah Rail Road. 1834. 8vo.

26 ANNUAL Message of the Executive, to the Legislature of Maryland, December Session, 1834. Annapolis, 1834. 8vo.

27 REPORT of the Committee on Internal Improvement, to whom was referred the Memorial of the Baltimore and Susquehanna Rail Road Company. Feb. 1834. 8vo.

28 HOUSE of Delegates. December Session, 1834. Report on Steam Towing Company. 8vo.

29 MEMORIAL to the General Assembly of Maryland, in behalf of the Chesapeake and Ohio Canal. 1835. 8vo.

30 REPORT of the Committee on Ways and Means, on the Bill to provide for the completion of the "Chesapeake and Ohio Canal to Cumberland," and the Bill for the completion of the "Baltimore and Susquehanna Rail Road to the Borough of York." March 4, 1835. Annapolis, 1835. 8vo.

31 REPORT of the Committee on Internal Improvement, to which was referred the Memorial invoking further aid to the Chesapeake and Ohio Canal. Feb. 23, 1835. 8vo.

32 BANK Statements. Western Shore Treasury, Annapolis, Jan. 15, 1835. 8vo.

33 REPORT of the Select Committee relative to the establishment of a State Bank and a National Currency, Jan. 26, 1835. 8vo.

34 REPORT of the Treasurer of the Western Shore, concerning the Tax for Colonization. Jan. 30, 1835. 8vo.

35 REPORT of the Committee on Lotteries; to the House of Delegates. Feb. 9, 1835. 8vo.

36 REPORT of the Treasurer of the Western Shore, in obedience to an order of the House of Delegates, Jan. 28, 1835. 8vo.

37 REPORT of the Committee to whom was referred several Memorials praying for the establishment of a real Estate Bank. Feb. 28, 1835. 8vo.

38 REPORT of the Committee of Claims, to the Legislature of Maryland. Annapolis, 1835. 8vo.

39 REPORT of the Committee . . appointed to prepare plans for the new buildings to be erected in the yard of the Maryland Penitentiary. Baltimore, 1835. 8°

40 REPORT of the Committee of Claims, to the Legislature of Maryland. Annapolis, 1835. 8°

41 DOCUMENT, N° 1, Copy of a Correspondence between Governor Thomas, of Maryland, and Governor Tazewell, of Virginia, in relation to the unsettled divisional boundary lines between the two States. Annapolis, 1835. 8°

42 MEMORIAL (of a Convention of Citizens of Maryland, Virginia, etc.) to the General Aſſembly of Maryland, in behalf of the Chesapeake and Ohio Canal. [Baltimore, 1835.] 8°

43 PROCEEDINGS of the Conventions of the Province of Maryland, held at Annapolis in 1774, '75 and '76. Baltimore, 1836. 8°

44 AN ACT . . for the Promotion of Internal Improvement, paſſed June 4, 1836. [Annapolis, 1836.] 8°

45 ACTS relating to the Chesapeake and Ohio Canal Company, paſſed . . at December Seſſion, 1838. [Annapolis, 1839.] 8°

46 DOCUMENT L. Mr. Wharton. Report of the Select Committee, appointed by the House of Delegates to report a Bill to abolish the Office of State Geologist. [Annapolis, 1839.] 8vo.

47 PROCEEDINGS of the Twentieth Annual Seſſion of the Evangelical Lutheran Synod of Maryland. Baltimore, 1839. 8vo.

48 THE CONSTITUTION of the State of Maryland, reported and adopted by the Convention of Delegates assembled at the city of Annapolis, Nov. 4, 1850, and . . ratified by the people, . . June, 1851, . . with marginal notes and an appendix by E. O. Hinkley. Baltimore, 1851. 8°

49 MESSAGE from the Governor of Maryland [P. F. Thomas] transmitting the reports of the Joint Commiſſioners [H. G. S. Key, J. P. Eyre, and G. R. Riddle] and of Lt. Col. Graham, United States Engineers, in relation to the intersection of the boundary lines of the States of Maryland, Pennsylvania, and Delaware. Washington, 1850. 8°

MARYLAND ACADEMY OF THE FINE ARTS. Charter and By-Laws, etc. Baltimore, 1838. 12°

MARYLAND GAZETTE (THE). N° 1275. Annapolis, 1770. Fol.

MARYLAND GAZETTE (The): N° 1345 to 2272. June 20, 1771, to July 29, 1790. [Wanting N° 1-1344, 1346-1433, 1435-36, 1438-60, 1462-1555, 1557-61, 1563-1604, 1606, 1614-15, 1617-18, 1622-42, 1644-47, 1649-53, 1656, 1658-64, 1666-87, 1689-91, 1693, 1695, 1696, 1698-1705, 1707-11, 1713, 1715-1878, 1881, 1886, 1904, 1917, 1922-76, 1978-81, 1983, 1989-90, 2000, 2010-11, 2017, 2022, 2032, 2038, 2041, 2045-47, 2049-2060, 2062-2063, 2066-2124, 2148, 2150, 2163-64, 2253, 2258, and all after 2272.] Annapolis, 1771-90. Fol.

MARYLAND HISTORICAL SOCIETY. Journal of C. Carroll during his visit to Canada in 1776 as one of the Commiſſioners from Congreſſ: with a Memoir and Notes, by B. Mayer. Baltimore, 1845. 8vo.

2 KENNEDY, J. P. Discourse on the life and character of George Calvert, the first Lord Baltimore: being the second annual addreſſ. Baltimore, 1845. 8vo.

3 HARRIS, J. M. Discourse on the life and character of Sir Walter Raleigh, being the third annual addreſſ. Baltimore, 1846. 8vo.

4 DONALDSON, Thomas. American Colonial History: an Addreſſ made by T. Donaldson, being the fourth annual addreſſ. Baltimore, 1849. 8°

5 BROWN, George William. The Origin and Progreſſ of Civil Liberty

in Maryland; a discourse delivered April 12, 1850, being the fifth annual addreſs to that aſsociation. Baltimore, 1850. 8°

6 MAYER, Brantz. Tah-Gah-Jute; or Logan and Captain M. Cresap: a discourse by B. Mayer. Baltimore [1851]. 8°

MARYLAND JOURNAL (THE) and Baltimore Advertiser. Nᵒ 140 to 1266. Jan. 22, 1777 to July 29, 1790 [wanting Nᵒ 1-139, 141-165, 170, 173, 174, 176, 180, 183, 185, 186, 192-93, 196, 207, 230, 261, 275-76, 281-86, 288-99, 302-459, 461-463,470,474-76,496,500,502, 504, 506, 512, 516-18, 530-31, 534-41, 544, 550-61, 563, 565-83, 585, 587-95, 597-613, 615-95, 697-709, 711-12,715-19,723, 726-27, 738-789, 795, 798-99, 803, 822-23, 827, 831-32, 837-38, 840, 847-49, 851, 853-972, 983, 1006, 1040, 1048-54, 1094-95, 1097, 1116, 1139, 1159-62, 1213, 1227-28, 1262]. Baltimore,1777-90. Fol.

2 THE MARYLAND Journal and Baltimore Advertiser. Nᵒ 582 to 685. Baltimore, 1784. Fol.

MARYLAND STATE COLONIZATION SOCIETY. Third annual report. Baltimore, 1835. 8vo.

MASON, ARCHIBALD. Two Eſsays on Daniel's prophetic number of two thousand three hundred days; and on the Christian's duty to inquire into the Church's deliverance. Newburgh, printed from the Glasgow edition, 1820. 8°

MASON, CHARLES. A Discourse [on Heb. xi. 4] on the death of D. Webster. Boston, 1852. 8°

MASON, CYRUS. The Oration on the thirteenth anniversary of the American Institute; .. together with the list of premiums awarded at the fair. New York, 1840. 8°

MASON, ERSKINE. A Pastor's Legacy; being sermons on practical

subjeĉts, by E. Mason. With a ... memoir of the author, by the Rev. W. Adams. New York, 1853. 8°

MASON, FRANCIS, Rev. The Karen Apostle, or memoir of Ko-Thay-Byu, the first Karen convert, with an historical and geographical account of the nation,its traditions,precepts,rites, etc. . . . Revised by H. J. Ripley. . . Fourth thousand. Boston, 1847. 12°

MASON, GEORGE. George Mason, the Young Backwoodsman; or, "Don't give up the ship." A story of the Miſsiſsippi. By the author of "Francis Berrian" [Timothy Flint]. Boston, 1829. 12°

MASON, GEORGE. The Tariff Controversy, or the promotion of American industry in the farming, manufaĉturing, and mechanical walks of life. Wells River, Vt. 1842. 12°

MASON, JOHN M. D.D. The Writings of the late J. M. Mason. Seleĉted and arranged by Ebenezer Mason. New York, 1832. 8vo.

MASON, LOWELL. An Addreſs on Church Music. New York,1851. 8°

MASON, RICHARD. Mason's Farrier and Stud-Book. New edition. The Gentleman's New Pocket Farrier .. to which is added a prize eſsay on Mules; an appendix containing recipes for diseases of horses; .. annals of the turf, American stud-book, etc. With a supplement .. by J. S. Skinner. Philadelphia, 1849. 12°

MASON, WILLIAM POWELL. Reports of Cases argued and determined in the Circuit Court of the United States, for the first circuit. 5 vol. 1816 to 1830. Bost. 1824-31. 8vo.

2 AN ORATION delivered . . . July 4, 1827, in commemoration of American Independence, etc. Boston, 1827. 8°

MASSACHUSETTENSIS. The Origin of the American Contest with

Great Britain, or the present political state of the Maſſachuſetts Bay, in general, and the town of Boſton in particular. ... in a series of weekly eſſays published at Boston, under the signature of Maſſachuſtensis, a native of New England. New York, 1775. 8vo.

MASSACHUSETTS, *Colony and State of.* The general Laws and Liberties of the Maſſachuſets Colony: revised and reprinted by order of the General Court holden at Boston, May 15th, 1672. [Bound at the end are; Several Laws and Orders made at the General Court holden May 15, 1672; May 7th and Oct. 15th, 1673; and May 27th, 1674.] Cambridge, printed by Samuel Green, for John Uſher of Boston, 1672-74. Fol.

2 THE GENERAL Laws and Liberties of the Maſſachusetts Colony, revised and reprinted by order of the General Court holden at Boston, May 15, 1672. Cambridge, 1675. Fol.

3 A COPY of the Kings Majesties Charter for incorporating the Company of the Maſſachuſets Bay in New England in America. Granted .... 1628. Boston, Printed by S. Green, for Benj. Harris, 1689. 4to.

4 A PROCLAMATION for a general Fast .. given at the Council Chamber in Boston, the twenty-third day of August, 1701. [Boston, 1701.] s. sh. 8vo.

5 THE CHARTER granted by their Majesties .. to the inhabitants of the Province of the Maſſachusetts Bay, etc. (Acts and laws of His Majesty's Province of the Maſſachusetts Bay.) 2 pts. Boston, 1726-27. Fol°

6 TEMPORARY Acts and Laws of His Majesty's Province of the Maſſachusetts Bay in New England. Boston, 1742. Fol°

7 [*Begins*] In Provincial Congreſs, Watertown, May 5, 1775. [Resolution recommending that a new Provincial Congreſs be elected and con-

vened; followed by a resolution that General Gage has disqualified himself to serve this Colony as Governor, and that no obedience ought in future to be paid to his Writs.] [Watertown? 1775.] s. sh. 4to.

8 THE MILITIA Act; together with the rules and regulations for the militia, *etc.* Boston, 1776. 4°

9 AN ADDRESS of the Convention for framing a new Constitution of Government for the State of Maſſachusetts Bay to their constituents. [With the proposed Constitution.] 2 parts. Boston, 1780. 8°

10 DEBATES, resolutions, and other proceedings of the Convention of the Commonwealth of Maſſachusetts convened at Boston on the 9th of January, 1788, together with the yeas and nays on the decision of the grand question. Boston, 1788. 8vo.

11 THE LAWS of the Commonwealth of Maſſachusetts, paſſed from the year 1780 to .. 1800. ... To which is added, an appendix, *etc.* [Edited by N. Dane, G. R. Minot, and J. Davis.] 2 vol. Boston, 1801. 8°

12 A DEFENCE of the Legislature of Maſſachusetts; or the rights of New England vindicated. Bost. 1804. 8°

13 LETTER of the Justices of the Supreme Judicial Court to His Excellency the Governor, with two judiciary bills, drawn by them, which were communicated to the Hon. General Court, by meſſage, June, 1804. Boston, 1804. 8°

14 PRIVATE and special Statutes of the Commonwealth of Maſſachusetts, from the year 1780 to .. 1805; with an appendix, containing such statutes, of the above description, paſſed before ... 1780, as are referred to in acts paſſed since, and including the temporary acts, made perpetual, March 7, 1797. [Vol. 1-3. Revised and edited by P. Coffin and J. Davis. Continued to Feb. 1822. Vol. 4, 5, by A. Stearns and L. Shaw.] 5 vol. Boston, 1805-23. 8°

15 REGULATIONS of the Governor

and Council [for the Management of the State prison]. [Bost. 1806.] 8°

16 COMMONWEALTH of Maſſachusetts. An act for the more convenient administration of justice in the Supreme Judicial Court. [Boston, 1806.] 8°

17 LAWS for regulating and governing the Militia of the Commonwealth of Maſſachusetts. . To which is added, in an appendix, the United States Militia Acts, paſſed in Congreſs, May 8, 1792, and March 2, 1803. Boston, 1807. 12°

18 THE LAWS of the Commonwealth of Maſſachusetts, from Nov. 28, 1780, to Feb. 28, 1807. With the Constitutions of the United States of America and of the Commonwealth prefixed. . . 3 vol. Bost. 1807. 8vo.

19 PATRIOTISM and Piety: The Speeches of His Excellency Caleb Strong, Esq. to the Senate and House of Representatives of the Commonwealth of Maſſachusetts; with their answers; and other official publick papers of His Excellency; from 1800 to 1807. Newburyport, 1808. 12°

20 COMMONWEALTH of Maſſachusetts. [A meſſage of Governor James Sullivan, respecting Courts of General Seſſions of the Peace. Jan. 1808.] [Boston? 1808.] Fol°

21 COMMUNICATION of James Sullivan, the Governor, to the Hon. Council, relative to the removal of Sheriff Lithgow [Sheriff of the county of Kennebeck]; and the report and advice of Council thereon. (Feb. 15, 1808.) Printed by order of the General Court. [Boston,] 1808. 8°

22 REPORT of the Committee appointed by the House of Representatives . . . to take into consideration the Judiciary system. [With the draft of a proposed legislative act. Jan. 1808.] [Boston, 1808.] 8°

23 [Begins] Commonwealth of Maſſachusetts, Council Chamber, Jan. 30, 1808. The Committee, etc. [A report on certain transactions in

the county of Kennebeck, etc.] [Boston,] 1808. 8°

24 THE REPLY of the majority of the representatives from the State of Maſſachusetts, in Congreſs, to the resolutions and instructions of the Legislature of that State, on the subject of the embargo laws. Salem, 1808. 8°

25 COMMONWEALTH of Maſſachusetts. An act establishing a judicial department. [Boston, 1809.] 8°

26 COMMONWEALTH of Maſſachusetts, etc. [Report of the Committee appointed on the Memorial of S. Woods, complaining of certain conduct of S. Dana, Esq. in his office of county attorney for . . . Middlesex. Feb. 25, 1809.] [Boston, 1809.] 8°

27 HIS Excellency Governor Gore's Speech to the Legislature of Maſſachusetts . . June 7, 1809. [Boston, 1809.] 8°

28 REPORT [of the Committee to whom were referred sundry petitions on the subject of the embargo, etc. With a copy of the embargo law]. [Boston, 1809.] 8°

29 HIS Excellency Governor Gerry's Speech to the Legislature of Maſſachusetts . . June 7,1810. [Boston, 1810.] 8°

30 LEGISLATURE of Maſſachusetts. . . Speech [of Governor Gerry to the Legislature, June 7, 1811]. [Boston, 1811.] 8°

31 THE THIRD Census, or enumeration of the inhabitants of the United States, within the District of Maſſachusetts. [Washington? 1811.] Fol°

32 COMMISSIONERS to take into consideration the disturbances in the county of Lincoln, Commonwealth of Maſſachusetts, etc. [A report, addreſſed to the General Court, relating to disturbances in the county of Lincoln.] [Boston, 1811.] 8°

33 REPORT of the Committee of Valuation. [Boston, 1811.] 8°

34 SUPREME Judicial Court, Commonwealth of Maſſachusetts. [A report to the House of Representatives

on the question: Whether aliens are rateable polls within the intent and meaning of the Constitution? *etc.* [Boston, 1811.] 8°

35 DOCUMENTS respecting the Resolutions of the Legislature of Maſsachusetts, paſsed Feb. 15, 1812 [1809], containing a refutation of certain insinuations . . against . . H. G. Otis, and T. Bigelow, Esqrs. Published by order of the House of Representatives. [Boston, 1812.] 8°

36 SPEECH of Elbridge Gerry, the Governor of . . Maſsachusetts, to both Houses of the Legislature, . . Jan. 1812. Boston, 1812. 8°

37 COMMONWEALTH of Maſsachusetts . . An act, exempting certain polls from taxation. Sect. 1. [Boston, 1812.] 8°

38 COMMONWEALTH of Maſsachusetts. [Report of a committee to whom was referred the petition of certain officers of militia.] [Boston, 1812.] 8°

39 COMMONWEALTH of Maſsachusetts. [A report on certain proposed alterations in the constitution of the Commonwealth, touching the representation and election.] [Boston, 1812.] 8°

40 COMMONWEALTH of Maſsachusetts, *etc.* [Vote of the House on the retirement of Joseph Story from the chair, with his speech in acknowledgment thereof, Jan. 17, 1812.] [Boston, 1812.] 8°

41 COMMONWEALTH of Maſsachusetts. [A bill relating to the organization of districts for the election of President and Vice-president of the United States.] [Boston, 1812.] 8°

42 COMMONWEALTH of Massachusetts. [Report of a committee concerning the defalcations of T. J. Skinner, late Treasurer of the Commonwealth ; with various documents relating thereto.] [Boston, 1812.] 8°

43 COMMONWEALTH of Maſsachusetts. House of Representatives, June 15, 1812. [Report of a Com-

mittee on the state of the militia.] [Boston, 1812.] 8°

44 COMMONWEALTH of Maſsachusetts. Report of the committee of conference on the choice of electors of president and vice-president . . June 26, 1812. [Boston, 1812.] 8°

45 THE SPEECH of his Excellency Governor Strong, delivered before the Legislature of Maſsachusetts, Oct. 16, 1812 ; with the documents which accompanied the same. To which is added, the answer of the House of Representatives. Boston, 1812. 8°

46 PUBLIC Documents of the Legislature of Maſsachusetts : containing the speech of . . Governor Strong, with the answer of the Senate and House of Representatives ; reports of the several committees of both branches, . . and a remonstrance of the Legislature to Congreſs on the present . . war. Published by order of both houses. Boston, 1813. 8°

47 REPORT of the Committee of the House of Representatives of Massachusetts, on the subject of impreſsed seamen ; with the evidence and documents accompanying it. Published by order of the House of Representatives. Boston, 1813. 8°

48 REPORT of the Committee of the House of Representatives of Massachusetts, on the subject of impreſsed seamen ; with the evidence and documents accompanying it. Published by order of the House of Representatives. Boston, 1813. 8°

49 THE CHARTERS and general Laws of the colony and province of Maſsachusetts Bay. Boston, 1814. 8vo.

50 To Members of the General Court. [A memorial respecting the Merrimack and Boston Canal.] [Boston, 1814.] 8°

51 AN APPEAL to his Excellency the Governor, . . lieutenant-governor, . . council . . senate, and . . house of representatives, in general court assembled [respecting a Mr. Jenkins' system of writing, with various me-

morials and testimonials on the same subject]. [Boston, 1814.] 8°

52 COMMONWEALTH of Maſsachusetts. [Report of a Committee on a proposed system for the management of the lands of the Commonwealth in the Diſtrict of Maine.] [Boston, 1814.] 8°

53 COMMONWEALTH of Maſsachusetts. [Report of a committee appointed to revise the criminal code.] [Boston, 1814.] 8°

54 COMMONWEALTH of Maſsachusetts. [Report of a committee to whom were referred certain memorials and remonstrances from various towns in Maſsachusetts against the war and embargo.] [Boston, 1814.] 8°

55 COMMONWEALTH of Maſsachusetts. [Report of a committee concerning the incorporation of the Boston and Roxbury Mill Company.] [Boston, 1814.] 8°

56 IN the House of Representatives, February 8, 1774. [A grant of land, (being the township of Baldwin, Maine,) with subsequent confirmations, to S. Whittemore, A. Lawrence, and others, in lieu of a township originally granted to Captain John Flint.] [Boston, 1815.] 8°

57 EXTRACTS from the Minutes of the General [Congregational] Aſsociation of Maſsachusetts Proper, holden at Royalston, . . June, 1815. Boston, 1815. 8°

58 DESCRIPTION and historical sketch of the Maſsachusetts State Prison, with the statutes, rules and orders, for the government thereof. Published by order of the board of directors. Charleston, 1816. 8°

59 COMMONWEALTH of Maſsachusetts. In the House of Representatives, Jan. 18, 1816. [Report of committee appointed for the laying out, settlement, and improvement of the Commonwealth's lands in the Diſtrict of Maine.] [Boston, 1816.] 8°

60 COMMONWEALTH of Maſsachusetts. In Senate, Jan. 29, 1816. [Report of a committee appointed to

consider the propriety of erecting a monument to the memory of Washington.] [Boston, 1816.] 8°

61 REPORT [of "the committee appointed by a resolve of the legislature"] ön the Hallowell and Augusta Bank. Commonwealth of Maſsachusetts. [Boston, 1816.] 8°

62 COMMONWEALTH of Maſsachusetts. [Report of a committee of both houſes on the separation of the Diſtrict of Maine from Maſsachusetts Proper; with a proposed bill for that purpose.] [Boston, 1816.] 8°

63 COMMONWEALTH of Maſsachusetts. An Act concerning the separation of the Diſtrict of Maine from Maſsachusetts Proper, and forming the same into a separate and independent State. [Boston, 1816.] 8°

64 COMMONWEALTH of Maſsachusetts. [Report of the committee of both houses, to whom were referred the memorials and documents presented to the legislature concerning the separation of Maine.] [Boston, 1816.] 8°

65 REPORT of the Treasurer (J. T. APTHORP) June 6, 1816. To the Honorable House of Representatives of Maſsachusetts. [Boston, 1816.] 8°

66 COMMONWEALTH of Maſsachusetts. In the House of Representatives, Nov. 1816. [Resolutions on the subject of selling the Commonwealth's interest in the Boston and Union Banks.] [Boston, 1816.] 8°

67 [Begins] COMMONWEALTH of Maſsachusetts. [Report of a joint committee on the State prison.] [Boston, 1817.] 8°

68 COMMONWEALTH of Maſsachusetts. House of Representatives, February 7, 1818. [Report of the committee appointed to consider the case of Josiah Little, Esquire, a member of the house, arrested for debt.] [Boston, 1818.] 8°

69 COMMONWEALTH of Maſsachusetts. In the House of Representatives, February 9, 1818. [Report of

the committee appointed to inquire into the proceedings and conduct of the managers of all lotteries, authorized and in progress within this commonwealth.] [Boston, 1818.] 8°

70 COMMONWEALTH of Massachusetts. [Report of a committee of both houses on the Hallowell and Augusta bank.] [Boston, 1818.] 8°

71 To THE Honourable the Senate and the Honourable the House of Representatives. [Report of the committee appointed to take into consideration the several laws and bills relating to the Courts of Probate ; with a proposed bill to regulate the jurisdiction and proceedings of those courts.] [Boston, 1818.] 8°

COMMONWEALTH of Massachusetts. [Communication to the legislature from the Chief Justice, and two of the other justices of the Supreme Judicial Court, suggesting a modification of the laws respecting the right of appeals, etc.] [Boston, 1818.] 8°

73 COMMONWEALTH of Massachusetts. [Letter from A. Stearns, announcing his acceptance of the office of University Professor of Law, and enquiring whether the office is incompatible with a seat in the House of Representatives : with the report of a committee of the house appointed to consider the case.] Bost.[1818.]8°

74 SPEECHES of the Governors of Massachusetts, from 1765 to 1775; and the answers of the House of Representatives to the same ; with their resolutions and addresses for that period, and other public papers, relating to the dispute between this country and Great Britain, which led to the Independence of the United States. Boston, 1818. 8°

75 [Begins] COMMONWEALTH of Massachusetts. An act making further provision for the punishment of convicts, .. and the better regulation of the State prison. [Bost. 1818.] 8°

76 [Begins] COMMONWEALTH of Massachusetts. [A report of a joint

committee on the State prison, etc.] [Boston, 1818.] 8°

77 COMMONWEALTH of Massachusetts. To the Honourable the Senate, and the honourable the House of Representatives of the commonwealth of Massachusetts. [Report of the Committee appointed to revise the criminal code of the Commonwealth, presenting several bills for the consideration of the legislature.] [Boston, 1819.] 8°

78 [REPORT of the committee, to whom were referred the petitions concerning the separation of the District of Maine from Massachusetts Proper; with a proposed bill for that purpose.] [Boston, 1819.] 8°

79 THE GENERAL Laws of Massachusetts, from the adoption of the Constitution to Feb. 1822 [continued to June, 1831]; with the Constitutions of the United States and of this Commonwealth. Together with their respective amendments prefixed. Revised and published, by authority of the legislature, .. by A. Stearns and L. Shaw, .. commissioners. T. Metcalf, .. editor. 3 vol. Boston, 1823-32. 8°

80 REPORT of the Commissioners of the State of Massachusetts, on the routes of canals from Boston Harbour to Connecticut and Hudson Rivers. [With an appendix, separately paged.] Boston, 1826. 8°

81 HISTORY of the Gaols in this State ; with tables, showing the commitments for five years. [A report from a committee of the House of Representatives, Feb. 16, 1827. With an appendix, separately paged.] [Boston, 1827.] 8°

82 COMMONWEALTH of Massachusetts. [Report of the committee appointed to take into consideration the necessity of amending the constitution of the commonwealth, on account of the secession of Maine.] [Boston, 1820.] 8°

83 COMMONWEALTH of Massachusetts .. Report of the committee of

both houses of the legislature on the expenses and resources of the commonwealth, and papers accompanying the same. [Boston, 1820.] 8°

84 COMMONWEALTH of Maſſachusetts. [Report of a committee of both houses of the legislature on certain resolutions of the legislature of the State of Maryland, relative to the appropriation of a portion of the public lands of the United States to the support of common schools, etc.] [Boston, 1822.] 8°

85 REPORT of the Board of Directors of Internal Improvements on the practicability and expediency of a railroad from Boston to the Hudson River, and from Boston to Providence .. To which are annexed, the reports of the engineers, etc. 2 parts. Boston, 1829. 8°

86 REPORT of the Board of Commissioners of Internal Improvements in relation to the survey of a route for a canal from Boston to the Blackstone canal, and thence to the line of Connecticut, etc. [With a report on the same subject by J. Hayward.] Boston, 1829. 8°

87 PROCEEDINGS of the Anti-Masonic State Convention in Faneuil Hall, Boston, Dec. 30 and 31, 1829, and Jan. 1, 1830. Boston, 1830. 8vo.

88 AN EXAMINATION of the Banking System of Maſſachusetts, in reference to the renewal of the bank charters. Boston, 1831. 8°

89 JOURNAL of the Convention for framing a constitution of government for the State of Maſſachusetts Bay, from the commencement of their first seſſion, Sept. 1, 1770, to the close of their last seſſion, June 16, 1780; including a list of the members; with an appendix, etc. Boston, 1832. 8vo.

90 JOURNAL of the Proceedings of the National Republican Convention [of Maſſachusetts], held at Worcester, Oct. 11, 1832. Bost. 1832. 8°

91 FOURTH Anti-Masonic State Convention held at Boston, Sept. 11, 12, and 13, 1833. Boston, 1833. 8vo.

92 REPORT of the Commiſſioners appointed by an order of the House of Representatives, Feb. 29, 1832, on the subject of the pauper system of the commonwealth of Maſſachusetts. Boston, 1833. 8°

93 HOUSE. N° 18. Report. The Committee of Agriculture, to whom were referred the several petitions for the encouragement of the culture and manufacture of silk. [With the draft of an act for that purpose.] [Boston, 1833.] 8°

94 HOUSE. N° 73. Report, by a joint committee of the legislature of Maſſachusetts on Free-Masonry, March, 1834. [Boston.] 8vo.

95 DOCUMENTS printed by order of the Senate, and by order of the House of Representatives during the second seſſion of the General Court of Maſſachusetts, 1835. Boston, 1835. 8°

96 THE REVISED Statutes of the Commonwealth of Maſſachusetts, paſſed Nov. 4, 1835; to which are subjoined, an act in amendment thereof, and an act expreſſly to repeal the acts which are consolidated therein, both paſſed in February, 1836; and to which are prefixed, the constitutions of the United States and of the Commonwealth of Maſſachusetts. Printed and published by virtue of a resolve of Nov. 3, 1835, under the supervision and direction of T. Metcalf and H. Mann. Boston, 1836. 8°

97 SENATE, N° 87. Report on Secret Societies and Monopolies, by a joint committee of the legislature of Maſſachusetts, 1836. [Boston.] 8vo.

98 THE JOURNALS of each provincial Congreſs of Maſſachusetts in 1774 and 1775, and of the Committee of Safety; with an appendix, containing the proceedings of the county conventions; narratives of the events of the nineteenth of April, 1775: papers relating to Ticonderoga and Crown Point; and other documents illustrative of the early history of the American Revolution. Published un-

der the supervision of W. Lincoln. Boston, 1838. 8vo.

99 COMMISSIONERS for the Zoological and Botanical Survey of the State. Reports on the Fishes, Reptiles and Birds of Maſſachusetts. [By D. H. Storer, and W. B. O. Peabody.] Boston, 1839. 8°

100 ACTS and Resolves [annual] paſſed by the legislature of Maſſachusetts, 1839-1846. 9 vol. [1842 being in two parts]. Boston, 1839-46. 8°

101 SECOND (third, seventh, ninth, tenth and eleventh) Annual Report of the Board of Education. Together with the second (3rd, 7th, 9th and 11th) annual report of (H. Mann,) .. Secretary, etc. Boston, 1839-48. 8°

102 SENATE, N° 36. Third Report of the Agriculture of Maſſachusetts, on wheat and silk. By Henry Colman. Boston, 1840. 8°

103 COMMISSIONERS for the Zoological and Botanical Survey of the State. Reports on the herbaceous plants and on the quadrupeds of Massachusetts. [By C. Dewey and E. Emmons.] Cambridge, 1840. 8°

104 COMMISSIONERS for the Zoological and Botanical Survey of the State. Report on the Invertebrata of Maſſachusetts, comprising the Mollusca, Crustacea, Annelida, and Radiata. [By A. A. Gould.] Cambridge, 1841. 8°

105 COMMISSIONERS for the Zoological and Botanical Survey of the State. A Report on the Insects of Maſſachusetts injurious to vegetation. [By Thaddeus William Harris.] Cambridge, 1841. 8°

106 HOUSE .. N° 19. Papers relating to the coal mines of the State. [Boston, 1842.] 8°

107 Two Months abroad : or, a trip to England, France, Baden, Pruſſia, and Belgium. By a Rail-road Director of Maſſachusetts [i. e. E. H. Derby!—In a series of letters subscribed Maſſachusetts]. Boston, 1844. 8°

108 REMARKS on the Judiciary System of Maſſachusetts, and the neceſſity of a change ; with a review of certain recent decisions. By a Member of the Bar. [Boston, 1844!] 8°

109 ABSTRACT exhibiting the condition of the banks in Maſſachusetts. July, 1844. Prepared .. by J. G. Palfrey. Boston, 1844. 8°

110 ABSTRACT of the returns of the overseers of the poor in Maſſachusetts for the year ending November 1, 1844. Prepared by J. G. Palfrey. [Boston, 1844.] 8°

111 ABSTRACT of returns of the keepers of jails, and overseers of the Houses of Correction, for the year ending November 1, 1844. Boston, 1844. 8°

112 THIRD (and fourth) Annual Report, relating to the registry and returns of births, marriages and deaths in Maſſachusetts for the year ending May 1, 1844 (and April 30, 1845). By J. G. Palfrey. Boston, 1845-46. 8°

113 ABSTRACT of the returns of the overseers of the poor in Maſſachusetts, for the year ending Nov. 1, 1845. Prepared by J. G. Palfrey. [Boston, 1845.] 8°

114 ABSTRACT of returns of the keepers of jails and overseers of the Houses of Correction, for the year ending November 1, 1845. Boston, 1845. 8°

115 ABSTRACT of the returns of Insurance Companies incorporated with specific capital; also of mutual marine and mutual fire and marine insurance companies. Dec. 1, 1844. Prepared by J. G. Palfrey. Boston, 1845. 8°

116 ABSTRACT exhibiting the condition of the banks in Maſſachusetts. Nov. 1845: prepared .. by J. G. Palfrey. Boston, 1845. 8°

117 DOCUMENTS printed by order of the House of Representatives of .. Maſſachusetts, Seſſion 1845. Boston, 1845. 8°

118 DOCUMENTS printed by order of the Senate .. of Maſsachusetts. Seſsion 1845. Boston, 1845. 8°

119 REPORT of the Committee to prevent the Admiſſion of Texas as a Slave State. [Boston, 1845.] 8°

120 ABSTRACT of the returns of Insurance Companies, incorporated with specific capital; also of mutual marine, and mutual fire and marine insurance companies: exhibiting the condition of those institutions on the first day of December, 1845. Prepared by J. G. Palfrey. Boston, 1846. 8°

121 ABSTRACT from the returns of Agricultural Societies in Maſsachusetts for 1845, with selections of addreſſes at cattle shows and fairs. Boston, 1846. 8°

122 STATISTICS of the condition and products of certain branches of industry in Maſsachusetts for the year ending April 1, 1845. Prepared .. by J. G. Palfrey. Boston, 1846. 8°

123 DOCUMENTS printed by order of the House of Representatives .. of Maſsachusetts. Seſsion 1846. Boston, 1846. 8°

124 DOCUMENTS prepared and submitted to the General Court of 1846. By the Secretary of the Commonwealth. Boston, 1846. 8°

125 COMMISSIONERS for the Zoological and Botanical Survey of the State. A Report on the Trees and Shrubs .. in the Forests of Maſsachusetts. Published .. by the Commiſſioners on the Zoological and Botanical Survey of the State. [See EMERSON, G. B.] Boston, 1846. 8°

126 ABSTRACT of the Maſsachusetts School Returns for 1845-46. Boston, 1846. 8vo.

127 MESSAGE from His Excellency George N. Briggs, transmitting the Report of B. P. Poore, employed in France as Historical Agent of the Commonwealth of Maſsachusetts; with letters .. in relation to the subject. [Boston, 1848.] 8vo.

128 REPORT of a General Plan for the Promotion of Public and Personal Health; devised, prepared and recommended by the Commiſſioners appointed under a resolve of the legislature of Maſsachusetts, relating to a sanitary survey of the State. Boston, 1850. 8°

129 SENATE . . N° 22. Annual Reports of the Railroad Corporations in the commonwealth of Maſsachusetts, 1850. Boston, 1851. 8°.

130 THE RICH Men of Maſsachusetts: containing a statement of the reputed wealth of about two thousand persons, with brief sketches of nearly fifteen hundred characters. Second edition .. enlarged. Boston, 1852. 8°

131 RECORDS of the Governor and Company of the Maſsachusetts Bay in New England, printed by order of the legislature. Edited by Nathaniel B. Shurtleff. 5 vol. Boston, 1853-54. 4°

132 REPORT on Insanity and Idiocy in Maſsachusetts, etc. [With the report of the Committee on Charitable Institutions on the above statement.] 2 parts. Boston, 1855. 8vo.

133 EIGHTEENTH Annual Report of the Board of Education, together with the eighteenth annual Report of the Secretary of the Board. Boston, 1855. 8vo.

MASSACHUSETTS ANTI-SLAVERY SOCIETY. Thirteenth Annual Report, presented to the Maſsachusetts Anti-Slavery Society, by its Board of Managers. .. With an appendix. Boston, 1845. 8vo.

MASSACHUSETTS BAPTIST CONVENTION. Minutes of the Massachusetts Baptist Convention, held in Worcester, Oct. 26 and 27, 1825. (Oct. 29, 30, 1828; Oct. 26, 27, 1831; and Eighth Anniversary, Oct. 31 and Nov. 1, 1832.) 4 parts. Worcester [1825-32]. 8°

2 THE FORTY-FIRST Annual Report of the Maſsachusetts Baptist Convention. Boston. 1843. 8vo.

MASSACHUSETTS CENTINEL; [Continued under the title of] Columbian Centinel: Jan. 9, 1798 (N° 33 of vol. VIII) to Dec. 28, 1839 (whole N° 5814). 26 vol. [wanting vol. 1 to VII. and N° 1-32 of vol. VIII. and also a few numbers of the years 1797 and 1799. From N° 27 of vol. XIII to June 16, 1790, the title is changed to "Columbian Centinel." From N° 1623, Oct. 9, 1799, to N° 2133, Sept. 1, 1804, the title reads: "Columbian Centinel and Massachusetts Federalist;" and, after the latter date, "Columbian Centinel" only]. Boston, 1788-1839. Fol°

2 THE MASSACHUSETTS Centinel, Vol. 8, N° 6-25, 27-29, 31-32. Vol. 11, N° 18, 49-52. Vol. 12, N° 1-11, 13, 15-16. Boston, 1787-89. Fol.

MASSACHUSETTS CHARITA-BLE Mechanic Association. First (second, third, fourth) Exhibition and Fair of the Massachusetts Charitable Mechanic Association, at Faneuil and Quincy halls, in .. Boston, .. 1837 (1839, 1841, 1844). 4 parts. Boston, 1837-44. 8°

MASSACHUSETTS GAZETTE. N° 346, 349-56, 358 (March 2, 1769), 3510 (March 9, 1769), 362 (March 16), 364, a N° for March 30, 1769, N° 398, 400, 402, 406, 381, 418, 396, 397, 398, 938, 413. Boston, 1769. Fol.

MASSACHUSETTS GAZETTE. N° 270-271. Boston, 1786. Fol.

MASSACHUSETTS GAZETTE and Boston Post-Boy and the Advertiser. N° 645-50, 665-69, 682-84, 708, 745, 750, 754-55, 765-66, 790-91, 780, Jan. 1, 1770, Dec. 14, 1772. Boston, 1770-72. Fol.

MASSACHUSETTS GAZETTE and Boston Weekly Newsletter. N° 3458-3461, 3470, 3473, 3477-79, 3462, 3464, 3465-67, 3604-11. Jan. 11, 1770 to Dec. 17, 1772. Boston, 1770-72. Fol.

MASSACHUSETTS GAZETTE and Boston Weekly Newsletter. N° 3614-3754, Jan. 7, 1773, to Nov. 9, 1775 [wanting N° 3616-19, 3622-23, 3625, 3627, 3629, 3631, 3634-35, 3637-38, 3643, 3645-47, 3660-84, 3686, 3691-92, 3698, 3709, 3719-54]. Boston, 1773-75. Fol.

MASSACHUSETTS GENERAL HOSPITAL. Annual Report of the Board of Trustees. 1828, '29, '33, '34, 1836-43, 1845. [Boston, 1828-46.] 8vo.

2 ACTS, Resolves, by-laws, and rules and regulations. Boston, 1846. 8°

MASSACHUSETTS HISTORI-CAL SOCIETY. Laws and Regulations of the Massachusetts Historical Society. 8vo.

2 COLLECTIONS: First series. 10 vol. Boston and Cambridge, 1792-1809. 8vo.

3 COLLECTIONS. Second series. 10 vol. Boston, 1815-23. 8vo.

4 COLLECTIONS. Third Series. 10 vol. Cambridge, 1825-49. 8vo.

5 COLLECTIONS. Fourth series. Vol. 1. Boston [Cambridge printed], 1852. 8vo.

6 AN HISTORICAL Journal of the American war. Extracted from the publications of the Massachusetts Historical Society. Boston, 1795. 8°

7 THE MASSACHUSETTS Historical Society, [Circular Letter] to [Dr. Mitchel, of New York, Cor. Member]. 4°

MASSACHUSETTS HORTICUL-TURAL SOCIETY. Report of the transactions of the Massachusetts Horticultural Society, for .. 1837-38; with preliminary observations by J. L. Russell. Boston, 1839. 8vo.

2 TRANSACTIONS .. 1842-43. To which is added the address delivered before the Society .. 16 Sept. [1843] by J. E. Teschemacher, Esq. 2 parts [separately paged]. Boston, 1843. 8vo.

MASSACHUSETTS HUMANE SOCIETY. The Institution of the Humane Society of the Commonwealth of Maſsachusetts: with the rules of the Society. Boston, 1788. 8vo.

MASSACHUSETTS LUNATIC HOSPITAL. Report of Commiſsioners appointed under a resolve of the legislature of Maſsachusetts, to superintend the erection of a Lunatic Hospital at Worcester, and to report a system of discipline and government for the same. Made Jan. 4, 1832. Boston, 1832. 8vo.

2 SECOND (third, fourth, and seventh) Annual Report of the Trustees of the State Lunatic Hospital at Worcester. December 1834-39. Boston, 1835-40. 8vo.

MASSACHUSETTS MEDICAL SOCIETY. Medical papers communicated to the Maſsachusetts Medical Society. Boston, 1790. 8vo.

2 THE ACTS of Incorporation, together with the By-laws and Orders of the Maſsachusetts Medical Society. Salem, 1806. 8vo.

3 ADDRESS to the Community on the neceſsity of legalizing the study of anatomy. By order of the Maſsachusetts Medical Society. Boston, 1829. 8°

MASSACHUSETTS PEACE SOCIETY. A Circular Letter from the Maſsachusetts Peace Society, respectfully addreſsed to the various aſsociations, presbyters, aſsemblies and meetings of the ministers of religion in the United States. Cambridge, 1816. 8°

2 SIXTH (ninth, eighteenth, nineteenth and twentieth) Annual Report of the Maſsachusetts Peace Society. 5 parts. [Boston, 1822-36.] 8°

MASSACHUSETTS QUARTERLY REVIEW. [Edited by R. W. Emerson, T. Parker, and J. E. Cabot.] 3 vol. Boston, 1847-50. 8°

MASSACHUSETTS REGISTER and United States Calendar; for the year of our Lord 1801 (to 1845). 45 vol. Boston [1800-1844]. 12°

MASSACHUSETTS SABBATH SCHOOL SOCIETY. First (seventh, eighth, ninth, twelfth, thirteenth, fourteenth) Annual Report of the .. Society, etc. 7 parts. Boston, 1833-46. 8°

MASSACHUSETTS SABBATH SCHOOL UNION. Fourth (eighth and ninth) Annual Report of the Maſsachusetts Sabbath School Union, presented May 28, 1829 (May 28, 1833, and May 27, 1834). Boston, 1829-34. 8°

MASSACHUSETTS SOCIETY for Promoting Agriculture. Laws and Regulations of the Maſsachusetts Society for promoting Agriculture. By the Trustees. Boston, 1793. 8vo.

2 RULES and Regulations of the .. Society .. containing the names of its members .. several important communications, etc. By the Trustees. Boston, 1796. 8vo.

3 ON the Culture of Potatoes .. published by order of the Maſsachusetts Society, etc. Boston, 1798. 8vo.

4 PAPERS on Agriculture, consisting of communications made to the Society .. with extracts from various publications .. by the Trustees of the Society : [with the premiums offered by the Society, abstracts of the accounts and list of the members.] 9 parts. Boston, 1799-1810. 8vo.

5 THE MASSACHUSETTS Agricultural Repository and Journal. Published by the Trustees of the .. Society. Vol. 3 [a continuation of the Papers on Agriculture published by the Society]. Boston, 1814. 8°

6 INQUIRIES by the Agricultural Society. Boston, 1800. 8vo.

7 INQUIRIES by the Maſsachusetts Society for promoting Agriculture. [Boston, 1805 ?] 8°

MASSACHUSETTS SOCIETY for the Suppreſsion of Intemperance. Report of the Board of Counsel to the Maſsachusetts Society for the Suppreſſion of Intemperance, presented at their eighth anniversary, June 2, 1820. Boston, 1820. 12°

2 A LETTER to the Mechanics of Boston, respecting the formation of a City Temperance Society; from a committee of the Maſsachusetts Society for the Suppreſſion of Intemperance. Boston, 1831. 12°

MASSACHUSETTS' SPY (THE); or, Thomas's Boston Journal. N° 187. September 1, 1774. Boston, 1774. Fol.

MASSACHUSETTS STATE RECORD, New England Register and Year Book of General Information. (Edited by N. Capen. 1847-1851.) 5 vol. Boston, 1847-51. 12°

MATHER, ALLYN, *A.M.* The Character of a well accomplished Ruler described. A discourse [on Exodus xviii. 21]. New Haven [1776]. 8°

MATHER, COTTON. Memorable Providences, relating to Witchcrafts and Poſseſſions. . . With an appendix in vindication of a chapter in a late book of remarkable providences, *etc.* Boston, 1689. 8vo.

2 THE WONDERS of the Invisible World. Observations . . upon the nature, the number, and the operations of the Devils, *etc.* accompany'd with . . accounts of the . . molestations by dæmons and witchcrafts, which have lately annoy'd the country: and the trials of some . . malefactors executed upon occasion thereof. . . Some counsils, directing a due improvement of the . . things lately done by . . evil spirits, in our neighbourhood. . . Conjectures upon the . . events likely to befall . . New England. . . A . . narrative of a late outrage committed by . . witches in Swedeland . . and . . The Devil discovered: in a . . discourse upon . . temptations . . of the Wicked One. 2 parts. Boston, 1693. 8vo. .

3 LIFE of the Rev. Jonathan Mitchel. Boston, 1697. 12mo.

4 THOUGHTS for the Day of Rain; in two Eſsays: 1. The Gospel of the Rainbow; . . 2. The Saviour with his Rainbow, *etc.* Boston, 1712. 8vo.

5 MIRABILIA Dei; an Eſsay on the . . Interpositions of the Divine Providence to . . relieve distreſsed people . . especially relating to that twice-memorable Fifth of November. Boston, 1719. 12mo.

6 THE WORLD Alarm'd. A surprizing relation of a new burning island lately raised out of the sea, near Tercera; with a geographical and theological improvement of so astonishing an occurrence. And a brief history of the other ignivomous mountains at this day flaming in the world. In a letter to an honourable Fellow of the Royal Society at London. From a member of the same society at Boston. Boston: printed by B. Green, for S. Gerrish, and sold at his shop in Cornhill. 1721. 12mo.

7 A SERMON [on 2 Kings ii. 12] on the death of Rev. Increase Mather, D.D. Boston, 1723. 8vo.

8 PARENTATOR. Memoirs of Remarkables in the Life and the Death of the Ever-Memorable Dr. Increase Mather. Who expired Aug. 23, 1723. Boston: printed by B. Green, for Nathaniel Belknap, at the corner of Scarlet's Wharff, 1724. 8°

9 LIFE of the Rev. Jonathan Mitchel. Boston, 1724. 8vo.

10 VIRTUE in its Verdure. A Christian exhibited as a green olive tree in the house of God, with a character of . . Abigail Brown. Boston, 1725. 8vo.

11 RATIO Disciplinæ Fratrum Nov-Anglorum. A faithful account of the discipline profeſsed and practised in the churches of New England. With interspersed and instructive reflections on the discipline of the Primitive churches. Boston: printed for S. Gerrish in Cornhill. 1726. 8vo.

12 MAGNALIA Christi Americana:

or, the ecclesiastical history of New England, from its first planting in the year 1620, unto the Year of Our Lord 1696. In seven books. First American edition, from the London edition of 1702. 2 vol. Hartford, 1820. 8°

13 THE LIFE of the late Rev. and learned Dr. Cotton Mather, of Boston (New England). Philadelphia, 1829. 12mo.

MATHER, INCREASE. The Life and Death of . . Richard Mather. Teacher of the church in Dorchester in New England. Cambridge, 1670. 4to.

2 Κομητογραφια. Or a discourse concerning Comets; . . as also two sermons occasioned by the late blazing stars. 3 parts. [The " Two Sermons," being parts 2 and 3, have each a separate title-page and pagination but a continuous register. The date in the imprint of Nº 2 is 1682, and it is of the second edition; part 3 is without date.] Boston, 1683. 8vo.

3 AN ESSAY for the recording of illustrious providences. Wherein an account is given of many remarkable events, which have happened in this last age, especially in New England. Boston, 1684. 12mo.

4 THE DOCTRINE of Singular Obedience, as the duty and property of the true Christian: opened and applied. In a sermon [on Mat. v. 47]. Boston, 1707. 12°

5 A DISCOURSE concerning faith and fervency in Prayer. . . Together with a vindication of the only true scriptural mode of standing in singing the praises of God, etc. [With an epistle dedicatory, by J. Jacob.] MS. notes. [Boston, 1713?] 8vo.

6 SEVERAL Reasons proving that inoculating or transplanting the Small Pox is a lawful practice, and that it has been blessed by God for the saving of many a life. Boston, 1721. s. sh. fol.

7 SOME further Account from London of the Small Pox inoculated. The second edition. With some remarks on a late scandalous pamphlet, entituled, Inoculation of the Small Pox as practised in Boston. Boston, 1721. 8vo.

8 A CALL to the Tempted: a sermon [on Acts xvi. 27, 28] on the horrid crime of self-murder. Boston, 1723-4. 8°

9 CÆLESTINUS: a conversation in Heaven, quickened and assisted, with discoveries of things in the Heavenly World. Boston, 1723. 12mo.

MATHER, J. H. and BROCKETT, L. P. Geography of the State of New York; . . with statistical tables, and a separate description and map of each county, etc. Hartford, 1847. 12°

MATHER, SAMUEL, D.D. The Departure and Character of Elijah considered and improved: a sermon [on 2 Kings ii. 12] after the decease of . . . Cotton Mather, etc. Boston, 1728. 12°

2 AN ESSAY concerning Gratitude. Boston, 1732. 8vo.

3 THE FALL of the Mighty lamented: a funeral discourse [on 2 Sam. i. 19] upon the death of . . Wilhelmina Dorothea Carolina, Queen-Consort to his Majesty of Great Britain, etc. Boston, 1738. 8°

4 A DISSERTATION concerning the most remarkable name of Jehovah. Boston, 1760. 8°

5 THE LORD'S Prayer: or, a new attempt to recover the right version and genuine meaning of that prayer. Boston, 1766. 8°

6 ALL Men will not be Saved for ever: or, an attempt to prove that this is a scriptural doctrine, and to give a sufficient answer to the publisher of extracts in favour of the salvation of all men. Boston, 1782. 8°

7 ALL Men will not be Saved for ever: or, an attempt to prove that this is a scriptural doctrine, etc. The second edition. Boston, 1783. 8°

8 To the Author of a Letter to Doctor Mather. [A Letter rebuking him for his "haughty air" and "unbecoming treatment of the aged," etc.] By one of the readers. Boston, 1783. 8°

MATHEWS, CORNELIUS. The various Writings of C. Mathews: embracing The Motley Book, Behemoth, The Politicians, Poems on Man in the Republic, Wakondah, Puffer Hopkins, Miscellanies, Selections from Arcturus, International Copyright. New York, 1863 [1843]. 8°

2 MAN in the Republic: a series of poems. New York, 1846. 32°

3 MONEYPENNY, or the heart of the world. A romance of the present day. New York, 1850. 8°

MATHEWS, JOHN H. A Treatise on the doctrine of presumption and presumptive evidence, as affecting the title to real and personal property. With notes and references to American cases, by B. Rand. New York, 1830. 8°

MATHEWS, T. W. Letters to a Christian Friend; containing strictures on a Discourse on Reconciliation by .. J. C. Jones; and a justification of the doctrine of universal pardon. London, Boston [printed], 1854. 8vo.

MATTISON, H. Spirit Rapping Unveiled! an exposé of the origin, history, theology, and philosophy of certain alleged communications from the spirit world, by means of "spirit rapping," "medium writing," "physical demonstrations," etc. New York, 1853. 12°

MATURIN, EDWARD. Lyrics of Spain and Erin. Boston, 1850. 12°

2 BIANCA. A tale of Erin and Italy. New York, 1852. 12°

MAURY, MATTHEW FONTAINE. [Begins] Southern Literary Messenger, July, 1844. Paper on the gulf-stream and currents of the sea, read before the National Institute at its annual meeting, Apr. 2, 1844. Richmond, 1844. 8°

2 A NEW Theoretical and Practical Treatise on Navigation: in which the auxiliary branches of mathematics and astronomy .. are treated of; also, the theory and .. methods of finding time, latitude, and longitude, etc. [With an appendix of tables, separately paged.] Philadelphia, 1845. 8°

3 REFRACTION and other Tables, prepared especially for the reduction of observations at the National Observatory, Washington. Washington, 1846. 4°

4 ABSTRACT Log, for the use of American navigators; prepared under the direction of Commodore L. Warrington, etc. Washington, 1848. 4°

5 NOTICE to Mariners: [being routes to ports in the Pacific, Indian, and South Atlantic Oceans, etc.]. .. Second edition. Washing. 1850. 4to.

6 EXPLANATIONS and Sailing Directions to accompany the wind and current charts approved by Commodore L. Warrington, etc. Washington, 1851. 4°

7 LIEUT. Maury's Investigations of the Winds and Currents of the Sea. (From the appendix to the Washington Astronomical Observations for 1846,) etc. Washington, 1851. 4to.

8 FROM the Appendix to the Washington Astronomical Observations for 1846. (On the probable relation between Magnetism and the Circulation of the Atmosphere.) Washington, 1851. 4to.

9 EXPLANATIONS and Sailing Directions to accompany the Wind and Current Charts, approved by Commodore C. Morris, Chief of the Bureau of Ordnance and Hydrography, and published by authority of Hon. W. A. Graham, Secretary of the Navy. Fourth edition. Washing. 1852. 4°

10 EXPLANATIONS and Sailing Directions to accompany the Wind and Current Charts, approved by Commodore C. Morris, .. and published by authority of Hon. J. C. Dobbin. .. Sixth edition, enlarged and improved. Philadelphia, 1854. 4to. Charts. 1848. Fol.

MAXCY, JONATHAN. *First President of South Carolina College*. An Oration delivered in the Baptist Meeting-house in Providence, July 4, 1795, at the celebration of the nineteenth anniversary of American Independence. Providence, 1795. 8°

2 AN ORATION delivered in the first Congregational Meeting-house in Providence, .. 4 July, 1799. Providence, 1799. 4°

3 AMERICAN Eloquence; consisting of orations, addreſſes, and sermons; being the literary remains of the Rev. J. Maxcy. With a memoir of his life by R. Elton. [With an appendix, containing addreſſes, etc. by A. Meſſer.] New York, 1845. 8°

MAXWELL, JOHN S. The Czar, his Court and People; including a tour in Norway and Sweden. New York, 1848. 12°

MAY, ALEXANDER. Diſſertation on the unity of disease, as opposed to nosology. Philadelphia, 1800. 8vo.

MAY, SAMUEL J. Letters to .. J. Hawes .. in review of his Tribute to the Memory of the Pilgrims. [With an appendix.] Hartford, 1831. 8°

2 A DISCOURSE [on Ezek. xxii. 29] on Slavery in the United States, delivered in Brooklyn, July 3, 1831. Boston, 1832. 8°

3 A DISCOURSE on the Life and Character of .. Charles Follen, .. delivered before the Maſſachusetts Anti-Slavery Society, .. April 17, 1840. Boston. 8°

4 EMANCIPATION in the British West Indies, August 1, 1834. An addreſſ delivered in the first Presbyterian church in Syracuse, on the first of August, 1845. Syracuse, 1845. 8°

MAYER, BRANTZ. Mexico as it was and as it is. N. York, 1844. 8vo.

2 MEXICO, Aztec, Spanish and Republican: a historical, geographical, political, statistical and social account of that country from the period of the invasion to the present time; with a view of the ancient Aztec Empire .. a historical sketch of the late war; and notices of New Mexico and California. 2 vol. Hartford, 1852. 8°

MAYGRIER, J. P. Midwifery Illustrated. . . Translated from the French, with notes, by A. S. Doane. Fifth edition, with additional matter and plates. New York, 1845. 8°

MAYHEW, EXPERIENCE. A Letter to a Gentleman on that question, Whether saving grace be different in species from common grace, or in degree only ? Boston, 1847. 12°

MAYHEW, JONATHAN, D. D. Sermons, etc. Boston, 1755. 8°

2 A DISCOURSE [on Daniel iv. 18] occasioned by the death of King George II, and the happy accession of .. King George III, etc. Boston, 1761. 8°

3 POPISH Idolatry, a discourse [on 2 Cor. vi. 16] delivered in the chapel of Harvard College .. at the lecture founded by .. Paul Dudley. Boston, 1765. 8°

4 AN ECLOGUE sacred to the memory of the Rev. Dr. J. Mayhew, etc. [Boston, 1766.] 4to.

MAYNARD, WILLIAM H. A Speech delivered in the Senate of New York, 3 and 4 Feb. 1832, .. on the resolution against renewing the charter of the Bank of the United States. Albany, 1832. 8°

MAYNE, JOHN, M.D. A Dispensatory and Therapeutical Remembrancer; .. Revised, with the addition of the formulæ of the United States Pharmacopeia .. by R. E. Griffith. Philadelphia, 1848. 12°

MAYO, A. D. Graces and Powers of the Christian Life. Boston, 1852. 12°

2 A SERMON on Daniel Webster, preached at Gloucester, Maſſachusetts. Gloucester, 1852. 8°

MAYO, Robert. Political Sketches of eight years in Washington; in four parts, with annotations. Also a general appendix; and a series of charts, giving a comparative synopsis of the constitutions of the several states and the United States. Baltimore, 1839. 8vo.

2 A Synopsis of the Commercial and Revenue System of the United States .. accompanied with a supplement of historical and tabular illustrations of the origin, organization and practical operations of the treasury department .. with an appendix. 2 vol. Washington, 1847. 4°

MAYO, William Starbuck. The Berber: or the mountaineer of the Atlas. A Tale of the Sallee Rovers. London [New York printed], 1850. 8vo.

2 Romance Dust from the Historic Placer. [New York printed] London, 1851. 12°

MEAD, A. M., Mrs. Sketches by a Christian's way-side. Philadelphia, 1846. 12°

MEAGHER, Thomas Francis. Speeches on the Legislative Independence of Ireland. With introductory notes. New York, 1853. 12°

MEANS and Ends, or Self-training. By the author of "Redwood," "Hope Leslie," "Home," "Poor Rich Man," etc. [C. M. Sedgwick]. Second edition. New York, 1845. 12°

MEASE, James. An Essay on the disease produced by the bite of a mad dog, or other rabid animal. With a preface and appendix by J. C. Lettsom. Philadelphia, 1793. 8vo.

2 Observations on the Arguments of Professor Rush in favour of the inflammatory nature of the disease produced by the bite of a mad dog. Philadelphia, 1801. 8vo.

3 A Geological Account of the United States, comprehending a short description of their animal, vegetable and mineral productions, antiquities and curiosities. Philadel. 1807. 12°

4 The Picture of Philadelphia; with a compendious view of its societies, literary, benevolent, patriotic and religious. Philadel. 1811. 12°

5 Introductory Lecture upon Comparative Anatomy and the diseases of domestic animals. Philadelphia, 1814. 8vo.

6 Address on establishing a Pattern Farm in the vicinity of Philadelphia. Philadelphia, 1818. 8vo.

7 A Reply to the Criticisms by J. N. Barker, on the historical facts of the Picture of Philadelphia. Philadelphia, 1828. 8vo.

8 Observations on the Penitentiary System, and Penal Code of Pennsylvania, with suggestions for their improvement. Philadelphia, 1828. 8vo.

9 Picture of Philadelphia, giving an account of its origin, increase and improvements. Continued by T. Porter. 2 vol. Philadelphia, 1831. 12°

10 Thermometrical Observations as connected with navigation; etc. Philadelphia, 1841. 8°

MECHANIC'S MAGAZINE, and Register of Inventions and Improvements. Jan. 1833 to Dec. 1836. [Edited by J. Knight, D. K. Minor, and G. C. Schaeffer.] Vol. 1-8. New York, 1833-36. 8°

MECKELL, J. F. Manual of General .. Anatomy. Translated from the German into French by A. J. L. Jourdan and G. Breschet. Translated from the French, with notes, by A. Sidney Doane. 3 vol. Philadelphia, 1832. 8°

MED, a slave-child. Case of the Slave-child, Med: Report of the arguments of counsel and of the opinion of the Court, in the case of Commonwealth vs. Aves; tried and determined in the Supreme Judicial Court of Massachusetts. Boston, 1836. 8°

MEDBERY, MRS. R. B. Memoir of Mrs. S. E. York, formerly Miss S. E. Waldo, Miſsionary in Greece. Boston, 1853. 12mo.

MEDICAL AND AGRICULTURAL REGISTER (THE) for the years 1806 and 1807. .. Edited by D. Adams. Boston [1806-7]. 8°

MEDICAL REPOSITORY (THE). Conducted by S. L. Mitchill, .. E. Miller, .. and E. H. Smith. ... 6 vol. Second Hexade, 6 vol. Third Hexade, vol. 1-3. [Vols. 1 and 2 are of a second edition. From vol. 3 the name of E. H. Smith is omitted. From vol. 4 the title reads: "The Medical Repository and Review," etc.] New York, 1800-12. 8°

MEDICAL SOCIETY, NEW HAVEN. Cases and Observations by the .. Society. N. Haven, 1788. 8vo.

MEDICAL SOCIETY, NEW YORK. Report and addreſs, delivered by the president; together with the charter of the College of Physicians and Surgeons in the city of New York. New York, 1807. 8vo.

MEDORUS. Death; or, Medorus' dream. By the author of "Ahasuerus" [Robert Tyler]. New York, 1843. 12°

MEETING of Irishmen in New York. [From the American Truth Teller.] To the People of Ireland. New York [1825]. 8°

MEIGS, HENRY. American Institute. An addreſs on the subject of agriculture and horticulture. New York, 1845. 8°

2 AMERICAN Institute. 19th annual fair. Agricultural addreſs, .. also an addreſs to the band of blind musicians. New York, 1846. 8°

MEIGS, RETURN JONATHAN. Reports of cases argued and determined in the Supreme Court of Tenneſsee, during the years 1838-9. Nashville, 1839. 8°

MELANCTHON, PHILIP. The

Life of P. Melancthon. Philadelphia [1829]. 12mo.

MELISH, JOHN. Travels in the United States of America, in the years 1806-1811; including an account of paſsages betwixt America and Britain, and travels through various parts of Great Britain, Ireland, and Upper Canada. 2 vol. Philadel. 1812. 8°

2 THE TRAVELLER'S Directory through the United States: consisting of a geographical description of the United States, with topographical tables of the counties, towns, population, etc. and a description of the roads. 2 pts. Philadel. 1815-14. 8°

3 A GEOGRAPHICAL description of the United States, with the contiguous British and Spanish Poſseſsions, intended as an accompaniment to Melish's map of these countries. Philadelphia, 1816. 8°

4 THE NECESSITY of protecting and encouraging the manufactures of the United States, in a Letter to J. Monroe, Esq. Philadelphia, 1818. 8°

5 LETTER to James Monroe, Esq. President of the United States, on the State of the Country: with a plan for improving the condition of society. Philadelphia, 1820. 8°

6 THE TRAVELLER'S Directory through the United States, containing a description of the principal roads. To which is added, an Appendix, containing Post-Office Regulations, etc. Philadelphia, 1822. 12°

7 THE TRAVELLER'S Directory through the United States. .. Illustrated by appropriate maps. . A new edition, revised and enlarged. New York, 1825. 12°

8 A GEOGRAPHICAL description of the United States, with the contiguous countries, including Mexico and the West Indies; intended as an accompaniment to Melish's map of these countries. A new edition ... improved. New York, 1826. 8°

MELLEN, GRENVILLE. The Martyr's triumph; Buried valley; and other poems. Boston, 1833. 12°

2 A Book of the United States, exhibiting its geography, divisions, constitution, and government; . together with a condensed history of the land, . . the biography of . . the leading men, . . statistical tables, . . engravings, etc. New York, 1839. 8vo.

MELLICHAMPE; a Legend of the Santee. By the author of " The Yemassee," . . etc. [William Gilmore Simms]. 2 vol. New York,1836. 12°

MELSHEIMER, F. V. A Catalogue of insects of Pennsylvania. Part 1. Hanover, York Co. 1806. 8vo.

MELVILLE, Herman. Omoo: a narrative of Adventures in the South Seas. Third edition. New York, 1847. 12°

2 Pierre; or the ambiguities. New York, 1852. 12°

MEMES, John S. Memoirs of the Empress Josephine. New York, 1844. 12°

MEMOIRS of Sergeant Dale, his daughter, and the orphan Mary. Philadelphia, 1830. 12mo.

MEMORIAL for Sunday School Boys. Philadelphia, 1831. 12mo.

MEMORIAL for Sunday School Girls. Philadelphia, 1830. 12m.

MEMORY. Philadelphia, 1832. 12mo.

MEN. Distinguished Men of modern times. [Selected from the "Gallery of portraits," published by the Society for the diffusion of useful knowledge.] 2 vol. New York,1845. 12°

MEN of the Time, or sketches of living notables. N. York, 1852. 12°

MENEGHINE, Professor, of Pisa. Mineralogical notices. [From the " American Journal of Science and Arts." Vol. 14, July, 1852, pp. 60-65.] [New Haven, 1852.] 8vo.

MENGOUS, Peter. Narrative of a Greek soldier, containing anecdotes illustrating the character and manners of the Greeks and Turks in Asia Minor. New York, 1830. 12mo.

MENTOR. [Begins] Good news for the Church. [From Poulson's American Daily Advertiser.] [Philadelphia, 1834.] 8°

MERCANTILE LIBRARY ASSOCIATION, Baltimore. Constitution, rules and regulations of the Mercantile Library Association of Baltimore. Baltimore [1841]. 8vo.

MERCANTILE LIBRARY ASSOCIATION, Boston. Report of the board of directors of the Mercantile Library Association, from the origin of the institution, in 1820, to its incorporation, in 1845. Boston, 1845. 8vo.

2 Thirty-third (thirty-fourth) annual report of the Mercantile Library Association, etc. Boston, 1853-54. 8vo.

3 See Catalogues, N° 67, 89.

MERCANTILE LIBRARY ASSOCIATION, New York. The thirteenth (15th to the 19th, 21st to the 25th, and 32nd to 34th) annual report of the board of directors of the Mercantile Library Association of the city of New York. New York, 1834-55. 8vo.

2 Constitution, Bye-laws, and Regulations of the Mercantile Library Association. New York, 1844. 8vo.

3 Another edition. N. York, 1855. 8vo.

4 See Catalogues, N° 34, 83, 87.

MERCER, Charles F. Speech in the House of Representatives, on the Seminole war. [Washington, 1818!] 12°

MERCHANT'S MAGAZINE and Commercial Review. Freeman Hunt, editor. July, 1839, to June, 1850. Vol. 1-22. New York, 1839-50. 8°

[Continued as] Hunt's Merchant's Magazine, etc. Vol. 23-35. New York, 1850-56. 8°

MERRIAM, GEORGE. Merriam's American Reader ; . . containing extracts suited to excite a love of science and literature, etc. Second edition. Brookfield, 1829. 12°

MERRICK, PLINY. A Letter on speculative Free-Masonry, being his answer to Gen. Nathan Heard and Col. Gardner Burbank. Worcester, 1829. 8vo.

MERRICK, S. V. Report upon an examination of some of the gas manufactories in Great Britain, France, and Belgium, under a resolution passed by the Select and Common Council of the city of Philadelphia. Philadelphia, 1834. 8°

MERRICK, WILLIAM D. Speech , . on the sub-treasury bill ; delivered in the Senate, . . . Jan. 23, 1840. Washington, 1840. 8°

MERRILL, DANIEL. The Kingdom of God : a discourse [on Matt. vi. 10] delivered . . . before . . . the Governor, . . Council, etc. of . . New Hampshire, June 5, . . being the anniversary Election. Concord, 1817. 8°

MERRILL, THOMAS A. A Sermon [on 1 Tim. iv. 8] preached in the audience of . . Governor, . . Council, etc. of . . Vermont, . . on the day of the anniversary Election. · Middlebury, 1806. 8°

MERRILL, ELIPHALET, and MERRILL, PHINEHAS. A Gazetteer of the State of New Hampshire. 3 parts. . . Compiled from the best authorities by E. Merrill and P. Merrill. Exeter, 1817. 8°

MERRILL, PHINEHAS. (The Scholar's Guide) to arithmetic. . . . The fourth edition, corrected and improved by the author. Exeter, 1802. 12°

. MERRITT, TIMOTHY. A Discussion [with L. R. Paige] on Universal

Salvation, in three lectures and five answers against that doctrine. . . To which are added two discourses [on Gal. iii. 13, and Rev. ii. 14, 15] on the same subject, by . . W. Fisk. New York, 1836. 12°

MERRY MOUNT : a Romance of 'the Massachusetts Colony. [By John Lothrop Motley.] 2 vol. Boston and Cambridge, 1849. 12°

MERRYWEATHER, GEORGE. Kings, the Devil's Viceroys and Representatives on Earth. [New York,] 1838. 8°

METCALF, SAMUEL L. A New Theory of Terrestrial Magnetism. New York, 1833. 8°

METCALF, THERON. Digest of the cases decided in the Supreme Judicial Court of the Commonwealth of Massachusetts, from March, 1816, to October, 1823, inclusive, as contained in the five last volumes of Tyng's and the first of Pickering's Reports. . . To which is added, a digested index of the names of the cases in the eighteen volumes of Massachusetts Reports. Boston, 1825. 8°

2 REPORTS of cases argued and determined in the Supreme Judicial Court of Massachusetts, 1840-44. Vol. 1-7. Boston, 1843-45. 8°

METHODIST ALMANAC for . . 1845, . . containing all the customary calculations in equal or clocktime, fitted to the horizon and meridian of Philadelphia. . . By D. Young. New York [1844]. 12°

2 METHODIST Almanac for . . 1847: . . calculated in equal or clocktime, for Boston, New York, Philadelphia, Detroit, etc. by D. Young. . . Comprising also a summary view of methodism, . . etc. G. Peck, editor. New York [1846]. 12°

METHODIST EPISCOPAL CHURCH. The doctrines and discipline of the Methodist Episcopal Church in America. With explanatory notes, by T. Coke and F. Asbury. The tenth edition. Philadelphia, 1798. 12mo.

2 MINUTES of the Annual Conferences of the Methodist Episcopal Church, for the years 1773 (to 1845). 3 vol. New York, 1840 [-45.] 8°

METHODIST EPISCOPAL Church Miſsionary Society. Twenty-seventh annual report of the Missionary Society of the Methodist Episcopal Church. N.York, 1846. 8°

METHODIST EPISCOPAL Church Sunday School Union. Fifth annual report of the Sunday School Union. . . Also an arranged catalogue of the Sunday School publications and tracts. 2 parts. New York, 1845. 12°

METHODIST MAGAZINE (THE). Vol. 1-11. 1818-1828. [Edited by J. Soule and T. Mason. Continued as] The Methodist Magazine and Quarterly Review. Vol. 12-22: New series, vol. 1-11. 1830-1840; [and as] Methodist Quarterly Review. Edited by G. Peck, D.D. Vol. 23-30. Third series, vol. 1-8. 1841-48. Vol. 31-38. Fourth series, vol. 1-8. J. M'Clintock, editor. 1849-56. New York, 1818-56. 8°

METHODIST PREACHER: or, monthly sermons from living ministers. Edited by S. W. Willson. Vol.1. Boston, 1830. 8vo.

METHUSELAH. Antediluvian Antiquities. Fragments of the age of Methuselah. Translated by an American traveller in the East. Vol. 1. Boston, 1829. 12°

METROPOLITAN CATHOLIC ALMANAC and Laity's Directory, etc. 1853. Baltimore [1853]. 12°

MEURER, MORITZ. The Life of Martin Luther: related from original authorities,with16engravings. Translated from the German by a Pastor of the Evangelical Lutheran Church. New York, 1848. 8°

MEXICO. The Infidel; or the fall of Mexico. A romance. By the author of "Calavar" [R. M. Bird]. Second edition. 2 vol. Philadelphia, 1835. 12°

MEXICO in 1842: a description of the Country; its natural and political features; with a sketch of its history brought down to the present year; to which is added an account of Texas and Yucatan, and of the Santa Fé expedition. Illustrated with a new map. New York, 1842. 16°

MIAMI UNIVERSITY, OXFORD, Ohio. Laws relating to the Miami University, together with the ordinances of the president and trustees, and extracts from the journal of proceedings. To which is added, a table of the lots and lands belonging to the University. Cincinnati, 1833. 8°

2 THIRD triennial Catalogue of the officers and graduates, . . March, . . 1840. Oxford, Ohio, 1840. 12°

MICHAUX, FRANÇOIS ANDRÉ. The North American Sylva, or a description of the forest trees of the United States, Canada, and Nova Scotia. Considered particularly with respect to their use in the arts, etc. To which is added a description of the most useful of the European forest-trees. [Translated from the French by A. L. Hillhouse.] 3 vol. Philadelphia, 1817-19. 8vo.

2 THE NORTH American Sylva; or, a description of the forest trees of the United States, Canada, and Nova Scotia; considered particularly with respect to their use in the arts, and their introduction into commerce. To which is added, a description of the most useful of the European forest trees. . . Translated from the French (by A. L. Hillhouse). 3 vol. Paris and Philadelphia, 1819-18-19. 8vo.

3 THE NORTH American Sylva, or a description of the forest trees of the United States, Canada, and Nova Scotia. Considered particularly with respect to their use in the arts, and

their introduction into commerce. To which is added a description of the most useful of the European forest trees. . . With notes by J. J. Smith. 3 vol. Philadelphia, 1850. 8°

MICHELET, Jules. Modern History, from the French of M. Michelet. With an introduction by A. Potter. New York, 1843. 12°

MICHIGAN, *State of.* The Revised Statutes of the State of Michigan, passed at the adjourned Session of 1837 and the regular Session of 1838. Printed under the direction of E. B. Harrington and E. J. Roberts. Detroit, 1838. 8°

2 THE REVISED Statutes of the State of Michigan, passed and approved May 18, 1846. Printed under the superintendence of S. M. Green. Detroit, 1846. 8°

3 ACTS of the Legislature of the State of Michigan, passed at the annual Session, . . 1841 (to 1844; 1845 to 1847). With an appendix [to each vol.] containing the treasurer's annual report, etc.). 6 vol. Detroit, 1841-47. 8°

4 JOURNAL of the Senate of the State of Michigan, 1837 (1839, 1841, 1843 to 1847) 9 vol. Detroit, 1837-1847. 8°

5 EXECUTIVE Journal of the Senate of the State of Michigan at the annual Session of 1844. Detroit, 1844. 8°

6 JOURNAL of the House of Representatives of the State of Michigan, 1837 (adjourned Session, 1839, 1843, 1846-7.) 6 vol. Detroit, 1837-47. 8°

7 DOCUMENTS accompanying the Journal of the Senate, . . . Session 1839 (1840, 1841, 1843, 1844, 1845, 1846, 1847). Detroit, 1839-47. 8°

8 DOCUMENTS accompanying the Journal of the House of Representatives. Session 1840 (1841, 1842, 1843, 1845, 1846, 1847). Detroit, 1840-47. 8°

9 DOCUMENTS communicated to the Senate and House of Representatives,

Session 1842 (1843). Detroit, 1842-1843. 8°

10 JOINT Documents of the Senate and House of Representatives, Session 1844 (1845, 1846, 1847). 4 vol. Detroit, 1844-47. 8°

MICHIGAN BAPTIST CONVENTION. The fifth annual report of the Baptist Convention of the State of Michigan. Detroit, 1840. 8°

2 PROCEEDINGS of the eighth anniversary of the Baptist Convention, of the State of Michigan. Detroit, 1843. 8°

MICHIGAN STATE AGRICULTURAL SOCIETY. Transactions of the Michigan State Agricultural Society. [Edited by J. C. Holmes.] 1849-53. Lansing, 1849-54. 8vo.

MICKLE, ISAAC. Reminiscences of Old Gloucester: or incidents in the history of the counties of Gloucester, Atlantic and Camden, New Jersey. Philadelphia, 1845. 8°

MIDDLEBURY COLLEGE, MIDDLEBURY, *Vermont.* Catalogue of the officers and students of Middlebury College, and Vermont Academy of medicine in connexion. Oct. 1824. [Middlebury, 1824.] 8°

2 CATALOGUS senatus academici, et eorum qui munera et officia academica gesserunt, quique aliquovis gradu exornati fuerunt, in Collegio Medioburiensi, *etc.* Medioburiæ, 1841. 8°

MILBURN, MATTHEW M. The Cow: dairy husbandry and cattle breeding. Edited by A. Stevens. New York, 1852. 12°

MILES, GEORGE D. Memoir of E. M. Woodward. . . Second edition, with a preface, by the Rt. Rev. A. Potter, D.D. Philadel. 1852. 16°

MILES, GEORGE H. Mohammed, the Arabian Prophet. A Tragedy in five Acts [and in verse]. Boston, 1850. 12°

MILES, HENRY A. Lowell, as it was, and as it is. Lowell, 1845. 12mo.

2 THE GOSPEL Narratives; their origin, peculiarities, and transmission. Boston, 1848. 8°

MILES, JOHN. Reports of cases determined in the District Court for the city and county of Philadelphia, March, 1835, to Dec. 1840. 2 vol. Philadelphia, 1836-42. 8°

MILITARY AND NAVAL MA-GAZINE of the United States (The). Edited by B. Homans. 6 vol. (vol. 6 never completed). Washington, 1833-36. 8°

MILLARD, DAVID. A Journal of Travels in Egypt, Arabia Petræ (sic), and the Holy Land, during 1841-2. Rochester, 1843. 12°

MILLER, ADAM. Origin and Pro-greſs of the German Miſsions in the Methodist Episcopal Church, etc. Cincinnati, 1843. 12°

MILLER, BRANCH W. Reports of cases argued and determined in the Supreme Court of the State of Louis-iana. By B. W. Miller. Vol. 1-5. (Vol. 6-19, by T. Curry.) 19 vol. New Orleans, 1831-1842. 8°

MILLER, JONATHAN P. The Con-dition of Greece in 1827 and 1828, being an exposition of the misery to which the inhabitants have been re-duced by the destruction of their towns and villages and the ravages of their country. N. York, 1828. 12mo.

MILLER, MORRIS S. Speech [in the House of Representatives, on the Militia bill]. [Washington, 1815?] 8°

MILLER, ROBERT. A Diſſertation upon the action of cold upon the hu-man body, and its application to the cure of diseases. Philadel. 1807. 8vo.

MILLER, SAMUEL. Retrospect of the eighteenth Century. Revelations in Science, Arts and Literature. 3 vol. New York, 1805. 8vo.

2 THE GUILT, Folly, and Sources of Suicide : two discourses, preached in N. York, Feb. 1805. N. York, 1805. 8°

3 A SERMON [on Lam. ii. 1, 13] delivered at the request of a number of young gentlemen, who had as-sembled to expreſs their condolence with the inhabitants of Richmond on the late mournful dispensation. New York, 1812. 8°

4 MEMOIRS of the Rev. J. Rodgers, late pastor of the Wall street and Brick Churches in the city of New York. New York, 1813. 8°

5 A LETTER [subscribed, " a Uni-tarian of Baltimore"] to . . . Samuel Miller . . . on the charges against Unitarians, contained in his late ordi-nation sermon in Baltimore. From the Unitarian Miscellany. Second edition. Baltimore, 1821. 12°

6 A LETTER to a gentleman of Bal-timore in reference to the case of the Rev. Mr. Duncan [i.e. relative to his work upon Creeds]. Princeton Preſs [New Jersey], 1826. 8°

7 LETTERS on clerical manners and habits. New York, 1827. 12mo.

8 HOLDING fast the faithful word : a sermon [on Tit. i. 9] delivered . . at the installation of . . W. B. Sprague . . as pastor, etc. Albany, 1829. 8°

9 LETTERS concerning the consti-tution and order of the Christian mi-nistry : addreſsed to the members of the Presbyterian churches in the city of New York. To which is prefixed, a letter on the present aspect and bearing of the Episcopal controversy. Second edition. Philadel. 1830. 8°

10 LETTERS on clerical manners and habits : addreſsed to a student in the theological seminary, at Princeton, N. J. . Third edition, revised. Prince-ton, 1835. 12°

11 THE EARTH filled with the glory of the Lord : a sermon [on Numb. xiv. 20, 21] preached . . before the American Board of Commiſsioners for Foreign Miſsions, at their twenty-sixth annual meeting. Boston, 1835. 8°

MILLER, STEPHEN F. AND OTHERS.

Report of the Commiſſioners appointed to examine the bank of the State of Alabama. Tuscaloosa, 1845. 8°

MILLER, WILLIAM S. *of New York*. Speech . . . on the war and mail steamer bill; delivered in the House of Representatives, *etc*. Washington, 1847. 8°

MILLINGTON, JOHN. Elements of civil engineering : being an attempt to consolidate the principles of the various operations of the civil engineer, into one point of view for the use of students; *etc*. Philadelphia, 1839. 8°

MILLS, ABRAHAM. The literature and the literary men of Great Britain and Ireland. 2 vol. N. York,1851. 8°

MILLS, EDMUND. An oration in commemoration of the anniversary of American Independence, pronounced at the first Congregational meeting-house, in Sutton, . . . July 4, 1809. Sutton, 1809. 8°

MILLS, ROBERT. Statistics of South Carolina, including a view of the natural, civil, and military history general and particular. Charleston, 1826. 8°

MILLS, ROBERT. The American Pharos, or light-house guide; founded on official reports, *etc*. Washington, 1832. 8°
.2 GUIDE to the national executive offices and the Capitol of the United States. Illustrated by diagram plans, *etc*. Washington, 1842. 12°

MILLS, SAMUEL J. and SMITH, DANIEL. Report of a Miſſionary Tour through that part of the United States which lies west of the Allegany mountains. By Samuel J. Mills and Daniel Smith. Andover, 1815. 8vo.

MILMAN, HENRY HART. The history of the Jews, from the earliest period to the present time. 3 vol. New York, 1843. 12°

MILNE-EDWARDS, HENRI. Outlines of Anatomy and Physiology. Translated from the French . . by J. F. W. Lane. Boston, 1841. 8vo.

MILTIMORE, JAMES. A Discourse [on 1 Chron. xii. 32] delivered in Newmarket, at the particular request of a respectable musical choir, to a numerous aſſembly, convened for celebrating the birthday of . . Washington. Exeter, 1794. 8°
2 A SERMON [on Job xxix. 14] preached . . before . . the Governor, . . Council, *etc*. of . . . New Hampshire. Concord, 1806. 8°

MILTON, *Town of*. A Collection of papers relative to the transactions of the town of Milton, in the state of Maſſachusetts, to promote a general inoculation of the Cow-Pox or Kine-Pock as a never failing preventive against Small-Pox infection. Boston, 1809. 8vo.

MILTON, JOHN. The Prose Works of J. Milton. With a biographical introduction, by R. W. Griswold. 2 vol. New York, 1847. 8°
2 THE PARADISE Lost: with notes explanatory and critical. Edited by J. R. Boyd. New York, 1851. 12°
3 THE POETICAL Works of John Milton: with a life of the author; preliminary diſſertations on each poem, notes critical and explanatory . . . and a verbal index. Edited by C. D. Cleveland. Philadel. 1853. 12°

MINER, CHARLES. History of Wyoming, in a series of letters. Philadelphia, 1845. 8vo.

MINER, T. B. The American Bee Keeper's Manual; being a practical Treatise on the history and domestic economy of the Honey Bee. London [New York printed], 1849. 12mo.

MINIFIE, WILLIAM. A Text-book of geometrical drawing, for the use of mechanics and schools. . . Third edition. Baltimore, 1851. 8°

MINOR, B. B. An Appeal to the Legislature of Virginia in behalf of the Colonial History of Virginia; containing a proposition to procure materials from England for the completion of said history: From the "Southern Literary Meſſenger." Richmond, Virginia, 1844. 8vo.

MINOR, HENRY. Reports of Cases argued and determined in the Supreme Court of Alabama. May 1820 to July 1826. Vol. 1. [No more published.] New York, 1829. 8°

MINOT, GEORGE. Digest of the decisions of the Supreme Judicial Court of Maſſachusetts, reported in the seventeen volumes of Maſſachusetts Reports, the twenty-four volumes of Pickering's Reports, and the first four volumes of Metcalf's Reports. Edited by G. Minot. (Supplement . . comprising the cases reported in the last ten volumes of Metcalf's Reports and the first three volumes of Cushing's Reports.) Boston, 1844-52. 8°

MINOT, GEORGE RICHARDS. The History of the Insurrections in Massachusetts in the year 1786 and the Rebellion consequent thereon. Worcester, 1788. 8vo.
2 THE HISTORY of the Insurrections in Maſſachusetts, in the year seventeen hundred and eighty six, and the rebellion consequent thereon. Second edition. Boston, 1810. 8°
3 AN EULOGY on George Washington . . delivered before the inhabitants of Boston, etc. Boston, [1800.] 8°
4 CONTINUATION of the History of the Province of Maſſachusetts Bay, from 1748. With an introductory sketch of events from its original settlement. 2 vol. Boston, 1798-1803. 8vo.

MINUTE GUN (THE). [Edited and printed by Samuel Foster Haven, Jr. aged 14.] Vol. 1. Worcester, 1845-46. 16°

MIRIAM: a dramatick poem by the author of "Joanna of Naples," [i. e. Louisa J. Park, afterwards Mrs. Hall]. Second edition revised. Boston, 1849. 12°

MISCELLANIES. By the author of "Letters on the Eastern States." [William Tudor.] Boston, 1821. 12°

MISERIES. The Miseries of Human Life [by J. Beresford]: an old friend in a new dreſs. New York, 1853. 8°

MISSION. West India Miſſion. Philadelphia, 1834. 12mo.

MISSIONARY (THE). (P. H. Greenleaf, Editor.) N° 13-33. Burlington, N. J. 1835. Fol.
2 THE MISSIONARY. [Imperfect, comprising vol. v. N° 7-12; vol. vi. N° 1, 2, 7 and 8 to 12; vol. vii. N° 1-5, 7 and 8.] Burlington, 1848-50. Fol.

MISSIONARY HERALD. See PANOPLIST.

MISSISSIPPI, State of. A Digest of the Laws of Miſſiſſippi, comprising all the laws of a general nature, including the acts of the Seſſion of 1839. By T. J. Fox Alden and J. A. Van Hoesen. New York, 1822. 8°
2 PROCEEDINGS of the fifth annual meeting of the Convention of the Baptist denomination of the State of Miſſiſſippi. Jackson, 1841. 8vo.

MISSISSIPPI VALLEY. View of the Valley of the Miſſiſſippi, or the emigrant's . . guide to the West, etc. Philadelphia, 1832. 12°
2 VIEW of the Valley of the Miſſiſſippi, or the emigrant's and traveller's guide to the West. Second edition. Philadelphia, 1834. 12°

MISSOURI, State of. The revised Statutes of the State of Miſſouri, revised and digested by the eighth General Aſſembly, during the years 1834 and 1835. Together with the Constitutions of Miſſouri and of the

United States. . . Published under the direction of the superintendent appointed by the General Aſsembly for that purpose (A. A. King). St. Louis, 1835. 8°

2 REPORTS of Cases argued and decided in the Supreme Court of the State of Miſsouri, from 1821 to 1835. 3 vol. Saint Louis, 1843. 8°

3 PROCEEDINGS, and addreſs of the Anti-Jackson Convention of Miſsouri to their fellow citizens. Fayette [1828]. 8°

MITCHELL, DONALD G. Dream Life: a Fable of the Seasons. By Ik Marvel. New York, 1852. 12°

2 See LORGNETTE and MARVEL, Ik.

MITCHELL, REV. JOHN. Notes from Over- Sea: consisting of observations made in Europe in the years 1843 and 1844: addreſsed to a brother. 2 vol. New York, 1845. 12°

MITCHELL, NAHUM. History of the early settlement of Bridgewater in Plymouth County, Maſsachusetts, including an extensive Family Register. Boston, 1840. 8°

MITCHELL, ORMSBY MACKNIGHT. A course of Six Lectures on Astronomy, delivered in . . New York. Specially reported for the New York Tribune. New York, 1848. 8°

MITCHELL, S. AUGUSTUS. An Accompaniment to Mitchell's Map of the World, on Mercator's projection; containing an index to the various countries, etc. represented on the map, . . also, a general description of the five great divisions of the globe. Philadelphia, 1838. 8vo. Map, fol.

2 MITCHELL's Atlas of Outline Maps, intended to be filled up by pupils studying Mitchell's School Geography and Atlas. Philadelphia, 1839. 4°

3 MITCHELL's Geographical Reader: a system of modern geography, etc. Philadelphia, 1840. 12°

4 A KEY to the study of the Maps

comprising Mitchell's School Atlas, etc. Philadelphia, 1841. 12°. Atlas, 1839. 4°

5 MITCHELL's School Geography. . . Illustrated by an atlas of eighteen maps. Philadelphia, 1845. 12°. Atlas. 4°

6 KEY for exercise on Mitchell's series of outline maps for the use of academies and schools. Hartford, 1845. 12°

7 REVISED edition. Mitchell's Primary Geography. . . Illustrated by one hundred and twenty engravings, and fourteen maps. Philadelphia, 1846. Square 16°

MITCHELL, WILLIAM. The Claims of Africa: a discourse [on Psalm lxviii. 31] delivered at . . the annual meeting of the Vermont Colonization Society, etc. Burlington, 1843. 8°

MITCHILL, S. L. Outline of the Doctrines in Natural History, Chemistry, and Economics, now delivering in the College of New York. New York, 1792. 12mo.

2 THE LIFE, Exploits, and Precepts of Tammany, the famous Indian Chief. New York, 1795. 8vo.

3 EXPLANATIONS of the Synopsis of Chemical Nomenclature and arrangement: containing several important alterations of the plan originally reported by the French Academicians. New York, 1801. 8vo.

4 A CONCISE Description of Schooley's Mountain in New Jersey, with some experiments on the water of its chalybeate spring. New York, 1810. 8vo.

5 REPORT on the Fishes of New York. New York, 1814. 12mo.

6 A DISCOURSE on the State and Prospects of American Literature, before the New York Alpha of the Phi-Beta-Kappa Society. Albany, 1821. 8°

MIX, SILAS. An Oration delivered at the national celebration, at New

Haven, Con. July 3, 1830. New Haven [1830]. 8°

MOBILE DIRECTORY AND REGISTER for 1844... with a variety of .. statistical matter, *etc.* By E. T. Wood. Mobile, 1844. 12mo.

MOHAMMAD BAKIR BNU MOHAMMAD TAKI. The Life and Religion of Mohammed, as contained in the Sheeâh traditions of the Hyât-ul-Kuloob. Translated from the Persian by J. L. Merrick. Boston, 1850. 8°

MOHICANS. The Last of the Mohicans ; a narrative of 1757. By the author of " The Pioneers " [J. F. Cooper]. A new edition. 2 vol. Philadelphia, 1836. 12°

MONDAT, V. On Sterility in the Male and Female, its causes and treatment. Translated from the fifth French edition. New York, 1844. 12°

MON DROIT. Criticism on the Declaration of Independence, as a literary document. By Mon Droit. New York, 1846. 8vo.

MONELL, CLAUDIUS L. A Treatise on the Practice of the Supreme Court of the State of New York adapted to the Code of Procedure as amended by the Act of April 11, 1849, and of April 16, 1852, and the Rules of the Supreme Court. Second edition, with copious notes and references to the decisions of our courts and books of practice. Vol. 1. Albany [New York printed], 1853. 8vo.

MONET DE LAMARCK, JEAN BAPTISTE PIERRE ANTOINE DE. Lamarck's Genera of Shells, with a catalogue of species. Translated from the French by Augustus A. Gould. Boston, 1833. 12mo.

MONETTE, JOHN W. History of the Discovery and Settlement of the Valley of the Mifsifsippi, by .. Spain, France, and Great Britain, and the subsequent occupation, settle-

ment, and extension of Civil Government by the United States, until .. 1846. 2 vol. New York, 1846. 8°

MONEY AND BANKING, or their Nature and Effects considered. Together with a plan for the universal diffusion of their legitimate benefits without their evils. Cincinnati, 1839. 12mo.

MONGE, GASPARD, *Count de Peluze.* An Elementary Treatise on Statics .. with a biographical notice of the author. Translated from the French by W. Baker. Philadelphia, 1851. 12°

MONIKINS (THE). [A tale.] Edited by the author of " The Spy." [By J. F. Cooper.] 2 vol. Philadelphia, 1841. 12°

MONK, MARIA. Awful Disclosures of M. Monk, as exhibited in a narrative of her .. residence of five years as a novice, and two years as a black Nun, in the Hotel Dieu Nunnery at Montreal. New York, 1836. 12°

2 FURTHER Disclosures by M. Monk, concerning the Hotel Dieu Nunnery of Montreal ; also, her visit to Nun's Island, and disclosures concerning that secret retreat. Preceded by a reply to the Priest's Book, by Rev. J. J. Slocum. New York, 1837. 12°

MONKEY (THE). American Sunday School Union, Philadelphia, 1832. 12mo.

MONMONIER, JOHN F. AND MAC JILTON, JOHN N. High-School Literature : a selection of readings for the higher clafses of schools. Selected and arranged by J. F. Monmonier, and J. N. Mac Jilton. Second edition. New York, 1853. 12°

MONROE, JAMES, *Fifth President of the United States.* A View of the Conduct of the Executive in the Foreign Affairs of the United States, connected with the mifsion to the

French Republic, 1794-6. Illustrated by his instructions and correspondence and other authentic documents. Philadelphia, 1797. 8vo.

2 A NARRATIVE of a Tour of Observation, during the summer of 1817, by J. Monroe, through the northeastern and north-western departments of the Union, with a view to the examination of their military defences. With an appendix. Philadelphia, 1818. 12mo.

3 THE MEMOIR of J. Monroe, . . relating to his unsettled claims upon the people and government of the United States. Charlottesville, Va. 1828. 8°

MONROE, THOMAS B. Reports of Cases at common law and in equity, argued and decided in the Court of Appeals of the Commonwealth of Kentucky. (1824-1828.) 7 vol. Frankfort, 1825-30. 8°

MONTEFIORE, J. The American Trader's Compendium; containing the laws, customs, and regulations of the United States relative to commerce : including the most useful precedents adapted to general business. Philadelphia, 1811. 8°

MONTGOMERY, CORINNE, Mrs. Texas and her Presidents, with a glance at her climate and agricultural capabilities. New York, 1845. 12°

2 EAGLE Pass; or, Life on the Border. New York, 1852. 12°

MONTGOMERY, G. W. Narrative of a Journey to Guatemala, in Central America, in 1838. New York, 1839. 8°

MONTGOMERY, H. The Life of Major General Zachary Taylor. Auburn, N. Y. 1848. 12°

MONTGOMERY, JAMES. Lectures on General Literature, Poetry, etc. delivered at the Royal Institution in 1830 and 1831. New York, 1846. 12°

MONTGOMERY, JORGE. Ber-

nardo del Carpio, an historical novel, of the eighth century, from the Spanish of Don J. Montgomery. New York, 1834. 12°

MONTHLY American Journal of Geology and Natural Science, etc. July, 1831, to June, 1832. Conducted by G. W. Featherstonhaugh. Philadelphia, 1831-32. 8°

MONTHLY ANTHOLOGY and Boston Review, containing sketches and reports of philosophy, religion, history, arts and manners. (Edited by a society of gentlemen.) Nov. 1803 to Dec. 1810. 9 vol. Boston, 1804-1810. 8°

MONTHLY CHRONICLE of events, discoveries, improvements, and opinions. 3 vol. Boston, 1840-1843. 8°

MONTHLY JOURNAL (THE) of Agriculture, containing the best current productions in promotion of agricultural improvement, . . with original contributions . . J. S. Skinner, editor. July, 1845, to June, 1847. Vol. 1, 2. New York, 1845-47. 8°

MONTHLY MAGAZINE (THE) and American Review. April, 1799, to Dec. 1800. [Edited by C. B. Brown.] 3 vol. New York, 1799-1800. 8°

MONTHLY MILITARY REPOSITORY (THE)... By C. Smith. Vol. 1, 2. New York, 1796-97. 8°

MONTHLY MISCELLANY (THE) of Inquiry into the origin, design, and principles of physical evil; or the natural and moral history of death, cogitative and incogitative, etc. [By David Wells.] N° 1. April, 1848. New York, 1848. 8°

MONTHLY ROSE; a periodical conducted by the present and former members of the Albany Female Academy. Albany, 1845. 8°

MOONEY, THOMAS. A History of

Ireland, from its first settlement to the present time; including a particular account of its literature, music, architecture, and national resources; with .. sketches of its eminent men, interspersed with a great number of Irish melodies, etc. Boston, 1846. 8°

MOORE, ALFRED, AND OTHERS. Report of the Commissioners appointed to examine the branch of the bank of the State of Alabama, at Huntsville. Nov. 3, 1841. Tuscaloosa, 1841. 8°

MOORE, CHARLES W. Address delivered on the centennial anniversary of St. John's [Masonic] Lodge, N° 1, at Portsmouth, N(ew) H(ampshire), etc. [With an appendix.] Boston, 1836. 8°

MOORE, CLEMENT C. A Lecture introductory to the course of Hebrew instruction in the general theological seminary of the Protestant Episcopal Church in the United States. New York, 1825. 8°
  2 ADDRESS delivered before the alumni of Columbia College. New York, 1825. 8°
  3 A VISIT from St. Nicholas. [A story for children, in verse.] New York, 1848. 12°
  4 GEORGE CASTRIOT, surnamed Scanderberg, King of Albania. New York, 1850. 12°

MOORE, HUGH. Memoir of Col. Ethan Allen; containing the most interesting incidents connected with his private and public career. Plattsburgh, N. Y. 1834. 12°

MOORE, HUMPHRY. The reciprocal influence of knowledge, religion, and civil freedom, in supporting the union .. of the body politick: a sermon [on 1 Cor. xii. 21] preached .. before the constituted authorities of .. New Hampshire, on the anniversary Election. Concord, 1829. 8°

MOORE, J. HAMILTON. The young gentleman and lady's monitor, and English teacher's assistant; being a collection of select pieces from our best modern writers. . . The ninth edition. Hudson, N. Y. 1795. 12°

MOORE, JACOB BAILEY. Annals of the town of Concord, in .. New Hampshire, from its first settlement, in .. 1726, to .. 1823. With several biographical sketches. To which is added, a memoir of the Penacook Indians. Concord, 1824. 8°
  2 MEMOIRS of American Governors. Vol. 1. [all ever published]. New York, 1846. 8°

MOORE, JOHN. An inaugural Dissertation on digitales purpurea, or fox-glove, and its use in some diseases. Philadelphia, 1800. 8vo.

MOORE, MARTIN, A. M. Memoirs of the life and character of Rev. John Eliot, apostle of the North American Indians. Boston, 1822. 12°

MOORE, NATHANIEL F. Ancient Mineralogy, or an inquiry respecting mineral substances mentioned by the ancients. New York, 1834. 8°
  2 LECTURES on the Greek language and literature. New York, 1835. 12mo.
  3 AN HISTORICAL Sketch of Columbia College, in the city of New York. New York, 1846. 12°

MOORE, S. S. and JONES, T. W. The Traveller's Directory; or, a pocket companion .. from Philadelphia to New York, and from Philadelphia to Washington. . . From actual survey. Second edition. Philadelphia, 1804. 8°

MOORE, WILLIAM V. Indian Wars of the United States, from the discovery to the present time. From the best authorities. Philadelphia, 1840. 12mo.

MORAL REFORMER, and teacher on the human constitution, W. A. Allcott, editor. 2 vol. Boston, 1835-36. 8°

MORAN, BENJAMIN. The Foot-path and Highway; or wanderings of an American in Great Britain in 1851 and 1852. Philadelphia, 1853. 8°

MORAVIANS. Sketches of Moravian miſsions. Philadelphia, 1828. 12mo.

MORDECAI, ALFRED. Report of Experiments on Gunpowder, made at Washington Arsenal in 1843 and 1844. Washington, 1845. 8vo.

MORE, HANNAH. Considerations on religion and public education; with remarks on the speech of M. Dupont, etc. First American edition. Boston, 1794. 12°

2 THE SHEPHERD of Salisbury Plain. Philadelphia, 1830. 12mo.

3 THE PILGRIMS; an allegory. Philadelphia [1830?]. 12mo.

MOREAU, F. J. A practical Treatise on midwifery: exhibiting the present advanced state of the science. Translated from the French by T. F. Betton, and edited by B. P. Goddard. Philadelphia, 1844. 4°

MOREAU DE SAINT MÉRY, LOUIS ELIE. A topographical and political Description of the Spanish part of Saint Domingo. Translated from the French by W. Cobbett. 2 vol. Philadelphia, 1796. 8°

2 DESCRIPTION topographique, physique, civile, politique et historique de la partie Françoise de l'Isle Saint Domingue. 2 tom. Philadelphie, 1797-98. 4to.

MOREHEAD, JAMES T. Speech .. on the bill to incorporate the subscribers to the fiscal bank of the United States; delivered in the Senate, ..July 27, 1841. Washington, 1841. 8°

2 THE PRACTICE in civil Actions and Proceedings at law in Kentucky; together with various precedents of declarations, with practical notes. Louisville, 1846. 8°

MORFIT, CAMPBELL. Chemistry applied to the manufacture of soap and candles, .. based upon the most recent discoveries, etc. Philadelphia, 1847. 8°

2 CHEMICAL and Pharmaceutic Manipulations; .. containing a complete description of the most approved apparatus, .. by C. Morfit, aſsisted by A. Mucklé. Philadel. 1849. 8vo.

MORGAN, JOHN. Discourse upon the Institution of Medical Schools in America. Philadelphia, 1765. 4to.

MORGAN, LEWIS H. League of the Ho-dé-no-sau-nee, or Iroquois. Rochester, 1851. 8°

MORISON, JOHN H. Life of the Hon. Jeremiah Smith, LL.D. etc. Boston, 1845. 12°

MORISON, WILLIAM. A Sermon [on Rom. xiii. 3] delivered at Dover, ... New Hampshire, before the ... General Court, at the annual Election, etc. New Hampshire, 1792. 8°

MORMON. The Book of Mormon: an Account written by the hand of Mormon upon plates taken from the plates of Nephi. By Joseph Smith. Palmyra, N. Y. 1830. 8vo.

MORNING AND EVENING Meditations for every day in a month. Boston, 1847. 8°

MORNING COURIER and New York Enquirer. By J. W. Webb. June 5, 1838, and October 1, 1839. New York, 1838-39. Fol.

MORNING RIDE (THE). American Sunday School Union. Philadelphia [1830?]. 12mo.

MORNING WATCH: A Narrative [in verse]. N. York, 1850. 12°

MORRELL, ABBY JANE. Narrative of a Voyage to the Ethiopic and South Atlantic Ocean, Indian Ocean, Chinese Sea, North and South Pacific Ocean. New York, 1833. 12mo.

MORRELL, BENJAMIN. A Narrative of four Voyages to the South

Sea, North and South Pacific Ocean. Chinese Sea, Ethiopic and Southern Atlantic Ocean, Indian and Antarctic Ocean, 1822-31. With a sketch of the author's life. N. York, 1832. 8vo.

MORRELL, L. A. The American Shepherd: being a history of the sheep, with their breeds, management, and diseases... With an appendix, *etc.* New York, 1846. 12°

MORRIS, Caspar. Memoir of Miß Margaret Mercer. Philadelphia, 1848. 12°

2 Lectures on Scarlet Fever. Philadelphia, 1851. 8vo.

MORRIS, Edward Joy. Notes of a Tour through Turkey, Greece, Egypt, Arabia Petraea to the Holy Land. 2 vol. Philadelphia, 1842. 8°

MORRIS, Gouverneur. An Inaugural Discourse delivered before the New York Historical Society. New York, 1816. 8vo.

MORRIS, George P. The Deserted Bride, and other poems. New York, 1838. 8°

2 The Deserted Bride, and other poems. New York, 1843. 8°

3 American Melodies; containing a single selection from the productions of two hundred writers. Compiled by G. P. Morris. With illustrations, designed and engraved by L. P. Clover. N. York, 1841. 12mo.

4 The Whip-Poor-Will. [A series of engravings, accompanied by quatrains.] Philadelphia and New York [1846]. 8°

MORRIS, George P. and Willis, Nathaniel Parker. The Prose and Poetry of Europe and America; consisting of literary gems and curiosities... Compiled by G. P. Morris and N. P. Willis. Seventh edition. New York, 1848. 8°

MORRIS, Robert. The Lights and Shadows of Freemasonry. Consisting of masonic tales, songs, and sketches, *etc.* Louisville, 1852. 8°

MORRISON, William M. Morrison's Strangers' Guide to the city of Washington, and its vicinity. Washington City, 1842. 12mo.

MORSE, Jedediah. The American Geography, or a view of the present situation of the United States of America. Elizabeth Town, 1789. 8vo.

2 The Present Situation of other Nations of the world contrasted with our own: a sermon [on Deut. iv. 6, 8, 9] delivered at Charlestown, in the Commonwealth of Maßachusetts, Feb. 19, 1795. Boston, 1795. 8vo.

3 The Duty of Resignation under Afflictions, illustrated in a sermon [on Matt. xxvi. 42], occasioned by the death of the Hon. Thomas Rußell. Boston, 1796. 4to.

4 A Sermon [on Matt. xxvi. 42] on the death of the Hon. T. Rußell. Boston, 1796. 4to.

5 A Sermon [on Exod. xviii. 8, 9] preached at Charlestown, Nov. 29, 1798, on the anniversary thanksgiving in Maßachusetts. With an appendix, .. exhibiting proofs of the early existence, progreß, and deleterious effects of French intrigue and influence in the United States. Boston, Dec. 1798. 8°

6 An Address to the students at Phillips' Academy, in Andover. Charlestown, 1799. 8vo.

7 A Fast Sermon [on Psal. xi. 3]. exhibiting the present Dangers, and consequent Duties of the citizens of the United States of America. Charlestown, 1799. 8vo.

8 A Sermon [on Exod. xviii. 8, 9] preached November 29, 1798, on the anniversary thanksgiving in Maßachusetts, *etc.* With an appendix, exhibiting proofs of the early existence, progreß, and deleterious effects of French intrigue, *etc.* Second edition. Boston, 1799. 8vo.

9 A Sermon [on Proverbs xi. 7] preached before the Humane Society of Maßachusetts. Boston, 1801. 8vo.

10 A Sermon [on Psalm lxxvii. 5]

delivered before the Artillery Company in Boston, 1803. Charlestown, 1803. 8vo.

11 THE TRUE Reasons on which the election of a Hollis Profeßor of Divinity in Harvard College was opposed, etc. Charlestown, 1805. 8°

12 THE AMERICAN Gazetteer, exhibiting a full account of the civil divisions, rivers, harbours, Indian tribes, etc. of the American continent; also of the West India and other appendant islands: with a particular description of Louisiana. Third edition, revised and corrected. Boston, 1810. 8°

13 A SERMON [on Tit. iii. 1, and Joel ii. 1, 2] delivered at Charlestown, July 23, 1812, the day appointed to be observed in fasting and prayer throughout the Commonwealth, in consequence of a declaration of war with Great Britain. Charlestown, 1812. 8vo.

14 THE AMERICAN Universal Geography; or a view of the present state of all the kingdoms, states, and colonies in the known world. . . To which are added, an abridgement of the last census of the United States, a chronological table of remarkable events, etc. Sixth edition. 2 vol. Boston, 1812. 8°

15 AN APPEAL to the public, on the controversy respecting the revolution in Harvard College, and the events which have followed it; occasioned by the use which has been made of certain complaints and accusations of Miß Hannah Adams against the author. Charlestown, 1814. 8°

16 A REPORT to the Secretary of War of the United States on Indian affairs, comprising a narrative of a tour performed in 1820, under a commission from the President, . . for the purpose of ascertaining . . the actual state of the Indian tribes in our country. [With an appendix.] New Haven, 1822. 8vo.

17 ANNALS of the American Revolution; or a record of the causes and events which produced . . the American Republic. . . To which is prefixed, a summary account of the first settlement of the country, and some of the principal Indian wars; . . to which is added, remarks on the . . constitution of our national government; and an appendix, containing a biography of the principal military officers . . instrumental in achieving our independence. Compiled . . by J. Morse. Hartford, 1824. 8°

MORSE, JEDIDIAH, and PARISH, ELIJAH. A Compendious History of New England. [Charlestown? imprint erased.] 1804. 12mo.

MORSE, SIDNEY E. A new System of Modern Geography. Or a view of the present state of the world; with an appendix, containing statistical tables, etc. Boston, Sept. 1822. 8°

2 A SYSTEM of Geography, for the use of schools. Illustrated with more than fifty cerographic maps, and numerous wood-cut engravings. New York, 1846. 4°

MORTON'S Hope: or, the Memoirs of a Provincial. [By John Lothrop Motley.] 2 vol. New York, 1839. 12°

MORTON, NATHANIEL. New Englands Memorial: or, a brief Relation of the most memorable and remarkable paßages of the providence of God, manifested to the Planters of New England, in America; with special reference to the first Colony thereof, called New Plimouth. As also a nomination of divers of the most eminent Instruments deceased, both of Church and Common-wealth, improved in the first beginning and after-progreß of sundry of the respective jurisdictions in those parts; in reference unto sundry exemplary paßages of their lives, and the time of their death. Published for the use and benefit of present and future generations, by Nathaniel Morton, Secretary to the Court for the Jurisdiction of New Plimouth. Cam-

B B

bridge: printed by S. G. and M. J. for John Vsher of Boston. 1669. 4to.

2 NEW ENGLAND's Memorial; or, a brief relation of the most memorable and remarkable paſſages of the providence of God manifested to the Planters of New England in America: with special reference to the first Colony thereof, called New-Plimouth. As also a nomination of divers of the most eminent Instruments deceased, both of Church and Commonwealth, improved in the first beginning and after progreſs of sundry of the respective jurisdictions in those parts; in reference unto sundry exemplary paſſages of their lives, and the time of their death. Published for the use and benefit of present and future generations. By Nathaniel Morton, Secretary to the Court for the Jurisdiction of New-Plimouth. Boston, reprinted for Daniel Henchman, at the Corner Shop over-against the Brick-Meeting-House. 1721. 8vo.

3 NEW ENGLAND's Memorial. Fifth edition. Containing, besides the supplement to the second edition, additions in marginal notes, and an appendix. By John Davis. Boston, 1826. 8vo.

4 THE NEW England's Memorial: or, a brief relation of the . . providence of God, manifested to the planters of New England in America; with special reference to the first Colony thereof, called New Plymouth. Plymouth, reprinted, 1826. 12°

MORTON, SAMUEL GEORGE. Synopsis of the Organic Remains of the cretaceous Group of the United States, etc. Philadelphia, 1834. 8vo.

2 ILLUSTRATIONS of Pulmonary Consumption; its anatomical characters, causes, symptoms, and treatment. To which are added, some remarks on the climate of the United States, the West Indies, etc. Philadelphia, 1837. 8vo.

3 CRANIA Americana, or, a comparative view of the skulls of various aboriginal nations of North and South America. To which is prefixed, an eſſay on the varieties of the human species. Plates. Philadelphia, 1839. Fol.

4 (FROM the American Journal of Science and Arts, N° 2, vol. 38.) Crania Americana: or a comparative view of the skulls of various aboriginal nations of North and South America. By S. G. Morton. [A review of the work by G. Combe.] [New Haven, 1840.] 8°

5 AN INQUIRY into the distinctive characteristics of the aboriginal race of America. Second edition. Philadelphia, 1844. 8°

6 A MEMOIR of William Maclure. Second edition. Philadel. 1844. 8°

7 ON a supposed new species of Hippopotamus. [From the proceedings of the Academy of Natural Sciences of Philadelphia, for February, 1844.] [Philadelphia, 1844.] 8°

8 FROM the Philadelphia Saturday Courier. The ancient Egyptians: [a specimen of a work by S. G. Morton, entitled Crania Ægyptiaca, etc.] [Philadelphia, 1843?] 8°

9 CRANIA Ægyptiaca; or, observations on Egyptian Ethnography, derived from anatomy, history, and the monuments. From the transactions of the American Philosophical Society, vol. 9. Philadelphia, 1844. 4to.

10 SOME observations on the Ethnography and Archæology of the American aborigines. New Haven, 1846. 8°

11 AN ILLUSTRATED system of human anatomy, special, general, and microscopic. Philadel. 1849. 8vo.

MORTON, WILLIAM T.G. Statements, supported by evidence, of W. T. G. Morton, M.D. on his claim to the discovery of the anæsthetic properties of ether, submitted to the . . select committee appointed by the Senate of the United States. . . Jan. 21, 1853. (Report to the House of

Representatives . . vindicating the rights of C. T. Jackson to the discovery . . and disproving the claims of W. T. G. Morton [by Alexander Evans]. Report on the premiums for medicine and surgery of the French Academy of Science, for 1847-48. Testimony in relation to the claims of Dr. H. Wells, etc. [With a lithographed list of testimonials in favour of W. T. G. Morton.] 4 pts. Washington, 1853. 8vo.

MOSES, MYER. Full Annals of the Revolution in France, 1830. To which is added, a full account of the celebration of said revolution in . . New York, . . Nov. 25, 1830. 2 pts. New York, 1830. 8°

MOTH. Account of the wheat moth or Virginia fly, as it appeared in France, in 1755; and in the township of Lower Dublin, in 1802-4. Philadelphia, 1805. 8vo.

MOTHERS' Monthly Journal. (Vol. 1, 2.) Edited by Mrs. M. Kingsford. (Vol. 3, 4, edited by Mrs. H. C. Conant; vol. 5-11, edited by Mrs. E. C. Allen.) 11 vol. Jan. 1836 to Nov. 1846. [From vol. 8, downwards, the title reads: " The Mother's Journal, and family visitant."] Utica, 1836-46. 8°

MOTHER'S MAGAZINE, edited by Mrs. A. G. Whittelsey. (D. Mead, J. S. C. Abbott, and O. B. Bidwell.) Reprinted from the American edition. Sept. 1834, to Aug. 1849, 15 vol. London, 1834-49. 8vo.

MOTHERWELL, WILLIAM. Minstrelsy, ancient and modern; with an historical introduction and notes. 2 vol. Boston, 1846. 8°
2 THE POETICAL Works of W. Motherwell; with memoir by J. M'Conechy. A new edition, enlarged. Boston, 1847. 12°

MOTIER, MARIE JEAN PAUL ROCH YVES GILBERT, Marquis de La Fayette. Fayette in prison; or, misfor-

tunes of the great, a modern tragedy [in five acts, and in verse]. By a gentleman of Massachusetts. Worcester, 1802. 8°
2 PICTORIAL Life of General Lafayette, etc. Philadelphia, 1847. 16°

MOTT, LUCRETIA. Discourse on Woman . . delivered at the Assembly Buildings, December 17, 1849. Philadelphia, 1850. 8°

MOTT, VALENTINE. An experimental inquiry into the chemical and medical properties of the statice limonium of Linnæus. New York, 1806. 8vo.
2 TRAVELS in Europe and the East; embracing observations made during a tour . . in the year 1834 . . 1841. New York, 1842. 8°

MOULTRIE, WILLIAM. Memoirs of the American Revolution, so far as it related to the States of North and South Carolina and Georgia. 2 vol. New York, 1802. 8°

MOUNT AUBURN. The picturesque pocket Companion and Visitor's Guide through Mount Auburn: illustrated with upwards of sixty engravings on wood. Bost. 1839. 12°

MOUNTFORD, WILLIAM. Martyria: a legend, wherein are contained homilies, conversations, and incidents of the reign of Edward the Sixth. Written by W. Mountford, Clerk. First American edition, with an introduction [by F. D. H. i. e. F. D. Huntington]. Boston, 1846. 12°
2 THORPE, a quiet English town, and human life therein. Boston, 1852. 8°

MUDIE, ROBERT. A popular guide to the observation of nature; or, hints of inducement to the study of natural productions and appearances, in their connections and relations. New York, 1844. 12°

MUEHRY, ADOLPH. Observations

on the comparative state of Medicine in France, England, and Germany during a journey into these countries in the year 1835 . . Translated from the German by E. G. Davis. Philadelphia, 1838. 8°

MUELLER, JOHANNES VON. The History of the World : . . Translated from the German of . . J. von Müller . . Revised . . and illustrated by a notice of the life and writings of the author by Alexander H. Everett. 4 vol. Boston, 1840. 12mo.

MUENSCHER, A. Elements of dogmatic History. Translated from the German by James Murdock. New Haven, 1830. 12mo.

MUHLENBERG. HENRY. Catalogus plantarum Americæ septentrionalis huc usque cognitarum indigenarum et cicurum ; or a catalogue of the hitherto known native and naturalized plants of North America, etc. Lancaster, Pa. 1813. 8vo.

2 DESCRIPTIO uberior graminum et plantarum calamariarum Americæ septentrionalis indigenorum et cicurum. Philadelphiæ, 1817. 8vo.

3 CATALOGUS Plantarum Americæ Septentrionalis. Philadel. 1818. 8vo.

MUIR, JAMES, D.D. Ten Sermons. Alexandria, 1812. 12°

MULCHINOCK, WILLIAM PEMBROKE. The Ballads and Songs of W. P. Mulchinock. New York, 1851. 12°

MULFORD, ISAAC S. A civil and political History of New Jersey . . from its early discovery . . to the present time. Philadel. 1851. 8vo.

MULLALY, JOHN. The Milk Trade in New York and vicinity, giving an account of the sale of pure and adulterated milk . . With an introduction by R. T. Trall. N. York, 1853. 8°

MUNFORD, WILLIAM. Reports of Cases argued and determined in the Supreme Court of Appeals of Virginia, from March, 1810, to March, 1820. 6 vol. New York [and] Richmond, 1812-21. 8°

MUNK, EDWARD. The Metres of the Greeks and Romans. . . Translated . . by C. Beck and C. C. Felton. Boston, 1844. 12°

MUNN, LEWIS C. The American Orator ; with an appendix, containing the Declaration of Independence, with fac-similes of the autographs of the signers, etc. Boston, 1853. 12°

MUNTER, BALTHASAR. Count Struenzée, the sceptic and the Christian. Translated from the French [translation] of the German, by Mrs. J. H. Wilson. Boston, 1853. 12°

MURPHEY, A. D. Reports of cases argued and adjudged in the Supreme Court of North Carolina. 1804-1819. 3 vol. Raleigh, 1822-1845. 8°

MURPHY, JOHN M'LEOD, AND JEFFERS, W. N. the Younger. Nautical Routine and Stowage, with short rules in navigation. N. York, 1849. 8°

MURRAY, HUGH, F.R.S.E. An Historical and Descriptive Account of British America; comprehending Canada, Upper and Lower, Nova Scotia, New Brunswick, Newfoundland, Prince Edward Island, the Bermudas, and the fur countries ; etc. New York, 1842. 12°

MURRAY, HUGH, F.R.S.E. AND OTHERS. Historical and Descriptive Account of British India, from the most remote period to the present time ; including a narrative of the early Portuguese and English voyages, the revolutions in the Mogul empire, and the origin, progreſs, and establishment of the British power ; with illustrations of the zoology, botany, climate, geology, and mineralogy. . . By H. Murray, J. Wilson,

R. K. Greville, Prof. Jameson, W. Ainslie, W. Rhind, Prof. Wallace, and Capt. C. Dalrymple. 3 vol. New York, 1844. 12°

MURRAY, JOHN. Meſſages from the Superior State communicated by J. Murray, through J. M. Spear in . . 1852. Containing important inſtructions to the inhabitants of the earth . . prepared for publication, with a sketch of the author's earthly life and a brief description of the spiritual experience of the medium, by S. C. Hewitt. Boston, 1852. 12°

MURRAY, LINDLEY. Key to the exercises adapted to Murray's English Grammar, etc. New York, 1819. 12°

2 ENGLISH Grammar . . with an appendix, etc. New York, 1826. 12°

3 SEQUEL to the English Reader: or, elegant extracts in prose and poetry, etc. Philadelphia, 1829. 12°

4 MURRAY's System of English Grammar, improved and adapted to the present, mode of instruction in this branch of science. By E. Pond. Third edition. Worcester, 1830. 12°

5 MURRAY's Grammar of the English Language, altered and abridged. Printed [in emboſſed typography] at the New England Institution for the Education of the Blind. [Edited by S. G. Howe.] [Boston,] 1835. 4°

6 MURRAY's System of English Grammar Improved. . . Larger arrangement. By E. Pond. Sixth edition. Worcester, 1835. 12°

7 THE PRONOUNCING English Reader. . . The English Reader by Lindley Murray. To which, by the aid of a key, is scrupulously applied Mr. Walker's pronunciation of the claſſical proper names, etc. by T. Alger, Jun. Boston, 1835. 12°

8 MURRAY's . . English Exercises.

. . Revised . . by T. Alger. Boston, 1838. 12°

9 MURRAY's English Grammar Simplified. . . By A. Fisk. Hallowell, 1840. 8°

10 ALGER's . . Abridgement of Murray's English Grammar, with an appendix, etc. Boston and Philadelphia, 1842. 12°

MURRAY, NICHOLAS. Notes, historical and biographical, concerning Elizabeth-town, its eminent men, churches and ministers. Elizabeth-town, N. J. 1844. 8°

MURRAY, W. R. The Cyclopædia of Useful and Entertaining Knowledge . . illustrated with 350 engravings. Boston, 1850. 8°

MURRELL, WILLIAM MEACHAM. Cruise of the frigate Columbia around the world, under the command of Commodore G. C. Read, in 1838, 1839, and 1840. Boston, 1840. 12°

MUSE, JOSEPH E. An Addreſſ upon the dominant errors of the agriculture of Maryland, delivered . . before the Dorchester Agricultural Society, . . Oct. 29, 1827. Baltimore, 1828. 8°

MUZZY, HARRIET. Poems, moral and sentimental . . collected and arranged by C. M. Thayer. New York, 1821. 12°

MYERS, NED. Ned Myers; or, a life before the mast. Edited by J. F. Cooper. Philadelphia, 1843. 12°

MYERS, P. HAMILTON. The First of the Knickerbockers. A tale of 1673. . . Second edition. New York, 1849. 12°

2 THE EMIGRANT Squire. Philadelphia, 1853. 8°

MYRTLE, LEWIS. Cap Sheaf a fresh bundle. New York, 1853. 12°

ANTUCKET INQUIRER. S. Haynes Jenks, editor. Nº 73. Sept. 18, 1839. Nantuck. 1839. Fol.

NAPOLEON I. *Emperor of the French. The Life of Napoleon...* By the author of " Waverley," *etc.* [Sir W. Scott]. Abridged by an American gentleman. New York, 1827. 8º

2 THE COURT and Camp of Bonaparte. New York, 1842. 12º

3 NAPOLEON and the Marshals of the Empire. 2 vol. Philadelphia, 1848. 12º

NARRATIVE of Emily Graham. Philadelphia. 12mo.

NASH, J. A. The Progreſsive Farmer: a scientific treatise on agricultural chemistry, the geology of agriculture; on plants, animals, manners, and soils applied to practical agriculture. New York, 1853. 12º

NATIONAL ACADEMY OF DESIGN. Catalogue of the nineteenth (and twentieth) annual Exhibition. New York, 1844-45. 8vo.

NATIONAL ADVOCATE. Vol. 9. Nº 2454. July 30, 1821. New York, 1821. Fol.

NATIONAL ANTI-SLAVERY STANDARD. Vol. 8. Nº 13. New York, 1847. Fol.

NATIONAL CALENDAR for 1820 (to 1829). By Peter Force. [Continued as] The National Calendar, for 1830 (to 1836). 14 vol. Washington, 1820-36. 12mo.

NATIONAL CIRCULAR, addreſsed to the head of each family in the United States. [On abstinence from the use of ardent spirits.] Boston [1830 ?]. 8º

NATIONAL ECLECTIC MEDICAL ASSOCIATION. Transactions of the National Eclectic Medical Aſsociation, at its third annual meeting, held at Rochester, New York, May 11, 1852. Rochester, 1852. 8vo.

NATIONAL GAZETTE (THE) and Literary Register. April 5, 1820 to December 31, 1841. Philadelphia, 1820-41. Fol.

NATIONAL INSTITUTION for the Promotion of Science. Constitution and By-laws. May, 1840. Washington, 1840. 8vo.

2 BULLETIN (second bulletin) of the proceedings of the National Inſtitution for the Promotion of Science. Washington, 1841-42. 8vo.

3 THIRD Bulletin of the Proceedings of the National Institute for the Promotion of Science, Washington, D. C. February, 1842, to February, 1845. Also the Proceedings of the Meeting of April, 1844. Washington, 1845. 8vo.

NATIONAL OBSERVATORY, WASHINGTON. Astronomical Observations made during the year 1847 at the National Observatory, Washington: under the direction of M. F. Maury, .. Superintendent: Commodore L. Warrington, Chief of Bureau of Ordnance and Hydrography. Vol. 3. Published by authority of the Hon. J. C. Dobbin, Secretary of the Navy. Washington, 1853. 4to.

NATIONAL PORTRAIT GALLERY of distinguished Americans. 4 vol. 1834-39. See HERRING, James.

NATIONAL PREACHER (American National Preacher); or original monthly sermons from living ministers (of the United States). Edited by Austin Dickinson. Vol. 1-9. June, 1826, to May, 1835. New York, 1826-35. 8vo.

NATIONAL REGISTER (THE), a weekly paper, containing .. public documents; .. proceedings of Congreſs; statistical tables, .. eſsays, .. and biographical sketches: with summary statements of the current news and political events. By Joel K. Mead. March 2, 1816, to June 27, 1818. Vol. 1-5. Washington, 1816-18. 8°

NATURAL HISTORY. Selected from the Youth's Friend. Philadelphia, 1827. 12mo.

NATURALIST (THE), and Journal of Natural History, Agriculture, Education, and Literature, conducted by I. N. Loomis, T. Fanning, J. S. Fowler, and J. Eichbaum. August, 1846. Vol. 1. Nº 8. Franklin College, Nashville, Tenneſsee, 1846. 8°

NAUTILUS (THE) Self-inflating life preserver. [A description of the invention, with a series of testimonials as to its efficiency.] [New York, 1845.] s. sh. fol.

NAVAL MAGAZINE (THE). Edited by .. C. S. Stewart, aided by an advisory committee. Jan. 1836 to Nov. 1837. 2 vol. New York, 1836-1837. 8°

NAXERA, EMMANUEL. De Lingua

Othomitorum Diſsertatio. Philadelphia, 1835. 4to.

NAYLOR, CHARLES, of Pennsylvania. Speech .. on the bill imposing additional duties as depositaries, in certain cases, on public officers; delivered ... Oct. 13. 1837. Washington, 1837. 8°

NEAL, afterwards HAVEN, ALICE BRADLEY, Mrs. The Goſsips of Rivertown; with sketches in prose and verse. Philadelphia, 1850. 12°
  2 CONTENTMENT better than wealth. New York, 1853. 12°

NEAL, DANIEL. The History of the Puritans or Protestant Nonconformists, from the Reformation of 1517 to the Revolution in 1688. Comprising an account of their principles. .. Reprinted from the text of Dr. Toulmin's edition, with his life of the author and account of his writings. Revised, corrected and enlarged, with additional notes by J. O. Choules. 2 vol. New York, 1848. 8°

NEAL, JOHN. The Down-Easters, etc. 2 vol. New York, 1833. 12°

NEAL, JOSEPH C. Charcoal Sketches; or, scenes in a metropolis. Philadelphia, 1838. 12°
  2 PETER Ploddy, and other oddities. Philadelphia, 1844. 12°

NEANDER, JOHANN AUGUST WILHELM. The Epistle of Paul to the Philippians, practically explained, by Dr. A. Neander. Translated from the German by Mrs. H. C. Conant. New York, 1851. 12°
  3 THE FIRST Epistle of John practically explained by Dr. A. Neander. Translated from the German by H. C. Conant. New York, 1852. 8vo.

NEEDLE. The Rusty Needle. American Sunday School Union. Philadelphia, 1831. 12°

NEEDLES, EDWARD. An historical Memoir of the Pennsylvania Society for promoting the abolition of slavery .. compiled from the minutes of that society, *etc.* Philadelphia, 1840. 8°

NEFF, JACOB K. The Army and Navy of America: containing a view of the heroic adventures, battles .. and glorious achievements in the cause of freedom, from the period of the French and Indian wars to the close of the Florida war, .. enlivened by a variety of the most interesting anecdotes, *etc.* Philadel. [1845.] 8°

NEGRIS, ALEXANDER. A Grammar of the modern Greek Language; with an appendix, containing original .. prose and verse. Συνοπτικη της Απλοελληνικης διαλεκτου γραμματικη. *Romaic.* Boston, 1828. 8°

NEGRO. The Negro Christianized, an eſſay to excite and aſſist .. the instruction of negro servants in Christianity. Boston, 1706. 12mo.

NEGROES. Observations on the inslaving, importing, and purchasing of Negroes. With some advice thereon, extracted from the epistle of the yearly meeting of the people called Quakers, held at ·London, in the year 1748. Second edition. (The uncertainty of a death-bed repentance, *etc.*) Germantown, Pa. 1760. 4°

NEGRO PEW. The "Negro Pew:" being an inquiry concerning the propriety of distinctions in the House of God on account of colour. Boston, 1837. 12°

NEILSON, CHARLES. An original, compiled, and corrected account of Burgoyne's campaign, and the memorable battles of Bemis's Heights, Sept. 19, and Oct. 7, 1777, *etc.* Albany, 1844. 12°

NELL, WILLIAM C. Services of colored Americans in the wars of 1776 and 1812. Boston, 1851. 8°

NELSON, DAVID. The cause and cure of Infidelity: with an account of the author's conversion. New York, 1837. 12°

NELSON, E. The use of ardent Spirits in a profeſſing Christian a great sin: a discourse delivered before the Temperance Society in Woburn, Dec. 14, 1829 [on 1 Cor. vi. 19, 20]. Boston, 1830. 12°

NELSON, JOHN, *D.D.* Gatherings from a Pastor's Drawer. Worcester, Andover [printed]1852. 12mo.

NELSON, S. O. [*Begins*] Branch of the bank, *etc.* [A statement of the affairs of the branch bank of the State of Alabama at Decatur, Dec. 30, 1839.] [Tuscaloosa? 1840.] s. sh. Fol.

NEPOS, CORNELIUS. Cornelius Nepos, with notes historical and explanatory, by Charles Anthon. New York, 1852. 8°

NEUMAN, HENRY. Seoane's Neuman and Baretti, by Velasquez. A pronouncing Dictionary of the Spanish and English languages; composed from the Spanish dictionaries of the Spanish Academy, Terreros, and Salvà, upon the basis of Seoane's edition of Neuman and Baretti, and from the English dictionaries of Webster, Worcester, and Walker, with the addition of more than 8000 words, idioms, *etc.* by M. Velasquez de la Cadena. New York, 1853. 8°

NEVIN, ALFRED. Churches of the Valley: or, an historical sketch of the old Presbyterian congregations of Cumberland and Franklin counties, in Pennsylvania. Philadelphia, 1852. 12mo.

NEVIN, JOHN W. A Summary of Biblical Antiquities. 2 vol. Philadelphia [1829]. 12mo.

2 THE MYSTICAL Presence: a vindication of the reformed or Calvinistic doctrine of the Holy Eucharist. Philadelphia, 1846. 12°

NEVINS, WILLIAM. Select Remains of the Rev. W. Nevins. With a memoir. New York, 1836. 8°

2 SERMONS of the late Rev. W. Nevins. New York, 1837. 12°

NEWARK COLLEGE, NEWARK. *Delaware.* Catalogue of the academical department of Newark College . . 1842. Baltimore [1842]. 8°

NEWARK, NEW JERSEY. Directory of the city of Newark . . By B. T. Pierson, 1852. Newark, 1852. 12°

NEW BEDFORD, MASSACHU-SETTS. Report of the School Committee of . . New Bedford, . . for the year 1845-46 (and 1846-47). New Bedford, 1846-47. 8°

NEW BEDFORD DAILY MERCURY. Vol. 9. N° 2183. Sept. 18, 1839. New Bedford, 1839. Fol.

NEW BEDFORD DIRECTORY, *etc.* N° 7. New Bedford, 1852. 8°

NEWELL, C. History of the Revolution in Texas, particularly of the war of 1835 and '36 ; together with the latest geographical, topographical, and statistical accounts of the country. New York, 1838. 12°

NEWELL, D. The Life of Rev. George Whitfield. N. York [1846]. 12°

NEWELL, HARRIET, *Mrs.* The Life and Writings of H. Newell. Philadelphia, 1832. 12mo.

NEWELL, WILLIAM. A Discourse on the Cambridge Church-gathering in 1636, delivered in the first church, Feb. 22, 1846. Boston, 1846. 8vo.

NEW ENGLAND. A Confession of Faith owned and consented unto by the Elders and Messengers of the churches assembled at Boston in New England, May 2, 1680. Being the second session of that Synod. Boston ; printed by John Foster. 1680. 8vo.

2 THE PRESENT State of New Eng-land, impartially considered, in a letter to the clergy. [By F. L. i. e. John Palmer.] Boston, 1689. 4to.

3 THE REVOLUTION in New England justified, and the people there vindicated from the aspersions cast upon them by Mr. John Palmer, in his pretended answer to the Declaration, published by the inhabitants of Boston, and the country adjacent, on the day when they secured their late oppressors, who acted by an illegal and arbitrary commission from the late King James. Printed for Joseph Brunning, at Boston, in New England. 1691. 4°

4 A NARRATIVE of the proceedings of Sir Edmund Androsse and his complices, who acted by an illegal and arbitrary commission from the late King James, during his government in New England. By several gentlemen who were of his Council (W. Stoughton, T. Hinckley, W. Winthrop, B. Gedney, S. Shrimpton). [Bost.] printed in the year 1691. 4to.

5 OBSERVABLE Things. The History of ten years rolled away under the great calamities of a war with Indian salvages : Repeated and improved in a sermon, at Boston-Lecture, 27 d. 7 m. 1698. Judg. VI. 3, 5, 6. The children of the East came up against them ; and they entered into the land, to destroy it ; and Israel was greatly impoverished. Boston, printed for Samuel Phillips, at the Brick Shop. 1699. Small 8vo.

6 A LETTER about the present state of Christianity among the Christianized Indians of New England. Bost. 1705. 12mo.

7 A MEMORIAL of the present deplorable state of New England, with the many disadvantages it lyes under, by the male-administration of their present Governour, Joseph Dudley, Esq. and his son Paul, etc. Together with the several affidavits of people of worth, relating to several of the said Governour's mercenary and illegal proceedings, but particu-

larly his private treacherous correspondence with her Majesty's enemies the French and Indians. To which is added, a faithful but melancholy account of several barbarities lately committed upon her Majesty's subjects by the said French and Indians, in the east and west parts of New England. Faithfully digested from the several original letters, papers, and MSS. by Philopolites. Printed in the year MDCCVII. and sold by S. Phillips, N. Buttolph, and B. Elliot, booksellers in Boston. 4to.

8 EXAMINATION of the pretensions of New England to commercial preeminence. To which is added, a view of the causes of the suspension of cash payments at the banks. Philadelphia, 1814. 12°

9 THE FIRST Settlers of New England: or, conquest of the Pequods, Narragausets, and Pokanokets, as related by a mother to her children. By a lady of Maſſachusetts [L. M. Child]. Boston, 1829. 12°

10 THE PRESENT State of New England with respect to the Indian war; wherein is an account of the true reason thereof, together with most of the remarkable paſſages that have happened from the 20th of June till the 10th of November, 1675. Faithfully composed by a merchant of Boston, and communicated to his friend in London. [To which is added, a continuation of the state of New England, being a further account of the Indian war. Together with an account of the intended rebellion of the negroes in the Barbadoes.] Printed, London, 1675-6. Reprinted, Boston, 1833. 12°

11 RURAL LIFE in New England: a domestic romance. By the author of " Lights and shadows of factory life." New York. 8vo.

12 RICHES and Honour: a New England story . . Founded on fact. By the author of " The victim of Chancery," etc. N. York, 1847. 12°

13 SUPERNATURALISM in New Eng-

land, by the author of " The Stranger in Lowell" [John Greenleaf Whittier]. London [N. Y. printed], 1847. 8vo.

NEW ENGLAND ANTI-SLAVERY Society, afterwards MASSACHUSETTS Anti-Slavery Society. Constitution of the New England Anti-Slavery Society, with an address to the public. Boston, 1832. 8°

2 FIRST (Third) annual Report of the board of managers of the New England Anti-Slavery Society. With an appendix. Bost. 1833-35. 8°

3 FIFTH (to the fourteenth inclusive) annual Report of the board of managers of the Maſſachusetts Anti-Slavery Society . . With an appendix. Boston, 1837-46. 8°

NEW ENGLAND CHRONICLE; or the Eſſex Gazette. N° 392 & 393. Cambridge, 1776. Fol.

THE NEW ENGLAND FARMER, containing eſſays, original and selected, relating to agriculture and domestic economy, etc. [vol. 1-15, edited by T. G. Feſſenden. Vol. 16-24 by T. G. Feſſenden, H. Colman, A. Putnam, and J. Breck successively]. Vol. 1-24. Boston, 1823-46. 4°

NEW ENGLAND HISTORIC GENEALOGICAL SOCIETY. Circular number two of the New England Historic Genealogical Society. April, 1846. [Boston, 1846.] 8°

2 THE NEW England Historical and Genealogical Register; published quarterly under the direction of the New England Historic, Genealogical Society. Vol. 1, 1847 .. W. Cogswell, editor. Vol. 2-10, Samuel G. Drake, editor. Boston, 1847-56. 8°

NEW ENGLAND INSTITUTION for the Education of the Blind, afterwards THE PERKINS INSTITUTION and the Maſſachusetts Asylum for the Blind. Addreſs of the Trustees .. to the public. Boston, 1833. 8vo.

2 ANNUAL Report of the Trustees .. to the Corporation, 1834; 1836 to 1839. 5 parts. Bost. 1834-39. 8vo.

3 NINTH (to the nineetenth) Annual Report of the Trustees .. to the Corporation. Boston and Cambridge, 1841-51. 8°

NEW ENGLAND JOURNAL OF Medicine and Surgery, and the collateral branches of Science. Conducted by a number of physicians. Vol. 1-15. (Vol. 6-10, new series; vol. 11-15, third series; vol. 14, 15, conducted by W. Channing and J. Ware.) Boston, 1812-26. 8°

NEW ENGLAND MAGAZINE. By J. T. and E. Buckingham. July, 1831 to Dec. 1834. 7 vol. Boston [1831-34]. 8vo.

NEW ENGLANDER (THE). [Edited by E. R. Tyler and W. T. Bacon] 1843-56. 14 vol. New Haven, 1843-56. 8°

NEW ENGLAND PRIMER improved for the more easy attaining the true reading of English. To which is added the Affembly of Divines, and Mr. Cotton's Catechism. [Edited by George Livermore.] Boston, 1777. [Reprinted, Hartford, 1843.] 24°

NEWHALL, ISAAC. Letters on Junius, addreffed to John Pickering, showing that the author of that celebrated work was Earl Temple. (Appendix. An enquiry into the conduct of a late Right Hon. Commoner, etc.) Boston, 1831. 12mo.

NEWHALL, JOHN B. Sketches of Iowa, or the Emigrant's Guide; containing a description of the agricultural and mineral resources, geological features and statistics of the territory of Iowa; etc. New York, 1841. 12°

NEW HAMPSHIRE, Province and State of. Acts and Laws paffed by the General Court of Affembly of New Hampshire [1716, and continued to 1726], etc. Boston, 1716-26. Fol.

2 AN ADDRESS of the Convention for framing a constitution of government for the people of New Hampshire, to the freemen thereof, voted June, 1783. Portsmouth, 1783. 8°

3 THE PERPETUAL Laws of the State of New Hampshire, from the Seffion of the General Court, July 1776, to .. Dec. 1788, continued into the present year 1789... Printed from attested copies of the original acts. [Edited by J. Pickering and D. Humphreys.] Portsmouth, New Hampshire, 1789. 8°

4 REPORT [of a joint committee] concerning the pauper laws of New Hampshire. [Concord? 1821.] 8°

5 THE REVISED Statutes of the State of New Hampshire, paffed Dec. 23, 1842. To which are prefixed, the Constitutions of the United States and of .. New Hampshire. [Revised by S. D. Bell and C. J. Fox.] Concord, 1843. 8°

6 MESSAGE of the Governor, Isaac Hill, to both Houses of the Legislature, June Seffion, 1836. Concord, 1836. 8°

7 STATE of New Hampshire. An Act to establish the city of Manchester. [Manchester, 1846.] 8°

8 FESTIVAL of the Sons of New Hampshire, with the speeches of Meffrs. Webster, Woodbury, Wilder, etc. .. Celebrated in Boston, Nov. 7, 1849. Phonographic report by Dr. J. W. Stone. Boston, 1850. 8°

NEW HAMPSHIRE BOOK (THE): being specimens of the literature of the Granite State. Nashua [printed at Boston], 1842. 12°

NEW HAMPSHIRE GAZETTE (THE), and Historical Chronicle. N° 976. Annapolis, 1775. Fol.

NEW HAMPSHIRE HISTORICAL SOCIETY. Collections of the New Hampshire Historical Society. Vol. 1-5. Concord, 1824-37. 8vo.

NEW HAMPSHIRE REGISTER and United States Calendar, with an ephemeris, etc. (1814; 1816; 1818; 1821; 1822; 1824 to 1838, by John Farmer. The astronomical calcula-

tions, 1825-27, by D. Leavitt; 1839-
40, by J. B. Moore; 1841-44, by A.
Fowler; 1845-47, by G. P. Lyon).
28 parts. [1815, 1817, 1819, 1820,
1823, and 1831 are wanting.] Exeter
and Concord [1813-1846]. 12°

NEW HAMPSHIRE BAPTIST
CONVENTION. Proceedings of the
Baptist Convention of the State of
New Hampshire, .. at their ninth
annual meeting. .. June .. 1834.
Concord, 1834. 8°

2 PROCEEDINGS of the New Hampshire Baptist State Convention, etc.
Concord, 1843. 8vo.

NEW HAVEN, CONNECTICUT.
Report of the Committee appointed
to inquire into the condition of the
New Haven burying ground, and to
propose a plan for its improvement.
New Haven, 1839. 8°

2 [Begins] FRENCH Spoliations.
[Petition of the inhabitants of New
Haven to the General Assembly of
Connecticut, on the subject of French
spoliations.] [N. Haven, 1843.] 8vo.

NEW JERSEY, Province and
State of. The Acts of the General
Assembly of the Province of New
Jersey. From the .. second year of
.. Queen Anne to .. the twenty-fifth
year of King George Second [and
continued to the year 1761, the first
of George III.]: Collected and published by order of the General Assembly .. by S. Nevill. 2 vol. Woodbridge, New Jersey, 1752-61. Fol.

2 THE GRANTS, Concessions, and
Original Constitutions of the Province
of New Jersey; the acts passed during the proprietary governments, and
other material transactions before the
surrender thereof to Queen Anne;
the instrument of surrender, and her
formal acceptance thereof; Lord
Cornbury's commission and instructions consequent thereon. Published
by virtue of an Act of the Legislature
by A. Leaming and J. Spicer. Philadelphia [1757]. Fol°

3 ACTS of the General Assembly of

the Province of New Jersey, .. 1702
to 1776. Compiled and published by
S. Allinson. Burlington, 1776. Fol°

4 STATUTES of the State of New
Jersey revised and published under
the authority of the Legislature.
Trenton, 1847. 8°

5 ACTS of the Seventy-first (to the
77th) Legislature of the State of
New Jersey. Trenton, Somerville,
1847-53. 8°

6 ACTS incorporating the Delaware
and Raritan Railway Company, the
Camden and Amboy Railroad and
Transportation Company, and the
New Jersey Railroad and Transport-
ation Company. Trenton, 1849. 8°

7 ABSTRACT of the Population and
Statistics of New Jersey according to
the Census of 1850. Somerville,
1852. 8°

NEW JERSEY, Diocese of.
Journal of the Proceedings of the
fifty-first annual Convention of the
Protestant Episcopal Church, in the
State of New Jersey. Camden,
1834. 8vo.

2 FORM of Prayer and Thanks-
giving for the blessings of civil liberty;
to be used yearly in the Diocese of
New Jersey. 1834. 8vo.

3 JOURNAL of the fifty-fourth (56th)
annual Convention of the Protestant
Church of the State of New Jersey,
held at Burlington in 1837 (1839).
Burlington, 1837-39. 8vo.

4 JOURNAL of Proceedings of the
Sixty-third Annual Convention. Burlington, 1846. 8vo.

5 [Begins p. 49], APPENDIX. So
much of the proceedings of the Convention of the diocese of New Jersey,
in May, 1849, as relates to the charges
against the Bishop: as reported by
C. King, etc. [Burlington, 1849.] 8vo.

6 JOURNAL of the special Convention of the Protestant Episcopal
Church, in the State of New Jersey;
held .. on the 17th day of March,
1852. (Episcopal address .. by G.

W. Doane, Bishop of the Diocese.)
Burlington, 1852. 8vo.

7 JOURNAL of Proceedings of the
sixty-ninth annual Convention, held
in Trinity Church, Newark, on Wednesday, 26th, and Thursday, 27th of
May, 1852. Burlington, 1852. 8vo.

8 JOURNAL of Proceedings of an
adjourned Convention, held in Trinity
Church, Newark, 14 July, 1852.
Philadelphia, 1852. 8vo.

9 A PAPER addressed by the committee representing the Diocese of
New Jersey to the Bishops assembled
upon the presentment of the Bishop
of New Jersey (G. W. Doane), at
Camden, October 7, 1852. [New-
ark, 1852.] 8vo.

10 A FULL Report of the Proceedings of the special Convention of the
Diocese of New Jersey, held in St.
Mary's Church, Burlington, March
17, 1851, and reported in the Banner
of the Cross. Philadelphia, 1852. 8vo.

11 JOURNAL of Proceedings of a
special Convention, held in Trinity
Church, Newark, Oct. 27, 1852.
Philadelphia, 1853. 8vo.

NEW JERSEY BAPTIST STATE
CONVENTION. Minutes of the fifteenth
anniversary of the New Jersey Baptist State Convention; and of the seventh annual meeting of the New
Jersey Baptist Education Society.
New York, 1844. 8°

NEW JERSEY COLLEGE,
PRINCETON. Catalogus Collegii Neo-
Caesariensis. Princetoniae, 1839. 8°

2 CATALOGUE of the officers and
students of the College of New Jersey, for 1841-42. Princeton, 1842. 8°

NEW JERSEY HISTORICAL
SOCIETY. Collections of the New
Jersey Historical Society. Vol. 1.
WHITEHEAD (William A.) East Jersey under the proprietary governments: a narrative of events connected with the settlement and progress of the province, until the surrender of the government to the
crown in 1702... With an appendix,

containing " The model of the government of East New Jersey,".. by
G. Scot... Now first reprinted from
the original edition of 1685. [New
York], 1846. 8°

NEW JERSEY GAZETTE. N°
152 and 154. Trenton, 1780. Fol.

NEW JERSEY JOURNAL (THE).
N° 92-97. Chatham, 1780. Fol..

NEW JERUSALEM MAGA-
ZINE. 1827-1856. Vol. 1-28. Boston, 1828-56. 8°

NEWMAN, SAMUEL P. Elements of
Political Economy. Andover, 1835. 12°

2 A PRACTICAL System of Rhetoric,
or the principles and rules of style,
inferred from examples of writing.
To which is added, an historical dissertation on English style. Twelfth
edition. New York, 1843. 12°

NEW MIRROR (THE)... Edited
by G. P. Morris (and N. P. Willis).
April 8, 1843—Sept. 28, 1844. Vol.
1-3. New York, 1843-44. 8°

NEW NETHERLAND. Vertoogh
van Nieu Nederland [by Adrian van
der Donck]; and Breeden Raedt
aende Vereenichde Nederlandsche
Provintien [by J. A. G. W. C. i. e.
C. Melyn?]. Two rare Tracts printed
in 1649-50, relating to the administration of affairs in New Netherland.
Translated by Henry C. Murphy.
New York [privately printed for James
Lenox], 1854. 4to.

NEW ORLEANS COMMER-
CIAL BULLETIN. N° 251. Sept. 18,
1839. New Orleans, 1839. Fol.

NEW ORLEANS. Faithful Pic-
ture of the political situation of New
Orleans, at the close of the last and
the beginning of the present year,
1807. Boston, 1808. 8°

2 RULES and Regulations for the
government of the high school for
boys of the second Municipality, City
of New Orleans. N. Orleans, 1843. 8°

3 RULES and Regulations for the
government of the public schools,

within the second municipality, *etc.*
[New Orleans,] 1845.   12°

4 ANNUAL Reports [1842-44] of
the Council of Municipality number
two, of the City of New Orleans, on
the condition of its public schools.
New Orleans, 1845.   8°

5 ANNUAL Reports of the Council
of Municipality number two, of . . .
New Orleans, on the condition of its
public schools. N. Orleans, 1845. 8°

6 THE NEW Orleans Free Library.
[Being an addreſs to the citizens of
New Orleans on the subjeſt of the
Free Library, subscribed "a C." Together with the correspondence relative to the establishment of that library.] [New Orleans, 1852.]   8°

NEWPORT MERCURY (THE).
Nº 248-1300. June 6, 1763 to Sept.
4, 1786. [Imperfeſt, wanting Nº
249-508, 510-617, 619-73, 676-77,
679-88, 690-95, 697-748, 750-75,
779-81, 784,786, 791-97, 799, 802-
04,806, 811-14, 824, 826, 833, 836,
841-42,844,846-48, 851, 854, 859-
62, 864-65, 867-68, 872-78, 880-
85, 887-92, 894,896-900, 902-908,
910,912-15, 917-1126, 1222, 1294,
1296-1298.] Newport, 1763-86.
Fol.

NEWPORT, *Rhode Island.* The
Controversy touching the Old Stone
Mill in the Town of Newport, Rhode
Island, with remarks introduſtory and
conclusive. Newport, 1851.   12°

2 A HAND-BOOK of Newport and
Rhode Island. By the author of " Pen
and Ink Sketches," etc. [J. R. D. *i. e.*
John Dix, afterwards Roſs]. Newport, 1852.   12°

NEWTON, JOHN. Memoirs of
Eliza Cunningham, by John Newton ;
of Jane Lucy Benn, by Rev. Basil
Woodd ; and of Caroline Elizabeth
Smelt, by Rev. Dr. Waddell. Phila-
delphia, 1828. 12mo.

2 THE LIFE of J. Newton. Philadel.
1831. 12mo.

NEWTON, SIR ISAAC. Newton's
Principia. The Mathematical Principles of Natural Philosophy, . . translated into English by A. Motte. To
which is added Newton's System of
the World ; . . with a life of the author, by N. W. Chittenden. New
York, 1848. 8°

NEW WORLD (THE). A weekly
journal of popular literature, science,
music, and the arts, containing the
newest works by celebrated authors,
etc. Park Benjamin, editor. (Vol. 4.
P. B. and J. Aldrich, editors.) Vol. 1-
5. June, 1840, to Dec. 1842. New
York, 1840-42. Folº

NEW YORK, CITY OF.

1 THE CHARGE given by the Chief
Justice of the Province of New York
to the Grand Jury of the city of New
York, in March term, 1726-7. New
York, John Peter Zenger, 1727. 4to.

2 PROCEEDINGS at a numerous
meeting of the citizens of New York
[to oppose the colleſtion of the duty
on tea]. New York, 1773. s. sh. fol.

3 CHARTER for establishing an Hospital in the City of New York: granted
by the Rt. Hon. John, Earl of Dun-
more, July 13, 1771. New York,
1794. 4to.

4 MEMORIAL of the Merchants of
. . New York [to the President and
Congreſs of the United States of
America]. Jan. 6, 1806. Washing-
ton, 1806. 8°

5 THE MEMORIAL of the College
of Physicians and Surgeons in the
city of New York. 8vo.

6 DOCUMENTS relating to the Board
of Health. New York, 1806. 8vo.

7 THE PICTURE of New York ; or,
the traveller's guide through the
commercial metropolis of the United
States. By a gentleman residing in
this city [Samuel L. Mitchell]. New
York, 1807. 12°

8 AN ACCOUNT of the Free School
Society of New York. New York,
1814. 8vo.

9 INSTITUTION for the Deaf and

Dumb. Circular of the President and Directors and the Petition to the Mayor, Aldermen, and Commonalty of the City of New York, with their favourable Report and patronage, *etc.* New York, 1818. 8°

10 INSTITUTION for the Deaf and Dumb. Addreſs of the Directors to their fellow-citizens. New York, 1821. 8°

11 EIGHTH Annual Report of the Directors of the New York Institution for the instruction of the deaf and dumb, to the Legislature of the State of New York, for the year ending Dec. 31, 1826; accompanied by documents illustrating the .. state and condition of the institution, *etc.* New York, 1827. 8vo.

12 THE FIRST Annual Report of the Managers of the Society for the prevention of pauperism in the city of New York. New York, 1818. 8vo.

13 A REPRINTED Copy of a pamphlet published in New York. . . A clear and concise statement of New York and the surrounding country, containing a faithful account of . . . impositions .. practised upon British emigrants, *etc.* Belper, 1819. 12mo.

14 SOCIETY for the prevention of Pauperism. Report to the Managers by their Committee on Idleneſs and sources of employment. New York, 1819. 8°

15 SKETCH of the resources of the City of New York, with a view to its municipal government, population, *etc.* from the foundation of the city to the date of the latest statistical accounts. [By J. A. Dix !]. New York, 1827. 8°

16 SOCIETY for the Reformation of Juvenile Delinquents. Third annual report of the managers of the Society, *etc.* New York, 1828. 8°

17 THE PICTURE of New York; and Stranger's guide to the commercial metropolis of the United States. New York [1828]. 12°

18 CONVENTION of the friends of American Industry. Report on the production and manufacture of cotton [subscribed, P. T. Jackson]. Boston, 1832. 8°

19 REPORT of the " Union Committee" appointed by the signers of a memorial to Congreſs, held .. the 11th of February, 1834, at the Merchants' Exchange. N. York, 1834. 8°

20 REPORT of the Society for promoting the Gospel among Seamen in the Port of New York. 1843, 1846. 2 parts. New York, 1843-46. 8°

21 FIRST report of the Prison Aſsociation of New York. December, 1844. New York [1845]. 8°

22 SECOND Report of the Prison Aſsociation of New York: including the constitution and by-laws, *etc.* New York, 1846. 8vo.

23 REPORT of the Committee of Arrangements of the Common Council of the city of New York, upon the funeral ceremonies in commemoration of the death of Andrew Jackson, Ex-President of the United States. New York, 1845. 8°

24 REPORT on the Institutions for the deaf and dumb in Central and Western Europe, in the year 1844, to the Board of Directors of the New York Institution, by Rev. G. E. Day, delegate of the Board; and letter of instructions by H. P. Peet, Principal of the institution. [Documents appended to the Twenty-sixth annual report.] New York, 1845. 8°

25 ANNUAL Statement of the funds of the Corporation of the city of New York, for the year ending Dec. 31, 1844. . . . By the comptroller of the city of New York. N. York, 1845. 8°

26 PROCEEDINGS of the National Convention of farmers, gardeners, *etc.* held at the Lyceum of Natural History in the City of New York; .. in connection with the eighteenth annual fair of the American Institute. New York, 1846. 8°

27 MANUAL of the Corporation of the City of New York, for the years 1848 (1850-51). By D. T. Valentine. New York, 1848-51. 18°

28 NEW York as it is; being the counter part of the metropolis of America. [A description of a carved model of New York and Brooklyn, executed by E. Porter Belden, and others.] New York, 1849. 12°

29 [*Begins*] September 1850. The following rules and rates have been adopted by the Aſſociation of Fire Insurance Companies, at meetings held 21st June—3rd September, 1850. [New York, 1850.] 8°

30 LIFE in New York. By the author of " The Old White Meeting House." Second edition. New York, 1851. 12°

31 EXAMINATION of the validity of the pretended Charters of the City of New York in a review of the decision of the Superior Court, in the case of G. Furman, Ex. and others against the Mayor, Aldermen, and Commonalty of the City of New York. By B. S. New York, 1852. 8°

32 THIRTEENTH Annual Report of the Board of Education, for the year ending January 1, 1855. New York, 1855. 8vo.

NEW YORK, COLONY AND STATE OF.

1 ACTS of Aſſembly paſſed in the province of New York, from 1691 to 1725. Examined and compared with the originals in the Secretary's office. Printed and sold by William Bradford, printer to the King's most Excellent Majesty for the Province of New York, 1726. Fol.

2 LAWS of New York from . . 1691, to 1751 inclusive. New York, 1752. Fol°

3 LAWS of New York from Nòv. 11, 1752, to May 22, 1762. Published according to an order of the General Aſſembly. Digested by W. Livingston and W. Smith, Jun. Vol. 2. New York, 1762. Fol°

4 LAWS of the State of New York, paſſed at the first meeting of the eighth Seſſion of the Legislature of said State, Oct. 1784. New York, 1784. Fol°

5 LAWS of the State of New York, paſſed by the Legislature . . at their last meeting of the eighth Seſſion. New York, 1785. Fol.

6 LAWS of the State of New York. Paſſed by the Legislature of said State, at their ninth Seſſion. New York, 1786. Fol°

7 LAWS of the State of New York, comprising the constitution, and the acts of the Legislature since the revolution, from the first to the twelfth Seſſion inclusive. [Edited by S. Jones and R. Varick.] 2 vol. New York, 1789. Fol°

8 LAWS of the State of New York, comprising the constitution and the acts of the Legislature, since the Revolution, from the first to the twentieth Seſſion, inclusive. 3 vol. New York, 1798, '92, '97. 8°

9 LAWS of the State of New York [continued to 1809]. 5 vol. Albany, 1802-9. 8°

10 PUBLIC Laws of the State of New York, paſſed at the thirty-third Seſſion of the Legislature, . . 1810. Albany, 1810. 8°

11 LAWS of the State of New York, revised and paſſed at the thirty-sixth Seſſion of the Legislature [continued to the forty-seventh Seſſion inclusive]. With marginal notes and references [to the laws of the thirty-sixth Session], furnished by the revisors, W. P. Van Neſs and J. Woodworth. 6 vol. Albany, 1813-25. 8°

12 LAWS of the State of New York, respecting navigable communications between the Great Western and Northern Lakes and the Atlantic Ocean. New York, 1817. 8vo.

13 AN ACT to incorporate the members of the New York Institution for the instruction of the deaf and dumb. To which is added, the By-Laws, etc. New York, 1819. 8°

14 LAWS of the State of New York in relation to the Erie and Champlain Canals . . With the annual Reports of the Canal Commiſſioners, and other documents. . . Also . . maps deline-

ating the routes of the .. canals, *etc.*
2 vol. [With an appendix.] Albany,
1825. 8vo.

15 LAWS of the State of New York,
pafsed at the forty-eighth Sefsion of
the Legislature, .. 1825 (to the 79th
Sefsion, 1856, including the Laws
pafsed at the 2nd Meetings of the 50th
and 51st Sefsions.) 34 vol. Albany,
1825-56. 8°

16 THE REVISED Statutes of the
State of New York, pafsed during the
years 1827 and 1828. To which are
added, certain former acts which have
not been revised. Printed and published under the direction of the revisers [J. Duer, B. F. Butler, and J.
C. Spencer]. Albany, 1829. 8°

17 THE REVISED Statutes of the
State of New York, as altered by the
Legislature; including the statutory
provisions of a general nature, pafsed
from 1828 to 1835 inclusive; with
references to judicial decisions: To
which are added certain local acts,
pafsed before and since the revised
statutes; all the acts of general interest pafsed during the Sefsion of
1836; and an appendix, containing
extracts from the original reports of
the revisers to the Legislature, *etc.*
Prepared by and published under the
superintendence of the late revisers
(J. Duer, B. F. Butler, and J. C.
Spencer). 3 vol. Albany, 1836. 8vo.

18 THE REVISED Statutes of the
State of New York, *etc.* Prepared
by J. Duer, B. F. Butler, and J. C.
Spencer. Third edition. 2 vol. Albany,
1846. 8°

19 REVISED Statutes of the State
of New York. Fourth edition. By
Hiram Denio and William Tracy. 2
vol. Albany, 1852. 8°

20 JOURNAL of the Votes and Proceedings of the General Afsembly of
the Colony of New York; began ..
9 April, 1691, and ended .. 27 Sept.
1743. 2 vol. (Vol. 1, 1691-1743;
vol. 2, 1743-65.) [Edited by A.
Lott.] New York, 1764-6. Fol°

21 VOTES and Proceedings of the

Senate of the State of New York, at
their first Sefsion, held at Kingston,
Sept. 9, 1777 (-1778). Kingston,
1777 [-78]. Fol°. Also at the

2nd *Sefsion, Poughkeepsie,*	1778-79
3rd *Sefsion, Poughkeepsie,*	1779-80
4th *Sefsion, Poughkeepsie,*	1781
5th Sefsion, (*wants title*),	1781-82
6th *Sefsion, 1st Meeting,*	1783
6th Sefsion, 2d Meeting,	1783
7th Sefsion, 1st Meeting,	1784
7th Sefsion, 2d Meeting,	1784
8th Sefsion, 1st Meeting,	1784
8th Sefsion, 2d Meeting,	1785
9th Sefsion, at N. York,	1786
10th Sefsion, at N. York,	1787
11th Sefsion, Poughk'psie,	1788
12th Sefsion, at Albany,	1788-89
13th Sefsion, 1st Meeting,	1789
13th Sefsion, 2d Meeting,	1790
14th Sefsion, at N. York,	1791
15th Sefsion, at N. York,	1792
16th Sefsion, at N. York,	1792-93
17th Sefsion, at Albany,	1794
18th Sefsion, at Albany,	1795
19th Sefsion, at Albany,	1796
20th Sefsion, 1st Meeting,	1796
20th Sefsion, 2d Meeting,	1797
21st Sefsion, at Albany,	1798
22nd Sefsion, 1st Meeting,	1798
22nd Sefsion, 2d Meeting,	1799
23rd Sefsion, at Albany,	1800
24th Sefsion, at Albany,	1800-1
25th Sefsion, at Albany,	1802
26th Sefsion, at Albany,	1803
27th Sefsion, at Albany,	1804
28th Sefsion, 1st Meeting,	1804
28th Sefsion, 2d Meeting,	1805
29th Sefsion, at Albany,	1806
30th Sefsion, at Albany,	1807
31st Sefsion, at Albany,	1808
32nd Sefsion, at Albany,	1808-9
33rd Sefsion, at Albany,	1810
34th Sefsion, at Albany,	1811
35th Sefsion, at Albany,	1812
36th Sefsion, at Albany,	1812-13
37th Sefsion, at Albany,	1814
38th Sefsion, at Albany,	1814-15
39th *Sefsion, at Albany,*	1816
40th Sefsion, at Albany,	1816-17
41st Sefsion, at Albany,	1818
42nd Sefsion, at Albany,	1819
43rd Sefsion, at Albany,	1820
44th Sefsion, at Albany,	1820-21
45th Sefsion, at Albany,	1822
46th Sefsion, at Albany,	1823
47th Sefsion, at Albany,	1824
48th Sefsion, at Albany,	1825
49th Sefsion, at Albany,	1826
50th *Sefsion, 1st Meeting,*	1827
50th Sefsion, 2d Meeting,	1827
51st Sefsion, 1st Meeting,	1828
51st *Sefsion, 2d Meeting,*	1828

52nd Seſſion, at Albany,   1829
[Wanting thoſe Seſſions printed in Italics.]
Kingston, 1777; Poughkeepsie, 1781-82, and 1788; New York, 1784-87, 1789-92, 1795-96, and Albany 1794, 1796-1829. Fol°

22 THE VOTES and Proceedings of the Aſſembly of the State of New York, at their first Seſſion, begun and holden .. at Kingston, in Ulster County, .. 10 Sept. 1777. Kingston, 1777. Fol°. Also at the

2nd Seſſion, Poughkeepsie,	1778-79
3rd Seſſion, Poughkeepsie,	1779-80
4th Seſſion, Poughkeepsie,	1781
Reprinted Albany,	1820.
5th Seſſion, Poughkeepsie,	1781-2
6th Seſſion, Poughkeepsie,	1783
7th Seſſion, at N. York,	1784
8th Seſſion, 1st Meeting,	1784
8th Seſſion, 2d Meeting,	1785
9th Seſſion, at N. York,	1786
10th Seſſion, at N. York,	1787
11th Seſſion, Poughkeepsie,	1788
12th Seſſion, at N. York,	1788-89
13th Seſſion, 1st Meeting,	1789
13th Seſſion, 2d Meeting,	1790
14th Seſſion, at N. York,	1791
15th Seſſion, at N. York,	1792
16th Seſſion, at N. York,	1792-93
17th Seſſion, at Albany,	1794
18th Seſſion, at Albany,	1795
19th Seſſion, at Albany,	1796
20th Seſſion, 1st Meeting,	1796
20th Seſſion, 2d Meeting,	1797
21st Seſſion, at Albany,	1798
22nd Seſſion, 1st Meeting,	1798
22nd Seſſion, 2d Meeting,	1799
23rd Seſſion, at Albany,	1800
24th Seſſion, at Albany,	1800-01
25th Seſſion, at Albany,	1802
26th Seſſion, at Albany,	1803
27th Seſſion, at Albany,	1804
28th Seſſion, 1st Meeting,	1804
28th Seſſion, 2d Meeting,	1805
29th Seſſion, at Albany,	1806
30th Seſſion, at Albany, ·	1807
31st Seſſion, at Albany,	1808
32nd Seſſion, at Albany,	1808-09
33rd Seſſion, at Albany,	1810
34th Seſſion, at Albany,	1811
35th Seſſion, at Albany,	1812
36th Seſſion, at Albany,	1812-13
37th Seſſion, at Albany,	1814
38th Seſſion, at Albany,	1814-15
39th Seſſion, at Albany,	1816
40th Seſſion, at Albany,	1816-17
41st Seſſion, at Albany,	1818
42nd Seſſion, at Albany,	1819
43rd Seſſion, at Albany,	1820
44th Seſſion, at Albany,	1820-21
45th Seſſion, at Albany,	1822
46th Seſſion, at Albany,	1823

47th Seſſion, at Albany,	1824
48th Seſſion, at Albany,	1825
49th Seſſion, at Albany,	1826
50th Seſſion, 1st Meeting,	1827
50th Seſſion, 2d Meeting,	1827
51st Seſſion, 1st Meeting,	1828
51st Seſſion, 2d Meeting,	1828
52nd Seſſion, at Albany,	1829

[Wanting those printed in Italics.]
Poughkeepsie, New York and Albany,
1779-1830. Fol°

23 JOURNAL of the Senate of .. New York, at their fifty-third Seſſion .. 1830 (to the 79th Seſſion, 1856). 27 vol. Albany, 1830-56. 8°

24 JOURNAL of the Aſſembly of .. New York, at their fifty-third Seſſion, .. 1830 (to the 79th Seſſion, 1856). 32 vol. Albany, 1830-56. 8°

25 LEGISLATIVE Documents of the Senate and Aſſembly of .. New York. Fifty-third Seſſion. 1830. (N° 1-434.) 4 vol. Albany, 1830. 8°

26 DOCUMENTS of the Senate .. Fifty-fourth Seſſion. 1831. (N° 1-78.) Albany, 1831. 8°. Also at the

55th Seſſion, 1832, N° 1-118 in 2 vol.
56th Seſſion, 1833, N° 1-123 in 2 vol.
57th Seſſion, 1834, N° 1-126 in 2 vol.
58th Seſſion, 1835, N° 1- 89 in 2 vol.
59th Seſſion, 1836, N° 1-110 in 2 vol.
60th Seſſion, 1837, N° 1- 73 in 2 vol.
61st Seſſion, 1838, N° 1- 76 in 2 vol.
62nd Seſſion, 1839, N° 1-112 in 3 vol.
63rd Seſſion, 1840, N° 1-127 in 4 vol.
64th Seſſion, 1841, N° 1-100 in 3 vol.
65th Seſſion, 1842, N° 1-109 in 4 vol.
66th Seſſion, 1843, N° 1-122 in 3 vol.
67th Seſſion, 1844, N° 1-135 in 4 vol.
68th Seſſion, 1845, N° 1-126 in 3 vol.
69th Seſſion, 1846, N° 1-145 in 4 vol.
70th Seſſion, 1847, N° 1-155 in 4 vol.
71st Seſſion, 1848, N° 1-79 in 3 vol.
72nd Seſſion, 1849, N° 1-86 in 3 vol.
73rd Seſſion, 1850, N° 1-113 in 3 vol.
74th Seſſion, 1851, N° 1- in 3 vol.
75th Seſſion, 1852, N° 1-98 in 3 vol.
76th Seſſion, 1853, N° 1-86 in 3 vol.
77th Seſſion, 1854, N° 1-111 in 3 vol.
78th Seſſion, 1855, N° 1- in 3 vol.
69 vol. Albany, 1831-55. 8°

27 DOCUMENTS of the Aſſembly .. Fifty-fourth Seſſion. 1831. (N° 1-362.) 4 vol. Albany, 1831. 8°

28 DOCUMENTS of the Aſſembly .. Fifty-fifth Seſſion, 1832. (N° 1-338.) 4 vol. Albany, 1832. 8°. Also at the

55th Seſſion, 1832, N° 1-338, in 4 vol.
56th Seſſion, 1833, N° 1-334, in 4 vol.

57th Seſſion, 1834, Nº 1-401, in 4 vol.
58th Seſſion, 1835, Nº 1-399, in 5 vol.
59th Seſſion, 1836, Nº 1-329, in 4 vol.
60th Seſſion, 1837, Nº 1-334, in 4 vol.
61st Seſſion, 1838, Nº 1-367, in 6 vol.
62nd Seſſion, 1839, Nº 1-412, in 6 vol.
63rd Seſſion, 1840, Nº 1-363, in 8 vol.
64th Seſſion, 1841, Nº 1-305, in 7 vol.
65th Seſſion, 1842, Nº 1-199, in 7 vol.
66th Seſſion, 1843, Nº 1-135, in 5 vol.
67th Seſſion, 1844, Nº 1-205, in 7 vol.
68th Seſſion, 1845, Nº 1-252, in 7 vol.
69th Seſſion, 1846, Nº 1-226, in 6 vol.
70th Seſſion, 1847, Nº 1-264, in 8 vol.
71st Seſſion, 1848, Nº 1-216, in 7 vol.
72nd Seſſion, 1849, Nº 1-244, in 7 vol.
73rd Seſſion, 1850, Nº 1-199, in 9 vol.
74th Seſſion, 1851, Nº 1-159, in 6 vol.
75th Seſſion, 1852, Nº 1-129, in 7 vol.
76th Seſſion, 1853, Nº 1-134, in 6 vol.
77th Seſſion, 1854, Nº 1-151, in 6 vol.
78th Seſſion, 1855, Nº 1——, in 7 vol.
147 vol. Albany, 1832-55. 8º

29 JOURNAL of the Votes and Proceedings of the General Aſſembly of the Colony of New York, from 1766 to 1776 inclusive. Reprinted in pursuance of a joint resolution of the Legislature of the State of New York, etc. Albany, 1820. Folº

30 JOURNALS [and correspondence] of the Provincial Congreſs, Provincial Convention, Committee of Safety, and Council of Safety, of the State of New York. 1775-77. 2vol. Albany, 1842. Folº

31 INDEXES to the Journals of the Senate of New York; commencing with the first Seſſion of the Legislature, in 1777, and ending with the twenty-second Seſſion, in 1799, inclusive. Albany, 1814. Folº

32 INDEXES to the Journals of the House of Aſſembly of .. New York, commencing with the first Seſſion of the Legislature, in 1777, and ending with the eighteenth Seſſion, in 1795. Albany, 1814. Folº

33 LEGISLATIVE Bills [brought into the Senate and Aſſembly, from the fifty-sixth (1833) to the sixty-fifth Seſſion (1842), the bills of each Seſſion bound in one vol.] [Albany, 1833-42.] Folº

34 SENATE Bills, sixty-sixth Seſſion, 1843, to the sixty-ninth Seſſion,

1846. 4 vol. [Albany, 1843-46.] Folº

35 ASSEMBLY Bills, sixty-sixth Session, 1843, to sixty-ninth Seſſion, 1846. 4 vol. [Albany, 1843-46.] Folº

36 AN ACT to incorporate medical societies, for the purpose of regulating the Practice of Physic and Surgery in this State. New York, 1806. 8vo.

37 REPORT of the Proceedings of the Medical and Surgical Society of the University of the State of New York during the winter of 1809-10. New York, 1810. 8vo.

38 REPORT of the Proceedings of the Medical and Surgical Society of the University of the State of New York during the winter of 1810-11. New York, 1811. 8vo.

39 REPORT of the Commiſſioners appointed by joint resolutions of the Hon. the Senate and Aſſembly of the State of New York, of . . . 13 and 15 March, 1810, to explore the route of an inland navigation, from Hudson River to Lake Ontario and Lake Erie. New York, 1811. 8º

40 REPORT of the Commiſſioners appointed by an act of the Legislature of . . New York, entitled, "An act to provide for the improvement of the internal navigation of the State," etc. Albany, 1812. 8º

41 AN ADDRESS to the Public on the African School, lately established under the care of the Synod of New York and New Jersey. New York, 1816. 8vo.

42 REPORT of the Joint Committee of the Legislature of New York, on the subject of the canals from Lake Erie to the Hudson River, and from Lake Champlain to the same. Albany, 1817. 8vo.

43 REPORT of the Commiſſioners of the State of New York, on the canals from Lake Erie to the Hudson River, and from Lake Champlain to the same. (Appendix.) Albany, 1817. 8vo.

44 SPEECH of Governor Clinton to

the Legislature of the State of New York on the sixth day of January, 1819. Albany, 1819. 8vo.

45 ADDRESS of the General Committee of the Board of Agriculture of the State of New York, to the County Agricultural Societies. Albany, 1820. 8vo.

46 THE SPEECHES of the different Governors to the Legislature of the State of New York, commencing with those of George Clinton, and continued down to the present time. Albany, 1825. 8°

47 STATISTICAL Tables of the State of New York; containing complete lists of the counties, towns, senatorial and congreſsional diſtricts, population, etc. Compiled from the best authorities. New York, 1828. 12°

48 SKETCH of the geographical route of a great railway, by which it is proposed to connect the canals and navigable waters of the States of New York, Pennsylvania, Ohio, Indiana, Illinois, Miſſouri: and the Michigan, North West, and Miſſouri Territories. New York, 1829. 8°

49 ANNUAL Reports on the geological survey of the State of New York, for the year 1837, by L. C. Beck, T. A. Conrad, W. W. Mather, E. Emmons, L. Vanuxem, and J. Hall, together with a letter from J. E. De Kay, in relation to annual reports from the zoological and botanical departments, presented to the House of Aſſembly, New York, by the governor W. L. Marcy. [Albany, 1838.] 8vo.

50 STATE of New York, Nº 150. In Aſſembly, February 17, 1841. Communication from the Governor, transmitting several reports relative to the geological survey of the State. [Albany, 1841.] 8°

51 A GAZETTEER of the State of New York; .. also, statistical tables, including the census of 1840, and tables of distances. Albany, 1842. 8°

52 NATURAL History of New York. 19 vol. New York (and Albany), 1842-54. 4to. Containing

Part I. Zoology, by J. E. De Kay. 5 vol.
Part II. Flora, by John Torrey. 2 vol.
Part III. Mineralogy, by Lewis C. Beck.
Part IV. Geology, by William W. Mather, Ebenezer Emmons, Lardner Vanuxem, and James Hall. 4 parts.
Part V. Agriculture, by E. Emmons. 4 vol.
Part VI. Palæontology, by J. Hall. 3 vol.

53 THE NEW York Political Manual, containing the official Election returns for 1840-42: also, the census of the State of New York in 1840. Together with other useful information. Albany, 1843. 8°

54 MINUTES of the Convention of Delegates from the Synod of New York and Philadelphia and from the Aſſociations of Connecticut, from 1766 to 1775 inclusive. Hartford, 1843. 8vo.

55 THE NEW York Traveller; containing railroad, steamboat, canal-packet, and stage routes through the State of New York. Also, other information useful to travellers. New York, July, 1845. 12°

56 STATE of New York. Nº 98. In Senate, March 18, 1846. Report of the Secretary of State, of abstracts of convictions for criminal offences, and of the returns of sheriffs respecting the persons convicted. [Albany, 1846.] 8°

57 STATE of New York, Nº 180. In Aſſembly, March 25, 1847. Report of the Secretary of State (N. S. Benton), of abstracts of convictions for criminal offences, and of the returns of sheriffs respecting the persons convicted. [Albany, 1847.] 8°

58 FIRST Report of the Commissioners on Practice and Pleadings (A. Loomis, D. Graham, D. D. Field). Code of Procedure. (Supplement to the Code of Procedure. Temporary Act.—Second Report.—Third Report. —Fourth Report. Code of Criminal Procedure. The code of criminal procedure . . . reported complete.— The code of civil procedure . . . reported complete.) 7 pts. Albany, 1848-50. 8°

59 AMENDMENTS (paſſed April 16,

1852) to the Code of Procedure of New York. New York, 1852. 8vo.

60 THE DOCUMENTARY History of .. New York, arranged under the direction of Christopher Morgan, Secretary of State, by E. B. O'Callaghan. 4 vol. Albany, 1850-51. 4°

61 DOCUMENTS relative to the Colonial History of the State of New York, procured in Holland, England, and France by John R. Brodhead, Esq. Agent under and by virtue of an act of the Legislature: Edited by E. B. O'Callaghan. Vol. 3, 4, 5, 6, 7 and 9. Albany, 1855-56. 4to.

NEW YORK ANNUAL REGISTER. 1834. Containing an Almanac, etc. .. By E. Williams. Fifth year. New York, 1834. 12°

NEW YORK BAPTIST MISSIONARY CONVENTION. Proceedings of the twenty-first anniversary of the Baptist Missionary Convention of the State of New York. Utica, 1842. 8°

2 PROCEEDINGS of the twenty-second anniversary of the Baptist Missionary Convention of the State of New York, held with the Syracuse Baptist Church, etc. Few MS. notes. Utica, 1843. 8°

NEW YORK BIBLE SOCIETY. Eleventh (to the 22nd) annual report of the Young Men's New York Bible Society, auxiliary to the American Bible Society, with the Constitution, etc. 1834-1845. 12 parts. New York, 1834-46. 8°

NEW YORK BOOK of Poetry. New York, 1837. 8°

NEW YORK CITY HALL RECORDER (THE). .. 1816-1821; containing reports of the most interesting trials and decisions .. in the various courts of judicature. .. With notes and remarks, critical and explanatory. By D. Rogers. 6 vol. [Vol. 1 is a reprint, dated 1842.] New York, 1842, 1817-22. 8°

NEW YORK COLONIZATION SOCIETY. Fourteenth annual report of the Colonization Society of the State of New York. New York, 1846. 8vo.

NEW YORK COMMERCIAL ADVERTISER. August 16, 1832. New York, 1832. Fol.

NEW YORK DIRECTORY. Longworth's American Almanac [by A. Beers, from 1808 to 1818 inclusive], New York Register, and City Directory. 1800, 1801, 1803, 1805 to 1813, 1816 to 1819, 1821 to 1842. [The Almanacks from 1808 to 1818 have a special title-page, bearing the name of A. Beers as the writer. The volume for 1818 has no almanack.] New York, 1800-42. 12°

2 JONES's New York mercantile and general Directory for 1805-6. By J. F. Jones. New York [1805]. 8°

3 MERCEIN's City Directory, New York Register, and Almanac for the forty-fifth year of American Independence [1820-21], etc. New York, 1820. 12°

4 NEW York as it is, in 1835; containing a general description of the city and environs, list of officers, public officers, etc. Third year of publication. New York, 1835. 12°

5 NEW York as it is, etc. Sixth year of publication. New York, 1840. 12°

6 THE NEW York City and co-partnership Directory, for 1843 and 1844. 2 parts. [Continued as] The New York City Directory, for 1844 and 1845. Third publication. [And as] Doggett's New York City Directory, for 1845 and 1846. Fourth publication. New York, 1843-45. 8°

NEW YORK DISPENSARY. The Charter and Bye-laws of the New York Dispensary. New York, 1818. 8vo.

NEW YORK ECCLESIOLOGICAL SOCIETY. The New York Ecclesiologist. Vol. 1, 2. New York [1848-50]. 8°

NEW YORK EVENING POST (THE). N° 5941. July 9, 1821. New York, 1821. Fol.

NEW YORK EXHIBITION, Illustrated Record of the Industry of all Nations. [See B. SILLIMAN, Jun.] New York. 1855. Fol.

NEW YORK GAZETTEER (THE) and Country Journal. N° 12-72. [Continued under the title of] The New York Gazetteer; or, Daily Evening Post. N° 73. [Wanting N° 17, 18, 26, 28 to 70.] New York, 1784-86. Fol.

NEW YORK GAZETTE (THE) and the Weekly Mercury. N° 1124-1652. July 12, 1773, to June 16, 1783. [Wanting N° 1 to 1123, 1125 to 1136, 1138 to 1140, 1142 to 43, 1145, 1147, 1150 to 56, 1158 to 60, 1162, 1165-67, 1174, 1180, 1182, 1185-88, 1193, 1195 to 96, 1198 to 99, 1204 to 07, 1212, 1214, 1216, 1218 to 19, 1221 to 22, 1226 to 33, 1235 to 1305, 1307, 1310 to 1425, 1427 to 1515, 1517 to 1547, 1551 to 61, 1563, 1567 to 71, 1573 to 1580.] New York, 1773-83. Fol.

NEW YORK HISTORICAL SOCIETY. The Constitution and Byelaws of the New York Historical Society. New York, 1805. 8vo.

2 COLLECTIONS . . . for the years 1809, '14, '21, '26, '29. 5 Vol. [Vol. 4 and 5 comprise " The History of the late province of New York, from its discovery, etc. By the Hon. William Smith."] New York, 1811-29. 8vo.

3 COLLECTIONS. Second Series. Vol. 1. New York, 1841. 8vo.

4 PROCEEDINGS of the New York Historical Society, for the year 1843, 1844, 1845. New York, 1844-46. 8°

5 A MEMOIR on the North-Eastern boundary in connexion with Mr. Jay's Map. Together with a speech on the same subject, by the Hon. D. Webster, at a special meeting of the New York Historical Society. New York, 1843. 8vo.

6 THE CHARTER and By-laws of the New York Historical Society. Revised March, 1846. N. York, 1846. 8°

7 SEMI-CENTENNIAL Celebration. Fiftieth anniversary of the founding of the New York Historical Society. Nov. 20, 1854. New York, 1854. 8vo.

NEW YORK HOSPITAL. A brief Account of the New York Hospital. New York, 1804. 8vo.

NEW YORK INDIANS. A brief Exposition of the Claims of the New York Indians to certain lands at Green Bay, in the Michigan Territory. [Washington, 1830?] 8°

NEW YORK LIFE INSURANCE AND TRUST COMPANY. In Chancery, before the Chancellor: in the matter of the New York Life Insurance . . . Company. Answer and report, 1836. New York, 1837. 8°

NEW YORK MAGDALEN SOCIETY. First annual Report of the Executive Committee of the New York Magdalen Society. [New York, 1831?] 8°

NEW YORK MARINE BIBLE SOCIETY. Twentieth (to the twenty-third) Annual Report, with the constitution, of the . . Bible Society; instituted in . . New York, Feb. 12, 1817. 4 parts. New York, 1836-1839. 8°

NEW YORK MERCURY EXTRAORDINARY (THE). April 6, 1783. New York, 1783. Fol.

NEW YORK MIRROR (THE), and Ladies' Literary Gazette; being a repository of miscellaneous literary productions, in prose and verse. Edited by S. Woodworth and G. P. Morris. [The name of G. P. Morris alone occurs on the title-pages of vol. 2-8. After vol. 8 no name of editor occurs, and the second title is omitted.] Vol. 1-20. Aug. 2, 1823, to Dec. 31, 1842. New York, 1824-42. 4°

NEW YORK MORNING POST (THE). N° 128, for Aug. 5, 1783,

and 746 to 753, Aug. 8-16, 1786.
[Wanting N° 1-127, 129-745, and
all after N° 753.] New York, 1783-
86. Fol.

2 THE NEW York Morning Post.
N° 140, 143-45, 147-48, 163, 185.
New York, 1783-84. Fol.

NEW YORK PACKET (THE),
and the American Advertiser. N°
355, 356 to 357, 359 to 61, 619.
Feb. 1784 to Aug. 1786. New York,
1784-86. Fol.

NEW YORK QUARTERLY RE-
VIEW (THE). Edited by A. G. Rem-
ington. Vol. 1-5. New York, 1852,
1856. 8°

NEW YORK READER, N° 2.
Being selections in prose and poetry,
for the use of schools. New York
[1827]. 12°

NEW YORK REVIEW (THE)
and Quarterly Church Journal.
March, 1837, to April, 1842. 10
vol. New York, 1837-42. 8vo.

NEW YORK STANDARD. Ex-
tra. The Voice of the People, and
the facts in relation to the rejection of
Martin Van Buren by the United
States Senate. New York, 1832. 4°

NEW YORK STATE AGRI-
CULTURAL SOCIETY. Transactions ..
(together with an abstract of the proceedings of the County Agricultural
societies ; .. and the American Institute). 1841 to 1845. Vol. 1-5.
Albany, 1842-46. 8°

NEW YORK STATE LIBRARY.
Annual Reports of the Trustees of the
State Library [and annual catalogue]
1845-55. [Albany, 1845-55.] 8°

2 REPORT of the Joint Library
Committee of the Legislature of New
York, on the subject of international
exchanges. [With other documents.]
Albany, 1847. 8°

NEW YORK STATE LUNATIC
ASYLUM at Utica. [First] annual report of the managers of the State

Lunatic Asylum, made to the Legislature, January 31, 1845 (also the
3rd, 4th, and 5th reports). Albany,
1845-48. 8°

NEW YORK STATE PRISON.
A view of the New York State Prison.
New York, 1815. 8vo.

NEW YORK STATE REGIS-
TER (THE). 1845,1846. Edited by
O. L. Holley. 2 vol. New York,
1845-46. 8°

NEW YORK STATE SOCIETY
for the Promotion of Temperance.
Fourth annual report of the New York
State Society for the promotion of
temperance. Albany, 1833. 8°

NEW YORK SUNDAY SCHOOL
UNION SOCIETY. The second annual
report. New York, 1818. 8°

NEW YORK TIMES and Com-
mercial Intelligencer. N. T. Eldridge and D. Macleod, editors. Vol. 3.
N° 477. Sept. 26, 1839. New York,
1839. Fol.

NEW YORK TYPOGRAPHI-
CAL SOCIETY. Proceedings at the
Printers' Banquet, held by the New
York Typographical Society, on the
occasion of Franklin's birthday. New
York, 1850. 8°

NIAGARA. An account of a
Journey to Niagara, Montreal, and
Quebec, in 1765; or " 'Tis eighty
years since." New York, 1846. 8°

NIAGARA FALLS. The Niagara
Falls' Guide, etc. [By J. Faxon?]
Buffalo, 1848. 12°

NICHOLAS, GEORGE. A Letter
from George Nicholas, of Kentucky,
to his friend in Virginia, justifying
the conduct of the citizens of Kentucky, as to some of the late measures of the general government, etc.
Philadelphia, reprinted 1799. 8vo.

NICHOLLS, BENJAMIN ELLIOTT.
The Mine explored ; or, help to the
reading of the Bible. Philadelphia
[1853]. 12°

NICHOLS, F. A Treatise of practical Arithmetic and Book-keeping, etc. Boston, 1797. 12°.

NICHOLS, ICHABOD. An Oration, delivered . . July 4, 1805, at the North Meeting-house in Salem, Maſſachusetts. Salem, 1805. 8°

NICHOLS, JAMES. The Life of J. Arminius . . Compiled from his life and writings, as published by Mr. J. Nichols. By N. Bangs. New York, 1843. 12°

NICHOLS, REBECCA S. Bernice: or the curse of Minna, and other poems. Cincinnati, 1844. 12°

NICHOLSON, ASENATH, Mrs. Ireland's Welcome to the Stranger, or an excursion through Ireland in 1844 and 1845, for the purpose of personally investigating the condition of the poor. New York, 1847. 12°

2 ANOTHER copy. [Same edition, with a different title-page.] London, 1847. 12°

3 ANNALS of the Famine in Ireland in 1847, 1848, and 1849. [Edited by J. L.] New York, 1851. 12°

NICHOLSON, GEORGE W. S. Poems of the Heart. Philadelphia, 1850. 12°

NICHOLSON, JOSEPH H. Mr. Nicholson's Motion [in the House of Representatives of the United States of America, imposing restrictions on the commerce of Great Britain, and her dependencies, with the United States]. Feb. 10, 1806. Washington, 1806. 8°

NICHOLSON, PETER. The Carpenter's new Guide : being a complete book of lines for carpentry and joinery ; . . also, additional plans for various staircases . . by W. Johnston, etc. Thirteenth edition. Philadelphia, 1848. 4°

NICKLIN, PHILIP H. Remarks on literary property. Philadelphia, 1838. 12mo.

NICOLLET, J. N. Eſſay on meteorological observations, etc. [Washington, 1839.] 8°

NILES, HEZEKIAH. Principles and Acts of the Revolution in America; or an attempt to collect and preserve some of the speeches, orations, and proceedings, with sketches and remarks on men and things, and other fugitive or neglected pieces, belonging to the Revolutionary period in the United States, etc. Baltimore, 1822. 8°

2 JOURNAL of the proceedings of the Friends of domestic industry in general Convention, met at . . New York, etc. Baltimore, 1831. 8°

3 NILES. See WEEKLY REGISTER.

NILES, JOHN M. The Life of O. H. Perry. With an appendix, comprising a biographical memoir of the late Captain J. Lawrence, with brief sketches of the most prominent events in the lives of Commodores Bainbridge, Decatur, Porter, and Macdonough. A view of the rise, present condition, and future prospects of the Navy of the United States ; . . to which is added a biography of General Pike, and a view of the leading events in the life of General Harrison. Second edition, enlarged and improved. Hartford, 1821. 12°

2 SPEECH . . on the bill imposing additional duties, as depositaries in certain cases, on public officers, etc.; delivered in the Senate, . . Feb. 13, 1838. Washington, 1838. 8°

NINETEENTH CENTURY (THE): a Quarterly Miscellany. [Edited by C. C. Burr.] Jan. to Apr. 1848. Vol. 1. Philadelphia, 1848. 8°

NIX's Mate: an historical romance of America. By the author of Athenia of Damascus [Rufus Dawes]. New York, 1839. 12°

NOAH, MORDECAI MANUEL. Travels in England, France, Spain, and the Barbary States, 1813-15. New York, 1819. 8°

2 GLEANINGS from a Gathered Harvest. New York, 1845. 8°

NOBLE, JOHN. Noble's Instructions to Emigrants: an attempt to give a correct account of the United States of America, and offer some information .. to those who have a wish to emigrate to that Republic, etc. Boston, 1819. 8vo.

NOBLE, LOUIS L. The Course of Empire, Voyage of Life, and other pictures of T. Cole, N. A. With selections from his letters and miscellaneous writings: illustrative of his life, character, and genius. New York, 1853. 12°

NOBLE, OLIVER, M. A. Some Strictures upon the Sacred Story recorded in the Book of Esther, showing the power and oppression of State Ministers, .. in a discourse [on Esther viii. 11] .. in commemoration of the Massacre at Boston, etc. Newbury Port, 1775. 8°

NOCTES (THE) Ambrosianæ of "Blackwood." [By J. Wilson, J. G. Lockhart, etc.] 4 vol. Philadelphia, 1843. 8vo.

NORDHEIMER, ISAAC. A Grammatical Analysis of selections from the Hebrew Scriptures; with an exercise in Hebrew composition. New York, 1838. 8°
2 A CRITICAL Grammar of the Hebrew language. 2 vol. [Vol. 1 is of the second edition.] New York, 1842, 1841. 8°

NORFOLK AND PORTSMOUTH JOURNAL. Nov. 1786. Norfolk, 1786. Fol.

NORMAN, B. M. Rambles in Yucatan; or notes of travel through the Peninsula, including a visit to the ruins of Chi-Chen, Kabah, Zayi, and Uxmal. Second edition. New York, 1843. 8vo.
2 NORMAN's New Orleans and Environs, containing a brief historical sketch of the Territory and State of Louisiana, and the City of New Orleans, from the earliest period to the present time. New Orleans, 1845. 12°
3 RAMBLES by Land and Water, or notes of Travel in Cuba and Mexico; including a canoe voyage up the River Panuco, and researches among the ruins of Tamaulipas, etc. New York [printed; and] N. Orleans, 1845. 12°

NORRIS, MOSES, of New Hampshire. Speech ... on the right of members [i. e. of those elected by general ticket for New Hampshire, Georgia, Mississippi, and Missouri] to their seats in the House of Representatives, .. Feb. 10, 1844. [Washington, 1844.] 8°
2 SPEECH .. on the annexation of Texas; delivered in the House of Representatives, Jan. 24, 1845. Washington, 1845. 8°

NORRIS, SEPTIMUS. Norris's Hand-book for Locomotive Engineers and Machinists. Philadelphia, 1852. 12mo.

NORTH (THE) and South, or, slavery and its contrasts. A tale of real life. By the author of Way-marks in the Life of a Wanderer, etc. Philadelphia, 1852. 12mo.

NORTH, EDWARD. An Inaugural Dissertation on the rheumatic state of fever. Philadelphia, 1797. 8vo.

NORTH AMERICAN. [Begins] United States, August 10, 1831. To General Lafayette. [A letter signed " A North American," on the Three Days and French politics generally.] [New York? 1831.] 8vo.

NORTH AMERICAN REVIEW (THE) and Miscellaneous Journal. [Edited successively by W. Tudor; W. Phillips; J. Sparks; E. T. Channing; Hon. E. Everett, 1819-24; J. Sparks, 1825-29; A. H. Everett, 1829-34; J. G. Palfrey, 1835-43; F. Bowen, 1843-53; A. P. Peabody, 1854-56.] 83 vol. Boston, 1815-56. 8vo.

2 GENERAL Index to the first 25 volumes, 1815-27. Bost. 1829. 8vo.

NORTH CAROLINA, *State of.* Laws of the State of North Carolina, including the titles of such statutes and parts of statutes of Great Britain as are in force in said State; together with the second charter granted by Charles II to the proprietors of Carolina; the great deed of grant from the Lords Proprietors, *etc.* . . . with marginal notes and references. Revised . . by H. Potter, J. L. Taylor, and B. Yancey, Esqrs, and published . . under the superintendence of H. Potter. 2 vol. Raleigh, 1821. 8°

2 IN Senate, December 19, 1815. [Resolutions respecting the mode of electing representatives to Congress, passed in the Legislature of North Carolina, and resolutions thereupon in the Legislature of Massachusetts.] [Boston, 1816.] 8°

3 PROCEEDINGS and Debates of the Convention of North Carolina, called to amend the Constitution of the State, which assembled at Raleigh, June 4, 1835. To which are subjoined, the Convention Act and the amendments to the Constitution, together with the votes of the people. Raleigh, 1836. 8°

NORTH CAROLINA BAPTIST STATE CONVENTION. Proceedings of the tenth (eleventh, twelfth, and thirteenth) annual meeting of the Baptist State Convention of North Carolina, . . . Oct. 2-5, 1840 (to 1843). Raleigh, 1841-44. 8°

NORTHEND, CHARLES. Obstacles to the greater success of common schools. Boston, 1844. 12°

2 THE TEACHER and the Parent; a treatise upon common-school education. . . . Second edition. Boston, 1853. 12°

NORTHERN TRAVELLER (THE); containing the routes to Niagara, Quebec, and the Springs; with descriptions, and useful hints to strangers. New York, 1825. 12°

2 THE NORTHERN Traveller; containing the Hudson River guide, and tour to the Springs, Lake George, and Canada, passing through Lake Champlain, *etc.* New York, 1844. 12°

NORTHERN BAPTIST EDUCATION SOCIETY. Seventeenth (and eighteenth) Annual Report of the Northern Baptist Education Society, presented at the annual meeting held in Boston, May 25, 1831 (1832). Boston [1831-32]. 8°

NORTHMORE, THOMAS. Washington, or liberty restored, a poem, in ten books. Baltimore, 1809. 12°

NORTON, ALFRED. An Address delivered before the Mercantile Library Association. Boston, 1836. 8°

NORTON, ANDREWS. Inaugural Discourse, delivered before the University in Cambridge, August 10, 1819. Cambridge, 1819. 8vo.

2 A STATEMENT of Reasons for not believing the doctrines of Trinitarians concerning the nature of God and the person of Christ. Cambridge, 1833. 12°

3 REMARKS on Mr. Norton's "Statement of Reasons (for not believing the doctrines of Trinitarians," *etc.*). Boston, 1834. 8°

4 THE EVIDENCES of the genuineness of the Gospel. 3 vol. Boston, 1837-44. 8vo.

5 TRACTS concerning Christianity. Cambridge, 1852. 8°

NORTON, GEORGE HATLEY. An Inquiry into the nature and extent of the Holy Catholic Church. Philadelphia, 1853. 12mo.

NORTON, JOHN. The Heart of New England Rent at the Blasphemies of the present Generation; or a brief tractate concerning the doctrine of the Quakers, *etc.* Cambridge, 1659. 4to.

2 MEMOIR of John Cotton . . with a preface and notes by E. Pond. New York, 1842. 12°

NORTON, WILLIAM A. An Elementary Treatise on Astronomy. Containing a systematic exposition of the theory, and the more important practical problems, with tables. New York, 1839. 8vo.

NORTON, CHARLES B. Norton's Literary Advertiser. Vol. 1, [in 8 numbers. Continued under the title of] Norton's Literary Gazette. Vol. 2.3. N. York, 1852-53. Fol⁰. [Continued as] Norton's Literary Gazette and Publisher's Circular: New series, 1854-55. New York, 1854-55. 4⁰
   2 NORTON's Literary Almanack . . ; containing important literary information; etc. New York, 1852. 8⁰
   3 NORTON's Literary Register and Book-buyers' Almanack for 1853. New York, 1853. 12⁰
   4 NORTON's Literary and Educational Register. New York, 1854. 8⁰

NORWOOD, ABRAHAM. The Acts of the Elders, commonly called the Book of Abraham ; to which is appended, a chapter from the Book of Religious Errors, with notes of explanation. New edition. Boston, 1846. 16mo.

NOTICES. Mineralogical Notices. N⁰ 4. [From the " American Journal of Science and Arts," vol. 14, pp. 264-280.] [New Haven, 1852.] 8vo.

NOTT, ELIPHALET. An Address delivered to the candidates for the baccalaureate, in Union College, at the anniversary commencement, July 24, 1811. Albany, 1811. 8⁰

NOTT, HENRY JUNIUS, and MACCORD, DAVID JAMES. Reports of Cases determined in the Constitutional Court of South Carolina [from Nov. term 1817 to Nov. term 1820]. Second edition. 2 vol. Charleston, 1842. 8⁰

NOTT, JOSIAH C. Two Lectures on the natural history of the Caucasian and Negro races. Mobile, 1844. 12⁰

   2 TYPES of Mankind: or Ethnological Researches . . illustrated by selections from the inedited papers of S. G. Morton . . and by additional contributions from . . L. Agassiz, W. Usher, and . . H. S. Patterson. By J. C. Nott and G. R. Gliddon. London, Philadelphia [printed], 1854. 4to.

NOTT, SAMUEL. Ministers of the Gospel are Earthen Vessels : a sermon [on 2 Cor. iv. 7] preached at . . the funeral of A. Lee, D.D., Norwich, 1832. 8⁰

NOTT, SAMUEL, the Younger. On a proper Education for an agricultural people . . delivered before the American Institute of Instruction, at its annual meeting, Boston. [Boston, 1835.] 8⁰

NOURSE, J. D. Remarks on the past and its legacies to American Society. Louisville, Ky. 1847. 12⁰

NOVANGLUS and Massachusetensis; or, Political Essays, published in 1774 and 1775, on the principal points of controversy between Great Britain and her Colonies, the former by J. Adams, the latter by J. Sewall. To which are added, Letters by President Adams to the Hon. W. Tudor. Boston, 1819. 8⁰

NOYES, JOHN. An Oration, delivered in Brattleborough, July 4, 1811 [in commemoration of American Independence]. Brattleborough, 1811. 8⁰

NOYES, WILLIAM CURTIS. Court of Appeals [of the United States]. W. C. Noyes vs. H. Blakeman and A. M. his wife and E. Ruckman. Points on the part of the appellants. [New York? 1845.] 8⁰

NULLIFIER. Memoirs of a Nullifier, written by himself. [A political fiction.] By a native of the South [Dr. Cooper?] Columbia, 1832. 12⁰

NUNEZ CABECA DE VACA, ALVAR. The Narrative of Alvar Nuñez Cabeça de Vaca, translated [from the Spanish] by Buckingham Smith [with a prefatory notice by G. W. R. Jr. *i. e.* George Washington Riggs]. Washington, 1851. 4to.

NURSERY BOOK for a Child that Loves to Learn. American Sunday School Union, Philadelphia, 1832. 12°

NURSERY LESSONS designed for children eight or ten years old. American Sunday School Union, Philadelphia [1830?] 12°

NUTTALL, THOMAS. The Genera of North American Plants, and a catalogue of the species for the year 1817. 2 vol. Philadelphia, 1818. 12mo.

2 A JOURNAL of Travels into the Arakansa Territory, during the year 1819. Philadelphia, 1821. 8vo.

3 A MANUAL of the Ornithology of the United States and of Canada. The Water-birds. Boston, 1834. 12mo.

4 A MANUAL of the Ornithology of the United States and of Canada. The Land-birds. Second edition with additions. Boston, 1840. 12mo.

5 THE NORTH American Sylva; or a description of the forest trees of the United States, Canada and Nova Scotia, not described in the work of F. A. Michaux, and containing all the forest trees discovered in the Rocky Mountains, the Territory of Oregon, down to the shores of the Pacific and into the confines of California, as well as in various parts of the United States. Illustrated by 122 plates. 3 vol. Philadelphia, 1842-49. 8°

NYSTROM, J. W. A Treatise on Screw Propellers and their Steam-Engines. . . Accompanied with a treatise on bodies in motion in fluid, exemplified for propellers and vessels; also, a full description of a calculating machine. Philadelphia, 1852. 8vo.

 AKES, WILLI-
AM. Catalogue
of Vermont
plants. . . As
published in
Thompson's
History of Ver-
mont. [Bur-
lington, 1842?] 8°

OBERLIN, JOHN FREDERIC. The
Life of J. F. Oberlin. Philadelphia,
1830. 12mo.

OBOOKIAH, HENRY. Memoirs
of Henry Obookiah, a native of Owhy-
hee. Philadelphia, 1830. 12mo.

O'BRIEN, JOHN. A Treatise on
American military laws, and the practice of courts martial ; with suggestions for their improvement. Philadelphia, 1846. 8vo.

OBSERVATOR. The Observa-
tor's Trip to America, in a dialogue
between the Observator and his
countryman Roger. [Philadelphia,]
1726. 12mo.

OBSERVATOR, *Pseud.* Thoughts
on the increasing wealth and national
economy of the United States of
America. Washington, 1801. 8°

OBSERVER. An Inquiry into the
necefsity and general principles of
reorganization in the United States
Navy, with an examination of the true
sources of subordination. By an Observer. Baltimore, 1842. 8°

OBSERVER (THE) and Repertory
of original and selected Efsays, in
verse and prose, on topics of polite
literature, *etc.* (By Beatrice Ironside.)
2 vol. Baltimore, 1806-7. 8vo.

O'CALLAGHAN, E. B. History
of New Netherland ; or, New York
under the Dutch. N. York, 1846. 8°

2 JESUIT Relations of discoveries
and other occurrences in Canada and
the Northern and Western States of
the Union. 1632 to 1672. From the
proceedings of the New York Historical Society, Nov. 1847. New York,
1847. 8°

3 THE DOCUMENTARY History of
the State of New York. *See* NEW
YORK, N° 60. 4to.

4 DOCUMENTS relative to the colonial History of the State of New
York, etc. (The documents in Dutch
and French . . translated by E. B.
O'Callaghan.) *See* NEW YORK, N°61.

OCCIDENT (THE), and American
Jewish Advocate, a monthly periodical, devoted to the diffusion of knowledge on the Jewish literature and
religion. Edited by J. Leeser. Vol. 1.
Philadelphia, 5604 [1845]. 8vo.

OCCOM, SAMSON. A Sermon [on
Rom. vi. 23] at the execution of M.
Paul, an Indian, who had been guilty
of murder . . To which is added a
short account of the late spread of
the Gospel among the Indians. Also
observations on the language of the
Muhhekaneew Indians . . By J. Edwards. New Haven, 1788. 8vo.

OCEAN SCENES, or, the perils
and beauties of the deep ; being ac-

counts of the most popular voyages on record, remarkable shipwrecks, etc. New York, 1848. 12mo.

O'CONNELL, JAMES F. A Residence of eleven years in New Holland and the Caroline Islands : being the adventures of J. F. O'Connell. Edited from his verbal narration. Boston, 1836. 12mo.

ODIORNE, JAMES C. Opinions on speculative Masonry, relative to its origin, nature, and tendency. A compilation embracing recent and important documents. Boston, 1830. 12mo.

OGDEN, GEORGE W. Letters from the West, comprising a tour through the western country, and a residence of two summers in . . Ohio and Kentucky : originally written in letters to a brother. New Bedford, 1823. 12°

OGDEN, JOHN C. A Sermon [on Neh. v. 19] delivered before . . the . . Senate and . . House of Representatives of . . New Hampshire, at the annual Election. Concord, 1790. 12°

OGILBY, JOHN G. The Catholic Church in England and America : three lectures : 1. The church in England and America, apostolic and catholic. 2. The causes of the English reformation. 3. Its character and results. New York, 1844. 12°

OGLE, CHARLES. Remarks . . on the civil and diplomatic Appropriation Bill [with reference to the expenditure of the President, etc.] ; delivered in the House of Representatives, April 14, 1840. [Washington, 1840.] 8°

OHIO, State of. The Statutes of Ohio and of the North-Western Territory, adopted or enacted from 1788 to 1833 inclusive. Together with the ordinance of 1787 ; the constitutions of Ohio and of the United States, and various public instruments and acts of Congress : illustrated by a preliminary sketch of the history of Ohio, etc.

Edited by S. P. Chase. 3 vol. Cincinnati, 1833-35. 8vo.

2 STATUTES of the State of Ohio of a general nature in force Dec. 7, 1840 ; also, the statutes of a general nature passed by the General Assembly, at their thirty-ninth session, commencing Dec. 7, 1840. Collated, with references to . . decisions . . and to prior laws, by J. R. Swan. Columbus, 1841. 8°

3 VIEW of the Ohio State Fair Grounds, 1854 . . as prepared for the fifth annual fair of the Ohio State Agricultural Society. Cincinnati [1854]. s. sh. fol.

4 NINTH annual Report of the Board of Agriculture of the State of Ohio to the Governor. For the year 1854. Columbus, 1855. 8vo.

OHIO ANNUAL REGISTER (THE), containing a condensed history of the State, with a . . catalogue of all the public officers in the several counties of Ohio, etc. . . for the year 1835. By J. A. Bryan. Columbus [1835]. 12°

OHIO RIVER. Railroad from the banks of the Ohio River to the tide waters of the Carolinas and Georgia. [A series of reports, etc.] Cincinnati, 1835. 8°

OKIE, A. H. Homœopathy : with particular reference to a lecture by Oliver Wendell Holmes. Boston, 1842. 12mo.

OLCOTT, CHARLES. Iron Ships. Specification of Olcott's newly invented self-ballasting iron safety ships. Washington, 1835. 8°

2 Two Lectures on the subjects of slavery and abolition. Massillon, Ohio, 1838. 8°

OLDFIELD, TRAVERSE. "To Δαιμονιον," or the Spiritual Medium. Its nature illustrated by the history of its uniform mysterious manifestation when unduly excited. Boston, 1852. 12mo.

OLIN, STEPHEN. Travels in Egypt,

Arabia Petræa, and the Holy Land. 2 vol. New York, 1843. 8°

2 EARLY Piety the basis of elevated character. A discourse [on 1 John ii. 14] to the graduating clafs of Wesleyan University, August 1850. New York, 1851. 16mo.

3 THE WORKS of Stephen Olin. 2 vol. New York, 1853. 8°

OLIO, or, satirical poetic-hodge-podge, with an illustrative or explanatory dialogue in vindication of the motive. Addrefsed to good nature, humour, and fancy. Philadelphia, 1801. 8°

OLIVER, BENJAMIN LYNDE. Letters on the Kine Pox, and a variety of other medical subjects, written by B. L. Oliver, of Salem, and William Currie, of Philadelphia. Philadel. 1802. 8vo.

2 THE RIGHTS of an American Citizen; with a commentary on State rights and on the constitution and policy of the United States. Boston, 1832. 8°

3 THE LAW Summary; a collection of legal tracts on subjects of general application in businefs. Second edition, corrected and enlarged. Hallowell, 1833. 8°

4 FORMS of Practice; or American precedents in personal and real actions, interspersed with annotations. Second edition. Hallowell, 1840. 8°

5 FORMS in Chancery, admiralty, and at common law; adapted to the practice of the federal and State courts. Boston, 1842. 8°

6 PRACTICAL Conveyancing; a selection of forms of general utility, with notes interspersed. Fourth edition, corrected and enlarged, by P. Oliver. Hallowell, 1845. 8°

OLIVER, DANIEL, M.D. An Addrefs delivered in .. Dartmouth College, upon the induction of the author into the profefsorship of moral and intellectual philosophy, etc. Concord, 1825. 8°

2 FIRST Lines of Physiology; de-

signed for the use of students, etc. Boston, 1835. 8vo.

3 FIRST Lines of Physiology. Third edition. Boston, 1844. 8°

OLIVER, JAMES. Wreck of the Glide, with recollections of the Fijis and of Wallis Island. [Edited by W. G. D.] New York, 1848. 12°

OLIVER, PETER. A Speech delivered in the new Court-house in Plymouth, May 15, 1750, being the first term (of the Court of Common-Pleas, etc. in said county) after the death of Isaac Lothrop, Esq. etc. Boston, 1750. 4°

OLLENDORFF, HEINRICH GODE-FROY. A Key to the exercises in the new method of learning .. Italian. ... Edited by F. Forresti. New York, 1846. 12°

2 OLLENDORFF's New Method of learning ... the German language; to which is added, a systematic outline of German grammar, by G. J. Adler.. Seventh edition. New York, 1848. 12°

3 OLLENDORFF's New Method of learning ... the Italian language. ... With additions and corrections by F. For[r]esti. New York, 1848. 12°

4 A KEY to the exercises in Ollendorff's new method of learning to read, write, and speak the Spanish language: arranged on a new plan, .. by M. Velazquez and T. Simonné. New York, 1848. 12°

OLMSTED, DENISON. Letters on Astronomy, .. in which the elements of the science are familiarly explained in connexion with its literary history. Boston, 1842. 12°

2 LIFE and Writings of E. P. Mason; interspersed with hints to parents and instructors on the training and education of a child of genius. New York, 1842. 12°

3 AN INTRODUCTION to Natural Philosophy... Compiled from various authorities. .... Stereotype edition. New York, 1844. 8°

D D

OLMSTED, Francis Allyn. Incidents of a Whaling Voyage. To which are added observations on the scenery, manners, and customs and miſſionary Stations of the Sandwich and Society Islands. Accompanied by numerous lithographic prints. New York, 1841. 12°

OLMSTED, Frederick Law. Walks and Talks of an American Farmer in England. New York, 1852. 8°
2 A Journey in the seaboard Slave States, with remarks on their economy. New York, 1856. 8°

OLMSTED, Gideon. The whole Proceedings in the case of Olmsted and others versus Rittenhouse's Executrices; ... Together with the act of the Legislature of the State of Pennsylvania, and other matters in relation to this important subject. Collected and arranged by R. Peters, jun. Philadelphia, 1809. 8°

OLNEY, J. A.M. An Improved System of Arithmetic, for the use of families, schools, and academies. Hartford, 1839. 12°
2 A Practical System of Modern Geography.. Simplified and adapted to the capacity of youth... Revised and illustrated by a new and enlarged Atlas... Forty-ninth edition. New York, 1845. 12°, Atlas, 4°

OLSHAUSEN, H. Proof of the genuineneſs of the writings of the New Testament: Translated from the German, with Notes by D. Fosdick. Andover, 1838. 12mo.

ONDERDONK, Benjamin Tredwell, Bishop. A Sermon [on John v. 35] preached .. at the funeral of ... J. H. Hobart, bishop of .. New York, etc. New York, 1830. 8°
2 Works on Episcopacy. With a Preface by the [editor], B. T. Onderdonk, D.D. 2 vol. New York, 1831. 12mo.
3 Bishop Onderdonk's Statement. A statement of facts and circum-

stances connected with the recent trial of the Bishop of New York. New York, 1845. 8°
4 The Proceedings of the Court convened under the third Canon of 1844, in the city of New York, ... Dec. 10, 1844, for the trial of the Right Rev. B. T. Onderdonk, ... Bishop of New York; on a presentment made by the Bishops of Virginia, Tenneſſee, and Georgia. New York, 1845. 8°

ONDERDONK, Henry, the Younger. Documents and Letters intended to illustrate the revolutionary incidents of Queen's County [N. Y.] with connecting narratives, explanatory notes, and additions. New York, 1846. 12°

O'NEIL, Charles. The Military Adventures of C. O'Neil, .. a soldier in the army of Lord Wellington during the memorable Peninsular War and the Continental Campaigns from 1811 to 1815... Engravings. Worcester, Boston [printed], 1851. 12°

ONIS, Luis De. Memoir upon the negotiations between Spain and the United States of America, which led to the treaty of 1819, etc. Translated from the Spanish, with notes, by T. Watkins. Baltimore, 1821. 8°

ONLY SON, or, the history of Jonah Roſs and his mother. Philadelphia [1833]. 8vo.

OPAL (The): a pure gift for the holy days, 1845. Edited by Mrs. S. J. Hale. New York, 1845. 12°

OPDYKE, George. A Treatise on Political Economy. New York, 1851. 12°

ORD, George. Sketch of the life of Alexander Wilson, author of the American Ornithology. Philadelphia, 1828. 8vo.

ORDEAL (The): a critical journal of politicks and literature. Vol. 1. Boston, 1809. 8°

· OREGON. The Oregon Controversy reviewed. In four letters. By a friend of the Anglo-Saxons. New York, 1846. 8vo.

OREGON SPECTATOR. Vol. 1. N° 7. Oregon City, 1846. s. sh. Fol°

O'REILLY, HENRY. Settlement in the West. Sketches of Rochester, with incidental notices of Western New York. A collection of matters designed to illustrate the progreſs of Rochester during the first quarter-century of its existence... Arranged by H. O'Reilly. Rochester,1838. 12°

ORIGIN of the Material Universe, with a description of the manner of the formation of the earth and events connected therewith, from its existence in a fluid state to the time of the Mosaical narrative. Boston,1850. 12°

ORLANDOS, JOANNIS. Report of the evidence and reasons of the award between J. Orlandos and Andreas Luriottis, of the one part, and Le Roy, Bayard and Co. and G. G. and S. Howland, of the other part. By the arbitrators [J. Platt, H. C. De Rham, and A. Ogden]. New York, 1826. 8°

ORNE, HENRY. An Oration, pronounced at Boston, July 4, 1820. .... in commemoration of American Independence. Boston, 1820. 8°

ORPHAN (THE). American Sunday School Union. Philadelphia, 1831. 12mo.

ORR, J. W. Pictorial Guide to the Falls of Niagara: a manual for visiters, etc. Buffalo, 1845. 12°

ORR, J. W. and N. Orr's Book of Swimming; as practised and taught in civilized and savage nations, and used for the preservation of health and life. New York, 1846. 24°

OSBORN, SELLECK. An Oration,

commemorative of American Independence, delivered .. July 4, 1810. New Bedford, 1810. 8°

OSBORNE, MICHAEL, Rev. A Sermon [on Mark xv. 15, 16] preached at the first meeting of the Central Board of Foreign Miſsions. Richmond, 1834. 8°

OSGOOD, DAVID. A Discourse [on Psal. cxlvii. 20] delivered Feb. 19th, 1795, the day set apart for a general thanksgiving through the United States. Boston, 1795. 8vo.

2 A. DISCOURSE [on Gen. viii. 22] delivered on the day of annual thanksgiving, Nov. 19,1795. Boston,1795. 8vo.

3 A DISCOURSE [on Judges ix. 56, 57] delivered before the Lieutenant-Governor .. and the Legislature of Maſsachusetts, May 31, being the day of General Election. [Boston,] 1809. 8°

4 A DISCOURSE [on 2 Sam. xv. 6] delivered at Cambridge in the hearing of the University, April 8, 1810. Cambridge, 1810. 8°

OSGOOD, FRANCES SARGENT, Mrs. The Poetry of Flowers and Flowers of Poetry: to which are added, a simple treatise on botany, with familiar examples, and a copious floral dictionary. Edited by F. S. Osgood. New York, 1846. 12°

2 POEMS. Philadelphia, 1850. 8°

O'SULLIVAN, JOHN L. Report in favour of the abolition of the punishment of death, by law, made to the Legislature of the State of New York, April 14, 1841. Second edition. [With an appendix.] New York, 1841. 8°

OSWALD, JOHN. An Etymological Dictionary of the English Language... Revised and improved .. by J. M. Keagy. To which is appended, a key to the Latin, Greek, and other roots. Philadel. 1847. 12°

, OTEY, JAMES H., Bishop of Tenneßes. The Triennial Sermon before the . . Board of Miſsions of the Protestant Episcopal Church in the United States of America, preached in St. Stephen's Church, Philadelphia . . Sept. 6, 1838 [on Romans xv. 29]. Philadelphia, 1838. 8°

OTHELLO, a tragic Opera, in two acts. Italian and English. New York, 1826. 12°

OTIS, HARRISON GRAY. An oration, delivered July 4, 1788, at . . Boston, in celebration of the anniversary of American Independence. Boston, 1788. 4°

2 LETTER from the Hon. H. G. Otis to the Hon. W. Heath, as chairman of the Roxbury Committee for petitioning Congreſs against permitting merchant veſsels to arm. Boston, April 1798. 8°

3 MR. OTIS's Speech in Congreſs on the Sedition Law, with remarks by the "Examiner" on this important ſubject. Boston [1809!] 8°

4 EULOGY on Gen. A. Hamilton, pronounced at the request of the citizens of Boston, July 26, 1804. Second edition. Boston, 1804. 8°

5 OTIS's Letters in defence of the Hartford Convention and the people of Maſsachusetts. Boston, 1824. 8°

6 AN ADDRESS to the Members of the City Council, on the removal of the Municipal Government to the Old State House. Boston, 1830. 8°

OTIS, HARRISON GRAY, and MELLEN, PRENTISS. Commonwealth of Maſsachusetts. Letter from H. G. Otis and P. Mellen, . . to the Governor [with the report of a committee of the House of Representatives, to whom it was referred ; respecting the claim of the Commonwealth against the United States]. [Boston, 1818.] 8°

OVERMAN, FREDERICK. The Manufacture of Iron in all its various branches . . to which is added an eſsay on the manufacture of steel ;

with one hundred and fifty wood engravings, etc. Philadelphia, 1850. 8°

2 MECHANICS for the millwright, machinist, engineer, civil engineer, architect and student, etc. Philadelphia, 1851. 12°

3 THE MANUFACTURE of Steel : containing the practice and principles of working and making steel. A hand-book for blacksmiths, etc. Philadelphia, 1851. 12°

4 A TREATISE on Metallurgy ; comprising mining, and general and particular metallurgical operations, etc. New York, 1852. 8°

5 THE MOULDERS and Founders' Pocket Guide : a treatise on moulding and founding. . . With an appendix, containing receipts for alloys . . also tables on the strength and other qualities of cast metals. Philadelphia, 1852. 8vo.

OVERTON, JOHN. Tenneſsee Reports, or Cases ruled and adjudged in the Superior Courts of Law and Equity, and Federal Courts for the State of Tenneſsee. 2 vol. Knoxville (Tenneſsee), 1813-17. 8°

OVIDIUS NASO, PUBLIUS. Ovid's Metamorphoses. Translated by Dryden, Congreve, and other eminent persons. 2 vol. New York, 1815. 12°

2 EXCERPTA ex Scriptis P. Ovidii Nasonis. Accedunt notulæ Anglicæ et questiones [by B. A. Gould]. Editio stereotypa. Bostoniæ, 1841. 12°

OUR COUNTRY ; its capabilities, its perils, and its hope ; being a plea for the early establishment of Gospel institutions in the destitute portions of the United States. New York, 1842. 12°

OUSELEY, SIR WILLIAM GORE. Remarks on the statistics and political institutions of the United States, with some observations on the ecclesiastical system of America, her sources of revenue, etc. To which are added, statistical tables, etc. Philadelphia, 1832. 8°.

OUTLINES of Sacred History; from the creation of the world to the destruction of Jerusalem. . . New edition, enlarged and improved. Illustrated with thirty-four engravings on wood. Philadelphia, 1843. 12°

OWEN, DAVID DALE. Report of a geological reconnoisance of the State of Indiana: made in the year 1837, in conformity to an order of the Legislature. Indianapolis, 1839. 8°

2 REPORT of a geological Survey of Wisconsin, Iowa, and Minnesota; and incidentally of a portion of Nebraska Territory. Made under instructions from the United States Treasury department. (Geological report of a survey of a portion of Wisconsin and Minnesota by J. G. Norwood. Geological report on that portion of Wisconsin bordering on the South shore of Lake Superior, by C. Whittlesey. Geological report of local detailed observations, in the valleys of the Minnesota, Mißißippi and Wis-

consin rivers, by B. F. Shumard. Description of the remains of extinct mammalia and chelonia, from Nebraska Territory, by J. Leidy. Appendix illustrations.) 2 vol. Philaphia, 1852. 4°

OWEN, JOHN J. A Greek Reader .. adapted to Sophocles's and Kuhner's Grammars, with notes and a lexicon. New York, 1852. 8°

OWEN, ROBERT DALE. Hints on public Architecture, containing, among other illustrations, views and plans of the Smithsonian Institution; together with an appendix relative to building materials. Prepared, on behalf of the Building Committee of the Smithsonian Institution, by R. D. Owen, Chairman of the Committee. New York, 1849. 4°

OWEN, THOMAS. The Taylor Anecdote Book. Anecdotes and letters of Z. Taylor. With a brief life. New York, 1848. 8°

ABODIE, WILLIAM J. Calidore: a legendary poem. Boston, 1839. 8°

PACIFIC OCEAN. Three years in the Pacific; including notices of Brazil, Chile, Bolivia, and Peru. By an officer of the United States Navy [W. S. W. Ruschenberger]. Philadelphia, 1834. 8vo.

2 AN HISTORICAL Account of the Circumnavigation of the Globe, and of the progreſs of discovery in the Pacific Ocean, from the voyage of Magellan to the death of Cook. New York, 1845. 12°

PACIFICUS, PHILO, *Pseud.* A solemn Review of the Custom of War; showing that war is the effect of popular delusion, and proposing a remedy. Fifth edition. Cambridge, 1816. 8°

PACKARD, CLARISSA. Recollections of a Housekeeper. New York, 1838. 12mo.

PACKARD, FREDERICK A. Thoughts on the condition and prospects of popular education in the United States. By a Citizen of Pennsylvania [F. A. Packard]. Philadelphia, 1836. 8vo.

2 MEMORANDUM of a late visit to some of the principal hospitals, prisons, etc. in France, Scotland, and England, embraced in a letter to the acting Committee of the Philadelphia Society for alleviating the miseries of Public Prisons. Philadelphia, 1840. 8°

3 LETTER from F. A. Packard to the Governor of Pennsylvania, in relation to Public Schools in England. Harrisburg, 1841. 8°

PADDOCK, JUDAH. A Narrative of the Shipwreck of the ship Oswego, on the coast of South Barbary, and of the sufferings of the master and the crew while in bondage among the Arabs, *etc.* New York, 1818. 8vo.

PAGAN AND MOHAMMEDAN COUNTRIES. Condition and Character of Females in Pagan and Mohammedan countries. Bost. 1832. 12mo.

PAGE, DAVID P. Theory and Practice of Teaching; or, the motives and methods of good school-keeping. Seventh edition. Syracuse, 1847. 12°

PAIGE, ALONZO C. Reports of cases argued and determined in the Court of Chancery of the State of New York. Second edition. [Volumes 1, 4, 5, and 6 only, are of the second edition.] Vol. 1-10. Albany, 1839-45. 8°

PAIGE, LUCIUS R. Selections from eminent Commentators, who have believed in punishment after death; wherein they have agreed with Universalists in their interpretation of scriptures relating to punishment. Second edition. Boston, 1840. 12°

PAIGE, REED. A Sermon [on Rom. xiii. 4] preached .. before .. the Governor, .. Council, *etc.* of .. New Hampshire, at the annual Election, June 6, 1805. Concord [1805]. 8°

PAINE, ELIJAH. Reports of Cases

argued and determined in the Circuit Court of the United States for the Second Circuit. Vol. 1. New York, 1827. 8vo.

PAINE, ELIJAH AND DUER, W. The Practice in civil actions and proceedings at Law in the State of New York, in the Supreme Court and other Courts of the State; and also in the Courts of the United States. 2 vol. New York, 1830. 8°

PAINE, MARTYN. Medical and Physiological Commentaries. 2 vol. New York, 1840. 8vo.

2 A THERAPEUTICAL Arrangement of the Materia Medica, or the Materia Medica arranged upon physiological principles, and in the order of the general practical value which remedial agents hold under their several denominations, etc. New York, 1842. 12mo.

3 A LECTURE on the Philosophy of Digestion... Fourth edition. New York, 1844-5. 8vo.

4 THE INSTITUTES of Medicine. New York, 1847. 8vo.

5 A DISCOURSE on the soul and instinct physiologically distinguished from materialism... Enlarged edition. New York, 1849. 8vo.

6 MEMOIR [and remains] of R. T. Paine, by his parents (M. and Mary Ann Paine). New York, 1852. 8vo.

PAINE, ROBERT TREAT, Jun. Works, in verse and prose, with notes. To which are prefixed, sketches of his life, character, and writings. Boston, 1842. 8vo.

PAINE, THOMAS. Letter addressed to the Abbé Raynal on the affairs of North America, in which the mistakes in the Abbé's account of the Revolution of America are corrected and cleared up. Philadelphia printed, Boston reprinted, 1782. 8°

2 LETTER addressed to the Addressers, on the late proclamation [against the work entitled: "The Rights of Man"]. Philadel. 1793. 8°

3 PROSPECTS on the war, and paper currency... First American edition. Baltimore, 1794. 8°

4 THE DECLINE and Fall of the English system of finance. Philadelphia, 1796. 8°

5 THE DECLINE and Fall of the English system of finance... Second American edition. New York, 1796. 12°

6 LETTER to George Washington, .. on affairs public and private. [With an appendix.] Philadelphia, 1796. 8°

7 AN ORATION .. in commemoration of the dissolution of the treaties, and consular convention, between France and the United States of America. Boston, 1799. 8°

8 AGRARIAN Justice opposed to Agrarian law and to Agrarian monopoly, etc. Philadelphia [1800?]. 8°

PAINE, THOMAS, A.M. An Eulogy on the life of General George Washington... Written at the request of the citizens of Newburyport, and delivered at the first Presbyterian meeting-house in that town, Jan. 2, 1800. Newburyport, 1800. 8°

PAINE, WILLIAM, M.D. An Address to the members of the American Antiquarian Society, pronounced in King's Chapel, Boston, on their third anniversary, Oct. 23, 1815. Worcester, 1815. 8°

PAINTING. Handbook of young artists and amateurs in Oil-painting; being chiefly a compilation from the Manual of Bouvier. Appended a new explanatory and critical Vocabulary. New York, 1845. 12mo.

2 PAINTING, its rise and progress, from the earliest ages to the present time. With sketches of the lives and works of eminent artists, and a brief notice of the principal public galleries of art in Europe. By T. C. Boston, 1846. 12°

PALESKE, CHARLES G. Observations on the application for a law to incorporate " The Union Canal

Company," respectfully submitted to the members of. both houses of the Legislature of Pennsylvania. [Philadelphia, 1808.] 8°

PALESTINE. Scenes in Palestine. By a Pilgrim of 1851. Boston, 1852. 12°

PALEY, WILLIAM, *Archdeacon of Carlisle.* Paley's Theology with illustrations. Natural Theology: or evidences of the existence and attributes of the Deity, collected from the appearances of nature. . . Illustrated by the plates and by a selection from the notes of J. Paxton, with additional notes, original and selected for this edition, and a vocabulary of scientific terms, by J. Ware. Boston, 1840. 12°

2 PALEY's Natural Theology; with illustrative notes, *etc.* by Henry, Lord Brougham, and Sir C. Bell. . . . To which are added, preliminary observations and notes, by A. Potter. 2 vol. New York, 1842-45. 12°

PALFREY, JOHN GORHAM. A Sermon [on Exodus xviii. 21, 22] preached . . the Lord's day after the decease of . . J. Parker, Chief Justice of Massachusetts. Boston, 1830. 8°

2 AN ORATION pronounced before the Citizens of Boston, on the anniversary of the Declaration of American Independence, July 4, 1831. Boston, 1831. 8°

3 ELEMENTS of Chaldee, Syriac, Samaritan, and Rabbinical Grammar. Boston, 1835. 8vo.

4 ACADEMICAL Lectures on the Jewish Scriptures and Antiquities. 4 vol. Boston, 1838-52. 8vo.

5 A DISCOURSE on the life and character of the Rev. J. T. Kirkland, *etc.* Cambridge, 1840. 8°

6 LOWELL Lectures on the Evidences of Christianity. . . With a discourse on the life and character of J. Lowell, Jun. by E. Everett. 2 vol. Boston, 1843. 8vo.

7 ABSTRACT exhibiting the condition of the Banks in Massachusetts,

on the first Saturday of October, 1846. Prepared from official returns. Boston, 1846. 8°

8 ABSTRACT exhibiting the condition of the Institutions for savings in Massachusetts, on the last Saturday of October, 1846. Prepared from the official returns. Boston, 1846. 8°

9 ABSTRACT from the returns of Agricultural Societies in Massachusetts, for the year 1845, with selections from addresses at cattle-shows and fairs. Boston, 1846. 8°

10 SPEECH . . on the political aspect of the Slave Question. Delivered in the House of Representatives. Washington, 1848. 8vo.

11 THE RELATION between Judaism and Christianity, illustrated in notes on passages in the New Testament containing quotations from or references to the Old. Boston, 1854. 8vo.

12 *See* MASSACHUSETTS, N° 109-122.

PALISOT DE BEAUVOIS, AMBROISE MARIE FRANÇOIS JOSEPH, *Baron.* Catalogue raisonné du Museum de Mr. C. W. Peale. Philadelphie [1796 ?]. 8vo.

PALMER, AARON H. Letter to the Hon. C. J. Ingersoll, . . containing some brief notices respecting the present state, productions, trade, etc. of the Comoro Islands, Abyssinia, Persia, Burmah, Cochin China, the Indian Archipelago and Japan; and recommending that a special mission be sent by the government of the United States to make treaties, *etc.* New York [1846]. 8°

PALMER, JOHN. The present state of New England impartially considered, *etc.* [By F.L. *i. e.* J. P. *See* NEW ENGLAND, N° 2.] [1689.] 4to.

PALMER, J. C. Thulia: a tale of the Antarctic. [In verse.] New York, 1843. 8°

PALMER, JAMES N. Report of the Engineer upon the several definite locations for the Hartford and Springfield Railroad: with the Acts of Incorporation in Connecticut and Massachusetts. Second edition. Hartford, 1841. 8vo.

PALMER, JOEL. Journal of Travels over the Rocky Mountains to the mouth of the Columbia river, . . during . . 1845 and 1846; containing minute descriptions of the valleys of the Willamette, Umpqua, and Clamet; a general description of Oregon Territory, etc. Cincinnati, 1847. 8°

PALMER, N. B. Report of Mr. Palmer, agent of the State [of Indiana] appointed to examine the state and condition of the State Bank and branches. Dec. 1842. Indianapolis, 1842. 8°

PALMER, RAY. A Discourse [on Psalm ii. 1-12] . . on the state of the civilised world, as related to the kingdom of Christ: etc. Albany, 1852. 8°

PALMER, THOMAS H. The Historical Register; being a history of the late war with Great Britain, and a summary of the proceedings of Congress, including a collection of all the state papers and official documents published during that period, both British and American. 4 vol. Philadelphia, [1814]-1816. 8°

2 PRIZE Essay. The Teacher's Manual: being an exposition of an efficient and economical system of education, suited to the wants of a free people. Boston, 1843. 12°

PANCOAST, JOSEPH. A Treatise on operative surgery; comprising a description of the various processes of the art, including all the new operations. Philadelphia, 1844. 4to.

PANOPLIST (THE)(or the Christian's Armory), conducted by an association of friends to evangelical truth. Vol. 1-3. Boston, 1805-1808. 8° [Continued as] The Panoplist and Missionary Magazine united. Vol. 4-

13; new series, vol. 1, etc. [the numeration of the vols. as forming part of a new series is dropped after vol. 5, and the old numeration from the commencement resumed]. Boston, 1808-17. 8°. [Continued as] The Panoplist and Missionary Herald. Vol. 14-16. Boston, 1818-20. 8°. [Continued as] The Missionary Herald. Published at the expense of the American Board of Commissioners for Foreign Missions. Vol. 17-52. Boston, 1821-56. 8°

PARISH, ELIJAH. A new system of modern geography, with maps. Second edition. Newburyport, 1812. 12°

PARISIAN SIGHTS and French principles, seen through American spectacles. New York, 1852. 12°

PARK, EDWARDS A. The Preacher and Pastor, by Fenelon, Herbert, Baxter, Campbell. Edited and accompanied with an introductory essay by E. A. Park. Andover, 1845. 12°

PARK, MUNGO. The ·Life and Travels of Mungo Park. With the account of his death from the journal of Isaaco, the substance of later discoveries relative to his lamented fate, and the termination of the Niger. New York, 1845. 12°

PARK, ROSWELL. A Sketch of the history and topography of West Point and the United States Military Academy. Philadel. 1840. 12mo.

2 PANTOLOGY; or, a systematic survey of human knowledge; proposing a classification of all its branches, a synopsis of their leading facts and principles, and a select catalogue of books on all subjects. Philadelphia, 1842. 8vo.

3 PANTOLOGY; or, a systematic survey of human knowledge . . Fourth edition, corrected and brought down to the present time. Philadelphia, 1847. 8vo.

4 A HAND-BOOK for American Tra-

vellers in Europe, *etc.* Part 1. New York, 1853. 8°

PARKE, BENJAMIN, AND JOHNSON, OVID F. A Digest of the Laws of Pennsylvania, from . . 7 April, 1830, to 15 April, 1835; with explanatory notes . . Together with references to numerous judicial decisions. Harrisburg, 1836. 8°

PARKE, URIAH. The Farmer's and Mechanic's practical Arithmetic, *etc.* Hartford, 1840. 12°

PARKER, AMASA J. Speech [in the House of Representatives] . . on the amendment proposed by Mr. Howard, declaring that Mefàrs. Prentifs and Word were not entitled to seats in the 25th Congrefs. Washington, 1838. 8°

PARKER, DANIEL. Proscription delineated; or a development of facts appertaining to the arbitrary and oppreffive proceedings of the North [Congregationalist] Affociation of Litchfield County, in relation to the author. Hudson, 1819. 12°

PARKER, EDWARD L. The History of Londonderry, comprising the towns of Derry and Londonderry, N[ew] H[ampshire.] [Edited] With a memoir of the author [by E. P. Parker]. Boston, 1851. 8°

PARKER, HENRY W. Poems. Auburn, 1850. 12°

PARKER, JOEL, *LL. D.* An Addrefs delivered before the Affociation in Keene, for the promotion of temperance, Aug. 5, 1829. Keene, 1830. 12°

2 DANIEL Webster as a Jurist. An Addrefs to the students in the Law School of the University at Cambridge. . . Second edition. Cambridge, 1853. 8°

PARKER, JOEL, *D. D.* Sermons on various subjects. Philadelphia, 1852. 8°

PARKER, JOHN A. The quadra-

ture of the circle; containing demonstrations of the errors of geometry in finding the approximation in use, the quadrature of the circle and practical questions on the quadrature, applied to the astronomical circles. With an appendix. New York, 1851. 8°

PARKER, JOHN R. A Treatise upon the telegraphic science: with some remarks upon the utility of telegraphs; *etc.* Boston, 1835. 8°

PARKER, LEONARD M. An Oration, pronounced at Charlestown, Massachusetts, . . 4 July, 1816, by request of the republican citizens of Middlesex County, being the fortieth anniversary of American Independence. Boston, 1816. 8°

PARKER, NATHAN, *D.D.* A Sermon [on John viii. 12] preached . . before . . the . . council and . . legislature of . . New Hampshire, June 3, 1819, being the anniversary Election. Concord, 1819. 8ᵘ

PARKER, RICHARD GREENE. Progreffive Exercises in rhetorical reading, *etc.* Boston, 1835. 12°

2 PARKER's geographical questions . . prepared particularly for Worcester's Atlas, *etc.* Boston, 1842. 12°

3 NATIONAL School Series. Introductory leffons in reading and elocution. Part first. Leffons in reading, by R. G. Parker... Part second. Lessons in elocution, by J. C. Zachos, *etc.* New York, 1852. 12°

PARKER, RICHARD GREENE, AND FOX, CHARLES. Progreffive exercises in English grammar. Part I. . . Tenth edition. Boston, 1843. 12°

2 THE SAME, Part II. . . Fourth edition. Boston and N. York, 1839. 12°

3 THE SAME, Part III. *etc.* Boston, 1840. 12°

PARKER, S. D. Report of the arguments of the Attorney of the Commonwealth (S. D. Parker), at the trials of A. Kneeland, for blasphemy, in the Municipal and Supreme Courts in Boston, Jan. and May, 1834. Boston, 1834. 8°

PARKER, SAMUEL. Journal of an exploring tour beyond the Rocky Mountains, under the direction of the A. B. C. F. M. performed in the years 1835, '36, and '37· Ithaca, 1838. 12mo.

PARKER, THEODORE. The Critical and miscellaneous writings of T. Parker. Boston, 1843. 12°

2 A SERMON [on Exod. xv. 3, and 1 John, iv. 8] of war, preached at the Melodeon, etc. Boston, 1846. 8°

3 A SERMON of Merchants [on Ecclesiasticus xxvii. 2] preached .. Nov. 22, 1846. Boston, 1847. 8°

4 A LETTER to the people of the United States touching the matter of Slavery. Boston, 1848. 12°

5 THE THREE chief safeguards of society, .. a sermon [on Prov. xiv. 34]. Boston, 1851. 8°

6 SPEECHES, addresses, and occasional sermons. 2 vol. Boston, 1852. 12°

7 A DISCOURSE, occasioned by the death of D. Webster, preached .. at the Melodeon on Sunday, October 31, 1852. Boston, 1853. 8°

PARKHURST, JOHN L. A Systematic Introduction to English Grammar. . . Second edition, enlarged and improved. Concord, 1824. 12°

PARKMAN, FRANCIS, the Elder, D.D. A Discourse [on John v. 35] ... occasioned by the death of the Rev. J. T. Kirkland, etc. Boston, 1840. 8°

PARKMAN, FRANCIS, the Younger. The California and Oregon Trail; being sketches of Prairie and Rocky Mountain life. New York, 1849. 12°

2 HISTORY of the Conspiracy of Pontiac, and the war of the North American tribes against the English Colonies after the conquest of Canada. Boston, 1851. 8°

PARKS, GORHAM. Speech ... . on the bill regulating the public deposites: delivered in the House of Representatives, June 22, 1836. Washington, 1836. 8°

PARLEY, PETER, Pseud. [i.e. Samuel Griswold Goodrich]. Peter Parley's Tales of Animals, containing descriptions of three hundred quadrupeds, birds, fishes, reptiles, and insects. Revised edition, with questions and other improvements. Louisville, 1845. 12°

2 PETER Parley's Tales about the sun, moon, and stars. Philadelphia, 1845. 16°

3 THE TALES of Peter Parley about Asia. Revised edition. Philadelphia, 1846. 12°

4 THE TALES of Peter Parley about Africa. Revised edition. Philadelphia, 1845. 12°

PARRISH, JOHN. Remarks on the Slavery of the Black People; addressed to the Citizens of the United States. Philadelphia, 1806. 8vo.

PARRY, SIR WILLIAM EDWARD, Admiral. Three Voyages for the discovery of a North-West Passage from the Atlantic to the Pacific, and narrative of an attempt to reach the North Pole. 2 vol. New York, 1844-1845. 12°

PARSONS, HORATIO A. A Guide to travellers visiting the Falls of Niagara. . . Second edition, greatly enlarged. Buffalo, 183[5]. 12°

PARSONS, J. U. Analytical Geography, a system of teaching by single topics. Framingham, 1838. 16°

2 ANALYTICAL Vocabulary, or analytical system of teaching orthography. . Second edition. Framingham, and Boston, 1838. 12°

PARSONS, LEVI. The Dereliction and Restoration of the Jews: a sermon [on Hosea iii. 4, 5] preached .. before the departure of the Palestine

Miſſion. (The Holy Land an interesting field of miſsionary enterprise, a sermon [on Acts xx. 22] .. by P. Fisk.) 2 pts. Boston, 1819. 8°

PARSONS, Patty. Patty Parsons and the Plum-cake. American Sunday School Union, Philadel. [1830?]. 12°

PARSONS, S. B. The Rose: its history, poetry, culture, and claſsification. New York, 1847. 8°

PARTISAN (The): a tale of the [American]Revolution. By the author of "The Yemaſsee," .. etc. [William Gilmore Simms]. 2 vol. New York, 1835. 12°

PARTRIDGE, A. Prospectus of the American literary, scientifick, and military Academy. Windsor [1820]. 8°

PASTOR. The Patient Pastor. American Sunday School Union, Philadelphia, 1831. 12°

PASTORAL. A Pastoral for the Times: the Church's Chain of Authority from God, to minister in the Word and Sacraments. [By G. W. Doane.] Burlington, N.J. 1844. 8vo.
2 A Pastoral for the season of Confirmation: Baptism; Confirmation; the Supper of the Lord. [By G.W. Doane.] Burlington, 1844. 8vo.

PASTORINI, Sig. Pseud. [i.e. Charles Walmesley, Bishop of Rama]. The General History of the Christian Church, from her birth to her final triumphant state in Heaven: chiefly deduced from the Apocalypse of St. John, the Apostle and Evangelist. By Sig. Pastorini. Fourth American edition. New York, 1846. 12°

PATHFINDER Railway Guide for the New England States: A. E. Newton, editor. N° 23. Boston, 1851. 16mo.

PATRICK, William. Historical

Sketches of Canterbury, N(ew H(ampshire): a sermon [on Job viii. 8, 9] at the close of the thirtieth year of the author's ministry. Concord, 1834. 8°

PATROON. The Young Patroon, or Christmas in 1690. A Tale of New York, by the author of the "First of the Knickerbockers" [i.e. P. Hamilton Myers]. New York, 1849. 12°

PATTEN, Rev. William. On the Inhumanity of the Slave-Trade, and the importance of correcting it: a sermon [on Prov. xxiv. 11, 12] delivered in .*. Newport, Rhode Island, Aug. 12, 1792. Providence, 1793. 12°

PATTERSON, A. C. A View of American Unitarian Miſsions: with Thoughts on the Miſsionary Cause, and the interest of Unitarians in it. Boston, 1838. 12mo.

PATTIE, James O. Personal Narrative during an Expedition from St. Louis through the regions between that Place and the Pacific Ocean. With a description of the country and the various nations. Edited by T. Flint. Cincinnati, 1833. 8vo.

PATTISON, Granville Sharp. A Lecture delivered in Jefferson Medical College, Philadelphia, on the question "Has the parotid gland ever been extirpated?" Philadelphia, 1833. 8°

PAUL, afterwards PAUL JONES, John. Life and Correspondence of J. Paul Jones, including his narrative of the campaign of the Liman. From original letters and manuscripts in the poſseſsion of Miſs Janette Taylor. [Edited by S. Converse?]. New York, 1830. 8°
2 Life of Rear Admiral John Paul Jones, Chevalier of the Military Order of Merit, and of the Ruſsian Order of St. Anne, etc. Compiled from his original journals and correspondence: including an account

of his services in the American Revolution, *etc.* [Edited by B. Walker?] Philadelphia, 1847. 12°

PAULDING, James Kirke. The Backwoodsman: a poem. Philadelphia, 1818. 12°

2 Koninosmarke, or Old Times in the New World. 2 vol. New York, 1834-36. 12mo.

3 Letters from the South. By a Northern man. New edition. 2 vol. New York, 1835. 12mo.

4 Salmagundi; or the Whim-whams and opinions of Launcelot Langstaff and others. First Series. [By J. K. Paulding, Washington Irving, and William Irving.] New edition. 2 vol. New York, 1835. 12mo.

5 Salmagundi; Second Series. 2 vol. New York, 1835. 12mo.

6 The Diverting History of John Bull and Brother Jonathan. By Hector Bull-us. New edition. New York, 1835. 12mo.

7 A Life of Washington. 2 vol. New York, 1835. 12mo.

8 Slavery in the United States. New York, 1836. 12°

9 Tales of the Good Woman. By a Doubtful Gentleman. New edition. 2 vol. New York, 1836. 12mo.

10 The Book of Saint Nicholas. Translated from the original Dutch of Dominie Nicholas Aegidius Oudenarde. New York, 1836. 12mo.

11 The Dutchman's Fireside. A Tale. Fifth edition. 2 vol. New York, 1837.

12 The Merry Tales of the Three Wise Men of Gotham. New York, 1839. 12mo.

13 Affairs and Men of New Amsterdam, in the time of Governor Peter Stuyvesant, compiled from Dutch manuscript records of the period. New York, 1843. 12°

14 A Life of Washington. 2 vol. New York, 1845. 12°

PAULDING, James Kirke, and Paulding, William Irving. Ame-

rican Comedies: . . . Contents: The bucktails, or Americans in England; The noble exile; Madmen all, or the cure of love: Antipathies, or the enthusiasts by the ears. Philadelphia, 1847. 8°

PAXTON, J. D. Letters on Slavery; addressed to the Cumberland Congregation, Virginia. Lexington [Philadelphia printed], 1833. 12mo.

PAXTON, Philip. A Stray Yankee in Texas. New York, 1853. 12°

PAYNE, William W. Speech . . on the proposition to refund the fine to Gen. Jackson [imposed on him for declaring martial law at New Orleans, in 1815]; delivered in the House of Representatives, Jan. 28, 1843. [Washington, 1843.] 8°

PAYSON, Edward, D.D. Memoir, select thoughts, and sermons, of the late . . E. Payson. Compiled by . . A. Cummings. 3 vol. Portland, 1846. 8°

PAYSON, Seth. A Sermon [on Eccl. ix. 18] preached . . before . . the Governor, . . Council, *etc.* of . . . . New Hampshire [at the annual Election]. Portsmouth, 1799. 8°

PEABODY, Andrew Preston. The nature and influence of war: an address delivered before the American Peace Society, at its annual meeting, May 29, 1843. Boston, 1843. 8°

2 The Uses of Classical Literature: an address delivered before the United Literary Societies of Dartmouth College, *etc.* July 26, 1843. Boston, 1843. 8°

3 Lectures on Christian Doctrine. Second edition, with an introductory lecture on the Scriptures. Boston, 1844. 12°

4 Christian Consolations: sermons designed to furnish comfort and strength to the afflicted. Boston, 1847. 8°

PEABODY, Elizabeth P. Crimes

of the House of Austria against mankind; collected from accredited history, and edited by E. P. Peabody. New York, 1852. 8°

PEABODY, Ephraim. An addreſs delivered at the centennial celebration in Wilton [New Hampshire], .. With an appendix. Boston, 1839. 8°

2 A Discourse [on Matt. xviii. 5] delivered at the first public meeting of the New Bedford Orphan's Home, Dec. 7, 1842. Boston, 1842. 8vo.

PEABODY, Nathaniel. First Leſſons in Grammar, on the plan of Pestalozzi. By a teacher in Boston. Boston, 1830. 12°

PEABODY, Stephen. A sermon [on Exod. xviii. 21] delivered before the .. General Court of the State of New Hampshire, at the annual Election, etc. Concord, 1797. 8°

PEABODY, Oliver William Bourne. An Addreſs delivered before the Peace Society, of Exeter, N(ew) H(ampshire), at their annual meeting, etc. Exeter (New Hampshire), 1830. 8°

2 Address delivered at the consecration of the Springfield Cemetery, etc. Springfield, 1841. 8°

3 Sermons by .. W. B. O. Peabody, with a memoir by his [twin] brother [i. e. O. W. B. Peabody]. Second edition. Boston, 1849. 12°

• PEACOCK, Timothy, Pseud. The Adventures of T. Peacock, Esquire, or Freemasonry practically illustrated; comprising a practical history of Masonry, exhibited in a series of amusing adventureſ of a Masonic Quixot. By a member of the Vermont-bar [Daniel P. Thompson]. Middlebury, 1835. 12°

PEAKE, Thomas. A Compendium of the Law of Evidence. Walpole, N. H. 1804. 8°

2 A Compendium of the Law of Evidence .. The second American, from the second London edition, with

very considerable additions. Philadelphia, 1806. 8°

PEALE, C. W. Discourse introductory to a course of Lectures on the science of Nature. Philadelphia, 1800. 8vo.

2 Introduction to a course of Lectures on Natural History. Philadelphia, 1800. 8vo.

PEALE, Rembrandt. Portfolio of an Artist. Philadelphia, 1839. 12mo.

PEARSON, Eliphalet. A Letter to the Candid; occasioned by the publications of Rev. B. Whitman [on the Unitarian controversy in Maſſachusetts]. Boston, 1831. 8°

PEASE, John C., and NILES, John M. A Gazetteer of the States of Connecticut and Rhode Island. . . From original and authentic materials. 2 parts. Hartford, 1819. 8°

PECK, Jacob. Reports of Cases argued and adjudged in the Supreme Court of Errors and Appeals of the State of Tenneſſee, commencing Sept. term, 1822, and ending with May term, 1824. Knoxville, Tenneſſee, 1824. 8°

PECK, James H. Report of the trial of J. H. Peck, Judge of the United States District Court for the district of Miſſouri, before the Senate of the United States, on an impeachment preferred by the House of Representatives against him for high misdemeanours in office. By A. J. Stansbury. Boston, 1833. 8°

PECK, John, and Lawton, J. An Historical Sketch of the Baptist Missionary Convention of the State of New York; embracing a narrative of the origin and progreſs of the Baptist denomination in Central and Western New York. With .. biographical notices of the founders of the Convention, etc. Utica, 1837. 12°

PECK, John M. A Gazetteer of Illinois; in three parts. Jacksonville, 1834. 16mo.

2 A GAZETTEER of Illinois, in three parts, *etc.* Second edition, revised, corrected and enlarged. Philadelphia, 1837. 12mo.

3 A NEW Guide for Emigrants to the West; containing sketches of Michigan, Ohio, Indiana, Illinois, Miſſouri, Arkansas, with the Territory of Wisconsin, and the adjacent parts. Second edition. Boston, 1837. 12°

PECK, WILLIAM DANDRIDGE. A Catalogue of American and foreign Plants, cultivated in the Botanic Garden, Maſſachusetts. Cambridge, 1818. 8vo.

PEDDER, JAMES. Report made to the Beet Sugar Society of Philadelphia, on the culture in France of the beet root, and manufacture of sugar therefrom, with miscellaneous remarks on the same, and on the culture of the poppy and extraction of salad oil, *etc.* Philadelphia, 1836. 8°

PEERS, BENJAMIN O. American Education: or strictures on the nature, neceſſity and practicability of a system of National Education, suited to the United States. With an introductory letter, by Francis L. Hawks. New York, 1838. 12mo.

PEET, EDWARD W. The True Glory of the Church. A sermon, delivered in St. Paul's Church, Rahway, on the 150th anniversary of the Society for the Propagation of the Gospel in Foreign Parts. New York, 1851. 8°

PEIRCE, BENJAMIN. A History of Harvard University, from its foundation, in 1636, to the American Revolution. [Edited by J. Pickering.] Cambridge, 1833. 8°

2 AN ELEMENTARY Treatise on Sound; being the second volume of a course of natural philosophy, *etc.* Boston, 1836. 8°

3 AN ELEMENTARY Treatise on Plane Geometry. . . Printed for the use of the blind [in emboſſed typography]. Boston, 1840. 4°

4 AN ELEMENTARY Treatise on Plane and Solid Geometry. Boston, 1841. 12°

5 AN ELEMENTARY Treatise on Curves, Functions, and Forces. (Vol. 1, containing analytic geometry, and the differential calculus.) Boston, 1841. 12°

6 AN ELEMENTARY Treatise on Curves, Functions, and Forces. Volume second; containing calculus of imaginary quantities, residual calculus and integral calculus. Boston, 1846. 12°

7 AN ELEMENTARY Treatise on Plane and Spherical Trigonometry, with their applications to navigation, surveying, heights and distances, and spherical astronomy; and particularly adapted to explaining the construction of Bowditch's Navigator, *etc.* Third edition, with additions. Boston, 1845. 12°

8 AN ELEMENTARY Treatise on Algebra: to which are added exponential equations and logarithms. . . Fifth edition. Boston, 1845. 12°

PEIRCE, DAVID, *Auditor of Accounts for the State of Vermont.* Auditor's Report to the General Assembly of the State of Vermont, *etc.* [Oct. 12, 1842. With an appendix of reports]. [Woodstock? 1842.] 8°

2 ANNUAL Report of the Auditor of Accounts of the State of Vermont, made to the Legislature, Oct. 12, 1843. [With an appendix of documents.] Woodstock, 1843. 8°

3 ANNUAL Report of the Auditor, . . Oct. 10, 1844. Woodstock, 1844. 8°

4 ANNUAL Report of the Auditor, . . Oct. 9, 1845. Woodstock, 1845. 8°

PEIRCE, OLIVER B. The Grammar of the English language. New York, 1839. 12°

2 PEIRCE's Abridgement of the Grammar of English language. Boston, New York, and Watertown, 1840. 12°

PEIRSON, ABRAHAM. Some Helps

for the Indians; shewing them how to improve their natural reason, to know the true God, and the Christian Religion. 1. By leading them to see the Divine Authority of the Scriptures. 2. By the Scriptures, the Divine truths neceſſary to eternal salvation. By Abraham Peirson, Pastor of the Church at Branford. Examined and approved by that experienced gentleman (in the Indian language) Captain John Scott. Cambridge: Printed for Samuel Green, 1658. *English and Natick Indian.* 16mo.

PELLICO, Silvio. My Prisons, memoirs of Silvio Pellico. [Translated from the Italian. Edited, with notes, by A. Norton.] (Additions .. With a biographical notice of Pellico by P. Maroncelli. Translated from the Italian.) 2 vol. Cambridge, 1836. 12mo.

PENDER, Thomas. The Divinity of the Scriptures, from reason and external circumstances: a sermon [on 2 Tim. iii. 16]. New York, 1728. 8°

PENDLETON, John S. Speech .. on the Oregon question; delivered in the House of Representatives, .. Jan. 26, 1846. Washington, 1846. 8°

PENFEATHER, Amabel, *Pseud.* Elinor Wyllys; or the young folk of Longbridge. A tale, by Amabel Penfeather. Edited by J. F. Cooper. 2 vol. Philadelphia, 1846. 12°

PENHALLOW, Samuel. The History of the Wars of New England with the Eastern Indians. Or, a narrative of their continued perfidy and cruelty, from the 10th of August, 1703, to the peace renewed 13th of July, 1722, to their submiſſion 15th December, 1725. Which was ratified August 5, 1726. By Samuel Penhallow, Esqr. Boston: printed by T. Fleet for S. Gerrish, at the lower end of Cornhill, and D. Henchman, over-against the Brick Meeting-House in Cornhill, 1726. 8vo.

PENINGTON, John. An Examination of Beauchamp Plantagenet's

Description of the Province of New Albion. Philadelphia, 1840. 8°

2 Scraps, osteologic and archæological. Read before the Council of the Historical Society of Pennsylvania. Fifty copies printed. Philadelphia, 1841. 8vo.

PENNINGTON, William Sanford. Reports of cases argued and determined in the Supreme Court of Judicature of the State of New Jersey; from May term, 1806, to Sept. 1813, inclusive. Second edition, by J. Harrison. Camden, 1835. 8°

PENNSYLVANIA, *Province and State of.*

1 The Laws of the Province of Pennsilvania, collected into one volumn by order of the Governour and Aſſembly. Printed and sold by Andr. Bradford in Philadelphia, 1714. Fol.

2 Acts of the Province of Pennsylvania paſſed in the General Assembly held at Philadelphia, 1720 and 1721. Philadelphia, 1721. Fol.

3 A Collection of Charters and other publick acts relating to the Province of Pennsylvania, *etc.* B. Franklin, Philadelphia, 1740. Fol.

4 A True and impartial State of the Province of Pennsylvania; being a full answer to the pamphlets, intitled, " A brief state, and a brief view .. of the conduct of Pennsylvania." [With an appendix.] Philadelphia. 1759. 8vo.

5 The Charters and Acts of Assembly of the Province of Pennsylvania. (Appendix, *etc.*) 2 vol. Philadelphia, 1762. Fol°

6 The Acts of Aſſembly of the Province of Pennsylvania, carefully compared with the originals; and an appendix, containing such acts, and parts of acts, relating to property, as are expired, altered, or repealed; together with the royal, proprietary, city, and borough charters, and the original conceſſions of the Hon. W. Penn to the first settlers of the Pro-

vince. Published by order of Assembly. Philadelphia, 1775. Fol°

7 THE ACTS of the General Assembly of .. Pennsylvania; carefully compared with the originals, [and edited, by T. Mackean]; and an appendix, containing the laws now in force, pafsed between .. Sept. 30, 1775 and the Revolution; together with the Declaration of Independence, etc. Philadelphia, 1782. Fol°

8 AHIMAN Rezon abridged and digested: as a help to all .. free and accepted Masons. To which is added, a sermon [on 1 Pet. ii. 16] preached in .. Philadelphia, .. Dec. 28, 1778, .. by W. Smith, D. D. Philadelphia, 1783. 8°

9 CONSIDERATIONS upon the present test-law of Pennsylvania. Second edition. Philadelphia, 1785. 12mo.

10 COMPILATION of the Laws of the State of Pennsylvania, relative to the poor, from the year 1700 to 1795 inclusive. Published for the guardians of the poor. [Edited by W. Franklin.] (Ordinances, rules, and byelaws for the almshouse, and house of employment.) 2 parts. Philadelphia, 1796. 8°

11 LETTER from the Secretary [A. J. Dallas] of the Commonwealth of Pennsylvania, by direction of the Governor, relative to the late malignant fever: and report of the Board of the Marine and City Hospitals, in reply. Philadelphia, 1798. 8vo.

12 THE DISSENT of the minority of the House of Representatives of the Commonwealth of Pennsylvania, from the addrefs to the President of the United States, adopted by said house, December, 1798. [Philadelphia? 1799?] 8°

13 A BRIEF Account of the proceedings of the Committee, appointed by the yearly meeting of Friends of Pennsylvania, New Jersey, etc. for promoting the improvement of the Indian nation. Philadel. 1806. 8vo.

14 PETITION of sundry inhabitants of the eleventh Congrefsional district

of the State of Pennsylvania [in relation to the judicial power of the United States, under the Constitution, in controversies concerning land claims]. Washington, 1806. 8°

15 RESOLUTIONS .. proposing an amendment to the Constitution of the United States, relative to the terms of continuance in .. office of the judges of the .. Courts of the United States. (Feb. 11, 12, 1808.) Washington, 1808. 8°

16 MEMOIRS of a Life, chiefly pafsed in Pennsylvania, within the last sixty years, with occasional remarks upon the general occurrences, character, and spirit of that period. [By Alexander Graydon. See GRAYDON.] Harrisburgh, 1811. 12°

17 ADDRESS to the Citizens of Pennsylvania on the encouragement of Agriculture. Philadel. 1818. 8vo.

18 SOCIETY for promoting internal improvement in the Commonwealth. The first annual report of the acting Committee. Philadelphia, 1826. 8°

19 COMMISSIONERS appointed to revise the penal code. Report on punishments and prison discipline. Second edition. Philadel. 1828. 8°

20 ANTI-MASONIC State Convention. Proceedings at Harrisburg, Feb. 25, 1830, and May 25, 1831. [Harrisburg?] 1831. 8vo.

21 A CONCISE History of the Eastern Penitentiary of Pennsylvania, together with a detailed statement of the proceedings of the Committee appointed, 1834, for the purpose of examining into the economy and management of that institution. By a Member of the Legislature. Philadelphia, 1835. 8vo.

22 LETTERS on the comparative merits of the Pennsylvania and New York systems of Penitentiary discipline. By a Mafsachusetts Man. Boston, 1836. 8°

23 THE PRESENT State and Condition of the free people of color of the City of Philadelphia and adjoining districts, as exhibited by the report of

a Committee of the Pennsylvania Society for promoting the Abolition of Slavery. Philadelphia, 1838. 8°

24 MINUTES of the Provincial Council of Pennsylvania, from the organization to the termination of the Proprietary Government. 3 vol. Harrisburg, 1838. 8°

25 LETTERS and Papers relating chiefly to the Provincial History of Pennsylvania [by J. Swift, E. Shippen, and others ; edited by T. Balch ? With MS. corrections]. Philadelphia, 1855. 8vo.

PENNSYLVANIA CHRONICLE (THE). N° 192. Sept. 17, 1770. Philadelphia, 1770. Fol.

PENNSYLVANIA EVENING HERALD (THE). N° 127. April 12, 1786. Philadelphia, 1786. Fol.

PENNSYLVANIA EVENING POST. N° 303, 312, 313, 322, 325. Philadelphia, 1777. Fol.

PENNSYLVANIA GAZETTE (THE). N° 1336-1502. Aug. 1st 1754, to Oct. 1757. [Wanting N° 1353, 1379-81, 1393, 1395, 1444-47, 1468, 1469, 1475-76, 1491, 1493-95, 1497-99, 1501.] Philadelphia, 1754-57. Fol.

PENNSYLVANIA GAZETTE (THE). N° 2440, 2468-69, 2471, 2491, 2514-15, 2522, 2710, 2861, 2771, 2852, 2859, 2862-63, 2866-68, 2918. Sept. 27, 1775, to May 3, 1786. Philadel. 1775-86. Fol.

PENNSYLVANIA GAZETTE (THE). May 2, 1778. York Town, 1778. Fol.

PENNSYLVANIA HALL. History of Pennsylvania Hall, which was destroyed by a mob, . . May 17, 1838. Philadelphia, 1838. 8°

PENNSYLVANIA HOSPITAL. Some account of the Pennsylvania Hospital, from its first rise to . . May, 1754. Philadelphia, 1817. 8°

PENNSYLVANIA INQUIRER and Daily Courier. Vol. 20, N° 94. April 19, 1839. Philadel. 1839. Fol.

PENNSYLVANIA INSTITUTION for the Instruction of the Blind. [Exhibition, Nov. 1833.] [Philadelphia, 1833.] 8°

2 [FORM of application for admission.] [Philadelphia, 1833 ?] Fol°

3 [ADDRESS to the inhabitants of Pennsylvania.] [Philadelphia, 1834.] Fol°

4 FIRST Annual Report of the Managers, also the constitution, charter, and by-laws, 1834. [Philadelphia, 1834.] 8°

5 CONSTITUTION, charter, and by-laws and documents relating to the Pennsylvania institution for the instruction of the blind. [Philadelphia,] 1837. 8°

PENNSYLVANIA JOURNAL and the Weekly Advertiser (The). N° 1627, 1661, 1774, 1786, 1792, 1796, 1799, 1800, 1812, 1368, 1597, 1607, 1608, 1614, 1617, 1623, 1624, 1633, 1635, 2048. Feb. 9, 1774, to Jan. 25, 1786. Philadelphia, 1774-1786. Fol.

2 THE PENNSYLVANIA Journal and Weekly Advertiser. N° 1674 to 1760. Jan. 4, 1775, to Aug. 28, 1776 [wanting N° 1698]. Philadelphia, 1775-76. Fol.

PENNSYLVANIA LEDGER (THE), or the Virginia, Maryland, Pennsylvania, and New Jersey Weekly Advertiser. N° 84. Philadelphia, 1776. Fol.

PENNSYLVANIA MAGAZINE (THE), or American Monthly Museum. Jan. to Dec. 1775. Vol. 1. [N° 1 is of the second edition.] Philadelphia, 1775. 8vo.

PENNSYLVANIA PACKET AND General Advertiser (The). [Continued under the title of Pennsylvania Packet and Daily Advertiser.] N° 1612, 1616, 1618, 2124, 2256-9.

Oct. 1783 to May, 1786. Philadelphia, 1783-86. Fol.

PENNSYLVANIA SOCIETY. The constitution of the Pennsylvania Society for the Abolition of Slavery. Philadelphia, 1787. 8vo.

PENNSYLVANIA SOCIETY for promoting the culture of the Mulberry, and the raising of Silkworms. Constitution, etc. [Philadelphia, 1828.] 8vo.

PENNSYLVANIAN Examination of a tract on the alteration of the tariff written by T. Cooper, M.D. By a Pennsylvanian. Third edition. To which are added irrefragable arguments in favour of the protection of manufactures, by the same T. Cooper. Philadelphia, 1824. 12°
2 AN EXAMINATION of the Report of a Committee of the citizens of Boston and its vicinity opposed to a further increase of duties on importation. By a Pennsylvanian. Philadelphia, 1828. 8vo.

PEPPERGRASS, PAUL, Pseud. The Spaewife; or the Queen's secret: a story of the reign of Elizabeth. 2 vol. Baltimore, 1853. 8°

PEQUA RAILROAD AND IMPROVEMENT COMPANY. Report to the directors of the Pequa Railroad and Improvement Company. Philadelphia, 1849. 8°

PERCIVAL, JAMES GATES. Poems, by J. G. Percival. New York, 1823. 8vo.
2 REPORT on the Geology of the State of Connecticut. New Haven, 1842. 8vo.
3 THE DREAM of a Day, and other poems. New Haven, 1843. 12°

PERCIVAL, MARGARET. Margaret Percival in America: a tale. Edited by a New England Minister, A. B. Being a sequel to Margaret Percival: a tale [by Miss E. Sewell]

edited by the Rev... W. Sewell. Boston, 1850. 12°
2 MARGARET Percival in America. A tale. Edited by a New England Minister, A. B. being a sequel to M. Percival. A tale [by Miss E. Sewell], edited by .. W. Sewell, B. A. Second edition. Boston, 1850. 12°

PERDICARIS, G. A. The Greece of the Greeks. 2 vol. New York, 1845. 12°

PERIODICAL   PUBLICATIONS, etc. See.
ACADEMIES.
ADAM's Boston Directory, 1846. See BOSTON Directory.
ADVOCATE of Peace, Boston, 1837.
AFRICAN Repository, Washington, 1825.
ALBANY Argus, Albany, 1832.
ALBANY Directory.
ALLEGHANY Magazine, Meadville, Pennsylvania, 1816.
AMARANTH, Boston, 1853.
AMERICAN, New York, 1821.
AMERICAN Advertising Directory, New York, 1831.
AMERICAN Almanac, Boston, 1831.
AMERICAN Annals of Education. See AMERICAN Journal of Education. Boston.
AMERICAN Annual Register, New York, 1825.
AMERICAN Baptist Register, Philadelphia, 1852.
AMERICAN Biblical Repository. See BIBLICAL Repository.
AMERICAN Calendar and United States Register, Philadelphia, 1794.
AMERICAN Ephemeris and Nautical Almanac, Washington, 1852.
AMERICAN Farmer, Baltimore, 1821.
AMERICAN Gardener's Magazine, Boston, 1835; continued as MAGAZINE of Horticulture, Boston.
AMERICAN Journal and Library of Dental Science, New York, 1839.
AMERICAN Journal of Education, Boston, 1828.
AMERICAN Journal of Education, by H. Barnard, Hartford, 1856.

AMERICAN Journal of Insanity, Utica.
AMERICAN Journal of Science, by Silliman, New Haven, 1818.
AMERICAN Journal of the Medical Sciences, Philadelphia, 1828.
AMERICAN Labourer, New York, 1843.
AMERICAN Law Journal, Philadelphia, 1808.
AMERICAN Literary Magazine, by T. D. Sprague, Albany, 1847.
AMERICAN Magazine [by N. Webster], New York, 1787.
AMERICAN Magazine and Monthly Chronicle, Philadelphia, 1757.
AMERICAN Magazine of Useful Knowledge, Boston, 1839.
AMERICAN Mechanics' Magazine, New York, 1825.
AMERICAN Medical and Philosophical Register, New York, 1814.
AMERICAN Monthly Magazine, New York, 1833.
AMERICAN Monthly Magazine and Critical Review, New York, 1817.
AMERICAN Monthly Review, Cambridge, 1832.
AMERICAN Museum, Philadelphia, 1787.
AMERICAN National Preacher, New York, 1826. See NATIONAL Preacher.
AMERICAN Oriental Society, Journal, Boston, 1843.
AMERICAN Polytechnic Journal, Washington and New York.
AMERICAN Publishers' Circular, New York, 1855.
AMERICAN Pulpit, Boston, 1831; afterwards PROTESTANT Episcopal Pulpit, New York, 1832.
AMERICAN Pioneer, Cincinnati, 1843.
AMERICAN Quarterly Observer, Boston, 1833.
AMERICAN Quarterly Register, Andover and Boston, 1829; continuation of QUARTERLY Register. See AMERICAN Education Society.
AMERICAN Quarterly Review, Philadelphia, 1827.
AMERICAN Quarterly Temperance Magazine, Albany, 1833.
AMERICAN Railroad Journal, New York, 1832.

AMERICAN Register, or General Repository of History, etc. Philadelphia, 1807.
AMERICAN Register, or Summary Review of History, etc. Philadelphia, 1817.
AMERICAN Review and Literary Journal, New York, 1801.
AMERICAN Review and Whig Journal, New York, 1845; afterwards AMERICAN Whig Review.
AMERICAN Review of History, Politics, etc. Philadelphia, 1811.
AMERICAN Turf Register, Baltimore, 1830.
AMERICAN Weekly Meſsenger, Philadelphia, 1814.
AMERICAN Whig Review; continuation of AMERICAN Review and Whig Journal, New York, 1848.
ANALECTIC Magazine, Philadelphia, 1813.
ANNUAL Law Register, Burlington, New Jersey, 1822.
ANNUAL of Scientific Discovery, Boston, 1850.
ANTI-Masonic Review, New York, 1828.
ANTI-Slavery Examiner, New York, 1836.
ANTI-Slavery Record, New York, 1835.
ANTI-Slavery Reporter, New York, 1833.
APPLETON's Mechanics' Magazine, New York, 1850.
ARCTURUS, New York, 1841.
ARMY and Navy Chronicle, by B. Homans, Washington, 1834.
ARMY and Navy Chronicle and Scientific Repository, by W. Q. Force, Washington, 1843.
ASTRONOMICAL Journal, Cambridge, 1851.
ATLANTIC Journal and Friend of Knowledge, Philadelphia, 1832.
ATLANTIC Magazine, New York, 1824.
ATLANTIC Souvenir, Philadelphia, 183-?
BALTIMORE Book, 1838.
BALTIMORE Directory, 1845.
BALTIMORE Medical and Physical Recorder, 1809.

BALLOU's Pictorial; *continuation of* GLEASON's Pictorial, Boston.

BANKER's Almanac, Boston.

BANKER's Magazine, Baltimore,1847; and Boston, 1852.

BIBLICAL Repertory, Princeton and Philadelphia, 1825.

BIBLICAL Repository, Andover, 1831.

BIBLIOTHECA Sacra, Andover, 1843.

BOSTON Almanac, 1836.

BOSTON Book, Boston, 1837.

BOSTON Chronicle, Boston, 1768.

BOSTON Evening Post, Boston, 1769.

BOSTON Directory, 1798.

BOSTON Gazette, 1769.

BOSTON Journal of Philosophy, 1823.

BOSTON Journal of Natural History, 1837.

BOSTON Monthly Magazine, 1825.

BOSTON Notion, Boston, 1839.

BOSTON Post Boy, 1769; *afterwards* MASSACHUSETTS Gazette.

BOSTON Quarterly Review (Brownson's), 1838.

BOSTON Weekly News Letter, 1769.

BOWEN's Boston News Letter, 1826.

BROADWAY Journal, New York, 1845.

BROWNSON's Quarterly Review, Boston, 1844. *See* BOSTON Quarterly Review.

CALUMET; New Series of the HARBINGER of Peace, New York, 1831.

CANFIELD and Warren's Directory of Rochester, New York, 1845. *See* ROCHESTER Directory.

CENSUS Directory, Philadelphia, 1811. *See* PHILADELPHIA Directory.

CHARLESTON Medical Journal, 1853; *continuation of* SOUTHERN Journal of Medicine.

CHEROKEE Meſſenger, Cherokee, 1845.

CHILD of Pallas, Baltimore, 1800.

CHILD's Albany Directory, 1835. *See* ALBANY Directory.

CHILD's Paper, New York, *etc.* 1852.

CHRISTIAN Advocate, Philadelphia, 1823.

CHRISTIAN Baptist, Cincinnati, 1835.

CHRISTIAN Disciple, Boston, 1813; *afterwards* CHRISTIAN Examiner, Boston, 1824.

CHRISTIAN Examiner. *See* CHRISTIAN Disciple.

CHRISTIAN History, Boston, 1744.

CHRISTIAN Inquirer, New York, 1826.

CHRISTIAN Journal and Literary Register, New York, 1817.

CHRISTIAN Review, Boston, 1836.

CHRISTIAN Scholar's and Farmer's Magazine, Elizabeth's Town, New Jersey, 1789.

CHRISTIAN Spectator, New Haven. *See* QUARTERLY Christian Spectator.

CHURCH Review, New Haven, 1848.

CINCINNATI Buſineſſ Directory, 1844. *See* CINCINNATI Directory.

CINCINNATI, Covington, Newport, and Fulton Directory, 1849. *See* CINCINNATI Directory.

CINCINNATI Daily Whig, 1839.

CINCINNATI Directory, 1834.

CINCINNATI Weekly Whig, 1839.

COLLECTIONS, Topographical, Historical, *etc.* by Farmer and Moore, Concord, New Hampshire, 1823.

COLONIZATION Herald, Philadelphia, 1848.

COLONIZATIONIST, Boston, 1833.

COLUMBIAN Centinel, Boston. *See* MASSACHUSETTS Centinel.

COLUMBIAN Magazine, Philadelphia, 1786; *afterwards* UNIVERSAL Asylum and Columbian Magazine.

COLUMBIAN Phœnix, Boston, 1800.

COMMERCIAL Review of the South and West, by De Bow, New Orleans, 1846.

COMMON School Journal, Boston, 1839.

CONGRESSIONAL Globe, Washington, 1834.

CONNECTICUT Common School Journal, Hartford, 1838.

CONNECTICUT Evangelical Magazine, Hartford, 1800.

CONNECTICUT Gazette, New London, 1782.

CORONAL, New York, 1853.

CORSAIR, New York, 1839.

COVINGTON Directory. *See* CINCINNATI Directory.

CRITERION, New York, 1856.

CRITIC, New York, 1828.

CULTIVATOR, Albany, 1834.
DAILY Advertiser, New York, 1786.
DAILY Evening Transcript, Boston, 1839.
DAILY Herald, Newburyport, 1839.
DAILY Sun, Cincinnati, 1839.
DARTMOUTH, Hanover, N. H. 1840.
DAYSPRING, Boston, 1842.
DE BOW's Review, New Orleans, 1846. See COMMERCIAL Review of the South and West.
DEMOCRATIC Review. See UNITED States Magazine and Democratic Review, 1838.
DESILVERS Philadelphia Directory, 1828. See PHILADELPHIA Directory.
DEW Drop, Philadelphia, 1853.
DIAL, Boston, 1841.
DIRECTORIES. See the several Towns.
DOGGETT's New York City Directory. See NEW York Directory.
DUNLAP's Maryland Gazette, Baltimore, 1778.
DUNLAP's Pennsylvania Packet, Philadelphia, 1775; afterwards PENNSYLVANIA Packet.
DWIGHT's American Magazine, New York, 1845.
EASTERN Argus, Portland, 1839.
ECLECTIC Magazine, 1845. See LITERATURE of the World, 1841.
ECLECTIC Repertory, Philadelphia, 1811.
ELLYSON's Richmond Directory, 1845. See RICHMOND Directory.
EMERALD, Boston, 1806.
EMPORIUM of Arts and Sciences, Philadelphia, 1812.
EVENING Mirror, New York, 1844.
EXCHANGE Advertiser, Boston, 1786.
FEDERALIST, New York, 1788.
FINANCIAL Register of the United States, Philadelphia, 1837.
FOREIGN Missionary Chronicle, Pittsburgh, 1833.
FRANKLIN Journal, Philadelphia, 1826; afterwards JOURNAL of the Franklin Institute. See FRANKLIN Institute, Philadelphia.
FREEMAN's Journal, Philadelphia, 1783.

FRIEND, Philadelphia, 1820.
FRIEND of Peace, Cambridge, 1816.
FULTON Directory. See CINCINNATI Directory.
GALLERY of Illustrious Americans, New York, 1850.
GARDNER's Hartford Directory, 1838. See HARTFORD Directory.
GAZETTE of the State of Georgia, Savannah, 1785.
GEER's Hartford Directory, 1842. See HARTFORD Directory.
GEM of the Season, New York, 1848.
GEM of the Western World, New York, 1850.
GENERAL Repository and Review, Cambridge, 1812.
GEORGETOWN Directory. See WASHINGTON Directory.
GIFT, Philadelphia, 1836.
GIFT for all Seasons, New York, 1853.
GLEASON's Pictorial Drawing Room Companion, Boston, 1851; afterwards BALLOU's Pictorial, Boston.
GODEY's Lady's Book, Philadelphia. See LADY's Book.
GOOD Book, by C. Rafenesque, Philadelphia, 1840.
GREAT Metropolis, or Guide to New York, for 1848. See NEW York.
GREEN Mountain Repository, Burlington, Vt. 1832.
HARPER's New Monthly Magazine, New York, 1850.
HARTFORD Directory.
HESPERIAN, Columbus and Cincinnati, 1838.
HIEROPHANT, New York, 1844.
HOFFMAN's Albany Directory, 1838. See ALBANY Directory.
HOMŒOPATHIC Examiner, New York, 1845.
HUNT's Merchants' Magazine, New York, 1851. See MERCHANTS' Magazine, 1839.
IDLE Man, New York, 1821.
INDEPENDENT Chronicle, Boston, 1786.
INDEPENDENT Gazette and New York Journal, 1784.
INDEPENDENT Gazetteer and Chronicle of Freedom, Philadel. 1783.

INDEPENDENT Journal, New York, 1784.

INDEPENDENT Ledger, Boston, 1786.

INDIANA Annual Register, Indianapolis, 1844.

INTERNATIONAL Monthly Magazine, New York, 1850.

IRIS, an Illuminated Souvenir, Philadelphia, 1852.

JEW, by S. H. Jackson, New York, 1824.

JEWISH Chronicle, New York, 1844.

JEWISH Intelligencer, New York, 1837.

JONES' New York Mercantile Directory, 1805. *See* NEW York Directory.

JOURNAL of Health, Philadelphia, 1830.

JOURNAL of the American Institute, New York, 1836. *See* AMERICAN Institute.

JOURNAL of the American Oriental Society. *See* AMERICAN Oriental Society, 1843.

JOURNAL of the Franklin Institute, Philadelphia, 1826. *See* FRANKLIN Institute.

JOURNAL of the Rhode Island Institute of Instruction, Providence, 1846.

JUNIUS Tracts, New York, 1844.

KEEPSAKE, New York, 1853.

KENTUCKY State Register, Louisville, 1847.

KIMBALL and James' Business Directory of the Mississippi Valley, Cincinnati, 1844.

KING's Rochester Directory. *See* ROCHESTER Directory.

KNICKERBOCKER, New York, 1833.

LADY's Book, Philadelphia, 1830; *afterwards* GODEY's Lady's Book, 1840.

LADIES' Companion, New York, 1834.

LANTERN, New York, 1852.

LAW Reporter, Boston, 1839; *afterwards* MONTHLY Law Reporter, 1849.

LIBERATOR, Boston, 1839.

LILY of the Valley, Boston, 1853.

LITERARY and Scientific Repository, New York, 1820.

LITERARY and Theological Review, by L. Woods, jr. New York, 1834.

LITERARY Magazine and American Register, Philadelphia, 1803.

LITERARY Miscellany, Cambridge, 1805.

LITERARY World, New York, 1847.

LITERATURE of the World, New York, 1841; *afterwards* ECLECTIC Magazine, 1845.

LORGNETTE. New York.

LOUISIANA Law Journal. New Orleans, 1842.

LOUISVILLE Daily Journal.

LOUISVILLE Directory, Louisville Ky. 1832.

LOUISVILLE Journal, Louisville Ky. 1839.

LOWELL Directory, 1834.

LOWELL Offering, Lowell, 1841; *afterwards* NEW England Offering, 1848.

M'ELRAY's Philadelphia Directory, 1837. *See* PHILADELPHIA Directory.

MAGAZINE of Horticulture, by Hovey, Boston. *See* AMERICAN Gardener's Magazine.

MAGNOLIA, by H. W. Herbert, New York, 1836.

MAGNOLIA, by C. Arnold, Boston, 1852.

MANCHESTER Directory, Manchester, N. H. 1852.

MARYLAND Gazette, Annapolis, 1770.

MARYLAND Gazette, Baltimore, 1778. *See* DUNLAP's Maryland Gazette.

MARYLAND Journal and Baltimore Advertiser, 1777.

MASSACHUSETTS Agricultural Repository, Boston. *See* MASSACHUSETTS Society for Promoting Agriculture.

MASSACHUSETTS Centinel. Boston, 1787; *afterwards* COLUMBIAN Centinel, 1798.

MASSACHUSETTS Gazette, Boston, 1769.

MASSACHUSETTS Gazette, Boston, 1786.

MASSACHUSETTS Gazette and Boston Post Boy, Boston, 1770. *See* BOSTON Post Boy.

MASSACHUSETTS Gazette and Boston Weekly News Letter, Boston, 1770.

MASSACHUSETTS Quarterly Review, Boston, 1847.

MASSACHUSETTS Register and State Calendar, Boston, 1801.

MASSACHUSETTS SPY, Boston, 1774.

MASSACHUSETTS State Record, Boston, 1847.

MECHANIC's Magazine, New York, 1833.

MEDICAL and Agricultural Register, Boston, 1806.

MEDICAL Repository, New York, 1800.

MERCHANT's Magazine, New York, 1839; afterwards HUNT's Merchant's Magazine, 1851.

METHODIST Magazine, New York, 1818; afterwards METHODIST Quarterly Review.

METHODIST Preacher, Boston, 1830.

METHODIST Quarterly Review, Boston. See METHODIST Magazine.

MILITARY and Naval Magazine of the United States. Washington, 1833.

MINUTE Gun. Worcester, 1845.

MISSIONARY, Burlington, New Jersey, 1835.

MISSIONARY Herald, Boston. See PANOPLIST.

MOBILE Directory, 1844.

MONTHLY American Journal of Geology, Philadelphia, 1831.

MONTHLY Anthology, Boston, 1804.

MONTHLY Chronicle of Events, Boston, 1840.

MONTHLY Journal of Agriculture, New York, 1845.

MONTHLY Law Reporter, Boston. See LAW Reporter.

MONTHLY Magazine and American Review, New York, 1799.

MONTHLY Military Repository, New York, 1796.

MONTHLY Miscellany (by D. Wells), New York, 1848.

MONTHLY Rose, Albany, 1845.

MORNING Courier and New York Enquirer, 1838.

MORAL Reformer, Boston, 1835.

MOTHER's Magazine, (London).

MOTHERS' Monthly Journal, Utica, 1836; afterwards MOTHER's Journal and Family Visitant.

MUNSELL's Albany Directory, 1852. See ALBANY Directory.

NANTUCKET Inquirer, 1839.

NATIONAL Advocate, New York, 1821.

NATIONAL Anti-Slavery Standard, New York, 1847.

NATIONAL Gazette and Literary Advertiser, Philadelphia, 1820.

NATIONAL Preacher, New York, 1826.

NATIONAL Register, Washington, 1816.

NATURALIST, Franklin College, Nashville Ky. 1846.

NAVAL Magazine, New York, 1836.

NEWARK Directory, Newark, N. J. 1852.

NEW Bedford Daily Mercury, 1839.

NEW Bedford Directory, No. 7, 1852.

NEW England Chronicle, Cambridge, 1776.

NEW England Farmer, Boston, 1823.

NEW England Historical and Genealogical Register, Boston, 1847.

NEW England Journal of Medicine, Boston, 1812.

NEW England Magazine, Boston, 1831.

NEW England Offering, Lowell, 1848. See LOWELL Offering.

NEW Englander, New Haven, 1843.

NEW Hampshire Gazette, Annapolis.

NEW Jerusalem Magazine, Boston, 1828.

NEW Jersey Gazette, Trenton, 1780.

NEW Jersey Journal, Chatham, N. J.

NEW Mirror, New York, 1853.

NEW Orleans Commercial Bulletin, 1839.

NEWPORT Mercury, Newport, Rhode Island, 1763.

NEW YORK Annual Register, by E. Williams, 1834.

NEW YORK As it is, New York, 1835.

NEW YORK City and Partnership Directory, 1843. See NEW York Directory.

NEW YORK City Hall Recorder, New York, 1842.

NEW YORK Commercial Advertiser, 1832.

NEW YORK Directory.

NEW YORK Ecclesiologist, 1848. See NEW YORK Ecclesiological Society.

New York Evening Post, 1821.
New York Gazette, 1733.
New York Gazette and Weekly Mercury, 1773.
New York Gazetteer and Country Journal, 1784.
New York Mercury, Extraordinary, 1783.
New York Mirror, 1824.
New York Morning Post, 1783.
New York Packet, 1784.
New York Quarterly Review, 1852.
New York Review and Quarterly Church Journal, 1837.
New York Standard Extra, 1832.
New York State Register, New York, 1845.
New York Times and Commercial Intelligencer, 1839.
New World, New York, 1840.
Niles' Weekly Register, Baltimore, 1811. See Weekly Register.
Nineteenth Century, Philadelphia, 1848.
Norfolk and Portsmouth Journal, Norfolk, Virginia, 1786.
North American Review, Boston, 1815.
Norton's Literary Advertiser, New York, 1852; afterwards Norton's Literary Gazette.
Norton's Literary Almanac, New York, 1852; continued as Norton's Literary Register, 1853; then Norton's Literary and Educational Register, 1854; and now Norton's Literary Register and Annual Book List, 1856.
Observer and Repertory of Original and Select Essays, Baltimore, 1806.
Occident, Philadelphia, 1845.
Ohio Annual Register, Columbus, 1835.
Opal, New York, 1845.
Ordeal, a Critical Journal of Politics and Literature, Boston, 1809.
Oregon Spectator, Oregon City, 1846.
Panoplist, Boston, 1805; afterwards Panoplist and Missionary Magazine, 1808; then Panoplist and Missionary Herald, 1818; and now Missionary Herald, 1821.

Pathfinder Railway Guide, Boston, 1851.
Pennsylvania Chronicle, Philadelphia, 1770.
Pennsylvania Evening Herald, Philadelphia, 1786.
Pennsylvania Evening Post, Philadelphia, 1777.
Pennsylvania Gazette, Philadelphia, 1754.
Pennsylvania Gazette, Philadelphia, 1775.
Pennsylvania Gazette, York Town, 1778.
Pennsylvania Inquirer and Daily Courier, Philadelphia, 1839.
Pennsylvania Journal and Weekly Advertiser, Philadelphia, 1774.
Pennsylvania Ledger, Philadelphia, 1776.
Pennsylvania Magazine, Philadelphia, 1775.
Pennsylvania Packet, Philadelphia, 1779. See Dunlap.
Pennsylvania Packet and General Advertiser, Philadelphia, 1783; afterwards Pennsylvania Packet and Daily Advertiser.
Philadelphia Directory, 1802.
Philadelphia Index or Directory, 1823. See Philadelphia Directory.
Philadelphia Medical and Physical Journal, 1805.
Philadelphia Register and National Recorder, 1819.
Pittsburgh Directory, 1813.
Poet's Offering, Philadelphia, 1850.
Political Censor, Philadelphia, 1796.
Polyanthos, Boston, 1806.
Portfolio, Philadelphia, 1801.
Portland Directory, 1834.
Presbyterian Magazine, Philadelphia, 1851.
Princeton Review. See Biblical Repertory.
Protestant Episcopal Pulpit. See American Pulpit.
Providence Directory, 1852.
Providence Gazette, Providence, Rhode Island, 1776.
Public Ledger, Philadelphia, 1839.

PUTNAM's Monthly, New York, 1853.

QUARTERLY Christian Spectator, New Haven, 1829.

QUARTERLY Register and Journal of the American Education Society, Andover and Boston, 1827. *See* AMERICAN Education Society.

QUARTERLY Review of the American Protestant Association, Philadelphia, 1844.

QUARTERLY Theological Magazine, Burlington, New Jersey, 1813.

REGISTER of Officers and Agents of the United States, Washington.

REGISTER of Pennsylvania, by S. Hazard, Philadelphia, 1828.

REGISTER of the Army and Navy, Washington.

RELIGIOUS Cabinet. *See* UNITED States Catholic Magazine.

RELIGIOUS Magazine, Philadelphia, 1828.

RELIGIOUS Souvenir for 1839, Hartford, 1845.

REPUBLICAN Farmer, Bridgeport, 1839.

RHODE ISLAND Republican, Newport, 1839.

RICHMOND Directory, 1845.

RIVINGTON's New York Gazetteer, 1773.

ROBINSON and Jones' Cincinnati Directory, 1846. *See* CINCINNATI Directory.

ROBINSON's Directory of Philadelphia, 1817. *See* PHILADELPHIA Directory.

ROCHESTER Directory.

ROSE OF SHARON, Boston, 1853.

ROYAL American Gazette, New York, 1781.

ROYAL Gazette, New York, 1778.

ROYAL Gazette, Charleston, 1782.

ROYAL Georgia Gazette, New York, 1779.

RURAL Magazine, Rutland, Vermont.

SALEM Advertiser, Salem, Massachusetts, 1839.

SALEM Directory.

SARTAIN's Union Magazine. *See* UNION Magazine.

SAVANNAH Republican, Savannah, 1839.

SELECT Reviews and Spirit of Foreign Magazines, Philadelphia, 1809.

SILLIMAN's Journal. *See* AMERICAN Journal of Science, 1819.

SOUTH Carolina Gazette, Portsept, Charleston, 1740.

SOUTH Carolina Gazette, Charleston, 1783.

SOUTHERN Journal of Medicine, 1846; *afterwards* CHARLESTON Medical Journal, 1847.

SOUTHERN Literary Messenger, Richmond, 1835.

SOUTHERN Review, Charleston, 1828.

SPIRIT of the English Religious Magazines, Burlington, New Jersey, 1835.

STEPHENS' Philadelphia Directory, 1796. *See* PHILADELPHIA Directory.

STIMPSONS' Boston Directory, 1831. *See* Boston Directory.

STRANGER, Albany, 1814.

THEATRICAL Censor, Philadelphia, 1805.

THEOLOGICAL and Literary Journal, by D. N. Lord, New York, 1848.

TO-DAY, Boston, 1852.

TOKEN and Atlantic Souvenir, Boston, New York and Boston, 1835.

TROY Directory.

UNION Magazine, New York, 1847; *afterwards* SARTAIN's Union Magazine, Philadelphia.

UNITARIAN, Cambridge, 1834.

UNITARIAN Miscellany, Baltimore, 1822.

UNITED STATES Catholic Magazine, Baltimore, 1842.

UNITED STATES Digest, by J. P. Putnam, Boston, 1850.

UNITED STATES Law Journal, New Haven, 1822.

UNITED STATES Literary Gazette, Boston, 1825; *afterwards* UNITED STATES Review and Literary Gazette, 1827.

UNITED STATES Magazine and Democratic Review, Washington, 1838; *afterwards* DEMOCRATIC Review, New York.

UNITED STATES Review and Literary Gazette.

UNIVERSAL Asylum and Columbian Magazine. *See* COLUMBIAN Magazine.

UNIVERSALIST Quarterly and General Review, Boston, 1844.

VIRGINIA Gazette, or American Advertiser, Richmond, 1786.

VIRGINIA Gazette and Weekly Advertiser, Richmond, 1787.

WAR, New York, 1813.

WASHINGTON and Georgetown Directory, 1853.

WEEKLY Herald, New York, 1840.

WEEKLY Register, by H. Niles, Baltimore, 1811.

WESTERN Review, Lexington, 1820.

WOODWARD and Rowland's Pittsburgh Directory, 1852.

WORCESTER Magazine and Historical Journal, 1826.

YALE Banger, New Haven, 1850.

YALE Tomahawk, New Haven, 1850.

YANKEE, 1828; *afterwards* YANKEE and Boston Literary Gazette.

PERKINS, A. J. and FITCH, G. W. A Manual of the Origin and Meaning of Geographical Names. New York, 1852. 12°

PERKINS, CHARLES. An Oration, pronounced at the request of the citizens of Norwich, Conn. on the anniversary of American Independance, July 4th, 1822. Norwich, 1822. 8°

PERKINS, GEORGE R. Higher Arithmetic, designed for the use of high schools, academies, and colleges, *etc.* Utica, 1841. 12°

2 A TREATISE on Algebra, embracing, besides the elementary principles, all the higher parts usually taught in colleges, *etc.* Utica, 1842. 8°

3 PLANE Trigonometry and its application to mensuration and land surveying. Accompanied with all the necessary logarithmic and trigonometric tables. New York, 1852. 8°

PERKINS, JAMES HANDASYD. The Memoir and Writings of J. H. Perkins.

Edited by W. H. Channing. 2 vol. Boston, 1851. 12°

PERKINS, JUSTIN. A Residence of eight years in Persia, among the Nestorian Christians; with notices of the Muhammedans. Andover, 1843. 8vo.

PERKINS, LAFAYETTE. A Poem, delivered on the celebration of Independence; . . at Wilton, Maine. Hallowell, 1828. 8°

PERKINS, SAMUEL. The History of the Political and Military Events of the late war between the United States and Great Britain. New Haven, 1825. 8vo.

PERLEY, DANIEL. A Grammar of the English Language. Andover. 12°

PERLEY, IRA. Eulogy . . on the late D. Webster, pronounced before the executive and legislative departments of New Hampshire. Dec. 22, 1852. Concord, 1852. 8°

PERRY, GARDNER B. An Address to the Essex County Agricultural Society, delivered . . Sept. 7, 1832, at their annual cattle-show. Salem, Mass. 1833. 8°

PERRY, M. C. *Commodore.* A Paper by Commodore M. C. Perry, read before the American Geographical and Statistical Society. (The enlargement of geographical science a consequence to the opening of new avenues to commercial enterprise.) New York, 1856. 8vo.

PERRY, WILLIAM. Alger's Perry. The Orthoepical Guide to the English Tongue, being Perry's Spelling-book, revised and corrected, with Walker's pronunciation precisely applied on a new scale. . . By I. Alger. Boston, 1832. 12°

PETER, WILLIAM. Specimens of the poets and poetry of Greece and Rome, by various translators. Edited by W. Peter. Philadelphia, 1847. 8°

PETERS, John R. Miscellaneous remarks upon the government, history, religions, literature, agriculture, arts, trades, manners and customs of the Chinese; as suggested by an examination of the .. Chinese Museum in the Marlborough Chapel, Boston. Boston, 1845. 8°

PETERS, Richard. A Sermon [on John viii. 32] on Education. Wherein some account is given of the Academy, established in the city of Philadelphia, preach'd at the opening thereof; etc. B. Franklin and D. Hall. Philadelphia, 1751. 8vo.

PETERS, Richard, the Younger. Admiralty Decisions in the District Court of the United States for the Pennsylvania district, by the Hon. R. Peters, comprising also some decisions in the same court, by the late Francis Hopkinson, Esq. To which are added, Cases determined in other districts. .. With an appendix, etc. [Collected and edited by R. Peters, jun.] 2 vol. Philadelphia, 1807. 8°

2 A Discourse on Agriculture. Philadelphia, 1816. 8vo.

3 Reports of Cases argued and determined in the Supreme Court of the United States. 1828-43. 17 vol. Philadelphia, Boston, 1839-43. 8vo.

4 A Full and Arranged Digest of the decisions in common law, equity, and admiralty of the courts of the United States, from the organization of the government in 1789 to 1847, in the Supreme, Circuit, District, and Admiralty Courts; .. with an appendix containing the rules and orders of the Supreme Court, etc. 2 vol. Philadelphia, 1848. 8°

PETERS, Samuel, LL.D. A History of the Rev. Hugh Peters .. Member of the celebrated Assembly of Divines .. With an appendix. New York, 1807. 8°

PETERSBURG, Virginia. Resolutions of the inhabitants of .. Petersburg, etc. [concerning the violation of the commercial rights of neutrals.] (Feb. 8, 1806.) Washington, 1806. 8°

PETERSON, Charles J. A Naval Story of the War of 1812. .. Cruising in the last war. Philadelphia [1850]. 8°

PETIT, Joseph. Marengo, or the campaign of Italy by the army of reserve, under the command of the Chief Consul Bonaparte. Translated from the French of J. Petit. To which is added, a biographical notice of the life and military actions of General Desaix. With a map of the seat of war. By C. Foudras. Philadelphia, 1801. 8°

PETTIGRU, J. L. An Oration delivered before the Phi Kappa and Demosthenian Societies of the University of Georgia, etc. Athens, Ga. 1846. 8°

PHARMACOPŒIA (The) of the United States of America. By authority of the National Medical Convention, held at Washington, A.D. 1840. Philadelphia, 1842. 8vo.

PHELPS'S New York City Guide. New York, 1852. 12°

2 Phelps's Hundred Cities and large towns of America: with railroad distances throughout the United States, etc. New York, 1853. 8°

PHELPS, Almira, H. L. Address on the subject of Female Education in Greece, and general extension of Christian intercourse among females. Troy, 1833. 8°

PHELPS, Charles. An Address, delivered in Townshend, .. 4 July, 1811 [in celebration of American Independence]. Brattleboro', 1811. 8°

PHELPS, Elizabeth Stuart, Mrs. The Fireside Friend, or Female Student: being advice to young ladies on the important subject of education. With an appendix on moral and religious education; from the French of

Madame de Sauffure. Boston, 1840.
12mo.

2 THE LAST Leaf from Sunny Side.
By H. Trusta (Mrs. E. S. Phelps) ..
With a memorial of the author, by A.
Phelps. Boston [Andover printed],
1853. 12°

PHELPS, JOHN. The Legal
Claffic, or young American's first
book of rights and duties, etc. Amherst, 1835. 16°

PHELPS, SAMUEL S. Substance
of the Speech of Mr. Phelps .. on the
.. Tariff; delivered in the Senate ..
Feb. 16 and 19, 1844. Washington,
1844. 8°

2 MR. PHELPS's Appeal to the
People of Vermont, in vindication of
himself against the charges made
against him [by W. Slade,] upon the
occasion of his re-election to the
Senate of the United States, in relation to his course as a Senator. Middlebury, 1845. 8°

3 To the People of Vermont. Mr.
Phelps's rejoinder to Mr. Slade's
"Reply." [Washington? 1845.] 8°

PHENIX (THE); a collection of
old and rare fragments: viz. the
Morals of Confucius .. the Oracles of
Zoroaster .. Sanchoniatho's history
of the Creation .. the Voyages of
Hanno .. Hiempsal, history of the
African settlements .. and the choice
sayings of Publius Syrus. New York,
1835. 12mo.

PHI BETA KAPPA SOCIETY.
The New York Phi Beta Kappa Society. Circular to the Members in
relation to literary and scientific transactions. Schenectady, 1833. 8°

PHILADELPHIA, City of. Plain
Truth: or, serious considerations on
the present state of the city of Philadelphia and province of Pennsylvania.
[Second edition.] By a tradesman of
Philadelphia [i. e. B. Franklin]. Philadelphia, 1747. 8vo.

2 PROCEEDINGS of the Fœderal

Convention held at Philadelphia in
the year 1787. Philadel. 1787. 8vo.

3 THE CHARTER, Constitution and
Bye-Laws of the College of Physicians
of Philadelphia. Philadel. 1790. 8vo.

4 DES Prisons de Philadelphie.
Par un Européen. Philadelphie,
1796. 8vo.

5 MINUTES of the proceedings of
the fourth convention of delegates
from the Abolition Societies .. of the
United States affembled at Philadelphia .. May 1797. Philadelphia,
1797. 8°

6 REPRESENTATION of the Philadelphia Chamber of Commerce [in
relation to a bill depending in the
House of Representatives of the
United States of America, to regulate
the clearance of armed merchant ves-
sels]. Dec. 10, 1804. [Washington,
1804.] 8°

7 GUIDE to the Philadelphia Museum. [Philadelphia, 1804.] 8vo.

8 MEMORIAL of sundry manufacturers of hats, in .. Philadelphia
[with other documents relating to the
Indian fur trade, submitted to the
committee of commerce and manu-
factures]. Washington, 1806. 8°

9 MEMORIAL of the merchants and
traders of the city of Philadelphia
[to the President and Congress of the
United States of America]. Jan. 16,
1806. Washington, 1806. 8°

10 MEMORIAL of the members of the
Chamber of Commerce of Philadel-
phia, relative to the Bank of the United
States. Washington, 1810. 8°

11 LETTER to the Directors of the
Banks of Philadelphia on the curtail-
ment of discounts and the effects of
the organization of the Bank of the
United States. Philadelphia, 1816. 8°

12 [Begins] To the Hon. Senate
and House of Representatives of the
United States. Memorial of the Philadelphia Society for the promotion
of American Manufactures. [Phila-
delphia, 1818.] 8°

13 JOURNAL, acts, and proceedings
of the convention affembled at Phila-

delphia .. May 14, and diſſolved .. Sept. 17, 1787, which formed the Constitution of the United States. Boston, 1819. 8º

14 SECOND annual Report of the Comptrollers of the Public Schools, of the first school diſtrict of the State of Pennsylvania. Philadelphia, 1820. 8vo.

15 HOUSE of Refuge. [Resolution respecting one, Nov. 20, 1826.] 8vo.

16 AN ADDRESS from the managers of the House of Refuge to their fellow citizens, Philadelphia. Philadelphia, 1826. 8vo.

17 PHILADELPHIA in 1830-1 : or, a brief account of the various institutions and public objects in this metropolis, etc. Philadel. 1830. 12º

18 THE JOURNAL of the Free Trade Convention, held in Philadelphia, .. Sept. 30 to Oct. 7, 1831 ; and their addreſs to the people of the United States. To which is added, a sketch of the debates in the convention. Philadelphia, 1831. 8º

19 FRIENDS of Education in Greece. [Begins] Fellow citizens. [A circular inviting subscriptions, etc. for the establishment of an American seminary in Athens.] Philadelphia, 1831. s. sh. fol.

20 HISTORY of the Orphan Asylum in Philadelphia. Philadelphia [1831]. 12mo.

21 REPORT of the Committee to whom was referred sundry memorials against lighting the city with Gas. Philadelphia, 1833. 8º

22 PROCEEDINGS of the Aſſociation for establishing a School for the education of the Blind in Philadelphia and Pennsylvania, under J. R. Friedlander. Philadelphia [1833]. 8º

23 REPORT on the Debtors' Apartment of the Arch Street Prison, Philadelphia. Harrisburg, 1833. 8º

24 THE PHILADELPHIA Book, or specimens of metropolitan literature. Philadelphia, 1836. 12mo.

25 REPORTS of the Trustees of the Philadelphia gas works to the select

and common councils of the city of Philadelphia. To which are added, 1. The reports of committees of councils prior to the establishment of the Philadelphia gas works. 2. The report of S. V. Merrick on the gas works of Europe. 3. The ordinances of the select and common councils in relation to the works, etc. 9 parts. Philadelphia, 1838. 8º

26 THE ANNUAL Report of the Committee on Legacies and Trusts, made in common council, May 24, 1838. To which is appended a statement of all the devises, bequests, and grants made to the corporation of the city of Philadelphia, in trust. Philadelphia, 1838. 8vo.

27 A DESCRIPTIVE Catalogue of the Chinese collection in Philadelphia, with miscellaneous remarks upon the manners, customs, trade and governments of the Celestial Empire. Philadelphia, 1839. 8vo.

28 CHARTER and By-laws of the Society of the Sons of St. George. Together with an historical sketch of the reign and progreſs of the society, etc. Philadelphia, 1840. 8º

29 PERSECUTION of the Jews in the East ; containing the proceedings of a meeting held at the Synagogue Mikveh Israel, Philadelphia, 27th of Aug. 1840. Philadel. 1840. 8º

30 REPORT of the special committee appointed by the common council on a communication from the board of trustees of the Girard College .. Read August 27, 1840. Philadelphia, 1840. 8º

31 THE MERCANTILE Register, or busineſs man's guide ; containing a list of the principal busineſs establishments, including hotels and public institutions, in Philadelphia. Philadelphia, 1846. 8vo.

32 PROCEEDINGS of the National Convention of the friends of public education, held in Philadelphia, Oct. 17, 18, and 19, 1849. Philadelphia, 1849. 8º

33 THIRTY-SEVENTH annual Report

of " The Controllers of the public schools of the first school district of Pennsylvania," comprising the city and county of Philadelphia for the year ending Dec. 31, 1855, with their accounts. Philadel. 1856. 8vo.

PHILADELPHIA DIRECTORY. Stephens's Philadelphia Directory for 1796. Philadelphia [1796]. 12°

2 THE PHILADELPHIA Directory, city and county register, for 1802. To which is added an almanack by A. Shoemaker. By J. Robinson. Philadelphia [1802]. 12°

3 THE PHILADELPHIA Directory for 1805-(1811). By J. Robinson. Phi ladelphia [1805-11]. 12°

4 CENSUS Directory for 1811. . . To which is annexed an appendix . . and a perpetual calendar. Philadelphia, 1811. 12°

5 THE PHILADELPHIA Directory for 1816. By J. Robinson. Philadelphia [1816]. 12°

6 ROBINSON's Directory for 1817, being an alphabetical list of merchants, etc. of Philadelphia. [Philadelphia, 1817.] 12°

7 THE PHILADELPHIA Directory and Register for 1813-1819. By J. A. Paxton. [Philadel. 1813-19.] 12°

8 THE PHILADELPHIA Directory and Register for 1820. By E. Whitely. [Philadelphia, 1820.] 12°

9 THE PHILADELPHIA Index or Directory for 1823. By R. Desilver. [Philadelphia, 1823.] 12°

10 THE PHILADELPHIA Directory and Stranger's Guide for 1825. T. Wilson, editor. Philadel. 1825. 8°

11 DESILVER's Philadelphia Directory and Stranger's Guide for 1828 to 1831, 1833, 1835, and '36. Philadelphia, 1828-35. 8°

12 A. M'ELROY's Philadelphia Directory. 1837, 1839-1845. 8 vol. Philadelphia, 1837-45. 8°

13 M'ELROY's Philadelphia Directory. 1853. Philadelphia, 1853. 8°

14 See PHILADELPHIA, N° 31.

PHILADELPHIA MEDICAL

AND PHYSICAL JOURNAL. Collected and arranged by B. S. Barton. Vol. 1, Pt. 1, 2. Vol. 2. Pt. 1. Philadel. 1805. 8vo.

PHILADELPHIA MEDICAL SOCIETY. First Report of the Committee . . on quack medicines. . . Extracted from the North American Medical and Surgical Journal, . . for Jan. 1828. Philadelphia, 1828. 8°

PHILADELPHIA REGISTER and National Recorder (The). Jan. 1819, to June, 1821. 5 vol. [After vol. 1, the title: " Philadelphia Register" is dropped, and that of " National Recorder" alone retained.] Philadelphia [1819-21]. 8°

PHILADELPHIAD (THE); or new picture of the City [in verse]. Interspersed with a candid review and display of some first-rate modern characters . . delineated in a friendly and satirical manner, etc. Vol. 1. Philadelphia, 1784. 8°

PHILADELPHIAN, Pseud. [i. e. W. WILLIAMS]. A Hand-book for the stranger in Philadelphia, etc. By a Philadelphian. Philadel. 1849. 16°

PHILADELPHUS, Pseud. Letters addressed to Caleb Strong, Esq. late Governor of Massachusetts, showing that retaliation, capital punishments, and war, are prohibited by the Gospel ; . . not necessary to the safety of individuals or nations ; but, incompatible with their welfare ; inconsistent with the Christian character ; and contrary to the laws of Christ. New York, 1816. 8°

PHILANTHROPOS, Pseud. The Universal Peace-maker, or modern author's instructor. By Philanthropos. [A political tract.] Philadelphia, 1764. 8°

2 A LETTER to Aaron Burr . . . on the barbarous origin, the criminal nature, and the baneful effects of duels ; occasioned by his late fatal interview

with the deceased . . . General Alexander Hamilton. By Philanthropos. New York, 1804. 8°

3 A DISSERTATION on a Congreſs of Nations. By Philanthropos. Published by order of the American Peace Society. [New York?] 1832. 8°

PHILENIA, *a lady of Boston. Pseud.* [*i. e.* Mrs. Sarah Wentworth Apthorp Morton]. Ouâbi; or the virtues of nature. An Indian tale, in four cantos. By Philenia, a lady of Boston. Boston, 1790. 8°

PHILIP, UNCLE, *Pseud.* [*i.e.*Francis L. Hawks]. History of the United States: N° 1; or Uncle Philip's Conversations with the children about Virginia. New York, 1840. 12°

2 HISTORY of the United States: N° 2 ; or Uncle Philip's Conversations with the Children about New York. New York, 1844. 12°

3 HISTORY of the United States: N° 3; or, Uncle Philip's Conversations with the children about Maſsachusetts. 2 vol. N. York, 1844. 12°

4 HISTORY of the United States: N° 6 ; or Uncle Philip's Conversations with the children about New Hampshire. 2 vol. New York, 1844. 12°

5 EVIDENCES of Christianity; or Uncle Philip's Conversations with the Children about the truth of the Christian religion. N. York, 1844. 12°

6 THE LOST Greenland ; or, Uncle Philip's Conversations with the children about the lost colonies of Greenland. New York, 1844. 12°

7 NATURAL History; or, Uncle Philip's Conversations with the children about tools and trades among inferior animals. New York, 1844. 12°

8 THE AMERICAN Forest: or, Uncle Philip's Conversations with the children about the trees of America. New York, 1845. 12°

PHILLIPPO, JAMES M. Jamaica, its past and present state. Philadelphia [printed; and] N. York, 1843. 8°

PHILLIPS, JOHN. An Oration, pronounced July 4, 1794, at . . Boston, in commemoration of the anniversary of American Independence. Boston, 1794. 8°

PHILLIPS, P. Digest of Cases decided and reported in the Supreme Court of the State of Alabama, from 1st Alabama Reports to 7th Porter inclusive; with the rules of court and practice, and a table of titles and cases; To which are appended, the Declaration of Independence; the Constitution of the United States, *etc.* Mobile, 1840. 8°

2 DIGEST of Cases decided by the Supreme Court of the State of Alabama, from Minor to 7 Alabama Reports inclusive. Mobile, 1846. 8°

PHILLIPS, P. AND OTHERS. Report of the Commiſsioners appointed to examine the Bank of Mobile. Nov. 3, 1841. Tuscaloosa, 1841. 8°

PHILLIPS, STEPHEN C. *of Maſsachusetts.* Speech . . upon the bill for the relief of the sufferers by the fire at New York; delivered in the House of Representatives, Feb. 16, 1836. Washington, 1836. 8°

PHILLIPS, W. H. Phillips's United States Patent Fire Annihilator. [Statement of its advantages, with the opinions of the preſs as to its efficacy.] New York, 1851. 8°

PHILLIPS, WILLIAM, *F. L. S. etc.* An Elementary Treatise on Mineralogy; . . Fifth edition, from the fourth London edition, by R. Allan; containing the latest discoveries. . With numerous additions . . . by F. Alger. Boston, 1844. 12°

PHILLIPS, WILLARD. The Inventor's Guide, comprising the rules, forms, and proceedings, for securing patent rights. Boston, 1837. 12mo.

2 THE LAW of Patents for Inventions, including the remedies and legal proceedings in relation to Patent Rights. Boston, N. York, 1837. 8vo.

3 A TREATISE on the Law of Insurance. Second edition. 2 vol. Boston, 1840. 8°

PHILLIS, *a servant girl . . belonging to Mr. J. Wbeatley, of Boston.* An Elegiac Poem on the death of . . G. Whitefield, *etc.* Boston printed, Newport, Rhode Island, reprinted [1770]. 4°

PHILOSOPHY of the Plan of Salvation. A book for the times. By an American citizen. With an introductory eſſay by C. E. Stowe. Fourth thousand. Salem, 1845. 12°

2 PHILOSOPHY of the Plan of Salvation. A book for the times by an American Citizen [J. B. Walker]. With an introductory Eſſay by C. E. Stowe. Boston, 1851. 12°

PHILOSOPHY OF EVIL, showing its uses and its unavoidable neceſſity; by a series of familiar illustrations drawn from a philosophical examination of the most startling evils of life; *etc.* Philadelphia, 1845. 12°

PHILOSOPHY OF MODERN Miracles, or the Relations of Spiritual Causes to Physical Effects; with especial reference to the mysterious developments at Bridgeport and elsewhere. By a Dweller in the Temple. New York, 1850. 8°

PHOCION, *Pseud.* A Letter from Phocion to the considerate citizens of New York, on the politics of the day. New York, 1784. 8°

PHYSICIAN. A View of the metaphysical and physiological arguments in favour of Materialism. By a Physician. Philadel. 1824. 12mo.

2 DESULTORY Notes on the origin, uses, and effects of ardent spirit. By a Physician. Philadelphia, 1834. 8°

3 NOTES on Cuba; containing an account of its discovery and early history; a description of the face of the country, its population, resources, and wealth: its institutions, and the manners and customs of its inhabitants.

With directions to travellers visiting the island. By a Physician. Boston, 1844. 12mo.

PICKENS, FRANCIS W. Speech . . . in the House of Representatives, Jan. 21, 1836, on the abolition question. Published from the notes of H. G. Wheeler, revised . . . by the author. Washington, 1836. 8°

PICKERING, ELLEN. The Grumbler. A novel. From the London edition. New York [1846]. 8vo.

PICKERING, JOHN. An Oration delivered . . . . 4 July, 1804, at St. Peter's Church, in Salem, Maſſachusetts; in commemoration of the Independence of the United States. Salem, 1804. 8°

2 A VOCABULARY of Words and Phrases supposed to be peculiar to the United States of America. Boston, 1816. 8vo.

3 A VOCABULARY, or, collection of words and phrases which have been supposed to be peculiar to the United States of America. To which is prefixed an Eſſay on the present state of the English language in the United States. . . Now republished with . . . additions. Few MS. notes. Boston, 1816. 8vo.

4 AN ESSAY on the Pronunciation of the Greek Language. Cambridge, 1818. 4to.

5 AN Eſſay on a uniform Orthography for the Indian Languages of North America. Cambridge, 1820. 4to.

6 A LECTURE on the alleged uncertainty of the law; delivered before the Boston Society for the Diffusion of Useful Knowledge, March 5, 1830. . . From the American Jurist, for Oct. 1834. Boston, 1834. 8°

7 EULOGY on Nathaniel Bowditch, President of the American Academy of Arts and Sciences, including an Analysis of his scientific publications. Delivered before the Academy, May 29, 1838. Boston, 1838. 8°

8 A COMPREHENSIVE Lexicon of the Greek Language, adapted to the use of Colleges and Schools in the United States. Third edition, greatly enlarged, and improved. Boston, 1846. 8°

9 AN EXAMINATION of the testimony of the Four Evangelists, etc. (The Trial of Jesus, etc. by M. Dupin; translated from the French by J. Pickering.) Boston, 1847. 8°

PICKERING, JOHN, and OLIVER, Daniel. A Greek and English Lexicon; adapted to the authors read in the Colleges and Schools of the United States, and to other Greek Clasſics. Second edition, with many additions and improvements. Boston, 1829. 8°

PICKERING, OCTAVIUS. A Digest of Pickering's Reports, vol. 2-7; being a supplement to the digest of the previous volumes of the Maſſachusetts Reports; by L. Bigelow. Boston, 1830. 8°

2 A DIGEST of Pickering's Reports, from the second to the eighth volume inclusive. By W. Phillips and others. Boston, 1831. 8vo.

3 REPORTS of Cases argued and determined in the Supreme Judicial Court of Maſſachusetts. Second edition. Vol. 1, with notes and references, by E. Pickering. Vol. 2-10, with notes, etc. by J. C. Perkins. Boston, 1833-41. 8vo. Vol. 11-24, 1833-1842. 8vo.

PICKERING, THEOPHILUS. The Rev. Mr. Pickering's Letters to the Rev. N. Rogers and Mr. D. Rogers of Ipswich; with their Answer to Mr. Pickering's First Letter; as also his Letter to Mr. Davenport . . [relative to his behaviour, conduct, and doctrine]. Boston, 1742. 8vo.

PICKERING, TIMOTHY. Letter from the Hon. T. Pickering, a senator of the United States from the State of Maſſachusetts, exhibiting to his constituents a view of the imminent dan-ger of an unneceſſary and ruinous war, etc. Boston, 1808. 8°

2 [LETTER exhibiting to his constituents a view of the imminent danger of an unneceſſary and ruinous war: addreſſed to his Excellency J. Sullivan.] [New York, 1808.] 8°

3 LETTER, exhibiting to his constituents a view of the imminent danger of an unneceſſary and ruinous war: addreſſed to his Excellency J. Sullivan. Second edition, Bost. 1808. 8°

4 A REVIEW of the correspondence between the Hon. John Adams, late President of the United States, and the late William Cunningham, Esq. beginning in 1803 and ending in 1812. (Appendix.) Salem,1824. 8vo.

5 THE SUFFERING Greeks. To the inhabitants of the county of Eſſex. [An addreſs in behalf of the Greeks.] [Salem, 1828.] 8°

PICKET, A. The Juvenile Expositor, or American school claſs-book. N° 4, improved and enlarged; embracing radical and derivative orthography, etc. New York, 1827. 12°

PICKMAN, BENJAMIN. An Oration, pronounced Feb. 22, 1797, before the inhabitants of . . . Salem, in Maſſachusetts, aſſembled to commemorate the birthday of George Washington, President of the United States of America. Salem, 1797. 8°

PICTURE BOOK for little boys and girls. American Sunday School Union, Philadelphia [1830?]. 12°

PICTURES of the Country. Philadelphia [1832]. 12mo.

PICTURES and Painters. Eſſays upon Art: the old masters and modern artists. New York, 1849. 12°

PICTURES for the Little Ones at Home. New York, 1855. Fol.

PIDGEON, WILLIAM. Traditions of De-coo-dah, and Antiquarian Researches: comprising extensive explorations . . . of the . . . earthen remains of the Mound Builders in America; The Traditions of the last Prophet of the Elk Nation relative to their origin and use; and the evidences of an ancient population more numerous than the present aborigines. London, N. York printed, 1853. 8vo.

PIERCE, FRANKLIN, *President of the United States of America.* Speech . . in Senate . . . May 1, 1840, upon claims for seven years' half pay [by the heirs of officers engaged in the revolutionary war, *etc.*] [Washington, 1840.] 8°

2 THE LIFE of Gen[eral] F. Pierce, the Granite Statesman; with a biographical sketch of Hon. W. R. King, *etc.* Tenth thousand. New York, 1852. 12°

PIERCE, JOHN, *D.D.* Reminiscences of Forty Years; delivered 19 March, 1837; *etc.* Boston, 1837. 8°

PIERPONT, JOHN. Who goeth a Warfare at his own Charges? A discourse delivered before the . . Artillery Company of Massachusetts, on the celebration of their 190th anniversary, Boston, June 2, 1828. Boston, 1828. 12°

2 PIERPONT's Introduction . . . to the National Reader; a selection of easy lessons, *etc.* Boston, 1831. 12°.

3 THE NATIONAL Reader; a selection of exercises in reading and speaking. . . Twenty-eighth edition. New York [1835?]. 12°

4 THE AMERICAN First Class Book; or exercises in reading and recitation. . . Twenty-sixth edition. New York [1835?]. 12°

5 THE YOUNG Reader; to go with the spelling-book . . Fifteenth edition. Boston, 1839. 12°

6 AIRS of Palestine, and other poems. Boston, 1840. 8vo.

PIERRE and his Family; or, a story of the Waldenses. Philadelphia, 1827. 12mo.

PIERSON, H. W. American Missionary Memorial, including biographical and historical sketches. Edited by H. W. Pierson. New York, 1853. 8vo.

PIKE, ALBERT. Prose Sketches and Poems, written in the western country. Boston, 1834. 12°

PIKE, ALBERT. Reports of cases argued and determined in the Supreme Court of the State of Arkansas, . . in law and equity. Jan. 1837 to July, 1844. 5 vol. Little Rock, 1840-45. 8°

PIKE, JAMES. The English Spelling Book. . . The third edition. Boston, 1822. 12°

PIKE, NICHOLAS. A new and complete System of Arithmetic. . . Third edition. Revised, corrected, and improved, . . by N. Lord. Boston, 1808. 8°

2 A NEW and complete System of Arithmetic. . . Eighth edition: abridged for the use of schools, . . by N. Lord. New York, 1816. 12°

3 PIKE's System of Arithmetic abridged . . by D. Leavitt. Concord, 1830. 12°

PIKE, ZEBULON MONTGOMERY. An Account of a voyage up the Mississippi river, from St. Louis to its source; made under the orders of the War department by Lieut. Pike, . . in . . 1805 and 1806. Compiled from Mr. Pike's Journal. [Washington? 1806?] 8°

2 AN ACCOUNT of expeditions to the sources of the Mississippi, and through the western parts of Louisiana, to the sources of the Arkansaw, Kans, La Platte, and Pierre Jann, rivers; performed by order of the Government of the United States, during the years 1805-1807; and a tour through the interior parts of New Spain . . in . . 1807. [With three appendixes.] Philadelphia, 1810. 8°

PILGRIM, PETER. Peter Pil-

grim, or a rambler's recolleftions.
By the author of " Calavar," " Nick of
the Woods," *etc.* [R. M. Bird]. 2
vol. Philadelphia, 1838. 12°

PILLET, RENÉ MARTIN, *Major
General.* Views of England, during
a residence of ten years ; six of these
as a prisoner of war. Translated from
the French. Boston, 1818. 12mo.

PILOT (THE), a tale of the sea.
By the author of " The Pioneers,"
etc. [J. F. Cooper]. A new edition.
2 vol. Philadelphia, 1836. 12°

PINCKNEY, CHARLES. Three
Letters, written and originally published under the signature of a South
Carolina Planter... To which is added
an appendix. Philadelphia, 1799. 8°

PINCKNEY, H. L. An Addreſs
delivered before the Temperance Society of . . . Washington, *etc.* Washington, 1836. 8°

PINDAR, JONATHAN, *Pseud.* The
probationary Odes of J. Pindar, a
cousin of Peter, and candidate for the
post of Poet Laureat to the C. U. S.
[Congreſs of the United States]. Philadelphia, 1796. 12mo.

PINDAR, SUSAN. Legends of the
Flowers. New York, 1852. 12°

PINEVILLE. Chronicles of Pineville, embracing sketches of Georgia
scenes, incidents, and charafters. By
the author of " Major Jones' Courtship." Philadelphia, 1845. 12°

PINNOCK, WILLIAM. A comprehensive System of Modern Geography and History. Revised and enlarged, .. by E. Williams. New York,
1835. 12°

PIONEERS (THE), or the sources
of the Susquehanna ; a descriptive
tale. By the author of " The Spy"
[J. F. Cooper]. A new edition. 2
vol. Philadelphia, 1836. 12°

PIRATE'S OWN BOOK, or au-
thentic narratives of the lives .. of the

most celebrated sea robbers. With
historical sketches of the Joaſsamee,
Spanish, Ladrone, West India, Malay
and Algerine Pirates. Portland, 1837.
12°

PITCAIRN'S ISLAND. A De-
scription of Pitcairn's Island and its
inhabitants. With an authentic account of the mutiny of the ship
Bounty, and of the subsequent fortunes of the mutineers. [By J. Barrow.] New York, 1845. 12°

PITKIN, TIMOTHY. A statistical
View of .the commerce of the United
States of America: its conneftion with
agriculture and manufaftures, and an
account of the public debt, revenues,
and expenditure. With a brief review of the trade, agriculture, and
manufafture of the Colonies previous
to their independence. Hartf.1816. 8°

2 A STATISTICAL View of the commerce of the United States of America. New Haven, 1835. 8vo.

3 A POLITICAL and civil History of
the United States of America, from
1763 to 1797. 2 vol. New Haven,
1828. 8vo.

PITMAN, JOHN. A Discourse
delivered at Providence, Aug. 5,1836,
in commemoration of the first settlement of Rhode Island and Providence
Plantations: being the second centennial anniversary of the settlement of
Providence. Providence, 1836. 8vo.

PITRAT, JEAN CLAUDE. Americans warned of Jesuitism, or the Jesuits unveiled. New York, 1851. 12°

PITT, WILLIAM, *Earl of Cbatbam.*
Celebrated Speeches of Chatham,
Burke, and Erskine. To which is
added, the argument of Mr. Mackintosh in the case of Peltier. Selefted
by a member of the Philadelphia bar.
Philadelphia, 1841. 8°

PITTSBURGH, PENNSYLVANIA.
Bye-laws and Ordinances of the City
of Pittsburgh, *etc.* Pittsburgh, 1828.
8vo.

2 SECOND (third and fourth) annual

Report of the board of directors of the Western Foreign Missionary Society. 3 parts. Pittsburgh, 1834-1836. 8vo.

PITTSBURGH DIRECTORY. Woodward and Rowlands' Pittsburgh Directory, etc. 1852. Pittsburgh [1852]. 8°

PLANTER (The): or, thirteen years in the south. By a Northern Man. Philadelphia, 1853. 12°

PLATO. The Gorgias of Plato, chiefly according to Stallbaum's text; with notes by Theodore D. Woolsey. Boston, 1842. 12°

2 PLATO contra Atheos. Plato against the Atheists; or, the tenth book of the dialogue on laws, Gr. accompanied with critical notes, and followed by extended dissertations on some of the main points of the Platonic philosophy and theology, especially as compared with the holy Scriptures. By T. Lewis. New York, 1845. 12mo.

PLEA for a Miserable World: 1. An address .. delivered at the laying of the corner stone of the building erecting for the Charity Institution in Amherst, by Noah Webster. 2. A sermon [on 2 Kings vi. 1-3] delivered on the same occasion, by . . D. A. Clark. . . 3. A brief account of the origin of the Institution. Boston, 1820. 8°

PLEA for Religious Newspapers; a sermon [on 1 Timothy iv. 13] preached to his own people on the Lord's day, December 29, 1844, by a Connecticut Pastor [J. D. Hull]. Hartford, 1845. 8°

PLUMBE, John, the Younger. Sketches of Iowa and Wisconsin, taken during a residence of three years. St. Louis, 1839. 12mo.

PLUTARCH, or the delay of the Deity in the punishment of the wicked. .. With notes, by H. B. Hackett. Andover, 1844. 12mo.

PLYMOUTH COLONY. The Book of the General Laws of the Inhabitants of the Jurisdiction of New Plymouth, collected out of the Records of the General Court, .. revised: and with .. additions .. by the order .. of the General Court. .. reprinted, etc. Boston, 1685. Fol.

POCAHONTAS: an historical drama, in five acts [and in verse]; with an introductory essay and notes. By a Citizen of the West [R. Mackay?]. New York, 1837. 12°

POCAHONTAS, Pseud. Cousin Franck's Household, or scenes in the Old Dominion, by Pocahontas. Boston, 1853. 12°

POE, Edgar Allan. The Raven, and other poems. London [New York printed], 1846. 8vo.

2 THE WORKS of the late E. A. Poe: with notices of his life and genius. By N. P. Willis, J. R. Lowell, and R. W. Griswold. In two volumes. (The Literati, etc.) 3 vol. New York, 1850. 12°

POESCHE, Theodore, and GOEPP, Charles. The New Rome; or, the United States of the World. New York, 1853. 12°

POET. Confessions of a Poet. [A novel. By L. Osborn.] 2 vol. Philadelphia, 1835. 12°

POETRY. Sacred Poetry. Philadelphia, 1829. 12mo.

POETRY for home and school. First and second parts. Selected by the author of " Theory of teaching," etc. Second edition. Bost. 1846. 12°

POET'S OFFERING for 1850. Edited by Sarah Josepha Hale. Philadelphia, 1850. 8°

POINDEXTER, George. Mr. Poindexter's motion for an impeachment of Judge Bruin, of the Mississippi Territory [in the House of Re-

presentatives of the United States].
April 11, 1808. Washingt. 1808. 8°

POINSETT, Joel R. Discourse
on the objects and importance of the
National Institution for the Promotion
of Science, established at Washington,
1840, delivered at the first anniversary [with the constitution and bylaws of the institution]. Washington,
1841. 8°

POLISH EXILE. The Remembrances of a Polish Exile. (With introductory remarks by W.B.Sprague.)
Printed, Albany. Reprinted, Philadelphia, 1835. 12°

POLITICAL CENSOR (The);
or review of the most interesting
political occurrences relative to the
United States. By Peter Porcupine
[i. e. William Cobbett]. Philadelphia,
1796. 8vo.

POLITICAL ECONOMY; founded in justice and humanity. In a letter to a friend. By W. T. of Washington. Washington, 1804. 8vo.

2 Cursory views of the liberal and
restrictive systems of Political Economy; and of their effects in Great
Britain, France, Russia, Prussia, Holland, and the United States. With an
examination of Mr. Huskisson's system of duties on imports. By a citizen of Philadelphia. Fourth edition,
.. enlarged and improved. Philadelphia, Dec. 12, 1826. 8°

POLITICIAN'S REGISTER
(The); containing the result of the
elections which have taken place during the years 1836-1840, for President, members of Congress, and State
officers; etc. Second edition. Baltimore, 1840. 12°

POLO, Marco. The Travels of
Marco Polo, greatly amended and
enlarged from valuable early manuscripts recently published by the
French Society of Geography, and,
in Italy, by Count Baldelli Boni.
[Translated from the Italian.] With

copious notes, illustrating the routes
and observations of the author, and
comparing them with those of more
recent travellers. By H. Murray,
F.R.S.E. New York, 1845. 12°

POLYANTHOS (The): a monthly
magazine, consisting of original performances and selections from works
of merit. Dec. 1805, to July, 1807.
5 vol. Boston, 1806-1807. 12°

2 The Polyanthos, enlarged.
4 vol. Oct. 1812—Sept. 1814. Boston, 1812-14. 8°

POND, Enoch. A Treatise on..
Christian Baptism .. Designed as a
reply to the statements and reasons of
.. A. Judson, .. in his sermon preached in .. Calcutta, .. Sept. 12, 1812.
.. Second edition, revised, etc. Worcester, 1819. 12°

2 The young Pastor's Guide: or
lectures on pastoral duties. Bangor,
1844. 12°

3 Swedenborgianism reviewed.
Portland, 1846. 12°

4 Plato: his life, works, opinions,
and influence. Portland, 1847. 16°

5 Review of Dr. Bushnell's " God
in Christ." Bangor, 1849. 12°

6 The ancient Church, from the
captivity to the coming of Christ.
Boston, 1851. 16°

PONS, François Raimond Joseph
de. A Voyage to the eastern part of
Terra Firma, on the Spanish Main, in
South America... With a large map
of the country, etc. Translated by an
American gentleman[the introduction
translated by S. L. Mitchill]. 3 vol.
New York, 1806. 8°

PONTE, Lorenzo L. da. The
American Library of History. N° 1,
2. A History of the Florentine Republic, etc. New York, 1833. 12°

POOLE, William Frederick. An
Index to Periodical Literature. New
York, 1853. 8°

" POOR RICHARD." Poor
Richard's Almanac for 1850 (1851),

as written by B. Franklin, for the years 1736-37-38. The astronomical calculations by Prof. B. Peirce, adapted to Boston, New York, Philadelphia, Baltimore, Washington, and Charleston. To which is added, the continuation of the life of the great philosopher, written by himself. New York, 1849-50. 12°

POPKIN, JOHN SNELLING. A Memorial of the Rev. J. S. Popkin .. Edited by C. C. Felton. Cambridge, 1852. 12°

PORCUPINE, PETER, *Pseud.* [*i.e.* WILLIAM COBBETT]. The life and adventures of Peter Porcupine, with a full and fair account of all his authoring transactions. By Peter Porcupine himself. Philadel. 1796. 8vo.

PORTER, BENJAMIN F. Reports of Cases argued and adjudged in the Supreme Court of Alabama; June term, 1834, to June term, 1839. 9 vol. Tuscaloosa, 1835-40. 8°
2 MR. PORTER's Bill for the preservation of the sixteenth section grants, and to establish permanently in the State of Alabama a common school fund; etc. [Tuscaloosa, 1844.] s. sh. fol°

PORTER, DAVID. Journal of a Cruise made to the Pacific Ocean, in the years 1812-1814. Second edition. To which is now added the transactions at Valparaiso, etc. 2 vol. New York, 1822. 8vo.
2 MINUTES of Proceedings of the Courts of Inquiry and Court Martial in relation to Captain D. Porter, Washington, July, 1825. Washington, 1825. 8°

PORTER, EBENEZER, D.D. Analysis of the principles of rhetorical delivery, as applied to reading and speaking .. Third edition. Andover, 1830. 12°
2 LECTURES on Homiletics and Preaching, and on public prayer;

with sermons and letters. Andover, 1834. 8vo.
3 THE RHETORICAL Reader .. Fifty-third edition, with an appendix. Andover, 1840. 12°

PORTER, JACOB. Topographical description and historical sketch of Plainfield, in Hampshire county, Massachusetts, May 1834. Greenfield, 1834. 8vo.

PORTER, JAMES. A Compendium of Methodism: embracing the history and present condition of its various branches in all countries, with a defence of its .. peculiarities .. Third edition. Boston, 1852. 12°

PORTER, JOHN, *Rev.* The absurdity and blasphemy of substituting the personal righteousness of men in the room of the surety-righteousness of Christ... A sermon [on Isaiah lxiv. 6]. Boston, 1750. 8°
2 THE EVANGELICAL Plan, or an attempt to form right notions in the minds of the common people, and to establish them in the truths of the Gospel. Being the substance of several sermons from Rom. iii. 23, 24, etc. Boston, 1769. 8°

PORTER, NATHANIEL. A Discourse [on 1 Chron. xii. 32] delivered .. before the Legislature of .. New Hampshire, at the annual Election, June 7. Concord, 1804. 8°

PORTER, NOAH. Prize Essay. The necessity and means of improving the common schools of Connecticut. Hartford, 1846. 8vo.
2 THE EDUCATIONAL Systems of the Puritans and Jesuits compared. A premium essay, written for the Society for the promotion of Collegiate and theological Education at the West. New York, 1851. 12°

PORTER, WILLIAM H. Proverbs, arranged in alphabetical order. In two parts. (Part first. Common proverbs explained. Part second. Scriptural proverbs explained.) Boston, 1845. 8°

PORTER, WILLIAM T. The big bear of Arkansas, and other sketches, illustrative of characters and incidents in the south and south-west. [By various authors.] Edited by W. T. Porter. Philadelphia, 1847. 12°

2 A QUARTER Race in Kentucky, and other sketches, illustrative of scenes, characters, and incidents throughout " the Universal Yankee Nation." Edited by W. T. Porter. Philadelphia, 1847. 12°

PORTFOLIO (THE). By Oliver Oldschool, Esq. [i. e. Joseph Dennie]. Jan. 1801 to Dec. 1805. Vol. 1-5. Philadelphia, 1801-1805. 4°

2 THE PORTFOLIO. New Series. By Oliver Oldschool, Esq. Vol. 1-6. Jan. 1806 to Dec. 1808. Philadelphia, 1806-1808. 8°

3 THE PORTFOLIO, a monthly magazine . . conducted by Oliver Oldschool, Esq. assisted by a confederacy of men of letters. (New Series.) Jan. 1809 to Dec. 1812. Vol. 1-8. Philadelphia, 1809-1812. 8°

4 THE PORTFOLIO. Third series. Conducted by Oliver Oldschool, Esq. Jan. 1813 to Dec. 1815. Vol. 1-6. Philadelphia, 1813-15. 8°

5 THE PORTFOLIO. By Oliver Oldschool, Esq. (Fourth series.) Jan. 1816 to Oct.1827. Vol.1-22. [Edited by J. E. Hall.] Philadelphia, 1816-1827. 8°

PORTLAND DIRECTORY [for 1834, 1837, 1841, and '44] [the vols. for 1841 and 1844, by H. Harris]. Portland, 1834-44. 12°

2 THE PORTLAND Reference Book and City Directory for 1846. By S. B. Beckett. [Portland,] 1846. 12°

PORTUGAL. Who is the legitimate King of Portugal? A Portuguese question, submitted to impartial men. By a Portuguese residing in London. Translated from the Portuguese. [Washington? 1828?] 8°

POSSELLIER, A. J. J. called GOMARD. Manual of Bayonet Exercise, prepared for the use of the Army of the United States. By G. B. McClellan. [From the French of A. J. J. Possellier.] Printed by order of the War Department. Philadelphia, 1852. 12mo.

POST, ALFRED C. Observations on the cure of Strabismus, with engravings. . . . With an appendix on the new operation for the cure of stammering. New York, 1841. 12°

POST, HENRY A. V. A Visit to Greece and Constantinople in 1827-8. New York, 1830. 8vo.

POTATOES. On the Culture of Potatoes: extracted from communications made to the Board. . . Published by order of the Massachusetts Society for promoting Agriculture. Boston, 1798. 8vo.

POTHIER, ROBERT JOSEPH. A Treatise on maritime Contracts of letting to hire. . . Translated from the French, with notes and a' life of the author, by C. Cushing. Boston, 1821. 8°

2 TREATISE on the Contract of Sale. Translated from the French, by L. S. Cushing. Boston, 1839. 8vo.

POTTER, ALONZO. The Principles of Science applied to the domestic and mechanic arts, etc. Bost. [1840]. 12°

2 POLITICAL Economy: its objects, uses, and principles: considered with reference to the condition of the American people. With a summary, for the use of students. New York, 1841. 12°

3 HANDBOOK for readers and students; intended as a help . . . in the selection of works for reading, investigation, or professional study. 3 pts. New York, 1845. 12°

4 THE SCHOOL and the Schoolmaster: a manual for the use of teachers, employers, trustees, inspectors, etc. etc. of Common Schools. In two parts. Part 1, by A. Potter; Part

2, by G. B. Emerson. New York, 1846. 12°

POTTER, ELISHA R. A Brief Account of emissions of paper money, made by the colony of Rhode Island. Providence, 1837. 8°

2 SPEECH . . . on the memorial of the Democratic members of the Legislature of Rhode Island; delivered in the House of Representatives, March 7, 9, and 12, 1844. [Washington, 1844.] 8°

POTTER, NATHANIEL. An Essay on the medicinal properties and deleterious qualities of Arsenic. Philadelphia, 1796. 8vo.

POTTER, ZABDIEL W. Speech .. on the bill to provide for completing the Ches[apeake] and Ohio Canal to the town of Cumberland, delivered in the House of Delegates of Maryland, .. March 2, 1844. [Annapolis? 1844.] 8°

POTTS, GEORGE, D. D. No Church without a Bishop; or, the controversy between the Rev. Drs. Potts and Wainwright. With a preface by the latter, and an introduction and notes by an Anti-sectarian. New York, 1844. 8°

2 ADDRESS delivered at the University of Pennsylvania, before the Society of the Alumni, on the occasion of their annual celebration, Nov. 15, 1852. Philadelphia, 1853. 8°

POULTNEY, EVAN. A final Reply to the Libels of Evan Poultney, late President of the Bank of Maryland, and a further examination of the causes of the failure of that institution. Baltimore, 1835. 8vo.

POWELL, JOHN JOSEPH. Essay upon the Law of Contracts and Agreements. Sixth American edition, revised and corrected. 2 vol. New York, 1825. 8°

2 A TREATISE on the law of Mortgages. Reprinted from the sixth English edition, much enlarged and im-

proved, with copious notes, by T. Coventry. [With] notes and references to American cases, by B. Rand. 3 vol. Boston, 1828. 8°

POWELL, THOMAS. The Living Authors of England. [A series of critical essays on the writings of different authors, with extracts from their works.] New York, 1849. 12°

2 THE LIVING Authors of America. First series. New York, 1850. 8vo.

POWER, THOMAS. An Oration delivered . . . before the citizens of Boston on the sixty-fourth anniversary of American Independence. Boston, 1840. 8°

POWERS, DANIEL. A Grammar on an entirely new System. West Brookfield, 1845. 12°

POWERS, GRANT. A Sermon [on 2 Timothy, iv. 7, 8] delivered at the funeral of Rev. W. Andrews. Hartford, 1838. 8°

2 HISTORICAL Sketches of the discovery, settlement, and progress of events in the Coos country and vicinity; principally included between the years 1754 and 1785. Haverhill, N. H. 1841. 12°

POWERS, H. P. Female Education. An address delivered .. on the anniversary of the Newark Institute for young ladies, July 21, 1826. . . With an appendix. Newark, 1826. 8°

POYEN, CHARLES. Progress of Animal Magnetism in New England. Being a collection of Experiments, Reports, and Certificates from the most respectable sources. Preceded by a dissertation on the proofs of Animal Magnetism. Bost. 1837. 12mo.

PRAED, WINTHROP MACKWORTH. The Poetical Works of W. M. Praed. Now first collected by R. W. Griswold. New York, 1844. 12mo.

2 LILLIAN and other Poems. . Now first collected [by R. W. G. i. e. Rufus W. Griswold]. New York, 1852. 12°

PRAIRIE. The Prairie; a tale. By the author of " The Pioneers" and "The last of the Mohicans" [J. F. Cooper]. A new edition. 2 vol. Philadelphia, 1836. 12°

PRATT, Enoch. A Comprehensive History, ecclesiastical and civil, of Eastham, Wellfleet, and Orleans, county of Barnstable, Mass., from 1644 to 1844. Yarmouth, 1844. 8°

PRAY, Lewis G. The History of Sunday Schools, and of religious education, from the earliest times. Boston, 1847. 12°

PRAYERS for Children. Boston [1830?]. 12mo.

PRAYERS suitable for children and Sunday schools. Philadelphia, 1831. 12mo.

PRECAUTION, a novel. [By J. Fenimore Cooper.] 2 vol. New York, 1820. 12°

PRENTICE, George Denison. Biography of Henry Clay. Second edition, revised. New York, 1831. 12°

PRENTICE, Thomas. The vanity of zeal for fasts without true judgment, mercy and compassions. A sermon [on Zech. vii. 8-12], etc. Boston. 4°

PRENTISS, Samuel. An Oration, pronounced .. July 4, 1812, .. being the thirty-seventh anniversary of American Independence. Montpelier, Vt. 1812. 8°

2 Remarks .. in the Senate .. March 1, 1836, on the question of reception of a petition from the Society of Friends, praying for the abolition of slavery in the District of Columbia. Washington, 1836. 8°

3 Speech .. on the Mississippi contested election; delivered in the House of Representatives .. Jan. 17, 1838. Washington, 1838. 8°

4 Speech .. on the bankrupt bill ; delivered in the Senate, .. June 23, 1840. Washington, 1840. 8°

PRESBYTER, Pseud. [i.e. Samuel Henry Turner]. Strictures on Archdeacon Wilberforce's Doctrine. of the Incarnation, in a letter to a student of Divinity, subscribed, Presbyter. New York, 1851. 12°

PRESBYTERIAN CHURCH in the United States. The Constitution of the Presbyterian Church in the United States of America, containing the Confession of Faith, the catechisms, the government and discipline, and the directory for the worship of God. Ratified and adopted by the Synod of New York and Philadelphia, .. May 16, 1788, etc. Wilmington, 1801. 12°

2 Missionary Intelligence, being a part of the Report of the Standing Committee of Missions of the Presbyterian Church .. for 1811. Philadelphia, 1811. 8°

3 Minutes of the Board of Foreign Missions of the Presbyterian Church, held at Baltimore, October 31, 1837. New York, 1838. 8°

4 First (to the ninth) Annual Report of the Board of Foreign Missions of the Presbyterian Church in the United States. 9 parts. New York, 1838-46. 8°

5 Annual Report of the Board of Missions of the Presbyterian Church. 1839-46, 1848-52. Philadelphia, 1839-52. 8°

6 The Constitution of the Presbyterian Church in the United States of America. Containing the confession of faith, the catechisms, the form of government, the book of discipline, the directory for the worship of God and general rules for judicatories as ratified by the General Assembly of 1821, and concluded by the General Assemblies of 1826 and 1833. Philadelphia, 1850. 12°

7 A History of the Division of the Presbyterian Church in the United States of America. By a Committee of the Synod of New York and New Jersey. New York, 1852. 12°

8 Thirty-third Annual Report of the Board of Education of the Presbyterian Church in the United States of America, *etc.* Philadel. 1852. 8°

PRESBYTERIAN MAGAZINE (The). Edited by C. Van Renſſelaer. Vol. 1. Philadelphia, 1851. 8°

PRESCOTT, Abraham. Report of the Trial of A. Prescott, on an indictment for the murder of Mrs. S. Cochran, *etc.* Concord, 1834. 8°

PRESCOTT, Allen. Allen Prescott; or, the fortunes of a New England boy. By the author of the "Morals of Pleasure," *etc.* [Mrs. Theodore Sedgwick]. 2 vol. New York, 1834. 12°

PRESCOTT, Benjamin. A Letter to .. J. Gee in answer to his of June 3, 1743; addreſſed to N. Eells, Moderator of the late Convention of Pastors in Boston. Boston, 1743. 8°

PRESCOTT, Edward G. An Oration, delivered before the officers of the militia, and members of the Volunteer Companies of Boston and the vicinity, on the 4th of July, 1832, at their request. Boston, 1832. 8°

PRESCOTT, James. Report of the Trial by impeachment of J. Prescott, Esq. Judge of the Probate of Wills, *etc.* for the County of Middlesex, for misconduct and maladministration in office, before the Senate of Maſſachusetts, in the year 1821. With an appendix, containing an account of former impeachments in the same State. By O. Pickering and W. H. Gardiner. Boston, 1821. 8°

PRESCOTT, William Hickling. History of the Reign of Ferdinand and Isabella, the Catholic. By William H. Prescott. In three volumes. Second edition. 3 vol. Boston: American Stationers' Company, 1838. 8°

2 History of the Reign of Ferdinand and Isabella, the Catholic. Tenth edition. 3 vol. New York, 1845. 8°

3 History of the Conquest of Mexico, with a preliminary view of the ancient Mexican civilization, and the life of the Conqueror Hernando Cortés. 3 vol. New York, 1846. 8°

4 Reviews of a part of Prescott's "History of Ferdinand and Isabella," and of Campbell's "Lectures on Poetry." Boston, 1841. 12°

PRESIDENCY (The). [Political Eſſays, subscribed, An Old Man; directed against the re-election of General Jackson. By J. M. White? Reprinted from the Baltimore Chronicle.] [Baltimore, 1831.] 8°

PRESTON, Lyman. Preston's Complete Time Table: showing the number of days from any date in any given month to any date in any other month, *etc.* (Preston's tables of interest, computed at seven per cent. .. Together with calculations of rebate or discount.) 2 parts. New York, 1846. 8°

PRESTON, William C. *of South Carolina.* Speech .. on the Annexation of Texas; delivered in the Senate .. April 24, 1838. Washington, 1838. 8°

2 Eulogy on Hugh Swinton Legaré, *etc.* [Charleston, 1843.] 8°

3 Address to the students of the South Carolina College, *etc.* Columbia, 1846. 8°

PRESTON, William Scott. A practical treatise on the law of Legacies. New York, 1827. 8°

2 Slavery, as it relates to the negro or African race; examined in the light of circumstances, history, and the Holy Scriptures; with an account of the origin of the black man's colour, .. and .. strictures on abolition. Albany, 1843. 12°

PRIEST, Josiah. American Antiquities and discoveries in the West. .. Compiled from travels, authentic sources and the researches of antiquarian societies. Fourth edition. Albany, 1834. 8vo.

PRIESTLEY, Joseph. A description of a system of biography; with a catalogue of all the names inserted in it, and the dates annexed to them. A new edition, with improvements. Philadelphia, 1803. 8vo.

2 A General History of the Christian Church from the fall of the Western Empire to the present time. 4 vol. Northumberland, 1802-3. 8vo.

3 A General History of the Christian Church to the fall of the Western Empire. The second edition improved. 2 vol. Northumberland, 1803-1804. 8vo.

PRIGG, Edward. Report of the Case of E. Prigg against the Commonwealth of Pennsylvania, . . . in which it was decided that all the laws of the several states relative to fugitive slaves are unconstitutional and void. . . By R. Peters. Philadelphia, 1842. 8vo.

PRIME, Nathaniel S. A History of Long Island, from its first settlement by Europeans to the year 1845, with special reference to its ecclesiastical concerns. In two parts, etc. New York, 1845. 12°

PRIME, Samuel Irenæus. Thoughts on the death of little children. . . With an appendix selected from various authors. [Prose and verse.] Fourth edition. New York, 1853. 12mo.

2 Travels in Europe and the East. . . 2 vol. London, and New York [printed], 1855. 12mo.

PRINCE, John. Part of a Discourse [on Rev. x. 5, 6] delivered on the 29th of December (being the Sabbath after the melancholy news of the death of General Washington), upon the close of the year 1799, recommending the improvement of time. Salem [1800]. 8°

PRINCE, Thomas. A Sermon [on 1 Chron. xxix. 26, 28] on . . the death of his late Majesty King George

and the . . accession of . . George II. Boston, 1727. 8°

2 Mr. Prince's fast and thanksgiving sermons [on Psalm xviii. 7] on the earthquake. [Boston, 1727.] 8°

3 The Departure of Elijah lamented. A sermon [on ii. Kings 12, 13] occasioned by the . . decease of . . Cotton Mather. Boston, 1728. 12°

4 The Grave and Death destroyed, and believers ransomed and redeemed from them. A sermon [on Hosea xiii. 14], July 7, 1728, being the Lord's day after the decease and funeral of S. Prince. Boston, 1728. 8°

5 Civil Rulers raised up by God to feed his People. A sermon [on Psalm lxxviii. 1, 2] at the publick lecture in Boston. Boston, 1728. 8°

6 The People of New England put in mind of the righteous acts of the Lord to them and to their fathers, and reasoned with concerning them. A sermon [on 1 Samuel ii. 6, 7] before the . . General Assembly of . . Massachusetts, May 27, 1730. Being the anniversary for the Election of His Majesty's Council, etc. Boston, 1730. 8°

7 The Dying Prayer of Christ, for his peoples' preservation and unity. A sermon [on John xvii. 11] to the North Church in Boston, Jan. 25, 1731-32. Being a day of prayer for the divine direction in their choice of another colleague Pastor. Boston, 1732. 8°

8 A Chronological History of New England in the form of Annals: being a summary and exact account of the most material transactions and occurrences relating to this Country, in the order of time wherein they happened, from the discovery by Gosnold, . . 1602, to . . 1730, etc. Vol. 1. [Vol. 2. Nº 1-3, all ever printed, wanting.] Boston, 1736. 8vo.

9 A Funeral Sermon [on Acts vii. 59] on the Rev. Mr. N. Williams. Boston, 1738. 8°

10 Extraordinary Events the do-

ings of God and marvellous in pious eyes. Illustrated in a sermon [on Psalm cxviii. 23] on the general thanksgiving, occasioned by taking the City of Louisburg, on the Isle of Cape Breton, *etc.* Boston, 1745. 8°

11 THE PIOUS Cry to the Lord for help when the godly and faithful fail among them. A sermon [on Psalm xii. 1] on the death of T. Cushing. Boston, 1746. 8°

12 A SERMON [on Ezra ix. 13, 14] delivered .. August 14, 1746, being the day of thanksgiving for the . . . victory near Culloden, *etc.* Boston, 1746. 8°

13 EXTRAORDINARY Events the doings of God. . . Illustrated in a sermon [on Psalm cxviii. 23] .. occasioned by taking the City of Louisbourg. . . . Third edition. Boston, 1746. 8vo.

14 A SERMON [on Psalm xvi. 11] occasioned by the decease of Mrs. Martha Stoddard. Boston,1748. 8vo.

15 THE NATURAL and moral Government and Agency of God in causing droughts and rains. A sermon [on Psalm cvii. 33-35], Aug. 24, 1749, being the day of the general thanksgiving in the Province of the Maſſachusetts for the extraordinary reviving rains, *etc.* Boston, 1749. 8°

16 A CHRONOLOGICAL History of New England in the form of Annals. . . With an introduction containing a brief epitome of the most considerable transactions .. abroad, from the creation, *etc.* A new edition. Boston, 1826. 8°

PRINCE, WILLIAM ROBERT. A Treatise on the Vine; embracing its history from the earliest ages, *etc.* By W. R. Prince, aided by W. Prince. New York, 1830. 8°

2 PERIODICAL Pamphlet, 1844 and 1845. Prince's descriptive catalogue of fruit and ornamental trees, *etc.* cultivated and for sale at .. Prince's Linnæan Botanic Garden and Nur-

series, Flushing, Long Island. Thirty-fourth edition. New York, 1844. 8°

PRISON DISCIPLINE. A Vindication of the separate system of prison discipline from the misrepresentations of the North American Review, July, 1839. 8°

PRISON DISCIPLINE SOCIETY, BOSTON. First (3rd to 9th, 11th to 19th) annual Report of the Board of Managers, *etc.* Boston,1826-44. 8vo.

2 REPORTS, *etc.* 1826-54. 3 vol. Boston, 1855. 8vo.

PRIZE (THE): or, the story of George Benson and Wm. Sandford. Philadelphia [1830 ?]. 12mo.

PROCTER, BRYAN WALLER. Essays and Tales in .. Prose, by Barry Cornwall. 2 vol. Boston, 1853. 8°

PRODIGAL DAUGHTER (THE): or, a .. relation [in verse] how a gentleman of a vast estate, in Bristol, in England, had a proud and disobedient daughter, *etc.* Boston,1807. 12°

PROFFIT, GEORGE H. Speech .. on the general appropriation bill ; delivered in the House of Representatives, April 27, 1840. Washington, 1840. 8°

PROLIX, PEREGRINE, *Pseud.* A pleasant Peregrination through the prettiest parts of Pennsylvania. Performed by Peregrine Prolix. Philadelphia, 1836. 12°

PROLIX, PETER, *Pseud.* [i. e. PHILIP HOULBROOKE NICKLIN]. A pleasant Peregrination through the prettiest parts of Pennsylvania. Philadelphia, 1836. 12°

PROSPECT before us. Vol. 2. Part 2. Richmond, 1801. 8°

PROTESTANT CLERGY. New Themes for the Protestant Clergy: creeds without charity, theology without humanity, and Protestantism without Christianity. [By S. Colwell.] With notes by the editor, on the literature of charity, population, pauperism, political economy, and Protestantism. Philadelphia, 1851. 12°

2 NEW Themes condemned : or, thirty opinions upon " New Themes (for the Protestant Clergy [by S. Colwell]"), and its " Reviewer." With answers to 1. " Some notice of a Review, by a Layman." 2. " Hints to a Layman." 3. " Charity and the Clergy" [by the Reviewer, *i. e.* S. A. Allibone. *See* LAYMAN, N° 10]. Philadelphia, 1853. 12°

PROTESTANT EPISCOPAL

CHURCH. Canons for the Government of the Protestant Episcopal Church in the United States of America... To which are added the Constitution of the Church, and the course of ecclesiastical studies established by the House of Bishops, in the General Convention of 1804. New York, 1832. 8vo.

2 JOURNALS of the General Conventions of the Protestant Episcopal Church in the United States of America, from .. 1784 to .. 1814. .. Also first appendix, containing the constitution and canons, and second appendix, containing three pastoral letters. Philadelphia, 1817. 8°

3 JOURNAL of the Proceedings of the Bishops, Clergy, and Laity of the Protestant Episcopal Church in the United States of America, in a General Convention held in .. New York, .. 1817. Second edition. Philadelphia, 1820. 8°

4 JOURNAL of the Proceedings of the Bishops, Clergy, and Laity of the Protestant Episcopal Church in the United States of America, in a General Convention held in .. Philadelphia, ... A. D. 1820. Philadelphia, 1820. 8°

5 JOURNAL of the Proceedings of the Bishops, Clergy, and Laity of the Protestant Episcopal Church in the United States of America, in a General Convention held in .. Philadelphia, ... A. D. 1821. Philadelphia, 1821. 8°

6 JOURNAL of the Proceedings of the Bishops, Clergy, and Laity of the Protestant Episcopal Church in the United States of America, in a General Convention .. held in .. Philadelphia, .. A. D. 1823. New York, 1823. 8°

7 REPORT of the Committee on the Psalms in Metre, appointed by the General Convention of 1829. [With the Book of Psalms in metre.] New York, 1831. 8vo.

8 REVISION of the Canons of the Protestant Episcopal Church in the United States, by the Committee of the General Convention.. 1831. 8vo.

9 PROCEEDINGS of the .. Domestic and Foreign Miſsionary Society .. of the Protestant Episcopal Church in the United States of America, at meetings held in New York, during the Seſsion of the General Convention in Oct. 1832. Together with the report of the board of directors, *etc.* Philadelphia, 1832. 8°

10 PROCEEDINGS of the .. Society .. at meetings held in Philadelphia, in August and Sept. 1835. Together with the report of the board of directors .. and the treasurer's account, .. *etc.* Philadelphia, 1835. 8°

11 JOURNAL of the proceedings of the bishops, clergy, and laity, of the Protestant Episcopal Church in the United States of America, in a General Convention, held in the city of New York, .. October, .. 1832. To which are annexed, the Constitution of the said Church, together with the Canons, as revised and paſsed by this General Convention. 2 pts. [separately paged]. New York, 1832. 8°

12 PROCEEDINGS of the Board of Miſsions of the Protestant Episcopal Church in the United States of America, at their second annual meeting. .. Together with the reports of the domestic and foreign committees, *etc.* New York, 1837. 8°

13 JOURNAL of the Proceedings of the Bishops, Clergy, and Laity of the Protestant Episcopal Church in the

United States of America, in a General Convention, held in the City of New York, Oct. 1841. Together with the Constitution and Canons for the government of the Protestant Episcopal Church. New York, 1841. 8vo.

14 AURICULAR Confeſsion in the Protestant Episcopal Church: considered in a Series of Letters . . . by a Protestant Episcopalian. New York, 1850. 12°

PROTESTANT EPISCOPAL Historical Society. Collections of the Protestant Episcopal Historical Society for the year 1851. New York, 1851. 8°

PROTESTANT EPISCOPAL PULPIT. A series of original sermons [continuation of AMERICAN PULPIT, which see]. Vol. 2.

PROUD, ROBERT. The History of Pennsylvania, from its settlement in 1681, till after the year 1742. With an Introduction and Appendix. 2 vol. Philadelphia, 1797-8. 8vo.

PROVIDENCE ATHENÆUM. Charter, Constitution, and By-laws of the Athenæum. Providence,1836. 8vo.

2 FIRST (to 12th, 14th to 18th and 20th) Annual Report of the Directors of the Athenæum to the proprietors. 1837-55. Providence, 1842, and 1838-55. 8vo.

3 TWENTIETH Annual Report of the Directors of the Providence Athenæum, . . . Sept. 24, 1855. Providence, 1855. 8vo.

4 See CATALOGUES, N° 33, 42.

PROVIDENCE DIRECTORY (THE), containing the names of the inhabitants, etc. Providence, 1852. 12°

PROVIDENCE GAZETTE AND Country Journal (The). N° 659, 662. Providence, 1776. Fol.

PSI UPSILON SOCIETY. [A

Catalogue of the members of the several chapters of this Society, at various colleges and Universities in the United States of America.] [New Haven, 1842.] 8°

2 CATALOGUE of the Psi Upsilon fraternity. New York, 1844. 8°

PUBLIC LEDGER. Vol. 7, N° 149. Sept. 19, 1839. Philadelphia, 1839. Fol.

PUBLICOLA, Pseud. Features of Federalism: or, a brief history of the principles and views of the Federalists, etc. By Publicola. Wilmington, 1803. 8°

2 THIRTEEN Eſsays on the policy of manufacturing in this country. From the New York Morning Herald. Philadelphia, Jan. 29, 1830. 8°

PULTE, J. H. Woman's Medical Guide; containing Eſsays on the Physical, Moral, and Educational Development of Females, and the Homœopathic Treatment of their Diseases. Cincinnati, 1853. 8vo.

PUMPELLY, MARY H. Poems. New York, 1852. 8°

PUNCHARD, GEORGE. History of Congregationalism, from about A. D. 250 to 1616. Salem, 1841. 12°

PURITAN. The Puritan: a series of eſsays, critical, moral, and miscellaneous. By John Ollbug, Esq. 2 vol. Boston, 1836. 12°

PURSUIT OF KNOWLEDGE under Difficulties; its pleasures and rewards illustrated by memoirs of eminent men. [By G. L. Craik.] 2 vol. New York, 1844. 12°

PUTNAM, AARON. A Treatise wherein are contained several particular subjects [viz. Of the being of God: the Divinity of Christ; etc.] Hartford, 1804. 8°

PUTNAM, GEORGE. Spiritual Renewal, the great work of the Christian Church and Ministry: a sermon [on Ephes. iv. 23] delivered at the ordination of the Rev. F. D. Huntington, *etc.* Second edition. Boston, 1842. 8°

2 OUR Political Idolatry: a discourse [on Isa. x. 11] delivered .. on fast day, April 6, 1843. Boston, 1843. 8°

3 AN ORATION delivered .. before the Phi Beta Kappa Society in Harvard University, *etc.* Bost. 1844. 8°

PUTNAM, GEORGE PALMER. The World's Progreſs: a dictionary of dates. With tabular views of general history, and a historical Chart. Edited by G. P. Putnam. N. York, 1851. 12°

2 PUTNAM's Home Cyclopedia. In six volumes, each complete in itself. New York, 1850-53. 12° Contents,

 I. History and Chronology.
 II. General Literature and the Fine Arts. By George Ripley and Bayard Taylor.
 III. The Useful Arts. By Dr. T. Antisell.
 IV. Universal Biography. By Parke Godwin.
 V. Universal Geography, a comprehensive Gazetteer of the World. By T. C. Calcott.
 VI. Science, including Natural History, Botany, Geology, Mineralogy, etc. By Samuel St. John.

PUTNAM'S Monthly Magazine of American Literature, Science, and Art. 8 vol. New York, 1853-56. 8vo.

PUTNAM, J. M. English Grammar, with an improved Syntax, *etc.* Concord, 1831. 12°

PUTNAM, SAMUEL. Sequel to the Analytical Reader.. Second edition. Dover, 1831. 12°

2 PUTNAM's Reader. The Analytical Reader, containing leſſons in simultaneous reading and defining, *etc.* Portland, 1834. 12°

POWNALL, THOMAS. The Speech of Th-m-s P-wn-ll [Thomas Pownall] Esq. late G-v-rn-r of this province, in the H-se of C-mm-ns, in favor of America. [Boston, 1774?] 4°

PYM, ARTHUR GORDON. Narrative, comprising the details of a mutiny on board the American brig Grampus, the recapture of the veſſel, shipwreck, and subsequent sufferings. New York, 1838. 12mo.

UAKERS. Judgment given by 28 Quakers against G. Keith and his Friends. With answers to the judgment. Pennsylvania, 1694. 4to.

2 A COLLECTION of some writings of the most noted of the people called Quakers, in their times. Philadelphia, 1767. 8vo.

3 A SERIOUS Addreſs to such of the people called Quakers on the Continent of North America, as profeſs scruples relative to the present government: exhibiting the ancient real testimony of that people, concerning obedience to civil authority; .. By a native of Pennsylvania, *etc.* Second edition. Philadel. 1778. 8°

QUARTERLY Christian Spectator: conducted by an aſsociation of gentlemen. Vol. 1-9. New Haven, 1829-37. 8vo.

QUARTERLY REVIEW of the American Protestant Aſsociation. Edited by R. W. Griswold. Vol. 1, 2. Philadelphia, 1844-45. 8°

QUARTERLY (THE) Theological Magazine, and Religious Repository. Conducted principally by members of the Protestant Episcopal Church (vol. 3, 4, by C. H. Wharton and J. Abercrombie). 4 vol. Jan. 1813 to Oct. 1814. Vol. 1, 2. Burlington, N. J. Vol. 3, 4, Philadelphia, 1813-1814. 8°

QUINBY, GEORGE W. Marriage and the Duties of the Marriage Relations. Cincinnati, 1852. 8vo.

QUINCE, PETER, *Pseud.* [i. e. ISAAC STORY]. A Parnaſsian Shop, opened in the Pindaric style. By Peter Quince, Esq. [Satires, in verse.] Boston, 1801. 12°

QUINCY, JOSIAH, *Junior.* Observations on the Boston Port-Bill. Boston, 1774. 8vo.

QUINCY, JOSIAH, *President of Harvard University.* An Oration, pronounced July 4, 1798, at .. Boston, in commemoration of the anniversary of American Independence. Boston, 1798. 8°

2 A SPEECH, delivered in Congreſs, .. 15 April, 1806, while the House, in committee of the whole, were discuſsing the bill for fortifying the ports and harbours of the United States. Boston, 1806. · 8°

3 SPEECH on the joint resolutions in the House of Representatives of the United States, approving the conduct of the Executive in refusing to receive any further communication from F. J. Jackson. To which is added the Report by the Joint Committee of the Maſsachusetts Legislature on the subject of the foreign relations of the United States. Baltimore, 1810. 8°

4 AN ORATION delivered before the Washington Benevolent Society of Maſsachusetts . . 30 April, 1813, being the anniversary of the first

inauguration of President Washington. Boston, 1813. 8°

5 ADDRESS delivered at the fifth anniversary of the Massachusetts Peace Society, Dec. 25, 1820. Cambridge, 1821. 8°.

6 MEMOIR of the Life of J. Quincy, Jun. Boston, 1825. 8vo.

7 AN ORATION delivered on . . the fourth of July, 1826, . . the fiftieth anniversary of American Independence, before the Supreme Executive of the Commonwealth, and the city council and inhabitants of . . Boston. Boston, 1826. 8°

8 AN ADDRESS to the Board of Aldermen and Members of the Common Council of Boston, on the organization of the city government, Jan. 2, 1826. Boston, 1826. 8°

9 ADDRESS to the Board of Aldermen, of . . Boston, Jan. 3, 1829 . . on taking final leave of the office of Mayor. Boston, 1829. 8°

10 AN ADDRESS delivered at the dedication of Dane Law College in Harvard University, Oct. 23, 1832. Cambridge, 1832. 8°

11 REPORT of the President of Harvard University (J. Quincy), submitting for consideration a general plan of studies, conformably to a vote of the Board of Overseers, etc. Cambridge, 1830. 8°

12 AN ADDRESS to the Citizens of Boston, . . 17 Sept. 1830, the close of the second century from the first settlement of the city. Boston, 1830. 8°

13 CONSIDERATIONS relative to the library of Harvard University, respectfully submitted to the Legislature of Massachusetts. Cambridge, 1833. 8°

14 THE HISTORY of Harvard University. 2 vol. Cambridge, 1840. 8°

15 REMARKS on the nature and probable effects of introducing the voluntary system in the studies of Latin and Greek, proposed in certain resolutions of the President and Fellows of Harvard University, etc. Cambridge, 1841. 8°

16 SPEECH of J. Quincy, President of Harvard University, before the Board of Overseers of that institution, Feb. 25, 1845, on the minority report of the Committee of Visitation, presented to that Board by G. Bancroft, Esq., Feb. 6, 1845. Boston, 1845. 8°

17 SPEECH of J. Quincy, President of Harvard University, before the Board of Overseers of that institution, . . on the minority report of the Committee of Visitation presented . . by G. Bancroft. . . Second edition. Boston, 1845. 8°

18 MEMOIR of James Grahame, author of " The History of the United States of North America," etc. Boston, 1845. 8°

19 THE MEMORY of the late James Grahame, the historian of the United States, vindicated from the charges of " detraction " and " calumny " preferred against him by Mr. George Bancroft, and the conduct of Mr. Bancroft towards that historian stated and exposed. Boston, 1846. 8°

20 THE HISTORY of the Boston Athenæum, with biographical notices of its deceased founders. Cambridge, 1851. 8vo.

21 A MUNICIPAL History of the Town and City of Boston, during two centuries, etc. Boston, 1852. 8°

QUINCY, JOSIAH. An Oration, delivered July 4, 1832, before the City Council and inhabitants of Boston. Boston, 1832. 8°

2 LETTER to the Shareholders of the Vermont Central Railroad [relative to his conduct as treasurer of the company, etc.] Boston, 1852. 8°

QUINTILIANUS, MARCUS FABIUS. M. Fabii Quintiliani de institutione oratoria e libris excerpta, ex editione Spaldingii. Selegit et accuravit J. Alden. Bostoniæ, 1840. 12°

AE, JOHN. Statement of some new principles on the subject of Political Economy, exposing the fallacies of the system of Free Trade, and of .. other doctrines maintained in the "Wealth of Nations." Boston, 1834. 8vo.

RAFFENEAU-DELILLE, ALIRE. An Inaugural Dissertation on Pulmonary Consumption. New York, 1807. 8vo.

RAFFLES, THOMAS. · Memoirs of the Rev. Thomas Spencer. Philadelphia, 1831. 12mo.

RAFINESQUE, CONSTANTINE SAMUEL. Circular Address on Botany and Zoology; with the prospectus of two periodical works. Philadelphia, 1816. 12mo.

2 ICHTHYOLOGIA Ohiensis, or natural history of the fishes inhabiting the river Ohio, and its tributary streams; preceded by a physical description of the Ohio, and its branches. Lexington, Kentucky, 1820. 8vo.

3 ANCIENT History, or annals of Kentucky; with a survey of the ancient monuments of North America; and a tabular view of the principal languages and primitive nations of the whole earth. Frankfort, Kentucky, 1824. 8vo.

4 MEDICAL Flora, or Manual of the Medical Botany of the United States of North America. 2 vol. Philadelphia, 1828-30. 12°

5 THE PULMIST; or, introduction to the art of curing and preventing the consumption or chronic phthisis; a medical essay, etc. Philadelphia, 1829. 8vo.

6 EIGHT Figures, Twenty - five Cents. American manual of the grape vines and the art of making wine. . . With eight figures. Philadelphia, 1830. 12°

7 FLORA Telluriana pars prima (tertia, quarta). First, (third, fourth) part of the synoptical Flora Telluriana, .. with new natural classes, orders, and families, etc. Philadel. 1836. 8vo.

8 A LIFE of Travels and Researches in North America and South Europe. Philadelphia, 1836. 12°

9 THE PLEASURES and Duties of Wealth. Philadelphia, 1840. 8vo.

10 ANTIKON Botanikon, or botanical illustrations by self figures of 2500 trees and plants, chiefly American. Second part, centuries 6-10. [Philadelphia, 1840?] 8vo.

RAGUET, CONDY. The Principles of Free Trade, illustrated in a series of .. essays. Originally published in the Banner of the Constitution. Philadelphia, 1835. 8vo.

2 A TREATISE on Currency and Banking. Second edition. Philadelphia, 1840. 12°

RAMBLE, LINCOLN, Pseud. Dreamland, a vision of the new year. By Lincoln Ramble, Esq. New York, 1846. 12°

RAMBLE, ROBERT, Pseud. City Scenes. Boston [1850!]. 12°

2 ROBERT Ramble's Scenes in the Country. Boston [1850?]. 12°

RAMSAY, ALLAN. The Gentle Shepherd. A pastoral comedy [in five acts and in verse] .. with the life of the author [by W. Tennant]. (Remarks on the writings of A. Ramsay, by W. Tennant. An essay on Ramsay's Gentle Shepherd. By Lord Woodhouslee. A catalogue of the Scottish poets, from the earliest periods.) [Edited by W. Gowans.] L. P. 2 parts. New York, 1852. 4to.

RAMSAY, DAVID. The History of the Revolution in South Carolina, from a British Province to an Independent State. 2 vol. Trenton, 1785. 8vo.

2 THE HISTORY of the American Revolution. 2 vol. Philadelphia, 1789. 8°

3 A SKETCH of the soil, climate, weather, and diseases of South Carolina. Charlestown, 1796. 8vo.

4 A REVIEW of the Improvements, Progress and State of Medicine in the 18th century. Charleston, 1801. 8vo.

5 AN ORATION, on the cession of Louisiana to the United States, delivered on the 12th May, 1804. Charleston, 1804. 8vo.

6 THE LIFE of George Washington, etc. New York, 1807. 8°

7 THE LIFE of George Washington, first President of the United States. Second edition. Boston, 1811. 12°

8 THE HISTORY of South Carolina, from its first settlement in 1670 to 1808. 2 vol. Charleston, 1809. 8vo.

9 AN EULOGIUM upon B. Rush, M.D. .. Written at the request of the Medical Society of South Carolina, and delivered .. 10 June, 1813. Philadelphia, 1813. 8°

10 HISTORY of the United States, from their first settlement as English Colonies .. to .. 1808. ... Continued to the Treaty of Ghent, by S. S. Smith, D.D. .. and other .. gentlemen. Second edition, revised, etc. 3 vol. Philadelphia, 1818. 8vo.

11 UNIVERSAL History Americanised; or, an historical view of the world, from the earliest records to the year 1808; with a particular reference to the state of society, literature, religion, and form of government, in the United States of America. To which is annexed, a supplement, containing a brief view of history from .. 1808 to the battle of Waterloo. (History of the United States from their first settlement as English Colonies .. to .. 1808 .. Continued to the treaty of Ghent, by S. S. Smith, and other literary gentlemen. Second edition, revised and corrected. 3 vol.) 12 vol. Philadelphia, 1819-18. 8°

12 MEMOIRS of the Life of Martha Laurens Ramsay. With an appendix containing extracts from her diary, letters, etc. and also from letters written to her by her father H. Laurens. Fourth edition. Boston, 1827. 12mo.

RAMSAY, GEORGE. The Philosophy and Poetry of Love. New York, 1848. 8°

RAMSEY, J. G. M. The Annals of Tennessee to the end of the 18th century, etc. Philadelphia, 1853. 8°

RAMSEY, WILLIAM. The Drunkard's Doom. (The character and doom of the drunkard maker.) Philadelphia, 1845. 12°

RAMSHORN, LEWIS. Dictionary of Latin Synonyms. From the German, by Francis Lieber. Boston, 1839. 12mo.

RAND, ASA. The Teacher's Manual for instructing in English Grammar. ... Re-published from the Education Reporter, with amendments and additions. Boston, 1832. 12°

RANDALL, SAMUEL S. A digest of the common school system of the State of New York : together with the forms, instructions, and decisions of the superintendent ; an abstract of the various local provisions ap-

plicable to the several cities, *etc.*
Albany, 1844. 12mo.

2 THE EDUCATIONAL Reader; containing selections from a variety of standard English and American authors in prose and poetry: adapted to family and school reading. Albany, 1845. 12°

3 THE ELEMENTARY School Reader, or, moral class-book: designed for the use of schools and families. Albany, 1846. 12°

4 INCENTIVES to the cultivation of the science of Geology: designed for the use of the young. New York, 1846. 12mo.

5 THE COMMON School System of the State of New York, comprising the . . laws relating to common schools, . . instructions and forms for . . school officers, . . and local provisions . . To which is prefixed a historical sketch of the . . system. Prepared in pursuance of an Act of the Legislature, under the direction of the Hon. C. Morgan, *etc.* Troy, N. Y. 1851. .8°

RANDOLPH, EDMUND. A Vindication of Mr. Randolph's resignation [of the office of Secretary of State to the United States of America. Written by himself]. Philadelphia, 1795. 8°

RANDOLPH, JOHN. Mr. John Randolph's Motion [in the House of Representatives of the United States of America, in relation to the removal of the Judges of the United States]. Feb. 7, 1806. Washington, 1806. 8°

2 LETTERS to a Young Relative. Philadelphia, 1834. 8vo.

RANDOLPH, JOHN THORNTON. The Cabin and Pastor; or, slaves and masters. Embellished with magnificent illustrations, *etc.* Philadelphia [1852]. 12°

RANDOLPH, PEYTON. Reports of Cases argued and determined in the Court of Appeals of Virginia. (To which are added, Reports of

Cases decided in the General Court of Virginia.) 6 vol. Richmond, 1823-29. 8°

RANDOLPH AND ST. CLAIR, *Counties of.* Memorial of sundry inhabitants of the counties of Randolph and St. Clair in the Indiana Territory. Jan. 17, 1806. Washington, 1806. 8°

RANGERS (THE); or the Tory's Daughter. A tale, illustrative of the revolutionary history of Vermont and the Northern Campaign of 1777. By the author of " The Green Mountain Boys " [Daniel P. Thompson]. Third edition. 2 vol. Boston, 1851. 12°

RANKIN, ANDREW. An Address delivered before the Temperate Society, at Plymouth [Massachusetts], *etc.* Hanover, 1828. 8°

RANKIN, JOHN. Letters on American Slavery, addressed to Mr. T. Rankin. Fifth edition. Boston, 1838. 12°

RANLETT, WILLIAM H. The Architect; a series of original designs, for domestic and ornamental cottages and villas, connected with landscape gardening, adapted to the United States, *etc.* Vol. 1 (in 10 numbers). New York, 1847. 4°

RANTOUL, ROBERT. An Oration delivered before the Democrats and Antimasons, of the county of Plymouth, at Scituate, 4 July, 1836. Boston, 1836. 8°

2 HON. R. Rantoul Jr.'s Letters on the death penalty. [Boston, 1846.] 8°

RAPELJE, GEORGE. A Narrative of excursions, voyages, and travels, in America, Europe, Asia, and Africa. New York, 1834. 8vo.

RAPHALL, MORRIS JACOB. Post-Biblical History of the Jews; from the close of the Old Testament, about the year 420 B. C. E. till the destruction of the Second Temple, in the year 70 C. E. 2 vol. London [New York, printed], 1856. 12mo.

RASK, RASMUS CHRISTIAN. A compendious Grammar of the old Northern or Icelandic language: compiled and translated from the grammars of Rask, by George P. Marsh. Burlington, Vt. 1838. 12°

RATHBUN, GEORGE. Speech .. on the annexation of Texas; delivered in the House of Representatives, Jan. 22, 1845. [Washington, 1845.] 8°

RATTLEHEAD, DAVID, Pseud. The Life and Adventures of an Arkansaw Doctor. Philadelphia, 1851. 12°

RAU, GOTTLIEB LUDWIG. Organon of the Specific Healing Art. .. Translated from the German, with an essay on the present internal condition of the homœopathic school, by C. J. Hempel. N. York, 1847. 8vo.

RAUCH, FREDERICK A. Psychology, or a view of the human soul, including anthropology. 2nd edition. New York, 1841. 8vo.
2 PSYCHOLOGY; or, a view of the human soul; including anthropology. .. Third edition, revised and improved. New York, 1844. 12°

RAVENSCROFT, JOHN STARK. Bishop of North Carolina. To the members of the Protestant Episcopal Church, in .. St. James's, Mecklenburg county .. Discourse [on 1 Cor. xv. 58], etc. Richmond, 1824. 8°
2 THE WORKS of .. J. S. Ravenscroft .. To which is prefixed a memoir of his life, etc. 2 vol. N. York, 1830. 8vo.

RAUSSE, J. H. Pseud. [i. e. H. F. Franke]. Miscellanies to the Graefenberg water-cure; or, a demonstration of the advantages of the hydropathic method of curing diseases as compared with the medical.

Translated by C. H. Meeker. New York, 1848. 12°

RAWLE, WILLIAM. An Address delivered before the Philadelphia Society for promoting Agriculture. Philadelphia, 1819. 8vo.
2 A VIEW of the Constitution of the United States of America. Philadelphia, 1825. 8°
3 A VIEW of the Constitution of the United States of America. Second edition. .. Philadelphia, 1829. 8vo.
4 REPORTS of Cases adjudged in the Supreme Court of Pennsylvania. By W. Rawle, Jun. [assisted by P. McCall]. 5 vol. Philadel. 1829-36. 8°
5 REPORTS of Cases adjudged in the Supreme Court of Pennsylvania. By W. Rawle, Jun. C. B. Penrose, and F. Watts. 3 vol. Philadelphia, Harrisburg, [and] Carlisle (Pennsylvania), 1830-43-33. 8°

RAWLE, WILLIAM HENRY. A practical Treatise on the law of covenants for title. Philadel. 1852. 8vo.

RAWLINGS, AUGUSTUS. Eulogy on D. Webster, delivered before the students and friends of the Albany Medical College. Oct. 28th, 1852. Albany, 1852. 8°

RAWSON, JAMES. A Dictionary of synonymical terms of the English language. Philadelphia, 1850. 12°

RAY, ISAAC. A Treatise on the medical jurisprudence of Insanity. Boston, 1838. 8°
2 A TREATISE on the medical jurisprudence of Insanity. 2nd edition. Boston, 1844. 12mo.

RAYMOND, DANIEL. Thoughts on Political Economy; etc. Baltimore, 1820. 8°

RAYMOND, HENRY J. The Relations of the American scholar to his Country and his Times. An address delivered before the Associate Alumni of the University of Vermont, at

Burlington, August 6th, 1850. New York, 1850. 8°

RAYMOND, JAMES. Digested Chancery Cases, contained in the reports of the Court of Appeals of Maryland. Baltimore, 1839. 8°

RAYMOND, WILLIAM. Biographical Sketches of the distinguished men of Columbia county, including an account of the most important offices they have filled, etc. Albany, 1851. 8°

RAYNER, B. L. Life of Thomas Jefferson, with selections from his private correspondence. Bost. 1834. 8vo.

REA, JOHN. A Letter to W. Bainbridge, Esq. formerly commander of the United States' ship George Washington, relating to some transactions on board said ship, during a voyage to Algiers, Constantinople, etc. Philadelphia, 1802. 8°

READ, GEORGE C. Commodore. Around the World: a narrative of a voyage in the East India squadron, under Commodore G. C. Read. By an officer of the United States Navy. 2 vol. New York, 1840. 12mo.

READ, HARRIETTE FANNING. Dramatic Poems. Boston, 1848. 8°

READ, HOLLIS. The Christian Brahmun: or memoirs of the life, writings, and character of the converted Brahmun, Babajee. Including illustrations of the domestic habits and superstitions of the Hindoos, a sketch of the Deckan, and notices of India in general, and an account of the American mission at Ahmednuggur. 2 vol. New York, 1836. 12°

READ, THOMAS BUCHANAN. Poems: .. a new and enlarged edition. Philadelphia, 1853. 8°

READ, WILLIAM GEORGE. Oration delivered at the first commemoration of the landing of the Pilgrims of

Maryland, celebrated May 10, 1842, etc. Baltimore [1842]. 8°

READER. The Intelligent Reader: designed as a sequel to the Child's Guide. Springfield, 1846. 12°

REASONS why the present system of auctions ought to be abolished. New York, 1828. 8°

RECORD. Ecclesiastical Record. Boston, 1832. 12mo.

REDFIELD, ISAAC F. Charge to the Grand Jury in Washington county [Vermont]. Nov. term, 1842. Burlington, 1842. 8°

REDFIELD, JAMES W. Comparative physiognomy; or resemblances between men and animals. N. York, 1852. 8°

REDFIELD, W. C. On Whirlwind Storms: with replies to the objections and strictures of Dr. Hare. New York, 1842. 8vo.

RED RIVER OF LOUISIANA. Natural History of the Red River of Louisiana. Geology, by President E. Hitchcock and Dr. G. C. Shumard; palaeontology, by Dr. B.F. Shumard; zoology, by Captain R. B. Marcy, S. F. Baird, C. Girard, C. B. Adams, and Dr. G. C. Shumard; botany, by Dr. J. Torrey; ethnology, by Captain R. B. Marcy and Prof. W. W. Turner. Reprinted from the report of Captain R. B. Marcy. Washington, 1853. 8°

REDWOOD LIBRARY, NEWPORT, Rhode Island. Charter of the Redwood Library Company, granted A.D. 1747. Newport, 1816. 8vo.

REED, JOHN, D.D. A Sermon [on Matt. xxiii. 8-10] preached before the Convention of the Congregational Ministers in Boston. Boston, 1807. 8°

REED, JOHN, of Massachusetts. Speech .. on the Tariff Bill; delivered in the House of Representatives . . April 3, 1828. Washington, 1828. 8°

2 SPEECH . . in relation to the failure of the bill making appropriations for fortifications, at the last seffion of Congrefs ; delivered in the House of Representatives . . Jan. 27, 1836. Washington, 1836. 8°

3 SPEECH . . on the sub-treasury bill ; delivered in the House of Representatives . . June 27, 1840. Washington, 1840. 8°

REED, S. Extract from a Sermon [on 2 Cor. xiii. 9] delivered in the Church of the Holy Innocents, Albany . . February 1st, 1852, being the second anniversary of the opening of the said church by the rector [S. R. i. e. Sylvanus Reed]. Albany, 1852. 8°

REED, SAMPSON. Correspondences for children of the New Church. Second edition. Boston, 1842. 12°

REED, WILLIAM B. The Infancy of the Union, a discourse delivered before the New York Historical Society, Dec. 19, 1839. Philadelphia, 1840. 8°

2 ADDRESS before the Alumni of the University of Pennsylvania . . November 13th, 1849. Philadelphia, 1850. 8°

3 THE LIFE of Esther de Berdt, afterwards Esther Reed, of Pennsylvania. Privately printed. Philadelphia, 1853. 8vo.

REES, JAMES. Mysteries of City Life, or stray leaves from the world's book : being a series of tales, sketches, incidents, and scenes founded upon the notes of a home miffionary. Philadelphia, 1849. 12°

REESE, DAVID MEREDITH. A plain and practical Treatise on the epidemic Cholera, as it prevailed in the city of New York, in the summer of 1832, etc. New York, 1833. 8°

REGISTER [biennial] of Officers and Agents, civil, military, and naval, in the service of the United States, on the thirtieth day of September, 1817 ; (to 30 Sept. 1845) together with the names, force, and condition of all the ships and veffels belonging to the United States. [Wanting 1833, and having supplementary vol. 1829, and two editions of 1835 and 1841.] 15 vol. Washington, 1818-45. 8°

REGISTER OF PENNSYLVANIA (THE), devoted to the preservation of facts and documents, and other useful information, respecting the State of Pennsylvania. Edited by S. Hazard. Jan. 1828 to Dec. 1835. 16 vol. Philadelphia, 1828-36. 8vo.

REGISTER of the Army and Navy of the United States. By Peter Force. N° 1. 1830. Washington, 1830. 8°

REGNAULT, VICTOR. Elements of Chemistry, . . Translated from the French by T. R. Betton, and edited, with notes, by J. C. Booth and W. L. Faber. 2 vol. Philadel. 1852. 8vo.

RELICS from the Wreck of a former World ; or splinters gathered on the shores of a turbulent planet ; proving the vast antiquity and the existence of animal life before the appearance of man. With an appendix on the scenery in a patch of infinite space. To which is added, accounts of the most wonderful bodies that have fallen from Heaven. New York, 1847. 8°

RELIGION and its Image. Philadelphia [1830?]. 12mo.

RELIGIOUS CABINET. See UNITED States Catholic Magazine.

RELIGIOUS MAGAZINE (THE), or Spirit of the foreign theological journals and reviews. 4 vol. Jan. 1828 to June 1830. Philadelphia [1828-30]. 8°

RELIGIOUS SOUVENIR (THE) for 1839. Republished for 1845.

Edited by Mrs. Lydia H. Sigourney. Hartford, 1845. 12°

REMARKS on State Rights [with an appendix]. By a citizen of Maſſachusetts. Boston, 1824. 8°

REMARKS on Prisons and prison discipline. From the Christian Examiner, vol. iii. N° 3. Boston, 1826. 8°

REMARKS on Prayer Meetings. Republished from the Episcopal Register for the years 1827 and 1828. Philadelphia, 1829. 8°

RENO, LYDIA M. Early Buds. [Poems.] Boston and Cambridge, 1853. 12°

RENWICK, HENRY B. Lives of John Jay (by H. B. Renwick) and Alexander Hamilton (by J. Renwick). New York, 1845. 12°

RENWICK, JAMES. Inaugural Discourse, delivered .. 4 Jan. 1821, .. in Columbia College. New York, 1821. 8°

2 TREATISE on the Steam Engine. [With an appendix.] N. York, 1830. 8vo.

3 THE ELEMENTS of Mechanics. Philadelphia, 1832. 8vo.

4 APPLICATIONS of the Science of Mechanics to practical purposes. New York, 1841. 12mo.

5 FIRST Principles of Natural Philosophy, etc. New York, 1844. 12°

6 FIRST Principles of Chemistry, etc. New York, 1845. 12°

7 LIFE of Dewitt Clinton. New York, 1845. 12°

REPUBLICAN FARMER. N° 1536. Sept. 25th, 1839. Bridgeport, 1839. Fol.

RESOLUTION. The Good Resolution [a Sunday School tale]. Philadelphia [1834]. 12°

RETROSPECT, and other poems. Boston, 1846. 12°

REVELATION. Family Conversations on the evidences of Revelation. Philadelphia, 1830. 12mo.

REVERE, JOSEPH WARREN. A Tour of duty in California; including a description of the Gold Region, and an account of the voyage around Cape Horn; with notices of Lower California, the Gulf and Pacific Coasts, and the principal events attending the conquest of the Californias. .. Edited by J. N. Balestier. New York, 1849. 12°

REVIEW of Political Affairs during the last half year. By a Republican of Maſſachusetts. [Boston,] Sept. 1808. 12°

REVIEW. A Solemn Review of the custom of War. Hartf. 1829. 8°

2 REVIEW of Pamphlets on Slavery and Colonization. Second separate edition. New Haven, 1833. 8vo.

REYNOLDS, E. WINCHESTER. Our Campaign; or, thoughts on the career of life. Boston, 1851. 12°

REYNOLDS, JOHN. Recollections of Windsor Prison; containing sketches of its history and discipline; with strictures and reflections. Boston, 1834. 12mo.

REYNOLDS, JOHN N. Addreſs on the subject of a surveying and exploring expedition to the Pacific Ocean and South Seas, delivered in the Hall of Representatives. .. With correspondence and documents. New York, 1836. 8°

2 PACIFIC and Indian Oceans: or, the South Sea surveying and exploring expedition: its inception, progreſs, and objects. New York, 1841. 8vo.

RHEA, JOHN. Mr. Rhea's ... Motion [relative to registration of land titles within the territories ceded by France to the United States]. [Washington,] 1804. 8°

RHETT, Robert Barnwell. Remarks of Mefsrs. Rhett, Belser, and
A. V. Brown [in the House of Repre-
sentatives] on the constitutional power
of Congrefs to receive or reject petitions; and in favour of the retention
of the 25th rule, prohibiting the reception of abolition petitions. [Wash-
ington, 1845?] 8°

RHODE ISLAND, State of. The
Charter granted by .. King Charles
the Second to the Colony of Rhode
Island and Providence Plantations, in
America. Newport, 1730. Fol.
2 Acts and Laws of His Majesties
Colony of Rhode Island and Providence Plantation, in America [with a
table of the same prefixed]. Newport, 1730-[36]. Fol.
3 At the General Afsembly of the
Governor and Company of the English Colony of Rhode Island and Providence Plantations, ... in the year
1764, etc. An act for the establishment
of a college or university within this
Colony. Providence, 1803. 8°
4 Report of the Committee of the
General Afsembly of the State of
Rhode Island and Providence Plantations, at the February Sefsion, ..
1809, to enquire into the situation of
the Farmers' Exchange Bank in Glo-
cester, with the documents accompanying the same. [Providence?]
1809. 8°
5 The Close of the late Rebellion
in Rhode Island. An extract from a
letter by a Mafsachusetts man resident in Providence. Prov. 1842. 8°
6 School Laws of Rhode Island.
Acts relating to the public schools of
Rhode Island, with remarks and forms.
Providence, 1851. 8°

RHODE ISLAND ANTI-SLA-
VERY Convention. Proceedings of
the Rhode Island Anti-Slavery Convention, held in Providence, .. Feb.
1836. [With an appendix.] Providence, 1836. 8°

RHODE ISLAND BAPTIST
State Convention. [Thirteenth an-
niversary.] Minutes of the Rhode
Island Baptist State Convention, ..
April 11, 1838. Provid. 1838. 8vo.

RHODE ISLAND HISTORICAL
Society. Collections of the Rhode
Island Historical Society. Vol. 1-4.
Providence, 1827-38. 8°

RHODE ISLAND MEDICAL
Society. The Act of Incorporation,
together with the medical police, by-
laws, and rules of the Rhode Island
Medical Society. Providence, 1849.
8vo.
2 Fiske Fund Prize Difsertation of
the Rhode Island Medical Society.
Lefsons from the History of Medical
Delusions, by W. Hooker. New York,
1850. 12°

RHODE ISLAND REPUBLICAN.
New Series. Vol. 3. N° 48. Sept.
25, 1839. Newport, 1832. Fol.

RICCORD, F. W. Stories of
Ancient Rome... With illustrations.
New York, 1852. 12°

RICE, C. D. Illustrations of Physiology. Boston, 1851. 8vo.

RICE, E. L. Introduction to American Literature; or, the origin and
developement of the English language; with gems of poetry. Cincinnati, 1846. 12°

RICE, John H. Historical and
philosophical considerations on Religion; addrefsed to James Madison,
Esq. late President of the United
States. Richmond, 1832. 12°

RICE, N. L. Romanism not
Christianity: a series of popular lectures, in which Popery and Protestantism are contrasted; shewing the
incompatibility of the former with
freedom and free institutions. Second
edition. Cincinnati, 1847. 12°

RICE, William. A digested Index
of the Statute Law of South Carolina,
from the earliest period to the year
1836, inclusive. Charleston, 1838. 8°

2 REPORTS of cases in Chancery, argued and determined in the Court of Appeals and Court of Errors of South Carolina, from Dec. 1838, to May, 1839, both inclusive. Charleston, 1839. 8°

3 REPORTS of cases at law argued and determined in the Court of Appeals and Court of Errors of South Carolina. . . Dec. 1838 to May, 1839. Vol. 1. Charleston, 1839. 8°

RICHARDS, GEORGE. An Oration on the Independence of the United States of Federate America; pronounced at Portsmouth, New Hampshire, July 4, 1795. Portsmouth, 1795. 8°

RICHARDS, GEORGE. A Discourse [on Heb. vii. 4] occasioned by the death of D. Webster, delivered in Central Church, Boston. Boston, 1852. 8°

RICHARDS, JAMES. Lectures on mental philosophy and theology. By J. Richards. . . With a sketch of his life, by S. H. Gridley. New York, 1846. 8°

RICHARDS, T. ADDISON. Tallulah and Jocassee, or Romances of Southern Landscape, and other tales. Charleston, 1852. 8°

RICHARDSON, H. D. Domestic Fowl and ornamental Poultry; their natural history, origin, and treatment . . With illustrations, etc. New York, 1852. 12°

RICHARDSON, JAMES. An Oration, on the principles of liberty and independence; pronounced July 4, 1808; at . . Dedham . . in commemoration of the anniversary of American Independence. Dedham, July 8, 1808. 8°

RICHARDSON, JAMES. An Addreſs delivered before the members of the Norfolk Bar, etc. Boston, 1837. 8°

RICHARDSON, JOHN. A New

Theory on the causes of the motions of the Planetary bodies, belonging to the Solar system. Vincennes (Indiana), 1829. 8°

RICHARDSON, JOHN, Major. Matilda Montgomerie: or the prophecy fulfilled. A tale of the late American war. Being a sequel to "Wacousta." New York [1851]. 8°

2 WAU-NAN-GEE; or the maſsacre at Chicago; a romance of the American revolution. New York, 1852. 8°

RICHARDSON, JOSEPH. Richardson's American Reader . . A selection of leſſons for reading and speaking, wholly from American authors . . Third edition. Boston, 1823. 12°

RICHARDSON, LUTHER. An Oration, pronounced July 4, 1800, at . . Roxbury, in commemoration of American Independence. Boston [1800]. 8°

RICHARDSON, MERRILL. Common School Education. An addreſs delivered before the School Society, Plymouth, Dec. 12, 1842. Hartford, 1843. 8°

RICHMOND, LEGH. The Dairyman's Daughter; an authentic narrative communicated by a clergyman of the Church of England [i. e. L. Richmond]. Philadel. 1827. 12mo.

RICHMOND, Virginia. Particular account of the dreadful fire at Richmond, which destroyed the theatre, etc. To which is added, some observations on theatrical performances; and an eſſay from the Virginia Argus. Baltimore, 1812. 8°

RICHMOND DIRECTORY. Ellyson's Richmond Directory, and buſineſs reference-book for 1845-46. Richmond [1845]. 12°

RICKEY, ANNA S. Forest Flowers of the West. [In verse.] Philadelphia, 1851. 12°

RICORD, PHILIPPE. A Practical

Treatise on Venereal Diseases; or, critical and experimental researches on inoculation, applied to the study of these affections; with a therapeutical summary and special formulary... Translated from the French, by A. S. Doane. Third edition. New York, 1848. 8°

2 ILLUSTRATIONS of Syphilitic Disease .. translated from the French by T. F. Betton .. with the addition of a history of Syphilis and a complete bibliography and formulary of remedies, collated and arranged by P. B. Goddard: with 50 large quarto plates. Philadelphia, 1851. 4°

RIDDELL, JOHN L. A Monograph of the Silver Dollar, good and bad. Illustrated with fac-simile figures. The assays made by W. P. Hort. New Orleans, 1845. 8vo.

RIDDELL, W. P. A Genealogical Sketch of the Riddell Family, including a list of the descendants of the three brothers, Hugh, Gawn, and Robert, who came to America in 1737. New Orleans, 1852. 8°

RIDGELY, DAVID. Document, N° 7. Report (second, third report) of D. Ridgely to the Executive of Maryland, in relation to the collection of documents, papers, etc. ordered to be deposited in the Council Chamber. 3 parts. Annapolis, 1836. 8°

2 ANNALS of Annapolis, comprising sundry notices of that old city from the period of the first settlements in its vicinity in the year 1649 until the war of 1812; together with various incidents in the history of Maryland .. with an appendix containing a number of letters from General Washington and other distinguished persons which .. have never been published before. Compiled and edited by D. Ridgely. Baltimore, 1841. 12°

RIDNER, JOHN P. The Artist's Chromatic Hand-book. Being a practical treatise on pigments. .. To

which is added, a few remarks on vehicles and varnishes, etc. New York, 1850. 12°

RIEDESEL, MADAME DE, Baroness. Letters relating to the War of American Independence, and the capture of the German troops at Saratoga. Translated from the German. New York, 1827. 12mo.

RIGGS, ELIAS. A Manual of the Chaldee Language; containing a Chaldee Grammar, chiefly from the German of G. B. Winer; a chrestomathy; and a vocabulary. With an appendix. Boston, 1832. 4to.

RIKER, JAMES, the Younger. The Annals of Newtown, in Queen's County, New York. Containing its history from its first settlement, together with many interesting facts concerning the adjacent towns; also a particular account of numerous Long Island families, etc. New York, 1852. 8°

RILEY, JAMES. An Authentic Narrative of the Loss of the American Brig Commerce, wrecked on the western coast of Africa, in the month of August, 1815. With an account of the sufferings of her surviving officers and crew .. and observations historical, geographical, etc. New York, 1817. 8vo.

RIPLEY, EZRA, AND OTHERS. A History of the Fight at Concord, on the 19th of April, 1775, etc. By Rev. E. Ripley, with other citizens of Concord. Concord, 1827. 8°

RIPLEY, GEORGE. Specimens of Foreign Standard Literature. Edited by G. Ripley. 14 vol. Boston, 1838-42. 8°

RIPLEY, HENRY J. The Four Gospels; with notes, for teachers in Sabbath schools and Bible classes, and as an aid to family instruction. 2 vol. Boston, 1837. 12mo.

2 SACRED Rhetoric, or composition

and delivery of sermons .. to which are added, hints on extemporaneous preaching. By H. Ware. Boston, 1849. 12°

RIPLEY, R. S., *Major*. The War with Mexico. 2 vol. New York, 1849. 8°

RITCHIE, ELIZABETH. Leſſons of Life and Death; a memorial of S. Ball, who died in her eighteenth year. Philadelphia [1852]. 16°

RITNER, JOSEPH, *Governor of Pennsylvania*. Vindication of General Washington from the stigma of adherence to secret societies... Together with a letter to D. Webster and his reply. Boston, 1841. 8vo.

RIVERS, GUY. Guy Rivers; a tale of Georgia. By the author of " Martin Faber," " Atalantis," *etc.* [William Gilmore Simms]. Third edition. 2 vol. New York, 1837. 12°

RIVES, WILLIAM C. Speech of Mr. Rivers in opposition to the sub-treasury bill, and in support of˙ his substitute; delivered in the Senate .. Feb. 6, 7, 1838. [Washington,] 1838. 8°

2 DISCOURSE on the Character and Services of John Hampden, and the great struggle for popular and constitutional liberty in his time... Delivered before the Trustees, Faculty, and Students of Hampden Sydney College, .. 12 Nov. 1845. Richmond, 1845. 8vo.

RIVINGTON'S NEW YORK Gazetteer: or, the Connecticut, New Jersey, Hudsons River and Quebec Weekly Advertiser. N° 2-127. April 29, 1773; Sept. 21, 1775. [Wanting N° 1, 9-11, 14-15, 17-21, 27, 29, 35, 37, 39, 41, 42, 45, 46, 48, 50, 52, 53, 56, 60, 62, 66, 68, 72, 75, 79-83, 85-92, 94-96, 100-102, 105-108, 110, 115, 117-126, and all after 127.] New York, 1773-75. Fol.

ROATH, DAVID L. The Five Love

Adventures of S. Slug, and other sketches. New York, 1852. 12°

ROB OF THE BOWL: a legend of St. Inigoe's. By the author of " Swallow Barn," " Horse-shoe Robinson," *etc.* [John P. Kennedy]. 2 vol. Philadelphia, 1838. 12°

ROBACK, C. W. The Mysteries of Astrology and the Wonders of Magic. London, Boston [printed], 1854. 8vo.

ROBB, JOHN S. Streaks of Squatter Life, and Far-West Scenes. To which are added other miscellaneous pieces. Philadelphia, 1849. 12°

ROBBINS, ASHER. Oration delivered on the fourth of July, 1827, at Newport, Rhode Island. Providence, 1827. 8°

2 SPEECH .. on the resolutions respecting fortifications, and on the three million appropriation of the last session, delivered in the Senate .. Feb. 18, 1836. Washington, 1836. 8°

3 MR. ROBBINS's Speech on the subject of an institution to be founded on the Smithsonian legacy; delivered in the Senate, ... 10 Jan. 1839. Washington, 1839. 8°

ROBBINS, CHANDLER. A Discourse [on Rev. xiv. 13] preached before the Second Church and Society in Boston in commemoration of the life and character of their former pastor, H. Ware. Boston, 1843. 8°

2 A HISTORY of the Second Church, or Old North, in Boston. To which is added, a History of the New Brick Church. With engravings. Boston, 1852. 8°

ROBBINS, ELIZA. American Popular Leſſons, chiefly selected from the writings of Mrs. Barbauld, Miſs Edgeworth, and other approved writers. New York [1839]. 12°

2 CLASS-BOOK of poetry, for the use of schools or private instruction. New York, 1852. 8°

ROBBINS, ROYAL. Outlines of Ancient and Modern History, on a new plan; embracing biographical notices of illustrious persons, etc. 2 vol. Hartford, 1846. 12°

ROBBINS, THOMAS. An Historical View of the first Planters of New England. Hartford, 1815. 12°

ROBERT AND LOUISA; or, diligence rewarded. Philadelphia, 1830. 12mo.

ROBERT HAMET, the Lame Cobbler. Philadelphia [1833]. 12mo.

ROBERT, Margaret, and Maria. Philadelphia [1832]. 12mo.

ROBERTS, EDMUND. Embaſſy to the Eastern Courts of Cochin-China, Siam, and Muscat; in the United States Sloop-of-War Peacock, during 1832-3-4. New York, 1837. 8vo.

ROBERTS, JOB. The Pennsylvanian Farmer; being a ſelection from the most approved treatises on husbandry, interspersed with observations and experiments. Philadelphia, 1804. 12°

ROBERTSON, WYNDHAM, the Younger. Oregon, our right and title. Containing an account of the condition of the Oregon Territory, its soil, climate, and geographical position; together with a statement of the claims of Ruſſia, Spain, Great Britain, and the United States; accompanied with a map, prepared by the author. Washington, 1846. 8°

ROBERTSON, IGNATIUS LOYOLA. Sketches of Public Charaĉters. Drawn from the living and the dead, with notices of other matters. New York, 1830. 12mo.

ROBESPIERRE, FRANÇOIS MAXIMILIEN JOSEPH ISIDORE. National Convention. Report upon the principles of political morality which are to form the basis of the administration of the interior concerns of the repub-

lic .. [Translated from a copy printed by order of the Convention.] Philadelphia, 1794. 8°

ROBINS, THOMAS E. and SMEDES, W. C. An Inquiry into the validity of the bonds of the State of Miſſiſſippi, iſſued on behalf of the Union bank of Miſſiſſippi; and means of payment. New York, 1847. 8°

ROBINSON, ALFRED. Life in California... Illustrated with numerous engravings... To which is annexed a historical account of the origin, customs and traditions of the Indians of Alta-California. Translated from the original Spanish manuscript [of Father G. Boscana]. 2 pts. New York, 1846. 12°

ROBINSON, CONWAY. The concluding Argument of Conway Robinson, as counsel for the appellants, in the case of the Bank of Washington, v. Arthur, etc... wherein is discuſſed the rule on which courts of equity aĉt, when asked to interfere with securities alleged to be .. usurious, etc. Richmond, 1846. 8°

ROBINSON, EDWARD, D.D. The Harmony of the Gospels in Greek, with Newcome's notes. Andover, 1834. 8vo.

2 BIBLICAL Researches in Palestine. First supplement. [From the American Biblical Repository, July, 1842.] New York, 1842. 8vo.

3 A DICTIONARY of the Holy Bible. .. Illustrated with maps and engravings on wood. Third edition. Boston and New York, 1845. 12°

4 A GREEK and English Lexicon to the New Testament... A new edition, revised and in great part rewritten. London [New York printed], 1850. 8vo.

ROBINSON, FAYETTE. Mexico and her Military Chieftains, from the Revolution of Hidalgo to the present time. Philadelphia, 1847. 8°

2 AN ACCOUNT of the organization

of the army of the United States; with biographies of distinguished officers of all grades. 2 vol. Philadelphia, 1848. 8°

ROBINSON, Horatio N. A Treatise on Surveying and Navigation. Cincinnati, 1852. 8vo.

ROBINSON, James. Elementary Lessons in Intellectual Arithmetic, illustrated upon analytic and inductive principles. Boston, 1831. 12°

ROBINSON, John. The Testimony and Practice of the Presbyterian Church in reference to American Slavery; with an appendix containing the position of the General Assembly (New School) Free Presbyterian, and .... [other] Churches. Cincinnati, 1852. 8vo.

ROBINSON, Phinehas. Immortality, a poem, in ten cantos. New York, 1846. 12°

ROBINSON, Samuel, M. D. A Catalogue of American Minerals, with their localities, including all which are known to exist in the United States and British Provinces... With an appendix, containing additional localities and a tabular view. Boston, 1825. 8vo.

ROBINSON, William Davis. Memoirs of the Mexican Revolution: including a narrative of the expedition of General X. Mina. With some observations on the practicability of opening a commerce between the Pacific and Atlantic Oceans, and on the future importance of such commerce. Philadelphia, 1820. 8°

ROBINSON, William Erigena. St. Patrick and the Irish. An oration pronounced before the Hibernian Provident Society of New Haven, March 17, 1842. New Haven, 1842. 8°

ROCAFUERTE, Vicente. Ideas necesarias a todo pueblo Americano Independiente, que quiera ser libre. (Articulos de confederacion, y con-

stitucion de los Estados-Unidos de América.) Philadelphia, 1821. 12mo.

ROCCUS, Franciscus. A Manual of Maritime Law : consisting of a treatise on ships and freight, and a treatise on insurance. Translated from the Latin of Roccus, with notes, by J. R. Ingersoll. Philadelphia, 1809. 8°

ROCHESTER DIRECTORY. A Directory of the village of Rochester, 1827... To which is added, a sketch of the history of the village, from 1812 to 1827. Rochester, 1827. 12°

2 Directory of the City of Rochester. C. and M. Morse, publishers. Rochester, 1834. 12°

3 Directory of the City of Rochester for 1838. William Swift, Jun. publisher. Rochester, 1838. 8°

4 King's Rochester City Directory and Register, 1841. Rochester, 1840. 8°

5 A Directory and Gazetteer of the City of Rochester, for 1844. By J. L. Elwood and D. M. Dewey. Rochester, 1844. 8°

6 Canfield and Warren's Directory of the City of Rochester, for 1845-46. With a map. Rochester, 1845. 8°

ROCKWELL, Charles. Sketches of foreign travel and life at sea; including a cruise on board a man-of-war, as also a visit to Spain, Portugal, the South of France, Italy, Sicily, Malta, the Ionian Islands, Continental Greece, Liberia, and Brazil; and a treatise on the navy of the United States. 2 vol. Boston, 1842. 8°

ROCKWELL, John A. A Compilation of Spanish and Mexican Law, in relation to mines, and titles to real estate, in force in California, Texas, and New Mexico... Together with a digest of the Common Law, on the subject of mines and mining. Vol. 1. New York, 1851. 8°

ROCKWELL, Lathrop. A Sermon [on Proverbs x. 7] delivered at

the funeral of . . M. Griswold, Esq. etc. New London, 1802. 8°

RODMAN, Ella, Miß. The Catanese: or, the real and the ideal. New York, 1853. 12°

RODMAN, William W. An Examination of the Evidence in regard to infinitesimal doses. Waterbury, 1851. 12mo.

RODOLPHUS; A Franconia story, by the author of the Rollo Books [Jacob Abbott]. New York, 1852. 8°

ROE, Arthur S. To Love and to be Loved. A story. New York, 1851. 12°

2 Time and Tide, or strive and win. New York, 1852. 12°

ROEBUCK, Jarvis. Experiments and Observations on the Bile. Philadelphia, 1801. 8vo.

ROGERS, E. C. Philosophy of Mysterious Agents, Human and Mundane: or, the Dynamic laws and relations of man. Boston, 1853. 8vo.

ROGERS, Henry D. First annual Report of the State Geologist. (Second annual report on the geological exploration of the State of Pennsylvania. Third to the fifth annual report on the geological survey of the State of Pennsylvania.) 5 parts. Harrisburg, 1836-41. 8°

2 Address delivered at the meeting of the Aßociation of American Geologists and Naturalists, held at Washington, May, 1844. . . With an abstraEt of the proceedings at their meeting. 2 parts. New York, 1844. 8vo.

ROGERS, Henry J. Rogers' Marine Telegraph List of Merchant Vessels of 150 tons and upward employed in the commerce of the United States; furnished for the American code of signals. New York, 1855. 8°

2 Rogers' American Code of Marine Signals, designed for communicating important information between

vessels at sea and off the coast, during periods of calms, light winds, storms, or rough weather. Second edition. Baltimore, 1855. 8°

ROGERS, John. Three Sermons on different subjeEts and occasions, etc. Boston, 1756. 8°

ROGERS, John, of New London. A Looking-glaß for the Presbyterians at New London, to see their worship and worshippers weighed in the balance and found wanting. With a true account of what the people called Rogerenes have suffered in that town from the 10th of June, 1764, to the 13th of December, 1766. Providence, 1767. 8vo.

ROGERS, M. L. Catalogue of the East Hartford Claßical and English School, for the year ending Aug. 19, 1846. Hartford, 1846. 12mo.

ROGERS, Robert, Major. Reminiscences of the French War; containing Rogers' expeditions with the New England rangers, under his command, as published in London in 1765; with notes and illustrations. To which is added an account of the life and military services of Maj. Gen. John Stark; with notices and anecdotes of other officers distinguished in the French and Revolutionary war. Concord, N. H. 1831. 12°

ROGERS, Samuel. The Pleasures of Memory, in two parts, with some other poems. Boston, 1795. 12°

ROGERS, William, D. D. A Sermon [on 2 Sam. iii. 38] occasioned by the death of the Rev. Oliver Hart. Philadelphia, 1796. 8vo.

ROGERS, William M. An Addreß delivered at the dedication of the New Hall of Bradford Academy, etc. (History of Bradford Academy, etc.) Boston, 1841. 8°

ROHDEN, L. von. The Life, CharaEter, and AEts of John the Baptist, and the relation of his Ministry to the Christian Dispensation, based upon the " Johannes der Täufer" of L. von Rohden, by the Rev. W. C. Duncan. [Containing a translation of Von Rohden's work, with additions.] New York, 1853. 8vo.

ROMAN LEGISLATION. The origin, history, and influence of Roman Legislation. (From the New York Review, for Oct. 1839.) [New York, 1839.] 8°

ROMANS, BERNARD. A concise Natural History of East and West Florida; . . to which is added, by way of appendix, plain and easy directions to navigators over the Bank of Bahama, the coast of the two Floridas, the North of Cuba, and the dangerous Gulf Paſſage, etc. [With an appendix.] Vol. 1. New York, 1775. 8vo.

ROMANZE [by C. Mariotti]. Cambridge, 1838. 12mo.

ROMAYNE, NICHOLAS, M. D. Report and Addreſs delivered by the President to the Medical Society of the county of New York; together with the charter of the College of Physicians and Surgeons. New York, 1807. 8vo.

ROME. La Gran Quivera, or Rome unmasked. A poem. New York, 1852. 12°

ROME and the Abbey : a tale of conscience. By the author of Geraldine. New York, 1852. 12°

ROORBACH, ORVILLE A. Bibliotheca Americana. Catalogue of American publications, including reprints and original works, from 1820 to 1848. New York, 1849. 8°

2 SUPPLEMENT to the Bibliotheca Americana; comprising a list of books, . . which have been published in the United States within the past year. Also omiſsions and corrections of errors, . . which occurred in the former work. New York, 1850. 8vo.

3 BIBLIOTHECA Americana. Catalogue of American publications, including reprints . . from 1820 to 1852 inclusive, etc. (Supplement . . to May, 1855.) 2 vol. New York, 1852-55. 8vo.

ROOT, ERASTUS. An Introduction to Arithmetic, for the use of common schools . . (Revised, corrected, and enlarged.) Norwich, 1811. 12°

ROOT, JESSE. Reports of Cases adjudged in the Superior Court and Supreme Court of Errors [of the State of Connecticut], from July . . 1789, to June, 1793 [continued to January, 1798]; with a variety of cases anterior to that period. Prefaced with observations upon the government and laws of Connecticut. To which is subjoined, sundry law points adjudged, and rules of practice adopted, in the Superior Court. 2 vol. Hartford, 1798, 1802. 8°

ROSE, HEINRICH. Tabulæ atomicæ. The chemical tables for the calculation of quantitative analyses of H. Rose. Recalculated for the more recent determinations of atomic weights, and with other alterations and additions. By W. P. Dexter. Boston, 1850. 8°

ROSENBERG, CHARLES G. Jenny Lind in America. New York, 1851. 12°

ROSE OF SHARON (THE): a religious Souvenir . . . . Edited by Mrs. C. M. Sawyer, 1853. Boston, 1853. 8°

ROSICH. L'amante astuto: opera comica, in due atti. Poesia del Signor Rosich. Ital. and Engl. New York, 1825. 12°

ROSS, ANNA. Anna Roſs; a story. Philadelphia, 1827. 12mo.

ROSS, ARTHUR A. A Discourse, embracing the civil and religious history of Rhode-Island ; delivered April

4, 1838, at the close of the second century from the first settlement of the Island. Providence, 1838. 12°

ROSS, JAMES. A short, plain, comprehensive, practical Grammar; .. with an alphabetical vocabulary. Eighth edition, revised and improved. Philadelphia, 1827. 12°

ROSS, JOEL H. What I saw in New York; or a bird's-eye view of city life. Auburn, 1851. 8°

ROSS, JOHN. Letter from J. Rofs .. in answer to inquiries from a friend regarding the Cherokee affairs with the United States. Followed by a copy of the protest of the Cherokee Delegation laid before the Senate... 1836. [Washington, 1836.] 8°

2 MESSAGE of the principal chief (J. Rofs) [to the National Council of the Cherokees], and correspondence between the Cherokee Delegation and the Hon. W. Wilkins, Secretary of War. [Tahlequah, 1844?] 8°

ROSSI, HENRIETTE DE, Countefs. Life of H. Sontag, Countefs de Rofsi. With interesting sketches by Scudo, H. Berlioz, L. Boerne, etc. New York, 1852. 8°

ROTTECK, CHARLES VON. General History of the World until 1831. Translated from the German, and continued to 1840, by F. Jones. First American edition. 4 vol. Philadelphia, 1840-41. 8vo.

ROU, LOUIS. A Collection of some Papers concerning Mr. L. Rou's affair [his disputes with the French Protestant Consistory in New York], etc. New York, 1725. 4to.

ROUELLE, JOHN. A complete Treatise on the mineral waters of Virginia. Philadelphia, 1792. 8°

ROUSSEAU, JOHN BAPTISTE CLEMENT. An Inaugural Differtation on Absorption. Philadel. 1800. 8vo.

ROVER. The Red Rover, a tale.

By the author of " The Pilot," etc. [J. F. Cooper]. A new edition. 2 vol. Philadelphia, 1836. 12°

ROWAN, JOHN. Mr. Rowan's motion [in the House of Representatives of the United States of America] for an inquiry into the conduct of H. Innis, district judge of the United States for .. Kentucky. Mar. 21, 1808. [With the documents relative thereto.] Washington, 1808. 8°

ROWLAND, HENRY A. On the common maxims of infidelity. New York, 1850. 12°

2 THE EXCELLENCY of our Christian Polity: a Discourse [on Matt. xxviii. 20] delivered before the [Presbyterian] Synod of New York and New Jersey. New York, 1851. 8°

ROWLAND, WILLIAM F. Election Sermon on 2 Sam. xxiii. 3, preached before the General Court of New Hampshire, June 2. Exeter, 1796. 8°

2 A SERMON [on Gal. v. 14] delivered before the .. General Court of .. New Hampshire, at the annual Election .. June 8. Concord, 1809. 8°

ROWLANDSON, MARY. The Soveraignty and Goodnefs of God, together with the faithfulnefs of His Promises, displayed; being a narrative of the captivity and restauration of Mrs. Mary Rowlandson. Commended by her to all that desires to know the Lord's doings to and dealings with her; especially to her dear children and relations. The second edition, corrected and amended. Written by her own hand for her private use, and now made publick at the earnest desire of some friends, and for the benefit of the afflicted. Cambridge, printed by Samuel Green, 1682. 16mo.

2 THE SOVERAIGNTY and Goodnefs of God, together with the Faithfulnefs of His Promises displayed: being a narrative of the captivity and restau-

ration of Mrs. Mary Rowlandson; Commended by her to all that desire to know the Lord's doings to and dealings with her; especially to her dear children and relations. Written by her own hand for her private use, and now made publick at the earnest desire of some friends, and for the benefit of the afflicted. The second edition, carefully corrected and purged from abundance of errors which escaped in the former impression. Boston: printed by T. Fleet, for Samuel Phillips, at the Three Bibles and Crown, in King Street, 1720. 16mo.

ROWSON, SUSANNA. Miscellaneous Poems. Boston, 1804. 12°

ROXBURY, *Maſſachusetts*. Municipal Register, containing the city charter, with rules and orders of the city council, and a list of the officers of the city of Roxbury, for 1846-7. Roxbury, 1846. 12°
  2 ANNUAL Report .. for .. 1845-6. [Roxbury, 1846.] 8°

ROY, W. L. A complete Hebrew and English critical and pronouncing Dictionary. New York, 1837. Fol.

ROYAL AMERICAN GAZETTE. N° 342, 590, 591, 592, 594. Jan. 1781, to June, 1783. N. York, 1781-83. Fol.

ROYAL GAZETTE (THE). N° 200-739. Aug. 29, 1778, to Oct. 25, 1783 [wanting N° 1-199, 201-408, 410-420, 422, 424-426, 431-451, 453-457, 459-461, 464-493, 497-501, 503-519, 521-522, 525-526, 528, 534-535, 540-542-642, 644, 701, 703-726, 728-735, 737]. New York, 1778-1783. Fol.

ROYAL GAZETTE (THE). N° 143. July 13, 1782. [Charlestown] 1782. Fol.

ROYAL GEORGIA GAZETTE (THE). N° 30-31, 74-75, 79-80, 38, 85, 93-108. August 12, 1779—

March 22, 1781. New York, 1779-1781. Fol.

RUBETA. The Vision of Rubeta, an epic story of the island of Manhattan. [By Laughton Osborne.] Boston, 1838. 8vo.

RUECKERT, ERNST FERDINAND. Therapeutics of Homœopathy: or, outlines of succeſsful homœopathic cures .. Translated by C. J. Hempel. New York, 1846. 8vo.

RUECKERT, TH. J. A Treatise on Headaches .. based on [and translated from] T. J. Rückert's clinical experience in homœopathy. With introduction, appendix, synopsis, notes, directions, .. and fifty additional cases. By J. C. Peters. New York, 1853. 8vo.

RUFFIN, EDMUND. An Eſsay on Calcareous Manures. Second edition. Shellbanks, Va. 1835. 8°

RUFFIN, THOMAS. Reports of Cases argued and adjudged in the Supreme Court of North Carolina, during the years 1820 and 1821. The former part by T. Ruffin, the latter by F. L. Hawks. (Vol. 2-4: 1822-26. By F. L. Hawks.) 4 vol. Raleigh, 1843-45. 8°

RUFFNER, HENRY. The Fathers of the Desert; or an account of the origin and practice of monkery among heathen nations, *etc.* 2 vol. New York, 1850. 12°

RUFFNER, WILLIAM HENRY. Lectures on the Evidences of Christianity; delivered at the University of Virginia during the seſsion of 1850-1. [Edited by W. H. Ruffner.] N. York, 1852. 8°
  2 AFRICA's Redemption. A Discourse [on Psalm lxviii. 31] on African Colonization in its miſsionary aspects, and in its relation to slavery and abolition. Philadel. 1852. 8vo.

RUGER, WILLIAM. Ruger's Arith-

metick. A new system of arithmetick, *etc.* Watertown, 1829. 12°

RUMSAY, James. A short Treatise on the application of steam,
whereby is clearly shewn, from actual experiments, that steam may be
applied to propel boats or veſſels of
any burthen against rapid currents
with great velocity. Philadelphia,
1787. 8vo.

RUPP, J. Daniel. He pasa Ek-
klesia. An original History of the
religious Denominations at present
existing in the United States, containing authentic accounts of their
rise, progreſs, statistics, and doctrines. Compiled by J. D. Rupp.
Philadelphia, 1844. 8vo.

2 History of Lancaster County.
To which is prefixed, a brief sketch
of the early history of Pennsylvania.
Compiled from authentic sources.
Lancaster, Penn. 1844. 8°

RURAL MAGAZINE, or Vermont
Repository.. Jan. 1795, to Dec. 1796.
2 vol. Rutland [1795-96]. 8°

RUSCHENBERGER, William S.
W. A Voyage round the World ;
including an embaſſy to Muscat and
Siam, in 1835-6 and -7. Philadelphia, 1838. 8vo.

2 Ruschenberger's Series. First
books of natural history. Elements
of anatomy and physiology... From
the text of Milne Edwards and A.
Comte. With plates. Philadelphia,
1845. 12°

3 Ruschenberger's Series. First
books of natural history. Elements
of entomology... From the text of
Milne Edwards and A. Comte... With
plates. Philadelphia, 1845. 12°

4 Ruschenberger's Series. First
books of natural history. Elements
of mammalogy... From the text of
Milne Edwards and A. Comte... With
plates. Philadelphia, 1845. 12°

5 Ruschenberger's Series. First
books of natural history. Elements

of herpetology and of ichthyology...
From the text of Milne Edwards and
A. Comte. With plates. Philadel-
phia, 1845. 12°

6 Ruschenberger's Series. First
books of natural history. Elements
of ornithology... From the text of
Milne Edwards and A. Comte... With
plates. Philadelphia, 1845. 12°

7 Ruschenberger's Series. First
books of natural history. Elements
of conchology... From the text of
Milne Edwards and A. Comte... With
plates. Philadelphia, 1845. 12°

8 Ruschenberger's Series. First
books of natural history. Elements
of botany... From the text of Milne
Edwards and A. Comte.... With
plates. Philadelphia, 1845. 12°

9 Ruschenberger's Series. First
books of natural history. Elements
of geology... From the text of F. S.
Beudant,.. Milne Edwards and A.
Comte... With three hundred engravings. Philadelphia, 1846. 12°

10 Ruschenberger's Series : First
books of natural history : Elements
of anatomy and physiology (mammalogy; ornithology; herpetology; conchology; entomology; botany; geology); prepared for the use of schools
and colleges by W. S. W. Ruschenberger,.. from the text of Milne Edwards and A. Comte. 8 parts. Philadelphia, 1848-47. 12°

11 A Notice of the origin, progreſs, and present condition of the
Academy of Natural Sciences of Philadelphia... [Read before the Society,
Feb. 10, 1852.] Philadel. 1852. 8vo.

RUSH, Benjamin. An Oration
delivered before the American Philosophical Society at Philadelphia, containing an enquiry into the natural
history of medicine among the Indians in North America. Philadelphia. 8vo.

2 The New Method of Inoculating
for the Small Pox. Philadelphia, 1781.
12mo.

3 Observations upon the cause

and cure of the Tetanus. Philadelphia, 1785. 8vo.

4 AN ORATION delivered before the American Philosophical Society, Feb. 1786.

5 AN ENQUIRY into the effects of Public Punishments upon Criminals and upon Society. Philadelphia, 1787. 8vo.

6 CONSIDERATIONS on the Injustice and Impolicy of punishing Murder by death. Philadelphia, 1792. 8vo.

7 MEDICAL Inquiries and Observations. (Vol. 1. Second American edition.) 2 vol. Philadelphia, 1794, 1793. 8°

8 AN ACCOUNT of the bilious remitting yellow fever, as it appeared in the city of Philadelphia, in .. 1793. Second edition. Philadelphia, 1794. 8°

9 AN EULOGIUM, intended to perpetuate the memory of David Rittenhouse, late President of the American Philosophical Society; delivered Dec. 17, 1796. Philadelphia. 8vo.

10 AN EULOGIUM, intended to perpetuate the memory of David Rittenhouse, late President of the American Philosophical Society. Philadelphia, 1796. 8vo.

RUSH, JAMES. The Philosophy of the Human Voice. Philadelphia, 1833. 8vo.

2 THE PHILOSOPHY of the Human Voice: embracing its physiological history; together with a system of principles, by which criticism in the art of elocution may be rendered intelligible, and instruction definite and comprehensive... To which is added, a brief analysis of song and recitative. Third edition. Philadel. 1845. 8vo.

RUSH, JACOB. Charges and Extracts of Charges on moral and religious subjects. To which is annexed, the Act of the State of Pennsylvania respecting vice and immorality. New York, 1804. 12mo.

RUSH, RICHARD. Remarks on the loan of a million and a half of dollars,

proposed to be raised by the City of Washington, and the towns of Georgia and Alexandria. [1829.] 8vo.

2 LETTER and accompanying Documents from the Hon. R. Rush to J. Gales, Esq. Mayor of .. Washington, respecting the loan .. negotiated .. in Europe, for the said city, and the towns of Georgetown and Alexandria, under the authority of an act of Congress of the United States, etc. Washington, 1830. 8°

3 A LETTER on Free-Masonry to the Committee of the Citizens of York County, Pennsylvania. Boston, 1831. 8vo.

4 MEMORANDA of a Residence at the Court of London. ... Second edition, revised and enlarged. Philadelphia, 1833. 8°

5 MEMORANDA of a Residence at the Court of London, comprising incidents official and personal from 1819 to 1825; including negotiations on the Oregon question, and other unsettled questions between the United States and Great Britain. Philadelphia, 1845. 8°

RUSSELL, GEORGE R. The Merchant. An Oration before the Rhode Island Alpha of the Phi Beta Kappa Society at Providence, September 4, 1849. Boston, 1849. 8°

RUSSELL, J. Junior. The History of the War between the United States and Great Britain, which commenced in June, 1812, and closed in Feb. 1815; .. compiled chiefly from public documents, with an appendix, containing the correspondence which passed .. in treating for peace. To which is added, the treaty of peace, and a list of vessels taken from Great Britain during the war. Hartford, 1815. 8°

RUSSELL, JOHN LEWIS. A Discourse delivered before the Massachusetts Horticultural Society, on the celebration of its seventh anniversary, Sept. 17, 1835. Boston, 1835. 8vo.

RUSSELL, John Miller. An Oration, pronounced at Charlestown, July 4, 1797. Charlestown [1797]. 8°

RUSSELL, Michael. History and present Condition of the Barbary States; comprehending a view of their civil institutions, antiquities, arts, religion, literature, commerce, agriculture, and natural productions. New York, 1844. 12°

2 Life of Oliver Cromwell. 2 vol. New York, 1844-46. 12°

3 Polynesia; or, an historical account of the principal islands in the South Sea, including New Zealand, etc. New York, 1845. 12°

4 Nubia and Abyssinia: comprehending their civil history, antiquities, arts, religion, literature, and natural history. New York, 1845. 12°

5 Palestine, or the Holy Land; from the earliest period to the present time. New York, 1846. 12°

6 View of ancient and modern Egypt; with an outline of its natural history. New York, 1846. 12°

RUSSELL, William. Primary Reader: a selection of easy reading lessons. 2nd edition. Bost. 1843. 12°

2 Spelling-Book, or second course of lessons in spelling and reading, etc. Boston, 1845. 12°

3 Sequel to the Primary Reader of Russell's elementary series, etc. Boston, 1846. 12°

4 Pulpit Elocution, comprising suggestions on the importance of study; remarks on the effect of manner in speaking; the rules of reading, exemplified from the Scriptures, hymns, and sermons; etc. Andover, 1846. 12°

5 Harper's New York Class-book; comprising outlines of the geography and history of New York; biographical notices, etc. N. York, 1847. 12°

6 The University Speaker: a collection of pieces designed for college

exercises in declamation, etc. Boston and Cambridge, 1852. 12°

RUSSELL, William, and Goldsbury, John. Introduction to the American Common-School Reader and Speaker, etc. Boston, 1845. 12°

RUSSELL, William S. Guide to Plymouth, and Recollections of the Pilgrims. Boston, 1846. 8°

RUSSIAN. A Sketch of the internal condition of the United States of America, and of their political relations with Europe. By a Russian. Translated from the French, by an American, with notes. Baltimore, 1826. 8vo.

RUSSIAN VICTORIES. The Celebration of the Russian Victories, in Georgetown, District of Columbia; .. including the oration of Mr. Custis; etc. Georgetown, 1813. 8°

RUSTICUS, Pseud. A Friendly Debate, or a Dialogue between Rusticus and Academicus about the late performance of Academicus. [See Academicus.] Boston, 1722. 8°

RUTGERS COLLEGE, New Brunswick, New Jersey. Catalogue of the officers and alumni of Rutgers College. New Brunswick, 1840. 8°

2 Rutgers College. (View of the order of studies, and method of instruction.) N. Brunswick, 1841. 8°

RUTH LEE. Phil. 1829. 12mo.

RUTLEDGE, John. An Examination of the question, Who is the writer of two forged letters addressed to the President of the United States? Second edition. Washington, 1803. 8°

RYAN, George. Report of the Trial of G. Ryan at Charlestown, N. H. May, 1811, for highway robbery. Keene [1811]. 8°

RYAN, James. An elementary Treatise on Algebra, etc. Fourth edition, enlarged. New York, 1839. 12°

ABINE, LOREN-zo. The American Loyalists, or biographical sketches of adherents to the British crown in the war of the Revolution: alphabetically arranged; with a preliminary historical eſſay. Boston, 1847. 8°

SACO, José Antonio. Justa defensa de la Academia Cubana de Literatura contra los violentos ataques que se le han dado en el diario de la Habaña desde el 12 hasta el 23 de Abril del presente año (1834). New Orleans, 1834. 8vo.

SADLER, Thomas. The Silent Pastor; or consolation for the sick. [With alterations and additions by the American editor, J. F. W. W.] Boston, 1848. 12°

SAGE, Rufus B. Scenes in the Rocky Mountains, and in Oregon, California, New Mexico, Texas, and the grand prairies; or, notes by the way, during an excursion of three years, etc. Philadelphia, 1846. 8°

SAGE, Sylvester. A Sermon [on Prov. xiv. 34] delivered before . . . the Governor, . . Council, and House of Representatives of . . Vermont, . . on the day of the anniversary Election. Windsor, 1803. 8°

SAINT CLAIR, or the protégé; a tale of the Federal City. By J. E. T[uel]. Washington, 1846. 8°

SAINT CLAIR, Arthur, General. A Narrative of the manner in which the campaign against the Indians, 1791, was conducted; together with observations on the statements of the Secretary of War and the Quarter Master General, and the Reports of the Committees. Philadel. 1812. 8°

SAINT GEORGE, A. Mrs. A Sketch of the Life of the illustrious Washington, first President of the United States of America. New York, 1834. 8vo.

SAINT JOHN, Henry, Viscount Bolingbroke. The Works of Lord Bolingbroke. With a life, prepared expreſsly for this edition, containing additional information relative to his personal and public character, selected from the best authorities. 4 vol. Philadelphia, 1841. 8°

SAINT JOHN, James Augustus. The Lives of celebrated Travellers. 3 vol. New York, 1844. 12°

SAINT JOHN, John R. A true Description of the Lake Superior Country. . . . Also a minute Account of the Copper Mines and Working Companies. New York, 1846. 12mo.

SAINT JOHN, Samuel. Elements of Geology, intended for the use of students. New York, 1851. 12°

SAINT MARY'S HALL, Burlington, New Jersey. An Appeal to Parents for female education on Christian principles; with a prospectus of St. Mary's Hall, . . Burlington, New

Jersey. [By G. W. Doane.] Burlington, 1837. 4°

2 NOTICES of St. Mary's Hall. [Burlington! 1837!] 8vo.

3 THE WAY of the Church with Children; together with the Catalogue and Prospectus of St. Mary's Hall. Summer Term, 1848. Burlington, 1848. 12mo.

4 ST. MARY's Hall Register. Fifteenth Year. Burlington,1852. 12mo.

SALEM, MASSACHUSETTS. Memorial of the Inhabitants of . . Salem [on the violation by Great Britain of the rights of neutrals]. Jan. 20, 1806. Washington, 1806. 8°

2 IMPRESSED Seamen from Salem. From the Salem Gazette of March 30, 1813. [Salem, 1813.] s. sh. fol°

3 IMPRESSED Seamen from Salem. From the Salem Gazette of April 27, 1813. [Salem, 1813.] s. sh. fol°

4 REGULATIONS for the superintendence, government, and instruction of the public schools . . of Salem. Salem, 1842. 8°

5 ANNUAL Report of the School Committee of the City of Salem. Salem, 1851. 8°

SALEM ADVERTISER (THE). Vol. 8. N° 23. Sept. 18, 1839. Salem, 1839. Fol.

SALEM ATHENÆUM. See CATALOGUES, N° 12.

SALEM DIRECTORY. The Salem Directory and City Register; etc. [for 1837; 1842; 1846]. Salem, 1837-46. 12°

SALES LA TERRIERE, PIERRE DE. A Dissertation on the Puerperal fever. Boston, 1789. 8vo.

SALISBURY, EDWARD E. An Inaugural Discourse on Arabic and Sanskrit literature, delivered in New Haven,August 16,1843. New Haven, 1843. 8vo.

SALKELD, JOSEPH. Buds, Blossoms, and Fruit of the Church. By a candidate for orders in the Church (J. Salkeld). New York, 1843. 12°

SALLUSTIUS, CRISPUS CAIUS. Sallust's Jugurthine War and Conspiracy of Catiline. With an English Commentary and geographical and historical indexes, by C. Anthon. . . Ninth edition, corrected and enlarged. New York, 1846. 12°

SALTER, RICHARD. A Sermon [on Esth. x. 3] preached before the General Assembly of . . Connecticut, at Hartford, on the day of their anniversary Election. N.London,1768. 4°

SALTONSTALL, LEVERETT. Speech . . in reply to Mr. Parmenter, on the bill providing for the civil and diplomatic expenses of the government for . . . 1840; delivered in the House of Representatives, April 21, 1840. Washington, 1840. 8°

2 SPEECH . . . upon the tariff bills reported by the Committee of Ways and Means, and the Committee on Manufactures; delivered in the House of Representatives, June 17, 1842. Washington, 1842. 8°

SALVATION. Divine Glory brought to view in the condemnation of the ungodly: or the doctrine of future punishment illustrated and vindicated in reply to a late pamphlet, entitled Salvation for all Men. By a friend to truth [J. Eckley]. Boston, 1782. 8°

SAM, UNCLE, Pseud. Uncle Sam's recommendation of phrenology to his millions of friends in the United States. In a series of . . letters. New York. 1842. 12°

SAMARITAN. The Good Samaritan. New York. 4to.

SAMPSON, MARMADUKE B. Rationale of Crime, and its appropriate treatment; being a treatise on criminal jurisprudence considered in relation to cerebral organization. . . . From the second London edition, with notes and illustrations by E. W. Farnham. New York, 1846. 12°

SAMPSON, WILLIAM. Sampson's Discourse, and Correspondence with various learned Jurists upon the History of the Law; with the addition of several eſſays, tracts and documents relating to the subject. Compiled by P. Thompson. Washington City, 1826. 8vo.

SAMSON, G. W. The Providence of God in raising up under our Republican Institutions great and good men as our rulers; a discourse [on Judges ii. 18] delivered on Thanksgiving day, Nov. 25, 1852. Boston, 1853. 8°.

SANBORN, DYER H. Analytical Grammar of the English Grammar. . . In five parts. . . Second edition. Concord, N. H. 1840. 12°

SANBORN, EDWIN D. A Eulogy on Daniel Webster, delivered before the students of Phillips Academy, Andover, Maſſachusetts, etc. Hanover, N. H. 1853. 8°

SAND, GEORGES, Pseud. [i. e. MARIE AURORE DUDEVANT]. Consuelo. By G. Sand. Translated by F. G. Shaw. Third edition. 3 vol. Boston, 1847. 12°
2 CONSUELO .. translated from the French by F. Robinson. New York, 1851. 8°
3 THE COUNTESS of Rudolstadt. By G. Sand. [Sequel to "Consuelo."] .. Translated by F. G. Shaw. Second edition. 2 vol. Boston, 1847. 12°
4 THE USCOQUE, or the Corsair; .. Translated by J. Bauer. New York [1851?] 8°

SANDEAU, JULES. Money-bags and Titles: a hit at the follies of the age. Translated from the French of J. Sandeau. By L. Myers. Philadelphia, 1850. 12°

SANDERS, CHARLES W. Sanders's Spelling Book, etc. Andover and New York, 1839. 12°
2 SANDERS's Series. The School-Reader. Fourth book. . . Fourth edition. New York, 1842. 12°

3 PRIMARY Education; as connected with the use of Sanders's Series of school books, etc. New York [1845?] 8°

SANDERS, DANIEL CLARKE. A Sermon [on 2 Kings, iv. 13] preached before the Governor, the Council, and .. House of Representatives of .. Vermont, .. Oct. 11, .. on occasion of General Election. Vergennes, 1798. 8°
2 A CHARGE to the Graduates in the University of Vermont, .. at the public commencement, etc. Burlington, 1812. 8°

SANDERSON, JOHN. Sanderson's Biography of the Signers to the Declaration of Independence [of the United States of America]. Revised and edited by R. T. Conrad. Philadelphia, 1846. 8°

SANDS, ROBERT C. Writings, in prose and verse. With a memoir of the author. 2 vol. New York, 1834. 8vo.

SANDWICH ISLANDS. A Narrative of Five Youths from the Sandwich Islands, now receiving their education in this country. New York, 1816. 8vo.
2 REFUTATION of the Charges brought by the Roman Catholics against the American Miſſionaries at the Sandwich Islands. Boston, 1843. 8°

SANFORD, EZEKIEL. A History of the United States before the Revolution: with some account of the Aborigines. Philadelphia, 1819. 8°
2 THE WORKS of the British Poets, with Lives of the Authors. By E. Sanford [continued after vol. 24 by Robert Walsh, and vol. 18-21, and 23 edited by him]. 50 vol. Philadelphia, 1819-23. 12°

SANFORD, JAMES, AND OTHERS. Report of the Commiſſioners appointed to examine the Planters and Merchants Bank of Mobile. [Tuscaloosa, 1841.] 8°

2 REPORT of the Commissioners appointed to examine the Mobile Branch Bank. Tuscaloosa, 1846. 8°

3 REPORT of the Commissioners appointed to examine the Mobile Branch Bank. Tuscaloosa, 1846. 8°

SANSOM, JOSEPH. Sketches of Lower Canada, historical and descriptive, etc. New York, 1817. 12°

SANTON. The Prophecy of the Santon, and other poems. Worcester, 1847. 16°

SARGENT, EPES. Velasco: a tragedy, in five acts [and in verse]. New York, 1839. 12°

2 THE STANDARD Speaker; containing exercises in prose and poetry for declamation .. newly translated or compiled. . . A treatise on oratory and elocution. Notes, explanatory and biographical. . . Third edition. Philadelphia, 1852. 8°

SARGENT, JOHN OSBORNE. A Lecture on the late improvements in steam navigation and the arts of naval warfare; with a brief notice of Ericsson's caloric engine: delivered before the Boston Lyceum. New York, 1844. 8°

2 ANOTHER edition. New York and London, 1844. 8°

SARGENT, JOHN T. Theodore Parker, the Reform Pulpit, and the Influences that oppose it. A sermon [on Gen. xix. 9], etc. Boston, 1852. 8°

SARGENT, LUCIUS MANLIUS. Hubert and Ellen. With other poems, etc. Large paper. Boston, 1812. 8°

2 HUBERT and Ellen. With other poems. Boston, 1813. 8vo.

3 LETTER, on the "State of the Temperance Reform," to the Rev. C. Stetson, etc. Boston, 1836. 8°

4 TEMPERANCE Tales; new illustrated edition. 2 vol. Boston, 1852. 8°

SARGENT, WINTHROP. Papers in relation to the official conduct of Governour Sargent. Boston, Aug. 1, 1801. 8°

2 DIARY of Col. Winthrop Sargent, Adjutant General of the United States army during the campaign of 1791. Now first printed. End. This edition .. hath been privately printed .. for G. W. Jones, being the fourth of the series of Wormsloe quartos. The impression is limited to forty-six copies. Wormsloe, 1851. 4to.

SARGENT, WINTHROP, AND BARTON, BENJAMIN SMITH. Papers relative to certain American antiquities. Philadelphia, 1796. 4to.

SARONI, HERRMAN, S. Musical Vade Mecum: a manual of the science of music, etc. New York, 1852. 12mo.

SARTORIUS, ERNST. The Person and Work of Christ .. translated by Rev. V. S. Stearns. Boston, 1848. 12°

SAVAGE, JAMES. An Oration, delivered July 4, 1811, at the request of the Select men of Boston in commemoration of American Independence. Boston, 1811. 8°

SAVAGE, THOMAS S. A Description of the characters and habits of Troglodytes Gorilla. And of the Osteology of the same, by J. Wyman. Boston, 1847. 4to.

SAVAGE, TIMOTHY, Pseud? The Amazonian Republic, recently discovered in the interior of Peru. New York, 1842. 12°

SAVANNAH REPUBLICAN. N° 184. Vol. 36. Sept. 20, 1839. Savannah, 1839. Fol.

SAUNDERS, F. Memories of the Great Metropolis: or London from the Tower to the Crystal Palace. New York, 1852. 12°

SAWYER, LEICESTER AMBROSE. The Elements of Biblical Interpretation. . . Together with an analysis of the rationalistic and mystic modes of interpreting. New York, 1836. 12°

2 ELEMENTS of Moral Philosophy,

on the basis of the Ten Commandments; containing a complete system of moral duties. N. York, 1845. 12°

3 ELEMENTS of Mental Philosophy; containing a critical exposition of the principal phenomena and powers of the human mind. New York, 1846. 12°

SAWYER, MATTHIAS E. An Enquiry into the existence of the living principle and causes of animal life. Philadelphia, 1793. 8vo.

SAWYER, THOMAS J. Memoir of Rev. S. R. Smith. Boston, 1852. 12°

SAX, J. BRADFORD. The Organic Laws; or, the laws which govern the human organism. New York, 1851. 12°

SAXE, JOHN GODFREY. Progreſs: a satire. [In verse.] Second edition. New York, 1847. 8°

2 POEMS. Second edition. Boston, 1850. 16°

SAXTON, L. C. Fall of Poland; containing an analytical and a philosophical account of the causes which conspired in the ruin of that nation, together with a history of the country from its origin. 2 vol. New York, 1852. 8°

SAY, THOMAS. American Entomology, or descriptions of the insects of North America, illustrated by coloured figures. [Plates 1-6, with descriptions. No more was published of this edition.] Philadelphia, 1817. 8vo.

2 DESCRIPTION of the land and fresh water Shells of the United States, .. from Mitchell, Ames, and White's third edition of Nicholson's Encyclopedia. Philadelphia, 1819. 8vo.

3 AMERICAN Entomology, or descriptions of the insects of North America. Illustrated by coloured figures. Vol. 1-2. (A Gloſsary to Say's Entomology.) 3 vol. Philadelphia, 1824-25. 8vo.

4 A GLOSSARY to Say's Entomology. Philadelphia, 1825. 8vo.

5 AMERICAN Conchology. Vol. 1. Nº 1-4. New Harmony, 1830. 8vo.

6 DESCRIPTIONS of some new terrestrial and fluviatile Shells of North America. 1829, 1830, 1831. New Harmony, 1840. 8°

SAYMORE, SARAH EMERY. Hearts unveiled; or "I knew you would like him." New York, 1852. 12°

SCACCHI, ARCANGELO. Abstract of a paper on the Humite of Monte Somma, .. with observations by J. D. Dana. [From the "American Journal of Science and Arts." Second series. Vol. 14. Nº 41.] [New Haven, 1852.] 8vo.

SCAMMON, J. YOUNG. Reports of cases argued and determined in the Supreme Court of the State of Illinois (from Dec. term, 1832, to Dec. term, 1843). Vol. 1. Second edition, and vol. 2, Philadelphia, 1841. Vol. 3 and 4, Chicago, 1844. 8°

SCENES of Childhood. American Sunday School Union. Philadelphia, 1831. 12mo.

SCENES of Intemperance. Philadelphia [1832]. 12mo.

SCHAFF, PHILIPP. History of the Apostolic Church; with a general introduction to Church History. Translated [from the German] by E. D. Yeomans. London and New York [printed], 1854. 8vo.

SCHAUFFLER, W. G. Meditations on the last days of Christ; together with eight meditations on the seventeenth chapter of John. Boston, 1853. 12°

SCHENCK, PETER H. Frauds on the Revenue; addreſsed to the people of the United States, and to their representatives in Congreſs. N. York, 1830. 8°

SCHIEFERDECKER, C. C. Short Eſsay on the invariably succeſsful treatment of Cholera with water. Philadelphia, 1849. 8vo.

2 A SHORT Guide for the rational Treatment of Children, in health and disease, by water. Philadelphia, 1852. 12°

SCHILLER, JOHANN CHRISTOPH FRIEDRICH VON. Correspondence between Schiller and Goethe, from 1794 to 1805, translated by G. H. Calvert. Vol. 1. New York [printed] and London, 1845. 12°

SCHLEGEL, JOHAN FREDERICH WILHELM. Neutral Rights; or, an impartial examination of the right of search of neutral veſſels under convoy, and of a judgment pronounced by the English Court of Admiralty, the 11th June, 1799, in the case of the Swedish convoy, with some additions and correĉtions. . . Translated from the French. Philadel. 1801. 8°

SCHLEMIHL, PETER, *Pseud.* Peter Schlemihl in America. [A theological and satirical romance.] 1848. 8°

SCHMUCKER, S. M. The Errors of Modern Infidelity illustrated and refuted. Philadelphia, 1848. 12°

SCHMUCKER, S. S. Elements of popular Theology, with special reference to the doĉtrines of the Reformation, as avowed before the Diet at Augsburg, in 1530. Andover, 1834. 8vo.

2 ELEMENTS of popular Theology, with special reference to the doĉtrines of the Reformation, as avowed before the Diet at Augsburg, in 1530. Second edition. New York, 1834. 8°

3 PSYCHOLOGY, or elements of a new system of mental philosophy on the basis of consciouſneſſ and common sense. Second edition. New York, 1843. 12mo.

SCHOOL. American Sunday School Union. [Sixty-eight books for children, published by them.] Philadelphia, 1825-32. 16mo.

2 AN ADDRESS to the young people attending Sabbath Schools. Philadelphia [1830]. 12mo.

3 LESSONS for Infant Schools. Philadelphia, 1831. 12mo.

SCHOOL ATLAS. The Universal School Atlas, arranged on the induĉtive plan, and designed to render the study of geography both easy and instruĉtive ; containing thirty-four maps. Cincinnati, 1832. 4°

SCHOOL CHILDREN at Noon. American Sunday School Union. Philadelphia [1830 ?]. 12mo.

SCHOOLCRAFT, HENRY ROWE, A view of the Lead Mines of Missouri : including some observations on the mineralogy, geology, geography, antiquities, soil, climate, population, and produĉtions of Missouri and Arkansaw, and other sections of the Western Country. New York, 1819. 8vo.

2 NARRATIVE Journal of Travels, through the North-Western regions of the United States, extending from Detroit through the great chain of American Lakes to the sources of the Miſſiſſippi rivers, performed as a member of the expedition under Governor Caſſ, in the year 1820. . . Embellished with a map and eight copper-plate engravings. Albany, 1821. 8vo.

3 TRAVELS in the central portions of the Miſſiſſippi Valley, comprising observations on its mineral geography, internal resources, and aboriginal population. Performed in 1821. New York, 1825. 8°

4 NARRATIVE of an Expedition through the Upper Miſſiſſippi to Itasca Lake, the aĉtual source of this river ; embracing an exploratory trip through the St. Croix and Burntwood (or Broule) rivers, in 1832, *etc.* [with an appendix]. New York, 1834. 8vo.

5 ALGIC Researches ; comprising inquiries respeĉting the mental characĉteristics of the North American Indians. First series : Indian tales and legends. 2 vol. N. York, 1839. 12°

6 ONEÓTA, or characteristics of the red race of America. From original notes and manuscripts. 8 pts. New York, 1845. 8°

7 ONEÓta, or, characteristics of the red race of America. From original notes and manuscripts. New York and London, 1845. 8°

8 NOTES on the Iroquois : or, contributions to the statistics, aboriginal history, antiquities, and general ethnology of western New York. New York, 1846. Roy. 8vo.

9 NOTES on the Iroquois; or contributions to American history, antiquities, and general ethnology. Albany, 1847. 8°

10 HISTORICAL and Statistical Information respecting the history, condition, and prospects of the Indian Tribes of the United States: collected and prepared under the direction of the Bureau of Indian affairs, per act of Congress of March 3, 1847, by H. R. Schoolcraft, illustrated by S. Eastman, Captain U. S. Army. Part 1-3. Philadelphia, 1851-53. 4°

11 PERSONAL Memoirs of a residence of thirty years with the Indian tribes on the American frontiers . . 1812 to 1842. Philadel. 1851. 8°

12 SUMMARY Narrative of an exploratory Expedition to the sources of the Mississippi river in 1820: resumed and completed by the discovery of its origin in Itasca Lake, in 1832. With appendices. Philadelphia, 1855. 8vo.

SCHOTT, JAMES. A Statement by J. Schott [in relation to his duel with Pierce Butler—including the correspondence of the parties]. [Baltimore, 1844.] 8°

SCHRAMKE, T. Description of the New York Croton Aqueduct in English, German, and French, with twenty plates. New York and Berlin [printed], 1846. 4°

SCHROEDER, FRANCIS. Shores of the Mediterranean, with sketches of travel. 2 vol. London [New York printed], 1846. 12mo.

SCHROEDER, JOHN FREDERICK. The Intellectual and Moral Resources of Horticulture. An anniversary discourse, pronounced before the New York Horticultural Society. New York, 1828. 8°

SCHULTZ, CHRISTIAN, Junior. Travels on an inland voyage through the States of New York, Pennsylvania, Virginia, Ohio, Kentucky and Tennessee, and through the Territories of Indiana, Louisiana, Mississippi, and New Orleans, in 1807 and 1808. With maps and plates. 2 vol. New York, 1810. 8°

SCHWARZ, JOSEPH. A Descriptive Geography and brief Historical Sketch of Palestine . . translated by J. Leeser. Philadelphia, 1850. 8°

SCIPIO, Pseud. Scipio's Reflections on Monroe's View of the conduct of the Executive on the foreign affairs of the United States, connected with a mission to the French Republic in the years 1794, '95, '96. Boston, 1798. 12°

SCOTLAND. The Whigs of Scotland : or, the last of the Stuarts. An historical romance of the Scottish persecution. 2 vol. New York, 1833. 12°

SCOTT, JOSEPH. The United States Gazetteer. Philadel. 1795. 12°

2 A GEOGRAPHICAL Dictionary of the United States of North America, containing a general description of each State, etc. Philadel. 1805. 8°

SCOTT, SIR WALTER, Bart. The Field of Waterloo, a poem [with notes]. Boston, 1815. 8°

2 THE LADY of the Lake. . . Illustrated edition. Philadel. 1844. 8°

3 LETTERS on Demonology and Witchcraft, etc. New York, 1845. 12°

4 WAVERLEY Poetry: being the

poems scattered through the Waverley Novels, attributed to anonymous sources, but presumed to be written by Sir W. Scott. Boston, 1851. 12°

SCOTT, WINFIELD. Infantry-Tactics; or rules for the exercise and manœuvres of the United States Infantry. By Major-Gen. Scott. Washington, 1835. 12°

2 GENERAL Scott and his Staff: comprising memoirs of . . distinguished officers attached to General Scott's army . . and other officers distinguished in the conquest of California and New Mexico; interspersed with anecdotes of the Mexican war, etc. Philadelphia, 1848. 12°

3 LIFE and Public Services of Winfield Scott. Philadel. 1852. 12°

SCOTTISH FARMER (THE). Philadelphia, 1830. 12mo.

SCRIPTURE ILLUSTRATIONS. First series. Philadel. 1827. 12mo.

2 SCRIPTURE Illustrations. Second series. Philadelphia, 1827. 12mo.

SCRIPTURES. Stories from the Scriptures. By a Grandmother. Philadelphia, 1829. 12mo.

SCUDDER, JOHN, Rev. Letter from Dr. Scudder, of Ceylon, addressed . . to the young men in the colleges and seminaries of learning in the United States of America. [New York.] 8°

SEAGER, E. S. Mrs. The Education of Woman. An address read before the Young Ladies' Literary Society of the Genesee Wesleyan Seminary. Second edition. Buffalo, 1852. 8°

SEAMAN, EZRA C. Essays on the Progress of Nations, in productive industry, civilization, population, and wealth; illustrated by statistics, etc. New York, 1846. 8°

2 ESSAYS on the Progress of Nations, in civilization, productive industry, wealth and population. Illus-

trated by statistics, etc. New York, 1852. 12°

SEARS, BARNAS. The Ciceronian; or the Prussian method of teaching the elements of the Latin language adapted to the use of American schools. Boston, 1844. 12°

2 CLASSICAL Studies, Essays on Ancient Literature and Art, with the biography and correspondence of eminent philologists. By B. Sears, B. B. Edwards, and C. C. Felton. Boston, 1849. 12°

3 THE LIFE of Luther; with reference to its earlier periods and the opening scenes of the Reformation. Philadelphia [1850]. 8vo.

SEARS, M. The American Politician; containing the Declaration of Independence, the Constitution of the United States, the inaugural and first annual addresses and messages of all the presidents, and other . . state papers; together with a selection of . . statistical tables, and biographical notices of the signers of the Declaration of Independence, the several presidents, etc. Third edition. Boston, 1842. 8°

SEARSON, JOHN. Poems, chiefly adapted to rural entertainment in the United States of America. Philadelphia, 1797. 8vo.

SEATSFIELD, CHARLES. Life in the New World; or sketches of American society. By Seatsfield. Translated from the German by G. C. Hebbe and J. Mackay. New York [1844]. 8vo.

2 TOKEAH; or the white rose. Second edition. Philadel. 1845. 8°

3 NORTH and South; or, scenes and adventures in Mexico. By Seatsfield. . . Translated from the German, by J. T. H[eadley?] New York [1845!] 8vo.

SEAWORTHY, GREGORY, Pseud. Nag's Head; or Two Months among "The Bankers." A story of seashore life and manners. Philadelphia, 1850. 12°

2 BERTIE or Life in the Old Field. A humorous novel. By Capt. Gregory Seaworthy . . with a letter to the author from W. Irving. Philadelphia, 1851. 12°

SEDGWICK, CATHARINE MARIA, *Miſs*. Facts and Fancies, for school day-reading; a sequel to " Morals of Manners." New York and London, 1848. 16°

2 A NEW England Tale, and Miscellanies. New York, 1852. 12°

SEDGWICK, HENRY D. A Vindication of the Conduct and Character of H. D. Sedgwick against certain Charges made by the Hon. J. Platt, together with some statements and inquiries, intended, to elicit the reasons of the award in the case of the Greek Frigates. Second edition, with a postscript. New York, 1826. 8°

2 REFUTATION of the Reasons aſsigned by the arbitrators for their award in the case of the two Greek Frigates. New York, 1826. 8°

SEDGWICK, THEODORE. Public and Private Economy. 3 parts. New York, 1836-9. 12°

SEDGWICK, THEODORE, *Jr*. A Memoir of the Life of William Livingston. New York, 1833. 8vo.

SEEGER, C. L. An Oration, pronounced at Northampton [in Massachusetts], July 4, 1810, in commemoration of the anniversary of American Independence. Second edition. Northampton, 1810. 8°

SEGUENOT. A Letter from a Romish Priest [Seguenot] in Canada to one who was taken captive in her infancy and instructed in the Romish Faith, but afterward returned to this her native country. With an answer thereto, by a person to whom it was communicated. Boston, 1729. 12mo.

SEGUR, PHILIPPE PAUL DE, *Count*.

History of the Expedition to Ruſsia, undertaken by the Emperor Napoleon in the year 1812. (From the seventh London edition, with corrections and occasional notes by the American editor.) New York, 1845. 12°

SEIP, FREDERIC. A Diſsertation on Cataract. Philadel. 1800. 8vo.

SELBY, BENJAMIN. Report of the auditor of public accounts (B. Selby) to the Senate of Kentucky, made in compliance with a resolution of Dec. 17, 1839. Frankfort, 1840. 8°

SELECT REVIEWS, and Spirit of the Foreign Magazines. By E. Bronson, and others. 8 vol. Philadelphia, 1809-12. 8°

SELFRIDGE, THOMAS OLIVER. Trial of T. O. Selfridge . . for killing C. Austin, on the Public Exchange, in Boston, Aug. 4, 1806. Taken in shorthand, by T. Lloyd . . and G. Caines; *etc.* Second edition. Boston [1806]. 8°

2 A CORRECT Statement of the . . controversy between T. O. Selfridge and B. Austin; also a brief account of the catastrophe [resulting in the death of Charles Austin] in State Street, Boston, . . Aug. 4, 1806. . . Second edition. Charlestown, 1807. 8°

SELKIRK, ALEXANDER. The Solitary of Juan Fernandez (A. Selkirk): or the real Robinson Crusoe. By the author of Picciola [*i. e.* X. Boniface Saintine]. Translated from the French by A. T. Wilbur. Boston, 1851. 12°

SELLER, RICHARD. The Sufferings of R. Seller, on board the flagship Royal Prince, for his testimony to the unlawfulneſs of war. Philadelphia [1835?]. 16mo.

SEMMES, THOMAS. An Eſsay on the effects of lead, comprising a few experiments on the Saccharum Saturni, and its application in the cure of diseases. Philadelphia, 1801. 8vo.

SENECA INDIANS. The Case of the Seneca Indians, in the State of

New York. . . Printed for the information of the Society of Friends, by direction of the Joint Committees on Indian Affairs, of the four yearly meetings of Friends of Genesee, New York, Philadelphia, and Baltimore. Philadelphia, 1840.   8°

SENEX. Letters under the signatures of Senex and of a Farmer, comprehending an examination of the conduct of our Executive towards France and Great Britain, out of which the present crisis has arisen. Baltimore, 1809.   8°

SEQUEL to Easy Lessons. A selection of reading lessons for common schools. . . By the author of "The Literary and Scientific Class Book," etc.   Keene [1829!].   12°

SERGEANT, John, of Pennsylvania. An Oration delivered in Independence Square, in the City of Philadelphia, . . July 24, 1826, in commemoration of T. Jefferson and J. Adams.   Philadelphia, 1826.   8°

2 Select Speeches.   Philadelphia, 1832.   8°

3 An Address delivered at the request of the Managers of the Apprentices' Library Company of Philadelphia, November 23, 1832.   Philadelphia, 1832.   8°

SERGEANT, Thomas. Constitutional Law: being a view of the practice and jurisdiction of the Courts of the United States, and of constitutional points decided.   Second edition, with additions and improvements. Philadelphia, 1830.   8°

2 View of the land laws of Pennsylvania.   With notices of its early history and legislation.   Philadelphia, 1838.   8°

3 A Treatise upon the law of Pennsylvania relative to the proceeding by foreign attachment, with the acts of Assembly now in force in Pennsylvania on the subject of foreign and domestic attachments.   Second edi-

tion, with additions and improvements. Philadelphia, 1840.   8°

SERGEANT, Thomas, and Rawle, William. Reports of cases adjudged in the Supreme Court of Pennsylvania. Second edition, revised and corrected. 17 vol.   [Vol. 1, 3 and 12 only, are of the second edition.]   Philadelphia, 1844, 1829, 1820, '41, '46.   8°

SEVENTY-SIX SOCIETY.
1 The Examination of Joseph Galloway by a Committee of the House of Commons (with explanatory notes).   Edited by T. Balch. Philadelphia, 1855.   8vo.

2 Papers in relation to the case of Silas Deane. Now first published from the original manuscripts. [Edited by T. Balch?] Philadelphia, 1855. 8vo.

SEVER, Nicholas. Speech on the occasion of Col. Lothrop's death, etc.   Boston, 1750.   4°

SEVERANCE, Moses. The American Manual, or new English reader. . . For the use of schools. Cazenovia, N. Y. 1839.   12°

SEVILLE. Il Barbiere di Siviglia, dramma buffo per musica [in two acts].   (The barber of Seville, etc.) Ital. and Engl. New York, 1825. 12°

SEWALL, Joseph.   Jehovah is the King and Saviour of his people. A sermon [on Isaiah xxxiii. 22] . . upon the . . death of his late Majesty King George.   Boston, 1727.   8°

2 He that would keep God's commandments must renounce the society of Evil-Doers: a sermon [on Psalm cxix. 15] preached at Boston [Massachusetts], . . after a bloody and mortal duel. With a preface by the United Ministers of the town. Boston, 1728.   8vo.

SEWALL, Jotham, the Younger. A Memoir of the Rev. J. Sewall by his son J. Sewall. Boston, 1853. 8°

SEWALL, Samuel.   Proposals

touching the Accomplishment of Prophesies. Boston, 1713. 4to.

2 PHŒNOMENA quædam Apocalyptica ad aspectum Novi Orbis Configurata. Or some few lines towards a description of the New Heaven as it makes to those who stand upon the New Earth... The second edition. (The fountain opened: or the ... bleſſings .. to be dispensed at the National Conversion of the Jews [a sermon upon Zech. xiii. 1]. By .. S. Willard... The third edition.) 2 parts. Boston, Maſſachusetts, 1727. 4to.

SEWALL, SAMUEL, and DANE, NATHAN. A Communication [to the General Court of Maſſachusetts] .. accompanied with several bills for the regulation of the State Prison, and an alteration of the criminal laws of the Commonwealth [of Maſſachusetts]. Boston, 1805. 8°

SEWALL, THOMAS, M.D. An Eulogy on Dr. Godman, etc. [With specimens of his composition.] Washington, 1830. 8°

2 AN ADDRESS delivered before the Washington City Temperance Society, Nov. 15, 1830. Washington, 1830. 8°

3 AN EXAMINATION of Phrenology; in two lectures, delivered to the students of the Columbian College, etc. Washington, 1837. 8°

SEWARD, JAMES. Scripture exalted, and Priestcraft eradicated: or The Bible without note or comment, the only proper medium of Christian instruction. Boston, 1839. 8vo.

SEWARD, WILLIAM HENRY. Life and Public Services of J. Q. Adams, sixth President of the United States. With the eulogy delivered before the Legislature of New York. Auburn, 1850. 12°

2 THE WORKS of William Henry Seward. Edited by George E. Baker. 3 vol. New York, 1853. 8°

SEYBERT, ADAM. An Inaugural

Diſſertation: being an attempt to disprove the doctrine of the putrefaction of the blood of living animals. Philadelphia, 1793. 8vo.

2 STATISTICAL Annals: embracing views of the population, commerce, navigation, fisheries, public lands, post office establishment, revenues, mint, military and naval establishments, expenditures, public debt and sinking fund, of the United States of America: Founded on official Documents: from March 4, 1789, to April 20, 1818. Philadel. 1818. 4to.

SEYMOUR, ALMIRA. The Emigrants; or first and final step. A true story. Boston and Cambridge, 1853. 16°

SEYMOUR, E. S. Sketches of Minnesota, the New England of the West. With incidents of travel in that Territory during the summer of 1849. With a map. New York, 1850. 12°

SFORZOSI, L. A Compendious History of Italy. Translated from the original Italian by N. Greene. New York, 1844. 12°

SGANGIN, I. An Elementary Course of Civil Engineering... Translated from the third French edition; with notes and applications adapted to the United States. Bost. 1828. 4°

SHADOW, BEN. Pseud. Echoes of a Belle; or, a voice from the Past. By Ben Shadow. N. York, 1853. 12°

SHAKSPEARE, WILLIAM. The Plays of William Shakspeare... Printed from the text of Isaac Reed. 6 vol. Boston, 1813. 12°

2 DRAMATIC Works and Poems, with notes, original and selected, and introductory remarks to each play, by Samuel Weller Singer, and a life of the poet, by C. Symmons. 2 vol. New York, 1834. 8vo.

3 THE DRAMATIC Works of W. Shakspeare, with a Life of the poet, and notes, original and selected.

[Edited by O. W. Peabody, the notes being taken chiefly from Singer's edition, and the life abridged from that by Dr. Symmons.] 7 vol. Boston, 1844. 8°

4 A SUPPLEMENT to the Plays of William Shakspeare, comprising the seven dramas which have been ascribed to his pen, but which are not included with his writings in modern editions, namely: The two noble kinsmen. The London Prodigal, Thomas Lord Cromwell, Sir John Oldcastle, The Puritan, or the widow of Watling Street, The Yorkshire Tragedy, the Tragedy of Locrine. Edited, with notes and an introduction to each play, by W. G. Simms. First American edition. New York, 1848. 8°

5 THE SHAKSPEARIAN Reader: a collection of the most approved plays of Shakspere .. revised, with introductory and explanatory notes, and a memoir of the author .. By J. W. S. Hows. New York, 1850. 12°

6 THE WORKS of Shakspeare, the text .. restored according to the first editions, with introductions, notes, original and selected, and a life of the poet. By the Rev. H. N. Hudson. Vol. 1-3. Boston, 1851, etc. 12°

SHALER, WILLIAM. Sketches of Algiers, political, historical, and civil, etc. Boston, 1826. 8° .

SHARP, DANIEL. A Sermon [on Ps. xc. 12] preached at the funeral of .. W. Eustis, .. late Governor of .. Maſſachusetts, etc. Boston, 1825. 8°

. SHATTUCK, LEMUEL. The History of the town of Concord, Middlesex county, Maſſachusetts; and of the adjoining towns, Bedford, Acton, Lincoln, and Carlisle, etc. Boston, Concord [Cambridge printed], 1835. 8vo.

2 REPORT to the Committee of the City Council appointed to obtain the census of Boston for the year 1845, embracing collateral facts and statist-

ical researches, illustrating the history and condition of the population, and their means of progreſs and prosperity. Boston, 1846. 8°

SHAW, BENJAMIN, AND OTHERS. Trial of B. Shaw, J. Alley .. J. Buffum, and P. Sprague, for riots and disturbance of public worship, in the Society of Quakers at Lynn, Maſſachusetts, etc. Salem, 1822. 8°

SHAW, CHARLES. A topographical and historical description of Boston, from the first settlement of the town to the present period, with some account of its environs. Boston, 1817. 12°

SHAW, JOSHUA. United States Directory, for the use of travellers and merchants, giving an account of the principal establishments of busineſs and pleasure throughout the Union. [Philadelphia, 1822.] 12°

SHAW, LEMUEL. A Discourse delivered before the officers and members of the Humane Society of Massachusetts, June 11, 1811. Boston, 1811. 8vo.

2 ADDRESS delivered before the bar of Berkshire, on the occasion of his first taking his seat as Chief Justice of the Supreme Judicial Court, Sept. term, 1830. From the American Jurist N° 9, January, 1831. Boston, 1831. 8°

SHAW, SAMUEL. The Journals of .. S. Shaw, the first American Consul at Canton. With a life of the author, by J. Quincy. Boston, 1847. 8°

SHEA, JOHN AUGUSTUS. Poems .. Collected by his son. New York, 1846. 12°

SHEA, JOHN GILMARY. Discovery and Exploration of the Miſſiſſippi Valley; with the original narratives of Marquette, Allouez, Membré, Hennepin, and Anastase Douay; with a fac-simile of the newly-discovered map of Marquette. N. York, 1852. 8°

SHELLEY, PERCY BYSSHE. Queen

SHE

Mab, a philosophical poem. New York [London], 1821. 12mo.

SHELTON, Frederic William. Salander and the Dragon. A romance of Hartz Prison. N. York, 1851. 16°

2 The Rector of St. Bardolph's; or, Superannuated. N. York, 1853. 12mo.

SHEPARD, Charles Upham. Treatise on Mineralogy: second part. Consisting of descriptions of the species, and tables illustrative of their natural and chemical affinities. 2 vol. New Haven, 1835. 12mo.

2 A Report on the geological Survey of Connecticut. New Haven, 1837. 8vo.

SHEPHERD. The Shepherd and his Flock. Philadel. [1830?] 12mo.

SHEPLEY, John. Reports of Cases argued and determined in the Supreme Judicial Court of . . Maine. By J. Shepley. Vol. 1-11, Maine Reports, vol. xiii-xxiv. Reports of cases, etc. By John Appleton. Vol. 2 [vol. 1 of Appleton's Reports, being vol. xix of the Maine Reports, wanting] Maine Reports, vol. xx. Hallowell, 1838-46. 8°

SHEPPARD, John H. Counsellor at Law. An Address delivered before Lincoln [Masonic] Lodge, Wiscasset. [With notes.] . . Third edition. Boston, 1831. 8°

SHERBURNE, John Henry. Life and Character of the Chevalier J. P. Jones, a captain in the navy of the United States during their revolutionary war. Washington, 1825. 8°

2 The Tourist's Guide, or pencillings in England and on the Continent; with the expenses, conveyances, distances, sights, hotels, etc. and important hints to the tourist. Philadelphia, 1847. 12°

3 The Life and Character of John Paul Jones, a captain in the United States navy during the Revolutionary war. Second edition. New York, 1851. 8°

SHERMAN, Henry. An analytical digest of the Law of Marine Insurance; containing a digest of all the cases adjudged in this State, from the earliest reports down to the present time; with reference to an appendix of cases decided in the . . Courts of the United States, from the earliest period down to the year 1830. New York, 1844. 8°

SHERWOOD, Mrs. Clara Stephens; or, the White Rose. Philadelphia, 1827. 12mo.

2 The Hedge of Thorns. Philadelphia, 1827. 12mo.

3 Juliana Oakley. A tale. Philadelphia, 1827. 12mo.

4 Ermina; or, the second part of Juliana Oakley. Philadelphia, 1827. 12mo.

5 Mary Grant; or the secret fault. Philadelphia, 1827. 12mo.

6 Religious Fashion; or the history of Anna. Philadel. 1827. 12mo.

7 The Infant's Progress, from the valley of destruction to everlasting glory. Philadelphia, 1829. 12mo.

8 Susannah: or, the three guardians. Philadelphia, 1829. 12mo.

9 The Errand-Boy. Philadelphia, 1830. 12mo.

10 The Happy Choice; or, the potter's common. Philadelphia, 1830. 12mo.

11 The Shepherd of the Pyrenees. Philadelphia [1830]. 12mo.

12 The Children of the Hartz Mountains. Philadel. [1830]. 12mo.

13 The Broken Hyacinth, or, Ellen and Sophia. Philadelphia, 1832. 12mo.

SHEW, Joel. The Water-Cure Manual: . . Together with descriptions of diseases, and the hydropathic means to be employed therein; illustrated with cases, etc. New York, 1847. 12°

2 Midwifery and the Diseases of

Women; a descriptive and practical work. Shewing the superiority of water treatment, *etc.* New York, 1852. 12°

3 CHILDREN: their hydropathic management in health and disease... Illustrated with numerous cases. New York, 1852. 12mo.

SHIELDS, *Mr.* [*Begins*] In Senate of the United States, Jan. 30, 1851. .. (Report as to the relative efficiency of the repeating pistols, invented by Samuel Colt, and other inventors.) [Washington? 1851.] 8vo.

SHIELDS, BENJAMIN G. *of Alabama.* Speech .. on the bill to repeal the independent treasury; delivered in the House of Representatives, Aug. 7, 1841. Washington, 1841. 8°

SHIELDS, E. J. *of Tennessee.* Speech .. on the bill to change the organization of the Post Office department; .. delivered in the House of Representatives .... May 20, 1836. Washington, 1836. 8°

SHIPP, BARNARD. Fame and other poems. Philadel. 1848. 8vo.

2 THE PROGRESS of Freedom and other poems. New York, 1852. 12°

SHOSHONEE VALLEY; a romance. By the author of " Francis Berrian " [Timothy Flint]. 2 vol. Cincinnati, 1830. 12°

SHUCK, HENRIETTA. Scenes in China: or, sketches of the country, religion, and customs of the Chinese. Philadelphia, 1852. 16°

SHURTLEFF, J. B. The Governmental Instructor; or a brief and comprehensive view of the Government of the United States and of the State Governments. .. Revised edition. New York, 1849. 12°

SHURTLEFFE, NATHANIEL B. Records of .. Massachusetts-Bay, *etc.* *See* MASSACHUSETTS, N° 131.

SHURTLEFF, ROSWELL. A Ser-

mon [on Rom. xiii. 1-5] preached before .. the Governor, .. Council, and .. Legislature of .. New Hampshire, at the General Election, .. June, 1819. Concord, 1819. 8°

SIBLEY, JOHN LANGDON. A History of the Town of Union, in the County of Lincoln, Maine .. With a family register of .the settlers before .. 1800, *etc.* Boston, 1851. 12°

SICHEL, J. Spectacles: their uses and abuses in long and short sightedness; and the pathological conditions resulting from their irrational employment .. Translated from the French .. by H. W. Williams. Boston, 1850. 8°

SIDNEY, J. C. American Cottage and Villa Architecture, a series of views and plans of residences actually built .. with hints on landscape gardening, *etc.* Parts 1-4. New York, 1850. 4°

SIEBOLD, CARL THEODOR ERNST VON, AND STANNIUS, HERMANN. Comparative Anatomy by C. Theodor von Siebold and H. Stannius. Translated from the German, and edited with notes and additions .. by W. I. Burnett. Vol. 1. London, Bost. [printed], 1854. 8vo.

SIGOURNEY, LYDIA HUNTLEY, *Mrs.* Sketches. Philadel. 1834. 12°

2 ZINZENDORFF, and other poems. Second edition. New York, 1837. 12°

3 THE BOY's Reading Book; in prose and poetry, for schools. New York, 1840. 12°

4 PLEASANT Memories of pleasant lands. Boston, 1842. 12mo.

5 SELECT Poems .. Fourth edition. With illustrations. Philadelphia, 1843. 12°

6 POCAHONTAS, and other poems. New York, 1844. 12°

7 LETTERS to Mothers. Sixth edition. New York, 1845. 12°

8 LETTERS to Young Ladies. ..

Fourteenth edition. N. York, 1846. 12°

9 ILLUSTRATED Poems. Philadelphia, 1849. 8°

10 WHISPER to a Bride. Hartford, 1850. 12°

11 POEMS for the Sea. Hartford, 1850. 12°

12 LETTERS to my Pupils, with narrative and biographical sketches. Second edition. New York, 1851. 12°

13 EXAMPLES of Life and Death. New York, 1852. 12°

14 OLIVE Leaves. . . Illustrated. New York, 1852. 12°

15 THE FADED Hope [a life of A. M. Sigourney; with selections from his writings]. New York, 1853. 12°

SILK. Letter from the Secretary of the Treasury, transmitting the information required by a resolution of the House of Representatives, in relation to the growth and manufacture of silk, adapted to the different parts of the Union. Washington, 1828. 8vo.

SILLIMAN, AUGUSTUS E. A Gallop among American scenery: or, sketches of American scenes and military adventure. New York, 1843. 12°

SILLIMAN, BENJAMIN, the Elder. A Journal of Travels in England, Holland, and Scotland, and of two passages over the Atlantic in 1805 and 1806. Second edition. 2 vol. Boston, 1812. 12mo.

2 A JOURNAL of Travels in England, Holland, and Scotland, and of two passages over the Atlantic, in the years 1805 and 1806; with considerable additions, principally from the original manuscripts of the author. Third edition. 3 vol. New Haven, 1820. 12°

3 REMARKS made on a short tour between Hartford and Quebec, in the autumn of 1819. . . Second edition, with corrections and additions. New Haven, 1824. 12°

4 ELEMENTS of Chemistry in the order of the lectures given in Yale College. 2 vol. N. Haven, 1830. 8°

5 MANUAL of the cultivation of the sugar cane, and the fabrication and refinement of sugar. Prepared [by B. Silliman, with the assistance of C. U. Shepard, and others], under the direction of the hon. Secretary of the Treasury, in compliance with a resolution of the House of Representatives, of Jan. 25, 1830. Washing. 1833. 8°

6 ADDRESS delivered before the Association of American Geologists and Naturalists, at their meeting held in Boston, April 25-30, 1842, etc. New York, 1842. 8°

7 AN ADDRESS delivered before the Association of the alumni of Yale College, in New Haven, August 17, 1842. New Haven, 1842. 8vo.

SILLIMAN, BENJAMIN, the Younger. Report on the chemical examination of several waters for the city of Boston. Boston, 1845. 8vo.

2 FIRST Principles of Chemistry, for the use of colleges and schools. Fifth thousand. Philadel. 1847. 12°

SILLIMAN, BENJAMIN, the Younger, and GOODRICH, C. R. The World of Science, Art, and Industry, illustrated from examples in the New York Exhibition, 1853-54. Edited by Prof. B. Silliman, Jr. and C. R. Goodrich. With 500 illustrations under the superintendence of C. E. Döpler Eagre. [Originally published in numbers under the title, " Illustrated Record of the industry of all nations. New York Exhibition."] New York, 1854. Fol.

SILVESTRE DE SACY, ANTOINE ISAAC, Baron. Principles of General Grammar. . . . . Translated [from the French] by D. Fosdick, Jun. Andover [printed;] and New York, 1834. 8°

SIMCOE, JOHN GRAVES. Simcoe's Military Journal. A history of the operations of a partizan Corps, called the Queen's Rangers, commanded by Lieut. Col. J. G. Simcoe during the war of the American Revolution. Now first published with a Memoir of the author, and other additions. New York, 1844. 8vo.

SIMMONDS, Peter L. Sir John Franklin and the Arctic Regions: with detailed notices of the expeditions in search of the miſſing veſſels under Sir J. Franklin. . . To which is added an account of the American expedition under the patronage of H. Grinnell, Esq. with an introduction to the American edition by J. C. Lord. Buffalo, 1852. 8°

SIMMONS, James F. Speech . . upon the resolutions to postpone the bill introduced by Mr. M'Duffie to reduce the duties on imports; delivered in the . . . Senate, March 27, 1844. [Washington, 1844.] 8°

SIMMONS, James Wright. The Greek Girl; a tale, in two cantos. Boston and Cambridge, 1852. 12°

SIMMONS, S. S. and others. Report of the Inspectors of the Penitentiary, showing the names, ages, crimes, etc. of Convicts. Dec. 15, 1843. Tuscaloosa, 1843. 8°

SIMMS, Jeptha R. History of Schoharie County, and border wars of New York; containing also a sketch of the causes which led to the American Revolution; and interesting memoranda of the Mohawk Valley; together with much other historical and miscellaneous matter, never before published. Albany, 1845. 8°

SIMMS, William Gilmore. The Vision of Cortes, Cain, and other poems. Charleston, 1829. 12°

2 Southern Paſſages and Pictures. By the author of " Atalantis," . . etc. New York, 1839. 12°

3 The History of South Carolina, from its first European discovery to its erection into a republic: with a supplementary chronicle of events to the present time. Second edition. Charleston, 1842. 12°

4 The Sources of American Independence. An Oration on the sixty-ninth anniversary of American Independence; delivered at Aiken, South Carolina. Aiken, 1844. 8vo.

5 The Yemassee; a romance of Carolina. By the author of " Guy Rivers," . . etc. (W. G. Simms). New York, 1844. 12mo.

6 The Life of Francis Marion. New York, 1845. 12°

7 The Life of Captain John Smith, the founder of Virginia. Third edition. New York [1846]. 12°

8 The Lily and the Totem, or the Huguenots in Florida, etc. Second edition. New York, 1850. 12°

9 The Sword and the Distaff: or, " Fair, fat, and forty." A story of the South at the close of the Revolution. Philadelphia, 1853. 12°

10 Marie de Berniere: a tale of the Crescent City. (The Maroon. Maize in Milk.) Philadel. 1853. 12°

SIMONS, James. A New Principle of Tactics practised by the armies of the Republic of France; illustrated, and recommended to be practised by the . . . . armies of the United States. Charleston, 1797. 8°

SIMPSON, James H. Journal of a military reconnaiſſance from Santa Fé, New Mexico, to the Navajo Country, made with the troops under command of brevet lieutenant Colonel J. M. Washington . . in 1849. Philadelphia, 1852. 8°

SIMPSON, Stephen. The Author's Jewel, consisting of eſſays, miscellaneous, literary, and moral. Philadelphia, 1823. 12°

2 Biography of Stephen Girard, with his will affixed. . . Embellished with a handsome portrait. . . Second edition. Philadelphia, 1832. 12°

SIMPSON, William. The Practical Justice of the Peace and parish-officer of .. South Carolina. Charlestown, 1761. 4°

SIMS, James. Observations on the scarlatina anginosa, commonly called the ulcerated sore-throat. With some remarks by T. Bulfinch. Boston, 1796. 8vo.

SIMS, Thomas, *Fugitive Slave.* Trial of T. Sims on an iſſue of personal liberty on the claim of J. Potter of Georgia against ḥim as an alleged fugitive from service. Arguments of R. Rantoul, Jr. and C. G. Loring, with the decision of G. T. Curtis. Boston, April 7-11th, 1851. Phonographic Report by Dr. J. W. Stone. Boston, 1851. 8°

SINGLETON, Arthur. Letters from the South and West. Boston, 1824. 8°

SINGULARITY, Thomas, *Pseud.* Novellettes of a Traveller; or odds and ends from the knapsack of T. Singularity. Edited by H. J. Nott. 2 vol. New York, 1834. 8°

SITGREAVES,L.*Captain.* Thirty-second Congreſs. Second Seſſion. Senate. Report of an expedition down the Zuni and Colorado Rivers by Captain L. Sitgreaves... Illustrations. (Report on .. Natural History .. by S. W. Woodhouse. Zoology: mammals and birds, by S. W. Woodhouse; reptiles, by E. Hallowell; fishes, by S. F. Baird and C. Girard: Botany: by Profeſſor J. Torrey. Medical report; by S. W. Woodhouse.) Washington, 1853. 8vo.

SIXPENNY Glaſs of Wine. Philadelphia [1833]. 12mo.

SKIFF, F. Skiff's patent metallic air-tight and air-exhausted coffins, for sale at the ware-rooms, *etc.* New York, 1852. 8°

SKINNER, John S. The Dog and the Sportsman; embracing the uses, breeding, training, diseases, *etc.* of dogs, and an account of the different kinds of game, with their habits; also hints to shooters, *etc.* Philadelphia, 1845. 12°

SKINNER, Thomas H. The Elements of Power in public Speaking: an addreſs delivered Jan. 1, 1833, at his inauguration as Bartlet profeſſor of sacred Rhetoric in the theological seminary at Andover. By T. H. Skinner. Boston, 1833. 8°

2 Aids to preaching and hearing. New York, 1839. 12°

SLADE, William. Vermont State Papers, being a colleƈtion of records and documents conneƈted with the establishment of government by the people of Vermont; together with the Journal of the Council of Safety, the First Constitution, the early journals of the General Aſſembly, and the laws from 1779 to 1786 inclusive. To which are added, the proceedings of the first and second Councils of Censors. Middlebury, 1823. 8vo.

2 Masonic Penalties. [A series of eſſays, part of which was first published in the Vermont American.] Castleton, Vt. [1830]. 8°

3 Speech .. on the Tariff Bill, delivered in the House of Representatives, Jan. 29, 1833. [Washington, 1833.] 8°

4 Letters of Mr. Slade to Mr. Hallett [on the masonic controversy and the presidential Eleƈtion]. Feb. 1836. [Washington? 1836.] 8°

5 Speech .. on .. the abolition of Slavery and the Slave Trade within the Distriƈt of Columbia; delivered in the House of Representatives, Dec. 23, 1835. [Washington,] 1836. 8°

6 Speech .. on the abolition of Slavery and the Slave Trade in the Distriƈt of Columbia, delivered in the House of Representatives .. Dec. 20, 1837. To which is added, the intended conclusion of the speech suppreſſed by resolution of the House. [Washington, 1838.] 8°

7 Address delivered before the Young Men's Temperance Society of

Middlebury, Vermont, Nov. 23, 1842, on the occasion of the death of F. A. M. Ferre. Washington, 1843. 8°

8 Gov. Slade's reply to Senator Phelps' appeal. Burlington, 1846. 8°

9 To THE people of Vermont [in answer to a pamphlet entitled, "Mr. Phelps' rejoinder to Mr. Slade's reply," containing a retrospect of his personal career]. [Burlington, 1846.] 8°

SLAVE. The White Slave; or memoirs of a fugitive. [By R. Hildreth.] Boston, 1852. 8°

SLAVERY. Remarks upon a plan for the total abolition of slavery in the United States. By a citizen of New York. New York [1830?]. 8°

2 SOME Thoughts concerning domestic Slavery, in a letter. Baltimore, 1838. 12mo.

SLIDELL, afterwards MACKENZIE, ALEXANDER. Case of the Somers Mutiny. Defence of A. Slidell Mackenzie . . before the court-martial held at the Navy Yard, Brooklyn. New York, 1843. 8°

2 THE LIFE of Commodore O. H. Perry. (Fifth edition.) [With two appendixes.] New York, 1845. 12°

SLIDELL, THOMAS. Supreme Court. T. McCargo versus the New Orleans Insurance Company. [Brief for defendants in an action on a policy of insurance on certain slaves embarked on board the brig Creole. S. Benjamin and Conrad for defendants.] New Orleans [1842]. 8°

2 SUPREME Court. T. McCargo versus the Merchants' Insurance Company [of New Orleans. Brief for defendants; in an action on a policy of insurance on 19 slaves embarked on board the brig Creole. S. Benjamin and Conrad for defendants]. New Orleans [1842]. 8°

3 SUPREME Court. E. Lockett versus the Merchants' Insurance Company [of New Orleans]. Brief for defendants [in an action on a policy of insurance on 15 slaves, embarked on

board the brig Creole. T. Slidell, Benjamin, and Conrad for defendants]. New Orleans [1842]. 8°

4 THE UNITED States of America, vs. the president, directors, and company of the Bank of the United States. Bacon and others, and Robertson and others, intervenors. In the Supreme Court of Louisiana: Argument in behalf of the intervenors. [With an appendix of documents.] [New Orleans, 1844?] 8°

SLOAN, JAMES. An Oration delivered at a meeting of the Democratic Association of the county of Gloucester, held in the Court-House at Woodbury, on the fourth day of March, 1802. Trenton, 1802. 8°

2 MR. SLOAN's Motion [in the House of Representatives of the United States of America, relative to the impressment of American seamen to serve in the British navy]. Feb. 12, 1806. Washington, 1806. 8°

SLOAN, SAMUEL. The Model Architect, a series of original designs for cottages, villas . . etc.; accompanied by explanations, specifications, estimates, and . . details. Philadelphia [1852]. Fol°

SMEDES, WILLIAM C. AND MARSHALL T. A. Reports of Cases argued and determined in the High Court of Errors and Appeals for the State of Mississippi. Vol. 1-13. Bost. 1844-1850. 8°

SMELLIE, WILLIAM. The Philosophy of Natural History . . with an introduction, and various additions and alterations . . by J. Ware. Fifth edition. Boston, 1834. 12°

2 THE PHILOSOPHY of Natural History . . With an introduction, and various additions and alterations . . by J. Ware. Stereotype edition. Boston, 1846. 12°

SMILEY, THOMAS T. A complete Key to Smiley's new Federal Calculator, or scholar's assistant, etc. Philadelphia, 1835. 12°

2 THE ENCYCLOPÆDIA of Geography, *etc.* Philadelphia, 1839. 12° Atlas, 4°

3 THE NEW Federal Calculator, or scholar's affistant, *etc.* Philadelphia, 1843. 12°

SMILIE, JOHN. Mr. Smilie's Motion [in the House of Representatives of the United States of America, relative to its rules of procedure, *etc.*] Feb. 24, 1808. Washington, 1808. 8°

SMITH, AUGUSTUS W. An Elementary Treatise on Mechanics, embracing the theory of Statics and Dynamics, and its application to solids and fluids. New York, 1849. 8°

SMITH, C. BILLINGS. The Philosophy of Reform, in which are exhibited the design, principle, and plan of God, for the full developement of man, as a social, civil, intellectual and moral being; *etc.* N. York, 1846. 12°

2 A LIFE in earnest, encouraged in a course of lectures to young men. New Haven, 1848. 12°

SMITH, CALEB B. Speech . . on the Mexican war, delivered in the House of Representatives, . . July 16, 1846. Washington, 1846. 8°

SMITH, CHARLES ADAM. Christianity the source of Freedom; a sermon [on John viii. 36] delivered . . July 4, 1852. Albany, 1852. 8°

2 DISCOURSE delivered on the occasion of the birth of Washington before the National Guards of Easton, Pa. Albany, 1852. 8vo.

SMITH, DANIEL, *Rev.* Anecdotes and Illustrations of the Christian Ministry. . . With an introduction by . . D. W. Clark. New York, 1850. 16°

2 THE LADIES' Book of Anecdotes and Sketches of Character. Compiled by D. Smith, with an introduction by R. S. Foster. New York, 1851. 16°

SMITH, E. DELAFIELD. Oratory; a poem, delivered before the Eucleian and Philomathean Societies of the University of New York. New York, 1852. 8°

SMITH, E. PESHINE. A Manual of Political Economy. New York, 1853. 12°

SMITH, EDWARD DARRELL. Inaugural Differtation, being an attempt to prove that certain substances are conveyed, unchanged, into the circulation; or if changed, that they are recomposed and regain their active properties. Philadelphia, 1800. 8vo.

SMITH, ELI. Researches of the Rev. E. Smith and Rev. H. G. O. Dwight in Armenia: including a journey through Asia Minor and into Georgia and Persia, with a visit to the Nestorian and Chaldean Christians of Oormiah and Salmas. 2 vol. Boston, 1833. 12°

2 MISSIONARY Sermons and addreffes. New York, 1842. 12°

SMITH, ELIZABETH OAKES. *Mrs.* The Sinlefs Child, and other poems. Edited by J. Keese. New York, 1843. 12°

2 WOMAN and her needs. New York, 1851. 8°

3 HINTS on Drefs and Beauty. New York, 1852. 8°

4 SHADOW Land; or, the seer. New York, 1852. 8°

SMITH, ETHAN. A Differtation on the prophecies relative to Antichrist and the last times; exhibiting the rise, character, and overthrow of that terrible power: and a treatise on the seven apocalyptic vials. Charlestown, 1811. 8°

2 VIEW of the Hebrews; or the tribes of Israel in America. Second edition, improved and enlarged. Poultney, Vt. 1825. 12°

SMITH, FRANCIS GURNEY. Domestic Medicine, Surgery, and Materia Medica; with directions for the diet and management of the sickroom, *etc.* Philadelphia, 1851. 12mo.

SMITH, FRANCIS H. College Reform. Philadelphia, 1851. 12°

SMITH, GEORGE G. An Address delivered before the Massachusetts Charitable Mechanic Association, at the celebration of their twelfth triennial anniversary, .. October 6, 1842. Boston [1842]. 8°

SMITH, GEORGE W. A Defence of the system of solitary confinement of prisoners adopted by the State of Pennsylvania, with remarks on the origin, progress, and extension of this species of prison discipline. Philadelphia, 1833. 8°

SMITH, HEZEKIAH. The Doctrine of the Believer's Baptism, by immersion only; asserted and maintained against the attempts of Mr. J. Parsons, A. M. to invalidate it, in two sermons preached at Haverhill, etc. Boston, 1766. 8vo.

SMITH, H. J. Education: Part 1. History of education, ancient and modern; Part 2. A plan of culture and instruction, based on Christian principles, etc. 2 parts. New York, 1845. 12°

SMITH, HENRY H. Minor Surgery; or, hints on the every-day duties of the surgeon... Illustrated by engravings. Philadel. 1843. 12°

SMITH, HORATIO. Festivals, Games, and Amusements; ancient and modern. With additions [relating to America] by S. Woodworth. New York, 1844. 12°

SMITH, HUGH, M.D. Letters to Married Ladies. To which is added, a letter on corsets, and copious notes, by an American physician. New York, 1827. 12°

SMITH, SIR JAMES EDWARD. An Introduction to Physiological and Systematical Botany. By J. E. Smith. First American, from the second English edition; with notes, by J. Bigelow. Boston, 1814. 8°
2 A GRAMMAR of Botany, illustrative of artificial as well as natural

classification, with an explanation of Jussieu's system. .. To which is added, a reduction of all the genera contained in the Catalogue of North American Plants, to the natural families of the French Professor, by H. Muhlenberg. New York, 1822. 8°

SMITH, JEREMIAH, Chief Justice of New Hampshire. An Oration on the Death of George Washington; delivered at Exeter [in New Hampshire], Feb. 22, 1800. Exeter (New Hampshire), 1800. 8°

SMITH, JEROME V. C. Natural History of the Fishes of Massachusetts, embracing a practical essay on angling. Boston, 1833. 8vo.
2 THE CLASS Book of Anatomy, explanatory of the first principles of human organization, as the basis of physical education, etc. Seventh improved stereotype edition. Boston, 1843. 12°
3 PILGRIMAGE to Egypt, embracing a Diary of Explorations on the Nile; with observations illustrative of the manners .. of the people, and of the present condition of the antiquities and ruins. Boston, 1852. 8°

SMITH, CAPTAIN JOHN. The True Travels, Adventures, and Observations of Captaine J. Smith, in Europe, Asia, Africke, and America: beginning about the yeere 1593, and continued to this present 1629. (The generall historie of Virginia, New England, and the Summer Iles; etc.) 2 vol. From the London edition of 1629. Richmond, 1819. 8°

SMITH, JOHN, Prof. A Grammar of the Greek Language; .. with the rules of contraction, and the syntax and prosody complete: To which is subjoined, an appendix. Boston, 1809. 12°

SMITH, MRS. JOHN, Pseud. [i. e. T. S. ARTHUR!] Confessions of a Housekeeper. Philadel. 1851. 12°

SMITH, JOHN AUGUSTINE. Select Discourses on the Functions of the

Nervous System in opposition to Phrenology, Materialism and Atheism, To which is prefixed, a lecture on the diversities of the human character, arising from physiological peculiarities. New York, 1840. 12mo.

2 THE MUTATIONS of the Earth ; or an outline of the more remarkable physical changes, of which, . . this earth has been the subject and the theatre : including an examination into the scientific errors of the author of the Vestiges of Creation: being the anniversary discourse for 1846, delivered . . before the Lyceum of Natural History of New York, etc. New York, 1846. 8vo.

SMITH, JOHN C. Shall we Build ? a sermon [on Neh. ii. 18] delivered . . in view of building a new church edifice. Washington, 1840. 8°

SMITH, JOHN CALVIN. An Oration, pronounced at Sharon, on the anniversary of American Independence, July 4, 1798. Litchfield [Connecticut, 1798]. 8°

SMITH, JOHN CALVIN. THE Illustrated Hand-book: a new guide for travellers through the United States of America, etc. New York, 1846. 12°

2 THE ILLUSTRATED Hand-book, a new guide for travelers through the United States of America ; etc. New York, 1847. 12°

SMITH, JOHN JAY. A Summer's Jaunt across the Water ; including visits to England, Ireland, Scotland, France, Switzerland, Germany, Belgium, etc. 2 vol. Philadelphia, 1846. 12mo.

SMITH, JOHN JAY, AND WATSON, JOHN F. American Historical and Literary Curiosities ; consisting of fac-similes of original documents relating to the events of the Revolution, etc. etc. With a variety of reliques, antiquities, and modern autographs. Collected and edited by J. J. Smith

and J. F. Watson, assisted by an Association of American antiquarians. 2 parts. (Part 1, second edition.) Philadelphia, 1847. 4°

2 AMERICAN Historical and Literary Curiosities ; consisting of fac-similes, etc. . . Collected and edited by J. J. Smith and J. F. Watson. . . Fourth edition, with additions and alterations. New York, 1850. Fol.

SMITH, JOHN WILLIAM. A Compendium of Mercantile Law. . . . Greatly enlarged from the third and last English edition, by J. P. Holcombe and W. Y. Gholson. New York, 1847. 8°

SMITH, JOSHUA TOULMIN. The Northmen in New England, or America in the tenth century. Boston, 1839. 12°

SMITH, JOSIAH. The Divine Right of Private Judgment Vindicated. In answer to the Reverend Mr. H. Fisher's Postscript . . to his Preservative from Damnable Errors, etc. [An appendix by N. Bassett.] Boston, 1730. 8vo.

SMITH, JUNIUS. Essays on the Cultivation of the Tea Plant, in the United States of America. New York, 1848. 8vo.

SMITH, MATTHEW HALE. Universalism Examined, Renounced, Exposed; in a series of lectures, embracing the experience of the author during a ministry of twelve years, etc. Boston, 1842. 12°

SMITH, MICHAEL. A Geographical View of the Province of Upper Canada, and Promiscuous Remarks on the Government; in two parts ; with an appendix, containing a complete description of the Niagara Falls: and remarks relative to the situation of the inhabitants respecting the war ; and a concise history of its progress, to the present date. Third edition. Philadelphia, Oct. 1813. 12°

SMITH, NATHAN. Medical and

Surgical Memoirs. . . Edited, with addenda, by N. R. Smith. Baltimore, 1831. 8°

SMITH, OLIVER. Outlines of Nature. New York, 1847. 12°

SMITH, PRUDENCE, *Miß, Pseud.* Modern American Cookery. . . With a list of family medical recipes, and a valuable miscellany. New York, 1831. 16mo.

SMITH, R. A. Philadelphia as it is, in 1852. . . With illustrations and a map of the city and environs. Philadelphia, 1852. 8°

SMITH, ROBERT. Reflections upon the late Correspondence between Secretary Smith and F. J. Jackson, Esq. [By A. C. Hanson?] Baltimore, 1810. 8°

SMITH, ROSWELL C. Intellectual and Practical Grammar, *etc.* Boston and New York, 1832. 12°

2 SMITH's Introductory Arithmetic. The little federal Calculator, *etc.* Boston, 1832. 12°

3 A KEY to the "Practical and Mental Arithmetic." For the use of teachers. Boston, 1834. 12°

4 SMITH's New Grammar. English Grammar on the productive system, *etc.* One hundred and forty-third edition. Philadel. 1839. 12°

5 SMITH's Geography . . on the productive system. . . Accompanied by a large . . Atlas. Hartford, 1840. 12° Atlas. 4°

6 SMITH's New Arithmetic . . on the productive system ; accompanied by a key and critical blocks. . . Stereotype edition. Hartford, 1843. 12°

7 PRACTICAL and Mental Arithmetic, on a new plan, *etc.* Bath, N. Y. 1843. 12°

8 PRACTICAL and Mental Arithmetic, on a new plan, *etc.* Auburn, 1845. 12°

SMITH, SAMUEL, *of Burlington, New Jersey.* The History of the Colony of Nova-Cæsaria, or New Jersey, . . to the year 1721. With some particulars since, and a short view of its present state. [With an appendix.] Burlington, 1765. 8°

SMITH, SAMUEL B. Renunciation of Popery, by S. B. Smith, late a priest in the Roman Catholic Church. Philadelphia, 1833. 8°

SMITH, SAMUEL STANHOPE. Sermons. Corrected and revised by the author. Newark, 1799. 8°

2 AN ESSAY on the causes of the variety of complexion and figure in the human species. To which are added, animadversions on certain remarks made on the first edition of this Essay by Mr. C. White. . . Also, strictures on Lord Kaims' Discourse on the original diversity of mankind. Second edition, enlarged and improved. New Brunswick, 1810. 8°

3 THE LECTURES . . delivered . . in the College of New Jersey, on . . moral and political philosophy. 2 vol. Trenton, 1812. 8°

4 A COMPREHENSIVE View of the leading and most important principles of natural and revealed Religion. . . Second edition, with additions. New Brunswick, 1816. 8°

SMITH, SEBA. Powhatan ; a metrical romance, in seven cantos. New York, 1841. 12°

2 NEW Elements of Geometry. New York, 1850. 8°

SMITH, SOLOMON. · The Theatrical Apprenticeship and anecdotical Recollections of S. Smith, *etc.* Philadelphia, 1847. 12°

SMITH, THOMAS. The Chairman and Speaker's Guide ; being a digest of the rules for the orderly conduct of public debate and of public meetings, *etc.* New York, 1844. 12°

SMITH, THOMAS, *Rev.* Extracts from the Journals kept by the Rev. T. Smith. . . With an appendix containing a variety of other matters selecled by S. Freeman. 2 parts. Portland, 1821. 12°

SMITH, W. L. G. Life at the South: or " Uncle Tom's Cabin" as it is. Being narratives, scenes, and incidents in the real " Life of the Lowly." Buffalo, 1852. 12°

SMITH, WALTER, AND OTHERS. Report of the Commissioners appointed by the Governor to examine the Bank of Mobile. Tuscaloosa, 1843. 8°

SMITH, WILLIAM. History of New York, from the first discovery to the year 1732. .. With a continuation, from . . 1732 to . . 1814. Albany, 1814. 8°

2 THE HISTORY of the Province of New York, from its discovery to the appointment of Governor Colden in 1762. 2 vol. New York, 1829. 8vo.

SMITH, WILLIAM, D. D. Provost of the College of Philadelphia. The Works of William Smith. 2 vol. Philadelphia, 1803. 8°

2 FUNERAL Sermon [on Psalm xlii. 6] on the death of a beloved pupil, Mr. W. G. Martin. Philadelphia, 1754. 8vo.

3 HISTORY of the rise and progress of the Charitable Scheme for the relief of poor Germans in Pennsylvania. Philadelphia, 1755. 4to.

SMITH, WILLIAM, LL.D. of South Carolina. A Comparative View of the constitutions of the several States with each other, and with that of the United States: exhibiting in tables the prominent features of each constitution, . . with notes and observations. Philadelphia, 1796. 4°

SMITH, WILLIAM R. The Justice of the Peace; containing a brief treatise upon all the duties and powers of that officer; with . . directions how to proceed in civil and criminal cases; arranged under the laws of Alabama, as now in force. To which is added,

the complete constable; with numerous forms. New York, 1841. 8°

SMITH, WILLIAM S. The Trial of W. S. Smith and S. G. Ogden for misdemeanours, had in the Central Court of the United States for the New York district, in July, 1806; with a preliminary account of the proceedings . . in the preceding April term. By T. Lloyd, Stenographer. New York, 1807. 8°

SMITH, WORTHINGTON. Address on the subject of petitioning the General Assembly to abolish the traffic in ardent spirits, etc. St. Albans, Vt. 1833. 8°

SMITHSONIAN INSTITUTION, WASHINGTON.

1 SMITHSONIAN Contributions to Knowledge. Vol. 1-8. Washington, 1848-56. 4°

Containing in
Vol. I. 1848.
1. Advertisement.
2. List of Officers of the Smithsonian Institution.
3. Ancient Monuments of the Missississippi Valley. By E. G. Squier and E. H. Davis.
Vol. II. 1851.
1. Researches relative to the Planet Neptune. By S. C. Walker.
2. On the Vocal Sounds of Laura Bridgeman, the Blind Deaf Mute, of Boston, compared with the Elements of Phonetic Language. By Francis Lieber.
3. Microscopical Examination of Soundings made by the United States Coast Survey of the Atlantic Coast. By J. W. Bailey.
4. Contributions to the Physical Geography of the United States. By C. Ellet. Part 1.
5. Mosasurus and the three allied new Genera, Holcodus, Conosaurus, and Amphorosteus. By Robert W. Gibbes.
6. The Classification of Insects, from Embryological data. By Louis Agassiz.
7. On the Explosiveness of Nitre. By Robert Hare.
8. Microscopical Observations made in South Carolina, Georgia and Florida. By J. W. Bailey.
9. Aboriginal Monuments of the State of New York. By E. G. Squier.
10. Appendix.—Ephemeris of the Planet Neptune. By S. C. Walker.

arts. By James C. Booth and C. Morfit. Washington, 1851. 8°

8 SMITHSONIAN Reports. Notices
of public libraries in the United States
of America. Printed by order of
Congreſs, as an appendix to the
fourth annual Report of the Board of
Regents of the Smithsonian Institution. By Charles C. Jewett. Washington, 1851. 8°

9 A COLLECTION of Meteorological
tables, with other tables useful in
practical meteorology. Prepared . .
by A. Guyot. Washington, 1852. 8°

10 DIRECTIONS for collecting, preserving and transporting specimens
of natural history prepared for the
use of the Smithsonian Institution.
Washington, 1852. 8°

11 SMITHSONIAN Institution . . Registry of periodical phenomena, etc.
[Washington, 1852?] Folᵒ

12 LIST of Foreign Institutions in
correspondence with the Smithsonian
Institution. [Washington, 1852?] 4°

13 PORTRAITS of North American
Indians, with sketches of scenery, etc.
painted by J. M. Stanley; deposited
with the Smithsonian Institution. [A
catalogue by J. M. Stanley.] Washington, 1852. 8°

14 SMITHSONIAN Report. On the
construction of catalogues of libraries
and their publication by means of
separate, stereotyped titles. By
Charles C. Jewett. Second edition.
Washington, 1853. 8°

15 CATALOGUE of the described
Coleoptera of the United States. By
F. E. Melsheimer, M. D. Revised
by S. S. Haldeman and J. L. Le
Conte. Washington, 1853. 8°

16 THE ANNULAR Eclipse of May
26, 1854. Published under the authority of Hon. J. C. Dobbin, Secretary of the Navy. Washington,
Cambridge [printed], 1854. 8°

17 DIRECTIONS for collecting, preserving, and transporting specimens
of natural history. Prepared for the
use of the Smithsonian Institution.
[Second edition.] Washing. 1854. 8°

18 LIST of Foreign Institutions in
correspondence with the Smithsonian
Institution. [Washington, 1854.] 8°

19 REGISTRY of Periodical Phenomena, etc. Washington [1854?] Folᵒ

SMOLNIKAR, ANDREAS BERN-
ARDUS. Denkwurdige Ereigniſse im
Leben der A. B. Smolnikar, etc. 3
Bde. Stereot. Bd. 1. Cambridge,
1838. Bd. 2. Philadelphia, 1839.
Bd. 3. New York, 1840. 12mo.

SMUGGLER'S SON, and other
tales and sketches. In prose and
verse. By A. W. M[itchell]. Philadelphia, 1842. 12°

SMYTH, THOMAS. Ecclesiastical
Republicanism; or the Republicanism, liberality, and Catholicity of
Presbytery, in contrast with Prelacy
and Popery. Boston, 1843. 12mo.

2 PRESBYTERY and not prelacy the
Scriptural and primitive polity, etc.
Boston, 1843. 8°

3 THE EXODUS of the Church of
Scotland: and the claims of the Free
Church of Scotland to the sympathy
and aſſistance of American Christians.
[A sermon on 2 Cor. viii. 1-4.]
Charleston, 1843. 8vo.

SNELL, DANIEL W. The Ma-
nager's Aſſistant; being a condensed
treatise on the Cotton Manufacture;
. . to which are added, various calculations, tables, comparisons, etc.
Hartford, 1850. 12°

SNELL, THOMAS. An Oration,
pronounced at Brookfield, July 5,
1813, at the celebration of the Independence of the United States of
America. (A poem delivered at
Brookfield, July 5, 1813, before the
Washington Benevolent Societies, etc.
By C. Prentiſs.) 2 parts. Brookfield,
1813. 8°

SNELLING, ANNA L. Kabaosa;
or, the warriors of the West. A tale
of the last war. New York, 1842. 12°

SNELLING, HENRY H. The

History and Practice of the Art of Photography; or the production of pictures through the agency of light, *etc.* New York, 1851. 12°

SNELLING, WILLIAM J. The Polar Regions of the Western Continent explored; embracing a geographical account of Iceland, Greenland, the Islands of the Frozen Sea, and the northern parts of the American Continent... Together with the adventures, discoveries, dangers, and trials of Parry, Franklin, Lyon, and other navigators, in those regions. Boston, 1831. 8°

2 TRUTH, a Gift for Scribblers [in verse]. Second edition, with additions and emendations. Boston, 1832. 12°

3 TRIAL of W. J. Snelling, for a Libel on the Hon. B. Whitman, Senior Judge of the Police Court, *etc.* Boston, 1834. 12°

SNODGRASS, W. D. Discourses on the Apostolical Succession. Troy, N. Y., 1844. 12°

SNOW, CALEB H. A History of Boston, the Metropolis of Massachusetts. Boston, 1828. 4to.

SNOW, HENRY. Addreſs delivered to the graduates of the Union Literary Society of Miami University, *etc.* Oxford, Ohio, 1841. 8°

SNOWDROP (THE). Philadelphia [1830]. 12mo.

SNOWDEN, RICHARD. The History of North and South America, from its discovery to the death of General Washington. Revised, corrected .. improved .. [and continued] by C. W. Bazeley. Philadelphia, 1832. 12°

SOCIETY FOR PROMOTING AGRICULTURE, Philadelphia. Memoirs. 5 vol. Philadelphia, 1808-26. 8vo.

2 LAWS of the .. Society .. as revised and enacted at the annual meeting .. 14 Jan. 1812. To which

is prefixed, a list of the members of the Society. Philadelphia, 1812. 8°

3 ADDRESS to the Citizens of Pennsylvania, on the importance of a more liberal encouragement of agriculture. Accompanied with inquiries on agricultural subjects proposed by the .. Society .. with a view to form an exposé of the state of agriculture in Pennsylvania. Philadelphia, 1818. 8vo.

4 AN ADDRESS delivered before the Society .. at its anniversary meeting, Jan. 19, 1819. By W. Rawle. Philadelphia, 1819. 8°

5 CHARTER and by-laws of the Philadelphia Society for promoting agriculture. Germantown, 1840. 8°

SOCIETY FOR THE PROMOTION OF AGRICULTURE, ARTS, AND MANUFACTURES, instituted in the State of New York.

1 TRANSACTIONS. Vol. 1, parts 1 and 2. Albany, 1792-94. 4to.

2 TRANSACTIONS. Vol. 1. Second edition, revised. Albany, 1801. 8vo. [The Act of Incorporation having expired in 1804, the Society was re-incorporated and continued under the title of]

3 THE SOCIETY for the Promotion of the Useful Arts in the State of New York. Transactions. Vol. 2-4. Albany, 1807-19. 8vo. [This Society was in 1824 incorporated with the ALBANY Lyceum of Natural History, and its publications were thenceforward iſsued under the title of The ALBANY INSTITUTE, which *see.*]

SOMERVILLE, WILLIAM C. Letters from Paris, on the causes and consequences of the French Revolution. Baltimore, 1822. 8vo.

SOMMERS, CHARLES G. Memoir of the Rev. John Stanford... Together with an appendix, comprising brief memoirs of the Rev. J. Williams, the Rev. T. Baldwin, .. and the Rev. R. Furman. New York, 1835. 12°

[SONGS AND BALLADS, English and American. Printed in various parts of the United States, but chiefly for Leonard Deming, 62 Hanover St. Boston, and Middlebury, Vermont, 1830-1848 ?] 275 sheets, 4° and 2 in fol° viz:

Adventurous Sailor.
All the Blue Bonnets over the Border, and
    Old Grimes.
American Hero.
American Perry.
American Taxation.
Analyzation, and
    'Tis time enough yet.
Answer to "The New Looking Glass," and
    A Glass is good.
A Playing we will go, and
    Tom Hitch the Tailor.
Auld Lang Syne,
    Parody on Sweet Home, and
    My old horse.
Banks of Brandywine, and
    James Bird.
Banks of the Claudey,
    Tomorrow, and
    The dashing white Sergeant.
Battle of Bunker Hill.
Battle of the Potomac, with
    The Malays.
Battle of Stonnington, and
    The Banks of the Ohio.
Battle of Waterloo, and
    Tary Sailor.
Beautiful Boy, and
    Love and Sausages.
Beautiful Nancy, and
    The Cottager's Daughter.
Billy Barlow.
Blackbird, and
    Peggy Gordon.
Black-eyed Susan, and
    Mary's Dream.
Bloody Brother.
Blue Bell of Scotland,
    The Watchman, and
    I won't be a Nun.
Bold Boatswain, and
    Minstrel's Return.
Bold Northwestman, and
    Wandering Boys of Switzerland.
Bold Shoemaker,
    Green bushes, and
    Fight of Waterloo.
Bold Smuggler, and
    Lord Lovell.
Bonnets so blue, and
    Jacket so blue.
Bonny Breast-knots,
    John Anderson my Jo, and
    Crofs-keen Lawn.
Bonny Bunch of Roses, and
    Crofs-keen Lawn.

Bonny Doun, and
    True Yankee Boys.
Bounding Billows, and
    Bunch of Rushes.
Brandreth's Pills, and
    The Devil and Hackney Coachman.
Bride's Farewell,   [een,
    O saw ye the lass with the bonny blue
    Contentment, and
    Major André's Farewell.
Braintree and Quincey Law Case.
British Lamentation, and
    Green on the Cape.
Bucket (The),
    Bright Rosy Morning, and
    The Rose Tree.
Butter and Cheese, and
    Adieu to Cold Winter.
Buy a Broom,
    Love's Garland, and
    Highland Mary.
Captain Glen.
Captain James, and
    The Heart that never loved.
Captain James.
Captain Kidd.
Captain Mullegan,
    Bold Soldier, and
    Blue-eyed Mary.
Captain Ward,
    Charming Polly, and
    The Waterman.
Children of the Wood.
Chimney Sweep,
    Beggar Girl, and
    Crazy Jane.
Chit Chat for Gentlemen, and
    The Enterprise and Boxer.
Clar de Kitchen.
Coal black Rose.
Coal hole, and
    The Fire Ship.
Coal hole, and
    Gossip Jones.
Constitution and Guerriere,
    Coast of Barbary, and
    Days of Absence.
Cork Leg, and
    Oyster Maid.
Corydon and Caroline,
    Major André's Farewell, and
    Contentment.
Courting Song.
Crooked Rib, and
    The scolding Wife.
Cruel Father, or Edgar and Lucy.
Crying Family, and
    I'd be a Butterfly.
Dame Durden, and
    Tom Bolin.
Damsel's Tragedy, or Cruel Mother in Law.
Dandy Song.
Dawning of the Day, and
    The Merry Swiss Boy.
Dialogue between Death and a Lady.

Dictates of right Reason.
Dinah Crow.
Dinah Crow's Abolition.
Dream (A).
Drinking Song,
    Scolding Wife, and
    The Jolly Sailor.
Duskey Night,
    Jesse the flower o'Dumblane, and
    Donald the pride of Dumblane.
Enniskillen Dragoon, and
    Wild Rover.
Erin go bragh [Campbell's " Exile"],
    Land of Sweet Erin, and
    Come rest in this bosom.
Essence Pedler.
Exeter Lovers.
Exiles of Eden.
Factory Maid, and
    The Clove-hitch Knot.
Fair Eleanor, and
    The dashing white Sergeant.
False hearted Girl.
Farmer's Daughter, or Barley Maid.
Farmer's Song.
Father Abbey's Will.
Five Points, or the Butcher and Drover.
Freedom, and
    The Sawyer and Lawyer.
Freedom and Peace.
French Claims, and
    The Lass that Loves a Sailor.
Gaby Glum, and
    The Old Maid's Petition.
Garden Gate,
    Mermaid Song, and
    My Grandmother.
General Warren, and
    My Soldier Laddie.
George Reiley, and
    O! Say not, Woman's Love is bought.
Golden Bull, or tragical Love Song.
Good old Colony Times, and
    Bonny Boat.
Good Wife, and
    Star Spangled Banner.
Gosport Tragedy.
Great Britain, and
    Humors of Glen.
Great Sea Snake, and
    Gaffer Grey.
Green Garters,
    I won't let you, and
    Shoulder knot.
Growing Beauty,
    The Campbells are coming, and
    Landlady of France.
Gumbo Chaff.
Hail Columbia, and
    What's the Matter now?
Halifax Station, and
    The Banks of the Schuylkill.
Handsome Harry.
Happy Bachelor, and
    The Widow's Daughter.
Happy Child.

Happy Farmer,
    Wandering Mary, and
    Young Harry.
Happy Ship Carpenter.
Hard Times.
Harry Bluff, and
    The female Sailor.
Hebrew Daniel (The).
Henry and Julia.
Hickory Soldiers.
Hickory Tree.
Hints to a new married Sister, and
    It won't be my fault if I die an Old
Hornet and Peacock, and   [Maid.
    General Provost's Lamentation.
Hornet and Peacock, and
    The Battle of Plat-te-bug.
If I had a Donkey, and
    Sich a gitting up Stairs.
Inconstant Girl, and
    Young Edward.
Indian Chief, and
    Canadian Boat Song.
Indian Philosopher, and
    Auld Lang Syne (second part).
I never says nothing to Nobody.
Irish Girl, and
    Bona's Exile.
Jack Monroe, and
    Fair Sally.
Jackson's Dinner.
Jemmy and Nancy.
Jeremy Diddler, and
    The Hunter's Horn.
Jim Brown.
Jim Crow.
John and Polly, and
    Jack and Sally.
Johnny Bull, and
    Yankee Volunteers.
Johnny Bull.
Johnny Bull's big Guns, and
    Battle of Lake Erie.
Johnny Bull's big Guns,
    Joys of Scolding, and
    Dashing white Sergeant.
John Riley, and
    The Lowlands of Holland.
Jolly Butcher.
Jolly Yankee Jackets of blue,
    Oh no, we never mention her, and
    Bright Phœba.
Jonathan to Jemima.
Jovial Fellows,
    Buy a Broom, and
    Highland Mary.
Kate and her Lovers.
Kate and John, and
    Kitty of Coleraine.
Katy Mory, and
    Patty and Mistress.
Keys of Love, and
    Calomel Song.
Lady Washington's Lamentation,
    American Star, and
    Hurra! for the Bonnets of blue.

Lamentation for Gen. Washington.
Lafs that Loves a Sailor,
    Banish Sorrow, and
    Happy Fellow.
Last words of Polly Goold.
L, A, W, and
    Be gone dull Care.
Lawrence and Ludlow, with
    Jemmy Slain in the Wars.
Lawyer outwitted.
Lexington Miller, and
    Jonny Jarman.
Lincolnshire Poachers, and
    Grey Goose's wing.
Loch na Gar, and
    Old King Cole.
London Lawyer's Son.
Long tail blue.
Lord Bakeman.
Lord Lovell, and
    Nothing at all.
Lord Thomas and Fair Eleanor.
Lord Ullin's Daughter, and
    Friendship.
Lofs of the Ship Albion, and
    Bruce's Addrefs.
Lofs of the Ship Columbia.
Lofs of the U. S. Sloop Hornet.
Love in a Tub, or the Merchant outwitted
    by the Vintner.
Loveletter and Answer, and
    Father, Jerry, and I.
Lovely Ann, and
    Enniskillen Dragoon.
Maid's Subtle Arts, and
    Bay of Biscay.
Major André, and
    André's Farewell.
Major Longbow, and
    Betty Deary.
Major's only Son.
Manners and Customs of Ann Street.
Mary of the Wild Moor, and
    The Waterman.
Mechanic's Song (by Franklin), and
    The Peasant's Chorus in Paris and
Mellow Horn,   [London.
    Banks of the Dee, and
    The Sheffield Apprentice.
Midnight Poachers (Antimasonic), and
    You don't exactly suit me.
Mourning Orphan, and
    Lucinda Adieu.
Murder of Cilley, and
    Gofsip Chat.
Murder of Joseph White.
My Cigar, and
    The Journeyman Tailor.
Naval Triumph, and
    Patriotic Diggers.
New England,
    The Campbells are coming, and
    Landlady of France.
New Song (Antimasonic), and
    Farewell Addrefs.
Noble Lads of Canada.

Nobody, and
    The Dumb Wife.
North Merchant.
O'er the Hills and far away, and
    Sprig of Shillalah.
Oh! what a Row! or the adventures of a
    Steam Ship, and
    The Knight Errant.
Old Ben, the Yankee, and
    Lightly may the boat row.
Old England forty years ago.
Old Grimes, and
    The Gallant Hufsar.
Old Maids' last prayer, and
    Ranordine.
Old Tip, and
    The Penitent Joes.
O no, no! not I! I and
    The Lady Gay.
O saw ye the Lafs wi' the bonnie blue een?
    Minstrel's Return from the War, and
    All's Well.
O thou art all to me, love,
    Did you ever go a Trainin', and
    Lovely Nan.
Paddy Carey's fortune, and
    The Bewitching boy.
Paddy's Wedding, or Fun in Ireland.
Parliament of England, and
    Marseilles Hymn.
Paul Jones' Victory, and
    Adam and Eve.
Peace and Liberty,
    The Troubadour, and
    An Old Man.
Perry's Victory on Lake Erie, and
    An Old Bachelor's Last Prayer.
Perry's Victory.
Petition of a Drunkard's Horse.
Polly Hopkins.
Polly Hopkins and Tommy Tompkins.
Pompey Smash.
Poor Little Sailor Boy,
    The Green Mountains.
Poor Patrick O'Neal.
'Prentice Boy, and
    General Wolfe.
Pretty Deary.
Primrose Hill, and
    St. Patrick was a Gentleman.
Proud Pedlar, and
    Light House.
Push along Keep moving, and
    The Irish Robber.
Ralph Rosy's Rambles in search of Kitty
    Clover his Sweetheart.
Red haired Man's Wife, and
    Dick the Joiner.
Rival Beauties.
Rocks of Scilly.
Rolling Stone,
Rory O'More, and
    Nothing else to do.
Rosanna.
Rose of Allandale, and
    Yorkshire Fish-hook.

Rose of Ardee, and
　　The Washing day.
Roving Irishman, and
　　The Braes of Balquhither.
Rules and Regulations of the Yamacraw
　　Intemperance Society, Dec. 1831.
Rules and Regulations of the Boston In-
　　temperance Society, Feb. 1831.
Sally M'Guire.
Sambo's address to the Bredren, and
　　Ole Wirginny.
Sammy Sugarplumb, and
　　The tidy one.
Saw ye my hero George, and
　　Battle of Bunker Hill.
Sea faring Man, and
　　Oh! dear Grog.
Shannon Side, and
　　Love song about Murder.
Ship Beverley.
Ship Boston.
Short Catechism, and
　　New Looking Glass.
Silk Merchant's Daughter.
Silver Key.
Sittin on a Rail, or the Racoon Hunt.
Sly Young Crow, and
　　Barney Brallaghan.
Soldier's Return, and
　　Soldier's Bride.
Solomon of the West, and
　　Britannia's Lamentations.
Solomon's Temple, and
　　The grand Sweeper.
Something New Starts every Day, and
　　My Highland Home.
Stage Dream, and
　　Lavender Girl.
Star of the West,
　　Morgiana, and
　　The Busy fly.
Steam Arm.
Storm at Sea.
Story of Uncle Ben.
Sweet Helen the fair,
　　Vision of fancy, and
　　Bow, wow, wow.
Sweet Home, and
　　Death of Parker.
Sweet William of Plymouth.
Tall Young Oysterman, and
　　Young Mutineer.
Tea Table Chat.
Tea Tax, and
　　The Cottage on the Moor.
The Toast be dear Woman,
　　Bachelor's Hall, and
　　The bold Dragoon.
Tid, the Gray Mare, and
　　Sandy and Jenny.
Tidy one.
Times as they are.
Toper's return from the Bar, and
　　Prisoner for life.
Truxton's Victory, and
　　The Female Drummer.

Undaunted female, and
　　Bachelor's faith.
Union of St. John's, and
　　March to the Battlefield.
Vermont Whig Song, by that same old Coon.
Wake of Teddy the tiler.
Wedlock is a ticklish thing, and
　　The Bonnet of Straw.
Wezy pekooliar, and　　[Morning.
　　Behold! how brightly breaks the
Wha'll be King but Charlie?
　　Banks of Champlain, and
　　The Thorn.
What shall we do for change?
When shall we three meet again?
　　Meeting of the three friends.
Widdow's Daughter, and
　　Whip-poor will.
Widdow's Daughter.
Wild Rover, and
　　Yankee Ship.
Wife, Children and friends,
　　Bonny Barbara Allan.
William of the Fury, and
　　I'm a comical fellow.
William Reily.
William Tailor, and
　　The Inconstant Girl.
Will the Weaver, and
　　The female Soldier.
Will you let me? and I will let you,
　　And Woman Dr. and Cr.
Wooden breast-bone, and
　　Jackson's Victory.
Wooden Dishes.
Yankee Ship, and
　　The Fisherman's Girl.
Yankee's Return from Camp.
Yorkshire Irishman, and the
　　Young Girl's Resolution.
Young Ladies' Choice, and
　　The Rover's Choice.
Young Man's Dream,
　　Meeting of the Waters, and
　　The transported Irish Boy.
Young Sea Captain.
Zip Coon on the go-ahead Principle.

SOPHOCLES. The Antigone of
Sophocles, with notes. By T. D.
Woolsey. Third edition, revised. *Gr.*
Boston, 1841. 12°

2 THE ELECTRA of Sophocles, with
notes, .. by T. D. Woolsey. Third
edition, revised. *Gr.* Boston, 1841.
12°

3 THE AIAS of Sophokles, with
critical and explanatory notes. Cambridge, 1851. 12°

SOPHOCLES, E. A. A Romaic
Grammar, accompanied by a Chres-

SOU

SOU

2 A CATALOGUE of Greek Verbs, for the use of colleges. Hartford, 1844. 12°

SOU. The well-spent Sou; or, Bibles for the poor Negroes. Translated from the French by J. Porter. New Haven, 1830. 8vo.

SOULIE, FRÉDÉRIC. The Mysteries of the Heaths; or the Chateau de Chevalaine. Translated by G. Fleming. New York, 1844. 8°

SOUTH. Letters from the South, written during an excursion in the summer of 1816. By the author of "John Bull and Brother Jonathan" [James K. Paulding]. 2 vol. New York, 1817. 12°

SOUTH AMERICA. A View of South America and Mexico; comprising their history, political condition, geography, etc. By a Citizen of the United States. 2 vol. [wanting the maps]. N. York, 1826. 12°

SOUTHARD, SAMUEL L. Reports of cases, argued and determined in the Supreme Court of Judicature of the State of New Jersey. 2 vol. Trenton, 1819-20. 8°

2 ANNIVERSARY Addreſs, delivered before the Columbian Institute, ... 31 Dec. 1827. Washington, 1828. 8°

3 AN ADDRESS delivered before the Alumni Aſſociation of Naſſau Hall, on the day of the annual commencement of the College. Princeton, 1832. 8°

4 SPEECH .. on the removal of the deposites; delivered in the Senate, .. Jan. 8, 1834. Washington, 1834. 8°

5 AN ADDRESS delivered before the .. Societies of the College of New Jersey, Sept. 26, 1837. .. Second edition. Princeton, 1838. 8°

SOUTHARD, SAMUEL L. Rev. The "Mystery of Godlineſs." [A course of sermons, on 1 Tim. iii. 16.] New York, 1848. 8°

SOUTH CAROLINA, Province and State of. Acts paſſed by the General Aſſembly, ... at a Seſſions .. holden at Charlestown, Nov. 15, .. 1733. And .. continued by .. prorogations .. to May 29, 1736. Charlestown, 1736. Fol°

2 THE LAWS of the Province of South Carolina. In two parts. The first part containing all the perpetual acts in force, .. with the titles of such .. as are repealed, expired, or obsolete. ... The second part, containing all the temporary acts in force. ... To which is added the titles of all the private acts, and the two charters granted by .. Charles II to the Lords proprietors of Carolina. And also the Act of Parliament for establishing an agreement with seven of the said Lords proprietors for the surrender of their title and interest to his Majesty. Collected .. by N. Trott. Part 1, in 2 vol. Charlestown, 1736. Fol.

3 AN ACCOUNT of sundry goods imported, and sundry goods of the produce of this Province exported, from the several ports within the said Province, from the first of Nov. 1738, to the first of Nov. 1739, with the number of veſſels entered and cleared at each port. As also from whence arrived and where bound. Charlestown, 1739. s. sh. fol.

4 JOURNAL of the Provincial Congreſs of South Carolina, 1776. Charlestown, 1776. 8vo.

5 ACTS, ordinances, and resolves of the General Aſſembly of the State of South Carolina, paſſed in March, 1789. Charleston [1789]. Fol°. Also the

Acts paſſed, Feb. 1790.
Acts ratified, Feb. 1791.
Acts paſſed, Dec. 1791.
Acts paſſed, Dec. 1792.
Acts paſſed, Dec. 1793.
Acts paſſed, Apr. 1794.
Acts paſſed, Dec. 1794.
Charleston, 1790-95. Fol°

6 THE PUBLIC LAWS of the State of South Carolina, from its first establishment as a British province .. to .. 1790 inclusive. ... To which is added, the titles of all the laws .. which have

been paſſed in South Carolina .. to the present time, *etc.* [Edited] by J. F. Grimké. Philadelphia, 1790. 4°

7 REPORTS of judicial decisions in the Constitutional Court of the State of South Carolina; held at Charleston and Columbia, during the years 1812 .. 1816. To which is added, two cases determined in the Court of Equity in .. 1822. 2 vol. Charleston, 1823. 8°

8 REPORTS of cases determined in the Constitutional Court of South Carolina. By the State Reporter [Harper]. Vol.1. Columbia,1824. 8°

9 ORIGINAL Communications made to the Agricultural Society of South Carolina; and extracts from select authors on agriculture. Charleston, 1824. 8°

10 REPORTS of Equity cases, determined in the Court of Appeals of the State of South Carolina. By the State Reporter. Columbia, 1825. 8°

11 THE STATUTES at large of South Carolina; edited under the authority of the Legislature. Vol. 1-5, edited by Thomas Cooper, and vol. 6-10, edited by David J. M'Cord. [Containing laws from 1682 to Dec.1838.] 10 vols. [Wanting vol. 3 and 4.] Large paper. Columbia,1836-41. 8vo.

12 REPORTS of judicial decisions in the Constitutional Court of South Carolina, held at Charleston and Columbia, in 1817, 1818. A new edition. Two volumes in one. [By — Mills.] Charleston, 1837. 8vo.

13 REPORT of law cases determined in the Court of Appeals of South Carolina, Jan. term, 1836, April term, 1836, and Feb. term, 1837. Charleston, 1839. 8°

14 CHANCERY Cases determined in the Court of Appeals of South Carolina, April term, 1836, and February term, 1837. Charleston, 1839. 8°

15 REPORT of a Committee of the Board of Directors of the Planters' and Mechanics' Bank of South Carolina, to whom was referred the opinion of the solicitor of the Bank, on

the question, Whether the Bank, by a suspension of specie payments, has incurred a forfeiture of its charter. Charleston, 1841. 8°

16 THE BANK Case: a report of the proceedings in the cases of the Bank of South Carolina, and the Bank of Charleston, upon scire facias to vacate their Charters, for suspending specie payments, with the final argument and determination thereof, in the Court for the Correction of Errors of South Carolina, in .. 1842 and 1843. Printed by order of the Legislature of South Carolina. Charleston, November, 1844. 8vo.

17 THE POLITICAL Annals of South Carolina. By a Citizen [signing himself J. D. *i.e.* J. D. B. De Bow]. Charleston, 1845. 8°

SOUTH CAROLINA GAZETTE. Posts[c]ript to the South Carolina Gazette. N° 361 [relating to the reception of Mr. George Whitefield in New England, communicated by Josiah Smith]. Charlestown, 1740. s. sh. 4to.

SOUTH CAROLINA GAZETTE; and General Advertiser. N° 29 and 94. Charlestown, 1783-84. Fol.

SOUTHERN JOURNAL (THE) of Medicine and Pharmacy. Vol. 1. Edited by J. L. Smith and S. D. Sinkler. Vol. 2, by P. C. Gaillard and H. W. Desauſſure. [The title was then altered to:] The Charleston Medical Journal and Review. Vol. 3-4. Edited by P. C. Gaillard and H. W. Desauſſure. Vol. 5-11, by D. J. Cain and F. Peyre Porcher. Charleston, 1846-56. 8°

SOUTHERN LITERARY MESSENGER (THE): devoted to every department of literature and the fine arts. [Edited by T. W. White, vol. 2-8; by B. B. Minor, vol. 9-11.] [Continued as] The Southern and Western Literary Meſſenger. [B. B. Minor, editor.] Vol. 12-13. The Southern Literary Meſſenger, J. R.

Thompson, editor. Vol. 14-17. Richmond, 1835-51. 8°

SOUTHERN REVIEW (THE) [quarterly]. Feb. 1828 to Feb. 1832. Vol. 1-8. Charleston, 1828-32. 8vo.

SOUTHERNER. Sketches of the higher claſſes of colored society in Philadelphia. By a Southerner. Philadelphia, 1841. 12°

SOUTHEY, ROBERT. The Life of Nelson. New York, 1843. 12°

SOUTHGATE, HORATIO, *Bishop*. Encouragement to Miſſionary effort among Mohamedans. A sermon [on Isaiah lx. 7] by H. Southgate, Missionary . . to Persia, *etc.* To which are annexed, an account of the meeting held at the Church of the Ascension, . ᵥ April 3, 1836. With the addreſs . . by Mr. Southgate, *etc.* New York, 1836. 8°

2 NARRATIVE of a Tour through Armenia, Kurdistan, Persia, and Mesopotamia. With an introduction and occasional observations upon the condition of Mohammedanism and Christianity in those countries. 2 vol. New York, 1840. 12°

SOUTHWORTH, EMMA D. E. NEVITTE, *Mrs.* The Deserted Wife. New York, 1851. 8°

. 2 SHANNONDALE. New York, 1851. 8°

3 VIRGINIA and Magdalene; or, the foster-sisters. A novel. Philadelphia, 1852. 8°

4 THE CURSE of Clifton: a tale of expiation and redemption. 2 vol. Philadelphia, 1853. 12°

5 OLD Neighbourhoods and New Settlements, or Christmas evening legends. Philadelphia, 1853. 12°

SPAFFORD, HORATIO GATES. A Gazetteer of the State of New York; carefully written from original and authentic materials, arranged on a new plan, *etc.* [With an appendix.] Albany, 1813. 8°

2 A GAZETTEER of the State of New York: . . with appendix, *etc.* Albany, 1824. 8°

3 A POCKET Guide for the tourist and traveller along the line of the canals, and the interior commerce of the State of New York. New York, 1824. 12°

SPAIN. A Year in Spain. By a Young American [Alexander Slidell Mackenzie]. Third edition, enlarged. 3 vol. New York, 1836. 12°

2 SPAIN Revisited. By the author of "A year in Spain" [A. Slidell Mackenzie]. Second edition. 2 vol. New York, 1836. 12°

SPALDING, JOSHUA. A Sermon [on Ecclesiastes i. 5] . . on the death of General Washington. Salem [1800]. 8°

SPALDING, M. J. D'Aubigné's "History of the great Reformation in Germany and Switzerland" reviewed, or the Reformation in Germany examined in its instruments, causes and manner, and its influence on religion, government, literature, and general civilization. Baltimore, 1844. 12mo.

2 SKETCHES of the early Catholic Miſſions of Kentucky; from their commencement in 1787, to the jubilee, 1826-7: embracing a summary of the early history of the State, *etc.* Compiled from authentic sources, with the aſſistance of S. T. Badin, the first priest ordained in the United States. Louisville [1844]. 12mo.

SPALDING, WILLIAM. Italy and the Italian Islands; from the earliest ages to the present time. 3 vol. New York, 1845, '43. 12°

SPARKS, JARED. Letters on the ministry, ritual and doctrines of the Protestant Episcopal Church, addreſſed to the Rev. W. E. Wyatt, . . in reply to a sermon exhibiting some of the principal doctrines of the Protestant Episcopal Church in the United States. Baltimore, 1820. 8°

2 REVIEW of the Rev. J. Sparks' Letters on the Protestant Episcopal Church, in reply to the Rev. Dr. Wyatt's Sermon. Baltimore, 1820. 8°

3 AN INQUIRY into the comparative moral tendency of Trinitarian and Unitarian doctrines; in a series of letters to the Rev. Dr. Miller, of Princeton. Boston, 1823. 8°

4 A COLLECTION of essays and tracts in Theology, from various authors, with biographical and critical notices. 6 vol. Boston, 1823-1826. 12°

5 THE LIFE of John Ledyard, comprising selections from his journals and correspondence. Cambridge, 1828. 8°

6 THE LIFE of John Ledyard, the American traveller; comprising selections from his journals and correspondence. Second edition. Cambridge, 1829. 12°

7 THE DIPLOMATIC Correspondence of the American Revolution. Being the letters of Benjamin Franklin, Silas Deane, etc. Edited by Jared Sparks. 12 vol. Boston, 1829, 30. 8vo. See UNITED STATES, N° 101.

8 THE LIFE of Gouverneur Morris, with selections from his correspondence and miscellaneous Papers. 3 vol. Boston, 1832. 8vo.

9 THE LIBRARY of American Biography. Conducted by Jared Sparks. [First series] 10 vol. Second series 15 vol. Together 25 vol. Boston, 1834-48. 12mo.

CONTENTS.

20- Life of Nathaniel Greene, by G. W. Greene.

21. Life of Stephen Decatur, by A. S. Mackenzie.

22. Life of Edward Preble, by L. Sabine; Life of William Penn, by G. E. Ellis.

23. Life of Daniel Boone, by J. M. Peck; Life of Benjamin Lincoln, by F. Bowen.

24. Life of John Ledyard, by J. Sparks.

25. Life of William R. Davie, by F. M. Hubbard;
Life of Samuel Kirkland, by S. K. Lothrop;
Index to the second series, vol. 11-25.

10 THE LIFE of George Washington. Large paper. Boston, 1839. 8vo.

11 LIFE of George Washington. Abridged by the author. 2 vol. Boston, 1843. 12°

12 ADDRESSES at the inauguration of J. Sparks as President of Harvard College, Wednesday, June 20, 1849. Cambridge, 1849. 8°

13 LETTER to Lord Mahon, being an answer to his letter addreſsed to the editor of Washington's Writings. Boston, 1852. 8°

14 A REPLY to the Strictures of Lord Mahon and others on the mode of editing the writings of Washington. Cambridge, 1852. 8°

15 REMARKS on a " Reprint of the original Letters from Washington to J. Reed, during the American Revolution, referred to in the pamphlets of Lord Mahon and Mr. Sparks." Boston, 1853. 8vo.

16 See STANHOPE, P. H.

17 CORRESPONDENCE of the American Revolution; being letters of eminent men to George Washington, from the time of his taking command in the army to the end of his Presidency. Edited from the original manuscripts by J. Sparks. 4 vol. Boston [Cambridge, printed], 1853. 8vo.

SPELLING and Thinking combined; or, the spelling-book made a medium of thought: the sequel to " My first School-book." Boston, 1846. 12°

SPELLING-BOOK. The Synthetic Spelling-book, etc. Washington, 1834. 12°

SPENCER, ARTHUR. To the Public [An addreſs relative to the conduct of A. Spencer in becoming evidence against Capt. Maltby; followed by four letters by A. Spencer.] Boston [1774]. s. sh. fol.

SPENCER, JOHN C. The proceedings of the late Convention: a review of a pamphlet, by .. J. C. Spencer, entitled, Report to the Vestry of St. Peter's Church, Albany, of the lay delegates appointed by them, etc. [with reference to charges preferred against B. T. Onderdonk, bishop of the Episcopal Church in New York]. New York, 1846. 8°

SPENER, PHILIP JAMES. Memoirs of P. J. SPENER, compiled from the German. Philadel. [1830]. 12mo.

SPENSER, EDMUND. The poetical Works of E. Spenser. First American edition: with introductory observations on the Faerie Queene, and notes by the editor. [Together with " an eſsay on the life and writings of E. Spenser," by P. Masterman.] 5 vol. Boston, 1848. 8°

SPICER, TOBIAS. Autobiography of Rev. T. Spicer: containing incidents and observations; also some account of his visit to England. New York, 1852. 12°

SPINDLER, CARL. Archibald Werner; or the brother's revenge. A romantic tale .. Translated from the German. New York, 1849. 8°

SPIRIT of the English Religious Magazines. Nº 2-4. Burlington, 1835. 8vo.

SPOFFORD, JEREMIAH. A Gazetteer of Maſsachusetts: containing a general view of the State, with an historical sketch of the principal events, etc. Newburyport, 1828. 12°

SPOONER, LYSANDER. Illegality of the Trial of J. W. Webster. Boston, 1850. 8°

2 An ESSAY on the Trial by Jury. London, Boston printed, 1852. 8vo.

SPOONER, SHEARJASHUB. A biographical and critical Dictionary of painters, engravers, sculptors, and architects from ancient to modern times. With the monograms, ciphers, and marks used by distinguished artists. Nᵒ 1-6. New York, 1852. 8°

SPRAGUE, CHARLES. An Address delivered before the Massachusetts Society for the Suppression of Intemperance, etc. Boston, 1827. 8°

2 CURIOSITY : a poem, delivered at Cambridge, before the Phi Beta Kappa Society, Aug. 27, 1829. Boston, 1829. 8°

3 An ODE, pronounced before the inhabitants of Boston, Sept. 17, 1830, at the centennial celebration of the settlement of the city. Bost. 1830. 8°

4 WRITINGS: now first collected. New York, 1841. 8vo.

5 WRITINGS of C. Sprague, now first collected. Second edition. New York, 1843. 12°

6 THE POETICAL and prose Writings of C. Sprague. Boston, 1850. 12°

SPRAGUE, JOHN T. The origin, progress, and conclusion of the Florida war; to which is appended, a record of officers . . and privates . . killed in battle, etc. N. York, 1848. 8°

SPRAGUE, PELEG. An Oration pronounced at Worcester [in Massachusetts], July 4, 1815, the thirty-ninth anniversary of American independence. Worcester, 1815. 8°

2 SPEECH . . in the Senate . . 16 April, 1830, . . upon the subject of the removal of the Indians. Washington, 1830. 8°

3 SPEECH . . on the removal of the deposites; delivered in the Senate of the United States, Jan. 1834. Washington, 1834. 8°

SPRAGUE, WILLIAM, JUN. Of-

ficial Report upon the subject of Masonry. Providence, 1832. 8vo.

SPRAGUE, WILLIAM B. An Historical Discourse [on Deuteronomy xxxii. 7] delivered at West Springfield, December 2, 1824, the day of the annual thanksgiving. Hartford, 1825. 8°

2 CAUSES of an unsuccessful Ministry: two sermons [on Heb. iv. 2] addressed to the second Presbyterian congregation in . . Albany, etc. Albany, 1829. 8°

3 An ADDRESS delivered in the South Dutch Church, Albany, on the anniversary of the County Sabbath School Union. Albany, 1829. 12°

4 LECTURES on Revivals of Religion : with an introductory Essay by L. Woods. Also an Appendix consisting of Letters from Drs. Alexander, Wayland, Dana, etc. Albany, 1832. 8°

5 SERMON in behalf of the Polish Exiles. Albany, 1834. 8vo.

6 LECTURES illustrating the contrast between true Christianity and various other systems. New York, 1837. 12°

7 LETTERS to Young Men, founded on the history of Joseph. Albany, 1845. 12°

8 A SERMON [on 1 Samuel, vii. 12] . . containing sketches of the history of the Second Presbyterian Church and congregation, Albany. Albany, 1846. 8vo.

9 A DISCOURSE commemorative of the Rev. Thomas Chalmers. [On Matt. xxv. 15.] With a Letter from Dr. Chalmers to an American clergyman. Albany, 1847. 8vo.

10 A SERMON [on Acts x. 38] delivered . . the Sabbath morning after the death of D. Campbell. Albany, 1851. 8°

SPRING, GARDINER. Memoir of Samuel John Mills. Boston, 1829. 12mo.

2 A TRIBUTE to the Memory of . . Jeremiah Evarts, Secretary of the

American Board of Commiſſioners for Foreign Miſſions, *etc.* New York, 1831. 8°

3 MEMOIR of Samuel John Mills. Second edition. N. York, 1842. 12°

4 A DISSERTATION on the rule of faith, delivered at Cincinnati, Ohio, at the annual meeting of the American Bible Society, *etc.* N. York, 1844. 8°

5 THE ATTRACTION of the Croſs; designed to illustrate the leading truths, obligations, and hopes of Christianity. New York, 1846. 12°

6 THE BETHEL Flag: a series of short discourses to seamen. New York, 1848. 12°

7 A PASTOR's Tribute to one of his Flock. The memoirs of the late H. L. Murray; [with extraĉts from her diary and correspondence.] New York, 1849. 8°

8 FIRST Things: A series of Lectures on the great faĉts and moral leſſons first revealed to mankind. Second edition. 2 vol. New York, 1851. 12°

9 THE GLORY of Christ: illustrated in his Charaĉter and History, including the last Things of his Mediatorial Government. 2 vol. New York, 1852. 8vo.

SPRING, SAMUEL. The Monk's Revenge; or, the secret enemy: a tale of the later crusades. New York, 1847. 8°

SPRINGER, JOHN S. Forest Life and forest trees, comprising winter camp-life among the loggers, and wild-wood adventure, *etc.* New York, 1851. 8°

SQUIER, EPHRAIM GEORGE. American Archæological Researches, N° 1. The Serpent Symbol and the Worship of the Reciprocal Symbols of Nature in America. New York, 1851. 8°

2 NICARAGUA, its people, scenery, monuments, and the proposed interoceanic canal, with numerous original maps and illustrations. 2 vol. New York, 1852. 8°

3 ANOTHER Copy, with new title-page. London [New York printed], 1852. 8vo.

4 NOTES on Central America, particularly the States of Honduras and San Salvador .... and the proposed Honduras inter-oceanic railway. With original maps and illustrations. New York, 1855. 8vo.

5 *See* SMITHSONIAN INSTITUTION, N° 1.

STAGG, EDWARD. Thoughts and Feelings: in Verse. New York, 1847. 12mo.

2 POEMS. Saint Louis, 1852. 12°

STALLO, J. B. General Principles of the Philosophy of Nature: with an outline of some of its recent developements among the Germans, embracing the philosophical systems of Schelling and Hegel, and Oken's system of nature. Boston, 1848. 12°

STANFORD, JOHN. The Aged Christian's Cabinet; containing a variety of Eſſays, Conversations, and Discourses adapted to the improvement, consolation, and animation of aged Christians. N. York, 1829. 8°

STANFORD, RICHARD. Mr. Stanford's Motion relative to a receſſion of the territory of Columbia. Washington, 1805. 8°

STANHOPE, PHILIP HENRY. Review of Lord Mahon's History of the American Revolution. [By J. G. Palfrey.] From the North American Review for July, 1852. Boston, 1852. 8°

STANIFORD, DANIEL. Staniford's Praĉtical Arithmetic, .. for the use of schools and academies. Bost. 1818. 12°

2 THE ELEMENTS of English Grammar; designed for the use of schools. .. Third edition. Boston, 1821. 12°

STANLEY, GEORGE W. An Oration, delivered ... Aug. 8, 1805, in commemoration of the Independence of the United States, *etc.* New Haven, 1805. 8°

STANSBURY, ARTHUR J. Elementary Catechism on the Constitution of the United States. For the use of schools. Boston, 1831. 12°

2 TRIAL of the Rev. A. Barnes .. on a charge of heresy, *etc.* As reported .. by A. J. Stansbury. 1836. 12mo.

STANSBURY, DANIEL. Tables to facilitate the necessary calculations in Nautical Astronomy, more particularly intended to enable navigators to determine their longitude from lunar observations . . . to which is prefixed an explanation of the tables, with examples, *etc.* New York, 1821. 4°

STANSBURY, HOWARD. An Expedition to the Valley of the Great Salt Lake of Utah: including a description of its geography, natural history, and minerals, and an analysis of its waters. With an .. account of the Mormon Settlement. . . Also a reconnoissance of a new route through the Rocky Mountains, and two . . . maps. Philadelphia, 1852. 8°

STANSBURY, P. A Pedestrian Tour of two thousand three hundred miles in North America. . . . Embellished with views. New York, 1822. 12°

STANTON, HENRY B. Sketches of Reform and Reformers of Great Britain and Ireland. New York, 1849. 12°

STAPLES, WILLIAM R. The Documentary History of the Destruction of the Gaspee. Compiled for the Providence Journal. Prov.1845. 4to.

STARK, ANN ELIZA. Memoir of A. E. Stark. Philadelphia. 12mo.

STATE PRISONS and the Penitentiary System vindicated, with observations on managing and conducting these Institutions. . . Also, some particular remarks and documents relating to the Massachusetts State Prison. By an officer of this establishment. Charlestown, 1821. 8°

STEAM for the Million: an elementary outline treatise on the nature and management of steam, and the principles and arrangement of the engine ; .. with an appendix, containing notes on expansive steam, station bills for sea steamers, *etc.* Philadelphia, 1847. 8°

STEAMBOAT DISASTERS and Railroad Accidents in the United States. To which are appended, accounts of recent shipwrecks, fires at sea, *etc.* Revised and improved. Worcester, 1846. 8°

STEARNS, ASAHEL. Commonwealth of Massachusetts. [Letter from A. Stearns, announcing his acceptance of the office of University Professor of Law, and enquiring whether the office is incompatible with a seat in the House of Representatives: with the report of a Committee of the House appointed to consider the case.] [Boston, 1818.] 8°

2 A SUMMARY of the law and practice of real actions ; with an appendix of practical forms. Second edition, with additions. Hallowell, 1831. 8°

STEARNS, CHARLES. The Ladies' Philosophy of Love, a poem, in four cantos. Written in 1774. Leominster, Mass. 1797. 4°

2 DRAMATIC Dialogues for the use of Schools. Leominster, 1798. 12°

STEARNS, JONATHAN F. A Sermon [on 2 Samuel iii. 38-39] occasioned by the death of Daniel Webster, delivered in the first Presbyterian Church, Newark, New Jersey. Newark, 1852. 8°

STEARNS, JOHN G. An Inquiry into the nature and tendency of speculative Free-masonry. With an appendix ; to which is added Plain Truth, a dialogue, and the author's reasons. Fifth edition. Utica, 1829. 8vo.

STEARNS, William A. The Great Lamentation. A sermon [on Genesis l. 10] in commemoration of D. Webster... Second edition. Boston and Cambridge, 1852. 8°

STEBBINS, Rufus P. An Addreß delivered before the Peace Society of Amherst College, July 4, 1838. Amherst, 1838. 8°

STEEL, John H. An Analysis of the Mineral Waters of Saratoga and Ballston... Together with a history of.. these celebrated watering places, etc. Saratoga Springs, 1838. 12°

STEELE, Allen. " The Episcopal Church defended" [a work by J. A. Bolles] reviewed: being a vindication of Methodist Episcopacy; with corrections of the errors and misrepresentations contained in the work reviewed. Batavia, 1843. 8vo.

STEELE, C. M. Mrs. A Mother's Thoughts on parental responsibility illustrated by opposite modes of home education. N.York,1852. 8°

STEELE, Eliza R. The Sovereigns of the Bible. N.York,1852. 8°

STEELL, Thomas Edward. A Dißertation on the use of the Digitalis Purpurea in the cure of certain diseases. New York, 1811. 8vo.

STEINER, Ignace. An Elementary Reader, German and English; based upon the affinity of the languages... Second edition, revised and corrected. New York, 1847. 12°

STENOGRAPHY made easy. [Boston, 1830?] 8vo.

STEPHENS, Ann S. Mrs. The Old Homestead. Edited and copyrighted by C. M. M'Lachlan [who has done nothing but put his name on a new title-page]. London [Boston printed], 1855. 12mo.

STERLING, John Canfield. Defence of J. C. Sterling on his trial upon presentment for alleged schismatical conduct, in the Protestant Episcopal Church in the United States of America. Second edition. New York, 1852. 8°

STERNE, Laurence. The Works of L. Sterne. With a life of the author, written by himself. Philadelphia, 1848. 8°

STETSON, Caleb. Two Discourses preached before the first Congregational Society in Medford; one [on 1 Chron. xvii. 1] upon leaving the old Church; and one [on 1 Cor. iii. 16] at the dedication of the new. Boston, 1840. 8°

STEUART, J. Bogota in 1836-7. Being a narrative of an expedition to the capital of New Grenada, and a residence there of eleven months. New York, 1838. 12mo.

STEVENS, A. M. A. Memorials of the introduction of Methodism into the Eastern States; comprising biographical notices of its early preachers, sketches of its first churches, and reminiscences of its early struggles and succeßes. Boston, 1848. 12°

STEVENS, Alexander H. A Dißertation on the proximate cause of inflammation, with an attempt to establish a rational plan of cure. Philadelphia, 1811. 8vo.

2 An Address to the claß of graduates of the College of Physicians and Surgeons of the University of .. New York, etc. New York, 1847. 8°

3 Annual Addreß delivered before the New York State Medical Society and Members of the Legislature at the Capitol, February 6, 1850. Albany, 1850. 8vo.

STEVENS, John, of Salem Chapel, Sobo. A new Selection of hymns, including also several original, etc. Few MS. notes. Boston [1813?]. 12°

STEVENS, Isaac I. Campaigns of the Rio Grande and of Mexico.

With notices of the recent work of Major Ripley. New York, 1851. 8°

STEVENS, WILLIAM. A System for the discipline of the artillery of the United States of America; or, the young artillerist's pocket companion. Vol. 1. New York, 1797. 12°

STEVENS, WILLIAM BACON. A Discourse delivered before the Georgia Historical Society, Savannah, . . Feb. 12, 1841 [on the origin and progress of Revolutionary proceedings in Georgia]. Savannah, 1841. 8°

STEVENSON, ROGER. Military Instructions for Officers detached in the Field, etc. Philadel. 1775. 12°

STEWARD, JAMES, D. D. History of the Discovery of America, of the landing of our forefathers at Plymouth, and of their most remarkable engagements with the Indians, in New England, 1620 to 1669. Brooklyn. 8°

STEWART, ALVAN. An Essay on the evils of intemperance, etc. Utica, 1833. 8°

STEWART, ANDREW. The National Union upheld and preserved by a national system of education : the annual address to the Franklin and Philo Literary Societies of Jefferson College, etc. Pittsburgh, 1835. 8°
2 REMARKS . . in defence of the protective policy; delivered in the House of Representatives . . 14 March and 27 May, 1846. Revised edition. [Washington, 1846.] 8°

STEWART, CHARLES S. Rev. Private Journal of a Voyage to the Pacific Ocean, and residence at the Sandwich Islands, in the years 1822, 1823, 1824, and 1825. New York, 1828. 8°
2 A VISIT to the South Seas, in the U. S. ship Vincennes, during the years 1829 and 1830. With scenes in Brazil, Peru, Manilla, the Cape of Good Hope, and St. Helena. 2 vol. New York, 1831. 12°

3 SKETCHES of Society in Great Britain and Ireland. Second edition. 2 vol. Philadelphia, 1835. 12°
4 A RESIDENCE in the Sandwich Islands. Fifth edition, enlarged; including an introduction and notes, by Rev. W. Ellis, from the last London edition. Boston, 1839. 12°

STEWART, F. CAMPBELL. The Hospitals and Surgeons of Paris; an historical and statistical account of the civil hospitals of Paris; with miscellaneous information and biographical notices of some . . eminent . . living Parisian surgeons. New York, 1843. 8°

STEWART, GEORGE N. Reports of Cases argued and determined in the Supreme Court of Alabama, etc. 1827-1831. 3 vol. Tuscaloosa, 1830-35. 8°

STEWART, GEORGE N. AND PORTER, BENJAMIN F. Reports of Cases at law and in Equity, argued and determined in the Supreme Court of Alabama. Jan. term, 1831, to Jan. term, 1834. 5 vol. Tuscaloosa, 1836-37. 8°

STEWART, K. J. The Freemason's Manual : a companion for the initiated through all the degrees of Freemasonry . . with . . . engravings; etc. Philadelphia, 1851. 8°

STILES, EZRA. The United States elevated to glory and honour. A Sermon [on Deut. xxvi. 19] . . Second edition, corrected. Worcester, 1785. 12°
2 A HISTORY of three of the Judges of King Charles I, Major General Whalley, Major-General Goffe, and Colonel Dixwell; who . . fled to America and were secreted . . for near thirty years. With an account of Mr. T. Whale, of Narragansett, supposed to have been also one of the judges. Hartford, 1794. 12°

STILES, WILLIAM H. Austria in 1848-49 : being a history of the late political movements in Vienna, Milan, Venice, and Prague; with details of the campaigns of Lombardy and Novara; a full account of the revolution in Hungary, and historical sketches of the Austrian Government, etc. 2 vol. New York, 1852. 8°

STILLE, ALFRED. Elements of General Pathology: a practical treatise on the causes, forms, symptoms, and results of disease. Philadelphia, 1848. 12°

STILLING, HEINRICH. Theobald; or the Fanatic: a true history . . Translated by . . S. Schæffer. Philadelphia, 1846. 12°

2 THEORY of Pneumatology: in reply to the question, What ought to be believed or disbelieved concerning presentiments, visions, and apparitions, according to nature, reason, and Scripture . . translated from the German, with copious notes, by S. Jackson . . Edited by . . G. Bush. New York, 1851. 12°

STILLMAN, SAMUEL. An Oration delivered July 4th, 1789, in celebration of the anniversary of American Independence. Boston, 1789. 8vo.

2 A DISCOURSE [on Hosea xiv. 3] before the Members of the Boston Female Asylum, Sept. 25, 1801, being their first anniversary. Boston, 1801. 8°

3 SELECT Sermons on doctrinal and practical subjects, . . comprising several sermons never before published. To which is prefixed a biographical sketch of the author's life. Boston, 1808. 8°

STIRLING, MARY ELIZABETH. Light in the Valley. A memorial of M. E. Stirling, etc. Philadelphia, 1852. 16mo.

STITH, WILLIAM. The History of the first Discovery and Settlement of Virginia, being an essay towards a general history of this colony. (Appendix to the first part of the history of Virginia; containing a collection of . . charters.) Williamsburg, 1747. 8vo.

2 THE SAME, with a new title-page. London, 1753. 8vo.

3 THE NATURE and extent of Christ's Redemption. A Sermon [on Matt. vii. 13, 14] preached before the General Assembly of Virginia, etc. Williamsburg, 1753. 8vo.

STOCK, JOHN EDMONDS. An inaugural Essay on the effects of cold upon the human body. Philadelphia, 1797. 8vo.

STOCKTON, RICHARD. Speech . . in the House of Representatives . . 10 Dec. 1814, on a bill to authorise the President . . to call upon the several States for their quotas of 80,430 militia, etc. George-Town, 1814. 8°

STOCKTON, T. H. Sermon occasioned by the death of President Taylor, delivered at the Masonic Hall, Cincinnati, Aug. 1, 1850. Cincinnati, 1850. 8°

STODDARD, AMOS. Sketches, historical and descriptive, of Louisiana. Philadelphia, 1812. 8°

STODDARD, D. T. A Grammar of the Modern Syriac Language, as spoken in Oroomia, Persia, and in Koordistan. London, New Haven printed, 1855. 8vo.

STODDARD, RICHARD HENRY. Poems. Boston, 1852. 12°

2 ADVENTURES in Fairy-Land, etc. Boston, 1853. 8°

STODDARD, SOLOMON. An Answer to some Cases of Conscience respecting the Country. Boston, in New England, 1722. 4to.

2 QUESTION whether God is not angry with the country for doing so little towards the conversion of the Indians! [A Sermon on Rom. viii. 19.] Boston, 1723. 4to.

L L

STOECKHARDT, Julius Adolph. The Principles of Chemistry illustrated by simple experiments. Translated from the third German edition by C. H. Peirce. Cambridge, 1850. 12mo.

STOKES, J. The Cabinet maker and Upholsterer's Companion, etc. Philadelphia, 1850. 12°

STOKES, William, M.D. Lectures on the theory and practice of physic .. Second American edition. With numerous notes and twelve additional lectures, by J. Bell, M.D. Philadelphia, 1840. 8°

STONE, Andrew L. A Sermon [on Eccles. xii. 5] preached .. on .. the Sunday succeeding the death of D. Webster. Boston, 1853. 8°

STONE, Eliab. A Discourse [on 2 Tim. iv. 6] .. in which the warnings of death are considered as excitements to review life. Second edition. Boston, 1811. 8°

STONE, John S. The bearings of modern Commerce on the progress of modern Missions: [a Sermon on Isaiah lx. 9.] The annual Sermon before the .. Board of Missions of the Protestant Episcopal Church in the United States. N. York, 1839. 8°

2 The Mysteries opened ; or scriptural views of preaching and the Sacraments, as distinguished from certain theories concerning baptismal regeneration and the real presence. New York, 1844. 12°

STONE, W. D. and others. Bank Reports. Bank of the State of Alabama. Reports on its affairs and position, and on those of its several branches. 4 parts. [Tuscaloosa, 1837.] 8°

STONE, William Leete. Letters on Masonry and Anti-Masonry, addressed to the Hon. John Quincy Adams. New York, 1832. 8vo.

2 Tales and Sketches. 2 vol. New York, 1834. 12°

3 Matthias and his impostures: or the progress of fanaticism, illustrated by the extraordinary case of Robert Matthews and some of his forerunners and followers. Third edition. New York, 1835. 12mo.

4 Letter to Dr. A. Brigham on Animal Magnetism : being an account of a remarkable interview between the author and Miss L. Brackett while in a state of somnambulism. New York, 1837. 8vo.

5 The Life and Times of Red-Jacket, or Sa-Go-Ye-Wat-Ha, being the sequel to the History of the Six Nations. New York, 1841. 8vo.

6 Border Wars of the American Revolution. 2 vol. New York, 1846. 12°

STONINGTON BAPTIST ASSOCIATION. Minutes of the Stonington Baptist Association, held at Chester, .. Connecticut, Oct. 19 and 20, 1813. [Chester, 1813.] 8°

STORIES and Hymns for little Children. American Sunday School Union, Philadelphia, 1833. 12mo.

STORIES for young Persons. By the author of " The Linwoods," .. etc. [C. M. Sedgwick]. New York, 1844. 12°

STORR, Professor. An Elementary Course of Biblical Theology. translated from the work of Professors Storr and Flatt, with additions by S. S. Schmucker. 2 vol. Andover, 1826. 4to.

STORROW, Charles S. A Treatise on Water-works for conveying and distributing supplies of water: with tables and examples. Boston, 1835. 12°

STORY. The Little Story Book. Philadelphia [1834]. 12mo.

STORY, Isaac. An Oration on the anniversary of the Independence of the United States of America, pronounced at Worcester, July 4, 1801. Worcester, July, 1801. 8°

STORY, JOSEPH. The Power of Solitude, a poem, in two parts. A new and improved edition. · Salem, 1804. 12°

2 AN ORATION, pronounced at Salem, .. 4 July, 1804, in commemoration of our national Independence. Salem, 1804. 8°

3 A SELECTION of Pleadings in civil actions, subsequent to the Declaration; with occasional annotations on the law of pleading. Salem [printed at Boston], Jan. 1805. 8°

4 A DISCOURSE pronounced before the Phi Beta Kappa Society, at the anniversary celebration on the thirty-first day of August, 1826. Boston, 1826. 8°

5 A DISCOURSE pronounced at the request of the Essex Historical Society, .. 18 Sept. 1828, in commemoration of the first settlement of Salem, in the State of Massachusetts. Boston, 1828. 8°

6 A DISCOURSE pronounced upon the inauguration of the author, as Dane Professor of law in Harvard University... 25 Aug. 1829. Boston, 1829. 8°

7 A SELECTION of Pleadings in Civil Actions, with occasional annotations. A second edition, with additions, by B. L. Oliver, Jun. Boston, 1829. 8°

8 AN ADDRESS delivered on the dedication of the Cemetery at Mount Auburn, Sept. 24, 1831. To which is added an appendix, containing a historical notice .. of the place, etc. Boston, 1831. 8°

9 A DISCOURSE, pronounced at the funeral obsequies of J. H. Ashmun, Royall Professor of law in Harvard University; etc. Cambridge,1833. 8°

10 COMMENTARIES on the Constitution of the United States; 3 vol. Boston, 1833. 8vo.

11 COMMENTARIES on the Consti-

tution of the United States; with a preliminary review of the constitutional history of the Colonies and States before the adoption of the Constitution. Abridged by the author. Boston, 1833. 8°

12 THE CONSTITUTIONAL Classbook: being a brief exposition of the Constitution of the United States. Boston, 1834. 12°

13 COMMENTARIES on the Conflict of Laws, foreign and domestic, in regard to contracts, rights, and remedies, and especially in regard to marriages, divorces, wills, successions, and judgments. Boston, 1834. 8vo.

14 THE MISCELLANEOUS Writings, literary, critical, juridical, and political, of J. Story. Now first collected. Boston, 1835. 8vo.

15 A DISCOURSE upon the life, character, and services of John Marshall, LL.D. Chief Justice of the United States of America. Boston, 1835. 8vo.

16 COMMENTARIES on Equity Jurisprudence, as administered in England and America. 2 vol. Boston, Cambridge [printed], 1836. 8°

17 COMMENTARIES on Equity Pleadings and the incidents thereto, according to the practice of the Courts of Equity of England and America. Boston, 1838. 8vo.

18 COMMENTARIES on Equity Jurisprudence, as administered in England and America. 2 vol. (Vol. 1. Second edition.) Boston,1839,6. 8vo.

19 A FAMILIAR Exposition of the Constitution of the United States, containing a brief Commentary on every clause. With an appendix containing important public Documents. Boston, 1840. 12mo.

20 A DISCOURSE delivered before the Society of the Alumni of Harvard University, etc. Boston, 1842. 8°

21 COMMENTARIES on the Law of Bills of Exchange, foreign and inland, as administered in England and America; with occasional illustrations from

the commercial law of the nations of Continental Europe. Bost. 1843. 8°

22 COMMENTARIES on the Law of Agency, as a branch of commercial and maritime jurisprudence, with occasional illustrations from the civil and foreign law. Second edition, revised, corrected, and enlarged. Boston, 1844. 8°

23 COMMENTARIES on Equity Pleadings, and the incidents thereof, according to the practice of the Courts of Equity of England and America. Third edition, revised, corrected, and enlarged. Boston, 1844. 8°

24 COMMENTARIES on the Law of Bailments, with illustrations from the civil and the foreign law. Fourth edition, revised, corrected, and enlarged. [Edited by W. W. Story.] Boston, 1846. 8°

25 COMMENTARIES on the Conflict of Laws, foreign and domestic, in regard to contracts, rights, and remedies, and especially in regard to marriages, divorces, wills, successions, and judgments. Third edition, revised, corrected, and greatly enlarged. [Edited by W. W. Story.] Boston, 1846. 8°

26 COMMENTARIES on the Law of Partnership, as a branch of commercial and maritime jurisprudence, with occasional illustrations from the civil and foreign law. Second edition. Boston, 1846. 8°

27 COMMENTARIES on Equity Jurisprudence, as administered in England and America. Fourth edition, revised, corrected, and enlarged. [Edited by W. W. Story.] Boston, 1846. 8°

28 THE MISCELLANEOUS Writings of J. Story... Edited by his son, W. W. Story. Boston, 1852. 8°

STORY, WILLIAM W. Reports of Cases argued and determined in the Circuit Court of the United States, for the first circuit. Vol. 1, 2. Boston, 1842-45. 8°

2 ADDRESS delivered before the Harvard Musical Association, ... at Cambridge, etc. Boston, 1842. 8°

3 A TREATISE on the Law of Contracts not under seal. Bost. 1844. 8°

4 LIFE and Letters of Joseph Story... Edited by .. W. W. Story. 2 vol. London, Boston printed. 1851. 8vo.

STOWE, CALVIN E. Introduction to the Criticism and Interpretation of the Bible, designed for the use of Theological Students. Bible Classes, and High Schools. In two volumes. Vol. 1. Cincinnati, 1835. 8vo.

STOWE, HARRIET ELIZABETH BEECHER, Mrs. The Mayflower: or, sketches of scenes and characters among the descendants of the Pilgrims. New York, 1844. 12°

2 UNCLE Tom's Cabin; or, Life among the Lowly... One hundred and tenth thousand. 2 vol. Boston. 1852. 12mo.

3 OHEIM Tom's Hütle, oder das Leben bei den Niedrigen... Uebersetzt von H. R. Hutten. Boston. Cambridge printed, 1853. 8vo.

STRAIN, ISAAC G. Cordillera and Pampa, Mountain and Plain. Sketches of a Journey in Chili, and the Argentine Provinces, in 1849. New York, 1853. 12°

STRANGER (THE): a Literary Paper. Vol. 1. Albany. 1814. 8°

STRANGER'S ASSISTANT and Schoolboy's Instructor ... in Arithmetic, etc. By a Citizen. New York, 1795. 8°

STRAUSE, J. Polyglot Pocket Book for English. German. French. Italian, Spanish, and Portuguese Conversation, for the use of students and travellers, etc. New York, 1851. 12°

STREET, ALFRED B. The Burning of Schenectady, and other poems. Albany, 1842. 12°

STREETER, S. F. The Teacher's Calling: an address delivered before the Maryland Institute of Education, September 24th, 1842. Baltimore [1842]. 8°

2 MARYLAND, two hundred years ago: a discourse, *etc.* [Baltimore,] 1852. 8°

STRETCH, L. M. The Beauties of History; or pictures of virtue and vice drawn from real life; designed for the instruction and entertainment of youth. Seventh edition. 2 vol. Springfield, 1794. 12°

STRICKLAND, WILLIAM. Reports on canals, railways, roads, and other subjects, made to the Pennsylvania Society for the Promotion of Internal Improvement. [With Plates.] Philadelphia, 1826. obl. fol°

STRICTURES on the Rev. Mr. Thatcher's Pamphlet, entitled, Observations upon the State of the Clergy of New England, *etc.* By J. S. Boston, 1784. 8°

STRONG, A. B. The American Flora, or history of plants and wild flowers; *etc.* Vol. 1. New York, 1847. 4°

STRONG, CALEB. Gov. Strong's Calumniator Reproved; or a review of a democratic pamphlet entitled: Remarks on the Governor's Speech. By No Bel-Esprit. Boston, 1814. 8°

STRONG, NATHANIEL T. A Further Illustration of the Case of the Seneca Indians in the State of New York, in a review of a pamphlet entitled "An Appeal to the Christian Community, by N. T. Strong." Printed by direction of the Joint Committee on Indian Affairs of the four yearly meetings of friends of Genesee, New York, Philadelphia, and Baltimore. Philadelphia, 1841. 8°

STRONG, THOMAS M. The History of the Town of Flatbush in King's County, Long Island. New York, 1842. 12°

STROUD, GEORGE M. A Sketch of the Laws relating to Slavery in the several States of the United States of America. Philadelphia, 1827. 8°

STUART, ALEXANDER H. H. Speech .. on the Tariff-Bill; delivered in the House of Representatives, .. 7 July, 1842. [Washington, 1842.] 8°

2 REMARKS .. on the Veto Message of the President, returning, with his objections, the bill extending the laws for laying and collecting the duties on imports; delivered in the House of Representatives, June 30, 1842. Washington, 1842. 8°

3 ANNIVERSARY address before the American Institute ... during the seventeenth annual fair. New York, 1844. 8°

STUART, ARABELLA W. Fourth thousand. The Lives of Mrs. A. H. Judson and Mrs. S. B. Judson, with a biographical sketch of Mrs. E. C. Judson, Missionaries to Burmah. Auburn, 1852. 12°

STUART, CHARLES B. The Naval Dry Docks of the United States... Second edition. New York, 1852. 4to.

2 THE NAVAL and Mail Steamers of the United States. .. Illustrated with thirty-six .. engravings. Second edition. New York, 1853. 4to.

STUART, JAMES. A Dissertation on the Salutary Effects of Mercury in Malignant Fevers. Philadelphia, 1798. 8vo.

STUART, MOSES. Letters to .. W. E. Channing, containing remarks on his Sermon (at the ordination of J. Sparks .. in Baltimore), *etc.* .. Second edition, .. enlarged. Andover, 1819. 8°

2 A LETTER to Professor Stuart, in answer to his letters to .. W. E. Channing, and in vindication of .. the New England and other clergy, from the unfounded aspersions cast on them, in said letters. Boston, 1819. 8°

3 A HEBREW Grammar; with a copious syntax and praxis. Andover, 1821. 8°

4 LETTERS on the Eternal Generation of the Son of God, addreſſed to .. S. Miller, D.D. [in reply to certain paſſages in his " Letters on Unitarianism"]. Andover, 1822. 8°

5 Two Discourses [on Isaiah liii. 5, 6] on the Atonement. Andover, 1824. 8°

6 A HEBREW Chrestomathy, designed as the first volume of a course of Hebrew study. Andover, 1829. 8°

7 COURSE of Hebrew Study adapted to the use of beginners. Vol. 2. [A sequel to the Hebrew Chrestomathy.] Andover, 1830. 8°

8 A LETTER to W. E. Channing .. on .. Religious Liberty; [in reply to certain paſſages in his works.] Second edition. Boston, 1830. 8°

9 A LETTER to W. E. Channing, on .. Religious Liberty. [Containing remarks on his " Discourses, Reviews and Miscellanies," also on the " Election Sermon."] Third edition. Boston, 1830. 8vo.

10 A HEBREW Chrestomathy, designed as an introduction to a course of Hebrew study. Second edition, with additions and corrections. Andover, 1832. 8°

11 Is the Mode of Christian Baptism prescribed in the New Testament? .. From the Bib. Repository, Vol. iii. N° 2. Andover, 1833. 8°

12 A GRAMMAR of the New Testament Dialect. Andover, 1836. 8vo.

13 LETTERS on the Divinity of Christ, addreſſed to the Rev. E. Channing, in answer to his sermon " On the Doctrines of Christianity," preached [at the ordination of J. Sparks,] .. With an introductory eſſay, by .. G. Fisk. [With an appendix.] Cambridge, 1836. 12°

14 CRITICAL History and Defence of the Old Testament Canon. Andover, 1845. 12mo.

15 SERMON [on Rom. xi. 25-31] at the ordination of .. W. G. Shauffler

as Miſſionary to the Jews; preached .. Nov. 14, 1831. ... Third edition. Boston, 1845. 8°

16 MISCELLANIES : consisting of 1, Letters to Dr. Channing on the Trinity; 2, Two Sermons on the Atonement; 3, Sacramental Sermon on the Lamb of God; 4, Dedication Sermon—Real Christianity; 5, Letter to Dr. Channing on Religious Liberty: 6, Supplementary notes and postscripts of new additional matter. Andover, 1846. 12°

17 SCRIPTURAL View of the Wine Question, in a letter to the Rev. Dr. Nott, etc. New York, 1848. 8°

18 HINTS on the Interpretation of Prophecy. .. Second edition, with additions and corrections. New York, 1851. 12mo.

STUDENTS. The Students. A drama, in five acts [and in verse]. New York, 1850. 12°

STURTEVANT, J. M. The Memory of the Just; a sermon [on Prov. x. 7] commemorative of the life and labours of the Rev. W. Kirby, etc. New York, 1852. 8°

STURTEVANT, T. D. Dickson and Swedenborg, on periodicity, cause, and cure of disease. New York, 1847. 12°

SUBSTANCES. Vegetable Substances used for the food of man. New York, 1844. 12°

SUGAR. Remarks on the manufacturing of Maple Sugar; with directions for its improvement. Philadelphia, 1790. 12mo.

SUGGS, SIMON. Some Adventures of Captain Simon Suggs, late of the Talapoosa Volunteers, together with " Taking the Census," and other Alabama sketches. By a Country Editor, etc. Philadelphia, 1851. 12°

SULLIVAN, FRANCIS STOUGHTON. Lectures on the Constitution and Laws of England : with a commentary on Magna Charta, and illustrations of many of the English Statutes. .. To which authorities are added, and a discourse is prefixed concerning the laws and government of England, by G. Stuart. First American edition. 2 vol. Portland, 1805. 8°

SULLIVAN, GEORGE. , An Oration pronounced at Exeter [in New Hampshire] .. 4 July, 1800, in commemoration of the anniversary of American Independence. Exeter, New Hampshire, 1800. 8°

2 SPEECH .. at the late Rockingham Convention, with the memorial and resolutions, and report of the Committee of Elections. Exeter [1812]. 8°

3 AN ADDRESS of Members of the House of Representatives of the Congrefs ·of the United States, to their constituents, on the subject of the war with Great Britain; [subscribed by G. Sullivan and others.] Hartford, reprinted, 1812. 8°

4 SUPREME Court of the United States : J. [or rather S.] B. Stone, ads. the United States of America. Argument for defendant [in an action for violation of the Act of Congrefs providing for the better security of the lives of pafsengers in steamvefsels, etc.] New York, 1840. 8°

SULLIVAN, JAMES. Observations upon the Government of the United States of America. Bost. 1791. 8°

2 THE HISTORY of the District of Maine, etc. with a map. Boston, 1795. 8vo.

3 THE HISTORY of Land Titles in Mafsachusetts. Boston, 1801. 8°

4 INTERESTING Correspondence between .. Governour Sullivan and Col. Pickering ; in which the latter vindicates himself against the groundlefs charges and insinuations made by the Governour and others. [Published by Col. Pickering.] Boston, 1808. 8°

SULLIVAN, RICHARD. Addrefs delivered before the .. patrons of the Mafsachusetts General Hospital, etc. [With an appendix.] Boston, 1819. 8°

2 ADDRESS delivered at the seventh anniversary of the Mafsachusetts Peace Society, Dec. 25, 1822. Cambridge, 1823. 8°

SULLIVAN, T. R. Sermons on Christian Communion, designed to promote the growth of the religious affections, by living ministers. Edited by T. R. Sullivan. Boston, 1848. 12°

SULLIVAN, WILLIAM. An Oration, pronounced, July 4, 1803, at .. Boston, in commemoration of the anniversary of American Independence. Boston, 1803. 8°

2 AN ORATION delivered before the Washington Benevolent Society of Mafsachusetts, .. 30 April, 1812, being the anniversary of the first inauguration of President Washington. Boston, 1812. 8°

3 THE MORAL Clafs Book, .. intended for schools... Second (stereotype) edition, with additions and corrections. Boston, 1833. 12°

4 INTRODUCTORY Discourse delivered before the American Institute of Instruction, etc. Boston, 1833. 8°

5 THE MORAL Clafs Book, or the law of morals ; derived from the created universe, and from revealed religion. Third (stereotype) edition, with additions and corrections. [Boston,] 1838. 12°

6 HISTORICAL Causes and Effects, from the fall of the Roman Empire, 476, to the Reformation, 1517. Boston, 1838. 12°

7 THE POLITICAL Clafs Book. .. With an appendix upon studies for practical men ; with notices of books suited to their use. By G. B. Emerson. New edition, with amendments and additions. Boston, 1839. 12°

8 ANOTHER Copy [of the edition of 1839, with a different title-page]. Boston, 1841. 12°

9 THE PUBLIC Men of the Revolution; including events from the peace of 1783 to the peace of 1815;

in a series of letters. . . With a biographical sketch of the author, and additional notes and references by his son, J. T. S. Sullivan. Philadelphia, 1847. 8°

SULLY, *Pseud.* Remarks on the Report of the Legislature on our foreign relations. Boston, 1810. 8°

SUMMERFIELD, CHARLES, *Pseud.* [i. e. THEODORE FOSTER ?]. The Desperadoes of the South-west: containing an account of the Cane-Hill murders; together with the lives of several of the most notorious regulators and moderators of that region. New York, 1847. 8°

SUMMERFIELD, JOHN. A Sermon [on Luke vi. 36] in behalf of the New York Institution for the instruction of the deaf and dumb. To which is added, an appendix with information relative to the Institution. New York, 1822. 8vo.

SUMMERS, GEORGE W. Speech .. on the veto on the provisional tariff bill; delivered in the House of Representatives, July 1, 1842. Washington, 1842. 8°

SUMNER, BRADFORD. An Oration delivered .. July 4, 1828, in commemoration of American Independence, before the Supreme Executive of the Commonwealth, *etc.* Boston, 1828. 8°

2 AN ADDRESS delivered at the fifteenth anniversary of the Massachusetts Peace Society, Jan. 19, 1831. Boston, 1831. 8°

SUMNER, CHARLES. Reports of cases argued and determined in the Circuit Court of the United States for the first circuit; from May term, 1829, to Oct. term, 1839. 3 vol. Boston, 1836-41. 8vo.

2 THE TRUE Grandeur of Nations: an oration delivered before the authorities of the city of Boston, July 4, 1845 [in commemoration of American Independence]. Second edition. Boston, 1845. 8vo.

3 THE TRUE Grandeur of Nations: an oration delivered before the authorities of the city of Boston, July 4, 1845. Third edition. Boston, 1846. 8vo.

4 THE SCHOLAR, the Jurist, the Artist, the Philanthropist. An address before the Phi Beta Kappa Society of Harvard University, at their anniversary, Aug. 27, 1846. Second edition. Boston, 1846. 8°

5 WHITE Slavery in the Barbary States: a lecture before the Boston Mercantile Library Association, *etc.* Boston, 1847. 8°

6 THE LAW of Human Progress. An oration before the Phi Beta Kappa Society of Union College, Schenectady, July 25, 1848. Boston, 1849. 8°

7 ORATIONS and Speeches. 2 vol. Boston, 1850. 8°

8 WHITE Slavery in the Barbary States. Boston, 1853. 12°

SUMNER, CHARLES PINCKNEY. The Compass; a poetical performance at the Literary Exhibition at Harvard University. By Charles P. Sumner. Boston, 1795. 12mo.

2 A LETTER on speculative Free-Masonry. Being an answer to a letter on that subject by the Suffolk Committee. Boston, 1829. 8vo.

SUMNER, WILLIAM H. An Inquiry into the importance of the Militia to a free commonwealth; in a letter from W. H. Sumner to John Adams, late President of the United States; with his answer. Boston, 1823. 8°

2 A PAPER on the militia, presented to the Hon. J. Barbour, Secretary of War, in Nov. 1826. . . . Taken from the documents submitted to the Board of officers relative to the re-organization of the militia. Washington, 1833. 8°

SUNDAY SCHOOL CHILDREN. Philadelphia [1830]. 12mo.

SUNDERLAND, LA ROY. Anti-Slavery Manual, containing a collection of facts and arguments on American slavery. Second edition, improved. New York, 1837. 12°

SUNLIGHT upon the Landscape, and other poems. By a Daughter of Kentucky. Cincinnati, 1853. 12°

SUPERIOR, LAKE. Life on the Lakes : being tales and sketches collected during a trip to the pictured Rocks of Lake Superior. By the author of Legends of a Log Cabin. 2 vol. New York, 1836. 12°

SUPERNUMERARY. A Peep behind the Curtain. By a Supernumerary. Boston [1850]. 12°

SUPERSTITIONS. Popular Superstitions. Philadel. [1832]. 12mo.

SUTHERLAND, JOEL B. A Manual of legislative practice and order of business in deliberative bodies. Second edition. Philadel. 1830. 12°

SUTHRON. Prairiedom. Rambles and scrambles in Texas or New Estremadura. By a Suthron. With a map. New York, 1845. 12°

SWAIN, JAMES. The Moral Diagraph, or the art of conversing through a wall. Philadelphia, 1829. 12mo.

SWAN, WILLIAM D. The Primary School Reader. Part first. Philadelphia, 1844. 12°
2 THE PRIMARY School Reader. Part second. Boston, 1845. 12°
3 THE PRIMARY School Reader, Part third, etc. Boston, 1845. 12°
4 QUESTIONS adapted to Emerson's arithmetic. Part third. Boston, 1845. 12°
5 THE GRAMMAR School Reader; consisting of selections in prose and poetry, etc. designed to follow the primary school reader, part third. Boston, 1845. 12°
6 THE DISTRICT School Reader; or, exercises in reading and speaking, etc. Boston, 1846. 8°
7 THE INSTRUCTIVE Reader; or, a

course of reading in natural history, science, and literature; designed for the use of schools. Philadelphia, 1848. 12mo.

SWEDENBORG, EMANUEL, Baron. Life of Emanuel Swedenborg, with some account of his writings; together with a brief notice of the rise and progress of the New Church. Boston, 1831. 12mo.
2 THE LAST Judgment, and the Babylon destroyed; so that all the predictions in the Apocalypse are at this day fulfilled. Translated from the Latin. Boston, 1840. 12mo.
3 A SKETCH of Swedenborg and Swedenborgians. Reprinted from the London Penny Cyclopædia. Boston, 1842. 16mo.
4 A DICTIONARY of correspondences, representatives, and significatives derived from the word of the Lord. Extracted from the writings of E. Swedenborg. (Principally an abridgment of the work compiled by G. Nicholson.) Boston, 1841. 12mo.

SWEETSER, WILLIAM, M. D. A Treatise on Consumption. Boston, 1836. 8vo.
2 MENTAL Hygiene; or, an examination of the intellect and passions. Designed to show how they affect and are affected by the bodily functions, and their influence on health and longevity. . . Second edition, rewritten and enlarged. New York, 1850. 12°

SWETT, JOHN A. A Treatise on the Diseases of the Chest. New York, 1852. 8°

SWETT, SAMUEL. History of the Bunker Hill Battle, with a Plan. . . Third edition, with notes and likenesses of the principal officers. [Wanting the "Likenesses."] Boston, 1827-25. 8°

SWIFT, JOSEPH G. Report on the Baltimore and Susquehanna railroad. . . . Also the annual report of the president and directors to the stockholders. Baltimore, 1828. 8°

SWIFT, ZEPHANIAH. A Digest of the law of evidence in civil and criminal cases. And a treatise on bills of exchange and promissory notes. Hartford, 1810. 8°

SWISSHELM, JANE G. Letters to Country Girls. N. York, 1853. 12°

SWORDS'S POCKET ALMANACK, Churchman's Calendar, and Ecclesiastical Register, for . . 1835. New York [1834]. 32mo.

2 SWORDS's Pocket Almanack, 1847, containing Lists of the Clergy in each diocese. Vol. 32. New York [1846]. 32mo.

3 SWORDS's Pocket Almanack, for . . 1853, containing lists of Bishops and Clergy in each Diocese, and other statistical information concerning the Protestant Episcopal Church in the United States. New York, 1853. 32mo.

SYLVESTRE DE SACY, A. J. Principles of General Grammar. Translated by D. Fosdick, Jun. Andover and New York, 1834. 12mo.

SYNTAX, JONATHAN, *Pseud.* Trial of Jonathan Syntax, for the murder of the " King's English;" before the Supreme Court of Linguists, *etc.* New York, 1835. 12°

SYSTEM. A Short System of Practical Arithmetic, *etc.* Hallowell, 1807. 12°

ABLES. Mathematical Tables; comprising logarithms of numbers, logarithmic sines, tangents and secants, natural sines, meridional parts, etc. Stereotype edition. Boston, 1830. 8°

TACITUS, Pseud. A Series of Letters addressed to Thomas Jefferson, Esq. President of the United States, concerning his official conduct and principles; with an appendix of important documents and illustrations. By Tacitus. Philadelphia, 1802. 8°

TACITUS, CAIUS CORNELIUS. Caii Cornelii Taciti Historiarum libri quinque. Accedit de moribus Germanorum libellus: Julii Agricolæ vita: de oratoribus dialogus. Cum excerptis variorum notis. Editio quarta. J. L. Kingsley, .. editore. New York, 1844. 12°

2 THE GERMANIA and Agricola... With notes for colleges, by W. S. Tyler. Lat. New York and London, 1847. 12°

TAGGART, SAMUEL. Mr. Taggart's Addreſs to his constituents, on the subject of impreſſments. [Washington ? 1813.] 8°

TAHITI, receiving the Gospel. Philadelphia [1832]. 12mo.

TAHITI with the Gospel. Philadelphia [1834]. 12mo.

TAILFER, PATRICK. A True and Historical Narrative of the Colony of Georgia in America... Together with his Majesty's Charter, Representations of the people, Letters, etc. .. By P. Tailfer, Hugh Anderson, D. Douglas, and others, landholders in Georgia, etc. Charlestown, South Carolina [printed] and London [1741]. 8°

TALBOT and Vernon. A novel. [By D. L. Mac Connel.] New York, 1850. 12°

TALCOTT, GEORGE. Review of the Testimony given before the General Court Martial, upon the trial of Brig. General G. Talcott, in June and July, 1851; and of the proceedings of the Court. By a Counsellor at Law. To which is appended a copy of the record of the trial. Albany, 1851. 8°

TALES and Sketches. Second Series... By the author of Hope Leslie, etc. [C. M. Sedgwick]. New York, 1844. 12°

TALLEYRAND DE PERIGORD, CHARLES MAURICE DE, Bishop of Autun, Prince of Benevento. Memoir concerning the commercial relations of the United States with England. By citizen Talleyrand. Read at the National Institute, the 15th Germinal, in the year 5 [April 4, 1797]. To which is added, an eſſay upon the advantages to be derived from new colonies in the existing circumstances; by the same author, etc.

524 TAN TAP

[Translated from the French.] Boston, 1809. 8°

TALLMADGE, JAMES. American Institute; seventeenth annual fair. Agricultural convention... Remarks of the Hon. J. Tallmadge on the commercial policy of England, affecting the interests of American agriculture. Second edition. New York, 1844. 8°

TALLMADGE, NATHANIEL P. Speech .. on the bill to regulate the deposites of the public money: in Senate, June 17, 1836. [Washington, 1836.] 8°

TALVJ. Pseud. [i. e. THÉRÈSE ALBERTINE LOUISE VON JACOB, afterwards MRS. EDWARD ROBINSON]. Heloise, or the unrevealed secret. A tale. New York, 1850. 12°

2 HISTORICAL View of the Languages and Literature of the Slavic nations; with a sketch of their popular poetry. By Talvi. With a preface by E. Robinson. New York, 1850. 8°

3 LIFE's Discipline: a tale of the annals of Hungary. N. York, 1851. 12°

TANCRED. Il Tancredi. Tancred, an heroic opera, in two acts. Ital. and Engl. New York, 1825. 12°

TANGUY DE LA BOISSIERE, C. C. Observations on the Dispatch written the 16 Jan. 1797, by Mr. Pickering, Secretary of the United States of America, to Mr. Pinkney. Translated from the French by S. Chandler. Philadelphia, 1797. 8vo.

TANNEHILL, WILKINS. Sketches of the History of Literature, from the earliest period to the revival of letters in the fifteenth century. Nashville, 1827. 8°

TANNER, H. S. A New Universal Atlas. Philadelphia, 1836. Fol.

2 THE AMERICAN Traveller, or tourist's and emigrant's guide through the United States: containing brief notices of the several States, cities, principal towns, etc. with tables of

distances. Ninth edition. With .. a new map [map wanting]. New York, 1844. 12°

TANNER, T. S. A Description of the canals and railroads of the United States, comprehending notices of all the works of internal improvement throughout the several States. New York, 1840. 12°

TAPPAN, DAVID, D. D. A Discourse [on Eccl. xi. 9] delivered in the Chapel of Harvard College [Cambridge], designed chiefly for the younger members of the University. Boston, 1794. 8vo.

2 CHRISTIAN Thankfulness explained and enforced, in a sermon [on Col. iii. 15] at Charlestown [South Carolina], Feb. 19, 1795. Boston, 1795. 8vo.

3 SERMONS on important subjects. To which are prefixed, a biographical sketch of the author; and a sermon preached at his funeral by Dr. Holmes. Cambridge, 1807. 8°

4 LECTURES on Jewish Antiquities; delivered at Harvard University, in Cambridge [Massachusetts], A. D. 1802 and 1803. Camb. 1807. 8°

TAPPAN, HENRY P. Elements of Logic, together with an introductory view of philosophy in general, and a preliminary view of the Reason. New York, 1844. 12mo.

2 A DISCOURSE on Education, delivered at the anniversary of the Young Ladies' Institute, Pittsfield, Mass. etc. New York, 1846. 8°

3 UNIVERSITY EDUCATION. New York, 1851. 12°

4 A STEP from the New World to the Old, and back again; with thoughts on the good and evil in both. 2 vol. New York, 1852. 12°

5 ILLUSTRIOUS Personages of the Nineteenth Century. New York, 1853. 8°

TAPPAN, WILLIAM B. Memoirs of Captain James Wilson. Philadelphia, 1829. 12mo.

2 POEMS and Lyricks. Boston, 1842. 12°

TASSO, TORQUATO. The Jerusalem Delivered. . . . Translated into English Spenserian verse, with a life of the author, by J. H. Wiffen. First American from the last English edition. New York, 1846. 12°

TATEM, HENRY. Rev. H. Tatem's Reply to the summons of the R[hode] I[sland] [Masonic] Royal Arch Chapter. [Warwick, 1832.] 8°

TATOR, HENRY H. An Oration commemorative of the birthday of Washington, delivered . . on the 22 of February, 1851. Albany, 1851. 8°

2 AN ORATION commemorative of the character of Mrs. M. Washington. Albany, 1851. 8°

3 AN ORATION commemorative of the character of Alexander Hamilton. Albany, 1851. 8°

4 AN EULOGY commemorative of the character of H. Clay. Albany, 1852. 8°

TAYLER, THOMAS. The Law Glossary: being a selection of the Greek, Latin, Saxon, French, Norman, and Italian sentences, phrases, and maxims, found in the leading English and American reports and elementary works. With historical and explanatory notes. . . Third edition, revised and corrected. New York, 1845. 8°

TAYLOR, C. B. A universal History of the United States of America, embracing the whole period from the earliest discoveries to the present time, etc. Hartford, 1847. 12°

TAYLOR, E. E. L. The Christian Sanctuary in its relations to human interests and the Divine Glory. A Discourse delivered at the opening of . . the Strong Place Baptist Church, Brooklyn. New York, 1853. 12°

TAYLOR, GEORGE. The Indications of the Creator; or, the natural evidences of final cause. New York, 1851. 12°

TAYLOR, J. ORVILLE. The district School. [A treatise on education.] New York, 1834. 12°

2 THE DISTRICT School; or, national education. Philadelphia, 1835. 12mo.

3 THE DISTRICT School; or national education. Third edition. Philadelphia, 1835. 12mo.

4 THE FARMER'S School-book. . . Tenth edition. New York, 1838. 12°

TAYLOR, J. RICE. Ode, written for the celebration of the National Anniversary, at Kenyon College, July 4, 1839. Gambier, 1839. 12°

TAYLOR, JANE E. J. A Memoir of J. E. J. Taylor. Philadelphia, [1830?] 12mo.

TAYLOR, JAMES W. The Victim of Intrigue. A tale of Burr's Conspiracy. Cincinnati, 1847. 8°

TAYLOR, JEREMIAH BAYARD. Views A-foot; or Europe seen with knapsack and staff. Part 1, 2. With a preface by N. P. Willis. London [New York printed], 1847. 8vo.

2 PEDESTRIAN Tour in Europe. Views a-foot, or Europe seen with knapsack and staff, . . with a preface by N. P. Willis. Twelfth edition, with additions. New York, 1851. 12°

3 RHYMES of Travel. Ballads and poems. Second edition. New York, 1849. 12°

4 THE AMERICAN Legend. A poem before the Phi Beta Kappa Society of Harvard University. Cambridge, 1850. 12°

5 A BOOK of Romances, Lyrics, and Songs. Boston, 1852. 12°

6 PICTURES of Palestine, Asia Minor, Sicily, and Spain; or, the lands of the Saracen. London [New York printed], 1855. 8vo.

7 LIFE and Landscapes from Egypt to the Negro Kingdoms of the White Nile, being a journey to Central Africa . . With a map and illustrations. Second edition. London [New York printed], 1855. 8vo.

TAYLOR, John, *Rev.* A History of the Baptist Churches of which the author has been alternately a member; in which will be seen something of a journal of the author's life for more than fifty years, *etc.* Frankfort, Ky. 1823. 12mo.

TAYLOR, John. A Report of the Trial of the cause of J. Taylor *vs.* E. C. Delavan, prosecuted for an alleged libel, . . and Mr. Delavan's correspondence with the . . Albany City Temperance Society. Albany, 1840. 8°

TAYLOR, John, *of Caroline County, Virginia.* An Inquiry into the principles and policy of the Government of the United States. Fredericksburgh, 1814. 8°
2 Tyranny unmasked. [A treatise on the commerce and finances of the United States, and especially on the policy of protecting duties.] Washington City, 1822. 8°

TAYLOR, John Louis. Cases determined in the Superior Courts of Law and Equity of the State of North Carolina, from March term, 1799, to July term, 1802. Newbern [N. C.], 1802. 8°
2 North Carolina Reports: embracing "Cases determined in the Superior Courts of Law and Equity of the State of North Carolina. By J. L. Taylor." Also, "Reports of cases ruled and determined by the Court of Conference of North Carolina. By D. Cameron and W. Norwood." Second edition, with notes referring to subsequent enactments . . and decisions . . by W. H. Battle. Raleigh, 1844. 8°
3 North Carolina Reports, embracing "The Carolina Law Repository," containing "Opinions of American jurists, and reports of cases adjudged in the Supreme Court of North Carolina." Vols. I. and II. Also, " North Carolina term reports," or, Cases adjudged in the Supreme

Court of North Carolina, from July term, 1816, to January term, 1818. By J. L. Taylor. Second edition, with notes, . . marginal abstracts, *etc.* and a new index; by W. H. Battle. Raleigh, 1844. 8°

TAYLOR, Joseph. Oratio funebris in obitum E. Wigglesworth. (Portrait of the Doctor's character, inserted in the Boston Evening Post. Poetical essay, published in the Massachusetts Gazette, sacred to the memory of Dr. Wigglesworth.) Cambridge, 1775. 8°

TAYLOR, Richard Cowling. Two Reports on the coal lands, mines, and improvements of the Dauphin and Susquehanna Coal Company, *etc.* With an appendix, containing numerous tables and statistical information, and various maps, sections, and diagrams, *etc.* Philadelphia, 1840. 8°
2 Reports on the Washington Silver Mine in Davidson county, North Carolina . . With an appendix, containing assays of the ores, returns of silver and gold produced, and statements of the affairs of the Washington Mining Company. Philadel. 1845. 8°
3 Statistics of Coal. The geographical and geological distribution of fossil fuel, or mineral combustibles employed in the arts and manufactures. Their production, consumption, commercial distribution, prices, duties, and international regulations . . Including four hundred statistical tables, and eleven hundred analyses of mineral bituminous substances . . with coloured maps and diagrams. London, [and] Philadelphia, 1848. 8vo.

TAYLOR, Robert H. Poems. New York, 1848. 8°

TAYLOR, Samuel. An Essay, intended to establish a standard for an universal system of Stenography. Reprinted, Albany [1810]. 8vo.

TAYLOR, Timothy Alden. Memoir of the Rev. O. A. Taylor. Boston, 1853. 8vo.

TAYLOR, WILLIAM, AND OTHERS. Report of the Commiſsioners appointed to examine the Planters and Merchants bank of Mobile. Tuscaloosa, 1842. 8°

TAYLOR, WILLIAM COOKE. History of Ireland, from the Anglo-Norman invasion till the union of the country with Great Britain. With additions, by W. Sampson. 2 vol. [The original edition was published, in Constable's Miscellany, under the title : " History of the Civil Wars in Ireland."] New York, 1844. 12°

2 A MANUAL of Ancient and Modern History ; . . . Revised, with a chapter on the history of the United States, by C. S. Henry. . . Fifth edition . . corrected. N. York, 1847. 8°

TAYLOR, ZACHARY, *President of the United States.* General Taylor and his Staff: comprising memoirs of Z. Taylor . . and other distinguished officers . . interspersed with numerous anecdotes of the Mexican war, *etc.* Philadelphia, 1848. 12°

2 OBITUARY Addreſses delivered on the occasion of the death of Z. Taylor, in the Senate and House of Representatives . . with the funeral sermon by the Rev. S. Pyne, *etc.* Washington, 1850. 8°

TEACHER. The Little Grammarian, or, an easy guide to the parts of speech. . . By a Teacher. Illustrated with woodcuts. Boston and New York, 1829. 12°

2 YOUTHFUL Dialogues. By a teacher. Philadelphia [1830?] 12mo.

3 THE TEACHER's Parting Gift to a Sunday School boy. Philadelphia, 1832. 12mo.

4 CONVERSATIONS on Common Things ; or, guide to knowledge. With questions. For the use of schools and families. By a Teacher. . . . Fifth edition, revised, corrected, and stereotyped. Boston, 1834. 12°

5 THE VILLAGE School Geography. Embellished with numerous engravings and ten . . maps. By a Teacher. Hartford [1836]. 16°

6 THEORY of Teaching, with a few practical illustrations. By a teacher. Boston, 1841. 12°

TEFFT, B. F. Daniel Webster : his life and character. Rochester, 1852. 8°

TEMPLE, SAMUEL. Temple's Arithmetick. . . Tenth edition. Boston, 1827. 12°

TEMPLE, THEODORE. The Secret Discipline, mentioned in ancient ecclesiastical history, explained. [With a preface by S. L. Knapp.] New York, 1833. 12mo.

TEMPLE OF TRUTH ; or a Vindication of various paſsages and doctrines of the Holy Scriptures, lately impeached in a Deistical publication printed in Philadelphia [The Temple of Reason edited by D. Driscol] . . together with a reply to two theological lectures, delivered . . by Mr. Palmer. By J. Hargrove. Baltimore, 1801. 8vo.

TENESLES, NICOLA, *an Etchemin Indian.* The Indian of New England, and the North-Eastern provinces ; a sketch of the life of an Indian Hunter. Ancient Traditions relating to the Etchemin tribe, . . with vocabularies . . giving the names of . . . animals, birds, and fish, in the languages of the Etchemin and Micmacs . . . derived from Nicola Tenesles by a citizen of Middletown, Conn. [Joseph Barratt, M.D.] Middletown, Connecticut, 1851. 8vo.

TENNENT, GILBERT. Twenty-three Sermons upon the chief end of man, the divine authority of the sacred Scriptures, the being and attributes of God, and the doctrine of the Trinity. Philadelphia, 1744. 4°

TENNESSEE, *State of.* A Short

Description of the Tenneſſee Government, or the Territory of the United States South of the River Ohio, to accompany and explain a map of that country. Philadelphia, 1793. 8vo.

2 JOURNAL of the Convention of the State of Tenneſſee, convened for the purpose of revising and amending the Constitution thereof, held in Nashville. Nashville, 1834. 8°

3 A COMPILATION of the Statutes of Tenneſſee, of a general and permanent nature, from the commencement of the government to the present time. With references to judicial decisions, in notes. To which is appended a new collection of forms. By R. L. Caruthers and A. O. P. Nicholson. Nashville, 1836. 8vo.

TENSAS, MADISON. Odd Leaves from the life of a Louisiana " Swamp Doctor." Philadelphia, 1850. 12°

TERCEIRA. The World Alarm'd. A Surprizing Relation of a New Burning Island lately raised out of the Sea near Tercera; with .. a brief history of the other ignivomous mountains at this day .. in the world. In a letter to an Honourable Fellow of the Royal Society at London. From a member of the same Society at Boston [i.e. C. Mather]. Boston, 1721. 12mo.

TERRY, ADRIAN R. Travels in the Equatorial Regions of South America, in 1822. Hartford, 1834. 12mo.

TESCHEMACHER, J. E. An Addreſs delivered before the Maſſachusetts Historical Society, at their fourteenth anniversary, September 16, 1842. Boston, 1842. 8°

TEXAS. Constitution of the Republic of Texas. To which is prefixed, the Declaration of Independence, made in Convention, March 2, 1836. Washington, 1836. 8°

2 TEXAS: a brief account of the origin, progreſs, and present state of the Colonial settlements of Texas; together with an exposition of the causes which have induced the existing war with Mexico. Extracted from a work entitled: " A geographical .. account of Texas." Nashville, 1836. 8°

3 A VISIT to Texas, being the journal of a traveller; .. Second edition; with an appendix, containing a sketch of the late war. New York, 1836. 12°

4 THE WAR in Texas; a review of facts and circumstances, showing that this contest is .. set on foot .. with the view of re-establishing, extending, and perpetuating the system of slavery and the slave trade in the republic of Mexico. By a citizen of the United States. Philadelphia, 1836. 8°

5 THE WAR in Texas; a review of facts and circumstances, showing that this contest is a crusade against Mexico, set on foot and supported by slave-holders, land-speculators, &c. in order to re-establish, extend, and perpetuate the system of slavery and the slave-trade. [Second edition, revised and enlarged.] By a citizen of the United States. Philadelphia, 1837. 8°

6 LAWS of the Republic of Texas. 2 vol. Houston, 1838. 12mo.

7 LAWS of the Republic of Texas. Third to Ninth Congreſs. 8 vol. Houston, 1839-1845. 8vo.

8 TEXAS in 1840, or the Emigrant's guide to the New Republic; being the result of observation, enquiry, and travel in that beautiful country. By an emigrant, late of the United States... With an introduction by the Rev. A. B. Lawrence, of New Orleans. New York, 1840. 12°

9 THE TEXAN Revolution. Republished, with additions, from the Northampton (Maſſachusetts) Gazette. To which is added, a letter .. on the annexation of Texas, and the late outrage in California. [Northampton, 1842.] 8°

10 THOUGHTS on the proposed annexation of Texas to the United States.

First published in the New York Evening Post, under the signature of Veto. New York, 1844. 8vo.

11 JOURNAL of the Senate of the Ninth Congreſs of the Republic of Texas. Washington, 1845. 8vo.

12 APPENDIX to the Journals of the Ninth Congreſs. Washington, 1845. 8vo.

THACHER, J. S. B. An Oration delivered before the citizens of Natchez, Miſs. . . July 4, 1836 [in commemoration of American Independence]. Natchez, 1836. 12°

THACHER, JAMES. Observations on Hydrophobia, produced by the bite of a mad dog, or other rabid animal; with an examination of the various theories and methods of cure, etc. Plymouth, 1812. 8°

2 A MILITARY Journal during the American Revolutionary War from 1775 to 1783: with an appendix, containing biographical sketches of several general officers. Boston, 1823. 8vo.

3 THE AMERICAN Orchardist; or, a practical treatise on the culture and management of apple and other fruit trees, etc. Second edition, much improved. Plymouth, 1825. 12°

4 AMERICAN Modern Practice; or, a simple method of prevention and cure of diseases. . . To which is added, an appendix, containing an account of many domestic remedies recently introduced into practice, and some approved formulæ, applicable to the diseases of our climate. A new edition, improved. Boston, 1826. 8°

5 A MILITARY Journal during the American Revolutionary War, from 1775 to 1783; describing . . events and transactions of this period; with numerous historical facts and anecdotes, from the original manuscript. To which is added an appendix, containing biographical sketches of several general officers. Second edition, revised and corrected. Bost. 1827. 8°

6 AMERICAN Medical Biography:

or, memoirs of eminent physicians who have flourished in America. To which is prefixed a succinct history of medical science in the United States, from the first settlement of the country. 2 vol. Boston, 1828. 8°

7 A PRACTICAL Treatise on the management of bees; and the establishment of apiaries, with the best method of destroying and preventing the depredations of the bee moth. Boston, 1829. 12°

8 AN ESSAY on Demonology, Ghosts, and Apparitions, and Popular Superstitions. Also, an account of the witchcraft delusion at Salem, in 1692. Boston, 1831. 12mo.

9 HISTORY of the town of Plymouth [New England. With an appendix]. Boston, 1832. 12mo.

10 HISTORY of the town of Plymouth, from its first settlement in 1630 to the present time. With a concise history of the Aborigines of New England, and their wars with the English. Second edition. Boston, 1835. 12°

THACHER, MOSES. An Addreſs delivered before the members of the Anti-Masonic State Convention at Augusta, Maine, July 4, 1832. Hallowell, 1832. 8vo.

THACHER, PETER. An Oration . . to commemorate the bloody massacre at Boston, perpetrated March 5, 1770. Watertown, 1776. 4°

2 THE REST which remaineth to the people of God . . shewn in a sermon [on Hebrews iv. 9] preached at the New North Church in Boston, September 13, 1778. Being the day of the death of . . A. Eliot, D.D. Boston [1778]. 8°

3 A REPLY to the strictures of Mr. J. S. a layman, upon the pamphlet entitled, Observations upon the present state of the Clergy in New England, etc. Boston [1785!] 8°

4 A SERMON [on Ruth ii. 20] for the relief of the indigent Widows and Orphans of deceased ministers. Boston, 1795. 8vo.

5 A Sermon [on Job xxix. 11-13] occasioned by the death of the Hon. Thomas Ruſſell, Esq. Boston, 1796. 4to.

6 An Address to the Members of the Maſſachusetts Charitable Fire Society, at their annual meeting, in Boston. Boston, 1805. 8vo.

7 An Oration delivered before the inhabitants of the town of Boston, on the thirty-first anniversary of the Independence of the United States of America. Second edition. Boston, 1807. 8º

THACHER, Peter Oxenbridge. An Addreſſ .. before the members of the bar of the county of Suffolk, Massachusetts. Boston, 1831. 8º

2 A Charge to the Grand Jury of .. Suffolk .. Maſſachusetts .. at the opening of the Municipal Court of .. Boston, etc. L. P. Boston, 1835. 8º

THACHER, Thomas. A Discourse [on Luke vii. 12] delivered at Boston before the Humane Society. Boston, 1800. 8vo.

THACHER, Thomas A. A Discourse commemorative of Profeſſor James L. Kingsley, delivered by request of the faculty in the Chapel of Yale College. . To which is prefixed the addreſſ at the funeral .. by T. D. Woolsey. New York, 1852. 8º

THACKERAY, William Makepeace. Punch's Prize Novelists, the Fat Contributor, and Travels in London. New York, 1853. 8º

THATCHER. The Thatcher's Wife: or an account of Mary Camps. Philadelphia [1830?]. 12mo.

THATCHER, B. B. Indian Biography; 2 vol. New York, 1832. 12mo.

2 Indian Traits: being sketches of the manners, customs, and character of the North American natives. 2 vol. New York, 1833. 12mo.

3 Indian Biography: or, an his-

torical account of those individuals who have been distinguished among the North American natives as orators, warriors, statesmen, and other remarkable characters. 2 vol. New York, 1845. 12º

THE THEATRICAL CENSOR and Critical Miscellany. By Gregory Gryphon, Esq. Nº 1-17 [with the prospectus]. Philadel. 1805-6. 8vo.

THEBAUD, Aug. J. Pius VII and Napoleon. A Lecture delivered before the Catholic Institute of New York, etc. New York, 1852. 8vo.

THEOLOGICAL AND LITERARY Journal. Edited by David N. Lord. Vol. 1-8. New York, 1848-1856. 8º

THEORY OF AGENCY: or an eſſay on the nature, source, and extent of moral freedom. In two parts. With occasional observations and reflections. By a well-wisher to mankind. Boston, 1771. 8vo.

THINGS as they are: or notes of a Traveller through some of the Middle and Northern States. New York, 1834. 12º

THINGS new and old, for the glory of God, and everlasting benefit of all who read and understand them; or old revelations and prophecies, in several sermons, revised, enriched, embellished, and confirmed; .. By a descendant from one of the early puritanic governors. Portland, 1845. 8º

THOMAS and Ellen; or the Bible the best Book. American Sunday School Union, Philadel. [1830?] 12º

THOMAS, Antoine Leonard. Eſſay on the character, manners, and genius of Women in different ages; enlarged from the French .. by Mr. Ruſſell. 2 vol. Philadelphia, 1774. 12mo.

THOMAS, Daniel. A Letter, .. to J. Norton, of Weymouth, [Maſſ.

in relation to the Unitarian controversy].. Together with an appendix, containing some notes and remarks. Boston, 1815. 8°

THOMAS, EBENEZER S. Reminiscences of the last sixty-five years, commencing with the battle of Lexington. Also, sketches of his own life and times. 2 vol. Hartford, 1840. 8°

THOMAS, J. *M. D.* Travels in Egypt and Palestine. Philadelphia, 1853. 12°

THOMAS, JOHN J. The Fruit Culturist, adapted to the climate of the Northern States .. With engravings. New York, 1846. 12°

2 FARM Implements, and the principles of their construction and use ; an elementary.. treatise on mechanics and on natural philosophy generally, as applied to the ordinary practices of agriculture. London, New York [printed? 1855]. 8vo.

THOMAS, ISAIAH. A Specimen of I. Thomas's printing types ; .. chiefly manufactured by .. W. Caslon, of London. Worcester, Massachusetts, 1785. 4°

2 THE HISTORY of Printing in America. With a biography of printers, and an account of newspapers. To which is prefixed, a .. view of the discovery and progress of the art in other parts of the world. 2 vol. Worcester, 1810. 8vo.

3 COMMUNICATION from the President of the American Antiquarian Society (I. Thomas) to the members, Oct. 24, 1814. .. Together with the laws of the society, as revised. Worcester [1814]. 8°

THOMAS, R. *M.A.* The Glory of America ; comprising memoirs of the lives and glorious exploits of some of the distinguished officers engaged in the late war with Great Britain, *etc.* New York, 1836. 12°

THOME, JAMES A. AND KIM-

BALL, J. H. Emancipation in the West Indies : a six months' tour in Antigua, Barbadoes, and Jamaica, in the year 1837. N. York, 1838. 12°

THOMPSON, BENJAMIN F. History of Long Island ; containing an account of the discovery and settlement, with other interesting matters, to the present time. N. York, 1839. 8°

2 THE HISTORY of Long Island ; from its discovery and settlement to the present time. With .. notices of numerous individuals and families ; also a particular account of the different churches and ministers. Second edition, revised and greatly enlarged. 2 vol. New York, 1843. 8°

THOMPSON, DANIEL P. Locke Amsden, or the schoolmaster : a tale. By the author of " May Martin," *etc.* (D. P. Thompson). Bost. 1847. 12°

THOMPSON, GEORGE, *M. P.* Discussion on American Slavery between G. Thompson, Esq. . . . and Rev. R. J. Breckinridge .. holden in the Rev. Dr. Wardlaw's chapel, Glasgow, Scotland ; on the evenings of the 13th, 14th, 15th, 16th, 17th of June, 1836. Second American edition, with notes, by Mr. Garrison. Boston, 1836. 8°

2 LETTERS and Addresses by G. Thompson [on American Negro Slavery] during his mission in the United States, from Oct. 1, 1834, to Nov. 27, 1835. [Edited by W. L. Garrison.] Boston, 1837. 12°

THOMPSON, JOSEPH P. The Fugitive Slave Law ; tried by the Old and New Testaments. [Reprinted from the New Englander for Nov. 1850.] New York, 1850. 8°

2 MEMOIR of D. Hale, late editor of the Journal of Commerce. With selections from his miscellaneous writings. New York, 1850. 12°

3 HINTS to Employers ; or a plea for apprentices and clerks. N. York, 1851. 32°

4 CHRISTIANITY effential to liberty. A Sermon [on John viii. 32] in aid of Hungary, etc. New York, 1851. 8°

5 STRAY Meditations; or, voices of the heart, in joy and sorrow. New York, 1852. 12°

THOMPSON, LESLIE A. Manual or Digest of the Statute Law of the State of Florida, of a general and public character. Boston, 1847. 8°

THOMPSON, PETER. The Cottage Boy; or, the history of P. Thompson. Revised by the Committee of publication. American Sunday School Union, Philadelphia [1831 ?] 12mo.

THOMPSON, WADDY. Speech.. on the bill to authorize the iffue of treasury notes; delivered in the House of Representatives.. Jan. 21, 1841. Washington, 1841. 8°

2 RECOLLECTIONS of Mexico. New York and London, 1847. 8°

THOMPSON, WILLIAM, Rev. Memoirs of the Rev. S. Munson and the Rev. H. Lyman, late miffionaries to the Indian Archipelago, with the journal of their exploring tour. New York, 1843. 12°

THOMPSON, ZADOCK. The Youth's Affistant in practical Arithmetic. Woodstock, Vt. 1825. 8°

2 THE YOUTH'S Affistant in theoretic and practical Arithmetic.. Fourth edition. Burlington, Vt. 1832. 12°

3 HISTORY of Vermont, natural, civil, and statistical. 3 parts. Burlington, 1842. 8°

THOMSON, ADAM. A Discourse on the preparation of the body for the small-pox, and the manner of receiving the infection. Philadelphia, 1750. 4to.

THOMSON, JAMES B. Day and Thomson's series. Practical Arithmetic.. for schools and academies. By J. B. Thomson. New Haven, 1846. 12°

2 DAY and Thomson's series. Practical Arithmetic, uniting the inductive with the synthetic mode of instruction; also illustrating the principles of cancelation; etc. Second edition, revised and improved. New York, 1846. 12mo.

3 THOMSON's First Leffons. Mental Arithmetic, etc. Twenty-second edition, revised and enlarged. Auburn [printed at New York, 1846]. 12mo.

4 DAY and Thomson's series. Higher Arithmetic; or the science and application of numbers; combining the analytic and synthetic modes of instruction; etc. N. York, 1848. 12mo.

5 DAY and Thomson's series. Practical Arithmetic.. by J. B. Thomson. Sixty-eighth edition.. enlarged. New York, 1852. 12°

THOMSON, JOHN. An Enquiry concerning the liberty and licentiousnefs of the Prefs, and the uncontroulable nature of the human mind, etc. New York, 1801. 8°

THOMSON, JOHN LEWIS. Historical Sketches of the late war between the United States and Great Britain, blended with anecdotes illustrative of the individual bravery of the American sailors, soldiers, and citizens. Third edition. Philadelphia, 1816. 12°

2 HISTORICAL Sketches of the late war between the United States and Great Britain. Fifth edition. Philadelphia, 1818. 12°

3 HISTORY of the second war between the United States and Great Britain, declared in 1812, and terminated in 1815.. to which are added sketches of the military operations of the United States to the present time, including Black Hawk's war, the Seminole wars in Florida, and the war with Mexico. Philadelphia, 1848. 8°

THORBURN, GRANT. Forty Years' Residence in America, or the

doctrine of a particular Providence, exemplified in the life of G. Thorburn. Boston, 1834. 12mo.

2 LIFE and Writings of Grant Thorburn, prepared by himself. New York, 1852. 8°

THOREAU, HENRY DAVID. A Week on the Concord and Merrimack Rivers. Boston and Cambridge, 1849. 8°

THORNTON, T. C. *Rev.* An Inquiry into the history of Slavery; its introduction into the United States; causes of its continuance; and remarks upon the Abolition tracts of W. E. Channing. Washington City, 1841. 12°

THORNTON, WILLIAM. Cadmus, or a treatise on the elements of written language. Philadel. 1793. 8vo.

2 OUTLINES of a Constitution for United North and South Carolina. Washington, 1815. 8vo.

THORPE, J. B. The Mysteries of the Backwoods; or, sketches of the South West, including character, scenery, and rural sports. Philadelphia, 1846. 12°

2 OUR Army in the Rio Grande: .. with descriptions of the battles of Palo Alto and Resaca de la Palma, the bombardment of Fort Brown, and the ceremonies of the surrender of Matamoros; *etc.* Philadelphia, 1846. 12°

3 OUR Army at Monterey: . . . . with a description of the three days' battle and the storming of Monterey; *etc.* Philadelphia, 1847. 12°

THROOP, GEORGE H. Lynde Weiss. An Autobiography. Philadelphia, 1852. 12°

TIBBITS, GEORGE. A Memoir on the expediency and practicability of improving or creating home markets for the sale of agricultural productions and raw materials, by the introduction or growth of artizans and manufacturers. . . Third edition. To

which are added, four appendices. Albany printed; Philadelphia reprinted, 1827. 8°

TICKNOR, CALEB. The Philosophy of Living; or the way to enjoy life and its comforts. New York, 1844. 12°

TICKNOR, GEORGE. Remarks on changes lately proposed or adopted, in Harvard University. Second edition. [Cambridge,] 1825. 8°

2 HISTORY of Spanish Literature. 3 vol. New York, 1849. 8°

TIDYMANS, P. On the Abuse of the Pardoning Power [two letters by P. Tidyman and S. R. Wood]. Philadelphia, 1839. 8°

TIFFANY, OSMOND, *the Younger.* The Canton Chinese, or the American's Sojourn in the Celestial Empire. Boston, 1849. 12°

TILGHMAN, WILLIAM. Report of the Judges of the Supreme Court of Pennsylvania, of the English Statutes which are in force in the Commonwealth of Pennsylvania, *etc.* [Signed W. T. J. Yeates, T. Smith, H. H. Brackenridge.] Lancaster, 1809. 8°

2 AN ADDRESS delivered before the Philadelphia Society for promoting Agriculture. Philadelphia, 1820. 8vo.

TIMON, *Pseud.* [*i. e.* LOUIS MARIE DE LA HAYE, *Viscount de Cormenin*]. The Orators of France, by Timon. . . Translated by a member of the New York bar from the fourteenth Paris edition. With an essay on the rise of French revolutionary eloquence, and the orators of the Girondists, by J. T. Headley. Edited by G. H. Colton. New York, 1847. 12°

TIMONIUS, EMMANUEL. Some Account of what is said of Inoculating or transplanting the Small Pox, by the learned Dr. E. Timonius and Jacobus Pylarinus, with some remarks thereon. To which are added a few queries in

answer to the scruples of many about
the lawfulnels of this method. Published by Zabdiel Boylston. Boston,
1721. 8vo.

TIRRELL, ALBERT JOHN. Trial of
Albert J. Tirrell for the murder of
Mary Ann Bickford, in the Supreme
Judicial Court of Maflachusetts. . . .
Together with the lives of A. J. Tirrell
and M. A. Bickford. Reported .. by
J. E. P. Weeks. Boston, 1846. 8°

TIVOLI, J. DE, *Pseud?* A Guide
to the Falls of Niagara. . . With a ..
lithographic view, by A. Vaudricourt.
New York, 1846. 8vo.

TOCQUEVILLE, ALEXIS DE.
American Institutions and their influ-
ence. . . . with notes by Hon. J. C.
Spencer. New York, 1851. 12°

TO-DAY, a Boston Literary Journal. Edited by C. Hale. 2 vol.
Boston, 1852. 8°

TODD, JOHN, *Rev.* The Sabbath
School Teacher: designed to aid in
elevating and perfecting the Sabbath
School system. Northampton, 1837.
12°

  2 LECTURES to Children; familiarly
illustrating important truth. . Twelfth
edition. Northampton, 1841. 16°

  3 THE MORAL Influence, dangers,
and duties, connected with great cities.
Northampton, 1841. 12°

  4 THE STUDENT's Manual. . Thirteenth edition. Northampton, 1845.
8°

  5 HINTS to Undergraduates: an
Oration delivered at .. Union College,
etc. Boston, 1846. 8°

TODD, TIMOTHY. An Oration delivered at Manchester [Vermont] ..
17 Aug. 1795, in commemoration of
Bennington battle, etc. Rutland,
1795. 8°

TOFT, ELIZABETH. Memoir of E.
Toft, a Sunday Scholar in Hull. American Sunday School Union, Philadelphia, 1831. 12°

TOGNO, JOSEPH. Experiments
to establish a peculiar physico-organic
action inherent in the animal tiflues,
called Endosmose and Exosmose.
Philadelphia, 1829. 4to.

TOKEN AND ATLANTIC
SOUVENIR (THE): a Christmas and
New Year's present, 1834-42. Edited
by Samuel G. Goodrich, etc. [Want-
ing the volumes for 1828 to 1833;
1838, 1839, 1841, and all after
1842.] Boston, 1835-38, New York,
1841, and Boston, 1842. 12°

TOM, UNCLE. A Letter on "Uncle
Tom's Cabin," [by H. E. B. Stowe].
By the author of "Friends in Council," etc. [Arthur Helps]. Cambridge, 1852. 8°

TONE, THEOBALD WOLFE. Life
of T. W. Tone, written by himself,
and continued by his son [W. T. W.
Tone], with his political writings, fragments of his diary, and negotiations
to procure the aid of the French and
Batavian republics. Narrative of his
trial, defence before the court-martial, and death. 2 vol. Washington,
1826. 8vo.

TONE, WILLIAM THEOBALD
WOLFE. School of Cavalry; or system of organisation, instruction, and
manœuvres, proposed for the cavalry
of the United States. Georgetown,
D. C., 1824. 8°

TOOMBS, ROBERT. Speech ..
against the tariff bill, reported by the
committee of ways and means; delivered in the House of Representatives .. July 1, 1846. [Washing-
ton, 1846.] 8°

TOPLADY, AUGUSTUS MONTAGUE.
A Course of Family Prayer for each
day in the week. Boston, 1817. 8°

TORIES. Truth will out! The
foul charges of the Tories against the
editor of the Aurora [B. F. Bache?]
repelled by positive proof and plain

truth, and his base calumniators put to shame. [Philadelphia, 1798.] 8°

TORREY, H. W. An English-Latin Lexicon, prepared to accompany Leverett's Latin-English Lexicon. Boston, 1840. 8°

TORREY, JESSE, Jun. A Portraiture of domestic Slavery in the United States, with reflections on the practicability of restoring the moral rights of the slave; and a project of a colonial asylum for free persons of colour: including memoirs of facts on the interior traffic in slaves, and on kidnapping. Philadel. 1817. 8vo.

TORREY, JOHN, M.D. A Compendium of the Flora of the Northern and Middle States; containing generic and specific descriptions of all the plants, exclusive of the Cryptogamia, hitherto found in the United States, north of the Potomac. New York, 1826. 12°

TORREY, JOHN, AND GRAY, ASA. A Flora of North America: containing abridged descriptions of all known plants growing north of Mexico; arranged according to the natural system. Vol. 1 and vol. 2. parts 1-3 [all ever published]. New York, 1838-43. 8vo.

TORREY, SCHAUFAL. Trial for Libel: S. Torrey, plaintiff, R. M. Field, defendant. Woodstock, Connecticut, 1835.] 8°

TOTTEN, B.J. Naval Text-book. Letters to the midshipmen of the United States navy on rigging, and managing vessels of war. Also a set of stationing tables: a naval gun exercise, and a marine dictionary. Boston, 1841. 8vo.

TOTTEN, J. G. Essays on hydraulic and common mortar, and on lime-burning. Translated from the French of Gen. Treussart. M. Petot, and M. Courtois. With brief observations on common mortars, by

draulic mortars, and concretes, etc. By J.G. Totten. N. York, 1842. 8vo.

TOULMIN, T. L. Report of the President of the branch bank at Mobile (T. L. Toulmin): also, the expense account and indebtedness of members, etc. to said bank. Tuscaloosa, 1845. 8°

TOUSARD, LEWIS. Justification of Lewis Tousard, addressed to the National Convention of France. Written and published from the bloody prisons of the Abbaye, by himself, the 24th of January, 1793. Philadelphia, 1793. 8°

TOUSSEUD, A. Passional Zoology; or spirit of the beasts of France... Translated by M. E. Lazarus, etc. New York, 1852. 12mo.

TOWER, DAVID B. The gradual Reader. First step, or exercises in articulation.. Fifth edition. Boston, 1842. 12°

2 THE GRADUAL Speller and complete Enunciator. etc. New York, Boston, 1846. 12°

TOWER, F. B. Illustrations of the Croton Aqueduct. To which added an appendix by C. A. New York, 1843. 4to.

TOWER, R. An Appeal to the people of the State of New York in favour of the construction of the Chenango Canal: with and documents. Utica, 184

TOWN. Ithiel. A new plan for ships. Some steam and the results of construction: on the subject of navigating houses ocean with steam-ships; manage, etc. New York:

2 A description of ... improvement in the principle, con, and practice of bridges for roads, ¶ aqueducts... being general account of

over rivers, creeks, harbours, *etc.* New York, 1839. 4°

TOWN, SALEM. A system of speculative masonry; . . being a course of lectures, delivered before the Grand Chapter of the State of New York, *etc.* Second edition. Salem, N. Y. 1822. 12°

2 AN ANALYSIS of the derivative words in the English language ; or, a key to their precise analytic definitions, by prefixes and suffixes: *etc.* 21st edition, carefully revised, enlarged, *etc.* Auburn, N.Y. 1845. 12°

TOWNSEND, ALEXANDER. Oration, delivered July 4, 1810, at . . Boston, on the feelings, manners, and principles, that produced American Independence. Boston,1810. 8°

TOWNSEND, JOHN K. Narrative of a Journey acroſs the Rocky Mountains to the Columbia River, and a visit to the Sandwich Islands, Chili, *etc.* With a scientific appendix. Philadelphia, 1839. 8°

TOWNSEND, PETER S. An account of the Yellow Fever, as it prevailed in the city of New York, in the summer and autumn of 1822. New York, 1823. 8°

TOWNSEND, SHIPPIE. Gospel News . . being a brief attempt to consider the evidences of the truth of the Gospel, *etc.* Boston, 1794. 8vo.

TRACT. Second part of the Tract on Miſſions. Salem, 1845. 8vo.

TRACY, CALVIN. A new system of Arithmetic, *etc.* New Haven, 1840. 12°

TRACY, HERBERT. Herbert Tracy, or the trials of mercantile life, and the morality of trade. By a " Counting-house Man." N. York, 1851. 8°

TRACY, JOSEPH. Colonization and miſſions. A historical examination of the state of society in Western

Africa, as formed by Paganism and Muhammedanism, slavery, the slave trade, and piracy, and of the remedial influence of colonization and miſſions. Second edition, Boston, 1845. 8vo.

TRACY, URIAH. Mr. Tracy's Speech in the Senate, . . Dec. 2, 1803, on the . . [proposed] amendment to the Constitution. [Washington, 1803.] 8°

TRAFTON, M. *Rev.* Rambles in Europe : in a series of letters. Boston, 1852. 12°

TRALL, RUSSELL T. The Hydropathic Encyclopædia : a system of hydropathy and Hygiene. . . With numerous engraved illustrations. 2 vol. New York, 1852. 12°

TRANSYLVANIA UNIVERSITY. A Catalogue of the officers and students. February, 1821. Lexington, Ky. 1821. 8°

TRAUTWINE, JOHN C. A new method of calculating the cubic contents of excavations and embankments, by the aid of diagrams. Philadelphia, 1851. 8°

TRAVELLER. Sketches of history, life, and manners in the United States. By a traveller [Mrs. Anne Royall]. New Haven, 1826. 12mo.

TREADWELL, DANIEL. The relations of Science to the useful arts. A lecture, delivered to the American Academy of Arts and Sciences, Nov. 1852. Cambridge and Bost. 1855. 8°

TREATISE. A preliminary Treatise on the law of Repulsion, as a universal law of nature : in which the Mosaic history of creation is vindicated and sustained, and various natural phenomena (heretofore mysterious) clearly explained. Philadelphia, 1853. 8vo.

TREGO, CHARLES B. A Geography of Pennsylvania, with a separate description of each county, and questions for teachers. To which is appended a travellers' guide. Philadelphia, 1843. 12mo.

TRENT, JOSEPH. An Inquiry into the effects of light in Respiration. Philadelphia, 1800. 8vo.

TRESCOT, WILLIAM HENRY. The diplomacy of the Revolution, an historical study. N. York, 1852. 12°

TRIALS. Celebrated trials of all countries, and remarkable cases of criminal jurisprudence. Selected by a member of the Philadelphia bar [John Jay Smith]. Philadelphia, 1835. 8°

TRIPP, ALONZO. Crests from the Ocean World; or, experiences in a voyage to Europe, *etc.* Boston, 1853. 12°

TRIUMPH. The triumph of infidelity : a poem. Printed in the World [New York ?] 1788. 8°

TROUBAT, FRANCIS J. The Law of Commandatary and Limited Partnership in the United States. Philadelphia, 1853. 8vo.

TROY DIRECTORY. 1836-7 to 1842-3. 5 vol. Troy [1836-43]. 12°

TROY FEMALE SEMINARY. Catalogue of the Members for the Academic Year 1829-30. [Troy, N. Y. 1829.] 8°

TRUMBULL, BENJAMIN, *Rev.* A Plea in Vindication of the Connecticut Title to the Contested Lands, lying West of the Province of New York; addressed to the public. [With an appendix of documents.] New Haven, 1774. 8°

2 AN APPEAL to the Public, relative to the Unlawfulness of Marrying a Wife's Sister. [N. Haven] 1810. 8vo.

3 A GENERAL History of the United States of America, from 1492 to 1792, *etc.* Vol. 1 to 1765 [all ever published]. Boston, 1810. 8°

4 A GENERAL History of the United States of America; from 1492 to 1765. [The same as the preceding, with a new title, and the addition of the preface, and the concluding chapter, pp. 443-467.] Boston, 1810. 8°

5 A COMPLETE History of Connecticut, civil and ecclesiastical, from .. the year 1630 to the year 1764; .. in two volumes .. Vol. 1 with an appendix, containing the original Patent of New England, never before published in America. 2 vol. New Haven, 1818. 8vo.

TRUMBULL, HENRY. History of the Discovery of America; of the landing of our forefathers at Plymouth, and of their most remarkable engagements with the Indians in New England; *etc.* [A republication, with alterations and additions, of a work under the same title by Ja°. Steward, D.D.] Boston, 1822. 8°

2 HISTORY of the Discovery of America, of the landing of our forefathers at Plymouth, and of their most remarkable engagements with the Indians in New England, *etc.* Boston, 1836. 8°

TRUMBULL, JAMES HAMMOND. The Public Records of the Colony of Connecticut, prior to the Union with New Haven Colony, May 1665; transcribed and published .. under the supervision of the Secretary of State, with occasional notes, and an appendix; by J. H. Trumbull. Hartford, 1850. 8°

2 THE PUBLIC Records of the Colony of Connecticut, from 1665 to 1678. Transcribed and edited, in accordance with a resolution of the General Assembly. With notes and an appendix. Hartford, 1852. 8°

TRUMBULL, JOHN. M'Fingal: an epic poem. Philadelphia, 1791. 12mo.

2 M'FINGAL : a modern epic poem. With explanatory notes. Augusta, 1813. 12mo.

TRUMBULL, JOHN. Autobiography, reminiscences, and letters of J. Trumbull, from 1756 to 1841. New York [printed at New Haven], 1841. 8°

TRUMBULL, JONATHAN. An Addreſs of His Excellency Governor Trumbull to the General Aſſembly and the Freemen of the State of Connecticut; declining any further election to public office. With the resolution of the Legislature, in consequence thereof. New London, 1783. 4°

TRUSTA, H. *Pseud.* [i. e. MRS. ELIZABETH STUART PHELPS]. A Peep at "Number Five:" or, a chapter in the life of a city pastor. Boston, 1852. 12mo.

2 THE TELL-TALE: or, home secrets told by old travellers. Boston, 1853. 12°

TUCKER, ABRAHAM. The Light of Nature pursued... From the second London edition, revised and corrected. Together with some account of the life of the author. By Sir H. P. St. John Mildmay. 4 vol. Cambridge, 1831. 8°

TUCKER, DAVID H. Elements of the Principles and Practice of Midwifery. Philadelphia, 1848. 8°

TUCKER, GEORGE. The Life of Thomas Jefferson, third President of the United States. With parts of his correspondence never before published, and notices of his opinions on questions of civil government, national policy, and constitutional law. 2 vol. Philadelphia, 1837. 8°

2 THE THEORY of Money and Banks Investigated. Boston, 1839. 12mo.

3 PROGRESS of the United States in Population and Wealth in fifty years, as exhibited by the decennial census. New York, 1843. 8vo.

TUCKER, HENRY SAINT GEORGE. Lectures on Constitutional Law, for the use of the law claſſes at the University of Virginia. Richmond, 1843. 12°

TUCKER, JOSIAH, D.D. *Dean of Gloucester.* The True Intereſt of Britain, set forth in regard to the Colonies; *etc.* To which is added, by the printer, a few more words on the freedom of the preſs in America. Philadelphia, 1776. 8°

TUCKER, SAINT GEORGE. A Diſſertation on Slavery; with a proposal for the gradual abolition of it in the State of Virginia. Philadelphia, 1796. 8°

TUCKER, SAMUEL. Observations on the Medical Effects of Bodily Labour, in chronic diseases, and in debility. Philadelphia, 1806. 8vo.

TUCKERMAN, EDWARD. An Enumeration of North American Lichenes, with a preliminary view of the structure and general history of these plants, and of the Friesian system; to which is prefixed, an eſſay on the natural systems of Oken, Fries, and Eudlicher. Cambridge, 1845. 12°

2 A SYNOPSIS of the Lichenes of New England, the other Northern States and British America. Cambridge, 1848. 8°

TUCKERMAN, HENRY THEODORE. Rambles and Reveries. [A collection of eſſays.] New York, 1841. 12°

2 ARTIST Life: or sketches of American painters. New York, 1847. 12°

3 CHARACTERISTICS of Literature illustrated by the Genius of distinguished men. Philadel. 1849. 12°

4 THE LIFE of Silas Talbot, a Commodore in the navy of the United States. New York, 1850. 12°

5 THE OPTIMIST. New York, 1850. 12°

6 POEMS. Boston, 1851. 12°

7 CHARACTERISTICS of Literature illustrated by the genius of distinguished writers. Second series. Philadelphia, 1851. 12°

· 8 Sicily; a Pilgrimage. New York, 1852. 8°

TUCKERMAN, Joseph. A Funeral Oration occasioned by the death of Gen. George Washington, written at the request of the Boston Mechanic Association, and delivered before them, ... 22 Feb. 1800. Boston, 1800. 8vo.

2 First Series, N° 54. Mr. Tuckerman's Eighth Semi-annual Report of his service as a minister at large in Boston. Printed for the American Unitarian Association. Boston, Dec. 1831. 12°

3 Mr. Tuckerman's Tenth Semi-annual Report, as a minister at large in Boston. Published by the American Unitarian Association. Boston, 1832. 12°

4 A Letter to the Executive Committee of the Benevolent fraternity of churches, respecting their organization for the support of the ministry at large in Boston. [Boston, 1834.] 8°

5 A Letter respecting Santa Cruz as a winter residence for invalids, addressed to J. C. Warren. Boston, 1837. 8vo.

TUCKERMAN, Samuel P. The National Lyre; a new collection of Sacred Music, consisting of Psalm and Hymn Tunes, with a choice selection of Sentences, Anthems, and Chants, etc. Boston, 1848. Oblong 8°

TUCKEY, J. K. Narrative of an Expedition to explore the River Zaire, usually called the Congo, in South Africa, in 1816, under the direction of Captain J. K. Tuckey, R.N. To which is added, the Journal of Professor Smith; and some general Observations on the Country and its Inhabitants. Published by permission of the Lords of the Admiralty. With a Chart of the River Zaire. New York, 1818. 8vo.

TUDOR, William, the Elder, of Boston. An Oration delivered March 5, 1779, at . . Boston, to commemorate the bloody tragedy of March 5, 1770. Boston, 1779. 4°

2 A Gratulatory Address delivered July 5, 1790, before the Society of the Cincinnati, of the Commonwealth of Massachusetts. Boston, 1790. 4°

3 Another Copy, on Large Paper. Boston, 1790. 4°

TUDOR, William, the Younger. An Oration pronounced July 4, 1809, at the request of the Selectmen of the town of Boston, in commemoration of the Anniversary of American Independence. Boston, 1809. 8°

2 Letters on the Eastern States. Second edition. Boston, 1821. 8vo.

3 The Life of James Otis: containing also notices of some contemporary characters and events from 1760 to 1775. Boston, 1823. 8°

TUEL, J. E. The Moral for Authors, as contained in the autobiography of Eureka, a manuscript novel, and discovered by J. E. Tuel. New York, 1849. 8vo.

TUNER'S GUIDE: containing a complete treatise on tuning the Pianoforte, organ, melodeon, and seraphine; Together with a specification of defects and their remedies. Boston, 1852. 12°

TURELL, Ebenezer, Rev. Mr. Turell's Dialogue between a minister and his neighbour about the times. To which is added, An answer to Mr. J. Lee's remarks on a passage in the preface of his direction to his people, etc. Boston, 1742. 16°

2 Mr. Turell's brief and plain Exhortation to his people on the late fast, January 28, 1747-8. Boston, 1748. 8°

TURK. Il Turco in Italia; The Turk in Italy; opera buffa. In two acts. Ital. and Engl. New York, 1826. 12°

TURKEY. Sketches of Turkey in 1831 and 1832. By an American [James E. De Kay]. New York, 1833. 8vo.

TURNBULL, LAWRENCE. Lectures on the Electro-Magnetic Telegraph, with an Historical Account of its rise and progress, containing a list of the number of Telegraphic Lines of the World. . . . With an Appendix containing the Decisions of Judges Woodbury and Kane in the celebrated Telegraphic Trials. Philadelphia, 1852. 8vo.

TURNBULL, ROBERT. The Genius of Scotland; or sketches of Scottish scenery, literature, and religion. Third edition. N. York, 1847. 12°

2 CHRIST in History; or, the Central Power among Men. Boston, 1854. 8vo.

TURNBULL, ROBERT J. A Visit to the Philadelphia Prison . . . containing . . an account of the . . . improved state of the Penal Laws of Pennsylvania: with observations on the impolicy . . . . of capital punishments. Philadelphia, 1796. 8vo.

TURNER, G. Traits of Indian Character; as generally applicable to the aborigines of North America. 2 vol. Philadelphia, 1836. 12°

TURNER, GEORGE. The Case of Thomas W. Dorr, convicted of an offence under the act entitled, An act in relation to offences against the sovereign power of the State of Rhode Island, explained. Washing! 1845? 8°

TURNER, O. Pioneer History of the Holland Purchase of Western New York, embracing some account of the ancient remains, a brief history of our immediate predecessors, the Confederated Iroquois, . . a Synopsis of colonial history; some notices of the border wars of the Revolution; and a history of Pioneer Settlements under the auspices of the Holland Company, including Reminiscences

of the war of 1812, the origin, progress, and completion of the Erie Canal, etc. Buffalo, 1850. 8°

TURNER, SAMUEL H. D.D. A Sermon delivered before the Convention of the Diocese of New York, Oct. 19. New York, 1824. 8vo.

2 A COMPANION to the Book of Genesis. New York, 1846. 8vo.

3 BIOGRAPHICAL Notices of some of the most distinguished Jewish Rabbies, and translations of portions of their commentaries, and other works, with illustrative introductions and notes by S. H. Turner. New York, 1847. 12°

4 SPIRITUAL Things compared with spiritual, and explained to spiritual men; or, an attempt to illustrate the New Testament by parallel references. New York, 1848. 12mo.

5 ESSAY on our Lord's Discourse at Capernaum, recorded in the sixth Chapter of St. John. With strictures on Cardinal Wiseman's Lectures on the real presence, and notices of some of his errors. . . Second edition. New York, 1851. 12mo.

6 THOUGHTS on the origin, character, and interpretation of Scriptural Prophecy. In seven Discourses. . . With notes. New York, 1852. 12mo.

TURNER, SHARON. The Sacred History of the World, attempted to be philosophically considered, in a series of letters to a son. 3 vol. New York, 1842, 46, 44. 12°

TURNER, WILLIAM. Triumphs of "Young Physic:" or Chrono-Thermal Facts. N. York [1847]. 8vo.

TURNOVER, a Tale of New Hampshire. Boston, 1853. 12°

TUSTIN, SEPTIMUS. The Doubting Communicant encouraged. Second edition. Philadel. 1853. 16°

TUTHILL, LOUISA CAROLINE, Mrs. The Young Lady's Reader; arranged for examples in rhetoric: for

the higher clasſes in seminaries. . . .
Second edition. N. Haven, 1844. 12°

2 MY Wife. [A tale.] Boston,
1846. 8°

3 THE MIRROR of Life : edited by
Mrs. L. C. Tuthill. [A collection of
eſſays and tales, in prose and verse.]
Philadelphia [1847]. 8°

4 THE GIRLS' and BOYS' Miscellany [of Tales; in verse and prose].
Philadelphia, 1848. 4°

5 HISTORY of Architecture, from
the earliest times; its present condition in Europe and the United States;
with a biography of eminent architects, and a gloſſary of architectural
terms. Philadelphia, 1848. 8°

6 THE YOUNG Lady's Home. [A
tale.] Philadelphia, 1848. 12°

TUTTLE, WILLIAM. The Life of
W. Tuttle, compiled from an auto-
biography under the name of John
Homespun, edited and continued to
the close of his life by . . J. F. Tuttle.
New York, 1852. 12mo.

TWINKLING STAR (THE). Philadelphia [1830?]. 12mo.

TWO FRIENDS (THE); or, religion the best guide to youth. Philadelphia, 1830. 12mo.

TWO PRODIGALS (THE). Phi-
ladelphia, 1832. 12mo.

TYLER, B. M. Arithmetick, the-
oretically and practically illustrated.
Middletown, 1827. 12°

TYLER, BENNET. Religious Principle, the foundation of personal safety
and social happineſs: a sermon [on
Gen. xx. 11] preached . . on the . .
anniversary Election, in . . . New
Hampshire. Concord, 1824. 8°

2 MEMOIR of the life and character
of Rev. A. Nettleton, D.D. Second
edition. Hartford, 1845. 12°

TYLER, DANIEL P. Statistics of
the condition and products of certain
branches of Industry in Connecticut,

for the year ending Oct. 1, 1843.
Prepared from the returns of the as-
seſſors, by D. P. Tyler. Hartford,
1846. 8vo.

TYLER, E. R. Review of Dr.
Tyler's Strictures upon an article in
the Christian Spectator, on the means
of regeneration. First published in
the Christian Spectator for March,
1830. New Haven, 1830. 8°

TYLER, LEVI. Report of the
President of the Lexington and Ohio
Railroad (L. Tyler), to the Senate of
Kentucky, made in compliance with
a resolution of that body. [Frank-
fort, 1840.] 8°

TYLER, ROBERT. Ahasuerus, a
poem by a Virginian [R. Tyler]. New
York, 1842. 12mo.

TYLER, ROYALL. Reports of
cases argued and determined in the
Supreme Court of Judicature of the
State of Vermont; with cases of practice and rules of the Court; commencing with the nineteenth century
[from Jan. term, 1800, to June term,
1803]. 2 vol. New York, 1809-
1810. 8°

TYNG, REV. STEPHEN HENRY,
D.D. The Beloved Physician: a discourse [on Col. iv. 14] addreſſed to
medical students, etc. Philadelphia,
1844. 8°

2 LECTURES on the law and the
Gospel. Sixth thousand. New York,
1848. 8°

TYSON, JAMES L. Diary of a
Physician in California; being the
results of actual experience, including notes of the journey by land and
water, and observations on the climate, soil, resources of the country,
etc. New York, 1850. 8°

TYSON, JOB R. A Brief Survey
of the great extent and evil tendencies
of the lottery system, as existing in
the United States, etc. Philadelphia,
1833. 8°

2 DISCOURSE on the surviving rem-

nant of the Indian race in the United States. Philadelphia, 1836. 8°

3 DISCOURSE delivered before the Historical Society of Pennsylvania, February 21, 1842, on the Colonial History of the Eastern and some of the Southern States. Philadelphia, 1842. 8°

4 THE SOCIAL and Intellectual State of the Colony of Pennsylvania, prior to the year 1743. [Read before the American Philosophical Society], etc. Philadelphia, 1843. 8°

5 DISCOURSE on the two hundredth anniversary of the birth of W. Penn, delivered in the Independence Hall at Philadelphia, on the 24th October, 1844, before the Historical Society of Pennsylvania. Philadelphia, 1845. 8°

TYSON, PHILIP T. Geology and Industrial Resources of California. . . To which is added the official reports of Genls. Persifer F. Smith, and B. Riley; including the reports of Lieuts. Talbot, Ord, Derby, and Williamson, of their explorations in California and Oregon; and also of their examinations of routes for railroad communication eastward from those countries. Baltimore, 1851. 8°

TYTLER, ALEXANDER FRASER, Lord Woodhouselee. Universal History, from the creation of the world [to the close of the seventeenth century, by A. F. Tytler; continued] to the decease of George III, 1820, by E. Nares. Edited by an American. 6 vol. New York, 1845, 43. 12°

TYTLER, JAMES, M.A. of Brechin, Forfarshire. Proposals for publishing, by subscription, A New System of Geography, ancient and modern. Salem, 1802. 8°

TYTLER, PATRICK FRASER, Lord Woodhouselee. [Life of Sir W. Raleigh: forming a portion of Greenbank's Periodical Library. [Imperfect: containing only pp. 49–96.] Philadelphia, 1833.] 8°

2 HISTORICAL View of the progress of discovery on the more northern Coasts of America, from the earliest period to the present time. . . With descriptive sketches of the natural history of the North American regions, by J. Wilson. . . To which is added an appendix, containing remarks on a late memoir of S. Cabot, with a vindication of R. Hakluyt. New York, 1846. 12°

NDERWOOD, ALVAN. A Discourse [on Zep. iii. 14, 15] delivered .. April 13, .. the day recommended for a National Thanksgiving for peace. Hartford, 1815. 8°

UNGEWITTER, FRIEDRICH H. Europe, past and present: a comprehensive manual of European geography and history, .. and a copious index. New York, 1850. 12°

UNIACKE, CROFTON. A Letter to the Lord Chancellor, on the necessity and practicability of forming a code of the laws of England. To which is annexed the new bankrupt law; arranged in the method of Domat's civil law, .. proposed to be adopted as the form of the statute law of the realm. Boston, 1827. 8°

UNION COLLEGE, SCHENECTADY, *New York*. Nomina Senatus Academici, et eorum qui munera at officia academica gesserunt, quique aliquopiam gradu exornati sunt, in Collegio Concordiæ dedicato, *etc.* [1834 and 1843.] 2 parts. Schenectadiæ, 1834-43. 8°

2 CATALOGUE of the officers and students, ... 1837-38, 1841, and 1842. Schenectady, 1837-42. 8°

3 THE FIRST semi-centennial anniversary of Union College, celebrated July 22, 1845. [Edited by A. L. Linn, J. B. Nott, and T. C. Reed.] Schenectady, 1845. 8°

UNION MAGAZINE (THE) of Literature and Art.˙. Edited by Mrs. C. M. Kirkland. Vol. 1-3. New York, 1847-48. 8°. [Continued at Philadelphia, under the title of] Sartain's Union Magazine of literature and art. C. M. Kirkland and J. S. Hart, editors. Vol. 4-8 and vol. 9. N° 1, 2. Philadelphia, 1849-51. 8°

UNITARIAN. How I became a Unitarian, explained in a series of letters to a friend by a Clergyman of the Protestant Episcopal Church. Boston and New York, 1852. 8°

UNITARIANS. Impartial Review. A general brief view of the existing controversy between Unitarians and the Orthodox, so called; as it appears .. more particularly in a review in "The Christian Disciple," of Professor Stuart's Letters, and in Dr. Wood's Letters to Unitarians. By a Laical Observer. Portsmouth, N. H. 1820. 8°

UNITARIAN (THE). Conducted by B. Whitman [J. Whitman, and G. Nichols]. Jan. to Dec. 1834. Cambridge and Boston, 1834. 8°

UNITARIAN CONTROVERSY. Review of the Unitarian Controversy. Extracted from the Panoplist. [Boston, 1816.] 8°

UNITARIAN MISCELLANY and Christian Monitor. [Edited by J. Sparks, and F. W. P. Greenwood.] 5 vol. Baltimore, 1822-24. 8°

UNITED STATES OF AMERICA.

1 EXTRACTS from the votes and proceedings of the American Continental Congreſs, held at Philadelphia on the 5th of September, 1774, etc. New London, 1774. 4°

2 EXTRACTS from the votes and proceedings of the American Continental Congreſs, held at Philadelphia on the 5th of September, 1774, etc. New London, 1774. sm. 4°

3 A LETTER to the Inhabitants of the Province of Quebec. Extract from the minutes of the Congreſs. Philadelphia, 1774. 8°

4 A FEW Remarks upon some of the Votes and Resolutions of the Continental Congreſs held at Philadelphia in September, and the Provincial Congreſs held at Cambridge in Nov. 1774. By a Friend to Peace and good order. 1775. 8vo.

5 A DECLARATION by the Representatives of the United Colonies of North America, now met in general congreſs at Philadelphia, setting forth the causes and neceſſity of their taking up arms. Philadelphia, printed; Watertown, reprinted, 1775. 8°

6 WHAT think ye of the Congreſs now! or an enquiry, how far the Americans are bound to abide by and execute the decisions of the late Congreſs. New York, 1775. 8vo.

7 JOURNALS of Congreſs. Containing the Proceedings from Sept. 5, 1774, to Nov. 3, 1788. Published by order of Congreſs. 13 vol. 1777-1788. 8vo. viz:

VOL.
1. Sept. 5, 1774, to Jan. 1, 1776, R. Aitken. Philadelphia, 1777.
2. Jan. 1, 1776, to Jan. 1, 1777, J. Dunlap. York Town, 1778.
3. Jan. 1, 1777, to Jan. 1, 1778, J. Dunlap. Philadelphia, n. d.
4. Jan. 1, 1778, to Jan. 1, 1779, D. C. Claypoole. Philadelphia, n. d.
5. Jan. 1, 1779, to Jan. 1, 1780, D. C. Claypoole. Philadelphia, 1782.
6. For the year 1780, John Dunlap. n. p. n. d.

7. For the year 1781, D. C. Claypoole. Philadelphia, 1781.
8. 4 Nov. 1782, to Nov. 1783, D. C. Claypoole. Philadelphia, 1783.
9. 3 Nov. 1783, to 3 June, 1784, J. Dunlap. Philadelphia, n. d.
10. 1 Nov. 1784, to Nov. 5, 1785, J. Dunlap. Philadelphia, n. d.
11. 3 Nov. 1785, to 3 Nov. 1786, J. Dunlap. n. p. n. d.
12. 6 Nov. 1786, to 5 Nov. 1787, J. Dunlap. Philadelphia, 1787.
13. 5 Nov. 1787, to 3 Nov. 1788, J. Dunlap. Philadelphia, n. d.

8 A CIRCULAR Letter from the Congreſs of the United States of America to their constituents. Sept. 1779. Philadelphia, printed; Boston, reprinted, 1779. 8°

9 THE CONSTITUTIONS of the several Independent States of America; the Declaration of Independence; the Articles of Confederation between the said States; the Treaties between his Most Christian Majesty and the United States of America. Philad. 1781. 8°

10 CONSTITUTION des Treize Etats Unis de l'Amérique. Philadelphie [Paris printed?], 1783. 8vo.

11 THE DYING Legacy of an aged Minister of the everlasting gospel to the United States of North America. Boston, 1783. 8°

12 THE CONSTITUTION or frame of government, for the United States of America, as reported by the convention of delegates, from the United States, etc. Boston, 1787. 8°

13 JOURNAL of the Senate of the United States: 1789-1845. viz.

First Congreſs.
1st Seſs. Mar. 4, 1789, to Sep. 29, 1789
2d Seſs. Jan. 4, 1790, to Aug. 12, 1790
3d Seſs. Dec. 6, 1790, to Mar. 3, 1791
Second Congreſs.
1st Seſs. Oct. 24, 1791, to May 8, 1792
2d Seſs. Nov. 2, 1792, to Mar. 3, 1793
Third Congreſs.
1st Seſs. Dec. 2, 1793, to June 9, 1794
2d Seſs. Nov. 3, 1794, to Mar. 3, 1795
Fourth Congreſs.
1st Seſs. Dec. 7, 1795, to June 1, 1796*
2d Seſs. Dec. 5, 1796, to Mar. 3, 1797*
Fifth Congreſs.
1st Seſs. May 17, 1797, to July 10, 1797
2d Seſs. Nov. 13, 1797, to July 16, 1798
3d Seſs. Dec. 3, 1798, to Mar. 3, 1799

Sixth Congreſs.

1st Seſſ. Dec. 2, 1799, to Mar. 14, 1800*
2d Seſſ. Nov. 17, 1800, to Mar. 3, 1801*

Seventh Congreſs.

1st Seſſ. Dec. 7, 1801, to May 3, 1802*
2d Seſſ. Dec. 6, 1802, to Mar. 3, 1803*

Eighth Congreſs.

1st Seſſ. Oct. 17, 1803, to Mar. 27, 1804
2d Seſſ. Nov. 5, 1804, to Mar. 3, 1805*

Ninth Congreſs.

1st Seſſ. Dec. 2, 1805, to Apr. 21, 1806*
2d Seſſ. Dec. 1, 1806, to Mar. 3, 1817

Tenth Congreſs.

1st Seſſ. Oct. 26, 1807, to Apr. 25, 1808
2d Seſſ. Nov. 7, 1808, to Mar. 3, 1809*

Eleventh Congreſs.

1st Seſſ. May 22, 1809, to June 28, 1809*
2d Seſſ. Nov. 27, 1809, to May 1, 1810*
3d Seſſ. Dec. 3, 1810, to Mar. 3, 1811

Twelfth Congreſs.

1st Seſſ. Nov. 4, 1811, to July 6, 1812
2d Seſſ. Nov. 2, 1812, to Mar. 3, 1813*

Thirteenth Congreſs.

1st Seſſ. May 21, 1813, to Aug. 2, 1813*
2d Seſſ. Dec. 6, 1813, to Apr. 18, 1814
3d Seſſ. Sept. 19, 1814, to Mar. 3, 1815

Fourteenth Congreſs.

1st Seſſ. Dec. 4, 1815, to Apr. 30, 1816
2d Seſſ. Dec. 2, 1816, to Mar. 3, 1817

Fifteenth Congreſs.

1st Seſſ. Dec. 1, 1817, to Apr. 20, 1818
2d Seſſ. Nov. 16, 1818, to Mar. 3, 1819

Sixteenth Congreſs.

1st Seſſ. Dec. 6, 1819, to May 15, 1820
2d Seſſ. Nov. 13, 1820, to Mar. 3, 1821

Seventeenth Congreſs.

1st Seſſ. Dec. 3, 1821, to May 8, 1822
2d Seſſ. Dec. 2, 1822, to Mar. 3, 1823

Eighteenth Congreſs.

1st Seſſ. Dec. 1, 1823, to May 26, 1824
2d Seſſ. Dec. 6, 1824, to Mar. 3, 1825

Nineteenth Congreſs.

1st Seſſ. Dec. 5, 1825, to May 22, 1826*
2d Seſſ. Dec. 4, 1826, to Mar. 3, 1827

Twentieth Congreſs.

1st Seſſ. Dec. 3, 1827, to May 26, 1828
2d Seſſ. Dec. 1, 1828, to Mar. 3, 1829

Twenty-firſt Congreſs.

1st Seſſ. Dec. 3, 1829, to May 31, 1830
2d Seſſ. Dec. 6, 1830, to Mar. 3, 1831*

Twenty-ſecond Congreſs.

1st Seſſ. Dec. 5, 1831, to July 16, 1832*
2d Seſſ. Dec. 3, 1832, to Mar. 3, 1833

Twenty-third Congreſs.

1st Seſſ. Dec. 2, 1833, to June 30, 1834*
2d Seſſ. Dec. 1, 1834, to Mar. 3, 1835*

Twenty-fourth Congreſs.

1st Seſſ. Dec. 7, 1835, to July 4, 1836
2d Seſſ. Dec. 5, 1836, to Mar. 3, 1837

Twenty-fifth Congreſs.

1st Seſſ. Sept. 4, 1837, to Oct. 16, 1837
2d Seſſ. Dec. 4, 1837, to June 9, 1838
3d Seſſ. Dec. 3, 1838, to Mar. 3, 1839

Twenty-ſixth Congreſs.

1st Seſſ. Dec. 2, 1839, to July 21, 1840
2d Seſſ. Dec. 7, 1840, to Mar. 3, 1841*

Twenty-ſeventh Congreſs.

1st Seſſ. May 31, 1841, to Sept. 13, 1841
2d Seſſ. Dec. 6, 1841, to Aug. 31, 1842
3d Seſſ. Dec. 5, 1842, to Mar. 3, 1843

Twenty-eighth Congreſs.

1st Seſſ. Dec. 4, 1843, to June 17, 1844
2d Seſſ. Dec. 2, 1844, to Mar. 3, 1845

New York, 1789-90; Philadelphia, 1791-1800; and Washington, 1801-1845. Each Seſſion in 1 volume, 1789-94 in fol°, and 1795-1845 in 8°   *wanting.

14 JOURNAL of the Houſe of Repreſentatives of the United States: 1789-1845: viz.

First Congreſs.

1st Seſſ. Mar. 4, 1789, to Sept. 29, 1789
2d Seſſ. Jan. 4, 1790, to Aug. 12, 1790
3d Seſſ. Dec. 6, 1790, to Mar. 3, 1791

Second Congreſs.

1st Seſſ. Oct. 24, 1791, to May 8, 1792*
2d Seſſ. Nov. 2, 1792, to Mar. 3, 1793*

Third Congreſs.

1st Seſſ. Dec. 2, 1793, to June 9, 1794
2d Seſſ. Nov. 3, 1794, to Mar. 3, 1795*

Fourth Congreſs.

1st Seſſ. Dec. 7, 1795, to June 1, 1796
2d Seſſ. Dec. 5, 1796, to Mar. 3, 1797

Fifth Congreſs.

1st Seſſ. May 15, 1797, to July 10, 1797
2d Seſſ. Nov. 13, 1797, to July 16, 1798
3d Seſſ. Dec. 3, 1798, to Mar. 3, 1799

Sixth Congreſs.

1st Seſſ. Dec. 2, 1799, to Mar. 14, 1800
2d Seſſ. Nov. 17, 1800, to Mar. 3, 1801

Seventh Congreſs.

1st Seſſ. Dec. 7, 1801, to May 3, 1802
2d Seſſ. Dec. 6, 1802, to Mar. 3, 1803

Eighth Congreſs.

1st Seſſ. Oct. 17, 1803, to Mar. 27, 1804
2d Seſſ. Nov. 5, 1804, to Mar. 3, 1805

Ninth Congreſs.

1st Seſſ. Dec. 2, 1805, to Apr. 21, 1806
2d Seſſ. Dec. 1, 1806, to Mar. 3, 1807

Tenth Congreſs.

1st Seſſ. Oct. 26, 1807, to Apr. 25, 1808
2d Seſſ. Nov. 7, 1808, to Mar. 3, 1809

Eleventh Congreſs.

1st Seſſ. May 22, 1809, to June 28, 1809
2d Seſſ. Nov. 27, 1809, to May 1, 1810*
3d Seſſ. Dec. 3, 1810, to Mar. 3, 1811

Twelfth Congreſs.

1st Seſſ. Nov. 4, 1811, to July 6, 1812
2d Seſſ. Nov. 2, 1812, to Mar. 3, 1813

Thirteenth Congreſs.

1st Seſs. May 21, 1813, to Aug. 2, 1813
2d Seſs. Dec. 6, 1813, to Apr. 18, 1814
3d Seſs. Sept. 19, 1814, to Mar. 3, 1815

Fourteenth Congreſs.

1st Seſs. Dec. 4, 1815, to Apr. 30, 1816
2d Seſs. Dec. 2, 1816, to Mar. 3, 1817

Fifteenth Congreſs.

1st Seſs. Dec. 1, 1817, to Apr. 20, 1818
2d Seſs. Nov. 16, 1818, to Mar. 3, 1819

Sixteenth Congreſs.

1st Seſs. Dec. 6, 1819, to May 15, 1820
2d Seſs. Nov. 13, 1820, to Mar. 3, 1821

Seventeenth Congreſs.

1st Seſs. Dec. 3, 1821, to May 8, 1822
2d Seſs. Dec. 2, 1822, to Mar. 3, 1823

Eighteenth Congreſs.

1st Seſs. Dec. 1, 1823, to May 26, 1824
2d Seſs. Dec. 6, 1824, to Mar. 3, 1825

Nineteenth Congreſs.

1st Seſs. Dec. 5, 1825, to May 22, 1826*
2d Seſs. Dec. 4, 1826, to Mar. 3, 1827

Twentieth Congreſs.

1st Seſs. Dec. 3, 1827, to May 26, 1828
2d Seſs. Dec. 1, 1828, to Mar. 3, 1829*

Twenty-first Congreſs.

1st Seſs. Dec. 3, 1829, to May 31, 1830*
2d Seſs. Dec. 6, 1830, to Mar. 3, 1831

Twenty-second Congreſs.

1st Seſs. Dec. 5, 1831, to July 16, 1832*
2d Seſs. Dec. 3, 1832, to Mar. 3, 1833

Twenty-third Congreſs.

1st Seſs. Dec. 2, 1833, to June 30, 1834*
2d Seſs. Dec. 1, 1834, to Mar. 3, 1835*

Twenty-fourth Congreſs,

1st Seſs. Dec. 7, 1835, to July 4, 1836
2d Seſs. Dec. 5, 1836, to Mar. 3, 1837

Twenty-fifth Congreſs.

1st Seſs. Sept. 4, 1837, to Oct. 16, 1837
2d Seſs. Dec. 4, 1837, to June 9, 1838
3d Seſs. Dec. 3, 1838, to Mar. 3, 1839

Twenty-sixth Congreſs.

1st Seſs. Dec. 2, 1839, to July 21, 1840
2d Seſs. Dec. 7, 1840, to Mar. 3, 1841*

Twenty-seventh Congreſs.

1st Seſs. May 31, 1841, to Sept. 13, 1841
2d Seſs. Dec. 6, 1841, to Aug. 31, 1842
3d Seſs. Dec. 5, 1842, to Mar. 3, 1843

Twenty-eighth Congreſs.

1st Seſs. Dec. 4, 1843, to June 17, 1844
2d Seſs. Dec. 2, 1844, to Mar. 3, 1845

New York, 1789-90; Philadelphia, 1791-1800; and Washington, 1801-1845. Each Seſion in 1 volume; 1789-92 in fol°, and 1793-1845 in 8°   *wanting.

15 THE CONGRESSIONAL Register; or, history of the proceedings and debates of the first House of Repreſentatives of the United States...

Taken in short-hand by T. Lloyd. Vol. 1. New York, 1789. 8°

16 REPORT of the Secretary of State (T. Jefferſon) on the ſubject of establishing a uniformity in the weights, measures, and coins of the United States. New York, 1790. 8°

17 RETURN of the whole number of Persons within the several Districts of the United States, according to an Act for the enumeration of the Inhabitants of the United States. Philadelphia, 1791. 8vo.

18 A MESSAGE of the President (George Washington) of the United States to Congreſs relative to France and Great Britain, delivered Dec. 5, 1793; with the papers therein referred to. To which are added the French originals. 3 parts [separately paged]. Published by order of the House of Representatives. Philadelphia, 1793. 8°

19 ACTS paſſed at the first Congreſs of the United States of America: begun and held at .. New York .. 4th of March, 1789. Philadelphia, 1795. 8°

20 THE Laws of the United States of America. 3 vol. Philadelphia, 1796. 8vo.

21 THE CONSTITUTIONS of the United States, according to the latest amendments; to which are annexed, the Declaration of Independence; and the Federal Constitution, with the amendments thereto, etc. Philadelphia, 1796. 12°

22 A COLLECTION of the Speeches of the President of the United States to both Houses of Congreſs, at the opening of every Seſſion, with their answers. Also the addreſſes to the President, with his answers: with an appendix, containing the Circular Letter of General Washington to the Governors of the several States, and his Farewell Orders to the armies of America, and the answer. Boston, 1796. 12°

23 A SELECTION of the Patriotic Addreſſes to the President of the

United States; together with the President's answers; presented in . . . 1798. Boston, 1798. 12°

24 INSTRUCTIONS to C. C. Pinckney, J. Marshall, and E. Gerry, Envoys .. to the French Republic, *etc.* Philadelphia, 1798. 8°

25 LETTER from the Secretary of State, inclosing abstracts of all the returns made to him by the collectors of the different ports, of registered and imprefsed seamen; together with a report, exhibiting abstracts of the communications received by him from the agents employed by virtue of the Act .. for the relief and protection of American Seamen, *etc.* 2 parts. [Philadelphia? 1799?] 8°

26 REGULATIONS for the order and discipline of the troops of the United States. [By F. W. von Steuben. Published by authority of Congrefs, 29 Mar. 1779.] Philadelphia, 1800. 12°

27 RETURN of the whole number of persons within the several districts of the United States, according to an act providing for the second census or enumeration of the inhabitants of the United States... Printed by order of the House of Representatives. [Washington? 1801.] Fol°

28 DEBATES on the Bill for repealing the Law " for the more convenient organization of the Courts of the United States," and a List of the Yeas and Nays. Albany, 1802. 8°

29 DEBATES in the Senate of the United States on the judiciary, during the first Sefsion of the Seventh Congrefs, *etc.* Philadelphia, 1802. 8°

30 MISSISSIPPI Question. Report of a debate in the Senate of the United States, on the 23rd, 24th, and 25th February, 1803, on certain resolutions concerning the violation of the right of deposit in the island of New Orleans. By W. Duane. Philadelphia, 1803. 8°

31 PUBLIC DOCUMENTS, Eighth Congrefs, Second Sefsion, 1804-1805. 2 vol. 8°

Containing in Volume 1,

1. Mefsage from the President (Thomas Jefferson) to both Houfes of Congrefs. 8 Nov. 1804. [With the accompanying documents.] 2 pts. Washington, 1804.

2. Report from the Committee of Commerce and Manufactures, .. on the .. petition of the President and Directors of the New York and Duchefs County State Companies, *etc.* 15 Nov. 1804. Washington, 1804.

3. Letter from the Secretary of the Navy (R. Smith) accompanying a report of the Commifsioners of the fund for Navy pensioners. (12 Nov. 1804.) [Washington, 1804.]

4. Mefsage from the President (Thomas Jefferson) .. accompanying sundry documents, exhibiting a statement of the destruction of the frigate Philadelphia; *etc.* 15 Nov. 1804. Washing. 1804.

5. Report, in part, of the Committee of Revisal .. on such matters of businefs as were depending and undetermined at the last Sefsion. 8 Nov. 1804. [Washington, 1804.]

6. Mr. Rhea's Motion [relative to registration of land titles within the territories ceded by France to the United States]. [Washington,] 1804.

7. Letter from the Secretary of the Treasury (A. Gallatin), transmitting a report and estimates .. for the service of the year 1805; also, a statement of the receipts and expenditures . . . for . . . 1804. 19 Nov. 1804. Washington, 1804.

8. Reports of the Committee of Commerce and Manufactures .. on the .. expediency of allowing, under proper regulations, a drawback of duties on goods, wares, and merchandise imported into .. New Orleans, .. and from thence exported to any foreign port or place. 27 Nov. 1804. [Washington, 1804.]

9. Report of the Committee to whom was referred .. the report of a select committee appointed .. to prepare and report articles of impeachment against S. Chase, one of the Afsociate Justices of the Supreme Court of the United States. 30 Nov. 1804. [Washington, 1804.]

10. Report from the Committee appointed .. to enquire into the expediency of extending the time for claimants to lands under the State of Georgia lying South of . . . Tennefsee, to register . . . their title, *etc.* [Washington,] 1804.

11. Memorial of the Citizens . . . of the Indiana Territory, praying for the interposition of Congrefs, to relieve them from certain opprefsions and embarrafsments. Washington, 1804.

12. Letter from the Mayor of Alexandria ..

(E. C. Dick) inclosing sundry resolutions of the citizens of . . . Alexandria, expressive of their disapprobation of a motion now depending before the House [of Representatives of the United States of America] to recede to the States of Virginia and Maryland . . parts of the . . District [of Columbia], etc. Washington, 1804.

13. Message from the President (Thomas Jefferson) . . communicating a report from the Surveyor of . . public buildings at . . Washington, etc. 6 Dec. 1804. Washington, 1804.

14. Motion respecting the establishment of a post road from Knoxville . . . to New Orleans, etc. [submitted to the House of Representatives of the United States of America]. Washington, 1804.

15. Report of the Committee of Elections . . on the petition of sundry citizens of . . Washington, in . . Pennsylvania, complaining of an undue election and return of J. Hoge, etc. 10 Dec. 1804. [Washington, 1804.]

16. Representation of the Philadelphia Chamber of Commerce [in relation to a bill depending in the House of Representatives of the United States of America; to regulate the clearance of armed merchant vessels]. 10 Dec. 1804. [Washington, 1804.]

17. 10 Dec. 1804. Referred, etc. [Reports from the Committee on proposed post roads, from Knoxville to New Orleans, and from Washington to Natchez and New Orleans. Washington, 1804.]

18. Report of the Committee of Claims, . . . on the . . petition of M. White and C. Hazen, executor and executrix of Moses Hazen, etc. 12 Dec. 1804. [Washington,] 1804.

19. Letter from G. W. Custis . . . enclosing sundry resolutions agreed to by the inhabitants of Alexandria relative to the recession of . . . part of the territory of Columbia, etc. 11 Dec. 1804. [Washington, 1804.]

20. Letter from the Secretary of the Treasury (A. Gallatin) inclosing abstracts . . from the Commissioners to make the valuations of lands and . . slaves in . . South Carolina, etc. (Nov. 24, 1804.) [Washington,] 1804.

21. Report of the Committee of Claims . . . on the . . petition of A. Elliott . . 14 Dec. 1804. [Washington, 1804.]

22. Report of the Committee appointed . . to enquire into the expediency of making provision, by law, for the completion of the public buildings belonging to the United States, near Philadelphia. 24 Dec. 1804. [Washington, 1804.]

23. Mr. Stanford's Motion relative to a recession of the territory of Columbia. Washington, 1805.

24. Letter from the Secretary of the Treasury (A. Gallatin) . . on the subject of lands south of the State of Tennessee [with other documents]. (21 Dec. 1804.) Washington, 1804.

25. Message from the President . . communicating the copy of a letter from R. O'Brien, late Consul of the United States at Algiers, giving some detail of transactions before Tripoli. 31 Dec. 1804. Washington, 1804.

26. Letter from the Secretary of the Treasury (A. Gallatin) . . inclosing sundry additional estimates . . for the year 1805. (Nov. 27, 1804.) Washington, 1804.

27. Letter from the Postmaster-General (G. Granger) . . including his report on the memorial of R. Henderson [respecting a contract for carrying mails], etc. 7 Jan. 1805. [Washington, 1805.]

28. Report of the Committee of Claims, on the Memorial of A. Murray, late Commander of the United States frigate Constellation, etc. 8 Jan. 1805. [Washington, 1805.]

29. Letter from the Surveyor of the Public Buildings at . . Washington (Dec. 30, 1804) . . accompanying a Bill making an appropriation for completing the south wing of the Capitol, etc. [Washington, 1804.]

30. Representation and Petition of the Representatives elected by the freemen of the Territory of Louisiana [addressed to the Congress of the United States of America]. (29 Sept. 1804.) Washington, 1805.

31. Letter from the Secretary of the Treasury (A. Gallatin) transmitting a statement of fees paid . . for legal advices . . by the collectors of the customs, etc. (Jan. 14, 1805). [With the statement.] Washington, 1805.

32. Translation of a Memorial in the French language of sundry citizens of the county of Wayne in the Indiana Territory [addressed to the Congress of the United States of America]. 17 Jan. 1805. Washington, 1805.

33. Letter from the Secretary of War (H. Dearborn) accompanying his report on the petition of sundry officers of the army, stationed at . . New Orleans, etc. (Jan. 15, 1805.) [Washington, 1805.]

34. Report of the Committee of Commerce and Manufactures . . on the . . memorial of sundry manufacturers of refined sugar in . . New York. 21 Jan. 1805. [Washington, 1805.]

35. Mr. Eustis's Motion [in the House of Representatives of the United States of America, relating to the Navy Yards of the United States]. 22 Jan. 1805. [Washington, 1805.]

36. Report from the Committee of Claims

on the petition of A. Scott, *etc.* 22 Jan. 1805. Washington, 1805.

37. Mr. Crowninshield's Motion [in the House of Representatives of the United States of America, relative to commercial restrictions]. 23 Jan. 1805. [Washington, 1805.]

38. Memorial of the Delegates appointed by various sections of the District of Columbia. 22 Jan. 1805. [Washington, 1805.]

39. Report of the Committee appointed . . on so much of the message of the President . . as relates to an amelioration of the form of government of the Territory of Louisiana; *etc.* 25 Jan. 1805. [Washington, 1805.]

40. Report of the Committee of Commerce and Manufactures . . on the . . petitions and memorials of a number of merchants, traders, and farmers . . of North Carolina. 28 Jan. 1805. Washington, 1805.

41. Message from the President communicating the report of the Directors of the Mint of the operations of that institution during the last year. 25 Jan. 1805. Washington, 1805.

42. Letter from the Secretary of the Treasury (A. Gallatin) accompanying a report and two statements, . . exhibiting the tonnage of vessels paying foreign duties entered in the several ports of the United States, during the years 1801, 1802, and 1803; *etc.* (Jan. 31, 1804.) Washington, 1805.

43. Report from the Committee to whom was referred . . . a petition of sundry British merchants and others, subjects of His Britannic Majesty within the United States [relative to legal jurisdiction, *etc.*] Washington, 1805.

44. Letter from the Treasurer of the United States (T. T. Tucker), accompanying his general accounts of receipts and expenditure . . from 1 Oct. 1803, to 30 Sept. 1804, inclusive. (Jan. 21, 1805.) [Washington, 1805.]

In Volume 2,

45. Report of the Committee to whom were referred . . the Memorials and Petitions of the Board of Trustees of Jefferson College in the Mississippi Territory, and of W. Dunbar, an inhabitant of . . said Territory, *etc.* 7 Feb. 1805. [Washington, 1805.]

46. Message from the President . . communicating information in part on the subject of a post road from . . . Washington to New Orleans, *etc.* Feb. 1, 1805. Washington, 1805.

47. Report of the Committee to whom was referred . . the memorials and petitions of sundry . . inhabitants of the District

of Columbia, for and against the building of a bridge across the Potomac river, *etc.* 4 Feb. 1805. [Washington, 1805.]

48. Letter from the Postmaster General (G. Granger), accompanying a report relative to [unproductive] post-roads, *etc.* 4 Feb. 1805. [Washington, 1805.]

49. Report, in part, from the Committee to whom was referred . . the memorial of the Legislative Council and House of Representatives of the Mississippi Territory. 9 Feb. 1805. Washington, 1805.

50. Letter from the Secretary of War (H. Dearborn) accompanying a report in relation to sundry claims to land for military services rendered in the late revolutionary war, *etc.* 4 Feb. 1805. [Washington, 1805.]

51. Report from the Committee of Claims . . on the . . . memorial of R. Taylor. 13 Feb. 1805. Washington, 1805.

52. Letter from the Secretary of the Treasury (A. Gallatin) accompanying his report on the petitions of J. M'Fadon, *etc.* (Feb. 13, 1805.) Washington, 1805.

53. Report from the Committee of Claims . . on the . . . petition of F. Mentges, *etc.* 16 Feb. 1805. Washington, 1805.

54. Report of the Committee to whom was recommitted . . the engrossed bill making farther provision for extinguishing the debts due from the United States. 19 Feb. 1805. [Washington, 1805.]

55. Report of the Committee of Claims . . . on the . . memorial of R. J. Meigs, jun. *etc.* 18 Feb. 1805. [Washington, 1805.]

56. Report from the Committee of Claims to whom were referred a Message from the President . . and other papers . . in relation to . . a claim for the restitution of the Danish brigantine Henrich. 20 Feb. 1805. Washington, 1805.

57. Report of the Committee of Commerce and Manufactures, . . on the . . petition of S. Philipson. 20 Feb. 1805. [Washington, 1805.]

58. Report of the Committee of Claims . . on the . . petition of O. Pollock, *etc.* 20 Feb. 1805. [Washington, 1805.]

59. Report of the Committee of Commerce and Manufactures, . . on the . . memorial of P. Nicklin and R. E. Griffith, *etc.* 20 Feb. 1805. [Washington, 1805.]

60. Report of the Committee of Claims . . . on the . . . petition of G. Little. 20 Feb. 1805. [Washington, 1805.]

61. Letter from the Secretary of the Treasury (A. Gallatin) transmitting a statement of the amount of duties and drawbacks on goods, wares and merchandize imported into the United States, and exported therefrom, during the years 1801, 1802, and 1803. 20 Feb. 1805.

[With the statement.] [Washington, 1805.]

62. Message from the President ... communicating further information in relation to a public road from ... Washington to New Orleans. 23 Feb. 1805. [Washington, 1805.]

63. Message from the President .. transmitting sundry documents (in the case of the [Danish] brig Heinrich). Feb. 5, 1805. [Washington, 1805.]

64. Message from the President .. transmitting a letter from Commodore Preble, giving a detailed account of the transactions of the vessels under his command, etc. [With the letter.] 20 Feb. 1845. [Washington, 1805.]

65. Letter from the Secretary of State (J. Madison) accompanied with a list of ... patents, etc. (18 Feb. 1805.) [Washington, 1805.]

66. Letter from the Secretary of War (H. Dearborn), accompanied with sundry documents, in relation to the .. public buildings on the banks of the Schuylkill near .. Philadelphia, etc. (Feb. 13, 1805.) Washington, 1805.

67. Report from the Committee appointed .. jointly .. to consider and report what business is necessary to be done by the Congress in their present session. 27 Feb. 1805. Washington, 1805.

68. Message from the President .. transmitting a statement of the militia of the several States. [With the statement.] 28 Feb. 1805. [Washington, 1805.]

69. Message from the President .. transmitting the annual account of the fund for defraying the contingent charges of government for the year 1804. 28 Feb. 1805. [With the account.] Washington, 1805.

70. A Treaty between the United States of America and the United tribes of Sac and Fox Indians. (3 Nov. 1804.) Washington, 1805.

71. A Treaty between the United States of America and the Delaware Tribe of Indians, concluded at Vincennes, 18 Aug. 1804, etc. Washington, 1804.

72. Message from the President .. transmitting copies of treaties .. concluded between the United States, and the Delaware tribe of Indians; the Piankeshaw tribe of Indians; and the United tribes of Sac and Fox Indians; on the 18 .. Aug. 27th .. of same month; and 3 .. Nov. ... 1805 [1804]. 13 Feb. 1805. Washington, 1805.

73. Message from the President ... accompanying copies of treaties concluded with the Delaware and Piankeshaw Indians for the extinguishment of their title to the lands therein described. 30 Nov. 1804. [Washington, 1804.]

74. In Senate, etc. Message of the President ... together with the treaty [with the Creek Indians] and documents accompanying it. Dec. 13, 1804. [Washington, 1804.]

75. In Senate, etc. Feb. 8, 1805. [A resolution, proposing an amendment of the Constitution of the United States in respect of the judicial power.] [Washington, 1805.]

76. In Senate .. Dec. 2, 1805. ... Message of the President .. with the documents (relative to complaints against arming the merchant ships and vessels of the United States). Jan. 31, 1805. [Washington, 1805.]

77. In Senate... Jan. 28, 1805. [A proposed resolution respecting tables of fees and compensation in legal proceedings in the several States.] [Washing. 1805.]

78. In Senate .. Feb. 8, 1805. [A proposed resolution relative to the procedure of the Senate in debate.] [Washington, 1805.]

79. In Senate, etc. Jan. 8, 1805. [Proposed resolutions with respect to the sale of public lands, etc.] [Washington, 1805.]

80. In Senate .. Nov. 21, 1804. . Resolution [proposed] expressive of the sense of Congress of the gallant conduct of Capt. S. Decatur, etc. [Washington, 1804.]

81. In Senate .. Jan. 8, 1805. [Report of a Committee respecting lands claimed by the United States, within the State of Tennessee.] [Washington, 1805.]

82. Report from the Committee of Claims, to whom were referred the representation and memorials of sundry citizens of Massachusetts, purchasers under the Georgia Company; of the agents for persons composing the New England Land Company, purchasers under the Georgia and Mississippi Company, etc. 18 Jan. 1805. Washington, 1805.

83. Message from the President ... accompanying certain articles of agreement and cession, which have been .. signed by the Commissioners of the United States, and the Commissioners of the State of Georgia, in pursuance of an act, intituled, .. "An act for amicable settlement of limits with the State of Georgia; etc." 26 April, 1802. [Washington, 1804.]

84. In Senate. ... Dec. 31, 1804. Additional rules of proceeding on trials of impeachment, etc. [Washing. 1804.]

85. In Senate .. Dec. 7, 1804. [Report of the Committee appointed to prepare and report proper rules of proceeding .. in cases of impeachment.] [Washington, 1804.]

86. Articles exhibited by the House of Representatives ... against S. Chase, one

of the Aſſociate Juſtices of the Supreme Court of the United States, in maintenance and support of their impeachment against him, *etc.* [Waſhing. 1805.]

87. The answer and pleas of S. Chaſe, one of the Aſſociate Juſtices of the Supreme Court . . to the articles of impeachment exhibited against him . . by the House of Repreſentatives of the United States, *etc.* Washington, 1805.

88. Replication by the Houſe . . to the anſwer of S. Chaſe, . . to the articles of impeachment, *etc.* (6 Feb. 1805.) [Washington, 1805.]

89. Exhibits accompanying the answer and plea of S. Chaſe, *etc.* [Waſhing. 1805.]

32 PUBLIC Documents, Ninth Congreſs, First Seſſion, 1805-1806. 3 vol. 8°

Containing in Volume 1,

1. Senate Documents, Dec. 6, 1805, to April 12, 1806. *Not numbered.*

In Volume 2,

2. Standing Rules and Orders of the House of Repreſentatives of the United States, eſtabliſhed at the first Seſſion of the ninth Congreſs. . (Supplement, *etc.*) 2 parts. Washington, 1805.

3. Meſſage from the President, . . containing his communication to both houſes of Congreſs, at the commencement of the first Seſſion of the ninth Congreſs. (Dec. 3, 1805.) Washington, 1805.

4. Mr. Gregg's Motion (in the House of Repreſentatives of the United States, relative to grants of land]. 6 Dec. 1805. [Washington, 1805.]

5. Documents accompanying a meſſage from the President, . . Dec. 6, 1805. Washington, 1805.

6. Report from the Committee of ways and means, to whom was referred . . . the petition of A. Benezet and others. Washington, 1805.

7. Report from the Committee of claims to whom were referred . . the Memorial of G. Little, together with a former report made thereon, *etc.* Washington, 1805.

8. Memorial of sundry manufacturers of hats, in . . Philadelphia. [With other documents, relating to the Indian fur trade, ſubmitted to the Committee of commerce and manufactures.] Washington, 1806.

9. Report from the Committee appointed . . to prepare and report . . ſtanding rules and orders of proceeding, *etc.* Washington, 1805.

10. Letter from the Secretary of the Treasury (A. Gallatin) . . accompanying a Bill ſupplementary to the " Act making

provision for the payment of claims of citizens of the United States on the government of France," *etc.* Washington, 1805.

11. Letter from the Secretary of the Treasury (A. Gallatin) accompanied with a report and estimates of appropriation . . for the ſervice of the year 1806; also, a ſtatement of . . receipts and expenditures . . [for the year ending 30 Sept.] 1805. Washington, 1805.

12. Report from the Committee of commerce and manufactures . . on . . the bill for the relief of T. Armiſtead. Dec. 16, 1805. Washington, 1805.

13. Report from the Secretary of State (T. Jefferſon), on the privileges and reſtrictions on the commerce of the United States in foreign countries. 16 Dec. 1793. Washington, 1806.

14. Report from the Committee of claims . . on . . the petition of the Crew of the late United States frigate Philadelphia. Dec. 17, 1805. Washington, 1805.

15. Report, in part, from the Committee of revisal and unfinished buſineſs, on . . . buſineſs . . depending and undetermined at the last Seſſion. Dec. 17, 1805. Washington, 1805.

16. Report from the Committee of Elections, . . on the . . petition of T. Spalding, . . complaining of an undue election and return of C. Mead, *etc.* Dec. 18, 1805. Washington, 1805.

17. Further Report from the Committee of revisal and unfinished buſineſs. Dec. 18, 1805. Washington, 1805.

18. Report of the Committee of claims . . on . . the memorial of R. J. Meigs, junior, with the Report of the Committee of Claims the 18th of Feb. last. Dec. 20, 1805. Washington, 1805.

19. Report of the Committee appointed on . . so much of the Meſſage of the President . . . as relates to the aggreſſions committed on our coasts by foreign armed veſſels ; to the defence of our ports and harbors, *etc.* Dec. 23, 1805. Washington, 1805.

20. Another copy.

21. Report of the Committee of commerce and manufactures, . . on . . the petition of Isaac Claſon. Dec. 24, 1805. Washington, 1805.

22. Report of the Committee of claims . . on . . the petition of J. F. Randolph and R. M'Gillis. Dec. 24, 1805. Washington, 1805.

23. Meſſage from the President . . communicating a report of the Surveyor of the Public Buildings at . . Washington (B. H. Latrobe). Dec. 27, 1805. Washington, 1805.

24. Meſſage from the President . . transmitting a report made to him by the Se-

cretary of the Treasury (A. Gallatin), relative to .. balances due by the States indebted to the United States, *etc.* Dec. 31, 1805. Washington, 1805.

25. Letter from the Secretary of the Treasury (A. Gallatin) to the Chairman of the Committee of ways and means (J. Randolph). (Dec. 28, 1805.) Washington, 1806.

26. Report of the Secretary of State (J. Madison) on the Memorial of Peter Landais [respecting his capture of three British vessels in 1779, their transmission to Bergen as prizes, and subsequent seizure by the King of Denmark]. (31 Dec. 1805.) Washington, 1806.

27. Report of the Committee appointed .. to inquire into the expediency of .. amending the act entituled, "An act to provide for mitigating or remitting forfeitures, penalties, and disabilities, accrued in certain cases," *etc.* Jan. 2, 1806. Washington, 1806.

28. Report of the Committee appointed .. on so much of the message of the President .. as relates to the organisation and classification of the Militia, and to the augmentation of our land forces. Jan. 2, 1806. Washington, 1806.

29. Letter from the Secretary of the Treasury (A. Gallatin), dated 2 Jan. 1806, accompanying a bill declaring the consent of Congress to an Act of the State of South Carolina, *etc.* Wash. 1806.

30. Mr. Madison's Motion for commercial restrictions, in a Committee of the whole House [of Representatives] on the report of the Secretary of State (Mr. Jefferson) on the privileges and restrictions on the commerce of the United States in foreign countries. Jan. 3, 1794. Washington, 1806.

31. Memorial of the Merchants of New York [to the President and Congress]. Jan. 6, 1806. Washington, 1806.

32. Report of the Committee to whom was recommitted .. a resolution respecting William Eaton. Jan. 8, 1806. Washington, 1806.

33. Report of the Committee of commerce and manufactures .. on .. the petition of P. Nicklin and R. E. Griffith, *etc.* Jan. 1806. Washington, 1806.

34. Report of the Committee of ways and means, ... on the ... petition of S. Beebee, *etc.* Jan. 8, 1806. Washington, 1806.

35. Memorial of the Legislature of the State of Georgia. Washington, 1806.

36. Message from the President .. respecting the application of Hamet Caramalli, Ex-Bashaw of Tripoli. Jan. 13, 1806. [With the accompanying documents.] Washington, 1806.

37. Message from the President .. transmit-

ting the annual account of the fund for defraying the contingent charges of government for the year 1805. Jan. 15, 1806. [With the account.] Washington, 1806.

In Volume 3,

38. Message from the President .. communicating the report of the Director of the Mint (R. Patterson) of the operations of that institution, during the last year. Jan. 15, 1806. [With the report.] Washington, 1806.

39. Memorial of the merchants and traders of the city of Philadelphia [to the President and Congress of the United States of America]. Jan. 16, 1806. Washington, 1806.

40. Letter from the Chairman of the Committee of ways and means, to the Secretary of the Navy, respecting a deficiency in the naval appropriation for the year 1805. Dec. 12, 1805. Washington, 1806.

41. Letter from the Secretary of the Treasury (A. Gallatin), transmitting a statement of the amount of duties and drawbacks on goods, wares, and merchandise imported into the United States and exported therefrom during the years 1802, 1803 and 1804. Jan. 16, 1806. [With the statement.] Washington, 1806.

42. Memorial of sundry inhabitants of the counties of Randolph and St. Clair in the Indiana Territory. Jan. 17, 1806. Washington, 1806.

43. Message from the President .. respecting the violation of neutral rights; the depredations on the colonial trade and impressments of American seamen. Jan. 17, 1806. [With the accompanying documents.] Washington, 1806.

44. Report of the Committee to whom were referred .. the several memorials and petitions of citizens and inhabitants of the county of Alexandria, of the city of Washington, *etc.* Jan. 21, 1806. Washington, 1806.

45. Mr. Gray's Motion [relative to members of the House of Representatives who shall become contractors for the public service. Jan. 24, 1806]. Washington, 1806.

46. Letter from the Secretary of the Navy (R. Smith) inclosing an estimate of the annual expense of supporting in actual service, .. frigates and smaller vessels, *etc.* Washington, 1806.

47. Mr. Gregg's Motion [in the House of Representatives of the United States] to suspend commercial intercourse with Great Britain and her dependencies. Jan. 29, 1806. Washington, 1806.

48. Message from the President .. transmitting a memorial of the merchants of ..

ting a report made to him by the Secretary of War, relative to fortifications
erected at the several ports and harbours of the United States; .. and a
statement exhibiting the amount of
money disbursed on account of the
Navy, in each year, since the establishment [in 1798] of the Navy Department, *etc.* Feb. 18, 1806. Washington,
1806.

75. Report of the Committee to whom was
referred .. the petition of W. Levis and
H. Maxwell [relating to the journals of
Congreſs]. Feb. 19, 1806. Washington, 1806.

76. Report of the Committee on public lands,
who were directed .. " to inquire into
the expediency of providing, by law, for
the legal adjudication of claims .. of
lands," *etc.* Feb. 19, 1806. Washington, 1806.

77. Meſſage from the President .. transmitting copies of treaties lately made between the United States and sundry
tribes of Indians. (Feb. 3, 1806.) [With
the treaties.] Washington, 1806.

33 PUBLIC Documents, Ninth to
Thirteenth Congreſs, various, in 1 vol.
1807-1815. Fol.

Containing,

1. Letter from the Secretary of the Treasury
(A. Gallatin), transmitting a statement
of goods, wares, and merchandize, exported from the United States during
one year, prior to October, 1806. Feb.
26, 1807. Washington, 1807.

2. Letter from the Secretary of the Treasury
(A. Gallatin), transmitting the annual
statement of the district tonnage of the
United States, on the thirty-first day of
December, 1806; together with an explanatory Letter to him from the Register of the Treasury thereon. Dec.
24, 1807. Washington, 1807.

3. Letter from the Secretary of the Treasury
(A. Gallatin), transmitting a Letter from
the Comptroller of the Treasury, accompanied with a statement of the
emoluments of the officers employed in
the collection of the Customs, 1810.
Feb. 25, 1811. Washington, 1811.

4. Letter from the Secretary of the Treasury
(A. Gallatin), transmitting his annual
statement of the amount of duties and
drawbacks, on goods, wares, and merchandize imported into and exported
from the United States during 1808-
1810. Nov. 27, 1811. Washington,
1811.

5. Letter from the Secretary of the Treasury
(A. Gallatin), transmitting the annual
statement of the district tonnage of the

United States, 31st Dec. 1810. Dec.
16, 1811. Washington, 1811.

6. Letter from the Secretary of the Treasury
(A. Gallatin), transmitting his annual
report on the state of the Finances; in
obedience to the Act to establish the
Treasury Department. Dec. 5, 1812.
Washington, 1812.

7. Documents accompanying the Bill concerning the Naval Establishment. Feb.
21, 1812. Washington, 1812.

8. Letter from the Secretary of the Treasury
(G. W. Campbell), transmitting his annual report, prepared in obedience to
the Act supplementary to the Act, entitled " An Act to establish the Treasury Department." Sept. 26, 1814.
Washington, 1814.

9. Letter from the Secretary of the Treasury
(S. H. Smith), transmitting sundry
statements of the Revenue received
under existing laws. Oct. 15, 1814.
Washington, 1814.

10. Letter from the Secretary of the Treasury
(A. J. Dallas), transmitting a statement
of goods, wares and merchandize imported in American and foreign bottoms
from 1st Oct. 1812, to 30th Sept. 1813.
Jan. 9, 1815. Washington, 1815.

11. Letter from the Secretary of the Treasury
(A. J. Dallas), transmitting a statement
of the exports of the United States during the year ending 30th Sept. 1814.
Feb. 9, 1815. Washington, 1815.

12. Letter from the Secretary of the Treasury
(A. J. Dallas), transmitting sundry statements relating to the Mint Establishment. Feb. 23, 1815. Washington,
1815.

13. Letter from the Secretary of the Treasury
(A. J. Dallas), transmitting the annual
statement of the district tonnage of the
United States, on the 31st Dec. 1813;
together with an Explanatory Letter of
the Register of the Treasury. January
20, 1815. Washington, 1815.

34 PUBLIC Documents, Tenth Congreſs, First Seſſion, 1807-1808. 1
vol. 8°

Containing,

1. Letter from the Treasurer of the United
States (T. T. Tucker), accompanying
his general accounts of receipts and ex-
penditures; .. from 1 Oct. 1806 to 30
Sept. 1807, inclusive. (Jan. 16, 1808.)
Washington, 1808.

2. Letter from the Secretary of the Treasury
(A. Gallatin), transmitting a statement
of .. duties and drawbacks on goods,
wares, and merchandise imported into
the United States, and exported therefrom, during the years 1804, 1805, and
1806. Washington, 1805.

3. Mefsage from the President, .. communicating documents and information touching the official conduct of Brigadier General J. Wilkinson, *etc.* Jan. 20, 1808. Washington, 1808.

4. Letter from the Secretary of the Treasury (A. Gallatin), transmitting a report prepared in obedience to " An act regulating the currency of .. foreign coins in the United States." (Jan. 14, 1808.) Washington, 1808.

5. Report of the Committee of commerce and manufactures .. on the .. petitions and memorial of P. and J. W. Revere, *etc.* [relating to duties on copper]. Jan. 21, 1808. Washington, 1808.

6. Letter from the Secretary of State (J. Madison), transmitting a list of the .. clerks in the Department of State, during .. 1807, with the .. salary allowed to each, *etc.* (Jan. 22, 1808.) [With the list.] Washington, 1808.

7. Letter from the Secretary of the Treasury (A. Gallatin) to the Chairman of the committee of ways and means [with an additional estimate of naval expenditure]. (Jan. 19, 1808.) Washington, 1808.

8. Letter from the Secretary of War (H. Dearborn), transmitting a list of the .. Clerks .. in the .. War Department, during .. 1807, with the amount of salary, *etc.* (Jan. 22, 1808.) [With the list.] Washington, 1808.

9. Letter from the Secretary of the Navy (R. Smith) to the Chairman of the committee on .. the .. military and naval establishments. (Jan. 22, 1808.) Washington, 1808.

10. Mefsage from the President, .. transmitting a treaty made .. 17 Nov. 1807, between the United States and the Ottaway, Chippeway, Wyandot, and Pottawatamie nations of Indians. Jan. 30, 1808. [With the treaty.] Washington, 1808.

11. Mefsage from the President, ... transmitting a treaty of limits between the United States and the Choctaw nation of Indians. Jan. 30, 1808. [With the treaty.] Washington, 1808.

12. Report of the Committee of claims .. on the .. memorial of C. Minifie. Jan. 30, 1808. Washington, 1808.

13. Mr. G. W. Campbell's Motion, proposing an amendment to the Constitution of the United States relative to the judges, *etc.* Jan. 30, 1808. Washington, 1808.

14. Mefsage from the President of the United States, transmitting an official communication of certain orders of the British government, against the maritime rights of neutrals, bearing date .. 11 Nov. 1808 [1807]. (Feb. 2, 1808.) Washington, 1808.

15. Report of the Postmaster General (G. Granger) on the petition of S. Whiting [in reference to certain monies claimed by him for services rendered], *etc.* (Jan. 8, 1808.) Washington, 1808.

16. Mefsage from the President .. communicating farther information in pursuance of two resolutions of the House [of Representatives] of 13 Jan. [1808]. Feb. 4, 1808. Washington, 1808.

17. Resolution of the Committee of commerce and manufactures .. to authorize the disposition of certain charts of the coast of North Carolina. Feb. 5, 1808. Washington, 1808.

18. Letter from the Secretary of the Treasury (A. Gallatin).. on the .. claim of M. Smith and D. Gates, *etc.* (Dec. 4, 1807.) Washington, 1808.

19. Letter from the Secretary of War (H. Dearborn), enclosing his report on the petition of A. Deloseair, *etc.* (Feb. 5, 1808.) Washington, 1808.

20. Mr. Burwell's Motion [in the House of Representatives of the United States of America, relative to armaments]. Feb. 8, 1808. Washington, 1808.

21. Mefsage from the President .. communicating information relative to the commencement of war by the Dey of Algiers against the United States. Feb. 9, 1808. Washington, 1808.

22. Letter from the Secretary of the Navy (R. Smith) to the Chairman of the committee on ... military and naval establishments, respecting the number of seamen, *etc.* Washington, 1808.

23. Letter from the Secretary .. (A. Gallatin) to the Chairman of the committee of commerce and manufactures [relative to an embargo laid on all ships and vessels in the ports and harbours of the United States]. (January 16, 1808.) Washington, 1808.

24. Mefsage from the President .. communicating information that the late differences between the United States and the Dey of Algiers have been amicably adjusted. (Feb. 15, 1808.) Washington, 1808.

25. Report of the Committee of claims .. on the .. petition of J. Shattuck, *etc.* Feb. 17, 1808. Washington, 1808.

26. Mefsage from the President .. communicating an additional report of the .. Commissioners appointed .. to regulate the laying out and making a road from Cumberland, in .. Maryland, to the State of Ohio. Feb. 19, 1808. Washington, 1808.

27. Letter and Report from the Secretary (A. Gallatin) on the resolution of the House [of Representatives], requesting a statement of the amount of tonnage employed in the exportation of articles

the produce or manufacture of the United States. (Jan. 18, 1808.) Washington, 1808.

28. Document accompanying the bill extending the terms of credit on revenue bonds in certain cases. Feb. 23, 1808. Washington, 1808.

29. Mr. Smilie's Motion [in the House of Representatives relative to its rules, etc.]. Feb. 24, 1808. Washington, 1808.

30. Resolutions of the General Assembly of Pennsylvania proposing an amendment to the Constitution of the United States, relative to the terms of continuance in .. office of the judges of the .. Courts of the United States. (Feb. 11, 12, 1808.) Washington, 1808.

31. Report of the Committee of claims .. on the .. petition of sundry inhabitants of Knox County, in .. Kentucky. Feb. 25, 1808. Washington, 1808.

32. Letter from the assistant Postmaster General (A. Bradley) inclosing a report .. in relation to the mail route from Alexandria to Fredericksburg. (Feb. 25, 1808.) Washington, 1808.

33. Message from the President .. inclosing a letter .. from the Secretary of War in relation to an increase of the army of the United States, and .. the raising of .. volunteers. (Feb. 25, 1808.) Washington, 1808.

34. Resolution of the General Assembly of Virginia, proposing an amendment to the Constitution of the United States authorizing State legislatures to remove from office their Senators in ... Congress, etc. (Jan. 13, 1808.) Washington, 1808.

35. Mr. Clopton's motion, proposing an amendment to the Constitution of the United States [submitted to the House of Representatives of the United States of America]. Feb. 29, 1808. Washington, 1808.

36. Document accompanying the bill to punish conspiracies to commit treason against the United States. 2 March, 1808. Washington, 1808.

37. Letter from the Secretary of the Treasury (A. Gallatin) .. enclosing a .. representation from the Commissioners to investigate land titles in the Territory of Michigan. (Jan. 5, 1808.) Washington, 1808.

38. Report of the Committee of Claims ... on the .. petition of D. Cotton. Mar. 7, 1808. Washington, 1808.

39. Letter from the Secretary of War (H. Dearborn) transmitting an additional report in relation to invalid pensioners. (Mar. 3, 1808.) Washington, 1808.

40. Message from the President .. communicating information of the situation of sundry parcels of ground in and adjacent to ... New Orleans. Mar. 7, 1808. Washington, 1808.

41. Report of the Committee appointed to inquire if .. compensation ought to be made to Captain Pike and his companions, for their services in exploring the Mississippi river, etc. Mar. 9, 1808. Washington, 1808.

42. Letter from the Secretary of War (H. Dearborn), transmitting a further report in relation to invalid pensioners. Mar. 10, 1808. Washington, 1808.

43. Message from the President .. transmitting two decrees; one, of the Emperor of the French, dated 17 Dec. 1807; the other, of the King of Spain, dated 3 Jan. 1808, in violation of the maritime rights of neutrals. Mar. 17, 1808. Washington, 1808.

44. Report of the Committee .. on the ... military and naval establishments, etc. Mar. 18, 1808. Washington, 1808.

45. Documents accompanying the bill for the relief of I. Briggs [in relation to his claims for surveying public roads]. Washington, 1808.

46. Message from the President ... transmitting a report [by I. Williams] on the .. military academy established at West Point. Mar. 18, 1808. Washington, 1808.

47. Mr. Rowan's motion [in the House of Representatives of the United States of America] for an inquiry into the conduct of H. Innis, District judge of the United States for .. Kentucky. Mar. 21, 1808. [With the documents relative thereto.] Washington, 1808.

48. Message from the President .. respecting the execution of the Act for fortifying the ports and harbours of the United States. Mar. 25, 1808. Washington, 1808.

49. Message from the President .. transmitting a statement of the militia of the several States, etc. Mar. 25, 1808. Washington, 1808.

50. Report of the Committee appointed ... to inquire what compensation should be allowed for issuing commissions ... relative to claims ... under the Act to provide for persons .. disabled .. in the revolutionary war. Mar. 28, 1808. Washington, 1808.

51. Message from the President .. communicating the report of the Surveyor of public buildings at Washington (B. H. Latrobe). Mar. 25, 1808. Washington, 1808.

52. Letter from the Secretary of the Treasury (A. Gallatin) to the chairman of the Committee of Claims ... accompanying the Bill to authorize the ... treasury to pay ... certain bills drawn by J. Armstrong, etc. Washing. 1808.

53. Report of the Committee appointed . . . jointly . . to consider and report what business is necessary to be done by Congress in their present session, etc. Washington, 1808.

54. Mr. G. W. Campbell's motion [in the House of Representatives of the United States of America, relative to the commerce of neutrals]. April 8, 1808. Washington, 1808.

55. Report of the Committee appointed on the . . . petitions of sundry inhabitants of the Counties of Randolph and St. Clair [in the Indiana Territory]. Apr. 11, 1808. Washington, 1808.

56. Mr. Poindexter's motion for an impeachment of Judge Bruin of the Mississippi Territory [in the House of Representatives of the United States of America]. April 11, 1808. Washington, 1808.

57. Documents accompanying the Bill making a farther appropriation for the support of government during the year 1808. Apr. 13, 1808. Washington, 1808.

58. Amendments of the Senate to the Bill, intituled, An act concerning public contracts. Apr. 13, 1808. Washington, 1808.

59. Documents accompanying a bill making appropriations for the support of an additional military force for the year 1808. Apr. 18, 1808. Washington, 1808.

60. Letter from the Secretary of the Treasury (A. Gallatin), transmitting his report on the petition of E. de Butts, and others, etc. (Apr. 14, 1808.) Washington, 1808.

61. Report of the Committee . . on the . . . Bill to make good a deficit in the appropriation of 1807, . . . and for other purposes. Apr. 21, 1808. Washington, 1808.

62. Further information and papers laid before the House . . relative to Brigadier General Wilkinson. April 25, 1808. Washington, 1808.

63. Letter from the Secretary of the Treasury (A. Gallatin), accompanied with sundry statements, prepared in obedience to . . "An act establishing a Mint and regulating the coins of the United States." (Apr. 23, 1808.) Washington, 1808.

64. Report of the Committee to whom were referred . . two messages from the President of the United States in relation to differences between the Dey of Algiers and the United States. Apr. 25, 1808. Washington, 1808. ✦

35 PUBLIC Documents. Thirteenth Congress, Second Session, 1813-1814. 2 vol. Fol°

Containing in Volume 1,

1. Letter from the Acting Secretary of the Treasury (W. Jones) transmitting a statement of unsettled accounts remaining in the office of the auditor of the Treasury. (Dec. 8, 1813.) [With the statement.] Washington, 1813.

2. Letter from the Secretary of the Navy (W. Jones) transmitting a general statement of the unsettled accounts in the office of the accountant of the Navy department; etc. [With the Statement.] (Dec. 11, 1813.) Washington, 1813.

3. Letter from the Secretary of War (J. Armstrong), transmitting statements . . . of monies . . . transferred from . . appropriations for the . . military department, etc. (Dec. 11, 1813.) [With the statements.] Washington, 1813.

4. Letter from the Secretary of War (J. Armstrong), transmitting a statement of the expenditure . . . of such sums of money as have been drawn from the Treasury . . for the use of the military department, from 1 Oct. 1812, to 30 Sept. 1813, etc. (Jan. 1, 1814.) [With the statement.] Washington, 1814.

5. Letter from the Secretary of the Navy (W. Jones) transmitting an exhibit of the expenditures . . . on account of the Navy, from 1 Oct. 1812, to 30 Sept. 1813; . . and of the unexpended balances of former appropriations, etc. (Jan. 1, 1814.) [With the Exhibit.] Washington, 1814.

6. Message of the President of the United States, transmitting the report of the Director of the Mint (R. Patterson) of the operations of that establishment during the last year. (Jan. 6, 1814.) [With the report.] Washington, 1814.

7. Letter from the Secretary of War (J. Armstrong), transmitting a statement of the expenditure of monies appropriated for the military establishment, for the year 1813. (Jan. 6, 1814.) [With the Statement.] Washington, 1814.

8. Letter from the [Acting] Secretary of the Treasury (W. Jones), transmitting his annual report, etc. (Jan. 8, 1814.) [With the report.] Washington, 1814.

9. Letter from the [Acting] Secretary of the Treasury (W. Jones), transmitting two statements of . . importations . . from Oct. 1, 1811, to Sept. 30, 1812. (Jan. 8, 1814.) [With the Statements.] Washington, 1814.

10. Message from the President . . transmitting an account of the contingent expenses of the Government for the year

1813. Jan. 14, 1814. [With the account.] Washington, 1814.

11. Letter from the Acting Secretary of the Treasury (W. Jones) transmitting the annual statement of .. duties and drawbacks, .. for the years 1810, 1811, and 1812. (Jan. 15, 1814.) [With the Statement.] Washington, 1814.

12. Letter from the Secretary of the Navy (W. Jones), transmitting the annual report of the Commissioners of the Navy Pension Fund. (Jan. 14, 1814.) [With the report.] Washing. 1814.

13. Letter from the Secretary of War (J. Armstrong) transmitting a report on the claims of the several States and Territories, for .. the .. Militia, etc. (Jan. 24, 1814.) [With the report.] Washington, 1814.

14. Letter from the Secretary of State (J. Monroe), transmitting a list of .... patents .. issued .. from Jan. 1, 1813, to Jan. 1, 1814. (Jan. 1, 1814.) [With the list.] Washington, 1814.

15. Letter from the Acting Secretary of the Treasury (W. Jones) transmitting his annual statements of moneys paid ... during the year 1813, for miscellaneous claims; of Contracts; ... and of payments made by collectors in 1812, for the relief of sick and disabled seamen. (Feb. 3, 1814.) [With the statements.] Washington, 1814.

In Volume 2,

16. Letter from the Acting Secretary of the Treasury (W. Jones), transmitting a report of the names of Clerks employed in the several offices of the Treasury, etc. (Feb. 2, 1814.) [With the report.] Washington, 1814.

17. Letter from the Acting Secretary of the Treasury (W. Jones), transmitting a statement of the exports of the United States, during the year ending 30 Sept. 1813. (Feb. 4, 1814.) [With the statement.] Washington, 1814.

18. Report of the Commissioners of the Sinking Fund, accompanied with sundry statements, etc. (Feb. 5, 1814.) Washington, 1814.

19. Letter from the Postmaster General (G. Granger) transmitting reports relative to public contracts; and .. the clerks employed in his office during the year 1813. (Feb. 9, 1814.) [With the reports.] Washington, 1814.

20. Letter from the Secretary of the Treasury (G. W. Campbell), transmitting the annual statement of district tonnage of the United States on ... 31 Dec. 1812; etc. Feb. 22, 1814. [With the statement.] Washington, 1814.

21. Letter from the Secretary of War (J. Armstrong), transmitting a statement .. of the clerks employed in the War department, etc. (Feb. 25, 1814.) [With the statement.] Washington, 1814.

22. Letter from the Secretary of the Treasury (G. W. Campbell) transmitting a statement of the emoluments of the officers employed in the collection of the customs, etc. (Feb. 28, 1814.) [With the statement.] Washington, 1814.

23. Letter from the Secretary of the Treasury (G. W. Campbell) transmitting a statement ... of monies disbursed for expenses of intercourse with the Barbary powers during the year 1813, etc. (March 3, 1814.) [With the statement.] Washington, 1814.

24. Letter from the Secretary of War (J. Armstrong), transmitting a statement of contracts for the supply of rations to the army of the United States. (March 28, 1814.) [With the statement.] Washington, 1814.

25. Letter from the Comptroller of the Treasury (E. Bacon), transmitting the annual list of unsettled balances on the books of the Treasury and Navy departments. (April 4, 1814.) Washington, 1814.

26. Letter from the Secretary of the Treasury (G. W. Campbell) transmitting .. sundry statements, prepared in obedience to the "Act establishing a mint and regulating the coins of the United States." (April 7, 1814.) [With the statements.] Washington, 1814.

27. Letter from the Secretary of the Treasury (G. W. Campbell) transmitting a revised statement of the debt of the United States, on 1 Jan. 1813, etc. (Apr. 12, 1814.) [With the statement.] Washington, 1814.

28. Message from the President .. transmitting Reports of the Secretary of War and Secretary of the Navy, etc. Feb. 3, 1814. [With the reports.] Washington, 1814.

29. In Senate, etc. [Report of the assistant postmaster general on unproductive post roads. March 21, 1814.] [Washington, 1814.]

30. Message from the President .. transmitting lists of the ministers and Consuls of the United States, who have been appointed since the adoption of the Constitution by the respective Presidents .. in the recess of the Senate; also, copies of .. Commissions, etc. April 9, 1814. Washington, 1814.

36 PUBLIC Documents, Thirteenth Congress, Third Session, 1814-1815. 1 vol. Fol°

Containing,

1. Letter from the Secretary of the Treasury (G. W. Campbell), transmitting his annual report, *etc.* (Sept. 23, 1814.) [With the report.] Washington, 1814.

2. Letter from the Secretary of the Treasury (S. H. Smith), transmitting .. sundry statements of the revenue, *etc.* (Oct. 13, 1814.) [With the statements.] Washington, 1814.

3. Letter from the Paymaster General (R. Brent), ... giving an account of the moneys disbursed for bounties and premiums. (Sept. 24, 1814.) Washington, 1814.

4. Letter from the Secretary of War (J. Monroe), transmitting a statement of the men .. recruited for the army .. during the present year. Nov. 10, 1814. [With the statement.] Washington, 1814.

5. Letter from the Secretary of the Navy (W. Jones), transmitting a statement of contracts made by that department, during the years 1813 and 1814. ... With the statement, *etc.* (Nov. 30, 1814.) Washington, 1814.

6. Letter from the Secretary of the Navy (B. Homans), transmitting an exhibit of the expenditure of moneys of that department from 1 Oct. 1813 to 30 Sept. 1814; and of unexpended balances, *etc.* (Jan. 5, 1815.) [With the exhibit.] Washington, 1815.

7. Letter from the Secretary of the Navy (B. W. Crowninshield), accompanied with statements of .. salaries, *etc.* Jan. 1815. Washington, 1815.

8. Letter from the Secretary of the Treasury (A. J. Dallas), accompanied with a statement exhibiting the sums respectively paid to each clerk in the ... Treasury Department for .. the year 1814. (Jan. 19, 1815.) Washington, 1815.

9. Letter from the Secretary of the Treasury (A. J. Dallas), transmitting the annual statement of the district tonnage of the United States on .. 31 Dec. 1813, *etc.* (Jan. 19, 1815.) [With the statement.] Washington, 1815.

10. Letter from the Secretary of the Navy (B. W. Crowninshield), transmitting a report on the .. Navy Pension Fund. (Jan. 23, 1815.) [With the report.] Washington, 1815.

11. Letter from the Secretary of State (J. Monroe), transmitting a list of ... patents .. obtained from 31 Dec. 1813 to 1 Jan. 1815. (Jan. 1, 1815.) [With the list.] Washington, 1815.

12. Letter from the Secretary of the Treasury (A. J. Dallas), transmitting a statement of .. drawbacks .. during the years 1811, 1812, and 1813. (Feb. 2, 1815.) [With the statement.] Washington, 1815.

13. Letter from the Secretary of the Treasury (A. J. Dallas), transmitting sundry statements to accompany the report on the state of the finances, made to Congress on the 23rd of Sept. last. (Feb. 3, 1815.) [With the statements.] Washington, 1815.

14. Letter from the Secretary of the Treasury (A. J. Dallas), transmitting a statement of moneys paid at the Treasury during the year 1814 for miscellaneous claims; .. and a statement of contracts, *etc.* (Feb. 4, 1815.) [With the statements.] Washington, 1815.

15. Report of the Commissioners of the Sinking Fund .. transmitting sundry statements, *etc.* (Feb. 6, 1815.) Washington, 1815.

16. Letter from the Secretary of the Treasury (A. J. Dallas), transmitting a statement of the exports of the United States, during the year ending 30 Sept. 1814. (Feb. 8, 1815.) [With the statement.] Washington, 1815.

17. Letter from the Secretary of War (J. Monroe), transmitting statements of contracts made by the War Department during the year 1814, and by the Commissary General of Purchases from 1 Jan. 1814 to .. 1 Nov. following. (Jan. 30, 1815.) [With the statements.] Washington, 1815.

18. Letter from the Postmaster General (R. J. Meigs), transmitting a report of unproductive post-roads, and a list of contracts made in the year 1814. (Feb. 8, 1815.) [With the report.] Washington, 1815.

19. Letter from the Secretary at War (J. Monroe), transmitting a statement of the expenditure .. for the contingent expenses of the military establishment, for .. 1814. (Feb. 20, 1815.) [With the statement.] Washington, 1815.

20. Letter from the Secretary of the Treasury (A. J. Dallas), transmitting sundry statements relating to the Mint Establishment. (Feb. 22, 1815.) [With the statements.] Washington, 1815.

21. Letter from the Acting Comptroller of the Treasury (N. Lufborough), transmitting statements of the accounts in the Treasury and Navy Departments, which have remained more than three years unsettled, *etc.* (Feb. 23, 1815.) [With the statements.] Washington, 1815.

22. Message from the President .. transmitting a report of the Postmaster General [dated Feb. 27, 1815], *etc.* Feb. 28, 1814 [1815]. [With the report.] Washington, 1815.

23. Letter from the Postmaster General (R. J. Meigs), transmitting a list of the .. clerks employed in the General Post Office, and the salary received by each. (Feb. 27, 1815.) [With the list.] Washington, 1815.

37 PUBLIC Documents, Fourteenth Congreſs, First Seſsion, 1815-1816. 2 vol. Folᵒ

Containing in Volume 1,

1. Letter from the Secretary of the Treasury (A. J. Dallas), transmitting his annual report upon the state of the finances of the United States. Dec. 7, 1815. [With the report, and an appendix of documents.] Washington, 1815.

2. Letter from the Secretary of War (W. H. Crawford), transmitting statements showing the application of moneys .. for the support of the Military Establishment, since the last Seſsion of Congreſs. (Dec. 8, 1815.) [With the statements.] Washington, 1815.

3. Letter from the Comptroller of the Treasury (J. Anderson), transmitting a list of balances, .. on the books of receipts and expenditures, .. and on the revenue books, of the Treasury, etc. (Dec. 8, 1815.) [With the lists.] Washington, 1815.

4. Letter from the Secretary of the Navy (B. W. Crowninshield), transmitting a statement of the expenditures .. on account of the Navy Department, from 1 Oct. 1814 to 30 Sept. 1815, .. and of the unexpended balances, etc. (Dec. 14, 1815.) [With the statement.] Washington, 1815.

5. Letter from the Secretary of the Treasury (A. J. Dallas), transmitting two statements of .. importations .. from 1 Oct. 1813 to 30 Sept. 1814. (Dec. 18, 1815.) [With the statements.] Washington, 1815.

6. Letter from the Secretary of the Treasury (A. J. Dallas), transmitting the annual statement of the duties of customs for the year 1814; and the sales of public lands for the year ending 30 Sept. 1815; also, statements relating to the internal duties of direct tax, for .. 1814. (Dec. 20, 1815.) [With the statements.] 3 parts. Washington, 1815.

7. Letter from the Secretary of the Navy (B. W. Crowninshield), transmitting statements of moneys transferred .. in the Navy Department. (Dec. 18, 1815.) [With the statements.] Washington, 1815.

8. Letter from the Secretary of the Treasury (A. J. Dallas), transmitting .. a statement of .. duties and drawbacks, .. during the years 1812, 1813, and 1814.

(Dec. 27, 1815.) [With the statement.] Washington, 1815.

In Volume 2,

9. Letter from the Secretary of the Navy (B. W. Crowninshield), transmitting a statement of the contracts made by the United States' Navy Department, in the year 1815. (Jan. 1, 1816.) Washington, 1816.

10. Letter from the Secretary of the Treasury (A. J. Dallas), transmitting the estimates of appropriations for the service of the year 1816. (Jan. 2, 1816.) [With the estimates.] Washington, 1816.

11. Letter from the Secretary of War (W. H. Crawford), transmitting statements of the expenditure and application of such sums of money as have been drawn from the Treasury, .. for the use of the military department, from 1 Oct. 1814 to 30 Sept. 1815, etc. (Jan. 2, 1816.) [With the statements.] Washington, 1815.

12. Letter from the Postmaster General (R. J. Meigs), transmitting a list of contracts made by that department in the year 1815. [With the list.] (Jan. 15, 1816.) Washington, 1816.

13. Letter from the Comptroller of the Treasury (J. Anderson), transmitting a statement of the balances which have remained due more than three years, prior to the 30 Sept. last, on the books of the Accountant of the Navy Department. (Jan. 17, 1816.) Washington, 1816.

14. Letter from the Secretary of the Treasury (A. J. Dallas), transmitting the annual statement of the district tonnage of the United States, .. 31 Dec. 1814, etc. [With the statement.] (Jan. 20, 1816.) Washington, 1816.

15. Letter from the Secretary of the Treasury (A. J. Dallas), transmitting a statement of the valuation of lands, lots, and dwelling houses, and of slaves, in the several States, etc. Jan. 25, 1816. [With the statement.] Washington, 1816.

16. Letter from the Secretary of War (W. H. Crawford), transmitting the annual statement of contracts made by the War Department for the year 1815. (Jan. 23, 1816.) [With the statement.] Washington, 1816.

17. Letter from the Secretary of the Treasury (A. J. Dallas), transmitting statements of the receipts and expenditures of the Treasury of the United States, from 3 March 1789 to 31 March 1815, etc. (Jan. 25, 1816.) [With the statements.] Washington, 1816.

18. Letter from the Secretary of State (J. Monroe), transmitting a list of the

names of persons to whom patents have been granted, etc. [in 1815]. (Feb. 1, 1816.) [With the list.] Washington, 1816.

19. Letter from the Secretary of War (W. H. Crawford), to the Chairman of the Committee of Ways and Means, transmitting a detailed estimate of the sums necessary for the Ordnance Department for the year 1816. (3 Feb. 1816.) [With the estimate.] Washington, 1816.

20. Letter from the Secretary of the Treasury (A. J. Dallas), transmitting . . . comparative statements between the annual amount of the expenditures of the military and naval establishments, etc. Feb. 6, 1816. [With the statements.] Washington, 1816.

21. Report of the Commissioners of the Sinking Fund, shewing the measures which have been authorized by the Board subsequent to their last Report, of the 6th of February, . . so far as completed. (Feb. 7th, 1816.) Washington, 1816.

22. Letter from the Secretary of the Treasury (A. J. Dallas), presenting . . . a statement of the valuation of lands, lots, dwelling-houses, and slaves. (Feb. 13, 1816.) [With the statement.] Washington, 1816.

23. Letter from the Secretary of the Treasury (A. J. Dallas) transmitting a statement of the exports of the United States, during the year ending . . 30 Sept. 1815. (Feb. 14, 1816.) [With the statement.] Washington, 1816.

24. Letter from the Secretary of the Treasury (A. J. Dallas), transmitting a statement of the emoluments of the officers employed in the collection of the customs for . . 1815. (Feb. 22, 1816.) [With the statement.] Washington, 1816.

25. Letter from the Secretary of the Treasury, transmitting a statement of the additions which have been made to the funded public debt, and to the floating public debt, since . . . 30 Dec. last. [1815.] (Feb. 28, 1816.) [With the statement.] Washington, 1816.

26. Letter from the Postmaster General (R. J. Meigs) transmitting a list of the unproductive post-offices, for the year 1815. (Mar. 6, 1816.) [With the list.] Washington, 1816.

27. Message from the President of the United States, transmitting a statement of the militia of the United States, according to the latest returns received by the War Department. (March 9, 1816.) Washington, 1816.

28. Message from the President of the United States, transmitting a report of the Secretary of the Treasury (A. J. Dallas) of certain expenses which have been

incurred for public edifices and improvements in . . Washington under the authority of the United States ; . . March 11, 1816. Washington, 1816.

29. Letter from the Secretary of the Treasury (A. J. Dallas) transmitting in obedience to a resolution of the House of Representatives . . an abstract of the valuation of lands, slaves, and dwelling-houses in . . Maryland ; etc. (March 16, 1816.) Washington, 1816.

30. Letter from the Comptroller (J. Anderson) transmitting abstracts of the accounts on the books of the Accountant of the War Department, which . . remain unsettled. (March 18, 1816.) Washington, 1816.

31. Report of the Secretary of the Treasury, respecting the valuation of lands, lots, dwelling-houses, slaves, etc. in . . Pennsylvania, etc. (Mar. 20, 1816.) Washington, 1816.

32. Report of the Secretary of the Treasury, in relation to expenses in the prosecution of offences against the United States, etc. (Mar. 29, 1816.) Washington, 1816.

33. Letter from the Secretary of the Treasury, transmitting statements relative to the operations of the Mint of the United States for the year 1815. April 8, 1816. [With the statements.] Washington, 1816.

34. Letter from the Secretary of War (W. H. Crawford), transmitting statements of the . . . clerks employed in the . . . War Department, etc. April 11, 1816. [With the statements.] Washington, 1816.

35. Letter from the Secretary of the Treasury (A. J. Dallas), transmitting a statement of loans made to the United States, by banks within the same, since March 1, 1812. (12 Apr. 1816.) [With the statement.] Washington, 1816.

36. Message from the President (James Madison) of the United States, transmitting a report of the Secretary of State (J. Monroe) . . of the number of impressed American seamen confined in Dartmoor prison ; the number surrendered ; etc. April 29, 1816. [With the report.] Washington, 1816.

38 PUBLIC Documents, Fourteenth Congress, Second Session, 1816-1817. 3 vol. Fol°.

Containing in Volume 1,

1. Letter from the Secretary of the Treasury (W. H. Crawford), transmitting his annual report of the state of the finances. (Dec. 16, 1816.) [With the statement.] Washington, 1816.

J. Meigs), transmitting a list of contracts made by him, in the year 1816, for transporting the mails. (Feb. 13, 1817.) [With the list.] Washington, 1817.

24. Letter from the Postmaster General (R. J. Meigs), transmitting a list of unproductive post roads for the year 1817. (Feb. 19, 1817.) [With the list.] Washington, 1817.

25. Letter from the Comptroller of the Treasury (J. Anderson), transmitting a statement of balances, which have remained due for more than three years prior to Sept. 30, 1816, on the books of the Accountant of the Navy. [With the statement.] Washington, 1817. 8°

26. Letter from the Acting Secretary of War (G. Graham), transmitting a statement showing the expenditure of the moneys appropriated for the contingent expenses of the military establishment for the year 1816. [With the statement.] Washington, 1817.

27. Letter from the Secretary of the Treasury (W. H. Crawford), transmitting a statement of the emoluments and expenditures of the officers of the customs in the year 1816. (Feb. 24, 1817.) [With the statement.] Washington, 1817.

28. Letter from the Secretary of the Treasury W. H. Crawford), transmitting sundry statements relative to the operations of the Mint of the United States. (Feb. 27, 1817.) [With the statements.] Washington, 1817.

In Volume 3,

29. Letter from T. T. Tucker, Treasurer of the United States, transmitting his accounts for 1816. [With the accounts.] Washington, 1817.

30. Letter from the Secretary of the Treasury (W. H. Crawford), transmitting statements of the importations of goods, wares, and merchandise, in American and foreign vessels, etc. [With the statements.] Washington, 1817.

39 PUBLIC Documents published by the Congress of the United States of America, 1815-1845. Washington, 1815-1845. 8°

[N. B. Those marked with a * are wanting.]

14th Cong. 1st Sess. 1815-16.
House Documents, N° 1 to 90, in 2 vol.

14th Cong. 2nd Sess. 1816-17.
Senate Documents, N° 1 to 123, in 1 vol.
House Documents, N° 1 to 102, in 2 vol.

15th Cong. 1st Sess. 1817-18.
Senate Documents, N° 1 to 193, in 2 vol.
House Documents, N° 1 to 202, in 8 vol.
Reports of Committees [imperfect series], 1 vol.

15th Cong. 2d Sess. 1818-19.
Senate Documents, N° 1 to 102, in 2 vol.
House Documents, N° 1 to 150, in 8 vol.

16th Cong. 1st Sess. 1819-20.
Senate Documents, N° 1 to 135, in 2 vol.
House Documents, N° 1 to 123, in 9 vol.
Reports of Comm. N° 1 to 98, in 1 vol.

16th Cong. 2d Sess. 1820-21.
Senate Documents, N° 1 to 120, in 5 vol.
House Documents, N° 1 to 112, in 9 vol.
Reports of Comm. N° 1 to 70, in 1 vol.

17th Cong. 1st Sess. 1821-22.
Senate Documents, N° 1 to 95, in 3 vol.
House Documents, N° 1 to 134, in 9 vol.*
Reports of Comm. N° 1 to 111, in 2 vol.

17th Cong. 2d Sess. 1822-23.
Senate Documents, N° 1 to 43, in 2 vol.
House Documents, N° 1 to 111, in 9 vol.
Reports of Comm. N° 1 to 105, in 2 vol.

18th Cong. 1st Sess. 1823-24.
Senate Documents, N° 1 to 80, in 3 vol.
House Documents, N° 1 to 163, in 12 vol.*
Reports of Comm. N° 1 to 133, in 2 vol.*

18th Cong. 2d Sess. 1824-25.
Senate Documents, N° 1 to 45, in 4 vol.*
House Documents, N° 1 to 110, in 9 vol.*
Reports of Comm. N° 1 to 90, in 2 vol.*

19th Cong. 1st Sess. 1825-26.
House Documents, N° 1 to 102, in 5 vol.*
Senate Documents, N° 1 to 184, in 10 vol.*
Reports of Comm. N° 1 to 232, in 2 vol.*

19th Cong. 2d Sess. 1826-27.
Senate Documents, N° 1 to 72, in 3 vol.*
House Documents, N° 1 to 146, in 11 vol.*
Reports of Comm. N° 1 to 102, in 3 vol.*

20th Cong. 1st Sess. 1828-29.
Senate Documents, N° 1 to 207, in 5 vol.
House Documents, N° 1 to 288, in 7 vol.
Reports of Comm. N° 1 to 270, in 4 vol.

20th Cong. 2d Sess. 1828-29.
Senate Documents, N° 1 to 105, in 2 vol.
House Documents, N° 1 to 146, in 6 vol.*
Reports of Comm. N° 1 to 104, in 1 vol.

21st Cong. 1st Sess. 1829-30.
Senate Documents, N° 1 to 146, in 2 vol.*
House Documents, N° 1 to 381, in 4 vol.
Reports of Comm. N° 1 to 419, in 3 vol.

21st Cong. 2d Sess. 1830-31.
Senate Documents, N° 1 to 76, in 2 vol.
House Documents, N° 1 to 140, in 4 vol.
Reports of Comm. N° 1 to 119, in 1 vol.

22nd Cong. 1st Sess. 1831-32.
Senate Documents, N° 1 to 182, in 3 vol.*
House Documents, N° 1 to 308, in 8 vol.
[Wanting N° 83 to 308, vol. 3-7.]
Reports of Comm. N° 1 to 513, in 5 vol.*

22nd Cong. 2d Sess. 1832-33.
Senate Documents, N° 1 to 85, in 2 vol.
[Wanting N° 85, or vol. 2.]
House Documents, N° 1 to 148, in 3 vol.
Reports of Comm. N° 1 to 128, } 1 vol.
Resolutions   N° 1 to 3, }

23rd Cong. 1st Seſs. 1833-34.
Senate Documents, Nº 1 to 514, in 14 vol.*
House Documents, Nº 1 to 523, in 6 vol.*
Reports of Comm. Nº 1 to 560, in 5 vol.*

23rd Cong. 2d Seſs. 1834-35.
Senate Documents, Nº 1 to 154, in 4 vol.*
House Documents, Nº 1 to 199, in 5 vol.*
Reports of Comm. Nº 1 to 142, in 2 vol.*

24th Cong. 1st Seſs. 1835-36.
Senate Documenrs, Nº 1 to 430, in 6 vol.
House Documenrs, Nº 1 to 297, in 7 vol.
Reports of Comm. Nº 1 to 857, in 3 vol.

24th Cong. 2d Seſs. 1836-37.
Senate Documents, Nº 1 to 226, in 3 vol.
House Documents, Nº 1 to 189, in 4 vol.
Reports of Comm. Nº 1 to 327, in 3 vol.

25th Cong. 1st Seſs. 1837.
Senate Documents, Nº 1 to 37, in 1 vol.*
House Documents, Nº 1 to 54, ⎫ in 1 vol.
Reports of Comm. Nº 1 to 3, ⎭

25th Cong. 2d Seſs. 1837-38.
Senate Documents, Nº 1 to 509, in 6 vol.
House Documents, Nº 1 to 467, in 12 vol.
Reports of Comm. Nº 1 to 1068, in 4 vol.*

25th Cong. 3d Seſs. 1838-39.
Senate Documents, Nº 1 to 307, in 5 vol.
House Documents, Nº 1 to 253, in 6 vol.
Reports of Comm. Nº 1 to 325, in 2 vol.

26th Cong. 1st Seſs. 1839-40.
Senate Documents, Nº 1 to 621, in 8 vol.
House Documents, Nº 1 to 265, in 7 vol.
Reports of Comm. Nº 1 to 716, in 4 vol.

26th Cong. 2d Seſs. 1840-41.
Senate Documents, Nº 1 to 238, in 6 vol.*
House Documents, Nº 1 to 124, in 6 vol.*
Reports of Comm. Nº 1 to 249, in 1 vol.*

27th Cong. 1st Seſs. 1841.
Senate Documents, Nº 1 to 124, in 1 vol.
House Documents, Nº 1 to 63, ⎫ in 1 vol.
Reports of Comm. Nº 1 to 11, ⎭

27th Cong. 2d Seſs. 1841-42.
Senate Documents, Nº 1 to 444, in 5 vol.
House Documents, Nº 1 to 1106, in 5 vol.
Reports of Comm. Nº 1 to 293, in 6 vol.

27th Cong. 3rd Seſs. 1842-43.
Senate Documents, Nº 1 to 247, in 4 vol.
House Documents, Nº 1 to 220, in 8 vol.
Reports of Comm. Nº 1 to 296, in 4 vol.

28th Cong. 1st Seſs. 1843-44.
Senate Documents, Nº 1 to 243, in 7 vol.
House Documents, Nº 1 to 280, in 6 vol.*
Reports of Comm. Nº 1 to 582, in 3 vol.*

28th Cong. 2d Seſs. 1844-45.
Senate Documents, Nº 1 to 277, in 13 vol.
  [Wanting vol. 4, 5, 6, and 10.]
House Documents, Nº 1 to 239, in 5 vol.
Reports of Comm. Nº 1 to 438, in 1 vol.

40 SUPPLEMENT to the Digest of
the Revenue Laws paſſed during the
second Seſſion of the Eighth Congreſs, ending March 3, 1805. [See
ADDINGTON, L.] Philadelphia, 1805.
12mo.

41 MESSAGE from the President of
the United States, communicating
discoveries made in exploring the
Miſſouri, Red River and Washita, by
Captains Lewis and Clark, Doctor
Sibley and Mr. Dunbar. With a statistical account of the countries adjacent. Washington, 1806. 8vo.

42 CONSTITUTION of the United
States of America as proposed by the
Convention held at Philadelphia, Sept.
17, 1787, and since ratified by the
several States : with the amendments
thereto. Published by order of the
Senate. Washington, 1806. 8º

43 DOCUMENTS accompanying the
Meſſage of the President, .. November 8, 1808. Washington, 1808. 8º

44 ANALYSIS of the late correspondence between our Administration
[i. e. of the United States of America]
and Great Britain and France. With
an attempt to shew what are the real
causes of the failure of the negocia-
tion. Boston [1808 ?]. 8º

45 REPORT of the Secretary of the
Treasury (A. Gallatin) on the subject
of public roads and canals : made in
pursuance of a resolution of Senate of
March 2, 1807. Washing. 1808. 8º

46 THE CONSTITUTIONS of the
United States ; according to the latest
amendments. To which are prefixed,
the Declaration of Independence, the
Federal Constitution, and the Bill of
Rights of the State of Virginia. Winchester, 1811. 8º

47 RESPECTFUL Observations on ..
the bill in relation to " the establishment of a quartermaster's department," in lieu of the existing military
agencies so far as it may affect the
office of the purveyor of public supplies. [Washington, 1812 ?] 8º

48 REPORT of the Committee on
Indian affairs relative to excitements
on the part of British subjects of the
Indians, to commit hostility against the
United States, etc. Washing. 1812. 8º

49 AN ADDRESS by members of the House of Representatives to the Congreſs of the United States to their Constituents on the ſubject of the war with Great Britain. Reprinted from the Alexandria edition. Baltimore, 1812. 8°

50 To the Hon. the Senate and House of Representatives of the United States in Congreſs aſſembled, the Representatives of the Commonwealth of Maſſachusetts [concerning a war with Great Britain, etc.]. Few MS. notes. [Washington? 1812.] 8°

51 THE AMERICAN'S Guide. The Constitutions of the United States of America with the latest amendments: also the Declaration of Independence, Articles of Confederation, with the Federal Constitution and acts for the government of the Territories. New York, 1813. 12°

52 THOUGHTS in a series of letters, in answer to a question respecting the division of the States. By a Massachusetts Farmer. [Boston, 1813.] 8°

53 STATE Papers and Publick Documents, from the acceſſion of G. Washington to the Presidency, exhibiting a complete view of our foreign relations since that time. 1789 (to 1815). Vol. 1-8. [Vol. i, contains the papers 1789-96; ii, 1797; iii, 1797-1801; iv, 1801-06; v, 1806-08; vi, 1808-09; vii, 1809-11; viii, 1811-15. Vol. 4 is dated 1814.] Boston, 1815. 8vo.

54 AN ABSTRACT of the public documents, exhibiting the measures recommended by the administration, and the proceedings in relation to them in Congreſs, tending to subject the people of the United States to a military conscription, .. and a naval impreſſment. Georgetown, 1815. 8°

55 DEBATE in the House of Representatives on the Seminole War in January and February, 1819. Washington, 1819. 12°

56 CONSTITUTIONAL LAW: comprising the Declaration of Independ-

ence, the Articles of Confederation, the Constitution of the United States, and the Constitutions of the several States composing the Union. Washington, 1820. 12°

57 JOURNAL of the first Seſſion of the Senate of the United States of America, .. from March 4, 1789, to the third Seſſion of the thirteenth Congreſs, March 3, 1815. 5 vol. Washington, 1820-21. 8vo.

58 SECRET Journals of the acts and proceedings of Congreſs from the first meeting thereof (May 10, 1775) to the diſſolution of the Confederation, by the adoption of the Constitution of the United States. 4 vol. Boston, 1821-20. 8°

59 CENSUS for 1820. Published by authority of an Act of Congreſs, under the direction of the Secretary of State. Washington, 1821. Folo

60 CENSUS of the United States. [1820.] [Washington? 1820.] 8°

61 HISTORY of the United States of America: with a brief account of some of the principal Empires and States of ancient and modern times. With questions. [By Salma Hale.] Keene, N. H. 1822. 12°

62 JOURNALS of the American Congreſs from 1774 to 1788. 4 vol. Washington, 1823. 8vo.

63 DIGEST of Accounts of Manufacturing Establishments in the United States, and of their manufactures. Made under the direction of the Secretary of State, etc. Washington, 1823. Folo

64 A DIGEST of the commercial regulations of the different foreign nations, with which the United States have intercourse. Washing. 1824. 8°

65 DISCUSSION of the Greek question in the House of Representatives. [Boston, 1824.] 8°

66 INDEX to Documents and Reports, House of Representatives, United States, 1789-1839. Bound in 1 vol. Washington, 1824-39. 8°

1. Index to the Executive Communications made to the House of Representatives,

566 **U N I**

from the commencement of the present form of Government until the end of the 14th Congreſs, inclusive; also an index to all the printed reports, alphabetically arranged. Washington, 1824.

2. Index to the Executive Communications and Reports of Committees made to the House of Representatives, from Dec. 3, 1817, to March 3, 1823, 15th, 16th and 17th Congreſes. Washing. 1823.

3. A Digested Index to the Executive Documents and Reports of Committees of the House of Representatives, from the 18th to the 21st Congreſs, both included. Washington, 1832.

4. Index to the Executive Documents and Reports of Committees of the House of Representatives, from the 22nd to the 25th Congreſs, both included, commencing Dec. 1831, and ending March, 1839. Washington [1839].

67 A GENERAL Outline of the United States of North America, her resources and prospects. Philadelphia, 1825. 8vo.

68 INFANTRY Tactics; or, rules for the exercises and manœuvres of the infantry of the United States Army. 2 vol. Washington, 1825. 8°

69 INFANTRY Tactics; or rules for the exercises and manœuvres of the infantry of the United States Army. Second edition. Washing. 1825. 8°

70 MILITARY Laws of the United States; to which is prefixed the Constitution of the United States. Compiled and published under authority of the War Department; by Truman Croſs. Washington, 1825. 8°

71 REGISTER of Debates in Congreſs .. (Dec. 6, 1824 to Oct. 6, 1837). Together with an appendix, containing .. important state papers and public documents. .. To which are added, the laws enacted, etc. 14 vol. in 29 parts. Washing. 1825-37. 8°

72 LAWS of the United States, in relation to the naval establishment, and the marine corps; .. to the end of the first Seſſion of the nineteenth Congreſs. Washington, 1826. 12°

73 A CONNECTED View of the whole internal Navigation of the United States, natural and artificial. Philadelphia, 1826. 8vo.

74 JOURNAL of the House of Representatives of the United States, from the first Seſſion of the first Congreſs, March 4, 1789, to the third Seſſion of the thirteenth Congreſs, March 2, 1815. Reprinted by order of the House of Representatives. 9 vol. Washington, 1826. 8vo.

75 MESSAGE from the President of the United States, transmitting information in relation to the construction of a road from Little Rock to Cantonment Gibson. Washington, 1826. 8°

76 LETTER from the Secretary of War (J. Barbour) transmitting a Report of the chief engineer (A. Macomb), in relation to the road through Ohio, Indiana, and Illinois. Washington, 1826. 8°

77 LETTER from the Secretary of War (J. Barbour), transmitting a Report [by W. G. M'Neill] upon the subject of an extension of the national road from Cumberland to the District of Columbia. Washington, 1826. 8°

78 THE PUBLIC and General Statutes paſſed by the Congreſs of the United States of America, from 1789 to 1827 inclusive, whether expired, repealed, or in force; arranged in chronological order, with marginal references, and a copious index. To which is added the Constitution of the United States, and an appendix. Published under the inspection of J. Story. 3 vol. Boston, 1827. 8vo.

79 AN ACCOUNT of the receipts and expenditures of the United States; for the year 1826 (1827 and 1828). 3 vol. Washington, 1827. Fol°

80 LETTER from the Secretary of War (J. Barbour), transmitting a Report [by S. H. Long] of surveys of proposed routes of a national road from the City of Washington to Buffalo. Washington, 1827. 8°

81 LETTER from the Secretary of War (J. Barbour), transmitting Reports and Drawings [by J. Knight] relative to the national road from Wheeling to the seat of government in the State of Misouri. Washington, 1827. 8°

82 LETTER from the Secretary of War (J. Barbour), transmitting a Report [by J. Knight] on the subject of the national road between Zanesville and Columbus. Washington, 1826 [1827]. 8°

83 LETTER from the Secretary of War (J. Barbour), transmitting the information required by a resolution of the House of Representatives.. in relation to a canal from Lake Pontchartrain to the Mifsifsippi River. [With the report, plan, and estimate, by S. Bernard and W. T. Poufsin.] Washington, 1827. 8°

84 LETTER from the Secretary of War (J. Barbour), transmitting a Report and Map of the survey of Saugatuck Harbour and River [by J. Anderson]. Washington, 1827. 8°

85 LETTER from the Secretary of War (J. Barbour), transmitting a report, map, and estimate of the Chesapeake and Ohio Canal to Alexandria, in the District of Columbia [by J. Geddes]. Washington, 1828. 8°

86 MESSAGE from the President of the United States, transmitting the correspondence between this government and that of Great Britain on the subject of the claims of the two Governments to the territory west of the Rocky Mountains. Washing.1828. 8°

87 LETTER from the Secretary of War (J. Barbour), transmitting a Report [by J. J. Abert] of the surveys of the Kennebec River, and of contemplated routes for canals, connected with the waters of the said river. Washington, 1828. 8°

88 [LETTERS laid before the Senate, respecting obstructions at the mouth of the Pascagoula River.] [Washington, 1828.] 8°

89 MESSAGE from the President .. transmitting a copy of the opinion of the Attorney General (W. Wirt) upon the construction of the award of the Emperor of Rufsia under the treaty of Ghent, etc. Washington, 1828. 8°

90 LETTER from the Secretary of War (J. Barbour) transmitting the information required by a resolution of the House of Representatives, in relation to the works of internal improvement undertaken or projected by the general government from 1824 to 1826. Washington, 1828. 8°

91 LETTER from the Secretary of War (J. Barbour) transmitting a Report of the chief Engineer, accompanied by a report [by S. Bernard and W. T. Poufsin] upon the reconnoifsance of a route acrofs the Cumberland Mountains of the national road from Washington to New Orleans. Washington, 1828. 8°

92 CHESAPEAKE and Ohio Canal. Letter from the Secretary of War (J. Barbour) transmitting estimates of the cost of making a canal from Cumberland to George Town [by J. Geddes and N. S. Roberts]. Washington, 1828. 8°

93 OFFICIAL Record from the War Department, of the proceedings of the Court Martial, which tried, and the orders of Gen. Jackson for shooting, the six militia men; together with official letters ... showing that these American citizens were inhumanly and illegally mafsacred. Washington, 1828. 8° ·

94 OFFICIAL Record from the War Department of the proceedings of the Court Martial which tried, and the orders of General Jackson for shooting, the six militia men [J. Webb, and others], etc. Fourth edition. Washington, 1828. 8°

95 THE CONSTITUTION of the United States; .. the Rules of the Senate and of the House of Representatives; with Jefferson's Manual. Printed by order of the Senate, etc. Washington, 1828. 12°

96 A GEOGRAPHICAL View of the United States. Second edition. Boston, 1828. 8vo.

97 ESSAY on the warehousing system and government credits of the United States. Philadel. 1828. 8°

98 JOURNAL of the executive proceedings of the Senate of the United

States of America: from the commencement of the first to the termination of the nineteenth Congrefs.
Vol. 1-2. [Vol. 1, 1789 to 1805; vol.
2, 1805 to 1815; vol. 3, 1815 to 1829.
Vol. 3, wanting.] Washington, 1828.
8vo.

99 LAWS of the United States, Resolutions of Congrefs under the Confederation, treaties, proclamations,
Spanish regulations, and other documents respecting the public lands [to
March, 1833]. Compiled by M. St.
C. Clarke], in obedience to a resolution of the House of Representatives,
etc. [With an appendix, by J. M.
White, entitled: Documents relating
to the settlement and confirmation of
private land claims in Florida.] 2 vol.
Washington, 1828-36. 8vo.

100 AN ACCOUNT of memorials presented to Congrefs, during its last
sefsion, . . praying that the mails may
not be transported, nor post-offices
kept open, on the Sabbath. New
York, 1829. 8°

101 THE DIPLOMATIC Correspondence of the American Revolution;
Being the Letters of Benjamin Franklin, Silas Deane, and others, concerning the Foreign Relations of the
United States during the Revolution;
together with the Letters in reply
from the Secret Committee of Congrefs, and the Secretary of Foreign
Affairs; also the entire Correspondence of the French Ministers, Gerard
and Luzerne, with Congrefs. Edited
by Jared Sparks. 12 vol. Boston,
1829-30. 8vo.

102 BANK of the United States.
Congrefs, House of Representatives,
April 13, 1830. [A report from the
Committee of Ways and Means on
that part of the President's Mefsage
which related to the United States
Bank. With an appendix.] [Wash-
ington, 1830.] 8°

103 CIRCULAR from the Solicitor of
the Treasury, with regulations to be
observed by district attorneys, *etc.*
Washington, 1830. 8°

104 TABLE of the Post Offices in
the United States, arranged by States
and Counties, as they were Oct. 1,
1830; with a supplement, *etc.* Washington, 1831. 12°

105 FIFTH Census; or, enumeration of the inhabitants of the United
States, 1830. To which is prefixed,
a schedule of the whole number of
persons within the several districts of
the United States, taken according to
the acts of 1790, 1800, 1810, [and]
1820. Published by authority of an
Act of Congrefs. Washington, 1832.
Fol°

106 REVIEW of the Veto; containing an examination of the principles
of the President's Mefsage, and his
objections to the Bill to modify and
continue the Act rechartering the
Bank of the United States. Philadelphia, 1832. 8°

107 REVIEW of the Veto; containing an examination of the principles
of the President's Mefsage, and his
objections to the Bill to modify and
continue the Act rechartering the
Bank of the United States. [Phila-
delphia, 1832?] 8°

108 REPORTS of the Committee of
Inquiry appointed March 14, 1832,
by the House of Representatives at
Washington, concerning the Bank of
the United States. Washing. 1832. 8°

109 AMERICAN State Papers. Documents Legislative and Executive, of
the Congrefs of the United States,
from the First Sefsion of the First to
the Third Sefsion of the Thirteenth
Congrefs, inclusive. Commencing
March 3, 1789, and ending March 3,
1815. Selected and edited, under the
Authority of Congrefs, by Walter
Lowrie, Secretary of the Senate, and
Matthew St. Clair Clarke, Clerke of
the House of Representatives. 21 vol.
Washington, 1832-34. Fol.

These 21 volumes of State Papers are arranged in ten clafses: viz.

CLASS

1. Foreign Relations, including the Annual Mefsages of the Presidents,

(March 3, 1789, to 1st Seſsion, 17th Congreſs inclusive, May 8, 1822. 4 vol.)

2. Indian Affairs (March 3, 1789, to March 3, 1827. 2 vol.) comprising 1st, All documents accompanying Indian Treaties; 2nd, Indian Maſsacres and Depredations; 3rd, Indian Wars; 4th, Efforts made for their benefit in civilization, agriculture, and the Mechanical Arts.

3. Finances (March 3, 1789, to May 8, 1822. 3 vol.) embracing 1st, Public Debt, and Public Credit; 2nd, Revenue, direct and indirect taxation; 3rd, The Currency; 4th, The Mint; 5th, Bank of the United States; 6th, General principles of the annual estimates; 7th, General principles of the expenses of collecting revenue; 8th, The table of receipts and expenditures.

4. Commerce and Navigation (exclusive of External Matters embraced in the First Claſs) (March 4, 1789, to March 3, 1823. 3 vol.) embracing 1st, Imports and Exports: 2nd, Fisheries; 3rd, Light House establishment; 4th, Improvement of harbours, rivers, roads, and canals; 5th, Tonnage; 6th, Coasting Trade.

5. Military Affairs (March 3, 1789, to Feb. 28, 1825. 2 vol.) 1st, Army; 2nd, Military Academy; 3rd, Fortifications; 4th, Armament, Arms; 5th, National armories; 6th, Militia.

6. Naval Affairs (March 3, 1789, to March 5, 1825, 1 vol.)

7. Post Office Department (March 4, 1789, to March 2, 1833. 1 vol.)

8. Public Lands (March 3, 1789, to May 27, 1824. 3 vol.)

9. Claims (March 4, 1789, to March 3, 1823. 1 vol.)

10. Miscellaneous (March 3, 1789, to March 3, 1823. 2 vol.)

110 AMERICAN State Papers. Documents Legislative and Executive, of the Congreſs of the United States, in relation to the Public Lands, from the First Seſsion of the First Congreſs to the First Seſsion of the Twenty-third Congreſs; March 4, 1789, to June 15, 1834. Selected and edited, under the authority of the Senate of the United States, by Walter Lowrie, Secretary of the Senate. 5 vol. [Vol. I. March 4, 1789, to Feb. 27, 1809; II. June 12, 1809, to Feb. 14, 1815; III. Dec. 22, 1815, to May 26, 1824; IV. Dec. 7, 1824, to Jan. 2, 1828; v. Jan. 4, 1828, to Jan. 21, 1834.] Washington, 1834. Folº

The first three volumes, containing Nº 1-413, are merely a reprint of the three volumes of Class 8 of the preceding work, and vols. 4 and 5 are additional, being Nº 414 to 956.

111 THE DIPLOMATIC Correspondence of the United States of America, from the Signing of the Definitive Treaty of Peace, 10th September, 1783, to the adoption of the Constitution, March 4, 1789. Being the letters of the Presidents of Congreſs, the Secretary for Foreign Affairs—American Ministers at Foreign Courts, Foreign Ministers near Congreſs—Reports of Committees of Congreſs, and Reports of the Secretary for Foreign Affairs on various Letters and communications; together with letters from individuals on public affairs. Published under the direction of the Secretary of State, from the original Manuscripts in the Department of State, conformably to an Act of Congreſs, approved May 5, 1832. 7 vol. Washington, 1833-34. 8º

112 CONVENTION between the United States of America and the King of the Two Sicilies. Concluded October 14, 1832: Ratified 8th June, 1833. [Washington, 1833.] Folº

113 A DIGEST of the existing commercial regulations of foreign countries, with which the United States have intercourse, as far as they can be ascertained. Prepared under the direction of the Secretary of the Treasury, in compliance with a resolution of the House of Representatives of 3rd March, 1831. 3 vol. Washington, 1833-36. 8º

114 THE DEBATES and Proceedings in the Congreſs of the United States; with an appendix, containing important state papers and public documents, and all the laws of a public nature. . . March 3, 1789, to March 3, 1791, inclusive. Compiled from authentic materials by J. Gales. 2 vol. Washington, 1834. 8º

115 HISTORY of Congreſs. Vol. 1, from March 4, 1789, to March 3, 1793, exhibiting a claſſification of the proceedings of the Senate and the House of Representatives. Philadelphia, 1834. 8vo.

116 A SYSTEM of Tactics; or, rules for the exercises and manœuvres of the cavalry and light infantry and riflemen of the United States. By authority of the Department of War. Washington, 1834. 8°

117 PROTEST of the President (Andrew Jackson) against the recent unconstitutional proceedings of the Senate; etc. (April 15, 1834.) Washington, 1834. 8°

118 STATISTICAL View of the population of the United States, from 1790 to 1830 inclusive. Furnished by the Department of State, etc. Washington, 1835. Folº

119 GENERAL Regulations for the army of the United States; also, the rules and articles of war, and extracts from laws relating to them. Published by authority of the War Department. Washington, 1835. 8°

120 BY Authority. Infantry Tactics; or rules for the exercise and manœuvres of the United States Infantry. By Major General Scott. 3 vol. New York, 1835. 12°

121 SECRET Proceedings and Debates of the Convention aſſembled at Philadelphia, in the year 1787, for the purpose of forming the Constitution of the United States of America. From the notes taken by the late Robert Yates, and copied by John Lansing, Jun. Including the "Genuine Information" laid before the legislature of Maryland by Luther Martin, also other historical documents. Washington, 1836. 8vo.

122 TREATIES between the United States of America and the several Indian tribes, from 1778 to 1837... Compiled and printed .. under the supervision of the Commiſſioner of Indian Affairs (T. H. Crawford). Washington, 1837. 8°

123 TREATIES between the United States of America and the several Indian Tribes, from 1778 to 1837. New edition (superintended by C. A. Harris). Washington, 1837. 8vo.

124 A DIGEST of the Laws of the United States, including an abstract of the Judicial decisions relating to the Constitutional and Statutory Law. By T. F. Gordon. Philadelphia, 1837. 8vo.

125 FROM the National Intelligencer... Congreſs of the United States: in the House of Representatives, .. Jan. 11, 1837. [A report of a debate on the tariff.] [Washington, 1837.] 8°

126 [Begins] 25TH CONGRESS, 1st Seſſion, Doc. Nº 52, House of Representatives... Report of the Solicitor of the Treasury, in the case of W. B. Stokes and others, etc. [New York, 1837.] 8°

127 GENERAL Public Acts of Congreſs, respecting the sale and dispoſition of the public lands, with instructions iſſued .. by the Secretary of the Treasury and Commiſſioner of the General Land Office, and official opinions of the Attorney General on questions arising under the land laws. In two parts. Washington, 1838. 8°

128 RESOLUTIONS, Laws, and Ordinances, relating to the pay, half-pay, .. bounty lands, and other promises made by Congreſs to the officers and soldiers of the Revolution; to the settlement of the accounts between the United States and the several States; and to funding the revolutionary debt. [Edited by W. S. Franklin.] Washington, 1838. 8°

129 THE LIGHT Houses, Beacons, and Floating Lights of the United States, for 1838. Washing. 1838. 8°

130 CONVENTION between the United States of America and the Mexican Republic, concluded April 11th, 1839. [Washington, 1839.] Folº

131 TREATY of Commerce and Navigation between the United States of America and His Majesty the King

of the Netherlands. Concluded January 19, 1839; Ratifications exchanged May 23, 1839. [Washington, 1839.] Fol°

132 SKETCHES of United States Senators, of the Sefsion of 1837-'8. By "A looker on here in Verona" [J. Holan]. Washington, 1839. 12°

133 THE PUBLIC and General Statutes pafsed by the Congrefs of the United States of America, from 1789 to 1836 inclusive. To which is added the Constitution of the United States and an appendix. (From 1789 to 1827.) Published under the inspection of Joseph Story. Second edition, edited by G. Sharswood. 4 vol. [Vol. 1-3 only are of the second edition.] Philadelphia, 1840-39-37. 8vo.

134 REMARKS on the Home Squadron, and Naval School. By a Gentleman of New York. N. York, 1840. 8°

135 LETTER from the Secretary of the Treasury, transmitting a report from the Superintendent of the construction of standard weights and measures (F. R. Hafsler). (July, 1840.) [Washington, 1840.] 8°

136 REPORT from the Secretary of the Treasury, transmitting a report of .. F. R. Hafsler, Superintendent of the Coast Survey, and the fabrication of standard weights and measures, etc. (Ninth report, .. rendering account of the works of 1840.) [Washington, 1840.] 8°

137 By the President of the United States of America. A Proclamation. Whereas a Treaty of Commerce and Navigation between the United States of America and His Majesty the King of Hanover, was concluded and signed by their plenipotentiaries at Berlin, on the twentieth day of May, in the year of our Lord one thousand eight hundred and forty; which treaty—being in the English and French languages—is, word for word, as follows: [Washington, 1841.] Fol°

138 STATISTICS of the United States of America, as collected and returned by the marshals of the several judicial districts, under the thirteenth section of the act for taking the sixth census; corrected at the Department of State, June 1, 1840. Washington, 1841. Fol°

139 SIXTH Census or enumeration of the inhabitants of the United States, as corrected at the Department of State in 1840. Published, by authority of an Act of Congrefs, under the direction of the Secretary of State. Washington, 1841. Fol°

140 STATISTICS of the United States of America, as collected and returned by the Marshals of the several judicial districts, under the thirteenth section of the Act for taking the Sixth Census; corrected at the Department of State, June 1, 1840. Published by authority of an Act of Congrefs, under the direction of the Secretary of State. Washington, 1841. Fol°

141 COMPENDIUM of the enumeration of the inhabitants and statistics of the United States, as obtained at the Department of State, from the returns of the sixth census, by counties and principal towns, exhibiting the population, wealth and resources of the country; with tables of apportionment... To which is added, an abstract of each preceding census. Prepared at the Department of State. Washington, 1841. Fol°

142 THE ADDRESSES and Mefsages of the Presidents of the United States, from Washington to Harrison. To which is prefixed the Declaration of Independence, and Constitution of the United States, together with a portrait and memoir of W. H. Harrison. [Edited by E. Walker.] New York, 1841. 8vo.

143 STANDARD Weights and Measures. Letter from the Secretary of the Treasury, transmitting a report of F. R. Hafsler, respecting ounce-weights. [With a copy of the report, dated June, 1841.] [Wash. 1841.] 8°

144 A TREATY to settle and define the Boundaries between the Territories of the United States and the Pos-

seſsions of Her Britannic Majesty in North America; for the final suppreſsion of the African slave trade; and for the giving up of criminals, fugitive from justice, in certain cases. Concluded 9th August—Ratified 22nd August—Exchanged 13th October—Proclaimed 10th November, 1842. [Washington, 1842.] Folº

145 AN EXPOSITION of the unjust and injurious relations of the United States naval medical corps, by a Member. Baltimore, 1842. 8º

146 ORIGINAL Contraĉts for the Survey of the Coast [between the Treasury Department and F. R. Haſsler]. [Washington? 1842.] 8vo.

147 [*Begins*] MESSAGE of the President, communicating copies of Correspondence with the Government of Mexico. [Washington? 1842.] 8vo.

148 CENSUS of the United States, from 1790 to 1840. [Printed at different periods and brought together, with a colleĉtive title-page, in 1843. " The census of 1790, 1800, and " 1810, as contained in this book, are " abstraĉts only. . . The abstraĉts of " the above years were formed from " the originals, and were printed with " the census of 1830."—*Advertisement prefixed.*] Washing. 1843. Folº

149 MANUFACTURES and Statistics of the United States. Taken with the Census of 1810, 1820, 1830, 1840; as also, from other sources. Washington, 1843. 4º

150 HISTORY of Congreſs; exhibiting a claſsification of the proceedings of the Senate, and the House of Representatives, from March 4, 1789, to March 3, 1793; embracing the first term of the administration of General Washington. Philadel. 1843. 8vo.

151 PROCEEDINGS in the House of Representatives . . on the presentation of the sword of Washington, and the staff of Franklin, Feb. 7, 1843. [With an appendix, containing proceedings of the Senate on same occasion.] Washington, 1843. 8º

152 OREGON Territory. Report of the Committee. . . [To which is appended a Bill to extend the civil and criminal jurisdiĉtion of the courts of the Territory of the Iowa over the Territory of Oregon.] [Washington, 1844.] 8vo.

153 ADDENDA Nº 1, comprising aĉts of the first and second Seſsions of the twenty-eighth Congreſs, 1844, 1845. [Washington, 1845.] 8º

154 EXAMINATION of "A reply to ' Hints on the re-organization of the navy.'" New York, 1845. 8º

155 A REPLY to " Hints on the re-organization of the navy." [New York?], 1845. 8º

156 [*Begins*] 28TH CONGRESS, 2d Seſsion, Senate, 114. Report of the Secretary of the Navy, communicating a report of the plan and construĉtion of the depot of charts and instruments, etc. [by J. M. Gilliſs. Without title-page, in place of which there is a MS. title, which reads " A brief Account of the United States Naval Observatory,"etc.]. [Washington, 1845.] 8vo.

157 DIGEST of the Decisions of the Courts of Common Law and Admiralty in the United States. Boston, 1845-51. Roy. 8º 9 vol. viz.:

VOL.

   1. By Theron Metcalf and Jonathan C. Perkins. Boston, 1845.
   2. By George T. Curtis. Boston, 1846.
   3. By George T. Curtis. Boston, 1846.
   4 and 5. Supplement to the United States Digest. By John Phelps Putnam. Boston, 1851.
   6. Table of Cases contained in the three volumes and the two volumes of Supplement. By George P. Sanger. Boston, 1849.
   7. Annual Digest for 1847.
   8. Annual Digest for 1848.
   9. Annual Digest for 1849.

158 TREATY of Commerce and Navigation between the United States of America and Belgium, concluded November 10, 1845, Ratifications exchanged March 31, 1846. [Washington, 1846.] Folº

159 REPORT of the Secretary of War to the President, for 1845, and

accompanying documents. [A review of the State paper so entitled.] [New York! 1846!] 8°

160 TREATY of Commerce and Navigation between the United States of America and the Two Sicilies. Dated at Naples, 1st December, 1845. Ratified by the President, 14th April, 1846. Exchanged, 1st June, 1846. Proclaimed, 24th July, 1846. [Washington, 1846.] Fol°

161 [Begins] HEAD Quarters of the Army. General Orders, N° 38. .. The following Manual for Rifles with percussion locks having been adopted by the War Department is published, etc. [Wash. 1846.] 16°

162 PUBLIC Laws of the United States of America. Edited by George Minot. To be continued annually. Boston, 1846-1850. 8°

163 PRIVATE Laws of the United States of America. . . Edited by G. Minot. To be continued annually. Boston, 1847-50. 8°

164 TREATIES concluded. by the United States of America with Foreign Nations and Indian Tribes. . . Edited by G. Minot. To be continued annually. Boston, 1847-50. 8°

165 TREATY of Commerce and Navigation between the United States of America and His Majesty the King of Hanover; with the Declaration of Accession of His Royal Highness the Grand Duke of Oldenburg, under the twelfth Article of the Treaty. Dated at Hanover, 10th June, 1846. Ratified by the President, 8th January, 1847. Exchanged, 5th March, 1847. Proclaimed, 24th April, 1847. Declaration of Accession dated at Oldenburg, 10th March, 1847. [Washington, 1847.] Fol°

166 HISTORY of the war between the United States and Mexico. (From the commencement to the battle of Churubusco.) From the best authorities. Philadelphia, 1847. 8°

167 TREATY of Peace, Amity, Navigation, and Commerce, between the United States of America and the Republic of New Granada. Concluded and signed at Bogota, 12th December, 1846. Ratified by the President of the United States 10th June, 1848. Exchanged at Washington, 10th June, 1848. Proclaimed by the President of the United States, 12th June, 1848. [Washing. 1848.] Fol°

168 THIRTIETH Congress, First Session. Ex. Doc. N° 54. House of Representatives. Annual report of the Commissioner of patents (E. Burke) for the year 1847. [With an appendix of documents.] Washing. 1848. 8°

169 THRILLING Incidents of the Wars of the United States. Comprising the most striking and remarkable events of the Revolution, the French war, the Tripolitan war, etc. With three hundred engravings. By the author of " The Army and Navy of the United States" [J. K. Neff]. Philadelphia, 1848. 8°

170 REPORTS from the Secretary of the Treasury (G. M. Bibb) of scientific investigations in relation to sugar and hydrometers made under the superintendence of . . . A. D. Bache, by . . R. S. McCulloh. Revised edition, by order of the Senate. Washington, 1848. 8°

171 31ST CONGRESS, 1st Session. House of Representatives. Ex. Doc. N° 5. Message from the President of the United States to the two houses of Congress, at the commencement of the first Session of the thirty-first Congress. (Documents accompanying the Message of the President, etc.) 3 parts. Washington, 1849. 8°

172 SPECIAL Session. Senate. Report from the Secretary of War (G. W. Crawford) communicating in compliance with a resolution of the Senate, of the 21st February, 1849, a copy of the official journal of Lieutenant P. St. George Cooke, from Santa Fé to San Diego, etc. [Wash. 1849.] 8°

173 30TH CONGRESS, 2nd Session. Senate. Ex. Doc. N° 32. Report of the Secretary of the Treasury (R. J.

Walker) on the warehousing system. [Washington, 1849.] 8°

174 CONVENTION between the United States of America and Her Majesty the Queen of the United Kingdom of Great Britain and Ireland, for the Improvement of the Communication by Post between their respective Territories. Concluded and signed at London on the 15th Dec. 1848. Ratified by the President of the United States on the 6th January, 1849. Exchanged at London on the 26th January, 1849. Proclaimed by the President of the United States on the 15th February, 1849. [Washington, 1849.] Fol°

175 BY Authority of Congreſs. The public statutes at large of the United States of America, from . . 1789 to March, . . 1845. With references to the matter of each act and to the subsequent acts on the same subject, and copious notes of the decisions of the Courts of the United States. . With the Declaration of Independence, the Articles of Confederation, and the Constitution, etc. (Private laws. Indian treaties. Foreign treaties.) Edited by R. Peters. 9 vol. Boston, 1850-48-51. 8°

176 31ST CONGRESS, 1st Seſſion. House of Representatives. Ex. Doc. N° 69. Geological Report on the copper lands of Lake Superior land district, Michigan (by J. W. Foster and J. D. Whitney). Letter from the Secretary of the interior (Hon. T. Ewing) enclosing the geological report, etc. 2 parts. Washington, 1850-51. 8°

177 TIGRE Island and Central America. Meſſage from the President of the United States, transmitting documents in answer to a resolution of the House respecting Tigre Island, etc. [Washington, 1850.] 8°

178 REPORT of the Secretary of War (G. W. Crawford), communicating information in relation to the geology and topography of California. [Washington, 1850.] 8°

179 31ST CONGRESS, 1st Seſſion. Senate. Ex. Doc. N° 64. Reports of the Secretary of War (S. J. Anderson), with reconnaiſſances of routes from San Antonio to El Paso. By . . J. E. Johnston, . . W. F. Smith, . . F. T. Bryan, . . N. H. Michler, and . . S. G. French. . . Also the Report of Captain R. B. Marcy's route from Fort Smith to Santa Fé; and the Report of . . J. H. Simpson of an expedition into the Navajo country. And the report of . . W. H. C. Whiting's reconnaiſſances of the Western Frontier of Texas. Washing. 1850. 8°

180 31ST CONGRESS, 1st Seſſion. Senate. Ex. Doc. N° 42. Report of the Secretary of War, communicating the report of an exploration of the Territory of Minnesota, by Brevet Captain Pope. [Washington, 1850.] 8°

181 REPORT of the Naval Committee to the House of Representatives, August, 1850, in favor of the establishment of a line of mail steam ships to the Western Coast of Africa, and thence via the Mediterranean to London; designed to promote the emigration of free persons of color from the United States to Liberia. . . With an appendix added by the American Colonization Society. Washington, 1850. 8°

182 31ST CONGRESS, 1st Seſſion. House of Representatives. Ex. Doc. N° 15. Commerce and Navigation. Letter from the Secretary of the Treasury [Hon. W. M. Meredith], transmitting a report from the Register of the Treasury of the commerce and navigation of the United States for the last fiscal year (ending 30th June, 1849). Wash. 1850. 8°

183 31ST CONGRESS, 1st Seſſion. Senate. Ex. Doc. N° 2. Report of the Secretary of the Treasury [Hon. W. M. Meredith] on the state of the finances. [Washington, 1850.] 8°

184 PATENT Laws. [Washington, 1851.] 8°

185 REGULATIONS for the uniform and dreſs of the Army of the United

States. June, 1851. From the original text and drawings in the War Department. Second edition. Philadelphia, 1851. Fol°

186 31st Congress, 1st Session. Senate. Ex. Doc. N° 75. Report of the Secretary of State (D. Webster), communicating the Report of the Rev. R. R. Gurley, who was recently sent out by the government to obtain information in respect to Liberia. [Washington, 1851.] 8°

187 31st Congress, 2nd Session. Senate. Ex. Doc. N° 4. Report of the Secretary of the Treasury [Hon. T. Corwin] on the state of the finances. Washington, 1851. 8°

188 Information to persons having business to transact at the Patent Office. Washington, 1851. 8°

189 Report of the Commissioner of Patents (T. Ewbank), for the year 1850 and 1851, each in 2 parts; and 1853 and 1854 (Charles Mason, Commissioner). Washington, 1851-55. 8°

190 Table of Post Offices in the United States on the first day of January, 1851. Washington, 1851. 8°

191 31st Congress, 2nd Session. Senate. Ex. Doc. N° 23. Report of the Secretary of the Treasury [Hon. T. Corwin], in answer to a resolution of the Senate calling for information in relation to the trade and commerce of the British American Colonies with the United States and other countries since 1829. Washington, 1851. 8°

192 Letter from the Secretary of the Treasury (T. Corwin), communicating a report of the computation of tables, to be used with the hydrometer recently adopted for use in the United States Custom Houses... By R. S. M'Culloh. [Washing. 1851.] 8°

193 Abstract of the seventh census. Report of the Superintendent of Census [J. C. G. Kennedy]. Third edition. Philadelphia [1852]. 4to.

194 Acts of Congress relating to Steamboats. Collated by the Rolls at Washington. Boston, 1852. 8°

195 The Constitutions of the several States of the Union and the United States, including the Declaration of Independence and Articles of Confederation. New York, 1852. 8vo.

196 32nd Congress, 1st Session. Senate. Ex. Doc. N° 3. Annual Report of the Superintendent of the [United States of America] Coast Survey (A. D. Bache), shewing the progress of that work during the year ending November, 1851, 1852, 1853. 3 vol. Washington, 1852-54. 8vo.

197 32nd Congress, 2nd Session. Senate. Ex. Doc. N° 3. Sketches accompanying the Annual Report of the Superintendent of the United States Coast Survey, 1851. [Washington, 1852.] 4to.

198 Report of the Secretary of War (C. M. Conrad), communicating, in compliance with a resolution of the Senate, the report of Lieutenant Col. Graham on the subject of the boundary line between the United States and Mexico. [Washington, 1852.] 8°

199 Report of the officers constituting the Light House Board convened under instructions from the Secretary of the Treasury, to inquire into the condition of the Light-house establishment of the United States, etc. Washington, 1852. 8vo.

200 Regulations for the Uniform and Dress of the Navy and Marine Corps of the United States. From the original text and drawings in the Navy Department. Philadel. 1852. Fol°

201 Laws and Regulations for the government of the Post Office Department. Washington, 1852. 8°

202 Thirty-second Congress, First Session... The Select Committee to whom was referred the memorial of Dr. W. T. G. Morton, asking remuneration from Congress for the discovery of the anæsthetic or pain-subduing properties of sulphuric ether, report, etc. [Washington, 1852.] 8°

203 The Seventh Census. Report of Jos. C. G. Kennedy, late Superin-

tendent of the Census for Dec. 1, 1852, to which is appended the Report for December 1, 1851. Washington, 1853. 8°

204 THE SEVENTH Census of the United States, 1850, embracing a statistical view of each of the States and territories, arranged by counties, towns, etc... With an introduction, embracing the aggregate Tables for the United States, compared with every previous Census since 1790, .. and an appendix... J. D. B. De Bow, Superintendent. Washington, 1853. 4to.

205 COMMUNICATION from the Secretary of the Treasury (T. Corwin), transmitting .. the Report of J. D. Andrews on the trade and commerce of the British North American Colonies, and upon the trade of the great lakes and rivers; also notices of the internal improvements in each State, etc. Washington, 1853. 8vo.

206 ARMY Meteorological Register, .. from 1843 to 1854 inclusive, compiled from Observations made by the Officers of the Medical Department of the Army, at the Military Posts of the United States. Prepared [by R. H. Coolidge, with the assistance of L. Blodget] under the direction of .. T. Lawson. Published by authority. Washington, 1855. 4to.

UNITED STATES ALMANAC. 1828. Calculated by S. Smith. [Continued under the title of] Desilver's United States Almanac (for 1829-31; and 1835). Philadelphia, 1828-35. 8°

2 THE UNITED States Almanac; or complete Ephemeris for ... 1843-1844. By J. Downes. 2 vol. Philadelphia [1842-43]. 12mo.

UNITED STATES CATHOLIC MAGAZINE (The), [a continuation of the Religious Cabinet]. Edited by Rev. C. I. White. Vol. 2, 3. (Vol. 4, The United States Catholic Magazine, and Monthly Review. Edited by Rev. C. I. White, Very Rev. M. J. Spalding.) Baltimore, 1842-45. 8°

UNITED STATES LAW JOURNAL and Civilian's Magazine. Edited by several members of the bar. Vol. 1. New Haven, 1822-23. 8vo.

UNITED STATES LITERARY GAZETTE. Vol. 1. Boston, 1825. 4to. Vol. 2. 1826. 8vo. [Then united with the New York Review, and continued under the title of] The United States Review and Literary Gazette. 2 vol. Boston and New York [Cambridge printed], 1827. 8vo.

UNITED STATES MAGAZINE and Democratic Review. [Edited by John L. O'Sullivan.] Vol. 1-8. Washington, 1838-40. 8°. New Series. (Vol. 18-29, conducted by T. P. Kettell.) Vol. 9-31. New York, 1841-1852. 8°

UNITED STATES MILITARY ACADEMY, West Point, New York. A Catalogue of the Graduates of the United States Military Academy, from its establishment in 1801 to (June) 1848, giving the present rank of those in service and the subsequent pursuits of those who have left service as far as known, together with the regulations for the admission of Cadets, and a synopsis of the course of study pursued at that institution. New York, 1847. 12°

UNIVERSALISM False and Unscriptural. An essay on the duration and intensity of future punishment. Philadelphia [1851]. 12°

UNIVERSALIST COMPANION (The), with an almanac and register, containing the statistics of the denomination, for 1853. A. B. Grosh, Editor, etc. Boston, 1853. 12mo.

UNIVERSALIST QUARTERLY and General Review. Vol. 1-13. Boston, 1844-56. 8°

UNIVERSITY OF ALABAMA, Tuscaloosa. Report of the Trustees of the University of Alabama, and the Special Report of Col. F. Bugbee, one of the Trustees of the University. [Tuscaloosa? 1845.] 8°

-UNIVERSITY OF MARYLAND. [Memorial] of the Trustees of the University of Maryland, and the Trustees of Baltimore College, to the Legislature of Maryland. Baltimore, 1830. 8°

UNIVERSITY OF NASHVILLE, *Tenneßee.* Laws of the University. .. New edition. Nashville, 1840. 8°

UNIVERSITY OF NORTH CAROLINA, *Chapel Hill.* Catalogus Universitatis Carolinæ Septentrionalis. Raleigh, 1812. 12°

2 CATALOGUE of the trustees, faculty, and students. ... Sept. 1841. Raleigh, 1841. 12°

UNIVERSITY OF PENNSYLVANIA, *Philadelphia.* A Report made to the Board of Trustees, 4th Nov. 1834, concerning the Universities of Oxford and Cambridge. By P. H. Nicklin. Philadelphia, 1834. 8vo.

2 CATALOGUE of the trustees, officers, and students of the University of Pennsylvania. Philadelphia [1841]. 8vo.

3 GENERAL Catalogue of the medical graduates of the University of Pennsylvania; with an historical sketch of the origin, progreſs, and present state of the medical department... Third edition. Philadelphia, 1845. 8vo.

4 CATALOGUE of the medical graduates in the University of Pennsylvania, at the commencement held April 4th, 1845 (to 1850, Annual). 6 parts. [Philadelphia, 1845.] 8vo.

UNIVERSITY OF THE CITY OF NEW YORK. The Constitution and Statutes for the present government of the University. N. York, 1831. 8°

2 CATALOGUE of the officers, alumni, and students of the University .... 1839-40 (to 1843-44). 4 pts. New York, 1840. 8°

UNIVERSITY OF THE STATE OF NEW YORK. Annual (49th) Report of the Regents, *etc.* Feb. 29,

1836 (to the 68th Annual Report made .. March 1, 1855). Albany, 1836-55. 8°

2 INSTRUCTIONS from the Regents ... to the several academies subject to their visitation, prescribing the requisites and forms of academic reports, *etc.* Revised edition [by T. R. Beck]. Albany, 1845. 8°

3 FOURTH Annual Report of the Regents of the University, on the condition of the State Cabinet of Natural History, and the Historical and Antiquarian Collection, annexed thereto. Made to the Senate, Jan. 14, 1851. (Also the 6th to 8th Annual Reports, *etc.*) Albany, 1851-1855. 8°

UNIVERSITY OF VERMONT, *Burlington.* Catalogue of the officers and students of the University of Vermont ... Oct. 1823 (1834, 1835, 1839, 1844). 5 parts. [Burlington, 1823-44.] 8°

2 CATALOGUS Senatus academici, et eorum qui munera et officia gesserunt, quive alicujus gradus laurea donati sunt, in Universitate Viridimontana. Burlingtoniæ, 1843. 8°

UP-COUNTRY LETTERS [by Z. P.] [*i.e.* L. W. Mansfield]: Edited by Prof. B——, National Observatory. New York, 1852. 12°

UPDIKE, WILKINS. Memoirs of the Rhode Island bar. Bost. 1842. 12°

2 HISTORY of the Episcopal Church in Narragansett, Rhode Island; including a History of other Episcopal Churches in the State; with an appendix containing a reprint of a work now extremely rare, entitled, "America Diſſected," by the Rev. J. Macsparran, D.D. New York, 1847. 8vo.

UPHAM, CHARLES WENTWORTH. Letters on the Logos. Boston, 1828. 12mo.

2 PRINCIPLES of Congregationalism. The second century lecture of the first Church [on Psal. lxxviii. 1-7]. Salem, 1829. 8°

P P

3 LECTURES on Witchcraft, comprising a history of the delusion in Salem, in 1692. Boston, 1831. 12°

UPHAM, THOMAS C. Elements of Mental Philosophy. (Appendix of the varieties of intellectual character, by D. Stewart.) 2 vol. Portland and Boston, 1831. 8°

2 A PHILOSOPHICAL and practical Treatise on the Will. Portland[Brunswick printed], 1834. 8°

3 THE MANUAL of Peace, embracing, I. Evils and remedies of war, II. Suggestions on the law of nations, III. Consideration of a congress of nations. New York, Brunswick [printed], 1836. 8°

4 OUTLINES of imperfect and disordered mental action. New York, 1840. 12mo.

5 ELEMENTS of Mental Philosophy, embracing the two departments of the Intellect and the Sensibilities. 2 vol. New York, 1841. 12mo.

6 THE MANUAL of Peace; exhibiting the evils and remedies of War. Boston, 1842. 12mo.

7 OUTLINES of imperfect and disordered mental action. New York, 1843. 12°

8 LIFE, and religious opinions and experience, of Madame de la Mothe Guyon: together with some account of the personal history and religious opinions of Fenelon, Archbishop of Cambray. 2 vol. N. York, 1847. 12°

9 AMERICAN Cottage Life. A series of Poems illustrative of American Scenery, and of the associations, feelings, and employments of the American cottager and farmer. Second edition. Brunswick, 1850-51. 12°

UPHAM, TIMOTHY. Libel Trial: Report of the trial of T. Upham, vs. Hill and Barton, for an alleged libel. ... To which is added an appendix, etc. Concord, 1831. 8°

UPTON, JOHN. Inexhaustible Iron Mines: containing twenty square miles of iron ores, and superb ... timber, with anthracite coal: Report on the freehold estate of W. Carroll, .. Maryland. Baltimore [1841]. 8°

URQUHART, JOHN. Memoirs of John Urquhart. Philadelphia, 1832. 12mo.

URCULLU, JOSÉ DE. Urcullu's Spanish Grammar... According to the seventh Paris edition .... by F. Robinson. Philadelphia, 1848. 12°

2 GRAMATICA Inglesa reducida á veinte y dos lecciones ... Edicion priméra Americana de la septima de Paris, aumentada y revista por F. Robinson. Filadelfia, 1848. 12°

USHER, FREEMAN L. The Signal, proposing a society for the moral and religious improvement of the clergy. Boston, 1815. 12°

AIL, ALFRED. The American Electro Magnetic Telegraph : with the reports of Congreſs, and a description of all telegraphs known, employing electricity or galvanism. Philadelphia, 1845. 8vo.

2 DESCRIPTION of the American Electro-Magnetic Telegraph; now in operation between .. Washington and Baltimore, *etc.* Washington, 1845. 8°

VALMANN, CARL. Amadeus: or a night with the spirit. New York, 1853. 12°

VAN BUREN, MARTIN, *President of the United States of America.* [*Begins*] 20th Congreſs, 1st Seſſion. In Senate of the United States, May 22, 1828. Mr. Van Buren made the following report .. in relation to the division line between the State of Georgia and the Territory of Florida. [Washington, 1828.] 8°

2 THE VOICE of the People, and the Facts, in relation to the rejection of Martin Van Buren by the United States Senate. New York, 1832. 4to.

VANDENHOFF, GEORGE. A Plain System of Elocution. . . With exercises in prose and verse. . . Second edition. New York, 1845. 12°

2 THE ART of Elocution; from the simple articulation of the elemental sounds of language to the highest

tone of expreſſion in speech, attainable by the human voice. London [New York printed], 1846. 12mo.

VAN DOREN, WILLIAM HOWARD. Mercantile Morals; or, thoughts for young men entering mercantile life. New York, 1852. 12°

VAN DYKE, J. C. Comptroller's Annual Report. (Dec. 5, 1839.) [Tuscaloosa, 1839.] s. sh. fol°

2 REPORT of the Comptroller of Public Accounts (J. C. Van Dyke). Nov. 27, 1841. Tuscaloosa, 1841. 8°

3 REPORT of the Comptroller of Public Accounts (J. C. Van Dyke) in relation to the Contingent Fund. Tuscaloosa, 1841. 8°

4 REPORT. of the Comptroller of Public Accounts in relation to the Contingent Fund. Tuscaloosa, 1841. 8°

5 COMPTROLLER's Report, showing the disbursements from the Contingent Fund. Dec. 5, 1843. [Tuscaloosa, 1843.] 8°

6 COMPTROLLER's Report. Dec. 11, 1843. [Tuscaloosa, 1843.] 8°

7 REPORT of the Comptroller of the State of Alabama (J. C. Van Dyke), for the fiscal year ending Nov. 27, 1845. Tuscaloosa, 1845. 8°

8 COMPTROLLER's Annual Report on the Contingent Fund. (Dec. 3, 1845.) [Tuscaloosa, 1845.] 8°

VAN HEUVEL, J. A. El Dorado; being a narrative of the circumstances which gave rise to reports, in the sixteenth century, of the existence of a rich and splendid city in South America, to which that name was given, and which led to many enterprises in search of it; including a defence of Sir W. Raleigh, in regard to the relations made by him respecting it, *etc.* With a map. New York [1844]. 8°

VAN NESS, WILLIAM P. Reports of two cases determined in the Prize Court for the New York district. New York, 1814. 8°

VAN PATTEN, JOHN F. The Trial, and Life and Confessions of J. F. Van Patten, who was .. convicted of the murder of Mrs. M. Schermerhorn, *etc.* New York, 1825. 8°

VAN RENSSELAER, JEREMIAH. Lectures on Geology; being outlines of the science, delivered in the New York Athenæum, in .. 1825. New York, 1825. 8°

VAN RENSSELAER, SOLOMON. A Narrative of the affair of Queenstown; in the war of 1812. With a review of the Strictures on that event, in a book [by J. Armstrong] entitled, "Notices of the war of 1812." New York, 1836. 12°

VANS, WILLIAM. A Statement of Facts, relating to the demand of W. Vans, on the estates of Messrs. J. and R. Codman, at Boston, deceased. [Boston, 1814.] 8°

VAN SANTVOORD, GEORGE. Life of Algernon Sidney; with sketches of some of his contemporaries and extracts from his correspondence and political writings. N. York, 1851. 12°
2 TREATISE on the Principles of Pleading in Civil Actions under the New York Code of Procedure. Albany, 1852. 8vo.

VAN SCHAACK, HENRY C. Life of Peter Van Schaack, LL.D. embracing selections from his correspondence and other writings during the American Revolution and his exile in England. New York, 1842. 8°

VAN WINKLE, C. S. The Printer's Guide; or an introduction to the art of printing: including an essay on punctuation, and remarks on orthography. Third edition, with additions and alterations. New York, 1836. 12°

VARLE, CHARLES. A Complete View of Baltimore, with a statistical sketch of all the commercial, mercantile, .. and religious institutions .. in the same and in its vicinity for fifteen miles round; ... to which is added a detailed statement of an excursion on the Baltimore and Ohio Railroad to the Point of Rocks, *etc.* Baltimore, 1833. 12°

VARNUM, JOSEPH B. The Seat of Government of the United States. A review of the discussions, in Congress and elsewhere, on the site and plans of the Federal City; with a sketch of its present position and prospects. Read (in part) before the New York and Maryland Historical Societies. Also, a notice of the Smithsonian Institution. By Joseph B. Varnum, Jun. New York, 1848. 8°

VAUX, ROBERT. Memoirs of the Life of Anthony Benezet. Philadelphia printed, York reprinted, 1817. 12mo.
2 LETTER on the Penitentiary System of Pennsylvania, addressed to William Roscoe, Esq. Philadelphia, 1827. 8vo.
3 REPLY to two Letters of William Roscoe, Esq. on the Penitentiary System of Pennsylvania. Philadelphia, 1827. 8vo.

VELDE, CARL FRANZ VAN DER. Tales from the German [of C. F. Vander Velde]. Translated by N. Greene. 2 vol. Boston, 1837. 12°

VENETIAN HISTORY. Sketches from Venetian History. [By E. Smedley.] 2 vol. N. York, 1844. 12°

VERMONT, *State of.* Vermont Currency [Bill for] Two shillings and sixpence. Westminster, 1781. s. sh. 12°

2 VERMONT Currency [Bill for] Twenty shillings. Westminster, 1781. s. sh. 12°

3 STATUTES of the State of Vermont, paſſed by the Legislature in Feb. and Mar. 1787. Windsor, printed by George Hough and Alden Spooner, 1787. 4°

4 ACTS and Laws paſſed by the Legislature of .. Vermont, at their adjourned Seſſion at Bennington, Jan. 1791. Bennington [1791]. 8°

5 ACTS and Laws paſſed by the Legislature of .. Vermont, at their Seſſion at Rutland, in Oct. 1792. Rutland [1792]. 8° Also at the Seſſions at

Windsor,	Oct. 1793,	Windsor,	1793
Rutland,	Oct. 1794,	Bennington,	n. d.
Windsor,	Oct. 1795,	[Rutland],	n. d.
Rutland,	Oct. 1796,	Bennington,	1796
Rutland,	Feb. 1797,	Bennington,	1797
Vergennes,	Oct. 1798,	Bennington,	1799

[Wanting pages 81-88.]

Windsor,	Oct. 1799,	Rutland,	n. d.
Middlebury,	Oct. 1800,	Bennington,	n. d.
Burlington,	Oct. 1802,	Bennington,	1802
Westminst.	Oct. 1803,	Windsor,	1803
Windsor,	Jan. 1804,	Windsor,	1804
Danville,	Oct. 1805,	Windsor,	1805
Middlebury,	Oct. 1806,	Bennington,	n. d.
Woodstock,	Oct. 1807,	Randolph,	n. d.
Montpelier,	Oct. 1808,	Bennington,	n. d.
Montpelier,	Oct. 1810,	Danville,	n. d.
Montpelier,	Oct. 1811,	Rutland,	n. d.
Montpelier,	Oct. 1812,	Danville,	n. d.
Montpelier,	Oct. 1813,	Rutland,	n. d.
Montpelier,	Oct. 1814,	Windsor,	n. d.
Montpelier,	Oct. 1815,	Windsor,	n. d.
Montpelier,	Oct. 1816,	Windsor,	n. d.
Montpelier,	Oct. 1817,	Middlebury,	n. d.
Montpelier,	Oct. 1818,	Windsor,	n. d.
Montpelier,	Oct. 1819,	Rutland,	n. d.
Montpelier,	Oct. 1820,	Middlebury,	n. d.
Montpelier,	Oct. 1821,	Middlebury,	1821
Montpelier,	Oct. 1822,	Poultney,	1822
Montpelier,	Oct. 1823,	Bennington,	n. d.
Montpelier,	Oct. 1824,	Bennington,	n. d.
Montpelier,	Oct. 1825,	n. p.	n. d.

[Wanting pages 63-72.]

Montpelier,	Oct. 1826,	Bennington,	n. d.
Montpelier,	Oct. 1827,	Woodstock,	n. d.
Montpelier,	Oct. 1828,	Woodstock,	1828
Montpelier,	Oct. 1829,	Woodstock,	n. d.
Montpelier,	Oct. 1830,	Woodstock,	n. d.
Montpelier,	Oct. 1831,	Middlebury,	1831
Montpelier,	Oct. 1832,	Montpelier,	1832
Montpelier,	Oct. 1833,	Montpelier,	1833

Montpelier,	Oct. 1834,	Middlebury,	1834
Montpelier,	Oct. 1835,	Montpelier,	1835
Montpelier,	Oct. 1836,	Montpelier,	1836
Montpelier,	Oct. 1837,	Montpelier,	1837
Montpelier,	Oct. 1838,	Montpelier,	1838
Montpelier,	Oct. 1839,	Montpelier,	1839
Montpelier,	Oct. 1840,	Burlington,	1840
Montpelier,	Oct. 1841,	Montpelier,	1841
Montpelier,	Oct. 1842,	Montpelier,	1842
Montpelier,	Oct. 1843,	Montpelier,	1843
Montpelier,	Oct. 1844,	Burlington,	1844
Montpelier,	Oct. 1845,	Burlington,	1845
Montpelier,	Oct. 1846,	Burlington,	1846

6 A JOURNAL of the Proceedings of the General Aſſembly of the State of Vermont, at their stated Seſſion, held at Manchester, ... Oct. 1788. Windsor, 1789. 4°. Also at the Seſſions at

Castleton,	Oct. 1790,	Windsor,	1791
Bennington,	Jan. 1791,	Bennington,	1791
Windsor,	Oct. 1791,	Windsor,	n. d.
Rutland,	Oct. 1792,	Bennington,	n. d.
Windsor,	Oct. 1793,	Windsor,	1794
Rutland,	Oct. 1794,	Bennington,	n. d.
Windsor,	Oct. 1795,	Rutland,	n. d.
Rutland,	Oct. 1796,	Bennington,	1797
Middlebury,	Oct. 1800,	Bennington,	n. d.
Burlington,	Oct. 1802,	Bennington,	1803
Westminst.	Oct. 1803,	Windsor,	1804
Rutland,	Oct. 1804,	Bennington,	1805
Danville,	Oct. 1805,	Windsor,	1806
Middlebury,	Oct. 1806,	Bennington,	n. d.
Montpelier,	Oct. 1808,	Bennington,	1809
Montpelier,	Oct. 1809,	Randolph,	1810
Montpelier,	Oct. 1810,	Danville,	1811
Montpelier,	Oct. 1811,	Rutland,	n. d.
Montpelier,	Oct. 1812,	Danville,	1812
Montpelier,	Oct. 1814,	Windsor,	n. d.
Montpelier,	Oct. 1815,	Windsor,	n. d.
Montpelier,	Oct. 1817,	Rutland,	n. d.
Montpelier,	Oct. 1818,	Bennington,	n. d.
Montpelier,	Oct. 1819,	Bennington,	n. d.
Montpelier,	Oct. 1821,	Rutland,	n. d.
Montpelier,	Oct. 1822,	Montpelier,	n. d.
Montpelier,	Oct. 1824,	Montpelier,	n. d.
Montpelier,	Oct. 1825,	Bennington,	n. d.
Montpelier,	Oct. 1826,	Rutland,	n. d.
Montpelier,	Oct. 1827,	Woodstock,	n. d.
Montpelier,	Oct. 1828,	Woodstock,	n. d.
Montpelier,	Oct. 1829,	Woodstock,	n. d.
Montpelier,	Oct. 1830,	Woodstock,	n. d.
Montpelier,	Oct. 1831,	Woodstock,	n. d.
Montpelier,	Oct. 1832,	Danville,	n. d.
Montpelier,	Oct. 1833,	Danville,	n. d.
Montpelier,	Oct. 1834,	Rutland,	1834
Montpelier,	Oct. 1835,	Middlebury,	1835

7 JOURNAL of the Senate of the State of Vermont, Oct. Seſſion, 1836 to Oct. Seſſion, 1846. Montpelier [and] Windsor, 1836-46. 8°

8 JOURNAL of the House of Representatives of the State of Vermont, Oct. Sefsion, 1837 to Oct. Sefsion, 1846. Montpelier [and] Windsor, 1837-46. 8°

9 STATUTES of the State of Vermont; revised and established by authority in .. 1787; including those pafsed since that period until .. Jan. 1791; likewise, the several acts respecting sales by the Surveyor General. Bennington, 1791. 8°

10 LAWS of the State of Vermont; revised and pafsed by the Legislature, in .. 1797; together with the Declaration of Independence, the Constitution,.. and .. an appendix [separately paged] containing the several laws ... regulating ... locks, toll bridges, turnpike roads, etc. Rutland, 1798. 8°

11 THE LAWS of the State of Vermont, digested and compiled [by T. Tolman], .. coming down to, and including, the year 1807; with an appendix, containing titles of local acts, and an index of the laws in force. 2 vol. Randolph, 1808. 8°

12 REPORT of the Committee appointed by Act of the last Sefsion of the Legislature, to examine into and report the situation of the Vermont State Bank. Montpelier, 1812. 8°

13 THE LAWS of Vermont, of a publick and permanent nature: coming down to, and including, the year 1824. To which are prefixed, the Declaration of Independence, etc. Compiled .. by W. Slade. Windsor, 1825. 8°

14 JOURNAL of the Council of Censors, at their Sefsions at Montpelier and Burlington, .. June to Nov. 1827. Montpelier, 1828. 8°

15 REPORTS of cases argued and determined in the Supreme Court of .. Vermont. Reported by the judges of said Court, agreeably to a statute law of the State. Vol. 1-9. (New series: vol. 10, 11 [part 1], by G. B. Shaw; third series: vol. 11 [part 2] -14, by W. Weston; fourth series:

vol. 15, by W. Slade; new series: vol. 16-18, by P. T. Washburn.) 18 vol. St. Albans; Burlington [and] Woodstock, 1829-47. 8°

16 THE LAWS of Vermont, of a public and permanent nature,.. [from 1825 to 1834, inclusive]. Compiled .. by D. P. Thompson. Montpelier, 1835. 8°

17 JOURNAL of the Council of Censors, at their Sefsions holden at Montpelier and Middlebury, .. June, .. 1834 to Jan. 1835. Middlebury, 1835. 8°

18 PROCEEDINGS of the Baptist Convention of the [State of Vermont], with the reports of the Vermont branch of the N(orthern) B(aptist) E(ducation) Society (1836, 1840, 1841). 3 parts. Brandon, 1836-41. 8°

19 REPORT and Correspondence on the subject of a geological and topographical survey of the State of Vermont. [Montpelier,] 1838. 8°

20 THE REVISED Statutes of the State of Vermont, pafsed Nov. 19, 1839. To which are added several public acts now in force; and to which are prefixed the Constitutions of the United States and of the State of Vermont. Published by order of the Legislature. Burlington, 1840. 8°

21 JOURNAL of the Sefsions of the Council of Censors, of the State of Vermont, .. June, .. 1841 to Feb. 1842. Burlington, 1842. 8°

22 JOURNAL of the Convention, holden at Montpelier,.. 4 Jan. 1843, agreeable to the ordinance of the Council of Censors, etc. Montpelier, 1843. 8°

23 MESSAGE of the Governor .. to the Legislature of Vermont, Oct. 10, 1846. Montpelier, 1846. 8°

24 DIRECTORY and Rules of the Senate and House of Representatives, for October Sefsion, 1847. Montpelier, 1847. 12°

VERNON, THOMAS. Cases argued and adjudged in the High Court of Chancery, originally published by

order of the Court from the manuscripts of T. Vernon. [Edited by W.
Peere Williams and W. Melmoth.]
With references .. to later cases; together with tables .. by J. Raithby.
First American, from the third London edition, with references continued
to the present time. Brookfield,
Maſs. 1829. 8°

VERPLANCK, GULIAN CROM-
MELIN. Addreſs delivered before the
American Academy of Fine Arts.
New York, 1824. 8°

2 ESSAYS on the nature and uses
of the various evidences of revealed
religion. New York, 1824. 8°

3 AN ESSAY on the doctrine of
contracts; being an inquiry how contracts are affected in law and morals,
by concealment, error, or inadequate
price. New York [1825]. 8°

4 DISCOURSES and Addreſses on
subjects of American History, Arts,
and Literature. New York, 1833.
12mo.

5 A LECTURE, introductory to the
course of scientific lectures before
the Mechanics' Institute of the city of
New York. New York, 1833. 8°

6 THE RIGHT Moral Influence and
use of liberal Studies. A discourse
delivered after the annual commencement of Geneva College, August 7th,
1833, etc. New York, 1833. 12°

7 THE CONNECTION of Morals and
Learning, and their influence upon
each other. [In two discourses.] 2 pt.
New York, 1834, 33. 12°

8 THE ADVANTAGES and the Dangers of the American Scholar: a discourse delivered on the day preceding
the annual commencement of Union
College, July 26, 1836. New York,
1836. 8°

VERY, JONES. Eſſays and poems.
Boston, 1839. 8°

VESEY, WILLIAM. A Sermon
Preached in Trinity Church in New
York, In America, May 12, 1709.
At the Funeral of the Right Honorable

John Lord Lovelace, Barron of Hur-
ley, her Majesties Capt. General and
Governour in chief of the Provinces
of New York and New Jersey, and
the Territories and Tracts of Land
depending thereon in America, and
Vice Admiral of the same. By William Vesey, A.M. and Rector of the
City of New York. Printed and sold
by William Bradford at the Sign of
the Bible in New York, 1709. 4to.

VESTIGES. Remarks upon a recent work .. entitled The natural history of the vestiges of creation [i. e.
Vestiges of the natural history of
creation]. Philadelphia, 1846. 12°

2 ART. VIII.— Explanations:— a
sequel to the Vestiges of the Natural
history of Creation. By the author of
that work. New York: Wiley and
Putnam, 1846. 12°. pp. 142. [An
article on the "Vestiges" extracted
from vol. 62 of the North American
Review.] [Boston, 1846.] 8vo.

VETHAKE, HENRY, LL.D. An
Introductory Lecture on Political
Economy; etc. Princeton, 1831. 8°

2 THE PRINCIPLES of Political Economy. [With addenda.] Philadelphia,
1838. 8vo.

VEZE, JEAN DE. An Enquiry
into, and observations upon the causes
and effects of the epidemic disease
which raged in Philadelphia from ..
August till .. December, 1793. (Re-
cherches et observations sur les causes
et les effets de la maladie épidémique
qui a régné a Philadelphie, etc.) Eng.
and Fr. Philadelphia, 1794. 8vo.

VIAUD, PIERRE. The Surprising
yet real and true Voyages and Adventures of Monsieur P. Viaud, a
French Sea Captain. [Narrated by
himself.] (Translated from the French
by Mrs. Griffith.) To which is added,
The shipwreck, a sentimental and descriptive poem ... by W. Falconer.
2 pts. Philadelphia, 1774. 12mo.

VICE .... The Danger-

ous Vice . . . . [Vice Presi-
dent], a fragment [in verse] addreſſed
to all whom it may concern. By a
gentleman, formerly of Boston [Mr.
Church]. Columbia, 1789. 4°

VIDAURRE, M. L. Efeĉtos de
las facciones en los gobiernos nacientes.
En este libro se recopelan los principios fundamentales del gobierno de-
mocratico constitucional representa-
tivo. Boston, 1828. 8vo.

VIEW. A General View of the
Fine Arts, critical and historical.
With an introduĉtion by D. Hunting-
ton. New York, 1851. 12°

VIGNOLES, CHARLES. Obser-
vations upon the Floridas. New York,
1823. 8°

VILLAGE READER. The Village
Reader, designed for the use of
schools. By the compilers of the Easy
Primer, etc. Springfield, 1841. 12°

VINCENT DE PAUL, Saint. Spiritual Maxims . . arranged for every
day in the year by . . . . Dr. Walsh,
Bishop of Halifax. To which is added
a Nine Days' Devotion in honour of
St. Vincent of Paul, and Biographical
Notice of Mrs. Seton, Foundreſs . . .
of the Sisters of Charity in the United
States. New York, 1851. 16°

VINET, ALEXANDRE. Vital Christianity: eſſays and discourses on the
religions of man and the religion of
God. Translated, with an introduction, by R. Turnbull. Boſt. 1845. 12°
  2 MONTAIGNE; the Endleſs Study
and other Miscellanies . . translated,
with an Introduĉtion and Notes by R.
Turnbull. New York, 1850. 12°

VIREY, JULIEN JOSEPH. Natural
History of the Negro Race. Extraĉted
from the French [i. e. from the His-
toire Naturelle du genre humain, of
Dr. Virey] by J. H. Guenebault.
Charleston, 1837. 12°

VIRGILIUS MARO, PUBLIUS.

The Story of Æneas and Dido bur-
lesqued; from the fourth book of the
Æneid of Virgil. Charlestown, 1774.
12mo.
  2 PUBLII Virgilii Maronis Buoc-
lica, Georgica, et Æneis. Accedunt
clavis metrica, notulæ Anglicæ, et
quæstiones. Cura B. A. Gould. In
usum scholæ Bostoniensis. Bostoniæ,
1840. 12°
  3 PUBLII Virgilii Maronis Buco-
lica, Georgica, et Æneis. Virgil, with
English notes. . . by F. Bowen. Stereotype edition. Boston, 1843. 8°

VIRGINIA, Colony and State of.
  1 THE LOYAL Addreſs of the Clergy
of Virginia. [A Poem.] Williamsburgh: Printed for Fr. Maggot, at
the Sign of the Hickery Tree in Queen
Street. 1702. Single sheet. Fol.
  2 A COLLECTION of all the Aĉts of
Aſſembly, now in force in the Colony
of Virginia. With the titles of such
as are expir'd or repeal'd. And notes.
. . Examin'd with the Records, by a
Committee appointed for that purpose,
who have added many useful marginal notes, and references, and an ex-
aĉt Table. Williamsburg: Printed
by William Parks. 1733. Folº
  3 THE ACTS of Aſſembly, now in
force, in the colony of Virginia. . . .
Published by order of the General
Aſſembly. Printed by W. Rind, A.
Purdie, and J. Dixon. Williamsburg,
1769. Folº
  4 ACTS of the General Aſſembly,
10 Geo. III. With an Index. Williamsburg: Printed by William Rind.
1770. Folº
  5 THE PROCEEDINGS of the House
of Burgeſſes of Virginia, convened in
General Aſſembly, on Thursday the
first day of June, 1775, will fully appear in their journals, printed at large;
but as it was judged neceſſary that
the most material transaĉtions should
be seen in one conneĉted and distinĉt
point of view, the House ordered that
these should be published in a pamphlet, and they are contained in the

following sheets. Williamsburg: Printed by Alexander Purdie [1775]. 4to.

6 [Acts pasſed at a General Assembly of the Commonwealth of Virginia. October Sesſion 1783. (*Wants title.*) Richmond, 1783.] Folº. Also the Acts pasſed at a

General Asſembly, begun May 3, 1784
General Asſembly, begun Oct. 18, 1784
General Asſembly, begun Oct. 17, 1785
General Asſembly, begun Oct. 16, 1786
General Asſembly, begun Oct. 1787
[wanting the title].
General Asſembly, begun Oct. 20, 1788
General Asſembly, begun Oct. 19, 1789
General Asſembly, begun Oct. 18, 1790
General Asſembly, begun Oct. 17, 1791
General Asſembly, begun Oct. 1, 1792
General Asſembly, begun Oct. 21, 1793
General Asſembly, begun Oct. 11, 1794
General Asſembly, begun Dec. 7, 1801
General Asſembly, begun Dec. 6, 1802
General Asſembly, begun Dec. 5, 1803
General Asſembly, begun Dec. 3, 1804
General Asſembly, begun Dec. 2, 1805
General Asſembly, begun Dec. 1, 1806

7 A Memorial and Remonstrance, presented to the General Asſembly .. at their Sesſion in 1785, in consequence of a bill brought into that Asſembly for the establishment of religion by law. ([With] An act for establishing religious freedom.) Reprinted at Worcester, 1786. 16º

8 The Address of the Minority in the Virginia Legislature [*i.e.* of the General Asſembly], to the people of that State; containing a vindication of the constitutionality of the alien and sedition laws. [Richmond? 1799.] 8º

9 The Address of the Minority in the Virginia Legislature to the people of that State; containing a vindication of the constitutionality of the alien and sedition laws. 8º

10 A Tour through part of Virginia in the summer of 1808. In a series of Letters, including an account of Harper's Ferry, the Natural Bridge, *etc.* New York, 1809. 8º

11 Letters from Virginia. Translated from the French. [Written, in English, by Profesſor Tucker.] Baltimore, 1816. 12º

12 The Revised Code of the Laws of Virginia: being a collection of all such acts of the General Asſembly, of a public and permanent nature, as are now in force; with a general index. To which are prefixed, the Constitution of the United States; the Declaration of Rights; and the Constitution of Virginia. [Collected and revised by B. W. Leigh.] 2 vol. Richmond, 1819. 8º

13 The Statutes at large; being a collection of all the laws of Virginia, from the first sesſion of the legislature, in the year 1619 [to the year 1792, inclusive]. Published pursuant to an Act of the General Asſembly of Virginia... By W. W. Hening. 13 vol. New York, Richmond, [and] Philadelphia, 1823-19-23. 8º

14 Proceedings and Debates of the Virginia State Convention, of 1829-30. To which are subjoined, the new Constitution of Virginia, and the votes of the People. Richmond, 1830. 8º

15 Supplement to the Revised Code of the Laws of Virginia: being a collection of all the acts of the General Asſembly ... pasſed since the year 1819, with a general index. To which are prefixed the acts organizing a convention, the declaration of rights, and the amended Constitution of Virginia. Richmond, 1833. 8º

16 Acts of the General Asſembly of the Commonwealth of Virginia, begun and held at the Capitol in the City of Richmond, the third day of December, 1832. (Acts pasſed at a General Asſembly .. begun Dec. 2, 1833.) 2 vol. Richmond, 1833-34. 8vo.

17 Acts of the General Asſembly of Virginia, pasſed at the Sesſion of 1834-35. Commencing 1st Dec. 1834, and ending 12th March, 1835. Richmond, 1835. 8º. Also

Acts pasſed at the Sesſion of 1835-36
Acts pasſed at the Sesſion of 1836-37
Acts pasſed at the Extra Sesſion, 1837
Acts pasſed at the Sesſion of 1838

Acts paſſed at the Seſſion of 1839
Acts paſſed at the Seſſion of 1839-40
Acts paſſed at the Seſſion of 1841-42
Acts paſſed at the Seſſion of 1842-43
Acts paſſed at the Seſſion of 1843-44
Acts paſſed at the Seſſion of 1844-45
Acts paſſed at the Seſſion of 1845-46
Acts paſſed at the Seſſion of 1846-47
Acts paſſed at the Seſuon of 1847-48
Acts paſſed at the Seſſion of 1848-49
Acts paſſed at the Extra and Regular
                 Seſſions 1849-50
Acts paſſed at the Seſſion of 1850-51
Acts paſſed at the Seſſion of 1852
Acts paſſed at the Seſſion of 1852-53
           Richmond, 1836-53. 8°

18 THE STATUTES at Large of Virginia, from October Seſſion, 1792, to December Seſſion, 1806 [continued to Dec. 1807] inclusive ; . . . being a continuation of Hening. By S. Shepherd. 3 vol. Richmond, 1835-36. 8°

19 COLLECTION of all Acts of the General Aſſembly relating to the James River and Kanawha Company ; Together with the by-laws and resolutions of the Stockholders of the Company, etc. 3 pts. Richmond [1835 ?] 8°

20 THE CAVALIERS of Virginia, or the recluse of Jamestown. An historical romance of the Old Dominion. By the author of " The Kentuckian in New York" [— Caruthers]. 2 vol. New York, 1835. 8°

21 PROCEEDINGS of the twenty-second annual meeting of the Baptist General Aſſociation of Virginia, assembled at Lynchburg, Virginia, May 31st, 1845. [Lynchburg ? 1845.] 8vo.

22 THE VIRGINIA Report of 1799-1800 touching the alien and sedition laws ; Together with the Virginia resolutions of December 21, 1798. Richmond, 1850. 8°

VIRGINIA AND NORTH CAROLINA ALMANACK, 1802. Astronomical Part by I. Briggs. Editorial Part by Americanus Urban. (N° 3. [to which is added] The Annual Register and Virginian Repository.) Petersburg, 1802. 12°

VIRGINIA GAZETTE and Weekly Advertiser. Dec. 6, 1787. Richmond, 1787. Fol.

VIRGINIA GAZETTE ; or, the American Advertiser. N° 254. Richmond, 1786. Fol.

VIRGINIA HISTORICAL AND PHILOSOPHICAL SOCIETY. An Account of Discoveries in the West until 1519, and of Voyages to and along the Atlantic Coast of North America, from 1520 to 1573. Prepared for " The Virginia Historical and Philosophical Society" by Conway Robinson. Richmond, 1848. 8°

VIRGINIA SPRINGS. Letters descriptive of the Virginia Springs; etc. Edited, by Peregrine Prolix. Philadelphia, 1837. 12mo.

VIRGINIAN. The Kentuckian in New York, or the adventures of three Southerns. By a Virginian. 2 vol. New York, 1834. 12°

2 A BRIEF Enquiry into the true nature and character of our Federal Government : being a review of Judge Story's commentaries on the Constitution of the United States. By a Virginian. Petersburg, 1840. 8vo.

3 AHASUERUS, a poem. By a Virginian [Robert Tyler]. New York, 1842. 12°

VOGDES, WILLIAM. The first part of the United States Arithmetic. Philadelphia, 1845. 12°

VOYAGER [i.e. GEORGE HILL]. The Ruins of Athens, with other poems. By a Voyager. Washington, 1831. 8°

VOYAGES round the World, from the death of Captain Cook to the present time ; etc. N. York, 1844. 12°

VRIES, DAVID PIETERSEN DE. Voyages from Holland to America, A.D. 1632 to 1644. . . . Translated from the Dutch by Henry C. Murphy [and privately printed for James Lenox, Esq.] New York, 1853. 4to.

. A. *Farmer* [*i.e.* SAMUEL SEABURY, afterwards *Bishop of Connecticut*]. Free Thoughts on the Proceedings of the Continental Congreſs held at Philadelphia, Sept. 5, 1774; .. wherein their errors are exhibited .. in a letter to the Farmers .. of North America, *etc.* by a Farmer (A. W.). [New York?] 1774. 8°

2 A VIEW of the Controversy between Great Britain and her Colonies: including a mode of determining their present disputes, .. in a letter to the author of A full vindication of the measures of the Congreſs, .. by A. W., Farmer. New York, 1774. 8°

WACKER, JACOB DAVID. Eſſay on Hydrocephalus Internus. Philadelphia, 1806. 8vo.

WADSWORTH, CHARLES. A Sermon [on Psalm cvii. 22, Psalm xli. 17, Rom. xii. 1] preached ... on thanksgiving day, November 25, *etc.* Philadelphia, 1852. 8vo.

WAIF (THE). A Collection of Poems. [Edited by H. W. Longfellow.] Boston, 1846. 12°

WAINWRIGHT, JONATHAN MAYHEW, *Bishop*. A Discourse [on Isaiah xi. 9] on the occasion of forming the African Miſſion School Society, .. in Hartford, Connecticut, *etc.* Hartford, 1828. 8°

2 SERMONS upon Religious Education and filial duty. New York, 1829. 8°

3 INEQUALITY of Individual Wealth the ordinance of Providence, and essential to civilization. A sermon [on Deut. xv. 11] preached before his Excellency J. Davis, Governor, .. the honorable Council, and the Legislature of Maſſachusetts, on the annual Election, January 7, 1835. Boston, 1835. 8vo.

4 THE LAND of Bondage, its ancient monuments and present condition: being the journal of a tour in Egypt. New York, 1852. 8°

5 OUR Saviour with Prophets and Apostles, a series of eighteen highly finished steel engravings, designed expreſsly for this work, with descriptions by several American divines. Edited by J. M. Wainwright. New York, 1852. 8°

WAKEFIELD, PRISCILLA. Mental Improvement: or the beauties and wonders of nature and art: in a series of instructive conversations. Second American, from the fifth London edition. New Bedford, 1809. 12°

WALDENSES. The History of the Waldenses. Philadelphia, 1829. 12mo.

WALDO, S. PUTNAM. Memoirs of Andrew Jackson, Major General in the army of the United States, *etc.* Fifth edition, improved. Hartford, 1820. 12°

2 THE TOUR of J. Monroe, President of the United States, through the

Northern and Western States, in 1817; his tour in .. 1818; together with a sketch of his life, *etc.* Second edition. Hartford, 1820. 8°

3 THE LIFE and Character of Stephen Decatur; late Commodore and Post Captain in the navy of the United States, *etc.* Second edition, revised, with important additions, *etc.* Middletown, 1822. 12°

4 BIOGRAPHICAL Sketches of distinguished American naval heroes in the war of the Revolution, between the American Republic and the kingdom of Great Britain, *etc.* Hartford, 1823. 8°

WALKER, CHARLES. A Sermon [on Rom. xiv. 13] preached at the Centre Church, ... Dec. 28, 1845. Brattleboro, 1846. 12°

WALKER, EDWARD, AND SONS. The Art of Book Binding, .. including a descriptive account of the New York Book-bindery. N.York,1850. 8°

WALKER, JAMES, D. D. Addreſſes at the Inauguration of the Rev. J. Walker, as President of Harvard College. Cambridge, 1853. 8°

WALKER, JAMES M. The Theory of the Common Law. Boston,1852. 8°

WALKER, JONATHAN. Trial and Imprisonment of J. Walker, at Pensacola, Florida, for aiding slaves to escape from bondage. With an appendix, containing a sketch of his life. [Written by himself. With a preface by M. W. Chapman.] Anti Slavery Office, Boston, 1846. 12°

WALKER, ROBERT J. Reports of cases adjudged in the Supreme Court of Miſſiſſippi. June, 1818, to Dec. 1832. Natchez, 1834. 8°

2 LETTER .. relative to the reannexation of Texas; and in reply to the call of the people of Carroll county, Kentucky, to communicate his views on that subject. Philadelphia, 1844. 8°

3 ANOTHER edition. Washington, 1844. 8°

WALKER, T. Elements of Geometry, with practical applications. Second edition. Boston, 1829. 12°

WALKER, TIMOTHY. Introductory Lecture on the dignity of the Law as a profeſſion, delivered at the Cincinnati College, *etc.* Cincinnati, 1837. 8°

2 INTRODUCTION to American Law, designed as a first book for students. Second edition, enlarged and amended. Cincinnati, 1844. 8°

3 THE REFORM Spirit of the Day. An oration before the Phi Beta Kappa Society of Harvard University, July 18, 1850. Boston, 1850. 8°

4 ORATION on the Life and Public Services of D. Webster, delivered before the bar of Cincinnati, Nov. 22, 1852. Cincinnati, 1852. 8°

WALKER, WILLIAM J. *M.D.* An Eſſay on the Treatment of compound and complicated Fractures; being the annual addreſs before the Maſſachusetts Medical Society, in Boston, .. May 28, 1845. Boston, 1845. 8°

WALLACE, ADAM. Lives of Adam Wallace, and Walter Mill, Martyrs. Philadelphia, 1829. 12mo.

WALLACE, JOHN, *B. A.* An Oration delivered at New Salem, on the thirty-third anniversary of American Independence, July 4, 1809. Greenfield, 1809. 8°

2 AN ADDRESS delivered at Newbury, Vermont, July 4, 1823 [in commemoration of the Independence of the United States of America]. Haverhill, N. H. 1823. 8°

WALLACE, JOHN B. Reports of cases adjudged in the Circuit Court of the United States for the third circuit, 1801. Second edition. Philadelphia, 1838. 8°

WALLACE, JOHN WILLIAM. The Reporters, chronologically arranged : with occasional remarks upon their respective merits. Second edition, revised. Philadelphia, 1845. 8°

WALLACE, WILLIAM CLAY. A Treatise on the Eye; containing discoveries of the causes of near and far-sightedneſs, and of the affections of the retina, with remarks on the use of medicines as substitutes for spectacles. Second edition. New York, 1839. 12°

WALLIS, M. D. *Mrs.* Life in Feejee, or five years among the Cannibals. By a Lady (M. D. Wallis). [With an Introduction by C. W. Flanders.] Boston, 1851. 12°

WALLIS, S. TEACKLE. Addreſs delivered before the Reading Room Society of Saint Mary's College, Baltimore, at the annual commencement, July 20, 1841. Baltimore [1841]. 8°
2 LECTURE on the Philosophy of History, and some of the popular errors which are founded on it, delivered before the Calvert Institute, Jan. 24, 1844. Baltimore [1844]. 8°
3 GLIMPSES of Spain; or notes of an unfinished tour in 1847. New York, 1849. 8°

WALL STREET, *in the City of New York.* A Week in Wall Street, by one who knows. [A satire.] New York, 1841. 12°

WALN, ROBERT, *the Younger.* Life of the Marquis de la Fayette, Major General in the war of the Revolution. Philadelphia, 1825. 8°

WALSH, MICHAEL, *A. M.* The Mercantile Arithmetic, adapted to the commerce of the United States... A new edition, stereotyped, revised and enlarged. Boston, 1838. 12°

WALSH, ROBERT. An Appeal from the Judgments of Great Britain respecting the United States of America. Part first, containing an historical outline of their merits and wrongs as colonies; and strictures upon the calumnies of the British writers. Philadelphia, 1819. 8°
2 THE JACKSON Wreath, or national souvenir, .. containing a bio-graphical sketch of General Jackson until 1819, by R. Walsh, Jun. Esq.; with a continuation until the present day, embracing a view of the recent political struggle. By Dr. J. McHenry. Philadelphia, 1829. 8°
3 DIDACTICS: social, literary, and political. 2 vol. Philadel. 1836. 12°

WALSH, WILLIAM, *R. C. Bishop of Halifax, in Nova Scotia.* A Pastoral Letter for the Lent of 1851, addreſsed to the clergy and laity of the diocese of Halifax... To which is added a Letter on the Roman Catholic Episcopal oath in refutation of the injurious and unfounded aſsertions of the Rev. Dr. Cumming. New York, 1851. 8°
2 THE CATHOLIC Offering: a gift book for all seasons. New York, 1852. 12°

WALTER, THOMAS U. AND SMITH, JOHN JAY. A Guide to Workers in Metal and Stone: for the use of architects and designers, .. manufacturers, etc. [A series of designs.] 4 parts. Philadelphia, 1846. 4°

WALTER, WILLIAM. A Discourse delivered before the Humane Society of Maſsachusetts. Boston, 1798. 4to.

WALTON, IZAAK. The Complete Angler; .. and instructions, .. by C. Cotton. With copious notes, for the most part original; a bibliographical preface, giving an account of fishing and fishing-books, from the earliest antiquity to the time of Walton; and a notice of Cotton and his writings; by the American editor. To which is added, an appendix, including .. papers on American fishing, .. catalogue of books on angling, etc. Large paper. New York, 1847. 8°

WALTON (KATHARINE): or the rebel of Dorchester. An historical romance of the Revolution in Carolina. By the author of "Richard Hurdis," etc. [i. e. William Gilmore Simms]. Philadelphia, 1851. 8°

WALTON, W. C.   Narrative of a
Revival of Religion in the third Presbyterian Church of Baltimore.   With
remarks on subjects connected with
revivals in general. Baltimore, 1824.
12°

WAR (THE); being a faithful record of the transactions of the war
between the United States of America
and their territories, and the United
Kingdom of Great Britain and Ireland,
and the dependencies thereof, declared on the 18 June, 1812.   June
27, 1812, to June 14, 1814. 2 vol.
New York, 1813-14. 4°

WARD, FERDINAND DE W. *Missionary at Madras*.   India and the
Hindoos; being a popular view of the
geography, history,...and religion of
that ancient people; with an account
of Christian Missions among them.
New York, 1850.   12°

2 A CHRISTIAN Gift; or, pastoral
letters. Rochester, 1853. 16mo.

WARD, JAMES W. Woman; a
poem. Cincinnati, 1852. 8°

WARD, MALTHUS A. *M.D.* An
Address pronounced before the Massachusetts Horticultural Society, in
commemoration of its third annual
festival, Sept. 21, 1831. [With a
report of the Society's proceedings,
etc.] Boston, 1831. 8°

WARD, MATTHEW F. Letters
from three Continents... Second edition. New York, 1851. 12°

2 ENGLISH Items: or, microscopic
views of England and Englishmen.
New York, 1853. 12°

WARD, NATHANIEL. The Simple
Cobler of Aggawam in America.
Edited by D. Pulsifer. [Originally
published in 1647 under the pseudo-
nyme of Theodore de la Guard.]
Boston, 1843. 12mo.

WARD, WILLIAM. Memoir of the
Rev. William Ward, one of the Ser-
ampore Missionaries. Philadelphia
[1830?]. 12mo.

WARE, ASHUR. Reports of [Ad-
miralty]Cases argued and determined
in the District Court of the United
States for the District of Maine.
1822-39. Portland, 1839. 8°

WARE, HENRY, *the Elder*. An
Inquiry into the foundation, evidences,
and truths of Religion. 2 vol. Cambridge, 1842. 12°

2 LETTERS addressed to Trinitarians
and Calvinists; occasioned by Dr.
Wood's Letters to Unitarians. Second
edition. Cambridge, 1820. 8°

3 ANSWER to Dr. Wood's Reply,
in a second series of letters addressed
to Trinitarians and Calvinists. Cambridge, 1822. 8°

WARE, HENRY, *the Younger*.
Hints on Extemporaneous Preaching.
Third edition. Boston, 1831. 12°

2 THE WORKS of Henry Ware.
Vol. 1, 2. [Having also additional
title-pages, which read: " The miscellaneous writings of H. Ware."]
[Edited by Chandler Robbins.] Boston, 1846. 12°

3 THE PROSE Works of Henry
Ware. Edited by Chandler Robbins.
London [Boston printed], 1849. 8vo.

WARE, JOHN, *M.D.* Memoir of
the Life of Henry Ware, Jun. New
edition. 2 vol. Boston, 1846. 12°

2 HINTS to Young Men on the
true relation of the Sexes. Boston,
1850. 12°

WARE, WILLIAM. Sketches of
European Capitals. Boston, 1851.
12°

2 LECTURES on the Works and
Genius of Washington Allston. Boston, 1852. 12°

WARNER, F. ADDISON. Memoir
of F. A. Warner. By a Clergyman.
Philadelphia, 1831. 12mo.

WARNER, I. W. The Immi-
grant's Guide and Citizen's Manual:
a work for immigrants of all classes
to the United States of North America, *etc*. New York, 1848. 12°

WARNER, James F. A Universal Dictionary of Musical Terms: taken in part from Dr. Weber's Vocabulary of Italian words and phrases, but chiefly furnished from other sources, etc. Boston, 1842. 8°

2 RUDIMENTAL Leſſons in Music; containing the primary instruction requisite for all beginners in the art, whether vocal or instrumental. New York, 1845. 12°

3 RUDIMENTAL Leſſons in Music; containing the primary instruction requisite for all beginners in the art, whether vocal or instrumental. Third edition. New York, 1847. 12°

WARREN BAPTIST ASSOCIATION. Minutes of the Warren (Baptist) Aſſociation, held at .. Pawtucket (R. I.), Sept. 10 and 11, 1816. Boston [1816]. 8°

WARREN, EDWARD. Some Account of the Lethèon: or, Who is the discoverer? Third edition. Boston, 1847. 8vo.

WARREN, GEORGE WASHINGTON. City of Charlestown: the inaugural addreſs of the Mayor (G. W. Warren), .. upon the first organization of the City Government, etc. Charlestown, 1847. 8°

WARREN, JOHN, M.D. An Oration, delivered July 4, 1783, at .. Boston, in celebration of the anniversary of American Independence. Boston [1783]. 4°

2 AN EULOGY on the Abbé T. Ruſſell. Boston, 1796. 4to.

WARREN, JOHN C. Cases of Organic Diseases of the Heart, with diſſectionsand some remarks intended to point out the distinctive symptoms of these diseases. Boston, 1809. 8vo.

2 SURGICAL Observations on Tumours, with cases and operations. Boston [printed], London, 1839. 8vo.

3 PHYSICAL Education and the Preservationof Health. Boston, 1846. 12°

4 ETHERIZATION; with surgical remarks. Boston, 1848. 12°

5 ADDRESS before the American Medical Aſſociation at the anniversary meeting in Cincinnati. Boston, 1850. 8vo.

6 THE MASTODON Giganteus of North America. Boston, 1852. 4°

WARREN, JOHN ESAIAS. Para; or scenes and adventures on the banks of the Amazon. N. York, 1851. 12°

2 VAGAMUNDO: or, the Attaché in Spain... Second edition. New York, 1852. 12°

WARREN, JOSIAH. Equitable Commerce a new development of principles as substitutes for laws and government, for the harmonious adjustment and regulation of the pecuniary, intellectual, and moral intercourse of mankind, etc. New York, 1852. 12°

WARREN, MERCY, Mrs. Poems, dramatic and miscellaneous. Boston, 1790. 12mo.

2 HISTORY of the rise, progreſs, and termination of the American Revolution; interspersed with biographical, political, and moral observations. 3 vol. Boston, 1805. 8°

WARREN, OWEN G. Supernal Theology, and life in the Spheres, deduced from alleged spiritual manifestations. By O. G. Warren. The introduction and narrative portion of the work, by one of the Medical Faculty. New York, 1852. 8°

WARREN, WILLIAM. A Systematic View of Geography. . . . Third edition. Portland, 1843. 12°

WASHBURN, EMORY. A Lecture [on social claſſifications and divisions], read before the Worcester Lyceum, March 30, 1831. Worcester, 1831. 8°

2 SPEECH .. delivered in the House of Representatives of Maſſachusetts, Feb. 14, 1838, on the Bill to aid the construction of the Western Railroad. Springfield, 1838. 8°

3 SKETCHES of the Judicial History of Maſſachusetts, from 1630 to the Revolution in 1775. Boston, 1840. 8°

WASHINGTON, *Diſtrict of Columbia*. Acts of the Corporation of ... Washington, paſſed by the first Council. To which is prefixed, the act of incorporation. 2 pts. Washington, 1803. 8°. Also the

Acts paſſed at the 2nd Council, 1804
Acts paſſed at the 3rd Council, 1805
Acts paſſed at the 4th Council, 1806
Acts paſſed at the 5th Council, 1807
Acts paſſed at the 6th Council, 1808
Acts paſſed at the 7th Council, 1809
Acts paſſed at the 8th Council, 1810
Acts paſſed at the 9th Council, 1811
Laws paſſed at the 25th Council, 1827
Laws paſſed at the 26th Council, 1829
Laws paſſed at the 27th Council, 1830
Laws paſſed at the 28th Council, 1831
Laws paſſed at the 29th Council, 1832
Laws paſſed at the 30th Council, 1833
Laws paſſed at the 31st Council, 1833
Laws paſſed at the 32nd Council, 1835 ⎫
Laws paſſed at the 33rd Council, 1836 ⎬ vol. 4
Laws paſſed at the 34th Council, 1837 ⎪
Laws paſſed at the 36th Council, 1838 ⎭
Laws paſſed at the 38th Council, 1840 ⎫ vol. 5
Laws paſſed at the 39th Council, 1842 ⎭

Washington, 1804-42. 8°

2 A DIGESTED Index of the laws of the Corporation of . . Washington, to the twenty-sixth Council, inclusive. Prepared by D. A. Hall. Washington, 1829. 8°

3 LAWS relating to the City of Washington, paſſed at the first seſſion of the twenty-second Congreſſ. 1832. [Washington, 1832.] 8°

4 LAWS relating to the City of Washington and District of Columbia, paſſed at the 2nd seſſion of the twenty-second Congreſſ. 1833. [Washington, 1833.] 8°

5 LAWS relating to the City of Washington and District of Columbia, paſſed at the 1st seſſion of the twenty-third Congreſſ. 1834. [Washington, 1834.] 8°

6 LAWS relating to the City of Washington and District of Columbia, paſſed at the first seſſion of the twenty-fourth Congreſſ. [Washington,] 1836. 8°

7 COMMUNICATIONS from the Mayor, enclosing a report of the Commissioners of the Sinking Fund: also, a statement of the register, shewing the amount of the City debt, *etc*. Washington, 1837. 8°

8 LAWS relating to the City of Washington . . . . paſſed at the 2nd seſſion of the twenty-fifth Congreſſ. 1838. [Washington, 1838.] 8°

9 LAWS relating to the City of Washington . . . paſſed at the third seſſion of the twenty-fifth Congreſſ. 1839. [Washington, 1839.] 8°

10 LAWS relating to the City of Washington and District of Columbia, paſſed by the twenty-sixth Congreſſ. [Washington,] 1841. 8°

11 SCENES at Washington ; a story of the last generation. By a citizen of Baltimore. New York, 1848. 12°

12 ETIQUETTE at Washington ; together with the customs adopted by polite society in the other cities of the United States; to which is added an appendix, containing an accurate description of the public buildings in Washington. . . . Second edition, revised, . . by a citizen of Washington. Baltimore [and] Washing. 1850. 16°

13 THE WASHINGTON and Georgetown Directory . . Compiled . . by A. Hunter. [1853.] Washington, 1853. 8°

WASHINGTON COLLEGE, HARTFORD, *Connecticut*. Catalogue of the members of the Washington College Athenæum Society, and of the books in the library. . . . July, 1834. Hartford, 1834. 12°

2 STATEMENT of the course of study and instruction pursued at Washington College ; . . with a catalogue of the officers and students. Jan. 1835. [With an Appendix.] Hartford, 1835. 8°

3 CATALOGUE of the Officers and Students of Washington College. . . 1840-41. Washington, 1841. 8°

WASHINGTON COLLEGE,

CHESTERTOWN, *Maryland.* Regulations of Washington College. . . To which is prefixed an historical sketch of the College and addreſs to the public. Baltimore, 1844. 8°

WASHINGTON, BUSHROD. Reports of Cases argued and determined in the Court of Appeals of Virginia. [1790-96.] 2 vol. Richmond, 1798, 1799. 8°

2 REPORTS of Cases determined in the Circuit Court of the United States for the Third Circuit, comprising the Diſtricts of Pennsylvania and New Jersey; commencing at April Term. 1803 [to Oct. 1827]. [Edited by R. Peters.] 4 vol. Philadelphia, 1826-1829. 8vo.

WASHINGTON, GEORGE. The Journal of Major George Washington, sent by the Hon. Robt. Dinwiddie, Esq. Lt. Governor and Commander in Chief in Virginia, to the Commandant of the French forces on Ohio. Williamsburgh, 1754. 8vo.

2 LETTERS from General Washington to several of his friends, in June and July, 1776, in which is set forth an interesting view of American politics at that all-important period. Philadelphia, 1795. 8°

3 THE PRESIDENT's Addreſs to the People of the United States, Sept. 17, 1796, intimating his resolution of retiring from public service, *etc.* Philadelphia, 1796. 8vo.

4 EPISTLES domestic, confidential, and official, written about the commencement of the American Contest; *etc.* New York, 1796. 8vo.

5 ADDRESS of G. Washington . . . to the people of the United States preparatory to his declination. Baltimore, 1796. 12°

6 OFFICIAL Letters to the American Congreſs written during the war between the United Colonies and Great Britain. 2nd Boston edition. 2 vol. Boston, 1796. 12°

7 OFFICIAL Letters to the American Congreſs, written during the war between the United Colonies and Great Britain. 2 vol. New York, 1796. 8vo.

8 REMARKS occasioned by the late conduct of Mr. Washington as President of the United States. 1796. Philadelphia, 1797. 8vo.

9 SELECTIONS from the Correspondence of G. Washington and J. Anderson. Charlestown, 1800. 8°

10 THE ADDRESS of the late George Washington, when President, to the people of the United States, on declining being considered a candidate for their future suffrages. Salem, 1800. 8°

11 WASHINGTON's Monuments of Patriotism. Being a collection of interesting documents connected with the military command and civil administration of the American hero and patriot. To which is annexed, an eulogium on the character of General Washington, by W. Jackson. Philadelphia, 1800. 8°

12 LETTERS from his Excellency G. Washington to A. Young, Esq. F.R.S. and Sir J. Sinclair, Bart. M.P. containing an account of his husbandry, with his opinion on .various questions in agriculture, and many particulars of the rural economy of the United States. [Edited by A. Young.] Alexandria, 1803. 8°

13 PROCEEDINGS of the Aſsociation of Citizens to erect a monument in honour of Gen. G. Washington. Boston, 1811. 12°

14 THE CONDUCT of Washington compared with that of the present administration, in a series of letters and official documents, with notes. By a friend of truth and of honorable peace. Boston, 1813. 8°

15 LIFE of George Washington. American Sunday School Union, Philadelphia [1832]. 12mo.

16 THE WRITINGS of George Washington; being his correspondence, addreſses, meſsages, and other papers official and private: with a life of the author. By Jared Sparks. 12 vol. Boston, 1837. 8vo.

17 ILLUSTRATIONS of the principal events in the life of Washington. Edited by Jared Sparks. (N° 1. No more published.) Boston, 1842. 4°

18 REVOLUTIONARY Orders of Gen. Washington, iſſued during the years 1778, '80, '81, and '82. Selected from the MSS. of John Whiting . . and edited by . . . Henry Whiting. New York, 1844. 8°

19 LETTERS on Agriculture . . to Arthur Young . . and Sir John Sinclair, . . With statistical tables and remarks, by Thomas Jefferson, R. Peters, and other gentlemen, on the economy and management of farms in the United States. Edited by F. Knight. Washington, 1847. 4°

20 WASHINGTON and the Generals of the American Revolution. New edition, with corrections. Philadelphia, 1848. 12°

21 REPRINT of the original Letters from Washington to Joseph Reed, during the AmericanRevolution. Referred to in the Pamphlets of Lord Mahon and Mr. Sparks. By William B. Reed. Philadelphia, 1852. 8vo.

22 WASHINGTON's Farewell Addreſs to the people of the United States of America. [Edited by J. L. i.e. James Lenox.] New York, 1850. Fol.

WASHINGTON, GEORGE C. Communication from G. C. Washington, President of the Chesapeake and Ohio Canal Company to the Governor of Maryland; [on the affairs of the Company; with the Engineer's report; etc.] Annapolis, 1839. 8°

2 ANOTHER Edition. Annapolis [1839]. 8°

WASHINGTONIANSONGSTER. The Cold Water Melodies, and Washingtonian Songster. Boston, 1842. 12°

WATCH-CHAIN (THE). Philadelphia [1833]. 12mo.

WATERHOUSE, BENJAMIN, M.D. A Synopsis of a Course of Lectures on the theory and practice of medi-cine. In four parts. Part the first. Boston, 1786. 8°

2 THE RISE, Progreſs, and present State of Medicine; a discourse, delivered at Concord, July 6, 1791, before the Middlesex Medical Aſſociation, etc. Boston, 1792. 8°

3 PROGRESS of the New Inoculation in America. Cambridge, 1802. 8vo.

4 CAUTION to Young Persons concerning health. Cambridge, 1805. 8vo.

5 CAUTIONS to Young Persons concerning Health, shewing the evil tendency of the use of Tobacco. Cambridge, 1805. 8vo.

6 HEADS of a Course of Lectures on Natural History. Cambridge, 1810. 8vo.

7 THE BOTANIST: being the botanical part of a course of lectures on natural history, delivered in the University at Cambridge. Together with a discourse on the principle of vitality. Boston, 1811. 8°

8 AN ESSAY on Junius and his Letters; embracing a sketch of the life . . of W. Pitt, Earl of Chatham, etc. Boston [Cambridge printed], 1831. 8°

WATERMAN, afterwards ESLING, CATHARINE H. Flora's Lexicon: an interpretation of the language and sentiment of flowers: with an outline of botany, and a poetical introduction. Philadelphia [1839]. 12°

2 THE BROKEN Bracelet, and other poems. [Edited by J. F.] Philadelphia, 1850. 12°

WATERMAN, ELIJAH. An Oration delivered before the Society of Cincinnati, Hartford, July 4, 1794. Hartford, 1794. 8°

2 MEMOIRS of the Life and Writings of J. Calvin: together with a selection of letters written by him and other distinguished reformers: also, notes and biographical sketches of some of his cotemporaries. Boston, 1813. 8°

WATERMAN, Thomas W. The American Chancery Digest, being an analytical digested index of all the reported decisions in equity of the United States Courts and of the Courts of the several States to the present time. With notes and a copious index, also an introductory essay, comprising an historical sketch of the Court of Chancery, etc. Third edition. 3 vol. New York, 1851. 8°

WATERSTON, R. C. An Address delivered before the Sunday School Society of Newburyport, at their third anniversary, etc. Boston, 1835. 8°

2 On Moral and Spiritual Culture in Early Education, .. delivered before the American Institute of Instruction, etc. [Boston, 1836.] 8°

3 Thoughts on Moral and Spiritual Culture. Second edition, revised. Boston, 1844. 8°

WATERVILLE COLLEGE, Maine. Catalogue of the officers and students of Waterville College, and of the Clinical School of Medicine, at Woodstock, Vermont, connected with the college, 1830-1. Hallowell, 1830. 8°

2 Catalogus Senatus Academici, et eorum qui munera et officia gesserunt, quique alicujus gradus laurea donati sunt in Collegio Watervillensi, etc. Augustæ, 1837. 8°

WATER-WITCH, or the skimmer of the seas. A tale. By the author of The Pilot, etc. [J. F. Cooper]. A new edition. 2 vol. Philadelphia, 1838. 12°

WATKINS, Tobias. Anniversary Discourse delivered before the Columbian Institute, etc. Washington, 1826. 8°

WATSON, Elkanah. History of the rise, progress, and existing condition of the Western Canals in the State of New York, etc. Albany, 1820. 8°

WATSON, Henry C. Camp-Fires of the Revolution: or, the War

of Independence, illustrated by thrilling events and stories by the Old Continental Soldiers. Philadelphia, 1850. 8°

2 Heroic Women of History: comprising some of the most remarkable examples of female courage .. and self-sacrifice, etc. Philadel. 1852. 8°

3 Nights in a Block House; or, sketches of border life, etc. Philadelphia, 1852. 8°

4 The Old Bell of Independence: or, Philadelphia in 1776. Philadelphia [1852]. 12°

WATSON, John, M.D. Thermal Ventilation and other sanitary improvements applicable to public buildings, and recently adopted at the New York Hospital: a discourse delivered at the Hospital, February 8, 1851. New York, 1851. 8vo.

WATSON, John, and others. Statement of the cost of each species of Manufacture, carried on in the penitentiary. Tuscaloosa, 1844. 8°

WATSON, John F. Annals of Philadelphia. With an appendix. Philadelphia, 1830. 4to.

2 Historic Tales of the Olden Time: concerning the early settlement and advancement of New York City and State, etc. New York, 1832. 12°

3 Annals of Philadelphia and Pennsylvania, in the olden time; being a collection of memoirs, anecdotes, and incidents of the city and its inhabitants, and of the earliest settlements of the inland part of Pennsylvania, from the days of the founders. 2 vol. Philadelphia, 1844. 8vo.

4 Annals and Occurrences of New York City and State, in the olden time; being a collection of memoirs, anecdotes, and incidents, etc. Philadelphia, 1846. 8°

WATSON, John T. A Dictionary of Poetical Quotations; consisting of elegant extracts on every subject, compiled from various authors, and arranged under appropriate heads. Philadelphia, 1848. 12°

WATSON, RICHARD, *Bishop of Llandaff.* Strictures on Bishop Watson's "Apology for the Bible." By a Citizen of New York. New York, 1796. 12°

WATTERSTON, GEORGE. Gallery of American Portraits. Washington, 1830. 12°

2 AN ADDRESS delivered before the Columbian Horticultural Society, at the first annual exhibition, *etc.* (Proceedings of the Society, *etc.*) Washington, 1834. 8°

3 GALLERY of American Portraits. Third edition. Washington, 1836. 12°

WATTERSTON, GEORGE, AND VAN ZANDT, NICHOLAS B. Continuation of the Tabular Statistical Views of the United States, *etc.* Washington, 1833. 8°

WATTS, CHARLES. A Discourse on the Life and Character of the Hon. G. Mathews, late Presiding Judge of the Supreme Court of the State of Louisiana. New Orleans, 1837. 8°

WATTS, FREDERICK, and SERGEANT, HENRY J. Reports of Cases adjudged in the Supreme Court of Pennsylvania. 1841-45. 9 vol. Philadelphia, 1842-46. 8°

WATTS, ISAAC. Church Psalmody: a collection of psalms and hymns adapted to public worship. Selected from Dr. Watts and other authors. [Edited by L. Mason and D. Greene.] Boston, 1831. 12mo.

2 AN ARRANGEMENT of the Psalms, Hymns, and Spiritual Songs of Isaac Watts, to which is added a supplement of more than three hundred hymns from the best authors. . . By J. M. Winchell. Improved by the addition of two hundred hymns. Boston [1832]. 16mo.

WAYLAND, FRANCIS, *D.D.* The Moral Dignity of the Missionary Enterprise. A sermon [on Matthew xiii.

38] delivered before the Boston Baptist Foreign Mission Society, . . October 26, and before the Salem Bible Translation Society, . . November 4, 1823. Fourth edition. Boston, 1826. 8vo.

2 ENCOURAGEMENTS to Religious Effort: a sermon [on Matthew vi. 10] delivered at the request of the American Sunday School Union, May 25, 1830. Philadelphia, 1830. 12mo.

3 THE CERTAIN Triumph of the Redeemer, a sermon [on 1 Cor. xv. 25] delivered in the Murray Street Church, . . May 9, 1830. New York, 1830. 8vo.

4 INTRODUCTORY Discourse (before the Convention of Teachers assembled to form the American Institute of Instruction). [*See* AMERICAN INSTITUTE OF INSTRUCTION.] Boston, 1831. 8vo.

5 OCCASIONAL Discourses, including several never before published. Boston, 1833. 12°

6 THE MORAL Conditions of success in the Promulgation of the Gospel. An address delivered in the Baptist Meeting-house in Baldwin Place, Boston, . . . June 29, 1834. Boston, 1834. 8vo.

7 THE ELEMENTS of Political Economy. Abridged for the use of Academies. Boston, 1837. 12mo.

8 ELEMENTS of Moral Science. . . Third edition, revised. Boston, 1837. 12°

9 THE ELEMENTS of Political Economy. New York, 1837. 8vo.

10 A DISCOURSE, delivered at the opening of the Providence Athenæum, July 11, 1838. Providence, 1838. 8vo.

11 THE LIMITATIONS of Human Responsibility. Second edition. New York, 1838. 12mo.

12 ELEMENTS of Moral Science. Abridged and adapted to the use of schools and academies. Boston, 1839. 12mo.

13 A DISCOURSE in commemoration of the life and character of the Hon. Nicholas Brown. Boston, 1841. 8vo.

14 THOUGHTS on the present collegiate system in the United States. Boston, 1842. 12mo.

15 THE AFFAIRS of Rhode Island. A discourse [on Psalm xlvi. 1] delivered in the meeting house' of the first Baptist Church, Providence, May 22, 1842. Third edition. Providence, 1842. 8vo.

16 A DISCOURSE [on Psalm cxvi. 12, 13, 14] delivered in the first Baptist Church, Providence, on the day of public thanksgiving, July 21, 1842. Second edition. Providence, 1842.

17 THE CLAIMS of Whalemen on Christian Benevolence, a discourse [on Matthew xxv. 40] delivered in the Baptist Church, William Street, . . November 20, 1842. New Bedford, 1843. 8vo.

18 THE ELEMENTS of Political Economy. Boston, 1843. 12mo.

19 THE ELEMENTS of Moral Science. Boston, 1844. 8vo.

20 A DISCOURSE in commemoration of the life and services of W. G. Goddard. Providence, 1846. 8°

21 A MEMOIR of the life and labors of the Rev. A. Judson, D.D. 2 vol. Boston, 1853. 12mo.

22 THE ELEMENTS of Intellectual Philosophy. Boston, 1854. 8vo.

WAYLEN, EDWARD. A History of Prince George's Parish, Montgomery county. With a preliminary glance at the rise and establishment of the Episcopal Church in Maryland. Rockville, 1845. 12mo.

WEAVER, G. S. Lectures on Mental Science, according to the Philosophy of Phrenology. New York, 1852. 12mo.

2 HOPES and Helps for the Young of both Sexes, etc. New York, 1853. 12mo.

WEAVER, W. A. Register of the Officers and Agents, civil, military, and naval, in the service of the United States, Sept. 30, 1833. [See REGISTER.] Philadelphia, 1834. 8vo.

WEBBER, CHARLES WILKINS. Old Hicks the Guide ; or adventures in the Camanche country in search of a gold mine. New York, 1848. 12°

2 THE HUNTER-NATURALIST Romance of Sporting ; or, wild scenes and wild hunters. Vol. 1. Philadelphia [1851 ?]. 8°

3 ROMANCE of Natural History ; or, wild scenes and wild hunters. Philadelphia, 1852. 8°

4 TALES of the Southern Border. Parts 2 and 3. Philadelphia, 1852. 8°

5 TALES of the Southern Border. Philadelphia, 1853. 8°

6 WILD Scenes and Song-Birds. New York [printed, and] London, 1854 [1853]. 8vo.

7 YIEGER's Cabinet. Spiritual Vampirism : the history of Etherial Softdown and her friends of the " New Light." Philadelphia, 1853. 12°

WEBBER, SAMUEL. An Introduction to English Grammar, on an analytical plan, etc. Cambridge and Boston, 1832. 12°

WEBER, GOTTFRIED. An Attempt at a systematically arranged Theory of Musical Composition, by Godfrey Weber. Translated from the third . . German edition, with notes, by J. T. Warner. Second edition. Boston, 1842. 8vo.

2 THEORY of Musical Composition, treated with a view to a naturally consecutive arrangement of topics. Translated from the third German edition, with notes by J. T. Warner. 2 vol. London [Boston], 1846. 8vo.

WEBSTER, DANIEL. An Anniversary Addreſs delivered before the Federal gentlemen of Concord,...July 4, 1806 [in commemoration of American Independence]. Concord, N. H. 1806. 8°

2 AN ADDRESS delivered before the Washington Benevolent Society at Portsmouth [in New Hampshire], July 4, 1812 [in commemoration of American Independence]. Portsmouth [1812]. 8°

3 SPEECH .. delivered in the House of Representatives of the U[nited] States, .. 14 Jan. 1814, on a bill, making further provision for filling the ranks of the regular army, *etc.* Keene, 1814. 8°

4 SPEECH .. upon the tariff, delivered in the House of Representatives of the United States, April, 1824. [With a note, containing extracts from a speech delivered by Mr. Robinson, in the House of Commons.] Washington, 1824. 8°

5 MR. WEBSTER's Speech on the Greek Revolution. Washing.1824. 8°

6 AN ADDRESS delivered at the laying of the corner stone of the Bunker Hill Monument. Fourth edition. Boston, 1825. 8°

7 A DISCOURSE in commemoration of the lives and services of John Adams and Thomas Jefferson, delivered in Faneuil Hall, Boston, August 2, 1826. Boston, 1826. 8°

8 SPEECH . . . in reply to Mr. Hayne, of South Carolina; the resolution of Mr. Foot, of Connecticut, relative to the public lands being under consideration ; .. in the Senate, Jan. 26, 1830. Washington, 1830. 8°

9 SPEECH .. at the National Republican Convention, in Worcester, Oct. 12, 1832. Boston, 1832. 8°

10 MR. WEBSTER's Speeches in the Senate, upon the question of renewing the Charter of the Bank of the United States, .. May 25 and 28, 1832. Washington, 1832. 8°

11 SPEECH .. in the Senate .. on the President's veto of the bank bill, July 11, 1832. Boston, 1832. 8°

12 ADDRESS to the Citizens of Pittsburgh, July 9, 1833, by D. Webster [on the occasion of his visit to that place]. Boston, 1833. 8°

13 SPEECH .. in the Senate, in reply to Mr. Calhoun's speech, on the bill " further to provide for the collection of duties on imports," .. 16 Feb. 1833. Washing. 1833. 8°

14 REMARKS .. on the removal of the deposites, and on the subject of

a national bank; delivered in the Senate, .. Jan. 1834. Washington, 1834. 8°

15 MR. WEBSTER's Speech on the President's protest [against a resolution of the Senate, declaring that in the late executive proceedings in relation to the public revenue, the President had assumed a power not conferred by the Constitution, *etc.*] delivered in the Senate, .. May 7, 1834. Washington, 1834. 8°

16 SPEECH .. on moving for leave to introduce a bill to continue the Bank of the United States for six years, delivered in the Senate, .. March 18, 1834. Washington, 1834. 8°

17 REMARKS of Mr. Webster, on different occasions, on the removal of the deposites; and on the subject of a National Bank, delivered in the Senate, . . . Jan. and Feb. 1834. Washington, 1834. 8°

18 LEGISLATIVE Nomination of Daniel Webster for the Presidency. [Boston? 1835.] 8°

19 SPEECHES and Forensic Arguments. 2 vol. Boston, 1835. 8vo.

20 SPEECH of Mr. Webster .. on introducing his proposition for the distribution of the surplus revenue; in Senate .. May 31, 1836. Washington, 1836. 8°

21 SPEECH of Mr. Webster, in the Senate .. Jan. 4, 1836, on Mr. Benton's resolutions for appropriating the surplus revenue to national defence. Boston, 1836. 8°

22 MR. WEBSTER's Speech on the currency, and on the new plan for collecting and keeping the public moneys, delivered in the Senate . . . Sept. 28, 1837. Washing. 1837. 8°

23 MR. WEBSTER's Second Speech [in the Senate], on the sub-treasury bill, delivered March 12, 1838. [Washington, 1838.] 8°

24 MR. WEBSTER's Speech on the bill imposing additional duties as depositaries, in certain cases, on public officers, .. commonly called the sub-treasury bill; delivered in the Senate

.. March 12, 1838; and his speech of .. 22nd March, in answer to Mr. Calhoun. Boston, 1838. 8°

25 THE BEAUTIES of the Hon. Daniel Webster; selected and arranged, with a critical essay on his genius and writings, by J. Rees. New York, 1839. 12°

26 REMARKS of Mr. Webster and Mr. Wright, on the President's Message, the finances, and debts of the nation. (In Senate, Dec. 16, 1840.) [Washington, 1840.] 8°

27 ADDRESS, delivered at Bunker Hill, June 17, 1843, on the completion of the monument. Boston, 1843. 8°

28 MR. WEBSTER's Address at Andover, Nov. 9, 1843 [relative to banking, the currency, and the commercial system of the United States]. Boston, 1843. 8°

29 WEBSTER's Speech: A defence of the Christian religion, and of the religious instruction of the young: delivered in the Supreme Court of the United States, Feb. 10, 1844, in the case of Stephen Girard's will. New York, 1844. 8vo.

30 MR. WEBSTER's Remarks at the meeting of the Suffolk bar, on moving the resolutions occasioned by the death of .. Mr. Justice Story. Boston, 1845. 8°

31 MR. WEBSTER's Vindication of the treaty of Washington of 1842; in a speech delivered in the Senate .. 6 and 7 Apr. 1846. Washington, 1846. 8°

32 AN APPEAL to the Whig National Convention, in favor of the nomination of D. Webster to the Presidency; by a Whig from the start. [A series of papers republished from the New York Commercial Advertiser.] New York, 1848. 8°

33 MR. WEBSTER's Speech in the United States Senate, March 24, 1848, upon the war with Mexico. Boston, 1848. 8°

34 THE WORKS of Daniel Webster. (Biographical Memoir of the Public

Life of D. Webster, by Edward Everett.) 6 vol. Boston, 1851. 8°

35 MR. WEBSTER's Speeches at Buffalo, Syracuse, and Albany. May, 1851. New York, 1851.

36 PERSONAL Memorials of Daniel Webster. Philadelphia, 1851. 8°

37 AN ADDRESS delivered before the New York Historical Society, Feb. 23, 1852. New York, 1852. 8vo.

38 LIFE and Memorials of Daniel Webster. From the New York Daily Times. 2 vol. New York, 1853. 12°

39 A MEMORIAL of Daniel Webster from the city of Boston [consisting of an account of his illness and death, with an account of the proceedings of various public bodies in Boston thereupon. Edited by G. S. H. i.e. George S. Hillard]. Boston, 1853. 8°

WEBSTER, JOHN W. A Description of the island of St. Michael, comprising an account of its geological structure; with remarks on the other Azores or Western Isles. Boston, 1821. 8vo.

2 A MANUAL of Chemistry, on the basis of Professor Brande's; .. Compiled from the works of the most distinguished Chemists. .. Second edition, comprehending the recent discoveries, etc. Boston, 1828. 8°

3 REPORT of the case of J. W. Webster ... indicted for the murder of George Parkman ... before the Supreme Judicial Court of Massachusetts; including the hearing on the petition for a writ of error, the prisoner's confessional statements, etc. By G. Bemis, Esq. Boston, 1850. 8°

WEBSTER, NOAH. Dissertations on the English Language: with notes historical and critical. To which is added, ... an essay on a reformed mode of spelling, with Dr. Franklin's arguments on that subject. Boston, 1789. 8°

2 A COLLECTION of Essays and Fugitive Writings on moral, historical, political and literary subjects. Boston, 1790. 8°

3 EFFECTS of Slavery on morals and industry. Hartford, 1793. 8°

4 AN ORATION pronounced before the citizens of New Haven, on the anniversary of the Independence of the United States, July 4th, 1798. New Haven [1798]. 8°

5 A LETTER to the Governors, Instructors, and Trustees of the Universities and other Seminaries on the errors of English grammars. New York, 1798. 8°

6 A BRIEF History of Epidemic and Pestilential Diseases. 2 vol. Hartford, 1799. 8vo.

7 A PHILOSOPHICAL and Practical Grammar of the English Language. New Haven, 1807. 12°

8 THE AMERICAN Spelling Book. With the latest corrections. Concord, N. H. [1823?] 12°

9 LETTERS to a Young Gentleman commencing his education: To which is subjoined a brief history of the United States. N. Haven, 1823. 8°

10 AN IMPROVED Grammar of the English Grammar. Cincinnati, 1836. 12°

11 MISTAKES and Corrections: 1, Improprieties . . . . in the Common version of the Scriptures, . . 2, Explanations of prepositions, . . 3, Errors in English grammars; 4, Mistakes in the Hebrew Lexicon of Gesenius; . . 5, Errors in Butler's Scholar's Companion; . . . 6, Errors in Richardson's Dictionary. New Haven, 1837. 8°

12 OBSERVATIONS on Language, and on the errors of class-books; addressed to the members of the New York Lyceum; also, observations on commerce, addressed to the members of the Mercantile Library Association, in New York. New Haven, 1839. 12°

13 THE ELEMENTARY Spelling Book. Concord, N. H. 1840. 12°

14 AN AMERICAN Dictionary of the English Language; first edition in Octavo, containing the whole vocabulary of the Quarto, with corrections,

improvements, and several thousand additional words: to which is prefixed an introductory dissertation on the origin, history, and connection of the languages of western Asia and Europe, with an explanation of the principles on which languages are formed. 2 vol. New Haven, 1841. Imp. 8vo.

15 COMMENDATIONS of Dr. N. Webster's books. [With an essay by N. Webster on the state of English philology.] [N. Haven? 1841?] 8°

16 THE LAST Revised edition. The elementary Spelling-book. N. York, 1843. 12°

17 A COLLECTION of Papers on political, literary, and moral subjects. New York, 1843. 8°

18 AN AMERICAN Dictionary of the English Language; first edition in Octavo, containing the whole vocabulary of the Quarto, with corrections, improvements, and several thousand additional words: to which is prefixed an introductory dissertation on the origin, history, and connection of the languages of Western Asia and Europe, with an explanation of the principles on which languages are formed. 2 vol. Springfield, 1845. Imp. 8vo.

19 AN AMERICAN Dictionary of the English Language; .. by N. Webster, abridged from the quarto edition of the author. To which are added, a synopsis of words differently pronounced by different orthoëpists, and Walker's Key to the classical pronunciation of Greek, Latin, and Scripture proper names. Revised edition, with an appendix. 2 pts. New York, 1846. 8°

20 A HIGH School Pronouncing Dictionary of the English Language; abridged from the American Dictionary of N. Webster by William G. Webster. New York, 1848. 12°

21 AN AMERICAN Dictionary of the English Language; containing the whole Vocabulary of the first Edition, the entire corrections and improve-

ments of the second edition: to which is prefixed, an ,ntroductory Differtation on the origin, history, and connection of the languages of Western Asia and Europe, with an explanation of the principles on which Languages are formed. Revised and enlarged by C. A. Goodrich. With Pronouncing Vocabularies of Scripture, Classical, and Geographical names. Springfield, 1848. 4to.

22 ANOTHER copy, from duplicate stereotypeplates. London, 1848. 4to.

23 A DICTIONARY of the English Language, abridged from the Quarto Dictionary by N. Webster: revised and enlarged by C. A. Goodrich; . . containing several thousand additional words, the Accented Vocabularies of Walker's Key to the Classical Pronunciation of Greek, Latin, and Scripture Proper Names. . . With a Memoir of the Author. London [New York printed!] 1854 [1853]. 8vo.

WEBSTER, PELATIAH. Political Essays on the Nature and operation of Money, Public Finances, and other Subjects; published during the American War, and continued up to 1791. Philadelphia, 1791. 8vo.

WEBSTER, SAMUEL. The Misery and Duty of an oppress'd and enslav'd People represented in a sermon [on Nehemiah ix. 36-38]. Bost.1774. 8°

WEBSTER, WILLIAM G. An Elementary Dictionary of the English Language,etc. NewYork[1844]. 12°

WEEK. The First Day of the Week. Philadelphia, 1827. 12mo.

2 THE WEEK; or the practical duties of the fourth Commandment. Philadelphia, 1827. 12mo.

3 THE WEEK completed. Philadelphia, 1827. 12mo.

WEEKLY REGISTER (THE). Containing political, historical, geographical, scientifical, astronomical, statistical, and biographical, documents, essays, and facts. . . H. Niles,

editor. [Continued after vol. 5 as Niles' Weekly Register.] Sept. 1811 to Sept. 1836. Vol. 1-50. [The title page to vol. 1 is of the "Third Edition" and bears date 1816.] Baltimore, 1816 [1811-36]. 8vo. Niles' Weekly Register. W.O.Niles, Editor. Vol. 51-52. [Further continued as] Niles' National Register. W.O.Niles, Editor. Vol. 53-56; J. Hughes, Editor. Vol. 57-64. Baltimore[1836-43]. 4to.

2 GENERAL Index to the first twelve volumes, etc. Baltimore, 1818. 8vo.

WEEKLY HERALD. Vol. 4. N° 3. Jan. 18th, 1840. New York, 1840. Fol.

WEEMS, MASON L. The Life of George Washington, with curious anecdotes. Philadel. 1810. 12°

2 THE LIFE of B. Franklin; with many choice anecdotes and admirable sayings of this great man. Philadelphia, 1839. 12°

3 THE LIFE of G. Washington, with curious anecdotes, etc. Philadelphia, 1840. 12°

WEIR, JAMES. Long Powers: or the regulators. A romance of Kentucky. 2vol. Philadelphia,1850. 12°

2 SIMON Kenton: or, the Scout's Revenge. An historical novel. Philadelphia, 1852. 12°

WEISENGER, L. A. AND OTHERS. [Begins] Gentlemen of the Senate, etc. [A petition to the Senate, and House of Representatives of Alabama, for a grant from the public funds in aid of Madison College.] Tuscaloosa! 1845! s. sh. fol°

WEISS, JOHN. Modern Materialism. A discourse at the ordination of Mr. C. Lowe, etc. New Bedford, 1852. 8°

2 A DISCOURSE occasioned by the death of Daniel Webster, delivered in the Unitarian Church, New Bedford, Nov. 14, 1852. Boston and Cambridge, 1853. 8°

WELCH, BENJAMIN. Surgeons' Splints and improved apparatus for fractures. New York, 1852. 8vo.

WELCH, OLIVER. The American Arithmetic, adapted to the currency of the United States... Second edition, revised, corrected and improved. Exeter, 1814. 12°

WELD, EDWARD F. The Ransomed Bride: a tale of the Inquisition. New York, 1846. 8°

WELD, H. HASTINGS. Scenes in the Lives of the Apostles. [A series of poems, selected from various authors.] Edited by H. H. Weld. Philadelphia [1846]. 8°

2 SCENES in the Lives of the Patriarchs and Prophets. [A selection of sacred poetry by various authors.] Edited by H. H. Weld. Philadelphia [1847]. 8°

WELD, LEWIS. An Address delivered in the Capitol, in Washington City, Feb. 16, 1828, at an exhibition of three of the pupils of the Pennsylvania Institution for the education of the deaf and dumb. Washington, 1828. 8°

WELLER, JOHN B. Remarks .. in reply to Mr. Stuart, of Pennsylvania [on a proposition relative to the navigation of the Western waters; delivered in the] House of Representatives, Jan. 17 and 18, 1844. [Washington, 1844.] 8°

WELLS, D. Hampshire, ss. Between J. Bardwell, et al. plaintiffs in equity, and D. Ames, et al. defendants. Remarks of D. Wells, for the plaintiffs, on the reply of the defendants, in the argument on exceptions to the Master's report; [in a case of claim to erect and use a certain dam.] [Northampton, 1836?] 12°

WELLS, JOHN. An Oration delivered .. 4 July, 1798, .. before the young men of the city of New York, assembled to commemorate their National Independence. New York, 1798. 8°

WELLS, LUCY K. A Mother's Plea for the Sabbath; in a series of letters to an absent son; illustrated by facts. Third edition, with an introductory essay, by .. W. Warren. Portland, 1847. 12°

WELLS, W. H. *M.A.* Wells' School Grammar .. of the English language... Third thousand. Andover, 1846. 12°

WENDELL, JOHN L. Reports of Cases argued and determined in the Supreme Court of Judicature, and in the Court for the trial of Impeachments and the correction of Errors of the State of New York [from May term, 1828, to Oct. term, 1841]. 26 vol. Albany, 1829-42. 8vo.

2 A DIGEST of Cases decided and reported in the Supreme Court of Judicature, and in the Court for the correction of Errors, of the State of New York, from May, 1828, to May, 1835; with tables of the names of the cases reported. Albany, 1836. 8°

WESLEYAN UNIVERSITY, MIDDLETOWN, *Connecticut*. A Catalogue of the officers and students, 1839-40 (to 1842-43). 3 parts. Middletown, 1839-42. 8°

WEST. The far West; or, a tour beyond the mountains, *etc.* [By Edmund Flagg.] 2 vol. New York, 1838. 12°

WEST, CHARLES E. An Address delivered before the Patron and Pupils of the Buffalo Female Academy, at the dedication of Goodell Hall, .. 6th of July, 1852. Buffalo, 1852. 8°

WEST POINT. A Guide Book to West Point and vicinity; containing descriptive, historical, and statistical sketches of the United States Military Academy, and of other objects of interest. N. York, 1844. 12°

WESTERN LITERARY INSTITUTE, *Cincinnati*. Transactions of the fourth annual meeting of the Western Literary Institute, and College of Profeſsional Teachers; held in ... 1834. Cincinnati, 1835. 8vo.

2 TRANSACTIONS of the fifth annual meeting, .. held in .. 1835. Cincinnati, 1836. 8vo.

WESTERN RESERVE COLLEGE, HUDSON, *Ohio.* Catalogue of the officers, alumni, and students, .. Dec. 1834 (and Nov. 1839). 2 parts. Cleveland, 1834-39. 12°

WESTERN REVIEW and Miscellaneous Magazine, a monthly publication, devoted to literature and science. 4 vol. Lexington, 1820-21. 8°

WESTERN TRAVELLER (THE); from Albany and Troy to Buffalo and Niagara Falls, *etc.* N. York, 1844. 12°

WESTERN WORLD. Lays of the Western World. [By various authors.] Illuminated by T. W. Gwilt Mapleson. New York [1848?]. 4°

WESTERVELT, HARMAN C. American Progreſs: an addreſs delivered at the eighteenth annual fair of the American Institute. New York, 1845. 8°

2 FAIRS.—American Institute.—The Proteƈtion of American Industry. An addreſs delivered before the American Institute, during the nineteenth annual fair. New York, 1846. 8°

WESTMAN, HABAKKUK O. Transaƈtions of the Society of Literary and Scientific Chiffoniers; being eſſays on primitive arts in domestic life: the Spoon, with upwards of one hundred illustrations, *etc.* New York, 1844. 8°

WESTON, EZRA. An Addreſs delivered before the Maſsachusetts Horticultural Society, at their eighth anniversary, Sept. 17, 1836. [With a report of the Society's proceedings, *etc.*] Boston, 1836. 8vo.

WETHERELL, ELIZABETH, *Pseud.* [*i. e.* MISS SUSAN WARNER]. The wide, wide World. 2 vol. New York, 1851. 12°

WETMORE, ALPHONSO. Gazet-

teer of the State of Miſsouri. To which is added, an appendix, containing frontier sketches and illustrations of Indian charaƈter. St. Louis, 1837. 8°

WETMORE, WILLIAM. An Oration on the death of General George Washington, delivered at the request of the citizens of Castine, .. 22 Feb. 1800, *etc.* Castine [1800]. 8°

WETTE, WILHELM MARTIN LEBERECHT DE. A critical and historical Introduƈtion to the Canonical Scriptures of the Old Testament. From the German of W. M. L. de Wette. Translated and enlarged by T. Parker. 2 vol. Boston, 1843. 8vo.

WHARTON, CHARLES HENRY. A Concise View of the principal points of controversy between the Protestant and Roman Churches; containing, 1. A letter to the Roman Catholics of the City of Worcester, in England. 2. A reply .. by .. Archbishop Carroll. 3. An answer to .. Archbishop Carroll's reply. 4. A short answer to the appendix to The Catholic Question, decided in New York in 1813. 5. A few short remarks on Dr. O'Callagher's reply to the above answer. By Rev. C. H. Wharton. 5 parts. New York, 1817. 8°

2 THE REMAINS of the Rev. C. H. Wharton, with a memoir of his life, by G. W. Doane, Bishop of New Jersey. 2 vol. Philadel. 1834. 12mo.

WHARTON, ELIZA. The Coquette; or, the history of Eliza Wharton; a novel, founded on faƈt. By a Lady of Maſsachusetts. Charlestown, 1802. 12°

WHARTON, FRANCIS. State Trials of the United States during the administrations of Washington and Adams; with references historical and profeſsional, and preliminary notes on the politics of the times. Philadelphia, 1849. 8°

2 A TREATISE on the Criminal Law of the United States, comprising a

Digest of the Penal Statutes of the general Government, and of Maſſachusetts, New York, Pennsylvania and Virginia; with the decisions. . . Second edition.   Philadel. 1852. 8°

WHARTON, Thomas J. A Digest of the reported cases adjudged in the several courts held in Pennsylvania; together with some manuscript cases. Second edition.   Philadel. 1829. 8°

2 Reports of cases adjudged in the Supreme Court of Pennsylvania, in the Eastern Diſtrict. Dec. term, 1835, to March term, 1841. 6 vol. Philadelphia, 1836-41. 8°

WHEATON, Eber. Analytical Arithmetic, etc. New York,1828. 12°

WHEATON, Henry. A Digest of the Law of maritime captures and prizes. New York, 1815. 8°

2 Reports of cases argued and adjudged in the Supreme Court of the United States, from 1816 to 1827. 12 vol.   Philadelphia and New York, 1818-27. 8vo.

3 Some Account of the Life, Writings, and Speeches of William Pinkney. New York, 1826. 8°

4 A Digest of the decisions of the Supreme Court of the United States, from Feb. term, 1821, to Jan. term, 1829; and also of the cases in the Circuit and Diſtrict Courts of the United States, from the commencement of the reports; being a continuation of Wheaton's Digest. By Two Gentlemen of the New York bar. New York, 1829. 8°

5 Report of the copy-right case of Wheaton v. Peters, decided in the Supreme Court of the United States. With an appendix, containing the acts of Congreſs relating to copyright. New York, 1834. 8°

6 Elements of International Law. Third edition, revised and corrected. Philadelphia, 1846. 8°

7 The Progress and Prospects of Germany: a discourse before the Phi Beta Kappa Society of Brown University, etc. Boston, 1847. 8°

WHEATON, Nathaniel S. A Journal of a Residence .. in London; including excursions through various parts of England; and a short tour in France and Scotland; in the years 1823 and 1824. Hartford, 1830. 8°

WHEELER, Jacob D. Reports of criminal law cases decided at the City-hall of the city of New York; with notes and references; (containing, also, a view of the criminal laws of the United States.) 3 vol. New York, 1823-25. 8°

2 A Practical Treatise on the law of slavery; being a compilation of all the decisions made on that subject, in the several Courts of the United States, and State Courts. With copious notes and references to the statutes and other authorities, systematically arranged. New York, 1837. 8°

3 The American Chancery Digest; being a digested index of all the reported decisions in Equity, in the United States Courts, and in the Courts of the several States. Second edition. 2 vol. New York, 1841. 8°

WHEELER, John. A Sermon [on 2 Cor. x. 4, 5] preached before the Vermont Domestic Miſſionary Society, etc. Windsor, 1826. 8°

WHEELER, John H. Historical Sketches of North Carolina, from 1584 to 1851. Compiled from original records, official documents, and traditional statements. With biographical sketches, etc. 2 vol. Philadelphia, 1851. 8°

WHEELOCK, Eleazar. A plain and faithful Narrative of the original design, rise, progreſs, and present state of the Indian Charity School, at Lebanon, in Connecticut. (A continuation of the narrative, etc.) 2 parts. Boston, 1763-65. 8°

WHEELOCK, John, A. M. An Eſſay on the beauties and excellencies of Painting, Music, and Poetry; pronounced at the anniversary com-

mencement at Dartmouth College, . .
1774. Hartford [1774]. 8°

2 EULOGIUM on . . J. Smith, D. D.
Profeſſor of the learned languages at
Dartmouth College. By the President
[J. Wheelock]. Hanover, 1809. 8°

WHEELWRIGHT, JOHN.
Charges preferred against the New
York Female Benevolent Society and
the Auditing Committee in 1835 and
1836, by J. R. M'Dowall, . . . answered and refuted by himself!! in
his own journal!!! in the year 1833.
New York, 1836. 8°

WHELPLEY, SAMUEL. A Com-
pend of History, from the earliest
times; comprehending a general view
of the present state of the world, with
respeƈt to civilization, religion, and
government; and a brief diſſertation
on the importance of historical knowledge. Tenth edition, with corrections and . . additions, . . by Rev. J.
Emerson. 2 vol. Boston, 1831. 12°

WHIPPLE, EDWIN PERCY. Lectures on subjeƈts conneƈted with Literature and life. Second edition.
Boston, 1850. 12°

2 WASHINGTON and the Principles
of the Revolution. An oration delivered before the Municipal Authorities of the city of Boston, at the celebration of the Declaration of American
Independence, July 4, 1850. Second
edition. Boston, 1850. 12°

WHIPPLE, JOHN, LL.D. A Discourse in commemoration of the life
and services of Daniel Webster. Providence, 1852. 8°

WHIPPLE, THOMAS. Speech . .
on the proposition to amend the Constitution of the United States; delivered in the House of Representatives, . . March 26, 1826. Washington, 1826. 8°

WHITCOMB, SAMUEL. Two
Leƈtures on the advantages of a Republican condition of Society, for the
promotion of the arts and the cultivation of science. Boston, 1833. 8°

WHITE, C. H. A History of the
" Spiritual Knockings," being aſi authentic relation of faƈts, with the
author's personal experience, etc.
[Watertown, Maſſ.] 1852. 12mo.

WHITE, CHARLES, D.D. President
of Wabash College. Eſſays on Literature and Ethics. Boston, 1853. 12°

WHITE, CHARLES I. D.D. Discourse [on 1 Cor. ch. 12] delivered
at the funeral service of the late J.
Nenninger, etc. Baltimore, 1839. 8°

2 LIFE of Mrs. E. A. Seton, foundreſs and first superior of the sisters or
daughters of Charity in the United
States of America; with copious ex-
traƈts from her writings, and an historical sketch of the sisterhood, etc.
New York, 1853. 12mo.

WHITE, DANIEL APPLETON. An
Eulogy on the life and charaƈter of
Nathaniel Bowditch. Salem, 1838. 8°

2 AN ADDRESS delivered before
the Society of the Alumni of Harvard
University, Aug. 27, 1844. Cambridge, 1844. 8°

WHITE, E. Specimen of modern
and light face Printing Types and
Ornaments cast at the Thames Street
Letter foundry of E. White. New
York, 1831. 8°

WHITE, GEORGE S. Memoir of
Samuel Slater, the father of American
manufaƈtures, conneƈted with a history of the rise and progreſs of the
cotton manufaƈture in England and
America. With remarks on the moral
influence of manufaƈtories in the United States. . . Second edition. Philadelphia, 1836. 8°

WHITE, GILBERT. The Natural
History of Selborne. New York,
1843. 12°

WHITE, HENRY, B.A. Elements
of Universal History. . . Fifth American edition, with additions and questions, by J. S. Hart. Philadelphia,
1845. 12°

WHITE, HENRY, *Rev.* The Early History of New England, illustrated by numerous interesting incidents. Ninth edition. Concord, 1845. 12°

WHITE, HUGH L. Letter . . of H. L. White to the Legislature of Tennefsee, on declining to obey certain of their resolutions of instruction, and resigning the office of Senator of the United States. Washing. 1840. 8°

WHITE, JOHN, *Rev.* The Difsenting Gentleman's Answer to the Rev. Mr. White's " Three Letters ;" in which a separation from the establishment is fully justified, *etc.* The fifth edition. Boston, 1748. 8°

WHITE, JOHN, *Rev.* AND OTHERS. The Testimony of a number of New England Ministers, met at Boston, Sept. 25, 1745; profefsing the ancient faith of these churches. . . Reciting an excellent act concerning preaching lately made by the General Afsembly of the Church of Scotland. Boston, 1745. 8°

WHITE, JOHN, *Lieut.* History of a Voyage to the China Sea. Boston, 1823. 8vo.

WHITE, JOSEPH M. A New Collection of Laws, Charters, and Local Ordinances of the governments of Great Britain, France, and Spain, relating to the concefsions of land in their respective colonies; together with the laws of Mexico and Texas on the same subject. To which is prefixed Judge Johnson's Translation of Azo's and Manuel's Institutes of the civil law of Spain. 2 vol. Philadelphia, 1839. 8°

WHITE, PHINEHAS. An Oration delivered at Dummerston, Vt. July 4, 1815, in commemoration of the 39th anniversary of American Independence. [Dummerston, 1815.] 8°

WHITE, WILLIAM, *Bishop.* A Sermon [on Deut. viii. 10] on the due celebration of the festival, appointed as a thanksgiving for the fruits of the earth, *etc.* Philadelphia, 1786. 8vo.

2 COMPARATIVE Views of the controversy between the Calvinists and the Arminians. 2 vol. Philadelphia, 1817. 8°

3 MEMOIRS of the Protestant Episcopal Church in the United States of America. Philadelphia, 1820. 8vo.

4 AN ADDRESS, delivered before the trustees, faculty, and students of the General Theological Seminary of the Protestant Episcopal Church in the United States, . . on the occasion of the delivery of the testimonials to the students who had completed their course of studies, July 30, 1824. New York, 1824. 8vo.

5 MEMOIRS of the Protestant Episcopal Church in the United States of America. . . . Second edition. New York, 1836. 8vo.

WHITE, WILLIAM. A History of Belfast [Maine], with introductory remarks on Acadia. Belfast, 1827. 12°

WHITE, WILLIAM CHARLES. An Oration, pronounced at Worcester, on the anniversary of American Independence, July 4, 1804. Worcester, July 10, 1804. 8°

2 AN ORATION, in commemoration of the anniversary of American Independence, delivered in Boston, July 4, 1809, at the request of the Bunker Hill Afsociation. . . To which is added, an introductory addrefs, by D. Everett, Esq. Boston, 1809. 8°

3 A COMPENDIUM and Digest of the law of Mafsachusetts. 4 vol. Boston, 1809-11. 8°

4 AVOWALS of a Republican. Worcester, 1813. 8°

WHITE MOUNTAIN and Winnepifsiogee Lake Guide Book. Boston, 1846. 12°

WHITE MOUNTAINS. Guide to the White Mountains and Lakes of New Hampshire. Concord [1851]. 12°

WHITE SULPHUR SPRINGS. Six Weeks in Fauquier: being the substance of a series of familiar letters; illustrating the scenery, . . and general characteristics of the White Sulphur Springs, *etc.* By a Visiter. New York, 1839. 12°

WHITEFIELD, GEORGE. Three Letters. ... 1, 2. Concerning Archbishop Tillotson : 3. To the Inhabitants of Maryland, Virginia, .. and.. Carolina, concerning their Negroes. Philadelphia, printed by B. Franklin, 1740. 8vo.

2 THE QUERISTS : or an extract of sundry passages taken out of Mr. Whitefield's printed Sermons, Journals, and Letters : together with some scruples propos'd in proper queries raised on each remark. By some Church members of the Presbyterian persuasion. Third edition. Philadelphia printed, Charles Town reprinted, 1741. 12mo.

3 A LETTER ... to some Church Members of the Presbyterian persuasion, in answer to certain scruples and queries relating to some passages in his printed Sermons and other Writings. To which is added Two Letters from Nathaniel Lovetruth [B. Franklin ?] to Mr. Whitefield, containing exceptions to his 'foresaid Letter. 3d edition. Charles Town, S. C. 1741. 12mo.

4 A SHORT Address to persons of all denominations, occasioned by the alarm of an intended invasion... The fourth edition. London printed, Boston reprinted, 1756. 8°

5 OBSERVATIONS on some fatal mistakes [in] a book lately published and intitled, " The doctrine of Grace,".. by Dr. W. Warburton, Lord Bishop of Gloucester. London and Edinburgh printed, Boston reprinted, 1764. 8°

WHITLEY, HENRY. Excessive Cruelty to Slaves. Three months in Jamaica, in 1832 : comprising a residence of seven weeks on a sugar plantation. [Philadelphia? 1833?] 8°

WHITING, HENRY. Sannillac, a poem... With notes by Lewis Cass and Henry R. Schoolcraft. Boston, 1831. 12°

WHITING, SAMUEL. A Discourse [on Ps. cxxiv. 3] delivered before .. the : .. Council and House of Representatives of .. Vermont, .. Oct. 12, 1797, being the day of general Election. Rutland, 1797. 8°

WHITMAN, BENJAMIN. An Oration pronounced at Hanover, Massachusetts, on the anniversary of American Independence, July 4, 1803, *etc.* Boston, 1803. 8°

2 THE HEROES of the North, or the battles of Lake Erie and Champlain : two poems. Boston, 1816. 8°

WHITMAN, BERNARD. Review of .. Mr. Whitman's Discourse on Regeneration. Boston, 1828. 8°

2 NATIONAL Defence. A discourse preached before the .. Artillery Company [on 1 Cor. x. 15] June 1, 1829, being the 191st anniversary. Second edition. Cambridge, 1829. 12°

3 Two Letters to the Rev. Moses Stuart, on the subject of religious liberty. Boston, 1830. 8°

4 Two Letters to the Rev. M. Stuart [in reply to his Letter to Dr. Channing] on the subject of religious liberty. Second edition. Boston, 1831. 8°

5 REVIEW of Mr. Whitman's Letters to Professor Stuart on religious liberty. Second edition ; with an appendix not before published. Boston, 1831. 8°

6 A REPLY to the Review of Whitman's Letters to Professor Stuart, in the " Spirit of the Pilgrims," for March, 1831. By B. Whitman. Boston, 1831. 8°

7 A LETTER to an Orthodox Minister on revivals of religion... Second edition. Boston, 1831. 12°

WHITMAN, SAMUEL. The Nature and Design of the Baptism of Christ, illustrated in a sermon [on Luke xvi. 16]. Northamp. 1800. 8°

WHITMAN, ZACHARIAH G. An Historical Sketch of the ancient and honourable Artillery Company ; from its formation in the year 1637, to the present time. Compiled and arranged from ancient records. Bost. 1820. 8°

2 THE HISTORY of the ancient and honorable Artillery Company [of Boston, in Maſſachusetts]... Revised and enlarged... [Edited by S. A. Allen, G. M. Thacher, and G. H. Whitman]. Second edition. Boston, 1842. 8°

WHITMORE, WALTER. Wilburn, or the heir of the manor. A romance of the Old Dominion. Cincinnati [1851 ?] 8°

WHITNEY, PETER. The Transgreſſion of a Land punished by a multitude of rulers, considered in two discourses, etc. Boston, 1774. 8°

2 THE HISTORY of the County of Worcester, in the Commonwealth of Maſſachusetts. Worcester, 1793. 8°

WHITON, JOHN M. Sketches of the History of New Hampshire, from its settlement in 1623 to 1833 : comprising notices of the memorable events and interesting incidents of a period of two hundred and ten years. Concord, 1834. 12°

WHITTAKER, HENRY. Practice and Pleading under the Codes (of New York), original and amended, with Appendix of Forms. New York [Printed], and London. 1852. 8vo.

WHITTEMORE, THOMAS. Memoir of the Rev. Walter Balfour. Boston, 1852. 12°

WHITTIER, JOHN GREENLEAF. Legends of New England. [In prose and verse.] Hartford, 1831. 12°

2 LAYS of my Home, and other poems. Boston, 1843. 12°

3 POEMS... Illustrated by H. Billings. Boston, 1850. 8°

4 OLD Portraits and Modern Sketches. Boston, 1850. 8°

5 SONGS of Labor and other Poems. Boston, 1850. 12°

6 THE CHAPEL of the Hermits, and other poems. Boston, 1853. 12°

WHITTINGHAM, WILLIAM ROLLINSON, *Bishop of Maryland.* A Letter to the Right Rev. F. P. Kenrick [in reply to his " Letter on Christian Union."] New York, 1841. 8vo.

WHITTY, *Mrs.* A Mother's Journal, during the last illneſs of her daughter, S. Chisman. Philadelphia, 1831. 12mo.

WHITWELL, SAMUEL. An Oration delivered to the Society of the Cincinnati, in the Commonwealth of Maſſachusetts, July 4, 1789. Boston, 1789. 4°

WICKES, THOMAS. An Exposition of the Apocalypse, in a series of discourses. New York, 1851. 8°

WICKLIFFE, ROBERT. Speech ... on the veto power ; delivered in the House of Representatives [of Kentucky],.. 26 Jan. 1842. Lexington, 1842. 8°

2 SECOND Speech .. on the veto power ; delivered in .. the House of Representatives [of Kentucky] Jan. 1842. Lexington, 1842. 8°

WIDOW (THE) and her Son. Philadelphia [1833]. 12mo.

WIGGLESWORTH, EDWARD. The Sovereignty of God in the Exercises of his Mercy : and how he is said to harden the hearts of men. Consider'd in two publick lectures [on Rom. ix. 18] at Harvard College in Cambridge. Boston, 1741. 12°

2 THE AUTHORITY of Tradition considered [in a sermon on Matthew xv. 6], etc. Boston, 1778. 8°

3 THE HOPE of Immortality. A discourse [on 1 Peter I. 3] occasioned by the death of the Honorable J. Winthrop. Boston, 1779. 8vo.

WIGHT, *Isle of.* A Visit to the Isle of Wight. Philadelphia, 1828. 12mo.

WIGHTWICK, GEORGE. Hints to Young Architects, calculated to facilitate their practical operations ; ...

with additional notes, and hints to persons about building in the country, by A. J. Downing. . . First American edition. New York and London, 1847. 8°

WIGWAM (THE) and the Cabin. By the Author of " The Yemaſsee," " Guy Rivers," etc. [i. e. W. G. Simms]. 1st and 2nd Series. London [New York printed], 1845-1846. 8vo.

WIKOFF, HENRY. Napoleon Louis Bonaparte, First President of France. Biographical and personal sketches, etc. New York, 1849. 12°

2 MY COURTSHIP and its Consequences; and revelations from the Foreign Office. London [New York printed], 1855. 8vo.

WILBERFORCE, SAMUEL, Bishop of Oxford. A Reproof of the American Church, by the Bishop of Oxford; extracted from a " History of the Protestant Episcopal Church in America," by S. Wilberforce, with an introduction by an American churchman. New York, 1846. 8°

WILBUR, HERVEY. A Short Biblical Catechism, containing questions historical, doctrinal, practical, and experimental. Fifth edition. Exeter, 1814. 12°

2 A LEXICON of Useful Knowledge, for the use of schools and libraries. New York, 1830. 12°

WILBUR, JOSIAH. The Grammatical Key, . . with an atlas for parsing, etc. Bellows Falls, Vt. 1821. 12°

WILCOCKS, ALEXANDER, M.D. An Eſsay on the Tides: Theory of the two forces. Philadel. 1855. 8vo.

WILCOX, P. B. Condensed Reports of Decisions in the Supreme Court of Ohio, containing all the cases decided by the Court in bank, from its organization to Dec. term, 1831, with cases decided upon the Circuit; . . and including all the decisions in the four first volumes of Hammond's reports; . . . Edited by P. B. Wilcox (vol. 1-7; vol. 8, 9, Cases . . in bank . . Dec. term, 1837-39 by C. Hammond; [Vol. 10] Reports of cases . . in bank, by P. B. Wilcox; Vol. 11-13, Reports, etc. E. M. Stanton, reporter; Vol. 14, Reports, etc. H. Griswold, Reporter). 14 vol. Columbus, 1832-46. 8°

WILDE, Mr. Speech . . on the bill for removing the Indians from the East to the West side of the Miſsisippi; delivered in the House of Representatives, etc. Washing. 1830. 8°

WILDE, GEORGE C. An Oration delivered in Newburyport, on the forty-seventh anniversary of American Independence, July 4, 1823. Second edition. Newburyport, 1823. 8°

WILDE, RICHARD HENRY. Conjectures and Researches concerning the love, madneſs, and imprisonment of Torquato Taſso. 2 vol. New York, 1842. 12°

WILD FLOWERS; or, the Mayday walk. Philadel. [1827]. 12mo.

WILEY AND PUTNAM'S Library of Choice Reading. London [New York printed], 1845-46. 8vo.

CONTENTS. See

R R

16. Poe, E. A. The Raven.
17. Taylor, J. B. Views a-foot.
18. Wigwam and the Cabin.

WILEY, C. H. The North Carolina Reader: containing a history and description of North Carolina, selections in verse, etc. Philadelphia [1851]. 12°

2 LIFE in the South, a companion to Uncle Tom's Cabin... With .. illustrations. Philadelphia, 1852. 8°

WILKES, CHARLES, *Commander United States Navy.* Narrative of the United States Exploring Expedition, during the years 1838-1842. Vol. 1-5, and Atlas. Philadelphia, 1844. 4to. Also,

VOL.
6. Ethnography and Philology. By Horatio Hale. Philadelphia, 1846. 4to.
7. Zoophytes. By James D. Dana. 1846. 4to. Atlas. 1849. Fol.
8. Mammalia and Ornithology. By Titian R. Peale. 1848. 4to. Wanting the Atlas.
9. The Races of Man: and their geographical distribution. By Charles Pickering. 1848. 4to.
10. Geology. By James D. Dana. 1849. 4to. Atlas, 1849. Fol.
11. Meteorology. By C. Wilkes. 1851. 4to.
12. Mollusca and Shells. By A. A. Gould. 1852. 4to. Wanting the Atlas.
13, 14. Crustacea. By James D. Dana. Parts 1-2. 1852-53. 4to. Wanting the Atlas.
15. Botany. Part 1. By A. Gray. 1854. 4to. Wanting Atlas.
16. Botany. [Part 2?] By W. D. Brackenridge. 1854. 4to. Wanting the Atlas.

2 VOYAGE Round the World, embracing the principal events of the narrative of the United States Exploring Expedition... With .. engravings. Philadelphia, 1849. 8°

WILKES, GEORGE. Europe in a Hurry. New York, 1853. 8°

WILKINS, HENRY. An Original Essay on animal motion. Philadelphia, 1792. 8vo.

2 AN INAUGURAL Dissertation on the theory and practice of Emetics. Philadelphia, 1793. 8vo.

WILKINSON, JAMES, *General.* Burr's Conspiracy exposed and General Wilkinson vindicated against the slanders of his enemies on that important occasion. [Washington?] 1811. 8°

2 MEMOIRS of my own times. 3 vol. Philadelphia, 1816. 8°. Diagrams and plans in 4°

WILL, THE ROVER. Rambles in Chili and Life among the Araucanian Indians in 1836. Thomaston, 1851. 8°

WILLARD, D. Willard's History of Greenfield. Greenfield, 1838. 12°

WILLARD, EMMA, *Mrs.* Journal, and Letters from France and Great Britain. Troy, 1833. 12°

2 HISTORY of the United States, or republic of America. Philadelphia, 1843. 8°

3 HISTORY of the United States, or republic of America. [To which are added, the Constitution of the United States; and a series of questions on the history.] Philadelphia, 1844. 8°

4 UNIVERSAL History, in perspective. Second edition. New York, 1845. 8°

5 ABRIDGED History of the United States, or republic of America... Improved edition. N.York, 1846. 12°

6 A TREATISE on the motive powers which produce the circulation of the blood. New York, 1846. 8°

7 A TREATISE on the motive powers which produce the circulation of the blood. New York and London, 1846. 12°

8 LAST Leaves of American History, comprising histories of the Mexican War and California. New York, 1849. 12°

9 ABRIDGED History of the United States; or republic of America. New and enlarged edition. By Emma Willard. New York, 1854. 12°

WILLARD, JACOB. An Oration delivered in Leominster [Massachusetts], July 4, 1809, upon the anniversary of the Independence of the United States of America. Boston, 1809. 8°

WILLARD, JOSEPH, *D. D.* A thanksgiving Sermon [on Ps. cxviii. 27]. Boston, 1784. 8°

2 A SERMON [on John v. 35] delivered . . at the funeral of the Rev. Timothy Hilliard. Boston, 1790. 8°

3 AN ADDRESS, in Latin, by J. Willard, . . and a discourse, in English, by David Tappan, . . delivered before the University in Cambridge, Feb. 21, 1800, in solemn commemoration of Gen. G. Washington. [Cambridge,] 1800. 4°

WILLARD, JOSEPH. An Addreſs in commemoration of the two-hundreth anniversary of the incorporation of Lancaster, Maſſachusetts. With an appendix. Boston, 1853. 8vo.

WILLARD, SAMUEL. The Fountain Opened: or, the admirable bleſsings plentifully to be dispensed at the national conversion of the Jews. [A sermon] from Zech. xiii. 1. Second edition. [With an appendix, by the editor, S. Sewall.] Boston, 1722. 8°

WILLARD, SAMUEL. The Grand Iſsue: an ethico-political tract. Boston, 1851. 8°

WILLARD, SOLOMON. Plans and Sections of the Obelisk on Bunker's Hill. With the details of experiments made in quarrying the granite. Boston, 1843. 4to.

WILLETT, WILLIAM M. A Narrative of the Military Actions of Col. Marinus Willett; taken chiefly from his own manuscript. Prepared by.. W. M. Willett. New York, 1831. 8°

WILLETTS, JACOB. The Scholar's Arithmetic, designed for the use of schools in the United States. . . Fifty-fifth edition, corrected and improved. New York, 1844. 12°

WILLIAMS, A. D. The Rhode Island Free Will Baptist Pulpit. Boston, 1852. 12mo.

WILLIAMS, C. R. *Mrs.* The Neutral French; or, the exiles of Nova Scotia. [A romance.] Second edition. 2 vol. Provid.[1842?]. 12°

WILLIAMS, SIR EDWARD VAUGHAN. A Treatise on the law of executors and administrators. Second American . . edition. With notes, and references to the decisions of the courts of this country, by F. J. Troubat. 2 vol. Philadelphia, 1841. 8°

WILLIAMS, EDWIN. The Wheat Trade of the United States and Europe. New York [1846]. 8°

2 THE STATESMAN's Manual. The Addreſses and Meſsages of the Presidents of the United States, inaugural, annual and special, from 1789 to 1849; with a memoir of each of the presidents and a history of their administrations: also the Constitution of the United States and a selection of important documents and statistical information. Compiled from official sources. . . With portraits of the Presidents. 4 vol. New York, 1849. 8°

WILLIAMS, EPHRAIM. Reports of cases argued and determined in the Supreme Judicial Court of the Commonwealth of Maſsachusetts. Vol. 1, by E. Williams. (Vol. 2-17, by Dudley Atkins Tyng.) With notes and references to the English and American cases by B. Rand. 17 vol. [Some of which are of the first, and others of the second and third editions. Vol. 4 and 6 were printed at Exeter, and vol. 13 and 14 at Philadelphia.] Boston, Exeter, Philadelphia, 1838-'21-'41-'37. 8vo.

WILLIAMS, HANNAH, *Mrs.* The Divine Promises Considered, and the duty of Christians to be followers of those, who thro' faith and patience, inherit them. A funeral discourse [on Heb. vi. 12] occasion'd by the death of Mrs. H. Williams. [By Thomas Prince.] Boston, 1746. 8°

WILLIAMS, HENRY. Speech . .
on the independent treasury bill ; . .
in the House of Representatives, June
4, 1840. [Washington, 1840.] 8°

WILLIAMS, JOHN. Several Arguments, proving that Inoculation is
unlawfull. Second edition. Boston,
1721. 8vo.

2 AN ANSWER to a Pamphlet entitled, A Letter to a Friend in the
Country attempting a Solution of the
Scruples against Inoculation. Boston,
1722. 8vo.

WILLIAMS, JOHN. The Re-
deemed Captive, returning to Zion.
A faithful history of remarkable occurrences, in the captivity and the
deliverance of Mr. John Williams ;
Minister of the Gospel, in Deerfield,
who, in the desolation which befel
that Plantation, by an incursion of the
French and Indians, was by them
carried away, with his family, and his
neighbourhood, unto Canada. Whereto there is annexed a sermon preached
by him, upon his return, at the Lecture in Boston, Decemb. 5, 1706.
On those words, Luk. viii. 39, Return
to thine own house, and shew how
great things God hath done unto
thee. Boston in N. E. Printed by
B. Green, for Samuel Phillips, at the
Brick Shop, 1707. sm. 8vo.

2 THE REDEEMED Captive, returning to Zion. A faithful history of remarkable occurrences in the captivity
and deliverance, of John Williams ;
Minister of the Gospel in Deerfield,
who, in the desolation which befel
that plantation by an incursion of the
French and Indians, was by them
carried away, with his family, and his
neighbourhood, unto Canada. Drawn
up by himself. Whereto there is
annexed a sermon preached by him,
upon his return, at the lecture in
Boston, Dec. 5, 1706. On . . Luk.
viii. 39. . . Third edition. As also an
appendix, containing an account of
those taken captive at Deerfield, Feb.
29, 1703, 4, . . and of the mischief

done by the enemy in Deerfield, from
the beginning of its settlement to the
death of the Rev. Mr. Williams in
1729. With a conclusion to the
whole. By the Rev. Mr. Williams . .
and the Rev. Mr. Prince. Boston,
1758. 8vo.

3 THE REDEEMED Captive return-
ing to Zion, or a faithful history of . .
the captivity and deliverance of Mr.
J. Williams, . . drawn up by himself.
Annexed to which is, a sermon
preached by him on his return. An
appendix by the Rev. Mr. Williams,
of Springfield. An appendix by the
Rev. Mr. Taylor, of Deerfield. Some
observations, by the Rev. Mr. Prince,
of Boston. Subjoined to this is a
sermon, delivered in the first parish
in Springfield, on the 16th of October,
1775, . . by R. Breck. . . The sixth
edition, with additions. Greenfield,
1800. 12°

WILLIAMS, JOHN. Dr. John
Williams' Last Legacy, or the useful
family herbal, 1825. Middlebury,
1837. 12°

WILLIAMS, JOHN, M. A. The
Life and Actions of Alexander the
Great. New York, 1843. 12°

WILLIAMS, JOHN H. A Brief
History of the rise and progress of
the Independent Order of Odd Fellows in the United States. Boston,
1845. 8°

WILLIAMS, JOHN LEE. A View
of West Florida, embracing its geography, topography, etc. With an
appendix, treating of its antiquities,
land-titles and canals. Philadelphia,
1827. 8°

2 THE TERRITORY of Florida: or
sketches of the topography, civil and
natural history, of the country, the
climate, and the Indian tribes, from
the first discovery to the present time.
New York, 1837. 8°

WILLIAMS, JOHN S. Report of
the Engineer (J. S. Williams) to the
President of the Hanging Rock and

Lawrence Furnace Railroad Company; to which is added, a letter to R. Hamilton, Esq. on the resistance of curves, and proposing a remedy. Cincinnati, 1837. 8°

WILLIAMS, JONATHAN. Thermometrical Navigation; being a series of experiments and observations, tending to prove, that by ascertaining the relative heat of the sea-water, .. the paſſage of a ship through the gulph stream, and from deep water into soundings, may be discovered in time to avoid danger, etc. Philadelphia, 1799. 8vo.

WILLIAMS, NATHANIEL W. The Reign of Jesus Christ: a sermon [on Matt. vi. 10] delivered .. before .. the Governor, .. Council, and .. Legislature of .. New Hampshire, June 7, 1827. Concord, 1827. 8°

WILLIAMS, REUEL. Speech .. on the bill to provide for running and marking the North Eastern boundary line; delivered in the Senate, .. May 14, 1838. Washington, 1838. 8°

WILLIAMS, ROGER. George Fox digg'd out of his Burrowes, or an offer of disputation on fourteen proposals made ... unto G. Fox then present on Rhode Island in New England, by R. Williams. As also how (G. Fox .. departing) the disputation went on between J. Stubs, J. Burnet, and W. Edmundson on the one part, and R. Williams on the other. In which many quotations out of G. Fox and E. Burrowes' book .. are alleaged. With an appendix of some .. of G. Fox his .. answers to his opposites in that book quoted and replyed to by Roger Williams. 2 parts. Boston, 1676. 4to.

WILLIAMS, SAMUEL. The Natural and Civil History of Vermont. [With an appendix.] Walpole, N. H. 1794. 8vo.
2 THE NATURAL and Civil History of Vermont. Second edition, cor-

rected and much enlarged. 2 vol. Burlington, 1809. 8°

WILLIAMS, SMITH. The Supplement, or deficiency supplied; being a series of leſſons in direct reading, etc. Concord, N. H. 1841. 12°

WILLIAMS, S. WELLS. The Middle Kingdom; a survey of the geography, government, education, social life, arts, religion, etc. of the Chinese Empire and its inhabitants. 2 vol. New York [printed] and London, 1848. 12mo.

WILLIAMS, STEPHEN W. M.D. A Biographical Memoir of J. Goodhue, M.D. late President of the Berkshire Medical Institution; etc. delivered at the close of an introductory lecture, .. 20 Nov. 1829. Pittsfield [1829]. 8°
2 A BIOGRAPHICAL Memoir of the Rev. John Williams, first minister of Deerfield, Maſſachusetts. With a slight sketch of Ancient Deerfield, and an account of the Indian wars in that place and vicinity. With an appendix, containing the journal of the Rev. Dr. Stephen Williams, .. during his captivity, etc. Greenfield, 1837. 12°
3 AMERICAN Medical Biography: or, memoirs of eminent physicians, embracing principally those who have died since the publication of Dr. Thacher's work on the same subject. Greenfield, 1845. 8°

WILLIAMS, THOMAS. The Mercy of God; a centurial sermon [on Luke iv. 28] on the revival of religion, A. D. 1740; etc. Hartford, 1840. 8°

WILLIAMS, W. Appleton's Railroad and Steamboat Companion; being a traveller's guide through New England and the Middle States; with routes in the Southern and Western States, and also in Canada. .. By W. Williams. New York, 1847. 12°
2 APPLETON's New York City and Vicinity Guide .. With maps and engravings. New York, 1849. 12°

3 THE TRAVELLER's and Tourist's Guide through the United States of America, Canada, etc. With ... map; etc. Philadelphia, 1851. 18°

4 APPLETON's New and Complete United States Guide Book for Travellers... By W. Williams. New and revised edition. 2 pts. New York [printed], London, 1853. 8vo.

WILLIAMS, WILLIAM R. Increase of Faith neceſſary to the ſucceſs of Christian Miſſions: a sermon [on 2 Cor. x. 15, 16] delivered before the Board of Managers of the Baptist General Convention, etc. New York, 1834. 8°

2 MISCELLANIES [containing Discourses, Reviews, and Sermons]. Second edition. New York, 1850. 8°

3 RELIGIOUS Progreſs: Discourses on the Development of the Christian Character. [With an appendix.] Boston, 1850. 12°

WILLIAMS COLLEGE, WILLIAMSTOWN, Maſſachusetts. Catalogue of the officers and students of Williams College, and the Berkshire Medical Institution connected with it. 1830-31. (1832-33, 1833-34.) 3 parts. [Troy, N. Y. 1830.] 8°

2 COMMENCEMENT. Williams College, Aug. 20, 1834. [North Adams, 1834.] 8°

3 CATALOGUS senatus academici, eorum qui munera et officia academica geſſerunt, quique aliquovis gradu exornati fuerunt, in Collegio Gulielmensi, etc. Trojæ, 1841. 8°

WILLIAMSON, A. Rev. The Present Jews not the lawful Heirs of the Abrahamic Will. Letters to a Millenarian. New York, 1852. 16°

WILLIAMSON, HUGH. Observations on the Climate in different parts of America compared with the climate in corresponding parts of the other Continent; to which are added, remarks on the different complexions of the human race, with some account

of the Aborigines of America. New York, 1811. 8vo.

2 THE HISTORY of North Carolina. 2 vol. Philadelphia, 1812. 8°

WILLIAMSON, WILLIAM D. The History of the State of Maine; from its first discovery, A.D. 1602, to the separation, A.D. 1820, inclusive. 2 vol. Hallowell, 1832. 8vo.

WILLICH, ANTHONY FLORIAN MADINGER. The Domestic Encyclopædia; etc. First American edition; with additions.. by J. Mease. 5 vol. Philadelphia, 1803, 1804. 8°

WILLIS, NATHANIEL PARKER. Inklings of Adventure. By the author of "Pencillings by the Way" (N. P. Willis). Third edition. 2 vol. New York, 1836. 12°

2 AL'ABRI, or the tent pitch'd. [A series of letters and sketches,] [the text being the same as that of the prose of Willis's "Letters from under a Bridge."] New York, 1839. 12°

3 THE COMPLETE Works of N. P. Willis. New York, 1846. 8°

4 POEMS of early and after years. .. Illustrated by E. Leutze. Philadelphia, 1848. 8°

5 RURAL Letters and other Records of Thought at Leisure, written in the intervals of more hurried literary labor. New York, 1849. 12°

6 MEMORANDA of the Life of Jenny Lind. Philadelphia, 1851. 12°

7 HURRY-GRAPHS: or, Sketches of Scenery, Celebrities, and Society, taken from life... Second edition. New York, 1851. 12°

8 SUMMER Cruise in the Mediterranean, on board an American frigate [a reprint of a portion of "Pencillings by the Way"]. N. York, 1853. 12°

WILLIS, RICHARD S. An Addreſs delivered at the Commencement Concert of the Beethoven Club, Yale College, etc. New Haven, 1841. 8°

WILLISTON, E. B. Eloquence of the United States. Compiled by

E. B. Williston. 5 vol. Middletown, 1827. 8°

WILLISTON, SETH, *D. D.* Slavery not a scriptural ground of division in efforts for the salvation of the heathen. New York, 1844. 12°

WILLITOFT, or the days of James I. A tale. Baltimore, 1851. 12°

WILLOW LEAVES: or, whispers to the sorrowful. [In prose and verse.] Arranged for the Maſſachusetts Sabbath School Society, *etc.* Boston [1852]. 12°

WILLS, SAMUEL, *Rev.* The Seven Churches of Asia: an exposition of the Epistles of Christ to the Seven Churches, *etc.* N. York, 1852. 8vo.

2 THE SEVEN Churches of Asia: An Exposition of the Epistles of Christ to the Seven Churches of Asia Minor; with a succinct historical and geographical account of each place and Church. New York [printed] and London, 1854. 8vo.

3 CHRISTIAN Ordinances and Ecclesiastical Observances reconsidered. New York [printed], and London, 1854. 12mo.

WILLSON, GEORGE. A Practical and Theoretical System of Arithmetic. Fifth edition, revised and corrected. Canandaigua, 1838. 12°

WILLSON, MARCIUS. American History: comprising historical sketches of the Indian tribes; a description of American antiquities;.. history of the United States, with appendices showing its connection with European history; history of the present British provinces, .. of Mexico, and .. of Texas, *etc.* New York, 1847. 8°

WILSON, ALEXANDER. American Ornithology; or, the natural history of the birds of the United States. [Vols. 8 and 9 edited, with a Memoir of the Author, by George Ord.] 9 vol. Philadelphia, 1808-14. 4to.

2 WILSON's American Ornithology,

with notes by Jardine; To which is added, a synopsis of American birds, including those described by Bonaparte, Audubon, Nuttall and Richardson; by T. M. Brewer. Boston, 1840. 12°

WILSON, BIRD. Memoir of the life of the Rt. Rev. William White, D.D. bishop of the Protestant Episcopal Church in the State of Pennsylvania. Philadelphia, 1839. 8°

WILSON, CHARLES HENRY. The Wanderer in America, or Truth at home; comprising a statement of observations and facts relative to the United States and Canada. Northallerton, 1820. 12°

WILSON, GEORGE, *Pseud.* George Wilson and his Friend. [A Sunday School tale.] By the author of Jane and her Teacher. Philadel. 1830. 12°

WILSON (HARRY) the Newsboy. Written for the American Sunday-School Union. Philadel. [1851]. 16°

WILSON, JAMES. The Substance of a Speech ... explanatory of the general principles of the proposed Fæderal Constitution;.. in the Convention of the State of Pennsylvania, ..24 Nov. 1787. Philadel. 1787. 8°

2 COMMENTARIES on the Constitution of the United States of America, by James Wilson, LL.D. and Thomas M'Kean, LL.D. London [Philadelphia printed], 1792. 8vo.

WILSON, JAMES, *one of the Justices of the Supreme Court of the United States.* The Works of the Hon. J. Wilson. Published under the direction of Bird Wilson, Esq. 3 vol. Philadelphia, 1804. 8°

WILSON, JOHN. Specimens of the British Critics. By Christopher North (J. Wilson). Philadelphia, 1846. 12°

WILSON, SAMUEL F. AND OTHERS. Report of the Commiſſioners appointed to examine the branch of the Bank of the State of Alabama at Mobile. Nov. 10, 1841. Tuscaloosa, 1841. 8°

2 REPORT of the Commissioners appointed to examine the branch of the bank of the State of Alabama at Mobile. [With an appendix.] Tuscaloosa, 1842. 8°

3 REPORT of the Commissioners appointed to examine the branch bank of Mobile. Tuscaloosa, 1844. 8°

WILSON, STEPHEN L. 1845. Albany City Guide; being a general description of the public buildings . . and institutions of the capital of the Empire State . . Compiled and published by S. Wilson. Albany, 1845. 12°

WILSON, THOMAS. The Biography of the principal American military and naval heroes; comprehending details of their achievements during the Revolutionary and late wars. 2 vol. New York, 1817. 12°

2 PICTURE of Philadelphia, for 1824, containing the "Picture of Philadelphia for 1811, by J. Mease, M.D." with all its improvements since that period. Philadelphia, 1823. 12°

WILSON, W. CARUS. Youthful Memoirs. Philadelphia, 1829. 12mo.

WILSON, W. D. A Discourse on Slavery: delivered before the Anti-Slavery Society in Littleton, New Hampshire. Concord, 1839. 8vo.

WILSON, WILLIAM D. The Church Identified, by a reference to the History of its origin, perpetuation, and extension, into the United States. New York, 1850. 12°

WINCHESTER, SAMUEL G. The Spruce Street Lectures, delivered by several Clergymen during the autumn and winter of 1831-32. To which is added, A Lecture on the importance of Creeds and Confessions; with an Appendix. [Edited by S. G. Win-

chester. With an Introduction by A. Green.] Philadelphia, 1833. 8°

WINER, GEORGE B. Grammar of the Chaldee Language, as contained in the Bible and the Targums. Translated from the German by H. B. Hackett. Andover, 1845. 8vo.

WINES, E. C. Two Years and a half in the Navy; or, journal of a cruise in the Mediterranean and Levant, on board the United States frigate Constellation, in the years 1829, 1830, and 1831. 2 vol. Philadelphia, 1832-33. 12°

2 A TRIP to Boston, in a series of letters to the editor of the United States Gazette. By the author of "Two years and a half in the Navy" (E. C. Wines). Boston, 1838. 12°

3 A PEEP at China, in Mr. Dunn's Chinese Collection; with miscellaneous notices relating to the customs of the Chinese, and our commercial intercourse with them. Philadelphia, 1839. 8vo.

WINSLOW, CHARLES F. Cosmography; or, philosophical views of the universe. Boston, 1853. 8°

WINSLOW, HUBBARD. Christianity applied to our civil and social Relations. Boston, 1835. 12mo.

2 THE YOUNG Man's Aid to Knowledge, Virtue, and Happiness. . Fourth edition. Boston, 1842. 16°

WINSLOW, OCTAVIUS. A Discourse, delivered on relinquishing the pastoral care of the Central Baptist Church, New York. New York, 1836. 8vo.

2 OBJECTIONS to a Baptist version of the New Testament; by William T. Brantly, D.D. with additional reasons for preferring the English Bible as it is. New York, 1837. 8vo.

3 EXPERIMENTAL and Practical Views of the Atonement. New York, 1838. 12mo.

4 CHRIST the theme of the home missionary: an argument for home missions. New York, 1838. 12°

WINSOR, Justin. History of the town of Roxbury, Maſſachusetts, with Genealogical Registers. Bost. 1849. 8vo.

WINTER EVENINGS' CON-VERSATIONS. Winter Evenings' Conversations . . . between a father and his children, on the works of God. Third edition. Philadelphia, 1828. 12°

2 Winter Evenings' Conversations on the works of God. Philadelphia, 1832. 12°

WINTHROP, Edward. Letters on the Prophetic Scriptures. New York, 1850. 12°

WINTHROP, John. A Journal of the Transactions and Occurrences in the Settlement of Maſſachusetts, and the other New England Colonies, from the year 1630 to 1644: written by John Winthrop, first Governor of Maſſachusetts: and now first published from a correct copy of the original manuscript. Hartford, 1790. 8vo.

2 A History of New England from 1630 to 1649. From his original MSS. With notes; by James Savage. 2 vol. Boston, 1825. 8vo.

WINTHROP, John. Two Lectures on Comets by Profeſſor Winthrop, also an eſſay on comets by Andrew Oliver, Jun. Esq. with sketches of the lives of Profeſſor Winthrop and Mr. Oliver: likewise a supplement relative to the present comet of 1811. Boston, 1811. 12°

WINTHROP, Robert Charles. Speech . . . on the resolution offered by Mr. Fillmore, . . to refer that part of the President's Meſſage relative to the tariff, to the Committee on Manufactures; delivered in the House of Representatives, Dec. 30, 1841. Washington, 1842. 8°

2 Speech . . on the resolution of the Committee of Ways and Means, that the Exchequer plan ought not to be adopted; delivered in the House of Representatives, Jan. 25, 1843. Washington, 1843. 8°

3 Speech . . on the annexation of Texas; delivered in the House of Representatives, ... Jan. 6, 1842. Washington, 1845. 8°

4 An Address delivered before the Maine Historical Society at Bowdoin College . . September 5, 1849. Boston, 1849. 8°

5 Addresses and Speeches on various occasions. Boston, 1852. 8°

WIRT, William. The Letters of the British Spy. Fifth Edition: With the last corrections of the Author. Baltimore, 1813. 12°

2 Sketches of the Life and Character of Patrick Henry. Philadelphia, 1817. 8°

3 Sketches of the Life and Character of Patrick Henry. Philadelphia, 1818. 8vo.

4 The Letters of the British Spy. . . . Tenth edition, revised and corrected. To which is prefixed, a biographical sketch of the author. New York, 1844. 12°

5 Sketches of the Life and Character of Patrick Henry... Ninth edition, corrected by the author. Philadelphia, 1845. 8°

WISCONSIN STATE AGRI-CULTURAL Society. Transactions of the Wisconsin State Agricultural Society, with an abstract of the correspondence of the Secretary. [Edited by A. C. Ingham?] Vol. 1, 2. Madison, 1852-53. 8vo.

WISE, Henry A. Speech . . on the . . abolition of slavery within the district of Columbia; delivered in the House of Representatives, Dec. 22, 1835. [Washington,] 1835. 8°

2 Speech . . on the bill to incorporate the subscribers to the fiscal bank of the United States; delivered in the House of Representatives . . . Aug. 6, 1841. Washington, 1841. 8°

WISE, John. A System of Aeronautics, comprehending its earliest investigations and modern practice and art... With a brief history of the author's fifteen years' experience in aerial voyages; *etc.* 3 parts. Philadelphia, 1850. 8°

WISHART, GEORGE. Life of George Wishart (of Ritarrow), the martyr. Philadelphia, 1829. 12mo.

WISH-TON-WISH. The Wept of Wish-Ton-Wish: a tale. By the author of " The Pioneers" .. *etc.* [J. F. Cooper]. A new edition. 2 vol. Philadelphia, 1836. 12°

WISNER, BENJAMIN B. The History of the old South Church in Boston, in four sermons, delivered May 9 and 16, 1830, being the first and second Sabbaths after the completion of a century from the first occupancy of the present meeting-house. [With notes.] Boston, 1830. 8°

WISNER, WILLIAM. Incidents in the Life of a Pastor. New York, 1852. 12°

WITHERSPOON, JOHN. The Works of the Rev. J. Witherspoon .. late President of the College at Princeton, New Jersey. To which is prefixed, An Account of the Author's Life, in a sermon occasioned y his Death, by .. Dr. J. Rodgers. b. Second edition, revised and corrected. 4 vol. Philadelphia, 1802. 8vo.

WOLCOTT, OLIVER. An Address to the People of the United States, on the subject of the Report of a Committee of the House of Representatives, appointed to " examine and report whether monies drawn from the Treasury, have been faithfully applied," *etc.* Boston, 1802. 8°

WOOD, AMOS. A Sermon [on Isa. ix. 7] preached before .. the .. Council, ... Senate, and House of Representatives of .. New Hampshire, .. the day of the general Election. Portsmouth, 1794. 12°

WOOD, GEORGE. A Speech ... before a Committee of the friends of Daniel Webster, at Constitution Hall, New York ... 4th May, *etc.* [advocating the nomination of D. Webster as a candidate for the Presidency]. New York, 1852. 8°

WOOD, GEORGE B. The History of the University of Pennsylvania from its origin to 1827. Philadelphia, 1827. 8vo.

2 A TREATISE on the Practice of Medicine. 2nd edition. 2 vol. Philadelphia, 1849. 8vo.

WOOD, JOHN. A correct Statement of the various sources from which the history of the administration of J. Adams was compiled, and the motives for its suppression, by Col. Burr: with some observations on a narrative by a citizen of New York. New York, 1802. 8°

WOOD, SILAS. A Sketch of the first settlement of the several towns on Long Island; with their political condition, to the end of the American Revolution. A new edition. Brooklyn, 1828. 8°

WOODBRIDGE, WILLIAM C. Lecture on the best method of teaching Geography. 8vo.

2 [EDITOR's Address in] the American Annals of Education and Instruction, for 1831. Boston, 1831. 8vo.

3 AMERICAN Annals of Education and Instruction. [See AMERICAN JOURNAL OF EDUCATION.] Boston, 1832-33. 8vo.

4 VIEWS of the juvenile, youthful, and adult Population of the United States, in connection with the means of instruction. Boston, 1833. 8vo.

5 REPORT of the Committee on the propriety of studying the Bible in the institutions of a Christian country, presented to the Literary Convention at New York. Boston and New York, 1832. 8vo.

6 ON Vocal Music as a branch of common education. 1833. 8°

7 MODERN School Geography. . . With an atlas. . . Third edition. Hartford, 1846. 12°. Atlas. 4°

WOODBURY, LEVI. Speech . . in the Senate, . . Feb. 23, 1830, on Mr. Foot's resolution, proposing an inquiry into the expediency of abolishing the office of Surveyor General of public lands, etc. [Washington, 1830.] 8°

2 A DISCOURSE pronounced at the Capitol of the United States, in the Hall of Representatives, before the American Historical Society, at their second annual meeting, Jan. 20, 1837. Washington, 1837. 8°

3 SPEECH . . on the capital of the Fiscal Bank; delivered in the Senate, July 10, 1841. Washington, 1841. 8°

4 A LECTURE on the uncertainties of history, delivered . . before the Capitol Hill Institute, Dec. 17, 1842. Washington, 1843. 8°

5 LETTER . . on the annexation of Texas [in answer to the resolution of a public meeting held in Prince William County, in the State of Virginia]. [Washington,] 1844. 8°

6 AN ORATION before the Phi Beta Kappa Society of Dartmouth College. Hanover, 1844. 8°

7 SPEECH . . on the annexation of Texas; delivered in the Senate, . . Feb. 17, 1845. [Washing. 1845.] 8°

8 WRITINGS of Levi Woodbury, political, judicial and literary. Now first selected and arranged [by Charles L. Woodbury?]. 3 vol. Boston, Cambridge [printed], 1852. 8°

WOODMAN, DAVID. Guide to Texas Emigrants. Boston, 1835. 12°

WOODMAN, JONATHAN. A Discourse [on Ps. xxxiii. 12] delivered before the Legislature of Vermont, on the day of general Election, Oct. 9, 1828. Montpelier, 1828. 8°

WOODMAN, JOSEPH. A Sermon [on Hosea vii. 9] preached June 3,

1802, on the annual Election of the Governor, Council, etc. of New Hampshire. [Wanting the last leaf.] Concord, 1802. 8°

WOODRUFF, SAMUEL. Journal of a Tour to Malta, Greece, Asia Minor, Carthage, Algiers, Port Mahon, and Spain, in 1828. To which is appended an account of the distribution of . . provisions and clothing to the suffering Greeks, by the agents of the Greek Committee of . . New York, . . May, 1828. Hartford, 1831. 12°

WOODS, DANIEL B. Sixteen Months at the Gold Diggings. New York, 1851. 8°

WOODS, LEONARD, D. D. Envy wishes, then believes: an oration delivered at commencement, Harvard University, etc. Leominster, 1796. 8°

2 LETTERS to Unitarians, occasioned by the sermon of . . W. E. Channing, at the ordination of . . Jared Sparks. Andover, 1820. 8°

3 A SERMON [on 1 Sam. xxv. 1] occasioned by the death of the Rev. Samuel Worcester. Salem, 1821. 8°

4 A REPLY to Dr. Ware's Letters to Trinitarians and Calvinists. Andover, 1821. 8°

5 REMARKS on Dr. Ware's Answer [in relation to the Unitarian controversy]. Andover, 1822. 8°

6 LETTERS to . . N. W. Taylor [on various theological subjects; in reply to his " Concio ad clerum," of Sept. 10, 1828]. Andover, 1830. 8°

7 A REVIEW of Dr. Wood's Letters to Dr. Taylor, on the permission of sin. With remarks on Dr. Bellamy's treatise on the same subject. First published in the Quarterly Christian Spectator. New Haven, 1830. 8vo.

8 A SERMON [on Acts x. 38] on the death of J. Evarts, etc. Andover, 1831. 8°

9 AN ESSAY on native depravity. Boston, 1835. 8°

10 LECTURES on Church Government, containing objections to the

Episcopal scheme. New York, 1844. 12mo.

11 THEOLOGY of the Puritans. Boston, 1851. 8°

12 THE WORKS of Leonard Woods, D.D. 5 vol. Boston, 1851. 8°

WOODS, LEONARD, *D.D. the Younger*. A Eulogy on Daniel Webster, delivered by request of the City .. of Portland, Nov. 17, 1852. Brunswick, 1852. 8°

WOODWARD, SAMUEL B. Essays on asylums for inebriates. [Worcester, 1838.] 8°

WOODWORTH, FRANCIS C. Uncle Frank's Home Stories. 5 vol. New York, 1852. 12°. viz:
1. A Budget of Willow Lane Stories.
2. A Peep at our Neighbours.
3. The Little Mischief-maker.
4. The Boy's and Girl's Country Book.
5. The Strawberry Girl.

2 STORIES about Birds, with pictures to match. Auburn, 1853. 12°

WOODWORTH, SAMUEL. Melodies, Duets, Trios, Songs and Ballads, pastoral, amatory, sentimental, patriotic, religious and miscellaneous. Together with metrical epistles, tales and recitations. Third edition, comprising many late productions never before published. N. York, 1831. 12°

WOOLLEN MANUFACTURES. Statistics of the Woollen Manufactories in the United States. By the Proprietor of the condensing cards. New York, 1845. 12°

WOOLSEY, THEODORE DWIGHT. Discourses and Addresses at the ordination of the Rev. T. D. Woolsey, LL. D. to the ministry of the Gospel, and his inauguration as President of Yale College, Oct. 21, 1846. New Haven, 1846. 8°

2 AN INAUGURAL Discourse, delivered .. Oct. 21, 1846, on assuming the office of President of Yale College. New Haven, 1846. 8°

3 AN HISTORICAL Discourse pronounced before the graduates of Yale College, Aug. 14, 1850, one hundred and fifty years after the founding of that institution. With an appendix. New Haven, 1850. 8°

WORCESTER, *Massachusetts*. Report of the Selectmen of Worcester. Worcester, 1839. 8°

WORCESTER COUNTY, *Massachusetts*. Proceedings of a Convention of Delegates from forty-one towns in the County of Worcester, holden at Worcester, the 12th and 13th of August, 1812 [concerning the war with Great Britain, *etc.*]. Worcester, 1812. 8°

2 PROCEEDINGS of the Convention of Ministers of Worcester County, on the subject of Slavery; held at Worcester, Dec. 1837, and Jan. 1838. Worcester, 1838. 8°

WORCESTER BAPTIST ASSOCIATION. Minutes of the Worcester Baptist Association, held .. in Harvard (Mass.) Aug. 16 and 17, 1820. Worcester, Sept. 1820. 8°

2 SEVENTEENTH Anniversary. Minutes of the Worcester Baptist Association, held with the Baptist Church in Harvard, *etc.* Worcester, 1836. 8°

WORCESTER, JESSE. An Appeal to an impartial public, or a brief view of a controversy in the Church at Holles. [Holles,] 1811. 12°

WORCESTER, JOSEPH E. A Gazetteer of the United States, abstracted from the Universal Gazetteer of the author; with enlargement of the principal articles. Andover, 1818. 8°

2 A GEOGRAPHICAL Dictionary, or universal gazetteer, ancient and modern. 2 vol. Second edition. Boston, 1823. 8°

3 SKETCHES of the Earth and its Inhabitants. 2 vol. Boston, 1823. 12°

4 OUTLINES of Scripture Geography, with an Atlas. Boston, 1830-1834. 12°

5 A PRONOUNCING and Explanatory

Dictionary of the English Language. New York, London [1832]. 8vo.

6 An Historical Atlas, etc. Seventh edition. Boston, 1835. Fol°

7 An Epitome of Geography, with an Atlas. Boston, 1838. 12°. Atlas. 1828. 4°

8 Elements of ancient classical and Scripture Geography: with an Atlas [which is wanting]. Boston, 1844. 12°

9 Elements of Geography, modern and ancient. With a modern and an ancient Atlas... Revised and improved edition. Boston, 1844. 12°. Modern Atlas. 4°. Ancient Atlas. 4°

10 Elements of History, ancient and modern: with a chart and tables of history, etc. Boston, 1846. 12°

11 A Pronouncing, Explanatory, and Synonymous Dictionary of the English Language. London [Cambridge printed], 1856. 8vo.

WORCESTER, Leonard. Letters and Remarks occasioned by a sermon delivered by .. Aaron Bancroft, .. in opposition to the doctrine of Election. Worcester, 1795. 8°

2 An Appeal to the conscience of .. S. Aiken, concerning his Appeal to the Churches. Montpelier, 1821. 8°

WORCESTER, N. A Synopsis of the symptoms, diagnosis, and treatment of the more common and important Diseases of the Skin, etc. Philadelphia, 1845. 8vo.

WORCESTER, Noah. Bible News of the Father, Son and Holy Ghost, as reported by .. Noah Worcester, .. not correct, in a letter [subscribed T. A.], etc. Boston, 1813. 8°

2 An Election Sermon [on Judg. iii. 11] delivered June 4, 1800, in presence of the Governor, .. Council, etc. [of New Hampshire]. Concord [1800]. 4°

3 Last Thoughts on important subjects, in 3 parts. 1. Man's liability to sin. 2. Supplemental Illustrations. 3. Man's capacity to obey. Cambridge, 1833. 8vo.

WORCESTER, S. T. Sequel to the Spelling Book. Boston, 1831. 12°

WORCESTER, Samuel. A Letter to .. W. E. Channing, on the subject of his Letter to .. S. C. Thacher, relating to the review in the Panoplist of American Unitarianism. Boston, 1815. 8°

2 A Second Letter to .. W. E. Channing on the subject of Unitarianism; [in reply to his " Remarks" on the former letter.] Bost. 1815. 8°

3 A Third Letter to ... W. E. Channing on ... Unitarianism; [in reply to remarks by him.] Boston, 1815. 8°

4 True Liberality: a sermon [on Isa. xxxii. 8] preached .. on the first anniversary of the American Society for Educating pious youth for the Gospel Ministry. Andover, 1816. 8°

5 Worcester's Spelling-book .. for the United States of America. Boston and New York, 1829. 12°

6 A Third Book for Reading and Spelling, etc. Twentieth edition. Boston, 1839. 12°

7 A Fourth Book of Lessons for Reading; with rules and instructions. Boston, 1844. 12°

8 An Introduction to the third Book for Reading and Spelling. Boston, 1846. 12°

WORCESTER, Thomas. Little Children of the Kingdom of Heaven, only by the blessing of Christ: a discourse [on Matt. xix. 13, 14], etc. Concord, 1803. 8°

2 Our Savior's Divinity, in primitive purity: a sermon [on Acts viii. 37], etc. Concord, 1810. 8°

WORCESTER MAGAZINE and Historical Journal. Oct. 1825 to Oct. 1826. (W. Lincoln and C. C. Baldwin, editors, etc.) 2 vol. Worcester, 1826. 8°

WORKMAN, James. Political Essays relative to the war of the French Revolution: viz... an answer to the two letters of the late .. E.

Burke against treating for peace with the French Republic; and a memorial .. for the conquest and emancipation of Spanish America, etc. Alexandria, 1801. 12°

2 Essays and Letters on various political subjects. Second American edition. New York, 1809. 12°

WRIFFORD, Allison. The Intellectual and Rhetorical Reader, etc. Concord, N. H. 1834. 12°

WRIGHT, A. D. Elements of the English Language; or, analytical orthography, etc. New York, 1839. 12°

WRIGHT, Benjamin H. and SULLIVAN, J. L. Report of B. Wright and J. L. Sullivan, Engineers, engaged in the survey of the route of the proposed canal from the Hudson to the head waters of the Lackawaxen River. Accompanied by other documents. Philadelphia, 1824. 8°

WRIGHT, Chester. A Sermon [on Ps. lxxxix. 15] preached on the day of general Election, .. before the .. Legislature of Vermont. Randolph, 1810. 8°

WRIGHT, Henry C. A Kiss for a blow: or, a collection of stories for children, showing them how to prevent quarrelling. Boston, 1848. 12°

WRIGHT, John C. Reports of cases at law and in Chancery, decided by the Supreme Court of Ohio, during the years 1831-1834. Taken from original minutes. Columbus, 1835. 8°

WRIGHT, Joseph W. Language and Belles Lettres; or philological lectures on the English language; comprising the peculiarities of its structure, idioms, and application. To which are added, practical dissertations on style, composition, and figurative language. N. York, 1844. 8vo.

WRIGHT, Silas. Speech .. on the proposition to amend the tariff; delivered in the House of Representatives, .. March 7, 1828. Washington, 1828. 8°

2 Speech .. on the motion of Mr. Webster, for leave to bring in a bill for prolonging the charter of the Bank of the United States; delivered in the Senate, March 20, 1834. Washington, 1834. 8°

WRIGHT, Stephen S. Narrative and Recollections of Van Dieman's Land, during a three years' captivity. .. Together with an account of the battle of Prescott; .. with a copious appendix, embracing facts and documents relating to the patriot war; now first given to the public, from the original notes and papers of Mr. Wright, and other sources, by C. Lyon. New York [1845?]. 8°

WRIGHT, Thomas, of Durham. The Universe and the Stars, being an original theory on the visible creation, founded on the laws of nature. First American edition, from the London edition of 1750, with notes by C. S. Rafinesque. Philadelphia, 1837. 8°

WRIGHT, William H. A brief Practical Treatise on Mortars: with an account of the processes employed at the public works in Boston harbor. Boston, 1845. 12mo.

WYATT, Thomas, M.A. A Manual of Conchology, according to the system laid down by Lamarck, with the late improvements by De Blainville. Exemplified and arranged for the use of students. By T. Wyatt. Illustrated by thirty-six plates, etc. New York, 1838. 8°

2 History of the Kings of France, .. from the foundation of the monarchy to Louis Philippe, etc. Philadelphia, 1846. 8°

3 Memoirs of the Generals, Commodores and other Commanders, who distinguished themselves in the American army and navy during the wars of the Revolution and 1812, and who were presented with medals by Congress for their gallant services. Illus-

trated by eighty-two engravings on
steel from the original medals. Philadelphia, 1848. 8°

4 THE SACRED Tableaux: or, remarkable incidents in the Old and
New Testament, illustrated, *etc.* With
descriptions by distinguished American writers. Edited by T. Wyatt.
Boston, 1848. 12°

WYCKOFF, ISAAC N. Anna the
Propheteſs; a funeral sermon occa-
sioned by the death of Mrs. Anna
Lansing. Albany, 1852. 8vo.

2 THE STABILITY of the Times: a
sermon [on Isaiah xxxiii. 6] delivered
on the 4th of July, 1852. Albany,
1852. 8°

WYMAN, MORRILL. A Practical
Treatise on Ventilation. Boston,
1846. 12°

WYNNE, JAMES. Lives of eminent Literary and Scientific Men of
America. New York, 1850. 12°

WYOMING. The Seven Brothers
of Wyoming, or the brigands of the
Revolution. New York [1853]. 8°

WYTHES, JOSEPH H. The Mi-
croscopist, or a complete manual on
the use of the microscope, *etc.* Philadelphia, 1851. 12°

XENOPHON. Ξενοφωντος Απομ-
νημονευματα. Xenophon's Memo-
rabilia of Socrates, with English notes,
by Alpheus S. Packard, Prof. of Rhetoric and Oratory and Claſsical Literature, Bowdoin College. Third edition. New York, 1843. 12°

ALE, CYRUS. War unreasonable and unscriptural: an addreſs before the Hartford County Peace Society; delivered . . November 11, 1832. Hartford, 1833. 8°

YALE, ELISHA. Eldership in the Church of God, *etc.* Albany, 1852. 12°

YALE BANGER (THE). Devoted to the interests of the Sophomore Claſs. Vol. 6. N° 1. [Yale College, New Haven,] 1850. Fol°

YALE COLLEGE, NEW HAVEN, *Connecticut.*

1 THE JUDGMENT of the Rector and Tutors of Yale College, concerning two of the students who were expelled; together with the reasons of it. New London, 1745. 4°

2 CATALOGUS [triennial] senatus academici et eorum qui munera et officia academica gefſerunt quique aliquovis gradu exornati fuerunt in Collegio Yalensi; *etc.* (1790; 1799; 1817; 1820; 1832; 1835; 1838; 1841, and 1844). 9 parts. Novi Portus, 1790-1844. 8°

3 CATALOGUE of the faculty and students of the Medical Institution of Yale College, Nov. 1814. New Haven, 1814. 8°

4 CATALOGUE [Annual] of the faculty and students of Yale College . . Nov. 1819 (1821; 1822; 1823;

1825; 1830-31; 1831-32; 1832-33; 1833-34; 1834-35; 1835-36; 1836-37; 1837-38; 1838-39; 1839-40; 1840-41; 1841-42; 1842-43; 1843-44; 1844-45; 1845-46, and 1846-47). 22 parts. New Haven, 1819-46. 8°

5 AN ADDRESS delivered at the formation of the Lycurgan Aſsociation, in Yale College. By a member of the junior claſs. New Haven, 1820. 4°

6 CATALOGUE of the members of the Connecticut Alpha of the Φ B K. New Haven, 1821. 8°

7 A CATALOGUE of the graduates of Yale College, from 1702 to 1827; the names alphabetically arranged, with the year of graduating prefixed to each. New Haven, 1827. 8vo.

8 REPORTS on the course of instruction in Yale College; by a Committee of the Corporation, and the Academical faculty. New Haven, 1830. 8°

9 A CIRCULAR explanatory of the recent proceedings of the Sophomore Claſs, in Yale College. New Haven, 1830. 8°

10 CATALOGUE of the subscriptions to the fund of one hundred thousand dollars for Yale College. New Haven, 1833. 8°

11 A CATALOGUE of the Connecticut Alpha of the Φ B K. New Haven, 1838. 8vo.

12 A CATALOGUE of the Society of brothers in Unity . . . founded 1768. New Haven, 1841. 8°

13 A TRIENNIAL Catalogue of the

theological department in Yale College . . . Aug. 1841. New Haven, 1841. 8°

14 A CATALOGUE of the Linonian Society of Yale College, . . founded September twelfth, 1753. [New Haven,] 1841. 8°

15 ORDER of Exercises at the junior Exhibition, Yale College, Tuesday, April 27, 1841. N. Haven, 1841. 8vo.

16 ORDER of Exercises at commencement, Yale College, August 18, 1842. New Haven, 1842. 8vo.

17 ORDER of Exercises at commencement, Yale College, August 17, 1843. New Haven, 1843. 8vo.

18 THE LAWS of Yale College : . . enacted by the president and fellows. New Haven, 1843. 8°

19 ORDER of Exercises at commencement, Yale College, August 15, 1844. New Haven, 1845. 8vo.

20 ORDER of Exercises at commencement, Yale College, August 21, 1845. New Haven, 1845. 8vo.

21 HYMN for the meeting of the Alumni, August 20, 1845. [New Haven, 1845.] s. sh. 8vo.

22 JUNIOR Exhibition, Yale College, April 22, 1845. N. Haven, 1845. 8vo.

23 JUNIOR Exhibition, Yale College, Apr. 28, 1846. N. Haven, 1846. 12mo.

24 THE GATHERED Alumni of Yale to their Alma Mater ; by a graduate of 1794. [E.B. i.e. E. Bacon.] Sung at the meeting of the Alumni, August 19th, 1846. [With a hymn by E. T. Fitch.] [N. Haven, 1846.] s. sh. fol.

25 See CATALOGUES, N° 23, 27, 38, 48, 65 and 66.

YALE TOMAHAWK. Devoted to the Clafs of Fifty-three. Vol. 4, N° 1. [Yale College, New Haven,] 1851. Fol°

YANKEE (THE). [Afterwards, from N° 34] The Yankee and Boston Literary Gazette. J. Neal and J. W. Miller, editors. Jan. 1 to Dec. 24, 1848. Portland, 1828. Fol°

YANKEE. The South West. [A narrative of travels.] By a Yankee

[J. H. Ingraham]. 2 vol. New York, 1835. 12°

YATES, JOHN V. N. and MOULTON, JOB W. History of the State of New York, including its aboriginal and colonial annals. Vol. 1, pt. 1-2. New York, 1824-26. 8°

YEATES, JASPER. Reports of cases adjudged in the Supreme Court of Pennsylvania : with some select cases at Nisi Prius and in the Circuit Courts. 4 vol. Philadelphia, 1817-1819. 8°

YEMASSEE ; a Romance of Carolina. [By William Gilmore Simms.] 3 vol. New York [printed, and] London, 1835. 12mo.

YEOMAN, THOMAS HARRISON. Consumption of the Lungs or Decline; the causes, symptoms, and rational treatment, with the means of prevention, revised by a Boston Physician. Boston and Cambridge, 1850. 12mo.

YERGER, GEORGE S. Reports of cases argued and determined in the Supreme Court of Tennefsee, from Dec. 1818, to Dec. 1837. 10 vol. Nashville, 1832-38. 8°

YOUNG, ALEXANDER. The Varieties of human greatnefs. A discourse [on 1 Chronicles, xxix. 12] on the life and character of the Hon. Nathaniel Bowditch. Bost. 1838. 8°

2 A DISCOURSE [from Daniel v. 11, 12] on the life and character of J. T. Kirkland. Boston, 1840. 8°

3 THE CHURCH, the Pulpit, and the Gospel. A discourse [on 1 Corinthians, i. 17] delivered at the ordination of the Rev. G. E. Ellis, as pastor of the Harvard Church, in Charlestown. Boston, 1840. 8°

4 CHRONICLES of the Pilgrim Fathers of the colony of Plymouth, from 1602 to 1625. Now first collected from original records and contemporaneous printed documents, and illustrated with notes. Boston, 1841. 8vo.

5 CHRONICLES of the Pilgrim Fa-

s s

thers of the Colony of Plymouth, from 1602 to 1625. Now first collected from original records and contemporaneous printed documents, and illustrated with notes. Second edition. Boston, 1844. 8°

6 The Stay and the Staff taken away. A discourse [on Isaiah iii. 1-3] occasioned by the death of the Hon. William Prescott. Boston, 1844. 8°

7 A Discourse [from Genesis xxxi. 41] on the twentieth anniversary of his ordination. Boston, 1845. 8°

8 Congregationalism Vindicated. A discourse delivered at the Dudleian Lecture, in the chapel of Harvard College. Boston, 1846. 8°

9 Chronicles of the First Planters of the Colony of Maſſachusetts Bay, from 1623 to 1636, now first collected from Original Records and contemporaneous manuscripts, and illustrated with notes. Bost. 1846. 8°

YOUNG, Augustus. Unity of Purpose, or rational analysis: being a treatise designed to disclose physical truths, and to detect and expose popular errors. Boston, 1846. 8°

YOUNG, Ebenezer. Speech .. on the bill to reduce and otherwise alter the duties on imports; delivered in the House of Rep[resentative]s .. Jan. 28, 1833. Waſhing. 1833. 8°

YOUNG, Edward. Night Thoughts on Life, Death, and Immortality.... With a memoir of the author, a critical view of his writings, and explanatory notes by J. R. Boyd. New York, 1851. 8°

2 Another Copy. Large and fine paper. New York, 1851. 8°

YOUNG, Philip. History of Mexico; her civil wars, her colonial and revolutionary annals, from the .... Spanish Conquest, 1520, to .. 1847; including an account of the war with the United States, its causes and military achievements. Cincin. 1847. 8°

YOUNG MEN'S INSTITUTE, Hartford, *Connecticut*. The Eighth annual report of the Executive Committee. Hartford, 1846. 8vo.

2 See Catalogues, N° 58.

YOUNG SOLDIER (The). Philadelphia, 1832. 12mo.

YOUTH'S ALMANAC for the year 1846. Astronomical Calculations by T. H. Safford. Bradford [1845]. 8vo.

ZEISBERGER, David. Delaware Indian and English Spelling book, for the Schools of the Miſſion of the United Brethren; with some short historical accounts from the Old and New Testament, *etc.* [MS. notes by P. S. Duponceau]. Philadelphia, 1806. 12°

ADDENDA.

ARNOT, William. Laws from Heaven for life on earth: illustrations of the Book of Proverbs. London, Philadelphia, 1857 [1856]. 8vo.

BARROW, David, and others. Testimony of Christ's Second Appearing exemplified. .. History of the progreſſive work of God. .... Antichrist's Kingdom, or Churches contrasted with the Church of Christ's First and Second Appearing. Published by the United Society called Shakers. 4th edit. [Edited by B. S. Youngs and C. Green.] Albany, 1856. 8vo.

BOSTON, *Maſſachusetts*.
34 City Document. N° 37. Report of the Trustees of the Public Library .. July, 1852 (1853, 1854.) 3 parts. Boston, 1852-54. 8vo.

BRITTAN, S. B. The Telegraph's Answer to Rev. A. Mahan. New York, 1855. 12mo.

BROWN, ISAAC V. Memoir of the Rev. R. Finley; ... with brief sketches of some of his cotemporaries; and numerous notes. New Brunswick, N. J. 1819. 8°

BRYAN, DANIEL. The Mountain Muse: comprising the adventures of Daniel Boone, and the power of virtuous and refined beauty. [In verse.] Harrisonburg, Va. 1813. 12mo.

COMSTOCK, JOHN L.
10 ELEMENTS of Geology; including fossil botany and palæontology. A popular treatise .. designed for the use of schools and general readers. New York, 1847. 12mo.

CONNECTICUT, State of.
76 RULES of the House of Representatives in the General Assembly of Connecticut. [Hartford, 1833?] 8vo.

77 RULES of the Senate and Joint Rules of proceeding for the Senate and House of Representatives of Connecticut. Hartford, 1835. 8vo.

78 RULES of the Senate and Joint Rules of proceeding of the Senate and House of Representatives, etc. Session 1843. Hartford, 1843. 8vo.

79 ROLL of the Senate. May Session, 1843. [Hartford, 1843.] 8vo.

80 LEGISLATIVE Roll and Lodgings, May Session, 1843. Hartf. 1843. 8vo.

81 LEGISLATIVE Roll: Rules of the House of Representatives, Joint Rules of Proceedings, and Joint Standing Committees. Session 1844. New Haven, 1844. 8vo.

82 LEGISLATIVE Roll: Rules of the House of Representatives, Joint Rules, etc. Session 1845. Hartf. 1845. 8vo.

83 TABULAR Statement of the number of Representatives from the several Counties and Towns in Connecticut, and of the taxes paid by each; with the numerical ratio of the Representation to the Population and Taxation. Hartford, 1845. 8vo.

84 LEGISLATIVE Roll: Joint Standing Committees, Rules of the House, etc. Session 1846. N. Hav. 1846. 8vo.

DOANE, GEORGE WASHINGTON.
58 AN APPEAL to parents for female education on Christian principles; with a prospectus of St. Mary's Hall, Green Bank, Burlington, New Jersey. Fifth edition. Burlington, 1841. 8vo.

59 THE CHURCH'S Opportunity the Church's Duty: the sermon before the Convention of the diocese of New Jersey [on Gal. vi. 6-10.] Burlington, 1847. 8vo.

DUPONCEAU, PETER STEPHEN.
9 A DISCOURSE on the necessity and the means of making our national literature independent of that of Great Britain. Philadelphia, 1834. 8vo.

HART, JOHN S.
2 THE RELATIONS of the English language to the Teutonic and classic branches of the Indo-European family of languages, with remarks on the study of the Anglo-Saxon. N. York [1855]. 8vo.

HAWKS, FRANCIS L. LL.D. D.D.
3 NARRATIVE of the expedition of an American squadron to the China Seas and Japan, performed in the years 1852, 1853, and 1854, under the command of Commodore M. C. Perry... Compiled from the original notes and journals of Commodore Perry and his officers. . . by F. L. Hawks. Vol. 1. Washing. 1856. 4to.

HULL, J. H. English Grammar, by lectures. .. Third edition, revised and corrected by the author. New Brunswick, N. J. 1827. 12°

HUNTT, HENRY. A Visit to the Red Sulphur Spring of Virginia, during the summer of 1837; with observations on the waters. Phil. 1839. 12°

JAY, JOHN. America Free or America Slave. An address on the state of the country, delivered at Bedford, Westchester County, New York. [New York, 1856.] 8vo.

LEA, Isaac.
16 Description of a new mollusk from the red sandstone near Pottsville, Pa. [Read before the Academy of Nat. Sciences.] Phil. 1855. 8vo.

MAC VICKAR, John.
3 Alumni Anniversary of Columbia College, New York. Addreſs delivered in the Collegiate Chapel. New York, 1837. 8vo.

MARYLAND, State of.
50 The Annual Report of (G. Mackubin)the treasurer of the W[estern] Shore [of Maryland], for Dec. Seſſion, 1834. Annapolis, 1834. 8°
51 The Annual Report of (G. Mackubin), the treasurer of the Western shore [of Maryland] for Dec. Seſſion, 1834. Annapolis, 1834. 8°

MASSACHUSETTS REGISTER: a State Record for .. 1852, containing a busineſs directory of the State, with a variety of useful information. Serial number, 86. By G. Adams. Boston, 1852. 8°

NEW YORK CHILDREN'S AID Society. First Annual Report of the ... Society. New York, 1854. 8vo.

NEW YORK, State of.
62 Second Annual Report of the Superintendent of Public Instruction [V. M. Rice.] Albany, 1856. 8vo.

OLDBUG, John, Pseud! The Puritan: a series of eſſays, etc. 2 vol. Boston, 1836. 12mo.

PALFREY, John Gorham.
13 Speech of Mr. P. on the bill creating a territorial government for Upper California, delivered in the House of Representatives, February 26, 1849. [Washington? 1849.] 8vo.

PONTE, Lorenzo da, the Elder. Il Don Giovanni, dramma buffo, in due atti...La parte poetica della tra-

duzione da L. [L.] da Ponte, Jun. Ital. and Engl. N. Jorca, 1826. 12°

PRESTON and BEST. A Grammar of the Bakĕle language, with Vocabularies. By the Miſſionaries of the A. B. C. F. M. (Preston and Best) Gaboon Station, Western Africa. N. York, 1854. 8vo.

RICHMOND, John W. Rhode Island Repudiation ; or the history of the revolutionary debt of Rhode Island. 2nd edit. Provid. 1855. 8vo.

SMITHSONIAN INSTITUTION. Catalogue of North American Reptiles in the Museum of the Smithsonian Institution. Part 1. Serpents. By Spencer F. Baird and C. Girard. Washington, 1853. 8vo.

STUART, Moses.
19 A Grammar of the New Testament dialect. Andover, 1834. 8°

TREADWELL, Daniel.
2 On the practicability of constructing cannon of great calibre, etc. ... [From the Memoirs of the American Academy.] Cambridge, 1856. 8vo.

UNITED STATES of America.
207 Perpetual War the Policy of Mr. Madison : being a candid examination of his late meſſage to Congreſs. .. by a New England farmer, author of a late pamphlet entitled, "Mr. Madison's War." Boston, 1812. 8vo.
208 Statistics of the United States of America, as collected and returned by the Marshals of the several judicial districts, under the thirteenth section of the Act for taking the sixth Census. Corrected at the Department of State, June 1, 1840. Washington, 1841. Oblong folio.

WATT, Robert. The Trials at large of R. Watt and D. Downe for High Treason, at Edinburgh. Philadelphia, 1794. 8vo.

CATALOGUE

OF THE CANADIAN AND OTHER

BRITISH NORTH AMERICAN

BOOKS IN THE LIBRARY OF

The BRITISH MUSEUM at

CHRISTMAS MdcccLvi

By HENRY STEVENS of Vermont

LONDON

Printed by Charles Whittingham at the Chiswick Press for

Henry Stevens 4 Trafalgar Square

1866

CATALOGUE OF CANADIAN BOOKS

IN THE LIBRARY OF THE

BRITISH MUSEUM.

Chriſtmas, 1856.

BUC

CAN

CADIAN RE-
CORDER. Vol.
27, Nº 27. July
6, 1839. Hali-
fax, 1839. Fol.

ARNOT,
WILLIAM. Sab-
bath School Teaching, in its principles and practice: an addreſs delivered at .. the Monthly meeting of
the United Sabbath School teachers
of Montreal, *etc.* Montreal, 1845. 8°

IGSBY, JOHN. Lo-
calities of Canadian
Minerals, with notes
and extracts, chiefly
collected from the
writings of J. Bigsby,
and published by order of the Literary and Historical Society of Quebec.
Quebec, 1827. 8vo.

BUCHANAN, JAMES, *British Consul at New York.* Reasons submitted
in favour of allowing a transit of merchandize through Canada to Michigan, without payment of duties: with
observations as to the importance of
the River St. Lawrence for extending
the trade of the Canadas and British
commerce. Toronto [1836]. 8vo.

BULLOCK, WILLIAM, *Rev.* Songs
of the Church. Halifax [Nova Sco-
tia], 1854. 12mo.

ANADA. Edits, ordon-
nances royaux, de-
clarations et arrets
du conseil d'état du
Roi concernant le
Canada ; mis par or-
dre chronologique. 2 vol. Quebec,
1803-1806. 4to.

2 A COMPLETE Index to the Or-
dinances and Statutes of Lower
Canada, to the 57th year of George
III, inclusive. Quebec, 1817. 8vo.

FIRST (to the ninth) Report of
the Committee of the House of Assembly on that part of the Speech
of His Excellency the Governor in
Chief which relates to the settlement of the Crown lands, with the
minutes of evidence taken before the
Committee. [The third, fourth, fifth,
and sixth reports are in French.]
Quebec, 1821-1825. 8vo.

4 A REPORT from the Special
Committee of the Legislative Council of the Province of Lower Canada,
appointed to enquire into and report
upon the establishments in this Pro-

vince for the reception and cure
of the insane, for the reception and
support of foundlings, and for the relief and cure of sick and infirm poor,
with the expences thereof, defrayed
out of the Provincial Revenue, *etc.*
Rapport, *etc. Eng. and Fren.* [Que-
bec, 1824.] Fol.

5 RAPPORT du Comité special de
la Chambre d'Aſſemblée du Bas Canada, nommé pour s'enquerir de l'état
actuel de l'éducation dans la Province
du Bas Canada. Quebec, 1824. 8vo.

6 REPORT of a Special Committee
appointed to enquire into the state
of education in this province. Quebec, 1824. 8vo.

7 A COLLECTION of the Acts
paſſed in the Parliament of Great
Britain, and of other public acts relative to Canada. Quebec, 1824. 4to.

8 ANALYSE d'un entretien sur la
conservation des establiſſemens du
Bas-Canada, des loix, des usages,
etc. de ses habitans. Par un Cana-
dien dans une lettre à un de ses
amis. Montreal, 1826. 8vo.

9 REPORT of the Special Committee, to whom was referred that
part of his Excellency's Speech
which referred to the organization
of the militia. Quebec, 1829. 8vo.

10 REPORTS and evidence of the
special committee of the House of
Aſſembly of Lower Canada. To
whom were referred the petition of
the inhabitants of the County of
York ... and other petitions praying
the redreſs of grievances. [Quebec],
1829. 8vo.

11 RAPPORT du Comité choisi sur
le gouvernement civil du Canada. . .
Re-imprime, par ordre de la Chambre d'Aſſemblée du Bas Canada.
French. Quebec, 1829. 8vo.

12 REPORTS of Commiſſioners
for roads and other internal communications for the Province of
Lower Canada. Rapports des Com-
miſſaires pour les chemins, *etc. Eng.
and French.* [Quebec, 1830]. Fol.

13 REPORTS from the Special

Committee on the petition of certain inhabitants of the district of
Gaspe, complaining of various grievances ; and other references. Rapport du Comité special, *etc. Eng.
and Fren.* Quebec, 1830. 8vo.

14 THE PROVINCIAL Statutes of
Lower Canada [from 31 Geo. III to
4 William IV]. Les Statuts Pro-
vinciaux du Bas-Canada. Vol. 1-14.
Quebec, 1830-31. 4to.

15 CENSUS and statistical returns
of the Province of Lower Canada,
1831. Recensement et retours statistiques de la Province du Bas Canada.
Eng. and Fren. [Quebec, 1831.]
Fol.

16 REPORT of the Standing Committee of Education and Schools.
Rapport du Comité permanent sur
l'éducation et les écoles. *Eng. and
Fren.* [Quebec, 1831.] Fol.

17 COPY of a Communication and
other papers received by the . . .
Speaker of the House of Aſſembly of
Lower Canada from the Hon. D. B.
Viger, appointed to proceed to Eng-
land and support the petitions of
complaint of the Aſſembly . . to the
Imperial Parliament. Copie d'une
communication, *etc. Engl. and Fr.*
[Quebec, 1832?] Fol.

18 QUERIES proposed to the medical practitioners of Lower Canada [re-
lative to the cases of cholera which
had come under their observation],
by the Committee of the House of
Aſſembly, to which is referred that
part of the speech of the Governor in
Chief which relates to the Act 2nd
Will. IVth, cap. 16. Questions sou-
mises aux médecins, *etc. Eng. and
Fr.* Quebec, 1833? Fol.

19 MESSAGE from the Governor
in Chief [to the House of Aſſembly
of Lower Canada] on the subject of
the writ of election, for the County
of Montreal. Received 13th Jan.,
1834. Meſſage de son Excellence le
Gouverneur en Chef, *etc. Fren. and
Eng.* [Quebec, 1834.] Fol.

20 Meſſage from the . . Governor

in Chief relating to the Supply Bill for the year 1833. Meſſage de son Excellence le Gouverneur-en-chef, *etc., Eng. and Fren.* [Quebec, 1834.] Fol.

21 REVIEW of the Report made in 1828 by the Canada Committee of the House of Commons. Originally published in the Montreal Herald. Montreal, 1835. 12mo.

22 [PROCLAMATION enforcing Quarantine—to which is added, Abſtract of the Provincial Act 35th Geo. III, C. 5.] Quebec, 1835. 8vo.

23 OBSERVATIONS on the proceedings and composition of the present House of Aſſembly of Lower Canada. Montreal, 1835. 8vo.

24 [COLLECTION of dispatches and documents laid before the Council by the Earl of Gosford, Governor in Chief.] [Quebec,] 1836. 8vo.

25 [ANNUAL Report of the Normal, Model and Common Schools in Upper Canada for the year 1852 (and 1853, 1854): with an appendix. By the chief Superintendent of Schools (E. Ryerson). Printed by order of the Legislative Aſſembly. 3 parts. Quebec, 1853-55. 8vo.

26 A GENERAL Statistical Abſtract, exhibiting the comparative state and progress of Education in Upper Canada . . . during the years 1842 to 1853 inclusive. Compiled from Returns in the Educational Department. Toronto, 1854. Single sheet fol.

CANADIAN ELECTIONS. What is the Result of the Canadian Elections?—fully answered. From the Daily Advertiser. 2nd Ed. Montreal, 1834. 8vo.

CANADIAN LITERARY News Letter and Booksellers' Advertiser. Nº 6-9 [wanting Nº 1 to 5]. Montreal, 1855. 4to.

CANADIAN MAGAZINE, and Literary Repository. July, 1823, to Dec. 1824. 3 vol. Montreal, 1823, 1824. 8°

CATALOGUES OF LIBRARIES.

1 CATALOGUE of English Books in the Library of the Legislative Council. Quebec, 20th December, 1821. (Catalogue des livres François; *etc.*) [Quebec, 1822.] 12mo.

2 REGULATIONS and Catalogue of the Quebec Garrison Library, *etc.* Quebec, 1827. 8vo.

3 CATALOGUE of Books in the Library of the House of Aſſembly. Quebec, 1831. 8vo.

4 CATALOGUE of Books added to the Library of the House of Aſſembly. 1831. [Quebec, 1832.] 8vo.

5 CATALOGUE of the Books in the Montreal Library. [With printed and MSS. additions inserted.] Montreal, 1833. 8vo.

6 CATALOGUE of the books in the Quebec Library. [Interleaved, with MSS. additions.] Quebec [1833]. 8vo.

7 CATALOGUE of the books in the Garrison Library of Quebec. [Quebec] 1833. 12mo.

8 CATALOGUE of English books in the Library of the Legislative Council, Quebec, 1st November, 1834. (Catalogue des livres François, *etc.*) [With MS. Additions.] [Quebec, 1834?] 12mo.

9 CATALOGUE of books in the Quebec Library. Catalogue des livres, *etc.* [With additions in MS.] Quebec [1835?] 8vo.

10 CATALOGUE des livres appartenant à la Bibliothèque de la Chambre d'Aſſemblée. Quebec, 1835. 8vo.

11 CATALOGUE of books in the various departments of science and general literature, for sale by Armour and Ramsay . . Montreal. Montreal, 1836. 12mo.

12 LIBRARY of the Legislative Aſſembly. Catalogue of books relating to the history of America forming part of the library of the Legislative Aſſembly, *etc.* Quebec, 1845. 8vo.

13 LIBRARY of the Legislative Council. Alphabetical Catalogue of the library, *etc.* [By W. A. Adamson?]

Authors and subjects. Montreal, 1845. 8vo.

14 CATALOGUE of the Library of the Literary and Historical Society of Quebec. Quebec, 1845. 8°

15 Library of the Legislative Assembly . . . Books added to the collection on the history of America, since . . 1845. Montreal, 1846. 8vo.

16 LIBRARY of the Legislative Assembly. Catalogue of books in the library of the Legislative Assembly of Canada. Montreal, 1846. 8vo.

17 LIBRARY of the Legislative Assembly. Supplement to the Catalogue of Books in the library of the Legislative Assembly, *etc.* Montreal, 1847. 8vo.

18 Library of the Legislative Assembly. Supplementary Catalogue of Books added to the collection on the history of America, during the year 1847. Montreal, 1848. 8vo.

CHAMBLY CANAL. A minute Statement relative to the works on the Chambly Canal, exhibiting the engineer's report, with a statement of the extra work performed by the contractors. Montreal, 1836. 8vo.

CHANT Patriotique du Canada. [With musical notes.] By F. R. A. [Quebec ?] 1836. Fol.

CHRISTIAN REPORTER and Temperance Advocate. New Series. Vol. 1. N° 28. Jan. 18th, 1840. Saint Johns, N.B. 1840. Fol.

CHRONICLE AND GAZETTE and Kingston Commercial Advertiser. Vol. 20, N° 80. Kingston, U.C. 1839. Fol.

CITY GAZETTE (THE). Vol. 31. N° 1568. Jan. 16, 1840. Saint Johns, N.B. 1840. Fol.

COLBORNE, JOHN, *Baron Seaton.* Addresses presented to his Excellency Major General Sir John Colborne, Lieut. Governor of Upper Canada, on the occasion of his leaving the province. Toronto, 1836. 8vo.

COLONIAL HERALD and Prince Edward's Island Advertiser.

Vol. 3, N° 143. April 25, 1840. Charlottetown, 1840. Fol.

COMMERCIAL NEWS and General Advertiser. Editor G. E. Fenety. Vol. 1. N° 57. Saint Johns, N.B. 1840. Fol.

COONEY, ROBERT. A Compendious History of the Northern part of the Province of New Brunswick, and of the District of Gaspe, in Lower Canada. Halifax, 1832. 8vo.

DES RIVIERES BEAUBIEN, HENRY. Traité sur les lois civiles du Bas Canada. 3 tom. Montreal, 1832-33. 8vo.

ESSON, H. A Sermon [on Ps. cxxii. 6-9] preached in the Presbyterian Church . . Montreal, 30th of November, 1835. [With notes.] Montreal, 1836. 8vo.

FARIBAULT, G. B. Catalogue d'ouvrages sur l'histoire de l'Amérique et en particulier sur celle du Canada, de la Louisiane, de l'Acadie, et autres lieux, ci-devant connus sous le nom de Nouvelle-France ; avec des notes bibliographiques, critiques, et littéraires. Quebec, 1837. 8vo.

FLEMING, PETER. Geometrical Solutions of the Quadrature of the Circle. Montreal, 1850. Fol.

GARNEAU, F. X. Histoire du Canada, depuis sa découverte jusqu'a nos jours. 2 tom. Quebec, 1845-46. 8vo.

GESNER, ABRAHAM. Remarks on the geology and mineralogy of Nova Scotia. Halifax, 1836. 8vo.

GIROD, AMURY. Notes diverses sur le Bas-Canada. Livr. 1. Village Debarrtzeh, 1835. 4to.

GLEANER (THE) and Northumberland, Kent, Gloucester, and Restigouche Schediasma. Vol. ii. N° 19. Jan. 21st, 1840. Chatham, N.B. 1840.

ALIBURTON, Thomas C. An historical and statistical Account of Nova Scotia. 2 Vol. Halifax, 1829. 8vo.

HALL, A. An Apology for British and Colonial Medical Degrees: or, Strictures on the Report of the Special Committee of the Legislative Affembly on the Laws relative to the Practice of Physic, Surgery, and Midwifery, in Lower Canada. Montreal, 1853. 8vo.

HALL, J. H. W. Scenes in a Soldier's Life: being a connected narrative of the principal events in Scinde, Beloochistan, and Affghanistan, during 1839-1843. Montreal, 1848. 16mo.

HAWKINS, Alfred. Picture of Quebec. With historical recollections. Quebec, 1834. 12mo.

HEAD, Sir Francis Bond, Bart. Meffages, Addreffes, etc, to Sir Francis B. Head, on his resignation of the government of Upper Canada. Toronto, 1838. 8vo.

HENEY, H. Commentaire, ou observations sur l'acte de la 31° année du règne de George III, chap. 31, communément appelé Acte Constitutionnel du haut et du Bas-Canada. (Notes) 2 part. Montreal, 1832. 8vo.

HOCHELAGA DEPICTA: the early history of Montreal. Edited by N. Bosworth. Montreal, 1839. 12°

HUBBARD, A. O. A Brief Examination of the nature and use of the drinks mentioned in the Scriptures; with some remarks as suggested by the connexion of the subject with the cause of temperance. Sherbrooke, 1838. 8°

NGLIS, Charles, Bishop of Nova Scotia. A Charge . . . to the Clergy of the Province of Quebec, at the primary Visitation . . 1789. Halifax, 1790. 4to.

AMES, William. An Inquiry into the merits of the principal naval actions between Great Britain and the United States; comprising an account of all British and American ships of war, reciprocally captured and destroyed since June 18, 1812. Halifax, 1816. 8vo.

JOURNAL OF EDUCATION. Vol. 6, N° 12, to Vol. 10, N° 1. [wanting many numbers]. Toronto, 1853-1857. 4to.

ERR, David Shank. Reports of Cases argued and determined in the Supreme Court of New Brunswick, Michaelmas Term, 1845. Vol. 3. N° 1. Saint John, 1846. 8vo.

KNIGHT, S. Forms of Prayer for the use of Christian families. To which is added a second series by the Rev. James Knight, A. M. Halifax, 1827. 12mo.

ESSEY, J. Four Sermons on the Priesthood of Christ. Halifax, 1827. 8vo.

LITERARY AND Historical Society of Quebec. By Laws, to which is prefixed the royal charter of incorporation of the Society. Quebec, 1832. 8vo.

2 Transactions. Vol. 3, pt. 4. May, 1837. Quebec, 8vo.

3 Report of the Council, 1836-37. Quebec, 8vo.

LOWER CANADA AGRICULtural Society. (Rules and Regulations. Addreff to the Public, etc.) Montreal, 1847. 8°

LOWER CANADA WATCHman. [Being a series of Papers reprinted from the Kingston Chronicle.] Kingston, U. C. 1829. 12mo.

ACKAY, ROBERT W.
S. The Stranger's
Guide to the Island
and City of Montreal,
etc. Montreal, 1848.
16°

MAC LANE, DAVID. The Trial
of David Mᶜ Lane for high treason,
at Quebec, 7th July, 1797. Quebec,
1797. 8vo.

MICMAC ALPHABET. Alpha-
bet Mikmaque [with spelling and
reading lessons.] Quebec, 1817. 12°

MONTREAL. Prospectus of the
plan and principles of a Society proposed to be formed in Montreal for
the attainment of universal religious
liberty and equality. Montreal,
1836. 8vo.

MONTREAL. Map of the City
of Montreal. . from recent Survey in
1834. By A. Jobin. Montreal, 1834.

MONTREAL DIRECTORY for
1845-6. By R. W. S. Mackay. Montreal [1845]. 12°

MONTREAL GAZETTE. Vol. 47.
N° 17. Feb. 9, 1839. Montreal,
1839. Fol.

MONTREAL HERALD AB-
STRACT. Vol. 5. N° 24. July 27,
1839. Montreal, 1839. Fol.

MONTREAL TRANSCRIPT, and
Commercial Advertiser. Vol. 4.
N° 53. Sept. 3rd, 1839. Montreal,
1839. Fol.

MONTREAL TRANSCRIPT and
General Advertiser. Vol. 3. N° 30.
Dec. 8th, 1838. Montreal, 1838.
Fol.

MORNING COURIER (THE).
Jan. 10th, 1840. Vol. 5. N° 94.
Montreal, 1840. Fol.

MOUNTAIN, GEORGE JEHOSA-
PHAT, *Lord Bishop of Montreal.* A
Charge, delivered to the Clergy of
the Diocese of Quebec, at his Primary
Visitation, completed in 1838. Que-
bec, 1839. 8vo.

EILSON, JOHN. Re-
port of the School
Visitor [J. Neilson]
for the counties Belle-
chafse, Ilet, Kamou-
raska and Rimouski
[addressed to the House of Assembly
of Lower Canada]. [Quebec, 1831.]
Fol.

NEWFOUNDLAND ALMA-
NACK, 1845. Compiled by J. Templeman. [St. John's, 1844.] 12mo.

NOVA SCOTIA. The Perpetual
Acts of the General Assemblies of his
Majesty's province of Nova Scotia, as
revised in the year 1783. [Revised
by J. Deschamps and J. Brenton.]
Halifax, 1784. Fol.

2 A GENERAL Description of Nova
Scotia. Halifax, 1823. 8°

3 THE STATUTES, rules, and ordinances of the University of King's
College at Windsor, in the Province
of Nova Scotia. Halifax, 4to.

NOVA SCOTIA GAZETTE and
the Weekly Chronicle. N° 296,
303-04. Halifax, 1776. Fol.

NOVA SCOTIA PACKET and
General Advertiser (The). N° 65-
66. Shelburne, 1786. Fol.

NOVA SCOTIA ROYAL GA-
ZETTE. Vol. 37. N° 38. Oct. 24,
1838. Halifax, 1838. Fol.

RIMER. A Primer
for the use of the
Mohawk Children, to
acquire the spelling
and reading of their
own: as well as to get
acquainted with the English Tongue,
which for that purpose is put on the
opposite page. Waerighwaghsawe
Iksaongoenwa Isiwaondad-derigh-
honny Kaghyadoghsera; Nayonde-
weyestaghk ayeweanaghnòdon
ayeghyà-dow Kaniyenkehága Ka-
weanondagh-kouh; Dyorheas-hà-
gas nitsinihadiwea-notea. Montreal, printed at Fleury Mesplets,
1781. 16mo.

PRINCE EDWARD ISLAND.
Acts of the General Assembly of Prince

Edward Island; comprising Parts First and Second, from the first Establishment of the Legislature to the fifty-seventh year of the reign of King George the Third, *etc.* Charlotte Town, 1817. 4to.

2 PUBLIC documents on various subjects connected with the interests of Prince Edward Island. Ordered by the House of Assembly to be printed. Charlottetown, 1841. 8vo.

3 CENSUS of the Population, and Statistical Returns, taken in 1841, together with a summary prepared by a Committee of the House of Assembly. Charlottetown, 1842. Fol.

UEBEC AND ITS ENVIRONS; being a picturesque guide to the stranger. [Quebec,] 1831. 8vo.

QUEBEC CITY. Plan of the City of Quebec. . . . By . . A. Hawkins. [Quebec,] 1840.

QUEBEC AUXILIARY BIBLE SOCIETY. Eleventh Report, 1835. Quebec, 1836. 8vo.

2 SIXTEENTH Annual Report, 1835. Quebec, 1835. 8vo.

QUEBEC DIRECTORY and Stranger's Guide to the City and Environs. 1844-5. By A. Hawkins. Quebec, 1844. 12°

QUEBEC GAZETTE (THE). 6th March, 1837. N° 5078. Quebec, 1837. Fol.

QUEBEC MERCURY. Vol. 33. N° 28 and Vol. 35. N° 20. Quebec, 1837-39. Fol.

AMSAY, GEORGE, *Earl of Dalhousie.* Memoirs of the administration of the government of Lower Canada, by the Right Honorable the Earl of Dalhousie, from June, 1820, till September, 1828. Quebec, 1829. 8vo.

RAND, S. T. A Short Statement of Facts relating to the history, manners . . . of the Micmac tribe of Indians in Nova Scotia and Prince Edward Island. Halifax, 1850. 8vo.

REINHARD, CHARLES DE. Report at Large of the Trial of C. De Reinhard for murder (committed in the Indian territories) at a Court of Oyer and Terminer held at Quebec, May, 1818. To which is annexed, a summary of A. McLellan's, indicted as an accessary. By W. S. Simpson. Montreal, 1819. 8°

RICHARDSON, JOHN, *Major.* Eight years in Canada, embracing a review of the administrations of Lords Durham and Sydenham, Sir C. Bagot and Lord Metcalfe; and including numerous interesting letters from Lord Durham, Mr. Chas. Butler, and other well-known public characters. Montreal, 1847. 8°

2 THE GUARDS in Canada; or, the Point of Honor: being a sequel to Major Richardson's "Eight Years in Canada." Montreal, 1848. 8°

ROLPH, THOMAS. A Brief Account, together with observations made during a visit in the West Indies, and a tour through the United States of America, 1832-3; together with a statistical account of Upper Canada. Dundas, U.C. 1836. 8°

ROY, JENNET. History of Canada. Montreal, 1847. 12mo.

ROYAL AMERICAN GAZETTE. N° 710, 711, 713, 714, 716-19. Shelburne, N.S. 1786. Fol.

ROYAL ARCTIC THEATRE, H.M.S. Assistance. [Two play bills (one printed on leather) and a song sung in the Pantomime of Zero. Together with a specimen of the means adopted for dispersing intelligence by balloons, consisting of a message printed on a slip of silk.] Griffith's Island Printing Office, 1851. Fol.

ROYAL GAZETTE. New Series.

Vol. 7. No. 27. Frederiƈton, N.B. 1840. Fol.

ROYAL GAZETTE. Vol. 9. N° 490. Dec.31,1839. Charlotte Town, P.E.I. 1839. Fol.

ENTINEL (THE) and New Brunswick General Advertiser. Vol. 3. N° 4. Jan. 25, 1840. Fredericton, 1840. Fol.

SIMCOE LAKE. Lake Simcoe. A sketch .. by Mr. Aitkin. Drawn. Quebec, 1800.

SMITH, WILLIAM. History of Canada; from its first discovery to 1791. 2 vol. Quebec, 1815. 8vo.

STANDARD (THE), or, Frontier Gazette. Vol. 7. N° 15. April 17th, 1840. Saint Andrews, N.B. 1840. Fol.

STANDARD (THE). New Brunswick, January 4th, 1840. Saint Andrews, N.B. 1840. Fol.

STANSER, Rev. Mr. Remarks on the Rev. Mr. Stanser's Examination of the Rev. Mr. Burke's Letter of instruƈtion to the C[atholic] M[iſsionaries] of Nova Scotia. Together with a reply to the Rev. Mr. Cochrán's Fiƒth and last letter to Mr. B. Published in the Nova Scotia Gazette; as also a short review [by E. Burke] of his former letters, and the replies which were made. Halifax, 1805. 8vo.

STEWART, CHARLES JAMES, Biſbop of Quebec. A Charge to the clergy of the diocese of Quebec. 1832. Quebec, 1834. 8vo.

STRATTON, THOMAS. Proofs of the Celtic origin of a great part of the Greek language; founded on a comparison of the Greek with the Gaelic or Celtic of Scotland. [MSS. correƈtions.] 2 copies. Kingston, 1840. 8vo.

2 ILLUSTRATIONS of the affinity of the Latin language to the Gaelic or Celtic of Scotland. MSS. correc-

tions.] 2 copies. [Toronto.] 1840. 8vo.

STRICKLAND, afterwards TRAILL, CATHERINE PARR. The Female Emigrant's Guide, and Hints on Canadian Housekeeping. Second [edition]. Toronto, 1854. 8vo.

STUART, GEORGE OKILL. Reports of cases argued and determined in the Courts of King's Bench and in the provincial Court of Appeals of Lower Canada. With .. cases in the Court of Vice Admiralty and on appeals from Lower Canada before the Lords of the Privy Council. Quebec, 1834. 8°

STUART, JAMES, Attorney General for the Province of Lower Canada. Copy of a Letter from J. Stuart to the Right Hon. . . Viscount Goderich relating to animadversions and imputations on his conduƈt and charaƈthr [sic] in certain proceedings of the Aſsembly of Lower Canada. Copie d'une lettre, etc. (Appendix.) Engl. and Fr. 2 pt. Quebec, 1832. Fol.

2 Copy of a Memorial from J. Stuart to . . . Lord Viscount Goderich. Copie d'un mémoire de J. S. etc. [Relative to his suspension by the Governor in Chief from the office of Attorney General. With numerous documents on the same subjeƈt.] Eng. and Fr. [Quebec, 1832?] Fol.

AYLOR, CHARLES. Remarks on the culture and preparation of hemp in Canada; etc. Remarques sur la culture et la préparation du chanvre, etc. Eng. and Fr. Quebec. 1806. 8°

TEMPLEMAN, JOSEPH. St. John's, Newfoundland .. Table shewing the mean temperature as also the mean height of the Barometer in each month in the five years ending 31st December, 1838, with the extremes of each, and the days on which such extremes occurred. Compiled from

Observations made by J. Templeman. St. John's [1839]. s. sh. fol.

2 St. John's Newfoundland. Table shewing the mean temperature and mean atmospheric pressure of each month in the eleven years, ending 1844. Compiled from observations made by J. Templeman. St. John's, 1845. Fol.

THOM, Adam. Remarks on the petition of the Convention and on the petition of the Constitutionalists. By Anti-Bureaucrat. Montreal, 1835. 18mo.

2 Anti-Gallic Letters, addressed to his Excellency the Earl of Gosford, Governor in Chief of the Canadas. By Camillus. Montreal, 1836. 12mo.

TIMES (The). Vol. 6. Nº 34, August 20th, 1839. Halifax, 1839. Fol.

TIMES (The), a weekly journal, etc. Vol. 3. Nº 24. Woodstock, N.B. 1840. Fol.

TIMES (The), and General Commercial Gazette. Vol. 8. Nº 22. Saint John's, N.B. 1840. Fol.

TRAVELLER. Notes upon Canada and the United States, from 1832 to 1840. By a Traveller [H. C. Todd?] 2nd ed. Toronto, 1840. 8º

NIVERSITY OF King's College, Windsor, Nova Scotia. The Statutes, rules, and ordinances, of the University of King's College, etc. Halifax, 1821. 4to.

IGER, Denis Benjamin. Remarks of . . . D. B. Viger relative to the grievances set forth in the address of the Commons of Lower Canada. Observations de D. B. Viger, etc. Engl. and Fr. [Quebec, 1832.] Fol.

2 Observations on a letter from J. Stuart to the Right Hon. Viscount Goderich, relating to animadversions and imputations on his conduct and character in certain proceedings of the Assembly of Lower Canada. Observations sur une lettre de J. Stuart. Engl. and Fr. 3 pts. [Quebec, 1832.] Fol.

3 Letters from the Hon. D. B Viger [appointed to proceed to England to support the petitions of complaint of the House of Assembly of Lower Canada]. to the Hon. L. J. Papineau, Speaker of the Assembly. Lettres, etc. Engl. and Fr. [Quebec, 1832.] Fol.

4 Divers Documents addressed to . . . L. J. Papineau, Speaker of the House of Assembly, by the Hon. D. B. Viger, appointed to proceed to England, and there to support the Petitions of the House to His Majesty, and to the two Houses of the Imperial Parliament. [Quebec, 1833.] Fol.

5 Observations contre la proposition faite dans le Conseil Legislatif le 4 de Mars, 1835, de rejeter le bill de l'Assemblée, pour la nomination d'un agent de la province. Montreal, 1835. 8vo.

6 Mémoires relatifs à l'emprisonnement de D. B. Viger. Montreal, 1840. 8vo.

7 The Ministerial Crisis of Mr. D. B. Viger and his position : being a Review of Mr. Viger's Pamphlet, entitled, " La Crise Ministerielle et M. D. B. Viger." Kingston, 1844.

EEKLY OBSERVER (The). Vol. 12. Nº 29. St. John's, N.B. 1840. Fol.

WILLSON, David. Letters to the Jews. Toronto, 1835. 12º

2 The Impressions of the Mind : to which are added, some remarks on Church and State Discipline, and the acting principles of life : [with " A Friend to Britain "] Toronto, 1835. 8º

WILTON, J. K. Scenes in a Soldier's Life; being a connected narrative of the principal military events

in Scinde, Beloochistan, and Affghanistan, during 1839-1843; *etc.* Montreal, 1848.   12°

OUNG, JOHN. The
Letters of Agricola,
on the principles of
vegetation and til-
lage.   [Reprinted
from the "Acadian
Recorder."]   Halifax, 1823.   8vo.

ENO.   The "Crise"
Metcalfe   and   the
Lafontaine   Baldwin
Cabinet   defended.
Letter to the Legis-
lative Aſſembly of
Canada.   Quebec, 1844.   12mo.

FINIS.

CATALOGUE OF THE MEXICAN

AND OTHER

SPANISH AMERICAN & WEST INDIAN

BOOKS IN THE LIBRARY OF

THE BRITISH MUSEUM AT

CHRISTMAS 1856

By HENRY STEVENS Ma Fsa Etc

LONDON

PRINTED BY CHARLES WHITTINGHAM AT THE CHISWICK

PRESS FOR HENRY STEVENS IV TRAFALGAR SQUARE

MDCCCLXVI

CATALOGUE OF SPANISH AMERICAN
BOOKS IN THE LIBRARY OF THE
BRITISH MUSEUM.

Chriſtmas, 1856.

BAD YLLANA, MANUEL, *Bishop of Arequipa.* Carta Pastoral con ocasion del Jubileo del Año Santo, para publicarle en la Capital de su Diocesi, a 16 de Marzo, 1777. Lima, 1777. 4to.

ACADEMIA DE MEDICINA. A los Señores direĉtor y catedraticos del Establecimiento de medicina de esta Capital en testimonio de gratitud, los alumnos del mismo. Mexico, 1836. 8vo.

2 REGLAMENTO de la Academia de Medicina de Mejico. Mejico, 1841. 8vo.

3 PERIÓDICO de la Academia de Medicina de Mejico. Segunda Serie. Tomo I. núm. 8. [Mexico], 1842. 8vo.

ACADEMIA DE PRIMERA EN-SENANZA. Idea historica de la fundacion de la Academia . . . con la oracion inaugural y oda leidas en su apertura. Mexico, 1827. 8vo.

ACADEMIA MEDICO-QUIRUR-GICA, PUEBLA. Ensayo para la materia medica Mexicana, arreglado por una comision nombrada por la Academia medico-quirurgica, *etc.* Puebla, 1832. 4to.

AGUILAR, JOSE MATEO. Panejirico de S. Ignacio de Loyola. [Edited by Y. A.] Lima, 1837. 4to.

AGUINALDO para el año de 1834, por el autor del " No me olvides." Lima, 1834. 8vo.

AGUIRRE, FRANCISCO LEON DE. Oracion funebre pronunciado en el aniversario de los militares que murieron en la gloriosa Jornada da Pichincha. Quito, 1824. 4to.

AGUIRRE, PEDRO ANTONIO DE. Transito Glorioſsimo de N. Srª la Santiſsima Virgen Maria; dixolo el R. P. Fr. Pedro Antonio de Aguirre de los Menores Descalços de N. S. P. S. Francisco Leĉtor de Prima de Theologia en su Religioſifsimo Convento de S. Diego de Mexico . . . 22 de Agosto Dominica 12. poſt Pentec. de 1694. Mexico, 1694. 4to.

B

ALAMEDA, *Mexico*. Decimas dedicadas a la sangria de la Alameda. Bueno estuvo el juramento, *etc*. [Mexico, 1824.] s. sh. 4to.

ALCON, Juan José. Diario de la Expedicion del Mariscal de Campo D. J. Ramirez sobre las provincias interiores de la Paz, Puro, Arequipa y Cuzco. Lima, 1815. 8vo.

ALDAMA Y GUEVARA, Joseph Augustin de. Arte de la Lengua Mexicana dispuesto por D. Joseph Augustin de Aldáma, y Guevára, Presbytero de el Arzobispado de Mexico. Mexico, 1754. 4to.

ALDAZORO, Santiago. Exposicion presentada a la Cámara de diputados, solicitando dispensa del pago de réditos por cinco años del Capital que reconoce al banco de avio, el ciudadano Santiago Aldazoro. Mégico, 1841. 8vo.

ALEGRE, Francisco Xavier. Historia de la compañía de Jesus en Nueva-España que estaba escribiendo el P. Francisco Javier Alegre al tiempo de su espulsion. Publicala.. C. M. de Bustamante. 3 tom. Mexico, 1841-2. 8vo.

ALEMAN, Mateo. Ortografia Castellana. A Don Iuan de Billela, del consejo del rei nuestro señor, presidente de la real audiencia de Guadalajara v:sitador jeneral de la Nueva España. Por Mateo Aleman, criado de su majestad. Mexico, 1609. 4to.

ALIAGA Y SANTA CRUZ, Juan. *Conde de San Juan de Lurigancho.* [Begins.] Recurso de D. Juan de Aliaga y Santa Cruz con motivo de lo que en el se expresa, y Decreto del Virey del Reyno. Lima, 1818. Fol.

ALMANACH Royal d' Hayti, pour ... 1816-17 ... par P. Roux. 2 parts. Cap. Henry [1815-16.] 8vo.

2 Almanach Royal d' Hayti, pour ... 1818, ... Par Buon. Sans-Souci, [1817]. 8vo.

ALMANACH NATIONAL de la République d' Haïti, pour l' année 1827. Port-au-Prince, 1826. 12mo.

ALMANACK da Corte do Rio de Janeiro para o anno de 1811. Rio de Janeiro, 1810. 16mo.

ALMONTE, Juan Nepomuceno. Noticia estadistica sobre Tejas. Mexico, 1835. 16mo.

ALPUCHE, Wenceslao. Poesias de D. Wenceslao Alpuche, con una noticia biografica, *etc*. Mérida de Yucatan, 1842. 8vo.

AMARO, Juan Romnaldo. Doctrina extraćtada de los catecismos Mexicanos de los padres Paredes, Carochi y Castaño ... traducida al Castellano ... por Juan Romnaldo Amaro ... va añadido ... el Preámbulo de la Confesion ... con un Modo Práćtico de contar, *etc*. *Mex*. and *Span*. Mexico, 1840. 16mo.

AMERICA. Manifestacion histórica y política de la revolucion de la America, y mas especialmente de la parte que corresponde al Perú y Rio de la Plata, *etc*. Buenos Ayres, 1818. 16mo.

1 Memoria interesante para servir à la historia de las persecuciones de la Iglesia en America. [By P. A. F. Cordova?] Lima, 1821. 4to.

3 Suplimento necesario para la lećtura e inteligencia del papel titulado: "Memoria interesante." [By E. A. d. O.] Lima. 4to.

ANGELIS, Pedro de. Coleccion de obras y documentos relativos a la historia antigua y moderna de las provincias del Rio de la Plata, illustrados con notas y dißertaciones. 6 tom. Buenos Aires, 1836-37. 4to.

ANNUARIO politico, historico e estatistico do Brazil 1847. Segundo anno. Rio de Janeiro, [1847.] 12mo.

ANTEGONIANUS, Agricola. *Pseud*. An eßay upon plantership, humbly inscribed to all the planters of the British Sugar Colonies in America. By an .old Planter. Second edition, correcled and enlarged. Antigua, 1750. 8vo.

ANTIGUA HERALD and Gazette. Nos. 399, 417, 419-29. [Saint John's,] 1839-40. Fol.

ARAMBURU, Martin de. Por la provincia de S. Hipolyto Martyr del Sagrado Orden de predicadores de Oaxaca; en los autos sobre que no imponga principal alguno en fincas del obispado de la Puebla sin consentimiento y licencia de la jurisdicçion ordinaria eclesiastica, etc. Mexico, 1771. Fol°

ARAUCANO (El). No. 462. Santiago, Chili, 1839. Fol.

ARELLANO, Jose Nicolas. Sermon (Prov. xiv. 34) predicado el 15 de Septiembre de 1845, vigesimo cuarto aniversario de nuestra independencia del gobierno Español, en . . . Guatemala. [Guatemala, 1845.] 8vo.

ARENALES, Jose. Noticias históricas y descriptivas sobre el gran pais del Chaco y Rio Bermejo, etc. Buenos Aires, 1833. 8vo.

ARENAS, Pedro de. Vocabulario Manual de las Lenguas Castellana, y Mexicana. En que se contienen las palabras, preguntas, y respuestas más comunes, y ordinarias que se suelen offrecer en el trato y communicacion entre Españoles, é Indios. Compuesto por Pedro de Arenas. Impreſso con licencia, y aprobacion. Mexico, 1611. 8vo.

ARGENTINE CONFEDERATION. Al Exercito de Buenos Ayres . . . los Gefes del Exercito Federal. [An Addreſs.] [Buenos Aires, 1830?] s. sh. 8vo.

2 Mensage del gobierno de Buenos Aires a la vigesima segunda legislatura. Buenos Aires, 1844. 8vo.

3 Message of the government of Buenos Ayres to the twenty-second legislature. Buenos Ayres, 1844. 8vo.

4 Coleccion de documentos oficiales sobre la mision de los ministros de S. M. Britanica, y S. M. el Rey de los Franceses cerca del gobierno de Buenos Aires, encargado de las relaciones exteriores de la Confederacion Argentina. Buenos Aires, 1845. Fol°

5 Correspondencia con los ministros de Inglaterra, y de Francia sobre los asuntos de la pacificacion, presentada a la H. Sala de Representantes por el gobierno de Buenos Aires; encargado de las relaciones exteriores de la Confederacion Argentina. Buenos Aires, 1846. Fol°

6 Message of the Government of Buenos Ayres to the twenty-sixth Legislature. Buenos Ayres, 1848. 8°

ARGENTINE LYRE. La lira Argentina, ó coleccion de las piezas poéticas dadas a luz en Buenos Ayres durante la guerra de su independencia. Buenos Ayres, 1824. 8vo.

ARGOTE Y CATALAT, Simon. Theses ex Universa philosophica atque ex primis Mathesis elementis desumpta. [Lima, 1787?] 8vo.

ARGUELLO, Manuel de. Sermon Panegyrico en la Celebridad de la Dedicacion del .Templo Nuevo de San Bernardo, titulo Maria de Guadalupe. Mexico, [1690?] 4to.

2 Sermon de la Dominica Septuagesima, en la Iglesia Cathedral de Mexico. Mexico, 1691. 4to.

3 Sermon Moral al Real Acuerdo de Mexico, al tempo que tomó poseſsion con publica entrada Joseph Sarmiento Valladares, Virrey, Governador, y Capitan General. Mexico, 1697. 4to.

ARISTA, General. Observaciones sobre la cuestion suscitada con motivo de la autorizacion concedida al General Arista para contratar la introducion de hilaza y otros efeclos prohibidos en la Republica. Mexico, 1841. 8vo.

ARRESE, Pedro Josef de. Rudimentos Fisico-Canonico-Morales. O Glosa al Edifto del Ylustrisimo

Señor Don Cayetano Francos, y Monroy Dignisimo Arzobispo de Guatemala, publicado en veinte y dos de Diciembre del año de 1785. Sobre el Bautismo de Fetos abortivos, y Operacion cesarea en las Mugeres, que mueren embarazadas. Compusola el Br. D. Pedro Josef de Arrese Clergio Presbitero, Secretario del mismo Ilustrisimo Señor Arzobispo, y Examinador Synodal del Arzobispado. Nueva Guatemala, 1786. 4to.

ARZU, MANUEL DE. Memoria presentada al congreso federal de centro-America al comenzar sus sesiones del año de 1826, per Manuel de Arzù. Imprenta de la Union Frente de Santa Rosa, [1826.] 4to.

ATENEO MEXICANO, *Mexico*. Reglamento del Atenéo Mexicano aprobado por la junta de gobierno en el año de 1843. México, 1843. 8vo.

AVENDANO SUAREZ DE SOUSA, PEDRO DE. [On Luke vi. 13. John vi. 55. and Matt. vi. 33.] del glorioso abbad S. Bernardo. Predicado .. à 24 de Agosto [1687] por el p. Pedro de Avendaño. Mexico, 1687. 4to.

2 SERMON [on John xxi. 20, and vi. 50.] que en la Fiesta que celebra la Compañia de Bethlem ... predicò el p. Pedro de Avendaño ... à 26 de Diziembre ... 1687. Mexico, 1688. 4to.

3 SERMON [on John xiv. 6.] del primer dia de pasqua, del Espiritu Santo, en su hospital de Mexico ... 26 de Mayo de 1697 ... dixolo D. Pedro de Avendaño Suarez de Sousa. Mexico, 1697. 4to.

4 SERMON [on Matt. xxv. 1.] de la esclarecida virgen, y inclita martyr de Christo Sta. Barbara, que ... predicò D. Pedro de Avendaño Suarez de Sousa, *etc*. Mexico, 1697. 4to.

AVILA, FRANCISCO DE. Arte de la Lengua Mexicana, y breves platicas de los Mysterios de N. Santa Fee Catholica, y otras para exortacion de su obligacion á los Indios. Compuesto por el P. F. Francisco de Avila, Predicador, Cura Ministro por su Magistad del Pueblo de la Milpan, y Lector del Idioma Mexicano, del Orden de los Menores de N. P. San Francisco. Dedicalo al M. R. P. F. Joseph Pedrasa. ... Mexico, 1717. 8vo.

AYRES DE CAZAL, MANOEL. Corografia Brazilica, ou Relação historico-geografica do Reino do Brazil, por hum presbitero secular do gram priorado do Crato (Manoel Ayres de Cazal.) 2 tom. Rio de Janeiro, 1817. 4to.

COROGRAPHIA Brasilica, ou Relação historico-geographica do Brasil. Nova Ediçāo, correcta, e emendada. 2 tom. Rio de Janeiro, 1833. 8vo.

AZCARATE, MIGUEL MARIA DE. Noticias estadísticas ... sobre los efectos de consumo introducidos en esta capital en el quinquenio de 1834 a 1838, *etc*. Mexico, 1839. Fol.

AZPILCUETA Y ARBURUA, ANTONIO NORBERTO DE. Explicacion, razon, y fundamento de las practicas de las reglas del Palmea, que deben saber los maestres ... de los navios, *etc*. Puerto de Santa Maria, 1751. 4to.

 F. L. C. Memoria analytica á cerca do Commercio d' escravos e á cerca dos malles da escravidão domestica. Por F. L. C. B. Rio de Janeiro, 1837. 8vo.

BAHAMA ISLANDS. Votes of the Honourable House of Assembly of the Bahama Islands. (Sept. 1794 to 19 March, 1796.) Nassau, New Providence, 1796. Fol.

2 VOTES of the Honourable House of Assembly of the Bahama Islands, (30th April to 18th December, 1800.)

2 parts. Nassau, New Providence, 1800-01. Fol.

3 VOTES of the Honourable House of Aſſembly of the Bahama Islands (6th Oct. to 10th Dec. 1801.) Nassau, New Providence, 1801. Fol.

4 VOTES of the Honourable House of Aſſembly of the Bahama Islands (13th Nov. 1804 to 14th Jan. 1805.) Naſſau, New Providence, 1805. Fol.

5 VOTES of the Honourable House of Aſſembly of the Bahama Islands (26th Feb. to 5th April, 1805.) Nassau, New Providence, 1805. Fol.

6 ACTS of Aſſembly of the Bahama Islands. From the year 1764 to the year 1799 inclusive. Vol. 1. Nassau New Providence, 1801. Fol.

7 ACTS of Aſſembly of the Bahama Islands. Vols. 1-3. Naſſau New Providence, 1806-14. Fol.

BALANZA general del comercio marítimo por los puertos de la re-república Mexicana en el año de 1825 (to 1828) formada por orden del gobierno, etc. 4 vols. Mexico, 1827-31. 8vo.

BALLON, MARIANO, Resp. Examen de Anatomia, Fisiologia, y Zoologia que presentan en la Real Universidad de San Marcos de Lima . . . los alumnos del Colegio de S. Fernando, M. Ballon, J. J. Morales, J. A. Miralla, J. Pequeño. Baxo la direccion de J. A. Fernandez. [Lima, 1812.] 4to.

BAQUIJANO Y CARRILLO, JOSEF DE. Relectio extemporanea ad explanationem legis Pamphilo xxxix. D. de Legatis et Fidei commissis III. . . . 1787. [Lima, 1787.] Fol.

2 ALEGATO que en la oposicion a la Catedra de Puma de Leyes de la Real Universidad de San Marcos de Lima dixo 1788. El Dr. Josef de Baquijano y Carrillo. [Lima, 1788.], Fol.

BARBA, ALVARO ALONSO. Arte de los metales, en que se enseña el verdadero beneficio de los de oro y plata por azogue: el modo de fundirlos todos, y como se han de refinar y apartar unos de otros . . Añadido con el tratado de las antiguas minas de España que escribió . . . A. Carrillo y Laso. Reimpreso, Lima, 1817. 4to.

BARBADIAN (THE). Nos. 1483-1605. Feb. 6th, 1839 to April 8th, 1840. [Bridge-Town,] 1839-40. Fol.

BARBADOES. Some Memoirs of the first Settlement of the Island of Barbadoes and other the Carribee Islands, with the succeſsion of the Governours and Commanders in chief of Barbadoes to the year 1741. Extracted from Antient Records, Papers, and Accounts taken from Mr. William Arnold, Mr. Samuel Bulkly, and Mr. John Summers, some of the first Settlers. Also some Remarks on the Laws and Constitution of Barbados. [With an Appendix.] Barbados, 1741. 12mo.

2 THE PRINCIPLES by which a currency is established, a coinage formed, and the money circulations of this Island may be restored and preserved. Barbados, 1791. 8vo.

BARBADOS GLOBE, and Colonial Advocate. New Series. Nos. 1127,1172, 1174,1290, 1324, 1330, 1335, 1337 to 1371, 1374 to 1398. Sept. 4, 1837 to April 9, 1840. Bridgetown, 1837-40. Fol.

BARBADOS MERCURY, and Bridge-Town Gazette. Nos. 5 to 133. Jan. 15, 1839 to April 7, 1840, [wanting Nos. 37, 40 to 48, 52, 55, 57 to 63, 110-111, 125-26, 131.] Bridgetown, 1839-40. Fol.

BARHAM, HENRY. Hortus Americanus, containing an account of the trees, shrubs, and other vegetable productions of South America and the West-India Islands, and particularly of the Island of Jamaica. To which is added a Linnæan index, etc. Kingston, Jamaica, 1794. 8vo.

BARQUERA, JUAN WENCESLAO. Oracion patriotica . . . por encargo

de la junta cívica, reunida . . . con el
. . . objeto de celebrar . . . el primer
grito de libertad en el Pueblo de Dolores, *etc.* México, 1825. 12mo.

BEAUMONT, PABLO DE LA PURIS-
SIMA CONCEPCION. Tratado de la
Agua Mineral caliente de San Bar-
tholome. [Mexico?] 1772. 4to.

BELENA, EUSEBIO BENTURA. Re-
copilacion sumaria de todos los autos
acordados de la real audiencia y sala
del crimen de esta Nueva España, y
providencias de su superior gobierno.
2 tom. Mexico, 1787. Fol.

BELIZE ADVERTISER. Nos.
40, 42, 45, 48, 49, 51 to 55, 58, 60,
61, 63 to 68. [Belize,] 1839-40. Fol.

BELLARMINO, ROBERTO. Declaracion copiosa de las quatro partes
mas eſſenciales, y neceſſarias de la
doctrina Christiana, . . . Por el emi-
nentiſſimo Cardenal Roberto Belar-
minio de la Compania de Iesus, con
las adiciones del Maestro Sebastian de
Lirio, . . . Traducida de lengua Castellana en la general del Inga por el
Bachiller Bartolome Iurado Palomino,
. . . Span. and Quichnan. Lima, 1649.
4to.

BELTRAN DE SANTA ROSA,
PEDRO. Arte de el Idioma Maya re-
ducido a succintas reglas, y semilex-
icon Yucateco por el R. P. F. Pedro
Beltran de Santa Rosa Maria, Ex-
Custodio, Lector, . . . Formólo, y Dic-
tólo, siendo Maestro de Lengua en el
Convento Capitular de N. S. P. S.
Francisco, de dicha Ciudad. Año de
1742 . . . Mexico, 1746. 4to.

BERBICE ADVERTISER, (THE).
Nos. 2823 to 3120. [Wanting 2824,
2826 to 2895, 2910-11, 2919 to 22,
2928 to 3045, 3047, 3051, 3056,
3058, 3060, 3062, 3066, 3081 to
83, 3087 to 90, 3094 to 98.] New
Amsterdam, British Guiana, 1837-40.
Fol.

BERMUDA GAZETTE (THE).

Nos. 95-102. St. George's, 1785.
Fol.

BERMUDEZ, JOSE MANUEL. Ora-
cion fúnebre del . . . Señor . . . J. D.
Gonzalez de la Reguera . . . Arzobispo de Lima. Lima, 1805. 4to.
2 VIDA de la gloriosa Virgen Do-
minicana Santa Rosa de Santa Maria
natural de Lima. Lima, 1827. 4to.

BERMUDEZ, PEDRO. Memoria
presentada à las Camaras de la Republica Peruana por el Ministro de
Estado en los departamentos de guerra y marina en el periodo constitucional de 1832. Lima, [1833?] 4to.

BERMUDIAN (THE). A com-
mercial, literary, and political weekly
Journal. Vol. 6, Nos. 1 to 52, vol.
7, Nos. 1 to 7, [wanting Nos. 1 to 5,
10 to 16, 19, 20, 25 to 28, 34 to 36,
43, 44 of vol. 6, and all after No. 7 of
vol. 7. Hamilton, [Bermuda] 1839-
40. Fol.

BERRIO DE MONTALBO,
LUIS. Al exᵐᵒ Señor don Garcia
Sarmiento de Sotomayor y Luna, . . .
en informe del nuevo beneficio qué se
ha dado a los metales ordinarios de
plata por azogue, y philosophia natural a q reduce el methodo y arte
de la mineria, para escusar a todos la
perdida y consumido de azogue ya
los artimoniosos, *etc.* Mexico, 1643.
Fol.

BERTONIO, LUDOVICO. Arte de
la Lengua Aymara, con una Silva de
Phrases de la misma lengua, y su
declaracion en Romance. Por el
Padre Ludovico Bertonio Italiano de
la Compañia de Iesus en la Provincia
de Peru . . . Impreſſo . . . en la Provincia de Chucuyto. 1612. 8vo.
2 CONFESSIONARIO muy copioso
en dos Lenguas, Aymara, y Española,
con una instruccion a cerca de los
siete Sacramentos de la Sancta Yglesia, y otras varias cosas, como puede
verse por la Tabla del mesmo libro.
Por el Padre Ludovico Bertonio Italiano de la Compañia de Iesus en la

Provincia del Peru . . . Impreſſo . . .
en la Provincia de Chucuyto, 1612.
8vo.

3 VOCABULARIO de la Lengua Aymara. Primera parte, donde por abe-
cedario se ponen en primer lugar
los Vocablos de la lengua Eſpañola
para buscar los que les corresponden
en la lengua Aymara. Compuesto por
el P. Ludovico Bertonio Italiano de la
Compañia de Iesus en la Provincia del
Piru, . . . 2 parts. Impreſſo . . . en
la Provincia de Chucuito. 1612. 4to.

BIBLE. Parafrase del Cap 17, del
Evanjelio de S. Juan. Por . . . D.
Justo Figuerola. Lima, 1831. 8vo.

2 BREVE idea del mérito de la
biblia de Vencé que en Méjico se
está publicando traducida al Español,
etc. [Edited by M. Galvan Rivera.]
Méjico, 1832. 8vo.

BIBLIOTECA (LA) Columbiana
Prospecto. Lima, [1821.] 4to.

BIENES, eclesiásticos. [On the
rights of the Church to temporal
poſſeſſions.] México, 1842. 8vo.

BOCANEGRA, MATHIAS DE.
Auto general de la Fee, celebrado
por . . . Don Iuan de Mañozca, Ar-
çobispo de Mexico, . . . Y por Doct.
D. Francisco de Estrada, y Escobedo,
Doct. D. Iuan Saenz de Mañozca,
Licenciado D. Bernabé de la Higue-
ra, y Amarilla, Y el Senor Fiscal
Doct. D. Antonio de Gabrola. En la
muy noble, y muy leal Ciudad de
Mexico, . . . El P. Mathias de Bo-
canegra de la Compañia de Iesus.
Mexico, [1649.] 4to.

BOLIVIA, REPUBLIC OF. Pro-
jecto de constitucion para la republica
de Bolivia, y Discurso del Libertador.
[Signed, Simon Bolivar.] Buenos
Aires, 1826. 8vo.

2 PROYECTO de constitucion para
la Republica de Bolivia y Discurso
del Libertador. Caracas, 1827-17.
8vo.

3 CÓDIGO civil Santa-Cruz. Paz
de Ayacucho, 1831. 4to.

4 CÓDIGO penal Santa Cruz. Paz
de Ayacucho, 1831. 4to.

BOMTEMPO, JOSE MARIA. Tra-
balhos medicos, etc. 2 parts [the first
beginning: "Memoria sobre algumas
enfermidades do Rio de Janeiro," and
the second: "Plano ou Regulamento
interino para os exercicios da Academia medico-cirurgica do Rio de Janeiro, etc.] Rio de Janeiro, [1825.]
4to.

BOOT, ADRIAN. Parecer del yn-
giniero Adrian Boot. Por orden del
exmo. Señor marques de guadal-
caçar virrey . . . desta nueva espana
en razon de la visita que se hizo . . .
al rededor de la laguna de mexo.
hasta acabar de ver todo el desaguen,
con toda la obra y obras que al presente esta hecho. [Manuscript.]
[Lima! 1615.] Fol.

BORDA Y OROSCO, JOSE AN-
TONIO. Relacion de las reales exequias . . . á la Memoria de la reyna
. . . Doña Isabel Farnesio, etc. (Oracion funebre que . . . dixo . . . el Doct.
T. de Orransia.) 2 parts. Lima,
1768. 4to.

BORGONO, JOSE MANUEL. De-
fensa del Coronel Don A. Gamarra,
presentada al consejo de oficiales
generales en 22 de Mayo de 1822,
por Don J. M. Borgono su defensor.
Lima, 1822. 4to.

BOTURINI BENADUCCI, LO-
RENZO. Tezcoco en los ultimos tiempos de sus antiguos reyes ó sea
relacion tomada de los manuscritos
inéditos de Boturini redactados por
. . . M. Veytia. Publicalos con notas
y adiciones para estudio de la jnven-
tud C. M. de Bustamante. Mexico,
1826. 8vo.

BOZA Y CARRILLO, ANTONIO
JOSEF. Prolusio academica pro stu-
diorum instauratione recitanda Limae
Regia . . . D. Marci Universitate.
Latin and Spanish. [Limae, 1816.]
4to.

BRANDIN, ABEL VICTORINO. De la Influencia de los Diferentes Climas del Universo sobre el hombre, y en particular, de la influencia de los climas de la America Meridional. Lima, 1826. 8vo.

BRASILSCHE GELT-SACK, waer in dat klaerlijck vertoont wort, waer dat de participanten van de West Indische Compagnie haer geldt ghebleven is. Gedruckt in Brasilien op 't Reciff in de Bree-Bijl. 1647. 4to.

BRASSEUR DE BOURBOURG, E. CHARLES. Lettres pour servir d'Introdučtion à l'Histoire Primitive des Nations civilisées de l'Amérique Septentrionale . . . cartas para servir de Introduccion a la Historia Primitiva de las Naciones civilizadas de la America Setentrional. *Fr.* and *Span.* Mexico. 1851. 4to.

BRAVO, NICOLAS, *Vice-president of the Republic of Mexico.* Manifiesto del Exmo. Señor D. Nicolas Bravo (a los estados y a todos los habitantes de la federacion Mexicana . . . 20 de abril de 1828). Mexico, 1828. 8vo.

BRAVO DE LAGUNAS Y CASTILLA, PEDRO JOSE. Voto Consultivo (sobre si se han de preferir en la venta, los trigos del distrito de esta ciudad de Lima, a los que se conducen por mar del reyno de Chili, *etc.*) Lima, 1755. 4to.

2 COLECCION legal de Cartas, Dictamenes y otros Papeles en Derecho. Los da a luz P. de Colmenares Fernandez de Cordova. Lima, 1761. 4to.

3 DISCURSO historico-juridico del Origen, Fundacion, Reedificacion, Derechos, y Exenciones del Hospital de San Lazaro de Lima: lo da a luz L. de Aparicio y Leon. Lima, 1761. 4to.

BRAZIL. Codigo Brasiliense, ou collecção das leis, alvarás, decretos, cartas regias, &c. promulgadas no Brasil desde a feliz chegada do principe regente N. S. a estes estados. Com hum indice chronologico. Tom.

1. desde 1808-1810 (tom 2. Ann. de 1811-13. Collecção das leis, *etc.* promulgadas . . . desde a feliz chegada de el Rey . . . ann. de 1811-16) [-1819.] 2 vols. Rio de Janeiro, 1811 [-19.] 4to.

2 CODIGO criminal do imperio do Brasil, *etc.* Segunda edicçao. Rio de Janeiro, 1830. 16mo.

3 HISTORIA da Revolução do Brasil com peças officiaes e fac simile da propria mão de Dom Pedro ; principiada por hum membro da camara dos Deputados, e concluida por I. F. Rio de Janeiro, 1831. 8vo.

BRICENO, D. B. Independencia de Venezuela, ó notas al impreso titulado Colombia ó Federacion de sus tres secciones, por D. B. Briceño. Caracas, 1832. 8vo.

BRITISH PACKET and Argentine News. (A. Brander, Responsible Editor.) Nos. 701-706. Buenos Ayres, 1840. Fol.

BROUGHTON, ARTHUR. Hortus Eastensis, or a catalogue of exotic plants in the garden of Hinton East, Esq. in the mountains of Liguanea, in the island of Jamaica . . . To which are added their English names, *etc.* Kingston [Jamaica], 1792. 4to.

2 HORTUS Eastensis, or a catalogue of exotic plants cultivated in the Botanic garden in the mountains of Liguanea, in Jamaica. St. Jago de la Vega, 1794. 4to.

BROWNE, HENRY. An addreſs delivered by the Rev. Henry Browne, on the occasion of the laying the foundation stone of St. Paul's Church, Annandale, St. Ann's, Jamaica. [With an introdučtion signed W. C. M.] Kingston, Jamaica, 1838. 8°

BUENOS-AYRES, Estatuto provisional para la direccion y administracion del Estado formado por la junta de observacion en Buenos Ayres, 1815. [Buenos Ayres, 1815.] 4to.

2 REPRESENTACION de los Hacen-

dados de B. A., al exmo. supremo Diredtor, para el restablecimiento de los Saladeros, exportacion libre de todos los frutos del pais, arreglo del abasto de carnes, y otros puntos de economia politica. Buenos-Ayres, 1817. 8vo.

BURON, JOSEPH DUARTE. Ilustracion de el derecho que compete a la santa iglesia cathedral metropolitana de esta ciudad de Mexico, para la percepcion del diezmo, que causa el fruto del maguey, el que por medio de su fermentacion pafsa naturalmente a la especie de pulque, ne cuya bebida usan los naturales de estos reynos, y no pocos de los Españoles, *etc.* Mexico, 1750. Folº

BUSCA-PIQUE (EL). Nos. 1, 2. Lima, 1838. 4to.

BUSTAMANTE, CARLOS MARIA DE. Historia Militar del General Don J. M. Morelos sacada en lo conducente a ella de sus declaraciones recibidas de orden del Virey de Mexico, cuando estuvo arrestado en la ciudadela de esta Capital. (Supplementa al Cuadro historico.) Mexico, 1825. 4º

2 NECESIDAD de la union de todos los Mexicanos contra las asechanzas de la nacion Española y liga Europea, comprobada con la historia de la antigua republica de Tlaxcallan. Mexico. 1826. 8vo.

3 SUPLEMENTO a la historia de las conquistas de H. Cortés escrita por Chimalpain [or rather translated by him into Mexican from the Spanish of F. Lopez de Gomára] ó sea: memoria sobre la guerra del Mixtón en el Estado de Xalisco, *etc. Span.* México, 1827. 8vo.

4 CAMPANAS del General F. M. Calleja comandante en gefe del ejercito real de operaciones llamado del centro. Mexico, 1828. 4º

5 MANANAS de la alameda de México. Publicalas para facilitar a las señoritas el estudio de la historia de

su pais C. M. de Bustamante. 2 tom. Mexico, 1835-36. 8vo.

6 EL GABINETE Mexicano durante el segundo periodo de la administracion del Exmo. Señor Presidente A. Bustamante, hasta la entrega del Mando al Exmo. Señor Presidente interino D. Antonio Lopez de Santa Anna, y continuacion del cuadro historico de la Revolucion Mexicana. Mexico, 1842. 8º

7 LA APARICION Guadalupana de Mexico vindicada de los defedtos que le atribuye ... J. B. Munoz en la disertacion que leyó en la academia de la historia de Madrid en 18 de Abril de 1794. Mexico, 1843. 4º

8 CUADRO historico de la Revolucion Mexicana, comenzada en 15 de Septiembre de 1810, por el ciudadano M. Hidalgo y Costilla ... Segunda édicion ... muy aumentada por el mismo antore. 5 tom. Mexico, 1843-46. 8º

9 [APUNTES para la historia] del General A. Lopez de Santa Anna hasta 6 de Diciembre de 1844. Mexico, 1844. 4º

10 CONTINUACION del cuadro historico; Historia del Emperador D. A. de Iturbide hasta su muerte y sus consecuencias; y establecimiento de la Republica popular federal. Mexico, 1846. 8º

11 CAMPANA sin gloria y guerra como la de los cacomixtles en las torres de las Iglesias tenida en el recinto de Mexico. Causada per haber persistido D. V. Gomez Farias, Vice-Presidente de la República Mexicana, en llevar adelante las leyes de 11 de Enero y 4 de Febrero de 1847, ... llamadas de Manos Muertes, *etc.* Mexico, 1847. 8º

12 EL NUEVO B. Diaz del Castillo ó sea Historia de la invasion de los Anglo-Americanos en Mexico. 2 tom. Mexico, 1847. 8º

BUSTAMANTE, JUAN. Viaje al viejo mundo por el Peruano Juan Bustamante, *etc.* Lima, 1845. 4to.

ABELLO, Manuel, and
Others. Pro publico
totius philosophiæ ex-
amine in hac ... Aca-
demia subeundo se-
quentia ex historia philosophiæ ...
exponunt candidati, qui subscribun-
tur Carolini. E. C. etc. [Lima, 1787?]
8vo.

CALENDARIO y guia de forasteros de Lima, para el año de 1826.
Por D. E. Carrasco. Lima [1825.]
12mo.

CALENDARIO manual y guia de
forasteros de Mexico para el año de
1829, por M. Galvan Rivera. [Mex-
ico, 1828.] 16mo.

CALENDARIO y guia de forasteros de la republica Boliviana para el
año de 1835. Paz de Ayacucho,
[1834.] 12mo.

CALLAO. Documentos relativos a
la rendicion del Callao. Lima, 1826.
4to.

CAMOENS, Luis de. Os Lusi-
adas, poema epico. Nova ediçāo
conforme á de 1572 publicada pelo
autor. 2 tom. Rio de Janeiro, 1821.
16mo.

CANO GUTIERREZ, Diego. Al
excelentissimo señor don Pedro de
Toledo y Leiva, marques de Mancera, virrey ... destos reynos, etc.
[A memorial respecting the working
of the Peruvian mines, the employment of the aborigines, etc.] [Lima?
1641?] Fol.

CAP FRANCOIS. Que ceux qui
ont une ame lisent ceci (Extrait d'une
lettre authentique du Cap François.)
[Containing an account of the Election of deputies to the States General.]
Au Cap, St. Domingue, 1789. 8vo.

CARDENAS, Juan de. Primera
Parte de los Problemas y secretos
marauillosos de las Indias. Compu-

esta por el Doctor Iuan de Cardenas
Medico. Dirigida al Illustrissimo
Señor Don Luys de Velasco, Virrey
dstanueua España. Mexico, 1591. 8vo.

CAROCHI, Horacio. Arte de la
Lengua Mexicana con la declaracion
de los adverbios della. Al Illustrissº.
y Reuerendissº. Señor Don Juan de
Mañozca Arçobispo de Mexico, del
Consejo de su Magestad, &c. Por el
Pedre Horacio Carochi Rector ...
Mexico, 1645. 4to.

2 Compendio del arte de la lengua
Mexicana del P. Horacio Carochi ...
dispuesto con brevedad, claridad, y
propriedad por el P. Ignacio de Pa-
redés, etc. Mexico, 1759. 4to.

CARPEGNA, Ramon. Prospecto
del establecimiento de educacion fundado con permiso del gobierno en la
ciudad de San Juan Bautista de Puerto Rico, etc. Puerto-Rico, 1832.
Fol.

2 Reglamento provisional ... por
el orden interior del establecimiento
de educacion. Puerto-Rico, 1832.
Fol.

3 Apertura del establecimiento de
educacion fundado en la ciudad de
S. Juan Bautista de Puerto Rico, etc.
Puerto-Rico, 1833. Fol.

CARRERA, Fernando de la.
Arte de la Lengua Yunga de los Valles del Obispado de Truxillo del Peru,
con un Confessonario, y todos las
Oraciones Christianas, traducidas en
la lengua, y otras cosas. Autor el
Beneficiado Don Fernando de la Carrera, natural de la dicha ciudad de
Truxillo, etc, Lima, 1644. 8vo.

CARRILLO, Fernando. Origen
y causa de los repartimientos de Indios, daños que resultaràn de quitar-
los a las labores de panes, y el medio
de que se podrà usar, para que no
aya juezes repartidores, que era de
donde nacian los daños a los naturales,
etc. [Mexico? 1632?] Fol.

CARVAJAL Y ROBLES, Ro-
DRIQO DE. Fiestas que celebro la ciu-
dad de los reyes del Piru, al naci-
miento del . . . principe . . . Baltasar
Carlos de Austria, *etc.* [In verse.]
Lima, 1632. 4°

CARVAJAL Y VARGAS MAN-
RIQUE DE LARA, JOSE MIGUEL, *Count
del Puerto.* Programma rerum quas
memoria didicit, quasque coram . . .
Academiæ doctoribus . . . recitabit J.
Carvajal y Vargas [Imperfect.] Limæ,
[1783.] 8vo.
2 BREVE resumen de los tratados,
y proposiciones que para materia de
su exàmen presenta al público . . .
José Miguel y Vargas Manriqve de
Lara. Lima [1787.] 8vo.

CARVALHO E MELLO, SEBAS-
TIAN JOSE DE, *Marquis de Pombal.*
Elogio do Illustrissimo e Excellentis-
simo Senhor Sebastiano Jose de Carvalho e Mello, *etc.* Rio de Janeiro,
1811. 4to.

CASASOLA, JOSE MARIA. Vindicacion del Lic. J. A. Lopez Salazar
. . . y diligencias judiciales con que
se terminó la causa criminal seguida
contra Juan Pablo Ortega y su
muger Ignacia Fortanell, por las calumnias . . . con que habian intentado infamar al mismo Lopez. Las
publica José Maria Casasola. Mexico,
1828. 8vo.

CASA Y PIEDRA, TOMAS JOSE
DE LA. Testimonios de gratitud á . . .
la Memoria del . . . Señor . . . J. D.
Gonzalez de la Reguera, *etc.* (Elogio
del Prelado difunto que . . . dixo . . .
V. Morales. Elogio del mismo Arzo-
bispo pronunciado . . . por . . . G. de
Zeballos y Calderon, Marques de
Casa-Calderon, *etc.*) Lima, 1805. 4to.

CASTANEDA, JUAN DE. Re-
formacion de las Tablas, y Quentas
de Plata y de la que tiene Oro . . .
Por Iuan de Castañeda, natural de
San Iuan de Pineda en Cataluña . . .
[Few MS. notes.] Mexico, 1688. 8vo.

CASTRO, FRANCISCO DE. La octava maravilla, y sin segundo milagro
de Mexico, perpetuado en las Rosas
de Guadalupe, y escrito heroyca-
mente en octavas por el P. F. de C.;
adjunta à las Espinas de la Passion
del Hombre Dios, discurridas en el
mismo metro por el P. J. Carnero,
etc. 2 parts. Mexico, 1729. 8°

CATALOGUE (A) of the more
valuable and rare plants in the public
Botanic Gardens in the mountain of
Liguanea, in Jamaica; also of medicinal and other plants, growing in South
and North America, the East Indies,
etc. [By A. Broughton.] [St. Jago
de la Vega,] 1794. 4to.

CAVO, ANDRES. Los tres siglos
de Mexico durante el gobierno Español hasta la entrada del ejército
Trigarante, obra escrita por Andres
Cavo. Publicala, con notas y suplemento C. M. de Bustamante, *etc.*
4 tom. [The "Suplemento" forms
tom III. and IV.] Mexico, 1836-38.
8vo.

CEPEDA, FERNANDO DE, *and*
CARILLO, F. ALFONSO. Relacion . . .
del Sitio en que esta fundada la . . .
Ciudad de Mexico . . . por . . . F. de
Cepeda . . . y F. A. Carrillo. Cor-
regida, ajustada, y concertada con el
Licenciado J. de Albares Serrano
(Relacion . . . contra ella por parte
de A. Urrutia de Vergara, *etc.*) Mex-
ico, 1637. Fol.

CERDAN Y PONTERO, AM-
BROSIO. Tratado general sobre las
aguas que fertilizan los valles de Lima.
Reimpreso, Lima, 1828. 4to.

CERVANTES, JUAN ATANASIO.
Satisfaccion y respuesta a los cargos
que por acusacion de . . . M. J. de
Andonaegui . . . y denuncia de A.
M. del Rio, se formaron contra . . .
Juan Velasquez . . . su procurador
Juan Atanasio Cervantes . . . en su
nombre. Mexico, 1777. Fol.

CERVANTES, Vicente de. Supplemento a la Gazeta de Literatura. Mexico, 2 de Julio de 1794. [Mexico, 1794.] 4to.

CEVALLOS, Bartholome de. Breve luctuosa descripcion de la solemne y magnifica translacion de la urna en que se depositó el cuerpo del Señor Joseph Damian de Cevallos Guerra. Conde de las Torres. Lima, 1744. 4to.

CEVALLOS, Pedro. Exposicion de los hechos y maquinaciones que han preparado la usurpacion de la Corona de España y los medios que el Emperador de los Franceses ha puesto en obra para realizarla. Impreso en Madrid. Reimpreso en Lima, 1809. 4to.

CHARLEMAGNE, Philemon. Royaume d'Hayti. Réfutation d'un ecrit de Charrault, ex-colon, intitulé : coup-d'œil sur St. Domingue. Par M. Philémon Charlemagne, etc. Cap-Henry, [1815.] 8vo.

CHARLES II. King of Spain. Metrica Panegyrica Descripcion de las plausibles fiestas, que . . . se celebraron en la . . . Ciudad de Mexico, al feliz casamiento de . . . C. Segundo con la Señora Maria Aña Palatina del Rhin, etc. Mexico, 1691. 4to.

CHAVERT, Juan Luis. Reflecciones medicas y obcervaciones sobre la fiebre amarilla. Mexico, 1828. 8vo.

CHIHUAHUA. Memoria presentada al . . . congreso constitucional de Chihuahua por el secretario del despacho de gobierno sobre el estado de la administracion pública. [Chihuahua,] 1827. Fol.

CHILI. Compendio de algunas de las muchas y graves razones en que se funda la prudente resolucion, que se ha tomado de cortar la guerra de Chile, haziendo la defensiva, y señalandole raya : y del poco funda-

mento que tiene la contraria opinion de proseguir la guerra como hasta aqui se ha seguido. Lima, 1611. Fol.

2 Proyecto de Constitucion provisoria para el Estado de Chile. Santiago de Chile, 1818. 8°

3 [Begins.] Copy of a Decree of the Chilian Government in favor of the " Pacific Steam Navigation Company" projected by Mr. W. Wheelwright. [Lima ? 1835.] Fol.

4 Lei sobre la organizacion i atribuciones de las municipalidades. Santiago de Chile, 1854. Fol.

CHOQUEHUANCA, Jose Domingo. Ensayo de Estadistica completa de los ramos economico-politicos de la Provincia de Azangaro en el Departamento de Puno de la Republica Peruana, del quinquenio desde 1825 hasta 1829 inclusive. Lima, 1833. Fol.

CHRISTIAN. DOCTRINE. Tercero Cathecismo y exposicion de la Doctrina Christiana, por Sermones. Para que los curas y otras ministros prediquen y enseñen a los Yndios y a las demas personas. Conforme a lo que en el sancto Concilio Provincial de Lima se proveyo. Span.-Quichua-Aymara. Ciudad de los Reyes, [Lima,] 1585. 4to.

2 Cartilla y Catecismo de la doctrina Cristiana. Lima, 1827. 4to.

3 Cartilla y Catecismo de la doctrina Cristiana. Lima, 1830. 4to.

CISNERUS, Diego. Sitio Naturaleza y Propriedades de la Ciudad de Mexico . . . Necefsidad de su cono cimieto para el exercicio de la Medicina . . . Por el Doctor Diego Cisneros Medico, etc. Mexico, 1618. 4to.

CIUDADANO. Manifiesto que ofrece, dedica y consagra a la magnanima nacion Peruana, un Ciudadano en contestacion al folleto titulado " Interesante," que se repartió en Arequipa el dia ocho de Octubre de este año, tres dias antes del sacrilego homicidio, intentado en la persona del ilustrisimo señor J. S. Goyeneche y Barreda, obispo de aquella diocesis; en el que se refuta solidamente el suplemento al Jenio del Rimac numero 283, dado a luz por J. A. Vijil, considerado reo del referido crimen. (Piezas principales que contiene el espediente seguido contra J. A. Vijil sobre el hecho de haberse presentado en el palacio del ilustrisimo . . . J. S. Goyeneche en la mañana del once de Octubre del presente año con el designio de asesinarle : Reimpreso.) Lima, 1834. 4to.

COCINA, VICENTE MANUEL. Opusculo filosófico sobre la historia del Derecho Romano, *etc.* Santjago, 1841. 8vo.

COLEGIO DE SAN ILDEFONSO. *Begins,* p. 3. Illmo. et Rmo. D.D.D. Fry, Josepho Calixto de Orihuela . . . Divi Ildefonsi Collegium . . . hocce amoris, studii, et congratulationis monimentum. [Subjects for examination of candidates in Theology. Preceded by Latin verses addressed to the Bishop of Orense.] [Imperfect: commencing at p. 3.] [Lima? 1830?] 4to.

COLMEIRO, MANUEL DE. Derecho administrativo Español. 2 tom. Madrid y Santiago, 1850. 8vo.

COLMEIRO, MIGUEL. Apuntes para la flora de las ˙dos Castillas. Madrid, Lima, 1849. 8vo.

COLOMBIA, *Republic of.* Republica de Colombia. El congreso ha acordado . . . la siguiente ley . . . Capitulo I. Del órden en la observancia de las leyes, *etc.* (Dada en Bogota a 1 de Mayo de 1825.—15.) [Bogota, 1825.] Fol.

2 LEY y reglamentos organicos de la ensenanza publica en Colombia acordados en el año de 1826.—16°. (de la independencia.) Bogota, 1826. 4to.

3 MENSAJE del vice-presidente de Colombia encargado del gobierno al congreso de 1827,—17°. (Bogotà enero 2 de 1827. Bogotà 12 de Mayo de 1827.) 2 parts. [Bogotà, 1827.] 4to.

4 NOTICIA sobre la geografia politica de Colombia proporcionada para la primera enseñanza de los niños. Caracas, 1830. 12mo.

COLONIAL REFORMER (THE). No. 2, Jan. 8, 1840. Spanish Town, Jamaica, 1840. Fol.

CONEJO, FLORENTINO. Acusacion que contra el . . . Auditor . . . F. Coñejo dirigen á la Suprema Corte Marcial M. Gomez Pedraza, M. Riva-Palacio, J. M. Lafragua, y M. Otero por los dictamenes que contra leyes espresas dió á la comandancia general de Mexico, en la causa que por conspiracion se siguió á los Acusadores. (*Exposicion al Publico—Documentos, etc.*) Mexico, 1843. 8vo.

CONOCIMIENTO (EL) de los tiempos. Ephemeride del año de 1739 . . . Con calendario delas fiestas, &c. Por el doct. D. P. de Peralta Barnuevo y Rocha. Lima, 1739. 12°

2 [EL CONOCIMIENTO de los tiempos . . . 1738. Imperfect at the beginning and the end.] [Lima, 1738.] 12°

3 [EL CONOCIMIENTO de los tiempos . . . 1750. Imperfect; wanting title-page, and all after leaf F. i.] [Lima, 1750.] 12°

4 EL CONOCIMIENTO de los tiempos . . . 1751 . . . Por el P. Juan Rer de la Compañia de Jesus. Lima, [1751.] 12°

5 EL CONOCIMIENTO de los tiempos . . . 1753 . . . Por el Padre J. Rer. (Experiencias physico-mathematicas á cerca de la naturaleza, y operaciones de el fuego.) Lima [1753.] 12°

6 EL CONOCIMIENTO de los tiempos . . . 1754 . . . Por el Padre J. Rer. Lima, [1754.] 12°

7 [EL CONOCIMIENTO de los tiem-

pos, *etc.* Wanting title-page, and having leaves 2 and 3 mutilated.] [Lima, 1762.] 12°.

8 EL CONOCIMIENTO de los tiempos ... 1765 ... Và al fin una descripcion de las provincias del obispado de Arequipa ... Por el doct. Don. C. Bueno. [Lima, 1765.] 12°

9 EL CONOCIMIENTO de los tiempos ... 1768. [Wanting all before leaf E. i.] [Lima, 1768.] 12°

10 EL CONOCIMIENTO de los tiempos ... 1770 ... Va al fin la descripcion del Obispado de la Paz. Por el doc. D. C. Bueno. [Wanting all after leaf H. iii.] [Lima, 1770.] 12°

11 EL CONOCIMIENTO de los tiempos ... 1771 ... Va al fin la descripcion del Obispado de Santa Cruz. Por el doct. Don C. Bueno. Lima, [1771.] 12°

12 EL CONOCIMIENTO de los tiempos ... 1775 ... Va al fin la descripcion del Obispado del Paraguay. Por el Doct. Don. C. Bueno. Lima, [1772.] 12°

13 EL CONOCIMIENTO de los tiempos ... 1773 ... Por el Doct. Don C. Bueno. Lima, [1773.] 12°

14 EL CONOCIMIENTO de los tiempos ... 1774 ... Va al fin la descripcion del Obispado del Tucuman. Por el doct. D. C. Bueno. Lima, [1774.] 12°

15 EL CONOCIMIENTO de los tiempos ... 1775 ... Va al fin la descripcion de la provincia del Chaco. Por el doct. D. C. Bueno. Lima, [1775.] 12°

16 EL CONOCIMIENTO de los tiempos ... 1776 ... Va al fin la descripcion del Obispado de Buenos-ayres. Por el doct. D. C. Bueno. Lima, [1776.] 12°

17 EL CONOCIMIENTO de los tiempos ... 1779 ... Va al fin una Guia de Forasteros para esta Ciudad de Lima. Por el doct. D. C. Bueno. [Lima, 1779.] 12°.

18 EL CONOCIMIENTO de los tiempos ... 1780 ... Va al fin una Guia de Forasteros para esta Ciudad[Lima.]

Por el doct. D. C. Bueno. [Lima, 1780.] 12°

19 EL CONOCIMIENTO de los tiempos ... 1787 ... Va al fin la Guia de Forasteros de esta Ciudad [Lima]. Por el doct. D. C. Bueno. [Lima, 1787.] 12°

20 EL CONOCIMIENTO de los tiempos ... 1788 ... Va al fin la Guia de Forasteros de esta Ciudad [Lima]. Por el doct. C. Bueno. [Lima, 1788.] 12°

21 [DESCRIPCION del Reyno del Perù, y de el de Chile por Obispados y provincias, y en igual conformidad de las del Rio de la Plata ... que en los 15 años contados de 1763 à 1772 y de 1774 à 1778 diò a luz en la Ciudad de los Reyes ... Don Cosme Bueno, *etc.*] [Lima, 1763-78.] 12mo.

The above is a MS. title prefixed to the book, which is a collection of 15 portions of a periodical, the above-named "El Conocimiento de los Tiempos," containing the descriptions set forth in the title, and also "Catalogo ... de los Virreyes, Governadores, *etc.* del Perù."

22 [DESCRIPCION del Reyno del Perù, *etc.*] MS. NOTE by R. Southey. [Lima, 1763-78.] 12mo.

This is another collection of duplicate portions of the same periodical, with the addition of three parts containing physical essays, from the same source.

CONSOLADOR (EL), o el modo de comportarse en los varios periodos de la vida, sin hacerse odioso a Dios ni a los hombres. [Preliminary number of a periodical. By F. Ayuso.] Lima, 1821. 4to.

CORDOBA, PEDRO TOMAS DE. Memorias geograficas, historicas, economicas y estadisticas de la isla de Puerto-Rico. 6 tom. Puerto-Rico, 1831-33. 8vo.

CORDOVA, PEDRO DE. Doctrina xpiana pa instrucion & informaciõ de los indios : por mañera de hystoria. Compuesta por el muy reverendo padre fray Pedro de Cordova : de buena memoria : primero fundador d' la orden de los Predicadores ē las yslas del mar Oceano : y por otros religio sos doctos d' la misma ordē. La ql dotrina fué vista y examinada y apruada por el muy R. S. el licēciado Tello de Sādoval Inquisidor y Visitador en esta nueva España por su Magestad. La qual fice empressa en Mexico por mandado del muy R. S. dō fray Juā çumarragapmer obispo desta ciudad : del cōsejo de su Magestad &c. y a su costa. Año de M. d .xliiij. Cō preuilegio de su. S. C. C. M. 4to.

CORNWALL CHRONICLE (THE) and County Gazette. Edited by A. Holmes. Vol. 67, No. 50. Dec. 11, 1839. Montego Bay, Jamaica, 1839. Fol.

CORNWALL COURIER and Jamaica General Intelligencer. Vol. 17, No. 50. Dec. 11, 1839. Falmouth, Jamaica, 1839. Fol.

CORREO DE CARACAS. 1 Oct. 1839. Caracas, 1839. Fol.

CORTES, HERNANDO. Historia de Nueva España escrita por . . . Hernan Cortes, aumentada con otros documentos, y notas por . . . F. A. Lorenzana, arzobispo de Mexico. Mexico, 1770. Fol.

CORTIGUERA Y SANTIAGO, FRANCISCO DE. Protrepticum sive adhortatorium Carmen, recitandum in D. Marci Limana Universitate. Limae, 1828. 8vo.

COSTA CAMPOS, MAURICIO DA. Vocabulario Marujo on conhecimento de todos os cabos necefsarios ao navio ; do seu poliame e de todos os termos marujaes, etc. Rio de Janeiro, 1823. 4to.

COSTANSO, MIGUEL. Diario Historico de los Viages de Mar y Tierra hechos al Norte de la California, de Orden del . . . Marques de Croix. Executados por la Tropa al mando de G. Portola : y por los Paquebots al mando de V. Vila y J. Perez. [Mexico, 1770.] Fol.

COUTO, JOSE MARÍA. Pastoral

que el Dr. D. J. M. Couto, vicario capitular en sede vacante del obispado de Valladolid de Michoacan, dirige . . . a los . . . parrocos y demos eclesiasticos . . . su diócesis. México, 1825. 8vo.

CROKER, TEMPLE HENRY. Where am I? How came I here? What are my wants? What are my duties? . . . [Four Sermons on Heb. iv. 24, 25.] Bafseterre, St. Christopher's, [1790.] 4to.

CRONICA politica y literaria de Lima. No. 2, 3, 4. [No. 1 wanting.] Lima, 1827. 4to.

CUBA. Cuadro estadistico de la . . . Isla de Cuba correspondiente al año de 1827, Formado por una comision de gefes y oficiales, . . . bajo la direccion del . . . Señor . . . Don F. D. Vives, precedido de una descripcion historica, fisica, geografica y acompañada de . . . notas, etc. Habana, 1829. Fol.

2 ARANCELES generales para el cobro de derechos de introduccion y estraccion en todas las aduanas de los puertos habilitados de la . . . Isla de Cuba para el año de, 1835. Habana, [1834.] Fol.

3 ECSAMEN analítico de la Balanza general del comercio de la isla de Cuba en el año de 1834 . . . compuesto . . . por los editores del Noticioso . . . de la Habana, en los números 162 y 167 del mismo periódico. Reimpreso, etc. Habana, 1835. 12mo.

4 ECSAMEN analitico de la Balanza general del comercio de la isla de Cuba, (en el año de 1835) etc. compuesto . . . por los editores del Noticioso y Lucero de la Habana en el número 151 del mismo periódico, etc. Reimpreso. Habana, 1836. 12mo.

5 ECSAMEN analítico de la Balanza general del comercio de la isla de Cuba en el año de 1836. etc. Dispuesto por la Redaccion del Noticiso [sic] y Lucero, y publicado en el número 114 del mismo periódico. [Havannah, 1837.] 12mo.

CUEVAS, AGUIRRE Y ESPINO-
sa, Joseph Francisco de. Extraĉto
de los Autos de diligencias, y reconoci-
mientos de los rios, lagunas, vertientes
y desagues de la Capital de Mexico,
y su valle : de los caminos para su
comunicacion, y su comercio : de los
daños que se vieron : remedios que se
arbitraron, *etc.* Mexico, 1748. Fol.

 E. A. Los Indios qui-
eren ser libres y lo
seran con justicia. B.
P. [An addreſs to the
colored inhabitants of
Mexico, signed E. A. D.] [Mexico,
1829.] Fol.

DAG ****** De Saint Domingue et de son indépendance par M.
Dag ****** créole, colon proprié-
taire. Brochure ... réimprimée au
Port au Prince avec des notes mar-
ginales redigées par deux jeunes
Haïtiens. Haïti, 1824. 4to.

DAMAS, Claude Charles de,
Viscount. Mémoire de M. de Damas,
gouverneur de la Martinique, sur les
troubles de cette colonie. [Fort Royal,
Martinique ? 1791.] 4to.

DANCER, Thomas. A brief history of the late expedition against
Fort San Juan, so far as it relates to
the diseases of the troops : together
with some observations on climate,
infeĉtion, and contagion, *etc.* Kingston, [Jamaica,] 1781. 4to.

2 Catalogue of plants, exotic and
indigenous, in the Botanical Garden,
Jamaica, 1792. St. Jago de la Vega,
[1792.] 4to.

3 The Medical Aſsistant ; or Jamaica Praĉtice of Physic, *etc.* Kingston, Jamaica, 1801. 4to.

4 Some Observations respeĉting
the Botanical Garden. Jamaica, 1804.
8vo.

5 A Roland for an Oliver ; or a
Jamaica Review of the Edinburgh
Reviewers. [By T. Dancer, M. D. ;

being a defence of his work, entitled,
" The Medical Aſsistant," *etc.* against
a critique of it said to have appeared
in the Edinburgh Review, but in
reality a separate publication, written
by — Fitzgerald.] *MS. note.* St.
Jago de la Vega, 1809. 8vo.

DAVILA, Jose Maria Sancho.
[*Begins*] Habiendo meditado pre-
sentar al Congresa un Manifiesto que
calificase el merito de su qveja ...
cree suficiente públicar su recurso
impreso, *etc.* Lima, [1830 ?] Fol.

DECIMAS dedicadas a la constitucion infeliz de la nacion! [Mex-
ico, 1824 !] s. sh. 4to.

DELLANAVE, Antonio Vicente.
Historia do descobrimento e conquista
do imperio Mexicano. 2 tom. Rio
de Janeiro, 1821-23. 8vo.

DESCOURTILZ, J. T. Ornitho-
logie Brésilienne : ou, Histoire des
Oiseaux du Brèsil, remarquables par
leur Plumage, leur Chant, ou leurs Ha-
bitudes. Part 1. [Londres, printed.]
Rio de Janeiro, [1854.] Fol.

DES LIANNES, Jean Pierre.
Précis pour J. P. Desliannes ... contre
le Sieur Grenier ; [in a suit concerning lands, *etc.*]   Port au Prince,
[1790 ?] 8vo.

DIARIO de la Tarde ... No. 2440.
2 de Setiembre, 1839. Buenos Aires,
1839. Fol.

2 Diario de la Tarde comercial
politico y literario. Editor Respon-
sable. Pedro Pence, No. 2568. Buenos Ayres, 1840. Fol.

DIARIO de Mexico. Tom. 13.
No. 18,910. With a fragment of a
subsequent No. pp. 735-8. [Mexico,
1810.] 4to.

DIARIO del Gobierno. No. 2586
1 Sept. 1839. Mexico, 1839. Fol.

DIEGO de San Francisco. Relacion verdadera, y breve de la per-

secucion, y Martirios que padecieron por la confeſsion de nuestra Santa Fee Catholica en Iapon, quinze Religiosos de la Provincia de S. Gregorio, de los Descalços del Orden de . . . S. Francisco de las Islas Philipinas. Adonde tambien se trata de otros muchos Martires Religiosos de otras Religiones, *etc.* (Aɛta audientiæ publicæ a S. D. N. Paulo V . . . Regis Voxu Iapon Legatis, *etc.* . . .] 2 parts. Manila,[and] Mexici. 1625-26. 8vo.

DOMENICA COLONIST (The). Nos. 705-760. March 23rd, 1839—April 11th, 1840. [Wanting Nos. 706 to 717, 719-20, 725, 729, 732, 738 to 41, 747, 750, 758-59.] Roseau, 1839-40. Fol.

DOMINGUEZ Y ARGAIZ, Francisco Eugenio. Platicas de los principales mysterios de Nvestra Sta. Fee, con una breve exortacion al fin del modo con que deben excitarse al dolor de las culpas. Hecho en el Idioma Yucateco. Por el Doɛtor D. Francisco Eugenio Dominguez y Argaiz, *etc.* Mexico, 1758. 4to.

DOMINICAN (The). No. 5. Roseau, 1839. Fol.

DUPUY, Baron de. Première Lettre du Baron de Dupuy, . . . a M. M. Henry, auteur du Pamphlet intitulé : Considerations offertes aux Habitans d'Hayti, sur leur Situation actuelle et sur le Sort présumé qui les attend. Cap-Henry,[1814]. 8vo.

2 Deuxieme Lettre . . . à M. H. Henry, auteur du Pamphlet intitulé : Considerations offertes aux Habitans d'Hayti, sur leur Situation actuelle et sur le Sort présumé qui les attend, imprimé à Kingston, Jamaïque. Cap Henry, [1814]. 8vo.

 CHAVE, Balthasar de. Discursos de la Antiguedad de la Lengua Cantabra Bascongada. Cõpuestos por

Balthasar de Echave, natural de la Villa de Cumaya en la Prouincia de Guipuzcoa, y vezino de Mexico . . . Habla con las Provincias de Guipuzcoa y Vizcaya, *etc.* Mexico, 1607. 4to.

ECUADOR. Protocolo de las Conferencias y Notas de las comisiones del Ecuador y Nueva Granada, en la cuestion sobre limites de ambos estados. Guayaquil, 1832. Fol.

EGANA, Juan de. Memoria politica sobre si conviene en Chile la libertad de cultos. Reimpresa en Lima, con una breve apologia del Art. 8 y 9 de la constitucion politica del Peru de 1823, y con notas y adiciones en que se esclarecen algunos puntos de la Memoria y Apologia, y en que se responde a los argumentos del Sr J. M. Blanco à favor de la tolerancia . . . y a los discursos de otros tolerantistas. [By I. Moreno.] Lima, 1817. 4to.

EGARINIO, Nonato. El pueblo pide justicia contra el malvado Victoria. [An appeal to the Mexicans, signed N. E.] Mexico, 1829. s. sh. Fol.

EGUIARA ET EGUREN, Joannes Josephus de. Bibliotheca Mexicana sive eruditorum historia virorum, qui in America Boreali nati, vel alibi geniti, in ipsam Domicili aut Studijs asciti, quavis linguâ scripto aliquid tradiderunt : . . . Authore D. Joanne Josepho de Eguiara et Eguren, . . . Tomus Primus Exhibens Litteras A B C. Mexici, 1755. Fol.

ELESPURU, Juan Bautista. [*Begins.*] Ligero extraɛto de las causas que impedieron á la tercera division á ponerse en disposicion de hacer uso de las armas. Lima, 1831. Fol.

ELESPURU Y PINILLOS, Pedro. Heroicum Carmen . . . in Limana Universitate recitandum. Praes. J, P. de V. [Lima,] 1834. 8vo.

ENNERY, — D', *Comte.* Royaume d'Hayti ... Lettre du Comte d'Ennery, ... A son ami le C ... de R ..., à Londres, sur les Hauts faits et les prouesses militaires du Général Desfourneaux, à Hayti. Cap-Henry, [1815.] 8vo.

ESCUDERO, José Agustin de. Noticias estadisticas del estado de Chihuahua. Mexico, 1834. 8vo.

ESPARZA, Marcos de. Informe presentado al Gobierno supremo del estado por M. de Esparza a consecuencia de la visita que praticó en los partidos de Villanueva y Juchipila. Zacatecas, 1830. 4to.

ESTEVA, José Ygnacio. Contrata de tabacos para la siembra que ha de hacerse en los cantones de Orizava, Córdova y Jalapa el presente año de 1826 y levantarse el siguiente de 1827, celebranda por ... Jose Ignacio Esteva,*etc.* [Mexico, 1827.] Fol.

ESTEVANEZ DE AZEVEDO, Juan. Practica de reparticion, y buen uso de Indios, y Azoques, *etc.* Lima, 1650. Fol.

2 [*Begins.*] Excelentissimo Señor. J. Estevanez de Azevedo, dize, *etc.* [A Memorial to the Viceroy of Peru, suggesting improvements in the working of quicksilver mines.] [Lima, 1650.] Fol.

ESTEVES, Manuel Ruperto. Manifiesto que M. R. Esteves da á sus conciudadanos de los documentos en que se contienen las poderosas razones que lo han obligado á venir á esta capital, como diputado electo por la provincia de Huancané. Lima, 1832. 4to.

ESTEVEZ, José. Analisis de la Pildora que administra ... J. R. Ugarte. Habana, 1814. 4to.

ESTRADA MEDINILLA, Maria de. Relacion escrita por Doña M. de Estrado Medinilla, à una Religiosa monja prima suya. De la felix entrada en Mexico dia de S. Augustin, à 28 de Agosto de mil y seiscientos y quarenta añosdel ... Señor Don Diego Lopez Pacheco, Cabrera, y Bobadilla Marques de Villena, Virrey ... desta Nueua España. *In verse.* [Mexico? 1640?] 4to.

 ABRY, Joseph Antonio. Compendiosa demostracion de los crecidos adelantamientos, que pudiera lograr la Real Hacienda ... mediante la rebaja en el precio del Azoque, que se consume para el laborio de las Minas de este Reyno, *etc.*, con una previa impugnacion a las reflexiones del Contador D. J. de Villa-Señor y Sanchez, sobre el mismo assumpto. Mexico, 1743. 4to.

FALMOUTH POST (The) and Jamaica General Advertiser. [Edited by J. Castello.] No. 29. vol. 5. July 17th, 1839. Falmouth, Jamaica, 1839. Fol.

FEBRES, Andres. Arte de la Lengua general del Reyno de Chilé, con un dialogo Chileno Hispano muy curioso ; A que se añade la Doctrina Christiana, estoses, Rezo, Catecismo, ... en Lengua Chilena y Castellana : Y por fin un Vocabulario Hispano-Chileno y un Calepino Chileno-Hispano ... Compuesto por el P. Andres Febres, *etc.* Lima, 1765. 8vo.

2 Diccionario Hispano Chileno. Compuesto por el R. P. Misionero A. Febres. Enriquecido de ·voces i mejorado por ... A. Hernandez i Calzada ... Edicion hecha para el Servicio de la Misiones ... bajo la inspeccion del R. P. misionero Fr. M. Anjel Astraldi. Santiago, 1846. 4to.

3 Diccionario Chileno Hispano, compuesto por el R. P. Misionero A. Febres. Enriquecido de voces e me-

jorado por el R. Padre misionero Fra. Antonio Hernandez i Calzada . . . Edicion hecha ara el servicio de la misiones . . . bajo la inspeccion del R. P. M. A. Astraldi. Santiago, 1846. 4to.

FERDINAND VII. *King of Spain.* Guatemala por Fernando Septimo el dia 12 de Diciembre de 1808. [Oracion Eucaristica que pronuncio . . . El . . . Dr. . . . I. Sicilia y Montoya . . . en la . . . accion de Gracias . . . por la exaltacion del . . . Rey. D. Fernando VII. al Trono de las Españas.] 2 parts. [Guatemala? 1808.] 4to.

FERNANDEZ, IGNACIO. Breves apuntes ó bien sean reflecciones que con motivo de la gran cuestion que se ventila en el dia, sobre si le pertenece ó no, el patronato de las iglesias de la república federal de los Estados Unidos Mexicanos las escribía sosteniendo la parte afirmativa . . . Ignacio Fernandez. Mexico, 1827. 4to.

FERNANDEZ DE ECHE-VERRIA Y VEYTIA, MARIANO. Historia antígua de Méjico . . . La publica con varias notas y un apendice el C. F. Ortega. 3 tom. Mejico, 1836. 8vo.

FERNANDEZ DE MADRID, JOSE. Memoria sobre el comercio cultivo y elaboracion del tabaco de esta isla. [i.e. Cuba.] Habana, 1821. 4to.
2 ENSAYO analitico sobre la naturaleza, causas y curacion de las calenturas thermo-adynamica y thermo-ataxica, llamadas calentura amarilla de America, vomito prieto, etc. Habana, 1821. 4to.

FIGUEROA, JOAN DE. Opusculo de Astrologia en medicina, y de los terminos y partes de la Astronomia necesarias para el uso della. Lima, 1660. 4to.

FILALETES, *Pseud.* Cartas Peruanas entre Filaletes y Eusebio, ó preservativo contra el veneno de los libros impios y seductores que corren en el pais. Tom 1. [Imperfect, want-

ing all after "Carta VII."] Lima, [1822-3.] 1826. 8vo.

FLORENCIA, FRANCISCO DE. La milagrosa invencion de un tesoro escondido en un campo, que hallò un . . . Cazique, y escondiò en su casa . . . Patente ya en el Santuario de los Remedios en su admirable Imagen de N. Señora . . . Noticias de su origen, y venidas á Mexico, etc. [Mexico,] 1685. 4to.

FLORES, JOSE. Especifico nuevamente descubierto en el reyno de Goatemala, para la curacion radical del . . . Mal de Cancro, etc. Reimpreso. Mexico, 1782. 4to.

FOGUERAS, JUAN. Satisfacion que se da por el M. R. P. Fr. Juan Fogueras . . . sobre el derecho fundado á la devolucion que declaró de las elecciones del capitulo que se dexó de celebrar en la provincia de Santa Elena de la Florida, el dia 23 de Henero . . . de 1745, en que estaba legitimamente convocado, etc. Mexico, 1747. Folº

FONSANCII, FRADERICO. Carta familiar de un sacerdote, respuesta a un amigo suyo, en que le dà cuenta de la conquista espiritual del vasto imperio del Gran Thibet [abridged from a pamphlet by A. M. Herrero], y la mission que los padres Capuchinos tienen alli con sus singulares progressos hasta el presente . . . [With an introductory letter signed Ricardo Anffescinio; the anagram of Fraderico Fonsancij.] Mexico, 1765. 4to.

FRAILE (EL). Nos. 1, 2. [Lima, 1821.] 4to.

FREITAS, MANOEL JOSE DE. Compendio da Grammatica Ingleza e Portugueza, etc. Rio de Janeiro, 1820. 4to.

FRENCH PEOPLE. [*Begins.*] Liberté. Egalité. Peuple Français, etc. [An address to the French people, complaining of the maladministration and crimes of Polverel and Sonthonax, their commissaries or delegates at St. Domingo.] (Adreſſe des négociants de la ville du Port-au-Prince, *etc.*) [Port-au-Prince ? or Paris ? 1793?] 4to.

FREYRE, Emmanuel Maria de. Prolusio academica in Divi Marci Universitate recitanda. Limæ, 1827. 4to.

FREYRE, Ramon. El ciudadano Ramon Freyre á sus conciudadanos [giving an account of his political life and service done to the country.] Lima, 1831. Fol.

FRIAS, Felix. Nota dirijida a S. G. . . . Don T. Frias, ministro de relaciones esteriores de Bolivia, por Don F. F. Cónsul de la! misma República en Chile. Valparaiso, 1845. 8vo.

FULANO DE TAL. Indice de las materias y ſe de las erratas que se hallan con abundancia en la dedicatoria, de la obra intitulada : Compendio o extracto de las tropelias, *etc.* por Fulano de Tal. Lima, 1811. 4to,

FUNES, Gregorio. Ensayo de la Historia Civil del Paraguay, Buenos-Ayres y Tucuman. 3 tom. Buenos-Ayres. 1816-17. 4to.

ACETA del Gobierno de Costa Rica. Nos. 196 to 203. San José, 1852. Fol.
GACETA del Gobierno de Mexico. Nos. 1258, 1278-79. Gaceta extraordinaria . . . 11 de Marzo 1818. [The Gaceta extraordinaria bears the imprint of Cadiz.] [Mexico, 1818.] 4to.

GACETA MERCANTIL (La). No. 4866, 19 de Setiembre, 1839. Buenos Aires, 1839. Fol.

GACHUPINES. Antier empezó el degüello de los pobres Gachupines. Mexico, 1828. s. sh. Fol.

GAINZA, Gavino. Conclusion fiscal en el proceso militar formado contra . . . Gavino Gainza, como general en gefe del exército real en el reyno de Chile, en . . . 1814; y sentencia difinitiva pronunciada por el consejo de guerra, *etc.* Lima, 1816. 8vo.

GAMA, Jose Basilio da, *alias* Termindo Sipilio. O Uruguay, poema. Nova ediç. Rio de Janeiro, 1811. 8vo.

GAMARRA. Augustin, *President of Peru.* Redaccion de la correspondencia oficial entre A. Gamarra, y el Obispo del Cuzco [J. C. de Orihuela] sobre imputaciones enormes que hace aquel a individuos del Clero. Lima, 1825. 4to.
2 El Presidente de la Republica presenta al publico las razones en que se fundó para la prision del señor exdiputado Igoain, que se ha puesto en libertad con arreglo á lo decidido por el consejo de estado. Lima, 1832. 4to.

GANDARA, Manuel Maria. Exposicion que hace al supremo gobierno Don M. M. Gándara gobernador que fue del departamento de Sonora sobre su conducta politica y demás sucesos antiguos y recientes acaecidos en aquel Departamento. Mexico, 1842. 8vo.

GARCES DE PORTILLO, Pedro. [*Begins.*] El doctor P. Garces de Portillo, *etc.* [A memorial to the King of Spain's viceroy, setting forth the memorialist's services in Mexico, and praying for promotion.] [Mexico? 1640?] s. sh. Fol.

GARCES Y EGUIA, Jose. Nueva teórica y práctica del beneficio de los metales de oro y plata por fundicion y amalgamacion. Mexico, 1802. 4°

GARCIA DE LA RIESTRA, Isabel. Representacion que eleva

al soberano congreso Doña I. Garcia
de la Riestra, a nombre de su hijo el
coronel graduato Don F. Valle-Ri-
estra, por habérsele comprendido en
la conspiracion de que fue absuelto
por el consejo de estado el disputado
J. F. Iguain. Lima, 1832. 4to.

GARCIA DE PALACIO, Diego.
Instrucion Nauthica, para el buen uso,
y regimiento de las Naos, su traça
y govierno conforme à la altura de
Mexico. Cōpuesta por el Doƈtor Diego Garcia de Palacio, del cōsejo de
su Magestad, y su Oydor en la Real
audiēncia de la dicha Ciudad. Mexico, 1587. 4to.

GARCIA RODRIGUEZ, Vicente
Josef. Geografia Peruana. Notas
astronomicas, diseño o perfeƈto pro-
totipo de las . . . provincias del . . .
Reyno del Peru. Miscellanea curi-
osa . . . recogida . . . por V. J. Garcia Rodriguez. [ms. notes.] Lima,
1778. 8vo.

This volume consists merely of fragment-
ary pieces of various calendars.

GARRICH, Raimundo Pascual.
Balanza general del comercio de la
Isla de Cuba en el año de 1836 . . .
por don ‾R. P. Garrich. Habana,
1837. Fol.

GAYTAN DE TORRES, Man-
uel. Relacion, y vista de oios que
Don Manuel Gaytan de Torres . . .
haze a su Magestad en el Real Consejo de las Indias, por comiſsion que
para ello tuuo de las Minas de cobre
que ay en las Serranias de Cocorote,
provincia de Veneçuela. [Lima?]
Año 1621. Fol.

GAZETA DE LITERATURA.
Tom. 2. Nos. 33 to 44, 46, 47. Tom.
3. Nos. 3 to 10, 14, 22, 25, 27, 29 to
31, 35 to 37, 39, 40. Suplemento
30 de enero 1795. Mexico, [1792-
95.] 4to.

GAZETA DE MEXICO desde
primero de Henero de 1728, (hasta

fines de Diziembre de 1730) Nos. 1
to 37 (que ha escrito Juan Francisco
Sahagum de Arevato Ladren de
Guevara.) Mexico, 1728-30. 4to.

GOMEZ DE LA PARRA, Jo-
seph. Grano de trigo fecundo en
virtudes en la vida, fecundiſsimo por
la Succeſsion en la muerte, la Catholica Magestad del Rey . . . Carlos
Segvndo, que Dios aya: Aſsumpto
Panegyrico Funeral . . . (Genealo-
gia de los Catholicos Reyes de España,
. . . des de D. Pelayo hasta Señor D.
Phelipe V. su legitimo Heredero.)
2 parts. Puebla, 1701. 4to.

GOMEZ MARIN, Manuel. De-
fensa Guadalupana . . . contra la disertacion de D. J. B. Muñoz. Méjico,
1819. 4to.

GOMEZ PEDRAZA, Manuel.
Bosquejo historico de la revolucion de
tres dias en la capital de los Estados-
Unidos Mexicanos o sea las acusaciones de la conduƈta del ministro de la
guerra D. M. Gomez Pedraza. México, 1828. 12mo.

2 Acusation que contra el Sr.
auditor licenciado D. Florentino Conejo dirigen a la suprema corte marcial
M. Gomez Pedraza . . . y M. Otero,
por los diƈtamenes que contra leyes
espresas dió a la comandancia general de Mexico, en la causa que por
conspiracion se siguió a los acusadores, y esposicion de los mismos
sobre aquel suceso. Mexico, 1843.
8vo.

GONZAGA DE LA ENCINA,
Luis, Bishop of Arequipa. Ediƈto
pastoral, formado con el objeto de
procurar la pacificacion y bien espiritual y temporal de su diocesis, y de
la monarquia Española. Lima, 1815.
4to.

GONZALEZ, Manuel Jesus.
Manifiesto documentado que presenta á sus conciudadanos el presbitero M. J. Gonzalez, obligado por las

calumnias que le han inferido por la imprenta, sus gratuitos enemigos, presentandolo como criminal y como antipatriota. Lima, 1832. 4to.

GONZALEZ DE AZEVEDO, JUAN. [*Begins.*] Muy poderoso Señor, El capitan J. Gonzalez de Azevedo. [A memorial, addreſſed to the King of Spain, respecting the grievances suffered by the native inhabitants of Lima and Quito from the government.] [Lima? 1615?] Fol.

GONZALEZ DE LA REGUERA, JUAN DOMINGO, *Archbishop of Lima.* Fama postuma del . . . Señor . . . J. D. Gonzalez de la Reguera . . . por [J. M. Bermudez] Autor de la Oracion fúnebre (Carmen funereum quo . . . Memoriæ . . . J. De la R . . . ultimi honores ei exhibiti offeruntur, *etc.*) Lima, 1805. 4to.

GONZALEZ Y CRESPO, MARIANO JOSE. Observaciones praticas sobre las virtudes de las aguas Minero-Medicinales de Trillo. Por el Doctor D. Mariano José Gonzalez y Crespo, *etc.* Tom. 1. Guadalajara, 1847. 8vo.

GONZALEZ Y MORILLAS, JOSE MARIA. Monografia optalmologica, ó descripcion de todas las enfermedades que pueden padecer los organos de la vision y partes anexas. Tom. 1. Habana, 1848. 8vo.

GOUVEA PINTO, ANTONIO JOAQUIM DE. Manual de appellações e aggravos; ou deducção systematica dos principios mais solidos e necessarios relativos a su materia fundamentada nas leis deste reino. Bahia, 1816. 4to.

GRANADOS Y GALVEZ, JOSEPH JOAQUIN. Tardes Americanas: Gobierno Gentil y Catolico: Breve y particular noticia de Toda la Historia Indiana: Sucesos, casos notables, y cosas ignoradas, desde la entrada de la Gran Nacion Tulteca á

esta tierra de Anahuac, hasta los presentes tiempos. Trabajadas por un Indio, y un Español. Sacalas a luz El M. R. P. Fr. Joseph Joaquin Granados y Galvez, Predicador general de Jure, ex-Definidor de la Provincia de Michoacan, y Guardian que fué de los Conventos di Xiquilpan, Valladolid, Rioverde, y Custodio de todas sus Misiones, y las Dedica Al Excmô. Sr. D. Joseph de Galvez, Caballero de la Real distinguida Orden de Carlos III., del Consejo de Estado, Gobernador del Supremo de las Indias, y Secretario del Despacho universal de ellas. Mexico, 1778. 4to.

GRENADA (THE), Free Preſſ and Public Gazette. Nos. 680, 699 to 700, 706 to 708, 711, 714 to 716. 718 to 723, 726, 729, 731 to 735. [Saint George's,] 1839-40. 4to.

GRENADA, *Island of.* Récit des troubles survenus à la Grenade. [St. George? 1795?] 4to.

GUADALOUPE, *Island of.* Adreſſe de l'Aſſemblée coloniale de la Guadaloupe, aux Aſſemblées administratives de Saint-Domingue, envoyée aux députés de cette colonie à l'Aſſemblée nationale pour appuyer et renforcer la dénonciation solemnelle du Comte de la Luzerne, faite par la députation de Saint-Domingue. Cap François, [1790.] 8vo.

2 ADRESSE de l'Aſſemblée générale-Coloniale de la Guadeloupe á l'aſſemblée nationale [of France]. (Adreſſe à M. de Damas, par les députés de l'aſſemblée coloniale de Tabago.) Fort-Royal, Martinique, [1791.] s. sh. 4to.

GUANAXUATO. Memoria que el gobernador del estado de Guanajuato formó . . . para conocimiento del congreso del mismo estado todo por lo respectivo al año de 1826. México, 1827. Fol.

GUATEMALA Constitucion de la Republica Federal de Centro-America dada por la Asamblea Nacional Constituyente en 22 de Noviembre de 1824. Guatemala [1824]. Fol.

2 EL SUPREMO poder executivo, ... decretado lo que sigue ... Art. 1. Todos los extrangeros que quieran venir à cualquiera de las provincias unidas del centro de Amèrica ... podran hacerlo en los términos y de la manera que mejor les convenga, etç. [Guatemala, 1824.] Fol.

3 EL SUPREMO poder executivo ... decretado lo que sigue ... Art. 1. Todos los extrangeros, etc. [Guatemala, 1824.] Fol.

4 EL SUPREMO poder executivo ... decreta el presente reglamento. Capitulo I. Asiento de los que fueron esclavos, y de sus antiguos dueños, etc. [Wanting all after Capitulo IV. N. 28.] [Guatemala, 1824.] Fol.

5 EL SUPREMO poder executivo ... ha decretado lo que sigue. La asambléa nacional constituyente ... decreta. 1º Tendrán por ahora congresos, Guatemala, San Salvador, Honduras, Nicaragua, y Costarica, etc. [Guatemala, 1824.] Fol.

6 EL SUPREMO poder executivo ... ha decretado lo que sigue. La asambléa ... observando que la medida de continuar el uso del papel sellado, y aumentar su valor, fué adoptada con buen exito en otros paises libres ... decreta lo siguiente, etc. [Guatemala, 1824.] Fol.

7 EL SUPREMO poder executivo ... ha decretado lo que sigue. La asambléa nacional constituyente ... decreta ... Art. 1. Desde la publicacion de esta ley, en cada pueblo, son libros los esclavos de uno y otro sexo, etc. [Guatemala, 1824.] Fol.

8 DISCURSO del Presidente del poder executivo á la apertura del Congreso Federal de Guatemala en 25 de Febrero de 1825. Guatemala, 1825. 4to.

9 ESPOSICION presentada al congreso Federal al comenzar la sesion ordinária del año de 1826. Por el secretario de estado y del despacho de relaciones esteriores é interiores, etc. Guatemala, [1826.] Fol.

10 ESTADO de las introducciones de efeótos estrangeros habidas en la Aduana del Guatemala, en los seis meses corridos desde 1 de Enero a 30 de Junio de 1851, etc. [Guatemala, 1851.] s. sh. Fol.

11 TARIFA de aforos para la exaccion de derechos en las aduanas maritimas y fronterizas de la Republica de Guatemala. [Guatemala,] 1852. 8vo.

GUEMEZ, PACHECO, PADILLA Y HORCACITAS, JUAN VICENTE, *Count de Revilla Gigedo, Viceroy of Mexico.* Instruccion reservada que el Conde de Revilla Gigedo dió à su succesor en el mando, Marqués de Branciforte, sobre el gobierno de este continente en el tiempo que fue su Virey. Mexico, 1831. 8vo.

GUIA política, eclesiastica y militar del virreynato del Perú para el año de 1795. Compuesta ... por ... J. H. Unanue. [Lima, 1795.] 8vo.

GUIANA CHRONICLE (THE). Nos. 3209, 3225, 3369, 3396-97, 4401 to 5, 4515-16, 4520 to 24, 4532-33, 4536, 4537-38, 4542-43, 4545-46, 4554, 4558 to 61, 4564, 4568 (March 6th, 1840), 45690 (March 18, 1840), 45693, 45697. George-Town, 1839-40. Fol.

GUIANA TIMES (THE). Nos. 5 to 7 and 9. March 1840. Georgetown, Guiana, 1840. Fol.

GUILDING, JOHN. A Sermon [on 1 Peter ii. 17] preached before his excellency the Governor ... of the Island of Saint Vincent, on Thursday, the 28th day of December, 1809, being the day appointed ... for the observance of the Jubilee, in celebration of the fiftieth anniversary of our most gracious sovereign's accefsion to the throne. Saint Vincent, 1810. 4to.

GUTIERREZ DE LA-FUENTE, ANTONIO. Manifiesto que di en Trujillo en 1824, sobre los motivos que me obligaron á deponer á D. J. de la Riva-Agüero, *etc.* Lima, 1829. Fol.

2 Contestacion de los amigos del jeneral La-fuente a los cargos que le hace el presidente provisional de la republica en la razon motivada, sobre el uso de las facultades estraordinarias. Lima, 1834. 4to.

GUTIERREZ DE MEDINA, CHRISTOVAL. Viage de Tierra, y mar, . . . que hizo el Excellentiſsimo señor Marqves de Villena mi señor, yendo por virrey, y capitan General de la Nueua España, *etc.* (Razon de la fabrica Allegorica. Zodiaco Regio, *etc.*) 4 parts. Mexico, 1640. 4to.

GUTIERREZ ESTRADA, J. M. Carta dirigida al . . . presidente de la republica sobre la necesidad de buscar en una Convencion el posible remedio de los males que aquejan á la República, y opiniones del autor acerca del mismo asunto. Mexico, 1840. 8vo.

ARRO-HARRING. Poesie eines Scandinaven. Rio de Janeiro, 1843. 8vo.

HAVANNA. Reglamento para el Banco Real de Fernando VII. Habana, 1832. 8vo.

2 BALANZA mercantil de la Habana correspondiente al año de 1836. Habana, 1837. Fol.

HAVANA REPUBLICAN. Vol. 4. No. 16. Sept. 25, 1839, Havana, 1839. Fol.

HAYTI. Royaume d'Hayti. Manifeste du Roi. [Proclaiming the legitimacy of the independence of Hayti.] Cap-Henry, [1814.] 8vo.

2 RELATION de la Fête de S. M. la Reine d'Hayti, des Actes du Gouvernement qui ont en lieu durant cet Evénement, et de tout ce qui s'est paſſé a l'occasion de cette Fête. Cap-Henry, [1816?] 8vo.

3 PIÈCES Officielles relatives aux négociations du Gouvernement Français avec le Gouvernement Haïtien, pour traiter de la formalité de la Reconnaiſsance de l'Independance d' Haïti. Port-au-Prince, 1824. 4to.

4 CIRCULAIRES du President d' Haiti aux Commandans d'Arrondiſsement, sur l'Agriculture. Port-au-Prince, 1831. 16mo.

5 RELACION de la fiesta del aniversario de la independencia de Hayti celebrada el 1. de Enero de 1834, año 31 (de la independencia). [Saint Domingo, 1834.] 4to.

HERAS, BARTOLOME MARIA LAS, *Archbishop of Lima.* [*Begins.*] Exhortacion que hace el Arzobispo de Lima à su Diocesis para el donativo en favor de la nacion española y su Monarca Fernando VII. [Lima, 1809.] 4to.

2 [*Begins.*] Nos. D. B. M. de las Heras . . . a todos nuestros diocesanos. [Pastoral Letter against infidel publications.] [Lima, 1821.] 4to.

HERES, TOMAS DE. Esposicion que el general de brigada Tomas de Heres presenta al publico sobre las acusaciones que le hace F. Brandsen en un impreso publicado en Santiago de Chile. Lima, 1825. 4to.

2 MEMORIA que leyó, al congreso del Peru, el encargado interinamente del ministerio de estado en los departamentos de guerra y marina. Lima, 1825. 4to.

HERNANDEZ, FRANCISCO. Quatro Libros de la Naturaleza, y Virtudes de las plantas, y animales que estan recevidos en el uso de Medicina en la Nueva España, y la methodo, . . . y preparacion, que para administrallas se requiere con lo que el Doctor Francisco Hernandez escrivió en lengua Latina . . . Traduzido [sic], y aumentados . . . por . . . F. Ximenez, *etc.* Mexico, 1615. 4to.

HERRERA, Bartolome. Discurso en la Misa solemne con que el Dean y Cabeldo de la Iglesia Catedral celebró la confirmacion del Arzobispado del Señor Jorge de Benavente y Macoaga. Lima, 1835. 4to.

HERRERA, Francisco. Al mundo entero. [A Vindication of himself.] Lima, 1827. 4to.

HIGGINS, Bryan. Observations and advices for the improvement of muscovado sugar and rum. Part 2. [wanting parts 1 and 3.] St. Jago de la Vega, 1800. 8°

HILHOUSE, William. Indian Notices: or, sketches of the habits, characters, languages, etc. of the several nations [of British Guiana]. With remarks on their capacity for colonization, present government, etc. also the Ichthyology of the fresh waters of the interior. [Georgetown!] 1825. 8vo.

A copy of a small colonial edition, printed for private circulation. The words above, " of British Guiana," are supplied on the titlepage, in MS. by the author.

HOLGUIN, Diego Goncalez. Vocabulario de la lengua general de todo el Peru Llamada lengua Qquichua, o del Inca. Corregido y renovado conforme a la propriedad cortesana del Cuzco. Dividido en dos libros, . . . Compuesto por el Padre Diego Gonçalez Holguin de la Compañia de Jesus, natural de Caçeres. Ciudad de los Reyes. [i. e. Lima,] 1608. 4to.

HUC,—, and CHAZELLES, A. de, Count. Martinique et Guadeloupe. Conseils coloniaux. Seſsion de 1840. Rapports sur la question de l'emancipation. Fort-Royal, Martinique, 1841. 8vo.

HUERTA, Alonzo de. Arte de la Lengua Quechua general de los Yndios de este Reyno del Piru . . . Compuesto por el Doctor Alonso de Huerta Clerigo Presbytero Predicador de la dicha Lengua en esta

Sancta Yglesia Cathredal, . . . En los Reyes. [Lima,] 1616. 4to.

 CAZA, Isidro, and Gondra, Isidro. Coleccion de las Antiguedades Mexicanas que ecsisten en el Museo Nacional, y dan a luz Isidro Icaza é Isidro Gondra. Litografiadas por Frederico Waldeck, . . . 3 nums. Mexico, 1827. Fol.

INDIES. [Begins.] Luego que Dios crió el mundo fabricó su mayorasgo que fue aquella antigua yglesia que tanto quiso y amo, etc. [A sermon or diſsertation on the depravation of morals in the Spanish Indies, etc.] [Manuscript.] [Lima? 1645?] Fol.

INDIJENO (El). Nums. 1 to 5. 18 de Feb.—3 de Agos. de 1833. Ayacucho, 1833. 8vo.

INGENUO. Rebelion en Aznapuquio por varios gefes del exercito Español, para deponer del mando al dignifsimo Virrey del Peru . . . J. de la Pezuela. Escrita por el Ingenuo Rio de Janeiro. Lima. 1822. 4to.

INQUISITION, Tribunal of New Spain. Relacion del tercero Auto particular de Fee que el tribunal del santo officio de la Inquisicion de . . . la Nueva España, celebró . . . à los treinta del mes de Março de 1648. Mexico, 1648. 4to.

IRIS DE LA PAZ. Breves observaciones sobre un articulo del Iris de la Paz, de 26 de Diciembre de 1830, titulado: Sucesos internacionales. Los tres dias del Desagnadero. [With the extract from the Iris.] Lina [Lima], 1831. 4to.

ITURBIDE, Agustin de. Breve diseño crítico de la emancipacion y libertad de la nacion Mexicana, y de las causas que influyeron en sus . . . sucesos, acaecidos desde el grito de

Iguala hasta la . . . muerte del libertador, *etc.* [Edited by L. L. S. E. I. with a Spanish version of the preface to the English translation, published by J. Murray in 1824, entitled, A statement of some of the principal events, *etc.*] [pp. 1-14, following the title-page, are wanting.] Mexico, 1827. 12mo.

IXTLILXUCHITL, FERNANDO DE ALVA. Horribles crueldades de los conquistadores de México . . . ó sea memoria escrita por D. F. de A. Ixtlilxuchitl [or rather his " Décima tercia relacion, de la venida de los Españoles y principio de la ley evangélica.] Publicala por suplemento a la historia del padre Sahagun C. M. de Bustamante. Mexico, 1829. 8vo.

AMAICA. An Inquiry concerning the Trade, Commerce, and Policy of Jamaica, relative to the scarcity of Money . . . to which is added, a Scheme for establishing a Public Bank. St. Jago de la Vega, Jamaica, 1757. 4to.

2 ACTS of Affembly, paffed in the Island of Jamaica, from 1770 to 1783, inclusive. (An abridgment of the laws of Jamaica, *etc.*) 2 parts. Kingston, Jamaica, 1786. 4to.

3 ACTS of Affembly, paffed in the Island of Jamaica, from the year 1681 to the year 1769, inclusive. 2 vols. Kingston, Jamaica, 1787. Fol.

Vol. 2 contains likewise " An abridgment " of the Acts "—" Appendix containing laws " respecting slaves "—and " An abridgment " of the laws . . . in manner of an index," *etc.* : each having a distinct pagination.

4 ACTS of Affembly, paffed in the Island of Jamaica from the year 1784 to the year 1788, inclusive. (An abridgment of the Acts. Acts paffed in the years 1789 and 1790.) 2 parts. Kingston, Jamaica, 1789 [-90.] 4to.

5 THE LAWS of Jamaica : comprehending all the Acts in force, paffed between the 32nd year of the reign of

King Charles the Second and the 45th and 46th years of the reign of King George the Third. 8 vols. St. Jago de la Vega, Jamaica, 1792-1806. 4to.

6 JOURNALS of the Affembly of Jamaica. Vols. 1-14. Jamaica, 1811-29. Fol.

7 VOTES of the Honourable House of Affembly of Jamaica [in 12 vols.] Jamaica, 1819-30. Fol.

8 THE PRIVILEGES of Jamaica vindicated ; with an impartial narrative of the late dispute between the Governor and House of Representatives, upon the case of John Olyphant, Esq. New edition ; to which is added, a recent case of breach of privilege. Printed, 766. Reprinted, Jamaica, 1810. 8vo.

9 (PRINTED for the Chamber of Commerce.) Resolutions of the several parishes in the counties of Surry, Middlesex, and Cornwall, and of the Chamber of Commerce, Jamaica ; on the state of the Island consequent upon the admiffion of foreign Slave Sugar into the markets of Great Britain, *etc.* Jamaica, 1847. 8°

JAMAICA ALMANAC (THE), for . . . 1818. Kingstown, Jamaica, 1818. 12°

JAMAICA DESPATCH and Kingston Chronicle. Nos. 1215, 1654, 1658, 1665, 1668, 1677, 1708 to 1710, 1802-03, 1811, 1819, 1895 to 1905, 1907 to 1924, 1926 to 50, 1952 to 54; 1956 to 82, 1984 to 88, 1990, 1994, 1996-97, 1999 to 2057, 2059 to 2128. [Continued under the title of.] The Jamaica Despatch and Jamaica Gazette. Nos. 2129 to 2202, 2204-05, 2207 to 09, 2211 to 2223. Kingston ? Jamaica, 1836-40. Fol.

JAMAICA GAZETTE. Edited by T. Shannon and J. Lunan. Nos. 108, 118, 120 to 23, 125 to 27, 129 to 59. Dec. 1, 1838—Dec. 28, 1839. Kingston, Jamaica, 1838-39. Fol.

JAMAICA QUARTERLY

JOURNAL (THE), and Literary Gazette. Conducted by a Society of Gentlemen. No. 1. July 1818. No. 2. Dec. 1818. No. 2. vol. 2, July 1819. No. 1. vol. 3, Sept. 1819. Kingston, Jamaica, 1818-19. 8vo.

JAMAICA STANDARD. Vol 3. Nos. 267-68, 275, 304, 307, 316. Montego Bay, Jamaica, 1839. Fol.

2 JAMAICA Standard. Nos. 266 to 388, January 9, 1839—April 15, 1840 [wanting Nos. 269, 271, 274, 76, 77, 288, 291, 306, 356, 374.] Montego-Bay, Jamaica, 1839-40. Fol.

JOFRE, LINO. Traji-Comedia. La America libertada por el invicto Bolivar. En tres actos [and in verse.] Panama, 1825. 4to.

JORGE. Dialogo sobre los Diezmos entre Jorge y Dicelogo [By J. Moreno.] 2 parts Lima, 1826. 4to

2 DIALOGO sobre los diezmos entre Jorge y Diceologo (Continuacion del dialogo sobre los diezmos. Conclusion del dialogo sobre los diezmos, etc.) 3 parts. [Each part has a separate head title, pagination, and register. Wants the general title.] Lima, 1826. 8vo.

JUAN BAPTISTA, *Franciscan at Mexico.* A Iesu Christo S. N. ofrece este Sermonario en lengua Mexicana. Su indigno sieruo Fr. Ioan Baptista de la Orden del Seraphico Padre sanct Francisco, de la Provincia del sancto Evangelio. Primera Parte. Mexico, 1606. [The colophon is dated 1607.] 4to.

JUSTINIANUS, FLAVIUS, *Emperor.* Elucidationes ad quatuor libros Institutionum Justiniani locupletatæ legibus, decisionibusque juris Hispani a Doctore Jacobo Magro; continuavit, addidit Proœmium aliaque utilia, novissimasque Resolutionesnondum compilatas collectionibus legum Castellænec Indiarum Eusebius Bonaventura Beleña. 4 tom. Mexici, 1787-88. 4to.

RUGER, C. J. Rates of duties exacted at the custom-houses of the island of Cuba, on the principal articles of importation, and on exports, calculated in fixed numbers. Havana, 1837. 16mo.

D. Manifiesto sobre el debido culto de los corazones de Jesus y de Maria. Lima, 1813. 4to.

L., J. S. P. O Brasil, e a constituição de Portugal, ou ensaio para a resolução do problema da reuniāo dos Portuguezes de ambos os Hemisferios; por J. S. P. L. Rio de Janeiro, 1822. 4to.

LABARTA, NICASIO. Pastoral del cabildo gobernador del Arzobispado de México à sus diocesanos. Mexico, 1825. 4to.

L'ACUL, *Parish of* [*Hayti.*] Extrait des registres des délibérations de la paroisse de l'Acul. (Compte que rend à ses Commettans A. P. Laffon de Ladébat, de la conduite qu'il a tenue à l'assemblée Coloniale de S. Domingue, etc.) [Port-au-Prince? 1790.] 4to.

LANDABURU Y BELSUNCE, AGUSTIN DE. *Resp.* A de Landaburu et Belsunce... Logicæ, Arithmeticæ, et Algebræ extemporali Subeundo examine, subjectos propositiones propugnabit, Præs. H. Enanué. Lima, [1785.] 8vo.

2 ENSAYO sobre los primeros fundamentos de las Bellas Letras, Gramática latina, Mithologia y Poesia. *Lat. and Span.* [Imperfect; containing the dedication only.] [Lima,] 1785. 8vo.

3 THESES... in philosophia. *Præs.* J. H. Unanue. [Imperfect; containing the title-page only.] Limae, [1788.] 8vo.

LANUZA, Jose Maria. Proyecto de ley eclesiastica del diputado por Yucatan J. M. Lanuza presentado a su respectiva camara, *etc.* Mexico, 1829. 8vo.

LA PLATA, *United Provinces of.* Constitucion de las Provincias Unidas en Sud America Sancionada y Mandada publicar por el Soberano Congreso. General Constituyente. Buenos-Ayres, 1819. 4to.

LARRAINZAR, Manuel. Noticia histórica de Soconusco y su incorporacion a la República Mexicana. Mexico [Paris?], 1843. 12mo.

LARREA Y LOREDO, Juan de. Principios que siguió ... J. de Larrea y Loredo en el ministerio de hacienda y seccion de negocios eclesiasticos de que estuvo encargado. Lima, 1827. 8vo.

LARRETA, Clemente de. Oracion funebre en la solemne translacion de la Urna en que se havia depositado el cuerpo del Señor Joseph de Cevallos Guerra, Conde de las Torres, el 23 de Março, 1744. [Ps. xxiv. 9.] [Lima, 1744.] 4to.

LARRIVA, Jose Joaquin de. Panegirico de la Concepcion de Maria. Lima, 1816. 4to.

LASO, Benito. Esposicion que hace Benito Laso, diputado al Congreso por la provincia de Puno. Lima, 1826. 4to.

LEAZ DE AYALA, Matheo. [*Begins.*] El Capp.ᵃⁿ Matheo Leaz de Ayala ... en la causa criminal que trató contra un Domingo fuêtes q se nombra secretario de su mag.ᵈ *etc.* [A memorial complaining of unjust accusations, *etc.*] [Manuscript.] [Buenos Ayres? 1620?] Fol.

LEON, Martin de. Relacion de las exequias q elexᵐᵒ. sʳ. D. Iuan de mendoça y luna Marques de Montesclaros, Virrei del Piru hizó en la muer-te de la Reina Nuestra S. Doña Margarita ... Por el preßentado fray Martin de leon, de la orden de San Augustin. Limæ, 1612. 4to.

LEON PINELO, Didaco de. Hypomnema apologeticum pro Regali Academia Limensi in Lipsianam periodum ... Accedunt dißertatiunculæ gymnasticæ palæstricæ, canoico-legales, aut promiscuæ: ... Authore D. D. Didaco de Leon Pinelo ... Limæ, 1648. 4to.

LEON Y GAMA, Antonio de. Descripcion historica y cronologica de las dos piedras que con ocasion del nuevo empedrado que se esta formando en la plaza principal de Mexico, se hallaron en ella el año de 1790. Da la a luz con notas, biografia de su autor Carlos Maria de Bustamante. Segunda ediçion. Mexico, 1832. 4to.

LIBERAL (The). Nos. 170 to 289. Feb. 10, 1839—April 8, 1840. Wanting Nos. 203 to 207, 273-74, 286.] Bridgetown, Barbadoes, 1839-40. Fol.

LIBERAL (El). Nos. 281-82. 4, 10. de Agosto 1841. Caracas, 1841. Fol.

LIMA. Confeßionario para los curas de Indios con la instrucion contra sus Ritos: y Exhortacion para ayudar a bien morir: y summa de Privilegios; y forma de Impedimentos del Matrimonio. Compuesto y traduzido en las lenguas Quichua, y Amara. Por autoridad del Concilio Provincial de Lima, del año de 1583. En la cividad de los Reyes. [Lima], 1585. 4to.

2 Informe de los Señores contadores del Tribunal de cuentas; hecho al ... Marques de Mancera, Virrey de stos Reynos, sobre el papel que dieron à su Ex. el Prior, y Consules desta Ciudad de Lima, en razon del aßiento de los açogues, propuesto por el señor Doctor D. Sebastian de San-

doval, y Guzman, *etc.* Lima, 1640.
Fol.

3 [*Begins.*] COPIA de un memorial que dió el consuldo de Lima al Virrey Conde de Lermas, sobre los inconbenienttes grandes q se orijinan del asientto de los negros que ttiene ensi Domingo Grillo. 2 parts. [Manuscript.] Lima, 1672. Fol.

4 LIMA gozosa. Descripcion de las festibas demonstraciones, con que esta Ciudad ... celebró la Real Proclamacion de el nombre augusto del Catolico Monarcha Don Carlos III. Lima, 1760. 4to.

5 INSTRUCCION del metodo con que deben repartirse à los indios de los partidos comprehendidos en el distrito de la diputacion provincial de Lima, las tierras, *etc.* Lima, 1814. Fol.

6 [*Begins.*] MANIFIESTO imparcial de los acontecimientos de la capital del Peru desde la salida del Ejército expedicionario para los Puertos Intermedios, *etc.* Lima, 1823. Fol.

7 LA voz dll [del] Pastor, y el desengaño por conciencia, defensa que hacen los exclaustrados en Lima. Parte 1. [Lima, 1831.] 4to.

8 REFLECSIONES sobre un informe del Cabildo eclesiastico de Lima. Lima, 1831. 4to.

9 MANIFIESTO que la mayoria de la M. H. I. D. de Lima presenta al publico imparcial sobre las ocurrencias del ultimo periodo de sus sesiones. Lima, [1833.] 4to.

LIMONADE, — DE, *Count.* Relation des glorieux événemens qui ont porté leurs Majestés Royales sur le Trône d'Hayti, suivie de l'Histoire du couronnement et du Sacre du roi Henry 1er, et de la reine Marie-Louise. Par le Comte de Limonade. Cap-Henry, 1811. 8vo.

2 ROYAUME d'Hayti. L'Olivier de la Paix. [Signed, Comte de Limonade.] Cap-Henry, [1815.] 8vo.

3 ROYAUME d'Hayti. L'Olivier de la Paix. [Signed Comte de Limo-

nade.] [Another Edition.] Cap-Henry, [1815.] 8vo.

LISBOA, JOSE ANTONIO. Reflexões sobre o Banco do Brasil. Rio de Janeiro, 1821. 8vo.

LISSAUTE, PEDRO. Discurso pronunciado en la solemnidad del tercer aniversario de la apertura del instituto de Jalisco. Guadalajara, 1830. 8vo.

LITURGIES. A Selection of Psalms and Hymns, from the authorized metrical versions of the Psalms of David, and from the Hymns annexed to the Book of Common Prayer, with appropriate tunes. Recommended for the use of the ... Diocese of Barbados and the Leeward Islands. [By W. H. Coleridge, Bishop of Barbadoes?] Barbados, 1831. 12mo.

2 CONSAGRACION de la capilla y cimenterio Britanico [at Caracas] hecha conforme a los ritos y ceremonias de la Iglesia de Inglaterra por ... G. H. Coleridge, Obispo de Barbada, *etc.* Caracas, 1834. 4to.

3 FORM of Consecration of the British Chapel and Burial Ground [at Caracas] according to the rites and ceremonies of the Church of England. By ... W. H. Coleridge, Bishop of Barbados, *etc.* Caracas, 1834. 4to.

4 FORM of consecration of the British Chapel and burial ground, according to the rites and ceremonies of the Church of England, by ... W. H. Coleridge, D.D., Lord Bishop of Barbados and the Leeward Islands, *etc.* Caracas, 1834. Fol.

LIZARAZU, JUAN DE. Al excelentifsimo señor marques de Mancera. ... sobre la reducion general de los Indios de la mita del Cerro de Potosi, y entero della, uso de los Indios, conservacion de los ingenios, distribucion de los azogues, y repartimiento general. [Lima? 1640?] Fol.

2 MEMORIAL de todos los papeles. ... que por parte del licenciado ...

Juan de Lizarazu, presidente de la audiencia de la Plata, se han presentado, contra . . . Juan de Palacios, visitador de la dicha audiencia. [Lima? 1650?] Fol.

LLAVE, Paulus de la, and LEX-arza, Joannes. Novorum vegetabilium descriptiones. Fascic. 1-3. [Each fascic. has a distinct register and pagination. No more seems to have been published.] Mexici, 1824-25. 8vo.

LOPEZ, Juan Luis. Discurso juridico, historico-politico, en defensa, de la jurisdicion real ilustracion de la provision de veinte de Febrero del año pasado de 1684. . . . Sobre que en recibir los corregidores deste Reyno informaciones secretas de oficio, ò à instancia de parte en orden à averiguar como observan los Curas, y Doctrineros las disposiciones Canonicas, Synodales, Cedulas, y Ordenanças de su Magestad, etc. Por el Doctor Don Juan Luis Lopez, etc. Lima, 1685. Fol.

LOPEZ DE GOMARA, Francisco. Historia de las conquistas de H. Cortés escrita en Español por F. Lopez de Gomára traducida al Mexicano . . . por D. J. B. de San Anton Muñon Chimalpain Quauhtlehuanitzin. Publícala . . . con varias notas . . . C. M. de Bustamante. Span. 2 tom. Mexico, 1826. 8vo.

LOPEZ DE SANTA-ANA, Antonio, President of Mexico. Versos al cumple años del Sr. Presidente Santa-Anna. [Mexico, 1843!] s. sb. 8vo.

LOPEZ YEPES, Joaquin. Catecismo y declaracion de la doctrina cristiana en lengua otomí, con un vocabulario del mismo idioma. Span. and Otomi. Megico, 1826. 4to.

LORENZANA Y BUITRON, Francisco Antonio. Cartas Pastorales, y edictos del Illmo. Señor D. Francisco Antonio Lorenza, y Buitron,

Arzobispo de Mexico. Mexico, 1770. Fol.

LOYO, Manuel Cayetano de. Defensa hecha a favor de Dª. D. Salguero en la causa criminal que se le ha formado a mocion del protomedicato, por haber curado contra sus prohibiciones y las del juez de primera instancia. En recurso a la representacion nacional. Lima, 1831. 4to.

LOZANO, Pedro. Descripcion Chorographica del Terreno, Rios, Arboles, y Animales de las . . . Provincias del gran Chaco, Gualamba, . . . escrita por . . . Pedro Lozano la . . . dedica . . . A. Machoni. Cordoba, 1733. 4to.

LUNAN, John. Hortus Jamaicensis, or a Botanical description : . . . and an account of the virtues, etc. of its indigenous plants hitherto known, as also of the most useful exotics. 2 vols. Jamaica, 1814. 4to.

LUXAN, Mariano. Relacion funebre de las Reales Exequias que a la memoria de Doña Maria Barbara, Reyna de las Españas mandò celebrar en esta Capital de Los Reyes J. M. de Velasio. Lima, 1760. 4to.

 J. B. Disertacion contra la tolerancia religiosa, por J. B. M. Méjico, 1831. 8vo.

M., L. de. Adreße d'un Créole [L. de M.] aux colons de Saint-Domingue. Port-au-Prince, [1790.] 8vo.

MAGDALENA, Augustin de la. Arte de la lengua Tagala, sacado de diversos Artes por Fr. Augustin de la Magdalena. [Mexico,] 1679. 8vo.

MALAMOCO, Juan Guzman de. Esposicion sencilla y breve que J. G. de Malamoco hace del origen de la dilatada pricion que la sufrido, del orden observado en su jusgamiento y triunfo de su inocencia, manifestado en los documentos que se insertan. Lima, 1825. 4to.

MALDONADO, JUAN. Relacion verdadera de la gran batalla, q Don Frey Luys de Cardenas General de los Galeros de Malta tuuo cō dos navios de guerra, *etc.* Lima, 1624. 4to.

MALDOÑADO SOTOMAYOR, PEDRO VICENTE. Representacion que hace a su magestad el governador de la provincia de las Esmeraldas D. P. V. Maldonado sobre la apertura del Nuevo Camino, que ha descubierto à su costa, y expensas, y sin gasto alguno de la Real Hacienda, *etc.* (Descripcion del nuevo Camino . . . por Don Joseph de Astorga, *etc.*) [Quito! 1742!] Fol.

MALOUET, PIERRE VICTOR. Copies des pièces des agens du Gouvernement français, imprimées et publiées en vertu de la Proclamation de Sa Majesté, du 11 Novembre 1814, l'an onzième de l'indépendance d' Hayti. [Signed Malouet.] Cap-Henry, 1814. 8vo.

MANSO, —. Haviendo el ardiente anhelo del exmo. Señor Conde de Super Unda (Virrey, Governador, y Capitan General de estos Reynos del Peru) Propendido al reparo del Hospital de San Bartholome: [Complimentary Verses to the Viceroy,] *etc.* Lima, 1760. 4to.

MANUAL MEXICANO, de la admistracion de los santos Sacramentos, conforme al Manual Toledano. Compuesto en lengua Mexicana, por el Bachiller Francisco de Lorra Baquio Presbytero. Dirigido al Doctor Andres Fernandez de Hipença, . . . Mexico, 1634. 8vo.

MARBAN, PEDRO. Arte de la lengua Moxa, con su Vocabulario, y Cathecismo. Compuesto por el M. R. P. Pedro Marban, *etc.* 2 parts. [Lima, 1702.] 8vo.

Each part has a separate pagination. A previous edition was published at Madrid under the title of "Arte y Vocabulario de la lengua Morocosi."

MARIA ANTONIA DE BORBON. Exequias de la Serenísima Señora D. Maria Antonia de Borbon Princesa de Asturias. Lima, 1807. 4to.

MARY, VIRGIN. Defensa de la Carta publicada en el Investigador N. 59. sobre la devocion del corazon de María Santísima, y manifestacion de la Ignorancia, mala Fe, y vana religion del devoto escritor en su carta impresa en el Num. 5º. Tom. 2º. del citado diaro. Lima, 1813. 4to.

MATA, NICOLAS URBANO DE, *Bishop of La Paz.* Relacion summaria de la vida, y dichosa muerte del U. P. Cypriano Baraze de la compañia de Jesus, muerto á manos de barbaros en la misſion de los Moxos de la Provincia del Perù. Sacala a luz . . . Nicolas Urbano de Mata, Obispo de la Ciudad de la Paz. Lima, 1704. 4to.

MARTILLOS. Martillos o utilidad publica de estos establecimientos. Lima, 1832. 4to.

MARTINEZ DE LA PARRA, JUAN. Sermon Panegirico, [Math. 25 cap.] elogio sacro de San Eligio Obispo de Noyons, Abogado, y Patron de los Plateros. Dixólo el P. Juan Martinez de la Parra, Religioso de la Compañia de Jesus, . . . y dedican afectuoso al Capitan D. Domingo de Larrea, y Zarate, Cavallero del Orden de San Tiago. Mexico, 1686. 4to.

2 SERMO Panegyrico [Marci. cap. 16.] a las Virtudes, y Milagros de el prodigioso Apostol de la India Nuevo Thaumaturgo del Oriente. SanFrancisco Xavier. Predicado en su dia tres de Diziembre . . . 1689. Por el R. P. Juan Martinez de la Parra, Profeſto de la mesma Compañia, *etc.* Mexico, 1690. 4to.

MARTINEZ DE LEJARZA, JUAN JOSE. Analisis estadistico de la Provincia de Michaugan en 1822. Mexico, 1824. 4to.

MARTINEZ DE ZUNIGA, JOA-

QUIN. Historia de las Islas Philipinas. Sampaloe, 1803. 4to.

MARURE, ALEJANDRO. Bosquejo histórico de las revoluciones de Centro-America desde 1811 hasta 1834. Tomo primeiro. Guatemala, 1837. 8vo.

MAYHEW, WILLIAM. Catholic Faith and Discipline, A [n Ordination] Sermon [on 2 Tim. ii. 2.] Kingston, Jamaica, [1841.] 8vo.

MEJIA, JOSE MARIA. Contestacion del Alcalde primero J. M. Mejia al Editorial del N. 1 del Periodico intitulado "El Mosquito" publicado el dia 3 del presente (Enero de 1840) relativo al Estado de los fondos municipales. Mexico, 1840. 8vo.

MENDEZ Y LACHICA, TOMAS DE. Panegirico del Patriarca San Felipe Neri, pronunciado en la Iglesia de la Real Congregacion del Oratorio de Lima. Lima, 1818. 8vo.

MENENDEZ, BALDOMERO JOSE. Noticia alfabetica de las administraciones de correos de la Peninsula, Islas Baleares, Puerto Rico, Cuba y Filipinas. [Orihuela], 1842. 4to.

MERCURE des Isles du vent, ou Eßais Philosophiques etc. Rédigés par M. S. Beauregard. No 1er Janvier 1783. (Prospectus.) [Baße Terre, 1782.] Guadeloupe, 1783. 8vo.

MERCURIO (EL), de Valparaiso. No. 3167. 6 de Julio 1839. Valparaiso, 1839. Fol.

MERCURIO Peruano, de historia, literatura y noticias publicas que da à luz la Sociedad Academica de Amantes de Lima, y en su nombre J. Calero y Moreira. 12 tom. Lima, 1791-95. 4to.

MERCY, Order of. Sumario de las gracias, jubileos, indulgencias y beneficios que ganan los hermanos terceros, novicios y profesos en la santa y real Orden Tercera de Nuestra

Madre y Señora de la Merced. [Lima?] 1805. 4to.

MESA, BARTOLOME DE. Explicacion previa de los Carros y Mascara, con que la Nacion Indica de Lima, y sus Pueblos comarcanos celebra la feliz exultacion al trono de Carlos IV. Siendo Comisarios B. de Mesa, R. Landaburu y I. Gomez, 2ª Impresion. Lima, 1790. 4to.

MEXICO. El consulado de Mexico sobre la contratacion del peru con la nueba españa. [Manuscript.] [Lima? 1620?] Fol.

2 MOTIVOS piadosos para adelantar la devocion tierna de los dolores de la SS. Virgen esmerandose en el cordial afecto a N. Señora . . . y querida . . . Santa Ana Madre de la dignissima Madre de Dios . . . Que ofrece para desempeño suyo la Congregacion de N. Señora de los dolores de el colegio de S. Pedro y S. Pablo de la Compañia de esta ciudad de Mexico. Mexico, [1623.] 8vo.

3 PROPOSICION que la Ciudad de Mexico hizo en su Consistorio, en 28 de Setiembre á la junta General, que cóuocó de Religiones, Uniuersidad, y Cónsulado; Maestros, y Contadores; . . . Dispuesto por D. Fernando Carrillo su Escrivano mayor, Año de 1630. Few MS. notes. [Mexico], 1630. Fol.

4 AL REY nuestro Senor por la Provincia de compañia de Iesvs de la Nueva España. En satisfacion de un libro de el visitador Obispo D. Iuan de Pulafox y Mendoza. Publicado en nombre de el dean, y cabildo de su Iglesia Catedral de la Puebla de los Angeles. [Mexico, 1647.] 4to.

5 [Begins.] DON LUIS ENRIQUEZ DE GUZMAN, etc. [An ordinance respecting the working of the mines, &c.] (Mexico, 18 Mayo, 1651.) [Mexico? 1651?] Fol.

6 REALES aranzeles de los Ministros de la Real Audiencia, Sala del Crimen, Oficios de Govierno . . . formados dichós Oranzeles por los Senores Oy-

dores de esta Real Audiencia . . . M. Calderon de la Varca, y Balthazar de Tovar, *etc.* Mexico, 1727. Fol.

7 [*Begins.*] D. Carlos Francisco de Croix, *etc.* (Instruccion, y ordenanza para el establecimiento de la real fabrica de polvora de cuenta de S. M.) [Mexico? 1766.] Fol.

8 [*Begins.*] Don Carlos Francisco de Croix, *etc.* (Instruccion provincial para que el ramo de cruzada se administre de cuenta de la real hacienda. México, 13 Dic., 1767.) [México? 1767?] Fol.

9 Concilios Provinciales, primero, y segundo, celebrados en la . . . Ciudad de Mexico, . . . en los años de 1555, y 1565. Dalos a luz . . . Francisco Antonio Lorenzana, *etc.* Mexico, 1769. Fol.

10 Concilium Mexicanum Provinciale III. celebratum Mexici anno MDLXXXIV. . . . confirmatum Romæ die XXVII. Octobris anno MDLXXXIX. . . . typis mandatum cura, & expensis D. D. Francisci Antonij a Lorenzana Archipræsulis. (Statuta Ordinata a Sancto concilio Provinciali Mexicano III. anno domini MDLXXXV. *etc.*) [The " Statuta" has a distinct title-page and pagination.] Mexici, 1770. Fol.

11 Reglamento formado para el cuerpo de invalidos de Nueva España, por . . . Antonio Maria Bucareli y Ursúa virrey governador, *etc.* Mexico, 1774. Fol.

12 Reglamento provisional para el prest, vestuario, gratificationes, hospitalidad, recluta, disciplina, y total govierno de la tropa que debe guarnecer el presidio de nuestra señora del carmen de la isla de Tris en la laguna de Término, *etc.* 3 parts. Mexico, 1774. Fol.

13 Decretos del Congreso Constituyente del estado de Mexico revisados por el mismo Congreso é impresos de su orden. Tomo 1. México, 1824. 8vo.

14 Actas del Congreso Constituyente del estado libre de Mexico, revisadas por el mismo Congreso, è impresas de su orden. 10 tom. Toluca, 1824-31. 8vo.

15 El congreso constituyente del estado de Mexico a sus comitentes (para instruir en el punto mas interesante à los hombres religiosos y patriotas por principios.) Mexico, 1825. Fol.

16 Guia de hacienda de la Republica Mexicana. Parte legislativa. (Parte directiva y de oficinas.) 2 parts. Mexico, 1825. 16mo.

17 Dictamen de las comisiones ecclesiástica y de relaciones sobre las instrucciones que deben darse á nuestro enviado á Roma, *etc.* [Dated México, 45 de Febrero de 1826.] [Mexico, 1826.] Fol.

18 Documentos importantes tomados del espediente instruido a consecuencia de la representacion que varios electores a la junta general del estado hicieron a su congreso constituyente pidiendose anulen las elecciones verificadas en Toluca, *etc.* (Dictamen de la comision.) [The " Dictamen" has a separate pagination.] Mexico, 1826. 8vo.

19 Guia de la Hacienda de la Republica Mexicana. Año de 1826. Parte legislativa. 2 tom. [Mexico, 1826.] 12°

20 A los habitantes del Estado de Mexico su congreso constituyente (dirige la voz al poner en vuestras manos el depósito sagrado de la constitucion y las bases fundamentales de las libertades públicas.) [Mexico, 1827.] Fol.

21 Arancel general para las aduanas marítimas y de frontera de la Republica Mexicana. Mexico, 1827. Fol.

22 Constitucion politica del Estado de Mexico sancionada por su congreso constituyente en 14 de Febrero de 1827 publicada en 26 del mismo mes y año en la Ciudad de Tezcoco. Mexico, [1827.] 12mo.

23 Manifiesto de la administracion y progresos de los ramos de la hacienda federal Mexicana · desde Agosto de [18]24 á Diciembre de

D

[1]826. [Signed J. Y. Esteva.] Mexico, 1827. Fol.

24 MEMORIA de los ramos que son a cargo del gobierno del estado libre de Mexico leida al primer congreso constitucional en sesion del dia de 6 de Marzo de 1827. [Mexico,] 1827. Fol.

25 MEMORIA que . . . leyó el Secretario de Estado y del despacho universal de Justícia [M. Ramos Arizpe] . . . en la Cámara . . . en . . . enero de 1827, sobre los ramos del ministerio de su cargo. Mexico, 1827. Fol.

26 ACTAS del primer Congreso Constitucional de Mexico. Tom. 1-5. Tlalpam, 1827-29. 8vo.

27 MEMORIA en que el gobierno del estado libre de Mexico da cuenta al primer congreso constitucional de todos los ramos que han sido a su cargo en el año economico corrido desde 26 de Octubre de 1826 . . . presentada . . . 1828. [Signed L. de Zavala.] Tlalpam, 1828. Fol.

28 REGLAMENTO de Libertad de imprenta mandado observar en la República Mexicana. Mexico, 1828. 16mo.

29 BALANZA General del comercio maritimo por los puertos de la Republica Mexicana en el año de 1826 (-1827-1828) formada por orden del Gobierno. 3 vol. Mexico, 1828-31. 4to.

30 ACTA del pronunciamento de la gran M. por el restablecimiento de la constitucion y las leyes. Mexico, 1829. s. sh. Fol.

31 ACTAS del segundo Congreso Constitucional de Mexico. Tom. 1. Tlalpam, 1829. 8º

32 COLECCION de ordenes y decretos de la soberano Junta Provisional Gubernativa, y soberanos congresos generales de la nacion Mexicana. Segunda edicion, corregida y aumentada por una comision de la Camara de Diputados. 4 tom. Mexico, 1829. 4to.

33 DETALLE de la action dada por nuestras armas el dia 11 del pasado Setiembre en las costas de Tampico (de Tamanlipas). Mejico, 1829. Fol.

34 DICTAMEN de la comision de industria de la Camara de Diputados sobre el nuevo arbitrio para dar un grande aumento a la hacienda federal, etc. Mexico, 1829. 4to.

35 LAS traiciones del congreso con sangre se han de vengar [An addreſs to the Mexicans]. [Mexico, 1829.] Fol.

36 LAS victimas de la patria sacrificadas en las calles de Mexico ó clamores de la América por los patriotas que regaron con su sangre el árbol de la libertad en los dias 2, 3 y 4 del mes de Diciembre de 1828. Parte primera. Mexico, 1829. 8vo.

37 MEMORIA que . . . leyó el Secretario de Estado (J. J. Espinosa de los Monteros) . . . en la Cámara de Diputados . . . y en la de Senadores el dia 20 de Enero de 1829, sobre los ramos del Ministerio de su cargo. Mexico, 1829. Fol.

38 NUEVO arbitrio para dar un grande aumento a la hacienda federal, y para proporcionar al mismo tiempo ocupacion y medios de subsistir á la clase de gentes pobres de la República Mexicana. Mexico, 1829. 4to.

39 MANIFIESTO que el Vice-presidente de la republica Mexicana dirige a la nacion (Enero 4 de 1830.) Mexico, 1830. Fol.

40 MEMORIA de la secretaria de estado y del despacho de relaciones interiores y exteriores leida por el secretario del ramo en la cámara de Diputados el dia 12 de Febrero de 1830, etc. [Signed L. Alaman.] Mexico, 1830. Fol.

41 ACTAS . . . comprensivas de 13 de Agosto 1830 á 1º. de Febrero de 1831. Toluca, 1831. 8vo.

42 COLECCION de las leyes y decretos expedidos por el Congreso General de los Estados Unidos Mejicanos, en los años de 1829 y 1830, etc. Méjico, 1831. 4to.

43 Tarifas que deberán observar todos los administradores de la renta de correos de la república Mexicana para el cobro, de las cartas y pliegos, y papeles impresos que se versen tanto de lo interior de ella, como de otros paises, con arreglo á lo dispuesto en el soberano decreto de 18 de Mayo . . . de 1832. [Mexico, 1832.] s. sh. Fol.

44 Memoria en que el gobierno del estado libre de Mexico da cuenta al . . . congreso constitucional, de todos los ramos que han sido a su cargo en el ultimo año economico. Presentada el dia 30 de Marzo de 1833. Toluca, 1833. Fol.

45 [Begins.] Num. 1. Estado que manifiestan las Prefecturas ó Distritos del Estado, sus partidos, poblaciones donde hay Ayuntamiento y en las que no lo hay, etc. [Mexico, 1837?] Fol.

46 Memoria de la hacienda nacional de la Republica Mexicana presentada a las camaras por el ministro del Ramo en Julio de 1838. Segunda Parte. [Mexico, 1838.] Fol.

47 Memoria del ministerio de lo interior de la Republica Mexicana leida en las cameras de su congreso general en el mes de Enero de 1838. Mexico, 1838. Fol.

48 Memoria leida por el ministro de relaciones exteriores [L. G. Cuevas] a las cameras del congreso nacional en los dias de 29 y 30 . . . de Enero de 1838, etc. Mexico, 1838. Fol.

49 Reseña histórica del establecimiento de ciencias médicas de la capital de Mégico. Mégico, 1839. 8vo.

50 Manifiesto al publico que hace el ayuntamiento de 1840 acerca de la conducta que ha observado en los negocios municipales y del estado en que quedan los ramos de su cargo. Mexico, [1840.] 8vo.

51 Memoria de la hacienda nacional de la República Mexicana presentada à las càmaras por el ministro

del ramo en Julio de 1839. Primera Parte. Mexico, 1840. Fol.

52 Memoria del ministro de guerra y marina presentada a las cameras del congreso general Mexicano en Enero de 1840. Mexico, 1840. Fol.

53 [Begins.] El C. Luis Gonzaga Vieyra, etc. (Ordenamiento de arreglo de los estudios médicos, y exámenes de profesores y policia en ejercicio de las facultades de medicina, etc.) [Mexico, 1841.] 4to.

54 Iniciativa que la . . . junta departamental de Mexico eleva al soberano congreso pidiendo no se aprueben los contratos celebrados por el general Arista para importar a la republica la hilaza extrangera. Mexico, 1841. 8vo.

55 Martirologio de Algunos de los primeros insurgentes por la libertad e independencia de la America Mexicana, ó sea prontuario é indice alfabetico de varios individuos . . . de quienes se habla en las causas de las conspiraciones de abril y agosto de 1811 . . . Publícalo C. M. de Bustamante. Mexico, 1841. 4°

56 Memoria de la hacienda nacional de la republica Mexicana presentada à las cameras por el ministro del ramo en julio de 1841. Primera parte. Mexico, 1841. Fol.

57 Representacion que hace el ayuntamiento de esta capital a las augustas camaras en defensa de la industria agrícola y fabril de la República, atacada por la órden suprema sobre introduccion de efectos prohibidos. México, 1841. 8vo.

58 Arancel general de aduanas marítimas y fronterizas. Mexico, 1842. 8vo.

59 Comunicacion oficial del Supremo Gobierno provisional de Méjico, dirigida al del Estado, y dictámen de la comision especial, nombrada por la Cámara de diputados, contraido á la respuesta que debe dársele. Merida de Yucatan, 1842. Fol.

60 Decreto sobre arreglo de la renta de correos, espedido por el supremo

gobierno en 24 de Octubre de 1842. México, 1842. 8vo.

61 [*Begins.*] EL C. Luis Gonzaga Vieyra, *etc.* (Reglamento de Enseñanza y policia médicas.) [Mexico, 1842.] 8vo.

62 PROYECTO de constitucion que presenta al soberano congreso constituyente la mayoria de su comision especial, y voto particular de la minoria. Mexico, 1842. 8vo.

63 REGLAMENTO de la Sociedad (aprobado en junta general el dia 9 de Octubre de 1842). México, 1842. 8vo.

64 YTINERARIOS formados por la Administracion general de correos... en el que se expresan las leguas que hay de Administracion à Administracion de las carreras respectivas à que se arreglaràn todas las Administraciones de la renta, para la designacion de portes y ajusto de los extraordinarios. [Mexico, 1842.] Fol.

65 BASES orgánicas de la república Mexicana acordadas por la honorable junta legislativa, establecida conforme á los decretos de ... diciembre 1842 y sancionadas ... el dia 12 de junio año de 1843. México, 1843. 8vo.

66 EL C. Valentin Canalizo ... comandante general del departamento de México comunica lo siguiente, *etc.* A. Lopez de Santa-Anna ... Presidente provisional de la república Mexicana à los habitantes de ella, sabed : que ... he tenido á bien decretar ... amnistia a todos los que por delitos politicos se hallen actualmente detenidos, *etc.* 13 de junio de 1843. Mexico, 1843. *s. sh.* Fol.

67 REPRESENTACION dirigida al ... Presidente provisional de la República por la junta general directiva de la industria nacional sobre la importancia de esta, necesidad de su fomento y medios de dispensarselo. Megico, 1843. 8vo.

68 REPRESENTACION dirigida al supremo gobierno por la Direccion ...

contestando a lo que ha expuesto la Junta de Puebla sobre proveer de algodon à las fábricas de la república. [Signed L. Alaman.] Mègico, 1843. 8vo.

69 ARANCEL general de aduanas marítimas y fronterizas de la república Mejicana. [With a *s. sh.* published by " la comision encargada de la reforma del arencel general de aduanas marìtimas."] México, 1845. 8vo.

MILA' DE LA ROCA, JOSE R. Proyecto para proporcionar el laboreo de las minas del estado de Chihuahua. [Mexico? 1828.] Fol.

MINAS-GERAES. Falla dirigida á assemblèa legislativa provincial de Minas-Geraes na sessão ordinaria do anno de 1840 pelo presidente da provincia Bernardo Jacintho da Veiga. Ouro-Preto, 1840. 8vo.

MIRAFLORES. Manifiesto de las sesiones tenidas en el pueblo de Miraflores para las Transaciones intentadas con el General San Martin, *etc.* Lima, 1820. Fol.

MOJARRIETA, JOSE SERAPIO. Esposicion sobre el origen, utilidad, prerogativas, derechos y deberes de los sindicos procuradores generales de los pueblos, *etc.* Reimpresa. Santiago de Cuba, 1833. 4to.

MOLINA, ALONSO DE. Arte de la lengua Mexicana y Castellana, compuesta por el muy Reverendo padre fray Alonso de Molina de la orden de Señor sant Francisco. Mexico, 1571. 16mo.

2 VOCABVLARIO en Lengua Castellana y Mexicana, compuesto por el muy Reverendo Padre Fray Alonso de Molina, de la Orden del bienaventurado nuestro Padre sant Francisco. Dirigido al muy Excelente Senor Don Martin Enriquez, Visorrey destanueva España. 2 parts. Mexico, 1571. Fol.

3 Doctrina Christiana, y Cathecismo en Lengua Mexicana. Compuesta, por el P. Fr. Alonso de Molina, de la Orden del Glorioso Seraphico Padre San Francisco, Corregida fielmĕte, por su original. Reimpreſſa en Mexico: 1744. *Small* 8vo.

MOLINA, Christoval de. [*Begins.*] Exmo Señor, C. de Molina regidor desta ciudad de Mexico, *etc.* [A memorial respecting the aborigines of the province of New Spain or Mexico.] [Mexico? 1626?] Fol.

MONTAHN, E. C. Samlingar till en historisk Afhandling om Säteriet Stora Edh. 3 Del. Wexiö°, 1819. 4to.

MONTANA, Augustin de la. Comedia Nueva. Su titulo la bella casada y la fea cizaña [in three acts and in verse]. Santiago, 1789. 4to.

MONTEAGUDO, Bernardo. Ensayo sobre la necesidad de una federacion jeneral entre los estados Hispano-Americanos, y plan de su organizacion; obra póstuma. Lima, 1825. 4to.

MONTEMAYOR DE CUENCA, Juan Francisco de. Summaria Investigation de el origen, y privilegios, de los Ricos Hombres, o Nobles, Caballeros, Infanzones o Hijos, dalgo, y Señores de Vaſſalos de Aragon, y del absoluto poder que en ellos tienen. Parte Primera escribiola Don Iuan Francisco de Montemaior de Cuenca, *etc.* [Part I. apparently complete; the Introduction and the body of the work are separately paged.] [Mexico, 1644.] 4to.

MONTENEGRO COLON, Feliciano. Geografia general para el uso de la juventud de Venezuela. Tom 1-4. [No more published.] Caracas, 1833-37. 8vo.

MONTGOMERY; or, the West-Indian Adventurer. A Novel, by a Gentleman. 3 vols. Jamaica, 1812. 8vo.

MORA, Jose Maria. Memoria ... para informar sobre el origen y estado actual de las obras emprendidas para el desagüe de las lagunas del Valle de México, *etc.* México, [1823.] 4to.

2 Memoria ... sobre el origen y estado actual de las obras emprendidas para el desagüe de las lagunas del valle de México. México, 1823. 8vo.

MORALES, Francisco Jose de. [*Begins.*] Viva la Patria. Discursos politico-morales que hace el Amante del Cristianismo a sus compatriotas. [Preceded by a dedication to the Clergy of Lima.] [Lima, 1822.] 4to.

MORALES, Juan Baptista de. La Prometida declaracion venida de Espana, de las prodigiosas senales del monstruoso Pescado que se hallò en un rio de Polonia en Alemania, cuyo retrato embiò a España, este año de 1624. ... Por Iuan Baptista de Morales su Autor. Lima, 1625. Fol.

MORAN, Jose Maria. Relacion de las persecuciones ... que sufrieron ... las misiones del Reino de Tunkin, en la gran China, que están al cargo de los misioneros españoles de la provincia del Santísimo Rosario del órden de Predicadores de las Islas Filipinas en el Asia. México, 1842. 8vo.

MORE, Gerard. Informe en Derecho, sobre que la Compañia de el Real Aſſiento de la Gran Bretaña, establecida ... para la introduccion de Esclavos Negros, en estas Indias, debe declararse libre y exempta de la paga de los Reales Derechos ... en todos los Puertos y demàs Lugares de la tierra adentro da esta America, *etc.* Mexico, 1724. Fol.

MORENO, Francisco Javier. [*Begins.*] Copia de la representacion que ha hecho al Soberano Congreso D. Francisco Javier Moreno,

Presidente de la Alta camara de Justicia, en vindicacion de su legal manejo y procedimientos. Lima, 1823. Fol.

MORENO, Ignacio de, *Resp.* Pro publico juris naturæ, et gentium examine omnes, et singulos hic subjectos propositiones . . . propugnabit I. a Moreno, *Præs.* M. a Rivero. Limæ, 1787. 8vo.

MORENO, Jose Ignacio. Exhortacion a la sumision y concordia que hizo a sus feligreses . . . J. I. Moreno, *etc.* Lima, 1812. 4to.

2 Prospectus in summa rhetoricæ artis capita de quibus . . . G. Carrillo, D. Ferreira, T. Arevalo respondebunt, . . . D. D. D. J. I. Moreno, *etc.* [Lima,] 1819. 4to.

3 Refutacion al Papel [de J. I. Moreno] titulado Abuso del poder contra las Libertades de la Iglesia. Lima, 1831. 4to.

MORGA, Antonio de. Sucesos de las Islas Philipinas dirigidos a Don Christoval Gomez de Sandoval y Rojas Duque de Cea. Por el Doctor Antonio de Morga Alcalde del Crimende la Real Audiencia de la Nueva España Cōsultor del Sio Officio de la Inquisicion. Mexici ad Indos, 1609. 4to.

MORNING JOURNAL (The). Dec. 31st, 1838—April 21st, 1840. [Imperfect; several Nos. wanting.] Kingston, Jamaica, 1838-40. Fol.

MORTAJA (La), o Examen de la costumbre de sepultar los cadaveres con habito de religioso. Lima, 1829. 4to.

MOXO Y DE FRANCOLI, Benito Maria de, *Archbishop of La Plata.* Coleccion de varios papeles relativos a los sucesos de Buenos-Ayres . . . publicados por un amigo del autor. Lima, 1808. 4to.

2 Discurso, el 27 de Setiembre, 1808, con motivo de la solemne accion de gracias por la exaltacion del Señor Fernando VII. al trono. Buenos Ayres, 1808. 4to.

3 Homilia, el 12 de Octubre, 1808, para exhortar a sus diocesanos que rogasen por la felicidad del Rey y de la patria, y asistiesen a la procesion de Rogativa. Describese la procesion del 12 de Octubre y añadense algunas reflexiones. Buenos Ayres, 1809. 4to.

MUNIZ, Pedro. Carta de D. Pedro Muñiz al Caritativo defensor de D. Aparicio Vidaurrazaga. Segunda edicion corregida, *etc.* Lima, 1814. 4to.

MUNOZ, Miguel. Cartilla ó breve instruccion sobre la vacuna . . . escrita . . . para la conservacion de este precioso antidoto. México, 1840. 8vo.

MURGUIA Y GALARDI, Jose. Memoria estadistica de Oaxaca y descripcion del Valle del mismo nombre estractada de la que . . . trabajó J. Murguia y Galardi. Publicala . . . C. M. de Bustamente . . . con una descripcion del antigüo palacio de Mictla, *etc.* Veracruz, 1821. 4to.

MUSEO MEXICANO (El), ó Miscelanea pintoresca de Amenidades curiosas é instructivas. Tom 1. Mexico, 1843. 8vo.

ACIONAL (El). Agosto 22, 1839. Montevideo, 1839. Fol.

NACIONAL Y Pontificia Universidad de Megico. Suplemento a las constituciones de la Nacional y pontificia Universidad de Mégico, que comprende los decretos y Reglamentos que rigen en ella desde su restablecimiento en el año de 1834. Mégico, 1839. Fol.

NACIONAL Y PONTIFICIO

SEMINARIO PALAFOXIANO. Constitucion del . . . Seminario, etc. [La Puebla], 1826. 12mo.

NAPOLEON, *Emperor of the French.* Dialogo entre Napoleon y Murat, quando este se presento a aquel en Bayona, del regreso vergonzoso de España a Francia. Reimpreso en Buenos-Aires, 1808. 4to.

NASSY, J. C. Efsai historique sur la Colonie de Surinam, sa fondation, ses revolutions, ses progrès, avec la description, et l'etat actuel de la Colonie. Avec l'histoire de la nation Juive Portugaise et Allemande y établie. Redigé par les Regens et Representons de la dite nation Juive Portugaise [J. C. Nafsy; J. H. Le Barrios; S. H. Brandon; Mos. P. de Leon; S. H. de la Parra; Is. de la Parra.] 2 partes. Paramaribo, 1788. 8vo.

NAVARRETE, FRANCISCO ANTONIO. Relacion peregrina de la agua corriente que para beber y vivir goza la Ciudad de Santiago de Queretaro. Describense las Fiestas que dicha Ciudad hizo al ver logrado tan peregrino beneficio. Mexico, 1739. 4to.

NAVARRO MARTIN DE VILLODRES, DIEGO ANTONIO, *Bishop of La Concepcion de Chile.* Carta Pastoral, à todos los fieles habitantes de Valdivia y Osorno. Lima, 1814. 8vo.

NAVARRO Y NORIEGA, FERNANDO. Catalogo de los curatos y misiones que tiene la Nueva España . . . o sea la division eclesiastica de este reyno, etc. Mexico, 1813. 8vo.

NAVIA Y CASTRILLON, JUAN GARCIA. Relacion de los ingenios de açucar ganados y minas que ay en el baiamo y govierno de Cuba. [Manuscript.] [Santiago? 1617?] Fol.

NEGRETE, PEDRO CELESTINO. Apuntes en forma de defensa, preparados para estender la del general P. C. Negrete. Mexico, 1828. 4to.

NEVE Y MOLINA, LUIS DE. Reglas de Orthographia Diccionario, y arte del idioma othomi, breve instruccion para los principiantes, que dictó el Luis de Neve y Molina, etc. Mexico, 1767. 8vo.

NEW GRANADA. Edicto para manifestar al publico el indulto general concedido por . . . Don Carlos III. a todos los comprehendidos en las revoluciones acaecídas en el año pasado de 1781, etc. [Bogota? 1782,] Fol.

2 OBSERVACIONES sobre el comercio de la Nueva Granada con un apendice relativo al de Bogota, 2 parts. Bogota, 1831. 8vo.

3 INFORME del secretario de Estado (J. Acosta) del despacho de relaciones esteriores de la Nueva Granada al congreso constitucional de 1845. Bogota, [1845.] 8vo.

4 APENDICE al informe del secretario de Estado (J. Acosta) del despacho de relaciones esteriores de la Nueva Granada al congreso constitucional de 1845. Bogota, [1845.] 8vo.

NEW TIMES (THE). No. 197. March 8, 1839. Bridgetown, 1839. Fol.

NICOLAS DE LA TRINIDAD. Sermon [Math. cap 5.] a S. Antonio de Padua. En la Rogativa, que por el buen viage de la Flota hizó la Mifsion, en el Convento de N. P. S. Francisco de la Ciudad de Cadiz, Año de 1687. Predicolo, el Padre Fr. Nicolas de la Trinidad, etc. Mexico, 1691. 4to.

NOVELAS escolhidas de diversos autores. 2 vol. (Vol. 1. Historia de Roberto. Sapho no salto de Leucate. Sofronimo e Themira. Fatima e Zendar. Historia de Janny Lille. Historia de Emilia. Pedro. Vol. 2. Iddalina de Tokenbourg. Isaura. Carlota. Aventura notavel. O casamento de Alfredo. Leocadio. Zaira. Julieta e Claudina.) Rio de Janeiro, 1820. 12mo.

NUESTRA SEÑORA DEL CAR-

MEN. [*Begins.*] Relacion y Diario de las Operaciones del navio Nuestra Señora del Carmen, que salió del Puerto del Callao; y bolbió con la presa de un Navio Olandès de ilicite comercio. Lima, 1725. 4to.

 B. V. Grito de alarma en los Indios contra los blancos y castas. [Signed B.V.O.] Mexico, 1829. 8vo.

OAJACA. Memoria que el gobernador del estado de Oajaca presentó en la apertura de las sesiones ordinarias del segundo congreso constitucional del mismo, verificado el 2 de Julio de 1827. Oajaca, 1827. Fol.

2 Codigo civil para gobierno del estado libre de Oajaca. Oajaca, 1828. 4to.

OBSERVADOR. Prospecto del periodico titulado: el observador de Lima. Lima, 1825. 4to.

OFFICIAL GAZETTE (The) and General Advertiser. No. 1. [Bridgetown,] Barbadoes, 1840. Fol.

OLIVAN, Alejandro. Informe a la junta de gobierno del real consulado de agricultura y comercio de la siempre fiel Isla de Cuba, *etc.* Habana, 1831. 8vo.

OLMEDO, J. l. de. [*Begins.*] Ode al Jeneral Flores. Vencedor en Miñarica. Reimpreso en Lima, [1835.] Fol.

O PATRIOTA, Jornal Litterario, Politico, Mercantil, *etc.* do Rio de Janeiro. 6 Nos. Rio de Janeiro, 1813. 16mo.

2 Segunda Subscripção—6 Nos. Rio de Janeiro, 1813. 8vo.

3 Terceira Subscripção—6 Nos. Rio de Janeiro, 1814. 8vo.

With the autograph of R. Southey.

ORBEGOSO, Juan de. Reconocimiento del istmo de Tehuantepec,

hecho el año de 1825. Jalapa, 1831. 16mo.

ORBEGOSO, Luis Jose. [*Begins.*] El Presidente Provisorio del Estado Nor-Peruano a sus Compatriotas. Lima, 1837. Fol.

ORIHUELA, Jose Calixto de *Bishop of Cuzco.* Carta pastoral sobre las obligaciones del Cristianismo, y la oposicion de este al espiritu revolucionario de estos ultimos tiempos. Lima, 1820. 4to.

2 Carta pastoral sobre el nuevo estado del Peru, y sentimientos que en cuanta a el se deben tener. Cuzco, 1825. 4to.

3 Carta pastoral a sus diocesanos. Lima, 1833. 4to.

ORIZABA. Manifiesto a la nacion sobre la renta del tabaco. (La diputacion de cosecheros de tabaco de la villa de Orizava manifiesta á la nacion el gran tesoro que desprecia.) Mexico, 1827. Fol.

2 Suplemento al manifiesto de los cosecheros de tabaco de la villa de Orizava. Mexico, 1827. Fol.

OROZ, Francisco de. Apuntamientos del estado Antigo, y Moderno de Guancavelica. Que el Capitan Don Francisco de Oroz, . . . Dedica al Excellentiſsimo Señor D. Gaspar de Bracamonte y Guzman, *etc.* [Lima? 1660?] Fol.

ORTEGA Y PIMENTEL, Isidoro Jose. Fúnebre pompa, Magnificas exequias . . . á la memoria del . . . Doct. J. de Castañeda Velazquez y Salazar (Oracion fúnebre que . . . á la Memoria del . . . Doct. J. de Castañeda Velasquez y Salazar . . . dixo J. P. de Osorio y Balcon.) Lima, 1763. 4to.

ORTIZ DE ZEVALLOS, Ignacio. Representacion del D. D. I. Ortiz de Zevallos reclamando el despojo de la plaza de fiscal de la corte suprema de justicia. Lima, 1831. 4to.

ORUE, Domingo de, *General.*

[*Begins.*]   Nota que dirije el Jeneral de Brigada D. de Orue a los Secretarios de la Representacion Nacional para que se le conceda permiso de hablar en la barra. Lima, 1828. Fol.

OTERO, MIGUEL. [*Begins.*] Juicio imparcial que sirve de respuesta al papel de Da C. Maiz ... sobre el asesinato que proyectó su marido Don J. Moreno, *etc.* Lima, 1835. Fol.

 J. J. *Sacerdote del Obispado de Puebla.* Compendio del confesionario en Mexicano y Castellano, *etc.* por un Sacerdote del Obispado de Puebla. [By J. J. P.] *Mex.* and *Span.* [La Puebla,] 1840. 16mo.

PACHECO, ANTONIO. Programma rerum quas didiscerunt [*sic*] juvenes examinandi M. Dorado, J. M. Izene, *etc.* edocti a D. A. Pacheco ... 18 Martii 1823. Limæ, [1823.] 4to.

PADILLA, JUAN DE. [*Begins.*] Mandó que se imprimiesse este escrito el ... Conde de Alva ... Virrey ... del Peru. En la junta que se ha formado, por cedula de su Magestad, de 21 de Setiembre de 1660. años. Para conferir las materias y puntos de la Carta, que con la Cedula referida se remite, cerca de la enseñanza y buen tratamiento de los Indios. [A reply by D. de Leon Pinelo to a document by Juan de Padilla complaining of the treatment of the Indians in Spanish America, with the document itself.] [Lima, 1661 !] Fol.

PALACIOS, PRUDENCIO ANTONIO DE. Respuesta fiscal de el Sr. D. P. A. de Palacios ... dada en los autos, que se formaron sobre la aprobacion de la Synodo Diocesana, que por el año de 1722 celebrò ... J. Gomez de La Parada, obispo que entonces era de la provincia de Yucatán, *etc.* Mexico, 1751. Folº

PALLADIUM (THE), Saint Lucia Free Press. Edited by C. Wells. Nos. 15-16, 30, 32, 34-35, 38, 42-51, 79-83, 85-93. *Eng.* and *Fren.* Castries, 1839-40. Fol.

PALOU, FRANCISCO, *Friar.* Relacion historica de la vida y apostolicas tareas del ... fray J. Serra, y de las misiones que fundó en la California septentrional, y nuevos establecimientos de Monterey. México, 1787. 4to.

PANDO, JOSE MARIA DE. Epistola a Prospero [in verse.] Lima, 1826. 4to.

2 A sus conciudadanos J. M. de Pando. (Apendice.) Lima, 1826. 4to.

3 MANIFIESTO que presenta á la nacion sobre su conducta publica J. M. de Pando. Lima, 1827. 4to.

4 MEMORIA sobre el estado de la hacienda de la republica Peruana en fin del año de 1830, presentada al congreso. Lima, 1831. 4to.

5 APENDICE á la memoria presentada al congreso sobre el estado de la Hacienda publica en fin del ano de 1830. Lima, 1831. Fol.

PAPEL periodico de la ciudad de Santa Fe de Bogota. [Edited by M. del Socorro Rodriguez.] 266 Nos. [Bogota, 1791-97.] 4to.

PARAMO I SOMOZA, ANTONIO. Discurso que en la apertura de la Sociedad Economica ... de Santiago, pronunciò en el dia 15 de Febrero de 1784 el Señor Don A. Paramo i Somoza. [Santiago, 1784.] 4to.

PARCERO, MARCOS. La Monja de las Madres Sor Maria Josefa del Rosario ... breve compendio de su vida, *etc.* Reimpreso. Santiago, 1842. 8vo.

PARDO, FELIPE. Discurso pronunciado ante el supremo consejo de la guerra, defendiendo al señor contra-almirante Don E. Cortes, y al señor general de Brigada Don J. M.

Egusquiza, en la causa que se les formó de orden del supremo gobierno, a consecuencia de los sucesos del mes de Enero del presente año. Lima, 1834. 4to.

PAREDES, IGNACIO DE. Promptuario manual Mexicano que ... podrá ser utilissimo ... à los que aprenden la lengua para la expedicion. Contiene quarenta y seis platicas con sus exemplos, y morales exhortaciones, y seis sermones morales, acomodados à los seis Domingos de la Quaresma, etc. Añadese por fin un Sermon de Nuestra Santissima Guadalupana Señora con una breve narracion de su historia, etc. Mex. Mexico, 1759. 4to.

PAREJA, FRANCISCO. Cathecismo, y Examen para los que comulgan, en lengua Castellana, y Timuquana ... A ora en esta II. impression corregido, y enmēdado, y algo necessario añadido. Por el Padre Fr. Francisco Pareja, Religioso de la Orden de N. Seraphico P. S. Francisco, y Padre de la Provincia de Santa Elena de la Florida, natural de Auñon diocesi del Arçobispado de Toledo. Mexico, 1627. 8vo.

PARRA, ANTONIO. Descripcion de diferentes piezas de historia natural las mas del ramo maritimo, representadas en setenta y cinco laminas. Havana, 1787. 4to.

PASTOR, MANUEL. Año de 1828. Censo de la ... Ciudad de la Habana ... formado ... por Don M. Pastor. Habana, 1829. Fol.

PASTOR LARRINAGA, JOSE. Cartas historicas à un amigo, ò Apologia del Pichon Palomino que parió una muger, y se vió en esta Ciudad de los Reyes el 6 de Abril, 1804. Lima, 1812. 4to.

PATRIOTA. Contestacion al manifiesto que presenta a la nacion sobre su conducta publica J. M. de Pando. [Subscribed "Un Patriota."] [Lima, 1827!] 4to.

PAVON, ANTONIO. Selectiores ex universa philosophia, etc. propositiones. [Wanting all after p. 2.] Lima, [1781.] 8vo.

PAZOS KANKI, VICENTE. Copia de una Representacion, dirigida ... al ... Presidente ... de las [sic] República de las Provincias-Unidas del Rio de la Plata (Londres 14 de Noviembre de 1825.) [Buenos Ayres! 1826!] Fol.

PEDEMONTE, CARLOS. Discurso ... en la misa de accion de gracias celebrada en la Iglesia Catedral de Trujillo por la gloriosa marcha del ejército de la patria victorioso en Junin y aniversario de la entrada en Lima de S. E. el Libertador S. Bolivar, etc. Trujillo, 1824. 4to.

2 DISCURSO, que en el segundo dia del Octavario de Concepcion, y Anniversario de la batalla de Ayacucho, con motivo de la Jura de la Constitucion y Presidencia Vitalicia del Libertador en el Perú, pronunció. C. Pedemonte. Lima, 1826. 16mo.

3 MEMORIA del ministerio de gobierno y relaciones exteriores para el congreso de 1831. Lima, 1831. 4to.

PEHUENCHAN LETTERS. [Begins.] Cartas Pehuenches, ó Correspondencia de dos Indios naturales del Pire Maper. [By Dr. Egana!] [Santiago! 1819.] 4to.

PEINIER, — DE, Count. Correspondance avec l'assemblée général de la partie francoise de St. Domingue. Port–au–Prince, 1790. 8vo.

2 LETTRE de M. le Général (de Peinier) à M. Chachereau, avocat au conseil-supérieur de Saint-Domingue, et réponse de M. Chachereau. Port-au-Prince, [1790.] 8vo.

PENA, FRANCISCO JAVIER DE LA. Arenga civica que para el 16 de Septiembre de 1832 tenia preparada el ciudadano F. J. de la Pena, etc. Segunda edicion corregida, etc. México, 1842. 8vo.

PENA, MIGUEL. Defensa . . . en la causa del Coronel L. Infante ante la camara del Senado de Colombia. Caracas, 1826. 8vo.

PERALTA BARNUEVO ROCHA Y BENAVIDES, PEDRO DE. El Templo de la Fama vindicado. Lima, 1710. 4to.

2 IMAGEN politica del govierno del Señor D. Ladron de Guevara, Virrey del Perù, etc. desde que entró a governar hasta el presente. Lima, 1714. 4to.

3 FUNEBRE Pompa, demonstracion doliente, magnificencia triste, que en las altas exequias y tumulo en la Iglesia Metropolitana de Lima al Señor Francisco Farnese, Duque de Parma, mando hacer J. de Armendariz, Virrey. Lima, 1728. 4to.

4 HISTORIA de España vindicada; en que se haze su mas exacta descripcion de sus excelencias y antiguas Riquezas. Lima, 1730. Fol.

5 LIMA fundada, o conquista del Peru. Poema Heroico. En que se deccanta . . . la historia del descubrimiento y sugecion de sas provincias por . . . F. Pizarro . . . y se contiene la serie de los reyes, . . . que ha tenido, etc. Lima, 1732. 4to.

PEREIRA DE LEON, MOSES. Efsai historique sur la colonie de Surinam, sa fondation, ses révolutions, ses progrés, depuis son origine jusqu' à nos jours . . . avec l'histoire de la nation Juive Portugaise et Allemande y établie . . . Le tout redigé et mis en ordre par les régens et réprésentans de la dite nation Juive Portugaise (M. Pereira de L., S. H. de la Parra, I. de la Parra, D. de I. C. Nafsy, S. W. Brandon.) 2 parts. Paramaribo, 1788. 8vo.

PEREZ, FRANCISCO. Catecismo de la doctrina cristiana en lengua Otomi traducida literalmente al Castellano. México, 1834. 8vo.

PEREZ, MANUEL. Arte de el idioma Mexico. Por el P. Fr. Manuel Perez, . . . Dedicalo a la dicha Santifsima Provincia. Mexico, 1713. 4to.

PEREZ BOCANEGRA, JUAN. Ritual Formulario, e institucion de curas, para administrar a los naturales de este Reyno, los santos Sacramentos del Baptismo, Confirmacion, Eucarista, y Viatico, Penitencia, Extrema-uncion, y Matrimonio, con advertencias muy necefsarias. Por el Bachiller Iuan Perez Bocanegra, . . . Span. and Quichua. Lima, 1631. 4to.

PEREZ CALAMA, JOSEPH, Bishop of Quito. Edicto para la santa visita. Y la arenga à la Real Audiencia Gobernadora en el dia de Besa-Manos del Principe nuestro Señor. Quito, 1791. 4to.

2 EDICTO pastoral, sobre los puntos siguientes : Que los casados, divorciados sin la legitima autoridad de la Iglesia, estan en pecado mortal: y que los que administrae el bautismo, y Extrema-Uncion sin oleos nuevos, cometen sacrilegio. Quito, 1791. 4to.

PEREZ DE VARGAS, JOSEPH ISIDRO, Præs. Specimen de rebus ad grammaticen pertinentibus a Latini Musæi alumnis E. M. de Freyre et Santa Cruz, E. Quiroga, E. Ballesteros, J. M. Perla, G. Teran, exhibendum. Limæ, 1827. 4to.

2 SYNOPSIS rerum quas pro Latinæ linguæ examine subeundo explanandas exhibebunt Latini Musei alumni J. J. Perez de Vargas, E. de Olivares, P. Tapia, E. de Esquivel et Navia, E. de Suero, L. de Hurtado, J. de Ramirez, C. de Quincunilla et Malo de Molina, Z. Rojas, J. de Ortiz Zeballos, A. de la Barrera. Limæ, 1829. 4to.

3 METODO analitico que debera rigorosamente observarse en el examen de los Alumnos del Museo Latino. Lima, 1830. 8vo.

PERIODIQUITO (EL). No. 1 to 11. [Lima, 1838.] 4to.

PERU. [*Begins.*] Memorial de Personæ benemeritas en el Peru para Prelacias y Prebendas y beneficios. [Manuscript.] [Lima! 1625!] s. sh. Fol.

2 [*Begins.*] PRIMERAM⁺ᵒ q es mui necesſario q los beneficios de las Provincias del Peru se probean como dé antes por presentacion de su Magᵈ. por los ynconbenientes que sean seguido y se van seguiendo q son los siguientes, *etc.* [Manuscript.] [Lima? 1625?] Fol.

3 [*Begins.*] DON Pedro de Toledo y Leyva, *etc.* [An ordinance relating to the working of the Peruvian mines, *etc.* ' Lima, 20 de Mayo, 1644.'] [Lima, 1644.] Fol.

4 Tomo Primero de las Ordenanzas del Peru ... Recogidas, y coordenadas. Por el Lic. D. Thomas de Ballesteros, Relator del Govierno Superior, *etc.* Lima, 1685. Fol.

5 REAL Orden comunicada por el Excmo. S. Virey del Reyno al Excmo. Cabildo de esta capital, aprobando la ereccion del Regimiento de Voluntarios, *etc.* Lima, 1812. 4to.

6 EL PENSADOR del Peru. (Apéndice al pensador del Peru.) Lima, 1815. 4to.

7 QUADRO historico politico de la capital del Peru, desde el 8 de Setiembre de 1820, hasta fines de Junio, 1822; leido en la sociedad patriotica, por un individuo de ella. Lima, 1822. 4to.

8 LEY reglamentaria de elecciones de diputados a congreso, senadores, diputados departamentales y de los individuos de las municipalidades, sancionada por el congreso constituyente conforme a la constitucion politica de la Republica Peruana. 2 parts. Lima, 1825. 4to.

9 MANIFIESTO del Gobierno del Peru en contestacion al que ha dado el General Bolivar sobre los motivos que tiene para hacerle la guerra. Lima, 1828. Fol.

10 [*Begins.*] MEMORANDUM a los Señores del Congreso, para la question pendiente sobre ... si conforme a la constitucion que rije se puede o no proceder a la renovacion de los vocales de las Cortes de Justicia nombrados en propiedad antes de su promulgacion conforme à la Constitucion del año de 1823. Lima, 1831. 4to.

11 [*Begins.*] A LA M. H. Junta Departamental se hace presente. [A petition of the citizens of Peru concerning the mines.] Trujillo, 1832. Fol.

12 EL PRESIDENTE de la Republica presenta al publico las razones en que se fundó para la prision del Señor Ex-diputado Igoain, que se ha puesto en libertad con arreglo á lo decidido por el consejo de estado. Lima, 1832. 8vo.

13 [*Begins.*] Ejercito Unido Estado Mayor Jeneral. Boletin, num. 5. Cuzco, 1835. Fol.

14 [*Begins.*] COPY of the Licence of the Government of the North and South Peruvian States to Mr. W. Wheelwright . . . to navigate the coasts and parts thereof, *etc.* Lima, 1836. Fol.

15 DOCUMENTOS relativos a reclamos al gobierno del Peru sobre propriedades Britanicas tomadas por autoridades Peruanas, saqueadas durante conmociones militares ó civiles, ó robadas de los Almacenes de la aduana del Callao, desde 1º de Enero de 1835 hasta Diciembre de 1839. Lima, 1840. 8vo.

PERUANO. Refutacion del papel publicado en Chile con el titulo de Apelacion á la nacion Peruana escrito por F. Brandsen. [By T. de Heres.] (Contestacion que da el D. D. I. Ortis de Zevallos al papel intitulado Apelacion á la nacion Peruana.) [The head-title runs: " Carta de un Peruano a Mr. F. de Brandsen."] Lima, 1825. 4to.

PERUANO (EL). No. 3, tom. 2. 24 de Abril, 1839. Lima, 1839. Fol.

PETERKIN, JOSEPH. A Treatise

on Planting from the origin of the semen to ebullition, with a correct mode of distillation and amelioration on the whole process progressively. Dedicated to the planters of the Charribbee Islands. 2nd ed. St. Christophers, 1790. 4to.

PHILALETHES. [*Begins.*] Preservativo contra el veneno de los libros impios y seductores que corren en el pais. [Carta de Filaletes a Eusevio.] Lima, 1822. 4to.

PHILIP V, *King of Spain.* Solemne proclamacion y cabalgata real que el dia 5 de Octubre de este año de 1701 hizó la muy noble y leal Ciudad de los Reyes Lima, levantando pendones por el Rey Catholico D. Felipe V, *etc.* [Wanting the first three leaves of sig. A.] Lima, 1701. 4to.

PHILO-XYLON, *Pseud.* Letters of Philo-xylon. . . . on the subject of Negro Laws and Negro Government, on plantation, in Barbados. Barbados, 1798. 8vo.

POEY, FELIPE. Memorias sobre la historia natural de la Isla de Cuba, acompañadas de sumarios Latinos y extractos en Frances. Habana, 1851. 4to.

POLYPHEME (THE) and De Cordova's Advertiser. No. 89. Sept. 19th, 1838. Kingston, Jamaica, 1838. Fol.

PORT-AU-PRINCE. Notice sur la ville du Port-au-Prince. [Port-au-Prince, 1788 ?] 8vo.
2 EXTRAIT des registres des délibérations de la paroisse de la Croix-des-Bouquets. Port au Prince, [1790.] 8vo.
3 ADRESSE de la Garde nationale du Port-au-prince [to the French people, on the state of the colony of Saint Domingo, or Hayti.] Port-au-Prince, 1792. s. sh. 4to.
4 PRODUCTION historique des faits qui se sont passés dans la partie de l'

Ouest, depuis le commencement de la révolution de Saint Domingue, jusqu'au premier Février 1792, présentée par les gardes nationales du Port-au-Prince, à messieurs les commissaires civils. [With an address, or proclamation, by the French commissaries, separately paged.] Port-au-Prince, 1792. 4to.
5 BANDO de buen gobierno mandado observar en la Ciudad de Puerto Principe y su jurisdiccion, por A. Vazquez, *etc.* Puerto Principe, 1835. Fol.
6 INFORME de la comision del Camino de N. Puerto-Principe, 1836. 8vo.
7 CEDULA de propiedad y reglamentos administrativos de la compañia . . . publicados por acuerdo de la diputacion patriotica. Puerto-Principe, 1837. 8vo.

PORT OF SPAIN (THE) Gazette. Nos. 1399 to 1500. April 2nd 1839 to March 20th 1840. [Wanting Nos. 1401 to 1409, 1412, 1419 to 1426, 1428, 1434, 1436, 1438, 1442, 1445, 1449 to 50, 1452 to 54, 1456, 1460, 1468 to 79, 1488, 1491 to 92, 1497.] Port of Spain, 1839-40. Fol.

PORTO RICO. Reglamento sobre la educacion, trato y ocupaciones que deben dar a sus esclavos los hacendados o mayordomos de esta isla. [Porto Rico, 1826.] 4to.
2 RELACION circunstandiada [sic] de todas las obras publicas que se han emprendido y continuado en la Isla de Puerto-Rico en el año de 1828, *etc.* Puerto-Rico, 1829. 4to.
3 RELACION circunstanciada de todas las obras publicas que se han emprendido y continuado en la Isla de Puerto Rico en el año de 1830, por disposicion del . . . Sr. D. M. de la Torre, *etc.* Puerto-Rico, 1831. 4to.
4 RELACION circunstanciada de todas las obras publicas que se han emprendido y continuado en la Isla de Puerto Rico en el año de 1831, *etc.* Puerto Rico, 1832. 4to.

5 RELACION circunstanciada de todas las obras publicas que se han emprendido y continuado en la Isla de Puerto-Rico en el año de 1832, *etc.* Puerto-Rico, 1833. 4to.

PORTUGAL. Convenção entre ... o Principe Regente de Portugal e Elrey do Reino Unido da Grande Bretanha e Irlanda sobre o estabelecimento dos paquetes. *Port.* and *Eng.* L. P. Rio de Janeiro, 1810. Fol.

2 TRATADO de amizade e alliança entre ... o Principe Regente de Portugal e Elrey do Reino Unido da Grande Bretanha e Irlanda, *etc. Port.* and *Eng.* L. P. Rio de Janeiro, 1810. Fol.

3 TRATADO de commercio e navegação entre .. o Principe Regente de Portugal, e Elrey do Reino Unido da Grande Bretanha e Irlanda. *Port.* and *Eng.* L. P. Rio de Janeiro, 1810. Fol.

4 [*Begins.*] EU o Principe Regente. [Decree prolonging the Alto Douro wine company's charter for a further period of twenty years: Feb. 10, 1815.] [Rio Janeiro, 1815.] s. sh. Fol.

5 [*Begins.*] EU ELREI. [Decree increasing the duties on imports : April 25, 1818.] [Rio Janeiro, 1815.] Fol.

6 [*Begins.*] EU ELREI. [Decree introducing some modifications into the tariff: May 30, 1820.] [Rio Janeiro, 1820.] Fol.

POWER, SAMUEL. Lettres pour la justification du Rev. S. Power. Trinidad, 1830. 8vo.

PRADO, PABLO DE. Directorio espiritual en la lengua Española, y Quichua general del Inga. Compuesto por el Padre Pablo de Prado ... Lima, 1641. 12mo.

PREZEAU, — DE. Réfutation de la Lettre du général Français Dauxion Lavayße. [Urging the submißion of Hayti to the authority of Louis XVIII.] Par ... de Prézeau, *etc.* Cap-Henry, 1814. 8vo.

2 LETTRE du Chevalier de Prézeau, Secrétaire du Roi, *etc. etc.* A ses Concitoyens de partie de l'Ouest et du Sud. Cap-Henry, [1815.] 8vo.

3 REFUTATION. (Royaume d'Hayti. Réfutation d'un écrit des excolons, refugiés à la Jamaïque, intitule: Exposé de l'Etat actuel des choses dans la Colonie de Saint-Domingue. Par ... de Prezeau, *etc.*) Cap-Henry, 1815. 8vo.

PROSPERI, FELIX. La Gran defensa. Nuevo methodo de fortificacion dividido en tres ordenes: a Saber : Doble, Reforzado, y Sencillo, *etc.* Tom 1. Mexico, 1744. Fol°

PUEBLA DE LOS ANGELES. Octava Maravilla del Nuevo Mundo en la gran capilla del Rosario. Dedicada y aplaudida en el Convento de N. P. S. Domingo de la Ciudad de los Angeles. El dia 16 del Mes de Abril de 1690 ... Puebla, 1690. 4to.

2 ALEGACION de los derechos que por parte del promotor fiscal del obispado de la Puebla de los Angeles se hace a esta Real Audiencia, para que en conformidad de lo determinado en 16 de Mayo de 1770 se sirva declarar que en conocer y proceder el provisor de dicha Ciudad no hace fuerza en la causa que expresa. [By J. A. de Tapia.] Puebla de los Angeles, 1771. Fol°

3 MEMORIA presentada al congreso primero constitucional de Puebla de los Angeles por el secretario del despacho de gobierno sobre el estado de la administracion publica. Año de 1826. Mexico, [1827 ?] Fol.

PUENTE, FRANCISCO DE LA. Tratado breve de la antiguedad del linaie de Vera, y memoria de personas señaladas del, que se hallan en historias y papeles autenticos. (Parrafos que se an de añadir en este libro.) Lima, 1635. 4to.

UERETARO. Colleccion de los decretos y ordenes del primer congreso constitucional del estado de Queretaro(1825-27). [Queretaro, 1827.] 4to.

QUINTANILLA Y MALO DE MOLINA, CAMILLO DE. Prolusio academica, recitanda in D. Marci Limana Universitate. Limæ, 1829. 8vo.

QUINT FERNANDEZ DAVILA, DIEGO, Lieut. Col. Oraciones Funebres que en las Exequias del Señor G. F. de Campos. Obispo de La Paz dixeron la primera F. Carrasco, la segunda M. Fulgencio de Gamboa. Da a la prensa D. Quint Fernandez Davila. Lima, 1791. 4to.

QUIROS, ANSELMO. Contestacion al manifiesto que hace a la nacion de su conducta publica Don J. M. de Pando. Lima, 1827. 4to.

M. Articulo Corregido del Observador de la Republica Mexicana del 5 de Mayo 1830 [respecting the charges on the carriage of gold and silver between Mexico and Vera Cruz, subscribed M. R.] [Mexico? 1831.] 8vo.

RAIMOND, JULIEN. Rapport de J. Raimond, commißaire délégué par le gouvernement Français aux iles sous le vent, au ministre de la Marine [on the affairs of Saint Domingo]. Cap Français, [1797.] 4to.

RAMIRES DE ARELLANO, RAFAEL. [Begins.] Recurso del Dr. R. Ramires de Arellano en la Corte Superior de Justicia. [Lima, 1828.] Fol.

REAL COLEGIO SEMINARIO. [Begins.] Carta expresiva de la mas

fina lealtad al Soberano, remitida por el Real Colegio Seminario, etc. (Elog'º del mismo seminario al Excmo. Señor Don J. T. Abascal y Sousa, etc.) [Lima, 1806.] 4to.

REAL DE CURBAN, GASPARD DE. Aviso al publico. Obra interesante. [Prospectus of a translation into Spanish of the "Science du Gouvernement" of G. de Real de Curban.] Mexico, 1829. s. sh. Fol.

REAL JUNTA DE FOMENTO DE AGRICULTURA Y COMERCIO. Informe presentado a la Real Junta ... de esta Isla [Cuba] en sesion de 11 de Diciembre de 1833 en el espediente sobre translacion, reforma y ampliacion de la escuela nautica establecida en el pueblo de Regla refundiendola en un instituto cientifico con arreglo a las necesidades del pais. Por la diputacion inspectora de dicho establecimiento. [The fly-leaf has only the words " Instituto Cubano."] Habana, 1834. 8vo.

REAL SOCIEDAD ECONOMICA DE AMIGOS DEL PAIS DE LA HABANA. Estatutos de la Real Sociedad economica ... aprobados por el rey, etc. Habaña, 1833. 4to.

REAL SOCIEDAD PATRIOTICA. Esposicion de las tareas que han ocupado à la real sociedad patriotica durante los años de 1825 y 1826; leida en junta general de 15 de Diciembre por su secretario D. J. Santos Suarez, etc. Habana, 1827. 4to.

REAL SOCIEDAD PATRIOTICA DE LA HABANA, afterwards REAL SOCIEDAD ECONOMICA HAVANNA, CUBA DE LA HABANA. Memorias de la Sociedad ... Números 54-57 ... Junio—Setiembre (1824) sobre el influjo de los climas cálidos y principalmente del de la Habana, en la estacion del calor. Programa propuesto por la Sociedad ... desenvuelto y presentado por ... J. Fernandez de

Madrid. [pp. 471-588.] Habana, 1824. 4to.

2 RELACION historica de los beneficios hechos a la real sociedad economica, casa de benificencia y demas dependencias de aquel cuerpo por . . . F. D. Vives. Escrita por las comisiones reunidas de ambas corporaciones. Habana, 1832. Fol.

3 ESTADO general de la instruccion pública primaria de la Isla de Cuba en 1836, conforme á los datos reunidos por la seccion de Educacion de la Real Sociedad, etc. Habaña, 1836. obl. 4to.

4 MEMORIAS . . . redacltadas por una Comision de su seno, [from tom. 17-20] (compuesta de los Sres. H. J. J. Garcia y D. F. de Paula Serrano Segunda Epoca.) 20 tom. Habana, 1836-45. 8vo.

5 MEMORIAS Segunda Serie. Tom 1. etc Habana, 1846, etc. · 8vo.

6 MEMORIAS . . . (Segunda Epoca) Segunda Edicion. Habana, 1847, etc. 8vo.

REAL UNIVERSIDAD DE SAN MARCOS DE LIMA. Constituciones y ordenanzas antiguas, añadidas y modernas de la real universidad . . . Recogidas . . . por A. E. de Salazar y Zevallos, etc. [Lima,] 1735. Fol.

2 EL CIELO en el Parnaſbo, certamen poetico con que la R. U. de S. M. de L., y en su nombre su recltor A. E. de Salazar y Zevallos celebrò el recibimiento de S. E. [I. de Mendoza Sotomayor y Camano.] en sus escuelas. Y la relacion de la festiva pompa y solemne aclamacion de su entrada en esta Ciudad. Que describe P. de Peralta Barnuevo y Rocha. Lima, 1736. 4to.

3 ACTUACIONES literarias de la Vacuna. [Lima,] 1807. 4to.

4 COLECCION de las composiciones de eloquencia y poesía, con que la R. U. de San M. de Lima, celebró, en los dias 20 y 21 de Noviembre de 1816, el recibimiento de . . . Don Joaquin de La Pezuela y Sanchez Mu-

ñoz de Velasco, . . . virey . . . del Perü, etc. (Elogio . . . que . . . pronunció . . . J. Cavero y Salazar, etc. Sermon . . . que . . . dixó . . . J. J. Larriva y Ruiz. 3 parts. Lima, 1816. 4to.

REGISTRO TRIMESTRE 6 coleccion de memorias de historia, literatura, ciencias y artes, por una sociedad de literatos. Num. 1, 2, 4. [No. 3 wanting.] Mexico, 1832. 4to.

RELIGIOSO. [Begins.] Monicion caritativa de un Religioso, al autor del Num. 2, intitulado El Fraile. [Lima, 1812?] 4to.

REYES ANGEL, GASPAR DE LOS. Sermon [Matth. 19 cap.] al glorioso San Francisco de Borja Duque Quarto de Gandia. Tercero General de la Compañia de Jesus. Predicokó el P. Gaspar de los Reyes Angel de las mesma Compañia. Mexico, 1688. 4to.

RIBEIRO DE ANDRADA MACHADO E SILVA, ANTONIO CARLOS, and others. Projecſto de constituição para o imperio do Brasil. Rio de Janeiro, 1823. 16mo.

RIBEIRO DOS GUIMARAES PEIXOTO, DOMINGOS. Projecſto de Estatutos para a Escola de Medicina do Rio de Janeiro. Rio de Janeiro, 1836. 4to.

RIBERA, JUAN ANTONIO. Pompa funeral en las exequias del Rey Fernando VI. en esta Iglesia Metropolitana de Lima. Julio 1760. Lima, 1760. 4to.

RIBERA FLOREZ, DIONYSIO DE. Relacion Historiada de las exequias funerales de . . . Philippo II. nuestro Señor Hechas por el Tribunal del Sancſto officio de la Inquisicion desta Nueva España, etc. Mexico, 1600. 4to.

RIBERA Y COLINDRES, LUYS DE. Del Govierno arbitrario del Pirú. Don Luys de Ribera y Colindres vezino de Sevilla, y residente en la Ciudad de la Plata del Pirù. *Lat.* [Lima? 1622.] Fol.

RIGAUD, ANDRÉ, *General.* Mémoire du général de brigade A. Rigaud en réfutation des écrits calomnieux contre les citoyens de couleur de Saint-Domingue. Aux Cayes, [1797.] 4to.

RINCON, ANTONIO DEL. Arte Mexicana compuesta por el Padre Antonio del Rincon de la compañia de Iesus. Dirigido al Illustrifsimo y reverendifsimo S. don Diego Romano Obispo de Tlaxcallan, y del consijo de su Magestad, *etc.* Mexico, 1595. 8vo.

RIO, ANDRES DEL. Discurso geologico leido en el acto de mineralógia del seminario nacional di mineria. Mexico, 1843. 8vo.

RIO, ANDRÉS MANUEL DEL. Elementos de orictognosia, ó del conocimiento de los fósiles, dispuestos segun los principios de A. G. Wérner, para el uso del Real Seminario de mineria de Mexico. Primera parte. Mexico, 1795. 4to.

RIO, GUILLERMO DEL. Monumentos literarios del Peru. Lima, 1812. 4to.

RIO, MANUEL DEL. Memoria del ministerio de gobierno y relaciones exteriores para el congreso de 1832. Lima. 1832. 4to.

ROCAFUERTE, VICENTE. Ensayo sobre el nuevo sistema de carceles. Mexico, 1830. 8vo.

2 ENSAYO sobre tolerancia religiosa. Mexico, 1831. 8vo.

3 MENSAJE del Presedente de la Republica en la apertura de las camaras legislativas de 1839. [Quito, 1839.] 4to.

RODRIGUEZ DELGADO, AUGUSTIN, *Bishop of Nuestra Señora de la Paz.* Carta pastoral. Lima, 1735. 4to.

RODRIGUEZ MEDRANO, BALTHASAR. Manifiesto de su justicia que producen los dueños de haziendas y ranchos de magueyes : para que, in su consideracion, se sirva esta real audiencia de revocar... la sentencia dada ... en estos autos, a los 18 de Julio. .. 1747, absolviendo a los cosecheros del pulque blanco de la demanda puesta contra ellos por el ... dean y cabildo de esta stã Iglesia cathedral metropolitana, *etc.* Mexico, 1750. Folº

ROEL, JUAN. Defensa de D. J. Villamil, ciudadano de Bolivia, con motivo de la persecucion que ha sufrido en Lima. Lima, 1832. 4to.

ROJAS, JOSE M. DE. Proyecto para el restablecimiento de la circulacion de Vales, conciliando el provecho del erario y del publico con la justicia de los acreedores. Caracas, 1828. 8vo.

ROMANE, I. B. Epitre adrefsée à Mademoiselle F. Wright [in verse.] Port-au-Prince, [1830.] 4to.

ROMAY, TOMAS. Memoria sobre la introduccion y progresos de la Vacuna en la isla de Cuba. Havana, 1805, 4to.

ROME, *Church of.* Bula de . . . Gregorio XVI. sobre los asuntos de España, y otros documentos importantes. Mexico, 1842. 8vo.

ROXAS, IGNACIO DE. Prolusio Academica pro studiorum inauguratione, recitanda in D. Marci Limana Universitate. Præside J. P. de V. Limæ, 1833. 8vo.

ROYAL GAZETTE of British Guiana. Nos. 5002 to 5128, 5117 to 79, 5182, 5186-87, 5189 to 93, 5204, 5208, 5211, 5213, 5216, 5218-19, 5227-28, 5232 to 38, 5240-43, 5251, 5257 to 61, 5267 to 70. Georgetown, 1838 to 1840. Folio.

ROYAL GAZETTE (THE), and Jamaica Times. Vol. 60, No. 24. Vol. 61, No. 131. Vol. 62, No. 52.

[Continued under the title of] The Royal Gazette of Jamaica. Vol. 62, Nos. 53, 54, 55, 56. Kingston, 1838-40. Fol.

ROYAL GAZETTE (The). Bermuda commercial advertiser and recorder. No. 42, Vol. 12. Hamilton, 1839. Fol.

ROYAL ST. VINCENT GAZETTE (The). Vol. 14, No. 19. June 13th, 1839. Kingstown, 1839. Fol.

ROYAL ST. VINCENT GAZETTE (The), and Weekly Advertiser. Second Series. Vol. 22 and 23, Nos. 1143 to 1201. Feb. 23rd, 1839; April 4th, 1840. [Wanting Nos. 1144-61, 1171-73, 1175, 1178-79, 1184-86, 1196.] Kingstown, 1839-40. Fol.

ROZA, Simeon de la. Refutacion documentada de los comunicados dirijidos contra S. de la Rosa, sub-director de la fabrica de Polvora, en los numeros que se citan de la miscelanea. Lima, 1831. 4to.

RUFZ, E. Enquête sur le Serpent. [From " Les Antilles," a colonial Journal.] Saint-Pierre, Martinique, 1843. 8vo.

RUIZ DE MONTOYA, Antonio. Vocabulario de la lengua Guarini compuesto por el Padre Antonio Ruiz, de la Compañia de Jesus, revisto y augmentado por otro Religioso de la misma Compañia. [Buenos Ayres,] 1722. 4to.

2 Arte de la lengua Guarini por el P. Antonio Ruiz de Monfoya . . . con los escolios Anotaciones y Apendices del P. Paulo Restivo . . . del P. Simon Bandini y de otros. (Supplemento.) [Buenos Ayres,] 1724. 4to.

 . y L, M. C. Espresiones de sincero y tierno efecto, con que un prisionero de la isla de Esteves manifesta su gratitud a S. E. el Libertador S.

Bolivar, suplicandole fige su residencia en esta capitad del Peru. [Acrostic verses.] Lima, [1826?] s. sh. Fol.

SAENZ, Manuel. A la magestad catholica del rey nuestro Señor . . . recurso, y reverente suplica por el P. Lict. Fr. M. Saenz, Orden de San Augustin, en nombre de su provincia del santisimo nombre de Jesus de Philipinas . . . sobre el furtiva, y atentada reincorporacion del Padre Fr. M. Gutierrez, de la misma orden, â la provincia de Mexico, etc. [Mex]-ico, 1753 ?] Fol°]

SAGRA, Ramon de la. Historia economico-politica y estadistica de la Isla de Cuba, ó sea de sus progresos en la poblacion, la agricultura, el comercio y las rentas. [With an appendix.] Habana, 1831. 4to.

2 Memoria sobre el bejuco del Guaco. Habana, 1833. 4to.

3 Tablas necrologicas del Coleramorbus en la Ciudad de la Habana y sus arrabales. Habana, 1833. Obl.4to.

SAHAGUN, Bernardino de. Historia de la Conquista de Mexico escrita por . . . B. Sahagun . . . Publicala por separado de sus demas obras C. M. de Bustamente. Mexico, 1829. 8°

2 Historia general de las cosas de Nueva España que . . . escribió B. de Sahagun . . . Dala a luz con notas y suplementos C. M. de Bustamente, etc. 3tom. México, 1829, 30. 8vo.

3 La Aparicion de Ntra. Señora de Guadalupe de Mexico, comprobada con la refutacion del argumento negativo que presenta D. J. B. Muños fundandose en el testimonio del P. Fr. B. Sahagun, ó sea: Historia original de este escritor [entitled " Relacion de la conquista de esta Nueva-España," etc.] que altera la publicada en 1829. Publicala precediendo una disertacion sobre la aparicion Guadalupana, y con notas sobre la conquista de México, C. M. Bustamente. México, 1840. 8vo.

SAINT CHRISTOPHER, *Island cf.* Acts of Assembly passed in the Island of St. Christopher from the year 1711 to 1769. (The laws of the Leward Islands.) 2 parts. St. Christopher, 1769. Fol.

SAINT CHRISTOPHER Advertiser (The), and Weekly Intelligencer. Nos. 4926, 4937, 4941, 4943, 4945 to 47, 4949, 4954 to 4957, 4963 to 4966, 4968. Basseterre, 1839-40. Fol.

SAINT CHRISTOPHER Gazette (The), and Charibbean Courier. Nos. 1168, 1242, 1254, 1261 to 67, 1269, 1272-73, 1275, 1281-82, 1284 to 87, 1290 to 92, 1308. Basseterre, 1837-40. Fol.

SAINT DOMINGO. Extrait des délibérations de la paroisse du Fond-des-Nègres. [Relating to the proceedings of the General Assembly sitting at Saint-Marc.] [Port-au-Prince, 1790.] 12mo.

2 Extrait des registres des délibérations de l'assemblée provinciale du Sud et de la séance du 1er Mai 1790. [Comprising a report in reply to the resolutions of the parishes of Anse-à-Veau and Fond-des-Nègres.] Port-au-Prince, [1790.] 8vo.

3 Lettre de l'assemblée provinciale permanente du Nord de Saint Dominque à M. le gouverneur général, et arrêté de la dite Assemblée pour la dissolution de l'Assemblée de Saint-Marc. Port-au-Prince, 1790. 8vo.

4 Extrait des registres de Assemblée provinciale, *etc.* de l'ouest. [Containing a vote of thanks to M. Roume, who had been superseded by the new commissioners from France.] Port-au-Prince, [1792.] 8vo.

SAINT GEORGE'S CHRONICLE (The), Grenada Gazette. 5013, 5023 to 5026, 5028, 5030, 5033 to 5055, 5059 to 5069. [SaintGeorge's,] [Grenada,] 1839-40. Fol.

SAINT JAGO DE LA VEGA

Gazette (The) and Country Advertiser. Nos. 7, 28, 52 to 107. Spanish Town, 1839-40. Fol.

SAINT LUCIA, *Island of.* Adresse des planteurs et citoyens de l'Isle Sainte Lucie, à M. de Damas, gouverneur, et à l'assemblée Coloniale de la Martinique. Au Fort-royal Martinique, [1791.] 4to.

SAINT VINCENT CHRONICLE (The), and Public Gazette. Vol. 5 and 6. [Wanting Nos. 2, 12, 13, 39, 49 of vol. 5; No. 1, and all after No. 9 of vol. 6.] Kingstown, 1839-40. Fol.

SALA, Juan. Ilustracion del derecho real de España. 3 tom. Mejico, 1831-33. 8o

SALINAS, Buenaventura de. Memorial de las Historias del Nuevo Mundo Piru: Meritos, y Excelencias de la Ciudad de Lima, . . . Por el Padre F. Buenaventura de Salinas, *etc.* Lima, 1630. 4to.

SAN BARTOLOMÉ, José de. El duelo de la Inquisicion: á Pesame que un filosofo rancio dà a sus armados compatriotas, los verdaderos Españoles, por la extincion de tan santo y utilismo Tribunal. Van añadidas varias notas critico-morales; y una disertacion historico-legal sobre la memorable historia del Sr. B. Carranza. [Lima?] 1814. 4to.

SAN CARLOS DE MONTEREY. [Begins] Estracto de Noticias del Puerto de Monterrey, de la Mission y Presidio que se han establecido en el con la denominacion de San Carlos, y del suceso de las dos Expediciones de Mar y Tierra que a este fin se despacharon en el año . . . de 1769. [Mexico, 1770?] Fol.

SANCHEZ, Francisco, Principios de retórica y poetica. [Edited by C. M. de Bustamante.] Mexico, 1825. 12o

SANCHES, Juan. Sermon en la miſſa de accion de gracias por la reedificacion del Hospital de San Lazaro de Lima, el 23 Abril 1758. [Lima, 1758.] 4to.

SANCTIUS, Josephus Eusebius. Prolusio academica in Divi Marci Limana Universitate recitanda. Lima, 1831. 8vo.

SANDOVAL, Rafael. Arte de la lengua Mexicana por el Br. en Sagrada Teologia D. Rafael Sandoval . . . Mexico, 1810. 8vo.

SAN LUIS DE POTOSI. Constitucion politica del Estado libre de S. Luis Potosi. Mexico, 1826. 24mo.

SAN MARCOS. Tabla de las materias mas fundamentales et interesantes de las matematicas puras que han cursado en la real vniersidad de san Marcos, los años 1805 y 6. Lima, 1807. Fol.

SAN MARTIN, Jose de, General. Manifiesto de las Sesiones tenidas en el Pueblo de Miraflores, para las Transacciones intentadas con el General San Martin, y documentos presentados por parte de los Comisionados en ellas . . Lima, 1820. Fol.

2 Impugnacion al articulo inserto contra el fundador de la libertad del Peru, [Don J. de San Martin] . . . en . . . la Abeja republicana. Escrita . . . par los amigos de la libertad. Lima, 1823. Fol.

SANTA-CRUZ. Còdigo de Procederes Santa Cruz. Imprenta Chuquisaqueña, 1833. 4to.

The first work printed with types cast in Upper Peru by a native of that country.

SANTANDER, Francisco de Paula, Vice-President of Columbia. Noticia biografica del Señor General F. de P. Santander, del orden de los libertadores de Venezuela y Candinamarea : Vice-presidente encargado del poder ejecutivo de la republica de Colombia. Lima, 1827. 4to.

SANTIAGO. Comision de negocios constitucionales. Projecto de reglamento de elecciones. 1828. (Reglamento de elecciones.) [Santiago, (1828.] 4to.

SATELITE DEL PERUANO (El) o Redaccion Politica Liberal é Instructiva, por una Sociedad Filantropica. No. I. Lima, 1812. 4to.

SATURNINO DA COSTA Pereira, José. Diccionario topographico do Imperio do Brasil, Contendo a Descripção de todas as Provincias em geral, e particularmente de cada huma de suas Citades, etc. Rio de Janeiro, 1834. Obl. 4to.

SIERRA Y ROSSO, Ignacio. Poema pronunciado en la instalacion de la academia de jurisprudencia el 8 de Febrero de 1835. México, 1835. 8vo.

2 Representacion dirigida al Congreso nacional por . . . I. Sierra y Roſſo, como apoderado del . . . presidente de la Republica, etc. Mexico, 1837. 8vo.

3 Discurso, pronunciado en Mexico el 16 de Setiembre de 1838, etc. (júbilo . . . de la libertad de la patria.) Mexico, 1838. 8vo.

4 Discurso que por encargo de la junta patriótica pronunció . . . . . I. Sierra y Rosso, en la colocacion del pie que perdió en Veracruz. . . A. Lopez de Santa Anna, en la gloriosa jornada del 5 de Deciembre de 1838. Mexico, 1842. 8vo.

SILVA LISBOA, Jose da. Memoria da Vida, publica do Lord Wellington, Duque de Wellington. 2 parts. Rio de Janiero, 1815. 4to.

2 Estudos do Ben Commum e Economia Politica. Rio de Janeiro, 1819. 4to.

SILVA Y OLAVE, Joseph, Praeses. Prospectus rerum quas in Latino sermone recitaturi sunt in regia Divi Marci Academia alumni de universa grammatica examinandi. Lima, [1809.] 4to.

SOBREVIELA, Manuel. Relacion sumaria de los progresos de los Misioneros Franciscos Observantes del Colegio de Propaganda Fide de Santa Rosa de Ocopa, en el Valle de Xauxa, en los años de 787, 88, y 89 en las Montañas de Caxamarquilla, Huanuco, Tarma, Xauxa, Guanta, y Archipielago de Chiloé, etc. [Lima?] 1790. Fol.

SOCIEDAD ECONOMICA DE AMIGOS DEL PAIS EN LA PROVINCIA DE CARACAS. Memorias de la Sociedad . . . en 1830. Caracas, 1831. 8vo.

SOCIETY FOR THE ENCOURAGEMENT OF ARTS, MANUFACTURES, AND COMMERCE. Institution and first proceedings of the Society. . . established in Barbados, 1781. [With a continuation.] Barbados, [1781-84.] 8vo.

SOLIS Y VALENZUELA, Pedro DE. Panegyrico sagrado, en alabanza del serafin de las soledades SanBruno, Fundador, y patriarca de la sagrada Cartuxa. . . Pedro de Solis y Valenzuela. . . Lima, 1646. 4°

SONORA. Noticia breve de la expedicion militar de S. y C. su exîto feliz, y ventajoso estado en que por consecuencia de ella se han puesto ambas provincias. [Mexico, 1771.] Fol.

SOUZA AZEVEDO PIZARRO E ARANJO, Jose de. Memorias historicas do Rio de Janeiro e das provincias annexas a jurisdiçaõ do vicerei do Estado do Brasil. 9 tom. [Tom. 8 is in 2 parts.] Rio de Janeiro, 1820-22. 4to.

SPAIN, Charles IV, King. Ordenanza que para la division de la. . . Ciudad de Santiago de Queretaro en quartelas menores, creacion de alcaldes de ellos, y reglas para su gobierno, segun lo resulto por S. M. en Real Cédula de 17 de Junio de 1794 . . . ha extendido . . . J. I. Ruiz Calado, y aprobó S.E. en superior de-

cierto de 4 de Junio de 1796. México, [1796.] Fol.

SPAIN, Cortes. Coleccion de los decretos y ordenes de las Cortes de España que se reputan vigentes en lá republica de los Estados Unidos Mexicanos. Mexico, 1829. 4to.

SPAIN, Ferdinand VII. King. Real cedula de S. M. que contiene el reglamento para la poblacion y fomento del comercio, industria, y agricultura de la isla de Puerto Rico. —His Majesty's Royal decree, etc. Ordonnance Royale de Sa Majesté, etc. Span. Engl. and Fr. St. Thomas, [1815.] Fol.

2 Real cedula de S. M. que contiene el reglamento para la poblacion y fomento del Comercio . . . y Agricultura de la Isla de Puerto Rico. His Majesty's Royal decree, etc. Ordonnance Royale, etc. Span. Engl. and Fr. St. Thomas, [1816?] Fol.

3 Real cedula de 21 de Octubre de 1817 sobre aumentar la poblacion blanca de la Isla de Cuba. Impresa en Español, Ingles, y Frances. Reimpresa. Habana, 1828. Fol.

4 Real cedula [dated 30 de Julio de 1833] sobre privilegios de inventos artisticos é introduccion de máquinas estrangeras, etc. Habana, 1836. Fol.

SPAIN, Isabella II, Queen. Instruccion provisional para el gobierno de la mineria en los dominios Españoles precedida de los reales decretos a que se refieren sus disposiciones y añadidos al fin los particulares espedidos por S. M. para la isla de Cuba, etc. Cuba, 1835. 8vo.

SPANISH GOVERNMENT. Fastos militares de iniquidad, barbarie y despotismo del gobierno Español, ejicutados en las villas de Orizava y Córdoba en la guerra de once años, por causa de la independencia y libertad la Nacion Mexicana . . . Dalos a luz como documentos que, apoyan las relaciones del cuadro historico de la revolucion. . . J. M. Tornel. [Edited by C. M. de Busta-mante.] Mexico, 1843. 8°

SPANISH NATION. A la nacion Española el Pensador del Peru. [By J. Morales y Ugalde, according to a MS. note on the titlepage.] Lima, 1814. 4to.

SUN (THE). Nos. 14, 19 to 27. Feb. 19th to April 4th 1840. [Bridgetown, Barbadoes,] 1840. Fol.

AGLE, JOSE BERNARDO DE, *Marquis de Torre Tagle.* Manifiesto del Marquis de Torre-Ta-gle, sobre algunos su-cesos notables de su gobierno. (Do-cumentos justificativos.) Lima, 1824. 4to.

2 NARRACION que hace Don Jose Bernardo Tagle de sus servicios a la causa de America. Lima, [1830?] Fol.

TAPIA ZENTENO, CARLOS DE. Noticia de la lengua huastica, que en beneficio de sus nacionales, de orden del Ilmô. Sr. Arzobispo de esta Santa iglesia Metropolitana, y a sus expensas, da C. de Tapea Zenteno . . . con cathecismo y doctrina Chris-tiana, *etc.* Mexico, 1767. 4to.

TARAZONA, ALONSO DE. [*Be-gins.*] Copia de carta escrita y em-biada de la Ciudad de Malfeta al Pro-vincial de esta Corte dandole quenta de un caso horroroso que sucedió con unos Cavalleros. Impreßa en Ma-drid, Reimpreßa en Lima, 1715. 4to.

TAUNAY, THEODORE. Idylles Brésiliennes, écrites en vers latins par T. Taunay, et traduites en vers français par F. E. Taunay. Rio de Janeiro, 1830. 4to.

TELLO DE GUZMAN, MARIA. Por Doña Maria Tello de Guzman, y Felix Hernandez de Guzman su Hijo, y Alonso de Carrion. Con el Señor

Fiscal. Sobre el oficio de Escrivano publico y del Cabildo de la ciudad de los Reyes. [Lima, 1613?] Fol.

TERRAZAS, MATIAS. Sermon, en complimiento del voto que hizo el General Joaquin de la Pezuela, 1813. [Exod. xv.] Lima, 1814. 4to.

2 SERMON en la solemne misa de accion de gracias, con motivo de ha-berse recibido la noticia de la resti-tucion al trono de las Españas de Fernando VII. [Ps. cxvii. 22, 23.] Lima, 1815. 4to.

TEXEDA, PEDRO ALEXANDER DE. Representacion, que en nombre de los actuales curas beneficiados de la ciudad de Santa Fee Real, y Minas de Guanaxuato presenta al . . . obispo de Michoacan, el Dr. D. P. A. de Texeda. Mexico, 1764. Fol°

THIERY DE MENONVILLE, NICOLAS JOSEPH. Traité de la Cul-ture du Nopal, et de l'Education de la Cochenille, dans les Colonies Françaises, de l'Amérique ; précédé d'un voyage à Guaxaca. (Eloge de M. Thiery de Menonville, par M. Arthaud.) 2 parts. Cap Français, Paris, Bordeaux, 1787. 8vo.

TOBAGO CHRONICLE (THE) and Royal Gazette. Nos. 257, 261 to 63, 266 to 310. March 28th, 1839—April 2nd, 1840. Scarbo-rough, [Tobago], 1839-40. Fol.

TOBAGO GAZETTE and West India News. A No. for Feb. 11th, 1839, and Nos. 54, 58 to 68, 85, 87, 89 to 91. Scarborough, [To-bago,] 1839-40. Fol.

TOBIAS, MARIANO. Extrait du Journal des Isles de France et de Bourbon. [Consisting of a letter by Mariano Tobias . . . in which are narrated his services on two occa-sions, to some unfortunate French-men.] [Port Louis, 1787]. 8vo.

TORNEL, JOSE MARIA. Replica de varios Españoles el Señor Tornel, en su contestacion a las cuatro palabras. Mexico, 1841. 8vo.

2 DESAHOGO de D. J. M. Tornel, bajo la firma de J. Lopez de Santa-Anna. [A criticism on an official communication made by the latter 30th May, 1843.] Merida de Yucatan, 1843. 8vo.

TORRES RUBIO, DIEGO DE. Arte de la lengua Aymara. Compuesto por el Padre Diego de Torres Rubio de la Compañia de Iesus. Lima, 1616. 8vo.

2 ARTE, y vocabulario de la lengua Quiehua general de los Indios de el Perú. Que compusó el Padre D. de Torres Rubio, de la Compañia de Jesus, y Añadió el P. J. de Figueredo de la misma compañia. Ahora nuevamente corregido, y aumentado en muchos vocablos. Por un Religioso de la misma compañia, etc. . . . Reimpreſo en Lima, 1754. 8vo.

TREATISES. Eight practical Treatises on the cultivation of the Sugar Cane, written in consequence of the Earl of Elgin's offer of a prize of one hundred pounds, etc. Jamaica, 1843. 8vo.

TRINIDAD STANDARD (THE), and West India Journal. Nos. 119 to 231. Feb. 19th, 1839, to March 17th, 1840. [Wanting Nos. 124, 126 to 29, 133, 135 to 50, 154, 156-57, 159, 161, 168-69, 172-73, 175, 181 to 83, 186-87, 189, 191, 193, 200 to 204, 207-8, 212, 230.] Port of Spain, 1839-40. Fol.

NANUE, JOSEPH HIPOLITO. Guià politica, ecclesiàstica y militar del virreynato del Perù, para el año de 1793. [Lima, 1792.] 8vo.

2 DISCURSO sobre el Panteon que està construyendo en el convento grande de San Francisco el Guardian À Diaz. Lima, 1803. 4to.

3 OBSERVACIONES sobre el clima de Lima y sus influencias en los seres organizados, en especial el hombre. Lima, 1806. 8vo.

UNITED STATES OF AMERICA. [Begins.] Constitucion de los Estados-Unidos de America. [Translated by Dr. Villavicencio.] To which are added. . . Population-returns, etc. [Lima? 1812?] 4to.

ALDIVIA, LUYS DE. Arte y Gramatica general de la lengua que corre en todo el Reyno di Chile, con un Vocabulario, y Confeſsionario. Compuestos por el Padre Luis de Valdivia . . . Iuntamente con la Doctrina Christiana, y Cathecismo del Concilio de Lima . . . y dos traduciones del en la lengua de Chile. 3 parts. Lima, 1606. 8vo.

2 RELACION de lo que sucedió en el Reyno de Chile, despues q̃ el Padre Luys de Valdivia, de la Compañia de Iesus, entrò en el con sus ocho compeñeros Sacerdotes de la misma Compañia, al año de 1612. [Lima? 1613?] Fol.

VALENZUELA, BRUNO DE. Epitome breve de la vida y muerte del ilustriſsimo dotor Don. B. de Almansa . . . Arçobispo de . . . Santa Fè de Bogota . . . Hecho por . . . P. de Solis y Valençuela, . . . sacado de los escritos del Padre Don Bruno de Valenzuela, . . . Lima, 1646. 4°

VASTEY, J. L. DE, Baron. Le Système Colonial dévoilé. Par le Baron de Vastey. Cap-Henry, 1814. 8vo.

2 NOTES a M. le Baron de V. P. Malouet, . . . en refutacion du 4 ème Volume de son Ouvrage, intitulé: " Collection de Mémoires sur les Colonies, et particulièrement su Saint Domingue," etc. . . . Par . . . J. L. Vastey, etc. Cap-Henry, 1814. 8vo.

3 REFLEXIONS sur une lettre de Mazères . . . addreſsée à M. J. C. L.

Sismondé de Sismondi sur les Noirs et les Blancs, la Civilisation de l' Afrique, le Royaume d'Hayti, *etc.* Par le Baron de Vastey. Cap-Henry, 1816. 8vo.

4 REFLEXIONS politiques sur quelques Ouvrages et Journaux Français concernant Hayti. Par Monsieur le Baron de Vastey, Secrétaire du Roi, *etc.* A Sans-Souci, [Port-au-Prince,] 1817. 8vo.

5 ESSAI sur les causes de la Révolution et des guerres civiles d'Hayti, faisant suite aux Réflexions Politiques . . . Par . . . Baron de Vastey, . . . [With an Appendix of documents.] Sans-Souci, [Port-au-Prince,] 1819. 8vo.

VEGA, MANUEL DE LA. Historia del descubrimiento de la América Septentrional por C. Colón escrita por M. de la Vega. Dala a luz con varias notas para mayor inteligencia de la historia de las conquistas de H. Cortés [by F. Lopez de Gomara] que pusó en Mexicano Chimalpain, . . . C. M. de Bustamante. Mexico, 1826. 8vo.

VELASCO, ALONSO ALBERTO DE. Renovacion por si Miſta de la soberana Imagen de Christo Señor . . . que llaman de Ytzimiquilpan . . . colocada en la Iglesia del Convento de San Joseph . . . Ciudad de Mexico. Narracion Historica, . . Dispuesto por el S. Concilio Tridentino el Dᵉʳ Alonso Alberto de Velasco, *etc.* Mexico, 1688. 4to.

VENEZUELA. Sobre la organization y régimen de la Universidad de Caracas. [This is No. 23 of a series; pp. 255-317.] [Caracas, 1827.] 8vo.

2 CONSTITUCION del Estado de Venezuela. Caracas, 1830. 8vo.

3 EXPOSICION que dirige al congreso de Venezuela en 1832 el secretario de hacienda (S. Michelena) sobre los negocios de su cargo. Caracas, [1832] 4to.

4 EXPOSICION que presenta al con-

greso de Venezuela en 1832 el secretario de guerra y marina (C. Soublette) sobre los negocios de su cargo. Caracas, [1832.] 4to.

5 MEMORIA que presenta el Secretario del Interior (A. Narvarte) de los negocios de su departamento al Congreso de 1832. [Caracas, 1832.] 8vo.

6 EXPOSICION que dirige al congreso de Venezuela en 1833, el secretario de hacienda (S. Michelena) sobre los negocios de su cargo. Caracas, [1833.] 8vo.

7 MEMORIAS de los Secretarios de Estado del Gobierno de Venezuela al Congreso en 1841. Contiene tambien el Mensage del Poder Ejectivo y las contestaciones de las Cámaras. 6 parts. [Caracas, 1841.] 8vo.

8 EXPOSICION que dirige al congreso de Venezuela en 1844 el secretario de guerra y marina (R. Ardaneta). Caracas, 1844. 8vo.

9 MEMORIA que presenta a la legislatura de 1845 el ministro de relaciones exteriores del gobierno de Venezuela. (J. M. Manrique.) Caricas, 1845. 8vo.

VERA CRUZ. Constitucion politica del estado libre de Veracruz, sancionada por su congreso constituyente, en 3 de Junio de 1825. Jalapa, 1825. 4to.

2 MANIFIESTO del congreso de Veracruz a la nacion Mexicana. Mexico, 1827. Fol.

VERGARA, ANTONIO CAMILO. [*Begins*] Exortacion del D.D.A.C. Vergara, cura rector de la parroquia de San Lazaro y asociado à la orden del Sol, a sus amados feligreses. Lima, [1830 ?] Fol.

VETANCURT, AUGUSTIN DE. Vida, y Favores del Rey del cielo hechos al glorioso Patriarcha Señor San Joseph ; . . . padre putativo de Christo . . . trasuntada de las obras de la. V. M. Maria de Jesus de Agreda, y otros Autores por . . . Augustin de Vetancurt, *etc.* Mexico, 1700. 4to.

VICTORIA, Guadalupe. Derrotero de las islas Antillas, de las costas de Tierra Firme, y de las del seno Mexicano, corregido y aumentado y con un apéndice sobre las correntes del oceano Atlantico, etc. Mexico, 1828. 8°

VIDAURRE, Manuel L. de. Discurso contra la modificacion que presentaron los Ss. incargados del projecto de constitucion. Lima, 1827. 4to.

2 Discurso pronunciado por M. L. de V. ante la representacion nacional sobre la cuestion de legitimidad de las elecciones hechas por el anterior gobierno para las mitras vacantes en la republica. Lima, 1827. 4to.

VIGIL, Francisco de Paula G. A sus conciudadanos el disputado Vigil. Lima, 1833. 4to.

2 Defensa de la autoridad de los gobiernos y de los obispos contra las pretensiones de la Curia Romana. Prima parte. Tom. 1—6. [No more appears to have been published.] Lima, 1848-49. 4to.

3 Adiciones de la Defensa de la Autoridad de los Gobiernos contra las pretensiones de la Curia Romana. Lima, 1852. 4to.

4 Carta al Papa y analisis del Breve de 10 de Junio de 1851. . . . Segunda edicion. Lima, 1852. 8vo.

5 Compendio de la Defensa de la Autoridad de las Gobiernos contra las pretensiones de la Curia Romana. Lima, 1852. 4to.

VILLADA, Vicente Jose. Esposicion documentada de la instalacion y estado actual del colegio y escudas Lancasterianas del instituto literario del Estado libre y soberano de Mexico, en San Augustin de las Cuevas. [Mexico,] 1827. 8vo.

VILLAGOMEZ, Pedro de, Archbishop of Lima. Carta pastoral de exortacion e instruccion contra las idolatrias, de los Indios del Arcobispado de Lima por . . . Don Pedro de

Villagomez. A sus visatadores de las idolatrias, y a sus vicarios, y curas de las doctrinas de Indios. Lima, 1649. Fol.

VILLALOBOS, Baltasar de. Metodo de curar Tabardillos, y descripcion de la Fiebre epedemica, que por los años de 1796 y 97 afligió varias problaciones del partido de Chancay. Se pone al fin un Apendice que enseña el modo de exterminar en brevisimo tiempo toda Calentura intermitente. Lima, 1800. 4to.

VILLARAN, Emmanuel Gaspar de. Theses ex universa Theologia de promptæ. Præs J. de Zavalo y Peña. Limæ, [1805.] 4to.

2 Theses de Theologia Prolegomenis et fontibus quarum propugnationem . . . suscipient . . . B. Figueroa J. Landazuri, A. Rato, M. Taboada, J. Hevia, J. Fernandini, D. Mendiola, J. Gomes, P. Cano. Limæ, [1817.] 8vo.

VILLARAN, Manuel, and Devoti, Felix. Discursos pronunciados en la Real Universidad de San Marcos en ocasion del acto literario dedicado por esta à los ilustres militares que defendieron la Plaza y puerto del Callao en las invasiones de la esquadra insurgente de Chile. [Lima,] 1819. 4to.

VILLA-SEÑOR Y SANCHEZ, Jose Antonio de. Respuesta . . . à favor de la Real Hacienda . . . en que defiende no ser el precio del Azogue, el que dà motivo à que no se costeen las Minas de cortas leyes. Mexico, 1742. 4to.

2 Theatro Americano, descripcion general de los Reynos y Provincias de la Nueva-España, y sus juridicciones. 2 parts. Mexico, 1746-48. Fol.

VILLAVICENCIO, Juan Joseph de. Vida, y virtudes de el venerable, y apostolico padre Juan de Ugarte de la compañia de Jesus, missionero de las Islas Californias, y uno de sus primeros conquestadores. Mexico, 1752. 4to.

VIRGILIUS MARO, Publius. Los cuatro primeros libros de la Eneida de Virgilio traducidos del Francés [of N. F. Le Blond de Saint Martin] en Castellano . . . por C. M. de Bustamante. Mexico, 1830. 12°

VIVES, Francesco Dionisio. Bando de buen gobierno adicionado por . . . F. D. Vives presidente . . . de esta . . . ciudad é isla de Cuba, *etc.* Habana, 1828. 8vo.

VOZ DE LA PATRIA. [Edited by C. M. de Bustamante.] Tom. 2-5. [Tom. 4 has a supplement with a distinct title page: Mexico por dentro y fuera bajo el Gobierno de los Vireyes.] By B. L. M. de V. Mexico, 1830, 31. 4°

ATT, Alexander. A new theory of optics, as regards refraction of dense media and vision. [Kingston,] Jamaica, 1825, 8vo.

2 A new theory of physical astronomy, established upon Analogy and the Laws of Chemical Action. [Kingston,] Jamaica, 1825. 8vo.

WEEKLY REGISTER (The). Nos. 1285 to 1355. Dec. 11th, 1838 —April 14th, 1840. [Wanting Nos. 1 to 1284, 1286 to 1306, 1333 and all after 1355.] Saint John's 1839-40. Fol.

WEST INDIAN. The Rev. Mr. Cooper and his Calumnies against Jamaica, particularly his late pamphlet in reply to facts verified on oath. By a West Indian. Jamaica, 1825. 8°

2 Notes in defence of the Colonies. On the increase and decrease of the slave population of the British West Indies. By a West Indian. Jamaica, 1826. 8°

WEST INDIAN. No. 547. Bridgetown, [Barbadoes,] 1839. Fol.

WILES (James). Hortus Eastensis : or, a Catalogue of exotic plants cultivated in the Botanic Garden in the Mountains of Liguanea, in Jamaica, 1826. 4to.

WILSON, Belford Hinton. Documents relating to Steam Navigation in the Pacific. Lima, 1836. Fol.

WRIGHT, Benjamin H. Informe sobre el camino de hierro de Puerto-Principe a Nuevitas. Puerto-Principe, 1837. 4to.

AVIER DE ECHAGUE, Francisco. Carta Pastoral del Gobernador Eclesiastico del Arzobispado de Lima, dirigida á los parrocos y Clero. Lima, 1825. 4to.

XIMENES, Salvador, *Bishop of Popayan.* Carta pastoral que el . . . obispo de Popayan, dirige a sus diocesanos para manfestarles la obcecacion . . . de los partidarios de la rebelion . . . y exhortales a la fidelidad . . . debida a . . . Fernando VII. Lima, 1820. 12mo.

2 Carta pastoral . . . con motivo de su regreso á la Capital de su obispado despues de las agitaciones politicas. Año de 1822. [Popayan,] 1823. 12mo.

., Y. Y. de. Carta escrita por en párroco del obispado de Puebla [Signed Y. Y. de Y.] sobre la encíclica de . . . Leon XII. á los señores arzobispos de América, inserta en la Gazeta de México del miércoles 6 de Julio de 1825. [Mexico, 1825.] 4to.

YANACOCHA. La batalla de Yanacocha, canta lirico. Paz de Ayacucho, 1835. 8vo.

YUCATAN. [*Begins*]. Por los

hijos y nietos de conquistadores de Yucatan, sobre la confirmacion que piden de las ayudas de costa que las Gouernadores les han señalado, etc. [Yucatan? 1614.] Fol.

2 MEMORIAS de estadistica remitidas por el gobierno de Yucatan, a la Camara de Senadores del soberano congreso general con arreglo al articulo 161 numero 8º de la constitucion Federal de los Estados Unidos Mexicanos. [Merida de Yucatan,] 1827. 8vo.

3 COLLECION de leyes, decretos y ordenes del augusto Congreso del Estado libre de Yucatan... Segunda Edicion. Correjida y aumentada por una comision nombrada por la sesta Lejislatura constitucional. 2 tom. Merida, 1832. 8vo.

4 PROYECTO que comprende la division del territorio del Estado... de Yucatan, presentado al... congreso en la session... del... 21 de Setiembre de 1840. Merida de Yucatan, 1840. 16mo.

5 CONSTITUCION política del Estado de Yucatan, sancionada en 31 de Marzo de 1841. Merida de Yucatan, 1841. 16mo.

6 CONSTITUCION política del Estado de Yucatan, sancionada en 31 de Marzo de 1841. Merida de Yucatan, 1841. 8vo.

7 DICTAMEN de la comision especial nombrada por la Augusta camera de disputados para el asunto de independencia. Merida de Yucatan, 1841. 8vo.

8 MEMORIA presentada al Augusta congreso del estado de Yucatan, por el secretario general de gobierno en 29 y 30 de Setiembre de 1841. Merida de Yucatan. Fol.

9 PROYECTO de bases para la regeneracion politica de la republica presentado a la Legislatura de Yucatan, por su comision de reformas. Merida de Yucatan, 1841. 8vo.

10 [Begins] SECRETARIA general de gobierno. El gobernador del Estado de Yucatan, á sus habitantes,

sabed: que el Congreso ha decretado el siquiente Reglamento para el gobierno interior de los pueblos, etc. [Signed by A. Ibarra de Leon.] [Merida de Yucatan, 1841.] 8vo.

11 PROTESTA de Yucatan, contra las violencias del gobierno provisorio de Mexico dirigida al congreso constituyente de la república. [Signed S. Mendez.] Merida de Yucatan, 1842. 8vo.

12 REGLAMENTO de la milicia local del Estado de Yucatan. Merida de Yucatan, 1842. 16mo.

13 REPRESENTACION que el gobernador de Yucatan (S. Méndez, dirige al congreso constituyente de la Republica Mejicana en complimiento del acuerdo de la legislatura del Estado, de 2 de Junio de 1842. Merida de Yucatan, 1842. 8vo.

YUCATANESE. Observaciones sobre las iniciativas que han dirigido el Congreso General la honorable legislatura de Queretaro y la comision permanente de la de Jalasio, relativas a los negocios de Yucatan; y por apéndice, una coleccion de los opúsculos y articulos que se han publicado sobre este mismo asunto en el presente año. [By Un Yucateco, i.e. T. M. Gutierrez de Estrado?] Mejico, 1831. 8vo.

ACATECAS. Constitucion política del Estado libre de Zacatecas. Guadalajara, 1825. 12mo.

2 MEMORIA en que el gobierno del estado libre de los Zacatecas, da cuenta de los ramos de su administracion al congreso del mismo estado, con arreglo à lo dispuesto en el articulo 74 de la constitucion. Zacatecas, 1827. Fol.

3 DECRETO sobre el establicimiento de un banco en la capital del estado, con notas... Representacion del cabildo eclesiastico de Guadalajara contra dicho decreto, con notas diri-

gidas á refutar los errores y suposi-
ciones de aquella corporacion, *etc.*
Zacatecas, 1830.   4to.

ZAVALA, Lorenzo de, and Lobato, Jose Maria. Mejicanos: *etc.*

[A congratulatory addreſs to the
Mexicans on the ſucceſs of their
revolution.   Signed L. de Z. and J.
M. Lobato.]   Mexico, 1828.   Fol.

Finis.

CATALOGUE

OF THE

AMERICAN MAPS

IN THE LIBRARY OF

The BRITISH MUSEUM at

CHRISTMAS 1856

By HENRY STEVENS Gmb Ma Frgs Etc.

LONDON

Printed by CHARLES WHITTINGHAM at the
Chiswick Press for Henry Stevens
IV trafalgar square
MdcccLxvi

CATALOGUE OF AMERICAN MAPS
IN THE LIBRARY OF THE
BRITISH MUSEUM.

Chriſtmas, 1856.

LBANY, *New York.* Map of the Vicinity of Albany and Troy, from original Surveys by J. C. Sidney, aſsisted by W. Arrott. 2 sheets. [Philadel.?] 1851.

ALLEGHANY COUNTY, *Maryland.* Map of part of Alleghany County, Maryland, shewing the Coal Region and Proposed Railroad from the Mines of the Maryland Mining Company to the Basin of the Chesapeake and Ohio Canal at the Town of Cumberland. Copied and correcĭed by C. N. Hagner. Baltimore [1820?]

ALLEGHANY COUNTY, *Pennsylvania.* Map of Alleghany County, Pennsylvania, with the names of property holders, from acĭual surveys by Sidney and Neff and S. M. Rea. (View of the Court House, Pittsburg.) 2 sheets. Philadelphia, 1851.

ALLENTOWN. Plan of the Borough of Allentown, Lehigh County, Pennsylvania, from original Surveys

by A. E. Rogerson. 2 sheets. [Philadelphia?] 1850.

AMERICAN PILOT, containing the navigation of the Sea Coast of North America. Boston, 1803. Fol.

ARCTIC EXPEDITION. A Chart illustrative of the Cruise of the American Arcĭic Expedition in search of Sir J. Franklin in the years 1850 and '51· Fitted out by H. Grinnell, Esq. of New York, commanded by E. J. de Haven. . . Compiled by . . G. P. Welsh under the direcĭion of F. M. Maury. [New York, 1851?]

ATLANTIC OCEAN, *North.* Wind and Current Chart of the North Atlantic. By M I. Maury. Compiled from materials in the Bureau of Ordnance and Hydrography. . Drawn by Lieut. W. B. Whiting. 8 sheets. Washington, 1848.

2 WIND and Current Chart of the North Atlantic. By M. I. Maury. . . Compiled from materials in the Bureau of Ordnance and Hydrography. Drawn by Lieut. W. B. Whiting. 8 sheets. Washington, 1848. Fol.

3 THE SAME. 3rd edition. Series A. Washington, 1850. Fol.

4 PILOT CHART of the North Atlantic. By M. F. Maury. 2 sheets. Washington, 1849.

ATLANTIC OCEAN, South. Wind and Current Chart of the South Atlantic. By M. I. Maury. 4 sheets. Washington, 1848. Fol.

2 PILOT Chart of the South Atlantic. By M. F. Maury. [Washington,] 1850.

ATLAS. A new and elegant General Atlas; containing maps of each of the United States [of America]. Baltimore [1812?] 4to.

2 A COMPLETE Historical, Chronological, and Geographical American Atlas, being a guide to the History of North and South America and the West Indies, exhibiting an accurate account of the Discovery, Settlement, and Progrefs of their various Kingdoms, States, Provinces, etc. together with the wars, celebrated Battles and remarkable events to the year 1822. According to the plan of Le Sage's Atlas, and intended as a companion to Lavoisne's Improvement of that celebrated work. [Published by] H. C. Carey and I. Lea. Philadelphia, 1823.

3 A COMPLETE Historical, Chronological, and Geographical American Atlas, etc. etc. Published by H. C. Carey and I. Lea. 3rd edition. Philadelphia, London, Leipzig, and Paris, 1827.

4 AN ILLUSTRATED Atlas, Geographical, Statistical, and Historical, of the United States and the Adjacent Countries. By T. G. Bradford. Boston and Cincinnati, 1838. Fol.

5 SMILEY's Atlas for the use of Schools and Families. Boston, 1838.

6 A UNIVERSAL, Illustrated Atlas, exhibiting a Geographical, Statistical, and Historical View of the World. Edited by T. G. Bradford and S. G. Goodrich. Boston, 1842. Fol.

ATTLEBOROUGH. Map of Attleborough, Bristol County, Massa-

chusetts, from original Surveys by H. F. Walling. [Philadelphia?] 1850.

BALTIMORE. Map of the City and County of Baltimore, Maryland, from original surveys by I. C. Sidney and P. I. Browne. 2 sheets. Baltimore, 1850.

2 PLAN of the City of Baltimore, Maryland. Compiled from records and surveys by Sidney and Neff. 2 sheets. Camden, New Jersey, 1851.

BATH. Map of the compact part of the City of Bath, Lincoln County, Maine, from original surveys under the direction of H. F. Walling. [New York?] 1851.

BELLE VUE. Map of Bellevue, near Niagara Falls, New York. 1847. C. B. Stuart, Agent. P. S. Duval, lith. [New York? 1848?]

BETHLEHEM. Plan of the Township of Bethlehem, Northampton County, Pennsylvania. Surveyed by J. C. Sidney. Philadelphia, 1850.

BLACK ROCK HARBOUR. Harbors of Black Rock and Bridgeport. Founded upon a Trigonometrical Survey under the direction of F. R. Hafsler. . . Triangulation by I. Ferguson. Topography by C. M. Eakin. Hydrography by the party under the command of Lieut. G. S. Blake. A. D. Bache, Superintendent. Verified by A. A. Humphreys. With some additions by I. M. Wampler. New York, 1848.

BLOCKLEY. Map of Blockley Township, including all Public Places, Property Owners, etc. Original Surveys by S. M. Rea and I. Miller. Philadelphia [1850?]

BOSTON. Map of the City and Vicinity of Boston, Massachusetts, from original Surveys by F. G. Sidney. 2 sheets. Boston, 1852.

2 PLAN of the City of Boston and immediate neighbourhood, from ac-

tual Surveys by H. M'Intyre. 4 sheets. Boston and Philadelphia, 1852.

BRASIL. Pilot Chart of the Coast of Brazil. By Lieut. M. F. Maury. 1849. Second edition. Washington, 1850.

BRIDGEPORT, *Connecticut*. Extract from the United States Coast Survey. F. R. Haßler, Superintendent. Harbour of Bridgeport, Connecticut. Surveyed Nov. 1835, by A. D. Mackey, G. S. Blake, O. Tod, B. I. Moeller, T. A. Budd, and T. A. M. Craven. Drawn by T. A. M. Craven. [Washington? 1835?]

BRISTOL COUNTY, *Maßachusetts*. Map of Bristol County, Massachusetts, based on the trigonometrical Survey of the State, the details from original surveys under the direction of H. F. Walling. (Map of the City of New Bedford and the Village of Fair Haven.) 2 sheets. New Bedford, 1851.

BRISTOL COUNTY, *Rhode Island*. Map of Bristol County, Rhode Island, from original Surveys under the direction of H. F. Walling. (Plans of Warren and Bristol Villages.) Providence, 1851.

BURLINGTON COUNTY, *New Jersey*. Map of Burlington County, mostly from original surveys by I. W. Otley and R. Whiteford. (Plans of the City of Burlington and the town of Mount Holly.) 3 sheets. Philadelphia, 1849.

CALIFORNIA. A Series of Charts with sailing directions, embracing Surveys of the Farallones, Entrance to the Bay of San Francisco, Bays of San Francisco and San Pablo, Straits of Carquines and Luisun Bay, Confluence and Deltic branches of the Sacramento and San Joaquin Rivers and the Sacramento River (with the Middle Fork) to the American River, including the Cities of Sacramento and Boston, State of California. By C. Ringgold, aßisted by S. F. Blunt, S. R. Knox, W. P. Humphreys, I. H. Rowe, E. Cullberg, T. A. Emmet. Constructed, projected, and drawn, by F. D. Stuart, aßisted by C. Everett, A. H. Campbell, and J. Tyssowski. Fourth edition, with additions. Washington, 1852. 8vo.

CAMDEN. Map of the City of Camden, New Jersey, from original surveys by J. C. Sidney. Philadelphia, 1851.

CANADA. Map of the Provinces of Canada, New Brunswick, Nova Scotia, Newfoundland, and Prince Edward Island, with a large section of the United States, and exhibiting the Boundary of the British Dominions in North America according to the treaties of 1842 and 6. Compiled from the latest and most approved astronomical observations, authorities, and recent surveys. By I. Bouchette. A Roll. 6 sheets. New York, 1846.

2 MAP of the Eastern portion of British North America, including the Gulf of St. Lawrence and part of the New England States, compiled . . by H. F. Perley. N[ew] Y[ork], 1853.

CANALS. Map and Profile of the Proposed Canal from Lake Erie to Hudson River . . constructed by direction of the Canal Commißioners from the Maps of the Engineers in 1817. [New York? 1817?]

2 GEOLOGICAL Profile extending from the Atlantic to Lake Erie. . By A. Eaton. [New York, 1825.]

3 SURVEY for a Ship Canal around the Falls of Niagara, made under the direction of W. G. Williams, Capt. United States Topographical Engineers, aßisted by Lieuts. T. F. Drayton and I. G. Reed. Drawn by Capt. Williams and Lieut. White. [Washington?] 1835.

4 SURVEY for a Ship Canal around the Falls of Niagara, made and drawn

under the direction of Captain W.
G. Williams, United States Topographical Engineers, by Lieuts. T. F.
Drayton and I. G. Reed, United States
Army. 2 sheets. [Washing.? 1835?]

5 Survey for Ship Canal round
Niagara Falls. Profiles levelled and
surveyed under direction of Captain
W. G. Williams, United States Topographical Engineers, by Lieutenants
Drayton and Reed. Line, N° 1. from
Porter's Storehouse to Niagara River
at Lewiston. Drawn by Lieut. Drayton. Line, N° 1 [2, 3, and] 4. 3
sheets. [Washington? 1835?]

6 Survey for a Ship Canal to connect the Lakes Erie and Ontario.
Lockport Route surveyed under the
direction of Captain W. G. Williams,
United States Topographical Engs.
by Lieuts. T. F. Drayton and I. G.
Reed. 1835. 2 sheets. [Washington!] 1835.

7 [Plan of the Maryland Canal.]
[Baltimore? 1845?]

CAPTAINS ISLAND. Harbors
of Captains Island East and Captains
Island West, from a trigonometrical
survey under the direction of F. R.
Hasler . . . triangulation by J. Ferguson. . . . Topography by C. M.
Eakin. . . Hydrography by the party
under the command of Lieut. G. S.
Blake. Washington, 1849.

CAT AND SHIP ISLAND. Harbors from a trigonometrical Survey
under the direction of A. D. Bache. . .
Main triangulation by F. H. Yerdes.
Secondary Triangulation by J. E.
Hilgard. Topography by W. E.
Greenwell. Hydrography by the
party under the command of C. P.
Patterson. Washington, 1850.

CENTRAL AMERICA. A New
Map of Central America, shewing the
different lines of Atlantic and Pacific
Communication. (Isthmus of Panama. Map of the Isthmus of Tehuantepec in the Republic of Mexico.)
Published by I. Disturnell. New
York, 1850.

CLAREMONT. Map of the Town
of Claremont, Sullivan County, New
Hampshire, from surveys under the
direction of H. F. Walling. [Philadelphia?] 1851.

CLEVELAND. Map of the City
of Cleveland, Cuyahoga County?
Ohio. Surveyed, drawn, and published by John Slatter and B. Callan.
4 sheets. Philadelphia, 1852.

COLUMBIA COUNTY. Map of
Columbia County, New York. (Plan
of Chatham Four Corners. Plan of
the City of Hudson) from actual surveys by J. W. Otley; . . assisted by
F. W. Keenan. 2 sheets. Philadelphia, 1851.

CONCORD, *New Hampshire*.
Map of the Village of Concord, Merrimack County, New Hampshire,
from original surveys under the direction of H. F. Walling. J. Hanson,
Assistant Engineer. Concord, 1851.

CONNECTICUT. An improved
Reference Map of the Valley of the
Connecticut and Western Station of
New England. (Profile of the Farmington, and Hampshire and Hampden
Canals.) Surveys by D. Hurd, Esq.
Chief Engineer. Published by P.
Pierce. 2 sheets. New Haven, 1828.

DANVERS. Map of the Town
of Danvers, Massachusetts. By
H. M'Intyre. Philadelphia, 1852.

DELAWARE. A Map of the
State of Delaware, from original surveys. By I. Price and S. M. Rea,
assisted by H. Paxson. 2 sheets.
Philadelphia, 1850.

DELAWARE COUNTY. Map of
Delaware County, Pennsylvania. By
I. W. Ash, M.D. From original
Surveys, with the farm limits. 4
sheets. Philadelphia, 1848.

DIGHTON. Map of the Town
of Dighton, Massachusetts, from
Surveys by H. F. Walling. 2 sheets.
[Philadelphia?] 1850.

· DOVER, *New Hampshire*. Map of the Towns of Dover, Somersworth, and Rollinsford, Strafford County, New Hampshire, from original Surveys under the direction of H. F. Walling. J. Hanson, Assistant Engineer. [With Plans of the Villages of Great Falls, Salmon Falls, and Dover.] [New York?] 1851.

DUTCHESS COUNTY. Map of Dutchess County, New York, from original Surveys [by] J. C. Sidney. (Plan of Poughkeepsie.) Philadelphia, 1850.

EASTON. Plan of the Town of Easton, Northampton County, Pennsylvania, from original surveys by J. C. Sidney. Philadelphia, 1850.

EDGARTOWN HARBOUR. Edgartown Harbour. Founded upon a Trigonometrical Survey under the direction of A. D. Bache. . . Triangulation by C. M. Eakin. Topography by H. L. Whiting. Hydrography by the party under the command of Lieut. C. H. Davis. Views by O. A. Lawson. Verified by A. A. Humphreys. New York, 1848.

ERIE CANAL. Map illustrative of a Communication between the Great Lakes and Atlantic Ocean, by means of a Canal from Lake Erie to Hudson's River. By J. H. Eddy. [New York?] 1816.

ESSEX COUNTY. Map of Essex County, New Jersey, with the names of Property Holders, *etc.* from actual Surveys by I. C. Sidney. (Plan of the City of Newark.) 2 sheets. Newark, 1850.

FALL RIVER. Map of the Town of Fall River, Bristol County, Massachusetts. From Surveys by H. F. Walling. [Boston?] 1850.

FISHER'S ISLAND SOUND, founded upon a trigonometrical survey under the direction of F. R.

Hassler. . . Triangulation by W. H. Swift. Hydrography by the party under the command of G. S. Blake. Topography by F. H. Gerdes. Republished in 1847, with additions. [Washington,] 1847.

FITCHBURY. Map of the Town of Fitchbury, Massachusetts, from original Surveys under the direction of H. F. Walling. . . J. Hanson, Assistant Engineer. Philadelphia, 1851.

FLORIDA. Map of the Territory of Florida, from its Northern Boundary to Lat. 27° 30′ N. Connected with the Delta of the Mississippi. Annexed to the report of the Board of Internal Improvement, dated Feb. 19th, 1829, relating to the Canal contemplated to connect the Atlantic with the Gulf of Mexico; and describing the Inland Navigation parallel to the Coast from the Mississippi to the Bay of Espiritu Santo; and from St. Mary's Harbour to St. Augustine. Drawn and compiled by W. H. Swift, Lt. Artillery. [Washington? 1830?]

2 A MAP of the Seat of War in Florida. 1836. [Washington?] 1836.

3 MAP of the Seat of War in East Florida. Compiled from various data in the United States Topographical Bureau, under the direction of Col. I. I. Abert, United States Topographical Engineer, by W. H. Hood. 2 sheets. [Washington?] 1837.

4 MAP of the Seat of War in Florida. Compiled by order of the Honorable I. R. Poinsett, Secretary of War, under the direction of Col. I. I. Abert, United States Topographical Engineer, from the reconnoissances of the officers of the United States Army by W. Hood. Bureau of United States Topographical Engineers. Washington, 1838.

FLORIDA CHANNEL. Map of the Straits of Florida and Gulf of Mexico, to accompany a report from the Treasury Department by I. D. Andrews, in obedience to the resolution of the Senate of March 8th, 1851, from the archives of the United States Coast Survey. A. D. Bache, Superintendent. [New York?] 1852.

GALIEN, RIVER. Survey of the mouth of Galien River, Michigan. Surveyed by Lieuts. I. M. Berrien and E. Rose. Drawn by Lieut. Berrien. [Washington?] 1835.

GEOLOGY simplified and illustrated, with appropriate Views of the Scenery of each formation, chiefly from recent accurate sketches by P. Brannon, and explanatory and descriptive Tables by P. Brannon and T. Downes Bennett. Boston and Southampton, 1845.

GEORGIA. North and South Carolina and Georgia. [Map shewing the internal navigation.] [Philadelphia, 1826.]

GERMANTOWN, *Pennsylvania.* Map of the Township of Germantown. By I. C. Sidney. Philadel. [1850?]
2 MAP of the Township of Germantown, Philadelphia County, Pennsylvania, from actual and other surveys by A. E. Rogerson and E. J. Murphy. 2 sheets. [Philadelphia?] 1851.

GETTYSBURG. Plan of the Town of Gettysburg, Adams County, Pennsylvania, from actual survey by J. C. Sidney. [Philadelphia?] 1850.

GOSHEN TOWNSHIPS, *Pennsylvania.* Map of the East and West Goshen Townships and the Borough of West Chester [with views of the] Court House and Chester County Bank. Published by Smith and Wistar. Philadelphia, 1849.

GREAT SALT LAKE. Map of the Great Salt Lake and adjacent Country in the Territory of Utah, surveyed in 1849 and 1850, under the orders of Col. J. J. Abert by Capt. H. Stansbury .. aided by Lieut. J. W. Gunnison and A. Carrington.

Drawn by Lieut. Gunnison and C. Preuß. Philadelphia, 1852.

HARRISBURG, *Pennsylvania.* Plan of the Borough of Harrisburg, Dauphin County, Pennsylvania, from original surveys by J. C. Sidney. Philadelphia, 1850.

HART ISLAND. Hart and City Island Harbor of Refuge .. (Sachem's Head Harbor), from a trigonometrical survey under the direction of A. D. Bache. [Washington,] 1851.

HATTERAS INLET. Reconnoissance of Hatteras Inlet Harbor of Refuge, coast of North Carolina. By the Hydrographic party under the command of T. A. Jenkins. [Washington,] 1850.

HAVERHILL. Map of the Town of Haverhill, Essex County, Mass. from surveys under the direction of Henry F. Walling. [New York?] 1851.

HELL GATE and its approaches, from a Trigonometrical Survey under the direction of F. R. Haßler and A. D. Bache. Triangulation by E. Blunt. Topography by H. L. Whiting. Hydrography by the parties under the command of D. D. Porter and M. Woodhull. [New York,] 1851.

HOLMES HOLE. The Harbor of Holmes Hole, founded upon a Trigonometrical Survey under the direction of A. D. Bache... Triangulation by C. M. Eakin. Topography by H. L. Whiting. Hydrography by the party under the command of G. S. Blake. New York, 1847.

HUDSON RIVER. Panorama of the Hudson River, from New York to Albany. Drawn from nature and engraved by W. Wade. New York, 1845.
2 PANORAMA of the Hudson River, from New York to Albany. Drawn from nature, and engraved by W. Wade. New York, 1846. 12°

HUNTINGTON BAY, founded upon a Trigonometrical Survey under the direction of F. R. Hafsler. . . . Triangulation by E. Blunt. Topography by F. H. Gerdes. Hydrography by the party under the command of G. S. Blake. [Washington,] 1849.

ILLINOIS and Mifsouri. [Map showing the internal navigation.] [Philadelphia, 1826.]

INDIANA. Plan of the Northern Boundary Line of the State of Indiana. [Washington ? 1831 ?]

ISRAELITES. Map of the Journey of the Children of Israel from Egypt through the Desert to the Holy Land, and the dividing of the same into the twelve Tribes by their Lawgiver Moses, according to Scripture. With a portrait of the author, Rabbi Jachiel Bar Joseph. *Heb.* N[ew] Y[ork,] 1840.

JACKSON COUNTY, *Michigan.* Map of Jackson County, published under the direction of D. Houghton, . . S. W. Higgins, Topographer to Geological Survey, C. C. Douglafs and B. Hubbard, Afsistant Geologists. Detroit 1850]

JERUSALEM. Map of Jerusalem, from actual Survey by F. Catherwood, with additions and corrections from later Travellers, and from personal observation by J. P. Durbin. 2 sheets. [With an explanation.] Philadelphia [1850?]

JORDAN RIVER. Map of the River Jordan and the Dead Sea, and the Route of the Party under the command of Lieut. W. F. Lynch, United States Navy. Constructed under his superintendence by . . R. Aulick, . . from the joint labours of Lieut. Dale and himself. Drawn by G. Strickland. [London, 1849.]

KENTUCKY and Tennefsee. [Map showing the internal navigation.] [Philadelphia, 1826.]

LEAVENWORTH, *Fort.* Map of a Reconnaifsance between Fort Leavenworth, on the Mifsouri River, and the Great Salt Lake, in the Territory of Utah, made in 1849 and 1850, under the orders of Col. J. J. Abert, by Capt. Howard Stanbury, . . aided by Lieut. J. W. Gunnison and A. Carrington. Drawn by Lieut. Gunnison and C. Preufs. [This Map belongs to Stansbury's expedition to the Valley of the Great Salt Lakes of Utah. Philadelphia, 1852. 8°] Philadelphia, 1852.

LENAWEE COUNTY, *Michigan.* Map of Lenawee County, published under the direction of D. Houghton, S. W. Higgins, Topographer to Geological Survey, C. C. Douglafs and B. Hubbard, Afsistant Geologists. Washington [1850?]

LITCHFIELD. Map of the Town of Litchfield, Litchfield County, Connecticut. Surveyed and drawn by E. M. Woodford. 2 sheets. Philadelphia, 1852.

LITTLE EGG HARBOUR, founded upon a Trigonometrical Survey under the direction of F. R. Hafsler. . . Triangulation by C. Renard. . . Topography by G. M. Bache and B. F. Sands, and C. Renard. Hydrography by G. M. Baches. Verified by A. A. Humphreys. New York, 1846.

LIVINGSTON COUNTY. Map of Livingston County, New York, from actual Surveys by Rea and Otley. [With plans of the villages of Yeneseo, Mount Morris, Lima, Nunda and Dansville.] 2 sheets. Philadelphia, 1852.

LYNN. Plan of the City of Lynn, Mafsachusetts, from actual Surveys by H. M'Intyre. Philadelphia, 1852.

MAINE. Atlas accompanying Greenleaf's Map and Statistical Survey of Maine. Portland, 1829. Fol.

2 MAP of the Northern Part of the State of Maine, and of the adjacent British Provinces; showing the portion of that State to which Great Britain lays claim. Reduced from the official Map A. With corrections from the latest surveys, by S. L. Dashiell. Washington, 1830.

MARYLAND. [A mineralogical and geological outline Map of Maryland.] [Baltimore? 1835?]

2 MAP of the State of Maryland. Constructed .. by F. Lucás, jun. 4 sheets. Baltimore, 1841.

MIDDLESEX COUNTY. Map of Middlesex County, New Jersey. Entirely from original Surveys by J. W. Otley and J. Keily, assisted by the late A. C. Stansbie. (Plans of Perth, Amboy City and New Brunswick.) 2 sheets. Camden [1850?].

MIDDLETOWN. Map of the City of Middletown, Connecticut, from original surveys by R. Whiteford. Philadelphia, 1851.

MINNESOTA. Map of the Territory of Minnesota, exhibiting the route of the expedition to the Red River of the North, in the summer of 1849. By Capt. J. Pope. [Washington? 1850?]

MISSISSIPPI, Alabama, and Louisiana. [Map showing the internal navigation.] [Philadelphia, 1826.]

2 MAP, Plan, and Profiles annexed to the Report on a Canal destined to connect the Mississippi with Lake Pontchartrain. Drawn by Capt. W. T. Pouskin, Topographical Engineer. Georgetown, 1827.

3 HYDROGRAPHICAL Basin of the Upper Mississippi River, from astronomical and barometrical observations, surveys and information by J. N. Nicollet, in the years 1836, 37, 38, 39 and 40; assisted in 1838, 39 and 40 by Lieut. J. C. Fremont... Reduced and compiled under the direction of Col. J. J. Abert .. by Lieut. W. H. Emory. [Washington,] 1843.

MOBILE BAY. Entrance to Mobile Bay, from a trigonometrical survey under the direction of A. D. Bache. Main triangulation by F. H. Gerdes. Secondary triangulation by R. W. Fauntleroy. Topography by W. E. Greenwell. Hydrography by the party under the command of C. P. Patterson. [New York,] 1851.

MONMOUTH COUNTY. Map of Monmouth County, New Jersey, from original surveys. J. Lightfoot, Surveyor. (Plans of Freehold, Middletown Point, and Red Bank.) 2 sheets. Middletown Point, 1851.

MONROE COUNTY. Map of Monroe County, New York, by P. J. Browne. (Map of Brockport village.) 2 sheets. Addison, 1852.

MONTGOMERY COUNTY. Map of Montgomery County, Pennsylvania, from original surveys under the direction of W. E. Morris. (Plan of the Borough of Pottstown. Plan and view of the Borough of Norristown.] Philadelphia, 1849.

NANTUCKET HARBOR, from a trigonometrical survey under the direction of A. D. Bache... Triangulation by A. D. Bache and C. M. Eakin. Topography by H. L. Whiting... Hydrography by the party under the command of C. H. Davis. [Washington,] 1848.

NAZARETH. Map of the Townships of Upper and Lower Nazareth, Northampton County, Pennsylvania. By J. C. Sidney. Philadelphia, 1850.

NEW BEDFORD, *Massachusetts*. The Harbour of New Bedford, founded upon a trigonometrical survey under the direction of A. D. Bache. Triangulation by C. M. Eakin. Topography by H. L. Whiting. Hydrography under the direction of G. S. Blake. Verified by Lieut. A. A. Humphreys. New York, 1846.

NEW BRUNSWICK. Map of the City of New Brunswick, New

Jersey, from actual surveys by J. C. Sidney. Philadelphia, 1850.

NEW CASTLE COUNTY. Map of New Castle County, Delaware, from original surveys by S. M. Rea and J. Price. (Plan of the City of Wilmington.) 2 sheets. Philadelphia, 1849.

NEW ENGLAND COASTING PILOT, from Sandy Point of New York unto Cape Canso, in Nova Scotia, and all the Island Breton, the harbour of Louisbourg and forts, etc. By Capt. C. Southack. [New York? 1710?]

NEW HAVEN, Connecticut. New Haven Harbor. Founded upon a trigonometrical survey under the direction of F. R. Haſsler, Superintendent of the coast of the United States. Triangulation by J. Ferguson and E. Blunt. Topography by C. M. Eakin, W. M. Boyce and J. Farley. Hydrography by the party under the command of G. S. Blake. A. D. Bache, Superintendent. Verified by A. A. Humphreys and aſsistants. New York, 1846.

2 MAP of the City of New Haven and vicinity, from actual surveys by Hartley and Whiteford. 4 sheets. Philadelphia, 1851.

NEW HOPE. Plan of the Boroughs of New Hope, Pennsylvania, and Lambertville, New Jersey; including enlarged plans of the towns, from actual surveys by A. E. Rogerson and E. J. Murphy. 2 sheets. [Philadelphia?] 1850.

NEW LONDON. Plan of the City of New London, New London County, Connecticut, from original surveys by J. C. Sidney. 2 sheets. Philadelphia, 1850.

NEW LONDON, Harbour. The Harbor of New London. Founded upon a trigonometrical survey under the direction of F. R. Haſsler... Triangulation by E. Blunt. Topography

by F. H. Gerdes and T. B. Glück. Hydrography by the party under the command of G. S. Blake. A. D. Bache, Superintendent. Verified by A. A. Humphreys. New York, 1848.

NEWPORT COUNTY. Map of Newport County, Rhode Island, from original surveys by H. F. Walling, aſsisted by O. Harkneſs and J. Hanson. (Block Island.) [Philadelphia?] 1850.

NEW YORK, City of. A Map exhibiting the different stage routs, between the cities of New York, Baltimore, and parts adjacent. To which is added as an historical companion, the Operations of the British Army, from their landing at Elk River in 1777 to their embarkation at Neirsink in 1778. By J. Hills. Philadelphia, 1800.

2 ACTUAL Map and Comparative Plans, showing 88 years growth of the City of New York, by D. Longworth. (Plan of New York in 1729. Surveyed by J. Lyne.) New York, 1817.

3 NEW York. [A Bird's-eye View of New York.] Painted by Heine J. Kummer and Dopler. New York, 1851.

4 SIDNEY'S Map of twelve miles around New York, with the names of Property Holders, etc. 2 sheets. Philadelphia, 1849.

NEW YORK, State of. The State of New York, with part of the adjacent States. By J. H. Eddy. New York, 1818.

2 NEW York. (Profile of the Champlain Canal, from Lake Champlain to the Hudson River. Profile of Levels of the Grand Canal.) Drawn by the City of New York, to accompany the memoir of C. D. Colden. [New York, 1825.]

3 NEW York, New Jersey, and Pennsylvania. [Map showing the internal navigation.] [Philadelphia, 1826.]

4 GEOLOGICAL Map of the State of New York. By Legislative Authority. New York, 1842.

5 THE EMPIRE State of New York, with its counties, towns, cities, villages, internal improvements, *etc.* Published by S. A. Mitchell. 2 sheets. Philadelphia, 1850.

NEW YORK BAY. Map of New York Bay and Harbor, and the environs. Founded upon a trigonometrical survey under the direction of F. R. Haßler, Superintendent of the Survey of the Coast of the United States. Triangulation by J. Ferguson and E. Blunt. The Hydrography under the direction of T. R. Gedney, Lieut. United States Navy. The Topography by C. Renard, T. A. Jenkins and B. E. Sands. A. D. Bache, Superintendent. Views of the coast drawn by J. Farley. New York, 1845.

NIAGARA. Sketch of the Niagara Falls Suspension Bridge (now in progreß), shewing the Basket Ferry and the Temporary Towers of the Foot Bridge. Halloway, del. [Buffalo?] 1848.

NIAGARA COUNTY. Map of Niagara County, New York, from actual surveys by Franklin Gifford and Samuel Geil. (Plan of the village of Lewiston, plan of Lockport, plan of the village of Niagara Falls, plan of the village of Wilson.) 2 sheets. Philadelphia, 1852.

NORRISTOWN. Map of the Borough of Norristown, from actual surveys by L. E. Corson. Philadelphia [1850?]

NORTHAMPTON COUNTY. Map of Northampton County, Pennsylvania, by M. S. Henry. (Plan of the Borough of Easton. View of the Delaware Water Gap.) [Philadelphia,] 1850.

NORTH CAROLINA. North and South Carolina and Georgia. [Map showing the internal navigation.] [Philadelphia, 1826.]

NORWICH. Plan of the City of Norwich, New London County, Connecticut, from original survey by H. M'Intyre. 2 sheets. Philadelphia, 1850.

OHIO, Indiana, and Michigan. [Map showing the internal navigation.] [Philadelphia, 1826.]

2 MAP exhibiting the position of the several lines connected with the settlement of the Ohio Boundary Question. Arranged under the immediate direction of Capt. A. Talcott, United States Engineers, by Lieut. W. Hood, United States Army. [Washington? 1835?]

3 MAP exhibiting the position of the several lines connected with the settlement of the Ohio Boundary Question... [Washington? 1835?]

4 OHIO Boundary, Nº 1. South Bend of Lake Michigan. Map exhibiting the position occupied in the determination of the Latitude of the extreme south bend of Lake Michigan. Surveyed under the direction of Captain A. Talcott, United States Topographical Engineers, by Lieuts. W. Hood and W. Smith. [Washington?] 1835.

5 OHIO Boundary, Nº 2. Map exhibiting the positions occupied on the Maumee Bay and River; viz. Turtle Island, the North Cape, and that above Toledo; together with the position of the "East Line," in its paßage of the Maumee River. Surveyed under the direction of Capt. Talcott, United States Engineers, by Lieuts. Hood and R. E. Lee. Drawn by Lieut. J. R. Irwin. 2 sheets. [Washington?] 1835.

6 OHIO Boundary, Nº 3. South Bend of Lake Erie: Map exhibiting the position occupied in the determination of the most southerly point of the Boundary Line between the United States and Canada. Surveyed under the direction of Capt. A. Talcott, United States Engineers, by Lieuts. W. Hood and R. E. Lee. (Point

Pelé, Upper Canada.) Map exhibiting the second position occupied in the determination of the most southwardly point · of the Boundary Line between the United States and Canada. Surveyed under the direction of Capt. A. Talcott, United States Engineers, by Lieut. W. Hood and R. E. Lee. 2 sheets. [Washington?] 1835.

ONEIDA COUNTY. Map of Oneida County, New York, from actual surveys by A. E. Rogerson and E. J. Murphy. (Plan of the village of Remsen, Boonville, Camden, Vernon, Rome, Clinton, Waterville, Whitesborough, Yorkville, Clayville, New Hartford and Utica.) 2 sheets. Philadelphia, 1852.

ONONDAGA COUNTY. Map of Onondaga County, New York, from actual surveys by L. Fagan, under direction of Sidney and Neff. (Plan of Syracuse, New York.) Syracuse and Providence, 1852.

ONTARIO COUNTY. Map of Ontario County, New York, from actual surveys by H. F. Walling. [With plans of the villages of Naples, Victor, Geneva and Canandaigua.] 2 sheets. Philadelphia, 1852.

ORANGE COUNTY. Map of Orange County, New York, from actual surveys by J. C. Sidney. (Plan of Newburgh.) 4 sheets. Newburgh and Philadelphia, 1850.

ORLEANS COUNTY. Map of Orleans County, New York, from actual surveys by Lightfoot and Yeil. [With Plans of Albion and Medina, surveyed and drawn by S. Geil.] 2 sheets. Philadelphia, 1852.

OYSTER BAY. Oyster or Syosset Bay, founded upon a Trigonometrical Survey under the direction of F. R. Hassler... Triangulation by E. Blunt. Topography by A. D. Mackay and F. H. Gerdes. Hydrography by the party under the command of Lieut.

G. S. Blake. A. D. Bache, Superintendent. Verified by A. A. Humphreys. New York, 1847.

PENNSYLVANIA. A Map of the Province of Pennsylvania, containing the three Countyes of Chester, Philadelphia, and Bucks, as far as yet surveyed and laid out... By T. Holme, Surveyor General. (A Plan of Philadelphia.) Philadelphia and London, 1845.

2 MAP of the first and second Coal Fields in Pennsylvania, embracing Schuylkill County and parts of Carbon, Luzerne, Columbia, Northumberland, Dauphin, and Lebanon Counties, by S. B. Fisher and P. W. Sheafer. (Plans of the Borough of Orwigsburg and of Pottsville.) 3 sheets. Philadelphia, 1849.

3 MAP of Pennsylvania, constructed from the County Surveys authorized by the State and other original documents, revised and improved under the supervision of W. E. Morris. 6 sheets. Philadelphia, 1850.

PHILADELPHIA. Plan of the City of Philadelphia and its environs, taken from actual survey. Drawn under the direction of J. A. Paxton, by W. Strickland. [Philadelphia?] 1811.

2 MAP of the City and Liberties of Philadelphia. By J. Reed. Facsimile reproduced by the Anastatic Process. 200 copies only printed, and the plates destroyed. 3 sheets. Philadelphia, 1846.

3 MAP of the Circuit of ten miles around the City of Philadelphia. ... From original Surveys by J. C. Sidney. [With Views of] Girard College and Laurel Hill Cemetery. Philadelphia, 1847.

4 MAP of the City of Philadelphia, together with all the surrounding Districts, including Camden, New Jersey, from official records, plans of the District Surveyors and original surveys by J. C. Sidney. 6 sheets. Philadelphia, 1850.

5 MAP of the Vicinity of Philadelphia, from actual surveys. 2 sheets. Philadelphia, 1851.

6 PLAN of the City of Philadelphia, together with the surrounding districts. Compiled from J. C. Sidney's Map. Reduced and improved by J. W. Otley. 2 sheets. Philadelphia, 1852.

PLYMOUTH. Map of the Town of Plymouth, Litchfield County, Connecticut. Surveyed and drawn by E. M. Woodford. 2 sheets. Philadelphia, 1852.

PORTLAND. Map of the City of Portland, Cumberland County, Maine, from original surveys. H. F. Walling, Civil Engineer. [Philadelphia?] 1851.

PORTSMOUTH. Map of the City of Portsmouth, New Hampshire. From original surveys under the direction of H. F. Walling. [Philadelphia?] 1850.

PROVIDENCE, *Rhode Island.* A Map of the City of Providence, from actual survey by Cushing and Walling. [With a view of Providence.] Providence, 1849.

PROVIDENCE COUNTY. Map of Providence County, Rhode Island, with some of the adjacent Towns, from original surveys by H. F. Walling. [With Plan of the City of Providence, and Views of various Buildings in it.] 2 sheets. [Providence, Rhode Island?] 1851.

R ARITAN. Plan of the Township of Raritan, Hunterden County, New Jersey. Surveyed by J. C. Sidney. (Plan of Flemington.) Philadelphia, 1850.

READING. Plan of the City of Reading, Berks County, Pennsylvania, from actual surveys by J. C. Sidney. 2 sheets. Philadelphia, 1849.

REHOBOTH. Map of the Town of Rehoboth, Massachusetts, from original surveys under the direction of H. F. Walling. 2 sheets. Philadelphia, 1850.

RICHMOND'S ISLAND HARBOUR. Triangulation by A. D. Bache and C. O. Boutelle. Topography by A. W. Longfellow. Hydrography by the Party under the command of M. Woodhull. [New York,] 1851.

S ACO. Map of the Villages of Saco and Biddeford, York County, Maine, from original surveys. H. F. Walling, Civil Engineer; O. Harkness, Assistant Engineer. [Philadelphia?] 1851.

ST. ANDREW'S SHOALS. Reconnoissance of St. Andrew's Shoals at the entrance of St. Andrew's Sound, Georgia, by the party under the command of Lieut. J. Rodgers. . . A. D. Bache, Superintendent. [Washington,] 1850.

ST. CHARLES COUNTY, *Missouri.* [A Part of St. Charles County, Missouri.] St. Louis, 1835.

ST. CLAIR. Map of the Delta of the St. Clair. Surveyed, projected, and drawn by Lieut. J. N. Macomb and W. H. Warner, under the direction of Capt. W. G. Williams. 2 sheets. [New York?] 1842.

ST. LAWRENCE, RIVER. Map of the Basin of the St. Lawrence, shewing also the natural and artificial routes between the Atlantic Ocean and the interior of North America, by T. C. Keefer, for J. D. Andrews' report. N[ew] Y[ork,] 1853.

SALEM. A Map of the Counties of Salem and Gloucester, New Jersey, from original surveys by A. C. Stansbie, J. Keily, and S. M. Rea. (Plan of Salem. View of Woodbury.) 4 sheets. Philadelphia, 1849.

SENECA COUNTY. Topographical Map of Seneca County, New

York, made .. by William T. Gibson. (Fall of the Silver Thread, formerly Lodi Falls, Lodi, near Seneca Lake, Plans of Waterloo, Seneca Falls, and Ovid.) 2 sheets. [New York?] 1852.

SHEFFIELD ISLAND. Harbors of Sheffield Island and Cawkins Island, from a trigonometrical survey under the direction of F. R. Hasler. Triangulation by E. Blunt. Topography by C. M. Eakin. Hydrography by the party under the command of Lieut. G. S. Blake. [Washington,] 1848.

SOMERSET COUNTY. Map of Somerset County, New Jersey, entirely from original surveys by J. W. Otley and I. Keily. (Plan of Somerville.) 2 sheets. Camden, 1850.

SOUTH CAROLINA. Atlas of the State of South Carolina, by R. Mills. Baltimore, 1825.

SOUTH CAROLINA. North and South Carolina and Georgia. [Map showing the internal navigation.] [Philadelphia, 1826.]

SPRINGFIELD. Map of the Town of Springfield, Massachusetts, from actual survey by J. C. Sidney. Philadelphia, 1850.

SUPERIOR, Lake. Map of that part of the Mineral Lands adjacent to Lake Superior, ceded to the United States by the treaty of 1842 with the Chippewas. Comprising that district lying between Chocolate River and Fond du Lac, under the superintendency of General J. Stockton. Projected and drawn under the direction of Lieut. Col. G. Talcott .. by A. B. Gray, assisted by J. Seib. [Washington? 1845?]

2 Section and Diagram illustrating the Geology of the Region between the Northern Shores of Lakes Superior and Michigan. [New York? 1847?]

3 Geological Map of the Lake Superior Land District in the State of Michigan. By J. W. Foster and J. D. Whitney. [New York?] 1847.

TAMAQUA. A. D. Sweeney's Map of the Borough of Tamaqua, surveyed in June, 1849. [Philadelphia? 1850?]

TARPAULIN COVE. The Harbor of Tarpaulin Cove. Founded upon a Trigonometrical Survey under the direction of A. D. Bache. Triangulation by C. M. Eakin. Topography by W. M. Boyce. Hydrography by the party under the command of G. S. Blake. Verified by A. A. Humphreys. New York, 1847.

TAUNTON. Map of the Village of Taunton, Bristol County, Massachusetts. By H. F. Walling. Philadelphia, 1850.

TEHUANTEPEC. Map of the Isthmus of Tehuantepec .. shewing the proposed route of the Tehuantepec Railroad. Surveyed under the direction of Major J. G. Barnard. New York, 1851.

TENNESSEE. Map of the Western District of Tennessee. [Washington? 1832?]

2 Sketch of the Eleventh District of Western Tennessee. [Washington? 1835?]

THOMASTON. Chart exhibiting the position, form, and dimensions of a breakwater for the improvement of the Harbour at East Thomaston, Maine. [Washington? 1835?]

TORNADO. Plan exhibiting the Ravages of the Tornado of August 22nd, 1851, embracing so much of its course as is included between the base of Wellington Hill in Waltham, and Mystic River. By H. L. Eustis. Boston, 1853.

TORRINGTON. Map of the Town of Torrington, Lichfield County, Connecticut, from original surveys by J. Houston. (Wolcottville Village.) 2 sheets. Philadelphia, 1852.

UNION. Plan of the Townships of Union and Newton, County of Camden, from original surveys by J. C. Sidney. (Plan of Gloucester City.) Philadelphia, 1850.

UNITED STATES. A new and correct Map of the United States of North America. . . Compiled . . . by S. Lewis. Philadelphia, 1815.
2 MAP of the Country embracing the several Routes examined, with a View to a National Road from Washington to Buffalo. Del. by Lieut. Trimble. [Washington? 1820?]
3 A MAP of the United States of America. Published by H. S. Tanner. Philadelphia [1820?]
4 UNITED States. [Map showing the internal navigation.] [Philadelphia, 1826.]
5 [SPECIMENS of American Cerographic Maps, South Carolina, etc. Printed under the Steam Prefs, from plates in metallic relief, at the rate of 1200 maps in an hour; by S. E. Morse.] Oblong 4to. New York, 1843.
6 MAP of the Boundary Lines between the United States and the Adjacent British Provinces, from the mouth of the River St. Croix to the intersection of the Parallel of 45 Degrees of North Latitude with the River St. Lawrence near St. Regis, shewing the Lines as respectively claimed by the United States and Great Britain under the treaty of 1783, as awarded by the King of the Netherlands, and as settled in 1842 by the Treaty of Washington. Compiled by Lieut. T. J. Lee and W. M. C. Fairfax, under the direction of Major J. D. Graham. [Washington,] 1843.
7 RECONNOISSANCE of the Western Coast of the United States, from Monterey to the Columbia River; in three sheets . . by the Hydrographic Party under the command of W. P. M'Arthur. . . . W. A. Bartlett, Afsistant. Third edition. [Washington,] 1851.

8 MAP of the United States of America, the British Provinces, Mexico and the West Indies, showing the country from the Atlantic to the Pacific Ocean. Published by J. H. Cotton. 4 sheets. New York, 1851.
9 MAP of the Railroads in the United States in operation and progrefs, to accompany a report from the Treasury Department; by J. D. Andrews. N[ew] Y[ork, 1851?]

VERMONT. A Topographical Map of the State of Vermont, from actual survey. By W. Blodget. 4 sheets. Newhaven, 1789.

VIRGINIA, Maryland, and Delaware. [Map showing the internal navigation.] [Philadelphia, 1826.]

WASHINGTON. Plan of the City of Washington, in the Territory of Columbia, ceded by the States of Virginia and Maryland to the United States of America, and by them established as the seat of their Government after the year 1800. Philadelphia, 1792.
2 PLAN of the Hall of the House of Representatives of the United States. Drawn by D. H. Burr. [Washington? 1836?]
3 [HOUSE of Representatives.] [Washington? 1836?]
4 MAP of the City of Washington, District of Columbia. (Plan of Georgetown, Map of the District of Columbia.) J. Keily, Surveyor. Camden, 1851.

WASHTENAW COUNTY, Michigan. Map of Washtenaw County. Published under the direction of D. Houghton. . . S. W. Higgins, Topographer to Geological Survey. C. C. Douglafs and Bela Hubbard, Afsistant Geologists. [Detroit? 1850?]

WATERBURY. Map of the Town of Waterbury, Newhaven County, Connecticut, from actual survey by H. Irvine. (Village of Waterville.) 2 sheets. Philadelphia, 1852.

WESTERN TERRITORY. Map of the Western Territory, *etc.* [shewing the Lands afsigned to Emigrant Indians West of Arkansas and Missouri.] [Washington? 1835?]

2 MAP showing the Lands afsigned to Emigrant Indians West of Arkansas and Mifsouri. Prepared at the Topographical Bureau. R. Jones, Adj. Genl. [Washington,] 1836.

WEST CHESTER COUNTY. Map of West Chester County, New York, from actual surveys by Sidney and Neff. 2 sheets. Philadelphia, 1851.

WILKESBARRE. Plan of the Town of Wilkesbarre, Luzerne County, from original surveys by J. C. Sidney. Philadelphia, 1850.

WILMINGTON. Plan of the City of Wilmington, Delaware, from actual surveys by J. C. Sidney. Philadelphia, 1850.

WINCHESTER. Map of the Town of Winchester, Litchfield County, Connecticut, from original surveys by E. M. Woodford. 2 sheets. Philadelphia, 1852.

WOONSOCKETS. Map of the Vicinity of Woonsockets, Providence County, Rhode Island, from surveys under the direction of H. F. Walling. [Philadelphia?] 1851.

WORCESTER. Map of the City of Worcester, Worcester County, Mafsachusetts, from original Surveys by H. F. Walling. [Philadelphia?] 1851.

2 MAP of [the Environs of] the City of Worcester, Worcester County, Mafsachusetts. From actual Survey. [Philadelphia?] 1851.

WORLD. A Map of the World on Mercator's Projection, exhibiting the researches of the principal modern Travellers and navigators. Published by S. A. Mitchell. [New York,] 1838.

WRENTHAM. Map of the Town of Wrentham, Norfolk County, Massachusetts. [With Plan of Wrentham Centre], from surveys under the direction of H. F. Walling. [New York?] 1851.